The following is a sample chart of accounts. It does not represent a comprehensive chart of all the accounts used in this text but rather those accounts that are commonly used. This sample chart of accounts is for a company that generates both service revenue as well as sales revenue. It uses the perpetual approach to inventory. If a periodic system was used, the following temporary accounts would be needed to record inventory purchases: Purchases, Freight-In, Purchase Returns and Allowances, and Purchase Discounts.

Chart of Accounts

Assets	Liabilities	Equity	Revenues	Expenses
Cash	Notes Payable	Share Capital—Preference	Service Revenue	Administrative Expenses
Accounts Receivable	Accounts Payable	Share Capital—Ordinary	Sales Revenue	Amortization Expense
Allowance for Doubtful Accounts (Loss Allowance)	Unearned Service Revenue	Share Premium—Preference	Sales Discounts	Bad Debt Expense (Expected Credit Loss)
Interest Receivable	Salaries and Wages Payable	Share Premium—Ordinary	Sales Returns and Allowances	Cost of Goods Sold
Inventory	Interest Payable	Retained Earnings	Interest Revenue	Depreciation Expense
Supplies	Dividends Payable	Treasury Shares	Gain on Disposal of Plant Assets	Freight-Out
Prepaid Insurance	Income Taxes Payable	Dividends		Income Tax Expense
Land	Bonds Payable	Income Summary		Insurance Expense
Equipment	Mortgage Payable			Interest Expense
Accumulated Depreciation—Equipment				Loss on Disposal of Plant Assets
Buildings				Maintenance and Repairs Expense
Accumulated Depreciation—Buildings				Rent Expense
Copyrights				Salaries and Wages Expense
Goodwill				Selling Expenses
Patents				Supplies Expense
				Utilities Expense

Account Classification and Presentation

Account Title	Classification	Financial Statement	Normal Balance
A			
Accounts Payable	Current Liability	Statement of Financial Position	Credit
Accounts Receivable	Current Asset	Statement of Financial Position	Debit
Accumulated Depreciation—Buildings	Plant Asset—Contra	Statement of Financial Position	Credit
Accumulated Depreciation—Equipment	Plant Asset—Contra	Statement of Financial Position	Credit
Administrative Expenses	Operating Expense	Income Statement	Debit
Advertising Expense	Operating Expense	Income Statement	Debit
Allowance for Doubtful Accounts (Loss Allowance)	Current Asset—Contra	Statement of Financial Position	Credit
Amortization Expense	Operating Expense	Income Statement	Debit
B			
Bad Debt Expense (Expected Credit Loss)	Operating Expense	Income Statement	Debit
Bonds Payable	Non-Current Liability	Statement of Financial Position	Credit
Buildings	Plant Asset	Statement of Financial Position	Debit
C			
Cash	Current Asset	Statement of Financial Position	Debit
Copyrights	Intangible Asset	Statement of Financial Position	Debit
Cost of Goods Sold	Cost of Goods Sold	Income Statement	Debit
D			
Debt Investments	Current Asset/Long-Term Investment	Statement of Financial Position	Debit
Depreciation Expense	Operating Expense	Income Statement	Debit
Dividend Revenue	Investing Category Income	Income Statement	Credit
Dividends	Temporary Account Closed to Retained Earnings	Retained Earnings Statement	Debit
Dividends Payable	Current Liability	Statement of Financial Position	Credit
E			
Equipment	Plant Asset	Statement of Financial Position	Debit
F			
Freight-Out	Operating Expense	Income Statement	Debit
G			
Gain on Disposal of Plant Assets	Other Operating Income	Income Statement	Credit
Goodwill	Intangible Asset	Statement of Financial Position	Debit
I			
Income Summary	Temporary Account Closed to Retained Earnings	Not Applicable	(1)
Income Tax Expense	Income Tax Expense	Income Statement	Debit
Income Taxes Payable	Current Liability	Statement of Financial Position	Credit
Insurance Expense	Operating Expense	Income Statement	Debit
Interest Expense	Financial Category Expense	Income Statement	Debit
Interest Payable	Current Liability	Statement of Financial Position	Credit
Interest Receivable	Current Asset	Statement of Financial Position	Debit

(continues)

Account Title	Classification	Financial Statement	Normal Balance
Interest Revenue	Investing Category Income	Income Statement	Credit
Inventory	Current Asset	Statement of Financial Position (2)	Debit
L			
Land	Plant Asset	Statement of Financial Position	Debit
Loss on Disposal of Plant Assets	Other Operating Expense	Income Statement	Debit
M			
Maintenance and Repairs Expense	Operating Expense	Income Statement	Debit
Mortgage Payable	Non-Current Liability	Statement of Financial Position	Credit
N			
Notes Payable	Current Liability/ Non-Current Liability	Statement of Financial Position	Credit
P			
Patents	Intangible Asset	Statement of Financial Position	Debit
Prepaid Insurance	Current Asset	Statement of Financial Position	Debit
R			
Rent Expense	Operating Expense	Income Statement	Debit
Research and Development Expense	Operating Expense	Income Statement	Debit
Retained Earnings	Equity	Statement of Financial Position and Retained Earnings Statement	Credit
S			
Salaries and Wages Expense	Operating Expense	Income Statement	Debit
Salaries and Wages Payable	Current Liability	Statement of Financial Position	Credit
Sales Discounts	Revenue—Contra	Income Statement	Debit
Sales Returns and Allowances	Revenue—Contra	Income Statement	Debit
Sales Revenue	Revenue	Income Statement	Credit
Selling Expenses	Operating Expense	Income Statement	Debit
Service Revenue	Revenue	Income Statement	Credit
Share Capital—Ordinary	Equity	Statement of Financial Position	Credit
Share Capital—Preference	Equity	Statement of Financial Position	Credit
Share Investments	Current Asset/Long-Term Investment	Statement of Financial Position	Debit
Share Premium—Ordinary	Equity	Statement of Financial Position	Credit
Share Premium—Preference	Equity	Statement of Financial Position	Credit
Supplies	Current Asset	Statement of Financial Position	Debit
Supplies Expense	Operating Expense	Income Statement	Debit
T			
Treasury Shares	Equity—Contra	Statement of Financial Position	Debit
U			
Unearned Service Revenue	Current Liability	Statement of Financial Position	Credit
Utilities Expense	Operating Expense	Income Statement	Debit

(1) The normal balance for Income Summary will be credit when there is a net income, debit when there is a net loss. The Income Summary account does not appear on any financial statement.

(2) If a periodic system is used, Inventory also appears on the income statement in the calculation of cost of goods sold.

Financial Accounting with IFRS

Financial Accounting with IFRS

Sixth Edition

Jerry J. Weygandt PhD, CPA
University of Wisconsin—Madison
Madison, Wisconsin

Paul D. Kimmel PhD, CPA
University of Wisconsin—Madison
Madison, Wisconsin

WILEY

Financial Accounting with IFRS
International Adaptation

Sixth Edition

Founded in 1807, John Wiley & Sons, Inc. has been a valued source of knowledge and understanding for more than 200 years, helping people around the world meet their needs and fulfill their aspirations. Our company is built on a foundation of principles that include responsibility to the communities we serve and where we live and work. In 2008, we launched a Corporate Citizenship Initiative, a global effort to address the environmental, social, economic, and ethical challenges we face in our business. Among the issues we are addressing are carbon impact, paper specifications and procurement, ethical conduct within our business and among our vendors, and community and charitable support.
For more information, please visit our website: www.wiley.com/go/citizenship.

ISBN: 978-1-394-47023-5
ISBN: 978-1-394-47024-2 (ePub)
ISBN: 978-1-394-47026-6 (ePdf)

Printed and bound by CPI Group (UK) Ltd, Croydon, CR0 4YY

C9781394470235_120826

The manufacturer's authorized representative according to the EU General Product Safety Regulation is Wiley-VCH GmbH, Boschstr. 12, 69469 Weinheim, Germany, e-mail: Product_Safety@wiley.com.

BRIEF CONTENTS

FROM THE AUTHORS

Dear Student,

Why This Course? Remember your biology course in high school? Did you have one of those "invisible man" models (or maybe something more high-tech than that) that gave you the opportunity to look "inside" the human body? This accounting course offers something similar. To understand a business, you have to understand the financial insides of a business organization.

A financial accounting course will help you understand the essential financial components of businesses. Whether you are looking at a large multinational company like **Samsung** or **adidas** or a single-owner software consulting business or coffee shop, knowing the fundamentals of financial accounting will help you understand what is happening. As an employee, a manager, an investor, a business owner, or a director of your own personal finances—any of which roles you will have at some point in your life—you will make better decisions for having taken this course.

"Whether you are looking at a large multinational company like **Samsung** or **adidas** or a single-owner software consulting business or coffee shop, knowing the fundamentals of financial accounting will help you understand what is happening."

Why This Text? Your instructor has chosen this text for you because of our trusted reputation. We have worked hard to write a text that is engaging, timely, and accurate.

How to Succeed? We've asked many students and many instructors whether there is a secret for success in this course. The nearly unanimous answer turns out to be not much of a secret: "Do the homework." This is one course where doing is learning. The more time you spend on practicing and doing—using the various tools that this text and the Wiley online course provides—the more likely you are to learn the essential concepts, techniques, and methods of accounting.

Good luck in this course. We hope you enjoy the experience and that you put to good use throughout a lifetime of success the knowledge you obtain in this course. We are sure you will not be disappointed.

Jerry J. Weygandt
Paul D. Kimmel

AUTHOR COMMITMENT

JERRY J. WEYGANDT, PhD, CPA, is Arthur Andersen Alumni Emeritus Professor of Accounting at the University of Wisconsin—Madison. He holds a Ph.D. in accounting from the University of Illinois. Articles by Professor Weygandt have appeared in *The Accounting Review, Journal of Accounting Research, Accounting Horizons, Journal of Accountancy*, and other academic and professional journals. These articles have examined such financial reporting issues as accounting for price-level adjustments, pensions, convertible securities, stock option contracts, and interim reports. Professor Weygandt is author of other accounting and financial reporting texts and is a member of the American Accounting Association, the American Institute of Certified Public Accountants, and the Wisconsin Society of Certified Public Accountants. He has served on numerous committees of the American Accounting Association and as a member of the editorial board of the Accounting Review; he also has served as President and Secretary-Treasurer of the American Accounting Association. In addition, he has been actively involved with the American Institute of Certified Public Accountants and has been a member of the Accounting Standards Executive Committee (AcSEC) of that organization. He has served on the FASB task force that examined the reporting issues related to accounting for income taxes and served as a trustee of the Financial Accounting Foundation. Professor Weygandt has received the Chancellor's Award for Excellence in Teaching and the Beta Gamma Sigma Dean's Teaching Award. He is on the board of directors of M & I Bank of Southern Wisconsin. He is the recipient of the Wisconsin Institute of CPA's Outstanding Educator's Award and the Lifetime Achievement Award. In 2001 he received the American Accounting Association's Outstanding Educator Award.

PAUL D. KIMMEL, PhD, CPA, received his bachelor's degree from the University of Minnesota and his doctorate in accounting from the University of Wisconsin. He was an Associate Professor at the University of Wisconsin—Milwaukee for more than 25 years and is now a Senior Lecturer at the University of Wisconsin—Madison. He has public accounting experience with Deloitte & Touche (Minneapolis). He was the recipient of the UWM School of Business Advisory Council Teaching Award and the Reggie Taite Excellence in Teaching Award, and a three-time winner of the Outstanding Teaching Assistant Award at the University of Wisconsin. He is also a recipient of the Elijah Watts Sells Award for Honorary Distinction for his results on the CPA exam. He is a member of the American Accounting Association and the Institute of Management Accountants and has published articles in *Accounting Review, Accounting Horizons, Advances in Management Accounting, Managerial Finance, Issues in Accounting Education*, and *Journal of Accounting Education*, as well as other journals. His research interests include accounting for financial instruments and innovation in accounting education.

NEW TO THIS EDITION

The last few years have brought many changes to the teaching and learning environment. As a result, we scrutinized every chapter of *Financial Accounting* to make sure our text best meets the needs of today's students and instructors. The most significant changes throughout the text include:

- **NEW** discussion of data analytics integrated throughout the text, at an appropriate level of detail for introductory accounting students.
- **NEW** Data Analytics assignments at the end of selected chapters.
- **MORE** bulleted/numbered lists within the text discussion, to highlight key information for students.
- **UPDATED** fair value principle and historical cost principle to current value basis/historical cost basis per recent IFRS throughout.
- **ADDED** Answers to Insight box questions near the end of each chapter.

New and Revised Standards

The sixth edition reflects significant updates to international accounting standards and incorporates enhanced pedagogical features:

IFRS 18 – Presentation and Disclosure in Financial Statements

Issued by the IASB in April 2024, IFRS 18 supersedes IAS 1 and becomes mandatory for annual reporting periods beginning on or after January 1, 2027. This standard introduces a more structured approach to income statement presentation by requiring companies to classify income and expenses into five categories: operating, investing, financing, income tax, and discontinued operations. Two new mandatory subtotals—"operating profit or loss" and "profit or loss before financing and income taxes"—enhance comparability and transparency across companies and industries. Chapters 5, 13, and 15 have been comprehensively updated to reflect IFRS 18 requirements, including revised illustrations and updated terminology.

Amendments to IAS 7 – Statement of Cash Flows

Following the issuance of IFRS 18, consequential amendments to IAS 7 streamline cash flow reporting. Key changes include: (1) using the new "operating profit" subtotal as the starting point for the indirect method, eliminating certain reconciling items; (2) mandatory classification of dividends paid as financing activities; and (3) standardized classification of interest and dividends based on business activities—for non-financial companies, interest paid is classified as financing activities while interest and dividends received are classified as investing activities. Chapter 14 presents updated statement of cash flows illustrations reflecting these amendments.

Enhanced Practice Materials

DO IT! Exercises have been updated throughout.This enhancement strengthens the connection between theoretical concepts and practical application, better preparing students for examinations while deepening their understanding of core accounting principles.

Contemporary Business Examples

Real-world examples have been updated to reflect current business environments and emerging trends. These contemporary illustrations demonstrate how accounting principles operate in today's dynamic marketplace, helping students connect classroom learning with professional practice.

Expanded Coverage of Data Analytics and ESG

Beyond newly issued IFRS standards, this edition significantly expands coverage of data analytics applications in accounting, demonstrating how data-driven decision-making transforms the profession. Environmental, Social, and Governance (ESG) considerations have been strengthened throughout the text, reflecting the growing importance of sustainability reporting in contemporary accounting practice. These additions ensure students develop skills aligned with evolving industry demands and global business priorities.

Chapter-by-Chapter Changes

Chapter 1: Accounting in Action

- **NEW** discussion of how financial statement users can employ data analytics to improve decision-making.
- **NEW** discussion on the current value basis, and updated discussion of historical cost basis, per recent IFRS.
- **NEW** Helpful Hint on the two concepts of income under IFRS: net income and comprehensive income.
- **NEW** Data Analytics Insight, on how Netflix uses data analytics to estimate costs for future productions.
- **NEW** Ethics Insight, on the financial frauds that occurred at Toshiba.
- **UPDATED** Do IT!
- **NEW** and **UPDATED** Exercises
- **NEW** Problems

Chapter 2: The Recording Process

- **NEW** Helpful Hint, to reinforce student understanding of journals.
- **NEW** Investor Insight box
- **UPDATED** Multiple Choice Questions
- **NEW** and **UPDATED** Exercises
- **NEW** Problems

Chapter 3: Adjusting the Accounts

- **NEW** discussion, illustration, and end-of-chapter assignments of the five-step revenue recognition process.
- **NEW** Helpful Hint, on how adjusting entries have no effect on cash flows.
- **UPDATED** discussion for historical cost and current value bases.
- **UPDATED** Environmental, Social, and Governance (ESG) Insight on disposing of electronics safely.
- **NEW** Investor Insight Box

- **UPDATED** Do IT!
- **NEW** Accounting Across the Organization Box
- **NEW** ESG Insight Box
- **NEW** and **UPDATED** Exercises
- **NEW** Problems

Chapter 4: Completing the Accounting Cycle

- **UPDATED** discussion of worksheet to put its use more in context of the accounting cycle.
- **NEW** discussion of recent technology (robotic process automation) used in the closing process.
- **UPDATED** definitions of current assets and current liabilities per most recent IFRS.
- **NEW** and **UPDATED** Exercises
- **NEW** Problems

Chapter 5: Accounting for Merchandising Operations

- **NEW** section, "Data Analytics and Credit Sales," on how companies use data analytics to improve business decision-making regarding their policies on credit sales, sales returns and allowances, and sales discounts.
- **EXPANDED** discussion of FOB shipping point/FOB destination to ensure student understanding.
- **NEW** Appendix 5C, \"Adjusting Entries for Credit Sales with Returns and Allowances,\" and related EOC material.
- **NEW** Accounting Across the Organization box on how Alibaba uses personalized shopping pages to increase its e-commerce presence and revenue.
- **UPDATED** discussion of fair value to current value/net realizable value throughout.
- **NEW** Data Analytics in Action end-of-chapter problem on using data visualizations to analyze companies' profitability.
- **UPDATED** to incorporate IFRS 18 requirements (see New and Revised Standards section).
- **UPDATED** Do IT!
- **NEW** Accounting Across the Organization Box
- **NEW** and **UPDATED** Exercises
- **NEW** Problems

Chapter 6: Inventories

- **NEW** discussions on (1) write-down reversals and (2) how data analytics can benefit inventory management.
- **NEW** Data Analytics Insight on effectiveness of dashboards.
- **NEW** Accounting Across the Organization box on fashion companies' innovative methods for handling deadstock.
- **UPDATED** Accounting Across the Organization box (\"A Big Hiccup\") to include Covid-19 impacts on global automotive manufacturers.
- **NEW** illustration showing Walmart's recent inventory disclosure, using the retail inventory method.
- **UPDATED** Do IT!

- **UPDATED** Multiple Choice Questions
- **NEW** and **UPDATED** Exercises
- **NEW** Problems

Chapter 7: Fraud, Internal Control, and Cash

- **NEW** section on how data analytics helps improve internal controls.
- **UPDATED** discussion of over-the-counter, electronic, and check receipts per recent technology.
- **UPDATED** discussion of electronic banking per recent technology.
- **UPDATED** discussion of cash equivalents and restricted cash per recent standards.
- **NEW** Anatomy of a Fraud boxes on fraud due to the missing control of segregation of duties.
- **NEW** Data Analytics in Action end-of-chapter problems on using data visualizations to help understand fraud and using data analytics to determine the impact of internal control activities.
- **NEW** end-of-chapter cases on blockchain technology and the IASB.
- **UPDATED** Do IT!
- **NEW** and **UPDATED** Exercises
- **NEW** Problems

Chapter 8: Accounting for Receivables

- **NEW** section on data analytics and receivables management.
- **NEW** Data Analytics Insight on using data analytics to help with credit decisions and estimating uncollectible accounts.
- **NEW** discussion of IASB expected credit loss model, which requires that companies measure expected uncollectible accounts and record bad debt expense on all receivables, even those with a low risk of loss.
- **NEW** Data Analytics in Action end-of-chapter problems on using data visualization to analyze bad debts over time and using data analytics to evaluate notes receivable over time.
- **UPDATED** Real World Illustration
- **NEW** Ethics Insight Box
- **NEW** and **UPDATED** Exercises
- **NEW** Problems

Chapter 9: Plant Assets, Natural Resources, and Intangible Assets

- **UPDATED** definition of depreciation.
- **NEW** Data Analytics in Action end-of-chapter problem on using data visualization to analyze assets.
- **UPDATED** Do IT!
- **NEW** and **UPDATED** Exercises
- **NEW** Problems

Chapter 10: Current Liabilities

- **NEW** Accounting Across the Organization box on whether SAP's growing deferred income account is a good sign or bad.

- **NEW** end-of-chapter case on how Covid-19 has impacted microfinancing.
- **UPDATED** Do IT!
- **NEW** and **UPDATED** Exercises
- **NEW** Problems

Chapter 11: Non-Current Liabilities

- **NEW** Investor Insight on how Volkswagen issued debt to manage developing electric vehicles as well as Covid-19 issues, and the implications of that for the company's future.
- **UPDATED** Do IT!
- **NEW** Investment Insight Box
- **NEW** and **UPDATED** Exercises
- **NEW** Problems

Chapter 12: Corporations: Organization, Share Transactions, and Equity

- **NEW** discussion on hybrid forms of business organization.
- **UPDATED** discussion of statement of changes in equity, as now a required statement.
- **NEW** ESG Insight box on the upward trend of shareholder proposals on corporate responsibility.
- **NEW** Investor Insight, on how companies that pay dividends can increase investor wealth.
- **NEW** Data Analytics in Action end-of-chapter problems on using data visualizations to compare share prices and data analytics to compare the effect of share splits.
- **UPDATED** Do IT!
- **NEW** and **UPDATED** Exercises
- **NEW** Problems

Chapter 13: Investments

- **NEW** discussions on (1) the classification and measurement of investments, (2) accounting for bonds both to hold and to sell, (3) using fair value to account for share investments of less than 20%, and (4) accounting for debt investments classified as held-for-collection and selling.
- **UPDATED** discussion to include the three (previously two) categories of securities.
- **UPDATED** to incorporate IFRS 18 requirements (see New and Revised Standards section).
- **UPDATED** Do IT!
- **UPDATED** Illustrations
- **UPDATED** Solved Examples
- **NEW** Multiple-Choice Questions
- **UPDATED** Brief Exercises
- **NEW** Questions
- **NEW** and **UPDATED** Exercises
- **NEW** Problems

Chapter 14: Statement of Cash Flows

- **NEW** Accounting Across the Organization box on how companies are moving away from hypergrowth and instead focusing on growing profits and cash flows.
- **NEW** Data Analytics in Action end-of-chapter problems on using data visualizations and data analytics to analyze cash flows.
- **UPDATED** to incorporate amended IAS 7 requirements (see New and Revised Standards section).
- **UPDATED** Illustrations
- **NEW** Multiple-Choice Questions
- **UPDATED** Brief Exercises
- **NEW** Questions
- **NEW** and **UPDATED** Exercises
- **NEW** Problems

Chapter 15: Financial Statement Analysis

- **UPDATED** to include more bulleted lists to facilitate student understanding.
- **NEW** Data Analytics in Action end-of-chapter problems on using data visualizations to analyze companies over time and data analytics to compare companies' inventory turnover.
- **UPDATED** to incorporate IFRS 18 requirements (see New and Revised Standards section).
- **NEW** and **UPDATED** Exercises
- **NEW** Problems

PROVEN PEDAGOGICAL FEATURES

In this new edition, all content has been carefully reviewed and revised to ensure maximum student understanding. At the same time, the time-tested features that have proven to be of most help to students have been retained, such as the following.

Infographic Learning

Over half of the text is visual, providing students alternative ways of learning about accounting.

ILLUSTRATION 6.9 **Allocation of costs—average-cost method**

Cost of Goods Available for Sale

Date	Explanation	Units	Unit Cost	Total Cost
Jan. 1	Beginning inventory	10	HK$100	HK$ 1,000
Apr. 15	Purchase	20	110	2,200
Aug. 24	Purchase	30	120	3,600
Nov. 27	Purchase	40	130	5,200
	Total	100		**HK$12,000**

Step 1: Ending Inventory

HK$12,000	÷	100	=	HK$120
Units		**Unit Cost**		**Total Cost**
45		HK$120		**HK$5,400**

Step 2: Cost of Goods Sold

Cost of goods available for sale	HK$12,000
Less: Ending inventory	5,400
Cost of goods sold	**HK$ 6,600**

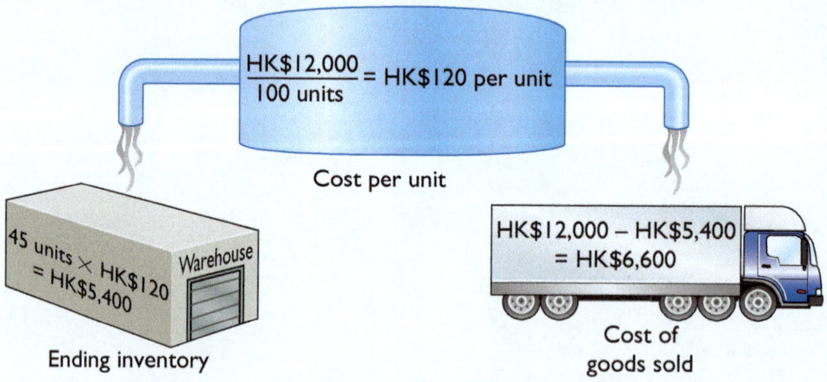

Real-World Decision-Making

Real-world examples, which illustrate engaging situations in companies, are provided throughout the text. Answers to the critical thinking questions posed to readers within the real-world examples are now available near the end of each chapter.

Environmental, Social, and Governance Insight

njgphoto/Getty Images

Got Junk?

Do you have an old computer or two that you no longer use? How about an old TV that needs replacing? Many people do. Approximately 163,000 computers and televisions become obsolete each day. Yet, in a recent year, only 11% of computers were recycled.

It is estimated that 75% of all computers ever sold are sitting in storage somewhere, waiting to be disposed of. Each of these old TVs and computers is loaded with lead, cadmium, mercury, and other toxic chemicals. If you have one of these electronic gadgets, you have a responsibility, and a probable cost, for disposing of it. Companies have the same problem, but their discarded materials may include lead paint, asbestos, and other toxic chemicals.

What accounting issue might this cause for companies? (Answer is available near the end of the chapter.)

DO IT! Exercises

DO IT! Exercises in the body of the text prompt students to stop and review key concepts. They outline the Action Plan necessary to complete the exercise as well as show a detailed solution.

ACTION PLAN

- **Make adjusting entries at the end of the period to recognize revenues for services performed and for expenses incurred.**
- **Don't forget to make adjusting entries for accruals. Adjusting entries for accruals will increase both a statement of financial position and an income statement account.**

DO IT! 3 | Adjusting Entries for Accruals

Mahindra Computer Services began operations on August 1, 2029. At the end of August 2029, management prepares monthly financial statements. The following information relates to August (amounts in thousands).

1. At August 31, the company owed its employees ₹800 in salaries and wages that will be paid on September 1.
2. On August 1, the company borrowed ₹30,000 from a local bank on a 15-year mortgage. The annual interest rate is 10%.
3. Revenue for services performed but unrecorded for August totaled ₹1,100.

Prepare the adjusting entries needed at August 31, 2029.

Solution

1. Salaries and Wages Expense	800	
Salaries and Wages Payable		800
(To record accrued salaries)		
2. Interest Expense	250	
Interest Payable		250
(To record accrued interest: ₹30,000 × 10% × $\frac{1}{12}$ = ₹250)		
3. Accounts Receivable	1,100	
Service Revenue		1,100
(To record revenue for services performed)		

Related exercise material: **BE3.9, DO IT! 3.3, E3.5, E3.6, E3.7, E3.8, E3.9, and E3.10.**

Review and Practice

Each chapter concludes with a Review and Practice section which includes a review of learning objectives, Decision Tools review, key terms glossary, practice multiple-choice questions with annotated solutions, practice brief exercises with solutions, practice exercises with solutions, and a practice problem with a solution.

Review and Practice

Practice Brief Exercises

Indicate why adjusting entries are needed.

1. **(LO 1)** The ledger of Dey Company includes the following accounts. Explain why each account may need adjustment.

a. Supplies.
b. Unearned Service Revenue.
c. Salaries and Wages Payable.
d. Interest Payable.

Solution

1. **a.** Supplies: to recognize supplies used during the period.
b. Unearned Service Revenue: to record revenue generated for services performed.
c. Salaries and Wages Payable: to recognize unpaid salaries and wages due to employees at the end of a reporting period.
d. Interest Payable: to recognize interest accrued but unpaid on notes payable.

Prepare adjusting entry for depreciation.

2. **(LO 2)** At the end of its first year, the trial balance of Denton Cleaners shows Equipment of £40,000 and zero balances in Accumulated Depreciation—Equipment and Depreciation Expense. Depreciation for the year is estimated to be £8,000. Prepare the adjusting entry for depreciation at December 31, post the adjustments to T-accounts, and indicate the statement of financial position presentation of the equipment at December 31.

Solution

2. Dec. 31	Depreciation Expense	8,000	
	Accumulated Depreciation—Equipment		8,000

Depreciation Expense

12/31	8,000		

Accum. Depreciation—Equipment

		12/31	8,000

Statement of financial position:

Equipment	£40,000	
Less: Accumulated depreciation—equipment	8,000	£32,000

Prepare adjusting entries for accruals.

3. **(LO 3)** You are asked to prepare the following accrual adjusting entries at December 31.

1. Services performed but not recorded are €4,200.
2. Utilities expenses incurred but not paid are €660.
3. Salaries and wages earned by employees of €3,000 are unpaid.

Use the following account titles: Accounts Receivable, Service Revenue, Salaries and Wages Expense, Salaries and Wages Payable, Utilities Expense, and Utilities Payable.

Digital study tools in Wiley's online course include the following.

Lecture PowerPoints

Lecture PowerPoints break down each section and learning objective in the text. The slides simplify major concepts in the text, making the concepts easier to understand. They provide additional explanation for activities, images, and figures to enhance student learning.

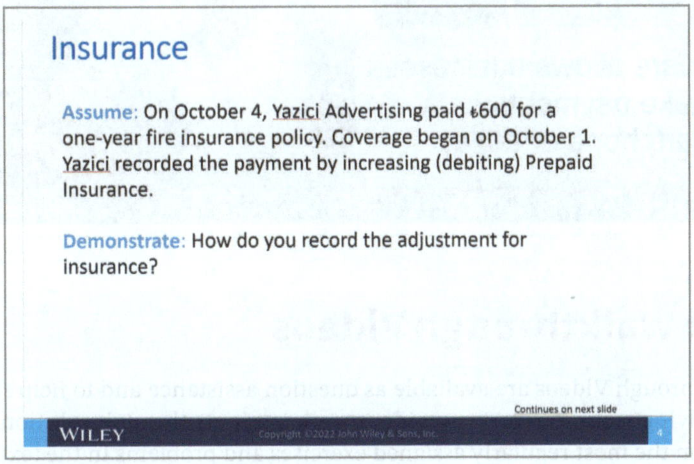

Accounting Animated Shorts

Short, animated videos engage students and simplify major concepts in the text, making the concepts easier to understand. They offer an alternative approach to understanding the written material.

Real-World Videos

Real-world videos feature both small businesses and larger companies to help students apply content and see how business owners apply concepts from the text in the real world. Many of the videos have associated questions available to be assigned.

Solution Walkthrough Videos

Solution Walkthrough Videos are available as question assistance and to help students develop problem-solving techniques. These videos walk students through solutions step-by-step and are based on the most regularly assigned exercises and problems in the text.

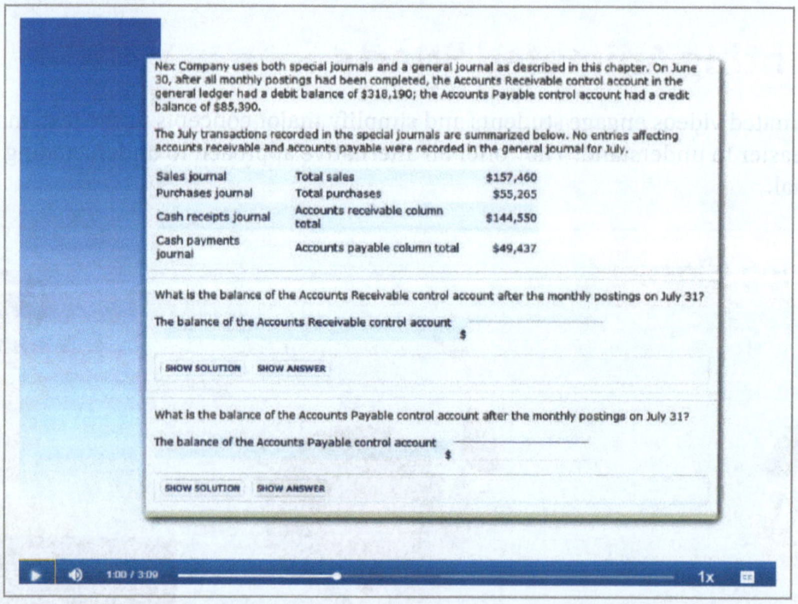

Gradable Excel Questions

Gradable Excel questions provide students an opportunity to practice Excel skills in the context of solving accounting problems.

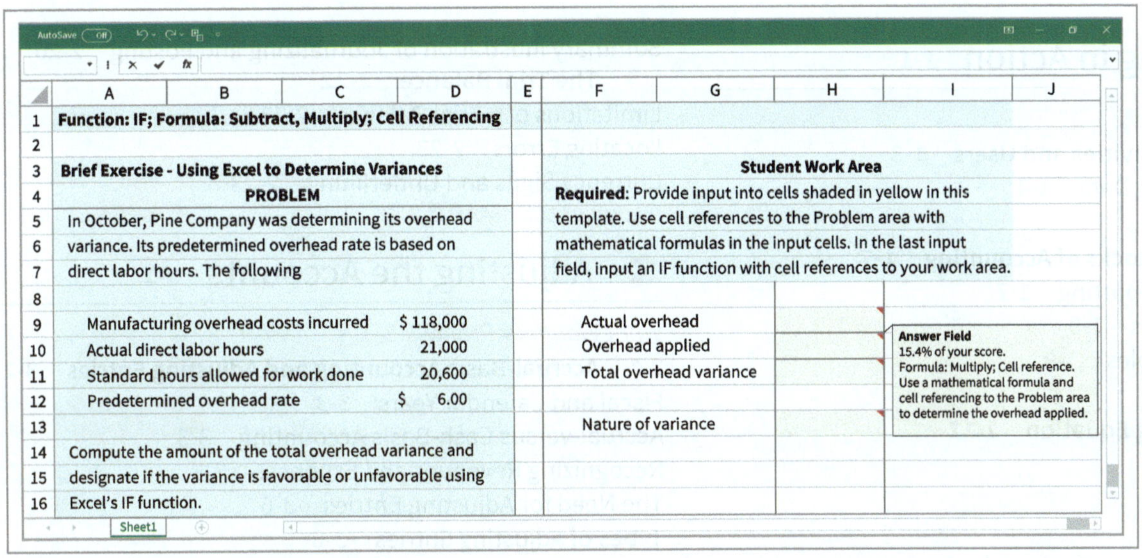

Other Learning Opportunities

Other learning opportunities in Wiley's online course include the following.

- **Accounting-Specific Data Analytics Module** offers interactive lessons, case studies, and videos. The module has been prepared using industry-validated content to help students develop the professional competencies needed for the changing workforce.
- **Matcha Creations** is a continuing case that spans across chapters and offers students the opportunity to see how a small business might use financial accounting to operate effectively.
- **Wiley Accounting Updates** (wileyaccountingupdates.com) provide faculty and students with weekly curated news articles and suggested discussion questions.
- **Flashcards and Crossword Puzzles** help students study and master basic vocabulary and concepts.
- **Student Practice** quickly and effectively assesses student understanding of the material they have just covered.

Now that you have the book, enhance it with the IFRS supplementary content at https://thbook.gitbook.io/weygandt6e

Use this QR code for a shortcut to https://thbook.gitbook.io/weygandt6e.

CONTENTS

Meet Our Contributor

In this new edition of *Financial Accounting*, the authors are pleased to welcome the assistance of Jack Cathey. A professor at the University of North Carolina—Charlotte, Jack assisted the authors with updating chapter content per the most recent IFRS as well as the current accounting environment. He also ensured that the company references are the most relevant and relatable to the student, focusing on well-known companies with tangible examples.

Additional Acknowledgments

Financial Accounting has benefited greatly from the input of those who have sent comments by letter or email, ancillary authors, and proofers. We greatly appreciate the constructive suggestions and innovative ideas of reviewers and the creativity and accuracy of the ancillary authors and checkers.

LuAnn Bean
Florida Institute of Technology

Jack Borke
University of Wisconsin—Platteville

Laura De Luca
Fanshawe College

Larry Falcetto
Emporia State University

Magdy Farag
California State Polytechnic University

Heidi Hansel
Kirkwood Community College

Kim Hurt
Central Community College

Derek Jackson
St. Mary's University

Ann Martel
University of Wisconsin—Milwaukee

Brigitte Muehlmann
Babson College

Christopher Nogot
Siena College of Taytay

Yvonne Phang
Borough of Manhattan Community College/CUNY

Laura Prosser
Black Hills State University

Rama Ramamurthy
Georgetown University

Alice Sineath
Forsyth Technical Community College

Lynn Stallworth
Appalachian State University

Diane Tanner
University of North Florida

Shelia Viel
University of Wisconsin—Milwaukee

Dick Wasson
Southwestern College

Catherine Wyatt
Lumina Datamatics

Lori Zaher
Bucks County Community College

We appreciate the exemplary support and commitment given to us by associate director Zoe Craig, acquisitions editor Victoria Pisto, senior product marketing manager Christina Koop Minarik, course content developer Alethia Marrero, editorial supervisor Terry Ann Tatro, senior course production operations specialist Rachel Conrad, and Subramaniam Vengatakrishnan at Lumina. All of these professionals provided innumerable services that helped the text take shape.

Finally, we appreciate suggestions and comments from users—instructors and students alike. We welcome your thoughts and ideas about the text.

Jerry J. Weygandt
Madison, Wisconsin

Paul D. Kimmel
Cedarburg, Wisconsin

CHAPTER 1

Accounting in Action

LEARNING OBJECTIVES After studying this chapter, you should be able to:

LO 1 Identify the activities and users associated with accounting.

LO 2 Explain the building blocks of accounting: ethics, principles, and assumptions.

LO 3 State the accounting equation, and define its components.

LO 4 Analyze the effects of business transactions on the accounting equation.

LO 5 Describe the five financial statements and how they are prepared.

Chapter Preview

The following Feature Story highlights the importance of having good financial information and knowing how to use it to make effective business decisions. Whatever your pursuits or occupation, the need for financial information is inescapable. You cannot earn a living, spend money, buy on credit, make an investment, or pay taxes without receiving, using, or dispensing financial information. Good decision-making depends on good information.

Accounting in Action

Accounting Activities and Users	The Building Blocks of Accounting	The Accounting Equation	Analyzing Business Transactions	Financial Statements
• Who uses accounting data • Data analytics	• Ethics in financial reporting • Accounting standards • Measurement principles • Assumptions	• Assets • Liabilities • Equity	• Accounting transactions • Transaction analysis • Summary of transactions	• Income statement • Retained earnings statement • Statement of financial position • Statement of cash flows • Comprehensive income statement

Practice

DO IT! 1 Basic Concepts

DO IT! 2 Building Blocks of Accounting

DO IT! 3 Equity Effects

DO IT! 4 Tabular Analysis

DO IT! 5 Financial Statement Items

Go to the Review and Practice section at the end of the chapter for a targeted summary and practice applications with solutions.
Additional tutorials and practice opportunities are available in the Wiley online course.

Feature Story Knowing the Numbers

Many students who take this course do not plan to be accountants. If you are in that group, you might be thinking, "If I'm not going to be an accountant, why do I need to know accounting?" In response, consider the quote from Harold Geneen, the former chairman of a major international company: "To be good at your business, you have to know the numbers—cold."

Success in any business comes back to the numbers. You will rely on them to make decisions, and managers will use them to evaluate your performance. That is true whether your job involves marketing, production, management, or information systems.

In business, accounting is the means for communicating the numbers. If you don't know how to read financial statements, you cannot really know your business.

Many companies spend significant resources teaching their employees basic accounting so that they can read financial statements and understand how their actions affect the company's financial results. Employers need managers in all areas of the company to be "financially literate."

Taking this course will go a long way to making you financially literate. In this text, you will learn how to read and prepare financial statements, and how to use basic tools to evaluate financial results.

Appendices A, B, and C of this text provide real financial statements of three companies from different countries that report using International Financial Reporting Standards (IFRS): **Taiwan Semiconductor Manufacturing Company (TSMC) Ltd.** (TWN), **Nestlé SA** (CHE), and **Delfi Limited** (SGP). Throughout this text, we increase your familiarity with financial reporting by providing numerous references, questions, and exercises that encourage you to explore these financial statements. In addition, we encourage you to visit each company's website where you can view its complete annual report.

Even though these three companies are based in three different countries, they all follow IFRS. This means they all follow the same basic accounting principles. As a result, their financial statements are very similar. Therefore, by learning these basic principles as presented in this text, you will be well equipped to begin understanding the financial results of companies around the world.

TPG/Shutterstock

1.1 Accounting Activities and Users

LEARNING OBJECTIVE 1

Identify the activities and users associated with accounting.

What consistently ranks as one of the top career opportunities in business? What frequently rates among the most popular majors on campus? Accounting.[1] Why do people choose accounting? They want to acquire the skills needed to understand what is happening financially inside an organization. Accounting is the financial information system that provides these insights. In short, to understand your organization, you have to know the numbers.

Accounting consists of three basic activities—it **identifies**, **records**, and **communicates** the economic events of an organization to interested users.

*Essential terms are printed in blue when they first appear, and are defined in the end-of-chapter **Glossary Review**.*

1. As a starting point to the accounting process, a company identifies the **economic events relevant to its business**. Examples of economic events are the sale of food and snacks by **Unilever** (GBR), the providing of telephone services by **Chunghwa Telecom** (TWN), and the manufacture of motor vehicles by **Tata Motors** (IND).
2. Once a company like Unilever identifies economic events, it **records** those events in order to provide a history of its financial activities. Recording consists of keeping a **systematic, chronological diary of events**, measured in monetary units. In recording, Unilever also classifies and summarizes economic events.
3. Finally, Unilever **communicates** the collected information to interested users by means of **accounting reports**. The most common of these reports are called **financial statements**.

To make the reported financial information meaningful, Unilever reports the recorded data in a standardized way. It accumulates information resulting from similar transactions. For example, Unilever accumulates all sales transactions over a certain period of time and reports the data as one amount in the company's financial statements. Such data are said to be reported **in the aggregate**. By presenting the recorded data in the aggregate, the accounting process simplifies a multitude of transactions and makes a series of activities understandable and meaningful.

A vital element in communicating economic events is the accountant's ability to **analyze and interpret** the reported information.

- Analysis involves use of ratios, percentages, graphs, and charts to highlight significant financial trends and relationships.
- Interpretation involves **explaining the uses, meaning, and limitations of reported data**.

Appendix A of this text shows the financial statements of **Taiwan Semiconductor Manufacturing Company (TSMC) Ltd.** (TWN). Appendix B illustrates the financial statements of **Nestlé SA** (CHE), and Appendix C includes the financial statements of **Delfi Limited** (SGP). We refer to these statements at various places throughout the text. (In addition, in the *A Look at U.S. GAAP* section at the end of each chapter, the U.S. company **Apple Inc.** is analyzed.)

At this point, these financial statements probably strike you as complex and confusing. By the end of this course, you'll be surprised at your ability to understand, analyze, and interpret them.

[1] The appendix to this chapter describes job opportunities for accounting majors and explains why accounting is such a popular major.

Illustration 1.1 summarizes the activities of the accounting process.

ILLUSTRATION 1.1 **The activities of the accounting process**

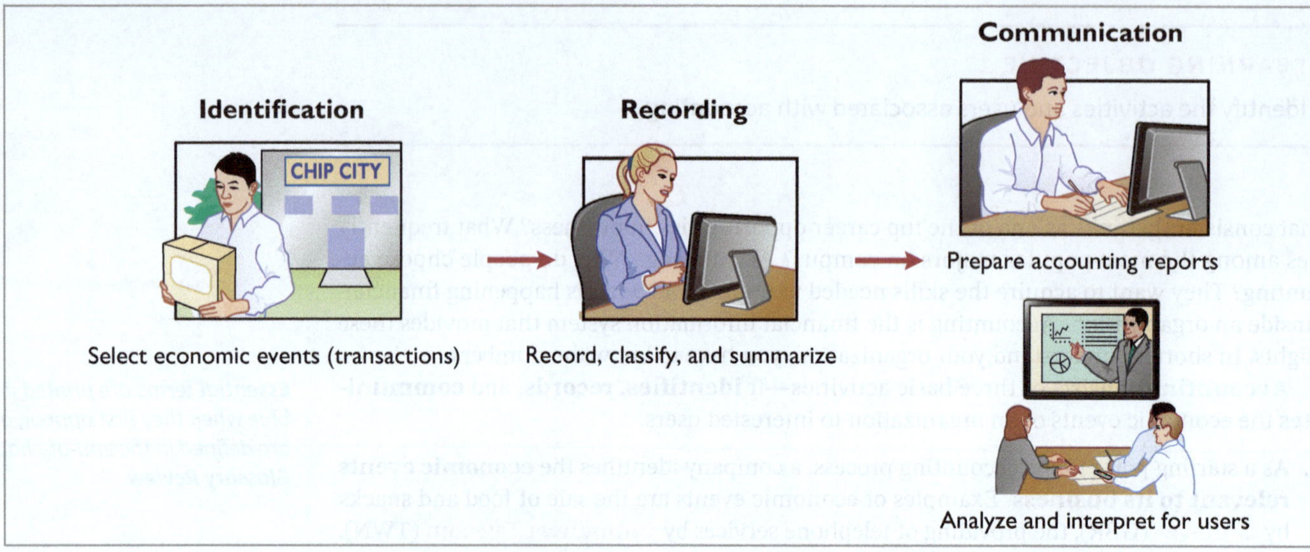

You should understand that the accounting process **includes** the bookkeeping function.

- **Bookkeeping** usually involves **only** the recording of economic events.
- It is therefore just one part of the accounting process.

In total, accounting involves **the entire process of identifying, recording, and communicating economic events.**[2]

Who Uses Accounting Data

The financial information that users need depends upon the kinds of decisions they make. There are two broad groups of users of financial information: internal users and external users.

Internal Users

Internal users of accounting information are managers who plan, organize, and run the business. These include marketing managers, production supervisors, finance directors, and company officers. In running a business, internal users must answer many important questions, as shown in **Illustration 1.2**.

ILLUSTRATION 1.2 **Questions that internal users ask**

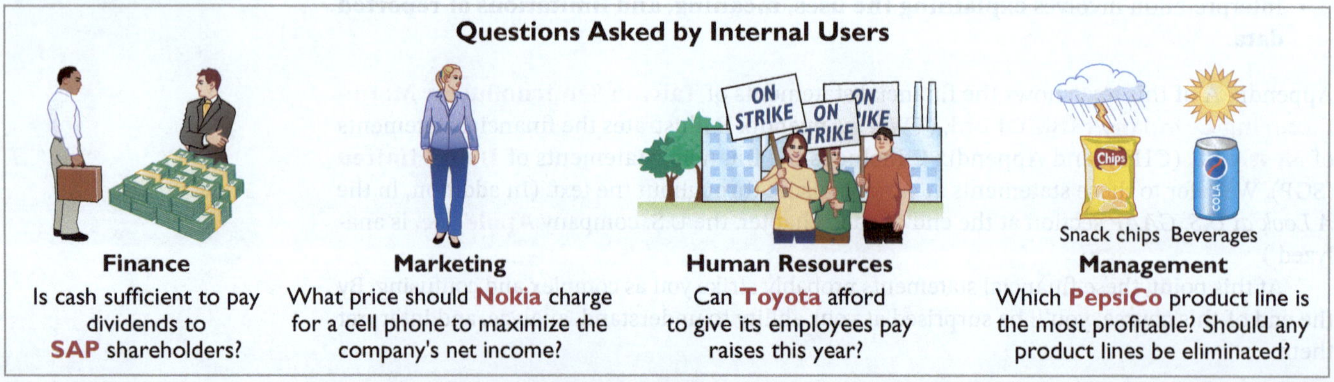

[2] The origins of accounting are generally attributed to the work of Luca Pacioli, an Italian Renaissance mathematician. Pacioli was a close friend and tutor to Leonardo da Vinci and a contemporary of Christopher Columbus. In his 1494 text *Summa de Arithmetica, Geometria, Proportione et Proportionalite*, Pacioli described a system to ensure that financial information was recorded efficiently and accurately.

To answer these and other questions, internal users need detailed information on a timely basis. **Managerial accounting** provides internal reports to help users make decisions about their companies. Examples are financial comparisons of operating alternatives, projections of income from new sales campaigns, and forecasts of cash needs for the next year.

External Users

External users are individuals and organizations outside a company who want financial information about the company. The two most common types of external users are investors and creditors.

- **Investors** (owners) use accounting information to decide whether to buy, hold, or sell ownership shares of a company.
- **Creditors** (such as suppliers and bankers) use accounting information to evaluate the risks of granting credit or lending money.

Illustration 1.3 shows some questions that investors and creditors may ask.

ILLUSTRATION 1.3 Questions that external users ask

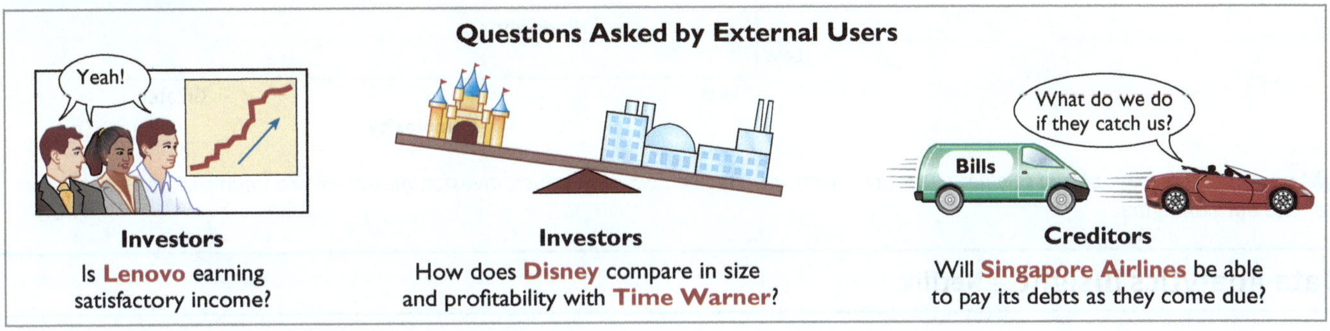

Financial accounting answers these questions. It provides economic and financial information for investors, creditors, and other external users. The information needs of external users vary considerably.

- **Taxing authorities**, such as the **State Administration of Taxation in the People's Republic of China** (CHN), want to know whether the company complies with tax laws.
- **Regulatory agencies**, such as the **Financial Services Authority of Indonesia** (IDN), want to know whether the company is operating within prescribed rules.
- **Customers** are interested in whether a company like **Tesla Motors, Inc.** (USA) will continue to honor product warranties and support its product lines.
- **Labor unions**, such as the **Indian National Trade Union Congress** (IND), want to know whether companies have the ability to pay increased wages and benefits to union members.

Data Analytics

Accounting software systems collect vast amounts of data about a company's economic events as well as its suppliers and customers. Business decision-makers take advantage of this wealth of data by using data analytics to gain insights and therefore make more informed business decisions.

Helpful Hints further clarify concepts being discussed.

- **Data analytics** involves analyzing data, often employing both software and statistics, to draw inferences.
- As both data access and analytical software improve, the use of data analytics to support decisions is becoming increasingly common at virtually all types of companies (see **Helpful Hint**).

HELPFUL HINT

Throughout this text, we will highlight examples where accounting information is used to support business decisions using data analytics.

Illustration 1.4 shows the four most common types of data analytics that help answer questions ranging from what happened and why did it happen, to what is likely to happen and what should we do about it? Analytics range from simple analysis that can be performed using spreadsheets with tools like pivot tables and graphs, to complex statistical software and even artificial intelligence. More complex analysis provides greater value to the business.

ILLUSTRATION 1.4

Four types of data analytics

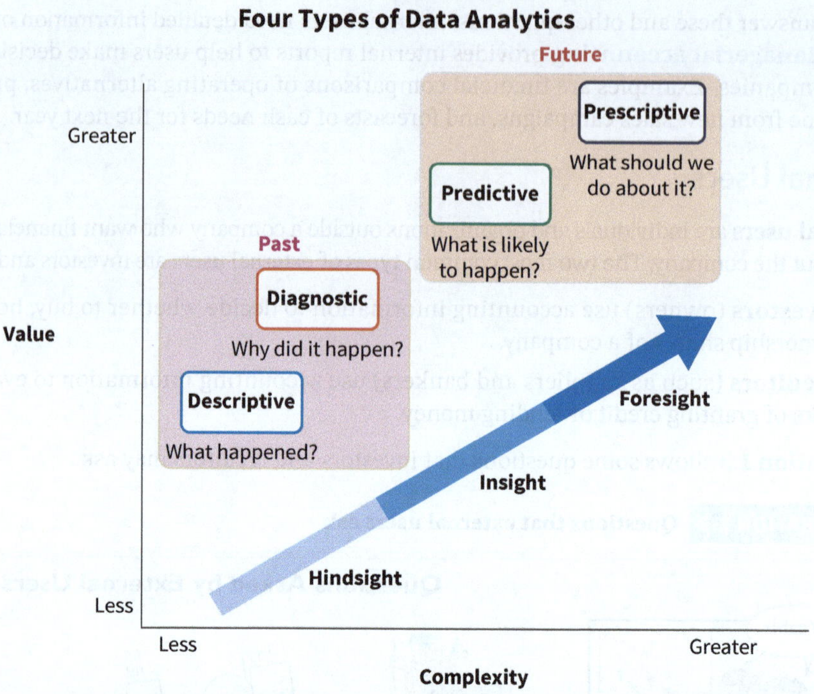

__Insight__ boxes provide examples of business situations from various perspectives—ethics; investor, global; environmental, social, and governance; and data analytics.

Data Analytics Insight Netflix

boumenjapet/Adobe Stock

Using Data Science to Create Art

Technology provides decision-makers and problem-solvers with access to a large volume of information called "big data." And **Netflix** (USA), the world's leading subscription streaming entertainment service, is tapping into this big data as part of its efforts to ramp up its original content production.

In a recent year, Netflix planned to spend $8 billion on content creation. Producing content involves a blend of creativity, technology, and business decisions, all of which result in costs. And by analyzing the large amounts of data from past productions, such as filming locations and production schedules, Netflix can more precisely estimate costs for future productions.

Further, consider that the production of a TV show or film involves hundreds of tasks. Here again, Netflix uses data science, in this case to visualize where bottlenecks might occur or where opportunities might exist to increase the efficiency of the production process.

Source: Based on Ritwik Kumar et al., "Data Science and the Art of Producing Entertainment at Netflix," *The Netflix Tech Blog* (March 26, 2018).

How can "big data" improve decision-making? (Answer is available near the end of the chapter.)

The __DO IT!__ exercises ask you to put newly acquired knowledge to work. They outline the Action Plan necessary to complete the exercise, and they show a Solution.

ACTION PLAN

- **Review the basic concepts discussed.**
- **Develop an understanding of the key terms used.**

DO IT! 1 | Basic Concepts

Indicate whether each of the five statements presented below is true or false. If false, indicate how to correct the statement.

1. The three steps in the accounting process are identification, recording, and communication.
2. Bookkeeping encompasses all steps in the accounting process.
3. Accountants prepare, but do not interpret, financial reports.
4. The two most common types of external users are investors and company officers.
5. Managerial accounting activities focus on reports for internal users.
6. Data analytics often employs both software and statistics to draw inferences.
7. Data analytics provides four types of data, including descriptive data mean what happened, diagnostic data mean why did it happen, predictive data mean what should we do about it, and prescriptive data mean what is likely to happen.
8. Employees must be internal users of accounting information.

Solution

1. True **2.** False. Bookkeeping involves only the recording step. **3.** False. Accountants analyze and interpret information in reports as part of the communication step. **4.** False. The two most common types of external users are investors and creditors. **5.** True. **6.** True. **7.** False. Predictive data mean what is likely to happen, and prescriptive data mean what should we do about it. **8.** False. When employees have decision-making authority over the company's affairs, they are internal users (ex : managers, including marketing managers, production supervisors, finance directors, and company officers etc.); otherwise, they are external users of accounting information.

Related exercise material: **DO IT! 1.1, E1.1, and E1.2.**

1.2 The Building Blocks of Accounting

LEARNING OBJECTIVE 2

Explain the building blocks of accounting: ethics, principles, and assumptions.

A doctor follows certain protocols in treating a patient's illness. An architect follows certain structural guidelines in designing a building. Similarly, an accountant follows certain standards in reporting financial information. These standards are based on specific principles and assumptions. For these standards to work, however, a fundamental business concept must be present—ethical behavior.

Ethics in Financial Reporting

People won't gamble in a casino if they think it is "rigged." Similarly, people won't invest in the securities market if they think share prices are rigged. In recent years, the financial press has been full of articles about financial scandals at **Mahindra Satyam** (IND), **Toshiba** (JPN), **Pou Sheng International** (HKG), **Siwei** (CHN), and other companies.

As the scandals came to light, mistrust of financial reporting in general grew. One article in the financial press noted that "repeated disclosures about questionable accounting practices have bruised investors' faith in the reliability of earnings reports, which in turn has sent share prices tumbling." Imagine trying to carry on a business or invest money if you could not depend on the financial statements to be honestly prepared. Information would have no credibility. There is no doubt that a sound, well-functioning economy depends on accurate and dependable financial reporting.

The standards of conduct by which actions are judged as right or wrong, honest or dishonest, fair or not fair, are **ethics**. Effective financial reporting depends on sound ethical behavior. To sensitize you to ethical situations in business and to give you practice at solving ethical dilemmas, we address ethics in a number of ways in this text:

1. A number of the *Feature Stories* and other parts of the text discuss the central importance of ethical behavior to financial reporting.
2. *Ethics Insight* boxes and marginal *Ethics Notes* highlight ethics situations and issues in actual business settings.
3. Many of the *Environmental, Social, and Governance Insight* boxes focus on ethical issues that companies face in measuring and reporting social and environmental issues.
4. At the end of the chapter, an *Ethics Case* simulates a business situation and asks you to put yourself in the position of a decision-maker in that case.

When analyzing these various ethics cases, as well as experiences in your own life, it is useful to apply the three steps outlined in **Illustration 1.5**.

ILLUSTRATION 1.5 **Steps in analyzing ethics cases and situations**

1. Recognize an ethical situation and the ethical issues involved.
Use your personal ethics to identify ethical situations and issues. Some businesses and professional organizations provide written codes of ethics for guidance in some business situations.

2. Identify and analyze the principal elements in the situation.
Identify the **stakeholders**—persons or groups who may be harmed or benefited. Ask the question: What are the responsibilities and obligations of the parties involved?

3. Identify the alternatives, and weigh the impact of each alternative on various stakeholders.
Select the most ethical alternative, considering all the consequences. Sometimes there will be one right answer. Other situations involve more than one right solution; these situations require an evaluation of each and a selection of the best alternative.

Ethics Insight Toshiba

nmann77/Adobe Stock

Loyalty to Your Employer Is Great, Until It Is Not

A common attribute of Japanese employees is a culture of strong loyalty to their employer. This loyalty arises out of a common practice of lifetime employment combined with a general cultural value of respect. While strong loyalty is a positive in many respects, it can create challenges in some circumstances.

For example, **Toshiba** (JPN), like many Japanese businesses, was severely affected by a series of events in the early 2000s. First, the company, along with the rest of the world, experienced the financial crisis and subsequent global recession in 2008 and 2009. Next, in 2011, an earthquake and subsequent tsunami in northern Japan triggered a significant recession in Japan. The company experienced a 14% decline in revenue from 2007 to 2013, and a 90% decline in profits over the same period.

In response to these events, company leadership began to pressure divisional and mid-level managers to achieve unreasonable financial goals. These managers, unable to meet the unreasonably high performance expectations and influenced by a strong culture of loyalty and respect, were left with little choice but to create profits where there were none. They committed a number of financial frauds, including unreasonable estimates and improper recording of transactions with suppliers.

In 2015, when these matters came to light, it was determined that reported revenues during this period had been overstated by ¥129 million and profits for the period has been overstated by ¥477 million.

Source: Based on Dennis Caplan, Saurav Dutta, and David Marchinko, "Unmasking the Fraud at Toshiba," *Issues in Accounting Education*, Vol. 34, No. 3 (August 2019).

What would you do if your company asked you to misreport an item? (Answer is available near the end of the chapter.)

Accounting Standards

In order to ensure high-quality financial reporting, accountants present financial statements in conformity with accounting standards that are issued by standard-setting bodies. Presently, there are two primary accounting standard-setting bodies—the **International Accounting Standards Board (IASB)** and the **Financial Accounting Standards Board (FASB)**.

- More than 150 countries follow standards referred to as **International Financial Reporting Standards (IFRS)**.
- IFRSs are determined by the IASB. The IASB is headquartered in London, with its board members drawn from around the world.
- Most companies in the United States follow standards issued by the FASB, referred to as **generally accepted accounting principles (GAAP)**.

As markets become more global, it is often desirable to compare the results of companies from different countries that report using different accounting standards. We provide at the end of each chapter a section called *A Look at U.S. GAAP*, to provide a comparison with IFRS.

Global Insight

Toru-Hanai/Pool/Getty Images

The Korean Discount

If you think that accounting standards don't matter, consider these events in South Korea. For many years, international investors complained that the financial reports of South Korean companies were inadequate and inaccurate. Accounting practices there often resulted in huge differences between stated revenues and actual revenues. Because investors did not have faith in the accuracy of the numbers, they were unwilling to pay as much for the shares of these companies relative to shares of comparable companies in different countries. This difference in share price was often referred to as the "Korean discount."

In response, Korean regulators decided that companies would have to comply with international accounting standards. This change was motivated by a desire to "make the country's businesses more transparent" in order to build investor confidence and spur economic growth. Many other Asian countries, including China, India, Japan, and Hong Kong, have also decided either to adopt international standards or to create standards that are based on the international standards.

Source: Based on Evan Ramstad, "End to 'Korea Discount'?" *Wall Street Journal* (March 16, 2007).

What is meant by the phrase "make the country's businesses more transparent"? Why would increasing transparency spur economic growth? (Answer is available near the end of the chapter.)

Measurement Principles

IFRS uses one of two measurement bases, the historical cost basis or the current value basis. Selection of which basis to use is generally determined by considering the qualitative characteristics of useful information, including relevance and faithful representation (see **Helpful Hint**). **Relevance** means that financial information is capable of making a difference in a decision. **Faithful representation** means that the numbers and descriptions match what really existed or happened—they are factual.

HELPFUL HINT

***Relevance* and *faithful representation* are two primary qualities that make accounting information useful for decision-making.**

Historical Cost

The **historical cost basis** records and reports assets at their cost. This is true not only at the time the asset is purchased, but also over the time the asset is held. For example, if Great Wall Manufacturing purchases land for ¥300,000 (amounts in thousands), the company initially reports it in its accounting records at ¥300,000. But what does Great Wall do if, by the end of the next year, the current value of the land has increased to ¥400,000? Under the historical cost basis, it continues to report the land at ¥300,000.

Current Value

The **current value basis** records and reports assets and other accounts at current value. Depending on the nature of the item being reported, current value is determined based on the item's fair value (the price received to sell an asset or settle a liability), value in use (the present value of the future cash flows associated with the item), or current cost (the current replacement cost of the item).

Current value information may be more useful than historical cost for certain types of assets and liabilities. For example, certain investment securities are reported at current value because market value information is usually readily available for these types of assets.

- In determining which measurement basis to use, companies weigh the factual nature of historical cost figures versus the relevance of current value.
- In general, even though IFRS allows companies to revalue property, plant, and equipment and other long-lived assets to current value, most companies choose to use cost.

Only in situations where assets are actively traded, such as investment securities, do companies apply the current value extensively.

Assumptions

Assumptions provide a foundation for the accounting process. Two main assumptions are the **monetary unit assumption** and the **economic entity assumption**.

Monetary Unit Assumption

The **monetary unit assumption** requires that companies include in the accounting records only transaction data that can be expressed in money terms. This assumption enables accounting to quantify (measure) economic events. The monetary unit assumption is vital to using the historical cost basis.

This assumption prevents the inclusion of some relevant information in the accounting records. For example, the health of a company's owner, the quality of service, and the morale of employees are not included. The reason: Companies cannot quantify this information in money terms. Though this information is important, companies record only events that can be measured in money. Throughout this text, we use a variety of currencies in our examples and end-of-chapter materials, such as the following.

Australia, dollar	$	Russia, ruble	₽
Brazil, real	R$	South Africa, rand	R
China, yuan renminbi	¥	South Korea, won	₩
Europe, euro	€	Switzerland, Swiss franc	CHF
Hong Kong, dollar	HK$	Taiwan, new dollar	NT$
India, rupee	₹	Turkey, lira	₺
Indonesia, rupia	Rp	United Kingdom, pound	£
Japan, yen	¥	United States, dollar	$

ETHICS NOTE

The importance of the economic entity assumption is illustrated by scandals involving Adelphia (USA). In this case, senior company employees entered into transactions that blurred the line between the employees' financial interests and those of the company. For example, Adelphia guaranteed over $2 billion of loans to the founding family.

Ethics Notes help sensitize you to some of the ethical issues in accounting.

Economic Entity Assumption

An economic entity can be any organization or unit in society. It may be a company (such as Maruti Suzuki (IND)), a governmental unit (the Indonesian province of Papua), a municipality (Beijing), or a temple (the Temple of the Six Banyan Trees). The **economic entity assumption** requires that the activities of the entity be kept separate and distinct from the activities of its owner and all other economic entities. To illustrate, Barb Su, owner of Barb's Bike Shop, must keep her personal living costs separate from the expenses of the business. Similarly, Maxway Cycles Co. (TWN) and Asia Bicycle Trading Company (TWN) are segregated into separate economic entities for accounting purposes (see **Ethics Note**).

Proprietorship A business owned by one person is generally a **proprietorship**. The owner is often the manager/operator of the business. Small service-type businesses (plumbing companies, beauty salons, and auto repair shops), farms, and small retail stores (antique shops, clothing stores, and used-book stores) are often proprietorships.

- Usually, only a relatively small amount of money (capital) is necessary to start in business as a proprietorship.
- The owner (proprietor) receives any profits, suffers any losses, and is personally liable for all debts of the business.

There is no legal distinction between the business as an economic unit and the owner, but the accounting records of the business activities are kept separate from the personal records and activities of the owner.

Partnership A business owned by two or more persons associated as partners is a **partnership**. In most respects a partnership is like a proprietorship except that more than one owner is involved.

- Typically, a partnership agreement (written or oral) sets forth such terms as initial investment, duties of each partner, division of net income (or net loss), and settlement to be made upon death or withdrawal of a partner.
- Each partner generally has unlimited personal liability for the debts of the partnership.
- Like a proprietorship, for accounting purposes the partnership transactions must be kept separate from the personal activities of the partners.

Partnerships are often used to organize retail and service-type businesses, including professional practices (lawyers, doctors, architects, and accountants).

Corporation A business organized as a separate legal entity under jurisdiction corporation law and having ownership divided into transferable shares is a **corporation**.

- The holders of the shares (shareholders) enjoy limited liability; that is, they are not personally liable for the debts of the corporate entity.
- Shareholders may transfer all or part of their ownership shares to other investors at any time (i.e., sell their shares). The ease with which ownership can change adds to the attractiveness of investing in a corporation.
- Because ownership can be transferred without dissolving the corporation, the corporation enjoys an unlimited life.

Although the combined number of proprietorships and partnerships in the world significantly exceeds the number of corporations, the revenue produced by corporations is much greater. Most of the largest companies in the world—for example, **ING** (NLD), **Royal Dutch Shell** (GBR and NLD), **Apple Inc.** (USA), **Fortis** (BEL), and **Toyota** (JPN)—are corporations.

Accounting Across the Organization

blublaf/E+/Getty Images

Spinning the Career Wheel

One question that students frequently ask is, "How will the study of accounting help me?" A working knowledge of accounting is desirable for virtually *every field* of endeavor. Some examples of how accounting is used in other careers include the following.

General management: Imagine running **Volkswagen** (DEU), **Saudi Telecom** (SAU), a **Subway** (USA) franchise, or a **Fuji** (JPN) bike shop. All general managers need to understand where the company's cash comes from and where it goes in order to make wise business decisions.

Marketing: Marketing specialists at a company like **Hyundai Motor** (KOR) develop strategies to help the sales force be successful. But making a sale is meaningless unless it is profitable. Marketing people must be sensitive to costs and benefits, which accounting helps them quantify and understand.

Finance: Do you want to be a banker for **Shanghai Commercial and Savings Bank** (TWN) or a financial analyst for **ICBC** (CHN)? These fields rely heavily on accounting. In all of them, you will regularly examine and analyze financial statements. In fact, it is difficult to get a good finance job without two or three courses in accounting.

Real estate: Are you interested in being a real estate broker for **Hong Kong Property Services** (HKG)? Because a third party—the bank—is almost always involved in financing a real estate transaction, brokers must understand the numbers involved: Can the buyer afford to make the payments to the bank? Does the cash flow from an industrial property justify the purchase price? What are the tax benefits of the purchase?

How might accounting help you? (Answer is available near the end of the chapter.)

DO IT! 2 | Building Blocks of Accounting

Indicate whether each of the five statements presented below is true or false. If false, indicate how to correct the statement.

1. Ethics are the standards of conduct by which actions are judged as right or wrong, honest or dishonest, fair or not fair.
2. The primary accounting standard-setting body headquartered in London is the International Accounting Standards Board (IASB).
3. An asset recorded using the historical cost basis results in recording assets at their cost. In later periods, however, the current value of the asset must be used if current value is higher than its cost.
4. Relevance means that financial information matches what really happened; the information is factual.
5. A business owner's personal expenses must be separated from expenses of the business to comply with accounting's economic entity assumption.
6. The monetary unit assumption enables companies to record all economic events, regardless of these economic information whether can be quantified.

ACTION PLAN

- **Review the discussion of ethics and financial reporting standards.**
- **Develop an understanding of the key terms used.**

Solution

1. True. **2.** True. **3.** False. Assets recorded using the historical cost basis are not adjusted in later periods to current value. They remain at their original cost. **4.** False. Faithful representation means that financial information matches what really happened; the information is factual. **5.** True. **6.** False. The monetary unit assumption requires companies record only events that can be measured in money.

Related exercise material: **DO IT! 1.2, E1.3, and E1.4.**

1.3 The Accounting Equation

LEARNING OBJECTIVE 3

State the accounting equation, and define its components.

The two basic elements of a business are what it owns and what it owes.

- **Assets** are the resources a business owns. For example, **adidas** (DEU) has total assets of approximately €15,176 billion. Liabilities and equity are the rights or claims against these resources. Thus, adidas has €15,176 billion of claims against its €15,176 billion of assets.
- Claims of those to whom the company owes money (creditors) are called **liabilities.**
- Claims of owners are called **equity.** adidas has liabilities of €8,721 billion and equity of €6,455 billion.

We can express the relationship of assets, liabilities, and equity as an equation, as shown in **Illustration 1.6.**

ILLUSTRATION 1.6
The basic accounting equation

Assets	=	Liabilities	+	Equity

This relationship is the **basic accounting equation.**

- Assets must equal the sum of liabilities and equity.
- Liabilities appear before equity in the basic accounting equation because they are paid first if a business is liquidated.

The accounting equation applies to all **economic entities** regardless of size, nature of business, or form of business organization. It applies to a small proprietorship such as a corner grocery store as well as to a giant corporation such as adidas. The equation provides the **underlying framework** for recording and summarizing economic events.

Let's look in more detail at the categories in the basic accounting equation.

Assets

As noted previously, **assets** are resources a business owns. The business uses its assets in carrying out such activities as production and sales.

- The common characteristic possessed by all assets is **the capacity to provide future services or benefits.**
- In a business, that service potential or future economic benefit eventually results in cash inflows (receipts).

For example, consider Taipei Pizza, a local restaurant. It owns a delivery truck that provides economic benefits from delivering pizzas. Other assets of Taipei Pizza are tables, chairs, sound system, cash register, oven, tableware, and, of course, cash.

Liabilities

Liabilities are claims against assets—that is, existing debts and obligations. Businesses of all sizes usually borrow money and purchase merchandise on credit. These economic activities result in payables of various sorts:

- Taipei Pizza, for instance, purchases cheese, sausage, flour, and beverages on credit from suppliers. These obligations are called **accounts payable**.
- Taipei Pizza also has a **note payable** to First Bank for the money borrowed to purchase the delivery truck.
- Taipei Pizza may also have **salaries and wages payable** to employees and **sales and real estate taxes payable** to the local government.

All of these persons or entities to whom Taipei Pizza owes money are its **creditors**.

Creditors may legally force the liquidation of a business that does not pay its debts. In that case, the law requires that creditor claims be paid **before** ownership claims.

Equity

The ownership claim on a company's total assets is **equity**. It is equal to total assets minus total liabilities. Here is why.

- The assets of a business are claimed by either creditors or shareholders. To find out what belongs to shareholders, we subtract creditors' claims (the liabilities) from the assets.
- The remainder is the shareholders' claim on the assets—equity. It is often referred to as **residual equity**—that is, the equity "left over" after creditors' claims are satisfied.

Equity generally consists of (1) share capital—ordinary and (2) retained earnings.

Share Capital—Ordinary

A company may obtain funds by selling ordinary shares to investors. **Share capital—ordinary** is the term used to describe the amounts paid in by shareholders for the ordinary shares they purchase.

Retained Earnings

Retained earnings is determined by three items: revenues, expenses, and dividends.

Revenues **Revenues are the gross increases in equity resulting from business activities entered into for the purpose of earning income** (see **Helpful Hint**).[3] Generally, revenues result from selling merchandise, performing services, renting property, and lending money.

> **HELPFUL HINT**
> **The effect of revenues is positive—an increase in equity coupled with an increase in assets or a decrease in liabilities.**

Revenues usually result in an increase in an asset. They may arise from different sources and are called various names depending on the nature of the business. Taipai Pizza, for instance, has two categories of sales revenues—pizza sales and beverage sales. Other titles for and sources of revenue common to many businesses are sales, fees, services, commissions, interest, dividends, royalties, and rent.

Expenses **Expenses** are the cost of assets consumed or services used in the process of earning revenue. **They are decreases in equity that result from operating the business** (see **Helpful Hint**). Like revenues, expenses take many forms and are called various names depending on the type of asset consumed or service used.

> **HELPFUL HINT**
> **The effect of expenses is negative—a decrease in equity coupled with a decrease in assets or an increase in liabilities.**

For example, Taipai Pizza recognizes the following types of expenses: cost of ingredients (flour, cheese, tomato paste, meat, mushrooms, etc.), cost of beverages, wages expense, utili-

---

[3] IFRS uses both the term income and the term revenue to refer to the increase in equity resulting from business activities entered into for the purpose of earning income. To avoid confusion, we will use the term revenue consistently in this text.

ties expense (electric, gas, and water expense), telephone expense, delivery expense (gasoline, repairs, licenses, etc.), supplies expense (napkins, detergents, aprons, etc.), rent expense, interest expense, and property tax expense.

Dividends Net income represents an increase in net assets which is then available to distribute to shareholders. The distribution of cash or other assets to shareholders is called a **dividend**.

- Dividends reduce retained earnings.
- However, dividends are **not expenses.**

A corporation first determines its revenues and expenses and then computes net income or net loss. If it has net income, and decides it has no better use for that income, a corporation may decide to distribute a dividend to its owners (the shareholders).

In summary, the principal sources (increases) of equity are investments by shareholders and revenues from business operations. In contrast, reductions (decreases) in equity result from expenses and dividends. These relationships are shown in **Illustration 1.7**.

ILLUSTRATION 1.7 Increases and decreases in equity

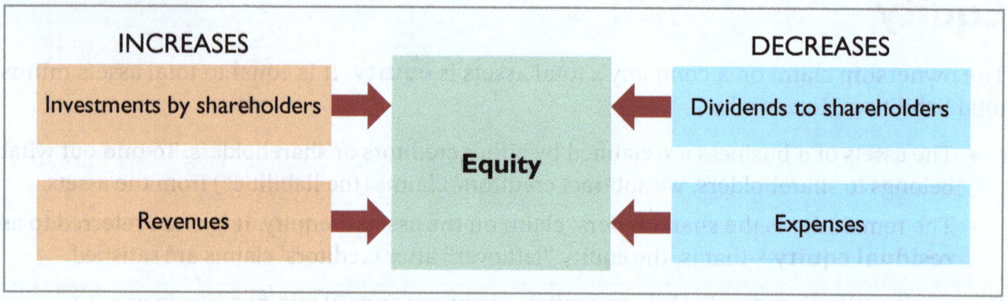

ACTION PLAN

- **Understand the sources of revenue.**
- **Understand what causes expenses.**
- **Review the rules for changes in equity: Investments and revenues increase equity. Expenses and dividends decrease equity.**
- **Recognize that dividends are distributions of cash or other assets to shareholders.**

DO IT! 3 | Equity Effects

Classify the following items as issuance of shares (I), dividends (D), revenues (R), or expenses (E). Then indicate whether each item increases or decreases equity.

a. Rent Expense.
b. Service Revenue.
c. Dividends.
d. Salaries and Wages Expense.
e. Investments by shareholders.
f. Purchase of equipment for cash.

Solution

a. Rent Expense is an expense (E); it decreases equity. **b.** Service Revenue is a revenue (R); it increases equity. **c.** Dividends is a distribution to shareholders (D); it decreases equity. **d.** Salaries and Wages Expense is an expense (E); it decreases equity. **e.** Investments by shareholders is the amounts paid by shareholders for the ordinary shares they purchase; it increases equity. **f.** Purchase of equipment for cash only effects the components of assets, no effect of equity.

Related exercise material: **BE1.1, BE1.2, BE1.3, BE1.4, BE1.5, BE1.6, DO IT! 1.3, and E1.5.**

1.4 Analyzing Business Transactions

LEARNING OBJECTIVE 4

Analyze the effects of business transactions on the accounting equation.

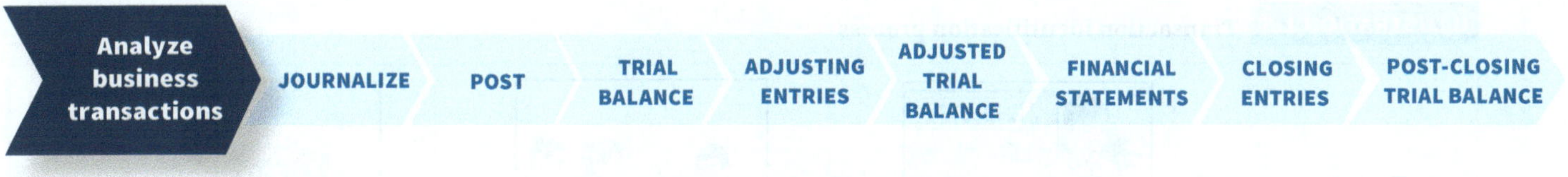

This ***accounting cycle graphic*** *illustrates the steps companies follow each period to record transactions and eventually prepare financial statements.*

The system of collecting and processing transaction data and communicating financial information to decision-makers is known as the **accounting information system**. Factors that shape an accounting information system include the nature of the company's business, the types of transactions, the size of the company, the volume of data, and the information demands of management and others.

Most businesses use computerized accounting systems—sometimes referred to as electronic data processing (EDP) systems. These systems handle all the steps involved in the recording process, from initial data entry to preparation of the financial statements. Many companies upgraded their accounting information systems to prevent cybersecurity attacks. In addition, companies are utilizing new technologies.

- Cloud-based storage permits employees to access records from different locations.
- Data automation and analytics tools help companies interpret large volumes of data to support enhanced decision-making and automating routine processes.

In order to remain competitive, companies continually improve their accounting systems to provide accurate and timely data for decision-making. For example, in a recent annual report, **Tootsie Roll** (USA) stated, "We also invested in additional processing and data storage hardware during the year. We view information technology as a key strategic tool, and are committed to deploying leading edge technology in this area."

Accounting information systems rely on a process referred to as **the accounting cycle**. As you can see from the graphic, the accounting cycle begins with the analysis of business transactions and ends with the preparation of a post-closing trial balance. We explain each of the steps, starting in this chapter and continuing in Chapters 2–4.

In this text, in order to emphasize the underlying concepts and principles, we focus on a manual accounting system. The accounting concepts and principles do not change whether a system is computerized or manual.

Accounting Transactions

Transactions (**business transactions**) are a business's economic events recorded by accountants. Transactions may be external or internal.

- **External transactions** involve economic events between the company and some outside enterprise. For example, Taipai Pizza's purchase of cooking equipment from a supplier, payment of monthly rent to the landlord, and sale of pizzas to customers are external transactions.
- **Internal transactions** are economic events that occur entirely within one company. The use of cooking and cleaning supplies are internal transactions for Taipai Pizza.

Companies carry on many activities that do not represent business transactions. Examples are hiring employees, responding to e-mails, talking with customers, and placing merchandise orders. Some of these activities may lead to business transactions. Employees will earn wages, and suppliers will deliver ordered merchandise.

A company must analyze each event to find out if it affects the components of the accounting equation. If it does, the company will record the transaction. **Illustration 1.8** demonstrates the transaction identification process.

Each transaction must have a dual effect on the accounting equation. For example, if an asset is increased, there must be a corresponding:

- Decrease in another asset, *or*
- Increase in a specific liability, *or*
- Increase in equity.

ILLUSTRATION 1.8 **Transaction identification process**

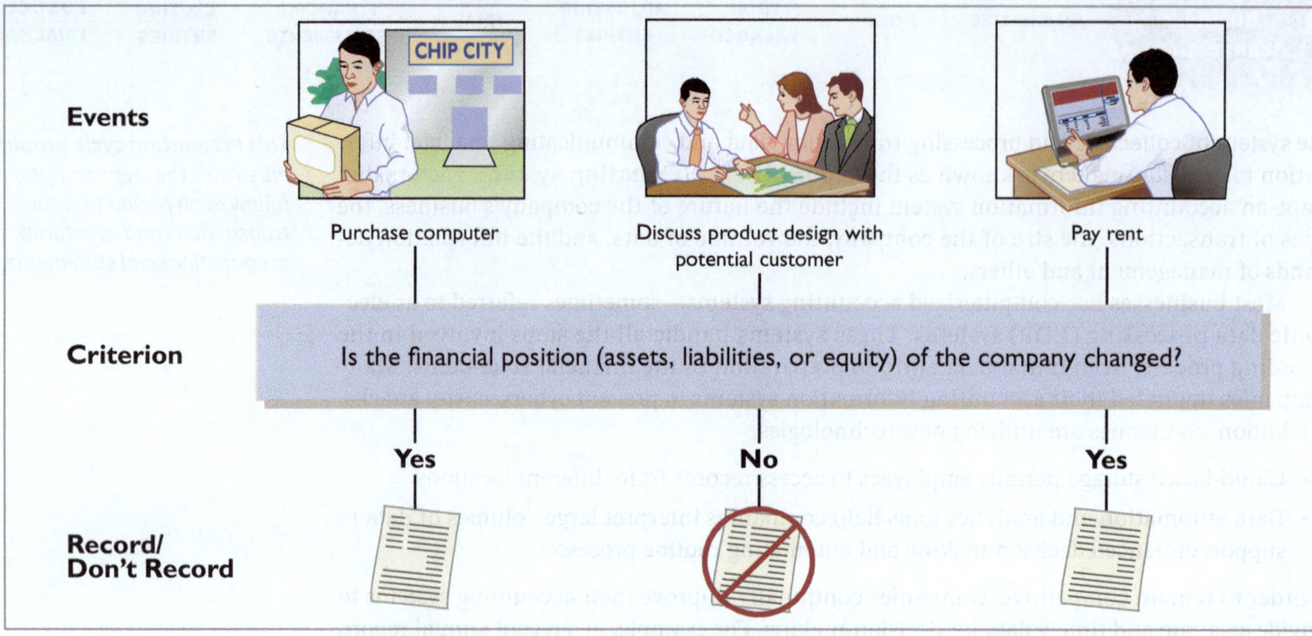

Two or more items could be affected. For example, as one asset is increased €10,000, another asset could decrease €6,000 and a liability could increase €4,000. Any change in a liability or ownership claim is subject to similar analysis.

Transaction Analysis

To demonstrate how to analyze transactions in terms of the accounting equation, we will review the business activities of Softbyte SA. As part of this analysis, we will expand the basic accounting equation. This will allow us to better illustrate the impact of transactions on equity. Recall that equity is comprised of two parts: share capital—ordinary and retained earnings.

- Share capital—ordinary is affected when the company issues new ordinary shares in exchange for cash.
- Retained earnings is affected when the company earns revenue, incurs expenses, or pays dividends.

Illustration 1.9 shows the **expanded accounting equation.**

ILLUSTRATION 1.9 **Expanded accounting equation**

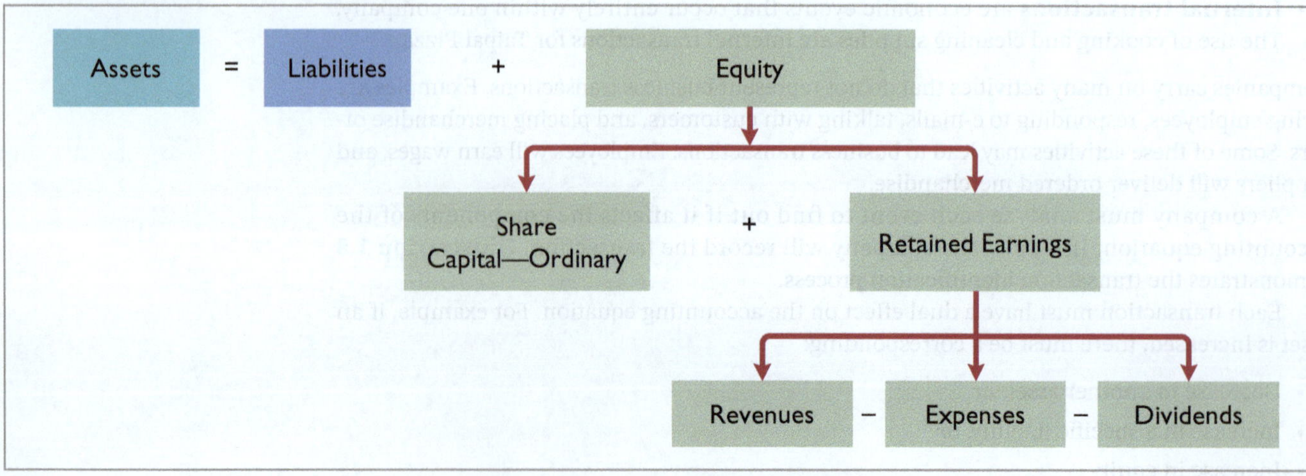

If you are tempted to skip ahead after you've read a few of the following transaction analyses, don't do it. Each has something unique to teach, something you'll need later (see **Helpful Hint**). (We assure you that we've kept them to the minimum needed!)

HELPFUL HINT

You will want to study these transactions until you are sure you understand them. They are not difficult, but understanding them is important to your success in this course. The ability to analyze transactions in terms of the basic accounting equation is essential in accounting.

Transaction (1). Investment by Shareholders Ray and Barbara Neal decide to start a smartphone app development company that they incorporate as Softbyte SA. On September 1, 2029, they invest €15,000 cash in the business in exchange for €15,000 of ordinary shares. The ordinary shares indicates the ownership interest that the Neals have in Softbyte SA. This transaction results in an equal increase in both assets and equity.[4]

Basic Analysis	The asset Cash increases €15,000, and equity identified as Share Capital—Ordinary increases €15,000.

Equation Analysis

	Assets	=	Liabilities	+	Equity	
	Cash	=			Share Capital	
(1)	+€15,000	=			+€15,000	Issued Shares

Observe that the equality of the basic equation has been maintained. Note also that the source of the increase in equity (in this case, issued shares) is indicated. Why does this matter?

- Because investments by shareholders do not represent revenues, and they are excluded in determining net income.
- Therefore, it is necessary to make clear that the increase is an investment rather than revenue from operations.

Additional investments (i.e., investments made by shareholders after the corporation has been initially formed) have the same effect on equity as the initial investment.

Transaction (2). Purchase of Equipment for Cash Softbyte SA purchases computer equipment for €7,000 cash. This transaction results in an equal increase and decrease in total assets, though the composition of assets changes.

Basic Analysis	The asset Cash decreases €7,000, and the asset Equipment increases €7,000.

Equation Analysis

	Assets			=	Liabilities	+	Equity
	Cash	+	Equipment	=			Share Capital
	€15,000						€15,000
(2)	−7,000		+€7,000				
	€ 8,000	+	€7,000	=			€15,000
	€15,000						

Observe that total assets are still €15,000. Share Capital—Ordinary also remains at €15,000, the amount of the original investment.

Transaction (3). Purchase of Supplies on Credit Softbyte SA purchases headsets (and other computer accessories expected to last several months) for €1,600 from Mobile Solutions. Mobile Solutions agrees to allow Softbyte to pay this bill in October.

- This transaction is a purchase on account (a credit purchase).
- Assets increase because of the expected future benefits of using the headsets and computer accessories, and liabilities increase by the amount due Mobile Solutions.

[4] For the illustrative equations that follow, we use the general account title "Share Capital" instead of "Share Capital—Ordinary" for space considerations.

Basic Analysis The asset Supplies increases €1,600, and the liability Accounts Payable increases €1,600.

Equation Analysis

	Assets					=	Liabilities	+	Equity
							Accounts		Share
	Cash	+	Supplies	+	Equipment	=	Payable	+	Capital
	€8,000				€7,000				€15,000
(3)			+€1,600				+€1,600		
	€8,000	+	€1,600	+	€7,000	=	€1,600	+	€15,000
			€16,600				€16,600		

Total assets are now €16,600. This total is matched by a €1,600 creditor's claim and a €15,000 ownership claim.

Transaction (4). Services Performed for Cash Softbyte SA receives €1,200 cash from customers for app development services it has performed. This transaction represents Softbyte's principal revenue-producing activity. Recall that **revenue increases equity**.

Basic Analysis The asset Cash increases €1,200, and equity increases €1,200 due to Service Revenue.

Equation Analysis

	Assets					=	Liabilities	+	Equity							
							Accounts		Share		Retained Earnings					
	Cash	+	Supplies	+	Equipment	=	Payable	+	Capital	+	Rev.	−	Exp.	−	Div.	
	€8,000		€1,600		€7,000		€1,600		€15,000							
(4)	+1,200										+€1,200					Service Revenue
	€9,200	+	€1,600	+	€7,000	=	€1,600	+	€15,000	+	€1,200					
			€17,800						€17,800							

The two sides of the equation balance at €17,800. Service Revenue is included in determining Softbyte's net income.

- Note that we do not have room to give details for each individual revenue and expense account in this illustration. Thus, revenues (and expenses when we get to them) are summarized under one column heading for Revenues and one for Expenses.
- However, it is important to keep track of the category (account) titles affected (e.g., Service Revenue) as they will be needed when we prepare financial statements later in the chapter.

Transaction (5). Purchase of Advertising on Credit Softbyte SA receives a bill for €250 from *Programming News* for advertising on its website but postpones payment until a later date. This transaction results in an increase in liabilities and a decrease in equity.

Basic Analysis The liability Accounts Payable increases €250, and equity decreases €250 due to Advertising Expense.

Equation Analysis

	Assets					=	Liabilities	+	Equity							
							Accounts		Share		Retained Earnings					
	Cash	+	Supplies	+	Equipment	=	Payable	+	Capital	+	Rev.	−	Exp.	−	Div.	
	€9,200		€1,600		€7,000		€1,600		€15,000		€1,200					
(5)							+250						−€250			Advertising Expense
	€9,200	+	€1,600	+	€7,000	=	€1,850	+	€15,000	+	€1,200	−	€250			
			€17,800						€17,800							

The two sides of the equation still balance at €17,800. Retained Earnings decreases when Softbyte incurs the expense.

- Expenses do not have to be paid in cash at the time they are incurred.
- When Softbyte pays at a later date, the liability Accounts Payable will decrease and the asset Cash will decrease [see Transaction (8)].

The cost of advertising is an expense (rather than an asset) because Softbyte has used the benefits. Advertising Expense is included in determining net income.

Transaction (6). Services Performed for Cash and Credit Softbyte SA performs €3,500 of app development services for customers. The company receives cash of €1,500 from customers, and it bills the balance of €2,000 on account. This transaction results in an equal increase in assets and equity.

Basic Analysis	Three specific items are affected: The asset Cash increases €1,500, the asset Accounts Receivable increases €2,000, and equity increases €3,500 due to Service Revenue.

Equation Analysis

	Assets				= Liabilities +	Equity				
	Cash +	Accounts Receivable +	Supplies +	Equipment =	Accounts Payable +	Share Capital +	Retained Earnings Rev. −	Exp. −	Div.	
	€ 9,200		€1,600	€7,000	€1,850	€15,000	€1,200	€250		
(6)	+1,500	+€2,000					+3,500			Service Revenue
	€10,700 +	€2,000 +	€1,600 +	€7,000 =	€1,850 +	€15,000 +	€4,700 −	€250		
	€21,300				€21,300					

Softbyte recognizes €3,500 in revenue when it performs the services. In exchange for these services, it received €1,500 in Cash and Accounts Receivable of €2,000. This Accounts Receivable represents customers' promise to pay €2,000 to Softbyte in the future. When it later receives collections on account, Softbyte will increase Cash and will decrease Accounts Receivable [see Transaction (9)].

Transaction (7). Payment of Expenses Softbyte SA pays the following expenses in cash for September: office rent €600, salaries and wages of employees €900, and utilities €200. These payments result in an equal decrease in assets and equity.

Basic Analysis	The asset Cash decreases €1,700, and equity decreases €1,700 due to the following specific expenses: Rent Expense, Salaries and Wages Expense, and Utilities Expense.

Equation Analysis

	Assets				= Liabilities +	Equity				
	Cash +	Accounts Receivable +	Supplies +	Equipment =	Accounts Payable +	Share Capital +	Retained Earnings Rev. −	Exp. −	Div.	
	€10,700	€2,000	€1,600	€7,000	€1,850	€15,000	€4,700	€ 250		
(7)	−1,700							−600		Rent Exp.
								−900		Sal./Wages Exp.
								−200		Utilities Exp.
	€ 9,000 +	€2,000 +	€1,600 +	€7,000 =	€1,850 +	€15,000 +	€4,700 −	€1,950		
	€19,600				€19,600					

The two sides of the equation now balance at €19,600. Three lines are required in the analysis to indicate the different types of expenses that have been incurred.

Transaction (8). Payment of Accounts Payable Softbyte SA pays its €250 *Programming News* bill in cash. The company previously [in Transaction (5)] recorded the bill as an increase in Accounts Payable and a decrease in equity.

Basic Analysis This cash payment "on account" decreases the asset Cash by €250 and also decreases the liability Accounts Payable by €250.

Equation Analysis

	Assets				= Liabilities +	Equity			
	Cash	+ Accounts Receivable	+ Supplies	+ Equipment	= Accounts Payable	+ Share Capital	+ Retained Earnings Rev.	− Exp.	− Div.
	€9,000	€2,000	€1,600	€7,000	€1,850	€15,000	€4,700	€1,950	
(8)	−250				−250				
	€8,750 +	€2,000 +	€1,600 +	€7,000 =	€1,600 +	€15,000 +	€4,700 −	€1,950	
	€19,350				€19,350				

Observe that the payment of a liability related to an expense that has previously been recorded does not affect equity. Softbyte recorded the expense [in Transaction (5)] and should not record it again.

Transaction (9). Receipt of Cash on Account Softbyte SA receives €600 in cash from customers who had been billed for services [in Transaction (6)]. Transaction (9) does not change total assets, but it changes the composition of those assets.

Basic Analysis The asset Cash increases €600, and the asset Accounts Receivable decreases €600.

Equation Analysis

	Assets				= Liabilities +	Equity			
	Cash	+ Accounts Receivable	+ Supplies	+ Equipment	= Accounts Payable	+ Share Capital	+ Retained Earnings Rev.	− Exp.	− Div.
	€8,750	€2,000	€1,600	€7,000	€1,600	€15,000	€4,700	€1,950	
(9)	+600	−600							
	€9,350 +	€1,400 +	€1,600 +	€7,000 =	€1,600 +	€15,000 +	€4,700 −	€1,950	
	€19,350				€19,350				

Note that the collection of an account receivable for services previously billed and recorded does not affect equity. Softbyte already recorded this revenue [in Transaction (6)] and should not record it again.

Transaction (10). Dividends The company pays a dividend of €1,300 in cash to Ray and Barbara Neal, the shareholders of Softbyte SA. This transaction results in an equal decrease in assets and equity.

Basic Analysis The asset Cash decreases €1,300, and equity decreases €1,300 due to dividends.

Equation Analysis

	Assets				= Liabilities +	Equity				
	Cash	+ Accounts Receivable	+ Supplies	+ Equipment	= Accounts Payable	+ Share Capital	+ Retained Earnings Rev.	− Exp.	− Div.	
	€9,350	€1,400	€1,600	€7,000	€1,600	€15,000	€4,700	€1,950		
(10)	−1,300								−€1,300	Dividends
	€8,050 +	€1,400 +	€1,600 +	€7,000 =	€1,600 +	€15,000 +	€4,700 −	€1,950 −	€1,300	
	€18,050				€18,050					

Note that the dividend reduces retained earnings, which is part of equity. **Dividends are not expenses**. Like shareholders' investments, dividends are excluded in determining net income.

Summary of Transactions

Illustration 1.10 summarizes the September transactions of Softbyte SA to show their cumulative effect on the basic accounting equation. It also indicates the transaction number and the specific effects of each transaction. Finally, Illustration 1.10 demonstrates a number of significant facts:

1. Each transaction must be analyzed in terms of its effect on:
   a. The three components of the basic accounting equation.
   b. Specific types (kinds) of items within each component.
2. The two sides of the equation must always be equal.
3. The Share Capital—Ordinary and Retained Earnings columns indicate the causes of each change in the shareholders' claim on assets.

ILLUSTRATION 1.10 **Tabular summary of Softbyte SA transactions**

	Assets				= Liabilities +	Equity				
							Retained Earnings			
Transaction	Cash	+ Accounts Receivable	+ Supplies	+ Equipment	= Accounts Payable	+ Share Capital	+ Rev.	− Exp.	− Div.	
(1)	+€15,000					+ €15,000				Issued Shares
(2)	−7,000			+€7,000						
(3)			+€1,600		+€1,600					
(4)	+1,200						+€1,200			Service Revenue
(5)					+250			−€250		Adver. Expense
(6)	+1,500	+€2,000					+3,500			Service Revenue
(7)	−1,700							−600		Rent Expense
								−900		Sal./Wages Exp.
								−200		Utilities Expense
(8)	−250				−250					
(9)	+600	−600								
(10)	−1,300								−€1,300	Dividends
	€ 8,050	+ €1,400	+ €1,600	+ €7,000	= €1,600	+ €15,000	+ €4,700	− €1,950	− €1,300	
	€18,050				€18,050					

There! You made it through transaction analysis. If you feel a bit shaky on any of the transactions, it might be a good idea at this point to get up, take a short break, and come back again for a brief (10- to 15-minute) review of the transactions, to make sure you understand them before you go on to the next section.

DO IT! 4 | Tabular Analysis

Transactions made by Virmari & Co., a public accounting firm in France, for the month of August are shown below. Prepare a tabular analysis which shows the effects of these transactions on the expanded accounting equation, similar to that shown in Illustration 1.10.

1. The company issued ordinary shares for €25,000 cash.
2. The company purchased €7,000 of office equipment on credit.
3. The company received €8,000 cash in exchange for services performed.
4. The company paid €850 for this month's rent.
5. The company paid a dividend of €1,000 in cash to shareholders.

ACTION PLAN

- **Analyze the effects of each transaction on the accounting equation.**
- **Use appropriate category names (not descriptions).**
- **Keep the accounting equation in balance.**

Solution

	Assets			=	Liabilities	+	Equity						
									Retained Earnings				
Trans-action	Cash	+	Equipment	=	Accounts Payable	+	Share Capital	+	Rev.	−	Exp.	−	Div.
(1)	+€25,000						+€25,000						
(2)			+€7,000		+€7,000								
(3)	+8,000								+€8,000				Service Revenue
(4)	−850										−€850		Rent Expense
(5)	−1,000												−€1,000 Dividends
	€31,150	+	€7,000	=	€7,000	+	€25,000	+	€8,000	−	€850	−	€1,000
	€38,150				€38,150								

Related exercise material: **BE1.7, BE1.8, BE1.9, DO IT! 1.4, E1.6, E1.7, and E1.8.**

1.5 Financial Statements

LEARNING OBJECTIVE 5

Describe the five financial statements and how they are prepared.

HELPFUL HINT

The income statement, retained earnings statement, statement of cash flows, and comprehensive income statement are all for a *period* of time, whereas the statement of financial position is for a *point* in time.

Companies prepare five financial statements from the summarized accounting data (see **Helpful Hint**):

1. An **income statement** presents the revenues and expenses and resulting net income or net loss for a specific period of time.
2. A **retained earnings statement** summarizes the changes in retained earnings for a specific period of time.[5]
3. A **statement of financial position** (sometimes referred to as a *balance sheet*) reports the assets, liabilities, and equity of a company at a specific date.
4. A **statement of cash flows** summarizes information about the cash inflows (receipts) and outflows (payments) for a specific period of time.
5. A **comprehensive income statement** presents other comprehensive income items that are not included in the determination of net income. Note that IFRS contains two concepts of income: net income and comprehensive income. In later chapters, we will provide more insight into the differences between these two income concepts.

These statements provide relevant financial data for internal and external users. **Illustration 1.11** shows the first four financial statements from the above list of Softbyte SA (see **Helpful Hints**). (Illustration 1.11 assumes Softbyte has no other comprehensive income items.) A comprehensive income statement is presented in Illustration 1.13 for Softbyte.

Note that the statements shown in Illustration 1.11 are interrelated:

1. Net income of €2,750 on the **income statement** is added to the beginning balance of retained earnings in the **retained earnings statement.**
2. Retained earnings of €1,450 at the end of the reporting period shown in the **retained earnings statement** is reported on the **statement of financial position.**
3. Cash of €8,050 on the **statement of financial position** is reported on the **statement of cash flows.**

Also, explanatory notes and supporting schedules are an integral part of every set of financial statements. We illustrate these notes and schedules in later chapters of this text.

Be sure to carefully examine the format and content of each statement in Illustration 1.11. We describe the essential features of each in the following sections.

[5] Most companies prepare a statement of changes in equity, which includes the information for the retained earnings statement along with the sources of the changes in the other equity accounts.

ILLUSTRATION 1.11

Financial statements and their interrelationships

Softbyte SA
Income Statement
For the Month Ended September 30, 2029

Revenues		
Service revenue		€4,700
Expenses		
Salaries and wages expense	€900	
Rent expense	600	
Advertising expense	250	
Utilities expense	200	
Total expenses		1,950
Net income		**€2,750**

1

Softbyte SA
Retained Earnings Statement
For the Month Ended September 30, 2029

Retained earnings, September 1	€ 0
Add: Net income	**2,750**
	2,750
Less: Dividends	1,300
Retained earnings, September 30	**€1,450**

2

Softbyte SA
Statement of Financial Position
September 30, 2029

Assets

Equipment		€ 7,000
Supplies		1,600
Accounts receivable		1,400
Cash		**8,050**
Total assets		€18,050

Equity and Liabilities

Equity		
Share capital—ordinary	€15,000	
Retained earnings	**1,450**	€16,450
Liabilities		
Accounts payable		1,600
Total equity and liabilities		€18,050

3

Softbyte SA
Statement of Cash Flows
For the Month Ended September 30, 2029

Cash flows from operating activities		
Cash receipts from revenues		€ 3,300
Cash payments for expenses		(1,950)
Net cash provided by operating activities		1,350
Cash flows from investing activities		
Purchase of equipment		(7,000)
Cash flows from financing activities		
Sale of ordinary shares	€15,000	
Payment of cash dividends	(1,300)	13,700
Net increase in cash		8,050
Cash at the beginning of the period		0
Cash at the end of the period		**€ 8,050**

HELPFUL HINT

The heading of each statement identifies the company, the type of statement, and the specific date or time period covered by the statement.

HELPFUL HINT

The arrows in this illustration show the interrelationships of the four financial statements.

1. **Net income is computed first and is needed to determine the ending balance in retained earnings.**
2. **The ending balance in retained earnings is needed in preparing the statement of financial position.**
3. **The cash shown on the statement of financial position is needed in preparing the statement of cash flows.**

HELPFUL HINT

Note that final sums are double-underlined, and negative amounts (in the statement of cash flows) are presented in parentheses.

Income Statement

The income statement reports the success or profitability of the company's operations over a specific period of time. For example, Softbyte SA's income statement is dated "For the Month Ended September 30, 2029." It is prepared from the data appearing in the revenue and expense columns of Illustration 1.10. The heading of the statement identifies the company, the type of statement, and the time period covered by the statement.

- The income statement lists revenues first, followed by expenses.
- Then, the statement shows net income (or net loss).
- When revenues exceed expenses, **net income** results. When expenses exceed revenues, a **net loss** results.

Although practice varies, we have chosen to list expenses in order of magnitude in our illustrations. (We will consider alternative formats for the income statement in later chapters.)

Note that the income statement does not include investment and dividend transactions between the shareholders and the business in measuring net income. For example, as explained earlier, the cash dividend from Softbyte SA was not regarded as a business expense. This type of transaction is considered a reduction of retained earnings, which causes a decrease in equity.

Retained Earnings Statement

Softbyte SA's retained earnings statement reports the changes in retained earnings for a specific period of time. The time period is the same as that covered by the income statement ("For the Month Ended September 30, 2029"). Data for the preparation of the retained earnings statement come from the retained earnings columns of the tabular summary (Illustration 1.10) and from the income statement (Illustration 1.11).

- The first line of the statement shows the beginning retained earnings amount, followed by net income and dividends.
- The retained earnings ending balance is the final amount on the statement.
- The information provided by this statement indicates the reasons why retained earnings increased or decreased during the period. If there is a net loss, it is deducted with dividends in the retained earnings statement.

Statement of Financial Position

Softbyte SA's statement of financial position reports the assets, liabilities, and equity at a specific date (September 30, 2029). The company prepares the statement of financial position from the column headings and the month-end data shown in the last line of the tabular summary (Illustration 1.10).

- Observe that the statement of financial position lists assets at the top, followed by equity and then liabilities.
- Total assets must equal total equity and liabilities.

Softbyte SA reports only one liability, Accounts Payable, on its statement of financial position. In most cases, there will be more than one liability. When two or more liabilities are involved, a customary way of listing is as shown in **Illustration 1.12**.

ILLUSTRATION 1.12

Presentation of liabilities

Liabilities	
Notes payable	€10,000
Accounts payable	63,000
Salaries and wages payable	18,000
Total liabilities	**€91,000**

The statement of financial position is like a snapshot of the company's financial condition at a specific moment in time (usually the month-end or year-end).

Accounting Across the Organization — Vodafone

Chris Ison/AP Photos

A Wise End

Not every company uses December 31 as the accounting year-end. Some companies whose year-ends differ from December 31 are **Vodafone Group** (GBR), March 31; **Walt Disney Company** (USA), the Saturday closest to September 30; and **Diageo** (GBR), June 30. Why do companies choose the particular year-ends that they do?

Many companies opt to end the accounting year when inventory or operations are at a low. Compiling accounting information requires much time and effort by managers, so companies would rather do it when they aren't as busy operating the business. Also, inventory is easier and less costly to count when it is low.

What year-end would you likely use if you owned a ski resort and ski rental business? What if you owned a college bookstore? Why choose those year-ends? (Answer is available near the end of the chapter.)

Statement of Cash Flows

The statement of cash flows provides information on the cash receipts and payments for a specific period of time. The statement of cash flows reports (1) the cash effects of a company's operations during a period, (2) its investing activities, (3) its financing activities, (4) the net increase or decrease in cash during the period, and (5) the cash amount at the end of the period (see **Helpful Hint**).

> **HELPFUL HINT**
> **Investing activities pertain to investments made by the company, not investments made by the owners.**

Reporting the sources, uses, and change in cash is useful because investors, creditors, and others want to know what is happening to a company's most liquid resource. The statement of cash flows provides answers to the following simple but important questions.

1. Where did cash come from during the period?
2. What was cash used for during the period?
3. What was the change in the cash balance during the period?

As shown in Softbyte SA's statement of cash flows in Illustration 1.11, cash increased €8,050 during the period. Net cash provided by operating activities increased cash €1,350. Cash flow from investing activities decreased cash €7,000. And cash flow from financing activities increased cash €13,700. At this time, you need not be concerned with how these amounts are determined. Chapter 13 will examine in detail how the statement is prepared.

Comprehensive Income Statement

In some cases, Softbyte SA must prepare a comprehensive income statement in addition to its income statement. Softbyte prepares this second statement if it has other comprehensive income items.

- Other comprehensive income items are not part of net income but are considered important enough to be reported separately.
- Softbyte adds other comprehensive income to net income to arrive at comprehensive income.

Illustration 1.13 shows a comprehensive income statement, assuming that Softbyte SA has other comprehensive income of €600.

ILLUSTRATION 1.13
Comprehensive income statement

Softbyte SA
Comprehensive Income Statement
For the Month Ended September 30, 2029

Net income	€2,750
Other comprehensive income	600
Comprehensive income	€3,350

In this two statement format, the comprehensive income statement is reported directly after the traditional income statement. Examples of this two statement format can be seen in the financial statements of **Nestlé** and **Delfi Limited** in Appendices B and C, respectively.

IFRS does allow an alternative statement format in which the information contained in the income statement and the comprehensive income statement are combined in a single statement, referred to as a **statement of comprehensive income**. An example of this approach can be seen in the financial statements of TSMC in Appendix A. *In this text, we use the two statement approach.* We provide a more detailed discussion about the components of other comprehensive income in later chapters.

Environmental, Social, and Governance Insight

Marek Uliasz/
Getty Images

Beyond Financial Statements

Should we expand our financial statements beyond the income statement, retained earnings statement, statement of financial position, and statement of cash flows? Some believe we should take into account ecological and social performance, in addition to financial results, in evaluating a company. The argument is that a company's responsibility lies with anyone who is influenced by its actions. In other words, a company should be interested in benefiting many different parties, instead of only maximizing shareholders' interests.

A socially responsible business does not exploit or endanger any group of individuals. It follows fair trade practices, provides safe environments for workers, and bears responsibility for environmental damage. Granted, measurement of these factors is difficult. How to report this information is also controversial. But, many interesting and useful efforts are underway.

Throughout this text, we provide additional insights into how companies are attempting to meet the challenge of measuring and reporting their contributions to society, as well as their financial results, to shareholders.

Why might a company's shareholders be interested in its environmental and social performance? (Answer is available near the end of the chapter.)

ACTION PLAN

- **Remember the basic accounting equation: assets must equal liabilities plus equity.**
- **Review previous financial statements to determine how total assets, net income, and equity are computed.**

DO IT! 5 | Financial Statement Items

Presented below is selected information related to Li Fashions at December 31, 2029. Li reports financial information monthly.

Equipment	HK$10,000	Utilities Expense	HK$ 4,000
Cash	8,000	Accounts Receivable	9,000
Service Revenue	36,000	Salaries and Wages Expense	7,000
Rent Expense	11,000	Notes Payable	16,500
Accounts Payable	2,000	Dividends	5,000

a. Determine the total assets of Li at December 31, 2029.

b. Determine the net income that Li reported for December 2029.

c. Determine the equity of Li at December 31, 2029.

Solution

a. The total assets are HK$27,000, comprised of Equipment HK$10,000, Accounts Receivable HK$9,000, and Cash HK$8,000.

b. Net income is HK$14,000, computed as follows.

Revenues		
Service revenue		HK$36,000
Expenses		
Rent expense	HK$11,000	
Salaries and wages expense	7,000	
Utilities expense	4,000	
Total expenses		22,000
Net income		HK$14,000

c. The ending equity of Li Fashions is HK$8,500. By rewriting the accounting equation, we can compute equity as assets minus liabilities, as follows.

Total assets [as computed in (a)]		HK$27,000
Less: Liabilities		
Notes payable	HK$16,500	
Accounts payable	2,000	18,500
Equity		HK$ 8,500

Note that it is not possible to determine the company's equity in any other way because the beginning total for equity is not provided.

Related exercise material: **BE1.10, BE1.11, DO IT! 1.5, E1.9, E1.10, E1.11, E1.12, E1.13, E1.14, E1.15, E1.16, E1.17, and E1.18.**

Appendix 1A Career Opportunities in Accounting

LEARNING OBJECTIVE *6

Explain the career opportunities in accounting.

Why is accounting such a popular major and career choice?

- There are a lot of jobs. In many cities in recent years, the demand for accountants exceeded the supply. Not only are there a lot of jobs, but there are a wide array of opportunities. As one accounting organization observed, "accounting is one degree with 360 degrees of opportunity."
- It is obvious that accounting matters. Interest in accounting has increased, ironically, because of the attention caused by the turmoil over toxic (misstated) assets at many financial institutions. These widely publicized scandals revealed the important role that accounting plays in society. Most people want to make a difference, and an accounting career provides many opportunities to contribute to society.
- Recent internal control requirements dramatically increased demand for professionals with accounting training.

Accountants are in such demand that it is not uncommon for accounting students to have accepted a job offer a year before graduation. As the following discussion reveals, the job options of people with accounting degrees are virtually unlimited.

Public Accounting

Individuals in **public accounting** offer expert service to the general public, in much the same way that doctors serve patients and lawyers serve clients. A major portion of public accounting involves **auditing**. In auditing, an independent accountant such as a Chartered Accountant (CA) or a certified public accountant (CPA) examines company financial statements and provides an opinion as to how accurately the financial statements present the company's results and financial position in accordance with international financial reporting standards. Analysts, investors, and creditors rely heavily on these "audit opinions," which CAs and CPAs have the exclusive authority to issue.

Taxation is another major area of public accounting. The work that tax specialists perform includes tax advice and planning, preparing tax returns, and representing clients before governmental agencies.

A third area in public accounting is **management consulting**. It ranges from installing basic accounting software or highly complex enterprise resource planning systems, to performing support services for major marketing projects and merger and acquisition activities.

Many accountants are entrepreneurs. They form small- or medium-sized practices that frequently specialize in tax or consulting services.

Private Accounting

Instead of working in public accounting, you might choose to be an employee of a for-profit company such as **Sinopec** (CHN), **Google** (USA), or **Samsung** (KOR). In **private** (or **managerial**) **accounting**, you would be involved in activities such as cost accounting (finding the cost of producing specific products), budgeting, accounting information system design and support, and tax planning and preparation. You might also be a member of your company's internal audit team. In response to increased internal control requirements, the internal auditors' job of reviewing the company's operations to ensure compliance with company policies and to increase efficiency has taken on greater importance.

Alternatively, many accountants work for not-for-profit organizations such as the **International Red Cross** (CHE) or the **Bill and Melinda Gates Foundation** (USA), or for museums, libraries, or performing arts organizations.

Governmental Accounting

Another option is to pursue one of the many accounting opportunities in governmental agencies. For example, tax authorities, law enforcement agencies, and company regulators all employ accountants. There is also a very high demand for accounting educators at public colleges and universities and in local governments.

Forensic Accounting

Forensic accounting uses accounting, auditing, and investigative skills to conduct investigations into theft and fraud. It is listed among the top 20 career paths of the future. The job of forensic accountants is to catch the perpetrators of theft and fraud occurring at companies. This includes tracing money-laundering and identity-theft activities as well as tax evasion. Insurance companies hire forensic accountants to detect frauds such as arson, and law offices employ forensic accountants to identify marital assets in divorces.

The Review and Practice section provides opportunities for students to review key concepts and terms as well as complete multiple-choice questions, brief exercises, exercises, and a comprehensive problem. Detailed solutions are also included.

Review and Practice

Learning Objectives Review

1 Identify the activities and users associated with accounting.

Accounting is an information system that identifies, records, and communicates the economic events of an organization to interested users. The major users and uses of accounting are as follows. (a) Management uses accounting information to plan, organize, and run the business. (b) Investors (owners) decide whether to buy, hold, or sell their financial interests on the basis of accounting data. (c) Creditors (suppliers and bankers) evaluate the risks of granting credit or lending money on the basis of accounting information. Other groups that use accounting information are taxing authorities, regulatory agencies, customers, and labor unions.

2 Explain the building blocks of accounting: ethics, principles, and assumptions.

Ethics are the standards of conduct by which actions are judged as right or wrong. Effective financial reporting depends on sound ethical behavior.

Accounting is based on standards such as International Financial Reporting Standards (IFRS). IFRS generally uses one of two measurement principles. The monetary unit assumption requires that companies include in the accounting records only transaction data that can be expressed in terms of money. The economic entity assumption requires that the activities of each economic entity be kept separate from the activities of its owner(s) and other economic entities.

3 State the accounting equation, and define its components.

The basic accounting equation is:

Assets = Liabilities + Equity

Assets are resources a business owns. Liabilities are creditorship claims on total assets. Equity is the ownership claim on total assets.

The expanded accounting equation is:

Assets = Liabilities + Share Capital—Ordinary + Revenues − Expenses − Dividends

Share capital—ordinary is affected when the company issues new ordinary shares in exchange for cash. Revenues are the gross increase in equity resulting from business activities for the purpose of earning income. Expenses are the costs of assets consumed or services used in the process of earning revenue. Dividends are payments the company makes to its shareholders.

4 Analyze the effects of business transactions on the accounting equation.

Each business transaction must have a dual effect on the accounting equation. For example, if an individual asset increases, there must be a corresponding (1) decrease in another asset, (2) increase in a specific liability, or (3) increase in equity.

5 Describe the five financial statements and how they are prepared.

An income statement presents the revenues and expenses, and resulting net income or net loss, for a specific period of time. A retained earnings statement summarizes the changes in retained earnings for a specific period of time. A statement of financial position reports the assets, liabilities, and equity at a specific date. A statement of cash flows summarizes information about the cash inflows (receipts) and outflows (payments) for a specific period of time. A comprehensive income statement adds or subtracts any items of other comprehensive income to net income to arrive at comprehensive income.

*6 Explain the career opportunities in accounting.

Accounting offers many different jobs in fields such as public and private accounting, governmental, and forensic accounting. Accounting is a popular major because there are many different types of jobs, with unlimited potential for career advancement.

Glossary Review

Accounting The information system that identifies, records, and communicates the economic events of an organization to interested users. (p. 1-3).

Accounting information system The system of collecting and processing transaction data and communicating financial information to decision-makers. (p. 1-15).

Assets Resources a business owns. (p. 1-12).

***Auditing** The examination of financial statements by a certified public accountant in order to express an opinion as to the fairness of presentation. (p. 1-27).

Basic accounting equation Assets = Liabilities + Equity. (p. 1-12).

Bookkeeping A part of the accounting process that involves only the recording of economic events. (p. 1-4).

Comprehensive income statement A financial statement that presents items that are not included in the determination of net income, referred to as other comprehensive income. (p. 1-22).

Corporation A business organized as a separate legal entity under jurisdiction corporation law, having ownership divided into transferable shares. (p. 1-11).

Current value basis A measurement basis that results in reporting assets and liabilities at current value. (p. 1-9).

Data analytics The evaluation of data, often employing both software and statistics, to draw inferences. (p. 1-5).

Dividend A distribution of cash or other assets by a corporation to its shareholders. (p. 1-14).

Economic entity assumption An assumption that requires that the activities of the entity be kept separate and distinct from the activities of its owner and all other economic entities. (p. 1-10).

Equity The ownership claim on a company's total assets. (p. 1-13).

Ethics The standards of conduct by which actions are judged as right or wrong, honest or dishonest, fair or not fair. (p. 1-7).

Expanded accounting equation Assets = Liabilities + Share Capital—Ordinary + Revenues − Expenses − Dividends. (p. 1-16).

Expenses The cost of assets consumed or services used in the process of earning revenue. (p. 1-13).

Faithful representation Numbers and descriptions match what really existed or happened—they are factual. (p. 1-9).

Financial accounting The field of accounting that provides economic and financial information for investors, creditors, and other external users. (p. 1-5).

Financial Accounting Standards Board (FASB) A private organization that establishes generally accepted accounting principles (GAAP) in the United States. (p. 1-8).

***Forensic accounting** An area of accounting that uses accounting, auditing, and investigative skills to conduct investigations into theft and fraud. (p. 1-28).

Generally accepted accounting principles (GAAP) Common U.S. standards that indicate how to report economic events. (p. 1-8).

Historical cost basis A measurement basis that results in companies recording assets and other accounts at their cost. (p. 1-9).

Income statement A financial statement that presents the revenues and expenses and resulting net income or net loss of a company for a specific period of time. (p. 1-22).

International Accounting Standards Board (IASB) An accounting standard-setting body that issues standards adopted by many countries outside of the United States. (p. 1-8).

International Financial Reporting Standards (IFRS) International accounting standards set by the International Accounting Standards Board (IASB). (p. 1-8).

Liabilities Creditor claims on total assets. (p. 1-13).

***Management consulting** An area of public accounting ranging from development of accounting and computer systems to support services for marketing projects and merger and acquisition activities. (p. 1-27).

Managerial accounting The field of accounting that provides internal reports to help users make decisions about their companies. (p. 1-5).

Monetary unit assumption An assumption stating that companies include in the accounting records only transaction data that can be expressed in terms of money. (p. 1-10).

Net income The amount by which revenues exceed expenses. (p. 1-24).

Net loss The amount by which expenses exceed revenues. (p. 1-24).

Partnership A business owned by two or more persons associated as partners. (p. 1-10).

***Private (or managerial) accounting** An area of accounting within a company that involves such activities as cost accounting, budgeting, design and support of accounting information systems, and tax planning and preparation. (p. 1-28).

Proprietorship A business owned by one person. (p. 1-10).

***Public accounting** An area of accounting in which the accountant offers expert service to the general public. (p. 1-27).

Relevance Financial information that is capable of making a difference in a decision. (p. 1-9).

Retained earnings statement A financial statement that summarizes the changes in retained earnings for a specific period of time. (p. 1-22).

Revenues The gross increase in equity resulting from business activities entered into for the purpose of earning income. (p. 1-13).

Share capital—ordinary Amounts paid in by shareholders for the ordinary shares they purchase. (p. 1-13).

Statement of cash flows A financial statement that summarizes information about the cash inflows (receipts) and cash outflows (payments) for a specific period of time. (p. 1-22).

Statement of financial position (balance sheet) A financial statement that reports the assets, liabilities, and equity of a company at a specific date. (p. 1-22).

***Taxation** An area of public accounting involving tax advice, tax planning, preparing tax returns, and representing clients before governmental agencies. (p. 1-27).

Transactions The economic events of a business that are recorded by accountants. (p. 1-15).

Practice Multiple-Choice Questions

1. (LO 1) Which of the following is **not** a step in the accounting process?

a. Identification. **c.** Recording.
b. Economic entity. **d.** Communication.

2. (LO 1) Which of the following statements about users of accounting information is **incorrect**?

a. Management is an internal user.
b. Taxing authorities are external users.
c. Present creditors are external users.
d. Regulatory authorities are internal users.

3. (LO 2) The historical cost basis results in:

a. initially recording assets at cost and adjusting when the current value changes.
b. keeping activities of an entity separate and distinct from its owner.
c. recording and reporting assets at their cost.
d. including only transaction data capable of being expressed in terms of money in the accounting records.

4. (LO 2) Which of the following statements about basic assumptions is **correct**?

a. Basic assumptions are the same as accounting principles.
b. The economic entity assumption states that there should be a particular unit of accountability.
c. The monetary unit assumption enables accounting to measure employee morale.
d. Partnerships are not economic entities.

5. (LO 2) The three types of business entities are:

a. proprietorships, small businesses, and partnerships.
b. proprietorships, partnerships, and corporations.
c. proprietorships, partnerships, and large businesses.
d. financial, manufacturing, and service companies.

6. (LO 3) Net income will result during a time period when:

a. assets exceed liabilities.
b. assets exceed revenues.
c. expenses exceed revenues.
d. revenues exceed expenses.

7. (LO 3) As of December 31, 2029, Stoneland AG has assets of €3,500 and equity of €2,000. What are the liabilities for Stoneland AG as of December 31, 2029?

a. €1,500. **b.** €1,000. **c.** €2,500. **d.** €2,000.

8. (LO 4) Performing services on account will have the following effects on the components of the basic accounting equation:

a. increase assets and decrease equity.
b. increase assets and increase equity.
c. increase assets and increase liabilities.
d. increase liabilities and increase equity.

9. (LO 4) Which of the following events is **not** recorded in the accounting records?

a. Equipment is purchased on account.
b. An employee is terminated.
c. A cash investment is made into the business.
d. The company pays a cash dividend.

10. (LO 4) During 2029, Xia Lin Company's assets decreased ¥500,000 and its liabilities decreased ¥900,000. Its equity therefore:

a. increased ¥400,000. **c.** decreased ¥400,000.
b. decreased ¥1,400,000. **d.** increased ¥1,400,000.

11. **(LO 4)** Payment of an account payable affects the components of the accounting equation in the following way.

  a. decreases equity and decreases liabilities.

  b. increases assets and decreases liabilities.

  c. decreases assets and increases equity.

  d. decreases assets and decreases liabilities.

12. **(LO 5)** Which of the following statements is **false**?

  a. A statement of cash flows summarizes information about the cash inflows (receipts) and outflows (payments) for a specific period of time.

  b. A statement of financial position reports the assets, liabilities, and equity at a specific date.

  c. An income statement presents the revenues, expenses, assets, and liabilities for a specific period of time.

  d. A retained earnings statement summarizes the changes in retained earnings for a specific period of time.

13. **(LO 5)** On the last day of the period, Jim Otto Company buys a $900 machine on credit. This transaction will affect the:

  a. income statement only.

  b. statement of financial position only.

  c. income statement and retained earnings statement only.

  d. income statement, retained earnings statement, and statement of financial position.

14. **(LO 5)** The financial statement that reports assets, liabilities, and equity is the:

  a. income statement.

  b. retained earnings statement.

  c. statement of financial position.

  d. statement of cash flows.

*15. **(LO 6)** Services performed by a public accountant include:

  a. auditing, taxation, and management consulting.

  b. auditing, budgeting, and management consulting.

  c. auditing, budgeting, and cost accounting.

  d. internal auditing, budgeting, and management consulting.

Solutions

1. **b.** Economic entity is not one of the steps in the accounting process. The other choices are true because (a) identification is the first step in the accounting process, (c) recording is the second step in the accounting process, and (d) communication is the third and final step in the accounting process.

2. **d.** Regulatory authorities are external, not internal, users of accounting information. The other choices are true statements.

3. **c.** The historical cost basis results in assets being recorded at their cost. The other choices are incorrect because (a) historical cost basis assets are not adjusted for changes in current value, (b) describes the economic entity assumption, and (d) describes the monetary unit assumption.

4. **b.** The economic entity assumption states that there should be a particular unit of accountability. The other choices are incorrect because (a) basic assumptions are not the same as accounting principles, (c) the monetary unit assumption allows accounting to measure economic events, and (d) partnerships are economic entities.

5. **b.** Proprietorships, partnerships, and corporations are the three types of business entities. Choices (a) and (c) are incorrect because small and large businesses only denote the sizes of businesses. Choice (d) is incorrect because financial, manufacturing, and service companies are types of businesses, not business entities.

6. **d.** Net income results when revenues exceed expenses. The other choices are incorrect because (a) assets and liabilities are not used in the computation of net income; (b) revenues, not assets, are included in the computation of net income; and (c) when expenses exceed revenues, a net loss results.

7. **a.** Using a variation of the basic accounting equation, Assets − Equity = Liabilities, €3,500 − €2,000 = €1,500. The other choices are therefore incorrect.

8. **b.** When services are performed on account, assets are increased and equity is increased. The other choices are incorrect because when services are performed on account (a) equity is increased, not decreased; (c) liabilities are not affected; and (d) equity is increased and liabilities are not affected.

9. **b.** If an employee is terminated, this represents an activity of a company, not a business transaction. Assets, liabilities, and equity are not affected. Thus, there is no effect on the accounting equation. The other choices are incorrect because they are all recorded: (a) when equipment is purchased on account, both assets and liabilities increase; (c) when a cash investment is made into a business, both assets and equity increase; and (d) when a dividend is paid, both assets and equity decrease.

10. **a.** Using the basic accounting equation, Assets = Liabilities + Equity, −¥500,000 = −¥900,000 + Equity, so equity increased ¥400,000, not (b) decreased ¥1,400,000, (c) decreased ¥400,000, or (d) increased ¥1,400,000.

11. **d.** Payment of an account payable results in an equal decrease of assets (cash) and liabilities (accounts payable). The other choices are incorrect because payment of an account payable (a) does not affect equity, (b) does not increase assets, and (c) does not affect equity.

12. **c.** An income statement presents the revenues and expenses for a specific period of time but not assets and liabilities. The other choices are true statements.

13. **b.** This transaction will cause assets to increase by $900 and liabilities to increase by $900. The other choices are incorrect because this transaction (a) will have no effect on the income statement, (c) will have no effect on the income statement or the retained earnings statement, and (d) will affect the statement of financial position but not the income statement or the retained earnings statement.

14. **c.** The statement of financial position is the statement that reports assets, liabilities, and equity. The other choices are incorrect because (a) the income statement reports revenues and expenses, (b) the retained earnings statement reports details about equity, and (d) the statement of cash flows reports inflows and outflows of cash.

*15. **a.** Auditing, taxation, and management consulting are all services performed by public accountants. The other choices are incorrect because public accountants do not perform budgeting or cost accounting.

Practice Brief Exercises

Use basic accounting equation.

1. **(LO 3)** At the beginning of the year, Ortiz Eyewear had total assets of £900,000 and total liabilities of £440,000. Answer the following questions.
   a. If total assets decreased £100,000 during the year and total liabilities increased £80,000 during the year, what is the amount of equity at the end of the year?
   b. During the year, total liabilities decreased £100,000 and equity increased £200,000. What is the amount of total assets at the end of the year?
   c. If total assets increased £50,000 during the year and equity increased £60,000 during the year, what is the amount of total liabilities at the end of the year?

Solution

1. a. (£900,000 − £440,000) − £100,000 − £80,000 = £280,000 equity
   b. £900,000 − £100,000 + £200,000 = £1,000,000 total assets
   c. £440,000 − £60,000 + £50,000 = £430,000 total liabilities

Determine effect of transactions on basic accounting equation

2. **(LO 4)** Presented below are three business transactions. List the letters (a), (b), and (c) with columns for assets, liabilities and equity. For each column, indicate whether the transactions increased (+), decreased (−), or had no effect (NE) on assets, liabilities, and equity.
   a. Purchased equipment on account.
   b. Declared and paid cash dividends.
   c. Paid expenses in cash.

Solution

	Assets	Liabilities	Equity
2. a.	+	+	NE
b.	−	NE	−
c.	−	NE	−

Determine effect of transactions on basic accounting equation.

3. **(LO 4)** Follow the same format as in **Practice Brief Exercise 2**. Determine the effect on assets, liabilities, and equity for the following three transactions.
   a. Performed accounting services for clients for cash.
   b. Borrowed cash from a bank on a note payable.
   c. Paid cash for rent for the month.

Solution

	Assets	Liabilities	Equity
3. a.	+	NE	+
b.	+	+	NE
c.	−	NE	−

Determine where items appear on financial statements.

4. **(LO 5)** Indicate whether the following items would appear on the income statement (IS), statement of financial position (SFP), or retained earnings statement (RES).
   a. Dividends.
   b. Cash.
   c. Salaries and wages expense.
   d. Service revenue.
   e. Accounts payable.

Solution

4. **a.** Dividends RES
   b. Cash SFP
   c. Salaries and wages expense IS
   d. Service revenue IS
   e. Accounts payable SFP

5. **(LO 5)** Presented below in alphabetical order are statement of financial position items for Feagler Gardening at December 31, 2029. Prepare a statement of financial position following the format of Illustration 1.11.

Prepare a statement of financial position.

Accounts receivable	€12,500
Cash	38,000
Notes payable	40,000
Share capital—ordinary	10,500

Solution

5.

Feagler Gardening
Statement of Financial Position
December 31, 2029

Assets	
Accounts receivable	€12,500
Cash	38,000
Total assets	€50,500
Equity and Liabilities	
Equity	
Share capital—ordinary	€10,500
Liabilities	
Notes payable	40,000
Total equity and liabilities	€50,500

Practice Exercises

1. **(LO 3, 4)** Selected transactions for Fabulous Flora are listed below.

Analyze the effect of transactions.

   1. Issued ordinary shares for cash to start business.
   2. Purchased equipment on account.
   3. Paid salaries.
   4. Billed customers for services performed.
   5. Received cash from customers billed in (4).
   6. Paid dividends.
   7. Incurred advertising expense on account.
   8. Purchased additional equipment for cash.
   9. Received cash from customers when service was performed.

Instructions

List the numbers of the above transactions and describe the effect of each transaction on assets, liabilities, and equity. For example, the first answer is: (1) Increase in assets and increase in equity.

Solution

1. 1. Increase in assets and increase in equity.
   2. Increase in assets and increase in liabilities.
   3. Decrease in assets and decrease in equity.
   4. Increase in assets and increase in equity.
   5. Increase in assets and decrease in assets.
   6. Decrease in assets and decrease in equity.
   7. Increase in liabilities and decrease in equity.
   8. Increase in assets and decrease in assets.
   9. Increase in assets and increase in equity.

Analyze the effect of transactions on assets, liabilities, and equity.

2. **(LO 3, 4)** Alma's Payroll Services entered into the following transactions during May 2029.
   1. Purchased computers for $15,000 from Bytes of Data on account.
   2. Paid $3,000 cash for May rent on storage space.
   3. Received $12,000 cash from customers for contracts billed in April.
   4. Performed payroll services for Magic Construction Company for $2,500 cash.
   5. Paid Northern Ohio Power Co. $7,000 cash for energy usage in May.
   6. Shareholders invested an additional $25,000 in the business.
   7. Paid Bytes of Data for the computers purchased in (1) above.
   8. Incurred advertising expense for May of $900 on account.

Instructions

Indicate with the appropriate letter whether each of the transactions above results in:

a. an increase in assets and a decrease in assets.
b. an increase in assets and an increase in equity.
c. an increase in assets and an increase in liabilities.
d. a decrease in assets and a decrease in equity.
e. a decrease in assets and a decrease in liabilities.
f. an increase in liabilities and a decrease in equity.
g. an increase in equity and a decrease in liabilities.

Solution

2. 1. c	3. a	5. d	7. e
2. d	4. b	6. b	8. f

Practice Problem

Prepare a tabular summary and financial statements.

(LO 4, 5) Su Feng opens her own law office, Legal Services Ltd., on July 1, 2029. During the first month of operations, the following transactions occurred (NT$ in thousands).

1. Shareholders invested NT$10,000 in cash in exchange for ordinary shares of Legal Services Ltd.
2. Paid NT$800 for July rent on office space.
3. Purchased office equipment on account NT$3,000.
4. Performed legal services for clients for cash NT$1,500.
5. Borrowed NT$700 cash from a bank on a note payable.
6. Performed legal services for client on account NT$2,000.
7. Paid monthly expenses: salaries NT$500 utilities NT$300, and advertising NT$100.

Instructions

a. Prepare a tabular summary of the transactions. (Prepare using NT$ in thousands.)
b. Prepare the income statement, retained earnings statement, and statement of financial position at July 31, 2029, for Legal Services Ltd. (Prepare using NT$ in thousands.)

Solution

a.

	Assets			=	Liabilities		+	Equity				
									Retained Earnings			
Trans-action	Cash	+ Accounts Receivable	+ Equipment	=	Notes Payable	+ Accounts Payable	+	Share Capital	+ Rev.	− Exp.	− Div.	
1.	+NT$10,000*							+NT$10,000				**Issued Shares**
2.	−800									−NT$800		**Rent Expense**
3.			+NT$3,000			+NT$3,000						
4.	+1,500								+NT$1,500			**Service Revenue**
5.	+700				+NT$700							
6.		+NT$2,000							+2,000			**Service Revenue**
7.	−900									−500		**Sal./Wages Exp.**
										−300		**Utilities Expense**
										−100		**Advertising Expense**
	NT$10,500 +	NT$2,000 +	NT$3,000	=	NT$700 +	NT$3,000 +		NT$10,000 +	NT$3,500 −	NT$1,700		
	NT$15,500				NT$15,500							

*Amounts shown in thousands of NT$.

b.

Legal Services Ltd.
Income Statement
For the Month Ended July 31, 2029
(NT$ in thousands)

Revenues		
Service revenue		NT$3,500
Expenses		
Rent expense	NT$800	
Salaries and wages expense	500	
Utilities expense	300	
Advertising expense	100	
Total expenses		1,700
Net income		NT$1,800

Legal Services Ltd.
Retained Earnings Statement
For the Month Ended July 31, 2029
(NT$ in thousands)

Retained earnings, July 1	NT$ -0-
Add: Net income	1,800
Retained earnings, July 31	NT$1,800

Legal Services Ltd.
Statement of Financial Position
July 31, 2029
(NT$ in thousands)

Assets		
Equipment		NT$ 3,000
Accounts receivable		2,000
Cash		10,500
Total assets		NT$15,500
Equity and Liabilities		
Equity		
Share capital—ordinary	NT$10,000	
Retained earnings	1,800	NT$11,800
Liabilities		
Notes payable	700	
Accounts payable	3,000	3,700
Total equity and liabilities		NT$15,500

Questions

1. "Accounting is ingrained in our society and it is vital to our economic system." Do you agree? Explain.

2. Identify and describe the steps in the accounting process.

3. a. Who are internal users of accounting data?
   b. How does accounting provide relevant data to these users?

4. What uses of financial accounting information are made by (a) investors and (b) creditors?

5. What are the four most common types of data analytics, and what basic question does each address?

6. "Bookkeeping and accounting are the same." Do you agree? Explain.

7. Remmers Travel Agency purchased land for £85,000 cash on December 10, 2029. At December 31, 2029, the land's value has increased to £93,000. What amount should be reported for land on Remmers' statement of financial position at December 31, 2029? Explain.

8. What is the monetary unit assumption?

9. What is the economic entity assumption?

10. What are the three basic forms of profit-oriented business organizations?

11. Teresa Alvarez is the owner of a successful printing shop. Recently, her business has been increasing, and Teresa has been thinking about changing the organization of her business from a proprietorship to a corporation. Discuss some of the advantages Teresa would enjoy if she were to incorporate her business.

12. What is the basic accounting equation?

13. a. Define the terms assets, liabilities, and equity.
    b. What items affect equity?

14. Which of the following items are liabilities of Designer Jewelry Stores?

a. Cash.	f. Equipment.
b. Accounts payable.	g. Salaries and wages payable.
c. Dividends.	h. Service revenue.
d. Accounts receivable.	i. Rent expense.
e. Supplies.	

15. Can a business enter into a transaction in which only the left side of the basic accounting equation is affected? If so, give an example.

16. Are the following events recorded in the accounting records? Explain your answer in each case.
    a. The president of the company dies.
    b. Supplies are purchased on account.
    c. An employee is fired.

17. Indicate how the following business transactions affect the basic accounting equation.
    a. Paid cash for janitorial services.
    b. Purchased equipment for cash.
    c. Received cash in exchange for ordinary shares.
    d. Paid accounts payable in full.

18. Listed below are some items found in the financial statements of Min-Seo Promotions. Indicate in which financial statement(s) the following items would appear.

a. Service revenue.	d. Accounts receivable.
b. Equipment.	e. Retained earnings.
c. Advertising expense.	f. Salaries and wages payable.

19. In February 2029, Xia Sun invested an additional £10,000 in Midtown plc. Midtown's accountant, Jon Shin, recorded this receipt as an increase in cash and revenues. Is this treatment appropriate? Why or why not?

20. "A company's net income appears directly on the income statement and the retained earnings statement, and it is included indirectly in the company's statement of financial position." Do you agree? Explain.

21. Jardine plc had an equity balance of £158,000 at the beginning of the period. At the end of the accounting period, the equity balance was £198,000.
    a. Assuming no additional investment or distributions during the period, what is the net income for the period?
    b. Assuming an additional investment of £13,000 but no distributions during the period, what is the net income for the period?

22. Summarized operations for Carston Gardens for the month of July are as follows.

    Revenues recognized: for cash £30,000; on account £70,000.

    Expenses incurred: for cash £26,000; on account £40,000.

    Indicate for Carston Gardens (a) the total revenues, (b) the total expenses, and (c) net income for the month of July.

23. The basic accounting equation is Assets = Liabilities + Equity. Replacing the words in that equation with numeric amounts, what is TSMC's accounting equation at December 31, 2020? The financial statements of TSMC are presented in Appendix A.

Brief Exercises

Use basic accounting equation.

BE1.1 (LO 3) Presented below is the basic accounting equation (in thousands). Determine the missing amounts.

	Assets	=	Liabilities	+	Equity
a.	¥88,000		¥50,000		?
b.	?		¥45,000		¥70,000
c.	¥94,000		?		¥60,000

BE1.2 (LO 3) Given the accounting equation, answer each of the following questions. *Use basic accounting equation.*

a. The liabilities of Shumway Ltd. are £120,000 and the equity is £232,000. What is the amount of Shumway Ltd.'s total assets?

b. The total assets of Shumway Ltd. are £190,000 and its equity is £80,000. What is the amount of its total liabilities?

BE1.3 (LO 3) At the beginning of the year, Gilles Plumbers had total assets of €800,000 and total liabilities of €300,000. Answer the following questions. (Note that each situation is independent.) *Use basic accounting equation.*

a. If total assets increased €150,000 during the year and total liabilities decreased €60,000, what is the amount of equity at the end of the year?

b. During the year, total liabilities increased €100,000 and equity decreased €70,000. What is the amount of total assets at the end of the year?

c. If total assets decreased €80,000 and equity increased €120,000 during the year, what is the amount of total liabilities at the end of the year?

BE1.4 (LO 3) Use the expanded accounting equation to answer each of the following questions. *Solve expanded accounting equation.*

a. The liabilities of Kumar Company are ₹90,000. Share capital—ordinary is ₹150,000; dividends are ₹40,000; revenues, ₹450,000; and expenses, ₹340,000. What is the amount of Kumar's total assets?

b. The total assets of Kalim Company are ₹57,000. Share capital—ordinary is ₹35,000; dividends are ₹7,000; revenues, ₹52,000; and expenses, ₹35,000. What is the amount of the company's total liabilities?

c. The total assets of Siram Co. are ₹660,000 and its liabilities are equal to two-thirds of its total assets. What is the amount of Siram Co.'s equity?

BE1.5 (LO 3) Indicate whether each of the following items is an asset (A), liability (L), or part of equity (E). *Identify assets, liabilities, and equity.*

________ **a.** Accounts receivable.	________ **d.** Supplies.
________ **b.** Salaries and wages payable.	________ **e.** Share capital—ordinary.
________ **c.** Equipment.	________ **f.** Notes payable.

BE1.6 (LO 3) Classify each of the following items as dividends (D), revenue (R), or expense (E). *Classify items affecting equity.*

________ **a.** Advertising expense.	________ **e.** Dividends.
________ **b.** Service revenue.	________ **f.** Rent revenue.
________ **c.** Insurance expense.	________ **g.** Utilities expense.
________ **d.** Salaries and wages expense.	

BE1.7 (LO 4) Presented below are three business transactions. On a sheet of paper, list the letters (a), (b), and (c) with columns for assets, liabilities, and equity. For each column, indicate whether the transactions increased (+), decreased (–), or had no effect (NE) on assets, liabilities, and equity. *Determine effect of transactions on basic accounting equation.*

a. Purchased supplies on account.

b. Received cash for performing a service.

c. Paid expenses in cash.

BE1.8 (LO 4) Follow the same format as in BE1.7. Determine the effect on assets, liabilities, and equity of the following three transactions. *Determine effect of transactions on basic accounting equation.*

a. Shareholders invested cash in the business.

b. Payment of dividends.

c. Received cash from a customer who had previously been billed for services performed.

BE1.9 (LO 4) Presented below are three transactions. Mark each transaction as affecting shareholders' investment (I), dividends (D), revenue (R), expense (E), or not affecting equity (NE). *Determine effect of transactions on equity.*

________ **a.** Received cash for services performed.

________ **b.** Paid cash to purchase equipment.

________ **c.** Paid employee salaries.

BE1.10 (LO 5) In alphabetical order below are statement of financial position items for Grande Ltd. at December 31, 2029. Prepare a statement of financial position, following the format of Illustration 1.11. *Prepare a statement of financial position.*

Accounts payable	£90,000
Accounts receivable	62,500
Cash	49,000
Share capital—ordinary	21,500

Determine where items appear on financial statements.

BE1.11 (LO 5) Indicate whether the following items would appear on the income statement (IS), statement of financial position (SFP), or retained earnings statement (RES).

_______ **a.** Notes payable. _______ **d.** Cash.

_______ **b.** Advertising expense. _______ **e.** Service revenue.

_______ **c.** Share capital—ordinary.

DO IT! Exercises

Review basic concepts.

DO IT! 1.1 (LO 1) Indicate whether each of the five statements presented below is true or false. If false, indicate how to correct the statement.

1. The three steps in the accounting process are identification, recording, and examination.
2. The accounting process includes the bookkeeping function.
3. Managerial accounting provides reports to help investors and creditors evaluate a company.
4. The two most common types of external users are investors and creditors.
5. Internal users include human resources managers.

Identify building blocks of accounting.

DO IT! 1.2 (LO 2) Indicate whether each of the five statements presented below is true or false. If false, indicate how to correct the statement.

1. IFRS are issued by the FASB.
2. The standards of conduct by which actions are judged as loyal or disloyal are ethics.
3. The primary accounting standard-setting body in the United States is the Securities and Exchange Commission (SEC).
4. Using the historical cost basis means that companies record assets at their cost and continue to report them at their cost over the time the assets are held.
5. The monetary unit assumption requires that companies record only transactions that can be measured in money.

Evaluate effects of transactions on equity.

DO IT! 1.3 (LO 3) Classify the following items as investment by shareholders (I), dividends (D), revenues (R), or expenses (E). Then indicate whether each item increases or decreases equity.

1. Dividends.
2. Rent revenue.
3. Advertising expense.
4. Shareholders invest cash in business.

Prepare tabular analysis.

DO IT! 1.4 (LO 4) Transactions made by Callahan Ltd., a law firm, for the month of March are shown below. Prepare a tabular analysis which shows the effects of these transactions on the accounting equation, similar to that shown in Illustration 1.10.

1. The company performed R20,000 of services for customers, on credit.
2. The company received R20,000 in cash from customers who had been billed for services [in transaction (1)].
3. The company received a bill for R3,200 of advertising but will not pay it until a later date.
4. The company paid a dividend of R5,000 in cash to shareholders.

Determine specific amounts on the financial statements.

DO IT! 1.5 (LO 5) Presented below is selected information related to Tsui Repairs at December 31, 2029. Tsui reports financial information monthly (amounts in thousands).

Accounts Payable	HK$ 3,000	Salaries and Wages Expense	HK$16,500
Cash	6,500	Notes Payable	25,000
Advertising Expense	6,000	Rent Expense	10,500
Service Revenue	53,500	Accounts Receivable	13,500
Equipment	29,000	Dividends	7,500

a. Determine the total assets of Tsui Repairs at December 31, 2029.

b. Determine the net income that Tsui Repairs reported for December 2029.

c. Determine the equity of Tsui Repairs at December 31, 2029.

Exercises

E1.1 (LO 1) Genesis Company performs the following accounting tasks during the year.

Classify the three activities of accounting.

________ Analyzing and interpreting information.
________ Classifying economic events.
________ Explaining uses, meaning, and limitations of data.
________ Keeping a systematic chronological diary of events.
________ Measuring events in currency (such as euros or yen).
________ Preparing accounting reports.
________ Reporting information in a standard format.
________ Selecting economic activities relevant to the company.
________ Summarizing economic events.

Accounting is "an information system that **identifies**, **records**, and **communicates** the economic events of an organization to interested users."

Instructions

Categorize the accounting tasks performed by Genesis as relating to either the identification (I), recording (R), or communication (C) aspects of accounting.

E1.2 (LO 1) **a.** The following are users of financial statements.

Identify users of accounting information.

________ Customers.
________ Tax authorities.
________ Labor unions.
________ Marketing manager.
________ Production supervisor.
________ Financial regulators.
________ Store manager.
________ Suppliers.
________ Vice president of finance.

Instructions

Identify the users as being either **external users** or **internal users**.

b. The following questions could be asked by an internal user or an external user.

________ Can we afford to give our employees a pay raise?
________ Did the company earn a satisfactory income?
________ Do we need to borrow in the near future?
________ How does the company's profitability compare to other companies?
________ What does it cost us to manufacture each unit produced?
________ Which product should we emphasize?
________ Will the company be able to pay its short-term debts?

Instructions

Identify each of the questions as being more likely asked by an **internal user** or an **external user**.

E1.3 (LO 2) Angela Manternach, president of Manternach Designs, has instructed Carla Ruden, the head of the accounting department for Manternach Designs, to report the company's land in the company's accounting reports at its current value of €170,000 instead of its cost of €100,000. Manternach says, "Showing the land at €170,000 will make our company look like a better investment when we try to attract new investors next month."

Discuss how using the historical cost basis makes ethical decision-making either easier or more difficult.

Instructions

Explain the ethical situation involving Carla Ruden, identifying the stakeholders and the alternatives.

E1.4 (LO 2) The following situations involve accounting principles and assumptions.

Use accounting concepts.

1. Julia A/S owns buildings that are worth substantially more than they originally cost. In an effort to provide more relevant information, Julia reports the buildings at their current value in its accounting reports.

2. Dekalb Creations includes in its accounting records only transaction data that can be expressed in terms of money.
3. Omar Shariff, owner of Omar's Oasis, records his personal living costs as expenses of the business.

Instructions

For each of the three situations, determine if the accounting method used is correct or incorrect. If correct, identify which principle or assumption supports the method used. If incorrect, identify which principle or assumption has been violated.

Classify accounts as assets, liabilities, and equity.

E1.5 (LO 3) Diehl Cleaners has the following statement of financial position items.

Accounts payable	Accounts receivable
Cash	Notes payable
Equipment	Salaries and wages payable
Supplies	Share capital—ordinary

Instructions

Classify each item as an asset, liability, or equity.

Analyze the effect of transactions.

E1.6 (LO 4) Selected transactions for Spring Cruises are listed below.

1. Received cash investment from shareholders to start business in exchange for ordinary shares.
2. Paid monthly rent.
3. Purchased equipment on account.
4. Billed customers for services performed.
5. Paid dividends.
6. Received cash from customers billed in (4).
7. Incurred advertising expense on account.
8. Purchased additional equipment for cash.
9. Received cash from customers when service was performed.

Instructions

List the numbers of the above transactions and describe the effect of each transaction on assets, liabilities, and equity. For example, the first answer is: (1) Increase in assets and increase in equity.

Analyze the effect of transactions on assets, liabilities, and equity.

E1.7 (LO 4) Collins Computer Timeshare entered into the following transactions during May 2029.

1. Purchased computers for R$20,000 from Digital Equipment on account.
2. Paid R$4,000 cash for May rent on storage space.
3. Received R$17,000 cash from customers for contracts billed in April.
4. Performed computer services for Viking Construction for R$4,000 cash.
5. Paid Tri-State Power R$11,000 cash for energy usage in May.
6. Shareholders invested an additional R$29,000 in the business in exchange for ordinary shares.
7. Paid Digital Equipment for the computers purchased in (1) above.
8. Incurred advertising expense for May of R$1,200 on account.

Instructions

Indicate with the appropriate letter whether each of the transactions above results in:

a. An increase in assets and a decrease in assets.
b. An increase in assets and an increase in equity.
c. An increase in assets and an increase in liabilities.
d. A decrease in assets and a decrease in equity.
e. A decrease in assets and a decrease in liabilities.
f. An increase in liabilities and a decrease in equity.
g. An increase in equity and a decrease in liabilities.

E1.8 (LO 4, 5) **Writing** An analysis of the transactions made by Kang & Co., a public accounting firm, for the month of August is shown below.

Analyze transactions and compute net income.

	Assets				= Liabilities +	Equity				
		Accounts			Accounts	Share	Retained Earnings			
	Cash	+ Receivable	+ Supplies	+ Equipment	= Payable	+ Capital	+ Rev.	− Exp.	− Div.	
1.	+£15,000					+£15,000				Issued Shares
2.	−2,000			+£5,000	+£3,000					
3.	−750		+£750							
4.	+4,600	+£4,500					+£9,100			Service Revenue
5.	−1,500				−1,500					
6.	−2,000								−£2,000	Dividends
7.	−650							−£650		Rent Expense
8.	+450	−450								
9.	−3,900							−3,900		Sal./Wages Expense
10.					+500			−500		Utilities Expense

Instructions

a. Describe each transaction that occurred for the month.

b. Determine how much equity increased for the month.

c. Compute the amount of net income for the month.

E1.9 (LO 5) An analysis of transactions for Kang & Co. was presented in E1.8.

Prepare financial statements.

Instructions

Prepare an income statement and a retained earnings statement for August and a statement of financial position at August 31, 2029. Assume that August is the company's first month of business.

E1.10 (LO 5) Toth Company had the following assets and liabilities on the dates indicated.

Determine net income (or loss).

December 31	Total Assets	Total Liabilities
2028	$400,000	$260,000
2029	$480,000	$300,000
2030	$590,000	$400,000

Toth began business on January 1, 2028, with an investment of $100,000.

Instructions

From an analysis of the change in equity during the year, compute the net income (or loss) for:

a. 2028, assuming Toth paid $15,000 in dividends for the year.

b. 2029, assuming shareholders made an additional investment of $50,000 and Toth paid no dividends in 2029.

c. 2030, assuming shareholders made an additional investment of $15,000 and Toth paid dividends of $30,000 in 2030.

E1.11 (LO 5) Two items are omitted from each of the following summaries of statement of financial position and income statement data for two proprietorships for the year 2029, Greene's Goods and Solar Enterprises.

Analyze financial statements items.

	Greene's Goods	Solar Enterprises
Beginning of year:		
Total assets	€110,000	€129,000
Total liabilities	85,000	(c)
Total equity	(a)	80,000
End of year:		
Total assets	160,000	180,000
Total liabilities	120,000	50,000
Total equity	40,000	130,000
Changes during year in equity:		
Additional investment	(b)	25,000
Dividends	37,000	(d)
Total revenues	220,000	100,000
Total expenses	175,000	60,000

Instructions

Determine the missing amounts.

Prepare income statement, comprehensive income statement, and retained earnings statement.

E1.12 (LO 5) The following information relates to Karen Weigel Co. for the year 2029.

Retained earnings, January 1, 2029	$42,000	Advertising expense	$ 1,800
Dividends paid during 2029	6,000	Rent expense	10,400
Service revenue	63,600	Utilities expense	3,100
Salaries and wages expense	30,200	Other comprehensive income	460

Instructions

After analyzing the data, prepare (a) an income statement and (b) a comprehensive income statement for the year 2029.

Correct an incorrectly prepared statement of financial position.

E1.13 (LO 5) Lynn Dreise is the bookkeeper for Sanculi SpA. Lynn has been trying to get the statement of financial position of Sanculi to balance correctly. Sanculi's statement of financial position is shown as follows.

Sanculi SpA
Statement of Financial Position
December 31, 2029

Assets		Liabilities	
Equipment	€48,000	Share capital—ordinary	€50,000
Supplies	8,000	Retained earnings	17,500
Cash	14,000	Accounts payable	16,000
Dividends	5,000	Accounts receivable	(8,500)
Total assets	€75,000	Total equity and liabilities	€75,000

Instructions

Prepare a correct statement of financial position.

Compute net income and prepare a statement of financial position.

E1.14 (LO 5) Bear Park Ltd., a camping ground in the Lake District, has compiled the following financial information as of December 31, 2029.

Revenues during 2029—camping fees	£140,000	Notes payable	£ 60,000
Revenues during 2029—general store	47,000	Expenses during 2029	150,000
Accounts payable	11,000	Supplies on hand	2,500
Cash on hand	20,000	Share capital—ordinary	20,000
Original cost of equipment	105,500	Retained earnings	?
Current value of equipment	140,000		

Instructions

a. Determine Bear Park's net income for 2029.

b. Prepare a statement of financial position for Bear Park Ltd. as of December 31, 2029.

Prepare an income statement and comprehensive income statement.

E1.15 (LO 5) Presented below is financial information related to the 2029 operations of Delgado Cruises SA.

Maintenance and repairs expense	R$ 97,000
Utilities expense	10,000
Salaries and wages expense	144,000
Advertising expense	3,500
Ticket revenue	342,000
Other comprehensive income	4,200

Instructions

Prepare the 2029 income statement and comprehensive income statement for Delgado Cruises SA.

E1.16 (LO 5) Presented below is information related to Ling an Co.

Prepare a retained earnings statement.

Retained earnings, January 1, 2029	£ 23,000
Share capital—ordinary	10,000
Legal service revenue—2029	340,000
Total expenses—2029	211,000
Assets, January 1, 2029	95,000
Liabilities, January 1, 2029	62,000
Assets, December 31, 2029	168,000
Liabilities, December 31, 2029	80,000
Dividends—2029	64,000

Instructions

Prepare the 2029 retained earnings statement for Ling an Co.

E1.17 (LO 5) This information is for Java Growers for the year ended December 31, 2029 (amounts in thousands).

Prepare a cash flow statement.

Cash received from revenues from customers	Rp600,000
Cash received for issuance of ordinary shares	280,000
Cash paid for new equipment	95,000
Cash dividends paid	20,000
Cash paid for expenses	430,000
Cash balance 1/1/29	28,000

Instructions

Prepare the 2029 statement of cash flows for Java Growers.

E1.18 (LO 5) The statement of cash flows classifies each transaction as an operating activity, an investing activity, or a financing activity. Operating activities are the types of activities the company performs to generate profits. Investing activities include the purchase of long-lived assets such as equipment or the purchase of investment securities. Financing activities are borrowing money, issuing shares of stock, and paying dividends.

Identify cash flow activities.

Presented below are the following transactions.

1. Shareholders invested $20,000 cash in exchange for ordinary shares.
2. Issued note payable for $12,000 cash.
3. Purchased office equipment for $11,000 cash.
4. Received $15,000 cash for services performed.
5. Paid $1,000 cash for rent.
6. Paid $600 dividend.
7. Paid $5,700 cash for salaries.

Instructions

Classify each of these transactions as operating, investing, or financing activities.

Problems

P1.1 (LO 4) Fredonia Repair Inc. was started on May 1. A summary of May transactions is presented as follows.

Analyze transactions and compute net income.

1. Shareholders invested $10,000 cash in the business in exchange for ordinary shares.
2. Purchased equipment for $5,000 cash.
3. Paid $400 cash for May office rent.
4. Paid $300 cash for supplies.
5. Incurred $250 of advertising costs in the *Beacon News* on account.
6. Received $4,700 in cash from customers for repair service.
7. Declared and paid a $700 cash dividend.

8. Paid part-time employee salaries $1,000.
9. Paid utility bills $140.
10. Performed repair services worth $1,100 on account.
11. Collected cash of $120 for services billed in transaction (10).

Check figures provide a key number to let you know you are on the right track.

Instructions

a. Total assets $13,560

a. Prepare a tabular analysis of the transactions using the following column headings: Cash, Accounts Receivable, Supplies, Equipment, Accounts Payable, Share Capital—Ordinary, and Retained Earnings (with separate columns for Revenues, Expenses, and Dividends). Include margin explanations for any changes in equity. Revenue is called Service Revenue.

b. Net income $4,010

b. From an analysis of the Retained Earnings columns, compute the net income or net loss for May.

Analyze transactions and prepare income statement, retained earnings statement, and statement of financial position.

P1.2 (LO 4, 5) On August 31, the statement of financial position of La Brava Veterinary Clinic showed Cash $9,000, Accounts Receivable $1,700, Supplies $600, Equipment $6,000, Accounts Payable $3,600, Share Capital—Ordinary $13,000, and Retained Earnings $700. During September, the following transactions occurred.

1. Paid $2,900 cash for accounts payable due.
2. Collected $1,300 of accounts receivable.
3. Purchased additional equipment for $2,100, paying $800 in cash and the balance on account.
4. Recognized revenue of $7,300, of which $2,500 is collected in cash and the balance is due in October.
5. Declared and paid a $400 cash dividend.
6. Paid salaries $1,700, rent for September $900, and advertising expense $200.
7. Incurred utilities expense for month on account $170.
8. Received $10,000 from Capital Bank on a 6-month note payable.

Instructions

a. Ending cash $15,900

a. Prepare a tabular analysis of the September transactions beginning with August 31 balances. The column headings should be as follows: Cash + Accounts Receivable + Supplies + Equipment = Notes Payable + Accounts Payable + Share Capital—Ordinary + Retained Earnings + Revenues − Expenses − Dividends.

b. Net income $4,330
Total assets $29,800

b. Prepare an income statement for September, a retained earnings statement for September, and a statement of financial position at September 30, 2029.

Prepare income statement, retained earnings statement, and statement of financial position.

P1.3 (LO 5) On May 1, 2029, Park Flying School Ltd., a company that provides flying lessons, was started with an investment of ₩45,000 cash in the business. Following are the assets and liabilities of the company on May 31, 2029, and the revenues and expenses for the month of May (all amounts in thousands).

Cash	₩ 4,500	Notes Payable	₩ 28,000
Accounts Receivable	7,420	Rent Expense	1,000
Equipment	64,000	Maintenance and	
Service Revenue	6,800	Repairs Expense	400
Advertising Expense	500	Gasoline Expense	2,500
Accounts Payable	1,400	Utilities Expense	400

No additional investments were made in May, but the company paid dividends of ₩480,000 during the month.

Instructions

a. Net income ₩2,000
Total assets ₩75,920
b. Net income ₩1,400

a. Prepare an income statement and a retained earnings statement for the month of May and a statement of financial position at May 31. (Show numbers in thousands.)

b. Prepare an income statement and a retained earnings statement for May assuming the following data are not included above: (1) ₩900,000 worth of services were performed and billed but not collected at May 31, and (2) ₩1,500,000 of gasoline expense was incurred but not paid.

Analyze transactions and prepare financial statements.

P1.4 (LO 4, 5) Matt Stiner started a delivery service, Stiner Deliveries Ltd., on June 1, 2029. The following transactions occurred during the month of June.

June	1	Shareholders invested £10,000 cash in the business in exchange for ordinary shares.
	2	Purchased a used van for deliveries for £14,000. Matt paid £2,000 cash and signed a note payable for the remaining balance.
	3	Paid £500 for office rent for the month.

5 Performed services worth £4,800 on account.
9 Declared and paid £300 in cash dividends.
12 Purchased supplies for £150 on account.
15 Received a cash payment of £1,250 for services performed on June 5.
17 Purchased gasoline for £100 on account.
20 Received a cash payment of £1,500 for additional services performed.
23 Made a cash payment of £500 on the note payable.
26 Paid £250 for utilities.
29 Paid for the gasoline purchased on account on June 17.
30 Paid £1,000 for employee salaries.

Instructions

a. Show the effects of the above transactions on the accounting equation using the following format.

a. Total assets £25,800

	Assets				=	Liabilities		+	Equity			
										Retained Earnings		
Date	Cash	+ Accounts Receivable	+ Supplies	+ Equipment	=	Notes Payable	+ Accounts Payable		+ Share Capital	+ Rev.	− Exp.	− Div.

Include margin explanations for any changes in the Retained Earnings account in your analysis.

b. Prepare an income statement for the month of June.

b. Net income £4,450

c. Prepare a statement of financial position at June 30, 2029.

c. Cash £8,100

P1.5 (LO 4, 5) Financial statement information about four different companies is as follows.

Determine financial statement amounts and prepare retained earnings statement.

	Donatello Company	Leonardo Company	Michelangelo Company	Raphael Company
January 1, 2029				
Assets	$ 75,000	$110,000	(g)	$150,000
Liabilities	48,000	(d)	$ 75,000	(j)
Equity	(a)	60,000	45,000	100,000
December 31, 2029				
Assets	(b)	137,000	200,000	(k)
Liabilities	55,000	75,000	(h)	80,000
Equity	40,000	(e)	130,000	140,000
Equity changes in year				
Additional investment	(c)	15,000	10,000	15,000
Dividends	6,000	(f)	14,000	10,000
Total revenues	350,000	420,000	(i)	500,000
Total expenses	335,000	382,000	342,000	(l)

Instructions

a. Determine the missing amounts. (*Hint:* For example, to solve for (a), Assets − Liabilities = Equity = $27,000.)

b. Prepare the retained earnings statement for Leonardo Company. Assume beginning retained earnings was $20,000.

b. Retained earnings (ending) $7,000

c. Write an email explaining the sequence for preparing financial statements and the interrelationship of the retained earnings statement with the income statement and statement of financial position.

Expand Your Critical Thinking

Financial Reporting Problem: TSMC, Ltd. (TWN)

CT1.1 The financial statements of **TSMC** are presented in Appendix A. The complete annual report, including the notes to the financial statements, is available at the company's website.

Instructions

Refer to TSMC's financial statements and answer the following questions. (Use amounts as reported in New Taiwan dollars.)

a. What were TSMC's total assets at December 31, 2020? At December 31, 2019?

b. How much cash (and cash equivalents) did TSMC have on December 31, 2020?

c. What amount of accounts payable did TSMC report on December 31, 2020? On December 31, 2019?

d. What was TSMC's revenue in 2019? In 2020?

e. What is the amount of the change in TSMC's net income from 2019 to 2020?

Comparative Analysis Problem: Nestlé SA (CHE) vs. Delfi Limited (SGP)

CT1.2 **Nestlé**'s financial statements are presented in Appendix B. Financial statements of **Delfi Limited** are presented in Appendix C.

Instructions

Refer to the financial statements and answer the following questions.

a. Based on the information contained in these financial statements, determine the following for each company.

1. Total assets at December 31, 2020.
2. Accounts (trade) receivable, net at December 31, 2020.
3. Net sales for year ended December 31, 2020.
4. Net income (profit) for year ended December 31, 2020.

b. What percentage do receivables represent of total assets for the two companies? What percentage does net income represent of sales (revenue) for the two companies?

Real-World Focus

CT1.3 This exercise will familiarize you with the skills needed (other than accounting skills) to be a successful accountant.

Instructions

Search the Internet for "start here go places" to access resources for future accountants and then answer the following questions.

a. What are the four skill sets that are useful for success in accounting?

b. Why are these skill sets useful for a successful accounting career?

Decision-Making Across the Organization

CT1.4 Anya and Nick Ramon, local golf stars, opened the Chip-Shot Driving Range Ltd. on March 1, 2029, investing £25,000 of their cash savings in the business in exchange for ordinary shares. A caddy shack was constructed for cash at a cost of £8,000, and £800 was spent on golf balls and golf clubs. The company leased five acres of land at a cost of £1,000 per month and paid the first month's rent. During the first month, advertising costs totaled £750, of which £100 was unpaid at March 31, and £500 was paid to members of the high-school golf team for retrieving golf balls. All revenues from customers were deposited in the company's bank account. On March 15, the company paid a total of £1,000 in dividends. A £120 utility bill was received on March 31 but was not paid. On March 31, the balance in the company's bank account was £18,900.

Anya and Nick thought they had a pretty good first month of operations. But, their estimates of profitability ranged from a loss of £6,100 to net income of £2,480.

Instructions

With the class divided into groups, answer the following.

a. How could the Ramons have concluded that the company operated at a loss of £6,100? Was this a valid basis on which to determine net income?

b. How could the Ramons have concluded that the company operated at a net income of £2,480? (*Hint:* Prepare a statement of financial position at March 31.) Was this a valid basis on which to determine net income?

c. Without preparing an income statement, determine the actual net income for March.

d. What was the revenue recognized in March?

Communication Activity

CT1.5 Erin Danielle, the bookkeeper for Liverpool Ltd., has been trying to determine the correct statement of financial position for the company. The company's statement of financial position is shown below.

Liverpool Ltd.
Statement of Financial Position
For the Month Ended December 31, 2029

Assets		**Liabilities**	
Equipment	£25,500	Share capital—ordinary	£20,000
Cash	9,000	Accounts receivable	(5,000)
Supplies	3,000	Retained earnings	4,000
Accounts payable	(8,000)	Notes payable	10,500
	£29,500		£29,500

Instructions

Explain to Erin Danielle in an email why the original statement of financial position is incorrect, and what should be done to correct it.

All About You

CT1.6 Some people are tempted to make their finances look worse to get financial aid. Companies sometimes also manage their financial numbers in order to accomplish certain goals. Earnings management is the planned timing of revenues, expenses, gains, and losses to smooth out bumps in net income. In managing earnings, companies' actions vary from being within the range of ethical activity to being both unethical and illegal attempts to mislead investors and creditors.

Instructions

Provide responses for each of the following questions.

a. Discuss whether you think each of the following actions to increase the chances of receiving financial aid is ethical.

1. Spend the student's assets and income first, before spending parents' assets and income.
2. Accelerate necessary expenses to reduce available cash. For example, if you need a new car, buy it before applying for financial aid.
3. State that a truly financially dependent child is independent.
4. Have a parent take an unpaid leave of absence for long enough to get below the "threshold" level of income.

b. What are some reasons why a **company** might want to overstate its earnings?

c. What are some reasons why a **company** might want to understate its earnings?

d. Under what circumstances might an otherwise ethical person decide to illegally overstate or understate earnings?

Considering Environmental, Social, and Governance Reporting

CT1.7 Although **Clif Bar & Company** (USA) is not a public company, it does share its financial information with its employees as part of its open-book management approach. Further, although it does not publicly share its financial information, it does provide a different form of an annual report to external users. In this report, the company provides information regarding its sustainability efforts.

Instructions

Go to the Who We Are page at the Clif Bar website and identify the five aspirations.

Answers to Insight and Accounting Across the Organization Questions

Using Data Science to Create Art Q: How can "big data" improve decision-making? **A:** Companies analyze the large amounts of data now available to improve cost estimation for future projects as well as identify bottlenecks and opportunities to increase the efficiency of production processes.

Loyalty to Your Employer Is Great, Until It Is Not Q: What would you do if your company asked you to misreport an item? **A:** You would be placed in a difficult situation. However, although you might be pressured by your supervisor to make the company's financial statements look better than warranted, you can be prosecuted for fraudulent activities.

The Korean Discount Q: What is meant by the phrase "make the country's businesses more transparent"? Why would increasing transparency spur economic growth? **A:** Transparency refers to the extent to which outsiders have knowledge regarding a company's financial performance and financial position. If a company lacks transparency, its financial reports do not adequately inform investors of critical information that is needed to make investment decisions. If company transparency is increased, investors would be more willing to supply the financial capital that businesses need in order to grow, which would spur the country's economic growth.

Spinning the Career Wheel Q: How might accounting help you? **A:** You will need to understand financial reports in any enterprise with which you are associated. Accounting reports provide financial information about the resources, claims on resources, and the performance of an organization, which is important for any role in the organization. Whether you become a manager, doctor, lawyer, social worker, teacher, engineer, architect, or entrepreneur, a working knowledge of accounting is relevant.

A Wise End Q: What year-end would you likely use if you owned a ski resort and ski rental business? What if you owned a college bookstore? Why choose those year-ends? **A:** You most likely would choose a different year-end for a ski resort and ski rental business, which would be busiest during the coldest months of the year, versus a college bookstore, which would be busiest at the beginning and end of each semester. So for the ski resort and rental business, May 31 (or some other month not during the busy winter months) would make sense. For the college bookstore, June 30 or July 31 (or some other month not during the busy school months) would make sense.

Beyond Financial Statements Q: Why might a company's shareholders be interested in its environmental and social performance? **A:** Many companies now recognize that being a socially responsible organization is not only the right thing to do, but it also is good for business. Many investment professionals understand, for example, that environmental, social, and proper corporate governance of companies affects the performance of their investment portfolios. For example, **British Petroleum**'s (GBR) oil spill disaster is a classic example of the problems that can occur for a company and its shareholders. BP's share price was slashed, its dividend reduced, its executives replaced, and its reputation badly damaged. Socially responsible investment funds are now gaining momentum in the marketplace, such that companies now recognize this segment as an important investment group.

A Look at U.S. GAAP

LEARNING OBJECTIVE 7

Describe the impact of U.S. accounting standards on global financial reporting.

As indicated in the chapter, IFRSs, which are issued by the IASB, are used by most countries in the world. However, another major standard-setter resides in the United States: the Financial Accounting Standards Board (FASB). Prior to the creation of IFRS, the U.S. accounting standards, referred to as generally accepted accounting principles (GAAP), were used by companies in many countries.

Key Points

While the IASB and the FASB often work together on projects, it appears for the foreseeable future the two Boards will continue to exist independent of one another. It is therefore important for investors, accountants, and students to understand the key similarities and differences that exist between the standards.

Similarities

- GAAP is based on a conceptual framework that is similar to that used to develop IFRS.
- The three common forms of business organization that are presented in the chapter, proprietorships, partnerships, and corporations, are also found in the United States. Because the choice of

business organization is influenced by factors such as legal environment, tax rates and regulations, and degree of entrepreneurism, the relative use of each form will vary across countries.

- Transaction analysis is basically the same under IFRS and GAAP but, as you will see in later chapters, the different standards may impact how transactions are recorded.
- Financial frauds have occurred at companies such as **Satyam Computer Services** (IND), **Parmalat** (ITA), and **Royal Ahold** (NLD). They have also occurred at large U.S. companies such as **Enron**, **WorldCom**, and **AIG**.

Differences

- The Sarbanes-Oxley Act (SOX) mandates certain internal controls for large public companies listed on U.S. exchanges. There is a continuing debate as to whether non-U.S. companies should have to comply with this extra layer of regulation. Debate about international companies (non-U.S.) adopting SOX-type standards centers on whether the benefits exceed the costs. The concern is that the higher costs of SOX compliance are making the U.S. securities markets less competitive.
- U.S. regulators have recently eliminated the need for foreign companies that trade shares in U.S. markets to reconcile their accounting with GAAP.
- IFRS tends to be less detailed in its accounting and disclosure requirements than GAAP. This difference in approach has resulted in a debate about the merits of "principles-based" (IFRS) versus "rules-based" (GAAP) standards.

GAAP Practice

GAAP Self-Test Questions

1. Which of the following is **not** a reason why a single set of high-quality international accounting standards would be beneficial?
   - **a.** Mergers and acquisition activity.
   - **b.** Financial markets.
   - **c.** Multinational corporations.
   - **d.** GAAP is widely considered to be a superior reporting system.
2. The Sarbanes-Oxley Act determines:
   - **a.** international tax regulations.
   - **b.** internal control standards as enforced by the IASB.
   - **c.** internal control standards of U.S. publicly traded companies.
   - **d.** U.S. tax regulations.
3. IFRS is considered to be more:
   - **a.** principles-based and less rules-based than GAAP.
   - **b.** rules-based and less principles-based than GAAP.
   - **c.** detailed than GAAP.
   - **d.** None of the answer choices is correct.
4. Which of the following statements is **false**?
   - **a.** GAAP is based on a conceptual framework that is similar to that used to develop IFRS.
   - **b.** FASB and the IASB are working on a joint project related to the conceptual framework.
   - **c.** Non-U.S. companies that trade shares in U.S. markets must reconcile their accounting with GAAP.
   - **d.** Proprietorships, partnerships, and corporations are also found in countries that use IFRS.
5. Which of the following is **true**?
   - **a.** Financial frauds have not occurred in U.S. companies because GAAP has detailed accounting and disclosure requirements.
   - **b.** Transaction analysis is basically the same under GAAP and IFRS.
   - **c.** IFRS companies have agreed to adopt the Sarbanes-Oxley Act related to internal control in 2025.
   - **d.** Foreign companies that trade shares in U.S. markets must reconcile their accounting with the FASB.

GAAP Exercises

GAAP1.1 Who are the two key international players in the development of international accounting standards? Explain their role.

GAAP1.2 What might explain the fact that different accounting standard-setters have developed accounting standards that are sometimes quite different in nature?

GAAP1.3 What is the benefit of a single set of high-quality accounting standards?

GAAP1.4 Discuss the potential advantages and disadvantages that countries outside the United States should consider before adopting regulations, such as those in the Sarbanes-Oxley Act, that increase corporate internal control requirements.

GAAP Financial Reporting Problem: Apple Inc. (USA)

GAAP1.5 The financial statements of **Apple** are presented in Appendix D. The complete annual report, including the notes to its financial statements, is available at the company's website.

Instructions

Refer to Apple's financial statements to answer the following questions.

a. What were Apple's total assets at September 26, 2020? At September 28, 2019?

b. How much cash did Apple have on September 26, 2020?

c. What amount of accounts payable did Apple report on September 26, 2020? On September 28, 2019?

d. What were Apple's total revenues in 2020? In 2019? In 2018?

e. What is the amount of the change in Apple's net income from 2019 to 2020?

Answers to GAAP Self-Test Questions

1. d **2.** c **3.** a **4.** c **5.** b

CHAPTER **2**

The Recording Process

LEARNING OBJECTIVES After studying this chapter, you should be able to:

LO 1 Describe how accounts, debits, and credits are used to record business transactions.

LO 2 Indicate how a journal is used in the recording process.

LO 3 Explain how a ledger and posting help in the recording process.

LO 4 Prepare a trial balance.

Chapter Preview

In Chapter 1, we analyzed business transactions in terms of the accounting equation, and we presented the cumulative effects of these transactions in tabular form. Imagine a company like **Bank of Taiwan** (TWN) (as in the following Feature Story) using the same tabular format as Softbyte SA to keep track of its transactions. In a single day, Bank of Taiwan engages in thousands of business transactions. To record each transaction this way would be impractical, expensive, and unnecessary. Instead, companies use a set of procedures and records to keep track of transaction data more easily. This chapter introduces and illustrates these basic procedures and records.

The Recording Process

Accounts, Debits, and Credits

- The account
- Debits and credits
- Equity relationships
- Summary of debit/credit rules

The Journal

- The recording process
- The journal

The Ledger and Posting

- The ledger
- Posting
- Chart of accounts
- The recording process illustrated
- Summary illustration of journalizing and posting

The Trial Balance

- Limitations of a trial balance
- Locating errors
- Currency signs and underlining

Practice

DO IT! 1 Normal Account Balances

DO IT! 2 Recording Business Activities

DO IT! 3 Posting

DO IT! 4 Trial Balance

Go to the Review and Practice section at the end of the chapter for a review of key concepts and practice applications with solutions.
Additional tutorials and practice opportunities are available in the Wiley online course.

Feature Story Accidents Happen

How organized are you financially? Take a short quiz. Answer *yes* or *no* to each question:

- Does your wallet contain so many cash machine receipts that you've been declared a walking fire hazard?
- Do you verify the accuracy of your bank account about as often as you clean the space behind your refrigerator?
- Do you wait until your debit card is denied before checking the status of your funds?

If you think it is hard to keep track of the many transactions that make up *your* life, imagine what it is like for a major company like **Bank of Taiwan (BOT)** (TWN). If you had your life savings invested at BOT, you might be just slightly displeased if, when you checked your balance online, a message appeared on the screen indicating that your account information was lost.

To ensure the accuracy of your balance and the security of your funds, BOT, like all other companies large and small, relies on a sophisticated accounting information system. That's not to say that BOT or any other company is error-free. In fact, if you've ever overdrawn your bank account because you failed to track your debit card purchases properly, you may take some comfort from one accountant's mistake at **Fidelity Investments** (USA), one of the largest mutual fund investment firms in the world. The accountant failed to include a minus sign while doing a calculation, making what was actually a $1.3 billion loss look like a $1.3 billion—yes, *billion*—gain! Fortunately, like most accounting errors, it was detected before any real harm was done.

No one expects that kind of mistake at a company like Fidelity, which has sophisticated computer systems and top investment managers. In explaining the mistake to shareholders, a spokesperson wrote, "Some people have asked how, in this age of technology, such a mistake could be made. While many of our processes are computerized, accounting systems are complex and dictate that some steps must be handled manually by our managers and accountants, and people can make mistakes."

TPG/Shutterstock

2.1 Accounts, Debits, and Credits

LEARNING OBJECTIVE 1

Describe how accounts, debits, and credits are used to record business transactions.

The Account

An **account** is an individual accounting record of increases and decreases in a specific asset, liability, or equity item. For example, Softbyte SA (the company discussed in Chapter 1) would have separate accounts for Cash, Accounts Receivable, Accounts Payable, Service Revenue, Salaries and Wages Expense, and so on. (Note that whenever we are referring to a specific account, we capitalize the name.)

In its simplest form, an account consists of three parts:

1. A title.
2. A left or debit side.
3. A right or credit side.

Because the format of an account resembles the letter T, we refer to it as a **T-account**. **Illustration 2.1** shows the basic form of an account.

ILLUSTRATION 2.1

Basic form of account

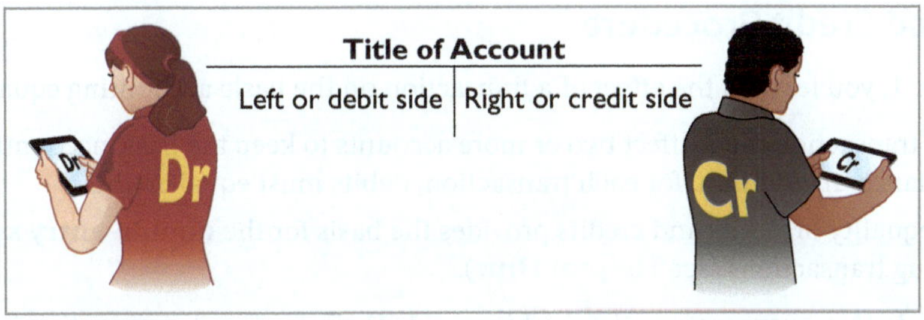

We use this form often throughout this text to explain basic accounting relationships.

Debits and Credits

The term **debit** indicates the left side of an account, and **credit** indicates the right side.

- They are commonly abbreviated as **Dr.** for debit and **Cr.** for credit. They **do not** mean increase or decrease, as is commonly thought.
- We use the terms **debit** and **credit** repeatedly in the recording process to describe **where** entries are made in accounts.
- For example, the act of entering an amount on the left side of an account is called **debiting** the account. Making an entry on the right side is **crediting** the account.

When comparing the totals of the two sides, an account shows a **debit balance** if the total of the debit amounts exceeds the credits. An account shows a **credit balance** if the credit amounts exceed the debits. Note the position of the debit side and credit side in Illustration 2.1.

The procedure of recording debits and credits in an account is shown in **Illustration 2.2** for the transactions affecting the Cash account of Softbyte SA. The data are taken from the Cash column of the tabular summary in Illustration 1.10.

ILLUSTRATION 2.2

Tabular summary and account form for Softbyte's Cash account

Tabular Summary

Cash
€15,000
−7,000
1,200
1,500
−1,700
−250
600
−1,300
€ 8,050

Account Form

Cash			
(Debits)	15,000	(Credits)	7,000
	1,200		1,700
	1,500		250
	600		1,300
Balance (Debit)	8,050		

Every positive item in the tabular summary represents a receipt of cash. Every negative amount represents a payment of cash. **Notice that in the account form, we record the increases in cash as debits and the decreases in cash as credits**. For example, the €15,000 receipt of cash (in blue) is debited to Cash, and the –€7,000 payment of cash (in red) is credited to Cash.

- Having increases on one side and decreases on the other reduces recording errors and helps in determining the totals of each side of the account as well as the account balance.
- The balance is determined by netting the two sides (subtracting one amount from the other).

Here, the account balance, a debit of €8,050, indicates that Softbyte had €8,050 more increases than decreases in cash. In other words, Softbyte started with a balance of zero and now has €8,050 in its Cash account.

Debit and Credit Procedure

HELPFUL HINT

Rules for accounting for specific events sometimes differ across countries. Despite the differences, the double-entry accounting system is the basis of accounting systems worldwide.

In Chapter 1, you learned the effect of a transaction on the basic accounting equation.

- Each transaction must affect two or more accounts to keep the basic accounting equation in balance. In addition, for each transaction, debits must equal credits.
- The equality of debits and credits provides the basis for the **double-entry system** of recording transactions (see **Helpful Hint**).

Under the double-entry system, the dual (two-sided) effect of each transaction is recorded in appropriate accounts. This system provides a logical method for recording transactions and also helps ensure the accuracy of the recorded amounts as well as the detection of errors. If every transaction is recorded with equal debits and credits, the sum of all the debits to the accounts must equal the sum of all the credits.

The double-entry system for determining the equality of the accounting equation is much more efficient than the plus/minus procedure used in Chapter 1. The following discussion illustrates debit and credit procedures in the double-entry system.

Dr./Cr. Procedures for Assets and Liabilities

In Illustration 2.2 for Softbyte, increases in Cash—an asset—are entered on the left side, and decreases in Cash are entered on the right side.

- We know that both sides of the basic equation (Assets = Liabilities + Equity) must be equal.
- It therefore follows that increases and decreases in liabilities have to be recorded **opposite from** increases and decreases in assets.
- Thus, increases in liabilities are entered on the right or credit side, and decreases in liabilities are entered on the left or debit side.

The effects that debits and credits have on assets and liabilities are summarized in **Illustration 2.3**.

ILLUSTRATION 2.3

Debit and credit effects—assets and liabilities

Debits	Credits
Increase assets	Decrease assets
Decrease liabilities	Increase liabilities

Asset accounts normally show debit balances. That is, debits to a specific asset account should exceed credits to that account. Likewise, **liability accounts normally show credit balances**. That is, credits to a liability account should exceed debits to that account. The **normal balance** of an account is on the side where an increase in the account is recorded. **Illustration 2.4** shows the normal balances for assets and liabilities.

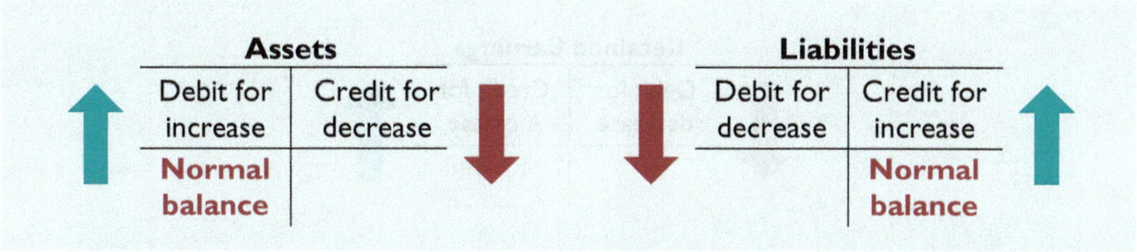

ILLUSTRATION 2.4

Normal balances—assets and liabilities

Knowing the normal balance in an account may help you trace errors. For example, a credit balance in an asset account such as Land or a debit balance in a liability account such as Salaries and Wages Payable usually indicates an error. Occasionally, though, an abnormal balance may be correct. The Cash account, for example, will have a credit balance when a company has overdrawn its bank balance by spending more than it has in its account.

Dr./Cr. Procedures for Equity

As Chapter 1 indicated, shareholders' investments and revenues increase equity. Dividends and expenses decrease equity. In a double-entry system, companies keep accounts for each of these types of transactions: share capital—ordinary, retained earnings, dividends, revenues, and expenses.

Share Capital—Ordinary Companies issue share capital—ordinary in exchange for the owners' investment paid in to the company.

- Credits increase the Share Capital—Ordinary account, and debits decrease it.
- When an owner invests cash in the business in exchange for ordinary shares, the company debits (increases) Cash and credits (increases) Share Capital—Ordinary.

Illustration 2.5 shows the rules of debit and credit for the Share Capital—Ordinary account.

Debits	Credits
Decrease Share Capital—Ordinary	Increase Share Capital—Ordinary

ILLUSTRATION 2.5

Debit and credit effects—share capital—ordinary

We can diagram the normal balance in Share Capital—Ordinary as shown in **Illustration 2.6**.

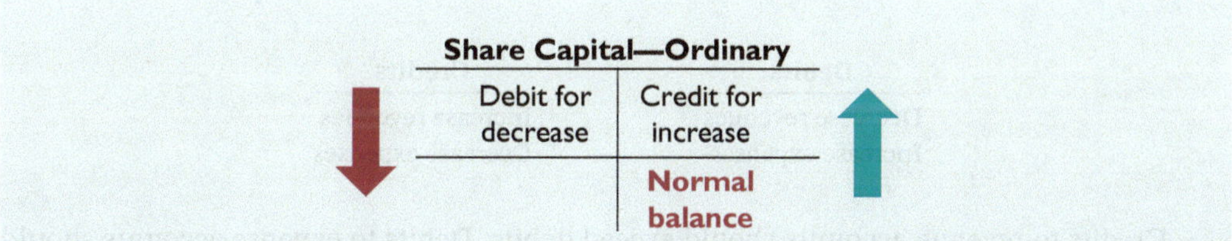

ILLUSTRATION 2.6

Normal balance—share capital—ordinary

Retained Earnings **Retained earnings** is net income that is kept (retained) in the business.

- Retained Earnings represents the portion of equity that the company has accumulated through the profitable operation of the business.
- Credits (net income) increase the Retained Earnings account, and debits (dividends or net losses) decrease it, as **Illustration 2.7** shows (see **Helpful Hint**).

HELPFUL HINT

The rules for debit and credit and the normal balances of share capital—ordinary and retained earnings are the same as for liabilities.

ILLUSTRATION 2.7

Debit and credit effects and normal balance—retained earnings

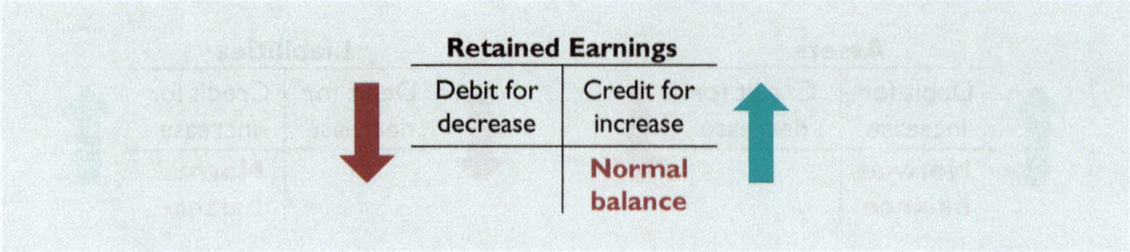

Dividends A **dividend** is a company's distribution to its shareholders. The most common form of a distribution is a **cash dividend.**

- Dividends reduce the shareholders' claims on retained earnings.
- Debits increase the Dividends account, and credits decrease it.

Illustration 2.8 shows that this account normally has a debit balance.

ILLUSTRATION 2.8

Debit and credit effect and normal balance—dividends

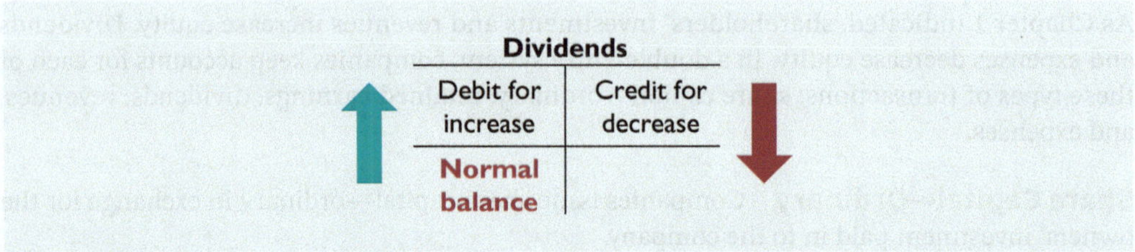

HELPFUL HINT

Because revenues increase equity, a revenue account has the same debit/credit rules as the Retained Earnings account. Expenses have the opposite effect.

Revenues and Expenses The purpose of earning revenues is to benefit the shareholders of the business.

- When a company recognizes revenues, equity increases. Therefore, **the effect of debits and credits on revenue accounts is the same as their effect on Retained Earnings**. That is, revenue accounts are increased by credits and decreased by debits (see **Helpful Hint**).
- Expenses have the opposite effect. Expenses decrease equity. Since expenses decrease net income and revenues increase it, it is logical that the increase and decrease sides of expense accounts should be the opposite of revenue accounts. Thus, expense accounts are increased by debits and decreased by credits.

Illustration 2.9 shows the rules of debits and credits for revenues and expenses.

ILLUSTRATION 2.9

Debit and credit effects—revenues and expenses

Debits	Credits
Decrease revenues	Increase revenues
Increase expenses	Decrease expenses

Credits to revenue accounts should exceed debits. Debits to expense accounts should exceed credits. Thus, revenue accounts normally show credit balances, and expense accounts normally show debit balances. **Illustration 2.10** shows the normal balances for revenues and expenses.

ILLUSTRATION 2.10

Normal balances—revenues and expenses

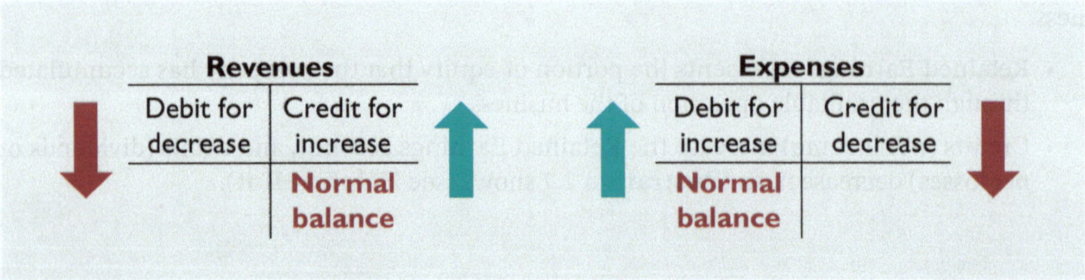

Investor Insight CTBC Brothers

Mandy Cheng/AFP/ Getty Images

Keeping Score

The **CTBC Brothers** (TWN) baseball team probably has these major revenue and expense accounts:

Revenues	Expenses
Admissions (ticket sales)	Players' salaries
Concessions	Administrative salaries
Television and radio	Travel
Advertising	Stadium maintenance

Do you think that the Manchester United (GBR) football (soccer) club would be likely to have the same major revenue and expense accounts as CTBC Brothers? (Answer is available near the end of the chapter.)

Equity Relationships

As Chapter 1 indicated, companies report share capital—ordinary and retained earnings in the equity section of the statement of financial position. They report dividends on the retained earnings statement. And they report revenues and expenses on the income statement. Dividends, revenues, and expenses are eventually transferred to retained earnings at the end of the period. As a result, a change in any one of these three items affects equity. **Illustration 2.11** shows the relationships related to equity.

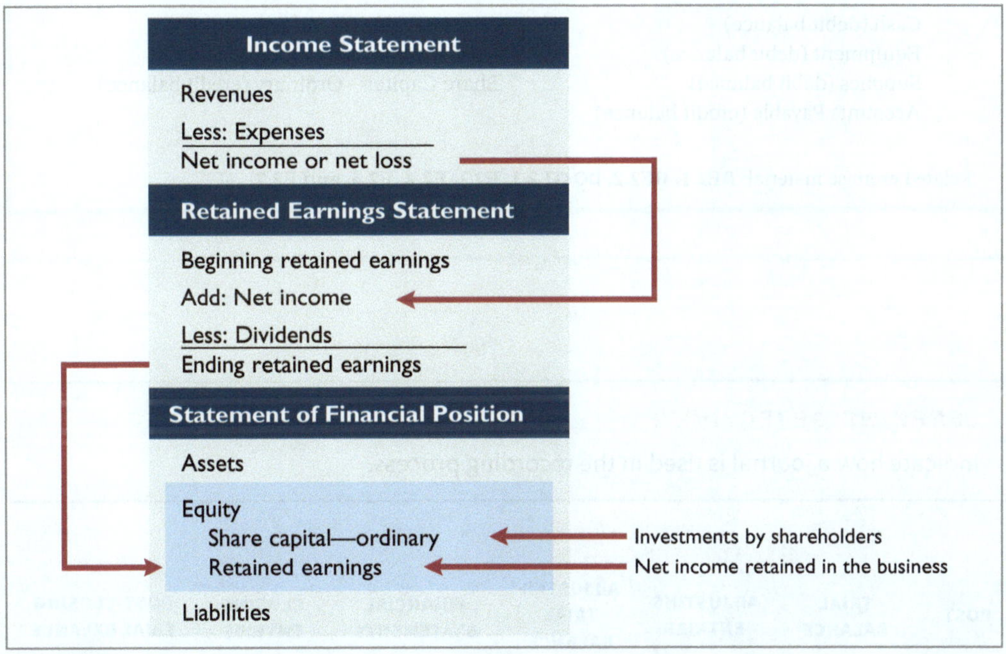

ILLUSTRATION 2.11
Equity relationships

Summary of Debit/Credit Rules

Illustration 2.12 shows a summary of the debit/credit rules and effects on each type of account. Study this diagram carefully. It will help you understand the fundamentals of the double-entry system.

ILLUSTRATION 2.12 Summary of debit/credit rules

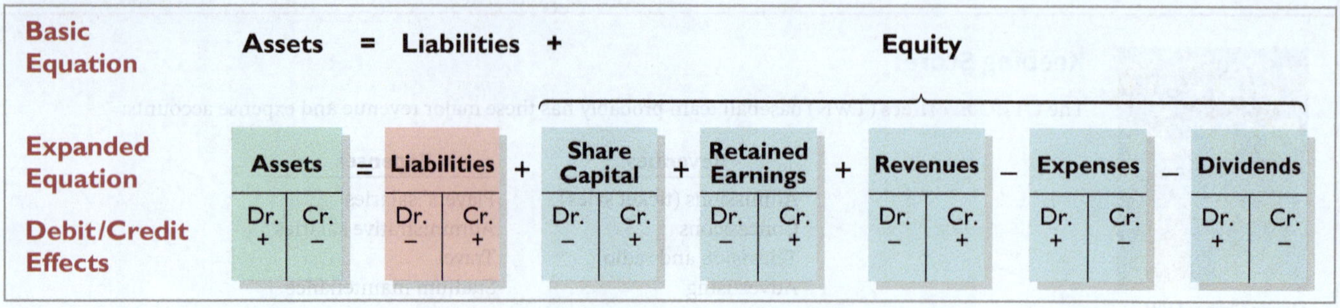

ACTION PLAN

- **Determine the types of accounts needed. Julie will need asset accounts for each different type of asset invested in the business and liability accounts for any debts incurred.**
- **Understand the types of equity accounts. Only Share Capital—Ordinary will be needed when Julie begins the business. Other equity accounts will be needed later.**

DO IT! 1 | Normal Account Balances

Julie Loeng has just rented space in a shopping mall. In this space, she will open a hair salon to be called "Hair It Is." A friend has advised Julie to set up a double-entry set of accounting records in which to record all of her business transactions.

Identify the statement of financial position accounts that Julie will likely need to record the transactions needed to open her business. Indicate whether the normal balance of each account is a debit or a credit.

Solution

Julie would likely need the following accounts in which to record the transactions necessary to ready her hair salon for opening day:

Cash (debit balance)
Equipment (debit balance)
Supplies (debit balance)
Accounts Payable (credit balance)
Notes Payable (credit balance) (if she borrows money)
Share Capital—Ordinary (credit balance)

Related exercise material: **BE2.1, BE2.2, DO IT! 2.1, E2.1, E2.2, E2.6, and E2.7.**

2.2 The Journal

LEARNING OBJECTIVE 2

Indicate how a journal is used in the recording process.

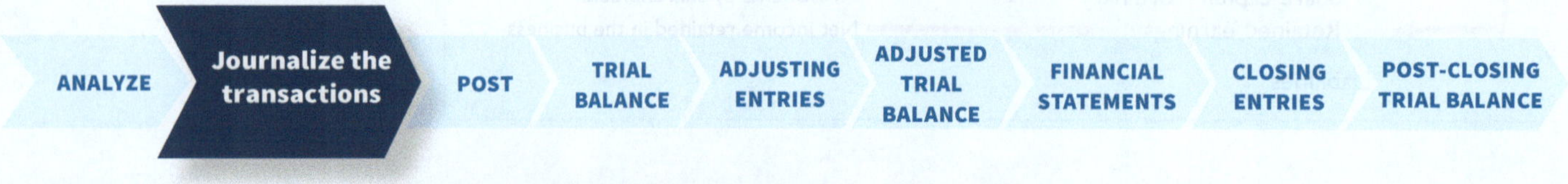

The Recording Process

Although it is possible to enter transaction information directly into the accounts, few businesses do so. Practically every business uses the basic steps shown in **Illustration 2.13** in the recording process (an integral part of the accounting cycle):

1. Analyze each transaction in terms of its effect on the accounts.
2. Enter the transaction information in a journal.
3. Transfer the journal information to the appropriate accounts in the ledger.

ILLUSTRATION 2.13 **The recording process**

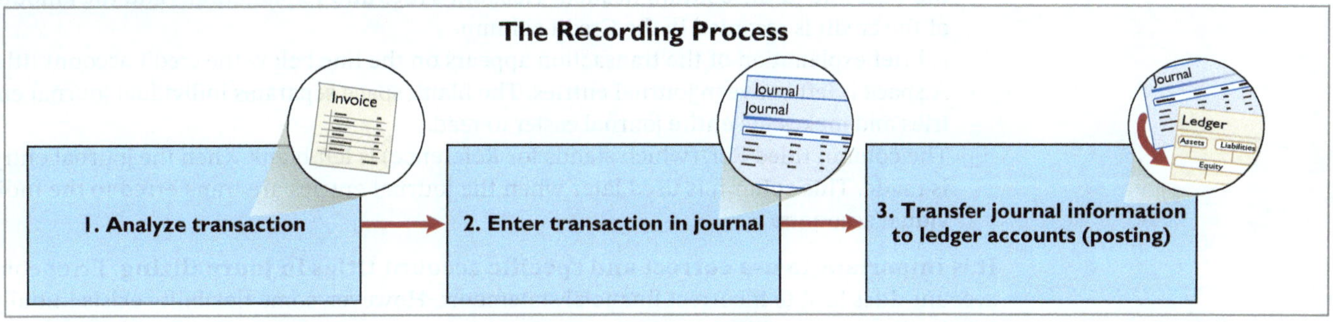

The steps in the recording process occur repeatedly (see **Ethics Note**). In Chapter 1, we illustrated the first step, the analysis of transactions, and will give further examples in this and later chapters. The other two steps in the recording process are explained in the next sections.

ETHICS NOTE

International Outsourcing Services, LLC was accused of submitting fraudulent store coupons to companies for reimbursement of as much as $250 million. Use of proper business documents reduces the likelihood of fraudulent activity.

The Journal

Companies initially record transactions in chronological order (the order in which they occur). Thus, the **journal** is referred to as the book of original entry. For each transaction, the journal shows the debit and credit effects on specific accounts (see **Helpful Hint**).

HELPFUL HINT

In a computerized system, journals are kept as files, and accounts are recorded in electronic databases.

Companies may use various kinds of journals, but every company has the most basic form of journal, a **general journal**. Typically, a general journal has spaces for dates, account titles and explanations, references, and two amount columns. See the format of the journal in Illustration 2.14. *Whenever we use the term "journal" in this text, we mean the general journal unless we specify otherwise.*

The journal makes several significant contributions to the recording process:

1. It discloses in one place the **complete effects of a transaction**.
2. It provides a **chronological record** of transactions.
3. It helps to **prevent or locate errors** because the debit and credit amounts for each entry can be easily compared.

Journalizing

Entering transaction data in the journal is known as **journalizing**. Companies make separate journal entries for each transaction. A complete entry consists of (1) the date of the transaction, (2) the accounts and amounts to be debited and credited, and (3) a brief explanation of the transaction.

Illustration 2.14 shows the technique of journalizing, using the first two transactions of Softbyte SA. Recall that on September 1, shareholders invested €15,000 cash in the corporation in exchange for ordinary shares, and Softbyte purchased computer equipment for €7,000 cash. The number J1 indicates that these two entries are recorded on the first page of the journal. **Illustration 2.14** shows the standard form of journal entries for these two transactions. (The boxed numbers correspond to explanations in the list below the illustration.)

ILLUSTRATION 2.14 **Technique of journalizing**

GENERAL JOURNAL — J1

Date	Account Titles and Explanation	Ref.	Debit	Credit
2029		[5]		
Sept. 1	[2] Cash		15,000	
[1]	[3] Share Capital—Ordinary			15,000
	[4] (Issued shares for cash)			
1	Equipment		7,000	
	Cash			7,000
	(Purchase of equipment for cash)			

[1] The date of the transaction is entered in the Date column.

[2] The debit account title (that is, the account to be debited) is entered first at the extreme left margin of the column headed "Account Titles and Explanation," and the amount of the debit is recorded in the Debit column.

3. The credit account title (that is, the account to be credited) is indented and entered on the next line in the column headed "Account Titles and Explanation," and the amount of the credit is recorded in the Credit column.
4. A brief explanation of the transaction appears on the line below the credit account title. A space is left between journal entries. The blank space separates individual journal entries and makes the entire journal easier to read.
5. The column titled Ref. (which stands for Reference) is left blank when the journal entry is made. This column is used later when the journal entries are transferred to the individual accounts.

It is important to use correct and specific account titles in journalizing. Erroneous account titles lead to incorrect financial statements. However, some flexibility exists initially in selecting account titles.

- The main criterion is that each title must appropriately describe the content of the account.
- Once a company chooses the specific title to use, it should record under that account title all later transactions involving the account. *In homework problems, you should use specific account titles when they are given.*
- When account titles are not given, you may select account titles that identify the nature and content of each account. The account titles used in journalizing should not contain explanations such as Cash Paid or Cash Received.

Simple and Compound Entries

Some entries involve only two accounts, one debit and one credit. (See, for example, the entries in Illustration 2.14.) This type of entry is called a **simple entry**. Some transactions, however, require more than two accounts in journalizing. An entry that requires three or more accounts is a **compound entry**.

To illustrate, assume that on July 1, Butler Shipping purchases a delivery truck costing £14,000. It pays £8,000 cash now and agrees to pay the remaining £6,000 on account (to be paid later). **Illustration 2.15** shows the compound entry.

ILLUSTRATION 2.15

Compound journal entry

GENERAL JOURNAL J1

Date	Account Titles and Explanation	Ref.	Debit	Credit
2029				
July 1	Equipment		14,000	
	Cash			8,000
	Accounts Payable			6,000
	(Purchased truck for cash with balance on account)			

In a compound entry, the standard format requires that all debits be listed before the credits.

Accounting Across the Organization Hain Celestial Group

Keith Homan/Shutterstock

It Starts with the Transaction

Recording financial transactions in a company's records should be straightforward. If a company determines that a transaction involves revenue, it records revenue. If it has an expense, then it records an expense. However, sometimes this is difficult to do.

For example, for more than a year, **Hain Celestial Group** (USA) (an organic food company) did not provide income information to investors and regulators. The reason given—the organic food company discovered revenue irregularities and said it could not release financial results until it determined when and how to record revenue for certain transactions. When Hain missed four deadlines for reporting earnings information, the food company suffered a 34% drop in its share price. As one analyst noted, it is hard to fathom why a seemingly simple revenue recognition issue took one year to resolve.

In other situations, outright fraud may occur. For example, regulators charged **Obsidian Energy** (CAN) for fraudulently moving millions of dollars in expenses from operating expenses to capital expenditure accounts. By understating reported operating expenses, Obsidian made it appear that it was managing its costs efficiently as well as increasing its income.

These examples demonstrate that "getting the basic transaction right" is the foundation for relevant and reliable financial statements. Starting with an incorrect or inappropriate transaction leads to distortions in the financial statements.

Sources: Based on Shawn Tully, "The Mystery of Hain Celestial's Accounting," *Fortune.com* (August 20, 2016); and Kelly Cryderman, "U.S. Charges Obsidian, Formerly Penn West, with Accounting Fraud," *The Globe and Mail* (June 28, 2017).

Why is it important for companies to record financial transactions completely and accurately? (Answer is available near the end of the chapter.)

DO IT! 2 | Recording Business Activities

As president and sole shareholder, Julie Loeng engaged in the following activities in establishing her beauty salon, Hair It Is.

1. Opened a bank account in the name of Hair It Is and deposited €20,000 of her own money in this account in exchange for ordinary shares.
2. Purchased equipment on account (to be paid in 30 days) for a total cost of €4,800.
3. Interviewed three applicants for the position of beautician.

In what form (type of record) should Hair It Is record these three activities? Prepare the entries to record the transactions.

ACTION PLAN

- **Understand which activities need to be recorded and which do not. Any that have economic effect should be recorded in a journal.**
- **Analyze the effects of transactions on asset, liability, and equity accounts.**

Solution

Each transaction that is recorded is entered in the general journal. The three activities would be recorded as follows.

1. Cash	20,000	
Share Capital—Ordinary		20,000
(Issued shares for cash)		
2. Equipment	4,800	
Accounts Payable		4,800
(Purchase of equipment on account)		

3. No entry because no transaction has occurred.

Related exercise material: **BE2.3, BE2.4, BE2.5, BE2.6, DO IT! 2.2, E2.3, E2.4, E2.5, E2.6, E2.7, E2.8, and E2.9.**

2.3 The Ledger and Posting

LEARNING OBJECTIVE 3

Explain how a ledger and posting help in the recording process.

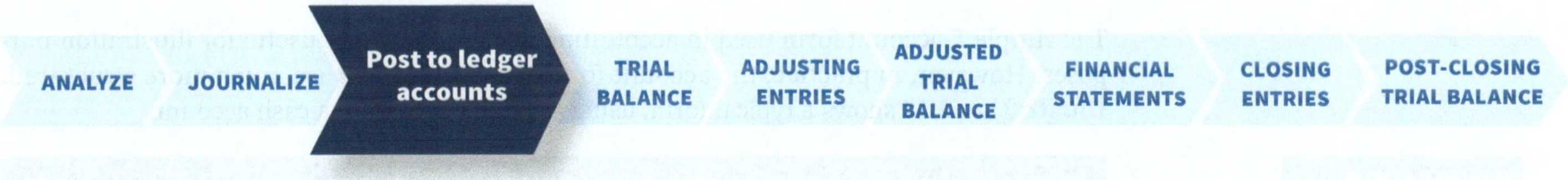

The Ledger

The entire group of accounts maintained by a company is the **ledger**.

- The ledger provides the balance in each of the accounts as well as keeps track of changes in these balances.
- Companies may use various kinds of ledgers, but every company has a general ledger.
- A **general ledger** contains all the asset, liability, and equity accounts, as shown in **Illustration 2.16**. *Whenever we use the term "ledger" in this text, we are referring to the general ledger unless we specify otherwise.*

The ledger provides the balance in each of the accounts. For example, the Cash account shows the amount of cash available to meet current obligations. The Accounts Receivable account shows amounts due from customers. Accounts Payable shows amounts owed to creditors. Each account is numbered for easier identification.

ILLUSTRATION 2.16 **The general ledger, which contains all of a company's accounts**

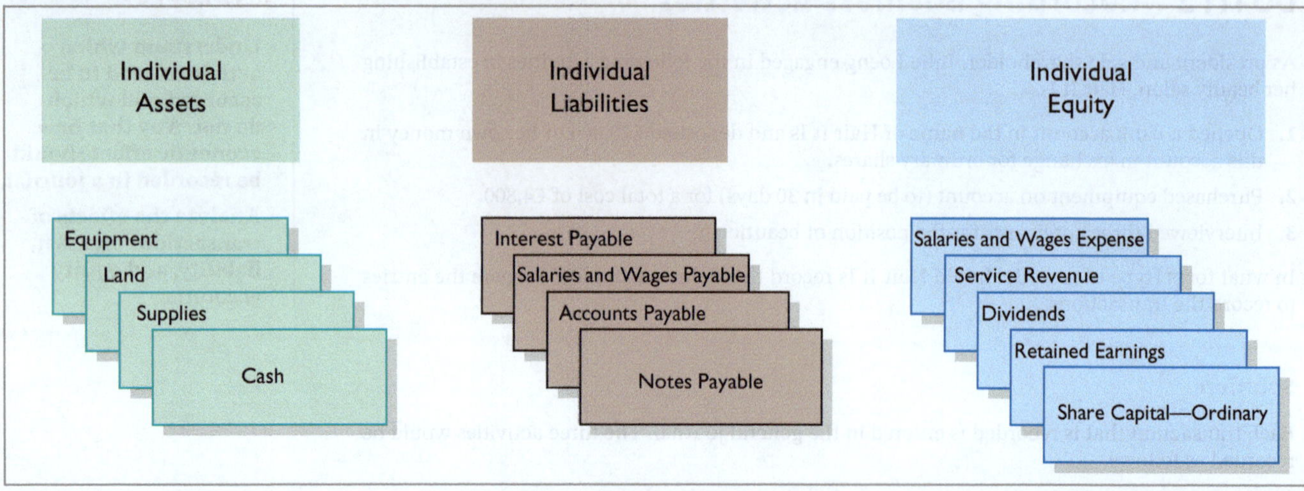

Ethics Insight Credit Suisse Group

iordani/Shutterstock

A Convenient Overstatement

Sometimes a company's investment securities suffer a permanent decline in value below their original cost. When this occurs, the company is supposed to reduce the recorded value of the securities on its statement of financial position ("write them down" in common financial lingo) and record a loss. It appears, however, that during the financial crisis of 2008, employees at some financial institutions chose to look the other way as the value of their investments skidded.

A number of securities traders that worked for the investment bank **Credit Suisse Group** (CHE) were charged with intentionally overstating the value of securities that had suffered declines of approximately $2.85 billion. One reason that they may have been reluctant to record the losses is out of fear that the company's shareholders and clients would panic if they saw the magnitude of the losses. However, personal self-interest might have been equally to blame—the bonuses of the traders were tied to the value of the investment securities.

Source: Based on S. Pulliam, J. Eaglesham, and M. Siconolfi, "U.S. Plans Changes on Bond Fraud," *Wall Street Journal Online* (February 1, 2012).

What incentives might employees have to overstate the value of these investment securities on the company's financial statements? (Answer is available near the end of the chapter.)

Standard Form of Account

The simple T-account form used in accounting texts is often very useful for illustration purposes. However, in practice, the account forms used in ledgers are much more structured. **Illustration 2.17** shows a typical form, using assumed data from a cash account.

ILLUSTRATION 2.17

Three-column form of account

CASH						NO. 101
Date		**Explanation**	**Ref.**	**Debit**	**Credit**	**Balance**
2029						
June	1			25,000		25,000
	2				8,000	17,000
	3			4,200		21,200
	9			7,500		28,700
	17				11,700	17,000
	20				250	16,750
	30				7,300	9,450

This format is called the **three-column form of account**. It has three money columns—debit, credit, and balance. The balance in the account is determined after each transaction. Companies use the explanation space and reference columns to provide special information about the transaction.

Posting

The procedure of transferring journal entries to the ledger accounts is called **posting**. This phase of the recording process accumulates the effects of journalized transactions into the individual accounts. Posting involves the following steps.

1. In the **ledger**, in the appropriate columns of the account(s) debited, enter the date, journal page, and debit amount shown in the journal.
2. In the reference column of the **journal**, write the account number to which the debit amount was posted.
3. In the **ledger**, in the appropriate columns of the account(s) credited, enter the date, journal page, and credit amount shown in the journal.
4. In the reference column of the **journal**, write the account number to which the credit amount was posted.

Illustration 2.18 shows these four steps using Softbyte SA's first journal entry. The boxed numbers indicate the sequence of the steps.

ILLUSTRATION 2.18

Posting a journal entry

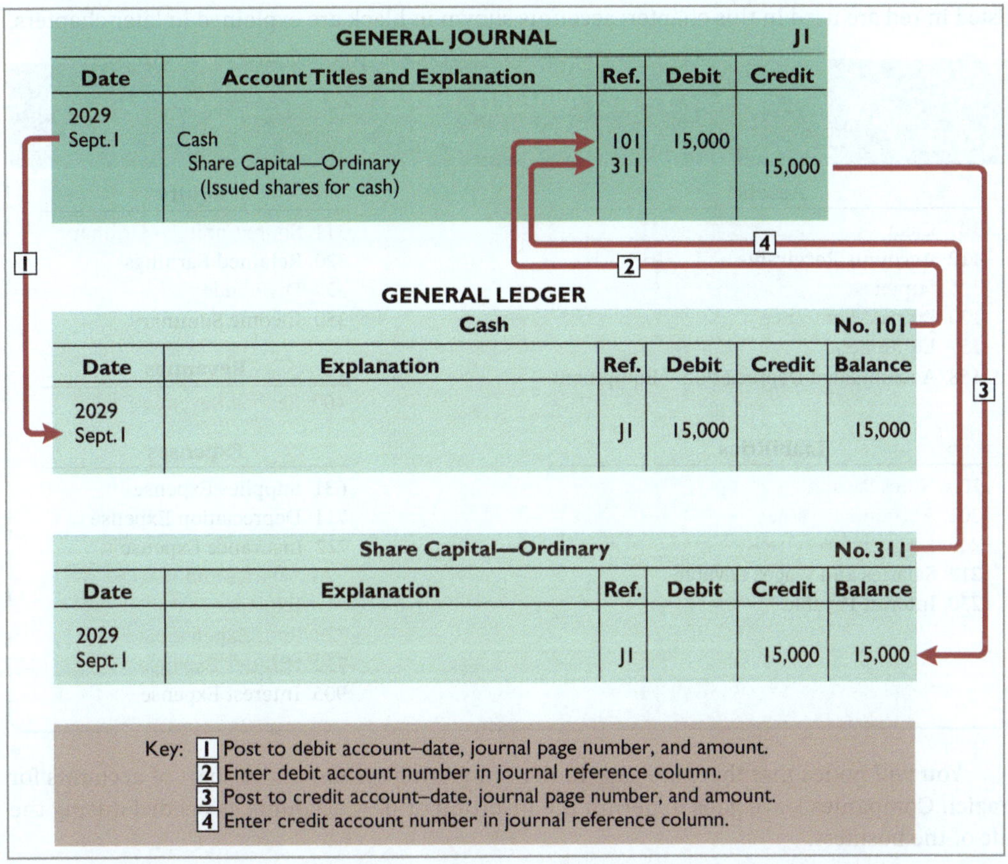

Posting should be performed in chronological order. That is, the company should post all the debits and credits of one journal entry before proceeding to the next journal entry. Postings should be made on a timely basis to ensure that the ledger is up-to-date. *In homework problems, you can journalize all transactions before posting any of the journal entries.*

The reference column of a ledger account indicates the journal page from which the transaction was posted. (After the last entry has been posted, the accountant should scan the reference column **in the journal**, to confirm that all postings have been made.) The explanation space of the ledger account is used infrequently because an explanation already appears in the journal.

Chart of Accounts

The number and type of accounts differ for each company. The number of accounts depends on the amount of detail management desires. For example, the management of one company may want a single account for all types of utility expense. Another may keep separate expense accounts for each type of utility, such as gas, electricity, and water. Similarly, a small company like Softbyte SA will have fewer accounts than a giant company like **Hyundai** (KOR). Softbyte may be able to manage and report its activities in 20 to 30 accounts, while Hyundai may require thousands of accounts to keep track of its worldwide activities.

- Most companies have a **chart of accounts**. This chart lists the accounts and the account numbers that identify their location in the ledger.
- The numbering system that identifies the accounts usually starts with the statement of financial position accounts and follows with the income statement accounts.

In this and the next two chapters, we explain the accounting for Yazici Advertising A.Ş. (a service company). Accounts 101–199 indicate asset accounts; 200–299 indicate liabilities; 301–399 indicate equity accounts; 400–499, revenues; 601–799, expenses; 800–899, other revenues; and 900–999, other expenses. **Illustration 2.19** shows Yazici's chart of accounts. Accounts listed in red are used in this chapter; accounts shown in black are explained in later chapters.

ILLUSTRATION 2.19

Chart of accounts

Yazici Advertising A.Ş.
Chart of Accounts

Assets	Equity
101 Cash	311 Share Capital—Ordinary
112 Accounts Receivable	320 Retained Earnings
126 Supplies	332 Dividends
130 Prepaid Insurance	350 Income Summary
157 Equipment	**Revenues**
158 Accumulated Depreciation—Equipment	400 Service Revenue
Liabilities	**Expenses**
200 Notes Payable	631 Supplies Expense
201 Accounts Payable	711 Depreciation Expense
209 Unearned Service Revenue	722 Insurance Expense
212 Salaries and Wages Payable	726 Salaries and Wages Expense
230 Interest Payable	729 Rent Expense
	732 Utilities Expense
	905 Interest Expense

You will notice that there are gaps in the numbering system of the chart of accounts for Yazici. Companies leave gaps to permit the insertion of new accounts as needed during the life of the business.

The Recording Process Illustrated

Illustrations 2.20 through **2.29** show the basic steps in the recording process, using the October transactions of Yazici Advertising A.Ş. Yazici's accounting period is a month. A basic analysis and a debit-credit analysis precede the journalizing and posting of each transaction. For simplicity, we use the T-account form in the illustrations instead of the standard account form. Study these transaction analyses carefully.

- **The purpose of transaction analysis is first to identify the type of account involved, and then to determine whether to make a debit or a credit to the account.**

- You should always perform this type of analysis before preparing a journal entry. Doing so will help you understand the journal entries discussed in this chapter as well as more complex journal entries in later chapters (see **Helpful Hint**).

ILLUSTRATION 2.20

Investment of cash by shareholders

Transaction: On October 1, C. R. Yazici invests ₺10,000 cash in an advertising company to be known as Yazici Advertising A.Ş.

Basic Analysis: The asset Cash increases ₺10,000; equity (specifically, Share Capital—Ordinary) increases ₺10,000.

Equation Analysis:

Assets	=	**Liabilities**	+	**Equity**	
Cash	=			Share Capital	
+10,000				+10,000	Issued Shares

Debit–Credit Analysis: Debits increase assets: debit Cash ₺10,000. Credits increase equity: credit Share Capital—Ordinary ₺10,000.

Journal Entry:

Oct. 1	Cash	101	10,000	
	Share Capital—Ordinary	311		10,000
	(Issued shares for cash)			

Posting:

Cash	101
Oct. 1 10,000	

Share Capital—Ordinary	311
	Oct. 1 10,000

Cash flow analyses show the impact of each transaction on cash.

Cash Flows
+10,000

HELPFUL HINT

Follow these steps:

1. **Determine what type of account is involved.**
2. **Determine what items increased or decreased and by how much.**
3. **Translate the increases and decreases into debits and credits.**

ILLUSTRATION 2.21

Purchase of office equipment

Transaction: On October 1, Yazici Advertising purchases office equipment costing ₺5,000 by signing a 3-month, 12%, ₺5,000 note payable.

Basic Analysis: The asset Equipment increases ₺5,000; the liability Notes Payable increases ₺5,000.

Equation Analysis:

Assets	=	**Liabilities**	+	**Equity**
Equipment	=	Notes Payable		
+5,000		+5,000		

Debit–Credit Analysis: Debits increase assets: debit Equipment ₺5,000. Credits increase liabilities: credit Notes Payable ₺5,000.

Journal Entry:

Oct. 1	Equipment	157	5,000	
	Notes Payable	200		5,000
	(Issued 3-month, 12% note for office equipment)			

Posting:

Equipment	157
Oct. 1 5,000	

Notes Payable	200
	Oct. 1 5,000

Cash Flows
no effect

ILLUSTRATION 2.22

Receipt of cash for future service

Many liabilities have the word "payable" in their title. But, note that Unearned Service Revenue is a liability even though the word *payable* is not used.

Cash Flows
+1,200

Transaction: On October 2, Yazici Advertising receives a ₺1,200 cash advance from R. Knox, a client, for advertising services that are expected to be completed by December 31.

Basic Analysis: The asset Cash increases ₺1,200; the liability Unearned Service Revenue increases ₺1,200 because the service has not been performed yet. That is, when Yazici receives an advance payment, it should record an unearned revenue (a liability) in order to recognize the obligation that exists. Note also that although many liabilities have the word "payable" in their title, unearned revenue is a liability because the obligation is satisfied by providing a product or performing a service.

Equation Analysis:

Assets	=	**Liabilities**	+	**Equity**
Cash	=	Unearned Service Revenue		
+1,200		+1,200		

Debit–Credit Analysis: Debits increase assets: debit Cash ₺1,200. Credits increase liabilities: credit Unearned Service Revenue ₺1,200.

Journal Entry:

Oct. 2	Cash	101	1,200	
	Unearned Service Revenue	209		1,200
	(Received cash from R. Knox for future service)			

Posting:

Cash	101
Oct. 1 10,000	
2 1,200	

Unearned Service Revenue	209
	Oct. 2 1,200

ILLUSTRATION 2.23

Payment of monthly rent

Cash Flows
−900

Transaction: On October 3, Yazici Advertising pays office rent for October in cash, ₺900.

Basic Analysis: Rent Expense increases ₺900 because the payment pertains only to the current month; the asset Cash decreases ₺900.

Equation Analysis:

Assets	=	**Liabilities**	+	**Equity**	
Cash	=			Expenses	
−900				−900	Rent Expense

Debit–Credit Analysis: Debits increase expenses: debit Rent Expense ₺900. Credits decrease assets: credit Cash ₺900.

Journal Entry:

Oct. 3	Rent Expense	729	900	
	Cash	101		900
	(Paid October rent)			

Posting:

Cash	101
Oct. 1 10,000	Oct. 3 900
2 1,200	

Rent Expense	729
Oct. 3 900	

ILLUSTRATION 2.24

Payment for insurance

Transaction

On October 4, Yazici Advertising pays ₺600 for a one-year insurance policy that will expire next year on September 30.

Basic Analysis

The asset Prepaid Insurance increases ₺600 because the payment extends to more than the current month; the asset Cash decreases ₺600. Payments of expenses that will benefit more than one accounting period are prepaid expenses or prepayments. When a company makes a payment, it debits an asset account in order to show the service or benefit that will be received in the future.

Equation Analysis

Assets		=	Liabilities	+	Equity
Cash +	Prepaid Insurance				
−600	+600				

Debit–Credit Analysis

Debits increase assets: debit Prepaid Insurance ₺600.
Credits decrease assets: credit Cash ₺600.

Journal Entry

Oct. 4	Prepaid Insurance	130	600	
	Cash	101		600
	(Paid one-year policy; effective date October 1)			

Posting

Cash		101	
Oct. 1	10,000	Oct. 3	900
2	1,200	4	600

Prepaid Insurance		130
Oct. 4	600	

Cash Flows
−600

ILLUSTRATION 2.25

Purchase of supplies on credit

Transaction

On October 5, Yazici Advertising purchases an estimated 3-month supply of advertising materials on account from Aero Supply for ₺2,500.

Basic Analysis

The asset Supplies increases ₺2,500; the liability Accounts Payable increases ₺2,500.

Equation Analysis

Assets	=	Liabilities	+	Equity
Supplies	=	Accounts Payable		
+2,500		+2,500		

Debit–Credit Analysis

Debits increase assets: debit Supplies ₺2,500.
Credits increase liabilities: credit Accounts Payable ₺2,500.

Journal Entry

Oct. 5	Supplies	126	2,500	
	Accounts Payable	201		2,500
	(Purchased supplies on account from Aero Supply)			

Posting

Supplies		126
Oct. 5	2,500	

Accounts Payable		201
	Oct. 5	2,500

Cash Flows
no effect

ILLUSTRATION 2.26

Hiring of employees

Event: On October 9, Yazici Advertising hires four employees to begin work on October 15. Each employee is to receive a weekly salary of ₺500 for a 5-day work week, payable every 2 weeks—first payment made on October 26.

Basic Analysis: A business transaction has not occurred. There is only an agreement between the employer and the employees to enter into a business transaction beginning on October 15. Thus, a debit–credit analysis is not needed because there is no accounting entry. (See transaction of October 26 for first entry.)

Cash Flows
no effect

ILLUSTRATION 2.27

Declaration and payment of dividend

Transaction: On October 20, Yazici Advertising's board of directors declares and pays a ₺500 cash dividend to shareholders.

Basic Analysis: The Dividends account increases ₺500; the asset Cash decreases ₺500.

Equation Analysis:

Assets	=	**Liabilities**	+	**Equity**
Cash	=			Dividends
−500				−500

Debit–Credit Analysis: Debits increase dividends: debit Dividends ₺500. Credits decrease assets: credit Cash ₺500.

Journal Entry:

Oct. 20	Dividends	332	500	
	Cash	101		500
	(Declared and paid a cash dividend)			

Posting:

Cash			101
Oct. 1	10,000	Oct. 3	900
2	1,200	4	600
		20	500

Dividends			332
Oct. 20	500		

Cash Flows
−500

ILLUSTRATION 2.28

Payment of salaries

Transaction	On October 26, Yazici Advertising owes employee salaries of ₺4,000 and pays them in cash. (See October 9 event.)
Basic Analysis	Salaries and Wages Expense increases ₺4,000; the asset Cash decreases ₺4,000.
Equation Analysis	**Assets** = **Liabilities** + **Equity** Cash = Expenses −4,000 −4,000 Salaries and Wages Expense
Debit–Credit Analysis	Debits increase expenses: debit Salaries and Wages Expense ₺4,000. Credits decrease assets: credit Cash ₺4,000.

Journal Entry

Date	Account	Ref.	Debit	Credit
Oct. 26	Salaries and Wages Expense	726	4,000	
	Cash	101		4,000
	(Paid salaries to date)			

Posting

Cash			101
Oct. 1	10,000	Oct. 3	900
2	1,200	4	600
		20	500
		26	4,000

Salaries and Wages Expense			726
Oct. 26	4,000		

Cash Flows
−4,000

ILLUSTRATION 2.29

Receipt of cash for services provided

Transaction	On October 31, Yazici Advertising receives ₺10,000 in cash from Copa Company for advertising services performed in October.
Basic Analysis	The asset Cash increases ₺10,000; the revenue account Service Revenue increases ₺10,000.
Equation Analysis	**Assets** = **Liabilities** + **Equity** Cash = Revenues +10,000 +10,000 Service Revenue
Debit–Credit Analysis	Debits increase assets: debit Cash ₺10,000. Credits increase revenues: credit Service Revenue ₺10,000.

Journal Entry

Date	Account	Ref.	Debit	Credit
Oct. 31	Cash	101	10,000	
	Service Revenue	400		10,000
	(Received cash for services performed)			

Posting

Cash			101
Oct. 1	10,000	Oct. 3	900
2	1,200	4	600
31	10,000	20	500
		26	4,000

Service Revenue			400
		Oct. 31	10,000

Cash Flows
+10,000

Summary Illustration of Journalizing and Posting

Illustration 2.30 shows the journal for Yazici Advertising A.Ş. for October.

ILLUSTRATION 2.30

General journal entries

GENERAL JOURNAL — PAGE J1

Date	Account Titles and Explanation	Ref.	Debit	Credit
2029				
Oct. 1	Cash	101	10,000	
	Share Capital—Ordinary	311		10,000
	(Issued shares for cash)			
1	Equipment	157	5,000	
	Notes Payable	200		5,000
	(Issued 3-month, 12% note for office equipment)			
2	Cash	101	1,200	
	Unearned Service Revenue	209		1,200
	(Received cash from R. Knox for future services)			
3	Rent Expense	729	900	
	Cash	101		900
	(Paid October rent)			
4	Prepaid Insurance	130	600	
	Cash	101		600
	(Paid one-year policy; effective date October 1)			
5	Supplies	126	2,500	
	Accounts Payable	201		2,500
	(Purchased supplies on account from Aero Supply)			
20	Dividends	332	500	
	Cash	101		500
	(Declared and paid a cash dividend)			
26	Salaries and Wages Expense	726	4,000	
	Cash	101		4,000
	(Paid salaries to date)			
31	Cash	101	10,000	
	Service Revenue	400		10,000
	(Received cash for services performed)			

Illustration 2.31 shows the ledger, with all balances in red.

ILLUSTRATION 2.31 **General ledger**

GENERAL LEDGER

Cash **No. 101**

Date	Explanation	Ref.	Debit	Credit	Balance
2029					
Oct. 1		J1	10,000		10,000
2		J1	1,200		11,200
3		J1		900	10,300
4		J1		600	9,700
20		J1		500	9,200
26		J1		4,000	5,200
31		J1	10,000		15,200

Supplies **No. 126**

Date	Explanation	Ref.	Debit	Credit	Balance
2029					
Oct. 5		J1	2,500		2,500

Prepaid Insurance **No. 130**

Date	Explanation	Ref.	Debit	Credit	Balance
2029					
Oct. 4		J1	600		600

Equipment **No. 157**

Date	Explanation	Ref.	Debit	Credit	Balance
2029					
Oct. 1		J1	5,000		5,000

Notes Payable **No. 200**

Date	Explanation	Ref.	Debit	Credit	Balance
2029					
Oct. 1		J1		5,000	5,000

Accounts Payable **No. 201**

Date	Explanation	Ref.	Debit	Credit	Balance
2029					
Oct. 5		J1		2,500	2,500

Unearned Service Revenue **No. 209**

Date	Explanation	Ref.	Debit	Credit	Balance
2029					
Oct. 2		J1		1,200	1,200

Share Capital—Ordinary **No. 311**

Date	Explanation	Ref.	Debit	Credit	Balance
2029					
Oct. 1		J1		10,000	10,000

Dividends **No. 332**

Date	Explanation	Ref.	Debit	Credit	Balance
2029					
Oct. 20		J1	500		500

Service Revenue **No. 400**

Date	Explanation	Ref.	Debit	Credit	Balance
2029					
Oct. 31		J1		10,000	10,000

Salaries and Wages Expense **No. 726**

Date	Explanation	Ref.	Debit	Credit	Balance
2029					
Oct. 26		J1	4,000		4,000

Rent Expense **No. 729**

Date	Explanation	Ref.	Debit	Credit	Balance
2029					
Oct. 3		J1	900		900

DO IT! 3 | Posting

Como SpA recorded the following transactions in a general journal during the month of March.

Mar. 4	Cash	2,280	
	Service Revenue		2,280
15	Salaries and Wages Expense	400	
	Cash		400
19	Utilities Expense	92	
	Cash		92

Post these entries to the Cash account of the general ledger to determine the ending balance in cash. The beginning balance in Cash on March 1 was €600.

ACTION PLAN

- **Recall that posting involves transferring the journalized debits and credits to specific accounts in the ledger.**
- **Determine the ending balance by netting the total debits and credits.**

Solution

Cash

3/1	600	3/15	400
3/4	2,280	3/19	92
3/31 Bal.	2,388		

Related exercise material: **BE2.7, BE2.8, DO IT! 2.3, E2.10, E2.11, E2.14, and E2.17.**

2.4 The Trial Balance

LEARNING OBJECTIVE 4

Prepare a trial balance.

ANALYZE | JOURNALIZE | POST | **Prepare a trial balance** | ADJUSTING ENTRIES | ADJUSTED TRIAL BALANCE | FINANCIAL STATEMENTS | CLOSING ENTRIES | POST-CLOSING TRIAL BALANCE

A **trial balance** is a list of accounts and their balances at a given time.

- Companies usually prepare a trial balance at the end of an accounting period.
- They list accounts in the order in which they appear in the ledger.
- Debit balances appear in the left column and credit balances in the right column. The totals of the two columns must equal.

The trial balance proves the mathematical equality of debits and credits after posting. Under the double-entry system, this equality occurs when the sum of the debit account balances equals the sum of the credit account balances. **A trial balance may also uncover errors in journalizing and posting.** For example, a trial balance may well have detected the error at **Fidelity Investments** (USA) discussed in the Feature Story. **In addition, a trial balance is useful in the preparation of financial statements**, as we will explain in the next two chapters.

The steps for preparing a trial balance are:

1. List the account titles and their balances in the appropriate debit or credit column.
2. Total the debit and credit columns.
3. Verify the equality of the two columns.

Illustration 2.32 shows the trial balance prepared from Yazici Advertising A.Ş.'s ledger. Note that the total debits equal the total credits.

ILLUSTRATION 2.32

A trial balance

Yazici Advertising A.Ş.
Trial Balance
October 31, 2029

	Debit	Credit
Cash	₺15,200	
Supplies	2,500	
Prepaid Insurance	600	
Equipment	5,000	
Notes Payable		₺ 5,000
Accounts Payable		2,500
Unearned Service Revenue		1,200
Share Capital—Ordinary		10,000
Dividends	500	
Service Revenue		10,000
Salaries and Wages Expense	4,000	
Rent Expense	900	
	₺28,700	₺28,700

A trial balance is a necessary checkpoint for uncovering certain types of errors. For example, if only the debit portion of a journal entry has been posted, the trial balance would bring this error to light.

Limitations of a Trial Balance

A trial balance does not guarantee freedom from recording errors, however (see **Ethics Note**). Numerous errors may exist even though the totals of the trial balance columns agree. For example, the trial balance may balance even when:

1. A transaction is not journalized.
2. A correct journal entry is not posted.
3. A journal entry is posted twice.
4. Incorrect accounts are used in journalizing or posting.
5. Offsetting errors are made in recording the amount of a transaction.

As long as equal debits and credits are posted, even to the wrong account or in the wrong amount, the total debits will equal the total credits. **The trial balance does not prove that the company has recorded all transactions or that the ledger is correct.**

ETHICS NOTE

An error is the result of an unintentional mistake; it is neither ethical nor unethical. An irregularity is an intentional misstatement, which is viewed as unethical.

Locating Errors

Errors in a trial balance generally result from mathematical mistakes, incorrect postings, or simply transcribing data incorrectly. What do you do if you are faced with a trial balance that does not balance? First, determine the amount of the difference between the two columns of the trial balance. After this amount is known, the following steps are often helpful.

1. If the error is €1, €10, €100, or €1,000, re-add the trial balance columns and recompute the account balances.
2. If the error is divisible by 2, scan the trial balance to see whether a balance equal to half the error has been entered in the wrong column.
3. If the error is divisible by 9, retrace the account balances on the trial balance to see whether they are incorrectly copied from the ledger. For example, if a balance was €12 and it was listed as €21, a €9 error has been made. Reversing the order of numbers is called a **transposition error**.
4. If the error is not divisible by 2 or 9, scan the ledger to see whether an account balance in the amount of the error has been omitted from the trial balance, and scan the journal to see whether a posting of that amount has been omitted.

Currency Signs and Underlining

Note that currency signs do not appear in journals or ledgers. Currency signs are typically used only in the trial balance and the financial statements.

- Generally, a currency sign is shown only for the first item in the column and for the total of that column.
- A single line (a totaling rule) is placed under the column of figures to be added or subtracted.
- Total amounts are double-underlined to indicate they are final sums.

Investor Insight Fannie Mae

Enviromatic/Getty Images

Why Accuracy Matters

While most companies record transactions very carefully, the reality is that mistakes still happen. For example, bank regulators fined **Bank One Corporation** (USA) (now **JPMorgan Chase**) $1.8 million because they felt that the unreliability of the bank's accounting system caused it to violate regulatory requirements.

Also, in recent years **Fannie Mae** (USA), the government-chartered mortgage association, announced a series of large accounting errors. These announcements caused alarm among investors, regulators, and politicians because they fear that the errors may suggest larger, undetected problems. This is important because the home-mortgage market depends on Fannie Mae to buy hundreds of billions of dollars of mortgages each year from banks, thus enabling the banks to issue new mortgages.

Finally, before a major overhaul of its accounting system, the financial records of **Waste Management, Inc.** (USA) were in such disarray that of the company's 57,000 employees, 10,000 were receiving pay slips that were in error.

The Sarbanes-Oxley Act was created to minimize the occurrence of errors like these by increasing every employee's responsibility for accurate financial reporting.

In order for these companies to prepare and issue financial statements, their accounting equations (debits and credits) must have been in balance at year-end. How could these errors or misstatements have occurred? (Answer is available near the end of the chapter.)

ACTION PLAN

- **Determine normal balances and list accounts in the order they appear in the ledger.**
- **Accounts with debit balances appear in the left column, and those with credit balances in the right column.**
- **Total the debit and credit columns to prove equality.**

DO IT! 4 | Trial Balance

The following accounts come from the ledger of Bali Beach Supply at December 31, 2029.

157	Equipment	R$88,000	311	Share Capital—Ordinary	R$20,000
332	Dividends	8,000	212	Salaries and Wages Payable	2,000
201	Accounts Payable	22,000	200	Notes Payable (due in 3 months)	19,000
726	Salaries and Wages Expense	42,000	732	Utilities Expense	3,000
112	Accounts Receivable	4,000	130	Prepaid Insurance	6,000
400	Service Revenue	95,000	101	Cash	7,000

Prepare a trial balance in good form.

Solution

Bali Beach Supply
Trial Balance
December 31, 2029

	Debit	Credit
Cash	R$ 7,000	
Accounts Receivable	4,000	
Prepaid Insurance	6,000	
Equipment	88,000	
Notes Payable		R$ 19,000
Accounts Payable		22,000
Salaries and Wages Payable		2,000
Share Capital—Ordinary		20,000
Dividends	8,000	
Service Revenue		95,000
Utilities Expense	3,000	
Salaries and Wages Expense	42,000	
	R$158,000	R$158,000

Related exercise material: **BE2.9, BE2.10, DO IT! 2.4, E2.11, E2.12, E2.13, E2.15, E2.16, and E2.17.**

Review and Practice

Learning Objectives Review

1 Describe how accounts, debits, and credits are used to record business transactions.

An account is a record of increases and decreases in specific asset, liability, and equity items. The terms debit and credit are synonymous with left and right. Assets, dividends, and expenses are increased by debits and decreased by credits. Liabilities, share capital—ordinary, and revenues are increased by credits and decreased by debits.

2 Indicate how a journal is used in the recording process.

The basic steps in the recording process are (a) analyze each transaction for its effects on the accounts, (b) enter the transaction information in a journal, and (c) transfer the journal information to the appropriate accounts in the ledger.

The initial accounting record of a transaction is entered in a journal before the data are entered in the accounts. A journal (a) discloses in one place the complete effects of a transaction, (b) provides a chronological record of transactions, and (c) prevents or locates errors because the debit and credit amounts for each entry can be easily compared.

3 Explain how a ledger and posting help in the recording process.

The ledger is the entire group of accounts maintained by a company. The ledger provides the balance in each of the accounts as well as keeps track of changes in these balances. Posting is the transfer of journal entries to the ledger accounts. This phase of the recording process accumulates the effects of journalized transactions in the individual accounts.

4 Prepare a trial balance.

A trial balance is a list of accounts and their balances at a given time. Its primary purpose is to prove the equality of debits and credits after posting. A trial balance also uncovers errors in journalizing and posting and is useful in preparing financial statements.

Glossary Review

Account A record of increases and decreases in specific asset, liability, or equity items. (p. 2-2).

Chart of accounts A list of accounts and the account numbers that identify their location in the ledger. (p. 2-14).

Compound entry A journal entry that involves three or more accounts. (p. 2-10).

Credit The right side of an account. (p. 2-3).

Debit The left side of an account. (p. 2-3).

Dividend A distribution by a company to its shareholders. (p. 2-6).

Double-entry system A system that records in appropriate accounts the dual effect of each transaction. (p. 2-4).

General journal The most basic form of journal. (p. 2-9).

General ledger A ledger that contains all asset, liability, and equity accounts. (p. 2-11).

Journal An accounting record in which transactions are initially recorded in chronological order. (p. 2-9).

Journalizing The entering of transaction data in the journal. (p. 2-9).

Ledger The entire group of accounts maintained by a company. (p. 2-11).

Normal balance An account balance on the side where an increase in the account is recorded. (p. 2-4).

Posting The procedure of transferring journal entries to the ledger accounts. (p. 2-13).

Retained earnings Net income that is kept (retained) in the business. (p. 2-5).

Simple entry A journal entry that involves only two accounts. (p. 2-10).

T-account The basic form of an account, consisting of (1) a title, (2) a left or debit side, and (3) a right or credit side. (p. 2-3).

Three-column form of account A form with columns for debit, credit, and balance amounts in an account. (p. 2-12).

Trial balance A list of accounts and their balances at a given time. (p. 2-22).

Practice Multiple-Choice Questions

1. **(LO 1)** Which of the following statements about an account is **true**?
   a. The right side of an account is the debit, or increase, side.
   b. An account is an individual accounting record of increases and decreases in specific asset, liability, and equity items.
   c. There are separate accounts for specific assets and liabilities but only one account for equity items.
   d. The left side of an account is the credit, or decrease, side.

2. **(LO 1)** Debits:
   a. increase both assets and liabilities.
   b. decrease both assets and liabilities.
   c. increase assets and decrease liabilities.
   d. decrease assets and increase liabilities.

3. **(LO 1)** A revenue account:
   a. is increased by debits.
   b. is decreased by credits.
   c. has a normal balance of a debit.
   d. is increased by credits.

4. **(LO 1)** Accounts that normally have debit balances are:
   a. assets, expenses, and revenues.
   b. assets, expenses, and share capital—ordinary.
   c. assets, liabilities, and dividends.
   d. assets, dividends, and expenses.

5. **(LO 1)** The expanded accounting equation is:
   a. Assets + Liabilities = Share Capital + Retained Earnings + Dividends + Revenues + Expenses.
   b. Assets = Liabilities + Share Capital + Retained Earnings + Dividends + Revenues – Expenses.
   c. Assets = Liabilities – Share Capital – Retained Earnings – Dividends – Revenues – Expenses.
   d. Assets = Liabilities + Share Capital + Retained Earnings + Revenues – Expenses – Dividends.

6. **(LO 1)** In accounting terminology, "every debit must have a or more credits, debits and credits must be equal," what do we call it?
   a. accounting equation.
   b. debit/credit rules.
   c. double-entry system.
   d. normal balance.

7. **(LO 2)** Which of the following is **not** part of the recording process?
   a. Analyzing transactions.
   b. Preparing an income statement.
   c. Entering transactions in a journal.
   d. Posting journal entries.

8. **(LO 2)** Which of the following statements about a journal is **false**?
   a. It is not a book of original entry.
   b. It provides a chronological record of transactions.
   c. It helps to locate errors because the debit and credit amounts for each entry can be readily compared.
   d. It discloses in one place the complete effect of a transaction.

9. **(LO 2)** The purchase of supplies on account should result in:
   a. a debit to Supplies Expense and a credit to Cash.
   b. a debit to Supplies Expense and a credit to Accounts Payable.
   c. a debit to Supplies and a credit to Accounts Payable.
   d. a debit to Supplies and a credit to Accounts Receivable.

10. **(LO 3)** The order of the accounts in the ledger is:
    a. assets, revenues, expenses, liabilities, share capital—ordinary, dividends.
    b. assets, liabilities, share capital—ordinary, dividends, revenues, expenses.
    c. share capital—ordinary, assets, revenues, expenses, liabilities, dividends.
    d. revenues, assets, expenses, liabilities, share capital—ordinary, dividends.

11. **(LO 3)** A ledger:
    a. contains only asset and liability accounts.
    b. should show accounts in alphabetical order.
    c. is a collection of the entire group of accounts maintained by a company.
    d. is a book of original entry.

12. **(LO 3)** Posting:
    a. normally occurs before journalizing.
    b. transfers ledger transaction data to the journal.
    c. is an optional step in the recording process.
    d. transfers journal entries to ledger accounts.

13. **(LO 3)** Before posting a payment of €5,000, the Accounts Payable of Green Grocers had a normal balance of €16,000. The balance after posting this transaction was:
    a. €21,000. **c.** €11,000.
    b. €5,000. **d.** cannot be determined.

14. **(LO 4)** A trial balance:
    a. is a list of accounts with their balances at a given time.
    b. proves the journalized transactions are correct.
    c. will not balance if a correct journal entry is posted twice.
    d. proves that all transactions have been recorded.

15. **(LO 4)** A trial balance will not balance if:
    a. a correct journal entry is posted twice.
    b. the purchase of supplies on account is debited to Supplies and credited to Cash.
    c. a £100 dividend is debited to Dividends for £1,000 and credited to Cash for £100.
    d. a £450 payment on account is debited to Accounts Payable for £45 and credited to Cash for £45.

16. **(LO 4)** The trial balance of Jeong Company had accounts with the following normal balances: Cash $5,000, Service Revenue $85,000, Salaries and Wages Payable $4,000, Salaries and Wages Expense $40,000, Rent Expense $10,000, Share Capital—Ordinary $42,000, Dividends $15,000, and Equipment $61,000. In preparing a trial balance, the total in the debit column is:
    a. $131,000. **c.** $91,000.
    b. $216,000. **d.** $116,000.

Solutions

1. **b.** An account is an individual accounting record of increases and decreases in specific asset, liability, and equity items. The other choices are incorrect because (a) the right side of the account is the credit side, not the debit side, and can be the increase or the decrease side, depending on the specific classification account; (c) there are also separate accounts for different equity items; and (d) the left side of the account is the debit side, not the credit side, and can be either

the decrease or the increase side, depending on the specific classification account.

2. **c.** Debits increase assets but they decrease liabilities. The other choices are incorrect because debits (a) decrease, not increase, liabilities; (b) increase, not decrease, assets; and (d) increase, not decrease, assets and decrease, not increase, liabilities.

3. **d.** A revenue account is increased by credits. The other choices are incorrect because a revenue account (a) is increased by credits, not debits; (b) is decreased by debits, not credits; and (c) has a normal balance of a credit, not a debit.

4. **d.** Assets, dividends, and expenses all have normal debit balances. The other choices are incorrect because (a) revenues have normal credit balances, (b) share capital—ordinary has a normal credit balance, and (c) liabilities have normal credit balances.

5. **d.** The expanded accounting equation is Assets = Liabilities + Share Capital + Retained Earnings + Revenues – Expenses – Dividends. The other choices are therefore incorrect.

6. **c.** (c) is correct, but (a) (b) (d) are wrong. (a) The accounting equation is "asset = liability + equity." (b) Debit/credit rules mean the following procedures: Increases in assets, expenses, and dividends are entered on the debit side, and decreases in assets, expenses, and dividends are entered on the credit side. Increases in liabilities, share capital, retained earnings and revenues are entered on the credit side, and decreases in liabilities, share capital, retained earnings and revenues are entered on the debit side. (d) The normal balance of an account is on the side where an increase in the account is recorded. For example, the normal balances of assets, expenses, and dividends normally show debit balances, but the normal balances of liabilities, share capital, retained earnings and revenues normally show credit balances.

7. **b.** Preparing an income statement is not part of the recording process. Choices (a) analyzing transactions, (c) entering transactions in a journal, and (d) posting journal entries are all part of the recording process.

8. **a.** The journal is a book of original entry. The other choices are all true statements.

9. **c.** The purchase of supplies on account results in a debit to Supplies and a credit to Accounts Payable. The other choices are incorrect because the purchase of supplies on account results in (a) a debit to Supplies, not Supplies Expense, and a credit to Accounts Payable, not Cash; (b) a debit to Supplies, not Supplies Expense; and (d) a credit to Accounts Payable, not Accounts Receivable.

10. **b.** The correct order of the accounts in the ledger is assets, liabilities, share capital—ordinary, dividends, revenues, expenses. The other choices are incorrect because they do not reflect this order. The order of the accounts in the ledger is (1) statement of financial position accounts: asset, liability, and equity accounts (Share Capital—Ordinary, Retained Earnings, and Dividends); and then (2) income statement accounts: revenues and expenses.

11. **c.** A ledger is a collection of all the accounts maintained by a company. The other choices are incorrect because a ledger (a) contains all account types—asset, liability, and equity accounts—not just asset and liability accounts; (b) usually shows accounts in account number order, not alphabetical order; and (d) is not a book of original entry because entries made in the ledger come from the journals (the books of original entry).

12. **d.** Posting transfers journal entries to ledger accounts. The other choices are incorrect because posting (a) occurs after journalizing, (b) transfers journal transaction data to the ledger; and (c) is not an optional step in the recording process.

13. **c.** The balance is €11,000 (€16,000 normal balance – €5,000 payment), not (a) €21,000 or (b) €5,000. Choice (d) is incorrect because the balance can be determined.

14. **a.** A trial balance is a list of accounts with their balances at a given time. The other choices are incorrect because (b) the trial balance does not prove that journalized transactions are mathematically correct; (c) if a journal entry is posted twice, the trial balance will still balance; and (d) the trial balance does not prove that all transactions have been recorded.

15. **c.** The trial balance will not balance in this case because the debit of £1,000 to Dividends is not equal to the credit of £100 to Cash. The other choices are incorrect because (a) if a correct journal entry is posted twice, the trial balance will still balance; (b) if the purchase of supplies on account is debited to Supplies and credited to Cash, Cash and Accounts Payable will be understated but the trial balance will still balance; and (d) since the debit and credit amounts are the same, the trial balance will still balance but both Accounts Payable and Cash will be overstated.

16. **a.** The total debit column = \$5,000 (Cash) + \$40,000 (Salaries and Wages Expense) + \$10,000 (Rent Expense) + \$15,000 (Dividends) + \$61,000 (Equipment) = \$131,000. The normal balance for assets, expenses, and Dividends is a debit. The other choices are incorrect because (b) revenue of \$85,000 should not be included in the total of \$216,000 and its normal balance is a credit; (c) the total of \$91,000 is missing the Salaries and Wages Expense of \$40,000, which has a normal balance of a debit; and (d) the total of \$116,000 is missing the Dividends of \$15,000, which has a normal balance of a debit.

Practice Brief Exercises

1. **(LO 1)** Transactions for Potter Designs for the month of May are presented below. Identify the accounts to be debited and credited for each transaction.

Identify accounts to be debited and credited.

May	1	Shareholders invested £22,000 in the business.
	6	Paid office rent of £900.
	12	Performed consulting services and billed client £4,400.
	18	Purchased equipment on account for £1,200.

Solution

1.

		Account Debited	Account Credited
May	1	Cash	Share Capital—Ordinary
	6	Rent Expense	Cash
	12	Accounts Receivable	Service Revenue
	18	Equipment	Accounts Payable

2. **(LO 2)** Using the data from **Practice Brief Exercise 1**, journalize the transactions (omit explanations).

Journalize transactions.

Solution

2.

May	1	Cash	22,000	
		Share Capital—Ordinary		22,000
	6	Rent Expense	900	
		Cash		900
	12	Accounts Receivable	4,400	
		Service Revenue		4,400
	18	Equipment	1,200	
		Accounts Payable		1,200

Post journal entries to T-accounts.

3. **(LO 3)** Selected transactions for Santana Outfitters are presented in journal form below. Post the transactions to T-accounts. Make one T-account for each account and determine each account's ending balance.

J1

Date		**Account Titles and Explanation**	**Ref.**	**Debit**	**Credit**
June	6	Cash		22,000	
		Share Capital—Ordinary			22,000
		(Issued shares for cash)			
	13	Accounts Receivable		8,200	
		Service Revenue			8,200
		(Billed for services performed)			
	14	Cash		3,700	
		Accounts Receivable			3,700
		(Received cash in payment of account)			

Solution

3.

Cash

6/6	22,000		
6/14	3,700		
Bal.	25,700		

Accounts Receivable

6/13	8,200	6/14	3,700
Bal.	4,500		

Service Revenue

		6/13	8,200
		Bal.	8,200

Share Capital—Ordinary

		6/6	22,000
		Bal.	22,000

Post journal entries to standard form of account.

4. **(LO 3)** Selected journal entries for Santana Outfitters are presented in **Practice Brief Exercise 3.** Post the transactions using the standard form of account.

Solution

4.

Cash

Date	Explanation	Ref.	Debit	Credit	Balance
June 6		J1	22,000		22,000
14		J1	3,700		25,700

Accounts Receivable

Date	Explanation	Ref.	Debit	Credit	Balance
June 13		J1	8,200		8,200
14		J1		3,700	4,500

Service Revenue

Date	Explanation	Ref.	Debit	Credit	Balance
June 13		J1		8,200	8,200

Share Capital—Ordinary

Date	Explanation	Ref.	Debit	Credit	Balance
June 6		J1		22,000	22,000

5. **(LO 4)** From the ledger accounts below, prepare a trial balance for Lee Investments at December 31, 2029. List the accounts in the order shown in the text. All account balances are normal (amounts in thousands).

Prepare a trial balance.

Accounts Receivable	¥10,000	Salaries and Wages Expense	¥ 2,300
Supplies	4,100	Rent Expense	1,200
Accounts Payable	3,500	Share Capital—Ordinary	10,200
Dividends	1,100	Cash	6,000
Service Revenue	11,000		

Solution

5.

Lee Investments
Trial Balance
December 31, 2029

	Debit	Credit
Cash	¥ 6,000	
Accounts Receivable	10,000	
Supplies	4,100	
Accounts Payable		¥ 3,500
Share Capital—Ordinary		10,200
Dividends	1,100	
Service Revenue		11,000
Salaries and Wages Expense	2,300	
Rent Expense	1,200	
	¥24,700	¥24,700

Practice Exercises

1. **(LO 2)** Presented below is information related to Provence Real Estate Agency (amounts in thousands).

Analyze and journalize transactions.

Oct. 1 Henri Bos begins business as a real estate agent with a cash investment of €30,000 in exchange for ordinary shares.
2 Paid rent, €700, on office space.
3 Purchases office equipment for €2,800, on account.
6 Sells a house and lot for Amit Das; bills Amit Das €4,400 for realty services performed.
27 Pays €1,100 on the balance related to the transaction of October 3.
30 Receives bill for October utilities, €130 (not paid at this time).

Instructions

Journalize the transactions. (You may omit explanations.)

Solution

1. **GENERAL JOURNAL**

Date	Account Titles and Explanation	Ref.	Debit	Credit
Oct. 1	Cash		30,000	
	Share Capital—Ordinary			30,000
2	Rent Expense		700	
	Cash			700
3	Equipment		2,800	
	Accounts Payable			2,800
6	Accounts Receivable		4,400	
	Service Revenue			4,400
27	Accounts Payable		1,100	
	Cash			1,100
30	Utilities Expense		130	
	Accounts Payable			130

Journalize transactions from account data and prepare a trial balance.

2. (LO 2, 4) The T-accounts below summarize the ledger of Depot Company at the end of the first month of operations (in U.S. dollars).

Cash — No. 101

Date	Debit	Date	Credit
4/1	16,000	4/15	700
4/12	1,200	4/25	1,600
4/29	900		
4/30	1,600		

Unearned Service Revenue — No. 209

Date	Debit	Date	Credit
		4/30	1,600

Accounts Receivable — No. 112

Date	Debit	Date	Credit
4/7	2,900	4/29	900

Share Capital—Ordinary — No. 311

Date	Debit	Date	Credit
		4/1	16,000

Supplies — No. 126

Date	Debit	Date	Credit
4/4	1,900		

Service Revenue — No. 400

Date	Debit	Date	Credit
		4/7	2,900
		4/12	1,200

Accounts Payable — No. 201

Date	Debit	Date	Credit
4/25	1,600	4/4	1,900

Salaries and Wages Expense — No. 726

Date	Debit	Date	Credit
4/15	700		

Instructions

a. Prepare the complete general journal (including explanations).

b. Prepare a trial balance at April 30, 2029.

Solution

2.

a. GENERAL JOURNAL

Date	Account Titles and Explanation	Ref.	Debit	Credit
Apr. 1	Cash	101	16,000	
	Share Capital—Ordinary	311		16,000
	(Issued shares for cash)			
4	Supplies	126	1,900	
	Accounts Payable	201		1,900
	(Purchased supplies on account)			
7	Accounts Receivable	112	2,900	
	Service Revenue	400		2,900
	(Billed customers for services performed)			
12	Cash	101	1,200	
	Service Revenue	400		1,200
	(Received cash for services performed)			
15	Salaries and Wages Expense	726	700	
	Cash	101		700
	(Paid salaries to date)			
25	Accounts Payable	201	1,600	
	Cash	101		1,600
	(Paid creditors on account)			
29	Cash	101	900	
	Accounts Receivable	112		900
	(Received cash in payment of account)			
30	Cash	101	1,600	
	Unearned Service Revenue	209		1,600
	(Received cash for future services)			

b.

Depot Company
Trial Balance
April 30, 2029

	Debit	Credit
Cash	$17,400	
Accounts Receivable	2,000	
Supplies	1,900	

Accounts Payable		$ 300
Unearned Service Revenue		1,600
Share Capital—Ordinary		16,000
Service Revenue		4,100
Salaries and Wages Expense	700	
	$22,000	$22,000

Practice Problem

Journalize transactions, post, and prepare a trial balance.

(LO 1, 2, 3, 4) A group of student-investors in Hong Kong opened Campus Laundromat Ltd. on September 1, 2029. During the first month of operations, the following transactions occurred.

Sept. 1 Shareholders invested HK$20,000 cash in the business in exchange for ordinary shares.
2 The company paid HK$1,000 cash for store rent for September.
3 Purchased washers and dryers for HK$25,000, paying HK$10,000 in cash and signing a HK$15,000, 6-month, 12% note payable.
4 Paid HK$1,200 for a one-year accident insurance policy.
10 Received a bill from the *Daily News* for online advertising of the opening of the laundromat HK$200.
20 Declared and paid a cash dividend to shareholders of HK$700.
30 The company determined that cash receipts for laundry services for the month were HK$6,200.

The chart of accounts for the company is the same as that for Yazici Advertising A.Ş. in Illustration 2.19 plus No. 610 Advertising Expense.

Instructions

a. Journalize the September transactions. (Use J1 for the journal page number.)
b. Open ledger accounts and post the September transactions.
c. Prepare a trial balance at September 30, 2029.

Solution

a. **GENERAL JOURNAL** **J1**

Date	Account Titles and Explanation	Ref.	Debit	Credit
2029				
Sept. 1	Cash	101	20,000	
	Share Capital—Ordinary	311		20,000
	(Issued shares for cash)			
2	Rent Expense	729	1,000	
	Cash	101		1,000
	(Paid September rent)			
3	Equipment	157	25,000	
	Cash	101		10,000
	Notes Payable	200		15,000
	(Purchased laundry equipment for cash and 6-month, 12% note payable)			
4	Prepaid Insurance	130	1,200	
	Cash	101		1,200
	(Paid one-year insurance policy)			
10	Advertising Expense	610	200	
	Accounts Payable	201		200
	(Received bill from *Daily News* for advertising)			

Date	Account Titles and Explanation	Ref.	Debit	Credit
2029				
Sept. 20	Dividends	332	700	
	Cash	101		700
	(Declared and paid a cash dividend)			
30	Cash	101	6,200	
	Service Revenue	400		6,200
	(Received cash for services performed)			

b.

GENERAL LEDGER

Cash — **No. 101**

Date	Explanation	Ref.	Debit	Credit	Balance
2029					
Sept. 1		J1	20,000		20,000
2		J1		1,000	19,000
3		J1		10,000	9,000
4		J1		1,200	7,800
20		J1		700	7,100
30		J1	6,200		13,300

Prepaid Insurance — **No. 130**

Date	Explanation	Ref.	Debit	Credit	Balance
2029					
Sept. 4		J1	1,200		1,200

Equipment — **No. 157**

Date	Explanation	Ref.	Debit	Credit	Balance
2029					
Sept. 3		J1	25,000		25,000

Notes Payable — **No. 200**

Date	Explanation	Ref.	Debit	Credit	Balance
2029					
Sept. 3		J1		15,000	15,000

Accounts Payable — **No. 201**

Date	Explanation	Ref.	Debit	Credit	Balance
2029					
Sept. 10		J1		200	200

Share Capital—Ordinary — **No. 311**

Date	Explanation	Ref.	Debit	Credit	Balance
2029					
Sept. 1		J1		20,000	20,000

Dividend — **No. 332**

Date	Explanation	Ref.	Debit	Credit	Balance
2029					
Sept. 20		J1	700		700

Service Revenue — **No. 400**

Date	Explanation	Ref.	Debit	Credit	Balance
2029					
Sept. 30		J1		6,200	6,200

Advertising Expense — **No. 610**

Date	Explanation	Ref.	Debit	Credit	Balance
2029					
Sept. 10		J1	200		200

Rent Expense — **No. 729**

Date	Explanation	Ref.	Debit	Credit	Balance
2029					
Sept. 2		J1	1,000		1,000

c.

Campus Laundromat Ltd.
Trial Balance
September 30, 2029

	Debit	Credit
Cash	HK$13,300	
Prepaid Insurance	1,200	
Equipment	25,000	
Notes Payable		HK$15,000
Accounts Payable		200
Share Capital—Ordinary		20,000
Dividends	700	
Service Revenue		6,200
Advertising Expense	200	
Rent Expense	1,000	
	HK$41,400	HK$41,400

Questions

1. Describe the parts of a T-account.

2. "The terms debit and credit mean increase and decrease, respectively." Do you agree? Explain.

3. Pete Harcourt, a fellow student, contends that the double-entry system means each transaction must be recorded twice. Is Pete correct? Explain.

4. Melissa Estes, a beginning accounting student, believes debit balances are favorable and credit balances are unfavorable. Is Melissa correct? Discuss.

5. State the rules of debit and credit as applied to (a) asset accounts, (b) liability accounts, and (c) the equity accounts (revenue, expenses, dividends, and share capital—ordinary).

6. What is the normal balance for each of the following accounts? (a) Accounts Receivable. (b) Cash. (c) Dividends. (d) Accounts Payable. (e) Service Revenue. (f) Salaries and Wages Expense. (g) Share Capital—Ordinary.

7. Indicate whether each of the following accounts is an asset, a liability, or an equity account and whether it has a normal debit or credit balance: (a) Accounts Receivable, (b) Accounts Payable, (c) Equipment, (d) Dividends, and (e) Supplies.

8. For the following transactions, indicate the account debited and the account credited.

   a. Supplies are purchased on account.

   b. Cash is received on signing a note payable.

   c. Employees are paid salaries in cash.

9. Indicate whether the following accounts generally will have (a) debit entries only, (b) credit entries only, or (c) both debit and credit entries.

   1. Cash.
   2. Accounts Receivable.
   3. Dividends.
   4. Accounts Payable.
   5. Salaries and Wages Expense.
   6. Service Revenue.

10. What are the basic steps in the recording process?

11. What are the advantages of using a journal in the recording process?

12. **a.** When entering a transaction in the journal, should the debit or credit be written first?

    b. Which should be indented, the debit or credit?

13. Describe a compound entry, and provide an example.

14. **a.** Should business transaction debits and credits be recorded directly in the ledger accounts?

    b. What are the advantages of first recording transactions in the journal and then posting to the ledger?

15. The account number is entered as the last step in posting the amounts from the journal to the ledger. What is the advantage of this step?

16. Journalize the following business transactions.

    a. Alberto Rivera invests €7,000 cash in the business in exchange for ordinary shares.

    b. Insurance of €800 is paid for the year.

    c. Supplies of €2,000 are purchased on account.

    d. Cash of €8,500 is received for services performed.

17. **a.** What is a ledger?

    b. What is a chart of accounts and why is it important?

18. What is a trial balance and what are its purposes?

19. Victor Grimm is confused about how accounting information flows through the accounting system. He believes the flow of information is as follows.

    a. Debits and credits posted to the ledger.

    b. Business transaction occurs.

    c. Information entered in the journal.

    d. Financial statements are prepared.

    e. Trial balance is prepared.

    Is Victor correct? If not, indicate to Victor the proper flow of the information.

20. Two students are discussing the use of a trial balance. They wonder whether the following errors, each considered separately, would prevent the trial balance from balancing.

    a. The bookkeeper debited Cash for €600 and credited Salaries and Wages Expense for €600 for payment of wages.

    b. Cash collected on account was debited to Cash for €800 and Service Revenue was credited for €80.

    What would you tell them?

21. What are the normal balances for **TSMC**'s Cash, Accounts Payable, and Interest Expense accounts?

Brief Exercises

BE2.1 (LO 1) For each of the following accounts, indicate the effects of (a) a debit and (b) a credit on the accounts and (c) the normal balance of the account.

Indicate debit and credit effects and normal balance.

1. Accounts Payable.
2. Advertising Expense.
3. Service Revenue.
4. Accounts Receivable.
5. Share Capital—Ordinary.
6. Dividends.

Identify accounts to be debited and credited.

BE2.2 (LO 1) Transactions for Thorn Consulting for the month of June are presented below. Identify the accounts to be debited and credited for each transaction.

June	1	Oleg Thorn invests €5,000 cash in a small welding business in exchange for ordinary shares.
	2	Purchases equipment on account for €3,600.
	3	€800 cash is paid to landlord for June rent.
	12	Sends a bill to K. Johnsen for €400 after completing welding work done on account.

Journalize transactions.

BE2.3 (LO 2) Using the data in BE2.2, journalize the transactions. (You may omit explanations.)

Identify and explain steps in recording process.

BE2.4 (LO 2) **Writing** Shea Jonas, a fellow student, is unclear about the basic steps in the recording process. Identify and briefly explain the steps in the order in which they occur.

Indicate basic and debit-credit analysis.

BE2.5 (LO 1) Gonzales SA, a financial advising company, has the following transactions during August of the current year, its first month of operations. Indicate (a) the effect on the accounting equation and (b) the debit-credit analysis as illustrated in the text.

Aug.	1	Shareholders invest R$9,000 in cash in exchange for ordinary shares.
	4	Pays insurance in advance for 6 months, R$2,100 cash.
	16	Receives R$3,600 from clients for services performed.
	27	Pays secretary R$1,000 salary.

Journalize transactions.

BE2.6 (LO 2) Using the data in BE2.5, journalize the transactions. (You may omit explanations.)

Post journal entries to T-accounts.

BE2.7 (LO 3) Selected transactions for Wang Enterprises are presented in journal form below. Post the transactions to T-accounts. Make one T-account for each account and determine each account's ending balance.

J1

Date		Account Titles and Explanation	Ref.	Debit	Credit
May	5	Accounts Receivable		5,400	
		Service Revenue			5,400
		(Billed for services performed)			
	12	Cash		4,200	
		Accounts Receivable			4,200
		(Received cash in payment of account)			
	15	Cash		3,000	
		Service Revenue			3,000
		(Received cash for services performed)			

Post journal entries to standard form of account.

BE2.8 (LO 3) Selected journal entries for Wang Enterprises are presented in BE2.7. Post the transactions using the standard form of account.

Prepare a trial balance.

BE2.9 (LO 4) From the ledger balances given below, prepare a trial balance for Amaro Company at June 30, 2029. List the accounts in the order shown in the text. All account balances are normal.

Accounts Payable $8,100, Cash $5,800, Share Capital—Ordinary $15,000, Dividends $1,200, Equipment $17,000, Service Revenue $10,000, Accounts Receivable $3,000, Salaries and Wages Expense $5,100, and Rent Expense $1,000.

Prepare a correct trial balance.

BE2.10 (LO 4) An inexperienced bookkeeper prepared the following trial balance. Prepare a correct trial balance, assuming all account balances are normal.

Chang Ltd.
Trial Balance
December 31, 2029

	Debit	Credit
Cash	£10,600	
Prepaid Insurance		£ 3,500
Accounts Payable		3,000
Unearned Service Revenue	2,200	
Share Capital—Ordinary		9,000
Dividends		4,500
Service Revenue		25,400
Salaries and Wages Expense	18,600	
Rent Expense		2,400
	£31,400	£47,800

DO IT! Exercises

Identify normal balances.

DO IT! 2.1 (LO 1) Tom Rast has just rented space in a strip mall. In this space, he will open a photography studio, to be called "Picture This!" A friend has advised Tom to set up a double-entry set of accounting records in which to record all of his business transactions.

Identify the statement of financial position accounts that Tom will likely need to record the transactions needed to open his business (a corporation). Indicate whether the normal balance of each account is a debit or credit.

Record business activities.

DO IT! 2.2 (LO 2) Tom Rast engaged in the following activities in establishing his photography studio, Picture This!:

1. Opened a bank account in the name of Picture This! and deposited £6,500 of his own money into this account in exchange for ordinary shares.
2. Purchased photography supplies at a total cost of £1,200. The business paid £400 in cash and the balance is on account.
3. Obtained estimates on the cost of photography equipment from three different manufacturers.

Prepare the journal entries to record the transactions. (You may omit explanations.)

Post transactions.

DO IT! 2.3 (LO 3) Tom Rast recorded the following transactions during the month of April.

April 3	Cash	3,400	
	Service Revenue		3,400
April 16	Rent Expense	700	
	Cash		700
April 20	Salaries and Wages Expense	250	
	Cash		250

Post these entries to the Cash T-account of the general ledger to determine the ending balance in cash. The beginning balance in cash on April 1 was £1,600.

Prepare a trial balance.

DO IT! 2.4 (LO 4) The following accounts are taken from the ledger of Chillin' Company at December 31, 2029.

200	Notes Payable	R$20,000	101	Cash	R$ 6,000
311	Share Capital—Ordinary	28,000	126	Supplies	7,000
157	Equipment	80,000	729	Rent Expense	4,000
332	Dividends	9,000	212	Salaries and Wages Payable	3,000
726	Salaries and Wages Expense	38,000	201	Accounts Payable	11,000
400	Service Revenue	90,000	112	Accounts Receivable	8,000

Prepare a trial balance in good form.

Exercises

Analyze statements about accounting and the recording process.

E2.1 (LO 1) Kim Yi has prepared the following list of statements about accounts.

1. An account is an accounting record of either a specific asset or a specific liability.
2. An account shows only increases, not decreases, in the item it relates to.
3. Some items, such as Cash and Accounts Receivable, are combined into one account.
4. An account has a left, or credit side, and a right, or debit side.
5. A simple form of an account consisting of just the account title, the left side, and the right side, is called a T-account.

Instructions

Identify each statement as true or false. If false, indicate how to correct the statement.

Identify debits, credits, and normal balances.

E2.2 (LO 1) Selected transactions for Acosta Decor, an interior design company, in its first month of business are as follows.

Jan.	2	Marie Acosta invested €10,000 cash in business in exchange for ordinary shares.
	3	Purchased a used car for €3,000 cash for use in business.
	9	Purchased supplies on account for €600.
	11	Billed customers €2,400 for services performed.
	16	Paid €350 cash for advertising.
	20	Received €900 cash from customers billed on January 11.
	23	Paid creditor €300 cash on balance owed.
	28	Declared and paid a €1,000 cash dividend.

Instructions

For each transaction, indicate the following.

a. The basic type of account debited and credited (asset, liability, equity).

b. The specific account debited and credited (Cash, Rent Expense, Service Revenue, etc.).

c. Whether the specific account is increased or decreased.

d. The normal balance of the specific account.

Use the following format, in which the January 2 transaction is given as an example.

	Account Debited				Account Credited			
Date	**(a) Basic Type**	**(b) Specific Account**	**(c) Effect**	**(d) Normal Balance**	**(a) Basic Type**	**(b) Specific Account**	**(c) Effect**	**(d) Normal Balance**
Jan. 2	Asset	Cash	Increase	Debit	Equity	Share Capital—Ordinary	Increase	Credit

Journalize transactions.

E2.3 (LO 2) Data for Acosta Decor are presented in E2.2.

Instructions

Journalize the transactions using journal page J1. (You may omit explanations.)

Analyze transactions and determine their effect on accounts.

E2.4 (LO 3) The following information relates to Yansheng Real Estate.

Oct.	1	Biao Yansheng begins business as a real estate agent with a cash investment of HK$17,000 in exchange for ordinary shares.
	2	Hires a part-time administrative assistant.
	3	Purchases supplies for HK$1,900, on account.
	6	Sells a house and lot for C. Chow; bills C. Chow HK$3,800 for realty services performed.
	27	Pays HK$1,300 on the balance related to the transaction of October 3.
	30	Pays the administrative assistant HK$2,500 in salary for October.

Instructions

Prepare the debit-credit analysis for each transaction as illustrated in the text.

Journalize transactions.

E2.5 (LO 2) Transaction data for Yansheng Real Estate are presented in E2.4.

Instructions

Journalize the transactions. (You may omit explanations.)

Analyze transactions and journalize.

E2.6 (LO 1, 2) Lennon Industries had the following transactions.

1. Borrowed €5,000 from the bank by signing a note.
2. Paid €3,900 cash for a computer.
3. Purchased €650 of supplies on account.

Instructions

a. Indicate what accounts are increased and decreased by each transaction.

b. Journalize each transaction. (Omit explanations.)

E2.7 (LO 1, 2) Ong Enterprises had the following selected transactions. *Analyze transactions and journalize.*

1. Shareholders invested NT$40,000 cash in the business in exchange for ordinary shares.
2. Paid office rent of NT$8,400.
3. Performed consulting services and billed a client NT$52,000.
4. Declared and paid a NT$7,500 dividend.

Instructions

a. Indicate the effect each transaction has on the accounting equation (Assets = Liabilities + Equity), using plus and minus signs.

b. Journalize each transaction. (Omit explanations.)

E2.8 (LO 2) Selected transactions for Sophie's Dog Care are as follows during the month of March. *Journalize a series of transactions.*

March	1	Paid monthly rent of $1,200.
	3	Performed services for $160 on account.
	5	Performed services for cash of $75.
	8	Purchased equipment for $600. The company paid cash of $90 and the balance was on account.
	12	Received cash from customers billed on March 3.
	14	Paid salaries and wages to employees of $525.
	22	Paid utilities of $72.
	24	Borrowed $1,500 from Grafton State Bank by signing a note.
	27	Paid $220 to repair service for plumbing repairs.
	28	Paid balance amount owed from equipment purchase on March 8.
	30	Paid $1,800 for six months of insurance.

Instructions

Journalize the transactions. (Omit explanations.)

E2.9 (LO 2) On April 1, Adventures Travel Agency began operations. The following transactions were completed during the month. *Record journal entries.*

1. Shareholders invested $24,000 in the business in exchange for ordinary shares.
2. Obtained a bank loan for $7,000 by issuing a note payable.
3. Paid $11,000 cash to buy equipment.
4. Paid $1,200 cash for April office rent.
5. Paid $1,450 for supplies.
6. Purchased $600 of advertising in the *Daily Herald*, on account.
7. Performed services for $18,000: cash of $2,000 was received from customers, and the balance of $16,000 was billed to customers on account.
8. Declared and paid a cash dividend of $400.
9. Paid the utility bill for the month, $2,000.
10. Paid *Daily Herald* the amount due in transaction (6).
11. Paid $40 of interest on the bank loan obtained in transaction (2).
12. Paid employees' salaries and wages, $6,400.
13. Received $12,000 cash from customers billed in transaction (7).

Instructions

Journalize the transactions. (Omit explanations).

E2.10 (LO 3) Alma Ortiz has prepared the following list of statements about the general ledger. *Analyze statements about the ledger.*

1. The general ledger contains all the asset and liability accounts but no equity accounts.
2. The general ledger is sometimes referred to as simply the ledger.
3. The accounts in the general ledger are arranged in alphabetical order.
4. Each account in the general ledger is numbered for easier identification.
5. The general ledger is a book of original entry.

Instructions

Identify each statement as true or false. If false, indicate how to correct the statement.

Post journal entries and prepare a trial balance.

E2.11 (LO 3, 4) Selected transactions from the journal of Kati Tillman, investment broker, are presented as follows.

Date	Account Titles and Explanation	Ref.	Debit	Credit
Aug. 1	Cash		6,000	
	Share Capital—Ordinary			6,000
	(Issued shares for cash)			
10	Cash		2,700	
	Service Revenue			2,700
	(Received cash for services performed)			
12	Equipment		5,000	
	Cash			800
	Notes Payable			4,200
	(Purchased office equipment for cash and notes payable)			
25	Accounts Receivable		1,600	
	Service Revenue			1,600
	(Billed clients for services performed)			
31	Cash		880	
	Accounts Receivable			880
	(Receipt of cash on account)			

Instructions

a. Post the transactions to T-accounts.

b. Prepare a trial balance at August 31, 2029.

Journalize transactions from account data and prepare a trial balance.

E2.12 (LO 2, 4) The T-accounts below summarize the ledger of Negrete Landscaping at the end of the first month of operations (amounts in €).

Cash			No. 101
4/1	14,000	4/15	1,300
4/12	900	4/25	1,500
4/29	400		
4/30	1,000		

Unearned Service Revenue			No. 209
		4/30	1,000

Accounts Receivable			No. 112
4/7	3,000	4/29	400

Share Capital—Ordinary			No. 311
		4/1	14,000

Supplies			No. 126
4/4	1,800		

Service Revenue			No. 400
		4/7	3,000
		4/12	900

Accounts Payable			No. 201
4/25	1,500	4/4	1,800

Salaries and Wages Expense			No. 726
4/15	1,300		

Instructions

a. Prepare the complete general journal (including explanations) from which the postings were made.

b. Prepare a trial balance at April 30, 2029.

Journalize transactions from account data and prepare a trial balance.

E2.13 (LO 2, 4) Presented below is the ledger for Shumway Co. (amounts in thousands of ¥).

Cash — No. 101

Date	Debit	Date	Credit
10/1	3,000	10/4	400
10/10	750	10/12	1,500
10/10	4,000	10/15	350
10/20	500	10/30	300
10/25	2,000	10/31	500

Accounts Receivable — No. 112

Date	Debit	Date	Credit
10/6	800	10/20	500
10/20	940		

Supplies — No. 126

Date	Debit	Date	Credit
10/4	400		

Equipment — No. 157

Date	Debit	Date	Credit
10/3	2,000		

Notes Payable — No. 200

Date	Debit	Date	Credit
		10/10	4,000

Accounts Payable — No. 201

Date	Debit	Date	Credit
10/12	1,500	10/3	2,000

Share Capital—Ordinary — No. 311

Date	Debit	Date	Credit
		10/1	3,000
		10/25	2,000

Dividends — No. 332

Date	Debit	Date	Credit
10/30	300		

Service Revenue — No. 400

Date	Debit	Date	Credit
		10/6	800
		10/10	750
		10/20	940

Salaries and Wages Expense — No. 726

Date	Debit	Date	Credit
10/31	500		

Rent Expense — No. 729

Date	Debit	Date	Credit
10/15	350		

Instructions

a. Reproduce the journal entries for the transactions that occurred on October 1, 10, and 20, and provide explanations for each.

b. Determine the October 31 balance for each of the accounts above, and prepare a trial balance at October 31, 2029.

Prepare journal entries and post using standard account form.

E2.14 (LO 2, 3) Selected transactions for Ling Couture during its first month in business are presented below.

Sept.	1	Shareholders invested NT$10,000 cash in the business in exchange for ordinary shares.
	5	Purchased equipment for NT$14,000 paying NT$4,000 in cash and the balance on account.
	25	Paid NT$3,000 cash on balance owed for equipment.
	30	Declared and paid a NT$900 dividend.

Ling's chart of accounts shows No. 101 Cash, No. 157 Equipment, No. 201 Accounts Payable, No. 311 Share Capital—Ordinary, and No. 332 Dividends.

Instructions

a. Journalize the transactions on page J1 of the journal. (Omit explanations.)

b. Post the transactions using the standard account form.

Analyze errors and their effects on trial balance.

E2.15 (LO 4) The bookkeeper for Kang Equipment Repair made a number of errors in journalizing and posting, as described below.

1. A credit posting of $525 to Accounts Receivable was omitted.
2. A debit posting of $750 for Prepaid Insurance was debited to Insurance Expense.
3. A collection from a customer of $100 in payment of its account owed was journalized and posted as a debit to Cash $100 and a credit to Service Revenue $100.
4. A credit posting of $415 to Property Taxes Payable was made twice.
5. A cash purchase of supplies for $250 was journalized and posted as a debit to Supplies $25 and a credit to Cash $25.
6. A debit of $625 to Advertising Expense was posted as $652.

Instructions

For each error:

a. Indicate whether the trial balance will balance.

b. If the trial balance will not balance, indicate the amount of the difference.

c. Indicate the trial balance column that will have the larger total.

Consider each error separately. Use the following form, in which error (1) is given as an example.

	(a)	(b)	(c)
Error	In Balance	Difference	Larger Column
(1)	No	$525	debit

Prepare a trial balance.

E2.16 (LO 4) The accounts in the ledger of Overnite Delivery Service contain the following balances on July 31, 2029 (amounts in thousands).

Accounts Receivable	¥ 7,640	Prepaid Insurance	¥ 1,968
Accounts Payable	8,394	Maintenance and Repairs Expense	961
Cash	?	Service Revenue	10,610
Equipment	45,360	Dividends	700
Gasoline Expense	758	Share Capital—Ordinary	38,000
Utilities Expense	523	Salaries and Wages Expense	4,428
Notes Payable	17,000	Salaries and Wages Payable	815

Instructions

Prepare a trial balance with the accounts arranged as illustrated in the chapter and fill in the missing amount for Cash.

Journalize transactions, post transactions to T-accounts, and prepare trial balance.

E2.17 (LO 2, 3, 4) Beyers Security provides security services. Selected transactions for Beyers are presented below.

Oct.	1	Received $66,000 cash in the business in exchange for ordinary shares.
	2	Hired part-time security consultant. Salary will be $2,000 per month. First day of work will be October 15.
	4	Paid one month of rent for building for $2,000.
	7	Purchased equipment for $18,000, paying $4,000 cash and the balance on account.
	8	Paid $500 for advertising.
	10	Received bill for equipment repair cost of $390.
	12	Provided security services for event for $3,200 on account.
	16	Purchased supplies for $410 on account.
	21	Paid balance due from October 7 purchase of equipment.
	24	Received and paid utility bill for $148.
	27	Received payment from customer for October 12 services performed.
	31	Paid employee salaries and wages of $5,100.

Instructions

a. Journalize the transactions. Do not provide explanations.

b. Post the transactions to T-accounts.

c. Prepare a trial balance at October 31, 2029. (*Hint:* Compute ending balances of T-accounts first.)

Identify key terms.

E2.18 (LO 1, 2, 3, 4) The following is a list of terms or phrases discussed in the chapter.

1. Credit
2. Journal
3. Ledger
4. Chart of accounts
5. Posting
6. Account
7. Trial balance
8. Accounting transactions
9. Debit

Instructions

Match each term or phrase to its description below.

a. A list of accounts and their balances at a given time.

b. An accounting record in which transactions are initially recorded in chronological order.

c. A record of all accounts maintained by a company and their amounts.

d. An individual accounting record of increases and decreases in specific asset, liability, equity, revenue, or expense items.

e. A list of the names of a company's accounts.

f. The right side of an account.

g. The procedure of transferring journal entry amounts to the ledger accounts.

h. The left side of an account.

i. Events that require recording in the financial statements because they affect assets, liabilities, or equity.

Problems

P2.1 (LO 1, 2) Feng Disc Golf Course was opened on March 1. The following selected events and transactions occurred during March (amounts in thousands).

Journalize a series of transactions.

Mar.	1	Lee Feng invested ¥20,000 cash in the business in exchange for ordinary shares.
	3	Purchased Rainbow Golf Land for ¥15,000 cash. The price consists of land ¥12,000, building ¥2,000, and equipment ¥1,000. (Make one compound entry.)
	5	Paid advertising expenses of ¥900.
	6	Paid cash ¥600 for a one-year insurance policy.
	10	Purchased golf discs and other equipment for ¥1,050 from Wang Company payable in 30 days.
	18	Received ¥1,100 in cash for golf fees (Feng records golf fees as service revenue).
	19	Sold 150 coupon books for ¥10 each. Each book contains 4 coupons that enable the holder to play one round of disc golf.
	25	Declared and paid a ¥800 cash dividend.
	30	Paid salaries of ¥250.
	30	Paid Wang Company in full.
	31	Received ¥2,700 cash for golf fees.

Feng Disc Golf uses the following accounts: Cash, Prepaid Insurance, Land, Buildings, Equipment, Accounts Payable, Unearned Service Revenue, Share Capital—Ordinary, Dividends, Service Revenue, Advertising Expense, and Salaries and Wages Expense.

Instructions

Journalize the March transactions.

P2.2 (LO 2, 3, 4) Julia Dumars is a licensed CPA. During the first month of operations of her business, Julia Dumars, Inc., the following events and transactions occurred.

Journalize transactions, post, and prepare a trial balance.

May	1	Shareholders invested $20,000 cash in exchange for ordinary shares.
	2	Hired a secretary-receptionist at a salary of $2,000 per month.
	3	Purchased $1,500 of supplies on account from Vincent Supply Company.
	7	Paid office rent of $900 cash for the month.
	11	Completed a tax assignment and billed client $2,800 for services performed.
	12	Received $3,500 advance on a management consulting engagement.
	17	Received cash of $1,200 for services performed for Orville Co.
	31	Paid secretary-receptionist $2,000 salary for the month.
	31	Paid 40% of balance due Vincent Supply Company.

Julia uses the following chart of accounts: No. 101 Cash, No. 112 Accounts Receivable, No. 126 Supplies, No. 201 Accounts Payable, No. 209 Unearned Service Revenue, No. 311 Share Capital—Ordinary, No. 400 Service Revenue, No. 726 Salaries and Wages Expense, and No. 729 Rent Expense.

Instructions

a. Journalize the transactions.

b. Post to the ledger accounts.

c. Prepare a trial balance on May 31, 2029.

c. Trial balance totals $28,400

P2.3 (LO 1, 2, 3, 4) Kochi Services was formed on May 1, 2029. The following transactions took place during the first month (amounts in thousands).

Journalize transactions, post, and prepare a trial balance.

Transactions on May 1:

1. Rahul Shah invested ₹40,000 cash in the company in exchange for ordinary shares.

2. Hired two employees to work in the warehouse. They will each be paid a salary of ₹3,050 per month.

3. Signed a 2-year rental agreement on a warehouse; paid ₹24,000 cash in advance for the first year.
4. Purchased furniture and equipment costing ₹30,000. A cash payment of ₹10,000 was made immediately; the remainder will be paid in 6 months.
5. Paid ₹1,800 cash for a one-year insurance policy on the furniture and equipment.

Transactions during the remainder of the month:

6. Purchased basic office supplies for ₹420 cash.
7. Purchased more office supplies for ₹1,500 on account.
8. Total revenues earned were ₹20,000–₹8,000 cash and ₹12,000 on account.
9. Paid ₹400 to suppliers for accounts payable due.
10. Received ₹3,000 from customers in payment of accounts receivable.
11. Received utility bills in the amount of ₹380, to be paid next month.
12. Paid the monthly salaries of the two employees, totaling ₹6,100.

Instructions

a. Prepare journal entries to record each of the events listed. (Omit explanations.)

b. Post the journal entries to T-accounts.

c. Prepare a trial balance as of May 31, 2029.

c. Trial balance totals ₹81,480

Prepare a correct trial balance.

P2.4 (LO 4) The trial balance of De Bortoli Co. shown below does not balance.

De Bortoli Co.
Trial Balance
June 30, 2029

	Debit	Credit
Cash		$ 3,340
Accounts Receivable	$ 2,812	
Supplies	1,200	
Equipment	2,600	
Accounts Payable		3,666
Unearned Service Revenue	1,100	
Share Capital—Ordinary		8,000
Dividends	800	
Service Revenue		2,480
Salaries and Wages Expense	3,200	
Utilities Expense	810	
	$12,522	$17,486

Each of the listed accounts has a normal balance per the general ledger. An examination of the ledger and journal reveals the following errors.

1. Cash received from a customer in payment of its account was debited for $580, and Accounts Receivable was credited for the same amount. The actual collection was for $850.
2. The purchase of a computer on account for $710 was recorded as a debit to Supplies for $710 and a credit to Accounts Payable for $710.
3. Services were performed on account for a client for $980. Accounts Receivable was debited for $980, and Service Revenue was credited for $98.
4. A debit posting to Salaries and Wages Expense of $700 was omitted.
5. A payment of a balance due for $306 was credited to Cash for $306 and credited to Accounts Payable for $360.
6. A dividend of $600 cash was debited to Salaries and Wages Expense for $600 and credited to Cash for $600.

Instructions

Trial balance totals $15,462

Prepare a correct trial balance. (*Hint:* It helps to prepare the correct journal entry for the transaction described and compare it to the mistake made.)

P2.5 (LO 4) The following trial balance of Scarlatti Corporation does not balance.

Prepare a correct trial balance.

Scarlatti Corporation
Trial Balance
April 30, 2029

	Debit	Credit
Cash	$ 5,912	
Accounts Receivable	5,240	
Supplies	2,967	
Equipment	6,100	
Accounts Payable		$ 7,044
Share Capital—Ordinary		8,000
Retained Earnings		2,000
Service Revenue		5,200
Office Expense	4,320	
	$24,539	$22,244

An examination of the ledger shows these errors.

1. Cash received from a customer on account was recorded (both debit and credit) as $1,580 instead of $1,850.
2. The purchase on account of a computer costing $1,900 was recorded as a debit to Office Expense and a credit to Accounts Payable.
3. Services were performed on account for a client, $2,250, for which Accounts Receivable was debited $2,250 and Service Revenue was credited $225.
4. A payment of $95 for telephone charges was entered as a debit to Office Expense and a debit to Cash.
5. The Service Revenue account was totaled at $5,200 instead of $5,280.

Instructions

From this information prepare a corrected trial balance.

P2.6 (LO 1, 2, 3, 4) The Sun Theater will begin operations in March. The Sun will be unique in that it will show only triple features of sequential theme movies. As of March 1, the ledger of Sun showed No. 101 Cash ₩3,000, No. 140 Land ₩24,000, No. 145 Buildings (concession stand, projection room, ticket booth, and screen) ₩10,000, No. 157 Equipment ₩10,000, No. 201 Accounts Payable ₩7,000, and No. 311 Share Capital—Ordinary ₩40,000. During the month of March, the following events and transactions occurred (amounts in thousands).

Journalize transactions, post, and prepare a trial balance.

Mar.	2	Rented the three *Kung Fu Panda* movies to be shown for the first 3 weeks of March. The film rental was ₩3,500; ₩1,500 was paid in cash and ₩2,000 will be paid on March 10.
	3	Ordered three *Batman* movies to be shown the last 10 days of March. It will cost ₩200 per night.
	9	Received ₩4,300 cash from admissions.
	10	Paid balance due on *Kung Fu Panda* movies rental and ₩2,100 on March 1 accounts payable.
	11	Sun Theater contracted with So Bin to operate the concession stand. Bin is to pay 15% of gross concession receipts, payable monthly, for the rental of the concession stand.
	12	Paid advertising expenses ₩900.
	20	Received ₩5,000 cash from customers for admissions.
	20	Received the *Batman* movies and paid the rental fee of ₩2,000.
	31	Paid salaries of ₩3,100.
	31	Received statement from So Bin showing gross receipts from concessions of ₩6,000 and the balance due to Sun Theater of ₩900 (₩6,000 × 15%) for March. Bin paid one-half the balance due and will remit the remainder on April 5.
	31	Received ₩9,000 cash from customers for admissions.

In addition to the accounts identified above, the chart of accounts includes No. 112 Accounts Receivable, No. 400 Service Revenue, No. 429 Rent Revenue, No. 610 Advertising Expense, No. 726 Salaries and Wages Expense, and No. 729 Rent Expense.

Instructions

d. Trial balance totals ₩64,100

a. Enter the beginning balances in the ledger. Insert a check mark (✓) in the reference column of the ledger for the beginning balance.

b. Journalize the March transactions. Sun records admission revenue as service revenue, rental of the concession stand as rent revenue, and film rental expense as rent expense.

c. Post the March journal entries to the ledger. Assume that all entries are posted from page 1 of the journal.

d. Prepare a trial balance on March 31, 2029.

Expand Your Critical Thinking

Financial Reporting Problem: TSMC, Ltd. (TWN)

CT2.1 The financial statements of **TSMC** are presented in Appendix A. The notes accompanying the statements contain the following selected accounts. The complete annual report, including the notes to the financial statements, is available at the company's website.

Accounts Payable	Income Tax Payable
Accounts Receivable	Finance Cost (Interest Expense)
Property, Plant, and Equipment	Inventories

Instructions

a. Answer the following questions.

1. What is the increase and decrease side for each account?
2. What is the normal balance for each account?

b. Identify the probable other account in the transaction and the effect on that account when:

1. Accounts Receivable is decreased.
2. Accounts Payable is decreased.
3. Inventories are increased.

c. Identify the other account(s) that ordinarily would be involved when:

1. Finance Cost (Interest Expense) is increased.
2. Property, Plant, and Equipment is increased.

Comparative Analysis Problem: Nestlé SA (CHE) vs. Delfi Limited (SGP)

CT2.2 **Nestlé**'s financial statements are presented in Appendix B. Financial statements of **Delfi Limited** are presented in Appendix C.

Instructions

a. Based on the information contained in the financial statements, determine the normal balance of the listed accounts for each company.

Nestlé	Delfi Limited
1. Inventories	1. Trade (Accounts) Receivable
2. Property, Plant, and Equipment	2. Cash and Cash Equivalents
3. Trade and Other Payables	3. Cost of Sales (Expense)
4. Finance Cost (Interest Expense)	4. Revenue

b. Identify the other account ordinarily involved when:

1. Trade (Accounts) Receivable is increased.
2. Salaries and Wages Payable (part of Other Payables) is decreased.
3. Property, Plant, and Equipment is increased.
4. Interest Expense (Finance Cost) is increased.

Real-World Focus

CT2.3 Much information about specific companies is available on the Internet. Such information includes basic descriptions of the company's location, activities, industry, financial health, and financial performance.

Instructions

Go to the **Yahoo! Finance** website and then type in a company name, or use the index to find company name. Choose **Profile** and then perform instructions (a)–(c) below. Next, click on the company's specific industry to identify competitors. Perform instructions (d)–(g) below.

a. What is the company's industry?

b. What was the company's total sales?

c. What was the company's net income?

d. What are the names of four of the company's competitors?

e. Choose one of these competitors.

f. What is this competitor's name? What were its sales? What was its net income?

g. Which of these two companies is larger by size of sales? Which one reported higher net income?

Decision-Making Across the Organization

CT2.4 Amy Torbert manages Hollins Riding Academy. The academy's primary sources of revenue are riding fees and lesson fees, which are paid on a cash basis. Hollins also boards horses for owners, who are billed monthly for boarding fees. In a few cases, boarders pay in advance of expected use. For its revenue transactions, the academy maintains the following accounts: No. 1 Cash, No. 5 Boarding Accounts Receivable, No. 27 Unearned Boarding Revenue, No. 51 Riding Revenue, No. 52 Lesson Revenue, and No. 53 Boarding Revenue.

The academy owns 10 horses, a stable, a riding corral, riding equipment, and office equipment. These assets are accounted for in accounts No. 11 Horses, No. 12 Building, No. 13 Riding Corral, No. 14 Riding Equipment, and No. 15 Office Equipment.

For its expenses, the academy maintains the following accounts: No. 6 Hay and Feed Supplies, No. 7 Prepaid Insurance, No. 21 Accounts Payable, No. 60 Salaries Expense, No. 61 Advertising Expense, No. 62 Utilities Expense, No. 63 Veterinary Expense, No. 64 Hay and Feed Expense, and No. 65 Insurance Expense.

Hollins maintains two equity accounts: No. 50 Share Capital—Ordinary and No. 51 Dividends.

During the first month of operations, an inexperienced bookkeeper was employed. Amy Torbert asks you to review the following eight entries of the 50 entries made during the month. In each case, the explanation for the entry is correct.

May 1	Cash	18,000	
	Share Capital—Ordinary		18,000
	(Invested £18,000 cash in business in exchange for ordinary shares)		
5	Cash	250	
	Riding Revenue		250
	(Received £250 cash for lessons performed)		
7	Cash	500	
	Boarding Revenue		500
	(Received £500 for boarding of horses beginning June 1)		
14	Riding Equipment	800	
	Cash		800
	(Purchased desk and other office equipment for £800 cash)		
15	Salaries Expense	440	
	Cash		440
	(Declared and paid cash dividends)		
20	Cash	148	
	Riding Revenue		184
	(Received £184 cash for riding fees)		

(continues)

May 30	Veterinary Expense	75	
	Accounts Payable		75
	(Received bill of £75 from veterinarian for services rendered)		
31	Hay and Feed Expense	1,500	
	Cash		1,500
	(Purchased an estimated 2 months' supply of feed and hay on account for £1,500)		

Instructions

With the class divided into groups, answer the following.

a. Identify each journal entry that is correct. For each journal entry that is incorrect, prepare the entry that should have been made by the bookkeeper.

b. Which of the incorrect entries would prevent the trial balance from balancing?

c. What was the correct net income for May, assuming the bookkeeper reported net income of £4,600 after posting all 50 entries (and the only errors occurred in the items listed above)?

d. What was the correct cash balance at May 31, assuming the bookkeeper reported a balance of £12,475 after posting all 50 entries (and the only errors occurred in the items listed above)?

Communication Activity

CT2.5 Shandler Home Cleaners has two recurring transactions: billing customers for services rendered and paying employee salaries. For example, on March 15, bills totaling €6,000 were sent to customers and €2,000 was paid in salaries to employees.

Instructions

Write an email to your instructor that explains and illustrates the steps in the recording process for each of the March 15 transactions. Use the format illustrated in the text under the heading, "The Recording Process Illustrated."

Ethics Cases

CT2.6 Ellynn Kole is the assistant chief accountant at Doman Circuits, a manufacturer of computer chips and cellular phones. The company presently has total sales of €20 million. It is the end of the first quarter. Ellynn is hurriedly trying to prepare a trial balance so that quarterly financial statements can be prepared and released to management and the regulatory agencies. The total credits on the trial balance exceed the debits by €1,000. In order to meet the 4 p.m. deadline, Ellynn decides to force the debits and credits into balance by adding the amount of the difference to the Equipment account. She chooses Equipment because it is one of the larger account balances; percentage-wise, it will be the least misstated. Ellynn "plugs" the difference! She believes that the difference will not affect anyone's decisions. She wishes that she had another few days to find the error but realizes that the financial statements are already late.

Instructions

a. Who are the stakeholders in this situation?

b. What are the ethical issues involved in this case?

c. What are Ellynn's alternatives?

CT2.7 If you haven't already done so, in the not-too-distant future you will prepare a résumé. In some ways, your résumé is like a company's annual report. Its purpose is to enable others to evaluate your past, in an effort to predict your future.

A résumé is your opportunity to create a positive first impression. It is important that it be impressive—but it should also be accurate. In order to increase their job prospects, some people are tempted to "inflate" their résumés by overstating the importance of some past accomplishments or positions. In fact, you might even think that "everybody does it" and that if you don't do it, you will be at a disadvantage.

Jay Ling, the president and CEO of a well-known electronics retailer, overstated his accomplishments by claiming that he had earned a bachelor's of science degree, when in fact he had not. Apparently, his employer had not done a background check to ensure the accuracy of his résumé. Should the company have fired him?

YES: The company is a publicly traded company. Investors, creditors, employees, and others doing business with the company will not trust it if its leader is known to have poor integrity. The "tone at the top" is vital to creating an ethical organization.

NO: Mr. Ling had been a company employee for 11 years. He had served the company in a wide variety of positions, and had earned the position of CEO through exceptional performance. While the fact that he lied 11 years earlier on his résumé was unfortunate, his service since then made this past transgression irrelevant. In addition, the company was in the midst of a massive restructuring, which included closing 700 of its 7,000 stores. It could not afford additional upheaval at this time.

Instructions

Write a response indicating your position regarding this situation. Provide support for your view.

All About You

CT2.8 Every company needs to plan in order to move forward. Its top management must consider where it wants the company to be in three to five years. Like a company, you need to think about where you want to be three to five years from now, and you need to start taking steps now in order to get there.

Instructions

Provide responses to each of the following items.

a. Where would you like to be working in three to five years? Describe your plan for getting there by identifying between five and 10 specific steps that you need to take.

b. In order to get the job you want, you will need a résumé. Your résumé is the equivalent of a company's annual report. It needs to provide relevant and reliable information about your past accomplishments so that employers can decide whether to "invest" in you. Do a search on the Internet to find a good résumé format. What are the basic elements of a résumé?

c. A company's annual report provides information about a company's accomplishments. In order for investors to use the annual report, the information must be reliable; that is, users must have faith that the information is accurate and believable. How can you provide assurance that the information on your résumé is reliable?

d. Prepare a résumé assuming that you have accomplished the five to 10 specific steps you identified in part (a). Also, provide evidence that would give assurance that the information is reliable.

Considering Environmental, Social, and Governance Reporting

CT2.9 Auditors provide a type of certification of company financial statements. Certification is used in many other aspects of business as well. For example, it plays a critical role in the sustainability movement. The February 7, 2012, issue of the *New York Times* contained an article by S. Amanda Caudill entitled "Better Lives in Better Coffee," which discusses the role of certification in the coffee business.

Instructions

Conduct an Internet search to locate and read the article, and then answer the following questions.

a. The article mentions three different certification types that coffee growers can obtain from three different certification bodies. Using financial reporting as an example, what potential problems might the existence of multiple certification types present to coffee purchasers?

b. According to the author, which certification is most common among coffee growers? What are the possible reasons for this?

c. What social and environmental benefits are coffee certifications trying to achieve? Are there also potential financial benefits to the parties involved?

Answers to Insight and Accounting Across the Organization Questions

Keeping Score Q: Do you think that the **Manchester United** (GBR) football (soccer) club would be likely to have the same major revenue and expense accounts as CTBC Brothers? **A:** Because their businesses are similar—professional sports—many of the revenue and expense accounts for the baseball and football teams might be similar.

It Starts with the Transaction Q: Why is it important for companies to record financial transactions completely and accurately? **A:** If companies fail to record transactions completely and accurately, financial statements will no longer be relevant and representationally faithful. And if investors cannot trust the resultant financial statements, a drop in the company's share price will often occur.

A Convenient Overstatement Q: What incentives might employees have to overstate the value of these investment securities on the company's financial statements? **A:** One reason that they may have been reluctant to record the losses is out of fear that the company's shareholders and clients would panic if they saw the magnitude of the losses. However, personal self-interest might have been equally to blame—the bonuses of the traders were tied to the value of the investment securities.

Why Accuracy Matters Q: In order for these companies to prepare and issue financial statements, their accounting equations (debits and credits) must have been in balance at year-end. How could these errors or misstatements have occurred? **A:** A company's accounting equation (its books) can be in balance yet its financial statements have errors or misstatements because entire transactions were not recorded, transactions were recorded at wrong amounts, transactions were recorded in the wrong accounts, and/or transactions were recorded in the wrong accounting period. Audits of financial statements uncover some but obviously not all errors or misstatements.

A Look at U.S. GAAP

LEARNING OBJECTIVE 5

Compare the procedures for the accounting process under IFRS and U.S. GAAP.

Companies that use GAAP follow the same set of procedures and records to keep track of transaction data as do IFRS companies. Thus, the material in Chapter 2 dealing with the account, general rules of debit and credit, and steps in the recording process—the journal, ledger, and chart of accounts—is the same under both GAAP and IFRS.

Key Points

- Both the IASB and FASB go beyond the basic definitions provided in this text for the key elements of financial statements, that is, assets, liabilities, equity, revenues, and expenses. The more substantive definitions, using the FASB definitional structure, are provided in the Chapter 1 *A Look at U.S. GAAP* section.
- For a period of time, the U.S. Securities and Exchange Commission (SEC) was considering adopting IFRS. During this period, the U.S. SEC indicated the following items should be considered in this decision.
  - Whether IFRS is sufficiently developed and consistent in application.
  - Whether the IASB is sufficiently independent.
  - Whether IFRS is established for the benefit of investors.
  - The issues involved in educating investors about IFRS.
  - The impact of a switch to IFRS on U.S. laws and regulations.
  - The impact on companies including changes to their accounting systems, contractual arrangements, company governance, and litigation.
  - The issues involved in educating accountants, so they can prepare statements under IFRS.
- It now appears that the SEC will not adopt IFRS but will permit foreign companies that have securities issued in U.S. markets to provide their financial information to the SEC using IFRS.

Similarities

- A trial balance under GAAP follows the same format as shown in the text.
- As shown in the text, currency signs are typically used only in the trial balance and the financial statements. The same practice is followed under GAAP, using the U.S. dollar. For example, the following income statement for **Apple Inc.** (USA) is denominated in its own currency—the U.S. dollar.

Apple Inc.
Consolidated Statement of Operations
For the Year Ended September 26, 2020
(in millions except per share data)

Net sales	$274,515
Cost of sales	169,559
Gross margin	104,956
Operating expenses:	
Research and development	18,752
Selling, general and administrative	19,916
Total operating expenses	38,668
Operating income	66,288
Other income/(expense), net	803
Income before provision for income taxes	67,091
Provision for income taxes	9,680
Net income	$ 57,411

Differences

- The statement of financial position is often called the balance sheet in the United States.
- Rules for accounting for specific events sometimes differ across countries. For example, IFRS companies rely less on historical cost and more on fair value than U.S. companies. Despite the differences, the double-entry accounting system is the basis of accounting systems worldwide.

GAAP Practice

GAAP Self-Test Questions

1. Which statement is **correct** regarding GAAP?
   a. GAAP reverses the rules of debits and credits, that is, debits are on the right and credits are on the left.
   b. GAAP uses the same process for recording transactions as IFRS.
   c. The chart of accounts under GAAP is different because revenues follow assets.
   d. None of the answer choices is correct.

2. A trial balance:
   a. is the same under GAAP and IFRS.
   b. proves that transactions are recorded correctly.
   c. proves that all transactions have been recorded.
   d. will not balance if a correct journal entry is posted twice.

3. One difference between GAAP and IFRS is that:
   a. IFRS uses accrual-accounting concepts and GAAP uses primarily the cash basis of accounting.
   b. GAAP uses a different posting process than IFRS.
   c. IFRS uses more fair value measurements than GAAP.
   d. the limitations of a trial balance are different between GAAP and IFRS.

4. The general policy for using proper currency signs (dollar, yen, pound, etc.) is the same for both GAAP and this text. This policy is as follows:
   a. Currency signs only appear in ledgers and journal entries.
   b. Currency signs are only shown in the trial balance.
   c. Currency signs are shown for all compound journal entries.
   d. Currency signs are shown in trial balances and financial statements.

GAAP Exercise

GAAP2.1 Describe some of the issues the U.S. SEC must consider in deciding whether the United States should adopt IFRS.

GAAP Financial Reporting Problem: Apple Inc. (USA)

GAAP2.2 The financial statements of **Apple** are presented in Appendix D. The complete annual report, including the notes to its financial statements, is available at the company's website.

Instructions

a. Apple has the following selected accounts:

Accounts Payable	Inventories
Accounts Receivable	Net Sales
Property, Plant, and Equipment, net	Research and Development

1. What is the increase and decrease side of each account?
2. What is the normal balance for each account?

b. Identify the probable other account in the transaction and the effect on that account when:

1. Accounts Receivable is decreased.
2. Accounts Payable is decreased.
3. Inventories is increased.

Answers to GAAP Self-Test Questions

1. b **2.** a **3.** c **4.** d

CHAPTER 3

Adjusting the Accounts

LEARNING OBJECTIVES

After studying this chapter, you should be able to:

LO 1 Explain the accrual basis of accounting and the reasons for adjusting entries.

LO 2 Prepare adjusting entries for deferrals.

LO 3 Prepare adjusting entries for accruals.

LO 4 Describe the nature and purpose of an adjusted trial balance.

Chapter Preview

In Chapter 1, you learned a neat little formula: Net income = Revenues – Expenses. In Chapter 2, you learned some rules for recording revenue and expense transactions. Guess what? Things are not really that nice and neat. In fact, it is often difficult for companies to determine in what time period they should report some revenues and expenses. In other words, in measuring net income, timing is everything.

Adjusting the Accounts

Accrual-Basis Accounting and Adjusting Entries	Adjusting Entries for Deferrals	Adjusting Entries for Accruals	Adjusted Trial Balance and Financial Statements
• Fiscal and calendar years • Accrual- vs. cash-basis accounting • Recognizing revenues and expenses • Need for adjusting entries • Types of adjusting entries	• Prepaid expenses • Unearned revenues	• Accrued revenues • Accrued expenses • Summary of basic relationships	• Preparing the adjusted trial balance • Preparing financial statements

Practice

DO IT! 1 Timing Concepts

DO IT! 2 Adjusting Entries for Deferrals

DO IT! 3 Adjusting Entries for Accruals

DO IT! 4 Trial Balance

Go to the Review and Practice section at the end of the chapter for a review of key concepts and practice applications with solutions.
Additional tutorials and practice opportunities are available in the Wiley online course.

Feature Story What Was Your Profit?

The accuracy of the financial reporting system depends on answers to a few fundamental questions: At what point has revenue been recognized? When have expenses really been incurred?

Unfortunately, all too often companies overstate their revenues. For example, during the dot-com boom, most dotcoms earned a large percentage of their revenue from selling advertising space on their websites. To boost reported revenue, some dot-coms began swapping website ad space. Company A would put an ad for its website on company B's website, and company B would put an ad for its website on company A's website. No money changed hands, but each company recorded revenue (for the value of the space that it gave the other company on its site). This practice did little to boost net income, and it resulted in no additional cash flow—but it did boost *reported revenue*. Regulators eventually put an end to this misleading practice.

Another type of transgression results from companies recording revenues or expenses in the wrong year. In fact, shifting revenues and expenses is one of the most common abuses of financial accounting. For example, **Tesco** (GBR), the large British grocery chain, was forced the lower its previously reported profits by £263 million, due to improper expense recognition related to its suppliers.

Perhaps one of the most unusual cases of reporting expenses in the wrong period was revealed by **Olympus Corporation** (JPN). The company admitted that it had covered up investment losses for more than a decade. It then tried to eliminate the losses from the books through a fraudulent process of overstating the price of some acquired assets and then writing down those assets in subsequent adjusting entries.

Unfortunately, revelations such as these have become all too common in the business world. It is no wonder that a survey of affluent investors reported that 85% of respondents believed that there should be tighter regulation of financial disclosures; 66% said they did not trust the management of publicly traded companies.

Why do so many companies violate basic financial reporting rules and sound ethics? Many speculate that executives are under increasing pressure to meet higher and higher earnings expectations. If actual results aren't as good as hoped for, some give in to temptation and "adjust" their numbers to meet market expectations.

TPG/Shutterstock

3.1 Accrual-Basis Accounting and Adjusting Entries

LEARNING OBJECTIVE 1

Explain the accrual basis of accounting and the reasons for adjusting entries.

If we could wait to prepare financial statements until a company ended its operations, no adjustments would be needed. At that point, we could easily determine its final statement of financial position and the amount of lifetime income it earned.

- However, most companies need feedback about how well they are performing during a period of time. For example, management usually wants monthly financial statements. Taxing agencies require all businesses to file annual tax returns.

- Therefore, **accountants divide the economic life of a business into artificial time periods**. This convenient assumption is referred to as the **time period assumption** (see **Alternative Terminology**).

ALTERNATIVE TERMINOLOGY

The time period assumption is also called the *periodicity assumption*.

Many business transactions affect more than one of these arbitrary time periods. For example, the airplanes purchased by **Cathay Pacific** (HKG) five years ago are still in use today. It would not make sense to expense the full cost of the airplanes at the time of purchase because they will be used for many subsequent periods. Instead, companies must therefore allocate the costs to the periods of use (what portion of the cost of the airplanes should be recorded as an expense each period?).

Time Period Assumption

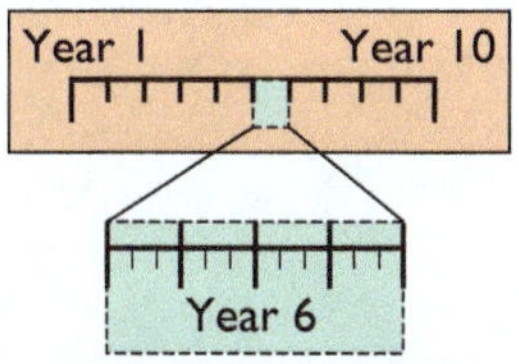

Fiscal and Calendar Years

Both small and large companies prepare financial statements periodically in order to assess their financial condition and results of operations. **Accounting time periods are generally a month, a quarter, or a year.**

- Monthly and quarterly time periods are called **interim periods**. Most large companies must prepare both quarterly and annual financial statements.
- An accounting time period that is one year in length is a **fiscal year**. A fiscal year usually begins with the first day of a month and ends 12 months later on the last day of a month.
- Many businesses use the **calendar year** (January 1 to December 31) as their accounting period. Some do not.

Companies whose fiscal year differs from the calendar year include **Sony** (JPN) and **India Adani** (IND), which both have fiscal years ending March 31. Sometimes a company's year-end will vary from year to year. For example, **JJB Sports**' (GBR) fiscal year ends on the Sunday before January 31, resulting in accounting periods of either 52 or 53 weeks.

Accrual- versus Cash-Basis Accounting

What you will learn in this chapter is **accrual-basis accounting**.

- Under the accrual basis, companies record transactions that change a company's financial statements **in the periods in which the events occur**. For example, using the accrual basis to determine net income means companies recognize revenues when they perform services (rather than when they receive cash). It also means recognizing expenses when incurred (rather than when paid).
- An alternative to the accrual basis is the cash basis. Under **cash-basis accounting**, companies record revenue at the time they receive cash. They record an expense at the time they pay out cash.

The cash basis seems appealing due to its simplicity, but it often produces misleading financial statements. For example, it fails to record revenue for a company that has performed services but has not yet received payment. As a result, the cash basis may not recognize revenue in the period that a performance obligation is satisfied.

Accrual-basis accounting is therefore in accordance with International Financial Reporting Standards (IFRS). Individuals and some small companies, however, do use cash-basis accounting. The cash basis is justified for small businesses because they often have few receivables and payables. Medium and large companies use accrual-basis accounting.

Recognizing Revenues and Expenses

It can be difficult to determine when to report revenues and expenses. The revenue recognition principle and the expense recognition principle help in this task.

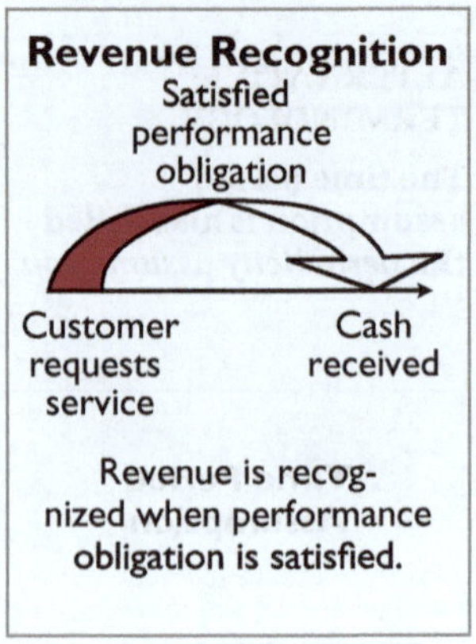

Revenue Recognition Principle

When a company agrees to perform a service or sell a product to a customer, it has a performance obligation.

- The **revenue recognition principle** requires that companies **recognize revenue in the accounting period in which the performance obligation is satisfied.**
- A company satisfies its performance obligation by performing a service or providing a good to a customer.

To illustrate, assume Soon Window Cleaners performs cleaning services for €100 on June 30, but customers do not pay until July 5. Under the revenue recognition principle, Soon records revenue on June 30 when it satisfies its performance obligation, which is when it performs the service, not in July when it receives the cash. At June 30, Soon would report a receivable on its balance sheet and revenue in its income statement for the service performed. The journal entries would be as follows.

June 30	Accounts Receivable	100	
	Service Revenue		100
July 5	Cash	100	
	Accounts Receivable		100

Five-Step Revenue Recognition Process—Sierra Travels Example

Revenue recognition results from a five-step process. This process can best be illustrated with an example. Assume that Sierra Travels signs a contract with the Lewis family to provide guide services for a one-week backpacking trip for €1,500. **Illustration 3.1** shows the five steps that Sierra follows to recognize revenue.

ILLUSTRATION 3.1 Five steps of revenue recognition

Step 1: Identify the contract with customers.	A contract is an agreement between two parties that creates enforceable rights or obligations. Sierra has a contract with the Lewis family to provide guide services.
Step 2: Identify the separate performance obligations in the contract.	Sierra has only one performance obligation—to provide guide services. If Sierra also agreed to sell the customer camping equipment, a separate performance obligation would exist for this promise.
Step 3: Determine the transaction price.	The transaction price is the amount of consideration that a company expects to receive from a customer in exchange for transferring a good or service. The transaction price for Sierra is €1,500.
Step 4: Allocate the transaction price to the separate performance obligations.	Sierra has only one performance obligation—to provide guide services to the Lewis family.
Step 5: Recognize revenue when each performance obligation is satisfied.	Sierra recognizes revenue of €1,500 for providing guide services to the Lewis family when it satisfies its performance obligation—the completion of the guided trip.

As indicated, Step 5 is when Sierra recognizes revenue related to providing the guide services to the Lewis family. At this point, Sierra completes the trip and satisfies its performance obligation.

Expense Recognition Principle

Accountants follow a simple rule in recognizing expenses: "Let the expenses follow the revenues." Thus, expense recognition is tied to revenue recognition. In the window cleaning example, this means that Soon should report the salary expense incurred in performing the June 30 cleaning service in the same period in which it recognizes the service revenue.

- The critical issue in expense recognition is when the expense makes its contribution to revenue.

- This may or may not be the same period in which the expense is paid. If Soon does not pay the salary incurred on June 30 until July, it would report salaries payable on its June 30 statement of financial position.
- This practice of expense recognition is referred to as the **expense recognition principle**. It requires that companies recognize expenses in the period in which they make efforts (consume assets or incur liabilities) to generate revenue.
- The term matching is sometimes used in expense recognition to indicate the relationship between the effort expended and the revenue generated.

Illustration 3.2 summarizes the revenue and expense recognition principles (see **Helpful Hint**).

It should be noted that in cases where an expense is not connected directly to revenue, it will be reported in the period in which it was incurred. For example, interest expense is a cost of borrowing and is not associated directly with revenue. Instead, it is reported in the period where the cost was incurred. Many general and administrative expenses are treated in this manner.

Expense Recognition

Efforts generated revenue

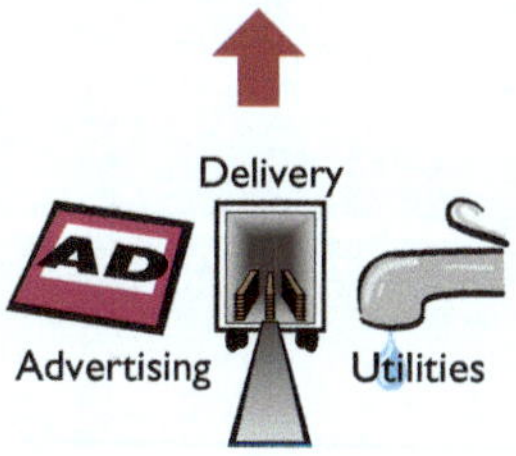

Expense is recognized when efforts are made to generate revenue.

ILLUSTRATION 3.2 **IFRS relationships in revenue and expense recognition**

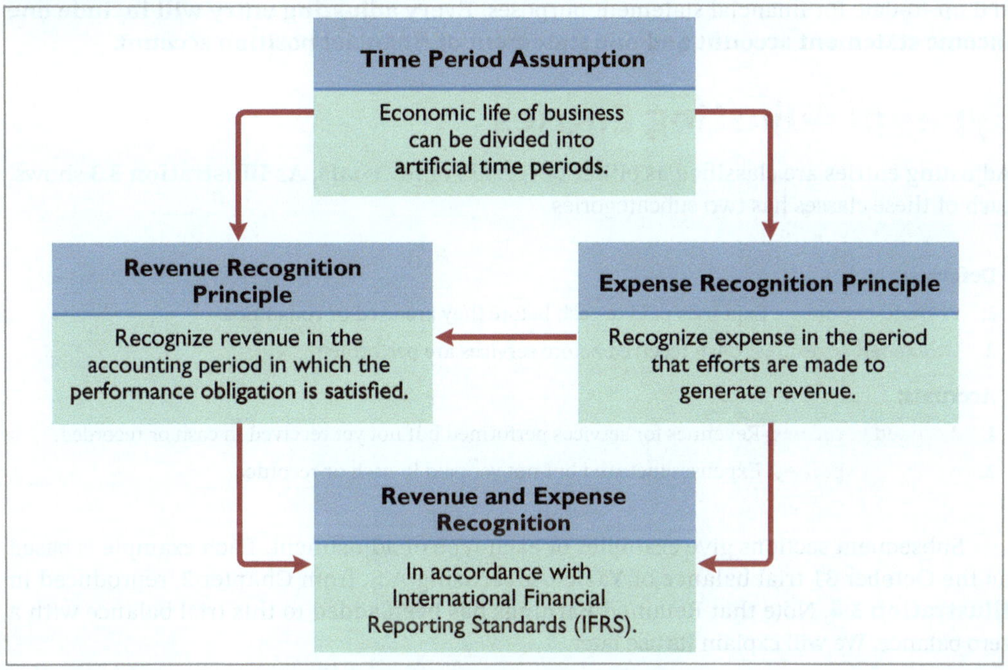

HELPFUL HINT

***Recognize* means to record or report.**

Investor Insight Apple Inc.

PhotoAlto/James Hardy/ Getty Images

Reporting Revenue Accurately

At one time, **Apple** (USA) was required to spread the revenues from iPhone sales over the two-year period following the sale of the phone. Accounting standards required this because Apple was obligated to provide software updates after the phone was sold. Since Apple had service obligations after the initial date of sale, it was forced to spread the revenue over a two-year period.

As a result, the rapid growth of iPhone sales was not fully reflected in the revenue amounts reported in Apple's income statement. A change in an accounting standard now enables Apple to report much more of its iPhone revenue at the point of sale. It was estimated that under the new rule revenues would have been about 17% higher and earnings per share almost 50% higher.

In the past, why was it argued that Apple should spread the recognition of iPhone revenue over a two-year period, rather than recording it upfront? (Answer is available near the end of the chapter.)

The Need for Adjusting Entries

In order for revenues to be recorded in the period in which services are performed and for expenses to be recognized in the period in which they are incurred, companies make adjusting entries. **Adjusting entries ensure that the revenue recognition and expense recognition principles are followed.**

Adjusting entries are necessary because the **trial balance**—the first pulling together of the transaction data—may not contain up-to-date and complete data. This is true for several reasons:

1. Some events are not recorded daily because it is not efficient to do so. Examples are the use of supplies and the earning of wages by employees.
2. Some costs are not recorded during the accounting period because these costs expire with the passage of time rather than as a result of recurring daily transactions. Examples are charges related to the use of buildings and equipment, rent, and insurance.
3. Some items may be unrecorded. An example is a utility service bill that will not be received until the next accounting period.

Adjusting entries are required every time a company prepares financial statements. The company analyzes each account in the trial balance to determine whether it is complete and up-to-date for financial statement purposes. **Every adjusting entry will include one income statement account and one statement of financial position account.**

Types of Adjusting Entries

Adjusting entries are classified as either **deferrals** or **accruals**. As **Illustration 3.3** shows, each of these classes has two subcategories.

ILLUSTRATION 3.3

Categories of adjusting entries

Deferrals:

1. **Prepaid expenses**: Expenses paid in cash before they are used or consumed.
2. **Unearned revenues**: Cash received before services are performed.

Accruals:

1. **Accrued revenues**: Revenues for services performed but not yet received in cash or recorded.
2. **Accrued expenses**: Expenses incurred but not yet paid in cash or recorded.

Subsequent sections give examples of each type of adjustment. Each example is based on the October 31 trial balance of Yazici Advertising A.Ş. from Chapter 2, reproduced in **Illustration 3.4**. Note that Retained Earnings has been added to this trial balance with a zero balance. We will explain its use later.

ILLUSTRATION 3.4

Trial balance

Yazici Advertising A.Ş.
Trial Balance
October 31, 2029

	Debit	Credit
Cash	ŧ15,200	
Supplies	2,500	
Prepaid Insurance	600	
Equipment	5,000	
Notes Payable		ŧ 5,000
Accounts Payable		2,500
Unearned Service Revenue		1,200
Share Capital—Ordinary		10,000
Retained Earnings		-0-
Dividends	500	
Service Revenue		10,000
Salaries and Wages Expense	4,000	
Rent Expense	900	
	ŧ28,700	ŧ28,700

We assume that Yazici uses an accounting period of one month. Thus, monthly adjusting entries are made. The entries are dated October 31.

DO IT! 1 | Timing Concepts

Below is a list of concepts in the left column, with a description of the concept in the right column. There are more descriptions provided than concepts. Match the description to the concept.

1. ______ Accrual-basis accounting.
2. ______ Calendar year.
3. ______ Time period assumption.
4. ______ Expense recognition principle.
5. ______ Cash-basis accounting.
6. ______ Interim periods.

a. Monthly and quarterly time periods.

b. Efforts (expenses) should be recognized in the period in which a company uses assets or incurs liabilities to generate results (revenues).

c. Accountants divide the economic life of a business into artificial time periods.

d. Companies record revenues when they receive cash and record expenses when they pay out cash.

e. An accounting time period that starts on January 1 and ends on December 31.

f. Companies record transactions in the period in which the events occur.

ACTION PLAN

- **Review the definitions of the timing concepts in the Glossary Review section.**
- **Study carefully the revenue recognition principle, the expense recognition principle, and the time period assumption.**

Solution

1. f **2.** e **3.** c **4.** b **5.** d **6.** a

Related exercise material: **BE3.1, DO IT! 3.1, E3.1, E3.2, and E3.3.**

3.2 Adjusting Entries for Deferrals

LEARNING OBJECTIVE 2

Prepare adjusting entries for deferrals.

To defer means to postpone or delay. **Deferrals** are expenses or revenues that are recognized at a date later than the point when cash was originally exchanged. The two types of deferrals are prepaid expenses and unearned revenues.

Prepaid Expenses

When companies record payments of expenses that will benefit more than one accounting period, they record an asset called **prepaid expenses** or **prepayments**. When expenses are prepaid, an asset account is increased (debited) to show the service or benefit that the company will receive in the future. Examples of common prepayments are insurance, supplies, advertising, and rent. In addition, companies make prepayments when they purchase buildings and equipment.

- **Prepaid expenses are costs that expire either with the passage of time** (e.g., rent and insurance) **or through use** (e.g., supplies).

- The expiration of these costs does not require daily entries, which would be impractical and unnecessary. Accordingly, companies postpone the recognition of such cost expirations until they prepare financial statements.
- At each statement date, they make adjusting entries to record the expenses applicable to the current accounting period and to show the remaining amounts in the asset accounts.

Prior to adjustment, assets are overstated and expenses are understated. Therefore, as shown in **Illustration 3.5**, **an adjusting entry for prepaid expenses results in an increase (a debit) to an expense account and a decrease (a credit) to an asset account.**

Let's look in more detail at some specific types of prepaid expenses, beginning with supplies.

ILLUSTRATION 3.5

Adjusting entries for prepaid expenses

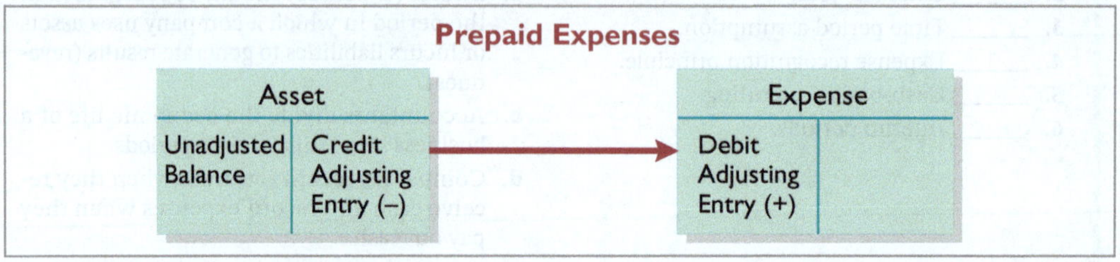

Supplies

The purchase of supplies, such as paper and envelopes, results in an increase (a debit) to an asset account. During the accounting period, the company uses supplies. Rather than record supplies expense as the supplies are used, companies recognize supplies expense at the **end** of the accounting period.

- At the end of the accounting period, the company counts the remaining supplies.
- The difference between the unadjusted balance in the Supplies (asset) account and the actual cost of supplies on hand represents the supplies used (an expense) for that period.

Recall from Chapter 2 that Yazici Advertising purchased supplies costing ₺2,500 on October 5. Yazici recorded the purchase by increasing (debiting) the asset Supplies. This account shows a balance of ₺2,500 in the October 31 trial balance. An inventory count at the close of business on October 31 reveals that ₺1,000 of supplies are still on hand. Thus, the cost of supplies used is ₺1,500 (₺2,500 – ₺1,000). This use of supplies decreases an asset, Supplies. It also decreases equity by increasing an expense account, Supplies Expense. This is shown in **Illustration 3.6**. (see **Helpful Hint**).

ILLUSTRATION 3.6 **Adjustment for supplies**

Basic Analysis	The expense Supplies Expense is increased ₺1,500; the asset Supplies is decreased ₺1,500.
Equation Analysis	(1) **Assets** = **Liabilities** + **Equity** Supplies –₺1,500 = Supplies Expense –₺1,500
Debit–Credit Analysis	Debits increase expenses: debit Supplies Expense ₺1,500. Credits decrease assets: credit Supplies ₺1,500.
Journal Entry	Oct. 31 Supplies Expense 631 1,500 Supplies 126 1,500 (To record supplies used)
Posting	

Supplies			126
Oct. 5	2,500	Oct. 31	Adj. 1,500
Oct. 31	Bal. 1,000		

Supplies Expense			631
Oct. 31	Adj. 1,500		
Oct. 31	Bal. 1,500		

HELPFUL HINT

Due to their nature, adjusting entries have no effect on cash flows. As a result, we do not show the cash flow effects in these illustrations.

After adjustment, the asset account Supplies shows a balance of ₺1,000, which is equal to the cost of supplies on hand at the statement date. In addition, Supplies Expense shows a balance of ₺1,500, which equals the cost of supplies used in October.

- If Yazici does not make the adjusting entry, October expenses are understated and net income is overstated by ₺1,500.
- Moreover, both assets and equity will be overstated by ₺1,500 on the October 31 statement of financial position.

Insurance

Companies purchase insurance to protect themselves from losses due to fire, theft, and unforeseen events. Insurance must be paid in advance, often for multiple months.

- The cost of insurance (premiums) paid in advance is recorded as an increase (debit) in the asset account Prepaid Insurance.
- At the financial statement date, companies increase (debit) Insurance Expense and decrease (credit) Prepaid Insurance for the cost of insurance that has expired during the period.

On October 4, Yazici Advertising paid ₺600 for a one-year fire insurance policy. Coverage began on October 1. Yazici recorded the payment by increasing (debiting) Prepaid Insurance. This account shows a balance of ₺600 in the October 31 trial balance. Insurance of ₺50 (₺600 ÷ 12) expires each month. The expiration of prepaid insurance decreases an asset, Prepaid Insurance. It also decreases equity by increasing an expense account, Insurance Expense.

As shown in **Illustration 3.7**, the asset Prepaid Insurance shows a balance of ₺550, which represents the unexpired cost for the remaining 11 months of coverage. At the same time, the balance in Insurance Expense equals the insurance cost that expired in October.

- If Yazici does not make this adjustment, October expenses are understated by ₺50 and net income is overstated by ₺50.
- Moreover, both assets and equity will be overstated by ₺50 on the October 31 statement of financial position.

Insurance

Oct. 4

Insurance purchased; record asset

Insurance Policy			
Oct ₺50	Nov ₺50	Dec ₺50	Jan ₺50
Feb ₺50	March ₺50	April ₺50	May ₺50
June ₺50	July ₺50	Aug ₺50	Sept ₺50
1 YEAR ₺600			

Oct. 31
Insurance expired; record insurance expense

ILLUSTRATION 3.7 **Adjustment for insurance**

Basic Analysis: The expense Insurance Expense is increased ₺50; the asset Prepaid Insurance is decreased ₺50.

Equation Analysis:

	Assets	=	Liabilities	+	Equity
(2)	Prepaid Insurance	=			Insurance Expense
	−₺50				−₺50

Debit–Credit Analysis: Debits increase expenses: debit Insurance Expense ₺50. Credits decrease assets: credit Prepaid Insurance ₺50.

Journal Entry:

Date	Account	Ref.	Debit	Credit
Oct. 31	Insurance Expense	722	50	
	Prepaid Insurance	130		50
	(To record insurance expired)			

Posting:

Prepaid Insurance			130
Oct. 4	600	Oct. 31	Adj. 50
Oct. 31	Bal. 550		

Insurance Expense			722
Oct. 31	Adj. 50		
Oct. 31	Bal. 50		

Depreciation

A company typically owns a variety of assets that have long lives, such as buildings, equipment, and motor vehicles. The period of service is referred to as the **useful life** of the asset.

Depreciation

Oct. 1

Equipment purchased; record asset

Equipment			
Oct ₺40	Nov ₺40	Dec ₺40	Jan ₺40
Feb ₺40	March ₺40	April ₺40	May ₺40
June ₺40	July ₺40	Aug ₺40	Sept ₺40
Depreciation = ₺480/year			

Oct. 31

Depreciation recognized; record depreciation expense

HELPFUL HINT

All contra accounts have increases, decreases, and normal balances opposite to the account to which they relate.

Because a building is expected to be of service for many years, it is recorded as an asset, rather than an expense, on the date it is acquired.

- As explained in Chapter 1, companies record such assets **at cost**, as required by the historical cost basis.
- To follow the expense recognition principle, companies allocate a portion of this cost as an expense during each period of the asset's useful life.
- **Depreciation** is the process of allocating the cost of an asset to expense over its useful life.

Need for Adjustment The acquisition of long-lived assets is essentially a long-term prepayment for the use of an asset. An adjusting entry for depreciation is needed to recognize the cost that has been used (an expense) during the period and to report the unused cost (an asset) at the end of the period. It is important to understand the following.

- Depreciation is an allocation concept, not a valuation concept.
- Depreciation allocates an asset's cost to the periods in which it is used.
- Depreciation does not attempt to report the actual change in the value of the asset.

For Yazici Advertising, assume that depreciation on the equipment is ₺480 a year, or ₺40 per month. As shown in **Illustration 3.8**, rather than decrease (credit) the asset account directly, Yazici instead credits Accumulated Depreciation—Equipment.

- Accumulated Depreciation is called a **contra asset account**.
- Such an account is offset against an asset account on the statement of financial position (see **Helpful Hint**). Thus, the Accumulated Depreciation—Equipment account offsets the asset Equipment.
- This account keeps track of the total amount of depreciation expense taken over the life of the asset.

To keep the accounting equation in balance, Yazici decreases equity by increasing an expense account, Depreciation Expense.

ILLUSTRATION 3.8 **Adjustment for depreciation**

Basic Analysis
The expense Depreciation Expense is increased ₺40; the contra asset Accumulated Depreciation—Equipment is increased ₺40.

Equation Analysis

Assets	=	Liabilities	+	Equity
Accumulated Depreciation—Equipment	=			Depreciation Expense
−₺40				−₺40

Debit–Credit Analysis
Debits increase expenses: debit Depreciation Expense ₺40.
Credits increase contra assets: credit Accumulated Depreciation—Equipment ₺40.

Journal Entry

Oct. 31	Depreciation Expense	711	40	
	Accumulated Depreciation—Equipment	158		40
	(To record monthly depreciation)			

Posting

Equipment			157
Oct. 1	5,000		
Oct. 31	Bal. 5,000		

Accumulated Depreciation—Equipment			158
		Oct. 31	Adj. 40
		Oct. 31	Bal. 40

Depreciation Expense			711
Oct. 31	Adj. 40		
Oct. 31	Bal. 40		

The balance in the Accumulated Depreciation—Equipment account will increase ₺40 each month, and the balance in Equipment remains ₺5,000.

Statement Presentation As indicated, Accumulated Depreciation—Equipment is a contra asset account. It is offset against Equipment on the statement of financial position. The normal balance of a contra asset account is a credit.

- A theoretical alternative to using a contra asset account would be to decrease (credit) the asset account by the amount of depreciation each period.
- But using the contra account is preferable for a simple reason: It discloses **both** the original cost of the equipment **and** the total cost that has been expensed to date.

Thus, in the statement of financial position, Yazici deducts Accumulated Depreciation—Equipment from the related asset account, as shown in **Illustration 3.9**.

ILLUSTRATION 3.9

Statement of financial position presentation of accumulated depreciation

Equipment	₺5,000
Less: Accumulated depreciation—equipment	40
	₺4,960

Book value is the difference between the cost of any depreciable asset and its related accumulated depreciation (see **Alternative Terminology**). In Illustration 3.9, the book value of the equipment at the statement of financial position date is ₺4,960. The book value and the current value of the asset are generally two different values. As noted earlier, **the purpose of depreciation is not valuation but a means of cost allocation.**

ALTERNATIVE TERMINOLOGY

Book value is also referred to as *carrying value*.

- Depreciation expense identifies the portion of an asset's cost that expired during the period (in this case, in October).
- The accounting equation shows that without this adjusting entry, total assets, total equity, and net income are overstated by ₺40 and depreciation expense is understated by ₺40.

Illustration 3.10 summarizes the accounting for prepaid expenses.

ILLUSTRATION 3.10

Accounting for prepaid expenses

Accounting for Prepaid Expenses

Examples	Reason for Adjustment	Accounts Before Adjustment	Adjusting Entry
Insurance, supplies, advertising, rent, depreciation	Prepaid expenses originally recorded in asset accounts have been used.	Assets overstated. Expenses understated.	Dr. Expenses Cr. Assets or Contra Assets

Unearned Revenues

When companies receive cash before services are performed, they record a liability by increasing (crediting) a liability account called **unearned revenues**. In other words, a **company now has a performance obligation** (liability) to transfer a service to one of its customers. Items like rent, magazine subscriptions, and customer deposits for future service may result in unearned revenues. Airlines such as **Cathay Pacific** (HKG) and **Garuda Indonesia** (IDN), for instance, treat receipts from the sale of tickets as unearned revenue until the flight service is provided.

- Unearned revenues are the opposite of prepaid expenses.
- Indeed, unearned revenue on the books of one company is likely to be a prepaid expense on the books of the company that has made the advance payment.

For example, if identical accounting periods are assumed, a landlord will have unearned rent revenue when a tenant has prepaid rent.

When a company receives payment for services to be performed in a future accounting period, it increases (credits) an unearned revenue (a liability) account to recognize the liability that exists. The company subsequently recognizes revenues when it performs the service.

During the accounting period, it is not practical to make daily entries as the company performs services. Instead, the company delays recognition of revenue until the adjustment process.

- The company then makes an adjusting entry to record the revenue for services performed during the period and to show the liability that remains at the end of the accounting period.
- Prior to adjustment, liabilities are overstated and revenues are understated. Therefore, the adjusting entry for unearned revenues results in a decrease (a debit) to a liability account and an increase (a credit) to a revenue account (see **Illustration 3.11**).

ILLUSTRATION 3.11

Adjusting entries for unearned revenues

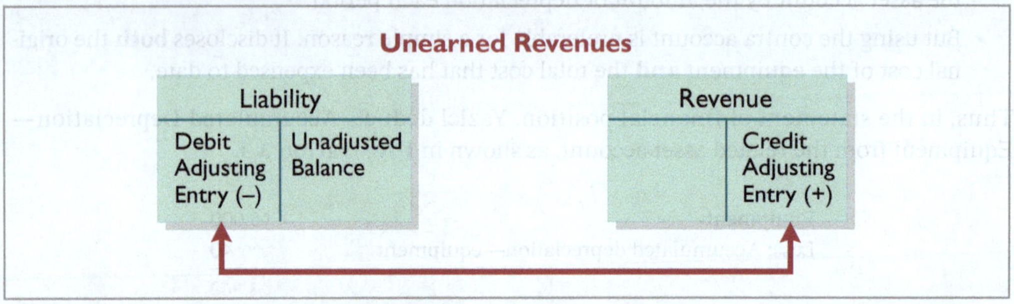

Yazici Advertising received ₺1,200 on October 2 from R. Knox for advertising services expected to be completed by December 31. Yazici credited the payment to Unearned Service Revenue. This liability account shows a balance of ₺1,200 in the October 31 trial balance. From an evaluation of the services Yazici performed for Knox during October, the company determines that it should recognize ₺400 of revenue in October. The liability (Unearned Service Revenue) is therefore decreased, and equity (Service Revenue) is increased.

As shown in **Illustration 3.12**, the liability Unearned Service Revenue now shows a balance of ₺800. That amount represents the remaining advertising services Yazici is obligated to perform in the future. At the same time, Service Revenue shows total revenue recognized in October of ₺10,400.

- Without this adjustment, revenues and net income are understated by ₺400 in the income statement.
- Moreover, liabilities will be overstated and equity will be understated by ₺400 on the October 31 statement of financial position.

ILLUSTRATION 3.12 **Service revenue accounts after adjustment**

Basic Analysis

The liability Unearned Service Revenue is decreased ₺400; the revenue Service Revenue is increased ₺400.

Equation Analysis

Assets	=	Liabilities	+	Equity
		Unearned Service Revenue		Service Revenue
		–₺400		+₺400

Debit–Credit Analysis

Debits decrease liabilities: debit Unearned Service Revenue ₺400.
Credits increase revenues: credit Service Revenue ₺400.

Journal Entry

Oct. 31	Unearned Service Revenue	209	400	
	Service Revenue	400		400
	(To record revenue for services performed)			

Posting

Unearned Service Revenue			209
Oct. 31	Adj. 400	Oct. 2	1,200
		Oct. 31	Bal. 800

Service Revenue			400
		Oct. 31	10,000
		31	Adj. 400
		Oct. 31	Bal. 10,400

Illustration 3.13 summarizes the accounting for unearned revenues.

ILLUSTRATION 3.13 Accounting for unearned revenues

Accounting for Unearned Revenues

Examples	Reason for Adjustment	Accounts Before Adjustment	Adjusting Entry
Rent, magazine subscriptions, customer deposits for future service	Unearned revenues recorded in liability accounts are now recognized as revenue for services performed.	Liabilities overstated. Revenues understated.	Dr. Liabilities Cr. Revenues

Accounting Across the Organization — Best Buy

skodonnell/iStock Unreleased/Getty Images

Turning Gift Cards into Revenue

Those of you who are marketing majors (and even most of you who are not) know that gift cards are among the hottest marketing tools in merchandising today. Customers purchase gift cards and give them to someone for later use. In a recent year, gift-card sales were expected to exceed $160 billion.

Although these programs are popular with marketing executives, they create accounting questions. Should revenue be recorded at the time the gift card is sold, or when it is redeemed? How should expired gift cards be accounted for? In the balance sheet for the year ended February 1, 2020, **Best Buy** (USA) reported unearned revenue related to gift cards of $281 million.

Suppose that Tyler Palmer purchases a $100 gift card at Best Buy on December 24, 2028, and gives it to his partner, Anisha Jin, on December 25, 2028. On January 3, 2029, Anisha uses the card to purchase a $100 smart speaker. When do you think Best Buy should recognize revenue and why? (Answer is available near the end of the chapter.)

DO IT! 2 | Adjusting Entries for Deferrals

The ledger of Hammond Deliveries, on March 31, 2029, includes these selected accounts before adjusting entries are prepared.

	Debit	Credit
Prepaid Insurance	€ 3,600	
Supplies	2,800	
Equipment	25,000	
Accumulated Depreciation—Equipment		€5,000
Unearned Service Revenue		9,200

An analysis of the accounts shows the following.

1. Insurance expires at the rate of €100 per month.
2. Supplies on hand total €800.
3. The equipment depreciates €200 a month.
4. During March, services were performed for €4,000 of the unearned service revenue.

Prepare the adjusting entries for the month of March.

ACTION PLAN

- **Make adjusting entries at the end of the period for revenues recognized and expenses incurred in the period.**
- **Don't forget to make adjusting entries for deferrals. Failure to adjust for deferrals leads to overstatement of the asset or liability and understatement of the related expense or revenue.**

Solution

1. Insurance Expense	100	
Prepaid Insurance		100
(To record insurance expired)		
2. Supplies Expense (€2,800 – €800)	2,000	
Supplies		2,000
(To record supplies used)		
3. Depreciation Expense	200	
Accumulated Depreciation—Equipment		200
(To record monthly depreciation)		
4. Unearned Service Revenue	4,000	
Service Revenue		4,000
(To record revenue for services performed)		

Related exercise material: **BE3.4, BE3.5, BE3.7, BE3.8, DO IT! 3.2, E3.8, E3.9, and E3.10.**

3.3 Adjusting Entries for Accruals

LEARNING OBJECTIVE 3

Prepare adjusting entries for accruals.

ANALYZE → JOURNALIZE → POST → TRIAL BALANCE → **Journalize and post adjusting entries: deferrals/accruals** → ADJUSTED TRIAL BALANCE → FINANCIAL STATEMENTS → CLOSING ENTRIES → POST-CLOSING TRIAL BALANCE

The second category of adjusting entries is **accruals**. Prior to an accrual adjustment, the revenue account (and the related asset account) or the expense account (and the related liability account) are understated. Thus, the adjusting entry for accruals will **increase both a statement of financial position and an income statement account**.

Accrued Revenues

Revenues for services performed but not yet recorded at the statement date are **accrued revenues**. Accrued revenues may accumulate (accrue) with the passing of time, as in the case of interest revenue. These are unrecorded because the earning of interest does not involve daily transactions. Companies do not record interest revenue on a daily basis because it is often impractical to do so. Accrued revenues also may result from services that have been performed but not yet billed nor collected, as in the case of commissions and fees. These may be unrecorded because only a portion of the total service has been performed and the clients will not be billed until the service has been completed.

- An adjusting entry records the receivable that exists at the statement of financial position date and the revenue for the services performed during the period.
- Prior to adjustment, both assets and revenues are understated.

As shown in **Illustration 3.14**, an adjusting entry for accrued revenues results in an increase (a debit) to an asset account and an increase (a credit) to a revenue account (see **Helpful Hint**).

ILLUSTRATION 3.14 **Adjusting entries for accrued revenues**

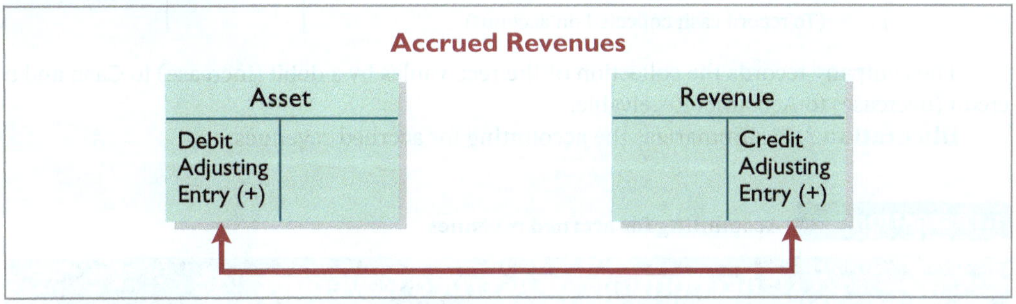

> **HELPFUL HINT**
> **For accruals, there may have been no prior entry, and the accounts requiring adjustment may both have zero balances prior to adjustment.**

In October, Yazici Advertising performed services worth ₺200 that were not billed to clients on or before October 31. Because these services were not billed, they were not recorded. The accrual of unrecorded service revenue increases an asset account, Accounts Receivable. It also increases equity by increasing a revenue account, Service Revenue, as shown in **Illustration 3.15**.

ILLUSTRATION 3.15 **Adjustment for accrued revenue**

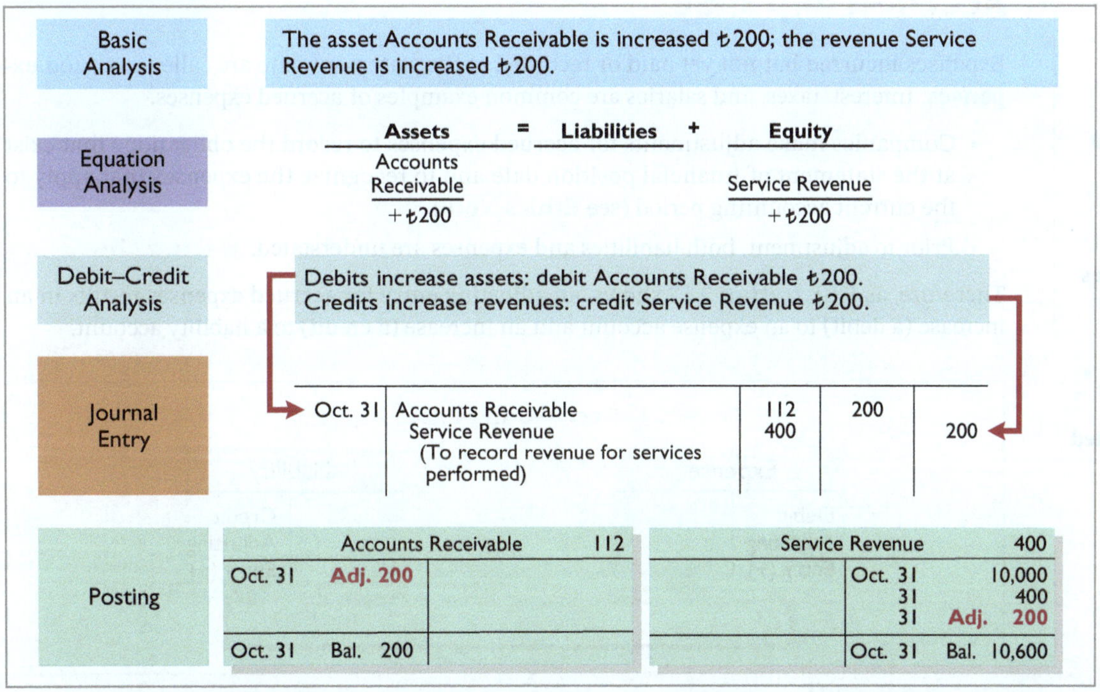

The asset Accounts Receivable shows that clients owe Yazici ₺200 at the statement of financial position date. The balance of ₺10,600 in Service Revenue represents the total revenue for services performed by Yazici during the month (₺10,000 + ₺400 + ₺200).

- Without the adjusting entry, assets and equity on the statement of financial position are understated.
- Moreover, revenues and net income on the income statement are understated.

On November 10, Yazici receives cash of ₺200 for the services performed in October and makes the following entry.

A	=	L	+	E
+200				
−200				

Cash Flows
+200

Nov. 10	Cash	200	
	Accounts Receivable		200
	(To record cash collected on account)		

The company records the collection of the receivables by a debit (increase) to Cash and a credit (decrease) to Accounts Receivable.

Illustration 3.16 summarizes the accounting for accrued revenues.

Equation analyses summarize the effects of transactions on the three elements of the accounting equation, as well as the effect on cash flows.

ILLUSTRATION 3.16 Accounting for accrued revenues

Accounting for Accrued Revenues

Examples	Reason for Adjustment	Accounts Before Adjustment	Adjusting Entry
Interest, rent, services	Services performed but not yet received in cash or recorded.	Assets understated. Revenues understated.	Dr. Assets Cr. Revenues

ETHICS NOTE

A report released by Fannie Mae's (USA) board of directors stated that improper adjusting entries at the mortgage-finance company resulted in delayed recognition of expenses caused by interest rate changes. The motivation for such accounting apparently was the desire to hit earnings estimates.

Accrued Expenses

Expenses incurred but not yet paid or recorded at the statement date are called **accrued expenses**. Interest, taxes, and salaries are common examples of accrued expenses.

- Companies make adjustments for accrued expenses to record the obligations that exist at the statement of financial position date and to recognize the expenses that apply to the current accounting period (see **Ethics Note**).
- Prior to adjustment, both liabilities and expenses are understated.

Therefore, as **Illustration 3.17** shows, an adjusting entry for accrued expenses results in an increase (a debit) to an expense account and an increase (a credit) to a liability account.

ILLUSTRATION 3.17

Adjusting entries for accrued expenses

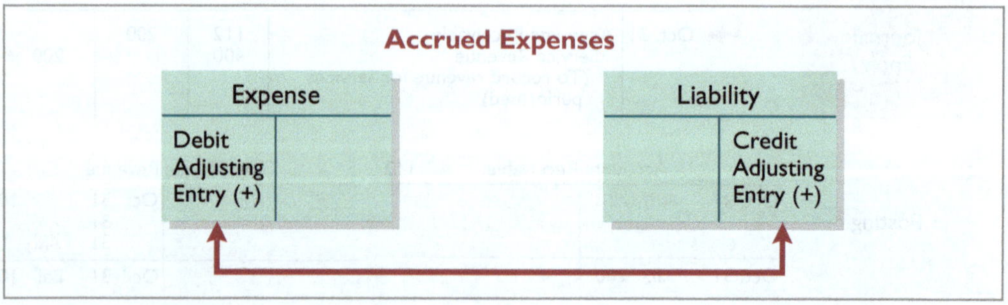

Let's look in more detail at some specific types of accrued expenses, beginning with accrued interest.

Accrued Interest

Yazici Advertising signed a three-month note payable in the amount of ₺5,000 on October 1. The note requires Yazici to pay interest at an annual rate of 12%.

The amount of the interest recorded is determined by three factors.

1. The face value of the note.
2. The interest rate, which is always expressed as an annual rate.
3. The length of time the note is outstanding.

For Yazici, the total interest due on the ₺5,000 note at its maturity date three months in the future is ₺150 (₺5,000 × 12% × $\frac{3}{12}$), or ₺50 for one month. **Illustration 3.18** shows the formula for computing interest and its application to Yazici for the month of October (see **Helpful Hint**).

HELPFUL HINT
In computing interest, we express the time period as a fraction of a year.

ILLUSTRATION 3.18
Formula for computing interest

Face Value of Note	×	Annual Interest Rate	×	Time in Terms of One Year	=	Interest
₺5,000	×	12%	×	$\frac{1}{12}$	=	₺50

As **Illustration 3.19** shows, the accrual of interest at October 31 increases a liability account, Interest Payable. It also decreases equity by increasing an expense account, Interest Expense.

ILLUSTRATION 3.19 **Adjustment for accrued interest**

Basic Analysis: The expense Interest Expense is increased ₺50; the liability Interest Payable is increased ₺50.

Equation Analysis:

Assets	=	Liabilities	+	Equity
		Interest Payable		Interest Expense
		+₺50		−₺50

Debit–Credit Analysis: Debits increase expenses: debit Interest Expense ₺50.
Credits increase liabilities: credit Interest Payable ₺50.

Journal Entry:

Date	Account	Ref.	Debit	Credit
Oct. 31	Interest Expense	905	50	
	Interest Payable	230		50
	(To record interest on notes payable)			

Posting:

Interest Expense			905
Oct. 31	Adj. 50		
Oct. 31	Bal. 50		

Interest Payable			230
		Oct. 31	Adj. 50
		Oct. 31	Bal. 50

Interest Expense shows the interest charges for the month of October. Interest Payable shows the amount of interest the company owes at the statement date. Yazici will not pay the interest until the note comes due at the end of three months. Companies use the Interest Payable account, instead of crediting Notes Payable, to disclose the two different types of obligations—interest and principal—in the accounts and statements.

- Without this adjusting entry, liabilities and interest expense are understated.
- Moreover, net income and equity are overstated.

Accrued Salaries and Wages

Companies pay for some types of expenses, such as employee salaries and wages, after the services have been performed. Yazici Advertising paid salaries and wages on October 26 for its employees' first two weeks of work. The next payment of salaries will not occur until November 9. As **Illustration 3.20** shows, three working days remain in October (October 29–31).

ILLUSTRATION 3.20
Calendar showing Yazici's pay periods

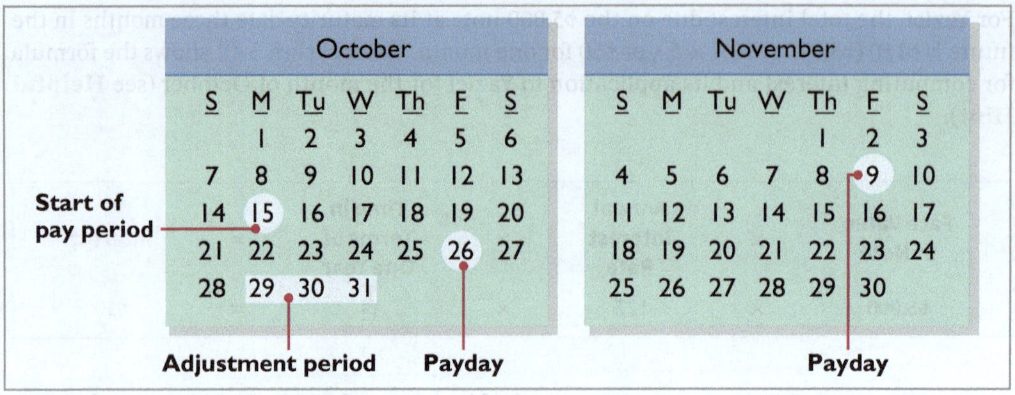

At October 31, the salaries and wages for these three days represent an accrued expense and a related liability to Yazici. The employees receive total salaries and wages of ₺2,000 for a five-day work week, or ₺400 per day. Thus, accrued salaries and wages at October 31 are ₺1,200 (₺400 × 3). This accrual increases a liability, Salaries and Wages Payable. It also decreases equity by increasing an expense account, Salaries and Wages Expense, as shown in **Illustration 3.21**.

ILLUSTRATION 3.21 **Adjustment for accrued salaries and wages**

Basic Analysis: The expense Salaries and Wages Expense is increased ₺1,200; the liability Salaries and Wages Payable is increased ₺1,200.

Equation Analysis:

Assets	=	Liabilities	+	Equity
		Salaries and Wages Payable		Salaries and Wages Expense
		+ ₺1,200		− ₺1,200

Debit–Credit Analysis: Debits increase expenses: debit Salaries and Wages Expense ₺1,200. Credits increase liabilities: credit Salaries and Wages Payable ₺1,200.

Journal Entry:

Oct. 31	Salaries and Wages Expense	726	1,200	
	Salaries and Wages Payable	212		1,200
	(To record accrued salaries and wages)			

Posting:

Salaries and Wages Expense		726		
Oct. 26		4,000		
31	Adj.	1,200		
Oct. 31	Bal.	5,200		

Salaries and Wages Payable				212
		Oct. 31	Adj.	1,200
		Oct. 31	Bal.	1,200

After this adjustment, the balance in Salaries and Wages Expense of ₺5,200 (13 days × ₺400) is the actual salary and wages expense for October. The balance in Salaries and Wages Payable of ₺1,200 is the amount of the liability for salaries and wages Yazici owes as of October 31.

- Without the ₺1,200 adjustment for salaries and wages, Yazici's expenses are understated ₺1,200.
- Moreover, its liabilities are understated ₺1,200.

Yazici pays salaries and wages every two weeks. Consequently, the next payday is November 9, when the company will again pay total salaries and wages of ₺4,000. The payment consists of

₺1,200 of salaries and wages payable at October 31 plus ₺2,800 of salaries and wages expense for November (7 working days, as shown in the November calendar × ₺400). Therefore, Yazici makes the following entry on November 9.

Nov. 9	Salaries and Wages Payable	1,200	
	Salaries and Wages Expense	2,800	
	Cash		4,000
	(To record November 9 payroll)		

A	=	L	+	E
		−1,200		
				−2,800
−4,000				

Cash Flows
−4,000

This entry eliminates the liability for Salaries and Wages Payable that Yazici recorded in the October 31 adjusting entry, and it records the proper amount of Salaries and Wages Expense for the period between November 1 and November 9.

Illustration 3.22 summarizes the accounting for accrued expenses.

ILLUSTRATION 3.22
Accounting for accrued expenses

Accounting for Accrued Expenses

Examples	Reason for Adjustment	Accounts Before Adjustment	Adjusting Entry
Interest, rent, salaries	Expenses have been incurred but not yet paid in cash or recorded.	Expenses understated. Liabilities understated.	Dr. Expenses Cr. Liabilities

Environmental, Social, and Governance Insight

njgphoto/Getty Images

Got Junk?

Do you have an old computer or two that you no longer use? How about an old TV that needs replacing? Many people do. Approximately 163,000 computers and televisions become obsolete each day. Yet, in a recent year, only 11% of computers were recycled.

It is estimated that 75% of all computers ever sold are sitting in storage somewhere, waiting to be disposed of. Each of these old TVs and computers is loaded with lead, cadmium, mercury, and other toxic chemicals. If you have one of these electronic gadgets, you have a responsibility, and a probable cost, for disposing of it. Companies have the same problem, but their discarded materials may include lead paint, asbestos, and other toxic chemicals.

What accounting issue might this cause for companies? (Answer is available near the end of the chapter.)

Summary of Basic Relationships

Illustration 3.23 summarizes the four basic types of adjusting entries. Take some time to study and analyze the adjusting entries. Be sure to note that **each adjusting entry affects one statement of financial position account and one income statement account**.

ILLUSTRATION 3.23
Summary of adjusting entries

Type of Adjustment	Accounts Before Adjustment	Adjusting Entry
Prepaid expenses	Assets overstated. Expenses understated.	Dr. Expenses Cr. Assets or Contra Assets
Unearned revenues	Liabilities overstated. Revenues understated.	Dr. Liabilities Cr. Revenues
Accrued revenues	Assets understated. Revenues understated.	Dr. Assets Cr. Revenues
Accrued expenses	Expenses understated. Liabilities understated.	Dr. Expenses Cr. Liabilities

Illustrations 3.24 and **3.25** show the journalizing and posting of adjusting entries for Yazici Advertising on October 31. The ledger identifies all adjustments by the reference J2 because they have been recorded on page 2 of the general journal. The company may insert a center caption "Adjusting Entries" between the last transaction entry and the first adjusting entry in the journal. When you review the general ledger in Illustration 3.25, note that the entries highlighted in red are the adjustments.

ILLUSTRATION 3.24

General journal showing adjusting entries

GENERAL JOURNAL J2

Date	Account Titles and Explanation	Ref.	Debit	Credit
2029	Adjusting Entries			
Oct. 31	Supplies Expense	631	1,500	
	Supplies	126		1,500
	(To record supplies used)			
31	Insurance Expense	722	50	
	Prepaid Insurance	130		50
	(To record insurance expired)			
31	Depreciation Expense	711	40	
	Accumulated Depreciation—Equipment	158		40
	(To record monthly depreciation)			
31	Unearned Service Revenue	209	400	
	Service Revenue	400		400
	(To record revenue for services performed)			
31	Accounts Receivable	112	200	
	Service Revenue	400		200
	(To record revenue for services performed)			
31	Interest Expense	905	50	
	Interest Payable	230		50
	(To record interest on notes payable)			
31	Salaries and Wages Expense	726	1,200	
	Salaries and Wages Payable	212		1,200
	(To record accrued salaries and wages)			

(1) Adjusting entries should not involve debits or credits to Cash.
(2) Evaluate whether the adjustment makes sense. For example, an adjustment to recognize supplies used should increase Supplies Expense.
(3) Double-check all computations.
(4) Each adjusting entry affects one statement of financial position account and one income statement account.

ILLUSTRATION 3.25 **General ledger after adjustment**

GENERAL LEDGER

Cash — No. 101

Date		Explanation	Ref.	Debit	Credit	Balance
2029						
Oct.	1		J1	10,000		10,000
	2		J1	1,200		11,200
	3		J1		900	10,300
	4		J1		600	9,700
	20		J1		500	9,200
	26		J1		4,000	5,200
	31		J1	10,000		15,200

Accounts Receivable — No. 112

Date		Explanation	Ref.	Debit	Credit	Balance
2029						
Oct.	31	Adj. entry	J2	200		200

Supplies — No. 126

Date		Explanation	Ref.	Debit	Credit	Balance
2029						
Oct.	5		J1	2,500		2,500
	31	Adj. entry	J2		1,500	1,000

Prepaid Insurance — No. 130

Date		Explanation	Ref.	Debit	Credit	Balance
2029						
Oct.	4		J1	600		600
	31	Adj. entry	J2		50	550

Equipment — No. 157

Date		Explanation	Ref.	Debit	Credit	Balance
2029						
Oct.	1		J1	5,000		5,000

Accumulated Depreciation—Equipment — No. 158

Date		Explanation	Ref.	Debit	Credit	Balance
2029						
Oct.	31	Adj. entry	J2		40	40

Notes Payable — No. 200

Date		Explanation	Ref.	Debit	Credit	Balance
2029						
Oct.	1		J1		5,000	5,000

Accounts Payable — No. 201

Date		Explanation	Ref.	Debit	Credit	Balance
2029						
Oct.	5		J1		2,500	2,500

Unearned Service Revenue — No. 209

Date		Explanation	Ref.	Debit	Credit	Balance
2029						
Oct.	2		J1		1,200	1,200
	31	Adj. entry	J2	400		800

Salaries and Wages Payable — No. 212

Date		Explanation	Ref.	Debit	Credit	Balance
2029						
Oct.	31	Adj. entry	J2		1,200	1,200

Interest Payable — No. 230

Date		Explanation	Ref.	Debit	Credit	Balance
2029						
Oct.	31	Adj. entry	J2		50	50

Share Capital—Ordinary — No. 311

Date		Explanation	Ref.	Debit	Credit	Balance
2029						
Oct.	1		J1		10,000	10,000

Retained Earnings — No. 320

Date		Explanation	Ref.	Debit	Credit	Balance
2029						

Dividends — No. 332

Date		Explanation	Ref.	Debit	Credit	Balance
2029						
Oct.	20		J1	500		500

Service Revenue — No. 400

Date		Explanation	Ref.	Debit	Credit	Balance
2029						
Oct.	31		J1		10,000	10,000
	31	Adj. entry	J2		400	10,400
	31	Adj. entry	J2		200	10,600

Supplies Expense — No. 631

Date		Explanation	Ref.	Debit	Credit	Balance
2029						
Oct.	31	Adj. entry	J2	1,500		1,500

Depreciation Expense — No. 711

Date		Explanation	Ref.	Debit	Credit	Balance
2029						
Oct.	31	Adj. entry	J2	40		40

Insurance Expense — No. 722

Date		Explanation	Ref.	Debit	Credit	Balance
2029						
Oct.	31	Adj. entry	J2	50		50

Salaries and Wages Expense — No. 726

Date		Explanation	Ref.	Debit	Credit	Balance
2029						
Oct.	26		J1	4,000		4,000
	31	Adj. entry	J2	1,200		5,200

Rent Expense — No. 729

Date		Explanation	Ref.	Debit	Credit	Balance
2029						
Oct.	3		J1	900		900

Interest Expense — No. 905

Date		Explanation	Ref.	Debit	Credit	Balance
2029						
Oct.	31	Adj. entry	J2	50		50

ACTION PLAN

- **Make adjusting entries at the end of the period to recognize revenues for services performed and for expenses incurred.**
- **Don't forget to make adjusting entries for accruals. Adjusting entries for accruals will increase both a statement of financial position and an income statement account.**

DO IT! 3 | Adjusting Entries for Accruals

Mahindra Computer Services began operations on August 1, 2029. At the end of August 2029, management prepares monthly financial statements. The following information relates to August (amounts in thousands).

1. At August 31, the company owed its employees ₹800 in salaries and wages that will be paid on September 1.
2. On August 1, the company borrowed ₹30,000 from a local bank on a 15-year mortgage. The annual interest rate is 10%.
3. Revenue for services performed but unrecorded for August totaled ₹1,100.

Prepare the adjusting entries needed at August 31, 2029.

Solution

1. Salaries and Wages Expense	800	
Salaries and Wages Payable		800
(To record accrued salaries)		
2. Interest Expense	250	
Interest Payable		250
(To record accrued interest: ₹30,000 × 10% × $\frac{1}{12}$ = ₹250)		
3. Accounts Receivable	1,100	
Service Revenue		1,100
(To record revenue for services performed)		

Related exercise material: **BE3.9, DO IT! 3.3, E3.5, E3.6, E3.7, E3.8, E3.9, and E3.10.**

3.4 Adjusted Trial Balance and Financial Statements

LEARNING OBJECTIVE 4

Describe the nature and purpose of an adjusted trial balance.

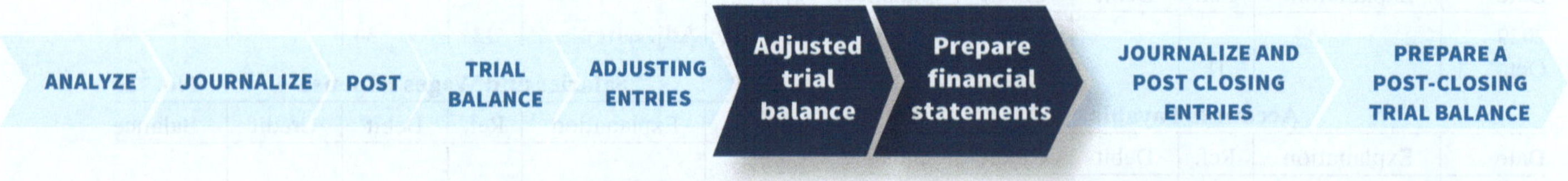

After a company has journalized and posted all adjusting entries, it prepares another trial balance from the ledger accounts. This trial balance is called an **adjusted trial balance.**

- The adjusted trial balance shows the balances of all accounts, including those adjusted, at the end of the accounting period.
- The purpose of an adjusted trial balance is to **prove the equality** of the total debit balances and the total credit balances in the ledger after all adjustments.
- Because the accounts contain all data needed for financial statements, the adjusted trial balance is the **primary basis for the preparation of financial statements.**

Preparing the Adjusted Trial Balance

Illustration 3.26 presents the adjusted trial balance for Yazici Advertising A.Ş. prepared from the ledger accounts in Illustration 3.25. The amounts affected by the adjusting entries are highlighted in red. Compare these amounts to those in the unadjusted trial balance in Illustration 3.4. In this comparison, you will see that there are more accounts in the adjusted trial balance as a result of the adjusting entries made at the end of the month.

ILLUSTRATION 3.26

Adjusted trial balance

Yazici Advertising A.Ş.
Adjusted Trial Balance
October 31, 2029

	Debit	Credit
Cash	₺15,200	
Accounts Receivable	**200**	
Supplies	**1,000**	
Prepaid Insurance	**550**	
Equipment	5,000	
Accumulated Depreciation—Equipment		₺ **40**
Notes Payable		5,000
Accounts Payable		2,500
Interest Payable		**50**
Unearned Service Revenue		**800**
Salaries and Wages Payable		**1,200**
Share Capital—Ordinary		10,000
Retained Earnings		-0-
Dividends	500	
Service Revenue		**10,600**
Salaries and Wages Expense	**5,200**	
Supplies Expense	**1,500**	
Rent Expense	900	
Insurance Expense	**50**	
Interest Expense	**50**	
Depreciation Expense	**40**	
	₺30,190	**₺30,190**

Preparing Financial Statements

Companies can prepare financial statements directly from the adjusted trial balance. Illustrations 3.27 and **3.28** present the interrelationships of data in the adjusted trial balance and the financial statements.

As Illustration 3.27 shows, companies prepare the income statement from the revenue and expense accounts. Next, they use the Retained Earnings and Dividends accounts and the net income (or net loss) from the income statement to prepare the retained earnings statement.

ILLUSTRATION 3.27 **Preparation of the income statement and retained earnings statement from the adjusted trial balance**

Yazici Advertising A.Ş.
Adjusted Trial Balance
October 31, 2029

Account	Debit	Credit
Cash	₺15,200	
Accounts Receivable	200	
Supplies	1,000	
Prepaid Insurance	550	
Equipment	5,000	
Accumulated Depreciation—Equipment		₺ 40
Notes Payable		5,000
Accounts Payable		2,500
Unearned Service Revenue		800
Salaries and Wages Payable		1,200
Interest Payable		50
Share Capital—Ordinary		10,000
Retained Earnings		–0–
Dividends	500	
Service Revenue		10,600
Salaries and Wages Expense	5,200	
Supplies Expense	1,500	
Rent Expense	900	
Insurance Expense	50	
Interest Expense	50	
Depreciation Expense	40	
	₺30,190	₺30,190

Yazici Advertising A.Ş.
Income Statement
For the Month Ended October 31, 2029

Revenues		
Service revenue		₺10,600
Expenses		
Salaries and wages expense	₺5,200	
Supplies expense	1,500	
Rent expense	900	
Insurance expense	50	
Interest expense	50	
Depreciation expense	40	
Total expenses		7,740
Net income		₺ 2,860

Yazici Advertising A.Ş.
Retained Earnings Statement
For the Month Ended October 31, 2029

Retained earnings, October 1	₺ –0–
Add: Net income	2,860
	2,860
Less: Dividends	500
Retained earnings, October 31	₺2,360

To statement of financial position

As Illustration 3.28 shows, companies then prepare the statement of financial position from the asset and liability accounts and the ending Retained Earnings balance as reported in the retained earnings statement.

ILLUSTRATION 3.28 **Preparation of the statement of financial position from the adjusted trial balance**

Yazici Advertising A.Ş.
Adjusted Trial Balance
October 31, 2029

Account	Debit	Credit
Cash	₺15,200	
Accounts Receivable	200	
Supplies	1,000	
Prepaid Insurance	550	
Equipment	5,000	
Accumulated Depreciation—Equipment		₺ 40
Notes Payable		5,000
Accounts Payable		2,500
Unearned Service Revenue		800
Salaries and Wages Payable		1,200
Interest Payable		50
Share Capital—Ordinary		10,000
Retained Earnings		–0–
Dividends	500	
Service Revenue		10,600
Salaries and Wages Expense	5,200	
Supplies Expense	1,500	
Rent Expense	900	
Insurance Expense	50	
Interest Expense	50	
Depreciation Expense	40	
	₺30,190	₺30,190

Yazici Advertising A.Ş.
Statement of Financial Position
October 31, 2029

Assets		
Equipment	₺5,000	
Less: Accumulated depreciation—equip.	40	₺ 4,960
Prepaid insurance		550
Supplies		1,000
Accounts receivable		200
Cash		15,200
Total assets		₺21,910
Equity and Liabilities		
Equity		
Share capital—ordinary	₺10,000	
Retained earnings	2,360	₺12,360
Liabilities		
Notes payable	5,000	
Accounts payable	2,500	
Unearned service revenue	800	
Salaries and wages payable	1,200	
Interest payable	50	9,550
Total equity and liabilities		₺21,910

Balance at Oct. 31 from retained earnings statement in Illustration 3.27

DO IT! 4 | Trial Balance

Kang Company was organized on April 1, 2029. The company prepares quarterly financial statements. The adjusted trial balance amounts at June 30 are shown below (amounts in millions).

	Debit		Credit
Cash	₩ 6,700	Accumulated Depreciation—Equipment	₩ 850
Accounts Receivable	600	Notes Payable	5,000
Prepaid Rent	900	Accounts Payable	1,510
Supplies	1,000	Salaries and Wages Payable	400
Equipment	15,000	Interest Payable	50
Dividends	600	Unearned Rent Revenue	500
Salaries and Wages Expense	9,400	Share Capital—Ordinary	14,000
Rent Expense	1,500	Service Revenue	14,200
Depreciation Expense	850	Rent Revenue	800
Supplies Expense	200		
Utilities Expense	510		
Interest Expense	50		
	₩37,310		₩37,310

a. Determine the net income for the quarter April 1 to June 30.

b. Determine the total assets and total liabilities at June 30, 2029, for Kang Company.

c. Determine the amount of retained earnings at June 30, 2029.

ACTION PLAN

- **In an adjusted trial balance, all asset, liability, revenue, and expense accounts are properly stated.**
- **To determine the ending balance in Retained Earnings, add net income and subtract dividends.**

Solution

a. The net income is determined by adding revenues and subtracting expenses. The net income is computed as follows (in millions).

Revenues		
Service revenue	₩14,200	
Rent revenue	800	
Total revenues		₩15,000
Expenses		
Salaries and wages expense	9,400	
Rent expense	1,500	
Depreciation expense	850	
Utilities expense	510	
Supplies expense	200	
Interest expense	50	
Total expenses		12,510
Net income		₩ 2,490

b. Total assets and liabilities are computed as follows (in millions).

Assets			**Liabilities**	
Equipment	₩15,000		Notes payable	₩5,000
Less: Accumulated depreciation—equipment	850	₩14,150	Accounts payable	1,510
Prepaid rent		900	Unearned rent revenue	500
Supplies		1,000	Salaries and wages payable	400
Accounts receivable		600	Interest payable	50
Cash		6,700		
Total assets		₩23,350	Total liabilities	₩7,460

c.

Retained earnings, April 1	₩ 0
Add: Net income	2,490
Less: Dividends	600
Retained earnings, June 30	₩ 1,890

Related exercise material: **BE3.11, BE3.12, DO IT! 3.4, E3.11, E3.12, and E3.19.**

Appendix 3A

Alternative Treatment of Deferrals

LEARNING OBJECTIVE *5

Prepare adjusting entries for the alternative treatment of deferrals.

In discussing adjusting entries for prepaid expenses and unearned revenues, we illustrated transactions for which companies made the initial entries to statement of financial position accounts. In the case of prepaid expenses, the company debited the prepayment to an asset account. In the case of unearned revenue, the company credited a liability account to record the cash received.

Some companies use an alternative treatment.

1. When a company prepays an expense, it debits that amount to an expense account.
2. When it receives payment for future services, it credits the amount to a revenue account.

In this appendix, we describe the circumstances that justify such entries and the different adjusting entries that may be required. This alternative treatment of prepaid expenses and unearned revenues has the same effect on the financial statements as the procedures described in the chapter.

Prepaid Expenses

Prepaid expenses become expired costs either through the passage of time (e.g., insurance) or through consumption (e.g., advertising supplies).

- If at the time of purchase the company expects to consume all or most of the supplies before the next financial statement date, it may choose to debit (increase) an expense account rather than an asset account.
- This alternative treatment is simply more convenient.

Assume that Yazici Advertising expects that it will use before the end of the month all of the supplies purchased on October 5. A debit of ₺2,500 to Supplies Expense (rather than to the asset account Supplies) on October 5 will eliminate the need for an adjusting entry on October 31. At October 31, the Supplies Expense account will show a balance of ₺2,500, which is the cost of supplies used between October 5 and October 31.

But what if the company does not use all the supplies? For example, what if an inventory of ₺1,000 of advertising supplies remains on October 31? Obviously, the company would need to make an adjusting entry. Prior to adjustment, the expense account Supplies Expense is overstated ₺1,000, and the asset account Supplies is understated ₺1,000. Thus, Yazici makes the following adjusting entry.

Oct. 31	Supplies	1,000	
	Supplies Expense		1,000
	(To record supplies inventory)		

A	=	L	+	E
+1,000				
				+1,000 Exp

Cash Flows
no effect

Illustration 3A.1 shows the accounts after the company posts the adjusting entry.

ILLUSTRATION 3A.1

Prepaid expenses accounts after adjustment

Supplies			Supplies Expense			
10/31 **Adj.**	**1,000**		10/5	2,500	10/31 **Adj.**	**1,000**
			10/31 **Bal.**	**1,500**		

After adjustment, the asset account Supplies shows a balance of ₺1,000, which is equal to the cost of supplies on hand at October 31. In addition, Supplies Expense shows a balance of ₺1,500. This is equal to the cost of supplies used between October 5 and October 31.

- Without the adjusting entry, expenses are overstated and net income is understated by ₺1,000 in the October income statement.
- Also, both assets and equity are understated by ₺1,000 on the October 31 statement of financial position.

Illustration 3A.2 compares the entries and accounts for advertising supplies in the two adjustment approaches.

ILLUSTRATION 3A.2

Adjustment approaches—a comparison

Prepayment Initially Debited to Asset Account (per chapter)				Prepayment Initially Debited to Expense Account (per appendix)			
Oct. 5	Supplies	2,500		Oct. 5	Supplies Expense	2,500	
	Accounts Payable		2,500		Accounts Payable		2,500
Oct. 31	Supplies Expense	1,500		Oct. 31	Supplies	1,000	
	Supplies		1,500		Supplies Expense		1,000

After Yazici posts the entries, the accounts appear as shown in **Illustration 3A.3**.

ILLUSTRATION 3A.3
Comparison of accounts

(per chapter)

Supplies

10/5	2,500	10/31 **Adj.**	**1,500**
10/31 **Bal.**	**1,000**		

Supplies Expense

10/31 **Adj.**	**1,500**		

(per appendix)

Supplies

10/31 **Adj.**	**1,000**		

Supplies Expense

10/5	2,500	10/31 **Adj.**	**1,000**
10/31 **Bal.**	**1,500**		

Note that the account balances under each alternative are the same at October 31: Supplies ₺1,000 and Supplies Expense ₺1,500.

Unearned Revenues

Unearned revenues are recognized as revenue at the time services are performed. Similar to the case for prepaid expenses, companies may credit (increase) a revenue account when they receive cash for future services.

To illustrate, assume that Yazici Advertising received ₺1,200 for future services on October 2. Yazici expects to perform the services before October 31.[1] In such a case, the company credits Service Revenue. If Yazici in fact performs the service before October 31, no adjustment is needed.

However, if at the statement date Yazici has not performed ₺800 of the services, it would make an adjusting entry (see **Helpful Hint**).

HELPFUL HINT
The required adjusted balances here are Service Revenue ₺400 and Unearned Service Revenue ₺800.

- Without the entry, the revenue account Service Revenue is overstated ₺800.
- The liability account Unearned Service Revenue is understated ₺800.

Thus, Yazici makes the following adjusting entry.

A	=	L	+	E
		+800		−800 Rev

Cash Flows
no effect

Oct. 31	Service Revenue	800	
	Unearned Service Revenue		800
	(To record unearned service revenue)		

Illustration 3A.4 shows the accounts after Yazici posts the adjusting entry.

ILLUSTRATION 3A.4
Unearned service revenue accounts after adjustment

Unearned Service Revenue

		10/31 **Adj.**	**800**

Service Revenue

10/31 **Adj.**	**800**	10/2	1,200
		10/31 **Bal.**	**400**

The liability account Unearned Service Revenue shows a balance of ₺800. This equals the services that will be performed in the future. In addition, the balance in Service Revenue equals the services performed in October.

- Without the adjusting entry, both revenues and net income are overstated by ₺800 in the October income statement.
- Also, liabilities are understated by ₺800 and equity is overstated by ₺800 on the October 31 statement of financial position.

[1] This example focuses only on the alternative treatment of unearned revenues. For simplicity, we have ignored the entries to Service Revenue pertaining to the immediate recognition of revenue (₺10,000) and the adjusting entry for accrued revenue (₺200).

Illustration 3A.5 compares the entries and accounts for initially recording unearned service revenue in (1) a liability account or (2) a revenue account.

ILLUSTRATION 3A.5
Adjustment approaches—a comparison

Unearned Service Revenue Initially Credited to Liability Account (per chapter)				Unearned Service Revenue Initially Credited to Revenue Account (per appendix)			
Oct. 2	Cash	1,200		Oct. 2	Cash	1,200	
	Unearned Service Revenue		1,200		Service Revenue		1,200
Oct. 31	Unearned Service Revenue	400		Oct. 31	Service Revenue	800	
	Service Revenue		400		Unearned Service Revenue		800

After Yazici posts the entries, the accounts appear as shown in **Illustration 3A.6**.

ILLUSTRATION 3A.6
Comparison of accounts

(per chapter)

Unearned Service Revenue

10/31 **Adj.**	**400**	10/2	1,200
		10/31 **Bal.**	**800**

Service Revenue

		10/31 **Adj.**	**400**

(per appendix)

Unearned Service Revenue

		10/31 **Adj.**	**800**

Service Revenue

10/31 **Adj.**	**800**	10/2	1,200
		10/31 **Bal.**	**400**

Note that the balances in the accounts are the same under the two alternatives: Unearned Service Revenue ₺800 and Service Revenue ₺400.

Summary of Additional Adjustment Relationships

Illustration 3A.7 provides a summary of basic relationships for deferrals.

ILLUSTRATION 3A.7 **Summary of basic relationships for deferrals**

Type of Adjustment	Reason for Adjustment	Account Balances Before Adjustment	Adjusting Entry
1. Prepaid expenses	(a) Prepaid expenses initially recorded in asset accounts have been used.	Assets overstated. Expenses understated.	Dr. Expenses Cr. Assets
	(b) **Prepaid expenses initially recorded in expense accounts have not been used.**	**Assets understated. Expenses overstated.**	**Dr. Assets Cr. Expenses**
2. Unearned revenues	(a) Unearned revenues initially recorded in liability accounts are now recognized as revenue.	Liabilities overstated. Revenues understated.	Dr. Liabilities Cr. Revenues
	(b) **Unearned revenues initially recorded in revenue accounts are still unearned.**	**Liabilities understated. Revenues overstated.**	**Dr. Revenues Cr. Liabilities**

Alternative adjusting entries **do not apply** to accrued revenues and accrued expenses because **no entries occur before companies make these types of adjusting entries.**

Appendix 3B Financial Reporting Concepts

LEARNING OBJECTIVE *6

Discuss financial reporting concepts.

This appendix provides a summary of the concepts used in this text. In addition, it provides other useful concepts which accountants use as a basis for recording and reporting financial information.

Qualities of Useful Information

The IASB developed a *Conceptual Framework for Financial Reporting*. The purpose of the framework is both to assist the IASB to develop standards based on consistent concepts and to aid financial statement preparers to develop accounting policies when there is no relevant standard.

- The framework begins by stating that the primary objective of financial reporting is to provide financial information that is **useful** to investors and creditors for making decisions about providing capital.
- Useful information should possess two fundamental qualities, relevance and faithful representation, as shown in **Illustration 3B.1**.

ILLUSTRATION 3B.1

Fundamental qualities of useful information

Relevance Accounting information has **relevance** if it would make a difference in a business decision. Information is considered relevant if it provides information that has **predictive value**, that is, helps provide accurate expectations about the future, and has **confirmatory value**, that is, confirms or corrects prior expectations. **Materiality** is a company-specific aspect of relevance. An item is material when its **size** makes it likely to influence the decision of an investor or creditor.

Faithful Representation **Faithful representation** means that information accurately depicts what really happened. To provide a faithful representation, information must be **complete** (nothing important has been omitted), **neutral** (is not biased toward one position or another), and **free from error**.

Enhancing Qualities

In addition to the two fundamental qualities, the IASB also describes a number of enhancing qualities of useful information. These include **comparability**, **verifiability**, **timeliness**, and **understandability**.

- **Comparability** results when different companies use the same accounting principles. Another type of comparability is consistency.
- **Consistency** means that a company uses the same accounting principles and methods from year to year.
- Information is **verifiable** if independent observers, using the same methods, obtain similar results.
- For accounting information to have relevance, it must be **timely**. That is, it must be available to decision-makers before it loses its capacity to influence decisions. For example, companies like **Tencent Holdings** (CHN) or **Asia Bicycle Trading Co.** (TWN) provide their annual reports to investors within 60 days of their year-end.
- Information has the quality of **understandability** if it is presented in a clear and concise fashion, so that reasonably informed users of that information can interpret it and comprehend its meaning.

Assumptions in Financial Reporting

To develop accounting standards, the IASB relies on some key assumptions, as shown in **Illustration 3B.2**. These include assumptions about the monetary unit, economic entity, time period, and going concern.

ILLUSTRATION 3B.2

Key assumptions in financial reporting

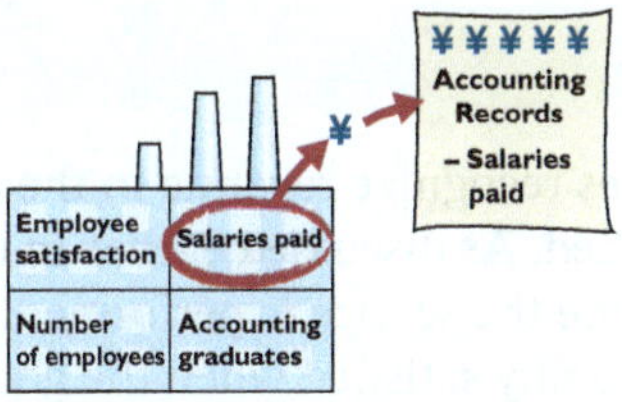

Monetary Unit Assumption The **monetary unit assumption** requires that only those things that can be expressed in money are included in the accounting records. This means that certain important information needed by investors, creditors, and managers, such as customer satisfaction, is not reported in the financial statements. This assumption relies on the monetary unit remaining relatively stable in value.

Economic Entity Assumption The **economic entity assumption** states that every economic entity can be separately identified and accounted for. In order to assess a company's performance and financial position accurately, it is important to not blur company transactions with personal transactions (especially those of its managers) or transactions of other companies.

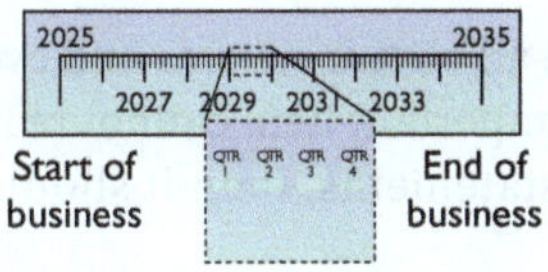

Time Period Assumption Notice that the income statement, retained earnings statement, and statement of cash flows all cover periods of one year, and the statement of financial position is prepared at the end of each year. The **time period assumption** states that the life of a business can be divided into artificial time periods and that useful reports covering those periods can be prepared for the business.

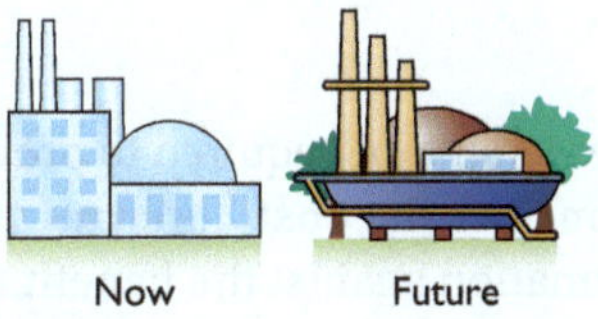

Going Concern Assumption The **going concern assumption** states that the business will remain in operation for the foreseeable future. This assumption is used to justify, for example, valuing property, plant, and equipment at historical cost and using depreciation to allocate the cost of the asset to expense over its useful life. Of course, many businesses do fail. When the going concern assumption is not valid, other accounting methods not covered in this text are used.

Principles in Financial Reporting

Measurement Bases

IFRS generally uses one of two measurement bases, the historical cost basis or the current value basis. Selection of which basis to follow generally relates to trade-offs between relevance and faithful representation.

Historical Cost Basis The **historical cost basis** (discussed in Chapter 1) dictates that companies record and continue to report assets at their cost. This is true not only at the time the asset is purchased but also over the time the asset is held. For example, if land that was purchased for €30,000 increases in value to €40,000, it continues to be reported at €30,000.

Current Value Basis The **current value basis** (discussed in Chapter 1) indicates that assets and liabilities should be reported at current value. Current value information may be more useful than historical cost for certain types of assets and liabilities. For example, certain investment securities are reported at current value because reliable market price information is often readily available for these types of assets.

In choosing between historical cost and current value, two qualities that make accounting information useful for decision-making are used—relevance and faithful representation.

- In determining which measurement basis to use, the factual nature of cost figures are weighed versus the relevance of current value.
- In general, most assets use the historical cost basis because current values may not be representationally faithful.
- Only in situations where assets are actively traded, such as investment securities, is the current value basis applied.

Revenue Recognition Principle

The **revenue recognition principle** requires that companies recognize revenue in the accounting period in which the performance obligation is satisfied. As discussed earlier in the chapter, in a service company, revenue is recognized at the time the service is performed. In a merchandising company, the performance obligation is generally satisfied when the goods transfer from the seller to the buyer (discussed in Chapter 5). At this point, the sales transaction is complete and the sales price established.

Expense Recognition Principle

The **expense recognition principle** (discussed earlier in the chapter) dictates that companies recognize expense in the period in which they make efforts to generate revenue. Thus, expenses follow revenues.

Full Disclosure Principle

The **full disclosure principle** requires that companies disclose all circumstances and events that would make a difference to financial statement users. If an important item cannot reasonably be reported directly in one of the four types of financial statements, then it should be discussed in notes that accompany the statements.

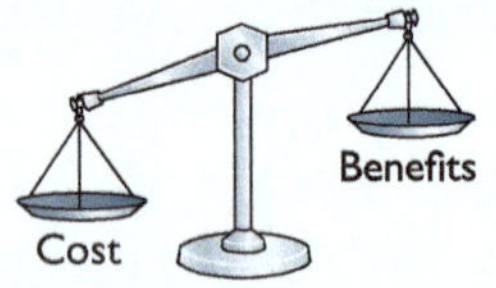

Cost Constraint

Providing information is costly. In deciding whether companies should be required to provide a certain type of information, accounting standard-setters consider the **cost constraint**. It weighs the cost that companies will incur to provide the information against the benefit that financial statement users will gain from having the information available.

Review and Practice

Learning Objectives Review

1 Explain the accrual basis of accounting and the reasons for adjusting entries.

The revenue recognition principle dictates that companies recognize revenue when a performance obligation has been satisfied. The expense recognition principle dictates that companies recognize expenses in the period when the company makes efforts to generate those revenues.

The time period assumption assumes that the economic life of a business is divided into artificial time periods. Accrual-basis accounting means that companies record events that change a company's financial statements in the periods in which those events occur, rather than in the periods in which the company receives or pays cash.

Companies make adjusting entries at the end of an accounting period. Such entries ensure that companies recognize revenues in the period in which the performance obligation is satisfied and recognize expenses in the period in which they are incurred. The major types of adjusting entries are deferrals (prepaid expenses and unearned revenues) and accruals (accrued revenues and accrued expenses).

2 Prepare adjusting entries for deferrals.

Deferrals are either prepaid expenses or unearned revenues. Companies make adjusting entries for deferrals to record the portion of the prepayment that represents the expense incurred or the revenue for services performed in the current accounting period.

3 Prepare adjusting entries for accruals.

Accruals are either accrued revenues or accrued expenses. Companies make adjusting entries for accruals to record revenues for services performed and expenses incurred in the current accounting period that have not been recognized through daily entries.

4 Describe the nature and purpose of an adjusted trial balance.

An adjusted trial balance shows the balances of all accounts, including those that have been adjusted, at the end of an accounting period. Its purpose is to prove the equality of the total debit balances and total credit balances in the ledger after all adjustments.

*5 Prepare adjusting entries for the alternative treatment of deferrals.

Companies may initially debit prepayments to an expense account. Likewise, they may initially credit unearned revenues to a revenue account. At the end of the period, these accounts may be overstated. The adjusting entries for prepaid expenses are a debit to an asset account and a credit to an expense account. Adjusting entries for unearned revenues are a debit to a revenue account and a credit to a liability account.

*6 Discuss financial reporting concepts.

To be judged useful, information should have the primary characteristics of relevance and faithful representation. In addition, it should be comparable, consistent, verifiable, timely, and understandable.

The **monetary unit assumption** requires that companies include in the accounting records only transaction data that can be expressed in terms of money. The **economic entity assumption** states that economic events can be identified with a particular unit of accountability. The **time period assumption** states that the economic life of a business can be divided into artificial time periods and that meaningful accounting reports can be prepared for each period. The **going concern assumption** states that the company will continue in operation long enough to carry out its existing objectives and commitments.

The **historical cost basis** states that companies should record and continue to report assets at their cost. The **current value basis** indicates that assets and liabilities should be reported at current value. The **revenue recognition principle** requires that companies recognize revenue in the accounting period in which the performance obligation is satisfied. The **expense recognition principle** dictates that efforts (expenses) be matched with results (revenues). The **full disclosure principle** requires that companies disclose circumstances and events that matter to financial statement users.

The **cost constraint** weighs the cost that companies incur to provide a type of information against its benefits to financial statement users.

Glossary Review

Accrual-basis accounting Accounting basis in which companies record transactions that change a company's financial statements in the periods in which the events occur. (p. 3-3).

Accruals Adjusting entries for either accrued revenues or accrued expenses. (p. 3-6).

Accrued expenses Expenses incurred but not yet paid in cash or recorded. (p. 3-16).

Accrued revenues Revenues for services performed but not yet received in cash or recorded. (p. 3-14).

Adjusted trial balance A list of accounts and their balances after the company has made all adjustments. (p. 3-22).

Adjusting entries Entries made at the end of an accounting period to ensure that companies follow the revenue recognition and expense recognition principles. (p. 3-6).

Book value The difference between the cost of a depreciable asset and its related accumulated depreciation. (p. 3-11).

Calendar year An accounting period that extends from January 1 to December 31. (p. 3-3).

Cash-basis accounting Accounting basis in which companies record revenue when they receive cash and an expense when they pay out cash. (p. 3-3).

***Comparability** Ability to compare the accounting information of different companies because they use the same accounting principles. (p. 3-30).

***Consistency** Use of the same accounting principles and methods from year to year within a company. (p. 3-30).

Contra asset account An account offset against an asset account on the statement of financial position. (p. 3-10).

***Cost constraint** Constraint that weighs the cost that companies will incur to provide the information against the benefit that financial statement users will gain from having the information available. (p. 3-32).

***Current value basis** A measurement basis that results in the assets and liabilities being reported at current value. (p. 3-31).

Deferrals Adjusting entries for either prepaid expenses or unearned revenues. (p. 3-6).

Depreciation The process of allocating the cost of an asset to expense over its useful life. (p. 3-10).

***Economic entity assumption** An assumption that every economic entity can be separately identified and accounted for. (p. 3-31).

Expense recognition principle The principle that companies recognize expense in the period in which they make efforts (consume assets or incur liabilities) to generate revenue. (pp. 3-5, 3-32).

***Faithful representation** Information that accurately depicts what really happened. (p. 3-30).

Fiscal year An accounting period that is one year in length. (p. 3-3).

***Full disclosure principle** Accounting principle that dictates that companies disclose circumstances and events that make a difference to financial statement users. (p. 3-32).

***Going concern assumption** The assumption that the company will continue in operation for the foreseeable future. (p. 3-31).

***Historical cost basis** A measurement basis that results in companies should record assets and other accounts at their cost. (p. 3-31).

Interim periods Monthly or quarterly accounting time periods. (p. 3-3).

***Materiality** A company-specific aspect of relevance. An item is material when its size makes it likely to influence the decision of an investor or creditor. (p. 3-30).

***Monetary unit assumption** An assumption that requires that only those things that can be expressed in money are included in the accounting records. (p. 3-31).

Prepaid expenses (prepayments) Expenses paid in cash before they are used or consumed. (p. 3-7).

***Relevance** The quality of information that indicates the information makes a difference in a decision. (p. 3-30).

Revenue recognition principle The principle that companies recognize revenue in the accounting period in which the performance obligation is satisfied. (pp. 3-4, 3-32).

***Timely** Information that is available to decision-makers before it loses its capacity to influence decisions. (p. 3-30).

Time period assumption An assumption that accountants can divide the economic life of a business into artificial time periods. (pp. 3-3, 3-31).

***Understandability** Information presented in a clear and concise fashion so that users can interpret it and comprehend its meaning. (p. 3-30).

Unearned revenues A liability recorded for cash received before services are performed. (p. 3-11).

Useful life The length of service of a long-lived asset. (p. 3-9).

***Verifiable** The quality of information that occurs when independent observers, using the same methods, obtain similar results. (p. 3-30).

Practice Multiple-Choice Questions

1. **(LO 1)** The revenue recognition principle states that:
   - **a.** revenue should be recognized in the accounting period in which a performance obligation is satisfied.
   - **b.** expenses should be matched with revenues.
   - **c.** the economic life of a business can be divided into artificial time periods.
   - **d.** the fiscal year should correspond with the calendar year.

2. **(LO 1)** The time period assumption states that:
   - **a.** companies must wait until the calendar year is completed to prepare financial statements.
   - **b.** companies use the fiscal year to report financial information.
   - **c.** the economic life of a business can be divided into artificial time periods.
   - **d.** companies record information in the time period in which the events occur.

3. **(LO 1)** Which of the following statements about the accrual basis of accounting is **false**?
   - **a.** Events that change a company's financial statements are recorded in the periods in which the events occur.
   - **b.** Revenue is recognized in the period in which services are performed.
   - **c.** This basis is in accordance with International Financial Reporting Standards.
   - **d.** Revenue is recorded only when cash is received, and expense is recorded only when cash is paid.

4. **(LO 1)** The principle or assumption dictating that efforts (expenses) should be recognized in the period in which a company consumes assets or incurs liabilities to generate revenue is the:
   - **a.** expense recognition principle.
   - **b.** cost assumption.
   - **c.** time period assumption.
   - **d.** revenue recognition principle.

5. **(LO 1)** Adjusting entries are made to ensure that:
   - **a.** expenses are recognized in the period in which they are incurred.
   - **b.** revenues are recorded in the period in which services are performed.
   - **c.** statement of financial position and income statement accounts have correct balances at the end of an accounting period.
   - **d.** All of the answer choices are correct.

6. **(LO 1)** Each of the following is a major type (or category) of adjusting entries **except**:
   - **a.** prepaid expenses.
   - **b.** accrued revenues.
   - **c.** accrued expenses.
   - **d.** recognized revenues.

7. **(LO 2)** The trial balance shows Supplies €1,350 and Supplies Expense €0. If €600 of supplies are on hand at the end of the period, the adjusting entry is:

a.	Supplies	600	
	Supplies Expense		600
b.	Supplies	750	
	Supplies Expense		750
c.	Supplies Expense	750	
	Supplies		750
d.	Supplies Expense	600	
	Supplies		600

8. **(LO 2)** Adjustments for prepaid expenses:
   - **a.** decrease assets and increase revenues.
   - **b.** decrease expenses and increase assets.
   - **c.** decrease assets and increase expenses.
   - **d.** decrease revenues and increase assets.

9. **(LO 2)** Accumulated Depreciation is:
   - **a.** a contra asset account.
   - **b.** an expense account.
   - **c.** an equity account.
   - **d.** a liability account.

10. **(LO 2)** Rivera Shipping computes depreciation on delivery equipment at ¥1,000 (amounts in thousands) for the month of June. The adjusting entry to record this depreciation is as follows.

a.	Depreciation Expense	1,000	
	Accumulated Depreciation—Rivera Shipping		1,000
b.	Depreciation Expense	1,000	
	Equipment		1,000
c.	Depreciation Expense	1,000	
	Accumulated Depreciation—Equipment		1,000
d.	Equipment Expense	1,000	
	Accumulated Depreciation—Equipment		1,000

11. **(LO 2)** Adjustments for unearned revenues:
    - **a.** decrease liabilities and increase revenues.
    - **b.** have an assets-and-revenues-account relationship.
    - **c.** increase assets and increase revenues.
    - **d.** decrease revenues and decrease assets.

12. **(LO 3)** Adjustments for accrued revenues:
    - **a.** have a liabilities-and-revenues-account relationship.
    - **b.** have an assets-and-revenues-account relationship.
    - **c.** decrease assets and revenues.
    - **d.** decrease liabilities and increase revenues.

13. **(LO 3)** Anika Winter earned a salary of €400 for the last week of September. She will be paid on October 1. The adjusting entry for Anika's employer at September 30 is:

a. No entry is required.

b. Salaries and Wages Expense	400	
Salaries and Wages Payable		400
c. Salaries and Wages Expense	400	
Cash		400
d. Salaries and Wages Payable	400	
Cash		400

14. **(LO 4)** Which of the following statements is **incorrect** concerning the adjusted trial balance?

a. An adjusted trial balance proves the equality of the total debit balances and the total credit balances in the ledger after all adjustments are made.

b. The adjusted trial balance provides the primary basis for the preparation of financial statements.

c. The adjusted trial balance lists the account balances segregated by assets and liabilities.

d. The adjusted trial balance is prepared after the adjusting entries have been journalized and posted.

*15. **(LO 5)** The trial balance shows Supplies NT$0 and Supplies Expense NT$1,500. If NT$800 of supplies are on hand at the end of the period, the adjusting entry is:

a. debit Supplies NT$800 and credit Supplies Expense NT$800.

b. debit Supplies Expense NT$800 and credit Supplies NT$800.

c. debit Supplies NT$700 and credit Supplies Expense NT$700.

d. debit Supplies Expense NT$700 and credit Supplies NT$700.

*16. **(LO 6)** Neutrality is an ingredient of:

	Faithful Representation	Relevance
a.	Yes	Yes
b.	No	No
c.	Yes	No
d.	No	Yes

*17. **(LO 6)** Which item is a constraint in financial accounting?

a. Comparability. **c.** Cost.

b. Materiality. **d.** Consistency.

Solutions

1. **a.** Revenue should be recognized in the accounting period in which a performance obligation is satisfied. The other choices are incorrect because (b) defines the expense recognition principle, (c) describes the time period assumption, and (d) a company's fiscal year does not need to correspond with the calendar year.

2. **c.** The economic life of a business can be divided into artificial time periods. The other choices are incorrect because (a) companies report their activities on a more frequent basis and not necessarily based on a calendar year; (b) companies report financial information more frequently than annually, such as monthly or quarterly, in order to evaluate results of operations; and (d) describes accrual-basis accounting.

3. **d.** Under the accrual basis of accounting, revenue is recognized when the performance obligation is satisfied, not when cash is received, and expense is recognized when incurred, not when cash is paid. The other choices are all true statements.

4. **a.** The expense recognition principle dictates that companies recognize expense in the period in which they make efforts to generate revenue. The other choices are incorrect because (b) there is no cost assumption, but the historical cost basis states that assets should be recorded and reported at their cost; (c) the time period assumption states that the economic life of a business can be divided into artificial time periods; and (d) the revenue recognition principle indicates that revenue should be recognized in the accounting period in which a performance obligation is satisfied.

5. **d.** Adjusting entries are made for the reasons noted in choices (a), (b), and (c). The other choices are true statements, but (d) is the best answer.

6. **d.** Unearned revenues, not recognized revenues, is one of the major categories of adjusting entries. The other choices all list one of the major categories of adjusting entries.

7. **c.** Debiting Supplies Expense for €750 and crediting Supplies for €750 (€1,350 − €600) will decrease Supplies and increase Supplies Expense. The other choices are incorrect because (a) will increase Supplies and decrease Supplies Expense and also for the wrong amounts, (b) will increase Supplies and decrease Supplies Expense, and (d) will cause Supplies to have an incorrect balance of €750 (€1,350 − €600) and Supplies Expense to have an incorrect balance of €600 (€0 + €600).

8. **c.** Adjustments for prepaid expenses decrease assets and increase expenses. The other choices are incorrect because an adjusting entry for prepaid expenses (a) increases expenses, not revenues; (b) increases, not decreases, expenses and decreases, not increases, assets; and (d) increases expenses, not decreases, revenues and decreases, not increases, assets.

9. **a.** Accumulated Depreciation is a contra asset account; it is offset against an asset account on the statement of financial position. The other choices are incorrect because Accumulated Depreciation is not (b) an expense account nor located on the income statement, (c) an equity account, or (d) a liability account.

10. **c.** The adjusting entry is to debit Depreciation Expense and credit Accumulated Depreciation—Equipment. The other choices are incorrect because (a) the contra asset account title includes the asset being depreciated, not the company name; (b) the credit should be to the contra asset account, not directly to the asset; and (d) the debit for this entry should be Depreciation Expense, not Equipment Expense.

11. **a.** Adjustments for unearned revenues will consist of a debit (decrease) to unearned revenues (a liability) and a credit (increase) to a revenue account. Choices (b), (c), and (d) are incorrect because adjustments for unearned revenues will increase revenues but will have no effect on assets.

12. **b.** Adjustments for accrued revenues will have an assets-and-revenues-account relationship. Choices (a) and (d) are incorrect because adjustments for accrued revenues have no effect on liabilities. Choice (c) is incorrect because these adjustments will increase, not decrease, both assets and revenues.

13. **b.** The adjusting entry should be to debit Salaries and Wages Expense for €400 and credit Salaries and Wages Payable for €400.

The other choices are incorrect because (a) if an adjusting entry is not made, the amount of money owed (liability) that is shown on the statement of financial position will be understated and the amount of salaries and wages expense will also be understated; (c) the credit account is incorrect as adjusting entries never affect cash; and (d) the debit account should be Salaries and Wages Expense and the credit account should be Salaries and Wages Payable. Adjusting entries never affect cash.

14. c. The accounts on the trial balance are segregated by the balance in the account—either debit or credit—not by whether they are assets or liabilities. All accounts in the ledger are included in the adjusted trial balance, not just assets and liabilities. The other choices are all true statements.

***15. a.** This adjusting entry correctly states the Supplies account at NT$800 (NT$0 + NT$800) and the Supplies Expense account at NT$700 (NT$1,500 – NT$800). The other choices are incorrect because (b) will cause the Supplies account to have a credit balance (assets have a normal debit balance) and the Supplies Expense account to be stated at NT$2,300, which is too high; (c) will result in a NT$700 balance in the Supplies account (NT$100 too low) and an NT$800 balance in the Supplies Expense account (NT$100 too high); and (d) will cause the Supplies account to have a credit balance (assets have a normal debit balance) and the Supplies Expense account to be stated at NT$2,200, which is too high.

***16. c.** Neutrality is one of the enhancing qualities that makes information more representationally faithful, not relevant. Therefore, choices (a), (b), and (d) are incorrect.

***17. c.** Cost is a constraint in financial accounting. The other choices are all enhancing qualities of useful information.

Practice Brief Exercises

Indicate why adjusting entries are needed.

1. **(LO 1)** The ledger of Dey Company includes the following accounts. Explain why each account may need adjustment.

a. Supplies.
b. Unearned Service Revenue.
c. Salaries and Wages Payable.
d. Interest Payable.

Solution

1. **a.** Supplies: to recognize supplies used during the period.
b. Unearned Service Revenue: to record revenue generated for services performed.
c. Salaries and Wages Payable: to recognize unpaid salaries and wages due to employees at the end of a reporting period.
d. Interest Payable: to recognize interest accrued but unpaid on notes payable.

Prepare adjusting entry for depreciation.

2. **(LO 2)** At the end of its first year, thc trial balance of Denton Cleaners shows Equipment of £40,000 and zero balances in Accumulated Depreciation—Equipment and Depreciation Expense. Depreciation for the year is estimated to be £8,000. Prepare the adjusting entry for depreciation at December 31, post the adjustments to T-accounts, and indicate the statement of financial position presentation of the equipment at December 31.

Solution

2. Dec. 31	Depreciation Expense	8,000	
	Accumulated Depreciation—Equipment		8,000

Depreciation Expense

12/31 8,000	

Accum. Depreciation—Equipment

	12/31 8,000

Statement of financial position:

Equipment	£40,000	
Less: Accumulated depreciation—equipment	8,000	£32,000

Prepare adjusting entries for accruals.

3. **(LO 3)** You are asked to prepare the following accrual adjusting entries at December 31.

1. Services performed but not recorded are €4,200.
2. Utilities expenses incurred but not paid are €660.
3. Salaries and wages earned by employees of €3,000 are unpaid.

Use the following account titles: Accounts Receivable, Service Revenue, Salaries and Wages Expense, Salaries and Wages Payable, Utilities Expense, and Utilities Payable.

Solution

3. Dec. 31	Accounts Receivable	4,200	
	Service Revenue		4,200
31	Utilities Expense	660	
	Utilities Payable		660
31	Salaries and Wage Expense	3,000	
	Salaries and Wages Payable		3,000

4. **(LO 1, 2, 3)** The trial balance for Blair Company includes the following statement of financial position accounts. Identify the accounts that may require adjustment. For each account that requires adjustment, indicate (a) the type of adjusting entry (prepaid expense, unearned revenue, accrued revenue, or accrued expense) and (b) the related account in the adjusting entry.

Analyze accounts in an unadjusted trial balance.

Accounts Receivable	Interest Payable
Supplies	Unearned Service Revenue
Prepaid Insurance	

Solution

4.

Account	Type of Adjustment	Related Account
Accounts Receivable	Accrued revenue	Service Revenue
Supplies	Prepaid expense	Supplies Expense
Prepaid Insurance	Prepaid expense	Insurance Expense
Interest Payable	Accrued expense	Interest Expense
Unearned Service Revenue	Unearned revenue	Service Revenue

5. **(LO 4)** The adjusted trial balance of Harmony Decorating includes the following accounts at December 31, 2029: Cash €12,000, Share Capital—Ordinary €22,000, Dividends €3,000, Service Revenue €41,000, Rent Expense €900, Salaries and Wages Expense €6,000, Supplies Expense €700, and Depreciation Expense €1,800. Prepare an income statement for the year.

Prepare an income statement from an adjusted trial balance.

Solution

5.

Harmony Decorating
Income Statement
For the Year Ended December 31, 2029

Revenues		
Service revenue		€41,000
Expenses		
Salaries and wages expense	€6,000	
Rent expense	900	
Depreciation expense	1,800	
Supplies expense	700	
Total expenses		9,400
Net income		€31,600

Practice Exercises

1. **(LO 2, 3)** Evan Watts, D.D.S., opened a dental practice on January 1, 2029. During the first month of operations, the following transactions occurred.

Prepare adjusting entries.

1. Watts performed services for patients totaling $2,400. These services have not yet been recorded.
2. Utilities expenses incurred but not paid prior to January 31 totaled $400.
3. Purchased dental equipment on January 1 for $80,000, paying $20,000 in cash and signing a $60,000, 3-year note payable. The equipment depreciates $500 per month. Interest is $600 per month.
4. Purchased a one-year malpractice insurance policy on January 1 for $12,000.
5. Purchased $2,600 of dental supplies. On January 31, determined that $900 of supplies were on hand.

Instructions

Prepare the adjusting entries on January 31. Account titles are Accumulated Depreciation—Equipment, Depreciation Expense, Service Revenue, Accounts Receivable, Insurance Expense, Interest Expense, Interest Payable, Prepaid Insurance, Supplies, Supplies Expense, Utilities Expense, and Utilities Payable.

Solution

1.

Jan. 31	Accounts Receivable	2,400	
	Service Revenue		2,400
	Utilities Expense	400	
	Utilities Payable		400
	Depreciation Expense	500	
	Accumulated Depreciation—Equipment		500
	Interest Expense	600	
	Interest Payable		600
	Insurance Expense ($12,000 ÷ 12)	1,000	
	Prepaid Insurance		1,000
	Supplies Expense ($2,600 – $900)	1,700	
	Supplies		1,700

Prepare correct income statement.

2. **(LO 2, 3, 4)** The income statement of Venden Movers for the month of July shows net income of £4,000 based on Service Revenue £8,700, Salaries and Wages Expense £2,500, Supplies Expense £1,700, and Utilities Expense £500. In reviewing the statement, you discover the following.

1. Insurance expired during July of £700 was omitted.
2. Supplies expense includes £250 of supplies that are still on hand at July 31.
3. Depreciation on equipment of £300 was omitted.
4. Accrued but unpaid wages at July 31 of £400 were not included.
5. Services performed but unrecorded totaled £650.

Instructions

Prepare a correct income statement for July 2029.

Solution

2.

Venden Movers
Income Statement
For the Month Ended July 31, 2029

Revenues		
Service revenue (£8,700 + £650)		£9,350
Expenses		
Salaries and wages expense (£2,500 + £400)	£2,900	
Supplies expense (£1,700 – £250)	1,450	
Utilities expense	500	
Insurance expense	700	
Depreciation expense	300	
Total expenses		5,850
Net income		£3,500

Practice Problem

Prepare adjusting entries from selected data.

(LO 2, 3) The Desai Lawn Care began operations on April 1. At April 30, the trial balance shows the following balances for selected accounts (amounts in thousands).

Prepaid Insurance	₹ 3,600
Equipment	28,000
Notes Payable	20,000
Unearned Service Revenue	4,200
Service Revenue	1,800

Analysis reveals the following additional data.

1. Prepaid insurance is the cost of a 2-year insurance policy, effective April 1.
2. Depreciation on the equipment is ₹500 per month.
3. The note payable is dated April 1. It is a 6-month, 12% note.
4. Seven customers paid for the company's 6-month lawn service package of ₹600 beginning in April. The company performed services for these customers in April.
5. Lawn services performed for other customers but not recorded at April 30 totaled ₹1,500.

Instructions

Prepare the adjusting entries for the month of April. Show computations.

Solution

GENERAL JOURNAL **J1**

Date		Account Titles and Explanation	Ref.	Debit	Credit
		Adjusting Entries			
Apr.	30	Insurance Expense		150	
		Prepaid Insurance			150
		(To record insurance expired: ₹3,600 ÷ 24 = ₹150 per month)			
	30	Depreciation Expense		500	
		Accumulated Depreciation—Equipment			500
		(To record monthly depreciation)			
	30	Interest Expense		200	
		Interest Payable			200
		(To record interest on notes payable: ₹20,000 × 12% × 1/12 = ₹200)			
	30	Unearned Service Revenue		700	
		Service Revenue			700
		(To record revenue for services performed: ₹600 ÷ 6 = ₹100; ₹100 per month × 7 = ₹700)			
	30	Accounts Receivable		1,500	
		Service Revenue			1,500
		(To record revenue for services performed)			

Note: All asterisked Questions, Exercises, and Problems relate to material in the appendices to the chapter.

Questions

1. **a.** How does the time period assumption affect an accountant's analysis of business transactions?

   b. Explain the terms fiscal year, calendar year, and interim periods.

2. Define two IFRSs that relate to adjusting the accounts.

3. What are the five steps of the revenue recognition process?

4. Susan Hardy, a lawyer, accepts a legal engagement in March, performs the work in April, and is paid in May. If Hardy's law firm prepares monthly financial statements, when should it recognize revenue from this engagement? Why?

5. Why do accrual-basis financial statements provide more useful information than cash-basis statements?

6. In completing the engagement in Question 4, Hardy pays no costs in March, £2,000 in April, and £2,500 in May (incurred in April). How much expense should the firm deduct from revenues in the month when it recognizes the revenue? Why?

7. "Adjusting entries are required by the historical cost basis of accounting." Do you agree? Explain.

8. Why may a trial balance not contain up-to-date and complete financial information?

9. Distinguish between the two categories of adjusting entries, and identify the types of adjustments applicable to each category.

10. What is the debit/credit effect of a prepaid expense adjusting entry?

11. "Depreciation is a valuation process that results in the reporting of the current value of the asset." Do you agree? Explain.

12. Explain the differences between depreciation expense and accumulated depreciation.

13. G. Phillips Company purchased equipment for Rs18,000. By the current statement of financial position date, Rs6,000 had been depreciated. Indicate the statement of financial position presentation of the data.

14. What is the debit/credit effect of an unearned revenue adjusting entry?

15. Whistler Cabinets performed services for a customer but has not yet recorded payment, nor has it recorded any entry related to the work. Which of the following accounts are involved in the adjusting entry: (a) asset, (b) liability, (c) revenue, or (d) expense? For the accounts selected, indicate whether they would be debited or credited in the entry.

16. A company fails to recognize an expense incurred but not paid. Indicate which of the following accounts is debited and which is credited in the adjusting entry: (a) asset, (b) liability, (c) revenue, or (d) expense.

17. A company makes an accrued revenue adjusting entry for NT$27,000 and an accrued expense adjusting entry for NT$21,000. How much was net income understated prior to these entries? Explain.

18. On January 9, a company pays €6,000 for salaries and wages of which €2,000 was reported as Salaries and Wages Payable on December 31. Give the entry to record the payment.

19. For each of the following items before adjustment, indicate the type of adjusting entry (prepaid expense, unearned revenue, accrued revenue, or accrued expense) that is needed to correct the misstatement. If an item could result in more than one type of adjusting entry, indicate each of the types.

    a. Assets are understated.
    b. Liabilities are overstated.
    c. Liabilities are understated.
    d. Expenses are understated.
    e. Assets are overstated.
    f. Revenue is understated.

20. One-half of the adjusting entry is given below. Indicate the account title for the other half of the entry.

    a. Salaries and Wages Expense is debited.
    b. Depreciation Expense is debited.
    c. Interest Payable is credited.
    d. Supplies is credited.
    e. Accounts Receivable is debited.
    f. Unearned Service Revenue is debited.

21. "An adjusting entry may affect more than one statement of financial position or income statement account." Do you agree? Why or why not?

22. Why is it possible to prepare financial statements directly from an adjusted trial balance?

*23. Dashan Company debits Supplies Expense for all purchases of supplies and credits Rent Revenue for all advanced rentals. For each type of adjustment, give the adjusting entry.

*24. **a.** What is the primary objective of financial reporting?

   b. Identify the characteristics of useful accounting information.

*25. Dan Fineman, the president of King Company, is pleased. King substantially increased its net income in 2029 while keeping its unit inventory relatively the same. However, Howard Gross, chief accountant, cautions Dan. Gross says that since King changed its method of inventory valuation, there is a consistency problem and it is difficult to determine whether King is better off. Is Gross correct? Why or why not?

*26. What is the distinction between comparability and consistency?

*27. Describe the constraint inherent in the presentation of accounting information.

*28. Quinn Becker is president of Better Books. She has no accounting background. Becker cannot understand why current value is not used as the basis for all accounting measurement and reporting. Discuss.

*29. What is the economic entity assumption? Give an example of its violation.

Brief Exercises

Identify the order of the five steps in the revenue recognition process.

BE3.1 (LO 1) Number the following steps of the revenue recognition process (from 1–5) to place in the correct order.

a. ________ Allocate the transaction price to the separate performance obligations.
b. ________ Identify the contract with customers.
c. ________ Identify the separate performance obligations in the contract.
d. ________ Recognize revenue when each performance obligation is satisfied.
e. ________ Determine the transaction price.

BE3.2 (LO 1) Transactions that affect net income do not necessarily affect cash. Identify the effect, if any, that each of the following transactions would have upon cash and net income. The first transaction has been completed as an example.

Identify impact of transactions on cash and net income.

	Cash	Net Income
a. Purchased $100 of supplies for cash.	–$100	$ 0
b. Recorded an adjusting entry to record use of $20 of the above supplies.		
c. Made sales of $1,300, all on account.		
d. Received $800 from customers in payment of their accounts.		
e. Purchased equipment for cash, $2,500.		
f. Recorded depreciation of building for period used, $600.		

BE3.3 (LO 1) The ledger of Althukair Company includes the following accounts. Explain why each account may require adjustment.

Indicate why adjusting entries are needed.

a. Prepaid Insurance.
b. Depreciation Expense.
c. Unearned Service Revenue.
d. Interest Payable.

BE3.4 (LO 2, 3) Gee Company accumulates the following adjustment data at December 31. Indicate (a) the type of adjustment (prepaid expense, accrued revenue, and so on), and (b) the status of accounts before adjustment (for example, "assets understated and revenues understated").

Identify the major types of adjusting entries.

1. Supplies of €150 are on hand.
2. Services performed but not recorded total €900.
3. Interest of €200 has accumulated on a note payable.
4. Rent collected in advance totaling €850 has been recognized as revenue.

BE3.5 (LO 2) Schramel Advertising's trial balance at December 31 shows Supplies £6,700 and Supplies Expense £0. On December 31, there are £2,100 of supplies on hand. Prepare the adjusting entry at December 31, and using T-accounts, enter the balances in the accounts, post the adjusting entry, and indicate the adjusted balance in each account.

Prepare adjusting entry for supplies.

BE3.6 (LO 2) At the end of its first year, the trial balance of Wolowitz Company shows Equipment €30,000 and zero balances in Accumulated Depreciation—Equipment and Depreciation Expense. Depreciation for the year is estimated to be €3,750. Prepare the annual adjusting entry for depreciation at December 31, post the adjustments to T-accounts, and indicate the statement of financial position presentation of the equipment at December 31.

Prepare adjusting entry for depreciation.

BE3.7 (LO 2) On July 1, 2029, Major Ltd. pays £15,120 to Orlow Insurance for a 3-year insurance contract. Both companies have fiscal years ending December 31. For Major Ltd., journalize and post the entry on July 1 and the annual adjusting entry on December 31.

Prepare adjusting entry for prepaid expense.

BE3.8 (LO 2) Using the data in BE3.7, journalize and post the entry on July 1 and the adjusting entry on December 31 for Orlow Insurance. Orlow uses the accounts Unearned Service Revenue and Service Revenue.

Prepare adjusting entry for unearned revenue.

BE3.9 (LO 3) The bookkeeper for Abduli Marble asks you to prepare the following accrual adjusting entries at December 31.

Prepare adjusting entries for accruals.

1. Interest on notes payable of €400 is accrued.
2. Services performed but not recorded total €2,300.
3. Salaries earned by employees of €900 have not been recorded.

Use the following account titles: Service Revenue, Accounts Receivable, Interest Expense, Interest Payable, Salaries and Wages Expense, and Salaries and Wages Payable.

BE3.10 (LO 2, 3) The trial balance of Beowulf Travel includes the following statement of financial position accounts, which may require adjustment. For each account that requires adjustment, indicate (a) the type of adjusting entry (prepaid expense, unearned revenue, accrued revenue, or accrued expense) and (b) the related account in the adjusting entry.

Analyze accounts in an unadjusted trial balance.

Accounts Receivable	Interest Payable
Prepaid Insurance	Unearned Service Revenue
Accumulated Depreciation—Equipment	

BE3.11 (LO 4) The adjusted trial balance of Kwun Photos at December 31, 2029, includes the following accounts: Share Capital—Ordinary ₩16,400, Dividends ₩7,000, Service Revenue ₩39,000, Salaries and Wages Expense ₩16,000, Insurance Expense ₩2,000, Rent Expense ₩4,000, Supplies Expense ₩1,500, and Depreciation Expense ₩1,300. Prepare an income statement for the year (amounts in thousands).

Prepare an income statement from an adjusted trial balance.

BE3.12 (LO 4) Partial adjusted trial balance data for Kwun Photos is presented in BE3.11. Prepare a retained earnings statement for the year assuming net income is ₩14,200 for the year and Retained Earnings is ₩7,240 on January 1 (amounts in thousands).

Prepare a retained earnings statement from an adjusted trial balance.

Prepare adjusting entries under alternative treatment of deferrals.

***BE3.13 (LO 5)** Eckholm Pet Grooming records all prepayments in income statement accounts. At April 30, the trial balance shows Supplies Expense HK$28,000, Service Revenue HK$92,000, and zero balances in related statement of financial position accounts. Prepare the adjusting entries at April 30 assuming (a) HK$4,000 of supplies on hand and (b) HK$30,000 of service revenue should be reported as unearned.

Identify characteristics of useful information.

***BE3.14 (LO 6)** The accompanying chart shows the qualitative characteristics of useful accounting information. Fill in the blanks.

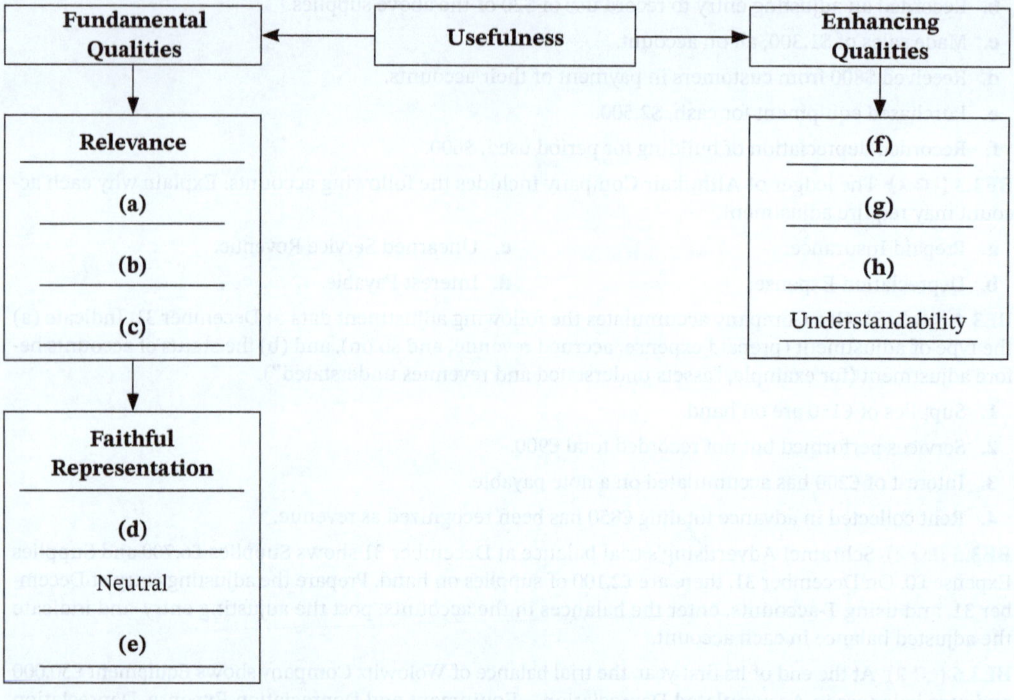

Identify characteristics of useful information.

***BE3.15 (LO 6)** Given the characteristics of useful accounting information, complete each of the following statements.

a. For information to be ______, it should have predictive value, confirmatory value, and be material.

b. ______ is the quality of information that gives assurance that the information accurately depicts what really happened.

c. ______ means using the same accounting principles and methods from year to year within a company.

Identify characteristics of useful information.

***BE3.16 (LO 6)** Here are some qualitative characteristics of useful accounting information:

1. Predictive value.
2. Neutral.
3. Verifiable.
4. Timely.

Match each qualitative characteristic to one of the following statements.

________ **a.** Accounting information should help provide accurate expectations about future events.

________ **b.** Accounting information cannot be selected, prepared, or presented to favor one set of interested users over another.

________ **c.** The quality of information that occurs when independent observers, using the same methods, obtain similar results.

________ **d.** Accounting information must be available to decision-makers before it loses its capacity to influence their decisions.

Define full disclosure principle.

***BE3.17 (LO 6)** Select the response that completes the following statement correctly. The full disclosure principle dictates that:

a. financial statements should disclose all assets at their cost.

b. financial statements should disclose only those events that can be measured in currency.

c. financial statements should disclose all events and circumstances that would matter to users of financial statements.

d. financial statements should not be relied on unless an auditor has expressed an unqualified opinion on them.

DO IT! Exercises

Identify timing concepts.

DO IT! 3.1 (LO 1) Below is a list of concepts in the left column, with a description of the concept in the right column. There are more descriptions provided than concepts. Match the description of the concept to the concept.

1. ______ Cash-basis accounting.
2. ______ Fiscal year.
3. ______ Revenue recognition principle.
4. ______ Expense recognition principle.

a. Monthly and quarterly time periods.
b. Accountants divide the economic life of a business into artificial time periods.
c. Efforts (expenses) should be recognized in the period in which a company uses assets or incurs liabilities to generate accomplishments (revenues).
d. Companies record revenues when they receive cash and record expenses when they pay out cash.
e. An accounting time period that is one year in length.
f. An accounting time period that starts on January 1 and ends on December 31.
g. Companies record transactions in the period in which the events occur.
h. Recognize revenue in the accounting period in which a performance obligation is satisfied.

Prepare adjusting entries for deferrals.

DO IT! 3.2 (LO 2) The ledger of Lafayette Ski School on March 31, 2029, includes the following selected accounts before adjusting entries.

	Debit	Credit
Prepaid Insurance	CHF 2,400	
Supplies	2,500	
Equipment	30,000	
Unearned Service Revenue		CHF9,000

An analysis of the accounts shows the following.

1. Insurance expires at the rate of CHF400 per month.
2. Supplies on hand total CHF1,600.
3. The equipment depreciates CHF480 per month.
4. During March, services were performed for two-fifths of the unearned service revenue.

Prepare the adjusting entries for the month of March.

Prepare adjusting entries for accruals.

DO IT! 3.3 (LO 3) Pegasus Computer Services began operations in July 2029. At the end of the month, the company prepares monthly financial statements. It has the following information for the month.

1. At July 31, the company owed employees €1,300 in salaries that the company will pay in August.
2. On July 1, the company borrowed €20,000 from a local bank on a 10-year note. The annual interest rate is 6%.
3. Service revenue unrecorded in July totaled €2,400.

Prepare the adjusting entries needed at July 31, 2029.

Calculate amounts from trial balance.

DO IT! 3.4 (LO 4) Ming Co. was organized on April 1, 2029. The company prepares quarterly financial statements. The adjusted trial balance amounts at June 30 are as follows.

	Debit		Credit
Cash	R$ 5,360	Accumulated Depreciation—Equipment	R$ 700
Accounts Receivable	580	Notes Payable	4,000
Prepaid Rent	1,120	Accounts Payable	790
Supplies	920	Salaries and Wages Payable	300
Equipment	12,000	Interest Payable	40
Dividends	500	Unearned Rent Revenue	400
Salaries and Wages Expense	7,400	Share Capital—Ordinary	11,200
Rent Expense	1,200	Service Revenue	11,360
Depreciation Expense	700	Rent Revenue	1,600
Supplies Expense	160		R$30,390
Utilities Expense	410		
Interest Expense	40		
	R$30,390		

a. Determine the net income for the quarter April 1 to June 30.

b. Determine the total assets and total liabilities at June 30, 2029, for Ming Co.

c. Determine the amount that appears for Retained Earnings at June 30, 2029.

Exercises

Determine point of revenue recognition.

E3.1 (LO 1) The following independent situations require professional judgment for determining when to recognize revenue from the transactions.

a. **Singapore Airlines** (SGP) sells you an advance-purchase airline ticket in September for your flight in December.

b. **Ultimate Electronics** (USA) sells you a home theater on a "no money down and full payment in three months" promotional deal.

c. The **Toronto Blue Jays** (CAN) sell season tickets online to games in the Skydome. Fans can purchase the tickets at any time, although the season doesn't officially begin until April. The major league baseball season runs from April through October.

d. **Barclays plc** (GBR) loans money on August 1. The loan and the interest are repayable in full in November.

e. In August, a customer orders a sweater from the **Target** (USA) website, paying with a Target credit card. The sweater arrives in September. Target sends a bill in October and receives payment in October.

Instructions

Identify when revenue should be recognized in each of the above situations.

Explain the time period assumption.

E3.2 (LO 1) Chloe Davis has prepared the following list of statements about the time period assumption.

1. Adjusting entries would not be necessary if a company's life were not divided into artificial time periods.
2. Taxing authorities require companies to file annual tax returns.
3. Accountants divide the economic life of a business into artificial time periods, but each transaction affects only one of these periods.
4. Accounting time periods are generally a month, a quarter, or a year.
5. A time period lasting one year is called an interim period.
6. All fiscal years are calendar years, but not all calendar years are fiscal years.

Instructions

Identify each statement as true or false. If false, indicate how to correct the statement.

Distinguish between cash and accrual basis of accounting.

E3.3 (LO 1) **Writing** On numerous occasions, proposals have surfaced to put governments on the accrual basis of accounting. This is no small issue. In many cases, significant unrecorded liabilities and losses would have to be recorded.

Instructions

a. What is the difference between accrual-basis accounting and cash-basis accounting?

b. Why would politicians prefer the cash basis over the accrual basis?

c. Explain in a letter why governments should adopt the accrual basis of accounting.

E3.4 (LO 1) Carillo Painting collected £108,000 from customers in 2029. Of the amount collected, £25,000 was for services performed in 2028. In addition, Carillo performed services worth £36,000 in 2029, which will not be collected until 2030.

Compute cash and accrual accounting income.

Carillo Painting also paid £72,000 for expenses in 2029. Of the amount paid, £30,000 was for expenses incurred on account in 2028. In addition, Carillo incurred £42,000 of expenses in 2029, which will not be paid until 2030.

Instructions

a. Compute 2029 cash-basis net income.

b. Compute 2029 accrual-basis net income.

E3.5 (LO 1, 2, 3) Yilmaz A.Ş. encounters the following situations:

Identify the type of adjusting entry needed.

1. Yilmaz collects ₺1,300 from a customer in 2029 for services to be performed in 2030.
2. Yilmaz incurs utilities expense that is not yet paid in cash or recorded.
3. Yilmaz's employees worked 3 days in 2029 but will not be paid until 2030.
4. Yilmaz performs services for customers but has not yet received cash or recorded the transaction.
5. Yilmaz paid ₺2,800 rent on December 1 for the 4 months starting December 1.
6. Yilmaz received cash for future services and recorded a liability until the service was performed.
7. Yilmaz performed consulting services for a client in December 2029. On December 31, it had not billed the client for services provided of ₺1,200.
8. Yilmaz paid cash for an expense and recorded an asset until the item was used up.
9. Yilmaz purchased ₺900 of supplies in 2029; at year-end, ₺400 of supplies remain unused.
10. Yilmaz purchased equipment on January 1, 2029; the equipment will be used for 5 years.
11. Yilmaz borrowed ₺12,000 on October 1, 2029, signing an 8% one-year note payable.

Instructions

Identify what type of adjusting entry (prepaid expense, unearned revenue, accrued expense, or accrued revenue) is needed in each situation at December 31, 2029.

E3.6 (LO 2, 3) Hwang Ltd. has the following balances in selected accounts on December 31, 2029.

Prepare adjusting entries from selected data.

Accounts Receivable	NT$ -0-
Accumulated Depreciation—Equipment	-0-
Equipment	7,000
Interest Payable	-0-
Notes Payable	10,000
Prepaid Insurance	2,100
Salaries and Wages Payable	-0-
Supplies	2,450
Unearned Service Revenue	32,000

All the accounts have normal balances. The information below has been gathered at December 31, 2029.

1. Hwang borrowed NT$10,000 by signing a 9%, one-year note on September 1, 2029.
2. A count of supplies on December 31, 2029, indicates that supplies of NT$900 are on hand.
3. Depreciation on the equipment for 2029 is NT$1,000.
4. Hwang paid NT$2,100 for 12 months of insurance coverage on June 1, 2029.
5. On December 1, 2029, Hwang collected NT$32,000 for consulting services to be performed from December 1, 2029, through March 31, 2030.
6. Hwang performed consulting services for a client in December 2029. The client will be billed NT$4,200.
7. Hwang pays its employees total salaries of NT$9,000 every Monday for the preceding 5-day week (Monday through Friday). On Monday, December 29, employees were paid for the week ending December 26. All employees worked the last 3 days of 2029.

Instructions

Prepare annual adjusting entries for the seven items described above.

Identify types of adjustments and account relationships.

E3.7 (LO 2, 3) Orwell Surf Shop accumulates the following adjustment data at December 31.

1. Services performed but unbilled total €3,000.
2. Supplies of €300 have been used.
3. Utilities expenses of €552 are unpaid.
4. Services performed of €260 collected in advance.
5. Salaries of €800 are unpaid.
6. Prepaid insurance totaling €350 has expired.

Instructions

For each of the above items indicate the following.

a. The type of adjustment (prepaid expense, unearned revenue, accrued revenue, or accrued expense).
b. The status of accounts before adjustment (overstatement or understatement).

Prepare adjusting entries from selected account data.

E3.8 (LO 2, 3) The ledger of Villa Rental Agency on March 31 of the current year includes the selected accounts, shown below, before adjusting entries have been prepared.

	Debit	Credit
Prepaid Insurance	€ 3,600	
Supplies	2,800	
Equipment	25,000	
Accumulated Depreciation—Equipment		€ 8,400
Notes Payable		20,000
Unearned Rent Revenue		10,200
Rent Revenue		60,000
Interest Expense	–0–	
Salaries and Wages Expense	14,000	

An analysis of the accounts shows the following.

1. The equipment depreciates €400 per month.
2. One-third of the unearned rent revenue was recognized as revenue during the quarter.
3. Interest of €500 is accrued on the notes payable.
4. Supplies on hand total €750.
5. Insurance expires at the rate of €300 per month.

Instructions

Prepare the adjusting entries at March 31, assuming that adjusting entries are made **quarterly**. Additional accounts are Depreciation Expense, Insurance Expense, Interest Payable, and Supplies Expense.

Prepare adjusting entries.

E3.9 (LO 2, 3) Lorena Manzone opened a dental practice on January 1, 2029. During the first month of operations, the following transactions occurred.

1. Performed services for patients who had dental plan insurance. At January 31, €785 of such services were performed but not yet recorded.
2. Utilities expenses incurred but not paid prior to January 31 totaled €650.
3. Purchased dental equipment on January 1 for €80,000, paying €30,000 in cash and signing a €50,000, 3-year note payable. The equipment depreciates €400 per month. Interest is €500 per month.
4. Purchased a one-year malpractice insurance policy on January 1 for €24,000.
5. Purchased €1,600 of dental supplies. On January 31, determined that €400 of supplies were on hand.

Instructions

Prepare the adjusting entries on January 31. Account titles are Accumulated Depreciation—Equipment, Depreciation Expense, Service Revenue, Accounts Receivable, Insurance Expense, Interest Expense, Interest Payable, Prepaid Insurance, Supplies, Supplies Expense, Utilities Expense, and Utilities Payable.

Prepare adjusting entries.

E3.10 (LO 2, 3) The trial balance for Yazici Advertising A.Ş. is shown in Illustration 3.4. Instead of the adjusting entries shown in the text at October 31, assume the following adjustment data.

1. Supplies on hand at October 31 total ₺500.
2. Expired insurance for the month is ₺120.
3. Depreciation for the month is ₺50.
4. Services related to unearned service revenue in October worth ₺600 were performed.
5. Services performed but not recorded at October 31 are ₺360.
6. Interest accrued at October 31 is ₺95.
7. Accrued salaries at October 31 are ₺1,625.

Instructions

Prepare the adjusting entries for the items above.

E3.11 (LO 1, 2, 3, 4) The income statement of Bjorn ASA for the month of July shows net income of €1,400 based on Service Revenue €5,500, Salaries and Wages Expense €2,300, Supplies Expense €1,200, and Utilities Expense €600. In reviewing the statement, you discover the following.

Prepare correct income statement.

1. Insurance expired during July of €500 was omitted.
2. Supplies expense includes €250 of supplies that are still on hand at July 31.
3. Depreciation on equipment of €150 was omitted.
4. Accrued but unpaid salaries and wages at July 31 of €400 were not included.
5. Services performed but unrecorded totaled €650.

Instructions

Prepare a correct income statement for July 2029.

E3.12 (LO 2, 3) This is a partial adjusted trial balance of Ramon Company.

Analyze adjusted data.

Ramon Company
Adjusted Trial Balance (partial)
January 31, 2029

	Debit	Credit
Supplies	$ 700	
Prepaid Insurance	1,560	
Salaries and Wages Payable		$1,060
Unearned Service Revenue		750
Supplies Expense	950	
Insurance Expense	520	
Salaries and Wages Expense	1,800	
Service Revenue		4,000

Instructions

Answer these questions, assuming the year begins January 1.

a. If the amount in Supplies Expense is the January 31 adjusting entry and $300 of supplies was purchased in January, what was the balance in Supplies on January 1?

b. If the amount in Insurance Expense is the January 31 adjusting entry and the original insurance premium was for one year, what was the total premium and when was the policy purchased?

c. If $2,500 of salaries was paid in January, what was the balance in Salaries and Wages Payable at December 31, 2028?

d. If $1,800 was received in January for services performed in January (no services are performed on credit), what was the balance in Unearned Service Revenue at December 31, 2028?

E3.13 (LO 2, 3) Selected accounts of Al-Kazaz Interiors are shown as follows.

Journalize basic transactions and adjusting entries.

Supplies Expense

7/31	900		

Supplies

7/1 Bal.	1,100	7/31	900
7/10	650		

Salaries and Wages Payable

		7/31	1,200

Accounts Receivable

7/31	500		

Unearned Service Revenue

7/31	1,150	7/1 Bal.	1,500
		7/20	1,000

Salaries and Wages Expense

7/15	1,200		
7/31	1,200		

Service Revenue

		7/14	2,200
		7/31	1,150
		7/31	500

Instructions

After analyzing the accounts, journalize (a) the July transactions and (b) the adjusting entries that were made on July 31. (*Hint:* July transactions were for cash.)

Prepare adjusting entries from selected account data.

E3.14 (LO 2, 3) The ledger of Yoon Lumber Supply on July 31, 2029, includes the selected accounts below before adjusting entries have been prepared.

	Debit	Credit
Notes Payable		₩ 20,000
Supplies	₩ 24,000	
Prepaid Rent	3,600	
Buildings	250,000	
Accumulated Depreciation—Buildings		140,000
Unearned Service Revenue		11,500

An analysis of the company's accounts shows the following.

1. The notes payable pay interest at a rate of 6% per year.
2. Supplies on hand at the end of the month totaled ₩18,600.
3. The balance in Prepaid Rent represents 4 months of rent costs.
4. Employees were owed ₩3,100 related to unpaid salaries and wages.
5. Depreciation on buildings is ₩6,000 per year.
6. During the month, the company satisfied obligations worth ₩4,700 related to the Unearned Services Revenue.
7. Unpaid maintenance and repairs costs were ₩2,300.

Instructions

Prepare the adjusting entries at July 31 assuming that adjusting entries are made monthly. Use additional accounts as needed.

Determine effect of adjusting entries.

E3.15 (LO 2, 3) On December 31, 2029, Waters Electricians prepared an income statement and statement of financial position, but failed to take into account three adjusting entries. The statement of financial position showed total assets €150,000, total liabilities €70,000, and equity €80,000. The incorrect income statement showed net income of €70,000.

The data for the three adjusting entries were:

1. Salaries and wages amounting to €10,000 for the last 2 days in December were not paid and not recorded. The next payroll will be in January.
2. Rent payments of €8,000 were received for two months in advance on December 1. The entire amount was credited to Unearned Rent Revenue when paid.
3. Depreciation expense for 2029 is €9,000.

Instructions

Complete the following table to correct the financial statement amounts shown (indicate deductions with parentheses).

Item	Net Income	Total Assets	Total Liabilities	Equity
Incorrect balances	€70,000	€150,000	€70,000	€80,000
Effects of:				
Salaries and Wages	______	______	______	______
Rent Revenue	______	______	______	______
Depreciation	______	______	______	______
Correct balances	______	______	______	______

Prepare and post transaction and adjusting entries for prepayments.

E3.16 (LO 2) Action Quest Games adjusts its accounts annually. The following information is available for the year ended December 31, 2029.

1. Purchased a 1-year insurance policy on June 1 for $1,800 cash.
2. Paid $6,500 on August 31 for 5 months' rent in advance.
3. On September 4, received $3,600 cash in advance from a company to sponsor a game night each month for a total of 9 months for the most improved students at a local school.
4. Signed a contract for cleaning services starting December 1 for $1,000 per month. Paid for the first 2 months on November 30. (*Hint:* Use the account Prepaid Cleaning to record prepayments.)
5. On December 5, received $1,500 in advance from a gaming club. Determined that on December 31, $475 of these games had not yet been played.

Instructions

a. For each of the above transactions, prepare the journal entry to record the initial transaction.

b. For each of the above transactions, prepare the adjusting journal entry that is required on December 31, (*Hint:* Use the account Service Revenue for item 3 and Maintenance and Repair Expense for item 4.)

c. Post the journal entries in parts (a) and (b) to T-accounts and determine the final balance in each account balance. (*Note:* Posting to the Cash account is not required.)

E3.17 (LO 3) Greenock Company has the following information available for accruals for the year ended December 31, 2029. The company adjusts its accounts annually.

Prepare adjusting and subsequent entries for accruals.

1. The December utility bill for $425 was unrecorded on December 31. Greenock paid the bill on January 11.
2. Greenock is open 7 days a week and employees are paid a total of $3,500 every Monday for a 7-day (Monday–Sunday) workweek. Assume December 31 is a Thursday, so employees will have worked 4 days (Monday, December 28–Thursday, December 31) that they have not been paid for by year-end. Employees will be paid next on January 4.
3. Greenock signed a $48,000, 5% bank loan on November 1, 2029, due in 2 years. No interest payments were made in 2029. Interest for 2029 was paid on January 1, 2030.
4. Greenock receives a fee from Pizza Shop next door for all pizzas sold to customers using Greenock's facility. The amount owed for December is $300, which Pizza Shop will pay on January 4. (*Hint:* Use the Service Revenue account.)
5. Greenock rented some of its unused warehouse space to a client for $6,000 a month, payable the first day of the following month. It received the rent for the month of December on January 2.

Instructions

a. For each situation, prepare the adjusting entry required at December 31. (Round all calculations to the nearest dollar.)

b. For each situation, prepare the journal entry to record the subsequent cash transaction in 2030.

E3.18 (LO 2, 3, 4) The trial balances before and after adjustment for Matusiak OAO at the end of its fiscal year are presented below.

Prepare adjusting entries from analysis of trial balances.

Matusiak OAO
Trial Balance
August 31, 2029

	Before Adjustment		After Adjustment	
	Dr.	**Cr.**	**Dr.**	**Cr.**
Cash	€10,400		€10,400	
Accounts Receivable	8,800		11,200	
Supplies	2,300		700	
Prepaid Insurance	4,000		2,500	
Equipment	14,000		14,000	
Accumulated Depreciation—Equipment		€ 3,600		€ 4,500
Accounts Payable		5,800		5,800
Salaries and Wages Payable		-0-		1,100
Unearned Rent Revenue		1,500		400
Share Capital—Ordinary		12,600		12,600
Retained Earnings		3,000		3,000
Service Revenue		34,000		36,400
Rent Revenue		11,000		12,100
Salaries and Wages Expense	17,000		18,100	
Supplies Expense	-0-		1,600	
Rent Expense	15,000		15,000	
Insurance Expense	-0-		1,500	
Depreciation Expense	-0-		900	
	€71,500	€71,500	€75,900	€75,900

Instructions

Prepare the adjusting entries that were made.

Prepare financial statements from adjusted trial balance.

E3.19 (LO 4) The adjusted trial balance for Matusiak OAO is given in E3.18.

Instructions

Prepare the income and retained earnings statements for the year and the statement of financial position at August 31.

Record transactions on accrual basis; convert revenue to cash receipts.

E3.20 (LO 2, 3) The following data are taken from the comparative statements of financial position of Cascade Billiards Club, which prepares its financial statements using the accrual basis of accounting.

Account Name	12/31/29 Balance	12/31/28 Balance
Accounts Receivable (from members)	$14,000	$ 9,000
Unearned Service Revenue	17,000	25,000

Members are billed based upon their use of the club's facilities. Unearned service revenues arise from the sale of gift certificates, which members can apply to their future use of club facilities. The 2029 income statement for the club showed that service revenue of $161,000 was recognized during the year.

Instructions

(*Hint:* You will probably find it helpful to use T-accounts to analyze these data.)

a. Prepare journal entries for each of the following events that took place during 2029.
1. Accounts receivable from 2028 were all collected.
2. Gift certificates outstanding at the end of 2028 were all redeemed.
3. An additional $38,000 worth of gift certificates were sold during 2029. A portion of these was used by the recipients during the year; the remainder was still outstanding at the end of 2029.
4. Services performed for members for 2029 were billed to members.
5. Accounts receivable for 2029 (i.e., those billed in item [4] above) were partially collected.

b. Determine the amount of cash received by the club, with respect to member services, during 2029.

Journalize adjusting entries.

***E3.21 (LO 5)** Vissar Foods has the following balances in selected accounts on December 31, 2029.

Service Revenue	€40,000
Insurance Expense	2,400
Supplies Expense	2,450

All the accounts have normal balances. Vissar Foods debits prepayments to expense accounts when paid, and credits unearned revenues to revenue accounts when received. The following information below has been gathered at December 31, 2029.

1. Vissar Foods paid €2,400 for 12 months of insurance coverage on June 1, 2029.
2. On December 1, 2029, Vissar collected €40,000 for consulting services to be performed from December 1, 2029, through March 31, 2030.
3. A count of supplies on December 31, 2029, indicates that supplies of €600 are on hand.

Instructions

Prepare the annual adjusting entries needed at December 31, 2029.

Journalize transactions and adjusting entries.

***E3.22 (LO 5)** At Cambridge Company, prepayments are debited to expense when paid, and unearned revenues are credited to revenue when cash is received. During January of the current year, the following transactions occurred.

Jan.	2	Paid $1,920 for fire insurance protection for the year.
	10	Paid $1,700 for supplies.
	15	Received $6,100 for services to be performed in the future.

On January 31, it is determined that $2,500 of the services were performed and that there are $650 of supplies on hand.

Instructions

a. Journalize and post the January transactions. (Use T-accounts.)

b. Journalize and post the adjusting entries at January 31.

c. Determine the ending balance in each of the accounts.

*E3.23 (LO 6) Presented below are the assumptions and principles discussed in Appendix 3B.

Identify accounting assumptions and principles.

1. Full disclosure principle.
2. Going concern assumption.
3. Monetary unit assumption.
4. Time period assumption.
5. Historical cost basis.
6. Economic entity assumption.

Instructions

Identify by number the accounting assumption or basis that is described below. Do not use a number more than once.

________ **a.** Is the rationale for why plant assets are not reported at liquidation value. (*Note:* Do not use the historical cost basis.)

________ **b.** Indicates that personal and business recordkeeping should be separately maintained.

________ **c.** Assumes that the monetary unit is the "measuring stick" used to report on financial performance.

________ **d.** Separates financial information into time periods for reporting purposes.

________ **e.** Measurement basis used when a reliable estimate of current value is not available.

________ **f.** Dictates that companies should disclose all circumstances and events that make a difference to financial statement users.

*E3.24 (LO 6) Weber Co. had three major business transactions during 2029.

Identify the assumption or principle that has been violated.

a. Reported at its current value of $260,000 merchandise inventory with a cost of $208,000 (in Canadian dollars).

b. The president of Weber Co., Austin Weber, purchased a truck for personal use and charged it to his expense account.

c. Weber Co. wanted to make its 2029 income look better, so it added 2 more weeks to the year (a 54-week year). Previous years were 52 weeks.

Instructions

In each situation, identify the assumption or principle that has been violated, if any, and discuss what the company should have done.

*E3.25 (LO 6) The following characteristics, assumptions, principles, or constraint guide the IASB when it creates accounting standards.

Identity financial accounting concepts and principles.

Relevance	Expense recognition principle
Faithful representation	Time period assumption
Comparability	Going concern assumption
Consistency	Historical cost basis
Monetary unit assumption	Full disclosure principle
Economic entity assumption	Materiality

Match each item above with a description below.

1. ________ Ability to easily evaluate one company's results relative to another's.
2. ________ Assumption that a company will continue to operate for the foreseeable future.
3. ________ The judgment concerning whether an item's size is large enough to matter to decision-makers.
4. ________ The reporting of all information that would make a difference to financial statement users.
5. ________ The practice of preparing financial statements at regular intervals.
6. ________ The quality of information that indicates the information makes a difference in a decision.
7. ________ A belief that items should be reported on the statement of financial position at the price that was paid to acquire them.
8. ________ A company's use of the same accounting principles and methods from year to year.
9. ________ Tracing accounting events to particular companies.
10. ________ The desire to minimize bias in financial statements.
11. ________ Reporting only those things that can be measured in monetary units.
12. ________ Dictates that efforts (expenses) be recognized in the period in which a company generates results (revenues).

Comment on the objective and qualitative characteristics of accounting information.

***E3.26 (LO 6) Writing** Speyeware International, headquartered in Vancouver, Canada, specializes in Internet safety and computer security products for both the home and commercial markets. In a recent statement of financial position, it reported a deficit of US$5,678,288. It has reported only net losses since its inception. In spite of these losses, Speyeware's shares have traded anywhere from a high of $3.70 to a low of $0.32 on the Canadian Venture Exchange (in Canadian dollars).

Speyeware's financial statements have historically been prepared in Canadian dollars. Recently, the company adopted the U.S. dollar as its reporting currency.

Instructions

a. What is the objective of financial reporting? How does this objective meet or not meet Speyeware's investors' needs?

b. Why would investors want to buy Speyeware's shares if the company has consistently reported losses over the last few years? Include in your answer an assessment of the relevance of the information reported on Speyeware's financial statements.

c. Comment on how the change in reporting information from Canadian dollars to U.S. dollars likely affected the readers of Speyeware's financial statements. Include in your answer an assessment of the comparability of the information.

Comment on the objective and qualitative characteristics of financial reporting.

***E3.27 (LO 6) Writing** A friend of yours, Mindy Gare, recently completed an undergraduate degree in science and has just started working with a biotechnology company. Mindy tells you that the company is trying to secure new sources of financing in order to proceed with the development of a new health-care product. Mindy said that her boss told her that the company must put together a report to present to potential investors.

Mindy thought that the company should include in this package the detailed scientific findings related to the Phase I clinical trials for this product. She said, "I know that the biotech industry sometimes has only a 10% success rate with new products, but if we report all the scientific findings, everyone will see what a sure success this is going to be! The president was talking about the importance of following some set of accounting principles. Why do we need to look at some accounting rules? What they need to realize is that we have scientific results that are quite encouraging, some of the most talented employees around, and the start of some really great customer relationships. We haven't made any sales yet, but we will. We just need the funds to get through all the clinical testing and get government approval for our product. Then these investors will be quite happy that they bought in to our company early!"

Instructions

a. What is accounting information?

b. Comment on how Mindy's suggestions for what should be reported to prospective investors conforms to the qualitative characteristics of accounting information. Do you think that the things that Mindy wants to include in the information for investors will conform to financial reporting guidelines?

Problems

Prepare adjusting entries, post to ledger accounts, and prepare an adjusted trial balance.

P3.1 (LO 2, 3, 4) Deanna Nardelli started her own consulting firm, Nardelli Consulting, on May 1, 2029. The trial balance at May 31 is as follows.

Nardelli Consulting
Trial Balance
May 31, 2029

Account Number		Debit	Credit
101	Cash	$ 4,500	
112	Accounts Receivable	6,000	
126	Supplies	1,900	
130	Prepaid Insurance	3,600	
149	Equipment	11,400	
201	Accounts Payable		$ 2,200
209	Unearned Service Revenue		2,000
311	Share Capital—Ordinary		20,000
400	Service Revenue		7,500
726	Salaries and Wages Expense	3,400	
729	Rent Expense	900	
		$31,700	$31,700

In addition to those accounts listed on the trial balance, the chart of accounts for Nardelli Consulting also contains the following accounts and account numbers: No. 150 Accumulated Depreciation—Equipment, No. 212 Salaries and Wages Payable, No. 631 Supplies Expense, No. 717 Depreciation Expense, No. 722 Insurance Expense, and No. 732 Utilities Expense.

Other data:

1. $900 of supplies have been used during the month.
2. Utilities expense incurred but not paid on May 31, 2029, $250.
3. The insurance policy for 2 years was purchased on May 1.
4. $400 of the balance in the unearned service revenue account remains unearned at the end of the month.
5. Assume May 31 is a Wednesday, and employees are paid on Fridays. Nardelli Consulting has two employees, who are paid $900 each for a 5-day work week.
6. The equipment has a 5-year life with no salvage value. It is being depreciated at $190 per month for 60 months.
7. Invoices representing $1,700 of services performed during the month have not been recorded as of May 31.

Instructions

a. Prepare the adjusting entries for the month of May. Use J4 as the page number for your journal.

b. Enter the totals from the trial balance as beginning account balances and place a check mark in the posting reference column. Post the adjusting entries to the ledger accounts.

c. Prepare an adjusted trial balance at May 31, 2029.

c. Adj. trial balance $34,920

P3.2 (LO 2, 3, 4) Lazy River Resort opened for business on May 1, 2029. Its trial balance before adjustment on May 31 is as follows.

Prepare adjusting entries, post, and prepare adjusted trial balance and financial statements.

Lazy River Resort
Trial Balance
May 31, 2029

Account Number		Debit	Credit
101	Cash	€ 3,400	
126	Supplies	2,080	
130	Prepaid Insurance	2,400	
140	Land	12,000	
141	Buildings	60,000	
149	Equipment	14,000	
201	Accounts Payable		€ 4,700
208	Unearned Rent Revenue		3,300
275	Mortgage Payable		40,000
311	Share Capital—Ordinary		41,380
332	Dividends	1,000	
429	Rent Revenue		10,300
610	Advertising Expense	600	
726	Salaries and Wages Expense	3,300	
732	Utilities Expense	900	
		€99,680	€99,680

In addition to those accounts listed on the trial balance, the chart of accounts for Lazy River Resort also contains the following accounts and account numbers: No. 142 Accumulated Depreciation—Buildings, No. 150 Accumulated Depreciation—Equipment, No. 212 Salaries and Wages Payable, No. 230 Interest Payable, No. 619 Depreciation Expense, No. 631 Supplies Expense, No. 718 Interest Expense, and No. 722 Insurance Expense.

Other data:

1. Prepaid insurance is a 1-year policy starting May 1, 2029.
2. A count of supplies shows €750 of unused supplies on May 31.
3. Annual depreciation is €3,600 on the buildings and €1,500 on equipment.
4. The mortgage interest rate is 6%. (The mortgage was taken out on May 1.)
5. Two-thirds of the unearned rent revenue is recognized as revenue.
6. Salaries of €750 are accrued and unpaid at May 31.

c. Adj. trial balance €101,055
d. Net income €4,795
Ending retained earnings €3,795
Total assets €91,925

Instructions

a. Journalize the adjusting entries on May 31.
b. Prepare a ledger using the three-column form of account. Enter the trial balance amounts and post the adjusting entries. (Use J1 as the posting reference.)
c. Prepare an adjusted trial balance on May 31.
d. Prepare an income statement and a retained earnings statement for the month of May and a statement of financial position at May 31.

Prepare adjusting entries and financial statements.

P3.3 (LO 2, 3, 4) Everett Co. was organized on July 1, 2029. Quarterly financial statements are prepared. The unadjusted and adjusted trial balances as of September 30 are shown as follows.

Everett Co.
Trial Balance
September 30, 2029

	Unadjusted		Adjusted	
	Dr.	Cr.	Dr.	Cr.
Cash	$ 8,700		$ 8,700	
Accounts Receivable	10,400		11,500	
Supplies	1,500		650	
Prepaid Rent	2,200		1,200	
Equipment	18,000		18,000	
Accumulated Depreciation—Equipment		$ -0-		$ 700
Notes Payable		10,000		10,000
Accounts Payable		2,500		2,500
Salaries and Wages Payable		-0-		100
Unearned Rent Revenue		1,900		1,050
Interest Payable		-0-		725
Share Capital—Ordinary		22,000		22,000
Dividends	1,600		1,600	
Service Revenue		16,000		17,100
Rent Revenue		1,410		2,260
Salaries and Wages Expense	8,000		8,725	
Rent Expense	1,900		2,900	
Depreciation Expense			700	
Supplies Expense			850	
Utilities Expense	1,510		1,510	
Interest Expense			100	
	$53,810	$53,810	$56,435	$56,435

Instructions

a. Journalize the adjusting entries that were made.
b. Prepare an income statement and a retained earnings statement for the 3 months ending September 30 and a statement of financial position at September 30.
c. If the note bears interest at 12%, how many months has it been outstanding? (The note and interest will be paid in 2 years.)

b. Net income $4,575
Ending retained earnings $2,975
Total assets $39,350

Prepare adjusting entries.

P3.4 (LO 2, 3) A review of the ledger of Lewis Company at December 31, 2029, produces the following data pertaining to the preparation of annual adjusting entries.

1. Insurance expense $6,800

1. Prepaid Insurance $15,200. The company has separate insurance policies on its buildings and its motor vehicles. Policy B4564 on the building was purchased on July 1, 2028, for $9,600. The policy has a term of 3 years. Policy A2958 on the vehicles was purchased on January 1, 2029, for $7,200. This policy has a term of 2 years.

2. Rent revenue $84,000

2. Unearned Rent Revenue $429,000. The company began subleasing office space in its new building on November 1, 2029. At December 31, the company had the following rental contracts that are paid in full for the entire term of the lease.

Date	Term (in months)	Monthly Rent Payment	Number of Leases
Nov. 1	9	$5,000	5
Dec. 1	6	$8,500	4

3. Notes Payable $40,000. This balance consists of a note for 6 months at an annual interest rate of 7%, dated November 1. Interest will be paid at note maturity. (Round to nearest dollar.)

3. Interest expense $467

4. Salaries and Wages Payable $0. There are eight salaried employees. Salaries are paid every Monday for the prior week. Five employees receive a salary of $600 each per week, and three employees earn $700 each per week. Assume December 31 is a Tuesday. Employees do not work weekends. All employees worked the last 2 days of December.

4. Salaries and wages expense $2,040

Instructions

Prepare the adjusting entries at December 31, 2029.

P3.5 (LO 2, 3, 4) On November 1, 2029, the account balances of Beck Equipment Repair were as follows.

Journalize transactions and follow through accounting cycle to preparation of financial statements.

No.		Debit	No.		Credit
101	Cash	£ 2,400	154	Accumulated Depreciation—Equipment	£ 2,000
112	Accounts Receivable	4,250	201	Accounts Payable	2,600
126	Supplies	1,800	209	Unearned Service Revenue	1,200
153	Equipment	12,000	212	Salaries and Wages Payable	700
			311	Share Capital—Ordinary	11,000
			320	Retained Earnings	2,950
		£20,450			£20,450

During November, the following summary transactions were completed.

Nov.	8	Paid £1,700 for salaries due employees, of which £700 is for October salaries.
	10	Received £3,620 cash from customers on account.
	12	Received £3,100 cash for services performed in November.
	15	Purchased equipment on account £2,000.
	17	Purchased supplies on account £700.
	20	Paid creditors on account £2,700.
	22	Paid November rent £400.
	25	Paid salaries £1,700.
	27	Performed services on account and billed customers for these services £2,200.
	29	Received £600 from customers for future service.

Adjustment data consist of:

1. Supplies on hand £1,400.
2. Accrued salaries payable £350.
3. Depreciation for the month is £200.
4. Services related to unearned service revenue of £1,220 were performed.

Instructions

a. Enter the November 1 balances in the ledger accounts.

b. Journalize the November transactions.

c. Post to the ledger accounts. Use J1 for the posting reference. Use the following additional accounts: No. 407 Service Revenue, No. 615 Depreciation Expense, No. 631 Supplies Expense, No. 726 Salaries and Wages Expense, and No. 729 Rent Expense.

d. Prepare a trial balance at November 30.

e. Journalize and post adjusting entries.

f. Prepare an adjusted trial balance.

g. Prepare an income statement and a retained earnings statement for November and a statement of financial position at November 30.

d. Trial balance £25,650
f. Adj. trial balance £26,200
g. Net income £1,770; Ending retained earnings £4,720
Total assets £19,250

***P3.6 (LO 2, 3, 4, 5)** Alpha's Graphics was organized on January 1, 2029, by Gabriel Alpha. At the end of the first 6 months of operations, the trial balance contained the following accounts.

Prepare adjusting entries, adjusted trial balance, and financial statements using appendix.

	Debit		Credit
Cash	€ 8,600	Notes Payable	€ 20,000
Accounts Receivable	14,000	Accounts Payable	9,000
Equipment	45,000	Share Capital—Ordinary	22,000
Insurance Expense	2,700	Service Revenue	58,100
Salaries and Wages Expense	30,000		
Supplies Expense	3,700		
Advertising Expense	1,900		
Rent Expense	1,500		
Utilities Expense	1,700		
	€109,100		€109,100

Analysis reveals the following additional data.

1. The €3,700 balance in Supplies Expense represents supplies purchased in January. At June 30, €1,300 of supplies are on hand.
2. The note payable was issued on February 1. It is a 6%, 6-month note.
3. The balance in Insurance Expense is the premium on a one-year policy, dated April 1, 2029.
4. Service revenues are credited to revenue when received. At June 30, services revenue of €1,300 are unearned.
5. Revenue for services performed but unrecorded at June 30 totals €2,000.
6. Depreciation is €2,250 per year.

Instructions

b. Adj. trial balance €112,725
c. Net income €19,000
Ending retained earnings €19,000
Total assets €71,800

a. Journalize the adjusting entries at June 30. (Assume adjustments are recorded every 6 months.)

b. Prepare an adjusted trial balance.

c. Prepare an income statement and retained earnings statement for the 6 months ended June 30 and a statement of financial position at June 30.

Expand Your Critical Thinking

Financial Reporting Problem: TSMC, Ltd. (TWN)

CT3.1 The financial statements of **TSMC** are presented in Appendix A. The complete annual report, including the notes to the financial statements, is available at the company's website.

Instructions

a. Using the consolidated financial statements and related information, identify items that may result in adjusting entries for prepayments.

b. Using the consolidated financial statements and related information, identify items that may result in adjusting entries for accruals.

Comparative Analysis Problem: Nestlé SA (CHE) vs. Delfi Limited (SGP)

CT3.2 Nestlé's financial statements are presented in Appendix B. Financial statements of **Delfi Limited** are presented in Appendix C. For Delphi, use the information in "The Group" columns.

Instructions

Based on information contained in these financial statements, determine the following for each company.

a. Net increase (decrease) in property, plant, and equipment (net) for the most recent fiscal year shown.

b. Increase (decrease) in marketing and administration expenses (Nestlé) and increase (decrease) in selling, distribution, and administrative expenses (Delfi) for the most recent fiscal year shown.

c. Increase (decrease) in non-current liabilities for the most recent fiscal year shown.

d. Increase (decrease) in profit for the most recent fiscal year shown.

e. Increase (decrease) in cash and cash equivalents for the most recent fiscal year shown.

Decision-Making Across the Organization

CT3.3 Happy Trails Park was organized on April 1, 2028, by Alicia Henry. Alicia is a good manager but a poor accountant. From the trial balance prepared by a part-time bookkeeper, Alicia prepared the following income statement for the quarter that ended March 31, 2029.

Happy Trails Park
Income Statement
For the Quarter Ended March 31, 2029

Revenues		
Rent revenue		£88,000
Operating expenses		
Advertising	£ 5,200	
Salaries and wages	28,800	
Utilities	750	
Depreciation	800	
Maintenance and repairs	4,000	
Total operating expenses		39,550
Net income		£48,450

Alicia thought that something was wrong with the statement because net income had never exceeded £20,000 in any one quarter. Knowing that you are an experienced accountant, she asks you to review the income statement and other data.

You first look at the trial balance. In addition to the account balances reported above in the income statement, the ledger contains the following additional selected balances at March 31, 2029.

Supplies	£ 6,200
Prepaid Insurance	7,500
Notes Payable	12,000

You then make inquiries and discover the following.

1. Rent revenue includes advanced rentals for summer occupancy £14,000.
2. There were £1,450 of supplies on hand at March 31.
3. Prepaid insurance resulted from the payment of a 1-year policy on January 1, 2029.
4. The mail on April 1, 2029, brought the following bills: advertising for week of March 24, £130; repairs made March 10, £260; and utilities, £120.
5. There are four employees, who receive wages totaling £300 per day. At March 31, 2 days' salaries and wages have been incurred but not paid.
6. The note payable is a 3-month, 10% note dated January 1, 2029.

Instructions

With the class divided into groups, answer the following.

a. Prepare a correct income statement for the quarter ended March 31, 2029.

b. Explain to Alicia the IFRSs that she did not follow in preparing her income statement and their effect on her results.

Communication Activity

CT3.4 In reviewing the accounts of Maribeth Ltd. at the end of the year, you discover that adjusting entries have not been made.

Instructions

Write an email to Maribeth Danon, the owner of Maribeth Ltd., that explains the following: the nature and purpose of adjusting entries, why adjusting entries are needed, and the types of adjusting entries that may be made.

Ethics Case

CT3.5 Watkin Exterminators is a pesticide manufacturer. Its sales declined greatly this year due to the passage of legislation outlawing the sale of several of Watkin's chemical pesticides. In the coming year, Watkin will have environmentally safe and competitive chemicals to replace these discontinued products. Sales in the next year are expected to greatly exceed any prior years. The decline in sales and profits appears to be a 1-year aberration. But even so, the company's president fears a large dip in the current year's profits. He believes that such a dip could cause a significant drop in the market price of Watkin's ordinary shares and make the company a takeover target.

To avoid this possibility, the company's president calls in Diane Leno, controller, to discuss this period's year-end adjusting entries. He urges her to accrue every possible revenue and to defer as many expenses as possible. He says to Diane, "We need the revenues this year, and next year can easily absorb expenses deferred from this year. We can't let our share price be hammered down!" Diane didn't get around to recording the adjusting entries until January 17, but she dated the entries December 31 as if they were recorded then. Diane also made every effort to comply with the president's request.

Instructions

a. Who are the stakeholders in this situation?

b. What are the ethical considerations of (1) the president's request and (2) Diane's dating the adjusting entries December 31?

c. Can Diane accrue revenues and defer expenses and still be ethical?

Answers to Insight and Accounting Across the Organization Questions

Reporting Revenue Accurately Q: In the past, why was it argued that Apple should spread the recognition of iPhone revenue over a two-year period, rather than recording it upfront? **A:** Apple promises to provide software updates over the life of the phone's use. Because this represents an unfulfilled performance obligation, it was argued that Apple should spread its revenue recognition over a two-year estimated life of the phone.

Turning Gift Cards into Revenue Q: Suppose that Tyler Palmer purchases a $100 gift card at Best Buy on December 24, 2028, and gives it to his partner, Anisha Jin, on December 25, 2028. On January 3, 2029, Anisha uses the card to purchase a $100 smart speaker. When do you think Best Buy should recognize revenue and why? **A:** According to the revenue recognition principle, companies should recognize revenue when the performance obligation is satisfied. In this case, revenue results when Best Buy provides the goods. Thus, when Best Buy receives cash in exchange for the gift card on December 24, 2028, it should recognize a liability, Unearned Sales Revenue, for $100. On January 3, 2029, when Anisha Jin exchanges the card for merchandise, Best Buy should recognize revenue and eliminate $100 from the balance in the Unearned Sales Revenue account.

Got Junk? Q: What accounting issue might this cause for companies? **A:** The statement of financial position should provide a fair representation of what a company owns and what it owes. If significant obligations of the company are not reported on the statement of financial position, the company's net worth (its equity) will be overstated. While it is true that it is not possible to estimate the **exact** amount of future environmental cleanup costs, it is becoming clear that companies will be held accountable. Therefore, it seems reasonable to accrue for environmental costs. Recognition of these liabilities provides a more accurate picture of the company's financial position. It also has the potential to improve the environment. As companies are forced to report these amounts on their financial statements, they will start to look for more effective and efficient means to reduce toxic waste and therefore reduce their costs.

A Look at U.S. GAAP

LEARNING OBJECTIVE 7

Compare the procedures for adjusting entries under IFRS and U.S. GAAP.

Measuring income, including the measurement of revenues and expenses in a manner that faithfully represents the economic activities of a business in a reliable manner, is a challenging task. Both the IASB and FASB have established and continue to develop their conceptual frameworks that will enable companies to better use the same principles to record transactions consistently over time. The objective of the conceptual framework project is to lead to standards that are more principles-based and internally consistent, which in turn will lead to the most useful financial reporting information.

Key Points

- As indicated above, both the IASB and FASB have established and are continuing to develop conceptual frameworks. Both frameworks are designed to address a common set of issues including the following.
  - What is the primary objective of financial reporting?
  - What are the qualitative characteristics that make accounting information useful?
  - What are the elements that make up the financial statements?
  - What basis should be used to measure and report, that is, should a historical cost or current value approach be used?
  - What criteria should be used to determine when revenue should be recognized and when expenses have been incurred?
  - What guidelines should be established for disclosing financial information?
- While the IASB and the FASB were working for a period of time to converge their conceptual frameworks, that project has become inactive.

Similarities

- Like IFRS, companies applying GAAP use accrual-basis accounting to ensure that they record transactions that change a company's financial statements in the period in which events occur.
- Similar to IFRS, cash-basis accounting is not in accordance with GAAP.
- GAAP also divides the economic life of companies into artificial time periods. Under both GAAP and IFRS, this is referred to as the *time period assumption*. GAAP requires that companies present a complete set of financial statements, including comparative information annually.
- The form and content of financial statements are very similar under GAAP and IFRS. Any significant differences will be discussed in those chapters that address specific financial statements.
- Revenue recognition fraud is a major issue in U.S. financial reporting. The same situation exists for most other countries as well.

Differences

- Prior to the issuance of a new joint revenue recognition standard by the IASB and the FASB, GAAP had more than 100 rules dealing with revenue recognition. Many of these rules were industry-specific. Revenue recognition under IFRS was determined primarily by a single standard, *IAS 18*. Despite this large disparity in the detailed guidance devoted to revenue recognition, the **general** revenue recognition principles required by IFRS were similar to those under GAAP.
- Internal controls are a system of checks and balances designed to detect and prevent fraud and errors. The Sarbanes-Oxley Act requires U.S. companies to enhance their systems of internal control. However, many foreign companies do not have this requirement.
- Under IFRS, revaluation to current value of items such as land and buildings is permitted. This is not permitted under GAAP.
- Under IFRS, the term "income" includes *both* revenues, which arise during the normal course of operating activities, and gains, which arise from activities outside of the normal sales of goods and services. The term income is not used this way under GAAP. Instead, under GAAP income refers to the net difference between revenues and expenses. Expenses under IFRS include both those costs incurred in the normal course of operations, as well as losses that are not part of normal operations. This is in contrast to GAAP, which defines each separately.

GAAP Practice

GAAP Self-Test Questions

1. GAAP:
   a. provides the same type of guidance as IFRS for revenue recognition.
   b. provides only general guidance on revenue recognition, compared to the detailed guidance provided by IFRS.
   c. allows revenue to be recognized when a customer makes an order.
   d. requires that revenue not be recognized until cash is received.
2. Which of the following statements is **false**?
   a. GAAP employs the time period assumption.
   b. GAAP employs accrual accounting.

c. GAAP requires that revenues and costs must be capable of being measured reliably.

d. GAAP uses the cash basis of accounting.

3. As a result of the revenue recognition project by the FASB and IASB:

a. revenue recognition places more emphasis on when the performance obligation is satisfied.

b. revenue recognition places more emphasis on when revenue is realized.

c. revenue recognition places more emphasis on when changes occur in related expenses.

d. revenue is no longer recorded unless cash has been received.

4. Which of the following is **false**?

a. Under IFRS, the term *income* describes both revenues and gains.

b. Under IFRS, the term *expenses* includes losses.

c. Under IFRS, firms do not engage in the closing process.

d. Previously, IFRS had fewer standards than GAAP that addressed revenue recognition.

5. Accrual-basis accounting:

a. is optional under GAAP.

b. results in companies recording transactions that change a company's financial statements in the period in which events occur.

c. has been eliminated as a result of the IASB/FASB joint project on revenue recognition.

d. is not consistent with the GAAP conceptual framework.

GAAP Exercises

GAAP3.1 Why might IFRS revalue land and buildings whereas under GAAP this practice is not permissible?

GAAP3.2 Under GAAP, do the definitions of revenues and expenses include gains and losses? Explain.

GAAP Financial Reporting Problem: Apple Inc. (USA)

GAAP3.3 The financial statements of **Apple** are presented in Appendix D. The complete annual report, including the notes to its financial statements, is available at the company's website.

Instructions

Visit Apple's company website and answer the following questions from its annual report.

a. Using the financial statements and related information, identify items that may result in adjusting entries for prepayments.

b. Using the financial statements and related information, identify items that may result in adjusting entries for accruals.

Answers to GAAP Self-Test Questions

1. a **2.** d **3.** a **4.** c **5.** b

CHAPTER 4

Completing the Accounting Cycle

LEARNING OBJECTIVES After studying this chapter, you should be able to:

LO 1 Prepare a worksheet.

LO 2 Prepare closing entries and a post-closing trial balance.

LO 3 Explain the steps in the accounting cycle and how to prepare correcting entries.

LO 4 Identify the sections of a classified statement of financial position.

Chapter Preview

Financial statements help employees understand what is happening in the business. In Chapter 3, we prepared financial statements directly from the adjusted trial balance. However, with so many details involved in the end-of-period accounting procedures, it is easy to make errors. One way to minimize errors in the records and to simplify the end-of-period procedures is to use a worksheet.

In this chapter, we will explain the role of the worksheet in accounting. We also will study the remaining steps in the accounting cycle, especially the closing process, again using Yazici Advertising A.Ş. as an example. Then, we will consider correcting entries and classified statements of financial position.

Completing the Accounting Cycle

The Worksheet	Closing the Books	The Accounting Cycle and Correcting Entries	Classified Statement of Financial Position
• Steps in preparing a worksheet • Preparing financial statements from a worksheet • Preparing adjusting entries from a worksheet	• Preparing closing entries • Posting closing entries • Preparing a post-closing trial balance	• Summary of the accounting cycle • Reversing entries • Correcting entries	• Intangible assets • Property, plant, and equipment • Long-term investments • Current assets • Equity • Non-current liabilities • Current liabilities

Practice

DO IT! 1 Worksheet

DO IT! 2 Closing Entries

DO IT! 3 Correcting Entries

DO IT! 4 Statement of Financial Position Classifications

Go to the Review and Practice section at the end of the chapter for a review of key concepts and practice applications with solutions.
Additional tutorials and practice opportunities are available in the Wiley online course.

Feature Story Speaking the Same Language

Recent events in the global capital markets underscore the importance of financial disclosure and transparency in markets around the world. As a result, many countries are examining their accounting and financial disclosure rules.

As indicated in the following graphic, financial regulators in over 150 countries now use the IFRSs issued by the International Accounting Standards Board (IASB).

What are the potential benefits of having countries use similar standards to prepare their financial statements? One benefit is that investors can compare the results of competing companies from different countries. A second benefit is it enhances efforts to finance growth. Companies (particularly in developing and emerging nations) need to raise funds from outside their borders. Companies that use IFRS gain credibility in the marketplace, which reduces financing costs.

The IASB's stated objectives are as follows.

- To develop a single set of high quality, understandable, enforceable and globally accepted international financial reporting standards (IFRSs) through its standard-setting body, the IASB.
- To promote the use and rigorous application of those standards.
- To take account of the financial reporting needs of emerging economies and small- and medium-sized entities (SMEs).
- To bring about convergence of national accounting standards and IFRSs to high-quality solutions.

Accounting standards may never be absolutely identical around the world. However, financial statement users have already benefitted from the increased comparability that has resulted from efforts to minimize differences in accounting standards.

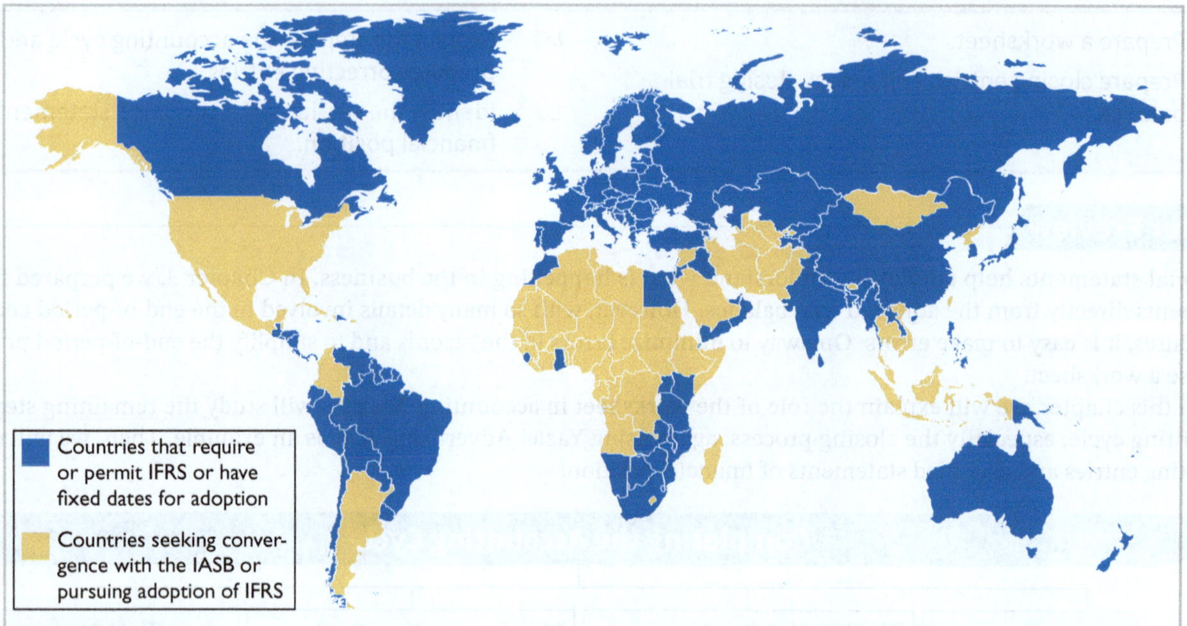

Source: PwC website.

TPG/Shutterstock

4.1 The Worksheet

LEARNING OBJECTIVE 1

Prepare a worksheet.

A **worksheet** is a multiple-column form used in the adjustment process and in preparing financial statements. As its name suggests, the worksheet is a working tool. **It is not a permanent accounting record**. It is neither a journal nor a part of the general ledger. The worksheet is merely a device used in preparing adjusting entries and the financial statements. Companies generally computerize worksheets using an electronic spreadsheet program such as **Microsoft** Excel.

Illustration 4.1 shows the basic form of a worksheet and the five steps for preparing it. Each step is performed in sequence.

- **The use of a worksheet is optional.**
- When a company chooses to use one, it prepares financial statements directly from the worksheet.
- It enters the adjustments in the worksheet columns and then journalizes and posts the adjustments after it has prepared the financial statements.

Thus, worksheets make it possible to provide the financial statements to management and other interested parties at an earlier date.

ILLUSTRATION 4.1 **Form and procedure for a worksheet**

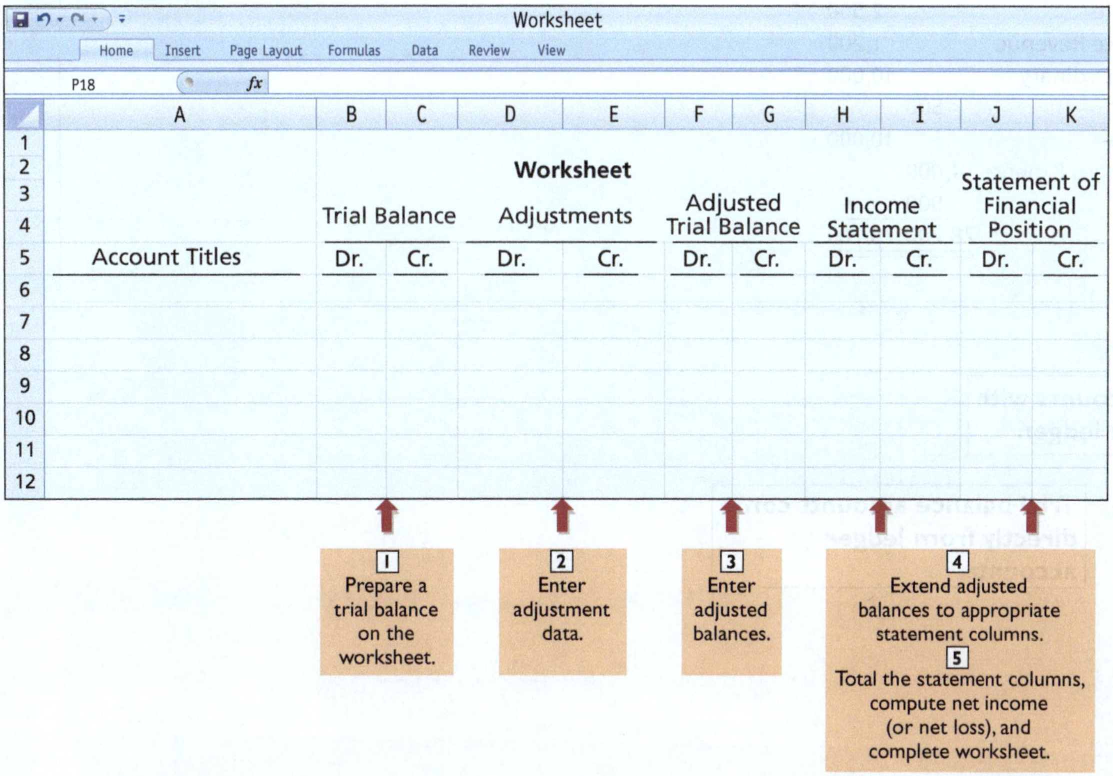

Steps in Preparing a Worksheet

We will use the October 31 trial balance and adjustment data of Yazici Advertising A.Ş. from Chapter 3 to illustrate how to prepare a worksheet. In the following pages, we describe and then demonstrate each step of the process.

Step 1 Prepare a Trial Balance on the Worksheet

The first step in preparing a worksheet is to enter all ledger accounts with balances in the account titles column and then enter debit and credit amounts from the ledger in the trial balance columns. **Illustration 4.2** shows the worksheet trial balance for Yazici Advertising. This trial balance is the same one that appears in Illustration 2.32 and Illustration 3.4.

ILLUSTRATION 4.2 **Preparing a trial balance**

Yazici Advertising

Home Insert Page Layout Formulas Data Review View

P18 *fx*

Yazici Advertising A.Ş.
Worksheet
For the Month Ended October 31, 2029

	Trial Balance		Adjustments		Adjusted Trial Balance		Income Statement		Statement of Financial Position	
Account Titles	Dr.	Cr.	Dr.	Cr.	Dr.	Cr.	Dr.	Cr.	Dr.	Cr.
Cash	15,200									
Supplies	2,500									
Prepaid Insurance	600									
Equipment	5,000									
Notes Payable		5,000								
Accounts Payable		2,500								
Unearned Service Revenue		1,200								
Share Capital—Ordinary		10,000								
Dividends	500									
Service Revenue		10,000								
Salaries and Wages Expense	4,000									
Rent Expense	900									
Totals	28,700	28,700								

Include all accounts with balances from ledger.

Trial balance amounts come directly from ledger accounts.

Step 2 Enter the Adjustments in the Adjustments Columns

As shown in **Illustration 4.3**, the second step when using a worksheet is to enter all adjustments in the adjustments columns. In entering the adjustments, use applicable trial balance accounts. If additional accounts are needed, insert them on the lines immediately below the trial balance totals. A different letter identifies the debit and credit for each adjusting entry. The term used to describe this process is **keying. Companies do not journalize the adjustments until after they complete the worksheet and prepare the financial statements**.

The adjustments for Yazici Advertising are the same as the adjustments in Illustration 3.24. They are keyed in the adjustments columns of the worksheet as follows.

a. Yazici debits an additional account, Supplies Expense, ₺1,500 for the cost of supplies used, and credits Supplies ₺1,500.

b. Yazici debits an additional account, Insurance Expense, ₺50 for the insurance that has expired, and credits Prepaid Insurance ₺50.

c. The company needs two additional depreciation accounts. It debits Depreciation Expense ₺40 for the month's depreciation, and credits Accumulated Depreciation—Equipment ₺40.

d. Yazici debits Unearned Service Revenue ₺400 for services performed, and credits Service Revenue ₺400.

e. Yazici debits an additional account, Accounts Receivable, ₺200 for services performed but not billed, and credits Service Revenue ₺200.

f. The company needs two additional accounts relating to interest. It debits Interest Expense ₺50 for accrued interest, and credits Interest Payable ₺50.

g. Yazici debits Salaries and Wages Expense ₺1,200 for accrued salaries, and credits an additional account, Salaries and Wages Payable, ₺1,200.

After Yazici has entered all the adjustments, the adjustments columns are totaled to prove their equality.

ILLUSTRATION 4.3 **Entering the adjustments in the adjustments columns**

Yazici Advertising

Home | Insert | Page Layout | Formulas | Data | Review | View

P18 fx

Yazici Advertising A.Ş.
Worksheet
For the Month Ended October 31, 2029

	A	B	C	D	E	F	G	H	I	J	K
5–6		Trial Balance		Adjustments		Adjusted Trial Balance		Income Statement		Statement of Financial Position	
7	Account Titles	Dr.	Cr.	Dr.	Cr.	Dr.	Cr.	Dr.	Cr.	Dr.	Cr.
8	Cash	15,200									
9	Supplies	2,500			(a) 1,500						
10	Prepaid Insurance	600			(b) 50						
11	Equipment	5,000									
12	Notes Payable		5,000								
13	Accounts Payable		2,500								
14	Unearned Service Revenue		1,200	(d) 400							
15	Share Capital—Ordinary		10,000								
16	Dividends	500									
17	Service Revenue		10,000		(d) 400						
18					(e) 200						
19	Salaries and Wages Expense	4,000		(g) 1,200							
20	Rent Expense	900									
21	Totals	28,700	28,700								
22											
23											
24	Supplies Expense			(a) 1,500							
25	Insurance Expense			(b) 50							
26	Accum. Depreciation—										
27	Equipment				(c) 40						
28	Depreciation Expense			(c) 40							
29	Accounts Receivable			(e) 200							
30	Interest Expense			(f) 50							
31	Interest Payable				(f) 50						
32	Salaries and Wages Payable				(g) 1,200						
33	Totals			3,440	3,440						
34											
35											
36											

Add additional accounts as needed to complete the adjustments:
(a) Supplies Used.
(b) Insurance Expired.
(c) Depreciation Expensed.
(d) Service Revenue Recognized.
(e) Service Revenue Accrued.
(f) Interest Accrued.
(g) Salaries Accrued.

Enter adjustment amounts in appropriate columns, and use letters to cross-reference the debit and credit adjustments.

Total adjustments columns and check for equality.

Step 3 Enter Adjusted Balances in the Adjusted Trial Balance Columns

As shown in **Illustration 4.4**, Yazici Advertising next determines the adjusted balance of an account by combining the amounts entered in the first four columns of the worksheet for each account. For example, the Prepaid Insurance account in the trial balance columns has a ₺600 debit balance and a ₺50 credit in the adjustments columns. The result is a ₺550 debit balance recorded in the adjusted trial balance columns. **For each account, the amount in the adjusted trial balance columns is the balance that will appear in the ledger after journalizing and posting the adjusting entries.** The balances in these columns are the same as those in the adjusted trial balance in Illustration 3.26.

After Yazici has entered all account balances in the adjusted trial balance columns, the columns are totaled to prove their equality. If the column totals do not agree, the financial statement columns will not balance and the financial statements will be incorrect.

ILLUSTRATION 4.4 **Entering adjusted balances in the adjusted trial balance columns**

Yazici Advertising

Yazici Advertising A.Ş.
Worksheet
For the Month Ended October 31, 2029

	A	B	C	D	E	F	G	H	I	J	K
5–6		Trial Balance		Adjustments		Adjusted Trial Balance		Income Statement		Statement of Financial Position	
7	Account Titles	Dr.	Cr.	Dr.	Cr.	Dr.	Cr.	Dr.	Cr.	Dr.	Cr.
8	Cash	15,200				15,200					
9	Supplies	2,500			(a) 1,500	1,000					
10	Prepaid Insurance	600			(b) 50	550					
11	Equipment	5,000				5,000					
12	Notes Payable		5,000				5,000				
13	Accounts Payable		2,500				2,500				
14	Unearned Service Revenue		1,200	(d) 400			800				
15	Share Capital—Ordinary		10,000				10,000				
16	Dividends	500				500					
17	Service Revenue		10,000		(d) 400		10,600				
18					(e) 200						
19	Salaries and Wages Expense	4,000		(g) 1,200		5,200					
20	Rent Expense	900				900					
21	Totals	28,700	28,700								
22											
23											
24	Supplies Expense			(a) 1,500		1,500					
25	Insurance Expense			(b) 50		50					
26	Accum. Depreciation—										
27	Equipment				(c) 40		40				
28	Depreciation Expense			(c) 40		40					
29	Accounts Receivable			(e) 200		200					
30	Interest Expense			(f) 50		50					
31	Interest Payable				(f) 50		50				
32	Salaries and Wages Payable				(g) 1,200		1,200				
33	Totals			3,440	3,440	30,190	30,190				

Combine trial balance amounts with adjustment amounts to obtain the adjusted trial balance. Total adjusted trial balance columns and check for equality.

Step 4 Extend Adjusted Trial Balance Amounts to Appropriate Financial Statement Columns

HELPFUL HINT

Every adjusted trial balance amount must be extended to one of the four statement columns.

As shown in **Illustration 4.5**, the fourth step is to extend adjusted trial balance amounts to the income statement and statement of financial position columns of the worksheet (see **Helpful Hint**). Yazici Advertising enters statement of financial position accounts in the appropriate statement of financial position debit and credit columns. For instance, it enters Cash in the statement of financial position debit column, and Notes Payable in the statement of financial position credit column. Yazici extends Accumulated Depreciation—Equipment to the statement of financial position credit column. The reason is that accumulated depreciation is a contra asset account with a credit balance.

Because the worksheet does not have columns for the retained earnings statement, Yazici extends the balance in Share Capital—Ordinary and Retained Earnings, if any, to the statement of financial position credit column. In addition, it extends the balance in Dividends to the statement of financial position debit column because it is an equity account with a debit balance.

ILLUSTRATION 4.5 **Extending the adjusted trial balance amounts to appropriate financial statement columns**

Yazici Advertising

Yazici Advertising A.Ş.
Worksheet
For the Month Ended October 31, 2029

	A	B	C	D	E	F	G	H	I	J	K
		Trial Balance		Adjustments		Adjusted Trial Balance		Income Statement		Statement of Financial Position	
7	Account Titles	Dr.	Cr.	Dr.	Cr.	Dr.	Cr.	Dr.	Cr.	Dr.	Cr.
8	Cash	15,200				15,200				15,200	
9	Supplies	2,500			(a) 1,500	1,000				1,000	
10	Prepaid Insurance	600			(b) 50	550				550	
11	Equipment	5,000				5,000				5,000	
12	Notes Payable		5,000				5,000				5,000
13	Accounts Payable		2,500				2,500				2,500
14	Unearned Service Revenue		1,200	(d) 400			800				800
15	Share Capital—Ordinary		10,000				10,000				10,000
16	Dividends	500				500				500	
17	Service Revenue		10,000		(d) 400		10,600		10,600		
18					(e) 200						
19	Salaries and Wages Expense	4,000		(g) 1,200		5,200		5,200			
20	Rent Expense	900				900		900			
21	Totals	28,700	28,700								
22											
23											
24	Supplies Expense			(a) 1,500		1,500		1,500			
25	Insurance Expense			(b) 50		50		50			
26	Accum. Depreciation—										
27	Equipment				(c) 40		40				40
28	Depreciation Expense			(c) 40		40		40			
29	Accounts Receivable			(e) 200		200				200	
30	Interest Expense			(f) 50		50		50			
31	Interest Payable				(f) 50		50				50
32	Salaries and Wages Payable				(g) 1,200		1,200				1,200
33	Totals			3,440	3,440	30,190	30,190				

Extend all revenue and expense account balances to the income statement columns.

Extend all asset and liability account balances, as well as Share Capital—Ordinary and Dividends account balances, to the statement of financial position columns.

Step 5 Total the Statement Columns, Compute the Net Income (or Net Loss), and Complete the Worksheet

As shown in **Illustration 4.6**, Yazici Advertising must now total each of the financial statement columns. The net income or loss for the period is the difference between the totals of the two income statement columns.

If total credits exceed total debits, the result is net income.

- In such a case, the company inserts the words "Net Income" in the account titles space.
- It then enters the amount in the income statement debit column and the statement of financial position credit column. **The debit amount balances the income statement columns; the credit amount balances the statement of financial position columns.**
- In addition, the credit in the statement of financial position column indicates the increase in equity resulting from net income.

What if total debits in the income statement columns exceed total credits?

- In that case, Yazici has a net loss.
- It enters the amount of the net loss in the income statement credit column and the statement of financial position debit column.

After entering the net income or net loss, Yazici determines new column totals.

The totals shown in the debit and credit income statement columns will match. So will the totals shown in the debit and credit statement of financial position columns. If either the income statement columns or the statement of financial position columns are not equal after the net income or net loss has been entered, there is an error in the worksheet.

ILLUSTRATION 4.6 **Computing net income or net loss and completing the worksheet**

Yazici Advertising

Home Insert Page Layout Formulas Data Review View

Yazici Advertising A.Ş.
Worksheet
For the Month Ended October 31, 2029

	A	B	C	D	E	F	G	H	I	J	K
5–6		Trial Balance		Adjustments		Adjusted Trial Balance		Income Statement		Statement of Financial Position	
7	Account Titles	Dr.	Cr.	Dr.	Cr.	Dr.	Cr.	Dr.	Cr.	Dr.	Cr.
8	Cash	15,200				15,200				15,200	
9	Supplies	2,500			(a) 1,500	1,000				1,000	
10	Prepaid Insurance	600			(b) 50	550				550	
11	Equipment	5,000				5,000				5,000	
12	Notes Payable		5,000				5,000				5,000
13	Accounts Payable		2,500				2,500				2,500
14	Unearned Service Revenue		1,200	(d) 400			800				800
15	Share Capital—Ordinary		10,000				10,000				10,000
16	Dividends	500				500				500	
17	Service Revenue		10,000		(d) 400		10,600		10,600		
18					(e) 200						
19	Salaries and Wages Expense	4,000		(g) 1,200		5,200		5,200			
20	Rent Expense	900				900		900			
21	Totals	28,700	28,700								
22											
23											
24	Supplies Expense			(a) 1,500		1,500		1,500			
25	Insurance Expense			(b) 50		50		50			
26	Accum. Depreciation—										
27	Equipment				(c) 40		40				40
28	Depreciation Expense			(c) 40		40		40			
29	Accounts Receivable			(e) 200		200				200	
30	Interest Expense			(f) 50		50		50			
31	Interest Payable				(f) 50		50				50
32	Salaries and Wages Payable				(g) 1,200		1,200				1,200
33	Totals			3,440	3,440	30,190	30,190	7,740	10,600	22,450	19,590
34											
35	Net Income							2,860			2,860
36	Totals							10,600	10,600	22,450	22,450

The difference between the totals of the two income statement columns determines net income or net loss.

Net income is extended to the credit column of the statement of financial position columns. (Net loss would be extended to the debit column.)

Preparing Financial Statements from a Worksheet

After a company has completed a worksheet, it has at hand all the data required for preparation of financial statements.

- The income statement is prepared from the income statement columns.
- The retained earnings statement and statement of financial position are prepared from the statement of financial position columns.

Illustration 4.7 shows the financial statements prepared from Yazici Advertising's worksheet. At this point, the company has not journalized or posted adjusting entries. Therefore, ledger balances for some accounts are not the same as the financial statement amounts.

The amount shown for Share Capital—Ordinary on the worksheet does not change from the beginning to the end of the period unless the company issues additional ordinary shares during the period. Because there was no balance in Yazici's Retained Earnings, the account is not listed on the worksheet. Only after dividends and net income (or loss) are posted to Retained Earnings does this account have a balance at the end of the first year of the business.

Using a worksheet, companies can prepare financial statements before they journalize and post adjusting entries.

- However, the completed worksheet is not a substitute for formal financial statements. The format of the data in the financial statement columns of the worksheet is not the same as the format of the financial statements.
- A worksheet is essentially a working tool of the accountant; companies do not distribute it to management and other parties.

ILLUSTRATION 4.7

Financial statements from a worksheet

Yazici Advertising A.Ş.
Income Statement
For the Month Ended October 31, 2029

Revenues		
Service revenue		₺10,600
Expenses		
Salaries and wages expense	₺5,200	
Supplies expense	1,500	
Rent expense	900	
Insurance expense	50	
Interest expense	50	
Depreciation expense	40	
Total expenses		7,740
Net income		₺ 2,860

Yazici Advertising A.Ş.
Retained Earnings Statement
For the Month Ended October 31, 2029

Retained earnings, October 1	₺ -0-
Add: Net income	2,860
	2,860
Less: Dividends	500
Retained earnings, October 31	₺2,360

(continues)

ILLUSTRATION 4.7
(continued)

Yazici Advertising A.Ş.
Statement of Financial Position
October 31, 2029

Assets		
Equipment	₺5,000	
Less: Accumulated depreciation—equipment	40	₺ 4,960
Prepaid insurance		550
Supplies		1,000
Accounts receivable		200
Cash		15,200
Total assets		₺21,910
Equity and Liabilities		
Equity		
Share capital—ordinary	₺10,000	
Retained earnings	2,360	₺12,360
Liabilities		
Notes payable	5,000	
Accounts payable	2,500	
Interest payable	50	
Unearned service revenue	800	
Salaries and wages payable	1,200	9,550
Total equity and liabilities		₺21,910

Preparing Adjusting Entries from a Worksheet

A worksheet is not a journal, and it cannot be used as a basis for posting to ledger accounts. To adjust the accounts, the company must journalize the adjustments and post them to the ledger.

HELPFUL HINT
Note that writing the explanation to the adjustment at the bottom of the worksheet is not required.

- The adjusting entries are prepared from the adjustments columns of the worksheet.
- The reference letters in the adjustments columns and the explanations of the adjustments at the bottom of the worksheet help identify the adjusting entries (see **Helpful Hint**).
- The journalizing and posting of adjusting entries follows the preparation of financial statements when a worksheet is used.

The adjusting entries on October 31 for Yazici Advertising are the same as those shown in Illustration 3.24.

ACTION PLAN

- **Statement of financial position: Extend assets to debit column. Extend liabilities to credit column. Extend contra assets to credit column. Extend Dividends account to debit column.**
- **Income statement: Extend expenses to debit column. Extend revenues to credit column.**

DO IT! 1 | Worksheet

Susan Elbe is preparing a worksheet. Explain to Susan how she should extend the following adjusted trial balance accounts to the financial statement columns of the worksheet.

Cash	Dividends
Accumulated Depreciation—Equipment	Service Revenue
Accounts Payable	Salaries and Wages Expense

Solution

Income statement debit column—Salaries and Wages Expense
Income statement credit column—Service Revenue
Statement of financial position debit column—Cash; Dividends
Statement of financial position credit column—Accumulated Depreciation—Equipment; Accounts Payable

Related exercise material: **BE4.1, BE4.2, BE4.3, DO IT! 4.1, E4.1, E4.2, E4.3, E4.5, and E4.6.**

4.2 Closing the Books

LEARNING OBJECTIVE 2

Prepare closing entries and a post-closing trial balance.

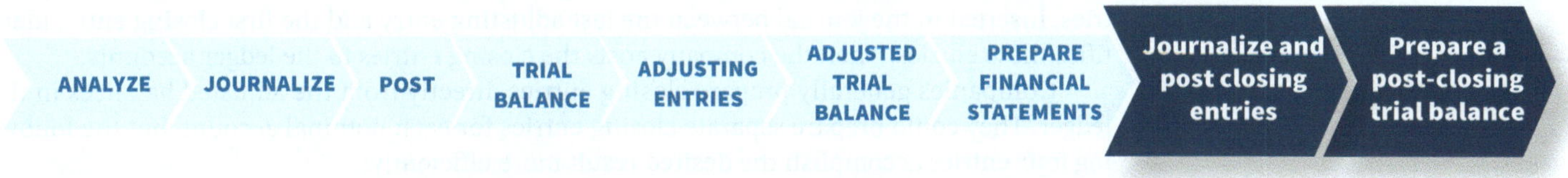

At the end of the accounting period, the company makes the accounts ready for the next period. This is called **closing the books**. In closing the books, the company distinguishes between temporary and permanent accounts.

- **Temporary accounts** relate only to a given accounting period. They include all income statement accounts and the Dividends account. **The company closes all temporary accounts at the end of the period.**
- **Permanent accounts** relate to one or more future accounting periods. They consist of all statement of financial position accounts, including equity accounts. **Permanent accounts are not closed from period to period.** Instead, the company carries forward the balances of permanent accounts into the next accounting period.

ALTERNATIVE TERMINOLOGY

Temporary accounts are sometimes called *nominal accounts*, and permanent accounts are sometimes called *real accounts*.

Illustration 4.8 identifies the accounts in each category (see **Alternative Terminology**).

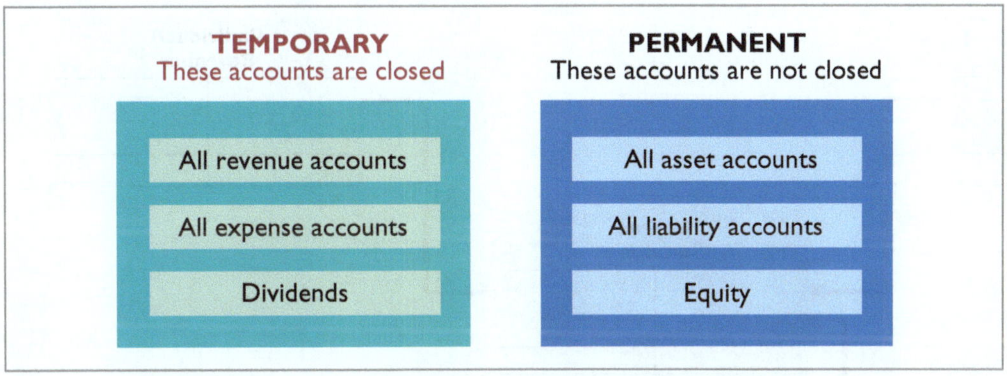

ILLUSTRATION 4.8

Temporary versus permanent accounts

Preparing Closing Entries

At the end of the accounting period, the company transfers temporary account balances to the permanent equity account, Retained Earnings, by means of closing entries.

- **Closing entries** formally recognize in the ledger the transfer of net income (or net loss) and Dividends to Retained Earnings. The retained earnings statement shows the results of these entries.
- **Closing entries also produce a zero balance in each temporary account.**
- The temporary accounts are then ready to accumulate data in the next accounting period separate from the data of prior periods. Permanent accounts are not closed.

Journalizing and posting closing entries is a required step in the accounting cycle (see Illustration 4.15). The company performs this step after it has prepared financial statements. In contrast to the steps in the cycle that you have already studied, companies generally journalize and post closing entries **only at the end of the annual accounting period**. Thus, all temporary accounts will contain data for the entire accounting period.

In preparing closing entries, companies could close each income statement account directly to Retained Earnings. However, to do so would result in excessive detail in the permanent Retained Earnings account.

- Instead, companies close the revenue and expense accounts to another temporary account, **Income Summary**.
- They then transfer the resulting net income or net loss from this account to Retained Earnings.

Companies **record closing entries in the general journal**. A center caption, Closing Entries, inserted in the journal between the last adjusting entry and the first closing entry, identifies these entries. Then the company posts the closing entries to the ledger accounts.

Companies generally prepare closing entries directly from the adjusted balances in the ledger. They could prepare separate closing entries for each nominal account, but the following four entries accomplish the desired result more efficiently:

HELPFUL HINT

Dividends are closed directly to Retained Earnings and not to Income Summary. Dividends are not an expense.

1. Debit each revenue account for its balance, and credit Income Summary for total revenues.
2. Debit Income Summary for total expenses, and credit each expense account for its balance.
3. Debit Income Summary and credit Retained Earnings for the amount of net income.
4. Debit Retained Earnings for the balance in the Dividends account, and credit Dividends for the same amount (see **Helpful Hint**).

Illustration 4.9 presents a diagram of the closing process. In it, the boxed numbers refer to the four entries required in the closing process.

ILLUSTRATION 4.9 **Diagram of closing process**

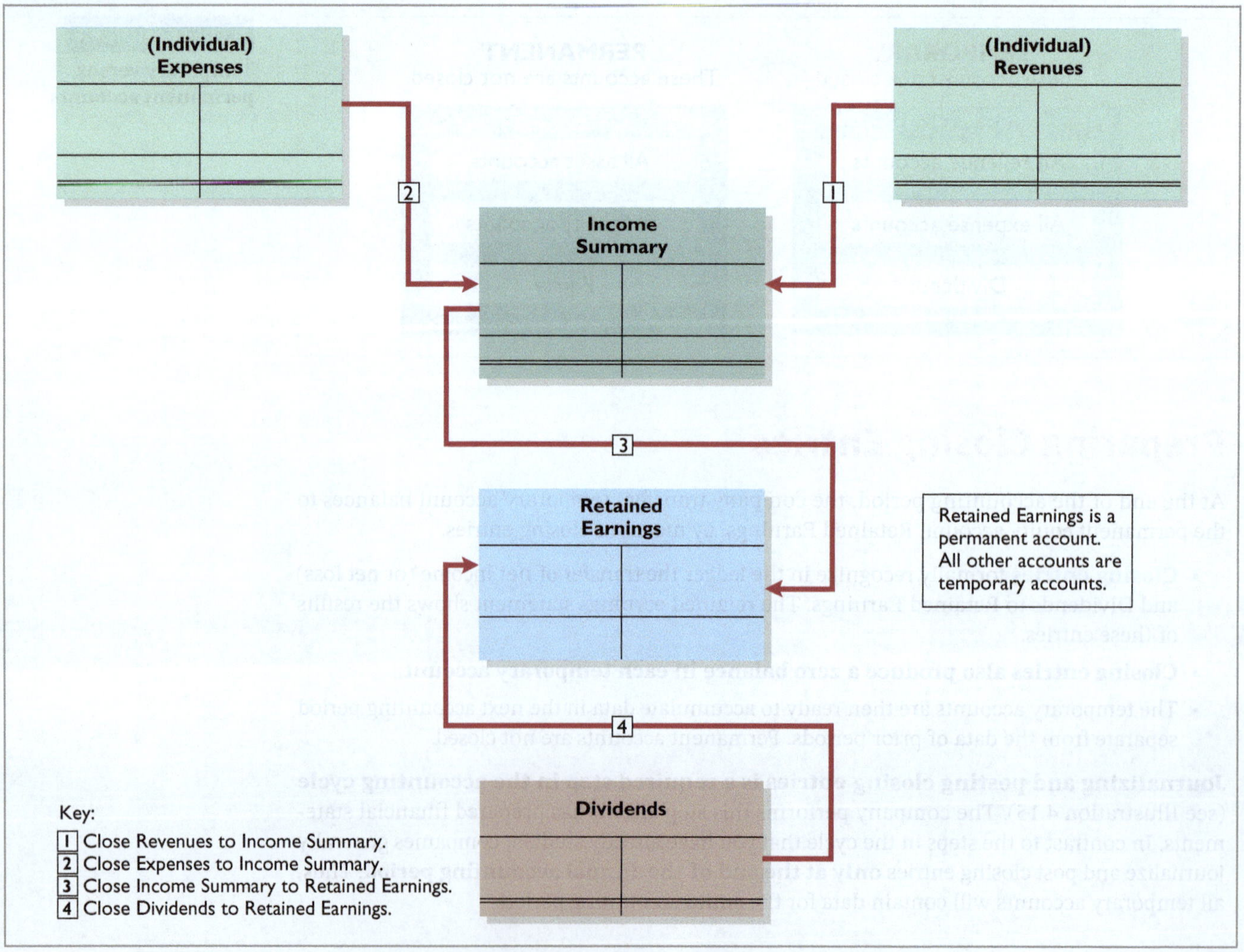

If there were a net loss (because expenses exceeded revenues), entry 3 in Illustration 4.9 would be reversed: there would be a credit to Income Summary and a debit to Retained Earnings.

Many companies have begun to employ **robotic process automation (RPA)** to improve their closing process. RPA involves the use of computer programs, instead of humans, to perform repetitive rules-based tasks. We will discuss other applications of RPA in later chapters.

Closing Entries Illustrated

In practice, companies generally prepare closing entries only at the end of the annual accounting period. However, to illustrate the journalizing and posting of closing entries, we will assume that Yazici Advertising closes its books monthly. **Illustration 4.10** shows the closing entries at October 31. (The numbers in parentheses before each entry correspond to the four entries diagrammed in Illustration 4.9.)

ILLUSTRATION 4.10

Closing entries journalized

GENERAL JOURNAL — J3

Date	Account Titles and Explanation	Ref.	Debit	Credit
	Closing Entries			
2029	(1)			
Oct. 31	Service Revenue	400	10,600	
	Income Summary	350		10,600
	(To close revenue account)			
	(2)			
31	Income Summary	350	7,740	
	Supplies Expense	631		1,500
	Depreciation Expense	711		40
	Insurance Expense	722		50
	Salaries and Wages Expense	726		5,200
	Rent Expense	729		900
	Interest Expense	905		50
	(To close expense accounts)			
	(3)			
31	Income Summary (₺10,600 – ₺7,740)	350	2,860	
	Retained Earnings	320		2,860
	(To close net income to retained earnings)			
	(4)			
31	Retained Earnings	320	500	
	Dividends	332		500
	(To close dividends to retained earnings)			

Note that the amounts for Income Summary in entries (1) and (2) are the totals of the income statement credit and debit columns, respectively, in the worksheet.

A couple of cautions in preparing closing entries.

1. Avoid unintentionally doubling the revenue and expense balances rather than zeroing them.
2. Do not close Dividends through the Income Summary account. **Dividends are not an expense, and they are not a factor in determining net income.**

Posting Closing Entries

Illustration 4.11 shows the posting of the closing entries and the underlining (ruling) of the accounts.

- Note that all temporary accounts have zero balances after posting the closing entries.

HELPFUL HINT

The balance in Income Summary before it is closed must equal the net income or net loss for the period.

- Realize that the balance in Retained Earnings represents the accumulated undistributed earnings of the corporation at the end of the accounting period. This balance is shown on the statement of financial position and is the ending amount reported on the retained earnings statement, as shown in Illustration 4.7.

Yazici Advertising uses the Income Summary account only in closing. It does not journalize and post entries to this account during the year (see **Helpful Hint**).

ILLUSTRATION 4.11 **Posting of closing entries**

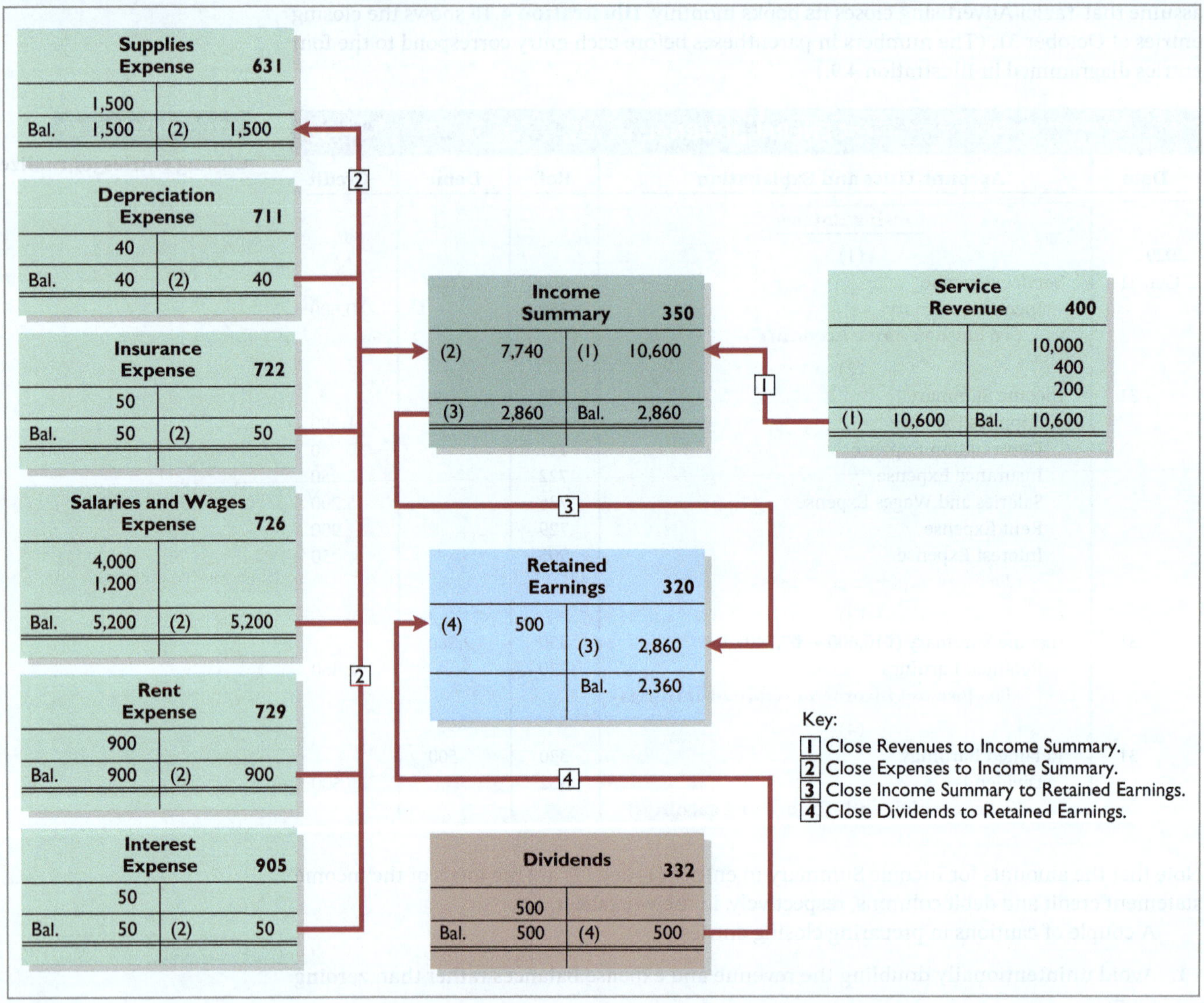

As part of the closing process, Yazici totals, balances, and double-underlines its temporary accounts—revenues, expenses, and Dividends, as shown in T-account form in Illustration 4.11. It does not close its permanent accounts—assets, liabilities, and equity (Share Capital—Ordinary and Retained Earnings). Instead, Yazici draws a single underline beneath the current-period entries for the permanent accounts. The account balance is then entered below the single underline and is carried forward to the next period (for example, see Retained Earnings).

Accounting Across the Organization

stevecoleimages/E+/
Getty Images

Transforming the Closing Process

Companies constantly look throughout their organization to find more efficient and effective ways to conduct business. The closing process is one of the areas where companies are always looking for improvement. The overall goal is to become more efficient by reducing the amount of time and effort that it takes to close the books each period, while ensuring that the closing process is as error-free as possible.

Like many aspects of business, new technologies are helping to improve the closing process. Companies now use software robots and processing mining to drive this forward. The robots work without the need for time off or even rest and do so with high accuracy. Process mining is used to identify and remove parts of the closing process that are slow or error-prone. The benefits to the business are not only a better closing process but freeing up time for the accounting staff to focus on higher-value activities, such as analysis and planning.

Source: Adapted from Nicolas Valette, Ludovic Deprez, and Camille Marchand, "Staying on Top of Your Financial Closing Process," *ey.com* (June 24, 2021).

Who else benefits from a shorter closing process? (Answer is available near the end of the chapter.)

Preparing a Post-Closing Trial Balance

After Yazici Advertising has journalized and posted all closing entries, it prepares another trial balance, called a **post-closing trial balance**, from the ledger.

- The post-closing trial balance lists permanent accounts and their balances after the journalizing and posting of closing entries.
- The purpose of the post-closing trial balance is **to prove the equality of the permanent account balances carried forward into the next accounting period.**
- Since all temporary accounts will have zero balances, **the post-closing trial balance will contain only permanent— statement of financial position—accounts.**

Illustration 4.12 shows the post-closing trial balance for Yazici Advertising A.Ş.

ILLUSTRATION 4.12
Post-closing trial balance

Yazici Advertising A.Ş.
Post-Closing Trial Balance
October 31, 2029

	Debit	Credit
Cash	₺15,200	
Accounts Receivable	200	
Supplies	1,000	
Prepaid Insurance	550	
Equipment	5,000	
Accumulated Depreciation—Equipment		₺ 40
Notes Payable		5,000
Accounts Payable		2,500
Unearned Service Revenue		800
Salaries and Wages Payable		1,200
Interest Payable		50
Share Capital—Ordinary		10,000
Retained Earnings		2,360
	₺21,950	₺21,950

Yazici prepares the post-closing trial balance from the permanent accounts in the ledger. **Illustration 4.13** shows the permanent accounts in Yazici's general ledger.

ILLUSTRATION 4.13 **General ledger, permanent accounts**

(Permanent Accounts Only)

GENERAL LEDGER

Cash **No. 101**

Date	Explanation	Ref.	Debit	Credit	Balance
2029					
Oct. 1		J1	10,000		10,000
2		J1	1,200		11,200
3		J1		900	10,300
4		J1		600	9,700
20		J1		500	9,200
26		J1		4,000	5,200
31		J1	10,000		**15,200**

Accounts Receivable **No. 112**

Date	Explanation	Ref.	Debit	Credit	Balance
2029					
Oct. 31	Adj. entry	J2	**200**		**200**

Supplies **No. 126**

Date	Explanation	Ref.	Debit	Credit	Balance
2029					
Oct. 5		J1	2,500		2,500
31	Adj. entry	J2		**1,500**	**1,000**

Prepaid Insurance **No. 130**

Date	Explanation	Ref.	Debit	Credit	Balance
2029					
Oct. 4		J1	600		600
31	Adj. entry	J2		**50**	**550**

Equipment **No. 157**

Date	Explanation	Ref.	Debit	Credit	Balance
2029					
Oct. 1		J1	5,000		**5,000**

Accumulated Depreciation—Equipment **No. 158**

Date	Explanation	Ref.	Debit	Credit	Balance
2029					
Oct. 31	Adj. entry	J2		**40**	**40**

Notes Payable **No. 200**

Date	Explanation	Ref.	Debit	Credit	Balance
2029					
Oct. 1		J1		5,000	**5,000**

Accounts Payable **No. 201**

Date	Explanation	Ref.	Debit	Credit	Balance
2029					
Oct. 5		J1		2,500	**2,500**

Unearned Service Revenue **No. 209**

Date	Explanation	Ref.	Debit	Credit	Balance
2029					
Oct. 2		J1		1,200	1,200
31	Adj. entry	J2	400		**800**

Salaries and Wages Payable **No. 212**

Date	Explanation	Ref.	Debit	Credit	Balance
2029					
Oct. 31	Adj. entry	J2		**1,200**	**1,200**

Interest Payable **No. 230**

Date	Explanation	Ref.	Debit	Credit	Balance
2029					
Oct. 31	Adj. entry	J2		**50**	**50**

Share Capital—Ordinary **No. 311**

Date	Explanation	Ref.	Debit	Credit	Balance
2029					
Oct. 1		J1		10,000	10,000

Retained Earnings **No. 320**

Date	Explanation	Ref.	Debit	Credit	Balance
2029					
Oct. 1					–0–
31	**Closing entry**	**J3**		**2,860**	**2,860**
31	**Closing entry**	**J3**	**500**		**2,360**

Note: The permanent accounts for Yazici Advertising are shown here. Illustration 4.14 shows the temporary accounts. Both permanent and temporary accounts are part of the general ledger. They are segregated here to aid in learning.

A post-closing trial balance provides evidence that the company has properly journalized and posted the closing entries. It also shows that the accounting equation is in balance at the end of the accounting period. However, like the trial balance, it does not prove that Yazici has recorded all transactions or that the ledger is correct. For example, the post-closing trial balance still will balance even if a transaction is not journalized and posted or if a transaction is journalized and posted twice.

The remaining accounts in the general ledger are temporary accounts, shown in **Illustration 4.14**. After Yazici correctly posts the closing entries, each temporary account has a zero balance. These accounts are double-underlined to finalize the closing process.

ILLUSTRATION 4.14 General ledger, temporary accounts

(Temporary Accounts Only)

GENERAL LEDGER

Dividends — No. 332

Date	Explanation	Ref.	Debit	Credit	Balance
2029					
Oct. 20		J1	500		500
31	Closing entry	J3		500	–0–

Income Summary — No. 350

Date	Explanation	Ref.	Debit	Credit	Balance
2029					
Oct. 31	Closing entry	J3		10,600	10,600
31	Closing entry	J3	7,740		2,860
31	Closing entry	J3	2,860		–0–

Service Revenue — No. 400

Date	Explanation	Ref.	Debit	Credit	Balance
2029					
Oct. 31		J1		10,000	10,000
31	Adj. entry	J2		400	10,400
31	Adj. entry	J2		200	10,600
31	Closing entry	J3	10,600		–0–

Supplies Expense — No. 631

Date	Explanation	Ref.	Debit	Credit	Balance
2029					
Oct. 31	Adj. entry	J2	1,500		1,500
31	Closing entry	J3		1,500	–0–

Depreciation Expense — No. 711

Date	Explanation	Ref.	Debit	Credit	Balance
2029					
Oct. 31	Adj. entry	J2	40		40
31	Closing entry	J3		40	–0–

Insurance Expense — No. 722

Date	Explanation	Ref.	Debit	Credit	Balance
2029					
Oct. 31	Adj. entry	J2	50		50
31	Closing entry	J3		50	–0–

Salaries and Wages Expense — No. 726

Date	Explanation	Ref.	Debit	Credit	Balance
2029					
Oct. 26		J1	4,000		4,000
31	Adj. entry	J2	1,200		5,200
31	Closing entry	J3		5,200	–0–

Rent Expense — No. 729

Date	Explanation	Ref.	Debit	Credit	Balance
2029					
Oct. 3		J1	900		900
31	Closing entry	J3		900	–0–

Interest Expense — No. 905

Date	Explanation	Ref.	Debit	Credit	Balance
2029					
Oct. 31	Adj. entry	J2	50		50
31	Closing entry	J3		50	–0–

Note: The temporary accounts for Yazici Advertising are shown here. Illustration 4.13 shows the permanent accounts. Both permanent and temporary accounts are part of the general ledger. They are segregated here to aid in learning.

DO IT! 2 | Closing Entries

Hancock Heating has the following balances in selected accounts of its adjusted trial balance.

Accounts Payable	€27,000	Dividends	€15,000
Service Revenue	98,000	Share Capital—Ordinary	42,000
Rent Expense	22,000	Accounts Receivable	38,000
Salaries and Wages Expense	51,000	Supplies Expense	7,000

Prepare the closing entries at December 31.

ACTION PLAN

- **Close revenue and expense accounts to Income Summary.**
- **Close Income Summary to Retained Earnings.**
- **Close Dividends to Retained Earnings.**

Solution

Dec. 31	Service Revenue	98,000	
	Income Summary		98,000
	(To close revenue account to Income Summary)		
31	Income Summary	80,000	
	Salaries and Wages Expense		51,000
	Rent Expense		22,000
	Supplies Expense		7,000
	(To close expense accounts to Income Summary)		

31	Income Summary (€98,000 – €80,000)	18,000	
	Retained Earnings		18,000
	(To close net income to retained earnings)		
31	Retained Earnings	15,000	
	Dividends		15,000
	(To close dividends to retained earnings)		

Related exercise material: **BE4.4, BE4.5, BE4.6, BE4.7, DO IT! 4.2, E4.4, E4.7, E4.8, and E4.11.**

4.3 The Accounting Cycle and Correcting Entries

LEARNING OBJECTIVE 3

Explain the steps in the accounting cycle and how to prepare correcting entries.

Summary of the Accounting Cycle

Illustration 4.15 summarizes the steps in the accounting cycle. You can see that the cycle begins with the analysis of business transactions and ends with the preparation of a postclosing trial balance. Companies perform the steps in the cycle in sequence and repeat them in each accounting period.

- Steps 1–3 may occur daily during the accounting period.
- Companies perform Steps 4–7 on a periodic basis, such as monthly, quarterly, or annually.
- Steps 8 and 9—closing entries and a post-closing trial balance—usually take place only at the end of a company's **annual** accounting period.

There are also two **optional steps** in the accounting cycle. As you have seen, companies may use a worksheet in preparing adjusting entries and financial statements. In addition, they may use reversing entries, as explained below.

Reversing Entries—An Optional Step

Some accountants prefer to reverse certain adjusting entries by making a **reversing entry** at the beginning of the next accounting period. A reversing entry is the exact opposite of the adjusting entry made in the previous period. **Use of reversing entries is an optional bookkeeping procedure; it is not a required step in the accounting cycle.** Accordingly, we have chosen to cover this topic in an appendix at the end of the chapter.

Correcting Entries—An Avoidable Step

Unfortunately, errors may occur in the recording process. Companies should correct errors, **as soon as they discover them**, by journalizing and posting **correcting entries**. If the accounting records are free of errors, no correcting entries are needed.

You should recognize several differences between correcting entries and adjusting entries.

- Adjusting entries are an integral part of the accounting cycle. Correcting entries, on the other hand, are unnecessary if the records are error-free.
- Companies journalize and post adjustments **only at the end of an accounting period.** In contrast, companies make correcting entries **whenever they discover an error** (see **Ethics Note**).

ETHICS NOTE

When companies find errors in previously released income statements, they restate those numbers.

ILLUSTRATION 4.15

Required steps in the accounting cycle

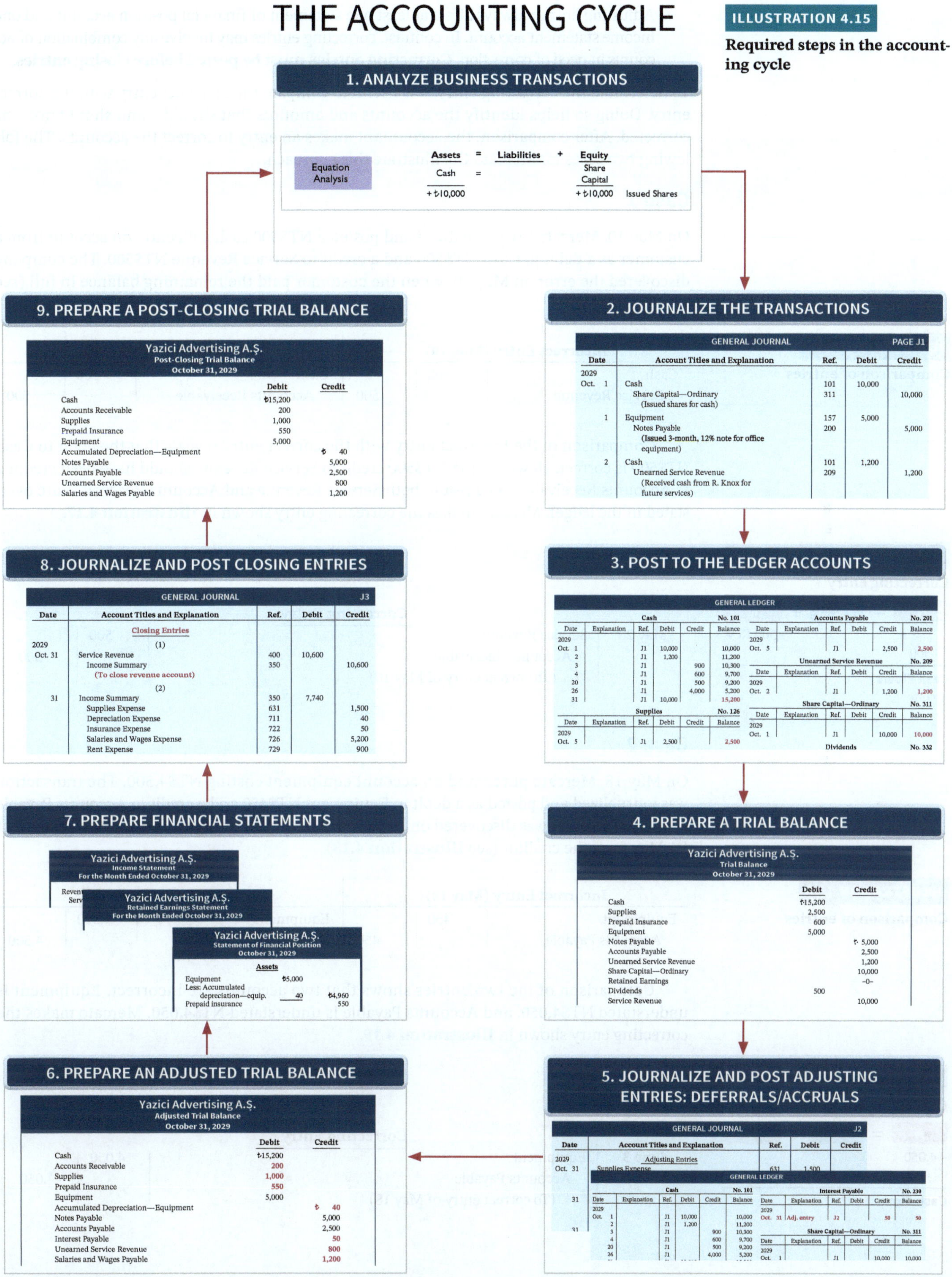

- Adjusting entries always affect at least one statement of financial position account and one income statement account. In contrast, correcting entries may involve any combination of accounts in need of correction. **Correcting entries must be posted before closing entries.**

To determine the correcting entry, it is useful to compare the incorrect entry with the correct entry. Doing so helps identify the accounts and amounts that should—and should not—be corrected. After comparison, the accountant makes an entry to correct the accounts. The following two cases for Mercato Co. illustrate this approach.

Case 1

On May 10, Mercato Co. journalized and posted a NT$500 cash collection on account from a customer as a debit to Cash NT$500 and a credit to Service Revenue NT$500. The company discovered the error on May 20, when the customer paid the remaining balance in full (see **Illustration 4.16**).

ILLUSTRATION 4.16
Comparison of entries

Incorrect Entry (May 10)			Correct Entry (May 10)		
Cash	500		Cash	500	
Service Revenue		500	Accounts Receivable		500

Comparison of the incorrect entry with the correct entry reveals that the debit to Cash NT$500 is correct. However, the NT$500 credit to Service Revenue should have been credited to Accounts Receivable. As a result, both Service Revenue and Accounts Receivable are overstated in the ledger. Mercato makes the correcting entry shown in **Illustration 4.17**.

ILLUSTRATION 4.17
Correcting entry

A	=	L	+	E
				−500 Rev
−500				

Cash Flows
no effect

Correcting Entry			
May 20	Service Revenue	500	
	Accounts Receivable		500
	(To correct entry of May 10)		

Case 2

On May 18, Mercato purchased on account equipment costing NT$4,500. The transaction was journalized and posted as a debit to Equipment NT$450 and a credit to Accounts Payable NT$450. The error was discovered on June 3, when Mercato received the monthly statement for May from the creditor (see **Illustration 4.18**).

ILLUSTRATION 4.18
Comparison of entries

Incorrect Entry (May 18)			Correct Entry (May 18)		
Equipment	450		Equipment	4,500	
Accounts Payable		450	Accounts Payable		4,500

Comparison of the two entries shows that two accounts are incorrect. Equipment is understated NT$4,050, and Accounts Payable is understated NT$4,050. Mercato makes the correcting entry shown in **Illustration 4.19**.

ILLUSTRATION 4.19
Correcting entry

A	=	L	+	E
+4,050				
		+4,050		

Cash Flows
no effect

Correcting Entry			
June 3	Equipment	4,050	
	Accounts Payable		4,050
	(To correct entry of May 18)		

Instead of preparing a correcting entry, **it is possible to reverse the incorrect entry and then prepare the correct entry**. This approach will result in more entries and postings than a correcting entry, but it will accomplish the desired result.

Investor Insight Nigerian Stock Exchange

Daniel Ernst/Adobe Stock Photos

How Can Accounting Aid African Growth?

The accuracy of a company's financial records is very important to investors, but other issues are also of concern. Recently, the **Nigerian Stock Exchange** adopted a company-governance system to assess the 190 companies that are listed on the exchange. The rating system requires the companies to answer questions about business ethics, audit procedures, internal controls, disclosure practices, and other matters. Africa's economy is growing rapidly, so it offers many opportunities to investors and companies.

But the accounting practices of many African companies lag behind those of companies in other parts of the world. In order to attract more outside investment and therefore lower the cost of financing projects, many African companies have adopted IFRS. One financial advisor said that while trying to help one African company, she found accounts that were commingled and assets that had not been recorded because they had been purchased with cash. She emphasized, however, that "just because they don't have the best accounting records doesn't mean they don't have a good business."

Source: Adapted from Kimberly S. Johnson, "Africa Makes Strides in Corporate Accounting, Governance," *Wall Street Journal Online* (November 17, 2014).

What benefit is likely to result if African companies improve their accounting practices and adopt IFRS? (Answer is available near the end of the chapter.)

DO IT! 3 | Correcting Entries

Sanchez Company discovered the following errors made in January 2029 (amounts in thousands).

1. A payment of Salaries and Wages Expense of $600 was debited to Supplies and credited to Cash, both for $600.
2. A collection of $3,000 from a client on account was debited to Cash $200 and credited to Service Revenue $200.
3. The purchase of supplies on account for $860 was debited to Supplies $680 and credited to Accounts Payable $680.

Correct the errors without reversing the incorrect entry.

ACTION PLAN

- **Compare the incorrect entry with correct entry.**
- **After comparison, make an entry to correct the accounts.**

Solution

1. Salaries and Wages Expense	600	
Supplies		600
2. Service Revenue	200	
Cash	2,800	
Accounts Receivable		3,000
3. Supplies ($860 – $680)	180	
Accounts Payable		180

Related exercise material: **BE4.8, BE4.9, DO IT! 4.3, E4.10, E4.12, and E4.13.**

4.4 Classified Statement of Financial Position

LEARNING OBJECTIVE 4

Identify the sections of a classified statement of financial position.

The statement of financial position presents a snapshot of a company's financial position at a point in time. To improve users' understanding of a company's financial position, companies often use a classified statement of financial position.

- A **classified statement of financial position** groups together similar assets and similar liabilities, using a number of standard classifications and sections.
- This is useful because items within a group have similar economic characteristics.

A classified statement of financial position generally contains the standard classifications listed in **Illustration 4.20**.

ILLUSTRATION 4.20
Standard statement of financial position classifications

Assets	Equity and Liabilities
Intangible assets	Equity
Property, plant, and equipment	Non-current liabilities
Long-term investments	Current liabilities
Current assets	

These groupings help financial statement readers determine:

1. Whether the company has enough assets to pay its debts as they come due.
2. The claims of short- and long-term creditors on the company's total assets.

HELPFUL HINT
Recall that the basic accounting equation is Assets = Liabilities + Equity.

Many of these groupings can be seen in the statement of financial position of Cheng Ltd. shown in **Illustration 4.21** (see **Helpful Hint**). In the sections that follow, we explain each of these groupings.

ILLUSTRATION 4.21
Classified statement of financial position

Cheng Ltd.
Statement of Financial Position
October 31, 2029
(NT$ in thousands)

Assets			
Intangible assets			
Patents			NT$ 3,100
Property, plant, and equipment			
Land		NT$10,000	
Equipment	NT$24,000		
Less: Accumulated depreciation—equipment	5,000	19,000	29,000
Long-term investments			
Investment in shares of Walters Corp.		5,200	
Investment in real estate		2,000	7,200
Current assets			
Prepaid insurance		400	
Supplies		2,100	
Inventory		3,000	
Notes receivable		1,000	
Accounts receivable		7,000	
Short-term investments		2,000	
Cash		6,600	22,100
Total assets			NT$61,400

ILLUSTRATION 4.21
(continued)

Equity and Liabilities

Equity		
Share capital—ordinary	NT$20,000	
Retained earnings	14,050	NT$34,050
Non-current liabilities		
Mortgage payable	10,000	
Notes payable	1,300	11,300
Current liabilities		
Notes payable	11,000	
Accounts payable	2,100	
Salaries and wages payable	1,600	
Unearned service revenue	900	
Interest payable	450	16,050
Total equity and liabilities		NT$61,400

Intangible Assets

Many companies have long-lived assets that do not have physical substance yet often are very valuable. We call these assets **intangible assets**.

- One significant intangible asset is goodwill.
- Others include patents, copyrights, and trademarks or trade names that give the company **exclusive right** of use for a specified period of time.

In Illustration 4.21, Cheng Ltd. reported intangible assets of NT$3,100. **Illustration 4.22** shows the intangible assets of **Nokia** (FIN) in a recent year (see **Helpful Hint**).

HELPFUL HINT
Sometimes intangible assets are reported under a broader heading called *"Other assets."*

ILLUSTRATION 4.22
Intangible assets section

Real World

Nokia
Statement of Financial Position (partial)
(in millions)

Intangible assets	
Capitalized development costs	€ 244
Goodwill	6,257
Other intangible assets	3,913
	€10,414

Environmental, Social, and Governance Insight — Nestlé SA

Simon Rawles/Alamy Stock Photo

Creating Value

Appendix B contains the financial statements of **Nestlé SA** (CHE). Those financial statements report on the company's profitability and financial position. In addition to these financial statements, Nestlé, like many other companies today, also reports its achievements with regard to other, non-financial goals.

In Nestlé's case, it calls these goals "Creating Shared Value." Nestlé has set objectives to help society in areas most directly related to its particular expertise: nutrition, water and environmental sustainability, and rural development. The company evaluates its progress in each area using objective measures. Examples of measures used are provided below.

Nutrition: Products meeting or exceeding Nutritional Foundation profiling criteria (as percentage of total sales) and products with increase in nutritious ingredients or essential nutrients.

Water and Environmental Sustainability: Reduce direct water withdrawals per tonne of product in every product category and also reduce greenhouse gas emissions per tonne of product in every product category.

Rural Development: Farmers trained through capacity-building programs and suppliers audited for food safety, quality, and processing.

To learn more about Nestlé's efforts to create shared value, go to the company's website.

What are some implications of Nestlé's decision to measure its non-financial results using objective measures and then publicly report these results? (Answer is available near the end of the chapter.)

ALTERNATIVE TERMINOLOGY

Property, plant, and equipment is sometimes called *fixed assets* or *plant assets*.

Property, Plant, and Equipment

Property, plant, and equipment are assets with relatively long useful lives that a company is currently using in operating the business. This category includes land, buildings, machinery and equipment, delivery equipment, and furniture (see **Alternative Terminology**). In Illustration 4.21, Cheng Ltd. reported property, plant, and equipment of NT$29,000.

Depreciation is the practice of allocating the cost of assets to a number of years.

- Companies systematically assign a portion of an asset's cost as an expense each year (rather than expensing the full purchase price in the year of purchase).
- The assets that the company depreciates are reported on the statement of financial position at cost less accumulated depreciation.
- The **accumulated depreciation** account shows the total amount of depreciation that the company has expensed thus far in the asset's life.

In Illustration 4.21, Cheng Ltd. reported accumulated depreciation of NT$5,000. **Illustration 4.23** presents the property, plant, and equipment of **Laclede Group** (KOR).

ILLUSTRATION 4.23

Property, plant, and equipment section

Real World

Laclede Group
Statement of Financial Position (partial)
(₩ in billions)

Property, plant, and equipment		
Land		₩ 2,604
Buildings	₩ 9,487	
Structures	1,568	
Machinery	36,956	
Vehicles	226	
Other	10,600	58,837
Less: Accumulated depreciation		32,617
		₩ 28,824

Long-Term Investments

Long-term investments are generally:

1. Investments in shares and bonds of other companies that are normally held for many years.
2. Non-current assets such as land or buildings that a company is not currently using in its operating activities.
3. Long-term notes receivable (see **Alternative Terminology**). In Illustration 4.21, Cheng Ltd. reported total long-term investments of NT$7,200 on its statement of financial position. **Alphabet Inc.** (USA) reported long-term investments in its statement of financial position, as shown in **Illustration 4.24**.

ALTERNATIVE TERMINOLOGY

Long-term investments are often referred to simply as *investments*.

ILLUSTRATION 4.24

Long-term investments section

Real World

Alphabet Inc.
Statement of Financial Position (partial)
(in thousands)

Long-term investments	
Non-marketable equity investments	$1,469

Current Assets

Current assets include cash, investments held for trading purposes, and assets that a company expects to convert to cash or use up within one year or its operating cycle, whichever is longer. In Illustration 4.21, Cheng Ltd. had current assets of NT$22,100. For most businesses, the cutoff for classification as current assets is one year from the statement of financial position date. For example, accounts receivable are current assets because the company will collect them and convert them to cash within one year. Supplies is a current asset because the company expects to use the supplies in operations within one year.

Some companies use a period longer than one year to classify assets and liabilities as current because they have an operating cycle longer than one year.

- The **operating cycle** of a company is the average time that it takes to purchase inventory, sell it on account, and then collect cash from customers.
- For most businesses, this cycle takes less than a year so they use a one-year cutoff.
- For other businesses, such as vineyards or airplane manufacturers, this period may be longer than a year.

Except where noted, we will assume that companies use one year to determine whether an asset or liability is current or non-current.

Common types of current assets are (1) cash, (2) investments (such as short-term government securities), (3) receivables (notes receivable, accounts receivable, and interest receivable), (4) inventories, and (5) prepaid expenses (supplies and insurance). **On the statement of financial position, companies usually list these items in the reverse order in which they expect to convert them into cash.** **Illustration 4.25** presents the current assets of **Tesco** (GBR).

ILLUSTRATION 4.25

Current assets section

Real World

Tesco
Statement of Financial Position (partial)
(£ in millions)

Current assets	
Inventories	£2,430
Trade and other receivables	1,311
Derivative financial instruments	97
Current tax assets	6
Short-term investments	360
Cash and cash equivalents	1,788
Total current assets	£5,992

As we explain later in the chapter, a company's current assets are important in assessing its short-term debt-paying ability.

Equity

The content of the equity section varies with the form of business organization.

- In a proprietorship, there is one capital account.
- In a partnership, there is a capital account for each partner.
- Corporations often divide equity into two accounts—Share Capital—Ordinary and Retained Earnings.

Corporations record shareholders' investments in the company by debiting an asset account and crediting the Share Capital—Ordinary account. They record in the Retained Earnings account income retained for use in the business. Corporations combine the Share Capital—Ordinary and Retained Earnings accounts and report them on the statement of financial position as **equity**. **Halie Capital Ltd.** reported its equity section as shown in **Illustration 4.26**.

ILLUSTRATION 4.26

Equity section

Halie Capital Ltd.
Statement of Financial Position (partial)
(in thousands)

Equity	
Share capital—ordinary	£ 685,934
Retained earnings	1,406,747
Total equity	£2,092,681

Non-Current Liabilities

Non-current liabilities are obligations that a company expects to pay **after** one year.

- Liabilities in this category include bonds payable, mortgages payable, long-term notes payable, lease liabilities, and pension liabilities.

- Many companies report long-term debt maturing after one year as a single amount in the statement of financial position and show the details of the debt in notes that accompany the financial statements. Others list the various types of non-current liabilities.

In Illustration 4.21, Cheng Ltd. reported non-current liabilities of NT$11,300. **Illustration 4.27** shows the non-current liabilities that **Siemens** (DEU) reported in its statement of financial position in a recent year.

ILLUSTRATION 4.27

Non-current liabilities section

Real World

Siemens
Statement of Financial Position (partial)
(in millions)

Non-current liabilities	
Long-term debt	€14,260
Pension plans and similar commitments	4,361
Provisions	2,533
Deferred tax liabilities	726
Other non-current liabilities	2,752
	€24,632

ETHICS NOTE

A company that has more current assets than current liabilities can increase the ratio of current assets to current liabilities by using cash to pay off some current liabilities. This gives the appearance of being more liquid. Do you think this move is ethical?

Current Liabilities

In the equity and liabilities section of the statement of financial position, the last grouping is current liabilities.

Current liabilities include liabilities related to the operations of the business as well as liabilities related to the financing of the business.

- Operating-related liabilities, for example, accounts payable and accrued expenses such as salaries and wages, are reported as current liabilities if they are due within one year or the operating cycle, whichever is longer (see **Ethics Note**).
- Financing-related liabilities such as interest payable and notes payable are treated as current if they are due within one year.
- In addition, any long-term debt that requires repayment within the next year is also a current liability.

As noted earlier, except where noted, we will assume that companies use one year to determine whether assets or liabilities are current or non-current.

In Illustration 4.21, Cheng Ltd. reported five different types of current liabilities, for a total of NT$16,050. **Illustration 4.28** shows the current liabilities section adapted from the statement of financial position of **Siemens** (DEU).

ILLUSTRATION 4.28

Current liabilities section

Real World

Siemens
Statement of Financial Position (partial)
(in millions)

Current liabilities	
Trade payables	€ 8,860
Current provisions	5,165
Other current financial liabilities	2,427
Income taxes payable	1,970
Current maturities for long-term debt	1,819
Other current liabilities	22,210
	€42,451

Users of financial statements look closely at the relationship between current assets and current liabilities. This relationship is important in evaluating a company's **liquidity**—its ability to pay obligations expected to be due within the next year. When current assets exceed current liabilities, the likelihood for paying the liabilities is favorable. When the reverse is true, short-term creditors may not be paid, and the company may ultimately be forced into bankruptcy.

Accounting Across the Organization

jorgeantonio/Getty Images

Managing Liquidity During a Global Pandemic

Companies face a constant challenge to manage their working capital and liquidity. Too much liquidity can be costly since liquid assets such as cash have a low rate of return. Too little liquidity can prevent the company for taking advantage of sales discounts, or even worse, cause them to miss payments that are due on their liabilities.

Given this backdrop, imagine how challenging liquidity management became during the Covid-19 global pandemic. For many companies, revenues dropped significantly, and accounts receivable were difficult to collect. Inventory swung widely–dropping quickly in industries such as medical protective equipment like masks and gloves, and building up quickly in industries like electronics and automotive production where production lines were essentially shut down early in the pandemic.

The Hackett Group (USA) assists large companies as they attempt to find the right balance. It reported that many large companies held onto their cash carefully during the pandemic, causing on average the amount of cash to go up by 40% compared to the pre-pandemic period. These companies did this by reducing capital expenditures and dividend payments along with tapping their short-term credit facilities.

Source: The Hackett Group.

What can various company managers do to ensure that working capital is managed efficiently to maximize net income? (Answer is available near the end of the chapter.)

DO IT! 4 | Statement of Financial Position Classifications

ACTION PLAN

- **Analyze whether each financial statement item is an asset, liability, or equity.**
- **Determine if asset and liability items are current or non-current.**

The following accounts were taken from the financial statements of Callahan Company.

________	Salaries and wages payable	________	Share investments (long-term)
________	Service revenue	________	Equipment
________	Interest payable	________	Accumulated depreciation—equipment
________	Goodwill	________	Depreciation expense
________	Debt investments (short-term)	________	Share capital—ordinary
________	Mortgage payable (due in 3 years)	________	Unearned service revenue

Match each of the following to its proper statement of financial position classification, shown below. If the item would not appear on a statement of financial position, use "NA."

Intangible assets (IA)	Equity (E)
Property, plant, and equipment (PPE)	Non-current liabilities (NCL)
Long-term investments (LTI)	Current liabilities (CL)
Current assets (CA)	

Solution

CL	Salaries and wages payable	LTI	Share investments (long-term)
NA	Service revenue	PPE	Equipment
CL	Interest payable	PPE	Accumulated depreciation—equipment
IA	Goodwill	NA	Depreciation expense
CA	Debt investments (short-term)	E	Share capital—ordinary
NCL	Mortgage payable (due in 3 years)	CL	Unearned service revenue

Related exercise material: **BE4.10, BE4.11, DO IT! 4.4, E4.3, E4.9, E4.14, E4.15, E4.16, and E4.17.**

Appendix 4A Reversing Entries

LEARNING OBJECTIVE *5

Prepare reversing entries.

After preparing the financial statements and closing the books, it is often helpful to reverse some of the adjusting entries before recording the regular transactions of the next period. Such entries are **reversing entries.**

- Companies make **a reversing entry at the beginning of the next accounting period**.
- Each reversing entry **is the exact opposite of the adjusting entry made in the previous period.**
- The recording of reversing entries is an **optional step** in the accounting cycle.

The purpose of reversing entries is to simplify the recording of a subsequent transaction related to an adjusting entry. For example, in Chapter 3, the payment of salaries after an adjusting entry resulted in two debits: one to Salaries and Wages Payable and the other to Salaries and Wages Expense. With reversing entries, the company can debit the entire subsequent payment to Salaries and Wages Expense. **The use of reversing entries does not change the amounts reported in the financial statements**. What it does is simplify the recording of subsequent transactions.

Reversing Entries Example

Companies most often use reversing entries to reverse two types of adjusting entries: accrued revenues and accrued expenses. To illustrate the optional use of reversing entries for accrued expenses, we will use the salaries expense transactions for Yazici Advertising as illustrated in Chapters 2, 3, and 4. The transaction and adjustment data are as follows.

1. October 26 (initial salary entry): Yazici pays ₺4,000 of salaries and wages earned between October 15 and October 26.
2. October 31 (adjusting entry): Salaries and wages earned between October 29 and October 31 are ₺1,200. The company will pay these in the November 9 payroll.
3. November 9 (subsequent salary entry): Salaries and wages paid are ₺4,000. Of this amount, ₺1,200 applied to accrued salaries and wages payable and ₺2,800 was earned between November 1 and November 9.

Illustration 4A.1 shows the entries with and without reversing entries.

The first three entries are the same whether or not Yazici uses reversing entries. The last two entries are different. The November 1 **reversing entry** eliminates the ₺1,200 balance in Salaries and Wages Payable created by the October 31 adjusting entry. The reversing entry also creates a ₺1,200 credit balance in the Salaries and Wages Expense account. As you know, it is unusual for an expense account to have a credit balance. The balance is correct in this instance, though, because it anticipates that the entire amount of the first salaries and wages payment in the new accounting period will be debited to Salaries and Wages Expense. This debit will eliminate the credit balance. The resulting debit balance in the expense account will equal the salaries and wages expense incurred in the new accounting period (₺2,800 in this example).

If Yazici makes reversing entries, it can debit all cash payments of expenses to the expense account. This means that on November 9 (and every payday) Yazici can debit Salaries and Wages Expense for the amount paid, without regard to any accrued salaries and wages payable. Being able to make the **same entry each time** simplifies the recording process. The company can record subsequent transactions as if the related adjusting entry had never been made.

Illustration 4A.2 shows the posting of the entries with reversing entries.

ILLUSTRATION 4A.1 **Comparative entries—without and with reversing**

Without Reversing Entries (per chapter)				With Reversing Entries (per appendix)			
	Initial Salary Entry				Initial Salary Entry		
Oct. 26	Salaries and Wages Expense	4,000		Oct. 26	(Same entry)		
	Cash		4,000				
	Adjusting Entry				Adjusting Entry		
Oct. 31	Salaries and Wages Expense	1,200		Oct. 31	(Same entry)		
	Salaries and Wages Payable		1,200				
	Closing Entry				Closing Entry		
Oct. 31	Income Summary	5,200		Oct. 31	(Same entry)		
	Salaries and Wages Expense		5,200				
	Reversing Entry				Reversing Entry		
Nov. 1	No reversing entry is made.			Nov. 1	**Salaries and Wages Payable**	**1,200**	
					Salaries and Wages Expense		**1,200**
	Subsequent Salary Entry				Subsequent Salary Entry		
Nov. 9	Salaries and Wages Payable	1,200		Nov. 9	**Salaries and Wages Expense**	**4,000**	
	Salaries and Wages Expense	2,800			**Cash**		**4,000**
	Cash		4,000				

ILLUSTRATION 4A.2 **Postings with reversing entries**

Salaries and Wages Expense

Debit		Credit	
10/26 Paid	4,000	10/31 Closing	5,200
31 Adjusting	1,200		
	5,200		
11/9 Paid	4,000	**11/1 Reversing**	**1,200**

Salaries and Wages Payable

Debit		Credit	
11/1 Reversing	**1,200**	10/31 Adjusting	1,200

A company can also use reversing entries for accrued revenue adjusting entries. For Yazici, the adjusting entry was Accounts Receivable (Dr.) ₺200 and Service Revenue (Cr.) ₺200. Thus, the reversing entry on November 1 is:

Nov. 1	Service Revenue	200	
	Accounts Receivable		200
	(To reverse October 31 adjusting entry)		

A	=	L	+	E
				−200 Rev
−200				

Cash Flows
no effect

When Yazici collects the accrued service revenue, it debits Cash and credits Service Revenue.

Review and Practice

Learning Objectives Review

1 Prepare a worksheet.

The steps in preparing a worksheet are as follows. (a) Prepare a trial balance on the worksheet. (b) Enter the adjustments in the adjustments columns. (c) Enter adjusted balances in the adjusted trial balance columns. (d) Extend adjusted trial balance amounts to appropriate financial statement columns. (e) Total the statement columns, compute net income (or net loss), and complete the worksheet.

2 Prepare closing entries and a post-closing trial balance.

Closing the books occurs at the end of an accounting period. The process is to journalize and post closing entries and then underline and balance all accounts. In closing the books, companies make separate entries to close revenues and expenses to Income Summary, Income Summary to Retained Earnings, and Dividends to Retained Earnings. Only temporary accounts are closed. A post-closing trial balance contains the balances in permanent accounts that are carried forward to the next accounting period. The purpose of this trial balance is to prove the equality of these balances.

3 Explain the steps in the accounting cycle and how to prepare correcting entries.

The required steps in the accounting cycle are (1) analyze business transactions, (2) journalize the transactions, (3) post to ledger accounts, (4) prepare a trial balance, (5) journalize and post adjusting entries, (6) prepare an adjusted trial balance, (7) prepare financial statements, (8) journalize and post closing entries, and (9) prepare a post-closing trial balance.

One way to determine the correcting entry is to compare the incorrect entry with the correct entry. After comparison, the company makes a correcting entry to correct the accounts. An alternative to a correcting entry is to reverse the incorrect entry and then prepare the correct entry.

4 Identify the sections of a classified statement of financial position.

A classified statement of financial position categorizes assets as intangibles; property, plant, and equipment; long-term investments; and current assets. Liabilities are classified as either non-current or current. There is also an equity section, which varies with the form of business organization.

***5 Prepare reversing entries.**

Reversing entries are the opposite of the adjusting entries made in the preceding period. Some companies choose to make reversing entries at the beginning of a new accounting period to simplify the recording of later transactions related to the adjusting entries. In most cases, only accrued adjusting entries are reversed.

Glossary Review

Classified statement of financial position A statement of financial position that contains standard classifications or sections. (p. 4-24).

Closing entries Entries made at the end of an accounting period to transfer the balances of temporary accounts to a permanent equity account, Retained Earnings. (p. 4-13).

Correcting entries Entries to correct errors made in recording transactions. (p. 4-20).

Current assets Assets, including cash, investments held for trading purposes, and assets that a company expects to convert to cash or use up within one year or its operating cycle, whichever is longer. (p. 4-26).

Current liabilities Obligations related to operations that a company expects to pay within the coming year or its operating cycle, whichever is longer, and obligations related to financing that will be paid in the next year. (p. 4-28).

Equity The ownership claims of shareholders on total assets. (p. 4-27).

Income Summary A temporary account used in closing revenue and expense accounts. (p. 4-14).

Intangible assets Long-lived assets that do not have physical substance. (p. 4-25).

Liquidity The ability of a company to pay obligations expected to be due within the next year. (p. 4-28).

Long-term investments Generally, (1) investments in shares and bonds of other companies that companies normally hold for many years; (2) non-current assets, such as land and buildings, not currently being used in operating activities; and (3) long-term notes receivable. (p. 4-26).

Non-current liabilities Obligations that a company expects to pay after one year. (p. 4-27).

Operating cycle The average time that it takes to purchase inventory, sell it on account, and then collect cash from customers. (p. 4-27).

Permanent (real) accounts Accounts that relate to one or more future accounting periods. Consist of all statement of financial position accounts. Balances are carried forward to the next accounting period. (p. 4-13).

Post-closing trial balance A list of permanent accounts and their balances after a company has journalized and posted closing entries. (p. 4-17).

Property, plant, and equipment Assets with relatively long useful lives and currently being used in operations. (p. 4-26).

Reversing entry An entry, made at the beginning of the next accounting period that is the exact opposite of the adjusting entry made in the previous period. (p. 4-20).

Temporary (nominal) accounts Accounts that relate only to a given accounting period. Consist of all income statement accounts and the Dividends account. All temporary accounts are closed at end of the accounting period. (p. 4-13).

Worksheet A multiple-column form that may be used in making adjustments and in preparing financial statements. (p. 4-3).

Practice Multiple-Choice Questions

1. **(LO 1)** Which of the following statements is **incorrect** concerning the worksheet?
   - **a.** The worksheet is essentially a working tool of the accountant.
   - **b.** The worksheet is distributed to management and other interested parties.
   - **c.** The worksheet cannot be used as a basis for posting to ledger accounts.
   - **d.** Financial statements can be prepared directly from the worksheet before journalizing and posting the adjusting entries.

2. **(LO 1)** In a worksheet, net income is entered in the following columns:
   - **a.** income statement (Dr) and statement of financial position (Dr).
   - **b.** income statement (Cr) and statement of financial position (Dr).
   - **c.** income statement (Dr) and statement of financial position (Cr).
   - **d.** income statement (Cr) and statement of financial position (Cr).

3. **(LO 1)** In the unadjusted trial balance of its worksheet for the year ended December 31, 2029, Kim Company reported Equipment of NT$120,000. The year-end adjusting entries require an adjustment

of NT$15,000 for depreciation expense for the equipment. After the adjusted trial balance is completed, what amount should be shown in the financial statement columns?

a. A debit of NT$105,000 for Equipment in the statement of financial position column.

b. A credit of NT$15,000 for Depreciation Expense in the income statement column.

c. A debit of NT$120,000 for Equipment in the statement of financial position column.

d. A debit of NT$15,000 for Accumulated Depreciation—Equipment in the statement of financial position column.

4. (LO 2) An account that will have a zero balance after closing entries have been journalized and posted is:

a. Service Revenue.

b. Supplies.

c. Prepaid Insurance.

d. Accumulated Depreciation—Equipment.

5. (LO 2) When a net loss has occurred, Income Summary is:

a. debited and Retained Earnings is credited.

b. credited and Retained Earnings is debited.

c. debited and Dividends is credited.

d. credited and Dividends is debited.

6. (LO 2) The closing process involves separate entries to close (1) expenses, (2) dividends, (3) revenues, and (4) income summary. The correct sequencing of the entries is:

a. (4), (3), (2), (1).

b. (1), (2), (3), (4).

c. (3), (1), (4), (2).

d. (3), (2), (1), (4).

7. (LO 2) Which types of accounts will appear in the post-closing trial balance?

a. Permanent (real) accounts.

b. Temporary (nominal) accounts.

c. Accounts shown in the income statement columns of a worksheet.

d. None of these answer choices is correct.

8. (LO 3) All of the following are required steps in the accounting cycle **except**:

a. journalizing and posting closing entries.

b. preparing financial statements.

c. journalizing the transactions.

d. preparing a worksheet.

9. (LO 3) The proper order of the following steps in the accounting cycle is:

a. prepare unadjusted trial balance, journalize transactions, post to ledger accounts, journalize and post adjusting entries.

b. journalize transactions, prepare unadjusted trial balance, post to ledger accounts, journalize and post adjusting entries.

c. journalize transactions, post to ledger accounts, prepare unadjusted trial balance, journalize and post adjusting entries.

d. prepare unadjusted trial balance, journalize and post adjusting entries, journalize transactions, post to ledger accounts.

10. (LO 3) When Lopez Company purchased supplies worth $600, it incorrectly recorded a credit to Supplies for $6,000 and a debit to Cash for $6,000. Before correcting this error:

a. Cash is overstated and Supplies is overstated.

b. Cash is understated and Supplies is understated.

c. Cash is understated and Supplies is overstated.

d. Cash is overstated and Supplies is understated.

11. (LO 3) Cash of €100 received at the time the service was performed was journalized and posted as a debit to Cash €100 and a credit to Accounts Receivable €100. Assuming the incorrect entry is not reversed, the correcting entry is:

a. debit Service Revenue €100 and credit Accounts Receivable €100.

b. debit Accounts Receivable €100 and credit Service Revenue €100.

c. debit Cash €100 and credit Service Revenue €100.

d. debit Accounts Receivable €100 and credit Cash €100.

12. (LO 4) The correct order of presentation in a classified statement of financial position for the following current assets is:

a. accounts receivable, cash, prepaid insurance, inventory.

b. prepaid insurance, inventory, accounts receivable, cash.

c. cash, accounts receivable, inventory, prepaid insurance.

d. inventory, cash, accounts receivable, prepaid insurance.

13. (LO 4) A company has purchased a tract of land. It expects to build a production plant on the land in approximately 5 years. During the 5 years before construction, the land will be idle. The land should be reported as:

a. property, plant, and equipment.

b. land expense.

c. a long-term investment.

d. an intangible asset.

14. (LO 4) In a classified statement of financial position, assets and liabilities are usually shown in the following order:

a. current assets, current liabilities, non-current liabilities, and non-current assets.

b. non-current liabilities, current liabilities, current assets, and non-current assets.

c. non-current liabilities, non-current assets, current liabilities, and non-current assets.

d. non-current assets, current assets, non-current liabilities, and current liabilities.

15. (LO 4) Current assets are listed:

a. in the reverse order of expected conversion to cash.

b. by importance.

c. by longevity.

d. by size.

***16. (LO 5)** On December 31, Kohl Company correctly made an adjusting entry to recognize $2,000 of accrued salaries payable. On January 8 of the next year, total salaries of $3,800 were paid. Assuming the correct reversing entry was made on January 1, the entry on January

8 will result in a credit to Cash $3,800 and the following debit(s):

a. Salaries and Wages Payable $1,800 and Salaries and Wages Expense $2,000.

b. Salaries and Wages Payable $2,000 and Salaries and Wages Expense $1,800.

c. Salaries and Wages Expense $3,800.

d. Salaries and Wages Payable $3,800.

Solutions

1. **b.** The worksheet is a working tool of the accountant; it is not distributed to management and other interested parties. The other choices are all true statements.

2. **c.** Net income is entered in the Dr column of the income statement and the Cr column of the statement of financial position. The other choices are incorrect because net income is entered in the (a) Cr (not Dr) column of the statement of financial position, (b) Dr (not Cr) column of the income statement and in the Cr (not Dr) column of the statement of financial position, and (d) Dr (not Cr) column of the income statement.

3. **c.** A debit of NT$120,000 for Equipment would appear in the statement of financial position column. The other choices are incorrect because (a) Equipment, less accumulated depreciation of NT$15,000, would total NT$105,000 under assets on the statement of financial position, not on the worksheet; (b) a debit, not credit, for Depreciation Expense would appear in the income statement column; and (d) a credit, not debit, of NT$15,000 for Accumulated Depreciation—Equipment would appear in the statement of financial position column.

4. **a.** The Service Revenue account will have a zero balance after closing entries have been journalized and posted because it is a temporary account. The other choices are incorrect because (b) Supplies, (c) Prepaid Insurance, and (d) Accumulated Depreciation—Equipment are all permanent accounts and therefore not closed in the closing process.

5. **b.** The effect of a net loss is a credit to Income Summary and a debit to Retained Earnings. The other choices are incorrect because (a) Income Summary is credited, not debited, and Retained Earnings is debited, not credited; (c) Income Summary is credited, not debited, and Dividends is not affected; and (d) Retained Earnings, not Dividends, is debited.

6. **c.** The correct order is (3) revenues, (1) expenses, (4) income summary, and (2) dividends. Therefore, choices (a), (b), and (d) are incorrect.

7. **a.** Permanent accounts appear in the post-closing trial balance. The other choices are incorrect because (b) temporary accounts and (c) income statement accounts are closed to a zero balance and are therefore not included in the post-closing trial balance. Choice (d) is wrong as there is a correct answer for this question.

8. **d.** Preparing a worksheet is not a required step in the accounting cycle. The other choices are all required steps in the accounting cycle.

9. **c.** The proper order of the steps in the accounting cycle is (1) journalize transactions, (2) post to ledger accounts, (3) prepare unadjusted trial balance, and (4) journalize and post adjusting entries. Therefore, choices (a), (b), and (d) are incorrect.

10. **d.** This entry causes Cash to be overstated and Supplies to be understated. Supplies should have been debited (increasing supplies) and Cash should have been credited (decreasing cash). The other choices are incorrect because (a) Supplies is understated, not overstated; (b) Cash is overstated, not understated; and (c) Cash is overstated, not understated, and Supplies is understated, not overstated.

11. **b.** The correcting entry is to debit Accounts Receivable €100 and credit Service Revenue €100. The other choices are incorrect because (a) Service Revenue should be credited, not debited, and Accounts Receivable should be debited, not credited; (c) Service Revenue should be credited for €100, and Cash should not be included in the correcting entry as it was recorded properly; and (d) Accounts Receivable should be debited for €100 and Cash should not be included in the correcting entry as it was recorded properly.

12. **b.** Companies list current assets in the following order: prepaid insurance, inventory, accounts receivable, and cash. Therefore, choices (a), (c) and (d) are incorrect.

13. **c.** Long-term investments include non-current assets such as land that a company is not currently using in its operating activities. The other choices are incorrect because (a) land would be reported as property, plant, and equipment only if it is being currently used in the business; (b) land is an asset, not an expense; and (d) land has physical substance and thus is a tangible property.

14. **d.** Usually in a classified statement of financial position, non-current assets are shown first followed by current assets, non-current liabilities, and current liabilities. The other choices are therefore incorrect.

15. **a.** Current assets are listed in the reverse order of expected conversion to cash (liquidity), not (b) by importance, (c) by longevity, or (d) by size.

*16. **c.** The use of reversing entries simplifies the recording of the first payroll following the end of the year by eliminating the need to make an entry to the Salaries and Wages Payable account. The other choices are incorrect because (a) Salaries and Wages Payable is not part of the payroll entry on January 8, and the debit to Salaries and Wages Expense should be for $3,800, not $2,000; and (b) and (d) the Salaries and Wages Expense account, not the Salaries and Wages Payable account, should be debited.

Practice Brief Exercises

Prepare closing entries from ledger balances.

1. **(LO 2)** The ledger of Xi Travel contains the following balances (amounts in thousands): Retained Earnings ¥40,000, Dividends ¥3,000, Service Revenue ¥65,000, Salaries and Wages Expense ¥39,000, and Maintenance and Repairs Expense ¥9,000. Prepare the closing entries at December 31.

Solution

1.	Dec. 31	Service Revenue	65,000	
		Income Summary		65,000
	31	Income Summary	48,000	
		Salaries and Wages Expense		39,000
		Maintenance and Repairs Expense		9,000
	31	Income Summary	17,000	
		Retained Earnings		17,000
	31	Retained Earnings	3,000	
		Dividends		3,000

2. **(LO 3)** At Shields Pharmaceuticals, the following errors were discovered after the transactions had been journalized and posted. Prepare the correcting entries.

Prepare correcting entries.

a. A cash sale to a customer for €780 was recorded as a debit to Cash €780 and a credit to Accounts Receivable €780.

b. The purchase of equipment on account for €1,730 was recorded as a debit to Equipment €1,370 and a credit to Accounts Payable €1,370.

Solution

2. a.	Accounts Receivable	780	
	Service Revenue		780
b.	Equipment (€1,730 – €1,370)	360	
	Accounts Payable		360

3. **(LO 4)** The statement of financial position debit column of the worksheet for Soon Cosmetics includes the following accounts (amounts in thousands): Accounts Receivable ₩25,000, Prepaid Insurance ₩7,000, Cash ₩8,000, Supplies ₩11,000, and Inventory ₩14,000. Prepare the current assets section of the statement of financial position, listing the accounts in proper sequence.

Prepare the current assets section of a statement of financial position.

Solution

3.

Soon Cosmetics
Statement of Financial Position (partial)

Current assets	
Prepaid insurance	₩ 7,000
Supplies	11,000
Inventory	14,000
Accounts receivable	25,000
Cash	8,000
Total current assets	₩65,000

Practice Exercises

1. **(LO 2)** Hercules Company ended its fiscal year on August 31, 2029. The company's adjusted trial balance as of the end of its fiscal year is shown as follows.

Journalize and post closing entries, and prepare a post-closing trial balance.

Hercules Company
Adjusted Trial Balance
August 31, 2029

No.	Account Titles	Debit	Credit
101	Cash	€10,900	
112	Accounts Receivable	6,200	
157	Equipment	10,600	
167	Accumulated Depr.—Equip.		€ 5,400
201	Accounts Payable		2,800
208	Unearned Rent Revenue		1,200
311	Share Capital—Ordinary		3,000
320	Retained Earnings		28,700
332	Dividends	12,000	
404	Service Revenue		42,400
429	Rent Revenue		6,100
711	Depreciation Expense	2,700	
720	Salaries and Wages Expense	37,100	
732	Utilities Expense	10,100	
		€89,600	€89,600

Instructions

a. Prepare the closing entries using page J15 in a general journal.

b. Post to Retained Earnings and No. 350 Income Summary accounts. (Use the three-column form.)

c. Prepare a post-closing trial balance at August 31, 2029.

Solution

1. a.

GENERAL JOURNAL **J15**

Date	Account Titles	Ref.	Debit	Credit
Aug. 31	Service Revenue	404	42,400	
	Rent Revenue	429	6,100	
	Income Summary	350		48,500
	(To close revenue accounts)			
31	Income Summary	350	49,900	
	Salaries and Wages Expense	720		37,100
	Utilities Expense	732		10,100
	Depreciation Expense	711		2,700
	(To close expense accounts)			
31	Retained Earnings (€49,900 – €48,500)	320	1,400	
	Income Summary	350		1,400
	(To close net loss to retained earnings)			
31	Retained Earnings	320	12,000	
	Dividends	332		12,000
	(To close dividends to retained earnings)			

b.

Retained Earnings **No. 320**

Date	Explanation	Ref.	Debit	Credit	Balance
Aug. 31	Balance				28,700
31	Close net loss	J15	1,400		27,300
31	Close dividends	J15	12,000		15,300

Income Summary **No. 350**

Date	Explanation	Ref.	Debit	Credit	Balance
Aug. 31	Close revenue	J15		48,500	48,500
31	Close expenses	J15	49,900		(1,400)
31	Close net loss	J15		1,400	0

c.

Hercules Company
Post-Closing Trial Balance
August 31, 2029

	Debit	Credit
Cash	€10,900	
Accounts Receivable	6,200	
Equipment	10,600	
Accumulated Depreciation—Equipment		€ 5,400
Accounts Payable		2,800
Unearned Rent Revenue		1,200
Share Capital—Ordinary		3,000
Retained Earnings		15,300
	€27,700	€27,700

2. **(LO 4)** The adjusted trial balance for Hercules Company is presented in **Practice Exercise 1**.

Prepare financial statements.

Instructions

a. Prepare an income statement and a retained earnings statement for the year ended August 31, 2029.

b. Prepare a classified statement of financial position at August 31, 2029.

Solution

2. **a.**

Hercules Company
Income Statement
For the Year Ended August 31, 2029

Revenues		
Service revenue	€42,400	
Rent revenue	6,100	
Total revenues		€48,500
Expenses		
Salaries and wages expense	37,100	
Utilities expense	10,100	
Depreciation expense	2,700	
Total expenses		49,900
Net loss		€ (1,400)

Hercules Company
Retained Earnings Statement
For the Year Ended August 31, 2029

Retained earnings, September 1, 2028		€ 28,700
Less: Net loss	€ 1,400	
Dividends	12,000	13,400
Retained earnings, August 31, 2029		€ 15,300

b.

Hercules Company
Statement of Financial Position
August 31, 2029

Assets		
Property, plant, and equipment		
Equipment	€10,600	
Less: Accumulated depreciation—equipment	5,400	€ 5,200
Current assets		
Accounts receivable	6,200	
Cash	10,900	17,100
Total assets		€22,300
Equity and Liabilities		
Equity		
Share capital—ordinary	€ 3,000	
Retained earnings	15,300	€18,300
Current liabilities		
Accounts payable	2,800	
Unearned rent revenue	1,200	4,000
Total equity and liabilities		€22,300

Practice Problem

Prepare worksheet and classified statement of financial position, and journalize closing entries.

(LO 1, 2, 4) At the end of its first month of operations, Pampered Pet Service has the following unadjusted trial balance.

Pampered Pet Service
August 31, 2029
Trial Balance

	Debit	Credit
Cash	NT$ 5,400	
Accounts Receivable	2,800	
Supplies	1,300	
Prepaid Insurance	2,400	
Equipment	60,000	
Notes Payable		NT$40,000
Accounts Payable		2,400
Share Capital—Ordinary		30,000
Dividends	1,000	
Service Revenue		4,900
Salaries and Wages Expense	3,200	
Utilities Expense	800	
Advertising Expense	400	
	NT$77,300	NT$77,300

Other data:

1. Insurance expires at the rate of NT$200 per month.
2. NT$1,000 of supplies are on hand at August 31.
3. Monthly depreciation on the equipment is NT$900.
4. Interest of NT$500 on the notes payable has accrued during August.

Instructions

a. Prepare a worksheet.

b. Prepare a classified statement of financial position assuming NT$35,000 of the notes payable are long-term.

c. Journalize the closing entries.

Solution

a.

Pampered Pet Service
Worksheet for the Month Ended August 31, 2029

Account Titles	Trial Balance Dr.	Trial Balance Cr.	Adjustments Dr.	Adjustments Cr.	Adjusted Trial Balance Dr.	Adjusted Trial Balance Cr.	Income Statement Dr.	Income Statement Cr.	Statement of Financial Position Dr.	Statement of Financial Position Cr.
Cash	5,400				5,400				5,400	
Accounts Receivable	2,800				2,800				2,800	
Supplies	1,300			(b) 300	1,000				1,000	
Prepaid Insurance	2,400			(a) 200	2,200				2,200	
Equipment	60,000				60,000				60,000	
Notes Payable		40,000				40,000				40,000
Accounts Payable		2,400				2,400				2,400
Share Capital—Ordinary		30,000				30,000				30,000
Dividends	1,000				1,000				1,000	
Service Revenue		4,900				4,900		4,900		
Salaries and Wages Expense	3,200				3,200		3,200			
Utilities Expense	800				800		800			
Advertising Expense	400				400		400			
Totals	77,300	77,300								
Insurance Expense			(a) 200		200		200			
Supplies Expense			(b) 300		300		300			
Depreciation Expense			(c) 900		900		900			
Accumulated Depreciation—Equipment				(c) 900		900				900
Interest Expense			(d) 500		500		500			
Interest Payable				(d) 500		500				500
Totals			1,900	1,900	78,700	78,700	6,300	4,900	72,400	73,800
Net Loss								1,400	1,400	
Totals							6,300	6,300	73,800	73,800

Explanation: (a) insurance expired, (b) supplies used, (c) depreciation expensed, and (d) interest accrued.

b.

Pampered Pet Service
Statement of Financial Position
August 31, 2029
(NT$ in thousands)

Assets

Property, plant, and equipment		
Equipment	NT$60,000	
Less: Accumulated depreciation—equipment	900	NT$59,100
Current assets		
Prepaid insurance	2,200	
Supplies	1,000	
Accounts receivable	2,800	
Cash	5,400	11,400
Total assets		NT$70,500

Equity and Liabilities

Equity		
Share capital—ordinary	NT$30,000	
Retained earnings	(2,400)*	NT$27,600
Non-current liabilities		
Notes payable		35,000
Current liabilities		
Notes payable	5,000	
Accounts payable	2,400	
Interest payable	500	7,900
Total equity and liabilities		NT$70,500

*Loss of NT$1,400 plus dividends of NT$1,000.

c.

Aug. 31	Service Revenue	4,900	
	Income Summary		4,900
	(To close revenue account)		
31	Income Summary	6,300	
	Salaries and Wages Expense		3,200
	Depreciation Expense		900
	Utilities Expense		800
	Interest Expense		500
	Advertising Expense		400
	Supplies Expense		300
	Insurance Expense		200
	(To close expense accounts)		
31	Retained Earnings (NT$6,300 – NT$4,900)	1,400	
	Income Summary		1,400
	(To close net loss to retained earnings)		
31	Retained Earnings	1,000	
	Dividends		1,000
	(To close dividends to retained earnings)		

Note: All asterisked Questions, Exercises, and Problems relate to material in the appendix to the chapter.

Questions

1. "A worksheet is a permanent accounting record and its use is required in the accounting cycle." Do you agree? Explain.

2. Explain the purpose of the worksheet.

3. What is the relationship, if any, between the amount shown in the adjusted trial balance column for an account and that account's ledger balance?

4. If a company's revenues are ¥125,000 and its expenses are ¥113,000, in which financial statement columns of the worksheet will the net income of ¥12,000 appear? When expenses exceed revenues, in which columns will the difference appear?

5. Why is it necessary to prepare formal financial statements if all of the data are in the statement columns of the worksheet?

6. Identify the account(s) debited and credited in each of the four closing entries, assuming the company has net income for the year.

7. Describe the nature of the Income Summary account and identify the types of summary data that may be posted to this account.

8. What are the content and purpose of a post-closing trial balance?

9. Which of the following accounts would not appear in the post-closing trial balance? Interest Payable, Equipment, Depreciation Expense, Dividends, Unearned Service Revenue, Accumulated Depreciation—Equipment, and Service Revenue.

10. Distinguish between a reversing entry and an adjusting entry. Are reversing entries required?

11. Indicate, in the sequence in which they are made, the three required steps in the accounting cycle that involve journalizing.

12. Identify, in the sequence in which they are prepared, the three trial balances that are used in the accounting cycles.

13. How do correcting entries differ from adjusting entries?

14. What standard classifications are used in preparing a classified statement of financial position?

15. What is meant by the term "operating cycle"?

16. Define current assets. What basis is used for arranging individual items within the current assets section?

17. Distinguish between long-term investments and property, plant, and equipment.

18. (a) What is the term used to describe the equity section of a corporation? (b) Identify the two equity accounts in a corporation and indicate the purpose of each.

19. Using **TSMC**'s annual report, determine its current liabilities at December 31, 2019, and December 31, 2020. Were current liabilities higher or lower than current assets in these two years?

*20. Cigale Company prepares reversing entries. If the adjusting entry for interest payable is reversed, what type of an account balance, if any, will there be in Interest Payable and Interest Expense after the reversing entry is posted?

*21. At December 31, accrued salaries payable totaled €3,500. On January 10, total salaries of €8,000 are paid. (a) Assume that reversing entries are made at January 1. Give the January 10 entry, and indicate the Salaries and Wages Expense account balance after the entry is posted. (b) Repeat part (a) assuming reversing entries are not made.

Brief Exercises

List the steps in preparing a worksheet.

BE4.1 (LO 1) The steps in using a worksheet are presented in random order below. List the steps in the proper order by placing numbers 1–5 in the blank spaces.

a. ______ Prepare a trial balance on the worksheet.
b. ______ Enter adjusted balances.
c. ______ Extend adjusted balances to appropriate statement columns.
d. ______ Total the statement columns, compute net income (loss), and complete the worksheet.
e. ______ Enter adjustment data.

Prepare partial worksheet.

BE4.2 (LO 1) The ledger of Walters Repair Shop includes the following unadjusted balances: Prepaid Insurance €3,000, Service Revenue €60,000, and Salaries and Wages Expense €25,000. Adjusting entries are required for (a) expired insurance €1,800; (b) services performed €1,100 are billed and not yet collected; and (c) accrued salaries payable €900. Enter the unadjusted balances and adjustments into a worksheet and complete the worksheet for all accounts. (*Note:* You will need to add the following accounts: Accounts Receivable, Salaries and Wages Payable, and Insurance Expense.)

Identify worksheet columns for selected accounts.

BE4.3 (LO 1) The following selected accounts appear in the adjusted trial balance columns of the worksheet for Lee Company: Accumulated Depreciation, Depreciation Expense, Share Capital—Ordinary, Dividends, Service Revenue, Supplies, and Accounts Payable. Indicate the financial statement column (income statement Dr., statement of financial position Cr., etc.) to which each balance should be extended.

Prepare closing entries from ledger balances.

BE4.4 (LO 2) The ledger of Desai Catering contains the following balances: Retained Earnings ₹30,000, Dividends ₹2,000, Service Revenue ₹58,000, Salaries and Wages Expense ₹39,000, and Supplies Expense ₹7,000. Prepare the closing entries at December 31.

Post closing entries; underline and balance T-accounts.

BE4.5 (LO 2) Using the data in BE4.4, enter the balances in T-accounts, post the closing entries, and underline and balance the accounts.

Journalize and post closing entries using the three-column form of account.

BE4.6 (LO 2) The income statement for Golden Golf Club for the month ending July 31 shows Service Revenue ¥17,800, Salaries and Wages Expense ¥9,600, Maintenance and Repairs Expense ¥2,500, and Net Income ¥5,700. Prepare the entries to close the revenue and expense accounts. Post the entries to the revenue and expense accounts, and complete the closing process for these accounts using the three-column form of account (amounts in thousands).

Identify post-closing trial balance accounts.

BE4.7 (LO 2) Using the data in BE4.3, identify the accounts that would be included in a post-closing trial balance.

List the required steps in the accounting cycle in sequence.

BE4.8 (LO 3) The steps in the accounting cycle are listed in random order below. List the steps in proper sequence, assuming no worksheet is prepared, by placing numbers 1–9 in the blank spaces.

a. _______ Prepare a trial balance.
b. _______ Journalize the transactions.
c. _______ Journalize and post closing entries.
d. _______ Prepare financial statements.
e. _______ Journalize and post adjusting entries.
f. _______ Post to ledger accounts.
g. _______ Prepare a post-closing trial balance.
h. _______ Prepare an adjusted trial balance.
i. _______ Analyze business transactions.

Prepare correcting entries.

BE4.9 (LO 3) At Raymond Ltd., the following errors were discovered after the transactions had been journalized and posted. Prepare the correcting entries.

1. A collection on account from a customer for £870 was recorded as a debit to Cash £870 and a credit to Service Revenue £870.
2. The purchase of store supplies on account for £1,510 was recorded as a debit to Supplies £1,150 and a credit to Accounts Payable £1,150.

Prepare the current assets section of a statement of financial position.

BE4.10 (LO 4) The statement of financial position debit column of the worksheet for Jolie Company includes the following accounts: Accounts Receivable $12,500, Prepaid Insurance $4,500, Cash $4,100, Supplies $5,200, and Debt Investments (short-term) $7,600. Prepare the current assets section of the statement of financial position, listing the accounts in proper sequence.

Classify accounts on statement of financial position.

BE4.11 (LO 4) The following are the major statement of financial position classifications:

Intangible assets (IA)	Equity (E)
Property, plant, and equipment (PPE)	Non-current liabilities (NCL)
Long-term investments (LTI)	Current liabilities (CL)
Current assets (CA)	

Match each of the following accounts to its proper statement of financial position classification.

_______ Accounts payable	_______ Income taxes payable
_______ Accounts receivable	_______ Debt investments (long-term)
_______ Accumulated depreciation—buildings	_______ Land
_______ Buildings	_______ Inventory
_______ Cash	_______ Patents
_______ Copyrights	_______ Supplies

Prepare reversing entries.

***BE4.12 (LO 5)** At October 31, Miras Transportation made an accrued expense adjusting entry of €3,300 for salaries. Prepare the reversing entry on November 1, and indicate the balances in Salaries and Wages Payable and Salaries and Wages Expense after posting the reversing entry.

DO IT! Exercises

Prepare a worksheet.

DO IT! 4.1 (LO 1) Jordan Carr is preparing a worksheet. Explain to Jordan how he should extend the following adjusted trial balance accounts to the financial statement columns of the worksheet.

Service Revenue	Accounts Receivable
Notes Payable	Accumulated Depreciation
Share Capital—Ordinary	Utilities Expense

Prepare closing entries.

DO IT! 4.2 (LO 2) Paloma Grooming shows the following balances in selected accounts of its adjusted trial balance (amounts in thousands).

Supplies	Rp32,000	Service Revenue	Rp108,000
Supplies Expense	6,000	Salaries and Wages Expense	40,000
Accounts Receivable	12,000	Utilities Expense	8,000
Dividends	22,000	Rent Expense	18,000
Share Capital—Ordinary	70,000		

Prepare the closing entries at December 31.

DO IT! 4.3 (LO 3) Hanson Stables has an inexperienced accountant. During the first month on the job, the accountant made the following errors in journalizing transactions. All entries were posted as made.

Prepare correcting entries.

1. The purchase of supplies for €650 cash was debited to Equipment €210 and credited to Cash €210.
2. A €500 cash dividend was debited to Salaries and Wages Expense €900 and credited to Cash €900.
3. A payment on account of €820 to a creditor was debited to Accounts Payable €280 and credited to Cash €280.

Prepare the correcting entries.

DO IT! 4.4 (LO 4) The following accounts were taken from the financial statements of Giles Company.

Match accounts to statement of financial position classifications.

______ Interest revenue	______ Share capital—ordinary
______ Utilities payable	______ Accumulated depreciation—equipment
______ Accounts payable	______ Equipment
______ Supplies	______ Salaries and wages expense
______ Bonds payable	______ Debt investments (long-term)
______ Goodwill	______ Unearned rent revenue

Match each of the accounts to its proper statement of financial position classification, as shown below. If the item would not appear on a statement of financial position, use "NA."

Intangible assets (IA)	Equity (E)
Property, plant, and equipment (PPE)	Non-current liabilities (NCL)
Long-term investments (LTI)	Current liabilities (CL)
Current assets (CA)	

Exercises

E4.1 (LO 1) The trial balance columns of the worksheet for Lim Acupuncture at June 30, 2029, are as follows (amounts in thousands).

Complete the worksheet.

Lim Acupuncture
Worksheet
For the Month Ended June 30, 2029

	Trial Balance	
Account Titles	**Dr.**	**Cr.**
Cash	2,320	
Accounts Receivable	2,440	
Supplies	1,880	
Accounts Payable		1,120
Unearned Service Revenue		240
Share Capital—Ordinary		3,600
Service Revenue		2,400
Salaries and Wages Expense	560	
Miscellaneous Expense	160	
	7,360	7,360

Other data:

1. A physical count reveals HK$500 of supplies on hand.
2. HK$100 of the unearned revenue is still unearned at month-end.
3. Accrued salaries are HK$210.

Instructions

Enter the trial balance on a worksheet and complete the worksheet.

Complete the worksheet.

E4.2 (LO 1) The adjusted trial balance columns of the worksheet for Tai Interiors are as follows (amounts in NT$).

Tai Interiors
Worksheet (partial)
For the Month Ended April 30, 2029

	Adjusted Trial Balance		Income Statement		Statement of Financial Position	
Account Titles	**Dr.**	**Cr.**	**Dr.**	**Cr.**	**Dr.**	**Cr.**
Cash	10,000					
Accounts Receivable	7,840					
Prepaid Rent	2,280					
Equipment	23,050					
Accumulated Depreciation—Equip.		4,900				
Notes Payable		5,700				
Accounts Payable		4,920				
Share Capital—Ordinary		25,960				
Dividends	3,650					
Service Revenue		17,590				
Salaries and Wages Expense	10,840					
Rent Expense	760					
Depreciation Expense	650					
Interest Expense	57					
Interest Payable		57				
Totals	59,127	59,127				

Instructions

Complete the worksheet.

Prepare financial statements from worksheet.

E4.3 (LO 1, 4) Worksheet data for Tai Interiors are presented in E4.2.

Instructions

Prepare an income statement, a retained earnings statement, and a classified statement of financial position.

Journalize and post closing entries and prepare a post-closing trial balance.

E4.4 (LO 2) Worksheet data for Tai Interiors are presented in E4.2.

Instructions

a. Journalize the closing entries at April 30.

b. Post the closing entries to Income Summary and Retained Earnings. Use T-accounts.

c. Prepare a post-closing trial balance at April 30.

Prepare adjusting entries from a worksheet, and extend balances to worksheet columns.

E4.5 (LO 1) The adjustments columns of the worksheet for Becker Company are shown below.

	Adjustments	
Account Titles	**Debit**	**Credit**
Accounts Receivable	1,100	
Prepaid Insurance		300
Accumulated Depreciation—Equipment		900
Salaries and Wages Payable		500
Service Revenue		1,100
Salaries and Wages Expense	500	
Insurance Expense	300	
Depreciation Expense	900	
	2,800	2,800

Instructions

a. Prepare the adjusting entries.

b. Assuming the adjusted trial balance amount for each account is normal, indicate the financial statement column to which each balance should be extended.

E4.6 (LO 1) Selected worksheet data for Wong Landscaping are presented below.

Derive adjusting entries from worksheet data.

Account Titles	Trial Balance		Adjusted Trial Balance	
	Dr.	**Cr.**	**Dr.**	**Cr.**
Accounts Receivable	?		34,000	
Prepaid Insurance	26,000		20,000	
Supplies	7,000		?	
Accumulated Depreciation—Equipment		12,000		?
Salaries and Wages Payable		?		5,600
Service Revenue		88,000		97,000
Insurance Expense			?	
Depreciation Expense			10,000	
Supplies Expense			4,500	
Salaries and Wages Expense	?		49,000	

Instructions

a. Fill in the missing amounts (all amounts in ¥).

b. Prepare the adjusting entries that were made.

E4.7 (LO 2) Kay Magill Company had the following adjusted trial balance.

Prepare closing entries and a post-closing trial balance.

Kay Magill Company
Adjusted Trial Balance
For the Year Ended June 30, 2029

Account Titles	Adjusted Trial Balance	
	Debit	**Credit**
Cash	$ 3,712	
Accounts Receivable	3,904	
Supplies	480	
Accounts Payable		$ 1,556
Unearned Service Revenue		160
Share Capital—Ordinary		4,000
Retained Earnings		1,760
Dividends	628	
Service Revenue		4,300
Salaries and Wages Expense	1,344	
Miscellaneous Expense	256	
Supplies Expense	1,900	
Salaries and Wages Payable		448
	$12,224	$12,224

Instructions

a. Prepare closing entries at June 30, 2029.

b. Prepare a post-closing trial balance.

E4.8 (LO 2) Huang Automotive ended its fiscal year on July 31, 2029. The company's adjusted trial balance as of the end of its fiscal year is as follows.

Journalize and post closing entries, and prepare a post-closing trial balance.

Huang Automotive
Adjusted Trial Balance
July 31, 2029

No.	Account Titles	Debit	Credit
101	Cash	NT$ 9,840	
112	Accounts Receivable	8,780	
157	Equipment	15,900	
158	Accumulated Depreciation—Equip.		NT$ 7,400
201	Accounts Payable		4,220
208	Unearned Rent Revenue		1,800
311	Share Capital—Ordinary		20,000
320	Retained Earnings		25,200
332	Dividends	16,000	
400	Service Revenue		64,000
429	Rent Revenue		6,500
711	Depreciation Expense	8,000	
726	Salaries and Wages Expense	55,700	
732	Utilities Expense	14,900	
		NT$129,120	NT$129,120

Instructions

a. Prepare the closing entries using page J15.

b. Post to Retained Earnings and No. 350 Income Summary accounts. (Use the three-column form.)

c. Prepare a post-closing trial balance at July 31.

Prepare financial statements.

E4.9 (LO 4) The adjusted trial balance for Huang Automotive is presented in E4.8.

Instructions

a. Prepare an income statement and a retained earnings statement for the year.

b. Prepare a classified statement of financial position at July 31.

Answer questions related to the accounting cycle.

E4.10 (LO 3) Ji-a Cho has prepared the following list of statements about the accounting cycle.

1. "Journalize the transactions" is the first step in the accounting cycle.
2. Reversing entries are a required step in the accounting cycle.
3. Correcting entries do not have to be part of the accounting cycle.
4. If a worksheet is prepared, some steps of the accounting cycle are incorporated into the worksheet.
5. The accounting cycle begins with the analysis of business transactions and ends with the preparation of a post-closing trial balance.
6. All steps of the accounting cycle occur daily during the accounting period.
7. The step of "post to the ledger accounts" occurs before the step of "journalize the transactions."
8. Closing entries must be prepared before financial statements can be prepared.

Instructions

Identify each statement as true or false. If false, indicate how to correct the statement.

Prepare closing entries.

E4.11 (LO 2) Selected accounts for Tamora's Salon are presented below. All June 30 postings are from closing entries.

Salaries and Wages Expense

6/10	3,200		
6/28	5,600		
Bal.	8,800	6/30	8,800

Service Revenue

		6/15	9,700
		6/24	8,400
6/30	18,100	Bal.	18,100

Retained Earnings

6/30	2,500	6/1	12,000
		6/30	5,000
		Bal.	14,500

Supplies Expense

6/12	600		
6/24	700		
Bal.	1,300	6/30	1,300

Rent Expense

6/1	3,000		
Bal.	3,000	6/30	3,000

Dividends

6/13	1,000		
6/25	1,500		
Bal.	2,500	6/30	2,500

Instructions

a. Prepare the closing entries that were made.

b. Post the closing entries to Income Summary.

E4.12 (LO 3) Andrew Clark Company discovered the following errors made in January 2029.

Prepare correcting entries.

1. A payment of Salaries and Wages Expense of $700 was debited to Equipment and credited to Cash, both for $700.

2. A collection of $1,000 from a client on account was debited to Cash $100 and credited to Service Revenue $100.

3. The purchase of equipment on account for $760 was debited to Equipment $670 and credited to Accounts Payable $670.

Instructions

a. Correct the errors by reversing the incorrect entry and preparing the correct entry.

b. Correct the errors without reversing the incorrect entry.

E4.13 (LO 3) Patel Company has an inexperienced accountant. During the first 2 weeks on the job, the accountant made the following errors in journalizing transactions. All entries were posted as made.

Prepare correcting entries.

1. A payment on account of $750 to a creditor was debited to Accounts Payable $570 and credited to Cash $570.

2. The purchase of supplies on account for $560 was debited to Equipment $56 and credited to Accounts Payable $56.

3. A $500 cash dividend was debited to Salaries and Wages Expense $500 and credited to Cash $500.

Instructions

Prepare the correcting entries.

E4.14 (LO 4) Writing The adjusted trial balance for Tsai Bowling Alley at December 31, 2029, contains the following accounts (amounts in thousands).

Prepare a classified statement of financial position.

	Debit		Credit
Buildings	¥128,800	Share Capital—Ordinary	¥100,000
Accounts Receivable	14,520	Retained Earnings	13,000
Prepaid Insurance	4,680	Accumulated Depreciation—Buildings	42,600
Cash	18,040	Accounts Payable	12,300
Equipment	62,400	Notes Payable	97,780
Land	65,000	Accumulated Depreciation—Equipment	18,720
Insurance Expense	780	Interest Payable	3,800
Depreciation Expense	7,360	Service Revenue	17,180
Interest Expense	3,800		¥305,380
	¥305,380		

Instructions

a. Prepare a classified statement of financial position; assume that ¥30,000 of the note payable will be paid in 2030.

b. Comment on the liquidity of the company.

E4.15 (LO 4) The following are the major statement of financial position classifications.

Classify accounts on statement of financial position.

Intangible assets (IA)	Equity (E)
Property, plant, and equipment (PPE)	Non-current liabilities (NCL)
Long-term investments (LTI)	Current liabilities (CL)
Current assets (CA)	

Instructions

Classify each of the following accounts taken from Faust Company's statement of financial position.

________ Accounts payable	________ Accumulated depreciation—equipment
________ Accounts receivable	________ Buildings
________ Cash	________ Land (in use)
________ Share capital—ordinary	________ Notes payable (due in 2 years)
________ Patents	________ Supplies
________ Salaries and wages payable	________ Equipment
________ Inventory	________ Prepaid expenses
________ Share investments (to be sold in 7 months)	

Prepare a classified statement of financial position.

E4.16 (LO 4) The following items were taken from the financial statements of J. Kung Enterprises. (All amounts are in thousands.)

Long-term debt	HK$ 1,000	Accumulated depreciation—equipment	HK$ 5,655
Prepaid insurance	650	Accounts payable	1,214
Equipment	11,500	Notes payable (due after 2030)	400
Share investments (long-term)	264	Share capital—ordinary	11,455
Debt investments (short-term)	3,690	Retained earnings	1,500
Notes payable (due in 2030)	500	Accounts receivable	1,696
Cash	2,668	Inventory	1,256

Instructions

Prepare a classified statement of financial position in good form as of December 31, 2029.

Prepare financial statements.

E4.17 (LO 4) These financial statement items are for Basten Tax Services at year-end, July 31, 2029.

Salaries and wages payable	£ 2,080	Notes payable (long-term)	£ 1,800
Salaries and wages expense	48,700	Cash	14,200
Utilities expense	22,600	Accounts receivable	9,780
Equipment	34,400	Accumulated depreciation—equipment	6,000
Accounts payable	4,100	Dividends	3,000
Service revenue	63,000	Depreciation expense	4,000
Rent revenue	8,500	Retained earnings (beginning of the year)	31,200
Share capital—ordinary	20,000		

Instructions

a. Prepare an income statement and a retained earnings statement for the year.

b. Prepare a classified statement of financial position at July 31.

Use reversing entries.

***E4.18 (LO 5)** Krantz Company pays salaries of $12,000 every Monday for the preceding 5-day week (Monday through Friday). Assume December 31 falls on a Tuesday, so Krantz's employees have worked 2 days without being paid at the end of the fiscal year.

Instructions

a. Assume the company does not use reversing entries. Prepare the December 31 adjusting entry and the entry on Monday, January 6, when Krantz pays the payroll.

b. Assume the company does use reversing entries. Prepare the December 31 adjusting entry, the January 1 reversing entry, and the entry on Monday, January 6, when Krantz pays the payroll.

Prepare closing and reversing entries.

***E4.19 (LO 2, 5)** On December 31, the adjusted trial balance of Cisneros Employment Agency shows the following selected data.

Accounts Receivable	$24,500	Service Revenue	$92,500
Interest Expense	8,300	Interest Payable	2,000

Analysis shows that adjusting entries were made to (1) accrue $5,000 of service revenue and (2) accrue $2,000 interest expense.

Instructions

a. Prepare the closing entries for the temporary accounts shown above at December 31.

b. Prepare the reversing entries on January 1.

c. Post the entries in (a) and (b), excluding the Income Summary account. Underline and balance the accounts. (Use T-accounts.)

d. Prepare the entries to record (1) the collection of the accrued revenue on January 10 and (2) the payment of all interest due ($2,000) on January 15.

e. Post the entries in (d) to the temporary accounts.

Problems

Prepare a worksheet, financial statements, and adjusting and closing entries.

P4.1 (LO 1, 2, 4) The trial balance columns of the worksheet for Lampert Roofing at March 31, 2029, are as follows.

Lampert Roofing
Worksheet
For the Month Ended March 31, 2029

Account Titles	Trial Balance Dr.	Trial Balance Cr.
Cash	4,500	
Accounts Receivable	3,200	
Supplies	2,000	
Equipment	11,000	
Accumulated Depreciation—Equipment		1,250
Accounts Payable		2,500
Unearned Service Revenue		550
Share Capital—Ordinary		10,000
Retained Earnings		2,900
Dividends	1,100	
Service Revenue		6,300
Salaries and Wages Expense	1,300	
Miscellaneous Expense	400	
	23,500	23,500

Other data:

1. A physical count reveals only $550 of roofing supplies on hand.
2. Depreciation for March is $250.
3. Unearned service revenue amounted to $210 at March 31.
4. Accrued salaries are $700.

Instructions

a. Enter the trial balance on a worksheet and complete the worksheet.

b. Prepare an income statement and a retained earnings statement for the month of March and a classified statement of financial position at March 31.

c. Journalize the adjusting entries from the adjustments columns of the worksheet.

d. Journalize the closing entries from the financial statement columns of the worksheet.

a. Adjusted trial balance $24,450
b. Net income $2,540
Total assets $17,750

P4.2 (LO 1, 2, 4) The adjusted trial balance columns of the worksheet for Nguyen Company are as follows.

Complete worksheet; prepare financial statements, closing entries, and post-closing trial balance.

Nguyen Company
Worksheet
For the Year Ended December 31, 2029

Account No.	Account Titles	Adjusted Trial Balance Dr.	Adjusted Trial Balance Cr.
101	Cash	5,300	
112	Accounts Receivable	10,800	
126	Supplies	1,500	
130	Prepaid Insurance	2,000	
157	Equipment	27,000	
158	Accumulated Depreciation—Equipment		5,600
200	Notes Payable		15,000
201	Accounts Payable		6,100
212	Salaries and Wages Payable		3,600
230	Interest Payable		600
311	Share Capital—Ordinary		11,000
320	Retained Earnings		2,000
332	Dividends	7,600	
400	Service Revenue		61,000
610	Advertising Expense	9,000	
631	Supplies Expense	4,000	
711	Depreciation Expense	5,600	
722	Insurance Expense	3,500	
726	Salaries and Wages Expense	28,000	
905	Interest Expense	600	
	Totals	104,900	104,900

Instructions

a. Net income $10,300
b. Current assets $19,600
Current liabilities $14,300

e. Post-closing trial balance $46,600

a. Complete the worksheet by extending the balances to the financial statement columns.

b. Prepare an income statement, a retained earnings statement, and a classified statement of financial position. (*Note:* $4,000 of the notes payable become due in 2030.)

c. Prepare the closing entries. Use J14 for the journal page.

d. Post the closing entries. Use the three-column form of account. Income Summary is No. 350.

e. Prepare a post-closing trial balance.

Prepare financial statements, closing entries, and post-closing trial balance.

P4.3 (LO 2, 4) The completed financial statement columns of the spreadsheet for Fleming Company are as follows.

Fleming Company
For the Year Ended December 31, 2029

Account No.	Account Titles	Income Statement Dr.	Income Statement Cr.	Statement of Financial Position Dr.	Statement of Financial Position Cr.
101	Cash			8,900	
112	Accounts Receivable			10,800	
130	Prepaid Insurance			2,800	
157	Equipment			24,000	
158	Accumulated Depreciation—Equip.				4,500
201	Accounts Payable				9,000
212	Salaries and Wages Payable				2,400
311	Share Capital—Ordinary				12,000
320	Retained Earnings				7,500
332	Dividends			11,000	
400	Service Revenue		60,000		
622	Maintenance and Repairs Expense	1,600			
711	Depreciation Expense	3,100			
722	Insurance Expense	1,800			
726	Salaries and Wages Expense	30,000			
732	Utilities Expense	1,400			
	Totals	37,900	60,000	57,500	35,400
	Net Income	22,100			22,100
		60,000	60,000	57,500	57,500

Instructions

a. Ending retained earnings $18,600
Total current assets $22,500

d. Post-closing trial balance $46,500

a. Prepare an income statement, a retained earnings statement, and a classified statement of financial position.

b. Prepare the closing entries.

c. Post the closing entries and underline and balance the accounts. (Use T-accounts.) Income Summary is account No. 350.

d. Prepare a post-closing trial balance.

Complete worksheet; prepare classified statement of financial position, entries, and post-closing trial balance.

P4.4 (LO 1, 2, 4) Rusthe Management Services began business on January 1, 2029, with a capital investment of $120,000. The company manages condominiums for owners (Service Revenue) and rents space in its own office building (Rent Revenue). The trial balance and adjusted trial balance columns of the worksheet at the end of the first year are as follows (amounts in $).

Rusthe Management Services
Worksheet
For the Year Ended December 31, 2029

Account Titles	Trial Balance Dr.	Trial Balance Cr.	Adjusted Trial Balance Dr.	Adjusted Trial Balance Cr.
Cash	13,800		13,800	
Accounts Receivable	28,300		28,300	
Prepaid Insurance	3,600		2,100	
Land	67,000		67,000	
Buildings	127,000		127,000	

(continues)

Account Titles	Trial Balance Dr.	Trial Balance Cr.	Adjusted Trial Balance Dr.	Adjusted Trial Balance Cr.
Equipment	59,000		59,000	
Accounts Payable		12,500		12,500
Unearned Rent Revenue		6,000		1,000
Mortgage Payable		120,000		120,000
Share Capital—Ordinary		130,000		130,000
Retained Earnings		14,000		14,000
Dividends	22,000		22,000	
Service Revenue		90,700		90,700
Rent Revenue		29,000		34,000
Salaries and Wages Expense	42,000		42,000	
Advertising Expense	20,500		20,500	
Utilities Expense	19,000		19,000	
Totals	402,200	402,200		
Insurance Expense			1,500	
Depreciation Expense			6,600	
Accumulated Depreciation—Buildings				3,000
Accumulated Depreciation—Equipment				3,600
Interest Expense			10,000	
Interest Payable				10,000
Totals			418,800	418,800

Instructions

a. Prepare a complete worksheet.

b. Prepare a classified statement of financial position. (*Note:* $45,000 of the mortgage note payable is due for payment next year.)

c. Journalize the adjusting entries.

d. Journalize the closing entries.

e. Prepare a post-closing trial balance.

a. Net income $25,100
b. Total current assets $44,200
e. Post-closing trial balance $297,200

P4.5 (LO 1, 2, 4) Anya Clark opened Anya's Cleaning Service on July 1, 2029. During July, the following transactions were completed.

Complete all steps in accounting cycle.

July	1	Shareholders invested €20,000 cash in the business in exchange for ordinary shares.
	1	Purchased used truck for €12,000, paying €4,000 cash and the balance on account.
	3	Purchased cleaning supplies for €2,100 on account.
	5	Paid €1,800 cash on a 1-year insurance policy effective July 1.
	12	Billed customers €4,500 for cleaning services.
	18	Paid €1,500 cash on amount owed on truck and €1,400 on amount owed on cleaning supplies.
	20	Paid €2,800 cash for employee salaries.
	21	Collected €3,400 cash from customers billed on July 12.
	25	Billed customers €6,000 for cleaning services.
	31	Paid €350 for the monthly gasoline bill for the truck.
	31	Declared and paid a €5,600 cash dividend.

The chart of accounts for Anya's Cleaning Service contains the following accounts: No. 101 Cash, No. 112 Accounts Receivable, No. 126 Supplies, No. 130 Prepaid Insurance, No. 157 Equipment, No. 158 Accumulated Depreciation—Equipment, No. 201 Accounts Payable, No. 212 Salaries and Wages Payable, No. 311 Share Capital—Ordinary, No. 320 Retained Earnings, No. 332 Dividends, No. 350 Income Summary, No. 400 Service Revenue, No. 631 Supplies Expense, No. 633 Gasoline Expense, No. 711 Depreciation Expense, No. 722 Insurance Expense, and No. 726 Salaries and Wages Expense.

Instructions

a. Journalize and post the July transactions. Use page J1 for the journal and the three-column form of account.

b. Prepare a trial balance at July 31 on a worksheet.

c. Enter the following adjustments on the worksheet and complete the worksheet.

1. Unbilled and uncollected revenue for services performed at July 31 were €2,700.
2. Depreciation on equipment for the month was €500.

b. Trial balance €37,700
c. Adjusted trial balance €41,900

3. One-twelfth of the insurance expired.
4. An inventory count shows €600 of cleaning supplies on hand at July 31.
5. Accrued but unpaid employee salaries were €1,000.

d. Net income €6,900
Total assets €29,500

d. Prepare the income statement and a retained earnings statement for July and a classified statement of financial position at July 31.

e. Journalize and post adjusting entries. Use page J2 for the journal.

f. Journalize and post closing entries and complete the closing process. Use page J3 for the journal.

g. Prepare a post-closing trial balance at July 31.

g. Post-closing trial balance
€30,000

Analyze errors and prepare correcting entries and trial balance.

P4.6 (LO 3) Dao Vang, CPA, was retained by Universal Cable to prepare financial statements for April 2029. Vang accumulated all the ledger balances per Universal's records and found the following.

Universal Cable
Trial Balance
April 30, 2029

	Debit	Credit
Cash	$ 4,100	
Accounts Receivable	3,200	
Supplies	800	
Equipment	10,600	
Accumulated Depreciation—Equip.		$ 1,350
Accounts Payable		2,100
Salaries and Wages Payable		700
Unearned Service Revenue		890
Share Capital—Ordinary		10,000
Retained Earnings		2,900
Service Revenue		5,450
Salaries and Wages Expense	3,300	
Advertising Expense	600	
Miscellaneous Expense	290	
Depreciation Expense	500	
	$23,390	$23,390

Dao Vang reviewed the records and found the following errors.

1. Cash received from a customer on account was recorded as $950 instead of $590.
2. A payment of $75 for advertising expense was entered as a debit to Miscellaneous Expense $75 and a credit to Cash $75.
3. The first salary payment in April was for $1,900, which included $700 of salaries payable on March 31. The payment was recorded as a debit to Salaries and Wages Expense $1,900 and a credit to Cash $1,900. (No reversing entries were made on April 1.)
4. The purchase on account of a printer costing $310 was recorded as a debit to Supplies and a credit to Accounts Payable for $310.
5. A cash payment of repair expense on equipment for $96 was recorded as a debit to Equipment $69 and a credit to Cash $69.

Instructions

a. Prepare an analysis of each error showing (1) the incorrect entry, (2) the correct entry, and (3) the correcting entry. Items 4 and 5 occurred on April 30, 2029.

b. Trial balance $22,690

b. Prepare a correct trial balance.

Comprehensive Accounting Cycle Review

Complete all steps in accounting cycle.

ACR4.1 Jaden Li opened Kleene Window Washing on July 1, 2029. During July, the following transactions were completed.

July	1	Shareholders invested NT$12,000 cash in the business in exchange for ordinary shares.
	1	Purchased used truck for NT$8,000, paying NT$2,000 cash and the balance on account.
	3	Purchased cleaning supplies for NT$900 on account.
	5	Paid NT$1,800 cash on a 1-year insurance policy effective July 1.
	12	Billed customers NT$3,700 for cleaning services performed.
	18	Paid NT$1,000 cash on amount owed on truck and NT$500 on amount owed on cleaning supplies.
	20	Paid NT$2,000 cash for employee salaries.
	21	Collected NT$1,600 cash from customers billed on July 12.
	25	Billed customers NT$2,500 for cleaning services performed.
	31	Paid NT$290 for maintenance of the truck during month.
	31	Declared and paid a NT$600 cash dividend.

The chart of accounts for Kleene Window Washing contains the following accounts: Cash, Accounts Receivable, Supplies, Prepaid Insurance, Equipment, Accumulated Depreciation—Equipment, Accounts Payable, Salaries and Wages Payable, Share Capital—Ordinary, Retained Earnings, Dividends, Income Summary, Service Revenue, Maintenance and Repairs Expense, Supplies Expense, Depreciation Expense, Insurance Expense, and Salaries and Wages Expense.

Instructions

a. Journalize the July transactions.

b. Post to the ledger accounts. (Use T-accounts.)

c. Prepare a trial balance at July 31.

d. Journalize the following adjustments.

1. Services performed but unbilled and uncollected at July 31 were NT$1,700.

2. Depreciation on equipment for the month was NT$180.

3. One-twelfth of the insurance expired.

4. A count shows NT$320 of cleaning supplies on hand at July 31.

5. Accrued but unpaid employee salaries were NT$400.

e. Post adjusting entries to the T-accounts.

f. Prepare an adjusted trial balance.

g. Prepare the income statement and a retained earnings statement for July and a classified statement of financial position at July 31.

h. Journalize and post closing entries and complete the closing process.

i. Prepare a post-closing trial balance at July 31.

f. Cash NT$5,410

g. Tot. assets NT$21,500

ACR4.2 Lars Linken opened Lars Cleaners on March 1, 2029. During March, the following transactions were completed.

Complete all steps in accounting cycle.

Mar.	1	Shareholders invested €15,000 cash in the business in exchange for ordinary shares.
	1	Borrowed €6,000 cash by signing a 6-month, 6%, €6,000 note payable. Interest will be paid the first day of each subsequent month.
	1	Purchased used truck for €8,000 cash.
	2	Paid €1,500 cash to cover rent from March 1 through May 31.
	3	Paid €2,400 cash on a 6-month insurance policy effective March 1.
	6	Purchased cleaning supplies for €2,000 on account.
	14	Billed customers €3,700 for cleaning services performed.
	18	Paid €500 on amount owed on cleaning supplies.
	20	Paid €1,750 cash for employee salaries.
	21	Collected €1,600 cash from customers billed on March 14.
	28	Billed customers €4,200 for cleaning services performed.
	31	Paid €350 for gas and oil used in truck during month (use Maintenance and Repairs Expense).
	31	Declared and paid a €900 cash dividend.

The chart of accounts for Lars Cleaners contains the following accounts: Cash, Accounts Receivable, Supplies, Prepaid Insurance, Prepaid Rent, Equipment, Accumulated Depreciation—Equipment, Accounts Payable, Salaries and Wages Payable, Notes Payable, Interest Payable, Share Capital—Ordinary, Retained Earnings, Dividends, Income Summary, Service Revenue, Maintenance and Repairs Expense, Supplies Expense, Depreciation Expense, Insurance Expense, Salaries and Wages Expense, Rent Expense, and Interest Expense.

Instructions

a. Journalize the March transactions.

b. Post to the ledger accounts. (Use T-accounts.)

c. Prepare a trial balance at March 31.

d. Journalize the following adjustments.

1. Services performed but unbilled and uncollected at March 31 were €200.
2. Depreciation on equipment for the month was €250.
3. One-sixth of the insurance expired.
4. An inventory count shows €280 of cleaning supplies on hand at March 31.
5. Accrued but unpaid employee salaries were €1,080.
6. One month of the prepaid rent has expired.
7. One month of interest expense related to the note payable has accrued and will be paid April 1. (*Hint:* Use the formula from Illustration 3.18 to compute interest.)

e. Post adjusting entries to the T-accounts.

f. Prepare an adjusted trial balance.

g. Prepare the income statement and a retained earnings statement for March and a classified statement of financial position at March 31.

h. Journalize and post closing entries and complete the closing process.

i. Prepare a post-closing trial balance at March 31.

f. Tot. adj. trial balance €31,960
g. Tot. assets €24,730

Journalize transactions and follow through accounting cycle to preparation of financial statements.

ACR4.3 On August 1, 2029, the following were the account balances of B&B Repair Services.

	Debit		Credit
Cash	$ 6,040	Accumulated Depreciation—Equipment	$ 600
Accounts Receivable	2,910	Accounts Payable	2,300
Notes Receivable	4,000	Unearned Service Revenue	1,260
Supplies	1,030	Salaries and Wages Payable	1,420
Equipment	10,000	Share Capital—Ordinary	16,300
		Retained Earnings	2,100
	$23,980		$23,980

During August, the following summary transactions were completed.

Aug.	1	Paid $400 cash for advertising in local newspapers. Advertising flyers will be included with newspapers delivered during August and September.
	3	Paid August rent $380.
	5	Received $1,200 cash from customers in payment on account.
	10	Paid $3,120 for salaries due employees, of which $1,700 is for August and $1,420 is for July salaries payable.
	12	Received $2,800 cash for services performed in August.
	15	Purchased store equipment on account $2,000.
	20	Paid creditors $2,000 of accounts payable due.
	22	Purchased supplies on account $800.
	25	Paid $2,900 cash for employees' salaries.
	27	Billed customers $3,760 for services performed.
	29	Received $780 from customers for services to be performed in the future.

Adjustment data:

1. A count shows supplies on hand of $960.
2. Accrued but unpaid employees' salaries are $1,540.
3. Depreciation on equipment for the month is $320.
4. Services were performed to satisfy $800 of unearned service revenue.
5. One month's worth of advertising services has been received.
6. One month of interest revenue related to the $4,000 note receivable has accrued. The 4-month note has a 6% annual interest rate. (*Hint:* Use the formula from Illustration 3.18 to compute interest.)

Instructions

a. Enter the August 1 balances in the ledger accounts. (Use T-accounts.)

b. Journalize the August transactions.

c. Post to the ledger accounts. B&B's chart of accounts includes Prepaid Advertising, Interest Receivable, Service Revenue, Interest Revenue, Advertising Expense, Depreciation Expense, Supplies Expense, Salaries and Wages Expense, and Rent Expense.

d. Prepare a trial balance at August 31.

e. Journalize and post adjusting entries.

f. Prepare an adjusted trial balance.

g. Prepare an income statement and a retained earnings statement for August and a classified statement of financial position at August 31.

h. Journalize and post closing entries and complete the closing process.

i. Prepare a post-closing trial balance at August 31.

f. Cash $2,020
Tot. adj. trial balance $32,580
g. Net loss $530

ACR4.4 At June 30, 2029, the end of its most recent fiscal year, Green River Computer Consultants' post-closing trial balance was as follows (amounts in thousands):

Record and post transaction, adjusting, and closing journal entries; prepare adjusted trial balance and financial statements.

	Debit	Credit
Cash	¥5,230	
Accounts receivable	1,200	
Supplies	690	
Accounts payable		¥ 400
Unearned service revenue		1,120
Share capital—ordinary		4,000
Retained earnings		1,600
	¥7,120	¥7,120

The company underwent a major expansion in July. New staff was hired and more financing was obtained. Green River conducted the following transactions during July 2029, and adjusts its accounts monthly.

July 1 Purchased equipment, paying ¥4,000 cash and signing a 2-year note payable for ¥20,000. The equipment has a 4-year useful life. The note has a 6% interest rate which is payable on the first day of each following month.
2 Shareholders invested ¥50,000 cash in the company in exchange for ordinary shares.
3 Paid ¥3,600 cash for a 12-month insurance policy effective July 1.
3 Paid the first 2 (July and August 2029) months' rent for an annual lease of office space for ¥4,000 per month.
6 Paid ¥3,800 for supplies.
9 Visited client offices and agreed on the terms of a consulting project. Green River will bill the client, Connor Productions, on the 20th of each month for services performed.
10 Collected ¥1,200 cash on account from Milani Brothers. This client was billed in June when Green River performed the service.
13 Performed services for Fitzgerald Enterprises. This client paid ¥1,120 in advance last month. All services relating to this payment are now completed.
14 Paid ¥400 cash for a utility bill. This related to June utilities that were accrued at the end of June.
16 Met with a new client, Thunder Bay Technologies. Received ¥12,000 cash in advance for future services to be performed.
18 Paid semi-monthly salaries for ¥11,000.
20 Performed services worth ¥28,000 on account and billed customers.
20 Received a bill for ¥2,200 for advertising services received during July. The amount is not due until August 15.
23 Performed the first phase of the project for Thunder Bay Technologies. Recognized ¥10,000 of revenue from the cash advance received July 16.
27 Received ¥15,000 cash from customers billed on July 20.

Adjustment data:

1. Adjustment of prepaid insurance.
2. Adjustment of prepaid rent.
3. Supplies used, ¥1,250.
4. Equipment depreciation, ¥500 per month.
5. Accrual of interest on note payable. (*Hint:* Use the formula from Illustration 3.18 to compute interest.)

6. Salaries for the second half of July, ¥11,000, to be paid on August 1.
7. Estimated utilities expense for July, ¥800.
8. Income tax for July, ¥1,200, will be paid in August. (*Hint:* Use the accounts Income Tax Expense and Income Taxes Payable.)

The chart of accounts for Green River Computer Consultants contains the following accounts: Cash, Accounts Receivable, Supplies, Prepaid Insurance. Prepaid Rent, Equipment, Accumulated Depreciation—Equipment, Accounts Payable, Notes Payable, Interest Payable, Income Taxes Payable, Salaries and Wages Payable, Unearned Service Revenue, Share Capital—Ordinary, Retained Earnings, Income Summary, Service Revenue, Supplies Expense, Depreciation Expense, Insurance Expense, Salaries and Wages Expense, Advertising Expense, Income Tax Expense, Interest Expense, Rent Expense, and Utilities Expense.

Instructions

a. Enter the July 1 balances in the ledger accounts. (Use T-accounts.)

b. Journalize the July transactions.

c. Post to the ledger accounts.

d. Prepare a trial balance at July 31.

e. Journalize and post adjusting entries for the month ending July 31.

f. Prepare an adjusted trial balance.

g. Net income ¥6,770
Tot. assets ¥99,670

g. Prepare an income statement and a retained earnings statement for July and a classified statement of financial position at July 31.

h. Journalize and post closing entries and complete the closing process.

i. Prepare a post-closing trial balance at July 31.

Expand Your Critical Thinking

Financial Reporting Problem: TSMC, Ltd. (TWN)

CT4.1 The financial statements of **TSMC** are presented in Appendix A. The complete annual report, including the notes to the financial statements, is available at the company's website.

Instructions

Answer the questions below using the statement of financial position and the notes to consolidated financial statements section.

a. What were TSMC's total current assets at December 31, 2019, and December 31, 2020?

b. Are assets that TSMC included under current assets listed in proper order? Explain.

c. How are TSMC's assets classified?

d. What were TSMC's total current liabilities at December 31, 2019, and December 31, 2020?

Comparative Analysis Problem: Nestlé SA (CHE) vs. Delfi Limited (SGP)

CT4.2 **Nestlé**'s financial statements are presented in Appendix B. Financial statements of **Delfi Limited** are presented in Appendix C.

Instructions

a. Based on the information contained in these financial statements, determine each of the following for Nestlé and Delfi at December 31, 2020.

1. Total current assets.
2. Net amount of property, plant, and equipment (land, buildings, and equipment).
3. Total current liabilities.
4. Total equity.

b. What conclusions concerning the companies' respective financial positions can be drawn from the companies' current assets and current liabilities?

Real-World Focus

CT4.3 Most companies have established home pages on the Internet, e.g., **Gitanjali Group** (IND) and **Wumart** (CHN).

Instructions

Examine the home pages of any two companies and answer the following questions.

a. What type of information is available?

b. Is any accounting-related information presented?

c. Would you describe the home page as informative, promotional, or both? Why?

Decision-Making Across the Organization

CT4.4 Whitegloves Janitorial Service was started 2 years ago by Jenna Olson. Because business has been exceptionally good, Jenna decided on July 1, 2029, to expand operations by acquiring an additional truck and hiring two more assistants. To finance the expansion, Jenna obtained on July 1, 2029, a £25,000, 10% bank loan, payable £10,000 on July 1, 2030, and the balance on July 1, 2031. The terms of the loan require the borrower to have £10,000 more current assets than current liabilities at December 31, 2029. If these terms are not met, the bank loan will be refinanced at 15% interest. At December 31, 2029, the accountant for Whitegloves Janitorial Service prepared the following statement of financial position.

Whitegloves Janitorial Service
Statement of Financial Position
December 31, 2029

Assets			**Equity and Liabilities**		
Property, plant, and equipment			Equity		
Equipment (net)	£22,000		Share capital—ordinary	£41,000	
Delivery trucks (net)	34,000	£56,000	Retained earnings	13,000	£54,000
Current assets			Non-current liabilities		
Prepaid insurance	4,800		Notes payable		15,000
Supplies	5,200		Current liabilities		
Accounts receivable	9,000		Notes payable	10,000	
Cash	5,500	24,500	Accounts payable	1,500	11,500
Total assets		£80,500	Total equity and liabilities		£80,500

Jenna presented the statement of financial position to the bank's loan officer on January 2, 2030, confident that the company had met the terms of the loan. The loan officer was not impressed. She said, "We need financial statements audited by a CA." A CA was hired and immediately realized that the statement of financial position had been prepared from a trial balance and not from an adjusted trial balance. The adjustment data at the statement of financial position date consisted of the following.

1. Unbilled janitorial services performed were £3,700.
2. Janitorial supplies on hand were £2,500.
3. Prepaid insurance was a 3-year policy dated January 1, 2029.
4. December expenses incurred but unpaid at December 31, £500.
5. Interest on the bank loan was not recorded.
6. The amounts for property, plant, and equipment presented in the statement of financial position were reported net of accumulated depreciation (cost less accumulated depreciation). These amounts were £4,000 for cleaning equipment and £5,000 for delivery trucks as of January 1, 2029. Depreciation for 2029, still unrecorded, was £2,000 for cleaning equipment and £5,000 for delivery trucks.

Instructions

With the class divided into groups, answer the following.

a. Prepare a correct statement of financial position.

b. Were the terms of the bank loan met? Explain.

Communication Activity

CT4.5 The accounting cycle is important in understanding the accounting process.

Instructions

Write an email to your instructor that lists the steps of the accounting cycle in the order they should be completed. End with a paragraph that explains the optional steps in the cycle.

Ethics Case

CT4.6 As the controller of Take No Prisoners Perfume, you discover a misstatement that overstated net income in the prior year's financial statements. The misleading financial statements appear in the company's annual report which was issued to banks and other creditors less than a month ago. After much thought about the consequences of telling the president, Fabien LaRue, about this misstatement, you gather your courage to inform him. Fabien says, "Hey! What they don't know won't hurt them. But, just so we set the record straight, we'll adjust this year's financial statements for last year's misstatement. We can absorb that misstatement better in this year than in last year anyway! Just don't make such a mistake again."

Instructions

a. Who are the stakeholders in this situation?

b. What are the ethical issues in this situation?

c. What would you do as a controller in this situation?

All About You

CT4.7 Companies prepare statements of financial position in order to know their financial position at a specific point in time. This enables them to make a comparison to their position at previous points in time, and gives them a basis for planning for the future. In order to evaluate your financial position, you may need to prepare a personal statement of financial position. Assume that you have compiled the following information regarding your finances. (*Note:* Some of the items might not be used in your personal statement of financial position.)

Amount owed on student loan balance (long-term)	€ 5,000
Balance in checking account	1,200
Investment (short-term)	3,000
Annual earnings from part-time job	11,300
Automobile	7,000
Balance on automobile loan (current portion)	1,500
Balance on automobile loan (long-term portion)	4,000
Home computer	800
Amount owed to you by younger brother	300
Balance in savings account	1,800
Annual tuition	6,400
Video and stereo equipment	1,250
Balance owed on credit card (current portion)	1,800

Instructions

Prepare a personal statement of financial position using the format you have learned for a classified statement of financial position for a company. For the equity account, use Owner's Capital.

Answers to Insight and Accounting Across the Organization Questions

Transforming the Closing Process Q: Who else benefits from a shorter closing process? **A:** Investors benefit from a shorter closing process. The shorter the closing, the sooner the company can report its financial results. This means that the financial information is timelier and therefore more relevant to investors.

How Can Accounting Aid African Growth? Q: What benefit is likely to result if African companies improve their accounting practices and adopt IFRS? **A:** High-quality reliable financial information is critical for investors and creditors. By improving the quality and reliability of financial information provided by the Nigerian companies, more capital can be attracted to invest in these companies, which in turn will support growth in the economy.

Creating Value Q: What are some implications of Nestlé's decision to measure its non-financial results using objective measures and then publicly report these results? **A:** Measuring and reporting are the foundations of accounting. The willingness of Nestlé to measure and report its progress in areas like nutrition and rural development will make the company more accountable and more likely to achieve these goals.

Managing Liquidity During a Global Pandemic Q: What can various company managers do to ensure that working capital is managed efficiently to maximize net income? **A:** Marketing and sales managers must understand that by extending generous repayment terms, they are expanding the company's receivables balance and slowing the company's cash flow. Production managers must strive to minimize the amount of excess inventory on hand. Managers must coordinate efforts to speed up the collection of receivables, while also ensuring that the company pays its bills (payables) on time but never too early.

A Look at U.S. GAAP

LEARNING OBJECTIVE 6

Compare the procedures for the accounting cycle under IFRS and U.S. GAAP.

The classified statement of financial position, although generally required internationally, contains certain variations in format when reporting under GAAP.

Key Points

- In general, GAAP follows the similar guidelines as this text for presenting items in the current asset section, except that under GAAP items are listed in order of liquidity, while under IFRS they are often listed in reverse order of liquidity. For example, under GAAP cash is listed first, but under IFRS it is listed last.
- Both GAAP and IFRS are increasing the use of fair value to report assets. However, at this point IFRS has adopted it more broadly. As examples, under IFRS companies can apply fair value to property, plant, and equipment; natural resources; and in some cases intangible assets.

Similarities

- Both IFRS and GAAP require disclosures about (1) accounting policies followed, (2) judgments that management has made in the process of applying the entity's accounting policies, and (3) the key assumptions and estimation uncertainty that could result in a material adjustment to the carrying amounts of assets and liabilities within the next financial year.
- Comparative prior-period information must be presented and financial statements must be prepared annually.

Differences

- IFRS requires that a company must make an explicit and unreserved statement that the financial statements comply with IFRS standards. No similar statement is required under GAAP.
- IFRS officially uses the term *statement of financial position* in its literature, while in the United States it is often referred to as the *balance sheet.*
- IFRS requires that specific items be reported on the statement of financial position, whereas no such general standard exists in GAAP. However, under GAAP, public companies must follow U.S. Securities and Exchange Commission (SEC) regulations, which require specific line items as well. In addition, specific GAAP standards mandate certain forms of reporting statement of financial position information. The SEC guidelines are more detailed than IFRS.
- IFRS requires that a complete set of financial statements must include comparative information from the preceding period. There is no similar requirement in GAAP. However, public companies following U.S. SEC regulations have a similar requirement.
- While IFRS companies often report non-current assets before current assets in their statements of financial position, this is never seen under GAAP. Also, some IFRS companies report the subtotal "net assets," which equals total assets minus total liabilities. This practice is also not seen under GAAP.
- A key difference in valuation is that under IFRS, companies, under certain conditions, can report property, plant, and equipment at cost or at fair value, whereas under GAAP this practice is not allowed.
- GAAP has many differences in terminology from what are shown in your text. For example, in the following sample balance sheet (statement of financial position), notice in the investment category that shares are called stock. In addition, the format used for statement of financial position presentation is often different between GAAP and IFRS.

Franklin Corporation
Balance Sheet
October 31, 2029

Assets			
Current assets			
Cash		$ 6,600	
Short-term investments		2,000	
Accounts receivable		7,000	
Notes receivable		1,000	
Inventory		3,000	
Supplies		2,100	
Prepaid insurance		400	$22,100
Long-term investments			
Investment in stock of Walters Corp.		5,200	
Investment in real estate		2,000	7,200
Property, plant, and equipment			
Land		10,000	
Equipment	$24,000		
Less: Accumulated depreciation—equipment	5,000	19,000	29,000
Intangible assets			
Patents			3,100
Total assets			$61,400
Liabilities and Stockholders' Equity			
Current liabilities			
Notes payable		$11,000	
Accounts payable		2,100	
Salaries and wages payable		1,600	
Unearned service revenue		900	
Interest payable		450	$16,050
Long-term liabilities			
Mortgage payable		10,000	
Notes payable		1,300	11,300
Stockholders' equity			
Common stock		20,000	
Retained earnings		14,050	34,050
Total liabilities and stockholders' equity			$61,400

GAAP Practice

GAAP Self-Test Questions

1. Which of the following statements is **false**?
   a. Assets equals liabilities plus stockholders' equity.
   b. Under IFRS, companies sometimes net liabilities against assets to report "net assets."
   c. Both GAAP and IFRS are increasing the use of fair value to report assets.
   d. Under GAAP, the statement of financial position is usually referred to as the statement of assets and equity.

2. A company has purchased a tract of land and expects to build a production plant on the land in approximately 5 years. During the 5 years before construction, the land will be idle. Under GAAP, the land should be reported as:
   a. land expense.
   b. property, plant, and equipment.
   c. an intangible asset.
   d. a long-term investment.

3. Current assets under GAAP are listed generally:
   a. by importance.
   b. in the reverse order of their expected conversion to cash.
   c. by order of liquidity.
   d. alphabetically.

4. Companies that use GAAP:

a. may report all their assets on their balance sheets at fair value.

b. often offset assets against liabilities and show net assets and net liabilities on their balance sheets, rather than the underlying detailed line items.

c. generally report current assets before non-current assets on their balance sheets.

d. do not have any guidelines as to what should be reported on their balance sheets.

5. Companies that follow GAAP to prepare a balance sheet generally use the following order of classification:

a. current assets, long-term assets, current liabilities, long-term liabilities, stockholders' equity.

b. long-term assets, long-term liabilities, current assets, current liabilities, stockholders' equity.

c. long-term assets, current assets, stockholders' equity, long-term liabilities, current liabilities.

d. stockholders' equity, long-term assets, current assets, long-term liabilities, current liabilities.

GAAP Exercises

GAAP4.1 In what ways does the format of a statement of financial of position under IFRS often differ from a balance sheet presented under GAAP?

GAAP4.2 What term is commonly used under GAAP in reference to the statement of financial position?

GAAP4.3 The balance sheet for Diaz Company includes the following accounts: Accounts Receivable $12,500; Prepaid Insurance $3,600; Cash $15,400; Supplies $5,200; and Short-Term Investments $6,700. Prepare the current assets section of the balance sheet, listing the accounts in proper sequence using GAAP.

GAAP4.4 Zurich Company recently received the following information related to the company's December 31, 2029, balance sheet.

Inventories	$ 2,700	Short-term investments	$ 120
Cash	13,100	Accumulated depreciation—	
Equipment	21,700	equipment	5,700
Investments in stocks		Accounts receivable	4,300
(long-term)	6,500		

Prepare the assets section of the company's classified balance sheet using GAAP.

GAAP4.5 The following information is available for Rego Bowling Alley at December 31, 2029, its first year of operation.

Buildings	$128,000	Interest Expense	$ 2,600
Accounts Receivable	7,540	Common Stock	112,000
Prepaid Insurance	4,680	Accumulated Depreciation—Buildings	42,600
Cash	18,040	Accounts Payable	12,300
Equipment	62,400	Notes Payable	95,000
Land	67,000	Accumulated Depreciation—Equipment	18,720
Insurance Expense	780	Interest Payable	2,600
Depreciation Expense	7,360	Service Revenue	15,180

Prepare a classified balance sheet using GAAP; assume that $13,900 of the notes payable will be paid in 2030.

GAAP4.6 Brian Hopkins is interested in comparing the liquidity and solvency of a U.S. software company with a Chinese competitor. Is this possible if the two companies report using different currencies?

GAAP Financial Reporting Problem: Apple Inc. (USA)

GAAP4.7 The financial statements of **Apple** are presented in Appendix D. The complete annual report, including the notes to its financial statements, is available at the company's website.

a. What were Apple's total current assets at September 26, 2020, and September 28, 2019?

b. Are the assets included in current assets listed in the proper order? Explain.

c. How are Apple's assets classified?

d. What were Apple's current liabilities at September 26, 2020, and September 28, 2019?

Answers to GAAP Self-Test Questions

1. d **2.** d **3.** c **4.** c **5.** a

CHAPTER **5**

Accounting for Merchandise Operations

LEARNING OBJECTIVES After studying this chapter, you should be able to:

LO 1 Describe merchandising operations and inventory systems.

LO 2 Record purchases under a perpetual inventory system.

LO 3 Record sales under a perpetual inventory system.

LO 4 Apply the steps in the accounting cycle to a merchandising company.

LO 5 Prepare financial statements for a merchandising company.

Chapter Preview

Merchandising is one of the largest and most influential industries in the world. It is likely that a number of you will work for a merchandiser. Therefore, understanding the financial statements of merchandising companies is important. In this chapter, you will learn the basics about reporting merchandising transactions. In addition, you will learn how to prepare and analyze a commonly used form of the income statement.

Accounting for Merchandise Operations

Merchandising Operations and Inventory Systems
- Operating cycles
- Flow of costs

Recording Purchases Under a Perpetual System
- Freight costs
- Purchase returns and allowances
- Purchase discounts
- Summary of purchasing transactions

Recording Sales Under a Perpetual System
- Sales returns and allowances
- Sales discounts
- Data analytics and credit sales

The Accounting Cycle for a Merchandising Company
- Adjusting entries
- Closing entries
- Summary of merchandising entries

Financial Statements for a Merchandiser
- Income statement
- Classified statement of financial position

Practice

DO IT! 1 Merchandising Operations and Inventory Systems

DO IT! 2 Purchase Transactions

DO IT! 3 Sales Transactions

DO IT! 4 Closing Entries

DO IT! 5 Financial Statement Classifications

Go to the Review and Practice section at the end of the chapter for a review of key concepts and practice applications with solutions.
Additional tutorials and practice opportunities are available in the Wiley online course.

Feature Story Who Doesn't Shop?

Carrefour (FRA), headquartered in France, is the largest retailer in Europe and the second largest retailer in the world. While 40% of its sales are in France, it operates stores under a variety of names in 32 countries in Europe, Asia, and Latin America, such as Carrefour Express, Dity, Ed, Minipreco, and Promocash. Its nearly 10,000 stores employ 471,000 people and generate sales of €112 billion.

Becoming an international titan hasn't always been easy. Carrefour has enjoyed some successful mergers and acquisitions. But, it has also experienced setbacks, including a failed effort to acquire a giant Brazilian retailer. It has had some success in increasing market share in emerging markets. But, by far the largest share of its sales are in Europe, which has experienced low consumer confidence in recent years due to the recession and debt crisis. As a result, Carrefour's increases in emerging markets have only served to offset declines in Europe.

Management has experienced upheaval, with three new chief executive officers during a seven-year period. Investors in recent years have withdrawn support for the company, resulting in a drop in Carrefour's share price of two-thirds in less than five years. At times, the company has struggled strategically. Recently, it decided to quit using temporary price cuts to promote products. Instead, Carrefour sets prices low on certain key items. It also decided to not set its prices as low as those of bargain stores, such as **E.Leclerc** (FRA). Carrefour's management felt that the additional services the company provides would enable it to charge slightly higher prices than bargain stores without losing customers. However, poor economic conditions made consumers extremely price-conscious. As a result, the company has seen a significant drop in customer traffic.

Nobody said retailing is easy, but at number two in the world, Carrefour has no intention of throwing in the towel. The company recently launched a makeover of 500 superstores in Europe, and it continues to look for expansion opportunities in countries that have good growth opportunities. Recently, the company opened its first store in India. Lars Olofsson, CEO of Carrefour, declared: "The opening of this first store marks Carrefour's entry into the Indian market and will be followed shortly by the opening of other Cash & Carry stores. This first step is essential to allow the Carrefour teams to fully understand the specificities of the Indian market and then build our presence in other formats."

TPG/Shutterstock

5.1 Merchandising Operations and Inventory Systems

LEARNING OBJECTIVE 1

Describe merchandising operations and inventory systems.

Metro (DEU), **Carrefour** (FRA), and **Tesco** (GBR) are called merchandising companies because they buy and sell merchandise rather than perform services as their primary source of revenue.

- Merchandising companies that purchase and sell directly to consumers are called **retailers**.
- Merchandising companies that sell to retailers are known as **wholesalers**.

For example, retailer **Walgreens** (USA) might buy goods from wholesaler **Grupo Casa SA de CV** (MEX). Retailer **Office Depot** (USA) might buy office supplies from wholesaler **Corporate Express** (NLD).

The primary source of revenue for merchandising companies is the sale of merchandise, often referred to simply as **sales revenue** or **sales**. A merchandising company has two categories of expenses: cost of goods sold and operating expenses.

1. **Cost of goods sold** is the total cost of merchandise sold during the period. This expense is directly related to the revenue recognized from the sale of goods.
2. **Operating expenses** are incurred in the process of earning sales revenue. Examples include advertising expense and rent expense. Note that operating expenses are a category of expenses, not a single line item on the income statement.

Illustration 5.1 shows the income measurement process for a merchandising company. The items in the two blue boxes are unique to a merchandising company; they are not used by a service company.

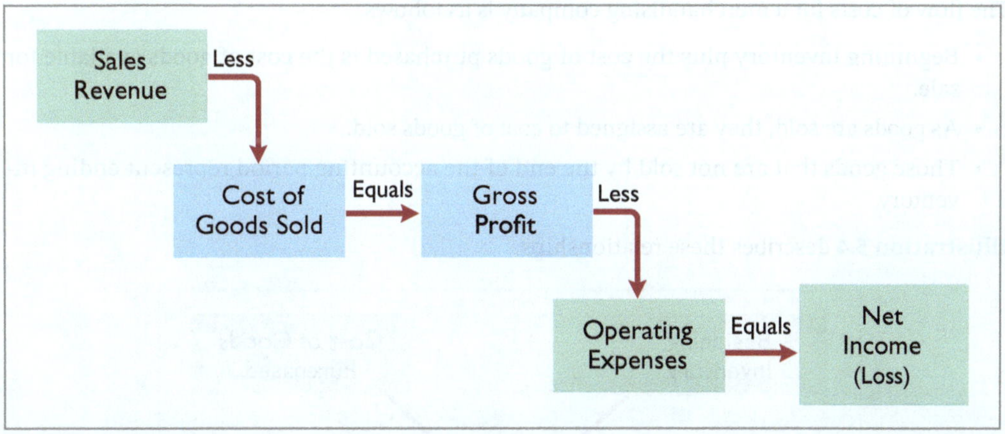

ILLUSTRATION 5.1

Income measurement process for a merchandising company

Operating Cycles

The operating cycle of a merchandising company ordinarily is longer than that of a service company. The purchase of merchandise inventory and its eventual sale lengthen the cycle. **Illustration 5.2** shows the operating cycle of a service company.

ILLUSTRATION 5.2

Operating cycle for a service company

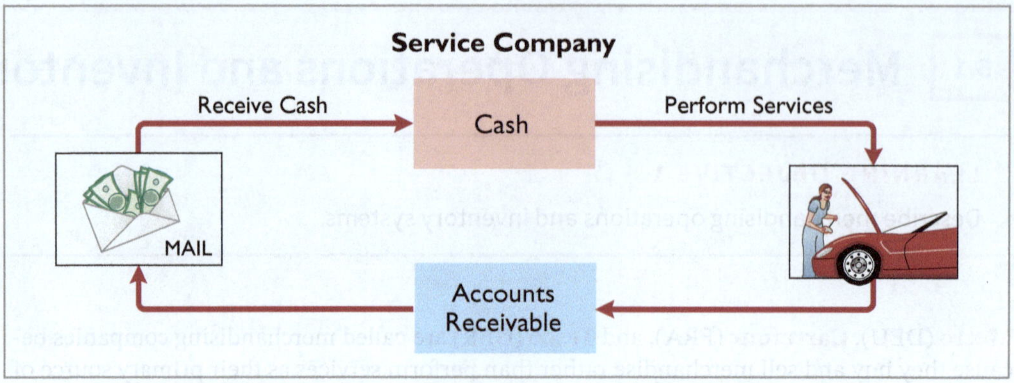

Illustration 5.3 shows the operating cycle of a merchandising company.

ILLUSTRATION 5.3

Operating cycle for a merchandising company

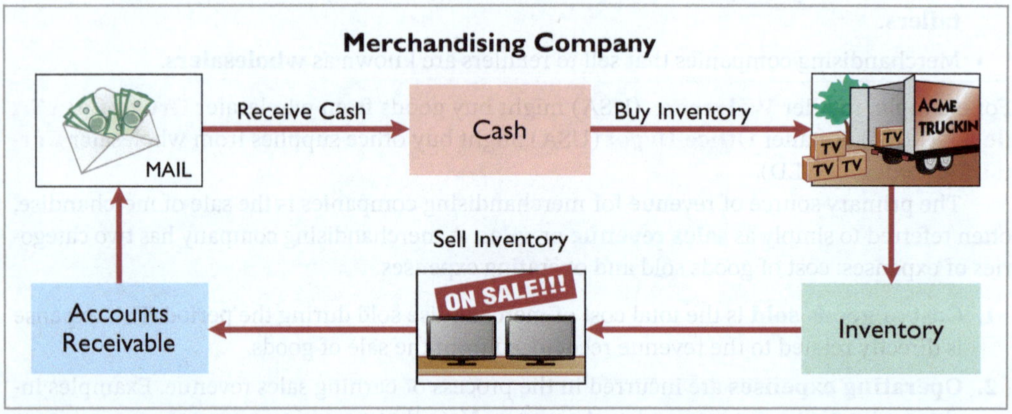

Note that the added asset account for a merchandising company is the Inventory account. Companies report inventory as a current asset on the statement of financial position.

Flow of Costs

The flow of costs for a merchandising company is as follows.

- Beginning inventory plus the cost of goods purchased is the cost of goods available for sale.
- As goods are sold, they are assigned to cost of goods sold.
- Those goods that are not sold by the end of the accounting period represent ending inventory.

Illustration 5.4 describes these relationships.

ILLUSTRATION 5.4

Flow of costs

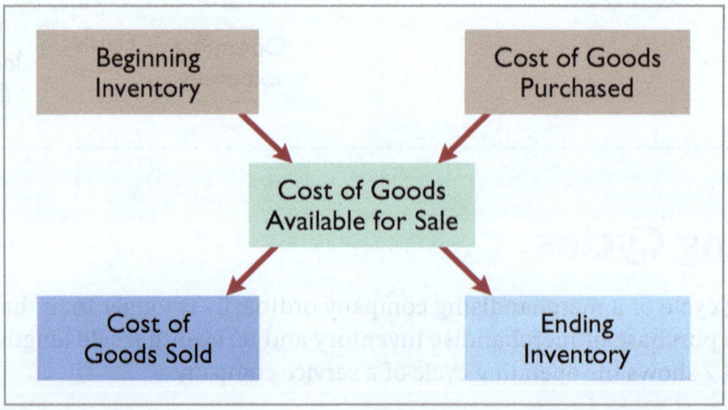

Companies use one of two systems to account for inventory: a **perpetual inventory system** or a **periodic inventory system**.

Perpetual System

In a **perpetual inventory system**, companies keep detailed records of the cost of each inventory purchase and sale (see **Helpful Hint**). These records continuously—perpetually—show the inventory that should be on hand for every item. For example, a **Toyota** (JPN) dealership has separate inventory records for each automobile, truck, and van on its lot and showroom floor. Similarly, a **Morrisons** (GBR) grocery store uses bar codes and optical scanners to keep a daily running record of every box of cereal and every jar of jelly that it buys and sells. Under a perpetual inventory system, a company determines the cost of goods sold **each time a sale occurs**.

HELPFUL HINT

Even under perpetual inventory systems, companies take a physical inventory count. This is done as a control procedure to verify inventory levels, in order to detect theft or "shrinkage."

Periodic System

In a **periodic inventory system**, companies do not keep detailed inventory records of the goods on hand throughout the period. Instead, they determine the cost of goods sold **only at the end of the accounting period**—that is, periodically. At that point, the company takes a physical inventory count to determine the cost of goods on hand.

To determine the cost of goods sold under a periodic inventory system, the following steps are necessary.

1. Determine the cost of goods on hand at the beginning of the accounting period.
2. Add to it the cost of goods purchased.
3. Subtract the cost of goods on hand as determined by the physical inventory count at the end of the accounting period.

Illustration 5.5 compares the sequence of activities and the timing of the cost of goods sold computation under the two inventory systems.

ILLUSTRATION 5.5

Comparing perpetual and periodic inventory systems

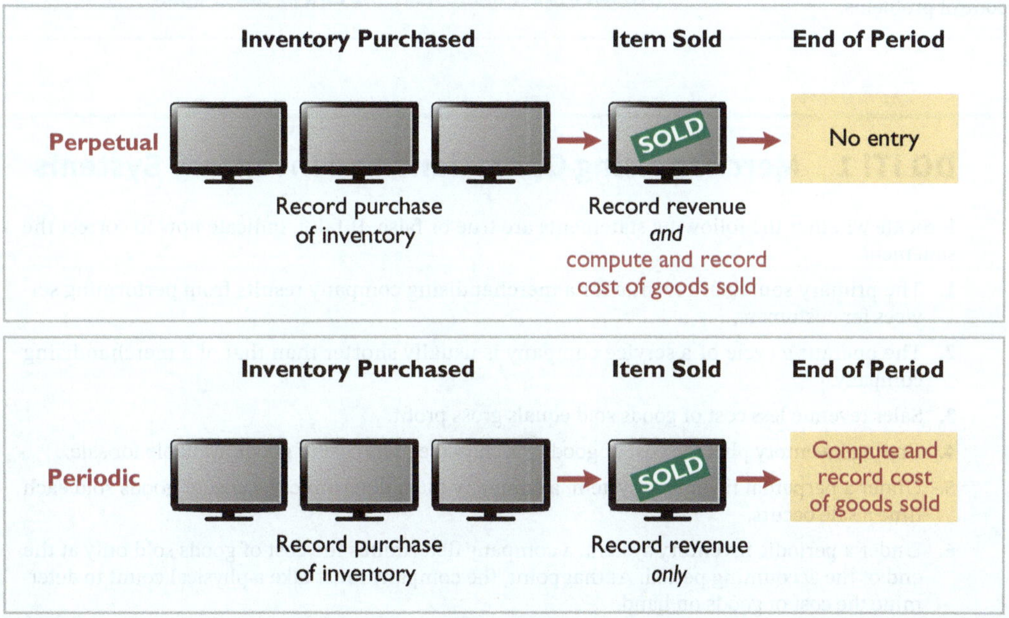

Advantages of the Perpetual System

Companies that sell merchandise with high unit values, such as automobiles, furniture, and major home appliances, have traditionally used perpetual systems. The growing use of computers and electronic scanners has enabled many more companies to install perpetual inventory systems. The perpetual inventory system is so named because the accounting records continuously—perpetually—show the quantity and cost of the inventory that should be on hand at any time.

A perpetual inventory system provides better control over inventories than a periodic system.

- Since the inventory records show the quantities that should be on hand, the company can count the goods at any time to see whether the amount of goods actually on hand agrees with the inventory records.
- If shortages are uncovered, the company can investigate immediately.

Although a perpetual inventory system requires both additional clerical work and expense to maintain the subsidiary records, a computerized system can minimize this cost. Much of **Amazon.com**'s (USA) success is attributed to its sophisticated inventory system.

Some businesses find it either unnecessary or uneconomical to invest in a computerized perpetual inventory system. Many small merchandising businesses now use basic accounting software, which provides some of the essential benefits of a perpetual inventory system. Also, managers of some small businesses still find that they can control their merchandise and manage day-to-day operations using a periodic inventory system.

Because of the widespread use of the perpetual inventory system, we illustrate it in this chapter. We discuss and illustrate the periodic system in Appendix 5B.

Investor Insight

Sportstock/Getty Images

Improving Its Share Appeal

Investors are often eager to invest in a company that has a hot new product. However, when a fast-growing snowboard-maker issued ordinary shares to the public for the first time, some investors expressed reluctance to invest in it because of a number of accounting control problems.

To reduce investor concerns, the company implemented a perpetual inventory system to improve its control over inventory. In addition, the company stated that it would perform a physical inventory count every quarter until it felt that its perpetual inventory system was reliable.

If a perpetual system keeps track of inventory on a daily basis, why do companies ever need to do a physical count? (Answer is available near the end of the chapter.)

ACTION PLAN

- **Review merchandising concepts.**
- **Understand the flow of costs in a merchandising company.**

DO IT! 1 | Merchandising Operations and Inventory Systems

Indicate whether the following statements are true or false. If false, indicate how to correct the statement.

1. The primary source of revenue for a merchandising company results from performing services for customers.
2. The operating cycle of a service company is usually shorter than that of a merchandising company.
3. Sales revenue less cost of goods sold equals gross profit.
4. Ending inventory plus the cost of goods purchased equals cost of goods available for sale.
5. Under a perpetual inventory system, a company must determine the cost of goods sold each time a sale occurs.
6. Under a periodic inventory system, a company determines the cost of goods sold only at the end of the accounting period. At that point, the company must take a physical count to determine the cost of goods on hand.

Solution

1. False. The primary source of revenue for a service company results from performing services for customers. **2.** True. **3.** True. **4.** False. Beginning inventory plus the cost of goods purchased equals cost of goods available for sale. **5.** True. **6.** True.

Related exercise material: **BE5.1, DO IT! 5.1, and E5.1.**

5.2 Recording Purchases Under a Perpetual System

LEARNING OBJECTIVE 2

Record purchases under a perpetual inventory system.

Companies purchase inventory using cash or credit (on account). They normally record purchases when they receive the goods from the seller. Every purchase should be supported by business documents that provide written evidence of the transaction. Each cash purchase should be supported by a canceled check or a cash register receipt indicating the items purchased and amounts paid. Companies record cash purchases by an increase in Inventory and a decrease in Cash.

- A **purchase invoice** should support each credit purchase.
- This invoice indicates the total purchase price and other relevant information.

However, the purchaser does not prepare a separate purchase invoice. Instead, the purchaser uses as a purchase invoice a copy of the sales invoice sent by the seller. In **Illustration 5.6**, for example, Sauk Stereo (the buyer) uses as a purchase invoice the sales invoice prepared by PW Audio Supply (the seller) (see **Helpful Hint**).

HELPFUL HINT

To better understand the contents of this invoice, identify these items:

1. **Seller**
2. **Invoice date**
3. **Purchaser**
4. **Salesperson**
5. **Credit terms**
6. **Freight terms**
7. **Goods sold: catalog number, description, quantity, price per unit**
8. **Total invoice amount**

ILLUSTRATION 5.6

Sales invoice used as purchase invoice by Sauk Stereo

INVOICE NO. 731

PW AUDIO SUPPLY
27 CIRCLE DRIVE
AMSTERDAM, THE NETHERLANDS 1081

SOLD TO
Firm Name Sauk Stereo
Attention of James Hoover, Purchasing Agent
Address 125 Main Street
Oslo Norway 283

Date 5/4/29	Salesperson Malone	Terms 2/10, n/30	FOB Shipping Point	
Catalog No.	Description	Quantity	Price	Amount
X572Y9820	Printed Circuit Board-prototype	1	2,300	€2,300
A2547Z45	Production Model Circuits	5	300	1,500
IMPORTANT: ALL RETURNS MUST BE MADE WITHIN 10 DAYS			TOTAL	€3,800

Sauk Stereo makes the following journal entry to record its purchase from PW Audio Supply an account. The entry increases (debits) Inventory and increases (credits) Accounts Payable.

A	=	L	+	E
+3,800				
		+3,800		

Cash Flows
no effect

May 4	Inventory	3,800	
	Accounts Payable		3,800
	(To record goods purchased on account from PW Audio Supply)		

Under the perpetual inventory system, companies record purchases of merchandise for sale in the Inventory account. Thus, **Carrefour** would increase (debit) Inventory for clothing, sporting goods, and anything else purchased for resale to customers.

Not all purchases are debited to Inventory, however. Companies record purchases of assets acquired for use and not for resale, such as supplies, equipment, and similar items, as increases to specific asset accounts rather than to Inventory. For example, to record the purchase of materials used to make shelf signs or for cash register receipt paper, Carrefour would increase (debit) Supplies.

Freight Costs

Freight terms are agreed to by the buyer and seller. They indicate who is responsible for paying the freight charges (shipping costs) and who is responsible for the risk of loss or damage to the merchandise during transport. Identifying which party bears the risk of loss or damage is an important factor in determining when the goods cease being an asset of the seller and become an asset of the buyer.

Freight terms are expressed as either FOB shipping point or FOB destination. The letters FOB mean **free on board** until the point where ownership is transferred.

- **FOB shipping point** means that ownership of goods passes to the buyer when the public carrier accepts the goods from the seller. The buyer is responsible for the freight costs from the shipping point to the buyer's destination (normally the buyer's place of business). The buyer is also responsible for any loss or damage that occurs along the way. In other words, the goods become part of the buyer's inventory at the point of shipping even though the goods will not arrive at the buyer's destination for several days or even weeks.
- **FOB destination** means that ownership of goods remains with the seller until the goods reach the buyer. The seller is responsible for delivering the goods to the destination. The seller pays the freight costs for transporting the goods to the buyer's destination and is responsible for any loss or damage that occurs along the way. As such, the goods would be included in the seller's inventory until they are delivered.

HELPFUL HINT
The buyer pays freight only when the shipping terms are FOB shipping point.

For example, the sales invoice in Illustration 5.6 indicates FOB shipping point. (see **Helpful Hint**). Thus, the buyer (Sauk Stereo) pays the freight charges. **Illustration 5.7** shows these shipping terms.

ILLUSTRATION 5.7 **Shipping terms**

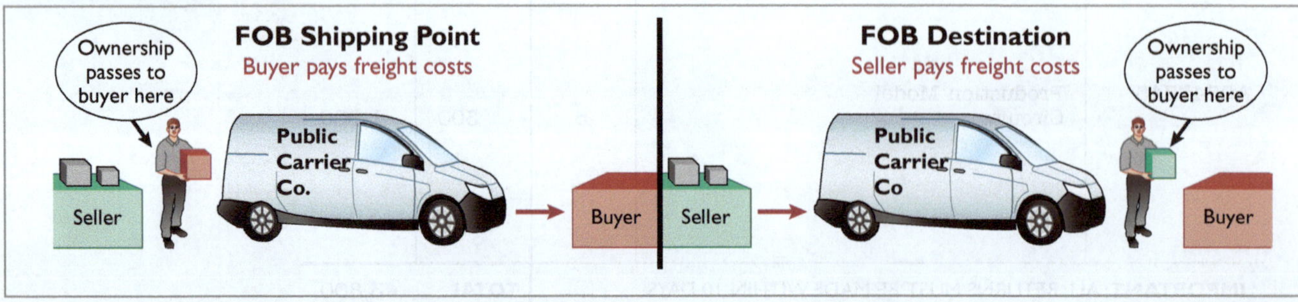

Freight Costs Incurred by the Buyer

When the buyer incurs the transportation costs, these costs are considered part of the cost of purchasing inventory. Therefore, the buyer debits (increases) the Inventory account. For example, if Sauk Stereo (the buyer) pays Acme Freight €150 for freight charges on May 6, the entry on Sauk Stereo's books is:

May 6	Inventory	150	
	Cash		150
	(To record payment of freight on goods purchased)		

A	=	L	+	E
+150				
−150				

Cash Flows
−150

Thus, any freight costs incurred by the buyer are part of the cost of merchandise purchased. The reason: Inventory cost should include all costs to acquire the inventory, including freight necessary to deliver the goods to the buyer. Companies recognize these costs as cost of goods sold when the inventory is sold.

Freight Costs Incurred by the Seller

In contrast, **freight costs incurred by the seller on outgoing merchandise are an operating expense to the seller**. These costs increase an expense account titled Freight-Out (sometimes called Delivery Expense). For example, if the freight terms on the invoice in Illustration 5.6 had required PW Audio Supply (the seller) to pay the freight charges, the entry by PW Audio Supply would be:

May 4	Freight-Out (or Delivery Expense)	150	
	Cash		150
	(To record payment of freight on goods sold)		

A	=	L	+	E
				−150 Exp
−150				

Cash Flows
−150

When the seller pays the freight charges, the seller will usually establish a higher invoice price for the goods to cover the shipping expense.

Purchase Returns and Allowances

A purchaser may be dissatisfied with the merchandise received because the goods are damaged or defective, of inferior quality, or do not meet the purchaser's specifications.

- The purchaser may return the goods to the seller for credit if the sale was made on credit, or for a cash refund if the purchase was for cash. This transaction is known as a **purchase return**.
- Or, the purchaser may choose to keep the merchandise if the seller is willing to grant an allowance (deduction) from the purchase price. This transaction is known as a **purchase allowance**.

Assume that Sauk Stereo returned goods costing €300 to PW Audio Supply on May 8. The following entry by Sauk Stereo for the returned merchandise decreases (debits) Accounts Payable and decreases (credits) Inventory.

May 8	Accounts Payable	300	
	Inventory		300
	(To record return of goods purchased from PW Audio Supply)		

A	=	L	+	E
		−300		
−300				

Cash Flows
no effect

Because Sauk Stereo increased Inventory when the goods were received, Inventory is decreased when Sauk Stereo returns the goods (or when it is granted an allowance).

Suppose instead that Sauk Stereo chose to keep the goods after being granted a €50 allowance (reduction in price). It would reduce (debit) Accounts Payable and reduce (credit) Inventory for €50.

Purchase Discounts

The credit terms of a purchase on account may permit the buyer to claim a cash discount for prompt payment.

- The buyer calls this cash discount a **purchase discount**.
- This incentive offers advantages to both parties: The purchaser saves money, and the seller is able to shorten the operating cycle by converting the accounts receivable into cash.

Credit terms specify the amount of the cash discount and time period in which it is offered. They also indicate the time period in which the purchaser is expected to pay the full invoice price.

HELPFUL HINT

The term *net* in "net 30" means the remaining amount due after subtracting any purchase returns and allowances and partial payments.

- In the sales invoice in Illustration 5.6 credit terms are 2/10, n/30, which is read "two-ten, net thirty" (see **Helpful Hint**).
- This means that the buyer may take a 2% cash discount on the invoice price less ("net of") any returns or allowances, if payment is made within 10 days of the invoice date (the **discount period**).
- Otherwise, the invoice price, less any returns or allowances, is due 30 days from the invoice date.

Alternatively, the discount period may extend to a specified number of days following the month in which the sale occurs. For example, 1/10 EOM (end of month) means that a 1% discount is available if the invoice is paid within the first 10 days of the next month.

When the seller elects not to offer a cash discount for prompt payment, credit terms will specify only the maximum time period for paying the balance due. For example, the invoice may state the time period as n/30, n/60, or n/10 EOM. This means, respectively, that the buyer must pay the net amount in 30 days, 60 days, or within the first 10 days of the next month.

When the buyer pays an invoice within the discount period, the amount of the discount decreases Inventory. Why? Because companies record inventory at cost, and by paying within the discount period, the buyer has reduced its cost. To illustrate, assume Sauk Stereo pays the balance due of €3,500 (gross invoice price of €3,800 less purchase returns and allowances of €300) on May 14, the last day of the discount period. Since the terms are 2/10, n/30, the cash discount is €70 (€3,500 × 2%), and Sauk Stereo pays €3,430 (€3,500 − €70). The entry Sauk Stereo makes to record its May 14 payment decreases (debits) Accounts Payable by the amount of the gross invoice price, reduces (credits) Inventory by the €70 discount, and reduces (credits) Cash by the net amount owed.

A	=	L	+	E
		−3,500		
−3,430				
−70				

Cash Flows
−3,430

May 14	Accounts Payable	3,500	
	Cash		3,430
	Inventory		70
	(To record payment within discount period)		

If Sauk Stereo failed to take the discount and instead made full payment of €3,500 on June 3, it would debit Accounts Payable and credit Cash for €3,500 each.

A	=	L	+	E
−3,500		−3,500		

Cash Flows
−3,500

June 3	Accounts Payable	3,500	
	Cash		3,500
	(To record payment with no discount taken)		

A merchandising company usually should take all available discounts. Passing up the discount may be viewed as **paying interest** for use of the money. For example, passing up the discount offered by PW Audio Supply would be comparable to Sauk Stereo paying an interest rate of 2% for the use of €3,500 for 20 days. This is the equivalent of an annual interest rate of approximately 36.5% (2% × 365/20). Obviously, it would be better for Sauk Stereo to borrow at prevailing bank interest rates of 6% to 10% than to lose the discount.

Summary of Purchasing Transactions

The following T-account (with transaction descriptions in red) provides a summary of the effect of the previous transactions on Inventory.

1. Sauk Stereo originally purchased €3,800 worth of inventory on account for resale (May 4).
2. It paid €150 in freight charges (May 6).
3. It returned €300 of goods (May 8).
4. It received a €70 discount off the balance owed because it paid within the discount period (May 14).

This results in a balance in Inventory of €3,580.

Inventory

Purchase	May 4	3,800	May 8	300	**Purchase return**
Freight-in	6	150	14	70	**Purchase discount**
Balance		3,580			

DO IT! 2 | Purchase Transactions

On September 5, Zhū Company buys merchandise on account from Gāo Company. The purchase price of the goods paid by Zhū is ¥15,000, and the cost to Gāo Company is ¥8,000. On September 8, Zhū returns defective goods with a selling price of ¥2,000. Record the transactions on the books of Zhū Company.

ACTION PLAN

- **Purchaser records goods at cost.**
- **When goods are returned, purchaser reduces Inventory.**

Solution

Sept. 5	Inventory	15,000	
	Accounts Payable		15,000
	(To record goods purchased on account)		
8	Accounts Payable	2,000	
	Inventory		2,000
	(To record return of defective goods)		

Related exercise material: **BE5.2, BE5.4, DO IT! 5.2, E5.2, E5.3, E5.4, and E5.11.**

5.3 Recording Sales Under a Perpetual System

LEARNING OBJECTIVE 3

Record sales under a perpetual inventory system.

In accordance with the revenue recognition principle, companies record sales revenue when the performance obligation is satisfied. Typically, the performance obligation is satisfied when the goods transfer from the seller to the buyer. At this point, the sales transaction is complete and the sales price established.

Sales may be made on credit or for cash. A **business document** should support every sales transaction, to provide written evidence of the sale.

- **Cash register documents** provide evidence of cash sales.
- A **sales invoice**, like the one shown in Illustration 5.6, provides support for a credit sale. The original copy of the invoice goes to the customer, and the seller keeps a copy for use in recording the sale.
- The invoice shows the date of sale, customer name, total sales price, and other relevant information.

The seller makes two entries for each sale.

1. **To record the sale**, seller increases (debits) Cash (or Accounts Receivable, if a credit sale), and also increases (credits) Sales Revenue.
2. **To record the cost of the merchandise sold**, the seller increases (debits) Cost of Goods Sold, and also decreases (credits) Inventory for the cost of those goods.

As a result, the Inventory account will show at all times the amount of inventory that should be on hand.

To illustrate a credit sales transaction, PW Audio Supply records its May 4 sale of €3,800 to Sauk Stereo (see Illustration 5.6) as follows (assume the merchandise cost PW Audio Supply €2,400).

A	=	L	+	E
+3,800				+3,800 Rev

Cash Flows
no effect

Date	Account Titles and Explanation	Debit	Credit
May 4	Accounts Receivable	3,800	
	Sales Revenue		3,800
	(To record credit sale to Sauk Stereo per invoice #731)		
4	Cost of Goods Sold	2,400	
	Inventory		2,400
	(To record cost of merchandise sold on invoice #731 to Sauk Stereo)		

A	=	L	+	E
				−2,400 Exp
−2,400				

Cash Flows
no effect

For internal decision-making purposes, merchandising companies may use more than one sales account. For example, PW Audio Supply may decide to keep separate sales accounts for its sales of TVs, Blu-ray players, and headsets. **Carrefour** might use separate accounts for sporting goods, children's clothing, and hardware—or it might have even more narrowly defined accounts. By using separate sales accounts for major product lines, rather than a single combined sales account, company management can more closely monitor sales trends and respond to changes in sales patterns more strategically. For example, if TV sales are increasing while Blu-ray player sales are decreasing, PW Audio Supply might reevaluate both its advertising and pricing policies on these items to ensure they are optimal.

On its income statement presented to outside investors, a merchandising company normally would provide only a single sales figure—the sum of all of its individual sales accounts. This is done for two reasons.

1. Providing detail on all of its individual sales accounts would add considerable length to its income statement.
2. Most companies do not want their competitors to know the details of their operating results.

However, **Microsoft** (USA) at one point expanded its disclosure of revenue from three to five types. The reason: The additional categories will better enable financial statement users to evaluate the growth of the company's consumer and Internet businesses.

At the end of "Anatomy of a Fraud" stories, which describe some recent real-world frauds, we discuss the missing control activities that would likely have prevented or uncovered the fraud.

Anatomy of a Fraud[1]

Holly Harmon was a cashier at a national superstore for only a short while when she began stealing merchandise using three methods.

1. Holly's husband or friends took UPC labels from cheaper items and put them on more expensive items. Holly then scanned the goods at the register.
2. Holly scanned an item at the register but then voided the sale and left the merchandise in the shopping cart.
3. Holly put goods into large plastic containers. She scanned the plastic containers but not the goods within them.

After Holly quit, a review of past surveillance tapes enabled the store to observe the thefts and to identify the participants.

Total take: $12,000

The Missing Controls

Human resource controls. A background check would have revealed Holly's previous criminal record. She would not have been hired as a cashier.

Physical controls. Software can flag high numbers of voided transactions or a high number of sales of low-priced goods. Random comparisons of video records with cash register records can ensure that the goods reported as sold on the register are the same goods that are shown being purchased on the video recording. Finally, employees should be aware that they are being monitored.

Source: Adapted from Wells, *Fraud Casebook* (2007), pp. 251–259.

Sales Returns and Allowances

We now look at the "flip side" of purchase returns and allowances, which the seller records as **sales returns and allowances**. These are transactions where the seller either accepts goods back from the buyer (a return) or grants a reduction in the purchase price (an allowance) so the buyer will keep the goods.

PW Audio Supply's entries to record credit for returned goods involve (1) an increase (debit) in Sales Returns and Allowances (a contra account to Sales Revenue) and a decrease (credit) in Accounts Receivable at the €300 selling price, and (2) an increase (debit) in Inventory (assume a €140 cost) and a decrease (credit) in Cost of Goods Sold, as shown below (assuming that the goods were not defective).

May 8	Sales Returns and Allowances	300	
	Accounts Receivable		300
	(To record credit granted to Sauk Stereo for returned goods)		
8	Inventory	140	
	Cost of Goods Sold		140
	(To record cost of goods returned)		

A = L + E
−300 Rev
−300
Cash Flows
no effect

A = L + E
+140
+140 Exp
Cash Flows
no effect

If Sauk Stereo returns goods because they are damaged or defective, then PW Audio Supply's entry to Inventory and Cost of Goods Sold should be for the net realizable value of the returned goods, rather than their cost. (Net realizable value is the estimated selling price in the ordinary course of business, less the estimated costs of completion and the estimated costs necessary to make the sale.) For example, if the returned goods were defective and had a net realizable value of €50, PW Audio Supply would debit Inventory for €50, and would credit Cost of Goods Sold for €50.

[1] The "Anatomy of a Fraud" stories in this text are adapted from *Fraud Casebook: Lessons from the Bad Side of Business*, edited by Joseph T. Wells (Hoboken, NJ: John Wiley & Sons, Inc., 2007). Used by permission. The names of some of the people and organizations in the stories are fictitious, but the facts in the stories are true.

What happens if the goods are not returned but the seller grants the buyer an allowance by reducing the purchase price?

- In this case, the seller debits Sales Returns and Allowances and credits Accounts Receivable for the amount of the allowance.
- An allowance has no impact on Inventory or Cost of Goods Sold.

Sales Returns and Allowances is a **contra revenue account** to Sales Revenue. This means that it is offset against a revenue account on the income statement. The normal balance of Sales Returns and Allowances is a debit. Companies use a contra account, instead of debiting Sales Revenue, to disclose in the accounts and in the income statement the amount of sales returns and allowances.

Disclosure of this information is important to management.

- Excessive returns and allowances may suggest problems—inferior merchandise, inefficiencies in filling orders, errors in billing customers, or delivery or shipment mistakes.
- A decrease (debit) recorded directly to Sales Revenue would obscure the relative importance of sales returns and allowances as a percentage of sales. It also could distort comparisons between total sales in different accounting periods.

At the end of the accounting period, if the company anticipates that sales returns and allowances will be material, the company should make an adjusting entry to estimate the amount of returns. In some industries, such as those relating to the sale of books and periodicals, returns are often material. The accounting for situations where returns must be estimated is described in more detail in Appendix 5C.

Accounting Across the Organization — Costco Wholesale

Jacob Wackerhausen/ Getty Images

The Point of No Return?

In most industries, sales returns are relatively minor. But returns of consumer electronics can really take a bite out of profits. At one time, the marketing executives at **Costco Wholesale** (USA) faced a difficult decision. Costco always prided itself on its generous return policy. Most goods had an unlimited grace period for returns. However, a new policy requires that certain electronics must be returned within 90 days of their purchase. The reason? The cost of returned products such as high-definition TVs, computers, and iPods cut an estimated 8¢ per share off Costco's earnings per share, which was $2.30.

Online sales have accentuated the return problem. Many retailers have found that to compete, they must offer free shipping for returned goods. However, to address the significant costs of returns, many retailers now encourage customers to return goods directly to stores. These retailers have benefited from the additional purchases that customers make once in the stores.

Source: Based on Kris Hudson, "Costco Tightens Policy on Returning Electronics," *Wall Street Journal* (February 27, 2007), p. B4; Loretta Chao, "More Retailers Offering Free Shipping on Returns," *Wall Street Journal* (October 11, 2015); and Erica Phillips, "Retailers Offer Myriad Returns Options to Retain Customers; Traditional and Online Retailers Are Expanding Returns Strategies, Aiming to Boost Convenience, Cut Costs," *Wall Street Journal Online* (December 27, 2017).

If a company expects significant returns, what are the implications for revenue recognition? (Answer is available near the end of the chapter.)

Sales Discounts

As mentioned in our discussion of purchase transactions, the seller may offer the customer a cash discount—called by the seller a **sales discount**—for the prompt payment of the balance due.

- Like a purchase discount, a sales discount is based on the invoice price less returns and allowances, if any.
- The seller increases (debits) the Sales Discounts account for discounts that are taken.

For example, PW Audio Supply makes the following entry to record the cash receipt on May 14 from Sauk Stereo within the discount period.

May 14	Cash	3,430	
	Sales Discounts	70	
	Accounts Receivable		3,500
	(To record collection within 2/10, n/30 discount period from Sauk Stereo)		

A = L + E
+3,430
−70 Rev
−3,500
Cash Flows
+3,430

Like Sales Returns and Allowances, Sales Discounts is a **contra revenue account** to Sales Revenue. Its normal balance is a debit. PW Audio Supply uses this account, instead of debiting Sales Revenue, to disclose the amount of cash discounts taken by customers. If Sauk Stereo does not take the discount, PW Audio Supply increases (debits) Cash for €3,500 and decreases (credits) Accounts Receivable for the same amount at the date of collection.

At the end of the accounting period, if the amount of potential discounts is material, the company should make an adjusting entry to estimate the discounts. This would not usually be the case for sales discounts but might be necessary for other types of discounts such as volume discounts, which are addressed in more advanced accounting courses.

The following T-accounts summarize the three sales-related transactions and show their combined effect on net sales.

Sales Revenue		Sales Returns and Allowances		Sales Discounts	
	3,800	300		70	

Net Sales
€3,430

Data Analytics and Credit Sales

Increased access to ever larger amounts of data about customers, suppliers, products, and virtually every other aspect of a business has resulted in a greater reliance by companies on data analytics to support business decisions. Credit sales, sales returns and allowances, and sales discounts all provide rich opportunities for the use of data analytics.

- Effectively analyzing data regarding current, as well as potential, customers can help a company expand its sales base while minimizing the risk of unpaid receivables.
- In recent years, U.S. companies such as **Best Buy**, **REI**, and **Costco** have all refined their customer return policies, sometimes with unique rules for specific product types, as a result of data analytics applied to their data on product returns.
- To achieve the optimal cost-benefit balance on sales discounts, companies statistically analyze past discount practices to determine how large the discount should be, how long the payment period should be, and other factors.

Further, **Amazon** (USA) now uses artificial intelligence to decide whether it would be more profitable to process a return or simply refund a customer's money without return of the product. Amazon also uses algorithms to detect fraudulent returns by cybercriminals.

DO IT! 3 | Sales Transactions

On September 5, Zhū Company buys merchandise on account from Gāo Company. The selling price of the goods is ¥15,000, and the cost to Gāo Company was ¥8,000. On September 8, Zhū returns defective goods with a selling price of ¥2,000 and a net realizable value of ¥300. Record the transactions on the books of Gāo Company.

ACTION PLAN

- **Seller records both the sale and the cost of goods sold at the time of the sale.**

- **When goods are returned, the seller records the return in a contra account, Sales Returns and Allowances, and reduces Accounts Receivable.**
- **Any goods returned increase Inventory and reduce Cost of Goods Sold. Defective or damaged inventory is recorded at net realizable value.**

Solution

Sept. 5	Accounts Receivable	15,000	
	Sales Revenue		15,000
	(To record credit sale)		
5	Cost of Goods Sold	8,000	
	Inventory		8,000
	(To record cost of goods sold on account)		
8	Sales Returns and Allowances	2,000	
	Accounts Receivable		2,000
	(To record credit granted for receipt of returned goods)		
8	Inventory	300	
	Cost of Goods Sold		300
	(To record net realizable value of goods returned)		

Related exercise material: **BE5.2, BE5.3, DO IT! 5.3, E5.3, E5.4, E5.5, and E5.11.**

5.4 The Accounting Cycle for a Merchandising Company

LEARNING OBJECTIVE 4

Apply the steps in the accounting cycle to a merchandising company.

Up to this point, we have illustrated the basic entries for transactions relating to purchases and sales in a perpetual inventory system. Now we consider the remaining steps in the accounting cycle for a merchandising company. Each of the required steps described in Chapter 4 for service companies apply to merchandising companies. Appendix 5A shows the use of a worksheet by a merchandiser (an optional step).

Adjusting Entries

A merchandising company generally has the same types of adjusting entries as a service company. However, a merchandiser using a perpetual system will require one additional adjustment to make the records agree with the actual inventory on hand. Here's why.

- At the end of each period, for control purposes, a merchandising company that uses a perpetual system will take a physical count of its goods on hand.
- The company's unadjusted balance in Inventory usually does not agree with the actual amount of inventory on hand. The perpetual inventory records may be incorrect due to recording errors, theft, or waste.
- Thus, the company needs to adjust the perpetual records to make the recorded inventory amount agree with the inventory on hand. **This involves adjusting Inventory and Cost of Goods Sold.**

For example, suppose that PW Audio Supply has an unadjusted balance of €40,500 in Inventory. Through a physical count, PW Audio Supply determines that its actual merchandise inventory at December 31 is €40,000. The company would make an adjusting entry as follows.

Dec. 31	Cost of Goods Sold	500	
	Inventory (€40,500 – €40,000)		500
	(To adjust inventory to physical count)		

A	=	L	+	E
−500				
				−500 Exp

Cash Flows
no effect

Closing Entries

A merchandising company, like a service company, closes to Income Summary all accounts that affect net income. In journalizing, the company credits all temporary accounts with debit balances, and debits all temporary accounts with credit balances, as the following shows for PW Audio Supply (see **Helpful Hint**). Note that PW Audio Supply closes Cost of Goods Sold to Income Summary.

Dec. 31	Sales Revenue	480,000	
	Income Summary		480,000
	(To close income statement accounts with credit balances)		
31	Income Summary	450,000	
	Cost of Goods Sold		316,000
	Salaries and Wages Expense		64,000
	Utilities Expense		17,000
	Advertising Expense		16,000
	Sales Returns and Allowances		12,000
	Sales Discounts		8,000
	Depreciation Expense		8,000
	Freight-Out		7,000
	Insurance Expense		2,000
	(To close income statement accounts with debit balances)		
31	Income Summary	30,000	
	Retained Earnings		30,000
	(To close net income to retained earnings)		
31	Retained Earnings	15,000	
	Dividends		15,000
	(To close dividends to retained earnings)		

HELPFUL HINT

The easiest way to prepare the first two closing entries is to identify the temporary accounts by their balances and then prepare one entry for the credits and one for the debits.

After PW Audio Supply has posted the closing entries, all temporary accounts have zero balances. Also, Retained Earnings has a balance that is carried over to the next period.

Summary of Merchandising Entries

Illustration 5.8 summarizes the entries for the merchandising accounts using a perpetual inventory system.

ILLUSTRATION 5.8 **Daily recurring and adjusting and closing entries**

	Transactions	Daily Recurring Entries	Dr.	Cr.
Sales Transactions	Selling merchandise to customers.	Cash or Accounts Receivable	XX	
		Sales Revenue		XX
		Cost of Goods Sold	XX	
		Inventory		XX
	Granting sales returns or allowances to customers.	Sales Returns and Allowances	XX	
		Cash or Accounts Receivable		XX
		Inventory	XX	
		Cost of Goods Sold		XX
	Paying freight costs on sales; FOB destination.	Freight-Out	XX	
		Cash		XX
	Receiving payment from customers within discount period	Cash	XX	
		Sales Discounts	XX	
		Accounts Receivable		XX
Purchase Transactions	Purchasing merchandise for resale.	Inventory	XX	
		Cash or Accounts Payable		XX
	Paying freight costs on merchandise purchased; FOB shipping point.	Inventory	XX	
		Cash		XX
	Receiving purchase returns or allowances from suppliers.	Cash or Accounts Payable	XX	
		Inventory		XX
	Paying suppliers within discount period.	Accounts Payable	XX	
		Inventory		XX
		Cash		XX
	Events	**Adjusting and Closing Entries**	**Dr.**	**Cr.**
	Adjust because book amount is higher than the inventory amount determined to be on hand.	Cost of Goods Sold	XX	
		Inventory		XX
	Closing temporary accounts with credit balances.	Sales Revenue	XX	
		Income Summary		XX
	Closing temporary accounts with debit balances.	Income Summary	XX	
		Sales Returns and Allowances		XX
		Sales Discounts		XX
		Cost of Goods Sold		XX
		Freight-Out		XX
		Expenses		XX

ACTION PLAN

- **Close all temporary accounts with credit balances to Income Summary by debiting these accounts.**
- **Close all temporary accounts with debit balances, except Dividends, to Income Summary by crediting these accounts.**

DO IT! 4 | Closing Entries

The trial balance of Celine's Sports Wear Shop at December 31 shows Inventory €25,000, Sales Revenue €162,400, Sales Returns and Allowances €4,800, Sales Discounts €3,600, Cost of Goods Sold €110,000, Rent Revenue €6,000, Freight-Out €1,800, Rent Expense €8,800, and Salaries and Wages Expense €22,000. Prepare the closing entries for the above accounts.

Solution

The two closing entries are:

Date	Account	Dr.	Cr.
Dec. 31	Sales Revenue	162,400	
	Rent Revenue	6,000	
	Income Summary		168,400
	(To close accounts with credit balances)		

31	Income Summary	151,000	
	Cost of Goods Sold		110,000
	Sales Returns and Allowances		4,800
	Sales Discounts		3,600
	Freight-Out		1,800
	Rent Expense		8,800
	Salaries and Wages Expense		22,000
	(To close accounts with debit balances)		

Related exercise material: **BE5.5, BE5.6, DO IT! 5.4, E5.6, E5.7, and E5.8.**

5.5 Financial Statements for a Merchandiser

LEARNING OBJECTIVE 5

Prepare financial statements for a merchandising company.

Merchandising companies widely use the classified statement of financial position introduced in Chapter 4. This section explains an income statement used by merchandisers and provides additional information related to the statement of financial position.

Income Statement

The income statement is a primary source of information for evaluating a company's performance. IFRS 18 requires companies to classify income and expenses into five categories—operating, investing, financing, income tax, and discontinued operations—based on their main business activities[2]. This structure provides useful information about financial performance and enhances comparability across companies and industries.

Income Statement Presentation of Sales

The income statement begins by presenting **sales revenue.** It then deducts contra revenue accounts—sales returns and allowances and sales discounts—from sales revenue to arrive at **net sales. Illustration 5.9** presents the sales section for PW Audio Supply, using assumed data.

ILLUSTRATION 5.9

Computation of net sales

PW Audio Supply
Income Statement (partial)

Sales		
Sales revenue		€480,000
Less: Sales returns and allowances	€12,000	
Sales discounts	8,000	20,000
Net sales		**€460,000**

This presentation discloses the key data about the company's principal revenue-producing activities.

Gross Profit

From Illustration 5.1, you learned that companies deduct cost of goods sold from sales revenue in order to determine **gross profit** (see **Alternative Terminology**). For this computation, companies use **net sales** (which takes into consideration Sales Returns and Allow-

ALTERNATIVE TERMINOLOGY

Gross profit is sometimes referred to as *gross margin*.

[2] Under IFRS 18, a company with a specified main business activity—investing in particular types of assets or providing financing to customers—must classify related income and expenses within the operating category, rather than the investing or financing categories. For example, investment and retail banks may both invest in assets and provide financing to customers as their main business activities.

ances and Sales Discounts) as the amount of sales revenue. On the basis of the sales data in Illustration 5.9 (net sales of €460,000) and cost of goods sold under the perpetual inventory system (assume €316,000), PW Audio Supply's gross profit is €144,000, computed as shown in **Illustration 5.10**.

ILLUSTRATION 5.10

Computation of gross profit

Net sales	€460,000
Cost of goods sold	316,000
Gross profit	**€144,000**

We also can express a company's gross profit as a percentage, called the **gross profit rate**. To do so, we divide the amount of gross profit by net sales. For PW Audio Supply, the **gross profit rate** is 31.3%, computed as shown in **Illustration 5.11**.

ILLUSTRATION 5.11

Gross profit rate formula and computation

Gross Profit	÷	Net Sales	=	Gross Profit Rate
€144,000	÷	€460,000	=	31.3%

- Analysts generally consider the gross profit **rate** to be more useful than the gross profit **amount**.
- The rate expresses a more meaningful (qualitative) relationship between net sales and gross profit.

For example, a gross profit of €1,000,000 may sound impressive. But if it is the result of a gross profit rate of only 7% when others in the industry get 20%, it is not so impressive. The gross profit rate tells how much of each euro of sales goes to gross profit.

Gross profit represents the **merchandising profit** of a company. It is not a measure of the overall profitability, because operating expenses are not yet deducted. But managers and other interested parties closely watch the amount and trend of gross profit.

- Managers compare current gross profit with amounts reported in past periods.
- They also compare the company's gross profit rate with rates of competitors and with industry averages.
- Such comparisons provide information about the effectiveness of a company's purchasing function and the soundness of its pricing policies.

Operating Expenses

Operating expenses are the next component in the income statement of a merchandising company. They are the expenses incurred in the process of earning sales revenue. Many of these expenses are similar in merchandising and service companies. At PW Audio Supply, operating expenses were €114,000. This €114,000 includes costs that were incurred for salaries, utilities, advertising, depreciation, freight-out, and insurance. The presentation of operating expenses is shown in **Illustration 5.12**.

ILLUSTRATION 5.12

Operating expenses

Operating expenses	
Salaries and wages expense	€ 64,000
Utilities expense	17,000
Advertising expense	16,000
Depreciation expense	8,000
Freight-out	7,000
Insurance expense	2,000
Total operating expenses	€114,000

Illustration 5.12 provides an opportunity to discuss two different presentation formats allowed by IFRS: **presentation by nature** and **presentation by function.**

- Presentation by nature provides very detailed information, with numerous line items, that reveal the nature of costs incurred by the company. In Illustration 5.12, the detailed information regarding costs incurred for salaries and wages, utilities, advertising, depreciation, freight-out, and insurance demonstrates presentation by nature.
- Presentation by function aggregates costs into groupings based on the primary functional activities in which the company engages. For example, at PW Audio Supply, operating expenses are those costs incurred to perform the operating functions of a merchandising business. If PW Audio Supply chose to present strictly by function, it would present its operating expenses as a single line item of €114,000.

However, if a presentation by function is used, IFRS requires disclosure of additional details regarding the nature of certain expenses that were included in the functional grouping. For example, depreciation and salary and wage costs are items specifically required to be disclosed. IFRS 18 allows companies to mix functional and natural classifications of operating expenses in the income statement when a mixed presentation provides the most useful structured summary of expenses.

Illustration 5.12 combines both a presentation by function and by nature to present operating expenses. It uses a functional grouping of operating expenses but also presents in detail the nature of the costs included in that functional grouping. *In your homework, you should use this approach.*

Operating Income (Operating Profit)

IFRS 18 introduces two new required subtotals on the face of the income statement: "operating profit (or loss)" and "profit (or loss) before financing and income taxes." The operating category typically includes income and expenses from a company's main business activities; therefore, **operating income (operating profit)** provides a complete picture of the results from a company's operations for the period. **Illustration 5.13** lists examples of categories of income and expenses.

ILLUSTRATION 5.13

Categories of income and expenses

Operating category	• Revenue from the sale of goods or services • Depreciation • Impairment of property, plant and equipment • Gains and losses on the disposal of property, plant and equipment
Investing category	• Interest revenue • Dividends revenue • Rental income
Financing category	• Interest expenses • Dividends
Income taxes category	• Tax expense
Discontinued operations category	• Income and expenses from discontinued operations

In addition, IFRS 18 requires companies to present **income before financing and income taxes (profit before financing and income taxes)** as a mandatory subtotal. This subtotal comprises operating profit or loss together with all income and expenses classified in the investing category, providing a picture of a company's performance before the effects of financing. **Illustration 5.14** shows this presentation for PW Audio Supply.

Interest Expense

Financing activities, which result in interest expense, represent distinctly different types of cost to a business. In evaluating the performance of a business, it is important to monitor its interest expense. As a consequence, interest expense, if material, must be disclosed on the face of the income statement. PW Audio Supply incurred interest expense of €1,800. Illustration 5.14 presents a complete income statement for PW Audio Supply. *Use this format when preparing your homework.*

ILLUSTRATION 5.14

Income statement

PW Audio Supply
Income Statement
For the Year Ended December 31, 2029

Sales		
Sales revenue		€480,000
Less: Sales returns and allowances	€12,000	
Sales discounts	8,000	20,000
Net sales		460,000
Cost of goods sold		316,000
Gross profit		144,000
Operating income and expenses		
Salaries and wages expense	64,000	
Utilities expense	17,000	
Advertising expense	16,000	
Depreciation expense	8,000	
Freight-out	7,000	
Insurance expense	2,000	
Casualty loss from vandalism	200	
Gain on sale of equipment	(600)	113,600
Operating income		30,400
Interest revenue		3,000
Income before financing and income taxes		33,400
Interest expense		1,800
Net income		€ 31,600

Comprehensive Income

Chapter 1 discussed the current value basis. IFRS requires companies to adjust the recorded values of certain types of assets and liabilities to their current values at the end of each reporting period. In some instances, the unrealized gains or losses that result from adjusting recorded amounts to current value are included in net income. However, in other cases, these unrealized gains and losses are not included in net income.

- These excluded items are reported as part of a more inclusive earnings measure, called **comprehensive income.**
- Examples of such items include certain adjustments to pension plan assets, gains and losses on foreign currency translation, and unrealized gains and losses on certain types of investments.
- Items that are excluded from net income but included in comprehensive income are either reported in a combined statement of net income and comprehensive income, or in a separate schedule that reports only comprehensive income.

Illustration 5.15 shows how comprehensive income is presented in a separate **comprehensive income statement**, assuming that PW Audio Supply had other comprehensive income of €2,300. *Use this format when preparing your homework.*

ILLUSTRATION 5.15

Separate statement of net income and comprehensive income

PW Audio Supply
Comprehensive Income Statement
For the Year Ended December 31, 2029

Net income	€31,600
Other comprehensive income	
Unrealized holding gain on investment securities	2,300
Comprehensive income	€33,900

Accounting Across the Organization — Alibaba

OceanProd/Adobe Stock

A Store with a Billion Items?

The rise of e-commerce has created some unique challenges and opportunities for businesses. Consider the challenge and opportunity face by **Alibaba** (CHN). Alibaba has become incredibly effective at attracting customers and sellers. It currently has a virtual store with over a billion different inventory items.

Since the store is virtual, physical space is not an issue. The problem is that consumers only have so much time to look for items. In response, using machine learning and artificial intelligence, Alibaba has built the ability to create customer-specific or personalized web pages. When customers search for an item, they will receive customized suggestions for additional items they may have an interest in based on their past purchases and the purchases of other customers.

How successful have Alibaba's efforts been? During a recent 11.11 Global Shopping Festival, Alibaba generated 6.7 billion personalized shopping pages, connecting consumers to 230,000 different merchants. The personalized shopping pages generated an additional 20% of recommended items sold compared to non-personalized pages.

Source: Adapted from "At Alibaba, Artificial Intelligence is Changing How People Shop Online," *alizila.com* (June 5, 2017).

Increased revenue has to be compared to increased costs. What sort of additional costs do you think Alibaba has to incur to offer personalized shopping pages? (Answer is available near the end of the chapter.)

Classified Statement of Financial Position

In the statement of financial position, merchandising companies report inventory as a current asset immediately above accounts receivable. Recall from Chapter 4 that companies generally list current asset items in the reverse order of their closeness to cash (liquidity). Inventory is less close to cash than accounts receivable because the goods must first be sold and then collection made from the customer. **Illustration 5.16** presents the assets section of a classified statement of financial position for PW Audio Supply (see **Helpful Hint**).

ILLUSTRATION 5.16

Assets section of a classified statement of financial position

PW Audio Supply
Statement of Financial Position (Partial)
December 31, 2029

Assets		
Property, plant, and equipment		
Equipment	€80,000	
Less: Accumulated depreciation—equipment	24,000	€ 56,000
Current assets		
Prepaid insurance	1,800	
Inventory	40,000	
Accounts receivable	16,100	
Cash	9,500	67,400
Total assets		€123,400

HELPFUL HINT

The €40,000 is the cost of the inventory on hand, not its expected selling price.

ACTION PLAN

- **Review the three major categories for income and expenses in IFRS 18—operating, investing, and financing—along with the requirements for two key subtotals: operating profit and profit before financing and income taxes.**
- **Add net income to beginning retained earnings and deduct dividends to arrive at ending retained earnings in the retained earnings statement.**
- **Review the major sections of the statement of financial position, income statement, and retained earnings statement.**

DO IT! 5 | Financial Statement Classifications

You are presented with the following list of accounts from the adjusted trial balance for merchandiser Gorman Company. Indicate in which financial statement (income statement, IS; statement of financial position, SFP; or retained earnings statement, RES) and under what classification each of the following would be reported.

Accounts Payable	Interest Expense
Accounts Receivable	Interest Payable
Accumulated Depreciation—Buildings	Inventory
Accumulated Depreciation—Equipment	Land
Advertising Expense	Notes Payable (due in 3 years)
Buildings	Property Taxes Payable
Cash	Salaries and Wages Expense
Depreciation Expense	Salaries and Wages Payable
Dividends	Sales Returns and Allowances
Equipment	Sales Revenue
Freight-Out	Share Capital—Ordinary
Gain on Disposal of Plant Assets	Utilities Expense
Insurance Expense	

Solution

Account	Financial Statement	Classification
Accounts Payable	SFP	Current liabilities
Accounts Receivable	SFP	Current assets
Accumulated Depreciation—Buildings	SFP	Property, plant, and equipment
Accumulated Depreciation—Equipment	SFP	Property, plant, and equipment
Advertising Expense	IS	Operating expenses
Buildings	SFP	Property, plant, and equipment
Cash	SFP	Current assets
Depreciation Expense	IS	Operating expenses
Dividends	RES	Deduction section
Equipment	SFP	Property, plant, and equipment
Freight-Out	IS	Operating expenses
Gain on Disposal of Plant Assets	IS	Other operating income
Insurance Expense	IS	Operating expenses
Interest Expense	IS	Financing category expenses
Interest Payable	SFP	Current liabilities
Inventory	SFP	Current assets
Land	SFP	Property, plant, and equipment
Notes Payable	SFP	Non-current liabilities
Property Taxes Payable	SFP	Current liabilities
Salaries and Wages Expense	IS	Operating expenses
Salaries and Wages Payable	SFP	Current liabilities
Sales Returns and Allowances	IS	Sales
Sales Revenue	IS	Sales
Share Capital—Ordinary	SFP	Equity
Utilities Expense	IS	Operating expenses

Related exercise material: **BE5.7, BE5.8, BE5.9, DO IT! 5.5, E5.9, E5.10, E5.12, E5.13, and E5.14.**

Appendix 5A Worksheet for a Merchandising Company

LEARNING OBJECTIVE *6

Prepare a worksheet for a merchandising company.

Using a Worksheet

As indicated in Chapter 4, a worksheet enables companies to prepare financial statements before they journalize and post adjusting entries. The steps in preparing a worksheet for a merchandising company are the same as for a service company. **Illustration 5A.1** shows the worksheet for PW Audio Supply (excluding non-operating items). The unique accounts for a

ILLUSTRATION 5A.1 **Worksheet for merchandising company**

PW Audio Supply

Home Insert Page Layout Formulas Data Review View

P18 fx

PW Audio Supply
Worksheet
For the Year Ended December 31, 2029

	A	B	C	D	E	F	G	H	I	J	K
5–6		Trial Balance		Adjustments		Adjusted Trial Balance		Income Statement		Statement of Financial Position	
7	Accounts	Dr.	Cr.	Dr.	Cr.	Dr.	Cr.	Dr.	Cr.	Dr.	Cr.
8	Cash	9,500				9,500				9,500	
9	Accounts Receivable	16,100				16,100				16,100	
10	INVENTORY	40,500			(a) 500	40,000				40,000	
11	Prepaid Insurance	3,800			(b) 2,000	1,800				1,800	
12	Equipment	80,000				80,000				80,000	
13	Accumulated Depreciation—Equipment		16,000		(c) 8,000		24,000				24,000
14	Accounts Payable		20,400				20,400				20,400
15	Share Capital—Ordinary		50,000				50,000				50,000
16	Retained Earnings		33,000				33,000				33,000
17	Dividends	15,000				15,000				15,000	
18	SALES REVENUE		480,000				480,000		480,000		
19	SALES RETURNS AND ALLOWANCES	12,000				12,000		12,000			
20	SALES DISCOUNTS	8,000				8,000		8,000			
21	COST OF GOODS SOLD	315,500		(a) 500		316,000		316,000			
22	Freight-Out	7,000				7,000		7,000			
23	Advertising Expense	16,000				16,000		16,000			
24	Salaries and Wages Expense	59,000		(d) 5,000		64,000		64,000			
25	Utilities Expense	17,000				17,000		17,000			
26	Totals	599,400	599,400								
27	Insurance Expense			(b) 2,000		2,000		2,000			
28	Depreciation Expense			(c) 8,000		8,000		8,000			
29	Salaries and Wages Payable				(d) 5,000		5,000				5,000
30	Totals			15,500	15,500	612,400	612,400	450,000	480,000	162,400	132,400
31	Net Income							30,000			30,000
32	Totals							480,000	480,000	162,400	162,400
33											

Key: (a) Adjustment to inventory on hand. (b) Insurance expired. (c) Depreciation expense. (d) Salaries and wages accrued.

merchandiser using a perpetual inventory system are shown in capital red letters. This worksheet assumes that the company did not have comprehensive income.

Trial Balance Columns

Data for the trial balance come from the ledger balances of PW Audio Supply at December 31. The amount shown for Inventory, €40,500, is the year-end inventory amount from the perpetual inventory system.

Adjustments Columns

A merchandising company generally has the same types of adjustments as a service company. As you see in the worksheet, adjustments (b), (c), and (d) are for insurance, depreciation, and salaries and wages. Yazici Advertising, as illustrated in Chapters 3 and 4, also had these adjustments. Adjustment (a) was required to adjust the perpetual inventory carrying amount to the actual count.

After PW Audio Supply enters all adjustments data on the worksheet, it establishes the equality of the adjustments column totals. It then extends the balances in all accounts to the adjusted trial balance columns.

Adjusted Trial Balance

The adjusted trial balance shows the balance of all accounts after adjustment at the end of the accounting period.

Income Statement Columns

Next, the merchandising company transfers the accounts and balances that affect the income statement from the adjusted trial balance columns to the income statement columns. PW Audio Supply shows sales of €480,000 in the credit column. It shows the contra revenue accounts Sales Returns and Allowances €12,000 and Sales Discounts €8,000 in the debit column. The difference of €460,000 is the net sales shown on the income statement (Illustration 5.14).

Finally, the company totals all the credits in the income statement column and compares those totals to the total of the debits in the income statement column. If the credits exceed the debits, the company has net income. PW Audio Supply has net income of €30,000. If the debits exceed the credits, the company would report a net loss.

Statement of Financial Position Columns

The major difference between the statements of financial position of a service company and a merchandiser is inventory. PW Audio Supply shows the ending inventory amount of €40,000 in the statement of financial position debit column. The information to prepare the retained earnings statement is also found in these columns. That is, the retained earnings beginning balance is €33,000. Dividends are €15,000. Net income results when the total of the debit column exceeds the total of the credit column in the statement of financial position columns. A net loss results when the total of the credits exceeds the total of the debit balances.

Appendix 5B Periodic Inventory System

LEARNING OBJECTIVE *7

Record purchases and sales under a periodic inventory system.

As described in this chapter, companies may use one of two basic systems of accounting for inventories: (1) the perpetual inventory system or (2) the periodic inventory system. In the chapter, we focused on the characteristics of the perpetual inventory system.

In this appendix, we discuss and illustrate the **periodic inventory system**. One key difference between the two systems is the point at which the company computes cost of goods sold. For a visual reminder of this difference, refer back to Illustration 5.5.

Determining Cost of Goods Sold Under a Periodic System

Determining cost of goods sold is different when a periodic inventory system is used rather than a perpetual system. As you have seen, a company using a **perpetual system** makes an entry to record cost of goods sold and to reduce inventory each time a sale is made.

- A company using a **periodic system** does not determine cost of goods sold until the end of the period.
- At the end of the period, the company performs a count to determine the ending balance of inventory.
- It then **calculates cost of goods sold by subtracting ending inventory from the cost of goods available for sale**.

Cost of goods available for sale is the sum of beginning inventory plus cost of goods purchased, as shown in **Illustration 5B.1**.

ILLUSTRATION 5B.1

Basic formula for cost of goods sold using the periodic system

	Beginning Inventory
+	Cost of Goods Purchased
	Cost of Goods Available for Sale
−	Ending Inventory
	Cost of Goods Sold

Another difference between the two approaches is that the perpetual system directly adjusts the Inventory account for any transaction that affects inventory (such as freight costs, returns, and discounts). The periodic system does not do this. Instead, it creates different accounts for purchases, freight costs, returns, and discounts. These various accounts are shown in **Illustration 5B.2**, which presents the calculation of cost of goods sold for PW Audio Supply using the periodic approach (see **Helpful Hint**).

ILLUSTRATION 5B.2

Cost of goods sold for a merchandiser using a periodic inventory system

PW Audio Supply
Cost of Goods Sold
For the Year Ended December 31, 2029

Cost of goods sold			
Inventory, January 1			**€ 36,000**
Purchases		€325,000	
Less: Purchase returns and allowances	€10,400		
Purchase discounts	6,800	17,200	
Net purchases		307,800	
Add: Freight-in		12,200	
Cost of goods purchased			**320,000**
Cost of goods available for sale			**356,000**
Less: Inventory, December 31			**40,000**
Cost of goods sold			**€316,000**

HELPFUL HINT

The far right column identifies the primary items that make up cost of goods sold of €316,000. The middle column explains cost of goods purchased of €320,000. The left column reports contra purchase items of €17,200.

Note that the basic elements from Illustration 5B.1 are highlighted in Illustration 5B.2. You will learn more in Chapter 6 about how to determine cost of goods sold using the periodic system.

The use of the periodic inventory system does not affect the form of presentation in the statement of financial position. As under the perpetual system, a company reports inventory in the current assets section.

Recording Merchandise Transactions

In a **periodic inventory system**, companies record revenues from the sale of merchandise when sales are made, just as in a perpetual system. Unlike the perpetual system, however, companies **do not attempt on the date of sale to record the cost of the merchandise sold**.

- Under a periodic system, companies take a physical inventory count at the **end of the period** to determine (1) the cost of the merchandise then on hand and (2) the cost of the goods sold during the period.
- And, **under a periodic system, companies record purchases of merchandise in the Purchases account rather than the Inventory account.**

Purchase returns and allowances, purchase discounts, and freight costs on purchases are recorded in separate accounts.

To illustrate the recording of merchandise transactions under a periodic inventory system, we will use purchase/sales transactions between PW Audio Supply and Sauk Stereo, as illustrated for the perpetual inventory system in this chapter.

Recording Purchases of Merchandise

HELPFUL HINT

Be careful not to debit purchases of equipment or supplies to a Purchases account.

On the basis of the sales invoice (Illustration 5.6) and receipt of the merchandise ordered from PW Audio Supply, Sauk Stereo records the €3,800 purchase as follows (see **Helpful Hint**).

May 4	Purchases	3,800	
	Accounts Payable		3,800
	(To record goods purchased on account from PW Audio Supply)		

Purchases is a temporary account whose normal balance is a debit.

Freight Costs

When the purchaser directly incurs the freight costs, it debits the account Freight-In (or Transportation-In). For example, if Sauk Stereo pays Acme Freight Company €150 for freight charges on its purchase from PW Audio Supply on May 6, the entry on Sauk Stereo's books is as follows.

May 6	Freight-In (Transportation-In)	150	
	Cash		150
	(To record payment of freight on goods purchased)		

Like Purchases, Freight-In is a temporary account whose normal balance is a debit. **Freight-In is part of cost of goods purchased.** The reason is that cost of goods purchased should include any freight charges necessary to bring the goods to the purchaser. Freight costs are not subject to a purchase discount. Purchase discounts apply only to the invoice cost of the merchandise.

Purchase Returns and Allowances

Sauk Stereo returns goods costing €300 to PW Audio Supply and prepares the following entry to recognize the return.

May 8	Accounts Payable	300	
	Purchase Returns and Allowances		300
	(To record return of goods purchased from PW Audio Supply)		

Purchase Returns and Allowances is a temporary account whose normal balance is a credit.

Purchase Discounts

On May 14, Sauk Stereo pays the balance due on account to PW Audio Supply, taking the 2% cash discount allowed by PW Audio Supply for payment within 10 days. Sauk Stereo records the payment and discount as follows.

May 14	Accounts Payable (€3,800 – €300)	3,500	
	Purchase Discounts (€3,500 × .02)		70
	Cash		3,430
	(To record payment within the discount period)		

Purchase Discounts is a temporary account whose normal balance is a credit.

Recording Sales of Merchandise

The seller, PW Audio Supply, records the sale of €3,800 of merchandise to Sauk Stereo on May 4 (sales invoice No. 731, Illustration 5.6) as follows.

May 4	Accounts Receivable	3,800	
	Sales Revenue		3,800
	(To record credit sales per invoice #731 to Sauk Stereo)		

Sales Returns and Allowances

To record the returned goods received from Sauk Stereo on May 8, PW Audio Supply records the €300 sales return as follows.

May 8	Sales Returns and Allowances	300	
	Accounts Receivable		300
	(To record credit granted to Sauk Stereo for returned goods)		

Sales Discounts

On May 14, PW Audio Supply receives payment of €3,430 on account from Sauk Stereo. PW Audio Supply honors the 2% cash discount and records the payment of Sauk Stereo's account receivable in full as follows.

May 14	Cash	3,430	
	Sales Discounts (€3,500 × .02)	70	
	Accounts Receivable (€3,800 – €300)		3,500
	(To record collection within 2/10, n/30 discount period from Sauk Stereo)		

Comparison of Entries—Perpetual vs. Periodic

Illustration 5B.3 summarizes the periodic inventory entries shown in this appendix and compares them to the perpetual-system entries from the chapter. Entries that differ in the two systems are shown in color.

Journalizing and Posting Closing Entries

For a merchandising company, like a service company, all accounts that affect the determination of net income are closed to Income Summary. Data for the preparation of closing entries may be obtained from the income statement columns of the worksheet. In journalizing, all debit column amounts are credited, and all credit columns amounts are debited. To close the merchandise inventory in a periodic inventory system:

1. The beginning inventory balance is debited to Income Summary and credited to Inventory.
2. The ending inventory balance is debited to Inventory and credited to Income Summary.

The two entries for PW Audio Supply are as follows.

	(1)		
Dec. 31	Income Summary	36,000	
	Inventory		36,000
	(To close beginning inventory)		
	(2)		
31	Inventory	40,000	
	Income Summary		40,000
	(To record ending inventory)		

ILLUSTRATION 5B.3 **Comparison of entries for perpetual and periodic inventory systems**

ENTRIES ON SAUK STEREO'S BOOKS

	Transaction	Perpetual Inventory System			Periodic Inventory System		
May 4	Purchase of merchandise on credit.	**Inventory**	**3,800**		**Purchases**	**3,800**	
		Accounts Payable		3,800	Accounts Payable		3,800
6	Freight costs on purchases.	**Inventory**	**150**		**Freight-In**	**150**	
		Cash		150	Cash		150
8	Purchase returns and allowances.	Accounts Payable	300		Accounts Payable	300	
		Inventory		**300**	**Purchase Returns and Allowances**		**300**
14	Payment on account with a discount.	Accounts Payable	3,500		Accounts Payable	3,500	
		Cash		3,430	Cash		3,430
		Inventory		**70**	**Purchase Discounts**		**70**

ENTRIES ON PW AUDIO SUPPLY'S BOOKS

	Transaction	Perpetual Inventory System			Periodic Inventory System		
May 4	Sale of merchandise on credit.	Accounts Receivable	3,800		Accounts Receivable	3,800	
		Sales Revenue		3,800	Sales Revenue		3,800
		Cost of Goods Sold	**2,400**		**No entry for cost of goods sold**		
		Inventory		**2,400**			
8	Return of merchandise sold.	Sales Returns and Allowances	300		Sales Returns and Allowances	300	
		Accounts Receivable		300	Accounts Receivable		300
		Inventory	**140**		**No entry**		
		Cost of Goods Sold		**140**			
14	Cash received on account with a discount.	Cash	3,430		Cash	3,430	
		Sales Discounts	70		Sales Discounts	70	
		Accounts Receivable		3,500	Accounts Receivable		3,500

Illustration 5B.4 shows the Inventory and Income Summary accounts after posting.

ILLUSTRATION 5B.4

Posting closing entries for merchandise inventory

Inventory

1/1	Bal.	36,000	12/31	Close	**36,000**
12/31	Close	**40,000**			
12/31	Bal.	40,000			

Income Summary

12/31	Close	**36,000**	12/31	Close	**40,000**

Often, the closing of Inventory is included with other closing entries, as shown for PW Audio Supply (see **Helpful Hint**). (*Close Inventory with other accounts in homework problems unless stated otherwise.*)

HELPFUL HINT
Except for merchandise inventory, the easiest way to prepare the first two closing entries is to identify the temporary accounts by their balances and then prepare one entry for the credits and one for the debits.

Dec. 31	**Inventory (Dec. 31)**	**40,000**	
	Sales Revenue	480,000	
	Purchase Returns and Allowances	10,400	
	Purchase Discounts	6,800	
	Income Summary		537,200
	(To record ending inventory and close accounts with credit balances)		
31	Income Summary	507,200	
	Inventory (Jan. 1)		**36,000**
	Sales Returns and Allowances		12,000
	Sales Discounts		8,000
	Purchases		325,000
	Freight-In		12,200
	Salaries and Wages Expense		64,000
	Freight-Out		7,000
	Advertising Expense		16,000
	Utilities Expense		17,000
	Depreciation Expense		8,000
	Insurance Expense		2,000
	(To close beginning inventory and other income statement accounts with debit balances)		
31	Income Summary	30,000	
	Retained Earnings		30,000
	(To transfer net income to retained earnings)		
31	Retained Earnings	15,000	
	Dividends		15,000
	(To close dividends to retained earnings)		

After the closing entries are posted, all temporary accounts have zero balances. In addition, Retained Earnings has a credit balance of €48,000: Beginning balance + Net income − Dividends (€33,000 + €30,000 − €15,000).

Using a Worksheet

As indicated in Chapter 4, a worksheet enables companies to prepare financial statements before journalizing and posting adjusting entries. The steps in preparing a worksheet for a merchandising company are the same as they are for a service company.

Trial Balance Columns

Data for the trial balance come from the ledger balances of PW Audio Supply at December 31. The amount shown for Inventory, €36,000, is the beginning inventory amount from the periodic inventory system.

Adjustments Columns

A merchandising company generally has the same types of adjustments as a service company. As you see in the worksheet in **Illustration 5B.5**, adjustments (a), (b), and (c) are for insurance, depreciation, and salaries and wages. These adjustments were also required for Yazici Advertising A.Ş., as illustrated in Chapters 3 and 4. The unique accounts for a merchandiser using a **periodic inventory system** are shown in capital red letters. Note, however, that the worksheet excludes non-operating items.

After all adjustment data are entered on the worksheet, the equality of the adjustment column totals is established. The balances in all accounts are then extended to the adjusted trial balance columns.

ILLUSTRATION 5B.5 **Worksheet for merchandising company—periodic inventory system**

PW Audio Supply

Home Insert Page Layout Formulas Data Review View

P18 fx

PW Audio Supply
Worksheet
For the Year Ended December 31, 2029

	Accounts	Trial Balance Dr.	Trial Balance Cr.	Adjustments Dr.	Adjustments Cr.	Adjusted Trial Balance Dr.	Adjusted Trial Balance Cr.	Income Statement Dr.	Income Statement Cr.	Statement of Financial Position Dr.	Statement of Financial Position Cr.
8	Cash	9,500				9,500				9,500	
9	Accounts Receivable	16,100				16,100				16,100	
10	INVENTORY	36,000				36,000		36,000	40,000	40,000	
11	Prepaid Insurance	3,800			(a) 2,000	1,800				1,800	
12	Equipment	80,000				80,000				80,000	
13	Accumulated Depreciation—Equipment		16,000		(b) 8,000		24,000				24,000
14	Accounts Payable		20,400				20,400				20,400
15	Share Capital—Ordinary		50,000				50,000				50,000
16	Retained Earnings		33,000				33,000				33,000
17	Dividends	15,000				15,000				15,000	
18	SALES REVENUE		480,000				480,000		480,000		
19	SALES RETURNS AND ALLOWANCES	12,000				12,000		12,000			
20	SALES DISCOUNTS	8,000				8,000		8,000			
21	PURCHASES	325,000				325,000		325,000			
22	PURCHASE RETURNS AND ALLOWANCES		10,400				10,400		10,400		
23	PURCHASE DISCOUNTS		6,800				6,800		6,800		
24	FREIGHT-IN	12,200				12,200		12,200			
25	Freight-Out	7,000				7,000		7,000			
26	Advertising Expense	16,000				16,000		16,000			
27	Salaries and Wages Expense	59,000		(c) 5,000		64,000		64,000			
28	Utilities Expense	17,000				17,000		17,000			
29	Totals	616,600	616,600								
30	Insurance Expense			(a) 2,000		2,000		2,000			
31	Depreciation Expense			(b) 8,000		8,000		8,000			
32	Salaries and Wages Payable				(c) 5,000		5,000				5,000
33	Totals			15,000	15,000	629,600	629,600	507,200	537,200	162,400	132,400
34	Net Income							30,000			30,000
35	Totals							537,200	537,200	162,400	162,400

Key: (a) Insurance expired. (b) Depreciation expense. (c) Salaries and wages accrued.

Income Statement Columns

Next, PW Audio Supply transfers the accounts and balances that affect the income statement from the adjusted trial balance columns to the income statement columns. The company shows Sales Revenue of €480,000 in the credit column. It shows the contra revenue accounts, Sales Returns and Allowances of €12,000 and Sales Discounts of €8,000, in the debit column. The difference of €460,000 is the net sales shown on the income statement (Illustration 5.9). Similarly, Purchases of €325,000 and Freight-In of €12,200 are extended to the debit column. The contra purchase accounts, Purchase Returns and Allowances of €10,400 and Purchase Discounts of €6,800, are extended to the credit columns.

The worksheet procedures for the Inventory account merit specific comment:

1. The beginning balance, €36,000, is extended from the adjusted trial balance column to the **income statement debit column**. From there, it can be added in reporting cost of goods available for sale in the income statement.
2. The ending inventory, €40,000, is added to the worksheet by an **income statement credit and a statement of financial position debit**. The credit makes it possible to deduct ending inventory from the cost of goods available for sale in the income statement to determine cost of goods sold. The debit means the ending inventory can be reported as an asset on the statement of financial position.

Illustration 5B.6 shows these two procedures.

ILLUSTRATION 5B.6

Worksheet procedures for inventories

		Income Statement			Statement of Financial Position	
		Dr.	Cr.		Dr.	Cr.
Inventory	**(1)**	**36,000**	**40,000** ←	**(2)** →	**40,000**	

The computation for cost of goods sold, taken from the income statement column in Illustration 5B.5, is as shown in **Illustration 5B.7** (see **Helpful Hint**).

ILLUSTRATION 5B.7

Computation of cost of goods sold from worksheet columns

Debit Column		**Credit Column**	
Beginning inventory	€ 36,000	Ending inventory	€40,000
Purchases	325,000	Purchase returns and allowances	10,400
Freight-in	12,200	Purchase discounts	6,800
Total debits	373,200	Total credits	€57,200
Less: Total credits	57,200		
Cost of goods sold	**€316,000**		

HELPFUL HINT

In a periodic system, cost of goods sold is a computation—it is not a separate account with a balance.

Finally, PW Audio Supply totals all the credits in the income statement column and compares these totals to the total of the debits in the income statement column. If the credits exceed the debits, the company has net income. PW Audio Supply has net income of €30,000. If the debits exceed the credits, the company would report a net loss.

Statement of Financial Position Columns

The major difference between the statements of financial position of a service company and a merchandising company is inventory. PW Audio Supply shows ending inventory of €40,000 in the statement of financial position debit column. The information to prepare the retained earnings statement is also found in these columns. That is, the retained earnings beginning balance is €33,000. Dividends are €15,000. Net income results when the total of the debit column exceeds the total of the credit column in the statement of financial position columns. A net loss results when the total of the credits exceeds the total of the debit balances.

Appendix 5C Adjusting Entries for Credit Sales with Returns and Allowances

LEARNING OBJECTIVE *8

Prepare adjusting entries for credit sales with returns and allowances.

Sales returns are common for many types of businesses. As noted in the chapter, at the end of the accounting period a company must estimate the amount of goods sold during the period that will be returned in subsequent periods and accrue for this amount.

To illustrate the accounting for an estimated return situation, assume that Rainbow Company began operations on January 1, 2029. On January 12, 2029, Rainbow sells 100 pairs of shoes for $100 each **on account** to Tanner Inc. Rainbow allows Tanner to return any unused shoes within 45 days of purchase. The cost of each product is $60. Rainbow records the sale as follows.

Accounts Receivable	10,000	
Sales Revenue (100 × $100)		10,000
Cost of Goods Sold	6,000	
Inventory (100 × $60)		6,000
(To record the sale of shoes and related cost of goods sold)		

On January 24, Tanner returns two pairs of shoes because they were the wrong color. Rainbow records the return as follows.

Sales Returns and Allowances	200	
Accounts Receivable (2 × $100)		200
Inventory	120	
Cost of Goods Sold (2 × $60)		120
(To record the return of shoes)		

On January 31, Rainbow prepares monthly financial statements and estimates that it is likely that only one more pair of shoes will be returned. Rainbow records two adjusting entries to account for this estimate.

- The first entry requires a debit to Sales Returns and Allowances and a credit to Refund Liability for the selling price of the estimated returns.
- The second entry requires a debit to Estimated Inventory Returns and a credit to Cost of Goods Sold for the cost of the estimated returns.

Rainbow makes the following adjusting entries to account for expected return at January 31, 2029.

Sales Returns and Allowances	100	
Refund Liability (1 × $100)		100
(To record expected sales return)		
Estimated Inventory Returns	60	
Cost of Goods Sold (1 × $60)		60
(To record the expected return of shoes and related reduction in Cost of Goods Sold)		

Refund Liability is a liability account. It reflects the estimated future amount owed to customers in response to future returned goods. The Estimated Inventory Returns account will generally be added to the Inventory account at the end of the reporting period.

On February 18, Tanner returns another pair of shoes to Rainbow. Assuming that Tanner has not already paid Rainbow for the shoes, Rainbow records the entry as follows.

Refund Liability	100	
Accounts Receivable (1 × $100)		100
Inventory	60	
Estimated Inventory Returns (1 × $60)		60
(To record the return of shoes)		

If Tanner had initially paid for the shoes in cash or paid its balance due on a credit purchase prior to returning the shoes on February 18, Rainbow would credit Accounts Payable rather than Accounts Receivable as shown in the following entry.

Refund Liability	100	
Accounts Payable (1 × $100)		100
Inventory	60	
Estimated Inventory Returns (1 × $60)		60
(To record the return of shoes)		

Review and Practice

Learning Objectives Review

1 Describe merchandising operations and inventory systems.

Because of inventory, a merchandising company has sales revenue, cost of goods sold, and gross profit. To account for inventory, a merchandising company must choose between a perpetual and a periodic inventory system.

2 Record purchases under a perpetual inventory system.

The company debits the Inventory account for all purchases of merchandise and freight-in, and credits it for purchase discounts and purchase returns and allowances.

3 Record sales under a perpetual inventory system.

When a merchandising company sells inventory, it debits Accounts Receivable (or Cash) and credits Sales Revenue for the selling price of the merchandise. At the same time, it debits Cost of Goods Sold and credits Inventory for the cost of the inventory items sold. Sales Returns and Allowances and Sales Discounts are debited and are contra revenue accounts.

4 Apply the steps in the accounting cycle to a merchandising company.

Each of the required steps in the accounting cycle for a service company applies to a merchandising company. A worksheet is again an optional step. Under a perpetual inventory system, the company must adjust the Inventory account to agree with the physical count.

5 Prepare financial statements for a merchandising company.

Under IFRS 18, the income statement classifies income and expenses into three major categories—operating, investing, and financing—and presents two mandatory subtotals: operating profit and profit before financing and income taxes. A comprehensive income statement adds or subtracts any items of other comprehensive income from net income to arrive at comprehensive income.

*6 Prepare a worksheet for a merchandising company.

The steps in preparing a worksheet for a merchandising company are the same as for a service company. The unique accounts for a merchandiser are Inventory, Sales Revenue, Sales Returns and Allowances, Sales Discounts, and Cost of Goods Sold.

*7 Record purchases and sales under a periodic inventory system.

In recording purchases under a periodic system, companies must make entries for (a) cash and credit purchases, (b) purchase returns and allowances, (c) purchase discounts, and (d) freight costs. In recording sales, companies must make entries for (a) cash and credit sales, (b) sales returns and allowances, and (c) sales discounts.

*8 Prepare adjusting entries for credit sales with returns and allowances.

Adjusting credit sales for returns and allowances requires two entries at the end of the period. The first entry requires a debit to Sales Returns and Allowances and a credit to Refund Liability for the selling price of the estimated returns. The second entry requires a debit to Estimated Inventory Returns and a credit to Cost of Goods Sold for the cost of the estimated returns. Refund Liability is a liability account and reflects the estimated future amount owed to customers in response to future returned goods. Estimated Inventory Returns will generally be added to the Inventory account at the end of the period.

Glossary Review

Comprehensive income An income measure that includes gains and losses that are excluded from the determination of net income. (p. 5-22).

Comprehensive income statement A statement that presents items that are not included in the determination of net income, referred to as other comprehensive income. (p. 5-22).

Contra revenue account An account that is offset against a revenue account on the income statement. (p. 5-14).

Cost of goods sold The total cost of merchandise sold during the period. (p. 5-3).

FOB destination Freight terms indicating that the seller places the goods free on board to the buyer's place of business, and the seller pays the freight. (p. 5-8).

FOB shipping point Freight terms indicating that the seller places goods free on board the carrier, and the buyer pays the freight costs. (p. 5-8).

Gross profit The excess of net sales over the cost of goods sold. (p. 5-19).

Gross profit rate Gross profit expressed as a percentage, by dividing the amount of gross profit by net sales. (p. 5-20).

Net sales Sales revenue less sales returns and allowances and less sales discounts. (p. 5-19).

Operating expenses Expenses incurred in the process of earning sales revenue. (p. 5-20).

Operating income (Operating profit) A subtotal comprises all income and expenses classified in the operating category. (p. 5-21).

Periodic inventory system An inventory system under which the company does not keep detailed inventory records throughout the accounting period but determines the cost of goods sold only at the end of an accounting period. (p. 5-5).

Perpetual inventory system An inventory system under which the company keeps detailed records of the cost of each inventory purchase and sale, and the records continuously show the inventory that should be on hand. (p. 5-5).

Purchase allowance A deduction made to the selling price of merchandise, granted by the seller so that the buyer will keep the merchandise. (p. 5-9).

Purchase discount A cash discount claimed by a buyer for prompt payment of a balance due. (p. 5-10).

Purchase invoice A document that supports each credit purchase. (p. 5-7).

Purchase return A return of goods from the buyer to the seller for a cash or credit refund. (p. 5-9).

Sales discount A reduction given by a seller for prompt payment of a credit sale. (p. 5-14).

Sales invoice A document that supports each credit sale. (p. 5-12).

Sales returns and allowances Transactions in which the seller either accepts goods back from the purchaser (a return) or grants a reduction in the purchase price (an allowance) so that the buyer will keep the goods. (p. 5-13).

Sales revenue (Sales) The primary source of revenue in a merchandising company. (p. 5-3).

Practice Multiple-Choice Questions

1. **(LO 1)** Gross profit will result if:
   a. operating expenses are less than net income.
   b. net sales are greater than operating expenses.
   c. net sales are greater than cost of goods sold.
   d. operating expenses are greater than cost of goods sold.

2. **(LO 2)** Under a perpetual inventory system, when goods are purchased for resale by a company:
   a. purchases on account are debited to Inventory.
   b. purchases on account are debited to Purchases.
   c. purchase returns are debited to Purchase Returns and Allowances.
   d. freight costs are debited to Freight-Out.

3. **(LO 3)** The sales accounts that normally have a debit balance are:
   a. Sales Discounts.
   b. Sales Returns and Allowances.
   c. Both Sales Discounts, and Sales Returns and Allowances.
   d. None of the answer choices is correct.

4. **(LO 3)** A credit sale of NT$7,500 is made on June 13, terms 2/10, net/30. A return of NT$500 is granted on June 16. The amount received as payment in full on June 23 is:
   a. NT$7,000.
   b. NT$6,860.
   c. NT$6,850.
   d. NT$6,500.

5. **(LO 2)** Which of the following accounts will normally appear in the ledger of a merchandising company that uses a perpetual inventory system?
   a. Purchases.
   b. Freight-In.
   c. Cost of Goods Sold.
   d. Purchase Discounts.

6. **(LO 3)** To record the sale of goods for cash in a perpetual inventory system:
   a. only one journal entry is necessary to record cost of goods sold and reduction of inventory.
   b. only one journal entry is necessary to record the receipt of cash and the sales revenue.
   c. two journal entries are necessary: one to record the receipt of cash and sales revenue, and one to record the cost of goods sold and reduction of inventory.
   d. two journal entries are necessary: one to record the receipt of cash and reduction of inventory, and one to record the cost of goods sold and sales revenue.

7. **(LO 4)** The steps in the accounting cycle for a merchandising company are the same as those in a service company **except**:
   a. an additional adjusting journal entry for inventory may be needed in a merchandising company.
   b. closing journal entries are not required for a merchandising company.
   c. a post-closing trial balance is not required for a merchandising company.
   d. an income statement is required for a merchandising company.

8. **(LO 5)** The income statement for a merchandising company shows each of the following features **except**:
   a. gross profit.
   b. cost of goods sold.
   c. a sales section.
   d. other comprehensive income.

9. (LO 5) If net sales are €400,000, cost of goods sold is €310,000, and operating expenses are €60,000, the gross profit is:

a. €30,000.

b. €90,000.

c. €340,000.

d. €400,000.

*10. (LO 6) In a worksheet using a perpetual inventory system, Inventory is shown in the following columns:

a. adjusted trial balance debit and statement of financial position debit.

b. income statement debit and statement of financial position debit.

c. income statement credit and statement of financial position debit.

d. income statement credit and adjusted trial balance debit.

*11. (LO 7) In determining cost of goods sold in a periodic system:

a. purchase discounts are deducted from net purchases.

b. freight-out is added to net purchases.

c. purchase returns and allowances are deducted from net purchases.

d. freight-in is added to net purchases.

*12. (LO 7) If beginning inventory is HK$600,000, cost of goods purchased is HK$3,800,000, and ending inventory is HK$500,000, cost of goods sold is:

a. HK$3,900,000.

b. HK$3,700,000.

c. HK$3,300,000.

d. HK$4,200,000.

*13. (LO 7) When goods are purchased for resale by a company using a periodic inventory system:

a. purchases on account are debited to Inventory.

b. purchases on account are debited to Purchases.

c. purchase returns are debited to Purchase Returns and Allowances.

d. freight costs are debited to Purchases.

Solutions

1. **c.** Gross profit will result if net sales are greater than cost of goods sold. The other choices are incorrect because (a) operating expenses and net income are not used in the computation of gross profit; (b) gross profit results when net sales are greater than cost of goods sold, not operating expenses; and (d) gross profit results when net sales, not operating expenses, are greater than cost of goods sold.

2. **a.** Under a perpetual inventory system, when a company purchases goods for resale, purchases on account are debited to the Inventory account, not (b) Purchases or (c) Purchase Returns and Allowances. Choice (d) is incorrect because freight costs are also debited to the Inventory account, not the Freight-Out account.

3. **c.** Both Sales Discounts and Sales Returns and Allowances normally have a debit balance. Choices (a) and (b) are both correct, but (c) is the better answer. Choice (d) is incorrect as both (a) and (b) are correct.

4. **b.** The full amount of NT$6,860 is paid within 10 days of the purchase (NT$7,500 − NT$500) − [(NT$7,500 − NT$500) × 2%]. The other choices are incorrect because (a) does not consider the discount of NT$140; (c) the amount of the discount is based upon the amount after the return is granted (NT$7,000 × 2%), not the amount before the return of merchandise (NT$7,500 × 2%); and (d) does not constitute payment in full on June 23.

5. **c.** The Cost of Goods Sold account normally appears in the ledger of a merchandising company using a perpetual inventory system. The other choices are incorrect because (a) the Purchases account, (b) the Freight-In account, and (d) the Purchase Discounts account all appear in the ledger of a merchandising company that uses a periodic inventory system.

6. **c.** Two journal entries are necessary: one to record the receipt of cash and sales revenue, and one to record the cost of goods sold and reduction of inventory. The other choices are incorrect because (a) only considers the recognition of the expense and ignores the revenue, (b) only considers the recognition of revenue and leaves out the expense or cost of merchandise sold, and (d) the receipt of cash and sales revenue, not reduction of inventory, are paired together, and the cost of goods sold and reduction of inventory, not sales revenue, are paired together.

7. **a.** An additional adjusting journal entry for inventory may be needed in a merchandising company to adjust for a physical inventory count, but it is not needed for a service company. The other choices are incorrect because (b) closing journal entries and (c) a post-closing trial balance are required for both types of companies. Choice (d) is incorrect because an income statement is required for both a merchandising company and a service company.

8. **d.** An other comprehensive income appears on the comprehensive income statement, not on an income statement. Choices (a) gross profit, (b) cost of goods sold, and (c) a sales section are all features of an income statement.

9. **b.** Gross profit = Net sales (€400,000) − Cost of goods sold (€310,000) = €90,000, not (a) €30,000, (c) €340,000, or (d) €400,000.

*10. **a.** In a worksheet using a perpetual inventory system, Inventory is shown in the adjusted trial balance debit column and in the statement of financial position debit column. The other choices are incorrect because the Inventory account is not shown in the income statement columns.

*11. **d.** In determining cost of goods sold in a periodic system, freight-in is added to net purchases. The other choices are incorrect because (a) purchase discounts are deducted from purchases, not net purchases; (b) freight-out is a cost of sales, not a cost of purchases; and (c) purchase returns and allowances are deducted from purchases, not net purchases.

*12. **a.** Beginning inventory (HK$600,000) + Cost of goods purchased (HK$3,800,000) − Ending inventory (HK$500,000) = Cost of goods sold (HK$3,900,000), not (b) HK$3,700,000, (c) HK$3,300,000, or (d) HK$4,200,000.

*13. **b.** Purchases for resale are debited to the Purchases account. The other choices are incorrect because (a) purchases on account are debited to Purchases, not Inventory; (c) Purchase Returns and Allowances are always credited; and (d) freight costs are debited to Freight-In, not Purchases.

Practice Brief Exercises

Compute the missing amounts in determining cost of goods sold.

1. **(LO 1)** Presented below are the components in determining cost of goods sold for (a) Frazier Hardware, (b) Todd Supplies, and (c) Abreu Beverages. Determine the missing amounts.

	Beginning Inventory	Purchases	Cost of Goods Available for Sale	Ending Inventory	Cost of Goods Sold
a.	£120,000	£150,000	?	?	£160,000
b.	£ 50,000	?	£125,000	£45,000	?
c.	?	£220,000	£330,000	£61,000	?

Solution

1. a. Cost of goods available for sale = £120,000 + £150,000 = £270,000
   Ending inventory = £270,000 – £160,000 = £110,000
   b. Purchases = £125,000 – £50,000 = £75,000
   Cost of goods sold = £125,000 – £45,000 = £80,000
   c. Beginning inventory = £330,000 – £220,000 = £110,000
   Cost of goods sold = £330,000 – £61,000 = £269,000

Journalize purchase transactions.

2. **(LO 2)** Prepare the journal entries to record the following transactions on Kowloon Group's books using a perpetual inventory system (amounts in thousands).
   a. On March 2, Totoro Equipment sold ₩800,000 of merchandise to Kowloon, terms 2/10, n/30.
   b. On March 6, Kowloon returned ₩100,000 of the merchandise purchased on March 2.
   c. On March 12, Kowloon paid the balance due to Totoro.

Solution

		Debit	Credit
2. a.	Inventory	800,000	
	Accounts Payable		800,000
b.	Accounts Payable	100,000	
	Inventory		100,000
c.	Accounts Payable (₩800,000 – ₩100,000)	700,000	
	Inventory (₩700,000 × 2%)		14,000
	Cash (₩700,000 – ₩14,000)		686,000

Prepare closing entries.

3. **(LO 4)** Cabrera Enterprise has the following account balances: Sales Revenue €300,000, Sales Returns and Allowances €10,000, Cost of Goods Sold €174,000, and Inventory €50,000. Prepare the entries to record the closing of these items to Income Summary.

Solution

		Debit	Credit
3.	Sales Revenue	300,000	
	Income Summary		300,000
	Income Summary	184,000	
	Cost of Goods Sold		174,000
	Sales Returns and Allowances		10,000

4. (LO 5) Assume Yoan Company has the following reported amounts: Sales revenue $400,000, Sales discounts $10,000, Cost of goods sold $234,000, and Operating expenses $60,000. Compute the following: (a) net sales, (b) gross profit, (c) income from operations, and (d) gross profit rate. (Round to one decimal place.)

Compute net sales, gross profit, income from operations, and gross profit rate.

Solution

4. **a.** Net sales = $400,000 − $10,000 = $390,000

   b. Gross profit = $390,000 − $234,000 = $156,000

   c. Income from operations = $156,000 − $60,000 = $96,000

   d. Gross profit rate = $156,000 ÷ $390,000 = 40%

Practice Exercises

1. (LO 2, 3) On June 10, Vareen Electronics purchased £8,000 of merchandise on account from Harrah Circuits, FOB shipping point, terms 3/10, n/30. Vareen pays the freight costs of £400 on June 11. Damaged goods totaling £300 are returned to Harrah for credit on June 12. The net realizable value of these goods is £70. On June 19, Vareen pays Harrah in full, less the purchase discount. Both companies use a perpetual inventory system.

Prepare purchase and sales entries.

Instructions

a. Prepare separate entries for each transaction on the books of Vareen Electronics.

b. Prepare separate entries for each transaction for Harrah Circuits. The merchandise purchased by Vareen on June 10 had cost Harrah £4,800.

Solution

1. **a.**

June 10	Inventory	8,000	
	Accounts Payable		8,000
11	Inventory	400	
	Cash		400
12	Accounts Payable	300	
	Inventory		300
19	Accounts Payable (£8,000 − £300)	7,700	
	Inventory (£7,700 × 3%)		231
	Cash (£7,700 − £231)		7,469

b.

June 10	Accounts Receivable	8,000	
	Sales Revenue		8,000
10	Cost of Goods Sold	4,800	
	Inventory		4,800
12	Sales Returns and Allowances	300	
	Accounts Receivable		300
12	Inventory	70	
	Cost of Goods Sold		70
19	Cash (£7,700 − £231)	7,469	
	Sales Discounts (£7,700 × 3%)	231	
	Accounts Receivable (£8,000 − £300)		7,700

Prepare an income statement.

2. **(LO 5)** In its income statement for the year ended December 31, 2029, Sun Ltd. reported the following condensed data.

Interest expense	NT$ 70,000	Net sales	NT$2,200,000
Operating expenses	725,000	Interest revenue	25,000
Cost of goods sold	1,300,000	Loss on disposal of plant assets	17,000

Instructions

Prepare an income statement.

Solution

2.

Sun Ltd.
Income Statement
For the Year Ended December 31, 2029

Net sales		NT$2,200,000
Cost of goods sold		1,300,000
Gross profit		900,000
Operating expenses		725,000
Loss on disposal of plant assets		17,000
Operating income		158,000
Interest revenue		25,000
Income before financing and income taxes		183,000
Interest expense		70,000
Net income		NT$ 113,000

Practice Problem

Prepare an income statement.

(LO 5) The adjusted trial balance columns of Falcetto SpA's worksheet for the year ended December 31, 2029, are as follows. (All amounts are in euros.)

	Debit		Credit
Cash	€ 14,500	Accumulated Depreciation—Equipment	€ 18,000
Accounts Receivable	11,100	Notes Payable	25,000
Inventory	29,000	Accounts Payable	10,600
Prepaid Insurance	2,500	Share Capital—Ordinary	70,000
Equipment	95,000	Retained Earnings	11,000
Dividends	12,000	Sales Revenue	536,800
Sales Returns and Allowances	6,700	Interest Revenue	2,500
Sales Discounts	5,000		
Cost of Goods Sold	363,400		
Freight-Out	7,600		
Advertising Expense	12,000		
Salaries and Wages Expense	56,000		
Utilities Expense	18,000		
Rent Expense	24,000		
Depreciation Expense	9,000		
Insurance Expense	4,500		
Interest Expense	3,600		
	€673,900		€673,900

Instructions

Prepare an income statement for Falcetto SpA.

Solution

Falcetto SpA Income Statement For the Year Ended December 31, 2029		
Sales		
Sales revenue		€536,800
Less: Sales returns and allowances	€ 6,700	
Sales discounts	5,000	11,700
Net sales		525,100
Cost of goods sold		363,400
Gross profit		161,700
Operating expenses		
Salaries and wages expense	56,000	
Rent expense	24,000	
Utilities expense	18,000	
Advertising expense	12,000	
Depreciation expense	9,000	
Freight-out	7,600	
Insurance expense	4,500	131,100
Operating income		30,600
Interest revenue		2,500
Income before financing and income taxes		33,100
Interest expense		3,600
Net income		€ 29,500

Note: Asterisked Questions, Exercises, and Problems relate to material in the appendices to the chapter.

Questions

1. (a) "The steps in the accounting cycle for a merchandising company are different from the accounting cycle for a service company." Do you agree or disagree? (b) Is the measurement of net income for a merchandising company conceptually the same as for a service company? Explain.

2. Why is the normal operating cycle for a merchandising company likely to be longer than for a service company?

3. (a) How do the components of revenues and expenses differ between merchandising and service companies? (b) Explain the income measurement process in a merchandising company.

4. How does income measurement differ between a merchandising and a service company?

5. When is cost of goods sold determined in a perpetual inventory system?

6. Distinguish between FOB shipping point and FOB destination. Identify the freight terms that will result in a debit to Inventory by the buyer and a debit to Freight-Out by the seller.

7. Explain the meaning of the credit terms 2/10, n/30.

8. Goods costing £2,500 are purchased on account on July 15 with credit terms of 2/10, n/30. On July 18, a £200 credit memo is received from the supplier for damaged goods. Give the journal entry on July 24 to record payment of the balance due within the discount period using a perpetual inventory system.

9. Karen Lloyd believes revenues from credit sales may be recorded before they are collected in cash. Do you agree? Explain.

10. (a) What is the primary source document for recording (1) cash sales, (2) credit sales. (b) Using XXs for amounts, give the journal entry for each of the transactions in part (a).

11. A credit sale is made on July 10 for €700, terms 2/10, n/30. On July 12, €100 of goods are returned for credit. Give the journal entry on July 19 to record the receipt of the balance due within the discount period.

12. Explain why the Inventory account will usually require adjustment at year-end.

13. Prepare the closing entries for the Sales Revenue account, assuming a balance of €180,000 and the Cost of Goods Sold account with a €125,000 balance.

14. What merchandising account(s) will appear in the post-closing trial balance?

15. Regis Co. has net sales of HK$1,090,000, cost of goods sold of HK$700,000, and operating expenses of HK$230,000. What is its gross profit and its gross profit rate?

16. Kim Ho Company reports net sales of ¥800,000, gross profit of ¥570,000, and net income of ¥240,000. What are its operating expenses?

17. Identify the distinguishing features of an income statement for a merchandising company.

18. Identify the sections of an income statement that relate to (a) operating activities, and (b) non-operating activities.

***19.** Indicate the columns of the worksheet in which (a) inventory and (b) cost of goods sold will be shown using a perpetual inventory system.

***20.** Identify the accounts that are added to or deducted from Purchases to determine the cost of goods purchased using a periodic inventory system. For each account, indicate whether it is added or deducted.

***21.** Goods costing NT$60,000 are purchased on account on July 15 with credit terms of 2/10, n/30. On July 18, a NT$6,000 credit was received from the supplier for damaged goods. Give the journal entry on July 24 to record payment of the balance due within the discount period, assuming a periodic inventory system.

***22.** What are the steps to record an end of period adjustment for credit sales with returns and allowances?

***23.** What treatment do Refund Liability and Estimated Inventory Returns receive in the financial statements?

Brief Exercises

Compute missing amounts in determining net income.

BE5.1 (LO 1) Presented below are the components in Clearwater Pools' income statement. Determine the missing amounts.

	Sales Revenue	Cost of Goods Sold	Gross Profit	Operating Expenses	Net Income
a.	£78,000	?	£30,000	?	£10,800
b.	£108,000	£55,000	?	?	£29,500
c.	?	£83,900	£79,600	£39,500	?

Journalize perpetual inventory entries.

BE5.2 (LO 2, 3) Giovanni Leather Goods buys merchandise on account from Gordon Tannery. The selling price of the goods is €780, and the cost of the goods is €560. Both companies use perpetual inventory systems. Journalize the transaction on the books of both companies.

Journalize sales transactions.

BE5.3 (LO 3) Prepare the journal entries to record the following transactions on Benson Ltd.'s books using a perpetual inventory system.

a. On March 2, Benson sold £800,000 of merchandise on account to Edgebrook Company, terms 2/10, n/30. The cost of the merchandise sold was £620,000.

b. On March 6, Edgebrook returned £120,000 of the merchandise purchased on March 2. The cost of the returned merchandise was £90,000.

c. On March 12, Benson received the balance due from Edgebrook.

Journalize purchase transactions.

BE5.4 (LO 2) From the information in BE5.3, prepare the journal entries to record these transactions on Edgebrook Company's books under a perpetual inventory system.

Prepare adjusting entry for merchandise inventory.

BE5.5 (LO 4) At year-end, the perpetual inventory records of Federer Sports showed merchandise inventory of CHF98,000. The company determined, however, that its actual inventory on hand was CHF96,100. Record the necessary adjusting entry.

Prepare closing entries for accounts.

BE5.6 (LO 4) Orlaida Bath Salts has the following account balances: Sales Revenue €192,000, Sales Discounts €2,000, Cost of Goods Sold €105,000, and Inventory €40,000. Prepare the entries to record the closing of these items to Income Summary.

Prepare sales section of income statement.

BE5.7 (LO 5) Yangtze Canoes provides the following information for the month ended October 31, 2029 (amounts in Chinese yuan): sales on credit ¥280,000, cash sales ¥100,000, sales discounts ¥5,000, sales returns and allowances ¥22,000. Prepare the sales section of the income statement based on this information.

Explain presentation in an income statement.

BE5.8 (LO 5) Writing Explain where each of the following items would appear on an income statement: (a) gain on sale of equipment, (b) interest expense, (c) casualty loss from vandalism, (d) cost of goods sold, and (e) depreciation expense.

Compute net sales, gross profit, income from operations, and gross profit rate.

BE5.9 (LO 5) Assume Jose Foods has the following reported amounts: Sales revenue €506,000, Sales returns and allowances €13,000, Cost of goods sold €342,000, Operating expenses €110,000. Compute the following: (a) net sales, (b) gross profit, (c) income from operations, and (d) gross profit rate. (Round to one decimal place.)

Identify worksheet columns for selected accounts.

***BE5.10 (LO 6)** Presented below is the format of the worksheet presented in Appendix 5A.

Trial Balance		Adjustments		Adjusted Trial Balance		Income Statement		Statement of Financial Position	
Dr.	Cr.	Dr.	Cr.	Dr.	Cr.	Dr.	Cr.	Dr.	Cr.

Indicate where the following items will appear on the worksheet: (a) Cash, (b) Inventory, (c) Sales revenue, and (d) Cost of goods sold.

Example:

Cash: Trial balance debit column; Adjusted trial balance debit column; and Statement of financial position debit column.

***BE5.11 (LO 7)** Assume that Kowloon Electronics uses a periodic inventory system and has these account balances (in thousands): Purchases ₩430,000; Purchase Returns and Allowances ₩13,000; Purchase Discounts ₩8,000; and Freight-In ₩16,000. Determine net purchases and cost of goods purchased.

Compute net purchases and cost of goods purchased.

***BE5.12 (LO 7)** Assume the same information as in BE5.11 and also that Kowloon Electronics has beginning inventory (in thousands) of ₩60,000, ending inventory of ₩86,000, and net sales of ₩680,000. Determine the amounts to be reported for cost of goods sold and gross profit.

Compute cost of goods sold and gross profit.

***BE5.13 (LO 7)** Prepare the journal entries to record these transactions on Huntington Kitchen's books using a periodic inventory system.

Journalize purchase transactions.

- **a.** On March 2, Huntington purchased £900,000 of merchandise on account from Saunder Cabinets, terms 2/10, n/30.
- **b.** On March 6, Huntington returned £184,000 of the merchandise purchased on March 2.
- **c.** On March 12, Huntington paid the balance due to Saunder.

***BE5.14 (LO 7)** Hall Music has the following merchandise account balances: Sales Revenue $180,000, Sales Discounts $2,000, Purchases $120,000, and Purchases Returns and Allowances $30,000. In addition, it has a beginning inventory of $40,000 and an ending inventory of $30,000. Prepare the entries to record the closing of these items to Income Summary using the periodic inventory system.

Prepare closing entries for merchandise accounts.

***BE5.15 (LO 7)** Presented below is the format of the worksheet using the periodic inventory system presented in Appendix 5B.

Identify worksheet columns for selected accounts.

Trial Balance		Adjustments		Adjusted Trial Balance		Income Statement		Statement of Financial Position	
Dr.	Cr.	Dr.	Cr.	Dr.	Cr.	Dr.	Cr.	Dr.	Cr.

Indicate where the following items will appear on the worksheet: (a) Cash, (b) Beginning inventory, (c) Accounts payable, and (d) Ending inventory.

Example:

Cash: Trial balance debit column; Adjustment trial balance debit column; and Statement of financial position debit column.

***BE5.16 (LO 8)** At December 31, 2029, Familla Company estimates that goods with a selling price of $1,400 and a cost of $650 that were sold on account during the current period will be returned during the next accounting period. Record the entry or entries required to adjust for this information.

Record entry for estimated sales returns.

DO IT! Exercises

DO IT! 5.1 (LO 1) Indicate whether the following statements are true or false. If false, indicate how to correct the statement.

Answer general questions about merchandisers.

1. A merchandising company reports gross profit but a service company does not.
2. Under a periodic inventory system, a company determines the cost of goods sold each time a sale occurs.
3. A service company is likely to use accounts receivable but a merchandising company is not likely to do so.
4. Under a periodic inventory system, the cost of goods on hand at the beginning of the accounting period plus the cost of goods purchased less the cost of goods on hand at the end of the accounting period equals cost of goods sold.

Record transactions of purchasing company.

DO IT! 5.2 (LO 2) On October 5, Lepik Flowers buys merchandise on account from Tamm Gardens. The selling price of the goods is €4,700, and the cost to Tamm is €3,100. On October 8, Lepik returns defective goods with a selling price of €650 and a net realizable value of €160. Record the transactions on the books of Lepik.

Record transactions of selling company.

DO IT! 5.3 (LO 3) Assume information similar to that in **DO IT! 5.2**. That is: On October 5, Lepik Flowers buys merchandise on account from Tamm Gardens. The selling price of the goods is €4,700, and the cost to Tamm is €3,100. On October 8, Lepik returns defective goods with a selling price of €650 and a net realizable value of €160. Record the transactions on the books of Tamm.

Prepare closing entries for a merchandising company.

DO IT! 5.4 (LO 4) The trial balance of Alagoas's Boutique at December 31 shows Inventory R$21,000, Sales Revenue R$156,000, Sales Returns and Allowances R$4,100, Sales Discounts R$3,000, Cost of Goods Sold R$92,400, Interest Revenue R$3,000, Freight-Out R$2,200, Utilities Expense R$7,400, and Salaries and Wages Expense R$19,500. Prepare the closing entries for Alagoas for these accounts.

Classify financial statement accounts.

DO IT! 5.5 (LO 5) Dorothea Publications is preparing its income statement, retained earnings statement, and classified statement of financial position. Using the column headings *Account*, *Financial Statement*, and *Classification*, indicate in which financial statement and under what classification each of the following would be reported.

Account	Financial Statement	Classification
Accounts Payable		
Accounts Receivable		
Accumulated Depreciation—Buildings		
Cash		
Casualty Loss from Vandalism		
Cost of Goods Sold		
Depreciation Expense		
Equipment		
Freight-Out		
Insurance Expense		
Interest Payable		
Inventory		
Land		
Notes Payable (due in 5 years)		
Share Capital—Ordinary		
Retained Earnings		
Dividends		
Property Taxes Payable		
Salaries and Wages Expense		
Salaries and Wages Payable		
Sales Returns and Allowances		
Sales Revenue		
Unearned Rent Revenue		
Utilities Expense		

Exercises

Answer general questions about merchandisers.

E5.1 (LO 1) Mr. Soukup has prepared the following list of statements about service companies and merchandisers.

1. Measuring net income for a merchandiser is conceptually the same as for a service company.
2. For a merchandiser, sales less operating expenses is called gross profit.
3. For a merchandiser, the primary source of revenues is the sale of inventory.
4. Sales salaries and wages is an example of an operating expense.
5. The operating cycle of a merchandiser is the same as that of a service company.

6. In a perpetual inventory system, no detailed inventory records of goods on hand are maintained.
7. In a periodic inventory system, the cost of goods sold is determined only at the end of the accounting period.
8. A periodic inventory system provides better control over inventories than a perpetual system.

Instructions

Identify each statement as true or false. If false, indicate how to correct the statement.

E5.2 (LO 2) Information related to Duffy Yachts is presented below.

Journalize purchase transactions.

1. On April 5, purchased merchandise on account from Thomas Nautical Supply for £25,000, terms 2/10, net/30, FOB shipping point.
2. On April 6, paid freight costs of £900 on merchandise purchased from Thomas.
3. On April 7, purchased equipment on account for £26,000.
4. On April 8, returned damaged merchandise to Thomas and was granted a £2,600 credit for returned merchandise.
5. On April 15, paid the amount due to Thomas in full.

Instructions

a. Prepare the journal entries to record these transactions on the books of Duffy under a perpetual inventory system.

b. Assume that Duffy paid the balance due to Thomas on May 4 instead of April 15. Prepare the journal entry to record this payment.

E5.3 (LO 2, 3) On September 1, Moreau Office Supply had an inventory of 30 calculators at a cost of €22 each. The company uses a perpetual inventory system. During September, the following transactions occurred.

Journalize perpetual inventory entries.

Sept.	6	Purchased with cash 90 calculators at €20 each from Roux Electronics.
	9	Paid freight of €180 on calculators purchased from Roux.
	10	Returned 3 calculators to Roux for €66 cash (including freight) because they did not meet specifications.
	12	Sold 28 calculators costing €22 (including freight) for €33 each on account to Village Book Store, terms n/30.
	14	Granted credit of €33 to Village Book Store for the return of one calculator that was not ordered.
	20	Sold 40 calculators costing €22 for €35 each on account to Holiday Card Shop, terms n/30.

Instructions

Journalize the September transactions.

E5.4 (LO 2, 3) On June 10, York Gifts purchased £7,600 of merchandise from Bianchi Designs, FOB shipping point, terms 2/10, n/30. York pays the freight costs of £400 on June 11. Damaged goods totaling £300 are returned to Bianchi for credit on June 12. The net realizable value of these goods is £70. On June 19, York pays Bianchi in full, less the purchase discount. Both companies use a perpetual inventory system.

Prepare purchase and sales entries.

Instructions

a. Prepare separate entries for each transaction on the books of York.

b. Prepare separate entries for each transaction for Bianchi. The merchandise purchased by York on June 10 had cost Bianchi £4,300.

E5.5 (LO 3) The following transactions are for Alonzo Company.

Journalize sales transactions.

1. On December 3, Alonzo Company sold $500,000 of merchandise to Arte Co., on account, terms 1/10, n/30. The cost of the merchandise sold was $330,000.
2. On December 8, Arte Co. was granted an allowance of $25,000 for merchandise purchased on December 3.
3. On December 13, Alonzo Company received the balance due from Arte Co.

Instructions

a. Prepare the journal entries to record these transactions on the books of Alonzo Company using a perpetual inventory system.

b. Assume that Alonzo Company received the balance due from Arte Co. on January 2 of the following year instead of December 13. Prepare the journal entry to record the receipt of payment on January 2.

Prepare sales section and closing entries.

E5.6 (LO 4, 5) The adjusted trial balance of Mendoza Auto Supply shows the following data pertaining to sales at the end of its fiscal year October 31, 2029: Sales Revenue €820,000, Freight-Out €16,000, Sales Returns and Allowances €28,000, and Sales Discounts €13,000.

Instructions

a. Prepare the sales section of the income statement.

b. Prepare separate closing entries for (1) sales, and (2) the contra accounts to sales.

Prepare adjusting and closing entries.

E5.7 (LO 4) Hezir Creations had the following account balances at year-end: Cost of Goods Sold ₺60,000, Inventory ₺15,000, Operating Expenses ₺29,000, Sales Revenue ₺117,000, Sales Discounts ₺1,300, and Sales Returns and Allowances ₺1,700. A physical count of inventory determines that merchandise inventory on hand is ₺14,200.

Instructions

a. Prepare the adjusting entry necessary as a result of the physical count.

b. Prepare closing entries.

Prepare adjusting and closing entries.

E5.8 (LO 4) Presented below is information related to Poulsen Industries for the month of January 2029.

Ending inventory per perpetual records	€ 21,600	Insurance expense	€ 12,000
		Rent expense	20,000
Ending inventory actually on hand	21,000	Salaries and wages expense	59,000
		Sales discounts	8,000
Cost of goods sold	208,000	Sales returns and allowances	13,000
Freight-out	7,000	Sales revenue	378,000

Instructions

a. Prepare the necessary adjusting entry for inventory.

b. Prepare the necessary closing entries.

Prepare an income statement.

E5.9 (LO 5) Presented below is information for Bach Chocolatiers for the month of March 2029.

Cost of goods sold	£212,000	Rent expense	£ 32,000
Freight-out	9,000	Sales discounts	7,400
Insurance expense	7,000	Sales returns and allowances	13,000
Salaries and wages expense	58,000	Sales revenue	380,000
		Other comprehensive income	2,200

Instructions

a. Prepare an income statement.

b. Prepare a comprehensive income statement.

c. Compute the gross profit rate.

Prepare an income statement.

E5.10 (LO 5) In its income statement for the year ended December 31, 2029, Mancini Films reported the following condensed data.

Operating expenses	€ 725,000	Interest revenue	€ 33,000
Cost of goods sold	1,256,000	Loss on disposal of plant assets	17,000
Interest expense	70,000	Net sales	2,200,000
		Other comprehensive income	8,300

Instructions

a. Prepare an income statement.

b. Prepare a comprehensive income statement.

E5.11 (LO 2, 3) An inexperienced accountant for Zoeng Ceramics made the following errors in recording merchandising transactions.

Prepare correcting entries for sales and purchases.

1. A HK$1,750 refund to a customer for faulty merchandise was debited to Sales Revenue HK$1,750 and credited to Cash HK$1,750.
2. A HK$1,400 credit purchase of supplies was debited to Inventory HK$1,400 and credited to Cash HK$1,400.
3. A HK$2,150 sales discount was debited to Sales Revenue.
4. A cash payment of HK$200 for freight on merchandise purchases was debited to Freight-Out HK$2,000 and credited to Cash HK$2,000.

Instructions

Prepare separate correcting entries for each error, assuming that the incorrect entry is not reversed. (Omit explanations.)

E5.12 (LO 5) In 2029, Endeaver Cameras had net sales of £860,000 and cost of goods sold of £533,200. Operating expenses were £221,000, and interest expense was £7,000.

Compute various income measures.

Instructions

a. Compute Endeaver's gross profit.
b. Compute the gross profit rate. Why is this rate computed by financial statement users?
c. What is Endeaver's income from operations and net income?
d. In what section of its classified statement of financial position should Endeaver report merchandise inventory?

E5.13 (LO 5) Financial information is presented here for two different companies.

Compute missing amounts and compute gross profit rate.

	Yoste Company	Noone Company
Sales revenue	$90,000	$ (d)
Sales returns and allowances	(a)	5,000
Net sales	84,000	100,000
Cost of goods sold	58,000	(e)
Gross profit	(b)	40,000
Operating expenses	14,380	(f)
Net income	(c)	17,000

Instructions

a. Fill in the missing amounts. Assume that there are no nonoperating activities.
b. Calculate the gross profit rate for each company. (Round to one decimal place.)

E5.14 (LO 5) Financial information is presented below for three different companies.

Compute missing amounts.

	Athena Cosmetics	Harry Grocery	Panama Wholesalers
Sales revenue	€90,000	€ (e)	€122,000
Sales returns and allowances	(a)	5,000	12,000
Net sales	86,000	95,000	(i)
Cost of goods sold	56,000	(f)	(j)
Gross profit	(b)	22,000	24,000
Operating expenses	15,000	(g)	18,000
Income from operations	(c)	(h)	(k)
Other operating expenses	(4,000)	(3,000)	(l)
Net income	(d)	11,000	5,000

Instructions

Determine the missing amounts.

***E5.15 (LO 6)** The following are selected accounts for Feisal Pet Supply as reported in the worksheet at the end of May 2029.

Complete worksheet for selected accounts.

Accounts	Adjusted Trial Balance		Income Statement		Statement of Financial Position	
	Dr.	Cr.	Dr.	Cr.	Dr.	Cr.
Cash	9,000					
Inventory	76,000					
Sales Revenue		460,000				
Sales Returns and Allowances	10,000					
Sales Discounts	9,000					
Cost of Goods Sold	288,000					

Instructions

Complete the worksheet by extending amounts reported in the adjusted trial balance to the appropriate columns in the worksheet. Do not total individual columns.

Prepare a worksheet.

***E5.16** **(LO 6)** The trial balance columns of the worksheet for Barbosa Apparel at June 30, 2029, are as follows.

Barbosa Apparel
Worksheet
For the Month Ended June 30, 2029

Account Titles	Trial Balance Debit	Trial Balance Credit
Cash	2,120	
Accounts Receivable	2,740	
Inventory	11,640	
Accounts Payable		1,120
Share Capital—Ordinary		4,000
Sales Revenue		42,800
Cost of Goods Sold	20,560	
Operating Expenses	10,860	
	47,920	47,920

Other data:

Operating expenses incurred on account, but not yet recorded, total R$1,640.

Instructions

Enter the trial balance on a worksheet and complete the worksheet.

Prepare cost of goods sold section.

***E5.17** **(LO 7)** The trial balance of Biju Medical Supplies at the end of its fiscal year, August 31, 2029, includes these accounts (amounts in thousands): Inventory Rp17,200; Purchases Rp149,000; Sales Revenue Rp190,000; Freight-In Rp5,000; Sales Returns and Allowances Rp3,000; Freight-Out Rp1,000; and Purchase Returns and Allowances Rp6,200. The ending inventory is Rp16,000.

Instructions

Prepare a cost of goods sold section for the year ending August 31 (periodic inventory).

Compute various income statement items.

***E5.18** **(LO 7)** On January 1, 2029, Scott Enterprises has an inventory of £50,000. At December 31, 2029, Scott had the following account balances.

Freight-in	£ 4,000
Purchases	509,000
Purchase discounts	6,000
Purchase returns and allowances	8,000
Sales revenue	840,000
Sales discounts	7,000
Sales returns and allowances	11,000

At December 31, 2029, Scott determines that its ending inventory is £60,000.

Instructions

a. Compute Scott's 2029 gross profit.

b. Compute Scott's 2029 operating expenses if net income is £130,000 and there are no non-operating activities.

***E5.19 (LO 7)** Below is a series of cost of goods sold sections for companies B, M, O, and S.

Prepare cost of goods sold section.

	B	M	O	S
Beginning inventory	$ 250	$ 120	$ 700	$ (j)
Purchases	1,500	1,080	(g)	43,590
Purchase returns and allowances	80	(d)	290	(k)
Net purchases	(a)	1,040	7,410	42,290
Freight-in	130	(e)	(h)	2,240
Cost of goods purchased	(b)	1,230	8,050	(l)
Cost of goods available for sale	1,800	1,350	(i)	49,530
Ending inventory	310	(f)	1,150	6,230
Cost of goods sold	(c)	1,230	7,600	43,300

Instructions

Fill in the lettered blanks to complete the cost of goods sold sections.

***E5.20 (LO 7)** This information relates to Olaf Decor.

Journalize purchase transactions.

1. On April 5, purchased merchandise on account from DeVito Group for €18,000, terms 2/10, net/30, FOB shipping point.
2. On April 6, paid freight costs of €820 on merchandise purchased from DeVito.
3. On April 7, purchased equipment on account for €30,000.
4. On April 8, returned some of April 5 merchandise, which cost €2,800, to DeVito.
5. On April 15, paid the amount due to DeVito in full.

Instructions

a. Prepare the journal entries to record these transactions on the books of Olaf using a periodic inventory system.
b. Assume that Olaf paid the balance due to DeVito on May 4 instead of April 15. Prepare the journal entry to record this payment.

***E5.21 (LO 7)** Presented below is information related to Chilean Industries.

Journalize purchase transactions.

1. On April 5, purchased merchandise on account from Graham Ltd. for £17,400, terms 2/10, net/30, FOB shipping point.
2. On April 6, paid freight costs of £800 on merchandise purchased from Graham.
3. On April 7, purchased equipment on account from Reed Manufacturing for £27,000.
4. On April 8, returned merchandise, which cost £4,000, to Graham.
5. On April 15, paid the amount due to Graham in full.

Instructions

a. Prepare the journal entries to record these transactions on the books of Chilean Industries using a periodic inventory system.
b. Assume that Chilean Industries paid the balance due to Graham on May 4 instead of April 15. Prepare the journal entry to record this payment.

***E5.22 (LO 7)** Presented below are selected accounts for Midler Stores as reported in the worksheet at the end of May 2029. Ending inventory is $75,000.

Complete worksheet.

Accounts	Adjusted Trial Balance		Income Statement		Statement of Financial Position	
	Dr.	Cr.	Dr.	Cr.	Dr.	Cr.
Cash	9,000					
Inventory	80,000					
Purchases	240,000					
Purchase Returns and Allowances		30,000				
Sales Revenue		450,000				
Sales Returns and Allowances	10,000					
Sales Discounts	5,000					
Rent Expense	42,000					

Instructions

Complete the worksheet by extending amounts reported in the adjusted trial balance to the appropriate columns in the worksheet. The company uses the periodic inventory system.

Record entry for estimated sales returns.

***E5.23 (LO 8)** At December 31, 2029, Highland Stores estimates that goods with a selling price of $4,700 and a cost of $1,870 that were sold on account during the current period will be returned during the next accounting period. On January 17, 2030, the goods were returned as estimated. The customer had not paid for the goods by the time of the return.

Instructions

Record the entry or entries required to adjust for this information, as well as the subsequent return.

Problems

Journalize purchase and sales transactions under a perpetual inventory system.

P5.1 (LO 2, 3) Ready-Set-Go distributes suitcases to retail stores and extends credit terms of 1/10, n/30 to all of its customers. At the end of June, Ready-Set-Go's inventory consisted of suitcases costing £1,200. During the month of July, the following merchandising transactions occurred.

July	1	Purchased suitcases on account for £1,620 from Trunk Manufacturers, FOB destination, terms 2/10, n/30. The appropriate party also made a cash payment of £100 for freight on this date.
	3	Sold suitcases on account to Satchel World for £2,200. The cost of suitcases sold was £1,400.
	9	Paid Trunk Manufacturers in full.
	12	Received payment in full from Satchel World.
	17	Sold suitcases on account to Lady GoGo for £1,400. The cost of the suitcases sold was £1,030.
	18	Purchased suitcases on account for £1,900 from Holiday Manufacturers, FOB shipping point, terms 1/10, n/30. The appropriate party also made a cash payment of £125 for freight on this date.
	20	Received £300 credit (including freight) for suitcases returned to Holiday Manufacturers.
	21	Received payment in full from Lady GoGo.
	22	Sold suitcases on account to Vagabond for £2,400. The cost of suitcases sold was £1,350.
	30	Paid Holiday Manufacturers in full.
	31	Granted Vagabond £200 credit for suitcases returned costing £120.

Ready-Set-Go's chart of accounts includes the following: No. 101 Cash, No. 112 Accounts Receivable, No. 120 Inventory, No. 201 Accounts Payable, No. 401 Sales Revenue, No. 412 Sales Returns and Allowances, No. 414 Sales Discounts, and No. 505 Cost of Goods Sold.

Instructions

Journalize the transactions for the month of July for Ready-Set-Go using a perpetual inventory system.

Journalize, post, and prepare a partial income statement.

P5.2 (LO 2, 3, 5) Winters Hardware Store completed the following merchandising transactions in the month of May. At the beginning of May, the ledger of Winters showed Cash of $8,000 and Share Capital—Ordinary of $8,000.

May	1	Purchased merchandise on account from Black Wholesale Supply for $8,000, terms 1/10, n/30.
	2	Sold merchandise on account $4,400, terms 2/10, n/30. The cost of the merchandise sold was $3,300.
	5	Received credit from Black Wholesale Supply for merchandise returned $200.
	9	Received collections in full, less discounts, from customers billed on May 2.
	10	Paid Black Wholesale Supply in full, less discount.
	11	Purchased supplies for cash $900.
	12	Purchased merchandise for cash $3,100.
	15	Received $230 refund for return of poor-quality merchandise from supplier on cash purchase.
	17	Purchased merchandise on account from Wilhelm Distributors for $2,500, terms 2/10, n/30, FOB shipping point.
	19	Paid freight on May 17 purchase $250.
	24	Sold merchandise for cash $5,500. The merchandise sold had a cost of $4,100.
	25	Purchased merchandise on account from Clasps, Inc. for $800, terms 3/10, n/30.
	27	Paid Wilhelm Distributors in full, less discount.
	29	Made refunds to cash customers for returned merchandise $124. The returned merchandise cost $90.
	31	Sold merchandise on account for $1,280 terms n/30. The cost of the merchandise sold was $830.

Winters Hardware's chart of accounts includes the following: No. 101 Cash, No. 112 Accounts Receivable, No. 120 Inventory, No. 126 Supplies, No. 201 Accounts Payable, No. 311 Share Capital—Ordinary, No. 401 Sales Revenue, No. 412 Sales Returns and Allowances, No. 414 Sales Discounts, and No. 505 Cost of Goods Sold.

Instructions

a. Journalize the transactions using a perpetual inventory system.

b. Enter the beginning cash and share capital—ordinary balances and post the transactions. (Use J1 for the journal reference.)

c. Prepare an income statement through gross profit for the month of May 2029.

c. Gross profit $2,828

P5.3 (LO 4, 5) Starz Department Store is located near the Towne Shopping Mall. At the end of the company's calendar year on December 31, 2029, the following accounts appeared in two of its trial balances.

Prepare financial statements and adjusting and closing entries.

	Unadjusted	Adjusted		Unadjusted	Adjusted
Accounts Payable	£ 76,300	£ 77,300	Inventory	£ 75,000	£ 75,000
Accounts Receivable	50,300	50,300	Mortgage Payable	80,000	80,000
Accumulated Depr.—Buildings	42,100	52,500	Prepaid Insurance	9,600	2,400
Accumulated Depr.—Equipment	29,600	42,700	Property Tax Expense		4,800
Buildings	290,000	290,000	Property Taxes Payable		4,800
Cash	23,800	23,800	Retained Earnings	64,600	64,600
Cost of Goods Sold	412,700	412,700	Salaries and Wages Expense	105,000	105,000
Depreciation Expense		23,500	Sales Commissions Expense	10,200	14,500
Dividends	24,000	24,000	Sales Commissions Payable		4,300
Equipment	110,000	110,000	Sales Returns and Allowances	8,000	8,000
Insurance Expense		7,200	Sales Revenue	724,000	724,000
Interest Expense	3,000	8,100	Share Capital—Ordinary	112,000	112,000
Interest Payable		5,100	Utilities Expense	11,000	12,000
Interest Revenue	4,000	4,000			

Instructions

a. Prepare an income statement, a retained earnings statement, and a classified statement of financial position. £16,000 of the mortgage payable is due for payment next year.

b. Journalize the adjusting entries that were made.

c. Journalize the closing entries that are necessary.

a. Net income £132,200
Retained earnings £172,800
Total assets £456,300

P5.4 (LO 2, 3, 4) At the beginning of the current season on April 1, the ledger of Granite Hills Pro Shop showed Cash $2,500, Inventory $3,500, and Share Capital—Ordinary $6,000. The following transactions were completed during April 2029.

Journalize, post, and prepare a trial balance.

Apr.	5	Purchased golf discs, bags, and other inventory on account from Arnie Co. $1,500, FOB shipping point, terms 3/10, n/60.
	7	Paid freight on the Arnie purchase $80.
	9	Received credit from Arnie Co. for merchandise returned $200.
	10	Sold merchandise on account for $1,340, terms n/30. The merchandise sold had a cost of $820.
	12	Purchased disc golf shirts and other accessories on account from Woods Sportswear $830, terms 1/10, n/30.
	14	Paid Arnie Co. in full, less discount.
	17	Received credit from Woods Sportswear for merchandise returned $30.
	20	Made sales on account to members for $810, terms n/30. The cost of the merchandise sold was $550.
	21	Paid Woods Sportswear in full, less discount.
	27	Granted an allowance to members for clothing that did not fit $80.
	30	Received payments on account from members $1,220.

The chart of accounts for the store includes the following: No. 101 Cash, No. 112 Accounts Receivable, No. 120 Inventory, No. 201 Accounts Payable, No. 311 Share Capital—Ordinary, No. 401 Sales Revenue, No. 412 Sales Returns and Allowances, and No. 505 Cost of Goods Sold.

Instructions

a. Journalize the April transactions using a perpetual inventory system.

b. Enter the beginning balances in the ledger accounts and post the April transactions. (Use J1 for the journal reference.)

c. Total debits $8,150

c. Prepare a trial balance on April 30, 2029.

Complete accounting cycle beginning with a worksheet.

***P5.5 (LO 4, 5, 6)** The trial balance of Rosiak Fashion Center contained the following accounts at November 30, the end of the company's fiscal year.

Rosiak Fashion Center
Trial Balance
November 30, 2029

	Debit	Credit
Cash	£ 8,700	
Accounts Receivable	27,700	
Inventory	44,700	
Supplies	6,200	
Equipment	133,000	
Accumulated Depreciation—Equipment		£ 23,000
Notes Payable		51,000
Accounts Payable		48,500
Share Capital—Ordinary		50,000
Retained Earnings		38,000
Dividends	8,000	
Sales Revenue		755,200
Sales Returns and Allowances	12,800	
Cost of Goods Sold	497,400	
Salaries and Wages Expense	136,000	
Advertising Expense	24,400	
Utilities Expense	14,000	
Maintenance and Repairs Expense	12,100	
Freight-Out	16,700	
Rent Expense	24,000	
Totals	£965,700	£965,700

Adjustment data:

1. Supplies on hand totaled £2,100.
2. Depreciation is £11,500 on the equipment.
3. Interest of £4,000 is accrued on notes payable at November 30.
4. Inventory actually on hand is £44,520.

Instructions

a. Adj. trial balance £981,200
Net loss £1,980

c. Gross profit £244,820
Total assets £181,520

a. Enter the trial balance on a worksheet, and complete the worksheet.

b. Journalize the adjusting entries.

c. Prepare an income statement and a retained earnings statement for the year, and a classified statement of financial position as of November 30, 2029. Notes payable of £6,000 are due in January 2030.

d. Journalize the closing entries.

e. Prepare a post-closing trial balance.

Determine cost of goods sold and gross profit under periodic approach.

***P5.6 (LO 5, 7)** At the end of Oates Department Store's fiscal year on November 30, 2029, these accounts appeared in its adjusted trial balance.

Freight-In	$ 5,060
Inventory	41,300
Purchases	613,000
Purchase Discounts	7,000
Purchase Returns and Allowances	6,760
Sales Revenue	902,000
Sales Returns and Allowances	20,000

Additional facts:

1. Per a physical count, merchandise inventory on November 30, 2029, is $36,200.
2. Note that Oates Department Store uses a periodic system.

Instructions

Prepare an income statement through gross profit for the year ended November 30, 2029.

Gross profit $272,600

***P5.7 (LO 7)** Writing Fons Apparel, a retail clothing operation, purchases all merchandise inventory on credit and uses a periodic inventory system. The Accounts Payable account is used for recording inventory purchases only; all other current liabilities are accrued in separate accounts. You are provided with the following selected information for the fiscal years 2026 through 2029, inclusive.

Calculate missing amounts and assess profitability.

	2026	2027	2028	2029
Inventory (ending)	€13,000	€ 11,300	€ 14,700	€ 12,200
Accounts payable (ending)	20,000			
Sales revenue		225,700	240,300	235,000
Purchases of merchandise inventory on account		141,000	150,000	132,000
Cash payments to suppliers		135,000	161,000	127,000

Instructions

a. Calculate cost of goods sold for each of the 2027, 2028, and 2029 fiscal years.

b. Calculate the gross profit for each of the 2027, 2028, and 2029 fiscal years.

c. Calculate the ending balance of accounts payable for each of the 2027, 2028, and 2029 fiscal years.

d. Sales declined in fiscal 2029. Does that mean that profitability, as measured by the gross profit rate, necessarily also declined? Explain, calculating the gross profit rate for each fiscal year to help support your answer. (Round to one decimal place.)

a. 2028 €146,600

c. 2028 Ending accts. payable €15,000

***P5.8 (LO 7)** At the beginning of the current season, the ledger of Village Tennis Shop showed Cash CHF2,500, Inventory CHF1,700, and Share Capital—Ordinary CHF4,200. The following transactions were completed during April.

Journalize, post, and prepare trial balance and partial income statement using periodic approach.

Apr.	4	Purchased racquets and balls from Hingis AG CHF860, terms 3/10, n/30.
	6	Paid freight on Hingis purchase CHF74.
	8	Sold merchandise to members CHF900, terms n/30.
	10	Received credit of CHF60 from Hingis for a racquet that was returned.
	11	Purchased tennis shoes from Volker Sports for cash CHF300.
	13	Paid Hingis in full.
	14	Purchased tennis shirts and shorts from Linzey Sportswear CHF700, terms 2/10, n/60.
	15	Received cash refund of CHF90 from Volker Sports for damaged merchandise that was returned.
	17	Paid freight on Linzey Sportswear purchase CHF25.
	18	Sold merchandise to members CHF1,200, terms n/30.
	20	Received CHF500 in cash from members in settlement of their accounts.
	21	Paid Linzey Sportswear in full.
	27	Granted an allowance of CHF25 to members for tennis clothing that did not fit properly.
	30	Received cash payments on account from members CHF630.

The chart of accounts for the tennis shop includes Cash, Accounts Receivable, Inventory, Accounts Payable, Share Capital—Ordinary, Sales Revenue, Sales Returns and Allowances, Purchases, Purchase Returns and Allowances, Purchase Discounts, and Freight-In.

Instructions

a. Journalize the April transactions using a periodic inventory system.

b. Using T-accounts, enter the beginning balances in the ledger accounts and post the April transactions.

c. Prepare a trial balance on April 30, 2029.

d. Prepare an income statement through gross profit, assuming inventory on hand at April 30 is CHF2,140.

c. Tot. trial balance CHF6,488
d. Gross profit CHF744

Inventory entries and prepare an income statement.

P5.9 (LO 2, 3, 4, 7) At the beginning of Gaoyang' fiscal year on January 1, 2029, Gaoyang company had a beginning inventory of 500 units at a cost of $30 per unit. Other inventory-related transactions are as follows:

1. Purchased 4,000 units on credit on March 5 at a cost of $30 per unit.
2. On May 10, a purchase return of 250 units occurred.
3. Sold 3,500 units on credit on July 7 at a price of $50 per unit.
4. On August 12, a sales return of 150 units occurred at a sales discount of $5,000.
5. Inventory count at the end of the period showed 600 units in stock.
6. Operating expenses incurred in year 2029 were $24,000.

Instructions

a. Journalize the necessary entries under the periodic inventory system and the perpetual inventory system.

b. Net income $29,000

b. Prepare an income statement for year 2029.

Comprehensive Accounting Cycle Review

ACR5 On December 1, 2029, Jurczyk Distributing had the following account balances.

	Debit		Credit
Cash	€ 7,200	Accumulated Depreciation—Equipment	€ 2,200
Accounts Receivable	4,600	Accounts Payable	4,500
Inventory	12,000	Salaries and Wages Payable	1,000
Supplies	1,200	Share Capital—Ordinary	30,000
Equipment	22,000	Retained Earnings	9,300
	€47,000		€47,000

During December, the company completed the following summary transactions.

Dec. 6	Paid €1,600 for salaries and wages due employees, of which €600 is for December and €1,000 is for November salaries and wages payable.
8	Received €2,100 cash from customers in payment of account (no discount allowed).
10	Sold merchandise for cash €6,600. The cost of the merchandise sold was €4,100.
13	Purchased merchandise on account from Gong Co. €9,000, terms 2/10, n/30.
15	Purchased supplies for cash €2,000.
18	Sold merchandise on account €12,000, terms 3/10, n/30. The cost of the merchandise sold was €8,400.
20	Paid salaries and wages €1,800.
23	Paid Gong Co. in full, less discount.
27	Received collections in full, less discounts, from customers billed on December 18.

Adjustment data:

1. Accrued salaries and wages payable €800.
2. Depreciation €200 per month.
3. Supplies on hand €1,700.

Instructions

a. Journalize the December transactions using a perpetual inventory system.

b. Enter the December 1 balances in the ledger T-accounts and post the December transactions. Use Cost of Goods Sold, Depreciation Expense, Salaries and Wages Expense, Sales Revenue, Sales Discounts, and Supplies Expense.

c. Journalize and post adjusting entries.

d. Totals €65,600

d. Prepare an adjusted trial balance.

e. Net income €840

e. Prepare an income statement and a retained earnings statement for December and a classified statement of financial position at December 31.

Data Analytics in Action

Using Data Visualization to Analyze Profitability Changes over Time

DA5.1 Data visualization can be used to understand profitability trends.

Excel

Example Even with the arrival of the global pandemic in 2020, **REI** (USA) continues to be a strong competitor in the outdoor gear industry. The pandemic, however, added to the shift in what, where, and when consumers buy. For example, more customers now buy online as some stores were temporarily closed. So how is REI doing? We can use the following column chart to visualize the company's performance.

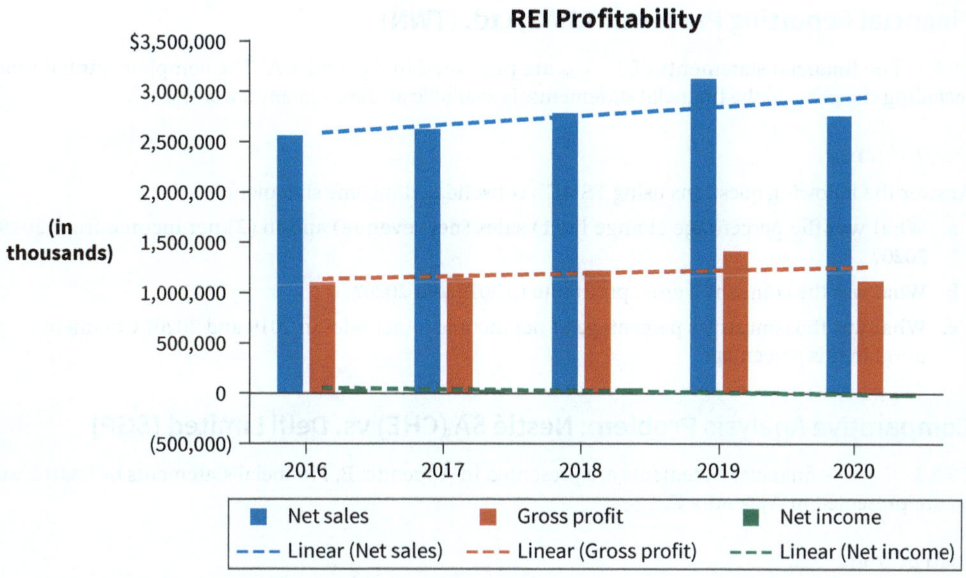

Source: REI website.

The chart illustrates REI's profitability from 2016 to 2020. We can see that REI's sales increased steadily for the first four years, with the largest dollar increase from 2018 to 2019. The pandemic caused a decline in sales as expected during 2020. Because gross profit is tied to sales, the company's gross profit resulted in a gradual increase as sales increased through 2019, with an expected drop in 2020. The slope of the trend lines shows that the sales increased at a greater rate than gross profit for the first four years, implying that cost of goods sold was increasing faster than sales. Despite the promising increase in gross profit through 2019, REI's net profit margin remained flat through 2019, indicating operating expenses must have been increasing.

For this case, you will use data from five years of REI's income statements to compute the percentage of net sales for each item on the income statements, prepare a clustered column chart by year to visualize each of the four subtotal percentages computed, and evaluate what the chart tells you about trends in sales and expenses. Because REI is a co-op in which members share in the company's profits, note that the company recognizes these distributions as expenses on its income statements.

Go to the Wiley online course for complete case details and instructions.

Using Data Visualization to Compare Companies' Profitability

DA5.2 **Caterpillar** (USA) is a manufacturer of construction and mining equipment, diesel and natural gas engines, industrial gas turbines, and diesel-electric locomotives. **Cummins** (USA) is a company that designs, manufactures, sells, and services diesel and natural gas engines and powertrain-related component products. **CNH Industrial** (USA) operates in the capital goods sector and designs, produces, and sells agricultural and construction equipment, trucks, commercial vehicles, buses, and specialty vehicles.

Excel

For this case, you will use financial information from these three companies to consider the implications if they each reuse existing materials. This action can reduce their cost of goods sold, which should cause their gross margin to increase. You will compute the gross profit ratio, as well as percentages of cost of goods sold, other expenses, and net income as compared to revenue, for the three companies. You will also prepare a clustered column chart by company showing cost of goods sold, other expenses, and net operating income as a percent of sales revenue, to compare the three companies. Finally, you will research their sustainability reports and consider in what ways Caterpillar, Cummins, and CNH Industrial promote rebuilding and recycling, and what impact recycling has on the companies' profitability.

Go to the Wiley online course for complete case details and instructions.

Expand Your Critical Thinking

Financial Reporting Problem: TSMC, Ltd. (TWN)

CT5.1 The financial statements of **TSMC** are presented in Appendix A. The complete annual report, including the notes to the financial statements, is available at the company's website.

Instructions

Answer the following questions using TSMC's consolidated income statement.

a. What was the percentage change in (1) sales (net revenue) and in (2) net income from 2019 to 2020?

b. What was the company's gross profit rate in 2019 and 2020?

c. What was the company's percentage of net income to net sales in 2019 and 2020? Comment on any trend in this percentage.

Comparative Analysis Problem: Nestlé SA (CHE) vs. Delfi Limited (SGP)

CT5.2 **Nestlé**'s financial statements are presented in Appendix B. Financial statements of **Delfi Limited** are presented in Appendix C.

Instructions

a. Based on the information contained in these financial statements, determine each of the following for each company.

1. Gross profit for the most recent fiscal year reported in the appendices.
2. Gross profit rate for the most recent fiscal year reported in the appendices.
3. Operating income for the most recent fiscal year reported in the appendices. (*Note:* Operating income may be described with alternative labels.)
4. Percentage change in operating income for the most recent fiscal year reported in the appendices.

b. What conclusions concerning the relative profitability of the two companies can you draw from these data?

Real-World Focus

CT5.3 No financial decision-maker should ever rely solely on the financial information reported in the annual report to make decisions. It is important to keep abreast of financial news. This activity demonstrates how to search for financial news on the Internet.

Instructions

Search the Internet for a financial-news article about **Nestlé** (CHE) or **Delfi Limited** (SGP) that sounds interesting to you and then answer the following questions.

a. What was the source of the article (e.g., Reuters, Businesswire, PR Newswire)?

b. Assume that you are a personal financial planner and that one of your clients owns shares in the company. Write a brief email to your client, summarizing the article and explaining the implications of the article for this investment.

Decision-Making Across the Organization

CT5.4 Three years ago, Debbie Sells and her brother-in-law Mike Mooney opened Family Department Store. For the first two years, business was good, but the following condensed income results for 2028 were disappointing.

Family Department Store Income Statement For the Year Ended December 31, 2028		
Net sales		£700,000
Cost of goods sold		553,000
Gross profit		147,000
Operating expenses		
Selling expenses	£100,000	
Administrative expenses	20,000	120,000
Net income		£ 27,000

Debbie believes the problem lies in the relatively low gross profit rate (gross profit divided by net sales) of 21%. Mike believes the problem is that operating expenses are too high.

Debbie thinks the gross profit rate can be improved by making both of the following changes. She does not anticipate that these changes will have any effect on operating expenses.

1. Increase average selling prices by 20%. This increase is expected to lower sales volume so that total sales will increase only 5%.
2. Buy merchandise in larger quantities and take all purchase discounts. These changes to selling and purchasing practices are expected to increase the gross profit rate from 21% to 24%.

Mike thinks expenses can be cut by making both of the following changes. He feels that these changes will not have any effect on net sales.

1. Cut 2029 sales salaries (selling expenses) of £60,000 in half and give sales personnel a commission of 2% of net sales.
2. Reduce store deliveries to one day per week rather than twice a week; this change will reduce 2029 delivery expenses (selling expenses) of £30,000 by 40%.

Debbie and Mike come to you for help in deciding the best way to improve net income.

Instructions

With the class divided into groups, answer the following.

a. Prepare a condensed income statement for 2029, assuming (1) Debbie's changes are implemented and (2) Mike's ideas are adopted.
b. What is your recommendation to Debbie and Mike?
c. Prepare a condensed income statement for 2029, assuming both sets of proposed changes are made.

Communication Activity

CT5.5 The following situation is in chronological order.

1. Dexter decides to buy a surfboard.
2. He calls Boardin Co. to inquire about its surfboards.
3. Two days later, he requests Boardin Co. to make a surfboard.
4. Three days later, Boardin Co. sends Dexter a purchase order to fill out.
5. He sends back the purchase order.
6. Boardin Co. receives the completed purchase order.
7. Boardin Co. completes the surfboard.
8. Dexter picks up the surfboard.
9. Boardin Co. bills Dexter.
10. Boardin Co. receives payment from Dexter.

Instructions

In an email to the president of Boardin Co., answer the following.

a. When should Boardin Co. record the sale?
b. Suppose that with his purchase order, Dexter is required to make a down payment. Would that change your answer?

Ethics Case

CT5.6 Anita Zurbrugg was just hired as the assistant treasurer of Yorktown Stores. The company is a specialty chain store with nine retail stores concentrated in one metropolitan area. Among other things, the payment of all invoices is centralized in one of the departments Anita will manage. Her primary responsibility is to maintain the company's high credit rating by paying all bills when due and to take advantage of all cash discounts.

Chris Dadian, the former assistant treasurer who has been promoted to treasurer, is training Anita in her new duties. He instructs Anita that she is to continue the practice of preparing all checks "net of discount" and dating the checks the last day of the discount period. "But," Chris continues, "we always hold the checks at least 4 days beyond the discount period before mailing them. That way, we get another 4 days of interest on our money. Most of our creditors need our business and don't complain. And, if they scream about our missing the discount period, we blame it on the mailroom or the post office. We've only lost one discount out of every hundred we take that way. I think everybody does it. By the way, welcome to our team!"

Instructions

a. What are the ethical considerations in this case?

b. Who are the stakeholders that are harmed or benefitted in this situation?

c. Should Anita continue the practice started by Chris? Does she have any choice?

Answers to Insight and Accounting Across the Organization Questions

Improving Its Share Appeal Q: If a perpetual system keeps track of inventory on a daily basis, why do companies ever need to do a physical count? **A:** A perpetual system keeps track of all sales and purchases on a continuous basis. This provides a constant record of the number of units in the inventory. However, if employees make errors in recording sales or purchases, or if there is theft, the inventory value will not be correct. As a consequence, all companies do a physical count of inventory at least once a year.

The Point of No Return? Q: If a company expects significant returns, what are the implications for revenue recognition? **A:** If a company expects significant returns, it should make an adjusting entry at the end of the year to increase Sales Returns and Allowances by the estimated amount of sales returns. This is necessary to not overstate the amount of revenue recognized in the period.

A Store with a Billion Items? Q: Increased revenue has to be compared to increased costs. What sort of additional costs do you think Alibaba has to incur to offer personalized shopping pages? **A:** Alibaba would incur the initial costs both to collect customer-level data and then use that data to develop and test the machine learning and artificial intelligence systems to provide personalized recommendations. After these systems are developed, there would be the ongoing cost of running these systems, collecting new data from each customer as they use the system, and refining these systems to make the company's predictions more accurate.

A Look at U.S. GAAP

LEARNING OBJECTIVE 9

Compare the accounting for merchandising under IFRS and U.S. GAAP.

The basic accounting entries for merchandising are the same under both GAAP and IFRS. The income statement is a required statement under both sets of standards. The basic format is similar although some differences do exist.

Key Points

IAS 1, "Presentation of Financial Statements," provides general guidelines for the reporting of income statement information. Subsequently, a number of international standards have been issued that provide additional guidance to issues related to income statement presentation. The following is a recent income statement for **Walmart Inc.** (USA). The income statement is presented in conformity with GAAP.

Real World

Walmart Inc.
Income Statement

(Amounts in millions except per share data)

Revenues:	
Net sales	$473,076
Membership and other income	3,218
	476,294
Costs and expenses:	
Cost of sales	358,069
Operating, selling, general and administrative expenses	91,353
Operating income	26,872
Interest:	
Debt	2,072
Capital leases	263
Interest income	(119)
Interest, net	2,216
Income from continuing operations before income taxes	24,656
Provision for income taxes:	
Current	8,619
Deferred	(514)
	8,105
Income from continuing operations	16,551
Income (loss) from discontinued operations, net of tax	144
Consolidated net income	16,695
Less consolidated net income attributable to noncontrolling interest	(673)
Consolidated net income attributable to Walmart	$ 16,022

Similarities

- Under both GAAP and IFRS, a company can choose to use either a perpetual or a periodic system.
- Inventories are defined by IFRS as held-for-sale in the ordinary course of business, in the process of production for such sale, or in the form of materials or supplies to be consumed in the production process or in the performing of services. The definition under GAAP is essentially the same.
- Similar to GAAP, comprehensive income under IFRS includes unrealized gains and losses (such as those on non-trading securities) that are not included in the calculation of net income.

Differences

- Under GAAP, companies generally classify income statement items by function. Classification by function leads to descriptions like administration, distribution (selling), and manufacturing. Under IFRS, companies may classify expenses by either nature or by function. Classification by nature leads to descriptions such as the following: salaries, depreciation expense, and utilities expense. If a company uses the functional-expense method on the income statement, disclosure by nature is required in the notes to the financial statements.
- Presentation of the income statement under GAAP follows either a single-step or multiple-step format. IFRS does not mention a single-step or multiple-step approach.
- Under IFRS, revaluation of land, buildings, and intangible assets is permitted. The initial gains and losses resulting from this revaluation are reported as adjustments to equity, often referred to as **other comprehensive income**. The effect of this difference is that the use of IFRS instead of GAAP results in more transactions affecting equity (other comprehensive income) but not net income.
- IFRS requires that two years of income statement information be presented, whereas GAAP has no similar requirement. However, public companies following U.S. Securities and Exchange Commission regulations are required to present three-year comparative income statements.

GAAP Practice

GAAP Self-Test Questions

1. Which of the following would **not** be included in the definition of inventory under GAAP?
   a. Photocopy paper held for sale by an office supply store.
   b. Stereo equipment held for sale by an electronics store.
   c. Used office equipment held for sale by the human relations department of a plastics company.
   d. All of the answer choices would meet the definition.

2. Which of the following would **not** be a line item of a company reporting costs by nature?
   a. Depreciation expense.
   b. Salaries and wages expense.
   c. Interest expense.
   d. Manufacturing expense.

3. Which of the following would **not** be a line item of a company reporting costs by function?
   a. Administration.
   b. Manufacturing.
   c. Utilities expense.
   d. Distribution.

4. Which of the following statements is **false**?
   a. GAAP specifically requires use of a multiple-step income statement.
   b. Under GAAP, companies can use either a perpetual or periodic system.
   c. IFRS does not specify a single-step or multiple-step approach.
   d. IFRS requires that 2 years of income statement information be presented.

5. Which of the following statements is **true**?
   a. IFRS does not permit the reporting of expenses classified by nature.
   b. Under both GAAP and IFRS, a company can choose to use either a perpetual or a periodic system.
   c. GAAP treats all items held for sale as inventory, regardless of whether they are held of sale in the ordinary course of business or not.
   d. GAAP permits the revaluation of property, plant, and equipment, whereas IFRS does not permit revaluation.

GAAP Exercises

GAAP5.1 Explain the difference between the "nature-of-expense" and "function-of-expense" classifications.

GAAP5.2 For each of the following income statement line items, state whether the item is a "by nature" expense item or a "by function" expense item.

________ Cost of goods sold.
________ Depreciation expense.
________ Salaries and wages expense.
________ Selling expenses.
________ Utilities expense.
________ Delivery expense.
________ General and administrative expenses.

GAAP5.3 Atlantis Company reported the following amounts in 2029: net income, $150,000; unrealized gain related to revaluation of buildings, $10,000; and unrealized loss on non-trading securities, $(35,000). Determine Atlantis's total comprehensive income for 2029.

GAAP Financial Reporting Problem: Apple Inc. (USA)

GAAP5.4 The financial statements of **Apple** are presented in Appendix D. The complete annual report, including the notes to its financial statements, is available at the company's website.

Instructions

(Round to one decimal place.)

a. What was the percentage change in (1) total revenue (net sales) and in (2) net income from 2018 to 2019 and from 2019 to 2020?

b. What was the company's gross profit margin rate in 2018, 2019, and 2020?

c. What was the company's percentage of net income to total revenue in 2018, 2019, and 2020?

Answers to GAAP Self-Test Questions

1. c **2.** d **3.** c **4.** a **5.** b

CHAPTER **6**

Inventories

LEARNING OBJECTIVES After studying this chapter, you should be able to:

LO 1 Discuss how to classify and determine inventory.

LO 2 Apply inventory cost flow methods and discuss their financial effects.

LO 3 Indicate the effects of inventory errors on the financial statements.

LO 4 Explain the statement presentation and analysis of inventory.

Chapter Preview

In the previous chapter, we discussed the accounting for merchandise inventory using a perpetual inventory system. In this chapter, we explain the methods used to calculate the cost of inventory on hand at the statement of financial position date and the cost of goods sold.

Inventories

Classifying and Determining Inventory
- Classifying inventory
- Determining inventory quantities

Inventory Methods and Financial Effects
- Specific identification
- Cost flow assumptions
- Financial statement and tax effects
- Using inventory cost flow methods consistently

Effects of Inventory Errors
- Income statement effects
- Statement of financial position effects

Inventory Statement Presentation and Analysis
- Presentation
- Lower of cost or net realizable value
- Financial analysis and data analytics

Practice

DO IT! 1 Rules of Ownership

DO IT! 2 Cost Flow Methods

DO IT! 3 Inventory Errors

DO IT! 4 LCNRV and Inventory Turnover

Go to the Review and Practice section at the end of the chapter for a review of key concepts and practice applications with solutions.
Additional tutorials and practice opportunities are available in the Wiley online course.

Feature Story "Where Is That Spare Bulldozer Blade?"

Let's talk inventory—big, bulldozer-size inventory. **Komatsu Ltd.** (JPN) is one of the world's largest manufacturers of giant construction and mining equipment. The company's name is actually somewhat ironic, since *komatsu* is Japanese for "small pine tree." But, there is nothing small about what Komatsu does. It produces many types of earthmoving equipment: excavators, forestry equipment for hauling giant logs, forklifts, metal presses, and lots of other really big things. It is the second largest seller of heavy equipment in the world.

How does a company remain profitable if it sells so many different products, many of them giant, all over the world? To be profitable, the company needs to effectively manage its inventory. Imagine what it costs Komatsu to have too many D575 bulldozers (the largest bulldozers in the world) sitting around in inventory. That is something the company definitely wants to avoid. On the other hand, the company must make sure that it has enough inventory readily available to meet demand, or it will lose sales.

Komatsu's inventory management expertise has helped it meet many challenges, including Japan's recent tsunami. In fact, Komatsu is so good at managing its own inventory that it actually has a division, **Komatsu Logistics**, that helps other companies address their inventory challenges. It offers a broad range of services such as disassembly, packing, storage, assembly, and international distribution. When you build equipment that is used to move mountains, everything else seems easy.

Sources: Company website; and Peter Marsh, "Komatsu Carries Strong Yen Load," *Financial Times* (October 25, 2010).

pressmaster/Adobe Stock

6.1 Classifying and Determining Inventory

LEARNING OBJECTIVE 1

Discuss how to classify and determine inventory.

Two important steps in the reporting of inventory at the end of the accounting period are the classification of inventory based on its degree of completeness and the determination of inventory amounts.

Classifying Inventory

How a company classifies its inventory depends on whether the firm is a merchandiser or a manufacturer. In a **merchandising** company, such as those described in Chapter 5, inventory consists of many different items. For example, in a grocery store, canned goods, dairy products, meats, and produce are just a few of the inventory items on hand. These items have two common characteristics.

1. They are owned by the company.
2. They are in a form ready for sale to customers in the ordinary course of business.

Thus, merchandisers need only one inventory classification, **merchandise inventory**, to describe the many different items that make up the total inventory.

In a **manufacturing** company, some inventory may not yet be ready for sale. As a result, manufacturers usually classify inventory into three categories: finished goods, work in process, and raw materials (see **Helpful Hint**).

HELPFUL HINT

Regardless of the classification, companies report all inventories under Current Assets on the statement of financial position.

- **Raw materials** are the basic goods that will be used in production but have not yet been placed into production.
- **Work in process** is that portion of manufactured inventory that has been placed into the production process but is not yet complete.
- **Finished goods inventory** is manufactured items that are completed and ready for sale.

For example, **Komatsu** (JPN) classifies earth-moving tractors completed and ready for sale as **finished goods**. It classifies the tractors on the assembly line in various stages of production as **work in process**. The steel, glass, tires, and other components that are on hand waiting to be used in the production of tractors are identified as **raw materials. Illustration 6.1** shows an adapted excerpt from Note 5 of Komatsu's annual report.

ILLUSTRATION 6.1

Composition of Komatsu's inventory

Real World

Komatsu
Notes to the Financial Statements
(yen in millions)

	March 31	
	2021	**2020**
Finished products, including finished parts held for sale	¥571,103	¥586,468
Work in process	159,515	153,082
Materials and supplies	63,234	65,759
Total	¥793,852	¥805,309

By observing the levels and changes in the levels of these three inventory types, financial statement users can gain insight into management's production plans.

- Low levels of raw materials and high levels of finished goods suggest that management believes it has enough inventory on hand and production will be slowing down—perhaps in anticipation of a recession.
- High levels of raw materials and low levels of finished goods probably signal that management is planning to step up production.

Many companies have significantly lowered inventory levels and costs using just-in-time inventory methods.

Under a **just-in-time (JIT) inventory** method, companies manufacture or purchase goods only when needed. **Dell** (USA) is famous for having developed a system for making computers in response to individual customer requests. Even though it makes each computer to meet each customer's particular specifications, Dell is able to assemble the computer and put it on a truck in less than 48 hours. The success of the JIT system depends on reliable suppliers. By integrating its information systems with those of its suppliers, Dell reduced its inventories to nearly zero. This is a huge advantage in an industry where products become obsolete nearly overnight.

The accounting concepts discussed in this chapter apply to the inventory classifications of both merchandising and manufacturing companies. Our focus here is on merchandise inventory. Additional issues specific to manufacturing companies are discussed as part of managerial accounting.

Accounting Across the Organization

New Africa/Adobe Stock

A Big Hiccup

JIT can save a company a lot of money, but it isn't without risk. An unexpected disruption in the supply chain can cost a company a lot of money. When facilities for **Taiwan Semiconductor Manufacturing** (TWN), the sole supplier of **Apple**'s (USA) A10 processor integral to a previous model of its iPhone7, were impacted by a 6.4-magnitude earthquake in southern Taiwan, the release of this cell phone model could have been delayed. Fortunately, both inventories of the fragile wafers used in the iPhone and the susceptible equipment used to produce them were not damaged.

Similarly, during the Covid-19 pandemic, a number of global automotive manufacturers, including **Renault** (FRA), **Volkswagen** (DEU), and **Daimler** (DEU), faced shortages of semiconductor chips used in digital automobiles. The impact on global car sales is estimated to be near 8 million cars, which is over 10% of the cars sold worldwide in the previous year's sales.

Sources: Adapted from Jonathan Webb, "The Taiwanese Earthquake That Nearly Flattened the Apple iPhone 7," *Forbes* (February 19, 2016); and Chuin-Wei Yap, William Boston, and Alistair MacDonald, "Global Supply-Chain Problems Escalate, Threatening Economic Recovery," *Wall Street Journal* (October 8, 2021).

What steps might the companies take to avoid such a serious disruption in the future? (Answer is available near the end of the chapter.)

Determining Inventory Quantities

No matter whether they are using a periodic or perpetual inventory system, all companies need to determine inventory quantities at the end of the accounting period. If using a perpetual system, companies take a physical inventory for the following reasons.

1. To check the accuracy of their perpetual inventory records.
2. To determine the amount of inventory lost due to wasted raw materials, shoplifting, or employee theft.

Companies using a periodic inventory system take a physical inventory for **two different purposes**: to determine the inventory on hand at the statement of financial position date, and to determine the cost of goods sold for the period.

Determining inventory quantities involves two steps: (1) taking a physical inventory of goods on hand and (2) determining the ownership of goods.

Taking a Physical Inventory

Companies take a physical inventory at the end of the accounting period. Taking a physical inventory involves actually counting, weighing, or measuring each kind of inventory on hand (see **Ethics Note**). In many companies, taking an inventory is a formidable task. Retailers such as **Esprit Holdings** (HKG), **Indomarco Prismatama** (IDN), or **Eslite Bookstore** (TWN) have thousands of different inventory items.

> **ETHICS NOTE**
>
> **In a famous fraud, a salad oil company filled its storage tanks mostly with water. The oil rose to the top, so auditors thought the tanks were full of oil. The company also said it had more tanks than it really did: It repainted numbers on the tanks to confuse auditors.**

- An inventory count is generally more accurate when goods are not being sold or received during the counting.
- Consequently, companies often "take inventory" when the business is closed or when business is slow.

Many retailers close after the holiday sales and returns—when inventories are at their lowest level—to count inventory. Jewelry retailer **Gitanjali Group** (IND), for example, has a year-end of March 31.

Determining Ownership of Goods

One challenge in computing inventory quantities is determining what inventory a company owns. To determine ownership of goods, two questions must be answered:

1. Do all of the goods included in the count belong to the company?
2. Does the company own any goods that were not included in the count?

Goods in Transit A complication in determining ownership is **goods in transit** (on board a truck, train, ship, or plane) at the end of the period. The company may have purchased goods that have not yet been received, or it may have sold goods that have not yet been delivered. To arrive at an accurate count, the company must determine ownership of these goods.

Goods in transit should be included in the inventory of the company that has legal title to the goods. Legal title is determined by the terms of the sale, as shown in **Illustration 6.2** and described below.

ILLUSTRATION 6.2 **Terms of sale**

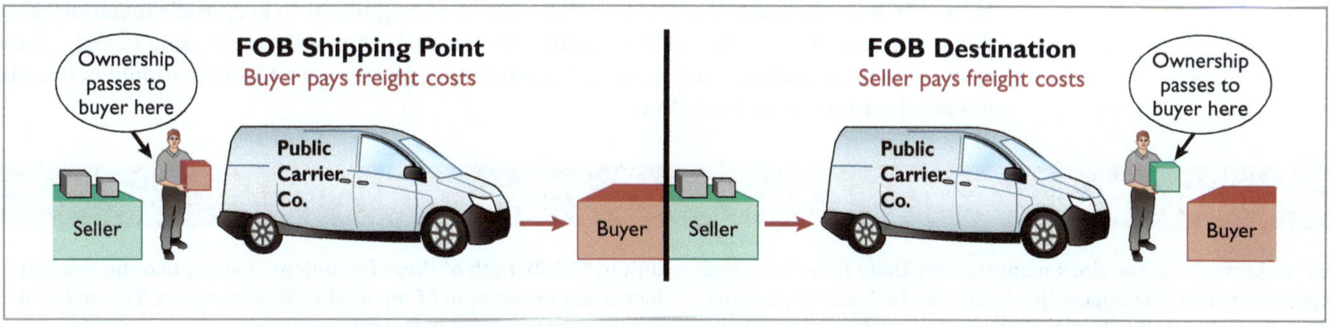

1. When the terms are **FOB (free on board) shipping point**, ownership of the goods passes to the buyer when the public carrier accepts the goods from the seller.
2. When the terms are **FOB destination**, ownership of the goods remains with the seller until the goods reach the buyer.

If goods in transit at the statement date are ignored, inventory quantities may be seriously miscounted. Assume, for example, that Hargrove Stores has 20,000 units of inventory on hand on December 31. It also has the following goods in transit.

1. Sales of 1,500 units shipped December 31 FOB destination.
2. Purchases of 2,500 units shipped FOB shipping point by the seller on December 31.

Hargrove has legal title to both the 1,500 units sold and the 2,500 units purchased. If the company ignores the units in transit, it would understate inventory quantities by 4,000 units (1,500 + 2,500).

As we will see later in the chapter, inaccurate inventory counts affect not only the inventory amount shown on the statement of financial position but also the cost of goods sold calculation on the income statement.

Ethics Insight

luanateutzi/Getty Images

Falsifying Inventory to Boost Income

Managers at a women's apparel maker were convicted of falsifying inventory records to boost net income—and consequently to boost management bonuses. In another case, executives at an electronics manufacturer were accused of defrauding lenders by manipulating inventory records. The indictment said the company classified "defective goods as new or refurbished" and claimed that it owned certain shipments "from overseas suppliers" when, in fact, the company either did not own the shipments or the shipments did not exist.

What effect does an overstatement of inventory have on a company's financial statements? (Answer is available near the end of the chapter.)

Consigned Goods In some lines of business, it is common to hold the goods of other parties and try to sell the goods for them for a fee, but without taking ownership of the goods. These are called **consigned goods**.

- For example, you might have a used car that you would like to sell. A used-car dealer might be willing to put the car on its lot and charge you a commission if it is sold.
- Under this agreement, the dealer **would not take ownership** of the car, which would still belong to you.
- Therefore, if an inventory count were taken, the car would not be included in the dealer's inventory because the dealer does not own it.

Many car, boat, and antique dealers sell goods on consignment to keep their inventory costs down and to avoid the risk of purchasing an item that they will not be able to sell. Today, even some manufacturers are making consignment agreements with their suppliers in order to keep their inventory levels low.

Anatomy of a Fraud

Ted Nickerson, CEO of clock manufacturer Dally Industries, had expensive tastes. To support this habit, Ted took out large loans, which he collateralized with his Dally Industries shares. If the price of Dally's shares fell, he was required to provide the bank with more shares. To achieve target net income figures and thus maintain the share price, Ted coerced employees in the company to alter inventory figures. Inventory quantities were manipulated by changing the amounts on inventory control tags after the yearend physical inventory count. For example, if a tag said there were 20 units of a particular item, the tag was changed to 220. Similarly, the unit costs that were used to determine the value of ending inventory were increased from, for example, $125 per unit to $1,250. Both of these fraudulent changes had the effect of increasing the amount of reported ending inventory. This reduced cost of goods sold and increased net income.

Total take: $245,000

The Missing Control

Independent internal verification. The company should have spot-checked its inventory records periodically, verifying that the number of units in the records agreed with the amount on hand and that the unit costs agreed with vendor price sheets.

Source: Adapted from Wells, *Fraud Casebook* (2007), pp. 502–509.

ACTION PLAN

- **Apply the rules of ownership to goods held on consignment.**
- **Apply the rules of ownership to goods in transit.**

DO IT! 1 | Rules of Ownership

Deng Imports completed its inventory count. It arrived at a total inventory value of ¥200,000 (amounts in thousands). As a new member of Deng's accounting department, you have been given the information listed below. Discuss how this information affects the reported cost of inventory.

1. Deng included in the inventory goods held on consignment for Falls Co., costing ¥15,000.
2. The company did not include in the count purchased goods of ¥10,000 which were in transit (terms: FOB shipping point).
3. The company did not include in the count sold inventory with a cost of ¥12,000 which was in transit (terms: FOB shipping point).
4. The company did not include in the count purchased goods of ¥8,000 which were in transit (terms: FOB Destination).
5. The company did not include in the count sold inventory with a cost of ¥6,000 which was in transit (terms: FOB Destination).

Solution

1. The goods of ¥15,000 held on consignment should be deducted from the inventory count. **2.** The goods of ¥10,000 purchased FOB shipping point should be added to the inventory count. **3.** Sold goods of ¥12,000 which were in transit FOB shipping point should not be included in the ending inventory. **4.** The goods of ¥8,000 purchased FOB destination should not be included in the ending inventory. **5.** Sold goods of ¥6,000 which were in transit FOB destination should be added to the inventory count.

Thus, inventory should be carried at ¥201,000 (¥200,000 – ¥15,000 + ¥10,000 + ¥6,000).

Related exercise material: **BE6.1, BE6.2, DO IT! 6.1, E6.1, and E6.2.**

6.2 Inventory Methods and Financial Effects

LEARNING OBJECTIVE 2

Apply inventory cost flow methods and discuss their financial effects.

Inventory is accounted for at cost.

- Cost includes all expenditures necessary to acquire goods and place them in a condition ready for sale. For example, freight costs incurred to acquire inventory are added to the cost of inventory, but the cost of shipping goods to a customer is a selling expense.
- After a company has determined the quantity of units of inventory, it applies unit costs to the quantities to compute the total cost of the inventory and the cost of goods sold. This process can be complicated if a company has purchased inventory items at different times and at different prices.

For example, assume that Crivitz Home Entertainment purchases three identical 50-inch TVs on different dates at costs of £720, £750, and £800. During the year, Crivitz sold two TVs at £1,200 each. These facts are summarized in **Illustration 6.3**.

ILLUSTRATION 6.3
Data for inventory costing example

Purchases			
February 3	1 TV	at	£720
March 5	1 TV	at	£750
May 22	1 TV	at	£800
Sales			
June 1	2 TVs	for	£2,400 (£1,200 × 2)

Cost of goods sold will differ depending on which two TVs the company sold. For example, it might be £1,470 (£720 + £750), or £1,520 (£720 + £800), or £1,550 (£750 + £800). In this section, we discuss alternative costing methods available to Crivitz.

Specific Identification

If Crivitz can positively identify which particular units it sold and which are still in ending inventory, it can use the **specific identification method** of inventory costing. For example, if Crivitz sold the TVs it purchased on February 3 and May 22, then its cost of goods sold is £1,520 (£720 + £800), and its ending inventory is £750 (see **Illustration 6.4**). Using this method, companies can accurately determine ending inventory and cost of goods sold.

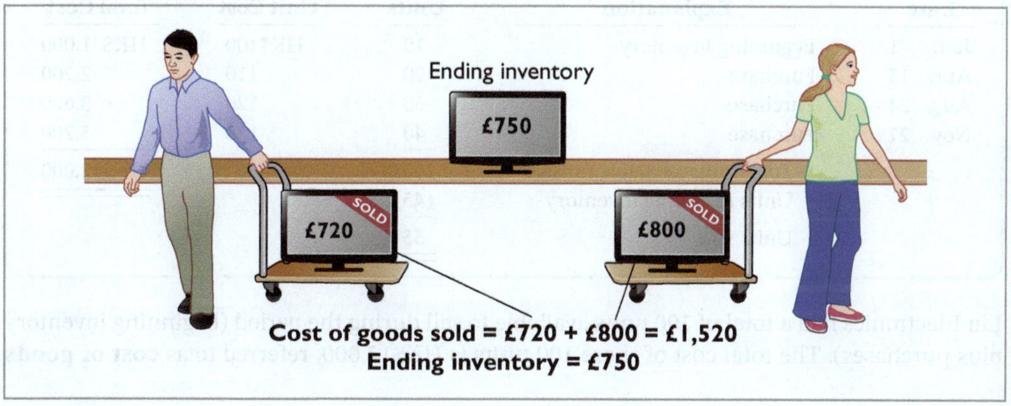

ILLUSTRATION 6.4
Specific identification method

ETHICS NOTE

A major disadvantage of the specific identification method is that management may be able to manipulate net income. For example, it can boost net income by selling units purchased at a low cost, or reduce net income by selling units purchased at a high cost.

Specific identification requires that companies keep records of the original cost of each individual inventory item.

- Historically, specific identification was possible only when a company sold a limited variety of high-unit-cost items that could be identified clearly from the time of purchase through the time of sale. Examples of such products are cars, pianos, or expensive antiques.
- Today, bar coding, electronic product codes, and radio frequency identification make it theoretically possible to do specific identification with nearly any type of product.

The reality is, however, that this practice is still relatively rare (see **Ethics Note**). Instead, rather than keep track of the cost of each particular item sold, most companies make assumptions, called **cost flow assumptions**, about which units were sold.

Cost Flow Assumptions

Because specific identification is often impractical, other cost flow methods are permitted. These differ from specific identification in that they **assume** flows of costs that may be unrelated to the physical flow of goods. There are two assumed cost flow methods:

1. First-in, first-out (FIFO).
2. Average-cost.

There is no accounting requirement that the cost flow assumption be consistent with the physical movement of the goods. Company management selects the appropriate cost flow method. However, once the cost flow assumption is chosen (or specific identification method is adopted), it must be applied to all inventories having a similar nature and use.

To demonstrate the two cost flow methods, we will use a **periodic** inventory system. We assume a periodic system because **very few companies use perpetual FIFO or average-cost** to cost their inventory and related cost of goods sold. Instead, companies that use perpetual systems often use an assumed cost (called a standard cost) to record cost of goods sold at the time of sale. Then, at the end of the period when they count their inventory, they **recalculate cost of goods sold using periodic FIFO or average-cost** as shown in this chapter and adjust cost of goods sold to this recalculated number. The cost of goods sold formula in a periodic system is as follows.

(Beginning Inventory + Purchases) − Ending Inventory = Cost of Goods Sold

To illustrate the two inventory cost flow methods, we will use the data for Lin Electronics' Astro condensers, shown in **Illustration 6.5**.

ILLUSTRATION 6.5

Data for Lin Electronics

Lin Electronics
Astro Condensers

Date	Explanation	Units	Unit Cost	Total Cost
Jan. 1	Beginning inventory	10	HK$100	HK$ 1,000
Apr. 15	Purchase	20	110	2,200
Aug. 24	Purchase	30	120	3,600
Nov. 27	Purchase	40	130	5,200
	Total units available for sale	100		HK$12,000
	Units in ending inventory	(45)		
	Units sold	55		

Lin Electronics had a total of 100 units available to sell during the period (beginning inventory plus purchases). The total cost of these 100 units is HK$12,000, referred to as **cost of goods**

available for sale. A physical inventory taken at December 31 determined that there were 45 units in ending inventory. Therefore, Lin sold 55 units (100 – 45) during the period.

To determine the cost of the 55 units that were sold (the cost of goods sold), we assign a cost to the ending inventory and subtract that value from the cost of goods available for sale.

- The value assigned to the ending inventory **will depend on which cost flow method we use**.
- No matter which cost flow assumption we use, though, the sum of cost of goods sold plus the cost of the ending inventory must equal the cost of goods available for sale—in this case, HK$12,000.

First-In, First-Out (FIFO)

The **first-in, first-out (FIFO) method** assumes that the **earliest goods** purchased are the first to be sold.

- FIFO often parallels the actual physical flow of merchandise. That is, it generally is good business practice to sell the oldest units first.
- Under the FIFO method, the **costs** of the earliest goods purchased are the first to be recognized in determining cost of goods sold. This does not necessarily mean that the oldest units **are** sold first, but that the costs of the oldest units are **recognized** first. (In a bin of picture hangers at the hardware store, for example, no one really knows, nor would it matter, which hangers are sold first.)

Illustration 6.6 shows the allocation of the cost of goods available for sale at Lin Electronics under FIFO.

ILLUSTRATION 6.6

Allocation of costs—FIFO method

Cost of Goods Available for Sale

Date	Explanation	Units	Unit Cost	Total Cost
Jan. 1	Beginning inventory	10	HK$100	HK$ 1,000
Apr. 15	Purchase	20	110	2,200
Aug. 24	Purchase	30	120	3,600
Nov. 27	Purchase	40	130	5,200
	Total	100		HK$12,000

Step 1: Ending Inventory

Date	Units	Unit Cost	Total Cost
Nov. 27	40	HK$130	HK$5,200
Aug. 24	5	120	600
Total	45		HK$5,800

Step 2: Cost of Goods Sold

Cost of goods available for sale	HK$12,000
Less: Ending inventory	5,800
Cost of goods sold	HK$ 6,200

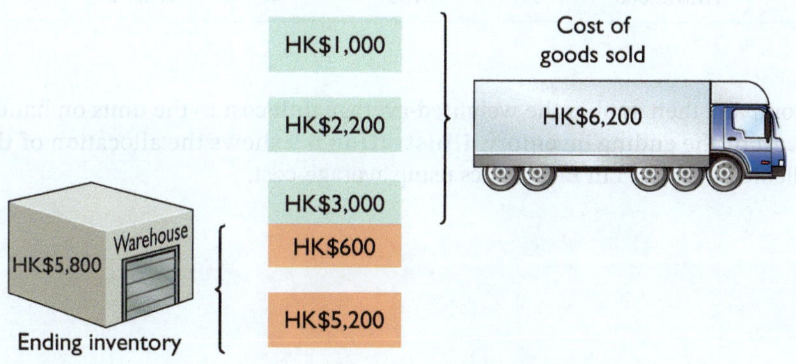

HELPFUL HINT

Note the sequencing of the allocation: (1) compute ending inventory, and (2) determine cost of goods sold.

Under FIFO, since it is assumed that the first goods purchased were the first goods sold, ending inventory is based on the prices of the most recent units purchased (see **Helpful Hint**). That is, **under FIFO, companies obtain the cost of the ending inventory by taking the unit cost of the most recent purchase and working backward until all units of inventory have been costed.**

- In Step 1, Lin Electronics prices the 45 units of ending inventory using the **most recent** prices. The last purchase was 40 units at HK$130 on November 27. The remaining 5 units are priced using the unit cost of the second most recent purchase, HK$120, on August 24.
- In Step 2, Lin Electronics calculates cost of goods sold by subtracting the cost of the units **not sold** (ending inventory) from the cost of all goods available for sale.

Illustration 6.7 demonstrates that companies also can calculate cost of goods sold by pricing the 55 units sold using the prices of the first 55 units acquired. Note that of the 30 units purchased on August 24, only 25 units are assumed sold. This agrees with our calculation of the cost of ending inventory, where 5 of these units were assumed unsold and thus included in ending inventory.

ILLUSTRATION 6.7

Proof of cost of goods sold

Date	Units	Unit Cost	Total Cost
Jan. 1	10	HK$100	HK$1,000
Apr. 15	20	110	2,200
Aug. 24	25	120	3,000
Total	55		HK$6,200

Average-Cost

The **average-cost method** allocates the cost of goods available for sale on the basis of the weighted-average unit cost incurred.

- The **weighted-average unit cost** is the average cost that is weighted by the number of units purchased at each unit cost.
- The average-cost method assumes that goods are similar in nature.

Illustration 6.8 presents the formula and a sample computation of the weighted-average unit cost.

ILLUSTRATION 6.8

Formula for weighted-average unit cost

Cost of Goods Available for Sale	÷	Total Units Available for Sale	=	Weighted-Average Unit Cost
HK$12,000	÷	100	=	HK$120

The company then applies the weighted-average unit cost to the units on hand to determine the cost of the ending inventory. **Illustration 6.9** shows the allocation of the cost of goods available for sale at Lin Electronics using average-cost.

ILLUSTRATION 6.9

Allocation of costs—average-cost method

Cost of Goods Available for Sale

Date	Explanation	Units	Unit Cost	Total Cost
Jan. 1	Beginning inventory	10	HK$100	HK$ 1,000
Apr. 15	Purchase	20	110	2,200
Aug. 24	Purchase	30	120	3,600
Nov. 27	Purchase	40	130	5,200
	Total	100		**HK$12,000**

Step 1: Ending Inventory

HK$12,000	÷	100	=	HK$120
		Unit Cost		**Total Cost**
Units				
45		HK$120		**HK$5,400**

Step 2: Cost of Goods Sold

Cost of goods available for sale	HK$12,000
Less: Ending inventory	5,400
Cost of goods sold	**HK$ 6,600**

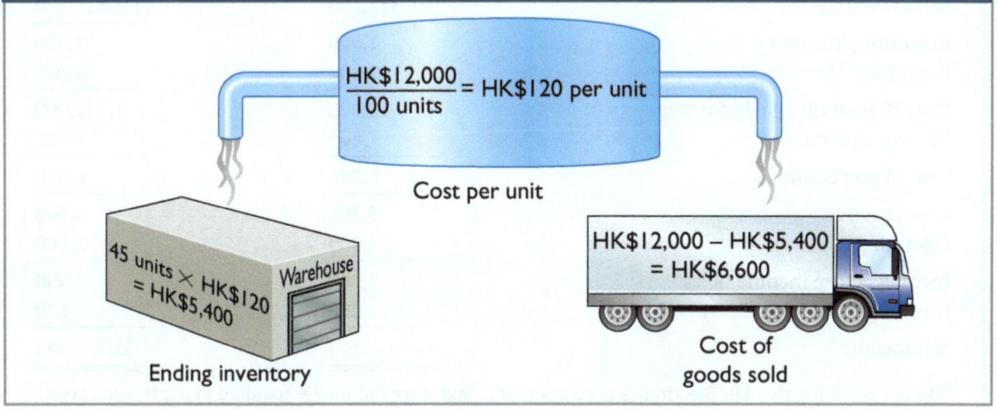

We can verify the cost of goods sold under this method by multiplying the units sold times the weighted-average unit cost (55 × HK$120 = HK$6,600). Note that this method does not use the average of the unit costs. That average is HK$115 (HK$100 + HK$110 + HK$120 + HK$130 = HK$460; HK$460 ÷ 4). The average-cost method instead uses the average **weighted by** the quantities purchased at each unit cost.[1]

Financial Statement and Tax Effects of Cost Flow Methods

Either of the two cost flow assumptions is acceptable for use. For example, **Lenovo** (CHN) uses the average-cost method, whereas **Yingli Solar** (CHN) uses average-costing for key raw materials and FIFO for the remainder of its inventories.

- A recent survey of IFRS companies indicated that approximately 60% of these companies use the average-cost method, with 40% using FIFO.
- Approximately 23% use both average-cost and FIFO for different parts of their inventory.

[1] A cost flow method that is used extensively in the United States is the last-in, first-out (LIFO) method. Under IFRS, LIFO is not permitted for financial reporting purposes because the IASB states that LIFO does not provide a reliable representation of recent cost levels of inventory. Appendix 6C discusses the basics of the LIFO method.

The reasons companies adopt different inventory cost flow methods are varied, but they usually involve one of three factors: (1) income statement effects, (2) statement of financial position effects, or (3) tax effects.

Income Statement Effects

To understand why companies choose either FIFO or average-cost, let's examine the effects of these two cost flow assumptions on the financial statements of Lin Electronics. The condensed income statements in **Illustration 6.10** assume that Lin sold its 55 units for HK$11,500, had operating expenses of HK$2,000, and is subject to an income tax rate of 30%.

ILLUSTRATION 6.10

Comparative effects of cost flow methods

Lin Electronics
Condensed Income Statements

	FIFO	Average-Cost
Sales revenue	HK$11,500	HK$11,500
Beginning inventory	1,000	1,000
Purchases	11,000	11,000
Cost of goods available for sale	12,000	12,000
Ending inventory	5,800	5,400
Cost of goods sold	6,200	6,600
Gross profit	5,300	4,900
Operating expenses	2,000	2,000
Income before income taxes*	3,300	2,900
Income tax expense (30%)	990	870
Net income	HK$ 2,310	HK$ 2,030

*We are assuming that Lin Electronics is a corporation, and corporations are required to pay income taxes.

Note the cost of goods available for sale (HK$12,000) is the same under both FIFO and average-cost. However, the ending inventories and the costs of goods sold are different. This difference is due to the unit costs that the company allocated to cost of goods sold and to ending inventory. Each dollar of difference in ending inventory results in a corresponding dollar difference in income before income taxes. For Lin, a HK$400 difference exists between cost of goods sold using FIFO versus average-cost.

In periods of changing prices, the cost flow assumption can have a significant impact on income and on evaluations based on income, such as the following.

1. In a period of inflation, FIFO produces a higher net income because the lower unit costs of the first units purchased are matched against revenues.
2. In a period of rising prices (as is the case in the Lin example), FIFO reports a higher net income (HK$2,310) than average-cost (HK$2,030).
3. If prices are falling, the results from the use of FIFO and average-cost are reversed. FIFO will report the lower net income and average-cost the higher.

To management, higher net income is an advantage. It causes external users to view the company more favorably. In addition, management bonuses, if based on net income, will be higher. Therefore, when prices are rising (which is usually the case), companies tend to prefer FIFO because it results in higher net income.

Statement of Financial Position Effects

A major advantage of the FIFO method is that in a period of inflation, the costs allocated to ending inventory will approximate their current cost. For example, for Lin Electronics, 40 of the 45 units in the ending inventory are costed under FIFO at the higher November 27 unit cost of HK$130.

Conversely, a shortcoming of the average-cost method is that in a period of inflation, the costs allocated to ending inventory may be understated in terms of current cost. The understatement becomes greater over prolonged periods of inflation if the inventory includes goods purchased in one or more prior accounting periods.

Tax Effects

We have seen that both inventory on the statement of financial position and net income on the income statement are higher when companies use FIFO in a period of inflation. Yet, some companies use average-cost. Why? The reason is that average-cost results in lower income taxes (because of lower net income) during times of rising prices. For example, at Lin Electronics, income taxes are HK$870 under average-cost, compared to HK$990 under FIFO. The tax savings of HK$120 makes more cash available for use in the business.

Using Inventory Cost Flow Methods Consistently

Whatever cost flow method a company chooses, it should use that method consistently from one accounting period to another. This approach is often referred to as the **consistency concept**, which means that a company uses the same accounting principles and methods from year to year.

- Consistent application enhances the comparability of financial statements over successive time periods.
- In contrast, using the FIFO method one year and the average-cost method the next year would make it difficult to compare the net incomes of the two years.

Although consistent application is preferred, it does not mean that a company may never change its inventory costing method. When a company adopts a different method, it should disclose in the financial statements the change and its effects on net income.

Global Insight

Mike Fuentes/
Bloomberg/Getty Images

Is LIFO Fair?

Many U.S. companies use last-in, last-out (LIFO) to value their inventories for financial reporting and tax purposes. LIFO assumes the latest goods purchased are the first goods sold. One reason why U.S. companies use LIFO relates to tax benefits. In a period of rising prices, companies using LIFO report lower income taxes (due to lower taxable income) and therefore higher cash flows. Critics say that LIFO provides an unfair "tax dodge."

As the U.S. Congress looks for more sources of tax revenue, some lawmakers favor the elimination of LIFO. Supporters of LIFO argue that the method is conceptually sound because it matches current costs with current revenues. In addition, they point out that this matching provides protection against inflation.

International accounting standards do not allow the use of LIFO. Because of this, the net income of oil companies such as **Shaanxi Yanching Petroleum** (CHN) and **Royal Dutch Shell** (GBR) are not directly comparable to U.S. companies, which makes analysis difficult.

Source: Adapted from David Reilly, "Big Oil's Accounting Methods Fuel Criticism," *Wall Street Journal* (August 8, 2006), p. C1.

What are the arguments for and against the use of LIFO? (Answer is available near the end of the chapter.)

ACTION PLAN

- **Understand the periodic inventory system.**
- **Allocate costs between goods sold and goods on hand (ending inventory) for each cost flow method.**
- **Compute cost of goods sold for each method.**

DO IT! 2 | Cost Flow Methods

The accounting records of Shumway Implements show the following data.

Beginning inventory	4,000 units at € 3
Purchases	6,000 units at € 4
Sales	7,000 units at €12

Determine the cost of goods sold during the period under a periodic inventory system using (a) the FIFO method and (b) the average-cost method.

Solution

Cost of goods available for sale = (4,000 × €3) + (6,000 × €4) = €36,000
Ending inventory = 10,000 − 7,000 = 3,000 units

a. FIFO: €36,000 − (3,000 × €4) = €24,000
b. Average cost per unit: [(4,000 @ €3) + (6,000 @ €4)] ÷ 10,000 = €3.60
Average-cost: €36,000 − (3,000 × €3.60) = €25,200

Related exercise material: **BE6.3, BE6.4, DO IT! 6.2, E6.3, E6.4, E6.5, E6.6, E6.7, and E6.9.**

6.3 Effects of Inventory Errors

LEARNING OBJECTIVE 3

Indicate the effects of inventory errors on the financial statements.

Unfortunately, errors occasionally occur in accounting for inventory.

- In some cases, errors are caused by failure to count or price the inventory correctly.
- In other cases, errors occur because companies do not properly recognize the transfer of legal title to goods that are in transit.

When errors occur, they affect both the income statement and the statement of financial position.

Income Statement Effects

The ending inventory of one period automatically becomes the beginning inventory of the next period. Thus, inventory errors affect the computation of cost of goods sold and net income in two periods.

The effects on cost of goods sold can be computed by first entering incorrect data in the formula in **Illustration 6.11** and then substituting the correct data.

ILLUSTRATION 6.11
Formula for cost of goods sold

Beginning Inventory + Cost of Goods Purchased − Ending Inventory = Cost of Goods Sold

If **beginning** inventory is understated, cost of goods sold will be understated. If **ending** inventory is understated, cost of goods sold will be overstated. **Illustration 6.12** shows the effects of inventory errors on the current year's income statement.

When Inventory Error:	Cost of Goods Sold Is:	Net Income Is:
Understates beginning inventory	Understated	Overstated
Overstates beginning inventory	Overstated	Understated
Understates ending inventory	Overstated	Understated
Overstates ending inventory	Understated	Overstated

ILLUSTRATION 6.12

Effects of inventory errors on current year's income statement

An error in the ending inventory of the current period will have a **reverse effect on net income of the next accounting period**. **Illustration 6.13** shows this effect.

- Note that the understatement of ending inventory in 2028 results in an understatement of beginning inventory in 2029 and an overstatement of net income in 2029.
- Over the two years, though, total net income is correct because the errors **offset each other**.

Notice that total income using incorrect data is €35,000 (€22,000 + €13,000), which is the same as the total income of €35,000 (€25,000 + €10,000) using correct data. Also note in this example that an error in the beginning inventory does not result in a corresponding error in the ending inventory for that period. The correctness of the ending inventory depends entirely on the accuracy of taking and costing the inventory at the statement of financial position date under the periodic inventory system (see **Ethics Note**).

ETHICS NOTE

Inventory fraud increases during recessions. Such fraud includes pricing inventory at amounts in excess of its actual value, or claiming to have inventory when no inventory exists. Inventory fraud usually overstates ending inventory, thereby understating cost of goods sold and creating higher income.

ILLUSTRATION 6.13 **Effects of inventory errors on two years' income statements**

Sample Company
Condensed Income Statements

	2028				2029			
	Incorrect		Correct		Incorrect		Correct	
Sales revenue		€80,000		€80,000		€90,000		€90,000
Beginning inventory	€20,000		€20,000		**€12,000**		**€15,000**	
Cost of goods purchased	40,000		40,000		68,000		68,000	
Cost of goods available for sale	60,000		60,000		80,000		83,000	
Ending inventory	**12,000**		**15,000**		23,000		23,000	
Cost of goods sold		48,000		45,000		57,000		60,000
Gross profit		32,000		35,000		33,000		30,000
Operating expenses		10,000		10,000		20,000		20,000
Net income		€22,000		€25,000		€13,000		€10,000

€(3,000) Net income understated

€3,000 Net income overstated

The errors cancel. Thus, the combined total income for the 2-year period is correct.

Statement of Financial Position Effects

Companies can determine the effect of ending inventory errors on the statement of financial position by using the basic accounting equation: Assets = Liabilities + Equity. Errors in the ending inventory have the effects shown in **Illustration 6.14**.

ILLUSTRATION 6.14

Effects of ending inventory errors on statement of financial position

Ending Inventory Error	Assets	Liabilities	Equity
Overstated	Overstated	No effect	Overstated
Understated	Understated	No effect	Understated

The effect of an error in ending inventory on the subsequent period was shown in Illustration 6.13.

- Note that if the error is not corrected, the combined total net income for the two periods would be correct.
- Thus, total equity reported on the statement of financial position at the end of 2029 will also be correct.

ACTION PLAN

- **An ending inventory error in one period will have an equal and opposite effect on cost of goods sold and net income in the next period.**
- **After two years, the errors have offset each other.**

DO IT! 3 | Inventory Errors

Visual Designs overstated its 2028 ending inventory by NT$22,000. Determine the impact this error has on ending inventory, cost of goods sold, and equity in 2028 and 2029.

Solution

	2028	2029
Ending inventory	NT$22,000 overstated	No effect
Cost of goods sold	NT$22,000 understated	NT$22,000 overstated
Equity	NT$22,000 overstated	No effect

Related exercise material: **BE6.5, DO IT! 6.3, E6.10, and E6.11.**

6.4 Inventory Statement Presentation and Analysis

LEARNING OBJECTIVE 4

Explain the statement presentation and analysis of inventory.

Presentation

As indicated in Chapter 5, inventory is classified in the statement of financial position as a current asset immediately above receivables. In a multiple-step income statement, cost of goods sold is subtracted from net sales. There also should be disclosure of:

1. The major inventory classifications.
2. The basis of accounting (cost, or lower of cost or net realizable value).
3. The cost method (FIFO or average-cost).

Lower of Cost or Net Realizable Value

The value of inventory for companies selling high-technology or fashion goods can drop very quickly due to continual changes in technology or fashions. These circumstances sometimes call for inventory valuation methods other than those presented so far.

For example, purchasing managers at **Ford** (USA) at one time decided to make a large purchase of palladium, a precious metal used in vehicle emission devices. They made this purchase because they feared a future shortage. The shortage did not materialize, and by the end of the year the price of palladium had plummeted. Ford's inventory was then worth $1 billion less than its original cost. Do you think Ford's inventory should have been stated at cost, in accordance with the historical cost basis, or at its lower net realizable value?

As you probably reasoned, this situation requires a departure from the cost basis of accounting. When the value of inventory is lower than its cost, companies must "write down" the inventory to its net realizable value. This is done by valuing the inventory at the **lower of cost or net realizable value (LCNRV)** in the period in which the price decline occurs.

- LCNRV is an example of the accounting concept of **prudence**, which means that the best choice among accounting alternatives is the method that is least likely to overstate assets and net income.
- Critics of accounting prudence argue that it introduces bias into accounting numbers. The can reduce the representational faithfulness as well as the relevance of financial reports.

Under the LCNRV basis, **net realizable value** refers to the net amount that a company expects to realize (receive) from the sale of inventory. Specifically, net realizable value is the estimated selling price in the normal course of business, less estimated costs to complete and sell.

Companies apply LCNRV to the items in inventory after they have used one of the inventory costing methods (specific identification, FIFO, or average-cost) to determine cost. To illustrate the application of LCNRV, assume that Gao TVs has the following lines of merchandise with costs and net realizable values as indicated. LCNRV produces the results shown in **Illustration 6.15**. Note that the amounts shown in the final column are the lower of cost or net realizable value amounts for each item.

ILLUSTRATION 6.15

Computation of lower of cost or net realizable value

	Units	Cost per Unit	Net Realizable Value per Unit	Lower of Cost or Net Realizable Value	
Flat-screen TVs	100	NT$600	NT$550	NT$ 55,000	(NT$550 × 100)
Wireless speakers	500	90	104	45,000	(NT$90 × 500)
Bluetooth headphones	850	50	48	40,800	(NT$48 × 850)
Smart watch accessories	3,000	5	6	15,000	(NT$5 × 3,000)
Total inventory				NT$155,800	

If, after an inventory item has been written down but before the item is sold, the value of the item recovers, the amount of the write-down is reversed. The amount of the reversal is limited to the amount of the original write-down. So, for example, if the net realizable value of the flatscreen TVs shown in Illustration 6.15 were to recover to NT$615 in the next period and the items were still held, a reversal would occur to write them back up to their cost of NT$600.

Financial Analysis and Data Analytics

The amount of inventory carried by a company has significant economic consequences. And inventory management is a double-edged sword that requires constant attention. On the one hand, management wants to have a great variety and quantity available so that customers have a wide selection and items are always in stock. But, such a policy may incur high carrying costs (e.g., investment, storage, insurance, obsolescence, and damage). On the other hand, low inventory levels lead to stock-outs and lost sales. Common ratios used to manage and evaluate inventory levels are inventory turnover and a related measure, days in inventory.

Inventory Turnover

Inventory turnover measures the number of times on average the inventory is sold during the period. Its purpose is to measure the liquidity of the inventory.

- The inventory turnover is computed by dividing cost of goods sold by the average inventory during the period.
- Unless seasonal factors are significant, average inventory can be computed from the beginning and ending inventory balances.

For example, **Esprit Holdings** (HKG) reported in a recent annual report a beginning inventory of HK$3,209 million, an ending inventory of HK$3,254 million, and cost of goods sold for the year ended of HK$12,071 million. **Illustration 6.16** shows the inventory turnover formula and computation for Esprit Holdings.

ILLUSTRATION 6.16

Inventory turnover formula and computation for Esprit Holdings (in millions)

Cost of Goods Sold	÷	Average Inventory	=	Inventory Turnover
HK$12,071	÷	$\frac{\text{HK\$3,209} + \text{HK\$3,254}}{2}$	=	3.7 times

A variant of the inventory turnover is **days in inventory**.

- Days in inventory measures the average number of days inventory is held.
- It is calculated as 365 divided by the inventory turnover.

For example, Esprit Holdings' inventory turnover of 3.7 times divided into 365 is approximately 99 days. This is the approximate time that it takes a company to sell the inventory once it arrives at the store.

There are typical levels of inventory in every industry. Companies that are able to keep their inventory at lower levels and higher turnovers and still satisfy customer needs are the most successful.

Accounting Across the Organization H&M

Ryan McVay/DigitalVision/ Cetty Images

Too Many Dresses or Too Few?

Prior to the disruption of the global supply chain that occurred in 2019 and 2020, fashion retailers such as **H&M** (SWE) were experiencing a sales boom. However, the combination of closed stores, closed factories, and changing consumer preferences have left many companies in the fashion industry with large amounts of deadstock. Deadstock are items that cannot be sold at their normal prices.

Deadstock is not new to the industry, but the levels that have built up recently are substantially higher than usual. In the past, many fashion brands such as **LVHM** (FRA) and **Burberry** (GBR) would destroy excess inventory. Now, with much higher levels of excess inventory, companies are launching new methods to dispose of deadstock. For example, LVMH launched a deadstock site called Nona Source to help sell its excess inventory.

Source: Adapted from Sophie Mellor, "Changing Fashions: Retailers Are Dealing with Deadstock More Openly," *Fortune* (April 29, 2021).

For fashion companies, what are the advantages and disadvantages of having excess inventory? (Answer is available near the end of the chapter.)

Data Analytics

Inventory management benefits greatly from data analytics. Companies such as **Walmart** (USA) collect massive amounts of data about every inventory item and every customer. They analyze customer habits, buying patterns, and sales trends. Using sophisticated models that incorporate economic variables, weather patterns, and many other factors, companies strive to optimize inventory levels to maximize sales while minimizing inventory holding costs.

For example, companies can use data analytics when determining if the net realizable value of certain products exceeds their costs. Furthermore, analytics can identify the last time a company sold a particular product, allowing the company to assess if that product is obsolete or damaged. By analyzing search histories on their websites and by examining sales order data, companies can track and anticipate changes in the demand for their products.

- This type of predictive analysis uses data to project expected sales.
- This, in turn, allows companies to plan future inventory purchasing decisions and to determine minimum and maximum desired quantities of inventory on hand at different times during the year.

Companies can also use other data analytics tools to ensure that the inventory on hand remains in optimal condition. For example, agribusiness companies are using data analytics to ensure that grain inventories are being stored in the best conditions possible. These systems use sensors to track the moisture and temperature of grain bins. Using weather data, these systems adjust the fan and air-circulation settings within the grain bins to ensure the grain is kept in optimal condition.

Data Analytics Insight Dashboards: Seeing Is Believing

Dashboards are a commonly employed tool for data analytics. Dashboards represent a collection of a variety of views of key measures that managers desire to monitor. If you have ever seen one, you know that a dashboard often consists of a number of worksheets. And because each worksheet is "live," the manager can manipulate variables or views.

For example, consider the Tableau dashboard shown here. Using this dashboard, the manager can evaluate how well the company is meeting customer demand by evaluating the fill rate (which shows the frequency of stock-outs). The manager can also easily see how efficiently the company is managing its inventory by evaluating the inventory turnover and days in inventory. This information can be evaluated by region, over time, and by product line.

What benefits does a dashboard such as this one provide to a manager for making decisions regarding inventory? (Answer is available near the end of the chapter.)

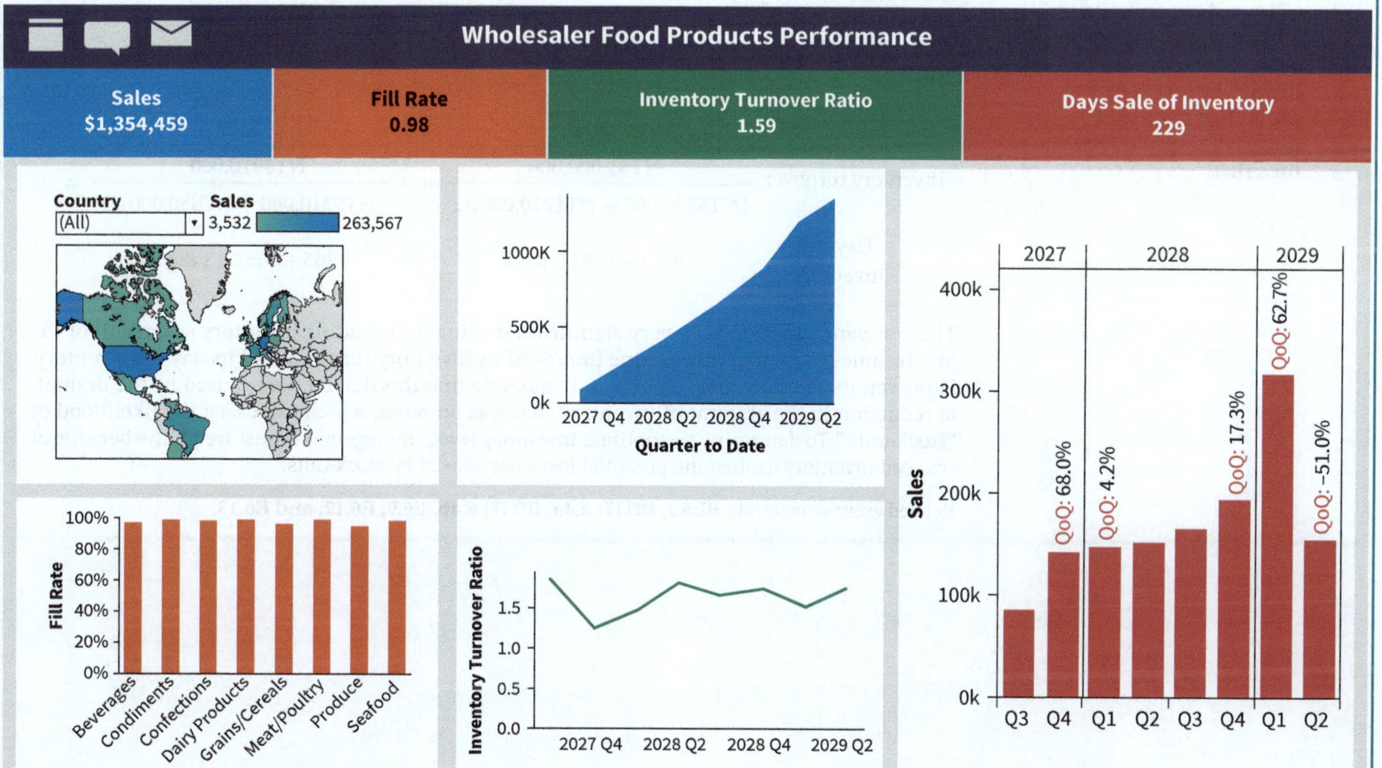

Source: Adapted from Tableau Public website.

DO IT! 4 | LCNRV and Inventory Turnover

ACTION PLAN

- **Determine whether cost or net realizable value is lower for each inventory type.**
- **Sum the lowest value of each inventory type to determine the total value of inventory.**

a. Poon Heaters sells three different types of home heating stoves (gas, wood, and pellet). The cost and net realizable value of its inventory of stoves are as follows (amounts in thousands).

	Cost	Net Realizable Value
Gas	NT$ 84,000	NT$ 79,000
Wood	250,000	280,000
Pellet	112,000	101,000

Determine the value of the company's inventory under the lower of cost or net realizable value approach.

Solution

The lowest value for each inventory type is gas NT$79,000, wood NT$250,000, and pellet NT$101,000. The total inventory value is the sum of these amounts, NT$430,000.

ACTION PLAN

- **To find the inventory turnover, divide cost of goods sold by average inventory.**
- **To determine days in inventory, divide 365 days by the inventory turnover.**
- **Just-in-time inventory reduces the amount of inventory on hand, which reduces carrying costs. Reducing inventory levels by too much has potential negative implications for sales.**

b. Early in 2029, Westmoreland Company switched to a just-in-time inventory system. Its sales revenue, cost of goods sold, and inventory amounts for 2028 and 2029 are shown below.

	2028	2029
Sales revenue	NT$2,000,000	NT$1,800,000
Cost of goods sold	1,000,000	910,000
Beginning inventory	290,000	210,000
Ending inventory	210,000	50,000

Determine the inventory turnover and days in inventory for 2028 and 2029. Discuss the changes in the amount of inventory, the inventory turnover and days in inventory, and the amount of sales across the two years.

Solution

	2028	2029
Inventory turnover	$\frac{\text{NT\$1,000,000}}{(\text{NT\$290,000} + \text{NT\$210,000})/2} = 4$	$\frac{\text{NT\$910,000}}{(\text{NT\$210,000} + \text{NT\$50,000})/2} = 7$
Days in inventory	$365 \div 4 = 91.3$ days	$365 \div 7 = 52.1$ days

The company experienced a very significant decline in its ending inventory as a result of the just-in-time inventory. This decline improved its inventory turnover and its days in inventory. However, its sales declined by 10%. It is possible that this decline was caused by the dramatic reduction in the amount of inventory that was on hand, which increased the likelihood of "stock-outs." To determine the optimal inventory level, management must weigh the benefits of reduced inventory against the potential lost sales caused by stock-outs.

Related exercise material: **BE6.7, DO IT! 6.4a, DO IT! 6.4b, E6.9, E6.12, and E6.13.**

Appendix 6A Inventory Cost Flow Methods in Perpetual Inventory Systems

LEARNING OBJECTIVE *5

Apply the inventory cost flow methods to perpetual inventory records.

What inventory cost flow methods can companies employ if they use a perpetual inventory system? Simple—they can use any of the inventory cost flow methods described in the chapter. To illustrate the application of the two assumed cost flow methods (FIFO and average-cost), we will use the data shown in **Illustration 6A.1** and in this chapter for Lin Electronics' Astro condensers.

ILLUSTRATION 6A.1
Inventoriable units and costs

Lin Electronics
Astro Condensers

Date	Explanation	Units	Unit Cost	Total Cost	Balance in Units
1/1	Beginning inventory	10	HK$100	HK$ 1,000	10
4/15	Purchases	20	110	2,200	30
8/24	Purchases	30	120	3,600	60
9/10	Sale	55			5
11/27	Purchases	40	130	5,200	45
				HK$12,000	

First-In, First-Out (FIFO)

Under perpetual FIFO, the company charges to cost of goods sold the cost of the earliest goods on hand **prior to each sale**. Therefore, the cost of goods sold on September 10 consists of the units on hand January 1 and the units purchased April 15 and August 24. **Illustration 6A.2** shows the inventory under a FIFO method perpetual system.

ILLUSTRATION 6A.2
Perpetual system—FIFO

Date	Purchases		Cost of Goods Sold	Balance (in units and cost)	
January 1				(10 @ HK$100)	HK$1,000
April 15	(20 @ HK$110)	HK$2,200		(10 @ HK$100) (20 @ HK$110)	HK$3,200
August 24	(30 @ HK$120)	HK$3,600		(10 @ HK$100) (20 @ HK$110) (30 @ HK$120)	HK$6,800
September 10			(10 @ HK$100) (20 @ HK$110) (25 @ HK$120) HK$6,200	(5 @ HK$120)	HK$ 600
November 27	(40 @ HK$130)	HK$5,200		(5 @ HK$120) (40 @ HK$130)	HK$5,800

Cost of goods sold

Ending inventory

The ending inventory in this situation is HK$5,800, and the cost of goods sold is HK$6,200 [(10 @ HK$100) + (20 @ HK$110) + (25 @ HK$120)].

Compare Illustrations 6.6 and 6A.2. You can see that the results under FIFO in a perpetual system are the **same as in a periodic system**. In both cases, the ending inventory is HK$5,800 and cost of goods sold is HK$6,200. Regardless of the system, the first costs in are the costs assigned to cost of goods sold.

Average-Cost

The average-cost method in a perpetual inventory system is called the **moving-average method**.

- Under this method, the company computes a new average **after each purchase** by dividing the cost of goods available for sale by the units on hand.
- The average cost is then applied to (1) the units sold, to determine the cost of goods sold, and (2) the remaining units on hand, to determine the ending inventory amount.

Illustration 6A.3 shows the application of the moving-average cost method by Lin Electronics (computations of the moving-average unit cost are shown after Illustration 6A.3).

ILLUSTRATION 6A.3

Perpetual system—average-cost method

Date	Purchases		Cost of Goods Sold	Balance (in units and cost)	
January 1				(10 @ HK$100)	HK$ 1,000
April 15	(20 @ HK$110)	HK$2,200		(30 @ HK$106.667)	HK$ 3,200
August 24	(30 @ HK$120)	HK$3,600		(60 @ HK$113.333)	HK$ 6,800
September 10			(55 @ HK$113.333)	(5 @ HK$113.333)	HK$ 567
			HK$6,233		
November 27	(40 @ HK$130)	HK$5,200		(45 @ HK$128.156)	HK$5,767

Cost of goods sold (HK$6,233)

Ending inventory (HK$5,767)

As indicated, Lin Electronics computes **a new average each time it makes a purchase**.

1. On April 15, after it buys 20 units for HK$2,200, a total of 30 units costing HK$3,200 (HK$1,000 + HK$2,200) are on hand. The average unit cost is HK$106.667 (HK$3,200 ÷ 30).
2. On August 24, after Lin Electronics buys 30 units for HK$3,600, a total of 60 units costing HK$6,800 (HK$1,000 + HK$2,200 + HK$3,600) are on hand. The average cost per unit is HK$113.333 (HK$6,800 ÷ 60).
3. On September 10, to compute cost of goods sold, Lin Electronics uses this unit cost of HK$113.333 in costing sales until it makes another purchase, when the company computes a new unit cost. Accordingly, the unit cost of the 55 units sold (on September 10) is HK$113.333, and the total cost of goods sold is HK$6,233.
4. On November 27, following the purchase of 40 units for HK$5,200, there are 45 units on hand costing HK$5,767 (HK$567 + HK$5,200) with a new average cost of HK$128.156 (HK$5,767 ÷ 45).

Compare this moving-average cost under the perpetual inventory system to Illustration 6.9 on showing the average-cost method under a periodic inventory system. Unlike FIFO, which results in the same cost for ending inventory under the perpetual and periodic systems, the moving-average method produces different costs.

Appendix 6B Estimating Inventories

LEARNING OBJECTIVE *6

Describe the two methods of estimating inventories.

In the chapter, we assumed that a company would be able to physically count its inventory. What if it cannot? What if the inventory were destroyed by fire or flood, for example? In that case, the company would use an estimate.

Two circumstances explain why companies sometimes estimate inventories.

1. A casualty such as fire, flood, or earthquake may make it impossible to take a physical inventory.
2. Managers may want monthly or quarterly financial statements, but a physical inventory is taken only annually.

The need for estimating inventories occurs primarily with a periodic inventory system because of the absence of perpetual inventory records.

There are two widely used methods of estimating inventories: (1) the gross profit method, and (2) the retail inventory method.

Gross Profit Method

The **gross profit method** estimates the cost of ending inventory by applying a gross profit rate to net sales. This method is relatively simple but effective.

- Accountants, auditors, and managers frequently use the gross profit method to test the reasonableness of the ending inventory amount. It will detect large errors.
- To use this method, a company needs to know its net sales, cost of goods available for sale, and gross profit rate. The company then can estimate its gross profit for the period.

Illustration 6B.1 shows the formulas for using the gross profit method.

ILLUSTRATION 6B.1
Gross profit method formulas

Step 1:	**Net Sales**	−	**Estimated Gross Profit**	=	**Estimated Cost of Goods Sold**
Step 2:	**Cost of Goods Available for Sale**	−	**Estimated Cost of Goods Sold**	=	**Estimated Cost of Ending Inventory**

To illustrate, assume that Kishwaukee Company wishes to prepare an income statement for the month of January. Its records show net sales of $200,000, beginning inventory $40,000, and cost of goods purchased $120,000. In the preceding year, the company realized a 30% gross profit rate. It expects to earn the same rate this year. Given these facts and assumptions, Kishwaukee can compute the estimated cost of the ending inventory at January 31 under the gross profit method as shown in **Illustration 6B.2**.

ILLUSTRATION 6B.2

Example of gross profit method

Step 1:	
Net sales	$200,000
Less: Estimated gross profit (30% × $200,000)	60,000
Estimated cost of goods sold	**$140,000**
Step 2:	
Beginning inventory	$ 40,000
Cost of goods purchased	120,000
Cost of goods available for sale	160,000
Less: Estimated cost of goods sold	140,000
Estimated cost of ending inventory	**$ 20,000**

The gross profit method is based on the assumption that the gross profit rate will remain constant. But, it may not remain constant due to a change in merchandising policies or in market conditions.

- In such cases, the company should adjust the rate to reflect current operating conditions.
- In some cases, companies can obtain a more accurate estimate by applying this method on a department or product-line basis.

Note that companies should not use the gross profit method to prepare financial statements at the end of the year. These statements should be based on a physical inventory count.

Retail Inventory Method

A retail store, such as **President Chain Store** (TWN), **Marks and Spencer plc** (GBR), or **Walmart** (USA), has thousands of different types of merchandise at low unit costs. In such cases, it is difficult and time-consuming to apply unit costs to inventory quantities. An alternative is to use the **retail inventory method** to estimate the cost of inventory.

- Most retail companies can establish a relationship between cost and sales price. The company then applies the cost-to-retail percentage to the ending inventory at retail prices to determine inventory at cost.
- Under the retail inventory method, a company's records must show both the cost and retail value of the goods available for sale.

Illustration 6B.3 presents the formulas for using the retail inventory method.

ILLUSTRATION 6B.3

Retail inventory method formulas

Step 1:	**Goods Available for Sale at Retail**	−	**Net Sales**	=	**Ending Inventory at Retail**
Step 2:	**Goods Available for Sale at Cost**	÷	**Goods Available for Sale at Retail**	=	**Cost-to-Retail Ratio**
Step 3:	**Ending Inventory at Retail**	×	**Cost-to-Retail Ratio**	=	**Estimated Cost of Ending Inventory**

We can demonstrate the logic of the retail method by using unit-cost data. Assume that Ortiz Inc. has marked 10 units purchased at $7 to sell for $10 per unit. Thus, the cost-to-retail ratio is 70% ($70 ÷ $100). If four units remain unsold, their retail value is $40 (4 × $10), and their cost is $28 ($40 × 70%). This amount agrees with the total cost of goods on hand on a per unit basis (4 × $7).

Illustration 6B.4 shows application of the retail method for Valley West. Note that it is not necessary to take a physical inventory to determine the estimated cost of goods on hand at any given time.

ILLUSTRATION 6B.4

Application of retail inventory method

	At Cost	At Retail
Beginning inventory	$14,000	$ 21,500
Goods purchased	61,000	78,500
Goods available for sale	$75,000	100,000
Less: Net sales		70,000
Step (1) Ending inventory at retail =		**$ 30,000**
Step (2) Cost-to-retail ratio = $75,000 ÷ $100,000 = 75%		
Step (3) Estimated cost of ending inventory = $30,000 × 75% = $22,500		

The retail inventory method also facilitates taking a physical inventory at the end of the year. Valley West can value the goods on hand at the prices marked on the merchandise and then apply the cost-to-retail ratio to the goods on hand at retail to determine the ending inventory at cost (see **Helpful Hint**).

HELPFUL HINT

In determining inventory at retail, companies use selling prices of the units.

The major disadvantage of the retail method is that it is an averaging technique. Thus, it may produce an incorrect inventory valuation if the mix of the ending inventory is not representative of the mix in the goods available for sale. Assume, for example, that the cost-to-retail ratio of 75% for Valley West consists of equal proportions of inventory items that have cost-to-retail ratios of 70%, 75%, and 80%. If the ending inventory contains only items with a 70% ratio, an incorrect inventory cost will result. Companies can minimize this problem by applying the retail method on a department or product-line basis.

While the gross profit method mentioned in the previous section may not be used for financial statement purposes, the retail inventory method is permitted. Since the retail inventory method uses current-period costs and prices to determine the cost-to-retail ratio, it is viewed as sufficiently close to cost to be used.

Appendix 6C LIFO Inventory Method

LEARNING OBJECTIVE *7

Apply the LIFO inventory costing method.

As indicated in the chapter, under IFRS, LIFO is not permitted for financial reporting purposes. In prohibiting LIFO, the IASB noted that use of LIFO results in inventories being recognized in the statement of financial position at amounts that bear little relationship to recent cost levels of inventories. Nonetheless, LIFO is used for financial reporting in the United States, and it is permitted for tax purposes in some countries. Its use can result in significant tax savings in a period of rising prices.

- The **last-in, first-out (LIFO) method** assumes that the **latest goods** purchased are the first to be sold.

- LIFO seldom coincides with the actual physical flow of inventory. (Exceptions include goods stored in piles, such as coal or hay, where goods are removed from the top of the pile as they are sold.)
- Under the LIFO method, the **costs** of the latest goods purchased are the first to be recognized in determining cost of goods sold.

Illustration 6C.1 shows the allocation of the cost of goods available for sale at Lin Electronics under LIFO. The number of units sold during November are 55 and therefore ending inventory is comprised of 45 units.

ILLUSTRATION 6C.1

Allocation of costs—LIFO method

Cost of Goods Available for Sale

Date	Explanation	Units	Unit Cost	Total Cost
Jan. 1	Beginning inventory	10	HK$100	HK$ 1,000
Apr. 15	Purchase	20	110	2,200
Aug. 24	Purchase	30	120	3,600
Nov. 27	Purchase	40	130	5,200
	Total	100		**HK$12,000**

Step 1: Ending Inventory

Date	Units	Unit Cost	Total Cost
Jan. 1	10	HK$100	HK$1,000
Apr. 15	20	110	2,200
Aug. 24	15	120	1,800
Total	45		**HK$5,000**

Step 2: Cost of Goods Sold

Cost of goods available for sale	HK$12,000
Less: Ending inventory	5,000
Cost of goods sold	**HK$ 7,000**

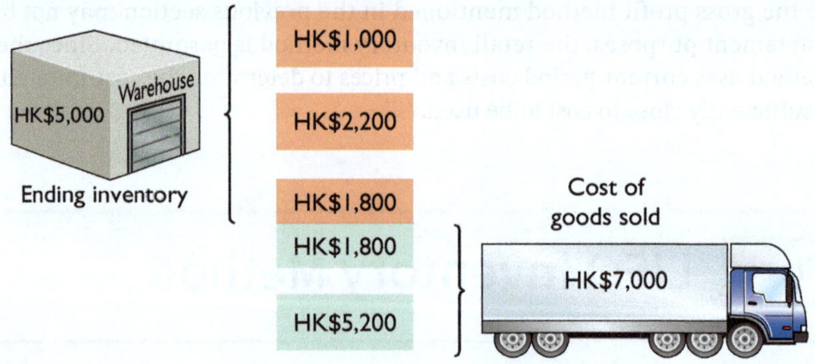

Under LIFO, since it is assumed that the first goods sold were those that were most recently purchased, ending inventory is based on the prices of the oldest units purchased. That is, **under LIFO, companies obtain the cost of the ending inventory by taking the unit cost of the earliest goods available for sale and working forward until all units of inventory have been costed.**

- In this example, Lin Electronics prices the 45 units of ending inventory using the **earliest** prices.
- The first purchase was 10 units at HK$100 in the January 1 beginning inventory. Then, 20 units were purchased at HK$110. The remaining 15 units needed are priced at HK$120 per unit (August 24 purchase).
- Lin Electronics calculates cost of goods sold by subtracting the cost of the units **not sold** (ending inventory) from the cost of all goods available for sale.

Illustration 6C.2 demonstrates that companies also can calculate cost of goods sold by pricing the 55 units sold using the prices of the last 55 units acquired. Note that of the 30 units purchased on August 24, only 15 units are assumed sold. This agrees with our calculation of the cost of ending inventory, where 15 of these units were assumed unsold and thus included in ending inventory.

ILLUSTRATION 6C.2

Proof of cost of goods sold

Date	Units	Unit Cost	Total Cost
Nov. 27	40	HK$130	HK$ 5,200
Aug. 24	15	120	1,800
Total	55		**HK$7,000**

Under a periodic inventory system, which we are using here, **all goods purchased during the period are assumed to be available for the first sale, regardless of the date of purchase.**

A major disadvantage of the LIFO method is that in a period of rising prices, the costs allocated to ending inventory may be significantly understated in the statement of financial position. For example, **Caterpillar** (USA) has used LIFO for over 50 years. Its statement of financial position shows ending inventory of $8,781 million. But, the inventory's actual current cost if FIFO had been used is $11,964 million.

One reason why U.S. companies use LIFO relates to tax benefits. In a period of rising prices, companies using LIFO report lower income taxes (because of lower taxable income) and therefore higher cash flows.

Review and Practice

Learning Objectives Review

1 Discuss how to classify and determine inventory.

Manufacturers usually classify inventory into three categories: finished goods, work in process, and raw materials. The steps in determining inventory quantities are (1) take a physical inventory of goods on hand and (2) determine the ownership of goods in transit or on consignment.

2 Apply inventory cost flow methods and discuss their financial effects.

The primary basis of accounting for inventories is cost. Cost of goods available for sale includes (a) cost of beginning inventory and (b) cost of goods purchased. The inventory cost flow methods are specific identification and two assumed cost flow methods—FIFO and average-cost.

Companies may allocate the cost of goods available for sale to cost of goods sold and ending inventory by specific identification or by a method based on an assumed cost flow. When prices are rising, the first-in, first-out (FIFO) method results in lower cost of goods sold and higher net income than average-cost. The reverse is true when prices are falling. In the statement of financial position, FIFO results in an ending inventory that is closer to current value. Inventory under average-cost is further from current value. Average-cost results in lower income taxes.

3 Indicate the effects of inventory errors on the financial statements.

In the income statement of the current year: (a) If beginning inventory is understated, net income is overstated. The reverse occurs if beginning inventory is overstated. (b) If ending inventory is overstated, net income is overstated. If ending inventory is understated, net income is understated. In the following period, its effect on net income for that period is reversed, and total net income for the two years will be correct.

In the statement of financial position: Ending inventory errors will have the same effect on total assets and total equity and no effect on liabilities.

4 Explain the statement presentation and analysis of inventory.

Inventory is classified in the statement of financial position as a current asset and is shown immediately above receivables. There also should be disclosure of (1) the major inventory classifications, (2) the basis of accounting, and (3) the cost method.

Companies use the lower of cost or net realizable value (LCNRV) basis when the net realizable value is less than cost. Under LCNRV, companies recognize the loss in the period in which the price decline occurs.

The inventory turnover is cost of goods sold divided by average inventory. To convert it to average days in inventory, divide 365 days by the inventory turnover.

*5 Apply the inventory cost flow methods to perpetual inventory records.

Under FIFO and a perpetual inventory system, companies charge to cost of goods sold the cost of the earliest goods on hand prior to each sale. Under the moving-average (average-cost) method and a perpetual system, companies compute a new average cost after each purchase.

*6 Describe the two methods of estimating inventories.

The two methods of estimating inventories are the gross profit method and the retail inventory method. Under the gross profit method, companies apply a gross profit rate to net sales to determine estimated cost of goods sold. They then subtract estimated cost of goods sold from cost of goods available for sale to determine the estimated cost of the ending inventory.

Under the retail inventory method, companies compute a cost-to-retail ratio by dividing the cost of goods available for sale by the retail value of the goods available for sale. They then apply this ratio to the ending inventory at retail to determine the estimated cost of the ending inventory.

*7 Apply the LIFO inventory costing method.

The LIFO (last-in, first-out) method, which is allowable under GAAP but not IFRS, assumes that the latest goods purchased are the first to be sold. LIFO seldom coincides with the actual physical flow of goods. This method matches costs of the most recently purchased items with revenues in the period. In periods of rising prices, use of the LIFO method results in lower income taxes and higher cash flows.

Glossary Review

Average-cost method Inventory costing method that uses the weighted-average unit cost to allocate to ending inventory and cost of goods sold the cost of goods available for sale. (p. 6-10).

Consigned goods Goods held for sale by one party although ownership of the goods is retained by another party. (p. 6-6).

Consistency concept Dictates that a company use the same accounting principles and methods from year to year. (p. 6-13).

Days in inventory Measure of the average number of days inventory is held; calculated as 365 divided by inventory turnover. (p. 6-18).

Finished goods inventory Manufactured items that are completed and ready for sale. (p. 6-3).

First-in, first-out (FIFO) method Inventory costing method that assumes that the costs of the earliest goods purchased are the first to be recognized as cost of goods sold. (p. 6-9).

FOB (free on board) destination Freight terms indicating that ownership of the goods remains with the seller until the goods reach the buyer. (p. 6-5).

FOB (free on board) shipping point Freight terms indicating that ownership of the goods passes to the buyer when the public carrier accepts the goods from the seller. (p. 6-5).

***Gross profit method** A method for estimating the cost of the ending inventory by applying a gross profit rate to net sales and subtracting estimated cost of goods sold from cost of goods available for sale. (p. 6-23).

Inventory turnover A ratio that measures the number of times on average the inventory sold during the period; computed by dividing cost of goods sold by the average inventory during the period. (p. 6-18).

Just-in-time (JIT) inventory Inventory system in which companies manufacture or purchase goods just in time for use. (p. 6-3).

***Last-in, first-out (LIFO) method** Inventory costing method that assumes the costs of the latest units purchased are the first to be allocated to cost of goods sold. This method is allowable under GAAP but not IFRS. (p. 6-25).

Lower of cost or net realizable value (LCNRV) basis A basis whereby inventory is stated at the lower of either its cost or its net realizable value. (p. 6-17).

***Moving-average method** A new average is computed after each purchase, computed by dividing the cost of goods available for sale by the units on hand. (p. 6-22).

Net realizable value Net amount that a company expects to realize (receive) from the sale of inventory. Specifically, it is the estimated selling price in the normal course of business, less estimated costs to complete and sell. (p. 6-17).

Prudence Concept that dictates that when in doubt, choose the method that will be least likely to overstate assets and net income. (p. 6-17).

Raw materials Basic goods that will be used in production but have not yet been placed into production. (p. 6-3).

***Retail inventory method** A method for estimating the cost of the ending inventory by applying a cost-to-retail ratio to the ending inventory at retail. (p. 6-24).

Specific identification method An actual physical flow costing method in which items still in inventory are specifically costed to arrive at the total cost of the ending inventory. (p. 6-7).

Weighted-average unit cost Average cost that is weighted by the number of units purchased at each unit cost. (p. 6-10).

Work in process That portion of manufactured inventory that has been placed into the production process but is not yet complete. (p. 6-3).

Practice Multiple-Choice Questions

1. **(LO 1)** Which of the following should **not** be included in the physical inventory of a company?
   - **a.** Goods held on consignment from another company.
   - **b.** Goods shipped on consignment to another company.
   - **c.** Goods in transit from another company shipped FOB shipping point.
   - **d.** All of the answer choices are correct.

2. **(LO 1)** As a result of a thorough physical inventory, Railway Ltd. determined that it had inventory worth €180,000 at December 31, 2029. This count did not take into consideration the following facts. Rogers Consignment currently has goods that would cost €35,000 on its sales floor that belong to Railway but are being sold on consignment by Rogers. The selling price of these goods is €50,000. Railway purchased €13,000 of goods that were shipped on December 27, FOB destination, that will be received by Railway on January 3. Determine the correct amount of inventory that Railway should report.
   - **a.** €230,000.
   - **b.** €215,000.
   - **c.** €228,000.
   - **d.** €193,000.

3. **(LO 1)** Cost of goods available for sale consists of two elements: beginning inventory and:
   - **a.** ending inventory.
   - **b.** cost of goods purchased.
   - **c.** cost of goods sold.
   - **d.** All of the answer choices are correct.

4. **(LO 2)** Tinker Bell Magic Shop has the following:

	Units	Unit Cost
Inventory, Jan. 1	8,000	£11
Purchase, June 19	13,000	12
Purchase, Nov. 8	5,000	13

If Tinker Bell has 9,000 units on hand at December 31, the cost of the ending inventory under FIFO is:
   - **a.** £99,000.
   - **b.** £108,000.
   - **c.** £113,000.
   - **d.** £117,000.

5. **(LO 2)** Davidson Electronics has the following:

	Units	Unit Cost
Inventory, Jan. 1	5,000	£ 8
Purchase, April 2	15,000	£10
Purchase, Aug. 28	20,000	£12

If Davidson has 7,000 units on hand at December 31, the cost of ending inventory under the average-cost method is:
   - **a.** £84,000.
   - **b.** £70,000.
   - **c.** £56,000.
   - **d.** £75,250.

6. **(LO 2)** In periods of rising prices, average-cost will produce:
   - **a.** higher net income than FIFO.
   - **b.** the same net income as FIFO.
   - **c.** lower net income than FIFO.
   - **d.** net income equal to the specific identification method.

7. **(LO 2)** Factors that affect the selection of an inventory costing method do **not** include:
   - **a.** tax effects.
   - **b.** statement of financial position effects.
   - **c.** income statement effects.
   - **d.** perpetual vs. periodic inventory system.

8. **(LO 3)** Atlantis Aquarium's ending inventory is understated NT$122,000. The effects of this error on the current year's cost of goods sold and net income, respectively, are:
   - **a.** understated, overstated.
   - **b.** overstated, understated.
   - **c.** overstated, overstated.
   - **d.** understated, understated.

9. **(LO 3)** Lee Athletics overstated its inventory by NT$500,000 at December 31, 2028. It did not correct the error in 2028 or 2029. As a result, Lee's equity was:
   - **a.** overstated at December 31, 2028, and understated at December 31, 2029.
   - **b.** overstated at December 31, 2028, and properly stated at December 31, 2029.
   - **c.** understated at December 31, 2028, and understated at December 31, 2029.
   - **d.** overstated at December 31, 2028, and overstated at December 31, 2029.

10. **(LO 4)** Rickety Company purchased 1,000 widgets and has 200 widgets in its ending inventory at a cost of HK$91 each and a net realizable value of HK$80 each. The ending inventory under LCNRV is:
   - **a.** HK$91,000.
   - **b.** HK$80,000.
   - **c.** HK$18,200.
   - **d.** HK$16,000.

11. **(LO 4)** Which of these would cause the inventory turnover to increase the most?
   - **a.** Increasing the amount of inventory on hand.
   - **b.** Keeping the amount of inventory on hand constant but increasing sales.
   - **c.** Keeping the amount of inventory on hand constant but decreasing sales.
   - **d.** Decreasing the amount of inventory on hand and increasing sales.

12. **(LO 4)** Carlos Cookware had beginning inventory of €80,000, ending inventory of €110,000, cost of goods sold of €285,000, and sales of €475,000. Carlos' days in inventory is:
   - **a.** 73 days.
   - **b.** 121.7 days.
   - **c.** 102.5 days.
   - **d.** 84.5 days.

13. **(LO 4)** The lower of cost or net realizable value rule for inventory is an example of the application of:

a. the prudence concept.
b. the historical cost principle.
c. the materiality concept.
d. the economic entity assumption.

*14. **(LO 5)** Songbird Records has sales of £150,000 and cost of goods available for sale of £135,000. If the gross profit rate is 30%, the estimated cost of the ending inventory under the gross profit method is:

a. £15,000. **c.** £45,000.
b. £30,000. **d.** £75,000.

*15. **(LO 6)** In a perpetual inventory system:

a. specific identification is always used.
b. average costs are computed as a simple average of unit costs incurred.
c. a new average is computed under the average-cost method after each sale.
d. FIFO cost of goods sold will be the same as in a periodic inventory system.

*16. **(LO 7)** Using the data in Question 4, the cost of the ending inventory under LIFO is:

a. £113,000. **c.** £99,000.
b. £108,000. **d.** £100,000.

Solutions

1. **a.** Goods held on consignment should not be included because another company has title (ownership) to the goods. The other choices are incorrect because (b) goods shipped on consignment to another company and (c) goods in transit from another company shipped FOB shipping point should be included in a company's ending inventory. Choice (d) is incorrect as there is a correct answer for this question.

2. **b.** The inventory held on consignment by Rogers should be included in Railway's inventory balance at cost (€35,000). The purchased goods of €13,000 should not be included in inventory until January 3 because the goods are shipped FOB destination. Therefore, the correct amount of inventory is €215,000 (€180,000 + €35,000), not (a) €230,000, (c) €228,000, or (d) €193,000.

3. **b.** Cost of goods available for sale consists of beginning inventory and cost of goods purchased, not (a) ending inventory or (c) cost of goods sold. Therefore, choice (d) is also incorrect.

4. **c.** Under FIFO, ending inventory will consist of 5,000 units from the Nov. 8 purchase and 4,000 units from the June 19 purchase. Therefore, ending inventory is (5,000 × £13) + (4,000 × £12) = £113,000, not (a) £99,000, (b) £108,000, or (d) £117,000.

5. **d.** Under the average-cost method, total cost of goods available for sale needs to be calculated in order to determine average cost per unit. The total cost of goods available is £430,000 = (5,000 × £8) + (15,000 × £10) + (20,000 × £12). The average cost per unit = (£430,000/40,000 total units available for sale) = £10.75. Therefore, ending inventory is (£10.75 × 7,000) = £75,250, not (a) £84,000, (b) £70,000, or (c) £56,000.

6. **c.** In periods of rising prices, average-cost will produce lower net income than FIFO, not (a) higher than FIFO or (b) the same as FIFO. Choice (d) is incorrect because, except by extraordinary coincidence, average-cost will not produce the same results as specific identification.

7. **d.** Perpetual vs. periodic inventory system is not one of the factors that affect the selection of an inventory costing method. The other choices are incorrect because (a) tax effects, (b) statement of financial position effects, and (c) income statement effects all affect the selection of an inventory costing method.

8. **b.** Because ending inventory is too low, cost of goods sold will be too high (overstated) and since cost of goods sold (an expense) is too high, net income will be too low (understated). Therefore, the other choices are incorrect.

9. **b.** Equity is overstated by NT$500,000 at December 31, 2028, and is properly stated at December 31, 2029. An ending inventory error in one period will have an equal and opposite effect on cost of goods sold and net income in the next period; after two years, the errors have offset each other. The other choices are incorrect because equity (a) is properly stated, not understated, at December 31, 2029; (c) is overstated, not understated, by NT$500,000 at December 31, 2028, and is properly stated, not understated, at December 31, 2029; and (d) is properly stated at December 31, 2029, not overstated.

10. **d.** Under the LCNRV basis, net realizable value is defined as the estimated selling price in the normal course of business, less estimated costs to complete and sell. Therefore, ending inventory would be valued at 200 widgets × HK$80 each = HK$16,000, not (a) HK$91,000, (b) HK$80,000, or (c) HK$18,200.

11. **d.** Decreasing the amount of inventory on hand will cause the denominator to decrease, causing inventory turnover to increase. Increasing sales will cause the numerator of the ratio to increase (higher sales means higher COGS), thus causing inventory turnover to increase even more. The other choices are incorrect because (a) increasing the amount of inventory on hand causes the denominator of the ratio to increase while the numerator stays the same, causing inventory turnover to decrease; (b) keeping the amount of inventory on hand constant but increasing sales will cause inventory turnover to increase because the numerator of the ratio will increase (higher sales means higher COGS) while the denominator stays the same, which will result in a lesser inventory increase than decreasing amount of inventory on hand and increasing sales; and (c) keeping the amount of inventory on hand constant but decreasing sales will cause inventory turnover to decrease because the numerator of the ratio will decrease (lower sales means lower COGS) while the denominator stays the same.

12. **b.** Carlos' days in inventory = 365/Inventory turnover = 365/[€285,000/(€80,000 + €110,000)/2)] = 121.7 days, not (a) 73 days, (c) 102.5 days, or (d) 84.5 days.

13. **a.** Prudence means that the best choice among accounting alternatives is the method that is least likely to overstate assets and net income. The other choices are incorrect because (b) historical cost means that companies value assets at the original cost; (c) materiality means that an amount is large enough to affect a decision-maker; and (d) economic entity means to keep the company's transactions separate from the transactions of other entities.

*14. **b.** COGS = Sales (£150,000) – Gross profit (£150,000 × 30%) = £105,000. Ending inventory = Cost of goods available for sale (£135,000) – COGS (£105,000) = £30,000, not (a) £15,000, (c) £45,000, or (d) £75,000.

*15. **d.** FIFO cost of goods sold is the same under both a periodic and a perpetual inventory system. The other choices are incorrect because (a) specific identification is not always used; (b) average costs are based on a moving average of unit costs, not an average of unit costs; and (c) a new average is computed under the average-cost method after each purchase, not sale.

*16. **d.** Under LIFO, ending inventory will consist of 8,000 units from the inventory at Jan. 1 and 1,000 units from the June 19 purchase. Therefore, ending inventory is (8,000 × £11) + (1,000 × £12) = £100,000, not (a) £113,000, (b) £108,000, or (c) £99,000.

Practice Brief Exercises

1. **(LO 2)** In its first month of operations, Moncada Stores made three purchases of merchandise in the following sequence: (1) 200 units at £7, (2) 300 units at £8, and (3) 150 units at £9. Assuming there are 220 units on hand, compute the cost of the ending inventory under the (a) FIFO method and (b) average-cost method. Moncada uses a periodic inventory system.

Compute ending inventory using FIFO and average-cost.

Solution

1. **a.** The ending inventory under FIFO consists of (150 units at £9) + (70 units at £8) for a total allocation of £1,910 (£1,350 + £560).

   b. The average cost of a unit in ending inventory is £7.92 (£5,150 ÷ 650). The average cost per unit is computed as follows:

200 units at £7 =	£1,400
300 units at £8 =	2,400
150 units at £9 =	1,350
650 units	£5,150

   Ending inventory is therefore £1,742.40 (220 × £7.92).

2. **(LO 3)** Avisail Leisure reports net income of €80,000 in 2029. However, ending inventory was overstated €9,000. What is the correct net income for 2029? What effect, if any, will this error have on total assets as reported in the statement of financial position at December 31, 2029?

Determine correct income statement amounts.

Solution

2. The overstatement of ending inventory caused cost of goods sold to be understated €9,000 and net income to be overstated €9,000. The correct net income for 2029 is €71,000 (€80,000 − €9,000). Total assets in the statement of financial position will be overstated by the amount that ending inventory is overstated, €9,000.

3. **(LO 4)** At December 31, 2029, the following information was available for Seng Holdings (all amounts in thousands): ending inventory ¥30,000, beginning inventory ¥42,000, cost of goods sold ¥240,000, and sales revenue ¥400,000. Calculate inventory turnover and days in inventory for Seng Holdings.

Compute inventory turnover and days in inventory.

Solution

3. Inventory turnover: $\dfrac{¥240{,}000}{(¥42{,}000 + ¥30{,}000)/2} = \dfrac{¥240{,}000}{¥36{,}000} = 6.67$

   Days in inventory: $\dfrac{365}{6.67} = 54.7$ days

Practice Exercises

1. **(LO 1)** Mika Sorbino, an auditor with Martinez Chartered Accountants, is performing a review of Sergei Group's inventory account. Sergei's did not have a good year and top management is under pressure to boost reported income. According to its records, the inventory balance at year-end was €650,000. However, the following information was not considered when determining that amount.

Determine the correct inventory amount.

   1. Included in the company's count were goods with a cost of €200,000 that the company is holding on consignment. The goods belong to Bosnia Enterprises.
   2. The physical count did not include goods purchased by Sergei with a cost of €40,000 that were shipped FOB shipping point on December 28 and did not arrive at Sergei's warehouse until January 3.

3. Included in the inventory account was €15,000 of office supplies that were stored in the warehouse and were to be used by the company's supervisors and managers during the coming year.
4. The company received an order on December 28 that was boxed and was sitting on the loading dock awaiting pick-up on December 31. The shipper picked up the goods on January 1 and delivered them on January 6. The shipping terms were FOB shipping point. The goods had a selling price of €40,000 and a cost of €30,000. The goods were not included in the count because they were sitting on the dock.
5. On December 29, Sergei shipped goods with a selling price of €80,000 and a cost of €60,000 to Oman Sales FOB shipping point. The goods arrived on January 3. Oman Sales had only ordered goods with a selling price of €10,000 and a cost of €8,000. However, a Sergei's sales manager had authorized the shipment and said that if Oman wanted to ship the goods back next week, it could.
6. Included in the count was €30,000 of goods that were parts for a machine that the company no longer made. Given the high-tech nature of Sergei's products, it was unlikely that these obsolete parts had any other use. However, management would prefer to keep them on the books at cost, "since that is what we paid for them, after all."

Instructions

Prepare a schedule to determine the correct inventory amount. Provide explanations for each item above, saying why you did or did not make an adjustment for each item.

Solution

1. Ending inventory—as reported	€650,000
1. Subtract from inventory: The goods belong to Bosnia Enterprises. Sergei is merely holding them as a consignee.	(200,000)
2. Add to inventory: The goods belong to Sergei when they were shipped.	40,000
3. Subtract from inventory: Office supplies should be carried in a separate account. They are not considered inventory held for resale.	(15,000)
4. Add to inventory: The goods belong to Sergei until they are shipped (Jan. 1).	30,000
5. Add to inventory: Oman Sales ordered goods with a cost of €8,000. Sergei should record the corresponding sales revenue of €10,000. Sergei's decision to ship extra "unordered" goods does not constitute a sale. The manager's statement that Oman could ship the goods back indicates that Sergei knows this overshipment is not a legitimate sale. The manager acted unethically in an attempt to improve Sergei's reported income by overshipping.	52,000
6. Subtract from inventory: IFRS requires that inventory be valued at the lower of cost or net realizable value. Obsolete parts should be adjusted from cost to zero if they have no other use.	(30,000)
Correct inventory	€527,000

Determine effects of inventory errors.

2. **(LO 3)** Tainan Hardware reported cost of goods sold as follows.

	2028	2029
Beginning inventory	NT$ 200,000	NT$ 300,000
Cost of goods purchased	1,500,000	1,750,000
Cost of goods available for sale	1,700,000	2,050,000
Ending inventory	(300,000)	(350,000)
Cost of goods sold	NT$1,400,000	NT$1,700,000

Tainan Hardware made two errors: (1) 2028 ending inventory was overstated NT$25,000, and (2) 2029 ending inventory was understated NT$55,000.

Instructions

Compute the correct cost of goods sold for each year.

Solution

2.

	2028	2029
Beginning inventory	NT$ 200,000	NT$ 275,000
Cost of goods purchased	1,500,000	1,750,000
Cost of goods available for sale	1,700,000	2,025,000
Corrected ending inventory	(275,000)[a]	(405,000)[b]
Cost of goods sold	NT$1,425,000	NT$1,620,000

[a]NT$300,000 – NT$25,000 = NT$275,000; [b]NT$350,000 + NT$55,000 = NT$405,000

Practice Problems

1. **(LO 2)** Englehart Foods has the following inventory, purchases, and sales data for the month of March.

Compute inventory and cost of goods sold using two cost flow methods in a periodic inventory system.

Inventory:	March 1	200 units @ €4.00	€ 800
Purchases:	March 10	500 units @ €4.50	2,250
	March 20	400 units @ €4.75	1,900
	March 30	300 units @ €5.00	1,500
Sales:	March 15	500 units	
	March 25	400 units	

The physical inventory count on March 31 shows 500 units on hand.

Instructions

Under a **periodic inventory system**, determine the cost of inventory on hand at March 31 and the cost of goods sold for March under (a) FIFO and (b) average-cost.

Solution

1. The cost of goods available for sale is €6,450, as follows.

Inventory:	March 1	200 units @ €4.00	€ 800
Purchases:	March 10	500 units @ €4.50	2,250
	March 20	400 units @ €4.75	1,900
	March 30	300 units @ €5.00	1,500
Total:			$6,450

Under a **periodic inventory system**, the cost of goods sold under each cost flow method is as follows.

a. **FIFO Method**

Ending inventory:

Date	Units	Unit Cost	Total Cost
March 30	300	€5.00	€1,500
March 20	200	4.75	950
			€2,450

Cost of goods sold: €6,450 – €2,450 = €4,000

b. **Average-Cost Method**

Average unit cost: €6,450 ÷ 1,400 = €4.607

Ending inventory: 500 × €4.607 = €2,303.50

Cost of goods sold: €6,450 – €2,303.50 = €4,146.50

*2. **(LO 5)** **Practice Problem 1** showed cost of goods sold computations under a periodic inventory system. Now let's assume that Englehart Foods uses a perpetual inventory system. The company has the same inventory, purchases, and sales data for the month of March as shown earlier:

Compute inventory and cost of goods sold using two cost flow methods in a perpetual inventory system.

Inventory:	March 1	200 units @ €4.00	€ 800
Purchases:	March 10	500 units @ €4.50	2,250
	March 20	400 units @ €4.75	1,900
	March 30	300 units @ €5.00	1,500
Sales:	March 15	500 units	
	March 25	400 units	

The physical inventory count on March 31 shows 500 units on hand.

Instructions

Under a **perpetual inventory system**, determine the cost of inventory on hand at March 31 and the cost of goods sold for March under (a) FIFO and (b) average-cost.

Solution

2. The cost of goods available for sale is €6,450, as follows.

Inventory:	March 1	200 units @ €4.00	€ 800
Purchases:	March 10	500 units @ €4.50	2,250
	March 20	400 units @ €4.75	1,900
	March 30	300 units @ €5.00	1,500
Total:			€6,450

Under a **perpetual inventory system**, the cost of goods sold under each cost flow method is as follows.

a. **FIFO Method**

Date	Purchases	Cost of Goods Sold	Balance	
March 1			(200 @ €4.00)	€ 800
March 10	(500 @ €4.50) €2,250		(200 @ €4.00) (500 @ €4.50)	€3,050
March 15		(200 @ €4.00) (300 @ €4.50) €2,150	(200 @ €4.50)	€ 900
March 20	(400 @ €4.75) €1,900		(200 @ €4.50) (400 @ €4.75)	€2,800
March 25		(200 @ €4.50) (200 @ €4.75) €1,850	(200 @ €4.75)	€ 950
March 30	(300 @ €5.00) €1,500		(200 @ €4.75) (300 @ €5.00)	€2,450
	Ending inventory €2,450	Cost of goods sold: €2,150 + €1,850 = €4,000		

b. **Moving-Average Cost Method**

Date	Purchases	Cost of Goods Sold	Balance	
March 1			(200 @ € 4.00)	€ 800
March 10	(500 @ €4.50) €2,250		(700 @ €4.357)	€3,050
March 15		(500 @ €4.357) €2,179	(200 @ €4.357)	€ 871
March 20	(400 @ €4.75) €1,900		(600 @ €4.618)	€2,771
March 25		(400 @ €4.618) €1,847	(200 @ €4.618)	€ 924
March 30	(300 @ €5.00) €1,500		(500 @ €4.848)	€2,424
	Ending inventory €2,424	Cost of goods sold: €2,179 + €1,847 = €4,026		

Note: Asterisked Questions, Exercises, and Problems relate to material in the appendices to the chapter.

Questions

1. "The key to successful business operations is effective inventory management." Do you agree? Explain.

2. An item must possess two characteristics to be classified as inventory by a merchandiser. What are these two characteristics?

3. Your friend Art Mega has been hired to help take the physical inventory in Jaegar Hardware Store. Explain to Art Mega what this job will entail.

4. a. Girard Company ships merchandise to Liu Company on December 30. The merchandise reaches the buyer on January 6. Indicate the terms of sale that will result in the goods being included in (1) Girard's December 31 inventory, and (2) Liu's December 31 inventory.

b. Under what circumstances should Girard Company include consigned goods in its inventory?

5. Topp Hat Shop received a shipment of hats for which it paid the wholesaler £2,970. The price of the hats was £3,000, but Topp was given a £30 cash discount and required to pay freight charges of £80. In addition, Topp paid £130 to cover the travel expenses of an employee who negotiated the purchase of the hats. What amount will Topp record for inventory? Why?

6. Explain the difference between the terms FOB shipping point and FOB destination.

7. Min-jun believes that the allocation of inventoriable costs should be based on the actual physical flow of the goods. Explain to Min-jun why this may be both impractical and inappropriate.

8. What is a major advantage and a major disadvantage of the specific identification method of inventory costing?

9. "The selection of an inventory cost flow method is a decision made by accountants." Do you agree? Explain. Once a method has been selected, what accounting requirement applies?

10. Which assumed inventory cost flow method:

a. usually parallels the actual physical flow of merchandise?

b. assumes that goods available for sale during an accounting period are identical?

c. assumes that the first units purchased are the first to be sold?

11. Beatriz Diaz is studying for the next accounting mid-term examination. What should Beatriz know about (a) departing from the cost basis of accounting for inventories and (b) the meaning of "net realizable value" in the lower of cost or net realizable value method?

12. Beethovan Music Center has 5 televisions on hand at the statement of financial position date. Each cost €100. The net realizable value is €90 per unit. Under the lower of cost or net realizable value basis of accounting for inventories, what value should be reported for the televisions on the statement of financial position? Why?

13. Maggie Stores has 20 toasters on hand at the statement of financial position date. Each cost £28. The net realizable value is £30 per unit. Under the lower of cost or net realizable value basis of accounting for inventories, what value should Maggie report for the toasters on the statement of financial position? Why?

14. Bakkar Kitchens discovers in 2029 that its ending inventory at December 31, 2028, was €7,600 understated. What effect will this error have on (a) 2028 net income, (b) 2029 net income, and (c) the combined net income for the 2 years?

15. Xu Fashions' statement of financial position shows Inventory HK$1,628,000. What additional disclosures should be made?

16. Under what circumstances might inventory turnover be too high? That is, what possible negative consequences might occur?

*17. How does the average-cost method of inventory costing differ between a perpetual inventory system and a periodic inventory system?

*18. When is it necessary to estimate inventories?

*19. Both the gross profit method and the retail inventory method are based on averages. For each method, indicate the average used, how it is determined, and how it is applied.

*20. Szabo Gourmet has net sales of €400,000 and cost of goods available for sale of €300,000. If the gross profit rate is 40%, what is the estimated cost of the ending inventory? Show computations.

*21. Park Shoe Shop had goods available for sale in 2029 with a retail price of €120,000. The cost of these goods was €84,000. If sales during the period were €90,000, what is the estimated cost of ending inventory using the retail inventory method?

*22. In a period of rising prices, the inventory reported in Kanth Company's statement of financial position is close to the current cost of the inventory. Phelan Company's inventory is considerably below its current cost. Identify the inventory cost flow method being used by each company. Which company has probably been reporting the higher gross profit?

*23. Why might the use of the LIFO method for costing inventories result in lower income taxes?

Brief Exercises

BE6.1 (LO 1) Lazio Antiques identifies the following items for possible inclusion in the taking of a physical inventory. Indicate whether each item should be included or excluded from the inventory taking.

Identify items to be included in taking a physical inventory.

a. Goods shipped on consignment by Lazio to another company.

b. Goods in transit from a supplier shipped FOB destination.

c. Goods sold but being held for customer pickup.

d. Goods held on consignment from another company.

BE6.2 (LO 1) Stallman Furniture took a physical inventory on December 31 and determined that goods costing €200,000 were on hand. Not included in the physical count were €25,000 of goods purchased from Pelzer Corporation, FOB shipping point, and €22,000 of goods sold to Alvarez Company for €30,000, FOB destination. Both the Pelzer purchase and the Alvarez sale were in transit at year-end. What amount should Stallman report as its December 31 inventory?

Determine ending inventory amount.

BE6.3 (LO 2) In its first month of operations, Tatung Electronics made three purchases of merchandise in the following sequence: (1) 300 units at NT$180, (2) 400 units at NT$210, and (3) 200 units at NT$240. Assuming there are 420 units on hand, compute the cost of the ending inventory under the (a) FIFO method and (b) average-cost method. Tatung uses a periodic inventory system. (Round average unit cost to two decimal places.)

Compute ending inventory using FIFO and average-cost.

Explain the financial statement effect of inventory cost flow assumptions.

BE6.4 (LO 2) The management of Muni Group is considering the effects of inventory-costing methods on its financial statements and its income tax expense. Assuming that the price the company pays for inventory is increasing, which method will:

a. Provide the higher net income?

b. Provide the higher ending inventory?

c. Result in the lower income tax expense?

d. Result in the more stable earnings over a number of years?

Determine correct income statement amounts.

BE6.5 (LO 3) Zammit Watches reports net income of €90,000 in 2029. However, ending inventory was understated €5,000. What is the correct net income for 2029? What effect, if any, will this error have on total assets as reported in the statement of financial position at December 31, 2029?

Determine the LCNRV valuation using inventory categories.

BE6.6 (LO 4) Blackburn Appliance Center accumulates the following cost and net realizable value data at December 31.

Inventory Categories	Cost Data	Net Realizable Value Data
Cameras	£12,000	£12,100
Camcorders	9,420	9,200
Blu-ray players	14,000	12,800

Compute the lower of cost or net realizable value valuation for the company's total inventory.

Compute inventory turnover and days in inventory.

BE6.7 (LO 4) At December 31, 2029, the following information was available for Tai Lin Goods: ending inventory HK$400,000, beginning inventory HK$580,000, cost of goods sold HK$2,842,000, and sales revenue HK$3,800,000. Calculate inventory turnover and days in inventory for Tai Lin.

Apply cost flow methods to perpetual inventory records.

***BE6.8 (LO 5)** Abbott's Department Store uses a perpetual inventory system. Data for product E2-D2 include the following purchases.

Date	Number of Units	Unit Price
May 7	50	£11
July 28	30	13

On June 1, Abbott's sold 30 units, and on August 27, 35 more units. Prepare the perpetual inventory schedule for the above transactions using (a) FIFO and (b) moving-average cost.

Apply the gross profit method.

***BE6.9 (LO 6)** At May 31, Chang Dancewear has net sales of ¥330,000 and cost of goods available for sale of ¥230,000. Compute the estimated cost of the ending inventory, assuming the gross profit rate is 45%.

Apply the retail inventory method.

***BE6.10 (LO 6)** On June 30, Lyon Fabrics has the following data pertaining to the retail inventory method: goods available for sale: at cost €35,000 and at retail €50,000, net sales €42,000, and ending inventory at retail €8,000. Compute the estimated cost of the ending inventory using the retail inventory method.

Compute the ending inventory using LIFO (periodic).

***BE6.11 (LO 7)** Data for Tatung Electronics are presented in BE6.3. Compute the cost of the ending inventory under the LIFO method, assuming there are 420 units on hand.

DO IT! Exercises

Apply rules of ownership to determine inventory cost.

DO IT! 6.1 (LO 1) Recife Apparel just took its physical inventory. The count of inventory items on hand at the company's business locations resulted in a total inventory cost of R$300,000. In reviewing the details of the count and related inventory transactions, you discover the following.

1. Recife sent inventory costing R$18,000 on consignment to Rio Company. All of this inventory is at Rio's showrooms on December 31.
2. The company did not include in the inventory count the goods (cost, R$20,000) that were purchased on December 28, terms FOB shipping point. The goods are in transit on December 31.
3. The company did not include in the inventory count the goods (cost, R$17,000) that were sold with terms of FOB shipping point. The goods are in transit on December 31.

Compute the correct December 31 inventory.

DO IT! 6.2 (LO 2) The accounting records of Connor Electronics show the following data.

Compute cost of goods sold under different cost flow methods.

Beginning inventory	3,000 units at £5
Purchases	8,000 units at £7
Sales	9,400 units at £10

Determine cost of goods sold during the period under a periodic inventory system using (a) the FIFO method and (b) the average-cost method. (Round unit cost to nearest tenth of a cent.)

DO IT! 6.3 (LO 3) Vanida Company understated its 2028 ending inventory by $27,000. Determine the impact this error has on ending inventory, cost of goods sold, and equity in 2028 and 2029.

Determine effect of inventory error.

DO IT! 6.4a (LO 4) Guo Hardware sells three different categories of tools (small, medium, and large). The cost and net realizable value of its inventory of tools are as follows.

Compute inventory value under LCNRV.

	Cost	Net Realizable Value
Small	HK$ 640,000	HK$ 730,000
Medium	2,900,000	2,600,000
Large	1,520,000	1,485,000

Determine the value of the company's inventory under the lower of cost or net realizable value approach.

DO IT! 6.4b (LO 4) Early in 2029, Lausanne Clocks switched to a just-in-time inventory system. Its sales, cost of goods sold, and inventory amounts for 2028 and 2029 are shown below.

Compute inventory turnover and assess inventory level.

	2028	2029
Sales	CHF3,120,000	CHF3,713,000
Cost of goods sold	1,200,000	1,425,000
Beginning inventory	180,000	220,000
Ending inventory	220,000	100,000

Determine the inventory turnover and days in inventory for 2028 and 2029. Discuss the changes in the amount of inventory, the inventory turnover and days in inventory, and the amount of sales across the two years.

Exercises

E6.1 (LO 1) Premier Bank and Trust is considering giving Alou Company a loan. Before doing so, management decides that further discussions with Alou's accountant may be desirable. One area of particular concern is the inventory account, which has a year-end balance of £297,000. Discussions with the accountant reveal the following.

Determine the correct inventory amount.

1. Alou sold goods costing £38,000 to Comerico Company, FOB shipping point, on December 28. The goods are not expected to arrive at Comerico until January 12. The goods were not included in the physical inventory because they were not in the warehouse.
2. The physical count of the inventory did not include goods costing £91,000 that were shipped to Alou FOB destination on December 27 and were still in transit at year-end.
3. Alou received goods costing £25,000 on January 2. The goods were shipped FOB shipping point on December 26 by Grant Co. The goods were not included in the physical count.
4. Alou sold goods costing £35,000 to Emerick Co., FOB destination, on December 30. The goods were received at Emerick on January 8. They were not included in Alou's physical inventory.
5. Alou received goods costing £44,000 on January 2 that were shipped FOB shipping point on December 29. The shipment was a rush order that was supposed to arrive December 31. This purchase was included in the ending inventory of £297,000.

Instructions

Determine the correct inventory amount on December 31.

E6.2 (LO 1) Kale Wilson, an auditor with Sneed Chartered Accountants, is performing a review of Platinum Stereos' inventory account. Platinum did not have a good year, and top management is under pres-

Determine the correct inventory amount.

sure to boost reported income. According to its records, the inventory balance at year-end was £740,000. However, the following information was not considered when determining that amount.

1. Included in the company's count were goods with a cost of £250,000 that the company is holding on consignment. The goods belong to Superior Ltd.
2. The physical count did not include goods purchased by Platinum with a cost of £40,000 that were shipped FOB destination on December 28 and did not arrive at Platinum's warehouse until January 3.
3. Included in the inventory account was £17,000 of office supplies that were stored in the warehouse and were to be used by the company's supervisors and managers during the coming year.
4. The company received an order on December 29 that was boxed and sitting on the loading dock awaiting pick-up on December 31. The shipper picked up the goods on January 1 and delivered them on January 6. The shipping terms were FOB shipping point. The goods had a selling price of £49,000 and a cost of £33,000. The goods were not included in the count because they were sitting on the dock.
5. Included in the count was £48,000 of goods that were parts for a machine that the company no longer made. Given the high-tech nature of Platinum's products, it was unlikely that these obsolete parts had any other use. However, management would prefer to keep them on the books at cost, "since that is what we paid for them, after all."

Instructions

Prepare a schedule to determine the correct inventory amount. Provide explanations for each item above, saying why you did or did not make an adjustment for each item.

Calculate cost of goods sold using specific identification and FIFO.

E6.3 (LO 2) On December 1, Discount Electronics has three DVD players left in stock. All are identical, all are priced to sell at NT$4,500. One of the three DVD players left in stock, with serial #1012, was purchased on June 1 at a cost of NT$3,000. Another, with serial #1045, was purchased on November 1 for NT$2,760. The last player, serial #1056, was purchased on November 30 for NT$2,520.

Instructions

a. Calculate the cost of goods sold using the FIFO periodic inventory method assuming that two of the three players were sold by the end of December, Discount Electronics' year-end.
b. If Discount Electronics used the specific identification method instead of the FIFO method, how might it alter its earnings by "selectively choosing" which particular players to sell to the two customers? What would Discount's cost of goods sold be if the company wished to minimize earnings? Maximize earnings?
c. Which of the two inventory methods do you recommend that Discount use? Explain why.

Compute inventory and cost of goods sold using FIFO and average-cost.

E6.4 (LO 2) Zhu Boards sells a snowboard, Xpert, that is popular with snowboard enthusiasts. The following information relates to Zhu's purchases of Xpert snowboards during September. During the same month, 121 Xpert snowboards were sold. Zhu's uses a periodic inventory system.

Date	Explanation	Units	Unit Cost	Total Cost
Sept. 1	Inventory	23	HK$ 970	HK$ 22,310
Sept. 12	Purchases	45	1,020	45,900
Sept. 19	Purchases	20	1,040	20,800
Sept. 26	Purchases	44	1,050	46,200
	Totals	132		HK$135,210

Instructions

a. Compute the ending inventory at September 30 and cost of goods sold using the FIFO and average-cost methods. Prove the amount allocated to cost of goods sold under each method. (Round all unit cost calculations for the average-cost method to the nearest cent and total cost to the nearest dollar.)
b. For both FIFO and average-cost, calculate the sum of ending inventory and cost of goods sold. What do you notice about the answers you found for each method?

Compute inventory and cost of goods sold using FIFO and average-cost.

E6.5 (LO 2) Zambian Co. uses a periodic inventory system. Its records show the following for the month of May, in which 68 units were sold.

			Units	Unit Cost	Total Cost
May	1	Inventory	30	€ 9	€270
	15	Purchases	22	11	242
	24	Purchases	38	12	456
		Totals	90		€968

Instructions

Compute the ending inventory at May 31 and cost of goods sold using the FIFO and average-cost methods. Prove the amount allocated to cost of goods sold under each method. (Round all unit cost calculations for the average-cost method to the nearest cent and total cost to the nearest euro.)

E6.6 (LO 2) Howsham Interiors reports the following for the month of June.

Compute inventory and cost of goods sold using FIFO and average-cost.

			Units	Unit Cost	Total Cost
June	1	Inventory	200	£5	£1,000
	12	Purchase	300	6	1,800
	23	Purchase	500	7	3,500
	30	Inventory	160		

Instructions

a. Compute the cost of the ending inventory and the cost of goods sold under (1) FIFO and (2) average-cost.

b. Which costing method gives the higher ending inventory? Why?

c. Which method results in the higher cost of goods sold? Why?

E6.7 (LO 2) Thaam Appliances had 100 units in beginning inventory at a total cost of NT$300,000. The company purchased 200 units at a total cost of NT$680,000. At the end of the year, Thaam had 75 units in ending inventory.

Compute inventory under FIFO and average-cost.

Instructions

a. Compute the cost of the ending inventory and the cost of goods sold under (1) FIFO and (2) average-cost.

b. Which cost flow method would result in the higher net income?

c. Which cost flow method would result in inventories approximating current cost in the statement of financial position?

d. Which cost flow method would result in Thaam paying less taxes in the first year?

E6.8 (LO 4) Kinshasa Camera Shop uses the lower of cost or net realizable value basis for its inventory. The following data are available at December 31.

Determine ending inventory under LCNRV.

Item	Units	Unit Cost	Net Realizable Value
Cameras:			
Minolta	8	₩170,000	₩156,000
Canon	6	150,000	152,000
Light meters:			
Vivitar	12	125,000	115,000
Kodak	14	115,000	135,000

Instructions

Determine the amount of the ending inventory by applying the lower of cost or net realizable value basis.

E6.9 (LO 4) Serebin Company applied FIFO to its inventory and got the following results for its ending inventory.

Compute lower of cost or net realizable value.

Cameras	100 units at a cost per unit of $65
Blu-ray players	150 units at a cost per unit of $75
iPods	125 units at a cost per unit of $80

The net realizable value of each of these products at year-end was cameras $71, Blu-ray players $67, and iPods $78.

Instructions

Determine the amount of ending inventory at lower of cost or net realizable value.

Determine effects of inventory errors.

E6.10 (LO 3) Bamburgh Hardware reported cost of goods sold as follows.

	2028	2029
Beginning inventory	€ 20,000	€ 30,000
Cost of goods purchased	150,000	175,000
Cost of goods available for sale	170,000	205,000
Ending inventory	30,000	35,000
Cost of goods sold	€140,000	€170,000

Bamburgh made two errors: (1) 2028 ending inventory was overstated €2,000, and (2) 2029 ending inventory was understated €6,000.

Instructions

Compute the correct cost of goods sold for each year.

Prepare correct income statements.

E6.11 (LO 3) Writing Wu Jewelry reported the following income statement data for a 2-year period.

	2028	2029
Sales revenue	HK$2,100,000	HK$2,500,000
Cost of goods sold		
Beginning inventory	320,000	440,000
Cost of goods purchased	1,730,000	2,040,000
Cost of goods available for sale	2,050,000	2,480,000
Ending inventory	440,000	520,000
Cost of goods sold	1,610,000	1,960,000
Gross profit	HK$ 490,000	HK$ 540,000

Wu uses a periodic inventory system. The inventories at January 1, 2028, and December 31, 2029, are correct. However, the ending inventory at December 31, 2028, was understated HK$60,000.

Instructions

a. Prepare correct income statement data for the 2 years.

b. What is the cumulative effect of the inventory error on total gross profit for the 2 years?

c. Explain in an email to the president of Wu what has happened, i.e., the nature of the error and its effect on the financial statements.

Compute inventory turnover, days in inventory, and gross profit rate.

E6.12 (LO 4) Writing This information is available for Sepia Photos for 2027, 2028, and 2029.

	2027	2028	2029
Beginning inventory	£ 100,000	£ 330,000	£ 400,000
Ending inventory	330,000	400,000	480,000
Cost of goods sold	900,000	1,120,000	1,300,000
Sales revenue	1,200,000	1,600,000	1,900,000

Instructions

Calculate inventory turnover, days in inventory, and gross profit rate for Sepia Photos for 2027, 2028, and 2029. Comment on any trends. (Round inventory turnover to two decimal places and days in inventory to the nearest whole day.)

Compute inventory turnover and days in inventory.

E6.13 (LO 4) The cost of goods sold computations for Gouda Company and Edam Company are shown below.

	Gouda Company	Edam Company
Beginning inventory	€ 47,000	€ 71,000
Cost of goods purchased	200,000	290,000
Cost of goods available for sale	247,000	361,000
Ending inventory	58,000	69,000
Cost of goods sold	€189,000	€292,000

Instructions

a. Compute inventory turnover and days in inventory for each company. (Round inventory turnover to two decimal places and days in inventory to the nearest whole day.)

b. Which company moves its inventory more quickly?

***E6.14 (LO 5)** Roselle TVs uses a perpetual inventory system. For its flat-screen television sets, the January 1 inventory was 3 sets at €600 each. On January 10, Roselle purchased 6 units at €648 each. The company sold 2 units on January 8 and 4 units on January 15.

Apply cost flow methods to perpetual records.

Instructions

Compute the ending inventory under (1) FIFO and (2) moving-average cost. (Round the unit cost to the nearest cent.)

***E6.15 (LO 5)** Howsham Ltd. reports the following for the month of June.

Calculate inventory and cost of goods sold using two cost flow methods in a perpetual inventory system.

Date	Explanation	Units	Unit Cost	Total Cost
June 1	Inventory	200	£5	$1,000
12	Purchase	300	6	1,800
23	Purchase	500	7	3,500
30	Inventory	160		

Instructions

a. Calculate the cost of the ending inventory and the cost of goods sold for (1) FIFO and (2) moving-average cost, using a perpetual inventory system. Assume a sale of 400 units occurred on June 15 for a selling price of £8 and a sale of 440 units on June 27 for £9.

b. How do the results differ from E6.6?

c. Why is the average unit cost not £6 [(£5 + £6 + £7) ÷ 3 = £6]?

***E6.16 (LO 5)** Information about Zhu Boards is presented in E6.4. Additional data regarding Zhu's sales of Xpert snowboards are provided below. Assume that Zhu uses a perpetual inventory system.

Apply cost flow methods to perpetual records.

Date	Explanation	Units	Unit Price	Total Revenue
Sept. 5	Sale	12	HK$1,990	HK$ 23,880
Sept. 16	Sale	50	2,030	101,500
Sept. 29	Sale	59	2,090	123,310
	Totals	121		HK$248,690

Instructions

a. Compute ending inventory at September 30 using FIFO and moving-average cost.

b. Compare ending inventory using a perpetual inventory system to ending inventory using a periodic inventory system (from E6.4).

c. Which inventory cost flow method (FIFO, moving-average cost) gives the same ending inventory value under both periodic and perpetual? Which method gives different ending inventory values?

***E6.17 (LO 6)** Brenda Company reported the following information for November and December 2029.

Use the gross profit method to estimate inventory.

	November	December
Cost of goods purchased	$536,000	$ 610,000
Inventory, beginning-of-month	130,000	120,000
Inventory, end-of-month	120,000	?
Net sales revenue	840,000	1,000,000

Brenda's ending inventory at December 31 was destroyed in a fire.

Instructions

a. Compute the gross profit rate for November.

b. Using the gross profit rate for November, determine the estimated cost of inventory lost in the fire.

***E6.18 (LO 6)** The inventory of Ipswich Books was destroyed by fire on March 1. From an examination of the accounting records, the following data for the first 2 months of the year are obtained: Sales Revenue £51,000, Sales Returns and Allowances £1,000, Purchases £31,200, Freight-In £1,200, and Purchase Returns and Allowances £1,800.

Determine merchandise lost using the gross profit method of estimating inventory.

Instructions

Determine the merchandise lost by fire, assuming:

a. A beginning inventory of £20,000 and a gross profit rate of 40% on net sales.

b. A beginning inventory of £30,000 and a gross profit rate of 32% on net sales.

Determine ending inventory at cost using retail method.

***E6.19 (LO 6)** Gepetto Shoe Store uses the retail inventory method for its two departments, Women's Shoes and Men's Shoes. The following information for each department is obtained.

	Women's Shoes	Men's Shoes
Beginning inventory at cost	$ 25,000	$ 45,000
Cost of goods purchased at cost	110,000	136,300
Net sales	178,000	185,000
Beginning inventory at retail	46,000	60,000
Cost of goods purchased at retail	179,000	185,000

Instructions

Compute the estimated cost of the ending inventory for each department under the retail inventory method.

Apply the LIFO cost method (periodic).

***E6.20 (LO 7)** Using the data in E6.6, compute the cost of the ending inventory and the cost of goods sold using LIFO periodic.

Apply the LIFO cost method (periodic).

***E6.21 (LO 7)** (a) Using the data in E6.7, compute the cost of the ending inventory and cost of goods sold using LIFO periodic. In addition, answer instructions (b), (c), and (d) from E6.7 as it relates to the three cost flow methods.

Problems

Determine items and amounts to be recorded in inventory.

P6.1 (LO 1) Anatolia Designs is trying to determine the value of its ending inventory at February 28, 2029, the company's year-end. The accountant counted everything that was in the warehouse as of February 28, which resulted in an ending inventory valuation of ₺48,000. However, she didn't know how to treat the following transactions so she didn't record them.

a. On February 26, Anatolia shipped to a customer goods costing ₺800. The goods were shipped FOB shipping point, and the receiving report indicates that the customer received the goods on March 2.

b. On February 26, Shira Inc. shipped goods to Anatolia FOB destination. The invoice price was ₺350. The receiving report indicates that the goods were received by Anatolia on March 2.

c. Anatolia had ₺620 of inventory at a customer's warehouse "on approval." The customer was going to let Anatolia know whether it wanted the merchandise by the end of the week, March 4.

d. Anatolia also had ₺400 of inventory on consignment at a Palletine craft shop.

e. On February 26, Anatolia ordered goods costing ₺780. The goods were shipped FOB shipping point on February 27. Anatolia received the goods on March 1.

f. On February 28, Anatolia packaged goods and had them ready for shipping to a customer FOB destination. The invoice price was ₺350; the cost of the items was ₺220. The receiving report indicates that the goods were received by the customer on March 2.

g. Anatolia had damaged goods set aside in the warehouse because they are no longer saleable. These goods cost ₺400 and Anatolia originally expected to sell these items for ₺600.

Instructions

For each of the preceding transactions, specify whether the item in question should be included in ending inventory and, if so, at what amount. For each item that is not included in ending inventory, indicate who owns it and what account, if any, it should have been recorded in.

Determine cost of goods sold and ending inventory using FIFO and average-cost with analysis.

P6.2 (LO 2) Dyna Distribution markets CDs of the performing artist King James. At the beginning of March, Dyna had in beginning inventory 1,500 King James CDs with a unit cost of €7. During March, Dyna made the following purchases of King James CDs.

March 5	3,500 @ €8	March 21	2,000 @ €10
March 13	4,000 @ €9	March 26	2,000 @ €11

During March, 10,000 units were sold. Dyna uses a periodic inventory system.

Instructions

a. Determine the cost of goods available for sale.

b. Determine (1) the ending inventory and (2) the cost of goods sold under the two assumed cost flow methods (FIFO and average-cost). Prove the accuracy of the cost of goods sold under the FIFO and average-cost methods. (Round the unit cost calculation to four decimal places.)

b. (2) Cost of goods sold:
FIFO €84,500
Average €89,615

c. Which cost flow method results in (1) the higher inventory amount for the statement of financial position and (2) the higher cost of goods sold for the income statement?

P6.3 (LO 2) Marlow Bed and Bath had a beginning inventory of 400 units of Product Kimbo at a cost of £8 per unit. During the year, purchases were:

Determine cost of goods sold and ending inventory using FIFO and average-cost with analysis.

Feb. 20	200 units at £9	Aug. 12	600 units at £11
May 5	500 units at £10	Dec. 8	300 units at £12

Marlow uses a periodic inventory system. Sales totaled 1,500 units.

Instructions

a. Determine the cost of goods available for sale.

b. Determine (1) the ending inventory and (2) the cost of goods sold under the two assumed cost flow methods (FIFO and average-cost). Prove the accuracy of the cost of goods sold under the FIFO and average-cost methods. (Round the unit cost calculation for average-cost to two decimal places.)

b. Cost of goods sold:
FIFO £14,400
Average £15,150

c. Which cost flow method results in (1) the lower ending inventory amount for the statement of financial position, and (2) the lower cost of goods sold for the income statement?

P6.4 (LO 2) Writing The management of Gisel Group is reevaluating the appropriateness of using its present inventory cost flow method. They request your help in determining the results of operations for 2029 if either the FIFO method or the average-cost method had been used. For 2029, the accounting records show the following data.

Compute ending inventory, prepare income statements, and answer questions using FIFO and average-cost.

Inventories		Purchases and Sales	
Beginning (10,000 units)	€22,800	Total net sales (225,000 units)	€865,000
Ending (15,000 units)		Total cost of goods purchased (230,000 units)	578,500

Purchases were made quarterly as follows.

Quarter	Units	Unit Cost	Total Cost
1	60,000	€2.30	€138,000
2	50,000	2.50	125,000
3	50,000	2.60	130,000
4	70,000	2.65	185,500
	230,000		€578,500

Operating expenses were €147,000, and the company's income tax rate is 32%.

Instructions

a. Prepare comparative condensed income statements for 2029 under FIFO and average-cost. Show computations of ending inventory. (Round the unit cost calculations to three decimal places.)

a. Net income:
FIFO €106,386
Average €104,907

b. Answer the following questions for management.

1. Which cost flow method (FIFO or average-cost) produces the more meaningful inventory amount for the statement of financial position? Why?
2. Which cost flow method (FIFO or average-cost) is more likely to approximate actual physical flow of the goods? Why?
3. How much additional cash will be available for management under average-cost than under FIFO? Why?

b. 3. €696

P6.5 (LO 2) You are provided with the following information for Senta Ltd. for the month ended October 31, 2029. Senta uses a periodic method for inventory.

Calculate ending inventory, cost of goods sold, gross profit, and gross profit rate under periodic method; compare results.

Date	Description	Units	Unit Cost or Selling Price
October 1	Beginning inventory	60	€24
October 9	Purchase	120	26
October 11	Sale	100	35
October 17	Purchase	70	27
October 22	Sale	65	40
October 25	Purchase	80	28
October 29	Sale	120	40

a. (iii) Gross profit:
FIFO €3,470
Average €3,395

Instructions

a. Calculate (i) ending inventory, (ii) cost of goods sold, (iii) gross profit, and (iv) gross profit rate under each of the following methods.
   1. FIFO.
   2. Average-cost. (Round the unit cost calculations to three decimal places.)

b. Compare results for the two cost flow assumptions.

Compare specific identification, FIFO and average-cost under periodic method; use cost flow assumption to influence earnings.

P6.6 (LO 2) You have the following information for Greco Diamonds. Greco Diamonds uses the periodic method of accounting for its inventory transactions. Greco only carries one brand and size of diamonds—all are identical. Each batch of diamonds purchased is carefully coded and marked with its purchase cost.

March	1	Beginning inventory 150 diamonds at a cost of €310 per diamond.
March	3	Purchased 200 diamonds at a cost of €350 each.
March	5	Sold 180 diamonds for €600 each.
March	10	Purchased 350 diamonds at a cost of €380 each.
March	25	Sold 400 diamonds for €650 each.

Instructions

a. Gross profit:
1. Maximum €164,100
2. Minimum €155,700

a. Assume that Greco Diamonds uses the specific identification method.
   1. Demonstrate how Greco Diamonds could maximize its gross profit for the month by specifically selecting which diamonds to sell on March 5 and March 25.
   2. Demonstrate how Greco Diamonds could minimize its gross profit for the month by selecting which diamonds to sell on March 5 and March 25.

b. Assume that Greco Diamonds uses the FIFO cost flow assumption. Calculate cost of goods sold. How much gross profit would Greco Diamonds report under this cost flow assumption?

c. Assume that Greco Diamonds uses the average-cost cost flow assumption. Calculate cost of goods sold. How much gross profit would the company report under this cost flow assumption? (Round the unit cost calculations to three decimal places.)

d. Which method should Greco Diamonds select? Explain.

Compute ending inventory, prepare income statements, and answer questions using FIFO and average-cost.

P6.7 (LO 2) **Writing** The management of Tudor Living asks your help in determining the comparative effects of the FIFO and average-cost inventory cost flow methods. For 2029, the accounting records provide the data shown below.

Inventory, January 1 (10,000 units)	£ 35,000
Cost of 120,000 units purchased	501,000
Selling price of 105,000 units sold	695,000
Operating expenses	130,000

Units purchased consisted of 40,000 units at £4.00 on May 10; 60,000 units at £4.20 on August 15; and 20,000 units at £4.45 on November 20. Income taxes are 28%.

Instructions

a. Gross profit:
FIFO £269,000
Average £262,075

a. Prepare comparative condensed income statements for 2029 under FIFO and average-cost. (Show computations of ending inventory.)

b. Answer the following questions for management in the form of a business email.
   1. Which inventory cost flow method produces the more meaningful inventory amount for the statement of financial position? Why?
   2. Which inventory cost flow method is more likely to approximate the actual physical flow of the goods? Why?
   3. How much more cash will be available for management under average-cost than under FIFO? Why?

Calculate cost of goods sold and ending inventory for FIFO and moving-average cost under the perpetual system; compare gross profit under each assumption.

***P6.8 (LO 5)** Tempo Ltd. is a retailer operating in Dartmouth, Nova Scotia. Tempo uses the perpetual inventory method. All sales returns from customers result in the goods being returned to inventory; the inventory is not damaged. Assume that there are no credit transactions; all amounts are settled in cash. You are provided with the following information for Tempo Ltd. for the month of January 2029.

Date	Description	Quantity	Unit Cost or Selling Price
December 31	Ending inventory	150	£19
January 2	Purchase	100	21
January 6	Sale	150	40
January 9	Sale return	10	40
January 9	Purchase	75	24
January 10	Purchase return	15	24
January 10	Sale	50	45
January 23	Purchase	100	26
January 30	Sale	160	50

Instructions

a. For each of the following cost flow assumptions, calculate (i) cost of goods sold, (ii) ending inventory, and (iii) gross profit.

1. FIFO.
2. Moving-average cost. (Round the unit cost calculations to three decimal places.)

b. Compare results for the two cost flow assumptions.

a. (iii) Gross profit:
FIFO £8,420
Average £8,266

***P6.9 (LO 5)** Dominican Appliance Mart began operations on May 1. It uses a perpetual inventory system. During May, the company had the following purchases and sales for its Model 25 Sureshot camera.

Determine ending inventory under a perpetual inventory system.

Date	Purchases: Units	Purchases: Unit Cost	Sales Units
May 1	7	NT$4,600	
4			4
8	8	NT$5,100	
12			5
15	6	NT$5,520	
20			3
25			5

Instructions

a. Determine the ending inventory under a perpetual inventory system using (1) FIFO and (2) moving-average cost. (Round the unit cost calculations to two decimal places.)

b. Which costing method produces (1) the higher ending inventory valuation and (2) the lower ending inventory valuation?

a. FIFO NT$22,080
Average NT$20,968

***P6.10 (LO 6)** Suzuki Company lost all of its inventory in a fire on December 26, 2029. The accounting records showed the following inventory-related data for November and December.

Compute gross profit rate and inventory loss using gross profit method.

	November	December (to 12/26)
Net sales	$600,000	$700,000
Beginning inventory	32,000	36,000
Purchases	389,000	420,000
Purchase returns and allowances	13,300	14,900
Purchase discounts	8,500	9,500
Freight-in	8,800	9,900
Ending inventory	36,000	?

Suzuki is fully insured for fire losses but must prepare a report for the insurance company.

Instructions

a. Compute the gross profit rate for November.

b. Using the gross profit rate for November, determine the estimated cost of the inventory lost in the fire.

a. Gross profit rate 38%

***P6.11 (LO 6)** Dixon Books uses the retail inventory method to estimate its monthly ending inventories. The following information is available for two of its departments at October 31, 2029.

Compute ending inventory using retail method.

	Hardcovers		Paperbacks	
	Cost	Retail	Cost	Retail
Beginning inventory	$ 420,000	$ 700,000	$ 280,000	$ 360,000
Purchases	2,135,000	3,200,000	1,155,000	1,540,000
Freight-in	24,000		12,000	
Purchase discounts	44,000		22,000	
Net sales		3,100,000		1,570,000

At December 31, Dixon Books takes a physical inventory at retail. The actual retail values of the inventories in each department are Hardcovers $790,000 and Paperbacks $335,000.

Instructions

a. Hardcovers: end. inv. $520,000

a. Determine the estimated cost of the ending inventory for each department at October 31, 2029, using the retail inventory method.

b. Compute the ending inventory at cost for each department at December 31, assuming the cost-to-retail ratios for the year are 65% for Hardcovers and 75% for Paperbacks.

Compare inventory turnover using FIFO and average-cost method.

***P6.12 (LO 2, 4, 5)** Tainan company was established at the beginning of year 2028, it reported the following inventory information for year 2028 and 2029:

	Purchases			
Year	**Units**	**Unit Cost**	**Sales Units**	**Sale Price Per Unit**
2028	3,000	$200	2,500	$250
2029	2,500	$176	2,000	$222

Instructions

Determine the inventory turnover and days in inventory for year 2029 using average-cost and FIFO method (Round the unit cost calculations to two decimal places.)

Apply the LIFO cost method (periodic).

***P6.13 (LO 7)** Using the data in P6.5, compute the cost of the ending inventory using the LIFO cost flow assumption. Assume that Senta Ltd. uses the periodic inventory system.

Comprehensive Accounting Cycle Review

ACR6 On December 1, 2029, Cambridge Printers had the account balances shown below.

	Debit		Credit
Cash	£ 4,650	Accumulated Depreciation—Equipment	£ 1,500
Accounts Receivable	3,900	Accounts Payable	3,000
Inventory	1,950*	Share Capital—Ordinary	20,000
Equipment	21,000	Retained Earnings	7,000
	£31,500		£31,500

*(3,000 × £0.65)

The following transactions occurred during December.

Dec. 3 Purchased 4,000 units of inventory on account at a cost of £0.72 per unit.

5 Sold 4,400 units of inventory on account for £0.92 per unit. (It sold 3,000 of the £0.65 units and 1,400 of the £0.72 units.)

7 Granted the December 5 customer £184 credit for 200 units of inventory returned costing £144. These units were returned to inventory.

17 Purchased 2,200 units of inventory for cash at £0.78 each.

22 Sold 2,000 units of inventory on account for £0.95 per unit. (It sold 2,000 of the £0.72 units.)

Adjustment data:

1. Accrued salaries payable £400.
2. Depreciation £200 per month.

Instructions

a. Journalize the December transactions and adjusting entries, assuming Cambridge uses the perpetual inventory method.

b. Enter the December 1 balances in the ledger T-accounts and post the December transactions. In addition to the accounts mentioned above, use the following additional accounts: Cost of Goods Sold, Depreciation Expense, Salaries and Wages Expense, Salaries and Wages Payable, Sales Revenue, and Sales Returns and Allowances.

c. Prepare an adjusted trial balance as of December 31, 2029.

d. Prepare an income statement for December 2029 and a classified statement of financial position at December 31, 2029.

e. Compute ending inventory and cost of goods sold under FIFO, assuming Cambridge uses the periodic inventory system.

f. Compute ending inventory and cost of goods sold under average-cost, assuming Cambridge uses the periodic inventory system.

Data Analytics in Action

Using Data Visualization to Analyze Changes over Time

DA6.1 Data visualization can be used to analyze company changes over time.

Excel

Example: Recall the Feature Story "Where Is That Spare Bulldozer Blade?" presented in the chapter. One competitor to **Komatsu Ltd.** (JPN) is **Caterpillar** (USA), which continues to enhance its inventory management by improving its product sustainability in two ways. First, it is rebuilding used parts to like-new condition. Second, the company is remanufacturing usable inventory parts when customers trade-in or dispose of their used equipment. These actions not only reduce inventory costs but also enable Caterpillar to participate in the circular economy, where manufacturers take responsibility for their products at the end of the product lives. As noted in its 2019 sustainability report, Caterpillar has a goal of 20% growth in both rebuilding and remanufacturing.

Has Caterpillar reached this goal? A line chart can help you visualize the company's progress over time. What information can you obtain by examining the following chart?

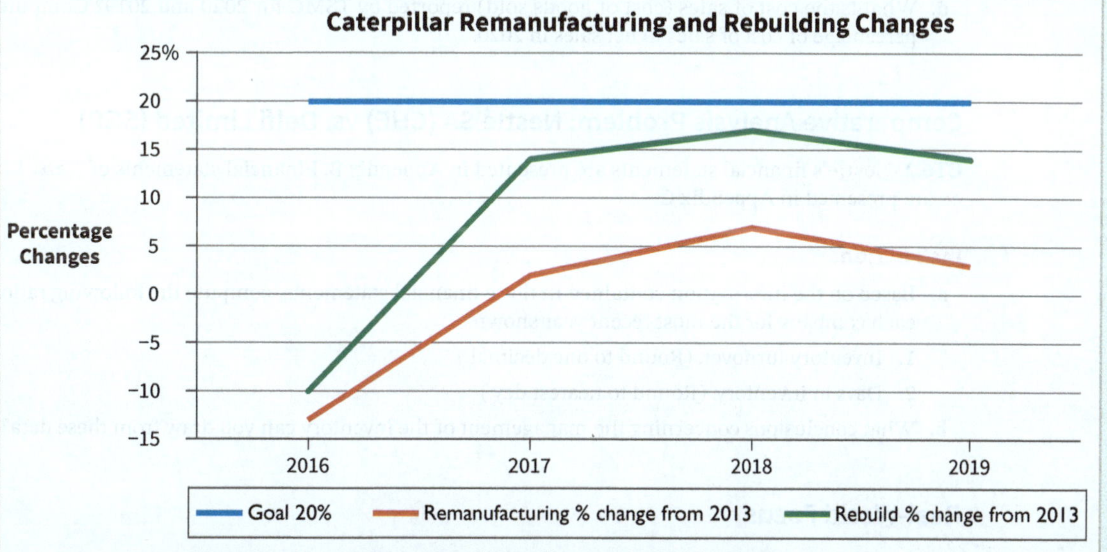

Source: Data from "ESG Data Center," *Caterpillar 2019 Sustainability Report.*

The chart indicates that while Caterpillar's goal has remained at 20%, the remanufacturing and rebuilding businesses are growing. The biggest increase in the growth of rebuilding occurred from 2016 to 2017. There was a decline from 2018 to 2019 in these initiatives as Caterpillar may have reached a peak that is leveling off due to new production that is more sustainable.

For this case, you will look more closely at specific Caterpillar data regarding its end-of-life returned materials and the percentage usable for recycling. You will create and analyze a combination column and line chart to determine how Caterpillar can increase its gross profit as it relates to these end-of-life materials.

Go to the Wiley online course for complete case details and instructions.

Using Data Analytics to Compare Companies' Inventory Turnover

Excel

DA6.2 Inventory turnover shows the number of times during the period a firm sells the entire financial value of its inventory. It is advantageous to turn over inventory more quickly to reduce the risk of obsolescence and spoilage. As such, companies often have a goal of increasing inventory turnover. For this case, you will use inventory turnover data for U.S. companies **Costco**, **Walmart**, **Target**, and **Amazon** to create and analyze scatter plots, as well as to calculate days' sales in inventory, to determine which company is managing its inventory levels most effectively.

Go to the Wiley online course for complete case details and instructions.

Expand Your Critical Thinking

Financial Reporting Problem: TSMC, Ltd. (TWN)

CT6.1 The notes that accompany a company's financial statements provide informative details that would clutter the amounts and descriptions presented in the statements. Refer to the financial statements of **TSMC** in Appendix A and the 2020 annual report's Notes to the Consolidated Financial Statements, available at the company's website.

Instructions

Answer the following questions. Complete the requirements in millions of new Taiwan dollars, as shown in TSMC's annual report.

a. What did TSMC report for the amount of inventories in its consolidated statement of financial position at December 31, 2020? At December 31, 2019?

b. Compute the new Taiwan dollar amount of change and the percentage change in inventories between 2019 and 2020. Compute inventory as a percentage of current assets at December 31, 2020.

c. How does TSMC value its inventories? Which inventory cost flow method does TSMC use? (See Notes to the Consolidated Financial Statements.)

d. What is the cost of sales (cost of goods sold) reported by TSMC for 2020 and 2019? Compute the percentage of cost of sales to net sales in 2020.

Comparative Analysis Problem: Nestlé SA (CHE) vs. Delfi Limited (SGP)

CT6.2 **Nestlé**'s financial statements are presented in Appendix B. Financial statements of **Delfi Limited** are presented in Appendix C.

Instructions

a. Based on the information contained in these financial statements, compute the following ratios for each company for the most recent year shown.

1. Inventory turnover. (Round to one decimal.)
2. Days in inventory. (Round to nearest day.)

b. What conclusions concerning the management of the inventory can you draw from these data?

Real-World Focus

CT6.3 A company's annual report usually will identify the inventory method used. Knowing that, you can analyze the effects of the inventory method on the income statement and statement of financial position.

Instructions

Answer the following questions based on the July 31, 2021, annual report of **Cisco** (USA), available online. Some questions will require you to consider information included in the notes to the financial statements.

a. At Cisco's fiscal year-end, what was the inventory on the balance sheet (statement of financial position)?

b. How has this changed from the previous fiscal year-end?

c. How much of the inventory was finished goods?

d. What inventory method does Cisco use?

CT6.4 All companies should take steps to prevent inventory theft. This exercise reviews ways that companies can reduce inventory-related frauds.

Instructions

Search online for the article entitled "6 Ways to Prevent Inventory Fraud in Your Business" by Darin Styles. Read the article and then answer the following questions.

a. What are the six steps outlined in the article?

b. What does the author describe as "segregation of duties"? What was the example given in the article?

c. What examples were given for "incorporating the element of surprise"?

d. Describe the method employing data analytics discussed in the article.

e. The article mentions "bill and hold arrangements." What legitimate reason might a customer have for requesting to purchase something using a bill-and-hold arrangement? What are the related fraud risks to the selling company?

Decision-Making Across the Organization

CT6.5 On April 10, 2029, fire damaged the office and warehouse of Ehlert Lighting. Most of the accounting records were destroyed, but the following account balances were determined as of March 31, 2029: Inventory (January 1, 2029), £80,000; Sales Revenue (January 1–March 31, 2029), £180,000; Purchases (January 1–March 31, 2029), £94,000.

The company's fiscal year ends on December 31. It uses a periodic inventory system.

From an analysis of the April bank statement, you discover cancelled checks of £4,200 for cash purchases during the period April 1–10. Deposits during the same period totaled £20,500. Of that amount, 60% were collections on accounts receivable, and the balance was cash sales.

Correspondence with the company's principal suppliers revealed £12,400 of purchases on account from April 1 to April 10. Of that amount, £1,900 was for merchandise in transit on April 10 that was shipped FOB destination.

Correspondence with the company's principal customers produced acknowledgments of credit sales totaling £37,000 from April 1 to April 10. It was estimated that £5,600 of credit sales will never be acknowledged or recovered from customers.

Ehlert Lighting reached an agreement with the insurance company that its fire-loss claim should be based on the average of the gross profit rates for the preceding 2 years. The financial statements for 2027 and 2028 showed the following data.

	2028	2027
Net sales	£600,000	£480,000
Cost of goods purchased	404,000	346,400
Beginning inventory	60,000	40,000
Ending inventory	80,000	60,000

Inventory with a cost of £17,000 was salvaged from the fire.

Instructions

With the class divided into groups, answer the following.

a. Determine the balances in (1) Sales Revenue and (2) Purchases at April 10.

***b.** Determine the average gross profit rate for the years 2027 and 2028. (*Hint:* Find the gross profit rate for each year and divide the sum by 2.)

***c.** Determine the inventory loss as a result of the fire, using the gross profit method.

Communication Activity

CT6.6 You are the controller of Classic Toys Ltd. Kathy McDonnell, the president, recently mentioned to you that she found an error in the 2028 financial statements, which she believes has corrected itself. She determined, in discussions with the Purchasing Department, that 2028 ending inventory was overstated by €1 million. Kathy says that the 2029 ending inventory is correct. Thus, she assumes that 2029 income is correct. Kathy says to you, "What happened has happened—there's no point in worrying about it anymore."

Instructions

You conclude that Kathy is incorrect. Write a brief, tactful email to Kathy, clarifying the situation.

Answers to Insight and Accounting Across the Organization Questions

A Big Hiccup Q: What steps might the companies take to avoid such a serious disruption in the future? **A:** The companies may need to consider more storage space to keep higher levels of inventory on hand to protect against future shortages. In addition, the companies might consider becoming less dependent on a single supplier in a single country.

Falsifying Inventory to Boost Income Q: What effect does an overstatement of inventory have on a company's financial statements? **A:** The statement of financial position looks stronger because inventory and retained earnings are overstated. The income statement looks better because cost of goods sold is understated and income is overstated.

Is LIFO Fair? Q: What are the arguments for and against the use of LIFO? **A:** Proponents of LIFO argue that it is conceptually superior because it matches the most recent cost with the most recent selling price. Critics contend that it artificially understates the company's net income and consequently reduces tax payments. Also, because most IFRS-based companies are not allowed to use LIFO, its use by U.S. companies makes analysis difficult.

Too Many Dresses or Too Few? Q: For fashion companies, what are the advantages and disadvantages of having excess inventory? **A:** An advantage of having a lot of inventory is that you reduce the likelihood that you will miss out on a opportunity to sell an item that a customer wants. Fashion trends are sometimes hard to spot. But by having a lot of inventory, you will be ready when a trend gets "hot." At the same time, excess inventory that is never sold creates waste and will potentially result in losses.

Dashboards: Seeing Is Believing Q: What benefits does a dashboard such as this one provide to a manager for making decisions regarding inventory? **A:** Dashboards provide a collection of views of key performance indicators all in one place. Dashboards are often dynamic, allowing the manager to perform "what if" analysis. Also, the dashboard enables the manager to zoom out or in to look at the whole company, divisions, regions, or particular product lines.

A Look at U.S. GAAP

LEARNING OBJECTIVE 8

Compare the accounting for inventories under IFRS and U.S. GAAP.

The major GAAP requirements related to accounting and reporting for inventories are the same as IFRS. The major difference is that GAAP permits the use of the LIFO cost flow assumption.

Key Points

- The requirements for accounting for and reporting inventories are more principles-based under IFRS. That is, GAAP provides more detailed guidelines in inventory accounting.
- IFRS requires companies to use the same cost flow assumption for all goods of a similar nature. GAAP has no specific requirement in this area.

Similarities

- The definitions for inventory are essentially similar under GAAP and IFRS. Both define inventory as assets held-for-sale in the ordinary course of business, in the process of production for sale (work in process), or to be consumed in the production of goods or services (e.g., raw materials).
- Who owns the goods—goods in transit or consigned goods—as well as the costs to include in inventory, are accounted for the same under GAAP and IFRS.
- Except for LIFO under GAAP, both IFRS and GAAP use the lower of cost or net realizable value for inventory valuation. Under GAAP, LIFO uses the market value instead of the net realizable value.

Differences

- Both GAAP and IFRS permit specific identification where appropriate. IFRS actually requires that the specific identification method be used where the inventory items are not interchangeable (i.e., can be specifically identified). If the inventory items are not specifically identifiable, a cost flow assumption is used. GAAP does not specify situations in which specific identification must be used.
- A major difference between GAAP and IFRS relates to the LIFO cost flow assumption. GAAP permits the use of LIFO for inventory valuation. IFRS prohibits its use. FIFO and average-cost are the only two acceptable cost flow assumptions permitted under IFRS.
- IFRS generally requires pre-harvest inventories of agricultural products (e.g., growing crops and farm animals) to be reported at the current value less cost of disposal. GAAP generally requires these items to be recorded at cost.

GAAP Practice

GAAP Self-Test Questions

1. Which of the following should **not** be included in the inventory of a company using GAAP?
   a. Goods held on consignment from another company.
   b. Goods shipped on consignment to another company.
   c. Goods in transit from another company shipped FOB shipping point.
   d. None of the answer choices is correct.

2. Which method of inventory costing is prohibited under IFRS?
   a. Specific identification.
   b. LIFO.
   c. FIFO.
   d. Average-cost.

GAAP Exercises

GAAP6.1 Briefly describe some of the similarities and differences between GAAP and IFRS with respect to the accounting for inventories.

GAAP6.2 LaTour Perfumes is based in France and prepares its financial statements in accordance with IFRS. In 2029, it reported cost of goods sold of €578 million and average inventory of €154 million. Briefly discuss how analysis of LaTour's inventory turnover (and comparisons to a company using GAAP) might be affected by differences in inventory accounting between IFRS and GAAP.

GAAP6.3 Franklin Company has the following four items in its ending inventory as of December 31, 2029. The company uses the lower of cost or market approach for its LIFO inventory valuation.

Item No.	Cost	Market
AB	$1,700	$1,400
TRX	2,200	2,300
NWA	7,800	7,100
SGH	3,000	3,700

Compute the lower of cost or market.

GAAP Financial Reporting Problem: Apple Inc. (USA)

GAAP6.4 The financial statements of **Apple** are presented in Appendix D. The complete annual report, including the notes to its financial statements, is available at the company's website.

Instructions

Answer the following questions. (Give the amounts in thousands of dollars, as shown in Apple's annual report.)

a. What did Apple report for the amount of inventories in its consolidated balance sheet at September 26, 2020? At September 28, 2019?

b. Compute the dollar amount of change and the percentage change in inventories between 2019 and 2020. Compute inventory as a percentage of current assets for 2020.

c. How does Apple value its inventory, and what cost flow assumption does it use?

d. What are the (product) cost of goods sold reported by Apple for 2020, 2019, and 2018? Compute the ratio of (product) cost of goods sold to net (product) sales in 2020.

Answers to GAAP Self-Test Questions

1. a **2.** b

CHAPTER 7

Fraud, Internal Control, and Cash

LEARNING OBJECTIVES After studying this chapter, you should be able to:

LO 1 Define fraud and the principles of internal control.
LO 2 Apply internal control principles to cash.
LO 3 Identify the control features of a bank account.
LO 4 Explain the reporting of cash.

Chapter Preview

As the following Feature Story about recording cash sales at **Nick's Steakhouse and Pizza** (CAN) indicates, control of cash is important to ensure that fraud does not occur. Companies also need controls to safeguard other types of assets. For example, Nick's undoubtedly has controls to prevent the theft of food and supplies, and controls to prevent the theft of tableware and dishes from its kitchen.

In this chapter, we explain the essential features of an internal control system and how it prevents fraud. We also describe how those controls apply to a specific asset—cash. The applications include some controls with which you may be already familiar, such as the use of a bank.

Fraud, Internal Control, and Cash

Fraud and Internal Control
- Fraud
- Internal control
- Principles of internal control activities
- Data analytics and internal controls
- Limitations of internal control

Cash Controls
- Cash receipts controls
- Cash disbursements controls
- Petty cash fund

Control Features of a Bank Account
- Making bank deposits
- Writing checks
- Electronic banking
- Bank statements
- Reconciling the bank account

Reporting Cash
- Cash equivalents
- Restricted cash

Practice

DO IT! 1 Control Activities
DO IT! 2a Control over Cash Receipts
2b Petty Cash Fund
DO IT! 3 Bank Reconciliation
DO IT! 4 Reporting Cash

Go to the Review and Practice section at the end of the chapter for a review of key concepts and practice applications with solutions.
Additional tutorials and practice opportunities are available in the Wiley online course.

Feature Story Minding the Money at Nick's

Nick Petros, the founder of **Nick's Steakhouse and Pizza** (CAN) in Calgary, came to Canada from Greece at age 17 with no money and speaking no English. For 25 years, he worked his way up the ranks in the restaurant industry, as a dishwasher, busboy, waiter, maître d', and then manager. In 1979, he combined his industry experience with a collection of his mother's homemade recipes to open his own restaurant. Nick's son Mark took over the business in 2000.

Over the course of a busy Friday or Saturday evening, up to 11 servers and three bartenders serve as many as 1,200 people in the 650-square-meter restaurant and bar. Mark Petros says his point-of-sale (POS) system helps him keep track of the orders, inventory, and money.

After taking a table's order, servers enter the items they require into one of six computer terminals located throughout the restaurant. The computer is preprogrammed with the item and its price so that the server simply presses a labelled button, for example, "Caesar salad" or "lasagna," to enter an order. The POS system sends the order information to the bar, salad station, or line cooks, and uses the information to track inventory. The servers collect payment from their tables. At the end of a shift, the POS system provides an employee report that itemizes the credit card, debit card, and cash sales that the server generated.

The bartenders and servers have a cash float of $400. The hosting staff also has a float to use for pickup orders and in case the servers need change for large bills. Mr. Petros explains, "When an employee with a float starts the shift, he or she makes sure that the cash on hand is equal to the float plus any orders taken so far that day. At the end of their shift, the same calculation is done to see if it balances out, or else they are responsible for the missing money."

Similarly, before the bartenders start their shift, they have to count the beer in the fridges and note the levels in partially full bottles of alcohol. Everything must correspond to the POS system. For example, if three beers are missing from the fridge, three beers should have been entered in the system. If they weren't, the bartender is responsible.

"There's never a discrepancy," says Mr. Petros. If there ever is one, he adds, it's easy to find the problem, usually an error in pushing a button or entering information.

TPG/Shutterstock

7.1 Fraud and Internal Control

LEARNING OBJECTIVE 1

Define fraud and the principles of internal control.

The Feature Story describes many of the internal control procedures used by **Nick's Steakhouse and Pizza** (CAN). These procedures are necessary to discourage employees from fraudulent activities.

Fraud

A **fraud** is a dishonest act by an employee that results in personal benefit to the employee at a cost to the employer. Examples of fraud reported in the financial press include the following.

- A bookkeeper in a small company diverted €750,000 of bill payments to a personal bank account over a three-year period.
- A shipping clerk with 28 years of service shipped $125,000 of merchandise to himself.
- A computer operator embezzled $21 million from **Wells Fargo Bank** (USA) over a two-year period.
- Drivers for a large Chinese ride-sharing service defrauded the company by partnering with customers who booked fake rides and then shared the driver's bonus received from the company for distances driven.

Why does fraud occur? The three main factors that contribute to fraudulent activity are depicted by the **fraud triangle** in **Illustration 7.1**.

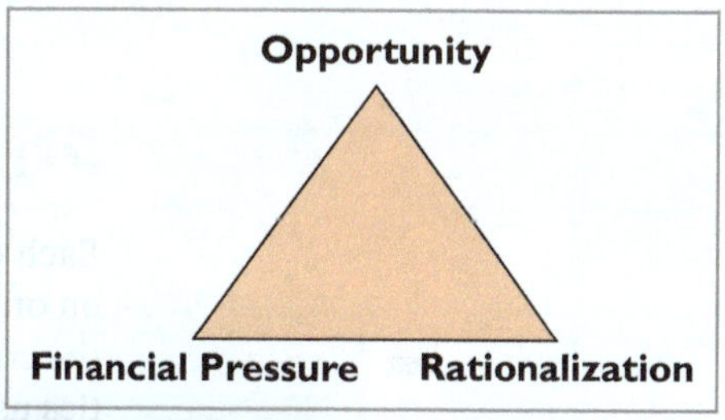

ILLUSTRATION 7.1 **Fraud triangle**

1. **Opportunity**. Opportunities to engage in fraud occur when the workplace lacks sufficient controls to deter and detect fraud. For example, inadequate monitoring of employee actions can create opportunities for theft and can embolden employees because they believe they will not be caught.
2. **Financial pressure**. Employees sometimes commit fraud because of personal financial problems caused by too much debt. Or, they might commit fraud because they want to lead a lifestyle that they cannot afford on their current salary.
3. **Rationalization**. In order to justify their fraud, employees rationalize their dishonest actions. For example, employees sometimes justify fraud because they believe they are underpaid while the employer is making lots of money. Employees feel justified in stealing because they believe they deserve to be paid more.

Internal Control

Internal control is a process designed to provide reasonable assurance regarding the achievement of company objectives related to operations, reporting, and compliance. In more detail, the purposes of internal control are to safeguard assets, enhance the reliability of accounting records, increase efficiency of operations, and ensure compliance with laws and regulations. Internal control systems have five primary components as listed below.[1]

1. **A control environment**. It is the responsibility of top management to make it clear that the organization values integrity and that unethical activity will not be tolerated. This component is often referred to as the "tone at the top."
2. **Risk assessment**. Companies must identify and analyze the various factors that create risk for the business and must determine how to manage these risks.
3. **Control activities**. To reduce the occurrence of fraud, management must design policies and procedures to address the specific risks faced by the company.
4. **Information and communication**. The internal control system must capture and communicate all pertinent information both down and up the organization, as well as communicate information to appropriate external parties.
5. **Monitoring**. Internal control systems must be monitored periodically for their adequacy. Significant deficiencies need to be reported to top management and/or the board of directors.

---

[1] Stephan J. McNally, "The 2013 COSO Framework and SOX Compliance," *Strategic Finance* (June 2013). The COSO definition of internal control is widely accepted around the world. See, for example, OECD, "Internal Control and Internal Audit: Ensuring Public Sector Integrity and Accountability" (April 2011).

Environmental, Social, and Governance Insight

BeholdingEye/Getty Images

And the Controls Are . . .

Internal controls are important for an effective financial reporting system. The same is true for sustainability reporting. An effective system of internal controls for sustainability reporting will help in the following ways: (1) prevent the unauthorized use of data; (2) provide reasonable assurance that the information is accurate, valid, and complete; and (3) report information that is consistent with overall sustainability accounting policies. With these types of controls, users will have the confidence that they can use the sustainability information effectively.

Some regulators are calling for even more assurance through audits of this information. Companies that potentially can cause environmental damage through greenhouse gases, as well as companies in the mining and extractive industries, are subject to reporting requirements. And, as demand for more information in the sustainability area expands, the need for audits of this information will grow.

Why is sustainability information important to investors? (Answer is available near the end of the chapter.)

Principles of Internal Control Activities

Each of the five components of an internal control system is important. Here, we will focus on one component, the control activities. The reason? These activities are the backbone of the company's efforts to address the risks it faces, such as fraud. The specific control activities used by a company will vary, depending on management's assessment of the risks faced. This assessment is heavily influenced by the size and nature of the company.

The six principles of control activities are as follows.

- Establishment of responsibility
- Segregation of duties
- Documentation procedures
- Physical controls
- Independent internal verification
- Human resource controls

We explain these principles in the following sections. You should recognize that they apply to most companies and are relevant to both manual and computerized accounting systems.

Establishment of Responsibility

Transfer of cash drawers

An essential principle of internal control is to assign responsibility to specific employees. **Control is most effective when only one person is responsible for a given task.**

To illustrate, assume that the cash on hand at the end of the day in an e-mart (KOR) supermarket is ₩100 short of the cash entered in the cash register. If only one person has operated the register, the shift manager can quickly determine responsibility for the shortage. If two or more individuals have worked the register, it may be impossible to determine who is responsible for the error.

Many retailers solve this problem by having registers with multiple drawers. This makes it possible for more than one person to operate a register but still allows identification of a particular employee with a specific drawer. Only the signed-in cashier has access to his or her drawer.

Establishing responsibility often requires limiting access only to authorized personnel, and then identifying those personnel. For example, the automated systems used by many companies have mechanisms such as identifying passcodes that keep track of who made a journal entry, who entered a sale, or who went into an inventory storeroom at a particular time. Use of identifying passcodes enables the company to establish responsibility by identifying the particular employee who carried out the activity.

Anatomy of a Fraud

Maureen Frugali was a training supervisor for claims processing at Colossal Healthcare. As a standard part of the claims-processing training program, Maureen created fictitious claims for use by trainees. These fictitious claims were then sent to the accounts payable department.

After the training claims had been processed, Maureen was to notify Accounts Payable of all fictitious claims, so that they would not be paid. However, she did not inform Accounts Payable about every fictitious claim. She created some fictitious claims for entities that she controlled (that is, she would receive the payment), and she let Accounts Payable pay her.

Total take: $11 million

The Missing Control

Establishment of responsibility. The healthcare company did not adequately restrict the responsibility for authorizing and approving claims transactions. The training supervisor should not have been authorized to create claims in the company's "live" system.

Source: Adapted from Wells, *Fraud Casebook* (2007), pp. 61–70.

Segregation of Duties

Segregation of duties is indispensable in an internal control system. There are two common applications of this principle:

1. Different individuals should be responsible for related activities.
2. The responsibility for recordkeeping for an asset should be separate from the physical custody of that asset.

The rationale for segregation of duties is this: **The work of one employee should, without a duplication of effort, provide a reliable basis for evaluating the work of another employee.** For example, the personnel that design and program computerized systems should not be assigned duties related to day-to-day use of the system. Otherwise, they could design the system to benefit them personally and conceal the fraud through day-to-day use.

Segregation of Related Activities **Making one individual responsible for related activities increases the potential for errors and irregularities.**

Purchasing Activities Companies should, for example, assign related **purchasing activities** to different individuals. Related purchasing activities include ordering merchandise, approving orders, receiving goods, authorizing payment, and paying for goods or services. Various frauds are possible when one person handles related purchasing activities:

- If a purchasing agent is allowed to order goods without obtaining supervisory approval, the likelihood of the purchasing agent receiving kickbacks from suppliers increases.
- If an employee who orders goods also handles the invoice and receipt of the goods, as well as payment authorization, he or she might authorize payment for a fictitious invoice.

These abuses are less likely to occur when companies divide the purchasing tasks.

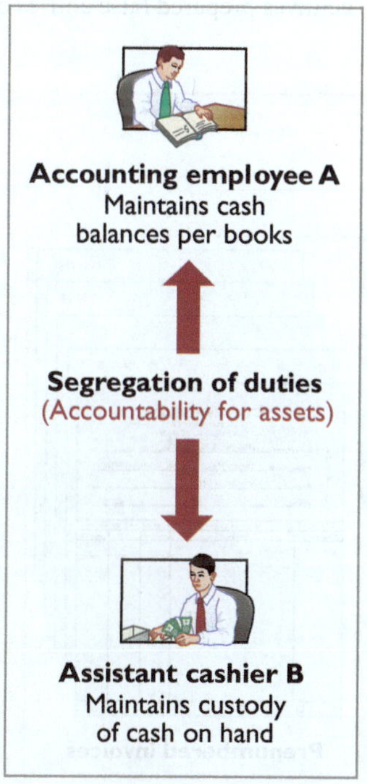

Sales Activities Similarly, companies should assign related **sales activities** to different individuals. Related selling activities include making a sale, shipping (or delivering) the goods to the customer, billing the customer, and receiving payment. Various frauds are possible when one person handles related sales activities:

- If a salesperson can make a sale without obtaining supervisory approval, he or she might make sales at unauthorized prices to increase sales commissions.
- A shipping clerk who also has access to accounting records could ship goods to himself.
- A billing clerk who handles billing and receipt could understate the amount billed for sales made to friends and relatives.

These abuses are less likely to occur when companies divide the sales tasks. The salespeople make the sale, the shipping department ships the goods on the basis of the sales order, and the billing department prepares the sales invoice after comparing the sales order with the report of goods shipped.

Anatomy of a Fraud

Ronald Lee was the owner of an aluminum casting business in Malaysia. After several years of successful operations, he began incurring extravagant expenditures for travel and other luxury items. In order to fund his new lifestyle, Ronald began to steal money from his own company. The scam was committed by the company making payments for aluminum ingots that were never received by the company.

The payments for the fraudulent orders were made by the company's controllers with full knowledge that they were not actual shipments received, which allowed the fraud to avoid being detected by the company's auditors. The payments were made to a company owned by Mr. Lee's cousin. The checks were made out to Cash, which allowed Mr. Lee to deposit them directly into his own account.

The fraud was discovered when an outside investor hired a forensic accountant to investigate the large losses being incurred by the company.

Total take: RM20,757,500

The Missing Control

Segregation of duties. While it is common for the controller to prepare and authorize checks, this person should not be responsible to reconcile the bank account. During the reconciliation it is possible that questions could be raised about large checks made out to cash.

Source: Adapted from Wells, *Fraud Casebook* (2011), pp. 265–272.

Segregation of Recordkeeping from Physical Custody The accountant should have neither physical custody of the asset nor access to it. Likewise, the custodian of the asset should not maintain or have access to the accounting records. **The custodian of the asset is not likely to convert the asset to personal use when one employee maintains the record of the asset, and a different employee has physical custody of the asset.** The separation of accounting responsibility from the custody of assets is especially important for cash and inventories because these assets are very vulnerable to fraud.

Anatomy of a Fraud

In some countries, it is common for a company to own its own bank. This bank loans money to its employees, collecting payments directly from the employees' paychecks. Such an arrangement was in place in Kenya when three executives decided to take advantage of the structure.

These executives began to make loans to themselves and also to members of the company's board. To cover their tracks, the executives prepared false entries on the records of the bank.

Total take: KSh1,669,500

The Missing Control

Segregation of duties. It is critical that the authorization, recordkeeping, and custody of assets stay separated. In this case, since the executives had both the authority to approve loans and also were responsible to keep the records for the bank, they were able to conceal their fraudulent behavior.

Source: Adapted from Wells, *Fraud Casebook* (2011), pp. 177–185.

Documentation Procedures

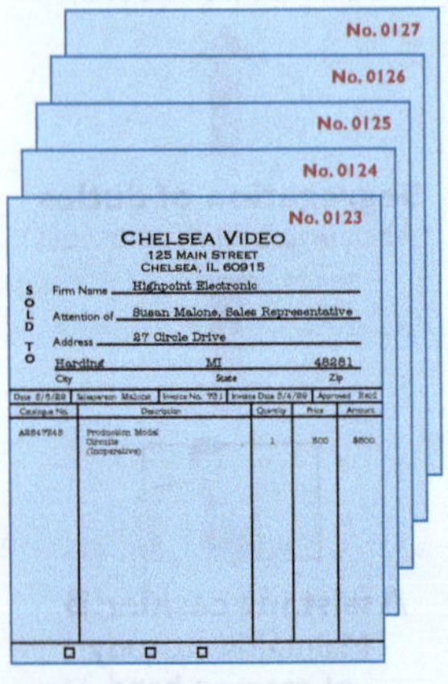

Prenumbered invoices

Documents provide evidence that transactions and events have occurred. For example, point-of-sale terminals are networked with a company's computing and accounting records, which results in direct documentation.

Similarly, a shipping document indicates that the goods have been shipped, and a sales invoice indicates that the company has billed the customer for the goods. By requiring signatures (or initials) on the documents, the company can identify the individual(s) responsible for the transaction or event. Companies should document transactions when they occur.

Companies should establish two procedures for documents.

1. Whenever possible, companies should use **prenumbered documents, and all documents should be accounted for**. Prenumbering helps to prevent a transaction from being recorded more than once, or conversely, from not being recorded at all.
2. The control system should require that employees **promptly forward source documents for accounting entries to the accounting department. This control measure helps to ensure timely recording of the transaction** and contributes directly to the accuracy and reliability of the accounting records.

Anatomy of a Fraud

To support their reimbursement requests for travel costs incurred, employees at Mod Fashions' design center were required to submit receipts. The receipts could include the detailed bill provided for a meal, the credit card receipt provided when the credit card payment is made, or a copy of the employee's monthly credit card bill that listed the item.

A number of the designers who frequently traveled together came up with a fraud scheme: They submitted claims for the same expenses. For example, if they had a meal together that cost €200, one person submitted the detailed meal bill, another submitted the credit card receipt, and a third submitted a monthly credit card bill showing the meal as a line item. Thus, all three received a €200 reimbursement.

Total take: €75,000

The Missing Control

Documentation procedures. Mod Fashions should require the original, detailed receipt. It should not accept photocopies, and it should not accept credit card statements. In addition, documentation procedures could be further improved by requiring the use of a company credit card (rather than a personal credit card) for all business expenses.

Source: Adapted from Wells, *Fraud Casebook* (2007), pp. 79–90.

Physical Controls

Use of physical controls is essential. **Physical controls** relate to the safeguarding of assets and enhance the accuracy and reliability of the accounting records. **Illustration 7.2** shows examples of these controls.

ILLUSTRATION 7.2 **Physical controls**

Physical Controls

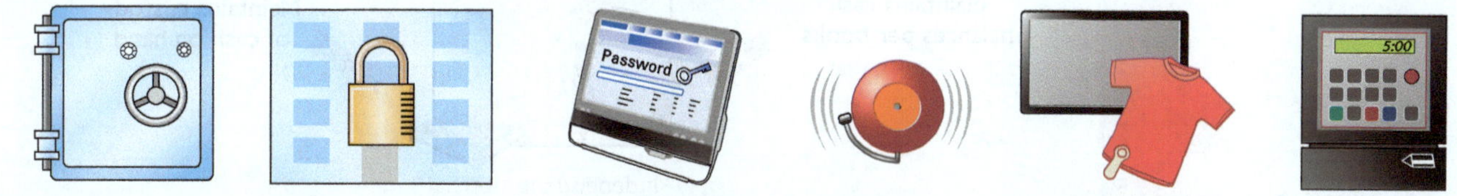

Safes, vaults, and safety deposit boxes for cash and business papers

Locked warehouses and storage cabinets for inventories and records

Computer facilities with passkey access or fingerprint or eyeball scans

Alarms to prevent break-ins

Security monitors and garment sensors to deter theft

Time clocks for recording time worked

Anatomy of a Fraud

At Centerstone Health, a large insurance company, the mailroom each day received insurance applications from prospective customers. Mailroom employees scanned the applications into electronic documents before the applications were processed. Once the applications were scanned, they could be accessed online by authorized employees.

Insurance agents at Centerstone Health earn commissions based upon successful applications. The sales agent's name is listed on the application. However, roughly 15% of the applications are from customers who did not work with a sales agent. Two friends—Alex, an employee in recordkeeping, and Parviz, a sales agent—thought up a way to perpetrate a fraud. Alex identified scanned applications that did not list a sales agent. After business hours, he entered the mailroom and found the hard-copy applications that did not show a sales agent. He wrote in Parviz's name as the sales agent and then rescanned the application for processing. Parviz received the commission, which the friends then split.

Total take: £240,000

The Missing Control

Physical controls. Centerstone Health lacked two basic physical controls that could have prevented this fraud. First, the mailroom should have been locked during non-business hours, and access during business hours should have been tightly controlled. Second, the scanned applications supposedly could be accessed only by authorized employees using their passwords. However, the password for each employee was the same as the employee's user ID. Since employee user-ID numbers were available to all other employees, all employees knew each other's passwords. Thus, Alex could enter the system using another employee's password and access the scanned applications.

Source: Adapted from Wells, *Fraud Casebook* (2007), pp. 316–326.

Independent Internal Verification

Most internal control systems provide for **independent internal verification**. This principle involves the review of data prepared by employees. To obtain maximum benefit from independent internal verification:

1. Companies should verify records periodically or on a surprise basis.
2. An employee who is independent of the personnel responsible for the information should make the verification.
3. Discrepancies and exceptions should be reported to a management level that can take appropriate corrective action.

Independent internal verification is especially useful in comparing recorded accountability with existing assets. The reconciliation of the electronic journal with the cash in the point-of-sale terminal at **Nick's Steakhouse and Pizza** is an example of this internal control principle. Other common examples are the reconciliation of a company's cash balance per books with the cash balance per bank, and the verification of the perpetual inventory records through a count of physical inventory. **Illustration 7.3** shows the relationship between this principle and the segregation of duties principle.

ILLUSTRATION 7.3

Comparison of segregation of duties principle with independent internal verification principle

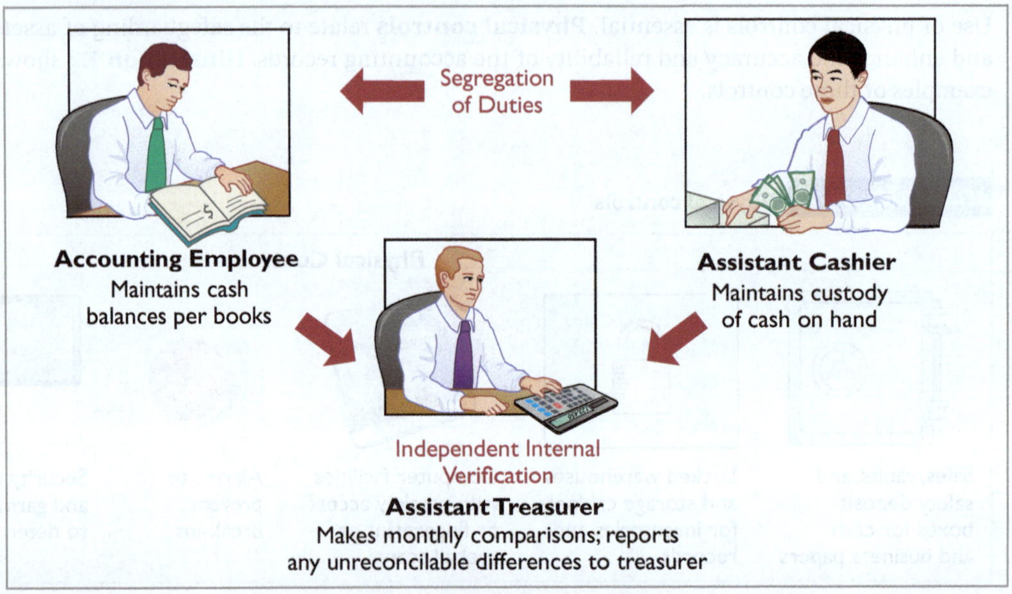

Anatomy of a Fraud

Bobbi Donnelly, the office manager for Mod Fashions' design center, was responsible for preparing the design center budget and reviewing expense reports submitted by design center employees. Her desire to upgrade her wardrobe got the better of her, and she enacted a fraud that involved filing expense-reimbursement requests for her own personal clothing purchases.

Bobbi was able to conceal the fraud because she was responsible for reviewing all expense reports, including her own. In addition, she sometimes was given ultimate responsibility for signing off on the expense reports when her boss was "too busy." Also, because she controlled the budget, when she submitted her expenses, she coded them to budget items that she knew were running under budget, so that they would not catch anyone's attention.

Total take: €275,000

The Missing Control

Independent internal verification. Bobbi's boss should have verified her expense reports. When asked what he thought her expenses for a year were, the boss said about €10,000. At €115,000 per year, her actual expenses were more than 10 times what would have been expected. However, because he was "too busy" to verify her expense reports or to review the budget, he never noticed.

Source: Adapted from Wells, *Fraud Casebook* (2007), pp. 79–90.

Large companies often assign independent internal verification to internal auditors. **Internal auditors** are company employees who continuously evaluate the effectiveness of the company's internal control systems. They review the activities of departments and individuals to determine whether prescribed internal controls are being followed. They also recommend improvements when needed. For example, **WorldCom** (USA) was at one time the second largest U.S. telecommunications company. The fraud that caused its bankruptcy (the largest ever when it occurred) involved billions of dollars. It was uncovered by an internal auditor.

Human Resource Controls

Human resource control activities include the following.

1. **Bond employees who handle cash.** **Bonding** involves obtaining insurance protection against theft by employees. It contributes to the safeguarding of cash in two ways. First, the insurance company carefully screens all individuals before adding them to the policy and may reject risky applicants. Second, bonded employees know that the insurance company will vigorously prosecute all offenders.
2. **Rotate employees' duties and require employees to take vacations.** These measures deter employees from attempting thefts since they will not be able to permanently conceal their improper actions. Many banks, for example, have discovered employee thefts when the employee was on vacation or assigned to a new position.
3. **Conduct thorough background checks.** Many believe that the most important and inexpensive measure any business can take to reduce employee theft and fraud is for the human resource department to conduct thorough background checks. Two tips: (1) Check to see whether job applicants actually graduated from the schools they list. (2) Never use telephone numbers for previous employers provided by the applicant. Always look them up yourself.

Anatomy of a Fraud

Ellen Lowry was the desk manager and Josephine Rodriguez was the head of housekeeping at the Excelsior Inn, a luxury hotel. The two best friends were so dedicated to their jobs that they never took vacations, and they frequently filled in for other employees. In fact, Josephine, whose job as head of housekeeping did not include cleaning rooms, often cleaned rooms herself, "just to help the staff keep up."

These two "dedicated" employees, working as a team, found a way to earn a little more cash. Ellen, the desk manager, provided significant discounts to guests who paid with cash. She kept the cash and did not register the guests in the hotel's computerized system. Instead, she took the room out of circulation "due to routine maintenance." Because the room did not show up as being used, it did not receive a normal housekeeping assignment. Instead, Josephine, the head of housekeeping, cleaned the rooms during the guests' stay.

Total take: $95,000

The Missing Control

Human resource controls. Ellen, the desk manager, had been fired by a previous employer after being accused of fraud. If the Excelsior Inn had conducted a thorough background check, it would not have hired her. The hotel fraud was detected when Ellen missed work for a few days due to illness. A system of mandatory vacations and rotating days off would have increased the chances of detecting the fraud before it became so large.

Source: Adapted from Wells, *Fraud Casebook* (2007), pp. 145–155.

Accounting Across the Organization

Stockbyte/Getty Images

Internal Control and the Role of Human Resources

Companies need to keep track of employees' degrees and certifications to ensure that employees continue to meet the specified requirements of a job. Also, to ensure proper employee supervision and proper separation of duties, companies must develop and monitor an organizational chart.

When one company went through this exercise, it found that out of 17,000 employees, there were 400 people who did not report to anyone. The company also had 35 people who reported to each other. In addition, if an employee complains of an unfair firing and mentions financial issues at the company, the human resource department must refer the case to the company audit committee and possibly to its legal counsel.

Why would unsupervised employees or employees who report to each other represent potential internal control threats? (Answer is available near the end of the chapter.)

Data Analytics and Internal Controls

Data analytics has dramatically changed many aspects of internal control practices. In the past, internal and external auditors tended to rely heavily on investigations of period-end samples of transactions to identify potential violations. Now, rather than wait for a period-end sample, many companies employ continuous monitoring of virtually every transaction. As a result, spikes in certain types of activity or developing trends are more quickly identified and investigated.

- **Many different aspects of journal entries can be monitored continuously**. For example, systems can automatically identify who recorded a particular journal entry. This helps to ensure that the segregation of duties control principle is not violated.
- **Large dollar amounts in risky areas can also be flagged and investigated quickly**. Recipients of payments can be easily screened to ensure, for example, that bonus amounts are correctly determined based on results and bonus formulas, and that bonuses are only paid to employees who are designated for bonus payments.

Limitations of Internal Control

HELPFUL HINT

Controls may vary with the risk level of the activity. For example, management may consider cash to be high risk and maintaining inventories in the stockroom as low risk. Thus, management would have stricter controls for cash.

Companies generally design their systems of internal control to provide **reasonable assurance** of proper safeguarding of assets and reliability of the accounting records. The concept of reasonable assurance rests on the premise that the costs of establishing control procedures should not exceed their expected benefit (see **Helpful Hint**).

To illustrate, consider shoplifting losses in retail stores. Stores could eliminate such losses by having a security guard stop and search customers as they leave the store. But store managers have concluded that the negative effects of such a procedure cannot be justified. Instead, they have attempted to control shoplifting losses by less costly procedures. They post signs saying, "We reserve the right to inspect all packages" and "All shoplifters will be prosecuted." They use hidden cameras and store detectives to monitor customer activity, and they install sensor equipment at exits.

No system of internal control is perfect. Generally, two major limitations are inherent in internal control systems.

1. **The human element**. A good system can become ineffective as a result of employee fatigue, carelessness, or indifference. For example, a receiving clerk may not bother to count goods received and may just "fudge" the counts. Occasionally, two or more individuals may work together to get around prescribed controls. Such **collusion** can significantly reduce the effectiveness of a system, eliminating the protection offered by segregation of duties. No system of internal control is perfect.
2. **The size of the business.** Small companies often find it difficult to segregate duties or to provide for independent internal verification.

ACTION PLAN

- **Familiarize yourself with each of the control activities.**
- **Understand the nature of the frauds that each control activity is intended to address.**

DO IT! 1 | Control Activities

Identify which control activity is violated in each of the following situations, and explain how the situation creates an opportunity for a fraud.

1. The person with primary responsibility for reconciling the bank account and making all bank deposits is also the company's accountant.
2. Wellstone Company's treasurer received an award for distinguished service because he had not taken a vacation in 30 years.
3. In order to save money spent on order slips and to reduce time spent keeping track of order slips, a local bar/restaurant does not buy prenumbered order slips.

Solution

1. Violates the control activity of segregation of duties. Recordkeeping should be separate from physical custody. As a consequence, the employee could embezzle cash and make journal entries to hide the theft.
2. Violates the control activity of human resource controls. Key employees must take vacations. Otherwise, the treasurer, who manages the company's cash, might embezzle cash and use his position to conceal the theft.

3. Violates the control activity of documentation procedures. If prenumbered documents are not used, then it is virtually impossible to account for the documents. As a consequence, an employee could write up a dinner sale, receive the cash from the customer, and then throw away the order slip and keep the cash.

Related exercise material: **BE7.1, BE7.2, BE7.3, BE7.4, DO IT! 7.1, E7.1, E7.2, E7.3, E7.5, and E7.6.**

7.2 Cash Controls

LEARNING OBJECTIVE 2

Apply internal control principles to cash.

Cash is the one asset that is readily convertible into any other type of asset. It also is easily concealed and transported, and is highly desired.

- Because of these characteristics, **cash is the asset most susceptible to fraudulent activities.**
- In addition, because of the large volume of cash transactions, numerous errors may occur in executing and recording them.

To safeguard cash and to ensure the accuracy of the accounting records for cash, effective internal control over cash is critical.

Cash Receipts Controls

Illustration 7.4 shows how the internal control principles explained earlier apply to cash receipts transactions. As you might expect, companies vary considerably in how they apply these principles. To illustrate internal control over cash receipts, we will examine control activities for a retail store with both over-the-counter and electronic and check receipts.

ILLUSTRATION 7.4 **Application of internal control principles to cash receipts**

Cash Receipts Controls

Establishment of Responsibility
Authorize only designated personnel to handle cash receipts (cashiers)

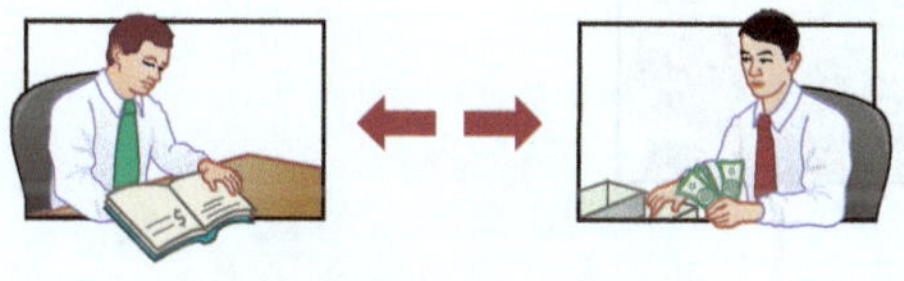

Segregation of Duties
Have different individuals handle cash and record cash receipts

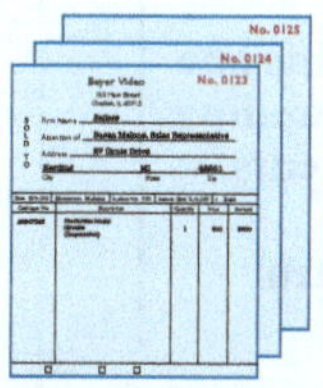

Documentation Procedures
Use remittance advice (mail receipts), cash register tapes, point-of-sale (POS) system reports, and deposit slips or confirmations

Physical Controls
Store cash in safes with limited access; use cash registers or point-of-sale (POS) terminals; deposit cash daily

Independent Internal Verification
Supervisors count cash receipts daily; accountant compares total receipts to bank deposits daily

Human Resource Controls
Bond personnel who handle cash; require employees to take vacations; conduct background checks

Over-the-Counter Receipts

In retail businesses, control of over-the-counter receipts centers on cash registers. With the increase in cloud-based computing, point-of-sale (POS) cash register systems have become affordable even for most small businesses. Most retail businesses receive payment with cash, credit cards, or debit cards. Staff members who operate cash registers (physical control) are each given cash, called "float" (assignment of responsibility) to make change for customers who pay cash. All sales must be entered into the register through the POS software, which records the sale (documentation) at the proper price, often simply by scanning a bar code.

- A big advantage of POS systems is that they update inventory records at the time of sale if the company is using a perpetual inventory system.
- This increases the company's ability to decrease employee theft by frequently reconciling inventory records with the actual amount of inventory on shelves.

At the end of a shift, staff members count the cash to ensure it agrees with the amount reported in the system, and then they report the count to a supervisor. A supervisor double-checks the amount (independent internal verification) and then prepares a deposit slip.

Access to the system should be restricted (physical control) so that cashiers cannot adjust the amount and type of sales recorded at the register to understate reported sales. Without these controls, the cashiers could hide the fact that they have taken cash. Employees must also ensure that the receipts are on-hand for sales made by debit or credit cards and that these match sales that were recorded with this type of payment. (For point-of-sale systems, the accounting department receives information on daily transactions and totals through the computer network.) **Illustration 7.5** summarizes this process (see **Helpful Hint**).

ILLUSTRATION 7.5

Control of over-the-counter receipts

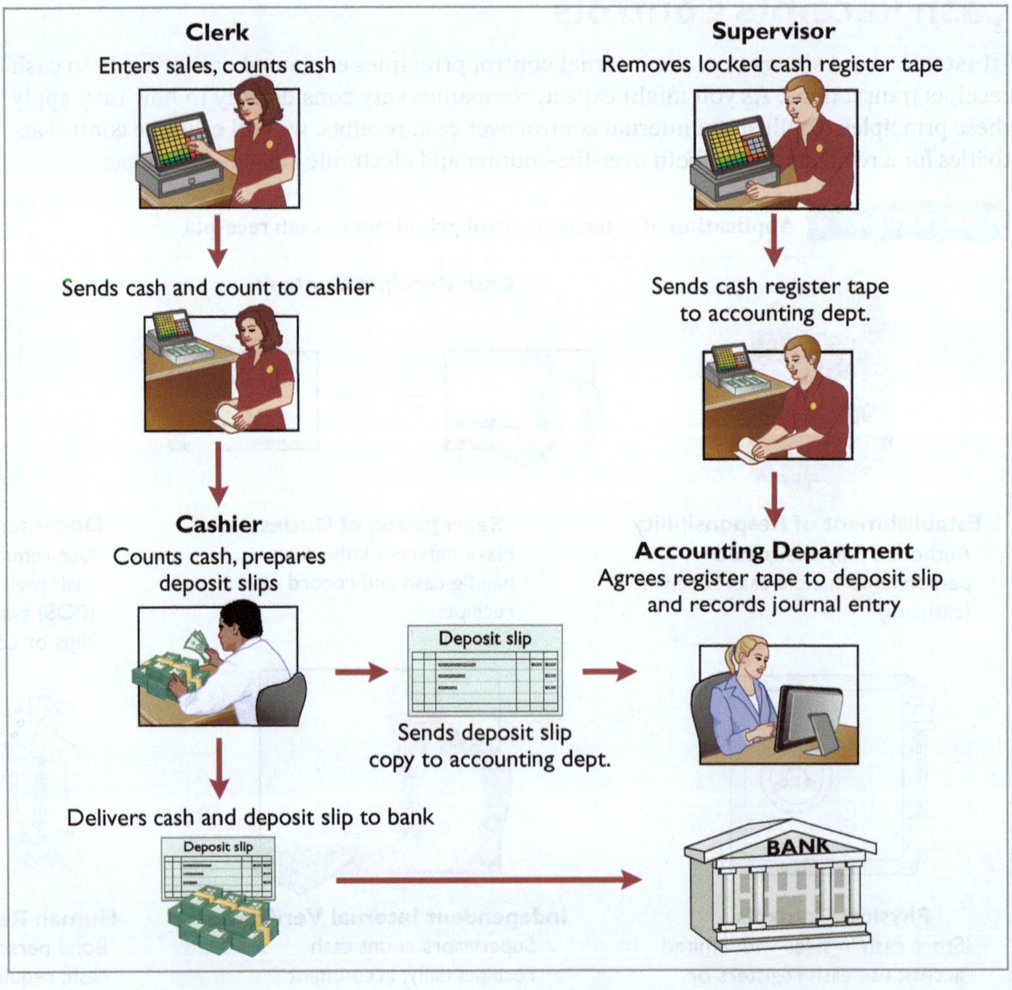

HELPFUL HINT

Flowcharts such as this one enhance the understanding of the flow of documents, the processing steps, and the internal control procedures.

This system for handling cash receipts uses an important internal control principle—segregation of recordkeeping from physical custody.

- The supervisor has access to the cash register tape but **not** to the cash.
- The clerk and the cashier have access to the cash but **not** to the register tape.
- In addition, the cash register tape provides documentation and enables independent internal verification.
- Use of these three principles of internal control (segregation of recordkeeping from physical custody, documentation, and independent internal verification) provides an effective system of internal control. Any attempt at fraudulent activity should be detected unless there is collusion among the employees.

In some instances, the amount deposited at the bank will not agree with the cash recorded in the accounting records based on the cash register tape. These differences often result because the clerk hands incorrect change back to the retail customer. In this case, the difference between the actual cash and the amount reported on the cash register tape is reported in a Cash Over and Short account. For example, suppose that the cash register tape indicated sales of ₺6,956 but the amount of cash was only ₺6,946. A cash shortfall of ₺10 exists. To account for this cash shortfall and related cash, the company makes the following entry.

Cash	6,946	
Cash Over and Short	10	
Sales Revenue		6,956
(To record cash shortfall)		

A	=	L	+	E
+6,946				
				−10
				+6,956

Cash Flows
+6,946

Cash Over and Short is an income statement item. It is reported as miscellaneous expense when there is a cash shortfall, and as miscellaneous revenue when there is an overage. Clearly, the amount should be small. Any material amounts in this account should be investigated.

Electronic Receipts

Electronic funds transfer (EFT) uses wire, telephone, or computers to transfer funds from one location to another. Examples of EFTs include the following.

- Direct deposit of payroll amounts to employees.
- Online bill payments for utilities and loans.
- Use of a debit card at point-of-sale (POS) terminals.

Not only do many businesses rely on EFTs as an efficient way to manage their cash, they also depend on their banks to maintain strong internal controls to safeguard it.

Because EFT does not involve employees handling cash, it reduces some of the opportunities for employee theft. However, opportunities still exist, especially in businesses that lack proper controls. Without assignment of responsibility or segregation of duties, an employee might redirect funds into a personal account and hide the theft with fraudulent accounting entries.

Check Receipts

Although the use of checks by retail customers has diminished significantly, checks continue to be used in business-to-business transactions. When a check is received at the time of sale, it will be included in the cash register and form part of an employee's reconciliation of daily sales to cash on hand.

- When a check is received in the mail, it is usually accompanied by a remittance advice, which is the detachable part of the invoice that customers are asked to send back with the check.
- Mailroom employees send the remittance advices to the accountants responsible for recording cash receipts, who then send the checks to another employee, who then deposits the checks at the bank (segregation of duties).

- The employee making the bank deposit should have no recordkeeping duties so that he or she is prevented from stealing the cash and covering up the theft by understating the value of cash receipt journal entries.

The person making the bank deposit will receive a bank-stamped deposit slip. Each day, an independent employee compares the amount of cash deposited per the deposit slip with the amount of cash receipts recorded that day to ensure the funds deposited were also recorded. If duties are segregated this way, no one employee would be able to steal and also be able to record the receipts to cover up the theft. The independent internal verification of the deposit slips further strengthens the controls over check receipts.

ACTION PLAN

- **Differentiate among the internal control principles of (1) establishing responsibility, (2) using physical controls, and (3) independent internal verification.**
- **Design an effective system of internal control over cash receipts.**

DO IT! 2a | Control over Cash Receipts

L. R. Cortez is concerned about the control over cash receipts in his fast-food restaurant, Big Cheese. The restaurant has two cash registers. At no time do more than two employees take customer orders and enter sales. Work shifts for employees range from 4 to 8 hours. Cortez asks your help in installing a good system of internal control over cash receipts.

Solution

Cortez should assign a separate cash register drawer to each employee at the start of each work shift, with register totals set at zero. Each employee should have access to only the assigned register drawer to enter all sales. Each customer should be given a receipt. At the end of the shift, the employee should do a cash count. A separate employee should compare the cash count with the register tape (or point-of-sale records) to be sure they agree. In addition, Cortez should install an automated point-of-sale system that would enable the company to compare orders entered in the register to orders processed by the kitchen.

Related exercise material: **BE7.5, BE7.6, BE7.7, BE7.8, DO IT! 7.2a, E7.2, E7.3, E7.4, E7.5, and E7.6.**

Cash Disbursements Controls

Companies disburse cash for a variety of reasons, such as to pay expenses and liabilities or to purchase assets. **Generally, internal control over cash disbursements is more effective when companies pay by check or electronic funds transfer (EFT) rather than by cash.** One exception is **payments for incidental amounts that are paid out of petty cash.**[2]

Companies generally issue checks only after following specified control procedures. **Illustration 7.6** shows how principles of internal control apply to cash disbursements.

Voucher System Controls

Most medium and large companies use vouchers as part of their internal control over cash disbursements. A **voucher system** is a network of approvals by authorized individuals, acting independently, to ensure that all disbursements by check are proper.

The system begins with the authorization to incur a cost or expense. It ends with the issuance of a check for the liability incurred. A **voucher** is an authorization form prepared for each expenditure. Companies require vouchers for all types of cash disbursements except those from petty cash.

- The starting point in preparing a voucher is to fill in the appropriate information about the liability on the face of the voucher. The vendor's invoice provides most of the needed information.

[2] We explain the operation of a petty cash fund in the next section.

ILLUSTRATION 7.6 **Application of internal control principles to cash disbursements**

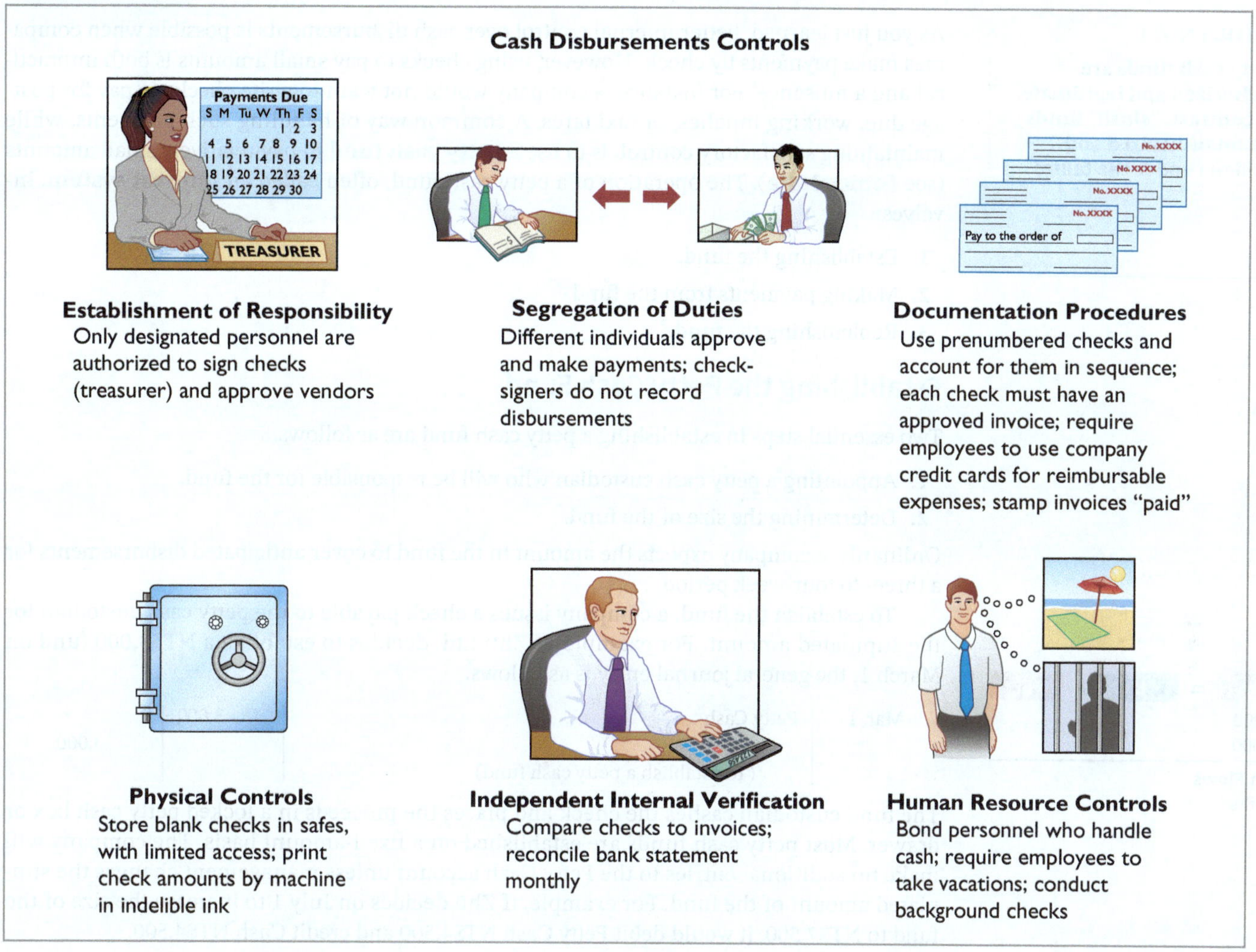

- Then, an employee in accounts payable records the voucher (in a journal called a **voucher register**) and files it according to the date on which it is to be paid.
- The company issues and sends a check on that date, and stamps the voucher "paid."
- The paid voucher is sent to the accounting department for recording (in a journal called the **check register**).

A voucher system involves two journal entries, one to record the liability when the voucher is issued and a second to pay the liability that relates to the voucher.

The use of a voucher system, whether done manually or electronically, improves internal control over cash disbursements in two ways.

1. The authorization process inherent in a voucher system establishes responsibility. Each individual has responsibility to review the underlying documentation to ensure that it is correct.
2. The voucher system keeps track of the documents that back up each transaction. By keeping these documents in one place, a supervisor can independently verify the authenticity of each transaction.

Petty Cash Fund

ETHICS NOTE

Petty cash funds are authorized and legitimate. In contrast, "slush" funds are unauthorized and hidden (under the table).

As you just learned, better internal control over cash disbursements is possible when companies make payments by check. However, using checks to pay small amounts is both impractical and a nuisance. For instance, a company would not want to write checks to pay for postage due, working lunches, or taxi fares. A common way of handling such payments, while maintaining satisfactory control, is to use a **petty cash fund** to pay relatively small amounts (see **Ethics Note**). The operation of a petty cash fund, often called an **imprest system**, involves:

1. Establishing the fund.
2. Making payments from the fund.
3. Replenishing the fund.[3]

Establishing the Petty Cash Fund

Two essential steps in establishing a petty cash fund are as follows.

1. Appointing a petty cash custodian who will be responsible for the fund.
2. Determining the size of the fund.

Ordinarily, a company expects the amount in the fund to cover anticipated disbursements for a three- to four-week period.

To establish the fund, a company issues a check payable to the petty cash custodian for the stipulated amount. For example, if Zhū Ltd. decides to establish a NT$3,000 fund on March 1, the general journal entry is as follows.

A	=	L	+	E
+3,000				
−3,000				

Cash Flows
no effect

Mar. 1	Petty Cash	3,000	
	Cash		3,000
	(To establish a petty cash fund)		

The fund custodian cashes the check and places the proceeds in a locked petty cash box or drawer. Most petty cash funds are established on a fixed-amount basis. The company will make no additional entries to the Petty Cash account unless management changes the stipulated amount of the fund. For example, if Zhū decides on July 1 to increase the size of the fund to NT$7,500, it would debit Petty Cash NT$4,500 and credit Cash NT$4,500.

Making Payments from the Petty Cash Fund

HELPFUL HINT

The petty cash receipt satisfies two internal control principles: (1) establishment of responsibility (signature of custodian), and (2) documentation procedures.

The petty cash custodian has the authority to make payments from the fund that conform to prescribed management policies. Usually, management limits the size of expenditures that come from petty cash. Likewise, it may not permit use of the fund for certain types of transactions (such as making short-term loans to employees).

Each payment from the fund must be documented on a prenumbered petty cash receipt (or petty cash voucher), as shown in **Illustration 7.7** (see **Helpful Hint**). The signatures of both the fund custodian and the person receiving payment are required on the receipt. If other supporting documents such as a freight bill or invoice are available, they should be attached to the petty cash receipt.

- The petty cash custodian keeps the receipts in the petty cash box until the fund is replenished.
- The sum of the petty cash receipts and the money in the fund should equal the established total at all times.
- Management can (and should) make surprise counts at any time (or use an independent person, such as an internal auditor) to determine the correctness of the fund.

The company does not make an accounting entry to record a payment when it is made from petty cash. It is considered both inexpedient and unnecessary to do so. Instead, the company recognizes the accounting effects of each payment when it replenishes the fund.

[3] The term "imprest" means an advance of money for a designated purpose.

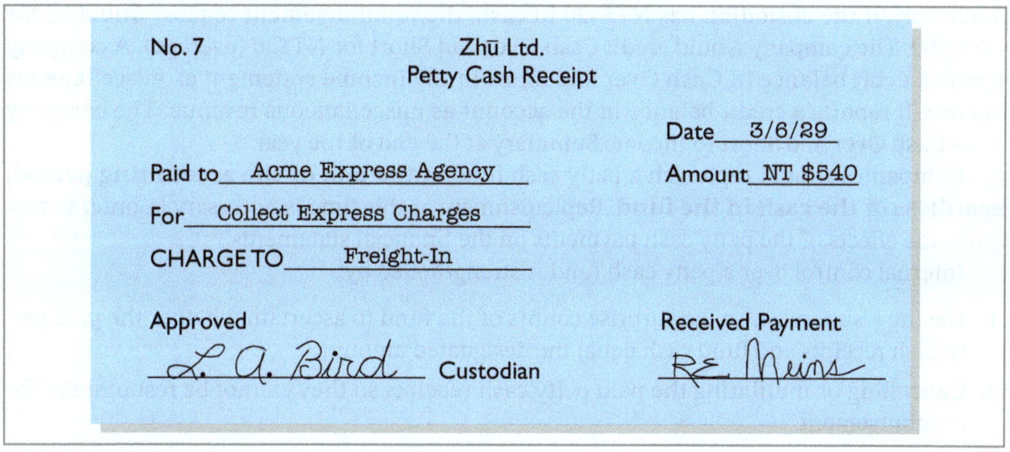
No. 7

Zhū Ltd.
Petty Cash Receipt

Date 3/6/29

Paid to Acme Express Agency

Amount NT $540

For Collect Express Charges

CHARGE TO Freight-In

Approved: L. A. Bird, Custodian

Received Payment: R. E. Mains

ILLUSTRATION 7.7
Petty cash receipt

Replenishing the Petty Cash Fund

When the money in the petty cash fund reaches a minimum level, the company replenishes the fund as follows (see **Helpful Hint**).

1. The petty cash custodian initiates a request for reimbursement. The individual prepares a schedule (or summary) of the payments that have been made and sends the schedule, supported by petty cash receipts and other documentation, to the treasurer's office.
2. The treasurer's office examines the receipts and supporting documents to verify that proper payments from the fund were made.
3. The treasurer then approves the request and issues a check to restore the fund to its established amount. At the same time, all supporting documentation is stamped "paid" so that it cannot be submitted again for payment.

HELPFUL HINT
Replenishing the petty cash fund involves three internal control procedures:
1. Segregation of duties.
2. Documentation procedures.
3. Independent internal verification.

To illustrate, assume that on March 15 Zhū Ltd.'s petty cash custodian requests a check for NT$2,610. The fund contains NT$390 cash and petty cash receipts for postage NT$1,320, freight-out NT$1,140, and miscellaneous expenses NT$150. The general journal entry to record the check is as follows.

Mar. 15	Postage Expense	1,320	
	Freight-Out	1,140	
	Miscellaneous Expense	150	
	Cash		2,610
	(To replenish petty cash fund)		

A = L + E
−1,320 Exp
−1,140 Exp
−150 Exp
−2,610
Cash Flows
−2,610

Note that the reimbursement entry does not affect the Petty Cash account.

- Replenishment changes the composition of the fund by replacing the petty cash receipts with cash.
- It does not change the balance in the fund.

HELPFUL HINT
Cash over and short situations result from mathematical errors or from failure to keep accurate records.

Occasionally, in replenishing a petty cash fund, the company may need to recognize a cash shortage or overage (see **Helpful Hint**). This results when the total of the cash plus receipts in the petty cash box does not equal the established amount of the petty cash fund. To illustrate, assume that Zhū's petty cash custodian has only NT$360 in cash in the fund plus the receipts as listed. The request for reimbursement would therefore be for NT$2,640, and Zhū would make the following entry.

Mar. 15	Postage Expense	1,320	
	Freight-Out	1,140	
	Miscellaneous Expense	150	
	Cash Over and Short	30	
	Cash		2,640
	(To replenish petty cash fund)		

A = L + E
−1,320 Exp
−1,140 Exp
−150 Exp
−30 Exp
−2,640
Cash Flows
−2,640

Conversely, if the custodian has NT$420 in cash, the reimbursement request would be for NT$2,580. The company would credit Cash Over and Short for NT$30 (overage). A company reports a debit balance in Cash Over and Short in the income statement as miscellaneous expense. It reports a credit balance in the account as miscellaneous revenue. The company closes Cash Over and Short to Income Summary at the end of the year.

Companies should replenish a petty cash fund **at the end of the accounting period, regardless of the cash in the fund**. Replenishment at this time is necessary in order to recognize the effects of the petty cash payments on the financial statements.

Internal control over a petty cash fund is strengthened by:

1. Having a supervisor make surprise counts of the fund to ascertain whether the paid petty cash receipts and fund cash equal the designated amount.
2. Cancelling or mutilating the paid petty cash receipts so they cannot be resubmitted for reimbursement.

Ethics Insight

Chris Fertnig/Getty Images

How Employees Steal

Occupational fraud is using your own occupation for personal gain through the misuse or misapplication of the company's resources or assets. This type of fraud is one of three types:

1. **Asset misappropriation,** such as theft of cash on hand, fraudulent disbursements, false refunds, ghost employees, personal purchases, and fictitious employees. This fraud is the most common but the least costly.
2. **Corruption,** such as bribery, illegal gratuities, and economic extortion. This fraud generally falls in the middle between asset misappropriation and financial statement fraud as regards frequency and cost.
3. **Financial statement fraud,** such as fictitious revenues, concealed liabilities and expenses, improper disclosures, and improper asset values. This fraud occurs less frequently than other types of fraud but it is the most costly.

The graph shows the frequency and the median loss for each type of occupational fraud. (Note that the sum of percentages exceeds 100% because some cases of fraud involved more than one type.)

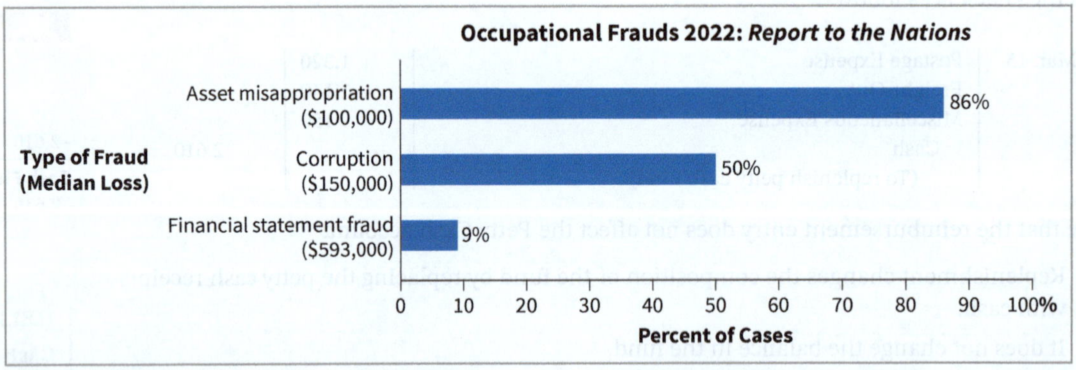

Source: Based on *2022 Report to the Nations on Occupational Fraud and Abuse*, Association of Certified Fraud Examiners, p. 9.

How can companies reduce the likelihood of occupational fraud? (Answer is available near the end of the chapter.)

DO IT! 2b | Petty Cash Fund

Bateer Company established a $50 petty cash fund on July 1. On July 30, the fund had $12 cash remaining and petty cash receipts for postage $14, office supplies $10, and delivery expense $15. Prepare journal entries to establish the fund on July 1 and to replenish the fund on July 30.

Solution

July 1	Petty Cash	50	
	Cash		50
	(To establish petty cash fund)		
30	Postage Expense	14	
	Supplies	10	
	Delivery Expense	15	
	Cash Over and Short		1
	Cash ($50 – $12)		38
	(To replenish petty cash)		

Related exercise material: **BE7.9, DO IT! 7.2b, E7.7, and E7.8.**

ACTION PLAN

- **To establish the fund, set up a separate general ledger account.**
- **Determine how much cash is needed to replenish the fund: subtract the cash remaining from the petty cash fund balance.**
- **Total the petty cash receipts. Determine any cash over or short—the difference between the cash needed to replenish the fund and the total of the petty cash receipts.**
- **Record the expenses incurred according to the petty cash receipts when replenishing the fund.**

7.3 Control Features of a Bank Account

LEARNING OBJECTIVE 3

Identify the control features of a bank account.

The use of a bank contributes significantly to good internal control over cash. A company safeguards its cash by using a bank as a depository and clearinghouse for checks received and checks written. The use of a bank checking account minimizes the amount of currency that must be kept on hand. It also facilitates control of cash because a double record is maintained of all bank transactions—one by the business and the other by the bank. The asset account Cash maintained by the company is the "flipside" of the bank's liability account for that company.

- A **bank reconciliation** is the process of comparing the bank's balance with the company's balance.
- It explains the differences to make them agree.

Many companies have more than one bank account. For efficiency of operations and better control, retailers like **Matahari Department Store** (IDN) and **Wumart** (CHN) often have regional bank accounts. Similarly, a company such as **ExxonMobil** (USA) with more than 100,000 employees may have a payroll bank account as well as one or more general bank accounts. In addition, a company may maintain several bank accounts in order to have more than one source for short-term loans.

Making Bank Deposits

An authorized employee, such as the head cashier, should make a company's bank deposits. Each deposit must be documented by a deposit slip (ticket), as shown in **Illustration 7.8**.

Deposit slips are prepared in duplicate. The bank retains the original; the depositor keeps the duplicate, machine-stamped by the bank to establish its authenticity.

ILLUSTRATION 7.8

Deposit slip

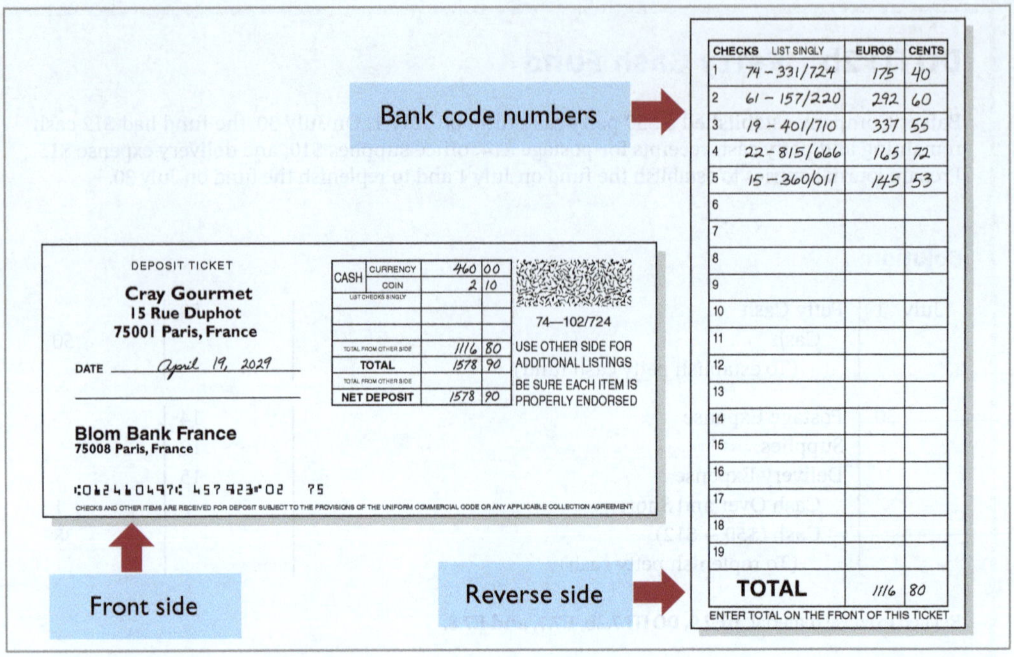

Writing Checks

A **check** is a written order signed by the depositor directing the bank to pay a specified sum of money to a designated recipient. There are three parties to a check:

1. The **maker** (or drawer) who issues the check.
2. The **bank** (or payer) on which the check is drawn.
3. The **payee** to whom the check is payable.

A check is a **negotiable instrument** that one party can transfer to another party by endorsement. Each check should be accompanied by an explanation of its purpose. In many companies, a remittance advice attached to the check, as shown in Illustration 7.9, explains the check's purpose.

ILLUSTRATION 7.9

Check with remittance advice

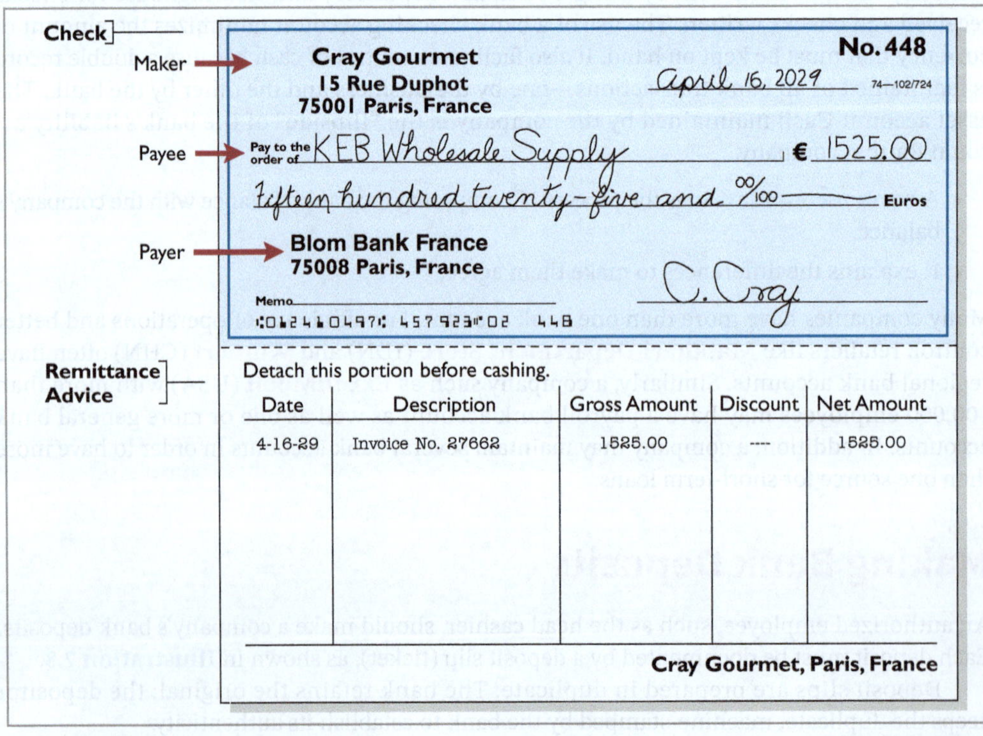

Electronic Banking

Most businesses today take advantage of electronic banking using a computer or mobile banking on a mobile device. Many banks have websites where customers can access their account information. Banks must ensure that these websites are secure and require users to have strong passwords and to change passwords frequently. Businesses must also incorporate strong internal controls, such as the following.

- Marking a check as deposited once a picture is taken and electronically submitted to the bank (called remote deposit capture) to ensure the check is not deposited twice (see **Illustration 7.10**).
- Safeguarding checks to ensure they are not stolen or misused.
- Documenting the use of the cash withdrawn from the ATM.

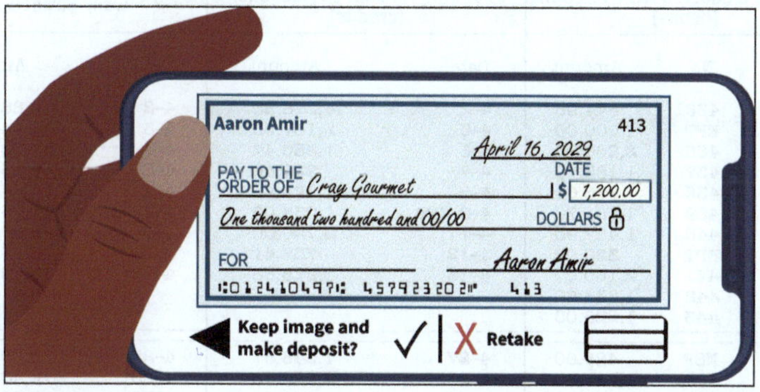

ILLUSTRATION 7.10

Mobile banking using a smart phone (check deposit)

Bank Statements

Each month, the company receives from the bank a **bank statement** showing its bank transactions and balances (see **Helpful Hint**).[4] For example, the statement for Cray Gourmet in **Illustration 7.11** shows the following.

1. Checks paid and other debits (such as debit card transactions or electronic funds transfers for bill payments) that reduce the balance in the depositor's account.
2. Deposits (by direct deposit, automated teller machine, or electronic funds transfer) and other credits that increase the balance in the depositor's account.
3. The account balance after each day's transactions.

HELPFUL HINT

Essentially, the bank statement is a copy of the bank's records sent to the customer or made available online for review.

Remember that **bank statements are prepared from the *bank's* perspective**. For example, **every deposit the bank receives is an increase in the bank's liabilities (an account payable to the depositor)**. Therefore, in Illustration 7.11, Blom Bank France **credits** to Cray Gourmet every deposit it received from Cray. The reverse occurs when the bank "pays" a check issued by Cray Gourmet on its checking account balance: Payment reduces the bank's liability and is therefore **debited** to Cray's account with the bank.

The bank statement lists in numerical sequence all paid checks along with the date the check was paid and its amount. Upon paying a check, the bank stamps the check "paid"; a paid check is sometimes referred to as a **canceled** check. In addition, the bank includes with the bank statement memoranda explaining other debits and credits it made to the depositor's account.

- A check that is not paid by a bank because of insufficient funds in a bank account is called an **NSF check** (not sufficient funds).
- The bank uses a debit memorandum when a previously deposited customer's check "bounces" because of insufficient funds.

[4] Our presentation assumes that a company makes all adjustments at the end of the month. In practice, a company may also make journal entries during the month as it reviews information from the bank regarding its account.

ILLUSTRATION 7.11

Bank statement

Blom Bank France
75008 Paris, France

ACCOUNT STATEMENT

Cray Gourmet
15 Rue Duphot
75001 Paris, France

Statement Date/Credit Line Closing Date
April 30, 2029

457923
ACCOUNT NUMBER

Balance Last Statement	Deposits and Credits		Checks and Debits		Balance This Statement
	No.	Total Amount	No.	Total Amount	
13,256.90	20	34,805.10	26	32,154.55	15,907.45

Amounts Deducted from Account (debits)			Amounts Added to Account (credits)		Daily Balance	
Date	No.	Amount	Date	Amount	Date	Amount
4-2	435	644.95	4-2	4,276.85	4-2	16,888.80
4-3	EFT	1,000.00	4-3	2,137.50	4-3	18,249.65
4-5	436	2,260.00	4-5	1,350.47	4-4	17,063.86
4-4	437	1,185.79	4-7	982.46	4-5	15,154.33
4-3	438	776.65	4-8	1,320.28	4-7	14,648.89
4-8	439	1,781.70	4-9 EFT	1,035.00	4-8	11,767.47
4-7	440	1,487.90	4-11	2,720.00	4-9	12,802.47
4-7	EFT	320.00	4-12	757.41	4-11	13,936.87
4-8	441	2,100.00	4-13	1,218.56	4-12	13,468.28
4-11	442	1,585.60				
4-12	443	1,226.00				
4-29	NSF	425.60	4-27	1,545.57	4-27	13,005.45
4-29	459	1,080.30	4-29	2,929.45	4-29	14,429.00
4-30	DM	120.00	4-30	2,128.60	4-30	15,907.45
4-30	DM	30.00				
4-30	461	500.15				

Symbols: **CM** Credit Memo **DM** Debit Memo **EC** Error Correction **INT** Interest Earned **NSF** Not Sufficient Funds **SC** Service Charge **EFT** Electronic Funds Transfer

- In such a case, the customer's bank marks the check NSF (not sufficient funds) and returns it to the depositor's bank. The bank then debits (decreases) the depositor's account, as shown by the symbol NSF in Illustration 7.11, and sends the NSF check and debit memorandum to the depositor as notification of the charge.

The NSF check creates an account receivable for the depositor and reduces cash in the bank account.

Reconciling the Bank Account

Because the bank and the company maintain independent records of the company's checking account, you might assume that the respective balances will always agree. In fact, the two balances are seldom the same at any given time, and both balances differ from the "correct or true" balance. Therefore, it is necessary to make the balance per books and the balance per bank agree with the correct or true amount—a process called **reconciling the bank account**. The need for reconciliation has two causes:

1. **Time lags** that prevent one of the parties from recording the transaction in the same period.
2. **Errors** by either party in recording transactions.

Time lags occur frequently. For example, several days may elapse between the time a company pays by check and the date the bank pays the check. Similarly, when a company uses the bank's night depository to make its deposits, there will be a difference of one day between the time the company records the receipts and the time the bank does so. A time lag also occurs whenever the bank mails a debit or credit memorandum to the company.

You might think that if a company never writes checks (for example, if a small company uses only a debit card or electronic funds transfers), it does not need to reconcile its account. However, **the possibility of errors or fraud still necessitates periodic reconciliation**. The incidence of errors or fraud depends on the effectiveness of the internal controls maintained by the company and the bank. Bank errors are infrequent. However, either party could accidentally record a €450 check as €45 or €540. In addition, the bank might mistakenly charge a check drawn by G. Dufour to the account of G. Dupont.

Reconciliation Procedure

In reconciling the bank account, it is customary to reconcile the balance per books and balance per bank to their adjusted (correct or true) cash balances.

- **To obtain maximum benefit from a bank reconciliation, an employee who has no other responsibilities related to cash should prepare the reconciliation.**
- When companies do not follow the internal control principle of independent internal verification in preparing the reconciliation, cash embezzlements may escape unnoticed.

Illustration 7.12 shows the reconciliation process. The starting point in preparing the reconciliation is to enter the balance per bank statement and balance per books on a schedule (see **Helpful Hint**). The following steps should reveal all the reconciling items that cause the difference between the two balances.

ILLUSTRATION 7.12

Bank reconciliation adjustments

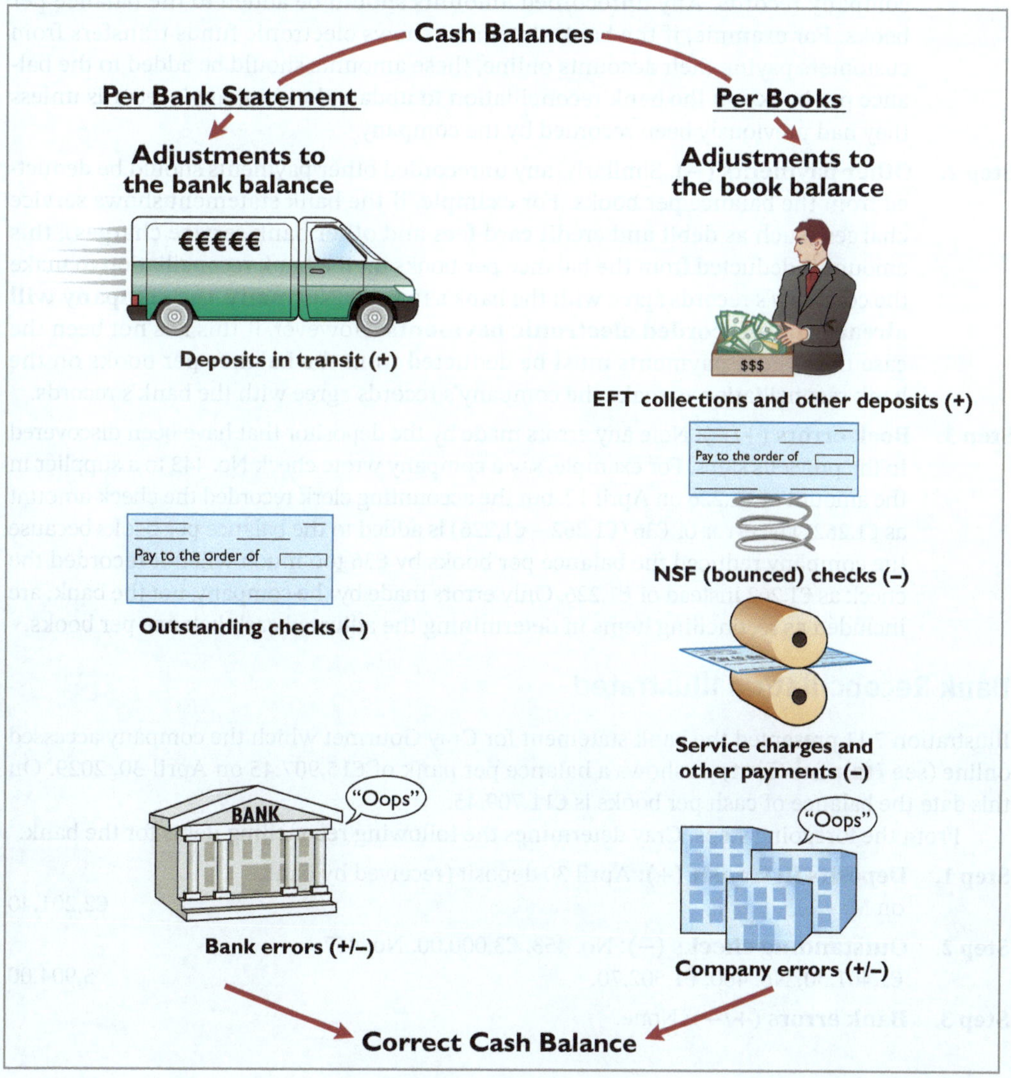

HELPFUL HINT

Deposits in transit and outstanding checks are reconciling items because of time lags.

Reconciling Items per Bank On the bank side of the reconciliation, the items to reconcile are deposits in transit (amounts added), outstanding checks (amounts deducted), and bank errors (if any). By adjusting the bank balance for these items, a company brings that balance up to date.

Step 1. **Deposits in transit (+).** Compare the individual deposits on the bank statement with the deposits in transit from the preceding bank reconciliation and with the deposits per company records or copies of duplicate deposit slips. Deposits recorded by the depositor that have not been recorded by the bank represent **deposits in transit**. Add these deposits to the balance per bank.

Step 2. **Outstanding checks (−).** Compare the paid checks shown on the bank statement or the paid checks returned with the bank statement with (a) checks outstanding from the preceding bank reconciliation, and (b) checks issued by the company recorded as cash payments. Issued checks recorded by the company that have not been paid by the bank represent **outstanding checks**. Deduct outstanding checks from the balance per bank.

Step 3. **Bank errors (+/−).** Note any errors made by the bank that were discovered in the previous steps. For example, if the bank processed a deposit of €1,693 as €1,639 in error, the difference of €54 (€1,693 − €1,639) is added to the balance per bank on the bank reconciliation. All errors made by the bank are reconciling items in determining the adjusted cash balance per the bank.

Reconciling Items per Books Reconciling items on the book side relate to amounts not yet recorded on the company's books and include adjustments from deposits and other amounts added, payments and other amounts deducted, and company errors (if any).

Step 1. **Other deposits (+).** Compare the other deposits on the bank statement with the company records. Any unrecorded amounts should be added to the balance per books. For example, if the bank statement shows electronic funds transfers from customers paying their accounts online, these amounts should be added to the balance per books on the bank reconciliation to update the company's records unless they had previously been recorded by the company.

Step 2. **Other payments (−).** Similarly, any unrecorded other payments should be deducted from the balance per books. For example, if the bank statement shows service charges (such as debit and credit card fees and other bank service charges), this amount is deducted from the balance per books on the bank reconciliation to make the company's records agree with the bank's records. **Normally, the company will already have recorded electronic payments**. However, if this has not been the case then these payments must be deducted from the balance per books on the bank reconciliation to make the company's records agree with the bank's records.

Step 3. **Book errors (+/−).** Note any errors made by the depositor that have been discovered in the previous steps. For example, say a company wrote check No. 443 to a supplier in the amount of €1,226 on April 12, but the accounting clerk recorded the check amount as €1,262. The error of €36 (€1,262 – €1,226) is added to the balance per books because the company reduced the balance per books by €36 too much when it recorded the check as €1,262 instead of €1,226. Only errors made by the company, not the bank, are included as reconciling items in determining the adjusted cash balance per books.

HELPFUL HINT

Note in the bank statement in Illustration 7.10 that the bank has paid checks No. 459 and 461, but check No. 460 is not listed. Thus, this check is outstanding. If a complete bank statement were provided, checks No. 453 and 457 also would not be listed. Cray obtains the amounts for these three checks from its cash payments records.

Bank Reconciliation Illustrated

Illustration 7.11 presented the bank statement for Cray Gourmet which the company accessed online (see **Helpful Hint**). It shows a balance per bank of €15,907.45 on April 30, 2029. On this date the balance of cash per books is €11,709.45.

From the foregoing steps, Cray determines the following reconciling items for the bank.

Step 1.	**Deposits in transit (+):** April 30 deposit (received by bank on May 1).	€2,201.40
Step 2.	**Outstanding checks (−):** No. 453, €3,000.00; No. 457, €1,401.30; No. 460, €1,502.70.	5,904.00
Step 3.	**Bank errors (+/−):** None.	

Reconciling items per books are as follows.

Step 1. **Other deposits (+):** Unrecorded electronic receipt from customer on account on April 9 determined from the bank statement. €1,035.00

Step 2. **Other payments (−):** The electronic payments on April 3 and 7 were previously recorded by the company when they were initiated. Unrecorded charges determined from the bank statement are as follows:

Returned NSF check on April 29	425.60
Debit and credit card fees on April 30	120.00
Bank service charges on April 30	30.00

Step 3. **Company errors (+):** Check No. 443 was correctly written by Cray for €1,226 and was correctly paid by the bank on April 12. However, it was recorded as €1,262 on Cray's books. 36.00

Illustration 7.13 shows Cray's bank reconciliation (see **Alternative Terminology**).

ILLUSTRATION 7.13
Bank reconciliation

Cray Gourmet
Bank Reconciliation
April 30, 2029

Cash balance per bank statement		€15,907.45
Add: Deposits in transit		2,201.40
		18,108.85
Less: Outstanding checks		
No. 453	€3,000.00	
No. 457	1,401.30	
No. 460	1,502.70	5,904.00
Adjusted cash balance per bank		**€12,204.85**
Cash balance per books		€11,709.45
Add: Electronic funds transfer received	€1,035.00	
Error in recording check No. 443	36.00	1,071.00
		12,780.45
Less: NSF check	425.60	
Debit and credit card fees	120.00	
Bank service charge	30.00	575.60
Adjusted cash balance per books		**€12,204.85**

ALTERNATIVE TERMINOLOGY

The terms adjusted cash balance, true cash balance, and correct cash balance are used interchangeably.

Entries from Bank Reconciliation

The depositor (that is, the company) next must record each reconciling item used to determine the **adjusted cash balance per books**. If the company does not journalize and post these items, the Cash account will not show the correct balance. The adjusting entries for the Cray Gourmet bank reconciliation on April 30 are as follows (see **Helpful Hint**).

HELPFUL HINT

These entries are adjusting entries. In prior chapters, we considered Cash an account that did not require adjustment because we had not yet explained a bank reconciliation.

Collection of Electronic Funds Transfer A payment of an account by a customer is recorded in the same way, whether the cash is received through the mail or electronically. The entry is as follows.

Apr. 30	Cash	1,035	
	Accounts Receivable		1,035
	(To record receipt of electronic funds transfer)		

A	=	L	+	E
+1,035				
−1,035				

Cash Flows
+1,035

A	=	L	+	E
+36				
		+36		

Cash Flows
+36

Book Error An examination of the cash disbursements journal shows that check No. 443 was a payment on account to Roux Foods, a supplier. The correcting entry is as follows.

Apr. 30	Cash	36	
	Accounts Payable		36
	(To correct error in recording check No. 443)		

A	=	L	+	E
+425.60				
−425.60				

Cash Flows
−425.60

NSF Check As indicated earlier, an NSF check becomes an accounts receivable to the depositor. The entry is as follows.

Apr. 30	Accounts Receivable	425.60	
	Cash		425.60
	(To record NSF check)		

Bank Charge Expense Fees for processing debit and credit card transactions are normally debited to the Bank Charge Expense account, as are bank service charges. We have chosen to combine and record these in one journal entry, as shown below, although they also could be journalized separately.

A	=	L	+	E
				−150 Exp
−150				

Cash Flows
−150

Apr. 30	Bank Charge Expense	150	
	Cash		150
	(To record charges for debit and credit card fees of €120 and bank service charges of €30)		

After Cray posts the entries, the Cash account will appear as in **Illustration 7.14**.

ILLUSTRATION 7.14
Adjusted balance in Cash account

Cash			
Apr. 30 Bal.	11,709.45	Apr. 30	425.60
30	1,035.00	30	150.00
30	36.00		
Apr. 30 Bal.	**12,204.85**		

The adjusted cash balance in the ledger should agree with the adjusted cash balance per books in the bank reconciliation in Illustration 7.13.

What entries does the bank make? If the company discovers any bank errors in preparing the reconciliation, it should notify the bank so the bank can make the necessary corrections on its records. The bank does not make any entries for deposits in transit or outstanding checks. Only when these items reach the bank will the bank record these items.

Investor Insight

Mary Altaffer/©AP/ Wide World Photos

Madoff's Ponzi Scheme

No recent fraud has generated more interest and rage than the one perpetrated by Bernard Madoff. Madoff was an elite New York investment fund manager who was highly regarded by securities regulators. Investors flocked to him because he delivered very steady returns of between 10% and 15%, no matter whether the market was going up or going down.

However, for many years, Madoff did not actually invest the cash that people gave to him. Instead, he was running a Ponzi scheme: He paid returns to existing investors using cash received from new investors. As long as the size of his investment fund continued to grow from new investments at a rate that exceeded the amounts that he needed to pay out in returns, Madoff was able to operate his fraud smoothly.

To conceal his misdeeds, Madoff fabricated false investment statements that were provided to investors. In addition, Madoff hired an auditor that never verified the accuracy of the investment records but automatically issued unqualified opinions each year. A competing fund manager warned the U.S. SEC a number of times over a nearly 10-year period that he thought Madoff was engaged in fraud. The U.S. SEC never aggressively investigated the allegations. Investors, many of which were charitable organizations, lost more than $18 billion. Madoff was sentenced to a jail term of 150 years.

How was Madoff able to conceal such a giant fraud? (Answer is available near the end of the chapter.)

DO IT! 3 | Bank Reconciliation

Deepika Kann owns Deepika Fine Fabrics. Deepika asks you to explain how she should treat the following reconciling items when reconciling the company's bank account: (1) a debit memorandum for an NSF check, (2) a credit memorandum received by the bank for an electronic funds transfer from one of the company's customers, (3) outstanding checks, and (4) a deposit in transit.

ACTION PLAN

- **Understand the purpose of a bank reconciliation.**
- **Identify time lags and explain how they cause reconciling items.**

Solution

Deepika should treat the reconciling items as follows.

1. NSF check: Deduct from balance per books.
2. Electronic funds transfer received by bank: Add to balance per books.
3. Outstanding checks: Deduct from balance per bank.
4. Deposit in transit: Add to balance per bank.

Related exercise material: **BE7.10, BE7.11, BE7.12, BE7.13, BE7.14, BE7.15, DO IT! 7.3, E7.9, E7.10, E7.11, E7.12, and E7.13.**

7.4 Reporting Cash

LEARNING OBJECTIVE 4

Explain the reporting of cash.

Cash consists of coins, currency (paper money), checks, money orders, and money on hand or on deposit in a bank or similar depository. Companies report cash in two different statements:

1. The statement of financial position, which reports the amount of cash available at a given point in time.
2. The statement of cash flows, which shows the sources and uses of cash during a period of time. (The statement of cash flows was introduced in Chapter 1 and will be discussed in much detail in Chapter 14.)

In this section, we discuss some important points regarding the presentation of cash in the statement of financial position.

When presented in a statement of financial position, cash on hand, cash in banks, and petty cash are often combined and reported simply as **Cash**. Because it is the most liquid asset owned by the company, cash is generally listed last in the current assets section of the statement of financial position.

Cash Equivalents

Many companies use the designation "Cash and cash equivalents" in reporting cash. (See **Illustration 7.15** for an example.) **Cash equivalents** are short-term, highly liquid investments that are both:

1. Readily convertible to known amounts of cash.
2. So near their maturity that their market value is relatively insensitive to changes in interest rates. (Generally, only investments with original maturities of three months or less qualify under this definition.)

ILLUSTRATION 7.15

Statement of financial position presentation of cash

Real World

Korean Air Lines, Inc.
Statement of Financial Position
(partial, in millions)

Assets	
Current assets	
Short-term investments	₩111,988
Cash and cash equivalents	**967,481**

ETHICS NOTE

Recently, some companies were forced to restate their financial statements because they had too broadly interpreted which types of investments could be treated as cash equivalents. By reporting these items as cash equivalents, the companies made themselves look more liquid.

Examples of cash equivalents are Treasury bills, commercial paper (short-term company notes), and money market funds. Cash equivalents are held for the purpose of meeting short-term cash commitments rather than for investment or other purposes (see **Ethics Note**).

Occasionally, a company will have a net negative balance in its bank account. In this case, the company should report the negative balance among current liabilities. For example, farm equipment manufacturer **Ag-Chem** (USA) at one time reported "Checks outstanding in excess of cash balances" of $2,145,000 among its current liabilities.

Restricted Cash

A company may have **restricted cash**, cash that is not available for general use but rather is restricted for a special purpose. For example, **Takung Art Co., Ltd.** (CHN) recently reported restricted cash of ¥25,676,519. The cash is earmarked for the purpose of buying and selling ownership units of artwork.

Restricted cash should be disclosed along with additional information about the nature of the restriction. In addition, the company must consider whether the nature of the restrictions result in the investment ceasing to qualify as highly liquid or readily convertible. In this case, the amount of restricted cash would no longer be included as in the total of Cash and cash equivalents.

ACTION PLAN

- **Understand how companies present cash and restricted cash on the statement of financial position.**
- **Review the designations of cash equivalents and restricted cash, and how companies typically handle them.**

DO IT! 4 | Reporting Cash

Indicate whether each of the following statements is true or false. If false, indicate how to correct the statement.

1. Cash and cash equivalents are comprised of coins, currency (paper money), money orders, and NSF checks.
2. The amount of restricted cash should be disclosed along with the nature of the restrictions.
3. A company may have a negative balance in its bank account. In this case, it should offset this negative balance against cash and cash equivalents on the statement of financial position.
4. Because cash and cash equivalents often includes short-term investments, accounts receivable should be reported as the last item on the statement of financial position.
5. Cash restricted for a special purpose is reported separately as a current asset or as a noncurrent asset, depending on when the cash is expected to be used.

Solution

1. False. NSF checks should be reported as receivables, not cash and cash equivalents. **2.** True. **3.** False. Companies that have a negative balance in their bank accounts should report the negative balance as a current liability. **4.** False. Cash equivalents are readily convertible to known amounts of cash, and so near maturity (less than 3 months) that they are considered more liquid than accounts receivable and therefore are reported after accounts receivable on the statement of financial position. **5.** True.

Related exercise material: **BE7.16, DO IT! 7.4, E7.14, and E7.15.**

Review and Practice

Learning Objectives Review

1 Define fraud and the principles of internal control.

A fraud is a dishonest act by an employee that results in personal benefit to the employee at a cost to the employer. The fraud triangle refers to the three factors that contribute to fraudulent activity by employees: opportunity, financial pressure, and rationalization. Internal control consists of all the related methods and measures adopted within an organization to safeguard its assets, enhance the reliability of its accounting records, increase efficiency of operations, and ensure compliance with laws and regulations.

The principles of internal control are establishment of responsibility, segregation of duties, documentation procedures, physical controls, independent internal verification, and human resource controls such as bonding and requiring employees to take vacations.

2 Apply internal control principles to cash.

Internal controls over cash receipts include (a) designating specific personnel to handle cash; (b) assigning different individuals to receive cash, record cash, and maintain custody of cash; (c) using remittance advices for mail receipts, cash register tapes for over-the-counter receipts, and deposit slips for bank deposits; (d) using company safes and bank vaults to store cash with access limited to authorized personnel, and using cash registers or point-of-sale terminals in executing over-the-counter receipts; (e) making independent daily counts of register receipts and daily comparison of total receipts with total deposits; and (f) bonding personnel that handle cash and requiring them to take vacations.

Internal controls over cash disbursements include (a) having specific individuals such as the treasurer authorized to sign checks and approve vendors; (b) assigning different individuals to approve items for payment, make the payment, and record the payment; (c) using prenumbered checks and accounting for all checks, with each check supported by an approved invoice; (d) storing blank checks in a safe or vault with access restricted to authorized personnel, and using a check-writing machine to imprint amounts on checks; (e) comparing each check with the approved invoice before issuing the check, and making monthly reconciliations of bank and book balances; and (f) bonding personnel who handle cash, requiring employees to take vacations, and conducting background checks.

Companies operate a petty cash fund to pay relatively small amounts of cash. They must establish the fund, make payments from the fund, and replenish the fund when the cash in the fund reaches a minimum level.

3 Identify the control features of a bank account.

A bank account contributes to good internal control by providing physical controls for the storage of cash. It minimizes the amount of currency that a company must keep on hand, and it creates a double record of a depositor's bank transactions. It is customary to reconcile the balance per books and balance per bank to their adjusted balances. The steps in the reconciling process are to determine deposits in transit and electronic funds transfers received by bank, outstanding checks, errors by the depositor or the bank, and unrecorded bank memoranda.

4 Explain the reporting of cash.

Companies list cash last in the current assets section of the statement of financial position. In some cases, they report cash together with cash equivalents. Cash restricted for a special purpose is reported separately as a current asset or as a non-current asset, depending on when the cash is expected to be used.

Glossary Review

Bank reconciliation The process of comparing the bank's balance of an account with the company's balance and explaining any differences to make them agree. (p. 7-19).

Bank statement A monthly statement from the bank that shows the depositor's bank transactions and balances. (p. 7-21).

Bonding Obtaining insurance protection against theft by employees. (p. 7-9).

Cash Resources that consist of coins, currency, checks, money orders, and money on hand or on deposit in a bank or similar depository. (p. 7-27).

Cash equivalents Short-term, highly liquid investments that can be converted to a specific amount of cash. (p. 7-27).

Check A written order signed by a bank depositor, directing the bank to pay a specified sum of money to a designated recipient. (p. 7-20).

Deposits in transit Deposits recorded by the depositor but not yet recorded by the bank. (p. 7-24).

Electronic funds transfer (EFT) A disbursement system that uses wire, telephone, or computers to transfer funds from one location to another. (p. 7-13).

Fraud A dishonest act by an employee that results in personal benefit to the employee at a cost to the employer. (p. 7-3).

Fraud triangle The three factors that contribute to fraudulent activity by employees: opportunity, financial pressure, and rationalization. (p. 7-3).

Internal auditors Company employees who continuously evaluate the effectiveness of the company's internal control system. (p. 7-8).

Internal control A process designed to provide reasonable assurance regarding the achievement of company objectives related to operations, reporting, and compliance. (p. 7-3).

NSF check A check that is not paid by a bank because of insufficient funds in a customer's bank account. (p. 7-21).

Outstanding checks Checks issued and recorded by a company but not yet paid by the bank. (p. 7-24).

Petty cash fund A cash fund used to pay relatively small amounts. (p. 7-16).

Restricted cash Cash that must be used for a special purpose. (p. 7-28).

Voucher An authorization form prepared for each payment in a voucher system. (p. 7-14).

Voucher system A network of approvals by authorized individuals acting independently to ensure that all disbursements by check are proper. (p. 7-14).

Practice Multiple-Choice Questions

1. **(LO 1)** Which of the following is **not** an element of the fraud triangle?
   a. Rationalization.
   b. Financial pressure.
   c. Segregation of duties.
   d. Opportunity.

2. **(LO 1)** An organization uses internal control to enhance the accuracy and reliability of accounting records and to:
   a. safeguard assets.
   b. prevent fraud.
   c. produce correct financial statements.
   d. deter employee dishonesty.

3. **(LO 1)** The principles of internal control do **not** include:
   a. establishment of responsibility.
   b. documentation procedures.
   c. management responsibility.
   d. independent internal verification.

4. **(LO 1)** Physical controls do **not** include:
   a. safes and vaults to store cash.
   b. independent bank reconciliations.
   c. locked warehouses for inventories.
   d. bank safety deposit boxes for important papers.

5. **(LO 1)** Which of the following control activities is **not** relevant when a company uses a computerized (rather than manual) accounting system?
   a. Establishment of responsibility.
   b. Segregation of duties.
   c. Independent internal verification.
   d. All of these control activities are relevant to a computerized system.

6. **(LO 2)** Permitting only designated personnel to handle cash receipts is an application of the principle of:
   a. segregation of duties.
   b. establishment of responsibility.
   c. independent internal verification.
   d. human resource controls.

7. **(LO 2)** The use of prenumbered checks in disbursing cash is an application of the principle of:
   a. establishment of responsibility.
   b. segregation of duties.
   c. physical controls.
   d. documentation procedures.

8. **(LO 2)** A company writes a check to replenish a €100 petty cash fund when the fund contains receipts of €94 and €4 in cash. In recording the check, the company should:
   a. debit Cash Over and Short for €2.
   b. debit Petty Cash for €94.
   c. credit Cash for €94.
   d. credit Petty Cash for €2.

9. **(LO 3)** The control features of a bank account do **not** include:
   a. having bank auditors verify the correctness of the bank balance per books.
   b. minimizing the amount of cash that must be kept on hand.
   c. providing a double record of all bank transactions.
   d. safeguarding cash by using a bank as a depository.

10. **(LO 3)** In a bank reconciliation, deposits in transit are:
    a. deducted from the book balance.
    b. added to the book balance.
    c. added to the bank balance.
    d. deducted from the bank balance.

11. **(LO 3)** The reconciling item in a bank reconciliation that will result in an adjusting entry by the depositor is:
    a. outstanding checks.
    b. deposit in transit.
    c. a bank error.
    d. bank service charges.

12. **(LO 4)** Which of the following items in a cash drawer at November 30 is **not** cash?
    a. Money orders.
    b. Coins and currency.
    c. An NSF check.
    d. A customer check dated November 28.

13. **(LO 4)** Which of the following statements correctly describes the reporting of cash?
    a. Cash cannot be combined with cash equivalents.
    b. Restricted cash need not be disclosed.
    c. Cash is listed last in the current assets section.
    d. The nature of the restrictions on cash need not be disclosed.

Solutions

1. **c.** Segregation of duties is not an element of the fraud triangle. The other choices are fraud triangle elements.

2. **a.** Safeguarding assets is one of the purposes of using internal control. The other choices are incorrect because while internal control can help to (b) prevent fraud, (c) produce correct financial statements, and (d) deter employee dishonesty, these are not the main purposes of using it.

3. **c.** Management responsibility is not one of the principles of internal control. The other choices are true statements.

4. **b.** Independent bank reconciliations are not a physical control. The other choices are true statements.

5. **d.** Establishment of responsibility, segregation of duties and independent internal verification are all relevant to a computerized system.

6. **b.** Permitting only designated personnel to handle cash receipts is an application of the principle of establishment of responsibility, not (a) segregation of duties, (c) independent internal verification, or (d) human resource controls.

7. **d.** The use of prenumbered checks in disbursing cash is an application of the principle of documentation procedures, not (a) establishment of responsibility, (b) segregation of duties, or (c) physical controls.

8. **a.** When this check is recorded, the company should debit Cash Over and Short for the shortage of €2 (total of the receipts plus cash in the drawer (€98) versus $100), not (b) debit Petty Cash for €94, (c) credit Cash for €94, or (d) credit Petty Cash for €2.

9. **a.** Having bank auditors verify the correctness of the bank balance per books is not one of the control features of a bank account. The other choices are true statements.

10. **c.** Deposits in transit are added to the bank balance on a bank reconciliation, not (a) deducted from the book balance, (b) added to the book balance, or (d) deducted from the bank balance.

11. **d.** Because the depositor does not know the amount of the bank service charges until the bank statements is received, an adjusting entry must be made when the statement is received. The other choices are incorrect because (a) outstanding checks do not require an adjusting entry by the depositor because the checks have already been recorded in the depositor's books, (b) deposits in transit do not require an adjusting entry by the depositor because the deposits have already been recorded in the depositor's books, and (c) bank errors do not require an adjusting entry by the depositor, but the depositor does need to inform the bank of the error so it can be corrected.

12. **c.** An NSF check should not be considered cash. The other choices are true statements.

13. **c.** Cash is listed last in the current assets section. The other choices are incorrect because (a) cash and cash equivalents can be appropriately combined when reporting cash on the statement of financial position, (b) restricted cash included in cash and cash equivalents must be disclosed, and (d) the nature of the restrictions is also disclosed when restricted cash is included in cash and cash equivalents.

Practice Brief Exercises

1. **(LO 2)** On May 31, Tyler Lighting's petty cash fund of £200 is replenished when the fund contains £7 in cash and receipts for postage £105, freight-out £49, and miscellaneous expense £40. Prepare the journal entry to record the replenishment of the petty cash fund.

Prepare entry to replenish a petty cash fund.

Solution

1.	May 31	Postage Expense	105	
		Freight-Out	49	
		Miscellaneous Expense	40	
		Cash		193
		Cash Over and Short		1

2. **(LO 3)** At August 31, Saladino Coffee has the following bank information: cash balance per bank ₺5,200, outstanding checks ₺1,462, deposits in transit ₺1,211, and a bank debit memo ₺110. Determine the adjusted cash balance per bank at July 31.

Prepare partial bank reconciliation.

Solution

2.	Cash balance per bank	₺5,200
	Add: Deposits in transit	1,211
		6,411
	Less: Outstanding checks	1,462
	Adjusted cash balance per bank	₺4,949

Explain the statement presentation of cash balances.

3. **(LO 4)** Zian Athletics has the following cash balances: Cash in Bank ¥18,762, Payroll Bank Account ¥8,000, Petty Cash ¥150, and Plant Expansion Fund Cash ¥30,000 to be used 2 years from now (amounts in thousands). Explain how each balance should be reported on the statement of financial position.

Solution

3. Zian should report Cash in Bank, Payroll Bank Account, and Petty Cash as current assets (usually combined as one Cash amount). Plant Expansion Fund Cash should be reported as a non-current asset, assuming the fund is not expected to be used during the next year.

Practice Exercises

Indicate good or weak internal control procedures.

1. **(LO 1, 2)** Listed below are five procedures followed by Lee Enterprises.
   1. Total cash receipts are compared to bank deposits daily by Wing Poon, who receives cash over the counter.
   2. Employees write down hours worked and turn in the sheet to the cashier's office.
   3. As a cost-saving measure, employees do not take vacations.
   4. Only the sales manager can approve credit sales.
   5. Three different employees are assigned one task each related to inventory: ship goods to customers, bill customers, and receive payment from customers.

Instructions

Indicate whether each procedure is an example of good internal control or of weak internal control. If it is an example of good internal control, indicate which internal control principle is being followed. If it is an example of weak internal control, indicate which internal control principles is violated. Use the table below.

Procedure	IC Good or Weak?	Related Internal Control Principle
1.		
2.		
3.		
4.		
5.		

Solution

1.

Procedure	IC Good or Weak?	Related Internal Control Principle
1.	Weak	Independent internal verification
2.	Weak	Physical controls
3.	Weak	Human resource controls
4.	Good	Establishment of responsibility
5.	Good	Segregation of duties

Prepare bank reconciliation and adjusting entries.

2. **(LO 3)** The information below relates to the Cash account in the ledger of Ong Trading (amounts in thousands).

Balance June 1—¥9,947; Cash deposited—¥37,120.
Balance June 30—¥10,094; Checks written—¥36,973.

The June bank statement shows a balance of ¥9,525 on June 30 and the following memoranda.

Credits		Debits	
Collection of electronic funds transfer	¥884	NSF check: R. Doll	¥245
Interest earned on checking accounts	¥26	Safety deposit box rent	¥35

At June 30, deposits in transit were ¥2,581, and outstanding checks totaled ¥1,382.

Instructions

a. Prepare the bank reconciliation at June 30.

b. Prepare the adjusting entries at June 30, assuming the NSF check was from a customer on account.

Solution

2. a.

Ong Trading Bank Reconciliation June 30		
Cash balance per bank statement		¥ 9,525
Add: Deposits in transit		2,581
		12,106
Less: Outstanding checks		1,382
Adjusted cash balance per bank		¥10,724
Cash balance per books		¥10,094
Add: Electronic funds transfer received	¥884	
Interest earned	26	910
		11,004
Less: NSF check	245	
Safety deposit box rent	35	280
Adjusted cash balance per books		¥10,724

b.

June 30	Cash	884	
	Accounts Receivable		884
30	Cash	26	
	Interest Revenue		26
30	Bank Charge Expense	35	
	Cash		35
30	Accounts Receivable (R. Doll)	245	
	Cash		245

Practice Problem

Prepare bank reconciliation and journalize entries.

(LO 3) Choi Group's bank statement for May 2029 shows the following data (amounts in thousands).

Balance 5/1	₩12,650	Balance 5/31	₩14,280
Debit memorandum:		Credit memorandum:	
NSF check	₩175	Collection of electronic funds transfer	₩505

The cash balance per books at May 31 is ₩13,319. Your review of the data reveals the following.

1. The NSF check was from Copple Co., a customer.
2. Outstanding checks at May 31 total ₩2,410.
3. Deposits in transit at May 31 total ₩1,752.
4. A Choi Group check for ₩352, dated May 10, cleared the bank on May 25. The company recorded this check, which was a payment on account, for ₩325.

Instructions

a. Prepare a bank reconciliation at May 31.

b. Journalize the entries required by the reconciliation.

Solution

a.

Choi Group
Bank Reconciliation
May 31, 2029

Cash balance per bank statement		₩14,280
Add: Deposits in transit		1,752
		16,032
Less: Outstanding checks		2,410
Adjusted cash balance per bank		₩13,622
Cash balance per books		₩13,319
Add: Electronic funds transfer received		505
		13,824
Less: NSF check	₩175	
Error in recording check (₩352 – ₩325)	27	202
Adjusted cash balance per books		₩13,622

b.

May 31	Cash	505	
	Accounts Receivable		505
	(To record receipt of electronic funds transfer)		
31	Accounts Receivable	175	
	Cash		175
	(To record NSF check)		
31	Accounts Payable	27	
	Cash		27
	(To correct error in recording check)		

Questions

1. A local bank reported that it lost $150,000 as the result of an employee fraud. Edward Jasso is not clear on what is meant by an "employee fraud." Explain the meaning of fraud to Edward and give an example of frauds that might occur at a bank.

2. Fraud experts often say that there are three primary factors that contribute to employee fraud. Identify the three factors and explain what is meant by each.

3. Identify the five components of a good internal control system.

4. "Internal control is concerned only with enhancing the accuracy of the accounting records." Do you agree? Explain.

5. What principles of internal control apply to most organizations?

6. In the corner grocery store, all sales clerks make change out of one cash register drawer. Is this a violation of internal control? Why?

7. Xi Ping is reviewing the principle of segregation of duties. What are the two common applications of this principle?

8. How do documentation procedures contribute to good internal control?

9. What internal control objectives are met by physical controls?

10. (a) Explain the control principle of independent internal verification. (b) What practices are important in applying this principle?

11. As the company accountant, the management of Faan Stores asks you to explain (a) the concept of reasonable assurance in internal control and (b) the importance of the human factor in internal control.

12. What principle(s) of internal control is (are) involved in making daily cash counts of over-the-counter receipts?

13. Assume that Kohl's (USA) installed new electronic cash registers in its department stores. How do cash registers improve internal control over cash receipts?

14. At Summato Wholesale, two mail clerks open all mail receipts. How does this strengthen internal control?

15. "To have maximum effective internal control over cash disbursements, all payments should be made by check." Is this true? Explain.

16. Deangelo Company's internal controls over cash disbursements provide for the treasurer to sign checks imprinted by a check-writing machine in indelible ink after comparing the check with the approved invoice. Identify the internal control principles that are present in these controls.

17. Explain how these principles apply to cash disbursements: (a) physical controls and (b) human resource controls.

18. (a) What is a voucher system? (b) What principles of internal control apply to a voucher system?

19. What is the essential feature of an electronic funds transfer (EFT) procedure?

20. (a) Identify the three activities that pertain to a petty cash fund and indicate an internal control principle that is applicable to each activity. (b) When are journal entries required in the operation of a petty cash fund?

21. "The use of a bank contributes significantly to good internal control over cash." Is this true? Why or why not?

22. Anna Korte is confused about the lack of agreement between the cash balance per books and the balance per bank. Explain the causes for the lack of agreement to Anna, and give an example of each cause.

23. Jung Ha Na asks your help concerning an NSF check. Explain to Jung (a) what an NSF check is, (b) how it is treated in a bank reconciliation, and (c) whether it will require an adjusting entry.

24. (a) "Cash equivalents are the same as cash." Do you agree? Explain. (b) Where and how should restricted cash funds be reported on the statement of financial position?

25. Riverside Fertilizer owns the following assets at the statement of financial position date.

Cash in bank savings account	€ 8,000
Cash on hand	850
Cash refund due from taxing authority	1,000
Checking account balance	14,000
Postdated checks	500

What amount should Riverside report as cash in the statement of financial position?

26. The financial statements of **TSMC** are presented in Appendix A. At what amount does the company report cash and cash equivalents in its 2020 consolidated statement of financial position?

Brief Exercises

Identify fraud triangle concepts.

BE7.1 (LO 1) Match each situation with the fraud triangle factor—opportunity, financial pressure, or rationalization—that best describes it.

a. An employee's monthly credit card payments are nearly 75% of his or her monthly earnings.

b. An employee earns minimum wage at a firm that has reported record earnings for each of the last five years.

c. An employee has an expensive gambling habit.

d. An employee has check-writing and signing responsibilities for a small company, as well as reconciling the bank account.

Indicate internal control concepts.

BE7.2 (LO 1) Ram Siram has prepared the following statements about internal control.

a. One of the objectives of internal control is to safeguard assets from employee theft, robbery, and unauthorized use.

b. One of the objectives of internal control is to enhance the accuracy and reliability of the accounting records.

Identify each statement as true or false. If false, indicate how to correct the statement.

Explain the importance of internal control.

BE7.3 (LO 1) Anusha Das is the new owner of Kolkata Parking. She has heard about internal control but is not clear about its importance for her business. Explain to Anusha the four purposes of internal control and give her one application of each purpose for Kolkata Parking.

Identify internal control principles.

BE7.4 (LO 1) The internal control procedures in Hamzah Electronics result in the following provisions. Identify the principles of internal control that are being followed in each case.

a. Employees who have physical custody of assets do not have access to the accounting records.

b. Each month, the assets on hand are compared to the accounting records by an internal auditor.

c. A prenumbered shipping document is prepared for each shipment of goods to customers.

Identify the internal control principles applicable to cash receipts.

BE7.5 (LO 2) Wu Hardware has the following internal control procedures over cash receipts. Identify the internal control principle that is applicable to each procedure.

a. All over-the-counter receipts are entered in cash registers.

b. All cashiers are bonded.

c. Daily cash counts are made by cashier department supervisors.

d. The duties of receiving cash, recording cash, and custody of cash are assigned to different individuals.

e. Only cashiers may operate cash registers.

Make journal entries for cash overage and shortfall.

BE7.6 (LO 2) The cash register tape for Bluestem Industries reported sales of $6,871.50. Record the journal entry that would be necessary for each of the following situations. (a) Cash to be accounted for exceeds cash on hand by $50.75. (b) Cash on hand exceeds cash to be accounted for by $28.32.

Make journal entry using cash count sheet.

BE7.7 (LO 2) While examining cash receipts information, the accounting department determined the following information: opening cash balance €160, cash on hand €1,125.74, and cash sales per register tape €980.83. Prepare the required journal entry based upon the cash count sheet.

Identify the internal control principles applicable to cash disbursements.

BE7.8 (LO 1, 2) Deutche Travel has the following internal control procedures over cash disbursements. Identify the internal control principle that is applicable to each procedure.

a. Company checks are prenumbered.

b. The bank statement is reconciled monthly by an internal auditor.

c. Blank checks are stored in a safe in the treasurer's office.

d. Only the treasurer or assistant treasurer may sign checks.

e. Check-signers are not allowed to record cash disbursement transactions.

Prepare entry to replenish a petty cash fund.

BE7.9 (LO 2) On March 20, Dody's petty cash fund of €100 is replenished when the fund contains €9 in cash and receipts for postage €52, freight-out €26, and travel expense €10. Prepare the journal entry to record the replenishment of the petty cash fund.

Identify the control features of a bank account.

BE7.10 (LO 3) Bei Yong is uncertain about the control features of a bank account. Explain the control benefits of (a) a check and (b) a bank statement.

Indicate location of reconciling items in a bank reconciliation.

BE7.11 (LO 3) The following reconciling items are applicable to the bank reconciliation for Ellington Company. Indicate how each item should be shown on a bank reconciliation: (a) outstanding checks, (b) bank debit memorandum for service charge, (c) bank credit memorandum for collecting a note for the depositor, and (d) deposits in transit.

Identify reconciling items that require adjusting entries.

BE7.12 (LO 3) Using the data in BE7.11, indicate (a) the items that will result in an adjustment to the depositor's records and (b) why the other items do not require adjustment.

Prepare partial bank reconciliation.

BE7.13 (LO 3) At July 31, Wenji Interiors has the following bank information (amounts in thousands): cash balance per bank ¥7,420, outstanding checks ¥762, deposits in transit ¥1,620, and a bank service charge ¥20. Determine the adjusted cash balance per bank at July 31.

Prepare partial bank reconciliation.

BE7.14 (LO 3) At August 31, Pratt Shipping has a cash balance per books of £9,500 and the following additional data from the bank statement: charge for printing Pratt Shipping checks £35, interest earned on checking account balance £40, and outstanding checks £800. Determine the adjusted cash balance per books at August 31.

Compute outstanding checks.

BE7.15 (LO 3) In the month of November, Fiesta Catering wrote checks in the amount of €9,750. In December, checks in the amount of €11,762 were written. In November, €8,800 of these checks were presented to the bank for payment, and €10,889 in December. What is the amount of outstanding checks at the end of November? At the end of December?

Explain the statement presentation of cash balances.

BE7.16 (LO 4) Zhang Company has the following cash balances: Cash in Bank $15,742, Payroll Bank Account $6,000, and Plant Expansion Fund Cash $25,000 to be used two years from now. Explain how each balance should be reported on the statement of financial position.

DO IT! Exercises

Identify violations of control activities.

DO IT! 7.1 (LO 1) Identify which control activity is violated in each of the following situations, and explain how the situation creates an opportunity for fraud or inappropriate accounting practices.

1. Once a month, the sales department sends sales invoices to the accounting department to be recorded.
2. Leah Hutcherson orders merchandise for Wular Lake Company; she also receives merchandise and authorizes payment for merchandise.
3. Several clerks at Great Foods use the same cash register drawer.

Design system of internal control over cash receipts.

DO IT! 7.2a (LO 2) Luo Yang is concerned with control over mail receipts at Yang's Tools. All mail receipts are opened by Rong Hu. Rong sends the checks to the accounting department, where they are stamped "For Deposit Only." The accounting department records and deposits the mail receipts weekly. Luo asks for your help in installing a good system of internal control over mail receipts.

DO IT! 7.2b (LO 2) Wilkinson Company established a $100 petty cash fund on August 1. On August 31, the fund had $7 cash remaining and petty cash receipts for postage $31, office supplies $42, and miscellaneous expense $16. Prepare journal entries to establish the fund on August 1 and replenish the fund on August 31.

Make journal entries for petty cash fund.

DO IT! 7.3 (LO 3) Roger Richman owns Richman Blankets. He asks you to explain how he should treat the following reconciling items when reconciling the company's bank account.

Explain treatment of items in bank reconciliation.

1. Outstanding checks.
2. A deposit in transit.
3. The bank charged to the company account a check written by another company.
4. A debit memorandum for a bank service charge.

DO IT! 7.4 (LO 4) Indicate whether each of the following statements is true or false (amounts in thousands).

Analyze statements about the reporting of cash.

1. A company has the following assets at the end of the year: cash on hand NT$40,000, cash refund due from customer NT$30,000, and checking account balance NT$22,000. Cash and cash equivalents is therefore NT$62,000.
2. A company that has received NSF checks should report these checks as a current liability on the statement of financial position.
3. Restricted cash is reported as part of cash and cash equivalents.
4. A company has cash in the bank of NT$50,000, petty cash of NT$400, and equity investments of NT$100,000. Total cash and cash equivalents is therefore NT$50,400.

Exercises

E7.1 (LO 1) Li Tung is the owner of Zhao Pizza. Zhao is operated strictly on a carryout basis. Customers pick up their orders at a counter where a clerk exchanges the pizza for cash. While at the counter, the customer can see other employees making the pizzas and the large ovens in which the pizzas are baked.

Identify the principles of internal control.

Instructions

Identify the six principles of internal control and give an example of each principle that you might observe when picking up your pizza. (*Note:* It may not be possible to observe all the principles.)

E7.2 (LO 1, 2) The following control procedures are used at Torres Company for over-the-counter cash receipts.

Identify internal control weaknesses over cash receipts and suggest improvements.

1. To minimize the risk of robbery, cash in excess of $100 is stored in an unlocked briefcase in the stockroom until it is deposited in the bank.
2. All over-the-counter receipts are processed by three clerks who use a cash register with a single cash drawer.
3. The company accountant makes the bank deposit and then records the day's receipts.
4. At the end of each day, the total receipts are counted by the cashier on duty and reconciled to the cash register total.
5. Cashiers are experienced; they are not bonded.

Instructions

a. For each procedure, explain the weakness in internal control, and identify the control principle that is violated.

b. For each weakness, suggest a change in procedure that will result in good internal control.

E7.3 (LO 1, 2) The following control procedures are used in Mendy Lang's Boutique for cash disbursements.

Identify internal control weaknesses over cash disbursements and suggest improvements.

1. The company accountant prepares the bank reconciliation and reports any discrepancies to the owner.
2. The store manager personally approves all payments before signing and issuing checks.
3. Each week, 100 company checks are left in an unmarked envelope on a shelf behind the cash register.
4. After payment, bills are filed in a paid invoice folder.
5. The company checks are unnumbered.

Instructions

a. For each procedure, explain the weakness in internal control, and identify the internal control principle that is violated.

b. For each weakness, suggest a change in the procedure that will result in good internal control.

Identify internal control weaknesses for cash disbursements and suggest improvements.

E7.4 (LO 2) Writing At Bun Company, checks are not prenumbered because both the purchasing agent and the treasurer are authorized to issue checks. Each signer has access to unissued checks kept in an unlocked file cabinet. The purchasing agent pays all bills pertaining to goods purchased for resale. Prior to payment, the purchasing agent determines that the goods have been received and verifies the mathematical accuracy of the vendor's invoice. After payment, the invoice is filed by the vendor name, and the purchasing agent records the payment. The treasurer pays all other bills following approval by authorized employees. After payment, the treasurer stamps all bills PAID, files them by payment date, and records the checks in the cash disbursements journal. Bun Company maintains one checking account that is reconciled by the treasurer.

Instructions

a. List the weaknesses in internal control over cash disbursements.

b. Write an email to the company treasurer indicating your recommendations for improvement.

Indicate whether procedure is good or weak internal control.

E7.5 (LO 1, 2) Listed below are five procedures followed by Eikenberry Hotels.

1. Several individuals operate the cash register using the same register drawer.
2. A monthly bank reconciliation is prepared by someone who has no other cash responsibilities.
3. Joe Cockrell writes checks and also records cash payment entries.
4. One individual orders inventory, while a different individual authorizes payments.
5. Unnumbered sales invoices from credit sales are forwarded to the accounting department every four weeks for recording.

Instructions

Indicate whether each procedure is an example of good internal control or of weak internal control. If it is an example of good internal control, indicate which internal control principle is being followed. If it is an example of weak internal control, indicate which internal control principle is violated. Use the table below.

Procedure	IC Good or Weak?	Related Internal Control Principle
1.		
2.		
3.		
4.		
5.		

Indicate whether procedure is good or weak internal control.

E7.6 (LO 1, 2) Listed below are five procedures followed by Rhone Bakery.

1. Employees are required to take vacations.
2. Any member of the sales department can approve credit sales.
3. Paul Jaggard ships goods to customers, bills customers, and receives payment from customers.
4. Total cash receipts are compared to bank deposits daily by someone who has no other cash responsibilities.
5. Time clocks are used for recording time worked by employees.

Instructions

Indicate whether each procedure is an example of good internal control or of weak internal control. If it is an example of good internal control, indicate which internal control principle is being followed. If it is an example of weak internal control, indicate which internal control principle is violated. Use the table below.

Procedure	IC Good or Weak?	Related Internal Control Principle
1.		
2.		
3.		
4.		
5.		

E7.7 (LO 2) Setterstrom Company established a petty cash fund on May 1, cashing a check for $100. The company reimbursed the fund on June 1 and July 1 with the following results.

Prepare journal entries for a petty cash fund.

June 1: Cash in fund $1.75. Receipts: delivery expense $31.25, postage expense $39.00, and miscellaneous expense $25.00.

July 1: Cash in fund $3.25. Receipts: delivery expense $21.00, entertainment expense $51.00, and miscellaneous expense $24.75.

On July 10, Setterstrom increased the fund from $100 to $130.

Instructions

Prepare journal entries for Setterstrom Company for May 1, June 1, July 1, and July 10.

E7.8 (LO 2) Horvath Furniture uses an imprest petty cash system. The fund was established on March 1 with a balance of €100. During March, the following petty cash receipts were found in the petty cash box.

Prepare journal entries for a petty cash fund.

Date	Receipt No.	For	Amount
3/5	1	Stamp Inventory	€39
7	2	Freight-Out	21
9	3	Miscellaneous Expense	6
11	4	Travel Expense	24
14	5	Miscellaneous Expense	5

The fund was replenished on March 15 when the fund contained €2 in cash. On March 20, the amount in the fund was increased to €175.

Instructions

Journalize the entries in March that pertain to the operation of the petty cash fund.

E7.9 (LO 3) Rachel Sells is unable to reconcile the bank balance at January 31. Rachel's reconciliation is shown here.

Prepare bank reconciliation and adjusting entries.

Cash balance per bank	$3,677.20
Add: NSF check	450.00
Less: Bank service charge	28.00
Adjusted balance per bank	$4,099.20
Cash balance per books	$3,975.20
Less: Deposits in transit	590.00
Add: Outstanding checks	770.00
Adjusted balance per books	$4,155.20

Instructions

a. What is the proper adjusted cash balance per bank?

b. What is the proper adjusted cash balance per books?

c. Prepare the adjusting journal entries necessary to determine the adjusted cash balance per books.

E7.10 (LO 3) On April 30, the bank reconciliation of Westbrook Company shows three outstanding checks: no. 254, $650; no. 255, $620; and no. 257, $410. The May bank statement and the May cash payments journal show the following.

Determine outstanding checks.

Bank Statement			Cash Payments Journal		
Checks Paid			Checks Issued		
Date	Check No.	Amount	Date	Check No.	Amount
5/4	254	$650	5/2	258	$159
5/2	257	410	5/5	259	275
5/17	258	159	5/10	260	890
5/12	259	275	5/15	261	500
5/20	261	500	5/22	262	750
5/29	263	480	5/24	263	480
5/30	262	750	5/29	264	560

Instructions

Using Step 2 in the reconciliation procedure, list the outstanding checks at May 31.

Prepare bank reconciliation and adjusting entries.

E7.11 (LO 3) The following information pertains to Crane Video (amounts in thousands).

1. Cash balance per bank, July 31, HK$7,263.
2. July bank service charge not recorded by the depositor HK$28.
3. Cash balance per books, July 31, HK$7,284.
4. Deposits in transit, July 31, HK$1,300.
5. Bank collected HK$700 note for Crane in July, plus interest HK$36, less fee HK$20. The collection has not been recorded by Crane, and no interest has been accrued.
6. Outstanding checks, July 31, HK$591.

Instructions

a. Prepare a bank reconciliation at July 31.
b. Journalize the adjusting entries at July 31 on the books of Crane Video.

Prepare bank reconciliation and adjusting entries.

E7.12 (LO 3) This information relates to the Cash account in the ledger of Howard Company.

Balance September 1—$16,400; Cash deposited—$64,000
Balance September 30—$17,600; Checks written—$62,800

The September bank statement shows a balance of $16,500 at September 30 and the following memoranda.

Credits		Debits	
Collection from customer of electronic funds transfer	$1,830	NSF check: H. Kane	$560
Interest earned on checking account	45	Safety deposit box rent	60

At September 30, deposits in transit were $4,738 and outstanding checks totaled $2,383.

Instructions

a. Prepare the bank reconciliation at September 30, 2029.
b. Prepare the adjusting entries at September 30, assuming the NSF check was from a customer on account.

Compute deposits in transit and outstanding checks for two bank reconciliations.

E7.13 (LO 3) The cash records of Dawes Ceramics show the following four situations.

For July:

1. The June 30 bank reconciliation indicated that deposits in transit total €920. During July, the general ledger account Cash shows deposits of €15,750, but the bank statement indicates that only €15,600 in deposits were received during the month.
2. The June 30 bank reconciliation also reported outstanding checks of €680. During the month of July, Dawes Ceramics' books show that €17,200 of checks were issued. The bank statement showed that €16,400 of checks cleared the bank in July.

For September:

3. In September, deposits per the bank statement totaled €26,700, deposits per books were €26,400, and deposits in transit at September 30 were €2,100.
4. In September, cash disbursements per books were €23,700, checks clearing the bank were €25,000, and outstanding checks at September 30 were €2,100.

There were no bank debit or credit memoranda. No errors were made by either the bank or Dawes Ceramics.

Instructions

Answer the following questions.

a. In situation (1), what were the deposits in transit at July 31?
b. In situation (2), what were the outstanding checks at July 31?
c. In situation (3), what were the deposits in transit at August 31?
d. In situation (4), what were the outstanding checks at August 31?

Show presentation of cash in financial statements.

E7.14 (LO 4) Kaur Artisans has recorded the following items in its financial records (amounts in thousands).

Cash in bank	₹ 42,000
Cash in plant expansion fund	100,000
Cash on hand	12,000
Highly liquid investments	34,000
Petty cash	500
Receivables from customers	89,000
Debt investments	61,000

The highly liquid investments had maturities of 3 months or less when they were purchased. The debt investments will be sold in the next 6 to 12 months. The plant expansion project will begin in 3 years.

Instructions

a. What amount should Kaur report as "Cash and cash equivalents" on its statement of financial position?

b. Where should the items not included in part (a) be reported on the statement of financial position?

E7.15 (LO 4) A new accountant at Wyne Glass is trying to identify which of the amounts shown below should be reported as part of the current asset "Cash and cash equivalents" in the year-end statement of financial position, as of April 30, 2029.

Identify reporting of cash.

1. $60 of currency and coin in a locked box used for incidental cash transactions.
2. $260 of April-dated checks that Wyne has received from customers but not yet deposited.
3. An $85 check received from a customer in payment of its April account, but postdated to May 1.
4. $2,500 in the company's checking account.
5. $4,800 in its savings account.
6. $75 of prepaid postage in its postage meter.
7. A $25 IOU from the company receptionist.

Instructions

a. What balance should Wyne report as its "Cash and cash equivalents" balance at April 30, 2029?

b. In what account(s) and in what financial statement(s) should the items not included in "Cash and cash equivalents" be reported?

E7.16 (LO 1, 2, 3, 4) The following is a list of words or phrases introduced in the chapter.

Identify concepts and principles of internal control.

1. Prenumbered documents
2. Custody of an asset should be kept separate from the record-keeping for that asset
3. Cash registers, garment sensors and burglar alarms are examples
4. Bonding employees
5. Collusion
6. Cash
7. Bank statement
8. Payee
9. Maker
10. Canceled checks
11. NSF checks
12. Outstanding checks
13. Petty cash receipt
14. Cash equivalents
15. Voucher system

Instructions

Match the word or phrase above with its description below.

________ **a.** Segregation of duties.
________ **b.** One to whom a check is payable.
________ **c.** Two or more employees circumventing prescribed procedures.
________ **d.** Prevent a transaction from being recorded more than once.
________ **e.** Checks which have been returned by the maker's bank for lack of funds.
________ **f.** Checks which have been paid by the depositor's bank.
________ **g.** Shows the depositor's bank transactions and balances.
________ **h.** Anything that a bank will accept for deposit.
________ **i.** Physical controls.
________ **j.** One who issues a check.
________ **k.** Insurance protection against misappropriation of assets.
________ **l.** An extensive network of approvals by authorized individuals.
________ **m.** Document indicating the purpose of a petty cash expenditure.
________ **n.** Issued checks that have not been paid by the bank.
________ **o.** Highly liquid investments.

Problems

Identify internal control principles over cash disbursements.

P7.1 (LO 1, 2) Bolz Office Supply recently changed its system of internal control over cash disbursements. The system includes the following features.

Instead of being unnumbered and manually prepared, all checks must now be prenumbered and prepared by using the new accounts payable software purchased by the company. Before a check can be issued, each invoice must have the approval of Kathy Moon, the purchasing agent, and Robin Self, the receiving department supervisor. Checks must be signed by either Jennifer Edwards, the treasurer, or Rich Woodruff, the assistant treasurer. Before signing a check, the signer is expected to compare the amount of the check with the amount on the invoice.

After signing a check, the signer stamps the invoice PAID and inserts the date, check number, and amount of the check within the stamp. The "paid" invoice is then sent to the accounting department for recording.

Blank checks are stored in a safe in the treasurer's office. The combination to the safe is known only by the treasurer and assistant treasurer. Each month, the bank statement is reconciled with the bank balance per books by the assistant chief accountant. All employees who handle or account for cash are bonded.

Instructions

Identify the internal control principles and their application to cash disbursements of Bolz Office Supply.

Identify internal control weaknesses in cash receipts and cash disbursements.

P7.2 (LO 1, 2) Rondelli School wants to raise money for a new sound system for its auditorium. The primary fund-raising event is a dance at which the famous disc jockey D.J. Sound will play classic and not-so-classic dance tunes. Matt Ballester, the music and theater instructor, has been given the responsibility for coordinating the fund-raising efforts. This is Matt's first experience with fund-raising. He decides to put the student choir in charge of the event; he will be a relatively passive observer.

Matt had 500 unnumbered tickets printed for the dance. He left the tickets in a box on his desk and told the choir students to take as many tickets as they thought they could sell for €5 each. In order to ensure that no extra tickets would be floating around, he told them to dispose of any unsold tickets. When the students received payment for the tickets, they were to bring the cash back to Matt and he would put it in a locked box in his desk drawer.

Some of the students were responsible for decorating the gymnasium for the dance. Matt gave each of them a key to the money box and told them that if they took money out to purchase materials, they should put a note in the box saying how much they took and what it was used for. After 2 weeks the money box appeared to be getting full, so Matt asked Jeff Kenney to count the money, prepare a deposit slip, and deposit the money in a bank account Matt had opened.

The day of the dance, Matt wrote a check from the account to pay the DJ. D.J. Sound, however, said that he accepted only cash and did not give receipts. So Matt took €200 out of the cash box and gave it to D.J. At the dance, Matt had Sam Copper working at the entrance to the gymnasium, collecting tickets from students, and selling tickets to those who had not prepurchased them. Matt estimated that 400 students attended the dance.

The following day, Matt closed out the bank account, which had €250 in it, and gave that amount plus the €180 in the cash box to Principal Finke. Principal Finke seemed surprised that, after generating roughly €2,000 in sales, the dance netted only €430 in cash. Matt did not know how to respond.

Instructions

Identify as many internal control weaknesses as you can in this scenario, and suggest how each could be addressed.

Journalize and post petty cash fund transactions.

P7.3 (LO 2) Kael Photography maintains a petty cash fund for small expenditures. These transactions occurred during the month of August.

Aug.	1	Established the petty cash fund by writing a check payable to the petty cash custodian for R$200.
	15	Replenished the petty cash fund by writing a check for R$175. On this date, the fund consisted of R$25 in cash and these petty cash receipts: freight-out R$74.40, entertainment expense R$36, postage expense R$33.70, and miscellaneous expense R$27.50.
	16	Increased the amount of the petty cash fund to R$400 by writing a check for R$200.
	31	Replenished the petty cash fund by writing a check for R$283. On this date, the fund consisted of R$117 in cash and these petty cash receipts: postage expense R$145, entertainment expense R$90.60, and freight-out R$46.40.

Instructions

a. Journalize the petty cash transactions.

b. Post to the Petty Cash account.

c. What internal control features exist in a petty cash fund?

Prepare a bank reconciliation and adjusting entries.

P7.4 (LO 3) On July 31, 2029, Keeds Company had a cash balance per books of $6,140. The statement from Dakota State Bank on that date showed a balance of $7,690.80. A comparison of the bank statement with the Cash account revealed the following facts.

1. The bank service charge for July was $25.
2. The bank collected $1,520 for Keeds Company through electronic funds transfer.
3. The July 31 receipts of $1,193.30 were not included in the bank deposits for July. These receipts were deposited by the company in a night deposit vault on July 31.
4. Company check No. 2480 issued to L. Taylor, a creditor, for $384 that cleared the bank in July was incorrectly entered as a cash payment on July 10 for $348.
5. Checks outstanding on July 31 totaled $1,860.10.
6. On July 31, the bank statement showed an NSF charge of $575 for a check received by the company from W. Krueger, a customer, on account.

Instructions

a. Prepare the bank reconciliation as of July 31.

b. Prepare the necessary adjusting entries at July 31.

a. Adjusted cash bal. $7,024.00

Prepare a bank reconciliation and adjusting entries from detailed data.

P7.5 (LO 3) The bank portion of the bank reconciliation for Shou Florists at November 30, 2029, was as follows (amounts in thousands).

Shou Florists
Bank Reconciliation
November 30, 2029

Cash balance per bank			HK$14,367.90
Add: Deposits in transit			2,530.20
			16,898.10
Less: Outstanding checks			
	Check Number	Check Amount	
	3451	HK$2,260.40	
	3470	720.10	
	3471	844.50	
	3472	1,426.80	
	3474	1,050.00	6,301.80
Adjusted cash balance per bank			HK$10,596.30

The adjusted cash balance per bank agreed with the cash balance per books at November 30. The December bank statement showed the following checks and deposits.

Bank Statement

Checks			Deposits	
Date	**Number**	**Amount**	**Date**	**Amount**
12-1	3451	HK$ 2,260.40	12-1	HK$ 2,530.20
12-2	3471	844.50	12-4	1,211.60
12-7	3472	1,426.80	12-8	2,365.10
12-4	3475	1,640.70	12-16	2,672.70
12-8	3476	1,300.00	12-21	2,945.00
12-10	3477	2,130.00	12-26	2,567.30
12-15	3479	3,080.00	12-29	2,836.00
12-27	3480	600.00	12-30	1,025.00
12-30	3482	475.50	Total	HK$18,152.90
12-29	3483	1,140.00		
12-31	3485	540.80		
	Total	HK$15,438.70		

The cash records per books for December showed the following.

Cash Payments Journal

Date	Number	Amount	Date	Number	Amount
12-1	3475	HK$1,640.70	12-20	3482	HK$ 475.50
12-2	3476	1,300.00	12-22	3483	1,140.00
12-2	3477	2,130.00	12-23	3484	798.00
12-4	3478	621.30	12-24	3485	450.80
12-8	3479	3,080.00	12-30	3486	889.50
12-10	3480	600.00	Total		HK$13,933.20
12-17	3481	807.40			

Cash Receipts Journal

Date	Amount
12-3	HK$ 1,211.60
12-7	2,365.10
12-15	2,672.70
12-20	2,954.00
12-25	2,567.30
12-28	2,836.00
12-30	1,025.00
12-31	1,690.40
Total	HK$17,322.10

The bank statement contained two memoranda:

1. A credit of HK$2,242 for the collection of Shou Florists of an electronic funds transfer.
2. A debit for the printing of additional company checks HK$85.

At December 31, the cash balance per books was HK$13,985.20, and the cash balance per the bank statement was HK$19,239.10. The bank did not make any errors, but **Shou Florists made two errors**.

Instructions

a. Adjusted balance per books HK$16,043.20

a. Using the steps in the reconciliation procedure described in the chapter, prepare a bank reconciliation at December 31, 2029.

b. Prepare the adjusting entries based on the reconciliation. (*Hint:* The correction of any errors pertaining to recording checks should be made to Accounts Payable. The correction of any errors relating to recording cash receipts should be made to Accounts Receivable.)

Prepare a bank reconciliation and adjusting entries.

P7.6 (LO 3) Timmins Grow-Fast spreads herbicides and applies liquid fertilizer for local farmers. On May 31, 2029, the company's Cash account per its general ledger showed a balance of £6,738.90.

The bank statement from Manchester Bank on that date showed the following balance.

MANCHESTER BANK

Checks and Debits	Deposits and Credits	Daily Balance
		5-31 6,968.00

A comparison of the details on the bank statement with the details in the Cash account revealed the following facts.

1. The statement included a debit memo of £40 for the printing of additional company checks.
2. Cash sales of £883.15 on May 12 were deposited in the bank. The cash receipts entry and the deposit slip were incorrectly made for £933.15. The bank credited Timmins for the correct amount.
3. Outstanding checks at May 31 totaled £276.25, and deposits in transit were £1,880.15.
4. On May 18, the company issued check No. 1181 for £685 to H. Moses, on account. The check, which cleared the bank in May, was incorrectly journalized and posted by Timmins for £658.
5. £2,690 was collected from a customer's note receivable by the bank for Timmins on May 31 through electronic funds transfer.
6. Included with the canceled checks was a check issued by Tomins to C. Pernod for £360 that was incorrectly charged to Timmins by the bank.
7. On May 31, the bank statement showed an NSF charge of £380 for a check issued by Sara Ballard, a customer, to Timmins on account.

Instructions

a. Adjusted cash bal. £8,931.90

a. Prepare the bank reconciliation at May 31, 2029.

b. Prepare the necessary adjusting entries for Timmins at May 31, 2029.

Prepare a comprehensive bank reconciliation with theft and internal control deficiencies.

P7.7 (LO 1, 2, 3) Daisey Company is a very profitable small business. It has not, however, given much consideration to internal control. For example, in an attempt to keep clerical and office expenses to a minimum, the company has combined the jobs of cashier and bookkeeper. As a result, Bret Turrin handles all cash receipts, keeps the accounting records, and prepares the monthly bank reconciliations.

The balance per the bank statement on October 31, 2029, was $18,380. Outstanding checks were No. 62 for $140.75, No. 183 for $180, No. 284 for $253.25, No. 862 for $190.71, No. 863 for $226.80, and No. 864 for $165.28. Included with the statement was a credit memorandum of $185 indicating the collection of a note receivable for Daisey Company by the bank on October 25. This memorandum has not been recorded by Daisey.

The company's ledger showed one Cash account with a balance of $21,877.72. The balance included undeposited cash on hand. Because of the lack of internal controls, Bret took for personal use all of the undeposited receipts in excess of $3,795.51. He then prepared the following bank reconciliation in an effort to conceal his theft of cash.

Cash balance per books, October 31		$21,877.72
Add: Outstanding checks		
No. 862	$190.71	
No. 863	226.80	
No. 864	165.28	482.79
		22,360.51
Less: Undeposited receipts		3,795.51
Unadjusted balance per bank, October 31		18,565.00
Less: Bank credit memorandum		185.00
Cash balance per bank statement, October 31		$18,380.00

Instructions

a. Adjusted cash bal. $21,018.72

a. Prepare a correct bank reconciliation. (*Hint:* Deduct the amount of the theft from the adjusted balance per books.)

b. Indicate the three ways that Bret attempted to conceal the theft and the dollar amount involved in each method.

c. What principles of internal control were violated in this case?

P7.8 (LO 3) A comparison of the bank statement with the Cash account for Company A on October 31, 2029 revealed the following facts:

Bank reconciliation and adjusting entries.

1. The balance of the "Cash" account on October 31 was $7,865, while the balance listed on the bank statement was $8,147.
2. The cash received on October 31, $1,984, had been deposited into the bank, but was not yet shown on the bank statement.
3. A customer of the Company A wrote a check for $320, which was returned due to insufficient funds. Company A did not make an entry when it received the returned check.
4. The bank statement on September 30 showed the following uncashed checks:

#721	$100	#765	$ 36
#728	2	#782	1,250

   Checking the bank statement on October 31, it is clear that checks #728 and #765 are still uncashed.
5. After checking the bank statement, it was found that the following checks issued in October had not been cashed:

#824	$ 65	#843	$818
#840	122	#844	90
#841	3	#845	463

6. A check for $1,000 was issued by Company B. The bank mistakenly attributed it to Company A and listed it on Company A's statement.
7. On October 30, the bank collected a non-interest-bearing note for $2,000 on behalf of Company A. After deducting a collection fee of $5, the amount was credited to the company's account, but Company A has not yet made an entry.
8. The bank statement included a deduction of $8, which was found to be the bank's expense for printing Company A's checkbook.

Adjusted cash bal. $9,532

Instructions

a. Prepare the bank reconciliation as of October 31, 2029.

b. Prepare the necessary adjusting entries at October 31, 2029.

Comprehensive Accounting Cycle Review

ACR7 On December 1, 2029, Papadopoulos Seasonings had the following account balances.

	Debit		Credit
Cash	€18,200	Accumulated Depreciation—	
Notes Receivable	2,200	Equipment	€ 3,000
Accounts Receivable	7,500	Accounts Payable	6,100
Inventory	16,000	Share Capital—Ordinary	50,000
Prepaid Insurance	1,600	Retained Earnings	14,400
Equipment	28,000		€73,500
	€73,500		

During December, the company completed the following transactions.

Dec. 7 Received €3,600 cash from customers in payment of account (no discount allowed).
12 Purchased merchandise on account from Spiro Co. €12,000, terms 1/10, n/30.
17 Sold merchandise on account €16,000, terms 2/10, n/30. The cost of the merchandise sold was €10,000.
19 Paid salaries €2,200.
22 Paid Spiro Co. in full, less discount.
26 Received collections in full, less discounts, from customers billed on December 17.
31 Received €2,700 cash from customers in payment of account (no discount allowed).

Adjustment data:

1. Depreciation €200 per month.
2. Insurance expired €400.

Instructions

a. Journalize the December transactions. (Assume a perpetual inventory system.)

b. Enter the December 1 balances in the ledger T-accounts and post the December transactions. Use Cost of Goods Sold, Depreciation Expense, Insurance Expense, Salaries and Wages Expense, Sales Revenue, and Sales Discounts.

c. The statement from Athens Bank on December 31 showed a balance of €26,130. A comparison of the bank statement with the Cash account revealed the following facts.

1. The bank collected a note receivable of €2,200 for Papadopoulos on December 15.
2. The December 31 receipts were deposited in a night deposit vault on December 31. These deposits were recorded by the bank in January.
3. Checks outstanding on December 31 totaled €1,210.
4. On December 31, the bank statement showed an NSF charge of €680 for a check received by the company from A. Quinn, a customer, on account.

Prepare a bank reconciliation as of December 31 based on the available information. (*Hint:* The cash balance per books is €26,100. This can be proven by finding the balance in the Cash account from parts (a) and (b).)

d. Journalize the adjusting entries resulting from the bank reconciliation and adjustment data.

e. Post the adjusting entries to the ledger T-accounts.

f. Prepare an adjusted trial balance.

g. Prepare an income statement for December and a classified statement of financial position at December 31.

f. Adj. cash balance €27,620

g. Net income €2,880

Data Analytics in Action

Using Data Visualization to Understand Fraud

DA7.1 Data visualization can be used to identify the occurrence of behavioral red flags.

Excel

Example: Most people who commit fraud leave clues, called red flags, that call attention to their actions. Sometimes, more than one red flag exists. Rarely, there are none.

Many of the red flags have common characteristics and can be divided into groups. For example, consider the following chart. Do you notice that several red flags are related to finances, while other red flags appear to have social and emotional ties? Both groups are tied to the pressure component of the fraud triangle, which will lead people to consider committing fraud.

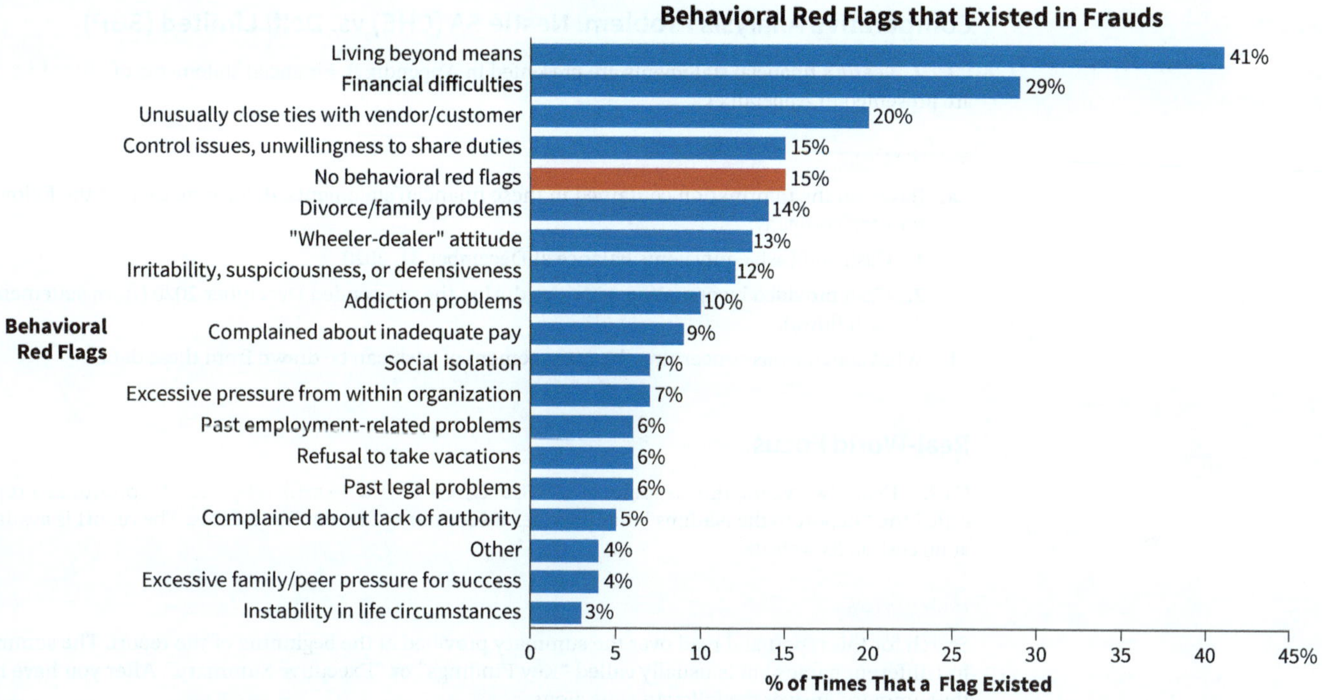

Source: Adapted from ACFE, "2018 Global Study on Occupational Fraud and Abuse," *Report to the Nations* (2018).

Unfortunately, even with 85% of incidents showing red flags (as noted in the chart, 15% of frauds indicated no red flags), much of the fraudulent activity is not identified until a loss has occurred. Nonetheless, it is important for managers to look out for red flags to help identify fraud situations as soon as possible.

For this case, you will use data that show internal controls in place and the impact on reducing the cost to the organization of the fraud. You will create a combo clustered column and line chart and then analyze it to determine which internal controls reduced the loss by the greatest percentage.

Go to the Wiley online course for complete case details and instructions.

Using Data Analytics to Determine the Impact of Internal Control Activities

DA7.2 Fraud not only costs an organization money but also time. For this case, you will use data that provides the percentage reduction of time and percent reduction of loss for various internal control activities. You will create and analyze a column chart to identify the controls that are most effective in reducing time and fraud.

Excel

Go to the Wiley online course for complete case details and instructions.

Expand Your Critical Thinking

Financial Reporting Problem: TSMC, Ltd. (TWN)

CT7.1 The financial statements of **TSMC** are presented in Appendix A. The complete annual report, including the notes to the financial statements, is available at the company's website.

Instructions

a. What data about cash and cash equivalents are shown in the consolidated statement of financial position?

b. In its notes to Consolidated Financial Statements, how does TSMC define cash equivalents?

Comparative Analysis Problem: Nestlé SA (CHE) vs. Delfi Limited (SGP)

CT7.2 **Nestlé's** financial statements are presented in Appendix B. Financial statements of **Delfi Limited** are presented in Appendix C.

Instructions

a. Based on the information contained in these financial statements, determine each of the following for each company:

1. Cash and cash equivalents balance at December 31, 2020.
2. Cash provided by operating activities during the year ended December 2020 (from statement of cash flows).

b. What conclusions concerning the management of cash can be drawn from these data?

Real-World Focus

CT7.3 Every two years, the **Association of Certified Fraud Examiners (ACFE)** produces a report called the "Report to the Nations" that provides a summary of recent fraud cases. The report is available at no cost on its website.

Instructions

Search for this report and read over the summary provided at the beginning of the report. The summary has different names but is usually called "Key Findings" or "Executive Summary." After you have read the summary, answer the following questions.

a. What does fraud cost businesses?

b. What are the most common types of fraud?

c. What is the most common method to detect fraud, and what can businesses do to make fraud detection more likely?

CT7.4 While blockchain technology is currently costly and complex, it has numerous potential benefits to improve internal control. An article by Ken Tysiac in the *Journal of Accountancy* entitled "Evaluating Blockchain and Internal Control Through a COSO Lens" discusses these potential benefits.

Instructions

Search online for the article and then describe the potential benefits of blockchain for each of the five primary components of internal control: (1) control environment, (2) risk assessment, (3) control activities, (4) information and communication, and (5) monitoring.

CT7.5 The **International Accounting Standards Board (IASB)** is a private organization established to develop a single set of high-quality, understandable, enforceable, and globally accepted financial reporting standards. The IASB conducts extensive research before issuing a new standard or amending an existing standard.

Instructions

Go to the IASB website to answer the following questions.

a. What are the important steps of the standard-setting process?

b. After a standard is issued, what steps does the IASB take to ensure that the standard is achieving its objective?

Decision-Making Across the Organization

CT7.6 The board of trustees of a local church is concerned about the internal accounting controls for the offering collections made at weekly services. The trustees ask you to serve on a three-person audit team with the internal auditor of a local college and a public accountant who has just joined the church.

At a meeting of the audit team and the board of trustees, you learn the following.

1. The church's board of trustees has delegated responsibility for the financial management and audit of the financial records to the finance committee. This group prepares the annual budget and approves major disbursements. It is not involved in collections or recordkeeping. No audit has been made in recent years because the same trusted employee has kept church records and served as financial secretary for 15 years. The church does not carry any fidelity insurance.
2. The collection at the weekly service is taken by a team of ushers who volunteer to serve one month. The ushers take the collection plates to a basement office at the rear of the church. They hand their plates to the head usher and return to the church service. After all plates have been turned in, the head usher counts the cash received. The head usher then places the cash in the church safe along with a notation of the amount counted. The head usher volunteers to serve for 3 months.
3. The next morning, the financial secretary opens the safe and recounts the collection. The secretary withholds £150–£200 in cash, depending on the cash expenditures expected for the week, and deposits the remainder of the collections in the bank. To facilitate the deposit, church members who contribute by check are asked to make their checks payable to "Cash."
4. Each month, the financial secretary reconciles the bank statement and submits a copy of the reconciliation to the board of trustees. The reconciliations have rarely contained any bank errors and have never shown any errors per books.

Instructions

With the class divided into groups, answer the following.

a. Indicate the weaknesses in internal accounting control over the handling of collections.

b. List the improvements in internal control procedures that you plan to make at the next meeting of the audit team for (1) the ushers, (2) the head usher, (3) the financial secretary, and (4) the finance committee.

c. What church policies should be changed to improve internal control?

Ethics Case

CT7.7 You are the assistant controller in charge of general ledger accounting at Hallasan Bottling. Your company has a large loan from an insurance company. The loan agreement requires that the company's cash account balance be maintained at ₩200,000 or more, as reported monthly (amounts in thousands).

At June 30, the cash balance is ₩80,000, which you report to Yoo Yun, the financial vice president. Yoo excitedly instructs you to keep the cash receipts book open for one additional day for purposes of the June 30 report to the insurance company. Yoo says, "If we don't get that cash balance over ₩200,000, we'll default on our loan agreement. They could close us down, put us all out of our jobs!" Yoo continues, "I talked to Oconto Distributors (one of Hallasan's largest customers) this morning. They said they sent us a check for ₩150,000 yesterday. We should receive it tomorrow. If we include just that one check in our cash balance, we'll be in the clear. It's in the mail!"

Instructions

a. Who will suffer negative effects if you do not comply with Yoo's instructions? Who will suffer if you do comply?

b. What are the ethical considerations in this case?

c. What alternatives do you have?

Answers to Insight and Accounting Across the Organization Questions

And the Controls Are... Q: Why is sustainability information important to investors? **A:** Investors, customers, suppliers, and employees want more information about companies' long-term impact on society. There is a growing awareness that sustainability issues can affect a company's financial performance. Proper reporting on sustainability issues develops a solid reputation for transparency and provides confidence to shareholders.

Internal Control and the Role of Human Resources Q: Why would unsupervised employees or employees who report to each other represent potential internal control threats? **A:** An unsupervised employee may have a fraudulent job (or may even be a fictitious person), for example, a person drawing a paycheck without working. Or, if two employees supervise each other, there is no real separation of duties, and they can conspire to defraud the company.

How Employees Steal Q: How can companies reduce the likelihood of occupational fraud? **A:** To reduce the occurrence of occupational fraud, a company should follow the procedures discussed in this chapter. For example, to reduce fraudulent disbursements, companies should require that only designated personnel sign checks, have different personnel approve payments and make payments, ensure that check-signers do not record disbursements, use prenumbered checks and match each check to an approved invoice, store blank checks securely, reconcile the bank statement, and stamp invoices PAID.

Madoff's Ponzi Scheme Q: How was Madoff able to conceal such a giant fraud? **A:** Madoff fabricated false investment statements that were provided to investors. In addition, his auditor never verified these investment statements even though the auditor issued an unqualified opinion each year.

A Look at U.S. GAAP

LEARNING OBJECTIVE 5

Compare the accounting for fraud, internal control, and cash under IFRS and U.S. GAAP.

Fraud can occur anywhere. And because the three main factors that contribute to fraud are universal in nature, the principles of internal control activities are used globally by companies. GAAP and IFRS are also very similar in accounting for cash. *IAS No. 1 (revised)*, "Presentation of Financial Statements," is the only standard that discusses issues specifically related to cash.

Key Points

- The fraud triangle discussed in this chapter is applicable to all international companies. Some of the major frauds on a U.S. basis are **Enron** (USA), **WorldCom** (USA), and more recently the Bernie Madoff Ponzi scheme.
- Internal controls are a system of checks and balances designed to prevent and detect fraud and errors. While most companies have these systems in place, many have never completely documented them, nor had an independent auditor attest to their effectiveness.
- Companies find that internal control review is a costly process but badly needed. One study estimates the cost to U.S. companies at over $35 billion. At the same time, examination of internal controls indicates lingering problems in the way companies operate.

Similarities

- Accounting scandals both in the United States and internationally have re-ignited the debate over the relative merits of GAAP, which takes a "rules-based" approach to accounting, versus IFRS, which takes a "principles-based" approach. The FASB announced that it intends to introduce more principles-based standards.
- The accounting and internal control procedures related to cash are essentially the same under both GAAP and this text. In addition, the definition used for cash equivalents is the same.
- Most companies report cash and cash equivalents together under GAAP, as shown in this text. In addition, GAAP follows the same accounting policies related to the reporting of restricted cash.
- GAAP and IFRS define cash and cash equivalents similarly as follows.
  - **Cash** is comprised of cash on hand and demand deposits.
  - **Cash equivalents** are short-term, highly liquid investments that are readily convertible to known amounts of cash and which are subject to an insignificant risk of changes in value.

Differences

- After numerous company scandals, the U.S. Congress passed the Sarbanes-Oxley Act (SOX). Under SOX, all publicly traded U.S. corporations are required to maintain an adequate system of internal control.
- As a result of SOX, company executives and boards of directors must ensure that internal controls are reliable and effective. In addition, independent outside auditors must attest to the adequacy of the internal control system.
- SOX created the Public Company Accounting Oversight Board (PCAOB) to establish auditing standards and regulate auditor activity.

GAAP Practice

GAAP Self-Test Questions

1. Non-U.S. companies that follow IFRS:
   a. do not normally use the principles of internal control activities described in this text.
   b. often offset cash with accounts payable on the statement of financial position.
   c. are not required to follow SOX.
   d. None of the answer choices is correct.

2. Which of the following is the correct accounting under GAAP for cash?
   a. Cash cannot be combined with cash equivalents.
   b. Demand deposits are not included as cash.
   c. Cash equivalents are short-term, highly liquid investments that can be converted into known amounts of cash and are so near maturity that their market value is not generally sensitive to interest rate changes.
   d. Cash on hand is not reported on the statement of financial position as Cash.

3. The Sarbanes-Oxley Act applies to:
   a. all U.S. companies listed on U.S. exchanges.
   b. all companies that list shares on any securities exchange in any country.
   c. all European companies listed on European exchanges.
   d. Both U.S. companies listed on U.S. exchanges and European companies listed on European exchanges.

4. High-quality accounting requires both high-quality accounting standards and:
   a. a reconsideration of SOX to make it less onerous.
   b. high-quality auditing standards.
   c. government intervention to ensure that the public interest is protected.
   d. the development of new principles of internal control activities.

5. Cash equivalents under GAAP:
   a. are significantly different than the cash equivalents discussed in the text.
   b. are generally disclosed separately from cash.
   c. may be required to be reported separately from cash in the future.
   d. None of the answer choices is correct.

GAAP Exercises

GAAP7.1 Some people argue that the internal control requirements of the Sarbanes-Oxley Act (SOX) put U.S. companies at a competitive disadvantage to companies outside the United States. Discuss the competitive implications (both pros and cons) of SOX.

GAAP7.2 State whether each of the following is true or false. For those that are false, explain why.

a. A proposed new financial accounting standard would not allow cash equivalents to be reported in combination with cash.

b. Perspectives on bribery and penalties for engaging in bribery are the same across all countries.

c. Cash equivalents are comprised of cash on hand and demand deposits.

d. SOX was created by the International Accounting Standards Board.

GAAP Financial Reporting Problem: Apple Inc. (USA)

GAAP7.3 The financial statements of **Apple** are presented in Appendix D. The complete annual report, including the notes to its financial statements, is available at the company's website.

Instructions

Using the financial statements and notes to the financial statements, answer these questions about Apple's internal controls and cash.

a. What comments, if any, are made about cash in the "Report of Independent Registered Public Accounting Firm"?

b. What data about cash and cash equivalents are shown in the consolidated balance sheet (statement of financial position)?

c. How are cash equivalents defined in the Notes to Consolidated Financial Statements?

d. Read the section of the report titled "Management's Report on Internal Control Over Financial Reporting." Summarize the statements made in that section of the report.

Answers to GAAP Self-Test Questions

1. c **2.** b **3.** a **4.** b **5.** c

CHAPTER **8**

Accounting for Receivables

LEARNING OBJECTIVES After studying this chapter, you should be able to:

LO 1 Explain how companies recognize accounts receivable.

LO 2 Describe how companies value accounts receivable and record their disposition.

LO 3 Explain how companies recognize, value, and dispose of notes receivable.

LO 4 Describe the statement presentation and analysis of receivables.

Chapter Preview

As indicated in the following Feature Story, receivables are a significant asset for many banks. Because a large portion of sales are credit sales, receivables are important to companies in other industries as well. As a consequence, companies must pay close attention to their receivables and manage them carefully. In this chapter, you will learn what journal entries companies make when they sell products, when they collect cash from those sales, and when they write off accounts they cannot collect.

Accounting for Receivables

Recognition of Accounts Receivable	Valuation and Disposition of Accounts Receivable	Notes Receivable	Presentation and Analysis
• Types of receivables • Recognizing accounts receivable	• Valuing accounts receivable • Disposing of accounts receivable	• Determining the maturity date • Computing interest • Recognizing notes receivable • Valuing notes receivable • Disposing of notes receivable	• Presentation • Analysis • Data analytics and receivables management

Practice

DO IT! 1 Recognizing Accounts Receivable

DO IT! 2a Bad Debt Expense

2b Factoring

DO IT! 3 Recognizing Notes Receivable

DO IT! 4 Analysis of Receivables

Go to the Review and Practice section at the end of the chapter for a review of key concepts and practice applications with solutions.
Additional tutorials and practice opportunities are available in the Wiley online course.

Feature Story Are You Going to Pay Me—or Not?

What is the only thing harder than making a sale? Answer: Collecting the cash. Just ask a banker, virtually any banker. Bankers around the world have been awash in "doubtful" loans for years. And, it may be many years before the mess is finally cleaned up.

If your business sells most of its goods on credit or is in the business of making loans, then accurately recording your receivables is one of your most important accounting tasks. At the end of every accounting period, companies are required to estimate how many of their receivables are "uncollectible." A significant decline in the amount of estimated doubtful loans can send a company's share price soaring. For example, **BNP Paribas** (FRA) reported a decline in the estimated provision for doubtful loans of more than 50%. The market reacted very favorably, with the company's share price rising by 5.3% in one day.

On the other hand, when a company announces an unexpected increase in its estimated doubtful loans, the securities market often reacts severely. For example, **BBVA** (ESP) announced that it was increasing its estimated provision for doubtful loans by €164 million. Its share price fell by 6% in a single day.

No bank is spared scrutiny of its estimated doubtful loans. In fact, it is likely that no number in a bank's financial statements receives more careful investigation by financial analysts and investors. Nearly three years after the beginning of the financial crisis, **Bank of America**'s (USA) share price was still in single digits (after hitting a high of $54 per share) primarily because of investor concern regarding its provision for doubtful loans. And, on the other side of the globe, in Iran, one banker suggested that as many as 20% of the loans held by that country's banks are doubtful.

Sources: Ben Hall, "Fall in Bad Loans Boosts BNP Paribas," *Financial Times Online* (August 2, 2010); Tracy Alloway, "BBVA, An Exercise in Spanish Banking Losses," *Financial Times Online* (February 3, 2011); and Najmeh Bozorgmehr, "Private Banks Open to Assist Tehran Insiders," *Financial Times Online* (May 9, 2011).

TPG/Shutterstock

8.1 Recognition of Accounts Receivable

LEARNING OBJECTIVE 1

Explain how companies recognize accounts receivable.

The term **receivables** refers to amounts due from individuals and companies.

- Receivables are claims that are expected to be collected in cash.
- The management of receivables is a very important activity for any company that sells goods or services on credit.

Receivables are important because they represent one of a company's most liquid assets. For many companies, receivables are also one of the largest assets. For example, receivables represent 43.7% of the current assets of telecommunications giant **Etisalat** (UAE). **Illustration 8.1** lists receivables as a percentage of total assets for five other well-known companies in a recent year.

ILLUSTRATION 8.1

Receivables as a percentage of assets

Company	Receivables as a Percentage of Total Assets
adidas (DEU)	9%
Hyundai (KOR)	3
Samsung (KOR)	9
Nestlé (CHE)	9
China Mobile Limited (HKG)	5

Types of Receivables

The relative significance of a company's receivables as a percentage of its assets depends on various factors: its industry, the time of year, whether it extends long-term financing, and its credit policies. To reflect important differences among receivables, they are frequently classified as (1) accounts receivable, (2) notes receivable, and (3) other receivables.

Accounts receivable are amounts customers owe on account. They result from the sale of goods and services. Companies generally expect to collect accounts receivable within 30 to 60 days. They are usually the most significant type of claim held by a company.

Notes receivable are a written promise (as evidenced by a formal instrument) for amounts to be received. The note normally requires the collection of interest and extends for time periods of 60–90 days or longer. Notes and accounts receivable that result from sales transactions are often called **trade receivables**.

Other receivables include non-trade receivables such as interest receivable, loans to company officers, advances to employees, and income taxes refundable (see **Ethics Note**). These do not generally result from the operations of the business. Therefore, they are generally classified and reported as separate items in the statement of financial position.

ETHICS NOTE

Companies report receivables from employees separately in the financial statements. The reason: Sometimes these receivables are not the result of an "arm's-length" transaction.

Recognizing Accounts Receivable

Recognizing accounts receivable is relatively straightforward.

- A service organization records a receivable when it performs service on account.
- A merchandiser records accounts receivable at the point of sale of merchandise on account. When a merchandiser sells goods, it increases (debits) Accounts Receivable and increases (credits) Sales Revenue.

Recall that sellers sometimes offer sales discounts to encourage early payment by the buyer. If the buyer pays during the discount period, the receivable balance will be satisfied with a smaller cash payment. Also, the buyer might find some of the goods unacceptable and choose to return the unwanted goods. When a buyer returns goods that it previously purchased on credit, the receivable balance is reduced.

To review, assume that Zhang Ltd. on July 1, 2029, sells merchandise on account to Li Stores for ¥1,000, terms 2/10, n/30 (amounts in thousands). On July 5, Li returns merchandise with a sales price of ¥100 to Zhang. On July 11, Zhang receives payment from Li for the balance due. The journal entries to record these transactions on the books of Zhang are as follows (see **Helpful Hint**). **(Cost of goods sold entries are omitted.)**

HELPFUL HINT

These entries are the same as those described in Chapter 5. For simplicity, we have omitted inventory and cost of goods sold from this set of journal entries and from end-of-chapter material.

July 1	Accounts Receivable	1,000	
	Sales Revenue		1,000
	(To record sales on account)		
July 5	Sales Returns and Allowances	100	
	Accounts Receivable		100
	(To record merchandise returned)		
July 11	Cash (¥900 – ¥18)	882	
	Sales Discounts (¥900 × .02)	18	
	Accounts Receivable		900
	(To record collection of accounts receivable)		

Some retailers issue their own credit cards. When you use a retailer's credit card (**IKEA** (SWE), for example), the retailer charges interest on the balance due if not paid within a specified period (usually 25–30 days).

To illustrate, assume that you use your IKEA credit card to purchase clothing with a sales price of €300 on June 1, 2029. IKEA will increase (debit) Accounts Receivable for €300 and increase (credit) Sales Revenue for €300 (cost of goods sold entry omitted) as follows.

A = L + E
+300
+300 Rev
Cash Flows
no effect

June 1	Accounts Receivable	300	
	Sales Revenue		300
	(To record sale of merchandise)		

Assuming that you owe €300 at the end of the month and IKEA charges 1.5% per month on the balance due, the adjusting entry that IKEA makes to record interest revenue of €4.50 (€300 × 1.5%) on June 30 is as follows.

A = L + E
+4.50
+4.50 Rev
Cash Flows
no effect

June 30	Accounts Receivable	4.50	
	Interest Revenue		4.50
	(To record sale of merchandise)		

Interest revenue is often substantial for many retailers.

Anatomy of a Fraud

Tasanee was the accounts receivable clerk for a large non-profit foundation that provided performance and exhibition space for the performing and visual arts. Her responsibilities included activities normally assigned to an accounts receivable clerk, such as recording revenues from various sources (donations, facility rental fees, and ticket revenue). However, she was also responsible for handling all cash and checks from the time they were received until the time she deposited them, as well as preparing the bank reconciliation.

Tasanee took advantage of her situation by falsifying bank deposits and bank reconciliations so that she could steal cash from the donations. Since nobody else logged the donations or matched the donation receipts to pledges prior to Tasanee receiving them, she was able to offset the cash that was stolen against donations that she received but didn't record. Her crime was made easier by the fact that her boss, the company's controller, only did a very superficial review of the bank reconciliation and thus didn't notice that some numbers had been cut out from other documents and taped onto the bank reconciliation.

Total take: $1.5 million

The Missing Controls

Segregation of duties. The foundation should not have allowed an accounts receivable clerk, whose job was to record receivables, to also handle cash, record cash, make deposits, and especially prepare the bank reconciliation.

Independent internal verification. The controller was supposed to perform a thorough review of the bank reconciliation. Because he did not, he was terminated from his position.

Source: Adapted from Wells, *Fraud Casebook* (2007), pp. 183–194.

Data Analytics Insight

Andrey Popov/Adobe Stock

They've Got Your Number

Offering credit to customers has costs, as some credit customers will ultimately not be able to pay the amounts owed. Companies can minimize these costs by effectively analyzing data regarding current and potential customers.

Traditionally, companies based credit decisions on a limited number of factors, such as the customer's payment history, credit history, and debt to assets ratio. In contrast, credit-granting decisions using big data can take into account hundreds or even thousands of data points. These can even include the customer's social media network, spending habits, criminal history, and cell phone information. As the CEO of one online lender stated, "all data is credit data."

Data analytics can also be used in estimating uncollectible accounts and to minimize bad debts. For example, companies can use data analytics to determine the normal payment patterns of specific customers and then automatically generate phone calls whenever these customers deviate from their normal payment patterns. Resolving accounts receivable issues earlier increases the likelihood of their being resolved favorably.

Source: Adapted from Mikella Hurley and Julius Adebayo, "Credit Scoring in the Era of Big Data," *Yale Journal of Law and Technology*, Volume 18, Issue 1 (2017).

Why might a company want to consider a customer's social media network when deciding whether to grant the customer credit? (Answer is available near the end of the chapter.)

DO IT! 1 | Recognizing Accounts Receivable

On May 1, Wilton sold merchandise on account to Bates for £50,000, terms 3/15, net 45. On May 4, Bates returns merchandise with a sales price of £2,000. On May 16, Wilton receives payment from Bates for the balance due. Prepare journal entries to record the May transactions on Wilton's books. (You may ignore cost of goods sold entries and explanations.)

ACTION PLAN

- **Prepare entry to record the receivable and related return.**
- **Compute the sales discount and related entry.**

Solution

May 1	Accounts Receivable	50,000	
	Sales Revenue		50,000
4	Sales Returns and Allowances	2,000	
	Accounts Receivable		2,000
16	Cash (£48,000 – £1,440)	46,560	
	Sales Discounts (£48,000 × .03)	1,440	
	Accounts Receivable		48,000

Related exercise material: **BE8.1, BE8.2, DO IT! 8.1, E8.1, E8.2, and E8.3.**

8.2 Valuation and Disposition of Accounts Receivable

LEARNING OBJECTIVE 2

Describe how companies value accounts receivable and record their disposition.

Valuing Accounts Receivable

Once companies record receivables in the accounts, the next question is: How should they report receivables in the financial statements? Companies report accounts receivable on the statement of financial position as an asset. But determining the **amount** to report is sometimes difficult because some receivables will become uncollectible.

Each customer must satisfy the credit requirements of the seller before the credit sale is approved. Inevitably, though, some accounts receivable become uncollectible. For example, a customer may not be able to pay because of a decline in its sales revenue due to a downturn in the economy. Similarly, individuals may be laid off from their jobs or faced with unexpected hospital bills.

ALTERNATIVE TERMINOLOGY
You will sometimes see Bad Debt Expense called Expected Credit Loss.

- Companies record credit losses as **Bad Debt Expense** (or Expected Credit Loss) (see **Alternative Terminology**).
- Such losses are a normal and necessary risk of doing business on a credit basis.

When the worldwide economy sharply contracted in the early months of the Covid-19 global pandemic, businesses closed. Many individuals either lost their jobs or had their incomes substantially reduced. As a result, many lenders experienced huge increases in their bad debt expense. For example, **Barclays plc** (GBR) increased its bad debt expense by over 250% from 2019 to 2020. During the same period, **CaixaBank SA** (ESP) increased its bad debt expense by over 450%.

Two methods are used in accounting for uncollectible accounts: (1) the direct write-off method and (2) the allowance method. The following sections explain these methods.

Direct Write-Off Method for Uncollectible Accounts

Under the **direct write-off method**, when a company determines a particular account to be uncollectible, it charges the loss to Bad Debt Expense. Assume, for example, that Warden Retail writes off as uncollectible M. E. Doran's NT$1,600 balance on December 12. Warden's entry is as follows.

A	=	L	+	E
				−1,600 Exp
−1,600				

Cash Flows
no effect

Dec. 12	Bad Debt Expense	1,600	
	Accounts Receivable		1,600
	(To record write-off of M. E. Doran account)		

Under this method, Bad Debt Expense will show only **actual losses** from uncollectibles. The company will report accounts receivable at its gross amount.

Use of the direct write-off method can reduce the relevance of both the income statement and the statement of financial position. Consider the following example. In 2029, Quick Buck Computers decided it could increase its revenues by offering computers to college students without requiring any money down and with no credit-approval process. It quickly sold one million computers with a selling price of HK$8,000 each. This increased Quick Buck's revenues and receivables by HK$8 billion.

The promotion was a huge success! The 2029 statement of financial position and income statement looked great. Unfortunately, during 2030, nearly 40% of the customers defaulted on their loans. This made the 2030 income statement and statement of financial position look terrible. **Illustration 8.2** shows the effect of these events on the financial statements if the direct write-off method is used.

ILLUSTRATION 8.2
Effects of direct write-off method

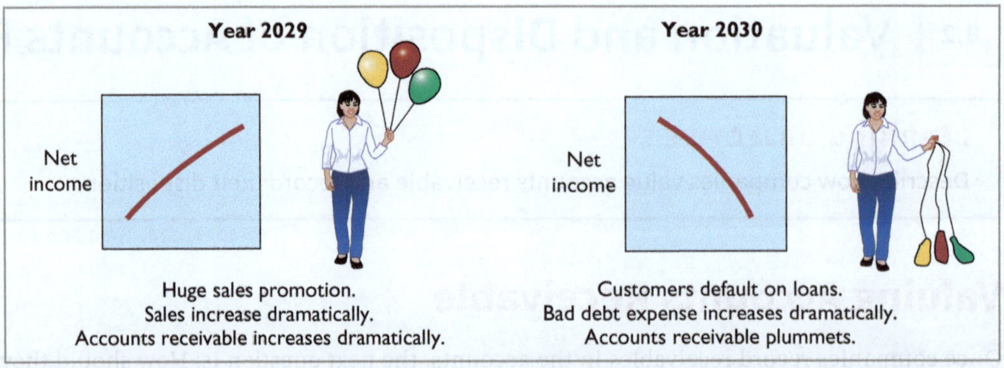

Under the direct write-off method, companies often record bad debt expense in a period different from the period in which they record the revenue. This is problematic for two reasons:

1. The method does not attempt to match bad debt expense to sales revenue in the income statement.
2. The direct write-off method does not show accounts receivable in the statement of financial position at the amount the company actually expects to receive.

Consequently, unless bad debt losses are insignificant, the direct write-off method is not acceptable for financial reporting purposes.

Allowance Method for Uncollectible Accounts

The **allowance method** of accounting for bad debts involves estimating uncollectible accounts at the end of each period. This provides better matching of expenses with revenues on the income statement. It also ensures that companies state receivables on the statement of financial position at their cash (net) realizable value. [1]

- **Cash (net) realizable value** is the net amount the company expects to receive in cash.
- It excludes amounts that the company estimates it will not collect.

Thus, this method reduces receivables in the statement of financial position by the amount of estimated uncollectible receivables.

Companies must use the allowance method for financial reporting purposes when bad debts are material in amount (see **Helpful Hint**). This method has three essential features:

1. Companies **estimate** uncollectible accounts receivable. They match this estimated expense **against revenues** in the same accounting period in which they record the revenues.
2. Companies debit estimated uncollectibles to Bad Debt Expense and credit them to Allowance for Doubtful Accounts (or Loss Allowance) (see **Alternative Terminology**) through an adjusting entry at the end of each period. Allowance for Doubtful Accounts is a contra account to Accounts Receivable.
3. When companies write off a specific account, they debit actual uncollectibles to Allowance for Doubtful Accounts and credit that amount to Accounts Receivable.

HELPFUL HINT

In this context, material means significant or important to financial statement users.

ALTERNATIVE TERMINOLOGY

You will sometimes see Allowance for Doubtful Accounts called Loss Allowance.

Recording Estimated Uncollectibles To illustrate the allowance method, assume that Hampson Furniture has credit sales of €1,200,000 in 2029. Of this amount, €200,000 of receivables remains uncollected at December 31. The credit manager estimates that €12,000 of these receivables will be uncollectible. The adjusting entry to record the estimated uncollectibles increases (debits) Bad Debt Expense and increases (credits) Allowance for Doubtful Accounts, as follows.

Dec. 31	Bad Debt Expense	12,000	
	Allowance for Doubtful Accounts		12,000
	(To record estimate of uncollectible accounts)		

A	=	L	+	E
				−12,000 Exp
−12,000				

Cash Flows
no effect

Hampson reports Bad Debt Expense in the income statement as an operating expense. Thus, the estimated uncollectibles are matched with sales in 2029. Hampson records the expense in the same year it made the sales.

Allowance for Doubtful Accounts shows the estimated amount of claims on customers that the company expects will become uncollectible in the future.

- Companies use a contra account instead of a direct credit to Accounts Receivable because they do not know which customers will not pay.
- The credit balance in the allowance account will absorb the specific write-offs when they occur.

---

[1] IFRS 9 requires companies to measure impairment of financial assets, including trade receivables, using the expected credit loss (ECL) model. The ECL model establishes a **three-stage impairment** framework based on the extent of deterioration in credit quality since initial recognition. If, at the reporting date, there has been no significant increase in credit risk, companies recognize 12-month ECL (Stage 1). If there has been a significant increase in credit risk but the financial instrument is not yet credit-impaired, companies recognize lifetime ECL (Stage 2). When a financial instrument becomes credit-impaired, companies continue to recognize lifetime ECL; however, interest revenue is calculated based on the net carrying amount (i.e., the gross carrying amount less the loss allowance), rather than the gross carrying amount (Stage 3).
For trade receivables that do not contain a significant financing component, IFRS 9 allows companies to use a simplified **"provision matrix"** to measure lifetime ECL. The provision matrix is an aging schedule-based tool that applies historical default rates over the expected life of the trade receivables, adjusted for forward-looking estimates.

As **Illustration 8.3** shows, the company deducts the allowance account from accounts receivable in the current assets section of the statement of financial position.

> **HELPFUL HINT**
> **Cash realizable value is sometimes referred to as accounts receivable (net).**

The amount of €188,000 in Illustration 8.3 represents the expected cash realizable value of the accounts receivable at the statement date (see **Helpful Hint**). **Companies do not close Allowance for Doubtful Accounts at the end of the fiscal year.**

ILLUSTRATION 8.3
Presentation of allowance for doubtful accounts

Hampson Furniture
Statement of Financial Position (partial)

Current assets		
Supplies		€ 25,000
Inventory		310,000
Accounts receivable	**€200,000**	
Less: Allowance for doubtful accounts	**12,000**	**188,000**
Cash		14,800
Total current assets		€537,800

Recording the Write-Off of an Uncollectible Account Companies use various methods of collecting past-due accounts, such as letters, calls, and legal action. When they have exhausted all means of collecting a past-due account and collection appears impossible, the company writes off the account. In the credit card industry, for example, it is standard practice to write off accounts that are 210 days past due. To prevent premature or unauthorized write-offs, authorized management personnel should formally approve each write-off. **To maintain segregation of duties, the employee authorized to write off accounts should not have daily responsibilities related to cash or receivables.**

To illustrate a receivables write-off, assume that the financial vice president of Hampson Furniture authorizes a write-off of the €500 balance owed by R. A. Ware on March 1, 2030. The entry to record the write-off is as follows.

A	=	L	+	E
+500				
−500				

Cash Flows
no effect

Mar. 1	Allowance for Doubtful Accounts	500	
	Accounts Receivable		500
	(Write-off of R. A. Ware account)		

The company does not increase bad debt expense when the write-off occurs.

- **Under the allowance method, companies debit every bad debt write-off to the allowance account rather than to Bad Debt Expense.**
- A debit to Bad Debt Expense would be incorrect because the company has already recognized the expense when it made the adjusting entry for estimated bad debts.
- Instead, the entry to record the write-off of an uncollectible account reduces both Accounts Receivable and Allowance for Doubtful Accounts.

After posting, the general ledger accounts appear as shown in **Illustration 8.4**.

ILLUSTRATION 8.4
General ledger balances after write-off

Accounts Receivable				Allowance for Doubtful Accounts			
Jan. 1 Bal.	200,000	Mar. 1	**500**	Mar. 1	**500**	Jan. 1 Bal.	12,000
Mar. 1 Bal.	199,500					Mar. 1 Bal.	11,500

A write-off affects **only statement of financial position accounts**—not income statement accounts. The write-off of the account reduces both Accounts Receivable and Allowance for Doubtful Accounts. Cash realizable value in the statement of financial position, therefore, remains the same, as **Illustration 8.5** shows.

ILLUSTRATION 8.5
Cash realizable value comparison

	Before Write-Off	After Write-Off
Accounts receivable	€200,000	€199,500
Allowance for doubtful accounts	12,000	11,500
Cash realizable value	**€188,000**	**€188,000**

Recovery of an Uncollectible Account Occasionally, a company collects from a customer after it has written off the account as uncollectible. The company makes two entries to record the recovery of a bad debt.

1. It reverses the entry made in writing off the account. This reinstates the customer's account.
2. It journalizes the collection in the usual manner.

To illustrate, assume that on July 1, R. A. Ware pays the €500 amount that Hampson had written off on March 1. Hampson makes the following entries.

(1)

July 1	Accounts Receivable	500	
	Allowance for Doubtful Accounts		500
	(To reverse write-off of R. A. Ware account)		

A = L + E
+500
−500

Cash Flows
no effect

(2)

July 1	Cash	500	
	Accounts Receivable		500
	(To record collection from R. A. Ware)		

A = L + E
+500
−500

Cash Flows
+500

Note that the recovery of a bad debt, like the write-off of a bad debt, affects **only statement of financial position accounts**. The net effect of the two entries above is a debit to Cash and a credit to Allowance for Doubtful Accounts for €500. Accounts Receivable and Allowance for Doubtful Accounts both increase in entry (1) for two reasons. First, the company made an error in judgment when it wrote off the account receivable. Second, after R. A. Ware did pay, Accounts Receivable in the general ledger and Ware's account in the subsidiary ledger should show the collection for possible future credit purposes.

Estimating the Allowance For Hampson Furniture in Illustration 8.3, the amount of the expected uncollectibles was given. However, in "real life," companies must estimate the amount of expected uncollectible accounts if they use the allowance method. Expected uncollectible accounts are estimated based on information about past events (loss experience), adjusted for current conditions and reasonable forecasts of factors that would affect uncollectible accounts. While much judgment is involved, the goal is to develop the best estimate of expected uncollectible receivables. **Illustration 8.6** shows an excerpt from the notes to **Unilever**'s (GBR) financial statements discussing its use of the allowance method.

ILLUSTRATION 8.6

Unilever's allowance method disclosure

Real World

Unilever Group

Notes to the Financial Statements

Trade and other current receivables—Allowance for doubtful accounts

Our historical experience of collecting receivables, supported by the level of default, is that credit risk is low across territories and so trade receivables are considered to be a single class of financial assets. Impairment for trade receivables are calculated for specific receivables with known or anticipated issues affecting the likelihood of recovery and for balances past due with a probability of default based on historical data as well as relevant forward-looking information.

Frequently, companies estimate the allowance as a percentage of the outstanding receivables. Under the **percentage-of-receivables basis**, management establishes a percentage relationship between the amount of receivables and expected losses from uncollectible accounts (see **Helpful Hint**).

HELPFUL HINT

Where appropriate, the percentage-of-receivables basis may use only a single percentage rate.

For example, suppose Steffen Ltd. has an ending balance in Accounts Receivable of £200,000 and an unadjusted credit balance in Allowance for Doubtful Accounts of £1,500. It estimates that 5% of its accounts receivable will eventually be uncollectible. It should report a balance in Allowance for Doubtful Accounts of £10,000 (.05 × £200,000). To increase the balance in Allowance for Doubtful Accounts from £1,500 to £10,000, the company debits

Allowance for Doubtful Accounts

	Dec. 31 Unadj. Bal. 1,500
	Dec. 31 Adj. 8,500
	Dec. 31 Bal. 10,000

(increases) Bad Debt Expense and credits (increases) Allowance for Doubtful Accounts by £8,500 (£10,000 − £1,500).

To more accurately estimate the ending balance in the allowance account, a company often prepares a schedule, called **aging the accounts receivable**.

- This schedule classifies customer balances by the length of time they have been unpaid.
- After the company arranges the accounts by age, it determines the expected bad debt losses by applying percentages, based on past experience, to the totals of each category.
- The longer a receivable is past due, the less likely it is to be collected. As a result, the estimated percentage of uncollectible debts increases as the number of days past due increases.

Illustration 8.7 shows an aging schedule for Xi Electronics (amounts in thousands) (see **Helpful Hint**). Note the increasing uncollectible percentages from 2% to 40%.

ILLUSTRATION 8.7

Aging schedule

Worksheet

	A	B	C	D	E	F	G
1					Number of Days Past Due		
2			Not				
3	Customer	Total	Yet Due	1–30	31–60	61–90	Over 90
4	T. E. Adert	¥ 600		¥ 300		¥ 200	¥ 100
5	R. C. Bortz	300	¥ 300				
6	B. A. Carl	450		200	¥ 250		
7	O. L. Diker	700	500			200	
8	T. O. Ebbet	600			300		300
9	Others	36,950	26,200	5,200	2,450	1,600	1,500
10		¥39,600	¥27,000	¥5,700	¥3,000	¥2,000	¥1,900
11	Estimated percentage uncollectible		2%	4%	10%	20%	40%
12	Total estimated uncollectible accounts	¥ 2,228	¥ 540	¥ 228	¥ 300	¥ 400	¥ 760
13							

HELPFUL HINT

The older categories have higher percentages because the longer an account is past due, the less likely it is to be collected.

Total estimated uncollectible accounts for Xi Electronics (¥2,228) represent the existing customer claims expected to become uncollectible in the future.

- This amount represents the **required balance** in Allowance for Doubtful Accounts at the statement of financial position date.
- Accordingly, **the amount of bad debt expense that should be recorded in the adjusting entry is the difference between the required balance and the existing balance in the allowance account.**
- The existing, unadjusted balance in Allowance for Doubtful Accounts is the net result of the beginning balance (a normal credit balance) less the write-offs of specific accounts during the year (debits to the allowance account).

For example, if the unadjusted trial balance shows Allowance for Doubtful Accounts with a credit balance of ¥528, then an adjusting entry for ¥1,700 (¥2,228 − ¥528) is necessary:

Dec. 31	Bad Debt Expense	1,700	
	Allowance for Doubtful Accounts		1,700
	(To adjust allowance account to total estimated uncollectibles)		

A	=	L	+	E
				−1,700 Exp
−1,700				

Cash Flows
no effect

After Xi posts the adjusting entry, its accounts appear as shown in **Illustration 8.8**.

Bad Debt Expense		Allowance for Doubtful Accounts	
Dec. 31 Adj. 1,700			Dec. 31 Unadj. Bal. 528
			Dec. 31 Adj. 1,700
			Dec. 31 Bal. 2,228

ILLUSTRATION 8.8
Bad debt accounts after posting

An important aspect of accounts receivable management is simply maintaining a close watch on the accounts. Studies have shown that accounts more than 60 days past due lose approximately 50% of their value if no payment activity occurs within the next 30 days. For each additional 30 days that pass, the collectible value halves once again.

Occasionally, the allowance account will have a **debit balance** prior to adjustment.

- This occurs because the debits to the allowance account from write-offs during the year **exceeded** the beginning balance in the account which was based on previous estimates for bad debts.
- In such a case, the company **adds the debit balance to the required balance** when it makes the adjusting entry.

Thus, if there was a ¥500 **debit** balance in the allowance account before adjustment, the adjusting entry would be for ¥2,728 (¥2,228 + ¥500) to arrive at a credit balance of ¥2,228 as shown below.

Dec. 31	Bad Debt Expense	2,728	
	Allowance for Doubtful Accounts		2,728
	(To adjust allowance account to total estimated uncollectibles)		

A	=	L	+	E
				−2,728 Exp
−2,728				

Cash Flows
no effect

After Xi posts the adjusting entry, its accounts appear as shown in **Illustration 8.9**.

Bad Debt Expense		Allowance for Doubtful Accounts	
Dec. 31 Adj. 2,728		Dec. 31 Unadj. Bal. 500	Dec. 31 Adj. 2,728
			Dec. 31 Bal. 2,228

ILLUSTRATION 8.9
Bad debt accounts after posting

The percentage-of-receivables basis provides an estimate of the **cash realizable value** of the receivables. The IASB now employs an expected credit loss model, which requires that companies must measure expected uncollectible accounts and record bad debt expense on all receivables, even those with a low risk of loss. Companies use sophisticated models employing data analytics to arrive at accurate estimates on a timely basis.

The note in **Illustration 8.10** regarding accounts receivable comes from the annual report of the storage and organization products company **The Container Store**.

ILLUSTRATION 8.10
The Container Store's note disclosure of accounts receivable

Real World

The Container Store Group, Inc.
Notes to the Financial Statements

Accounts receivable

Accounts receivable consist primarily of trade receivables, receivables from The Container Store, Inc.'s credit card processors for sales transactions, and tenant improvement allowances from The Container Store, Inc.'s landlords in connection with new leases. An allowance for doubtful accounts is established on trade receivables, if necessary, for estimated losses resulting from the inability of customers to make required payments. Factors such as payment terms, historical loss experience, and economic conditions are generally considered in determining the allowance for doubtful accounts. Accounts receivable are presented net of allowances for doubtful accounts of $326 and $57 at March 28, 2020 and March 30, 2019, respectively.

Ethics Insight

Christy Thompson/ Shutterstock

Cookie Jar Allowances

There are many pressures on companies to achieve earnings targets. For managers, poor earnings can lead to dismissal or lack of promotion. It is thus not surprising that management may be tempted to look for ways to boost their earnings number.

One way a company can achieve greater earnings is to lower its estimate of what is needed in its Allowance for Doubtful Accounts (sometimes referred to as "tapping the cookie jar"). For example, suppose a company has an Allowance for Doubtful Accounts of $10 million and decides to reduce this balance to $9 million. As a result of this change, Bad Debt Expense decreases by $1 million and earnings increase by $1 million.

Large banks such as **JPMorgan Chase** (USA), **Wells Fargo** (USA), and **Bank of America** (USA) recently decreased their Allowance for Doubtful Accounts by over $4 billion. These reductions came at a time when these big banks were still suffering from lower mortgage lending and trading activity, both of which led to lower earnings. They justified these reductions in the allowance balances by noting that credit quality and economic conditions had improved. This may be so, but it sure is great to have a cookie jar that might be tapped when a boost in earnings is needed.

How might investors determine that a company is managing its earnings? (Answer is available near the end of the chapter.)

ACTION PLAN

- **Estimate the amount the company does not expect to collect.**
- **Consider the existing balance in the allowance account when using the percentage-of-receivables basis.**
- **Report receivables at their cash (net) realizable value—that is, the amount the company expects to collect in cash.**

DO IT! 2a | Bad Debt Expense

Brule Group has been in business for 5 years. The unadjusted trial balance at the end of the current year shows Accounts Receivable $30,000, Sales Revenue $180,000, and Allowance for Doubtful Accounts with a debit balance of $2,000. Brule estimates bad debts to be 10% of accounts receivable. Prepare the entry necessary to adjust Allowance for Doubtful Accounts.

Solution

Brule should make the following entry to bring the debit balance in Allowance for Doubtful Accounts up to a normal, credit balance of $3,000 (10% × $30,000):

Bad Debt Expense [(10% × $30,000) + $2,000]	5,000	
Allowance for Doubtful Accounts		5,000
(To record estimate of uncollectible accounts)		

Related exercise material: **BE8.3, BE8.6, DO IT! 8.2a, E8.4, E8.5, E8.6, E8.7, and E8.8.**

Disposing of Accounts Receivable

In the normal course of events, companies collect accounts receivable in cash and remove the receivables from the books. However, as credit sales and receivables have grown in significance, the "normal course of events" has changed. Companies now frequently sell their receivables to another company for cash, thereby shortening the cash-to-cash operating cycle.

Companies sell receivables for two major reasons:

1. **Receivables may be the only reasonable source of cash.** When money is tight, companies may not be able to borrow money in the usual credit markets. Or if money is available, the cost of borrowing may be prohibitive.
2. **Billing and collection are often time-consuming and costly.** It is often easier for a retailer to sell the receivables to another party with expertise in billing and collection matters. Credit card companies such as **MasterCard** (USA) and **Visa** (USA) specialize in billing and collecting accounts receivable. MasterCard and Visa credit cards are issued by banks around the world, including **ICBC** (CHN), **BNP Paribas** (FRA), and **Barclays** (GBR).

Sale of Receivables to a Factor

A common sale of receivables is a sale to a factor. A **factor** is a finance company or bank that buys receivables from businesses and then collects the payments directly from the customers.

- Factoring is a multibillion dollar business, although factoring arrangements vary widely.
- Typically, the factor charges a commission to the company that is selling the receivables. This fee often ranges from 1–3% of the amount of receivables purchased.

To illustrate, assume that Keelung Jewelry factors NT$600,000 of receivables to Federal Factors (amounts in thousands). Federal Factors assesses a service charge of 2% of the amount of receivables sold. The journal entry to record the sale by Keelung Jewelry on April 2, 2029, is as follows.

Apr. 2	Cash	588,000	
	Service Charge Expense (2% × NT$600,000)	12,000	
	Accounts Receivable		600,000
	(To record the sale of accounts receivable)		

A	=	L	+	E
+588,000				
				−12,000 Exp
−600,000				

Cash Flows
+588,000

Under IFRS 18, if selling receivables is part of Keelung's main business activities, the related service charge expense is classified within the operating category of the income statement. If the company infrequently sells receivables, the service charge expense may be presented within other operating expenses.

National Credit Card Sales

Credit card use is becoming widespread around the world. **ICBC** is among the largest credit card issuers in the world. **Visa** and **MasterCard** are the credit cards that most individuals use. Three parties are involved when national credit cards are used in retail sales:

1. The credit card issuer, which is independent of the retailer.
2. The retailer.
3. The customer.

A retailer's acceptance of a credit card is another form of selling (factoring) the receivable.

Illustration 8.11 shows the major advantages of credit cards to the retailer. In exchange for these advantages, the retailer pays the credit card issuer a fee of 2–4% of the invoice price for its services (see **Ethics Note**).

ETHICS NOTE

In exchange for lower interest rates, some companies have eliminated the 25-day grace period before finance charges kick in. Be sure you read the fine print in any credit agreement you sign.

ILLUSTRATION 8.11

Advantages of credit cards to the retailer

Accounting for Credit Card Sales The retailer generally considers sales from the use of credit card sales as **cash sales**. The retailer must pay to the bank that issues the card a fee for processing the transactions. The retailer records the credit card slips in a similar manner as checks deposited from a cash sale.

To illustrate, Ling Lee purchases NT$6,000 of paper products for her restaurant from Wu Supplies using her Visa First Bank Card. First Bank charges a service fee of 3%. The entry to record this transaction by Wu Supplies on March 22, 2029, is as follows.

A	=	L	+	E
+5,820				
				−180 Exp
				+6,000 Rev

Cash Flows
+5,820

Mar. 22	Cash	5,820	
	Service Charge Expense	180	
	Sales Revenue		6,000
	(To record Visa credit card sales)		

Accounting Across the Organization Sogo Co., Ltd.

ArtBoyMB/Getty Images

How Does a Credit Card Work?

Most of you know how to use a credit card, but do you know what happens in the transaction and how the transaction is processed? Suppose that you use a **Visa** card to purchase some new ties at **Sogo Co., Ltd.** (TWN). You swipe your credit card (or insert if it is a chip card) which allows the information on the magnetic strip on the back of the card to be read. The salesperson then enters the amount of the purchase. The machine contacts the Visa computer, which routes the call back to the bank that issued your Visa card. The issuing bank verifies that the account exists, that the card is not stolen, and that you have not exceeded your credit limit. At this point, the receipt is printed.

Visa acts as the clearing agent for the transaction. It transfers funds from the issuing bank to Sogo's bank account. Generally, this transfer of funds, from sale to the receipt of funds in the merchant's account, takes two to three days.

In the meantime, Visa puts a pending charge on your account for the amount of the purchase; that amount counts immediately against your available credit limit. At the end of the billing period, Visa sends you an invoice (your credit card bill) which shows the various charges you made, and the amounts that Visa expended on your behalf, for the month. You then must "pay the piper" for your stylish new ties.

Assume that Sogo prepares a bank reconciliation at the end of each month. If some credit card sales have not been processed by the bank, how should Sogo treat these transactions on its bank reconciliation? (Answer is available near the end of the chapter.)

ACTION PLAN

- **Consider sale of receivables to a factor.**
- **Weigh cost of factoring against benefit of having cash in hand.**

DO IT! 2b | Factoring

Kell Wholesalers needs to raise €120,000 in cash to safely cover next Friday's employee payroll. Kell has reached its debt ceiling. Kell's present balance of outstanding receivables totals €750,000. Kell decides to factor €125,000 of its receivables on September 7, 2029, to alleviate this cash crunch. Record the entry that Kell would make when it raises the needed cash. (Assume a 1% service charge.)

Solution

Assuming that Kell factors €125,000 of its accounts receivable at a 1% service charge, it would make this entry:

Sept. 7	Cash	123,750	
	Service Charge Expense (1% × €125,000)	1,250	
	Accounts Receivable		125,000
	(To record sale of receivables to factor)		

Related exercise material: **BE8.7, DO IT! 8.2b, E8.9, E8.10, and E8.11.**

8.3 Notes Receivable

LEARNING OBJECTIVE 3

Explain how companies recognize, value, and dispose of notes receivable.

Companies may also grant credit in exchange for a formal credit instrument known as a promissory note. A **promissory note** is a written promise to pay a specified amount of money on demand or at a definite time. Promissory notes may be used in the following cases.

1. When individuals and companies lend or borrow money.
2. When the amount of the transaction and the credit period exceed normal limits.
3. In settlement of accounts receivable.

In a promissory note, the party making the promise to pay is called the **maker**. The party to whom payment is to be made is called the **payee**. The note may specifically identify the payee by name or may designate the payee simply as the bearer of the note.

In the note shown in **Illustration 8.12**, Calhoun plc is the maker and Wilma Ltd. is the payee. To Wilma Ltd., the promissory note is a note receivable. To Calhoun plc, it is a note payable (see **Helpful Hint**).

ILLUSTRATION 8.12

Promissory note

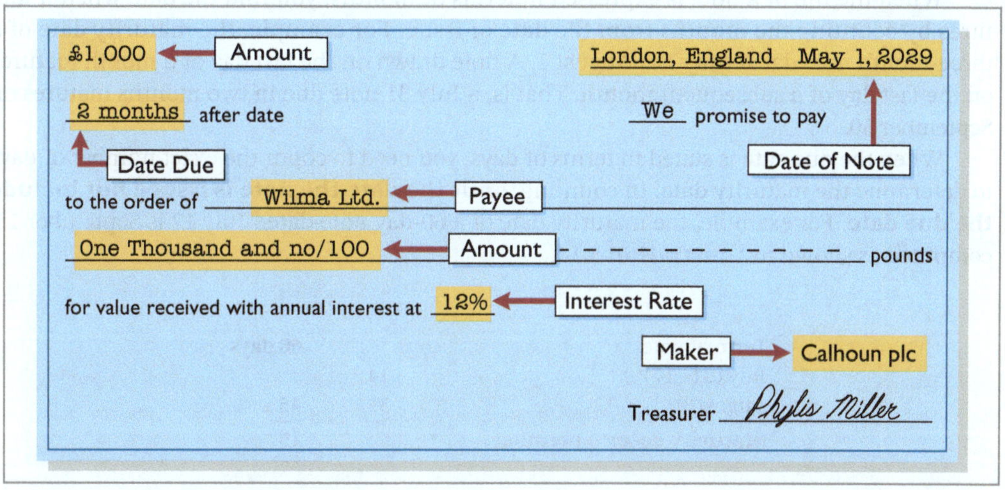

HELPFUL HINT

For this note, the maker, Calhoun plc, debits Cash and credits Notes Payable. The payee, Wilma Ltd. debits Notes Receivable and credits Cash.

Notes receivable give the holder a stronger legal claim to assets than do accounts receivable. Like accounts receivable, notes receivable can be readily sold to another party. Promissory notes are negotiable instruments (as are checks), which means that they can be transferred to another party by endorsement.

- Companies frequently accept notes receivable from customers who need to extend the payment of an outstanding account receivable. They often require such notes from high-risk customers.
- In some industries (such as the pleasure and sport boat industry), all credit sales are supported by notes.
- The majority of notes, however, originate from lending transactions.

The basic issues in accounting for notes receivable are the same as those for accounts receivable. On the following pages, we look at these issues. Before we do, however, we need to consider two issues that do not apply to accounts receivable: determining the maturity date and computing interest.

Determining the Maturity Date

Illustration 8.13 shows three ways of stating the maturity date of a promissory note.

ILLUSTRATION 8.13
Maturity date of different notes

When the life of a note is expressed in terms of months, you find the date when it matures by counting the months from the date of issue. For example, the maturity date of a three-month note dated May 1 is August 1. A note drawn on the last day of a month matures on the last day of a subsequent month. That is, a July 31 note due in two months matures on September 30.

When the due date is stated in terms of days, you need to count the exact number of days to determine the maturity date. In counting, **omit the date the note is issued but include the due date**. For example, the maturity date of a 60-day note dated July 17 is September 15, computed as shown in **Illustration 8.14**.

ILLUSTRATION 8.14
Computation of maturity date

Term of note		60 days
July (31–17)	14	
August	31	45
Maturity date: September		**15**

Computing Interest

Illustration 8.15 gives the basic formula for computing interest on an interest-bearing note.

ILLUSTRATION 8.15
Formula for computing interest

$$\text{Face Value of Note} \times \text{Annual Interest Rate} \times \text{Time in Terms of One Year} = \text{Interest}$$

HELPFUL HINT
The interest rate specified is the *annual* rate.

The interest rate specified in a note is an **annual** rate of interest (see **Helpful Hint**). The time factor in the formula in Illustration 8.15 expresses the fraction of a year that the note is outstanding.

- When the maturity date is stated in days, the time factor is often the number of days divided by 360.
- Remember that when counting days, omit the date that the note is issued but include the due date.
- When the due date is stated in months, the time factor is the number of months divided by 12.

Illustration 8.16 shows computation of interest for various time periods.

ILLUSTRATION 8.16

Computation of interest

Terms of Note	Interest Computation							
	Face	×	Rate	×	Time	=	Interest
៛ 730, 12%, 120 days	៛ 730	×	12%	×	120/360	=	៛ 29.20
៛1,000, 9%, 6 months	៛1,000	×	9%	×	6/12	=	៛ 45.00
៛2,000, 6%, 1 year	៛2,000	×	6%	×	1/1	=	៛120.00

There are different ways to calculate interest. For example, the computation in Illustration 8.16 assumes 360 days for the length of the year. Most financial institutions use 365 days to compute interest. *For homework problems, assume 360 days to simplify computations.*

Recognizing Notes Receivable

To illustrate the basic entry for notes receivable, we will use Calhoun plc's £1,000, two-month, 12% promissory note dated May 1. Assuming that Calhoun plc wrote the note to settle an open account, Wilma Ltd. makes the following entry for the receipt of the note.

May 1	Notes Receivable	1,000	
	Accounts Receivable		1,000
	(To record acceptance of Calhoun plc note)		

A	=	L	+	E
+1,000				
−1,000				

Cash Flows
no effect

The company records the note receivable at its **face value**, the value shown on the face of the note. No interest revenue is reported when the note is accepted because the revenue recognition principle does not recognize revenue until the performance obligation is satisfied. Interest is earned (accrued) as time passes.

If a company issues cash in exchange for a note, the entry is a debit to Notes Receivable and a credit to Cash in the amount of the loan.

Valuing Notes Receivable

Valuing short-term notes receivable is the same as valuing accounts receivable. Like accounts receivable, companies report short-term notes receivable at their **cash (net) realizable value**. The notes receivable allowance account is Allowance for Doubtful Accounts. The estimations involved in determining cash realizable value and in recording bad debt expense and the related allowance are done similarly to accounts receivable.

Disposing of Notes Receivable

Notes may be held to their maturity date, at which time the face value plus accrued interest is due. In some situations, the maker of the note defaults, and the payee must make an appropriate adjustment. In other situations, similar to accounts receivable, the holder of the note speeds up the conversion to cash by selling the receivables (as described earlier in this chapter).

Honor of Notes Receivable

A note is **honored** when its maker pays in full at its maturity date. For each interest-bearing note, the **amount due at maturity** is the face value of the note plus interest for the length of time specified on the note.

To illustrate, assume that Wolder Co. lends Higley Co. €10,000 on June 1, accepting a five-month, 9% interest note. In this situation, interest is €375 (€10,000 × 9% × $\frac{5}{12}$). The amount due, **the maturity value**, is €10,375 (€10,000 + €375). To obtain payment, Wolder (the payee) must present the note either to Higley (the maker) or to the maker's agent, such as a bank. If Wolder presents the note to Higley on November 1, the maturity date, Wolder's entry to record the collection is as follows.

A = L + E
+10,375
−10,000
+375 Rev
Cash Flows
+10,375

Nov. 1	Cash	10,375	
	Notes Receivable		10,000
	Interest Revenue (€10,000 × 9% × $\frac{5}{12}$)		375
	(To record collection of Higley note and interest)		

Accrual of Interest Receivable

Suppose instead that Wolder Co. prepares financial statements as of September 30. The timeline in **Illustration 8.17** presents this situation.

ILLUSTRATION 8.17

Timeline of interest earned

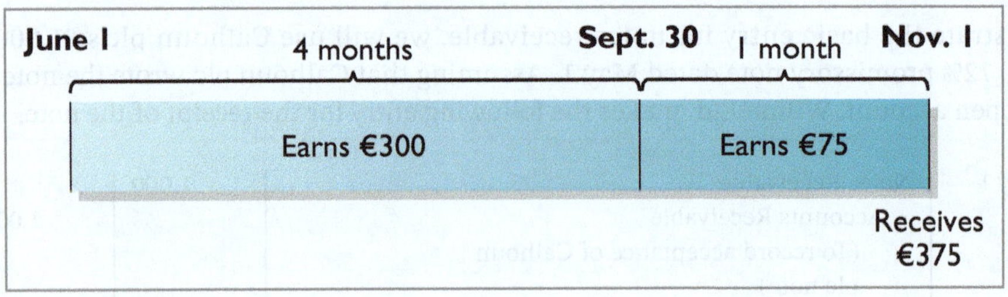

To reflect interest earned but not yet received, Wolder must accrue interest on September 30. In this case, the adjusting entry by Wolder is for four months of interest, or €300, as shown below.

A = L + E
+300
+300 Rev
Cash Flows
no effect

Sept. 30	Interest Receivable (€10,000 × 9% × $\frac{4}{12}$)	300	
	Interest Revenue		300
	(To accrue 4 months' interest on Higley note)		

At the note's maturity on November 1, Wolder receives €10,375. This amount represents repayment of the €10,000 note as well as five months of interest, or €375, as shown below. The €375 is comprised of the €300 Interest Receivable accrued on September 30 plus €75 earned during October. Wolder's entry to record the honoring of the Higley note on November 1 is as follows.

A = L + E
+10,375
−10,000
−300
+75 Rev
Cash Flows
+10,375

Nov. 1	Cash [€10,000 + (€10,000 × 9% × $\frac{5}{12}$)]	10,375	
	Notes Receivable		10,000
	Interest Receivable		300
	Interest Revenue (€10,000 × 9% × $\frac{1}{12}$)]		75
	(To record collection of Higley note and interest)		

In this case, Wolder credits Interest Receivable because the receivable was established in the adjusting entry on September 30.

Dishonor of Notes Receivable

A **dishonored (defaulted) note** is a note that is not paid in full at maturity.

- A dishonored note receivable is no longer negotiable, but the payee still has a claim against the maker of the note for both the note and the interest.
- Therefore, the note holder usually transfers the Notes Receivable account to an Accounts Receivable account.

To illustrate, assume that Higley Co. on November 1 indicates that it cannot pay at the present time. The entry to record the dishonor of the note depends on whether Wolder Co. expects eventual collection. If it does expect eventual collection, Wolder Co. debits the amount due (face value and interest) on the note to Accounts Receivable. It would make the following entry at the time the note is dishonored (assuming no previous accrual of interest).

Nov. 1	Accounts Receivable	10,375	
	Notes Receivable		10,000
	Interest Revenue		375
	(To record the dishonor of Higley note)		

A	=	L	+	E
+10,375				
−10,000				
				+375 Rev

Cash Flows
no effect

If instead on November 1 there is no hope of collection, the note holder would write off the face value of the note by debiting Allowance for Doubtful Accounts. No interest revenue would be recorded because collection will not occur.

Ethics Insight

STRDEL/AFP/Getty Images

Let the "Good Times" Roll

Following the 2008 global financial crisis, governments in India and elsewhere eased monetary and regulatory policies in an effort to encourage economic growth. India's state-controlled banking system became clogged with bad debt. While some in banking claim that irrational exuberance and inadequate evaluation of borrowers were to blame, others point to years of well-connected politicians and industrialists using their influence to get cheap loans.

For example, larger-than-life Indian tycoon Vijay Mallya used his political connections to borrow almost Rs 7,000 to finance **Kingfisher Airlines** (IND) and other projects, including his brewery and Formula 1 racing team. The self-appointed "King of the Good Times" fled the country after being accused of laundering money, bribing bank officials, and defaulting on loans.

Source: Adapted from Megha Bahree, "Vijay Mallya, Indian 'King of the Good Times,' Dethroned by Debt," *The New York Times* (April 28, 2016).

What factors should be considered in evaluating loan applications? (Answer is available near the end of the chapter.)

DO IT! 3 | Recognizing Notes Receivable

Gambit Stores accepts from Leonard Co. a $3,400, 90-day, 6% note dated May 10 in settlement of Leonard's overdue account. (a) What is the maturity date of the note? (b) What is the interest payable at the maturity date? (c) What entry does Gambit make at the maturity date, assuming Leonard pays the note and interest in full at that time?

ACTION PLAN

- **Count the exact number of days to determine the maturity date. Omit the date the note is issued, but include the due date.**
- **Compute the accrued interest.**
- **Prepare the entry for payment of the note and the interest.**

Solution

a. The maturity date is August 8, computed as follows.

Term of note:		90 days
May (31–10)	21	
June	30	
July	31	82
Maturity date: August		8

b. The interest payable at the maturity date is $51, computed as follows.

Face	×	Rate	×	Time	=	Interest
$3,400	×	6%	×	90/360	=	$51

c. Gambit Stores records this entry at the maturity date:

Cash	3,451	
Notes Receivable		3,400
Interest Revenue		51
(To record collection of Leonard note and interest)		

Related exercise material: BE8.8, BE8.9, BE8.10, DO IT! 8.3, E8.12, E8.13, and E8.14.

8.4 Presentation and Analysis

LEARNING OBJECTIVE 4

Describe the statement presentation and analysis of receivables.

If a company has significant receivables, analysts carefully review the company's financial statement disclosures to evaluate how well the company is managing its receivables.

Presentation

Companies should identify in the statement of financial position or in the notes to the financial statements each of the major types of receivables.

- Short-term receivables appear in the current assets section of the statement of financial position. Short-term investments appear after short-term receivables because these investments are more liquid (nearer to cash).
- Companies report both the gross amount of receivables and the allowance for doubtful accounts.

Under IFRS 18, companies classify bad debt expense (expected credit loss) and service charge expense within the operating category of the income statement. Interest revenue is classified in the investing category.

Analysis

Investors and company managers compute financial ratios to evaluate the liquidity of a company's accounts receivable. They use the **accounts receivable turnover** to assess the liquidity of the receivables.

- This ratio measures the number of times, on average, the company collects accounts receivable during the period.
- It is computed by dividing net credit sales (net sales less cash sales) by the average net accounts receivable during the year.
- Unless seasonal factors are significant, average net accounts receivable outstanding can be computed from the beginning and ending balances of net accounts receivable.

For example, in a recent year **Lenovo Group** (CHN) (which reported in U.S. dollars) had net sales of $38,707 million for the year. It had a beginning accounts receivable (net) balance of

$2,885 million and an ending accounts receivable (net) balance of $3,171 million. Assuming that Lenovo's sales were all on credit, its accounts receivable turnover is computed as shown in **Illustration 8.18**.

ILLUSTRATION 8.18
Accounts receivable turnover and computation

Net Credit Sales	÷	Average Net Accounts Receivable	=	Accounts Receivable Turnover
$38,707	÷	$\frac{\$2,885 + \$3,171}{2}$	=	12.8 times

The result indicates an accounts receivable turnover of 12.8 times per year. The higher the turnover, the more liquid the company's receivables.

A variant of the accounts receivable turnover that makes the liquidity even more evident is its conversion into an **average collection period** in terms of days. This is done by dividing the turnover into 365 days. For example, Lenovo's turnover of 12.8 times is divided into 365 days, as shown in **Illustration 8.19**, to obtain approximately 28.5 days. This means that it takes Lenovo on average 28.5 days to collect its accounts receivable.

ILLUSTRATION 8.19
Average collection period for receivables formula and computation

Days in Year	÷	Accounts Receivable Turnover	=	Average Collection Period in Days
365 days	÷	12.8 times	=	28.5 days

Companies frequently use the average collection period to assess the effectiveness of a company's credit and collection policies. The general rule is that the collection period should not greatly exceed the credit term period (that is, the time allowed for payment).

Data Analytics and Receivables Management

Opportunities abound to improve receivables management through data analytics. Software packages promise increases in working capital, improved revenues, and enhanced customer relations. Visualization software, which presents data in sophisticated graph format, enables managers to more quickly identify issues and obtain a deeper understanding of the factors that influence successful receivables management.

- Use of such software helps identify which currencies, sales representatives, customers, product lines, or geographic regions need closer attention.
- This sometimes enables management to do a more granular investigation of the cash-to-cash cycle time to evaluate which product lines are meeting company goals.

Data analytics of receivables is particularly valuable for predictive analysis which allows improved evaluation of customers' risk profiles. In many instances, the company can identify risky customers and take corrective action before problems arise. Software provided by companies such as **Workday** (USA) use artificial intelligence to forecast which customers are likely to pay late.

Finally, with Tableau or other visualization software, companies create dashboards that provide dynamic tracking and analysis of their receivables position. The Tableau dashboard shown in **Illustration 8.20** provides an accounts receivable aging schedule, total amount of receivables, number of outstanding invoices, percent of overdue invoices, and average collection time. With this dashboard, the manager can zoom in on detailed information about specific customers, as well as change the due date or time period covered.

ILLUSTRATION 8.20 **Tableau accounts receivable dashboard**

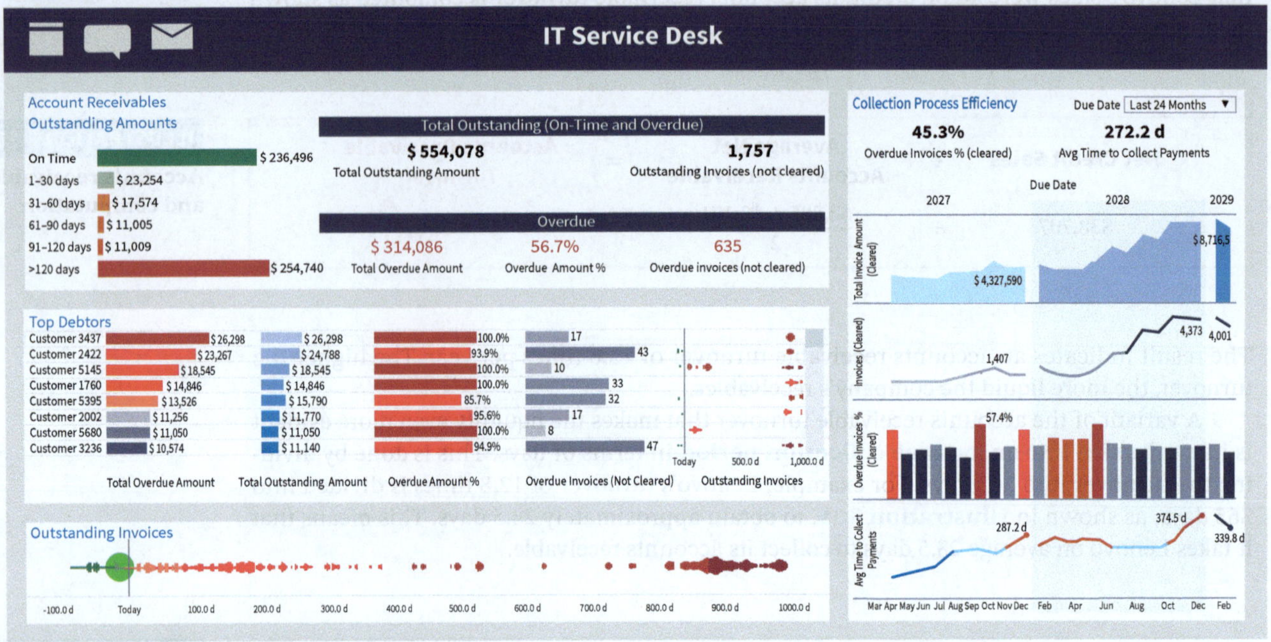

Source: Adapted from Tableau website.

ACTION PLAN

- **Review the formula to compute the accounts receivable turnover.**
- **Make sure that both the beginning and ending accounts receivable balances are considered in the computation.**
- **Review the formula to compute the average collection period in days.**

DO IT! 4 | Analysis of Receivables

In 2029, Nadal Racquets has net credit sales of €923,795 for the year. It had a beginning accounts receivable (net) balance of €38,275 and an ending accounts receivable (net) balance of €35,988. Compute Nadal's (a) accounts receivable turnover and (b) average collection period in days.

Solution

a.	Net credit sales	÷	Average net accounts receivable	=	Accounts receivable turnover
	€923,795	÷	$\frac{€38,275 + €35,988}{2}$	=	24.9 times
b.	Days in year	÷	Accounts receivable turnover	=	Average collection period in days
	365	÷	24.9 times	=	14.7 days

Related exercise material: **BE8.11, BE8.12, DO IT! 8.4, and E8.17.**

Review and Practice

Learning Objectives Review

1 Explain how companies recognize accounts receivable.

Receivables are frequently classified as (1) accounts, (2) notes, and (3) other. Accounts receivable are amounts customers owe on account. Notes receivable are claims for which lenders issue formal instruments of credit as proof of the debt. Other receivables include non-trade receivables such as interest receivable, loans to company officers, advances to employees, and income taxes refundable.

Companies record accounts receivable when they perform a service on account or at the point of sale of merchandise on account. Accounts receivable are reduced by sales returns and allowances. Cash discounts reduce the amount received on accounts receivable. When interest is charged on a past due receivable, the company adds this interest to the accounts receivable balance and recognizes it as interest revenue.

2 Describe how companies value accounts receivable and record their disposition.

There are two methods of accounting for uncollectible accounts: the allowance method and the direct write-off method. Companies use the percentage-of-receivables basis to estimate uncollectible accounts using the allowance method. The percentage-of-receivables basis emphasizes the cash realizable value of the accounts receivable. An aging schedule is often used with this basis.

When a company collects an account receivable, it credits Accounts Receivable. When a company sells (factors) an account receivable, a service charge expense reduces the amount received.

3 Explain how companies recognize, value, and dispose of notes receivable.

For a note stated in months, the maturity date is found by counting the months from the date of issue. For a note stated in days, the number of days is counted, omitting the issue date and counting the due date. The formula for computing interest is Face value × Interest rate × Time.

Companies record notes receivable at face value. In some cases, it is necessary to accrue interest prior to maturity. In this case, companies debit Interest Receivable and credit Interest Revenue.

Notes can be held to maturity. At that time, the face value plus accrued interest is due, and the note is removed from the accounts. In many cases, the holder of the note speeds up the conversion by selling the receivable to another party (a factor). In some situations, the maker of the note dishonors the note (defaults), in which case the company transfers the note and accrued interest to an account receivable or writes off the note.

4 Describe the statement presentation and analysis of receivables.

As with accounts receivable, companies report notes receivable at their cash (net) realizable value. The notes receivable allowance account is Allowance for Doubtful Accounts. The computation and estimations involved in valuing notes receivable at cash realizable value, and in recording the proper amount of bad debt expense and the related allowance, are similar to those for accounts receivable.

Companies should identify in the statement of financial position or in the notes to the financial statements each major type of receivable. Short-term receivables are considered current assets. Companies report the gross amount of receivables and the allowance for doubtful accounts. They report bad debt and service charge expenses in the income statement as operating (selling) expenses. Interest revenue appears in the investing category of the statement. Managers and investors evaluate accounts receivable for liquidity by computing a turnover ratio and an average collection period.

Glossary Review

Accounts receivable Amounts owed by customers on account. (p. 8-3).

Accounts receivable turnover A measure of the liquidity of accounts receivable; computed by dividing net credit sales by average net accounts receivable. (p. 8-20).

Aging the accounts receivable The analysis of customer balances by the length of time they have been unpaid. (p. 8-10).

Allowance method A method of accounting for bad debts that involves estimating uncollectible accounts at the end of each period. (p. 8-7).

Average collection period The average amount of time that a receivable is outstanding; calculated by dividing 365 days by the accounts receivable turnover. (p. 8-21).

Bad Debt Expense (Expected Credit Loss) An expense account to record uncollectible receivables. (p. 8-6).

Cash (net) realizable value The net amount a company expects to receive in cash. (p. 8-7).

Direct write-off method A method of accounting for bad debts that involves expensing accounts at the time they are determined to be uncollectible. (p. 8-6).

Dishonored (defaulted) note A note that is not paid in full at maturity. (p. 8-19).

Factor A finance company or bank that buys receivables from businesses and then collects the payments directly from the customers. (p. 8-12).

Maker The party in a promissory note who is making the promise to pay. (p. 8-15).

Notes receivable Written promise (as evidenced by a formal instrument) for amounts to be received. (p. 8-3).

Other receivables Various forms of non-trade receivables, such as interest receivable and income taxes refundable. (p. 8-3).

Payee The party to whom payment of a promissory note is to be made. (p. 8-15).

Percentage-of-receivables basis Management estimates what percentage of receivables will result in losses from uncollectible accounts. (p. 8-9).

Promissory note A written promise to pay a specified amount of money on demand or at a definite time. (p. 8-15).

Receivables Amounts due from individuals and other companies. (p. 8-2).

Trade receivables Notes and accounts receivable that result from sales transactions. (p. 8-3).

Practice Multiple-Choice Questions

1. **(LO 1)** Receivables are frequently classified as:
   - **a.** accounts receivable, company receivables, and other receivables.
   - **b.** accounts receivable, notes receivable, and employee receivables.
   - **c.** accounts receivable and general receivables.
   - **d.** accounts receivable, notes receivable, and other receivables.

2. **(LO 1)** Buehler Company on June 15 sells merchandise on account to Chaz Co. for $1,000, terms 2/10, n/30. On June 20, Chaz Co. returns merchandise worth $300 to Buehler Company. On June 24, payment is received from Chaz Co. for the balance due. What is the amount of cash received?
   - **a.** $700.
   - **b.** $680.
   - **c.** $686.
   - **d.** None of the answer choices is correct.

3. **(LO 2)** Hughes plc has a credit balance of £5,000 in its Allowance for Doubtful Accounts before any adjustments are made at the end of the year. Based on review and aging of its accounts receivable at the end of the year, Hughes estimates that £60,000 of its receivables are uncollectible. The amount of bad debt expense which should be reported for the year is:
   - **a.** £5,000.
   - **b.** £55,000.
   - **c.** £60,000.
   - **d.** £65,000.

4. **(LO 2)** Use the same information as in Question 3, except that Hughes has a debit balance of £5,000 in its Allowance for Doubtful Accounts before any adjustments are made at the end of the year. In this situation, the amount of bad debt expense that should be reported for the year is:
   - **a.** £5,000.
   - **b.** £55,000.
   - **c.** £60,000.
   - **d.** £65,000.

5. **(LO 2)** Accounts receivable at the end of the month are €800,000. Bad debts are expected to be 1.5% of accounts receivable. If Allowance for Doubtful Accounts has a credit balance of €1,000 before adjustment, what is the balance after adjustment?
   - **a.** €7,000.
   - **b.** €11,000.
   - **c.** €12,000.
   - **d.** €13,000.

6. **(LO 2)** At December 31, 2029, Carlson Enterprises had accounts receivable of ₺750,000. On January 1, 2029, Allowance for Doubtful Accounts had a credit balance of ₺18,000. During 2029, ₺30,000 of uncollectible accounts receivable were written off. Past experience indicates that 3% of accounts receivable become uncollectible. What should be the bad debt expense for 2029?
   - **a.** ₺10,500.
   - **b.** ₺22,500.
   - **c.** ₺30,000.
   - **d.** ₺34,500.

7. **(LO 2)** An analysis and aging of the accounts receivable of Prince Ltd. at December 31 reveals the following data.

Accounts receivable	£800,000
Allowance for doubtful accounts per books before adjustment	50,000
Amounts expected to become uncollectible	65,000

The cash realizable value of the accounts receivable at December 31, after adjustment, is:
   - **a.** £685,000.
   - **b.** £750,000.
   - **c.** £800,000.
   - **d.** £735,000.

8. **(LO 2)** Which of the following statements about Visa credit card sales is **incorrect**?
   - **a.** The credit card issuer makes the credit investigation of the customer.
   - **b.** The retailer is not involved in the collection process.
   - **c.** Two parties are involved.
   - **d.** The retailer receives cash more quickly than it would from individual customers on account.

9. **(LO 2)** Blinka Retailers accepted HK$500,000 of Citibank Visa credit card charges for merchandise sold on July 1. Citibank charges 4% for its credit card use. The entry to record this transaction by Blinka Retailers will include a credit to Sales Revenue of HK$500,000 and a debit(s) to:

a.	Cash	HK$480,000
	and Service Charge Expense	HK$20,000
b.	Accounts Receivable	HK$480,000
	and Service Charge Expense	HK$20,000
c.	Cash	HK$500,000
d.	Accounts Receivable	HK$500,000

10. **(LO 3)** One of the following statements about promissory notes is incorrect. The **incorrect** statement is:
   - **a.** The party making the promise to pay is called the maker.
   - **b.** The party to whom payment is to be made is called the payee.
   - **c.** A promissory note is not a negotiable instrument.
   - **d.** A promissory note is often required from high-risk customers.

11. **(LO 3)** Foti Co. accepts a $1,000, 3-month, 6% promissory note in settlement of an account with Bartelt Co. The entry to record this transaction is as follows.

a.	Notes Receivable	1,015	
	Accounts Receivable		1,015
b.	Notes Receivable	1,000	
	Accounts Receivable		1,000
c.	Notes Receivable	1,000	
	Sales Revenue		1,000
d.	Notes Receivable	1,030	
	Accounts Receivable		1,030

12. **(LO 3)** Ginter Ltd. holds Kolar Co.'s NT$10,000, 120-day, 9% note (amounts in thousands). The entry made by Ginter when the note is collected, assuming no interest has been previously accrued, is:

a.	Cash	10,300	
	Notes Receivable		10,300
b.	Cash	10,000	
	Notes Receivable		10,000
c.	Accounts Receivable	10,300	
	Notes Receivable		10,000
	Interest Revenue		300
d.	Cash	10,300	
	Notes Receivable		10,000
	Interest Revenue		300

13. **(LO 4)** Accounts and notes receivable are reported in the current assets section of the statement of financial position at:

a. cash (net) realizable value.

b. net book value.

c. lower-of-cost-or-net realizable value.

d. invoice cost.

14. **(LO 4)** Shin Industries had net credit sales during the year of ¥800,000 and cost of goods sold of ¥500,000 (amounts in thousands). The balance in accounts receivable at the beginning of the year was ¥100,000, and the end of the year it was ¥150,000. What were the accounts receivable turnover and the average collection period in days?

a. 4.0 and 91.3 days.

b. 5.3 and 68.9 days.

c. 6.4 and 57 days.

d. 8.0 and 45.6 days.

Solutions

1. **d.** Receivables are frequently classified as accounts receivable, notes receivable, and other receivables. The other choices are incorrect because receivables are not frequently classified as (a) company receivables, (b), employee receivables, or (c) general receivables.

2. **c.** Because payment is received within 10 days of the purchase, the cash received is $686 {[$1,000 − $300] − [($1,000 − $300) × 2%]}. The other choices are incorrect because (a) $700 does not consider the 2% discount; (b) the amount of the discount is based upon the amount after the return is granted ($700 × 2%), not the amount before the return of merchandise ($1,000 × 2%); and (d) there is a correct answer.

3. **b.** By crediting Allowance for Doubtful Accounts for £55,000, the new balance will be the required balance of £60,000. This adjusting entry debits Bad Debt Expense for £55,000 and credits Allowance for Doubtful Accounts for £55,000, not (a) £5,000, (c) £60,000, or (d) £65,000.

4. **d.** By crediting Allowance for Doubtful Accounts for £65,000, the new balance will be the required balance of £60,000. This adjusting entry debits Bad Debt Expense for £65,000 and credits Allowance for Doubtful Accounts for £65,000, not (a) £5,000, (b) £55,000, or (c) £60,000.

5. **b.** Accounts receivable times the percentage expected to default equals €12,000. Because a balance in Allowance for Doubtful Accounts is presently €1,000, the adjusting entry debits Bad Debt Expense for €11,000 (€12,000 − €1,000) and credits Allowance for Doubtful Accounts for €11,000, not (a) €7,000, (c) €12,000, or (d) €13,000.

6. **d.** The accounts written off during the year will result in a debit balance in the Allowance for Doubtful Accounts of ₺12,000 (₺30,000 − ₺18,000) at the end of the year. As indicated, 3% of accounts receivables are uncollectible, or ₺22,500 (₺750,000 × 3%). Given a debit balance of ₺12,000 in the allowance account at the end of the year, the adjusting entry at the end of the year is a debit to Bad Debt Expense for ₺34,500 (₺22,500 + ₺12,000) and a credit to Allowance for Doubtful Accounts of ₺34,500, not (a) ₺10,500, (b) ₺22,500, or (c) ₺30,000.

7. **d.** Accounts Receivable less the expected uncollectible amount equals the cash realizable value of £735,000 (£800,000 − £65,000), not (a) £685,000, (b) £750,000, or (c) £800,000.

8. **c.** There are three parties, not two, involved in Visa credit card sales: the credit card company, the retailer, and the customer. The other choices are true statements.

9. **a.** Credit card sales are considered cash sales. Cash is debited HK$480,000 for the net amount received (HK$500,000 − HK$20,000 for credit card use fee), and Service Charge Expense is debited HK$20,000 for the 4% credit card use fee (HK$500,000 × 4%). The other choices are therefore incorrect.

10. **c.** A promissory note is a negotiable instrument. The other choices are true statements.

11. **b.** Notes Receivable is recorded at face value ($1,000). No interest on the note is recorded until it is earned. Accounts Receivable is credited because no new sales have been made. The other choices are therefore incorrect.

12. **d.** Cash is debited for its maturity value [NT$10,000 + interest earned (NT$10,000 × 1/3 × 9%)], Notes Receivable credited for its face value, and Interest Revenue credited for the amount of interest earned. The other choices are therefore incorrect.

13. **a.** Accounts Receivable is reported in the current assets section of the statement of financial position at the gross amount less the allowance for doubtful accounts, not at (b) net book value, (c) lower-of-cost-or-net realizable value, or (d) invoice cost.

14. **c.** The accounts receivable turnover is 6.4 [¥800,000/(¥100,000 + ¥150,000)/2]. The average collection period in days is 57 days (365/6.4). The other choices are therefore incorrect.

Practice Brief Exercises

Record basic accounts receivable transactions.

1. **(LO 1)** Record the following transactions on the books of Gwok Toys (amounts in thousands).

a. On August 1, Gwok sold merchandise on account to Miguel Imports for NT$15,500, terms 1/10, n/30.

b. On August 8, Miguel returned merchandise worth NT$3,100 to Gwok.

c. On August 11, Miguel paid for the merchandise.

Solution

		Debit	Credit
1. a.	Accounts Receivable	15,500	
	Sales Revenue		15,500
b.	Sales Returns and Allowances	3,100	
	Accounts Receivable		3,100
c.	Cash (NT$12,400 − NT$124)	12,276	
	Sales Discounts (NT$12,400 × 1%)	124	
	Accounts Receivable (NT$15,500 − NT$3,100)		12,400

Prepare entry using percentage-of-receivables method.

2. **(LO 2)** Sanchez Vineyards uses the percentage-of-receivables basis in 2029 to record bad debt expense. It estimates that 3% of accounts receivable will become uncollectible. Sales revenues are €900,000 for 2029, and sales returns and allowances are €50,000. At December 31, 2029, the balance in accounts receivable is €139,000, and the allowance for doubtful accounts has a credit balance of €3,000. Prepare the adjusting entry to record bad debt expense in 2029.

Solution

2. Bad Debt Expense [(€139,000 × 3%) − €3,000]	1,170	
Allowance for Doubtful Accounts		1,170

Prepare entry for notes receivable exchanged for account receivable.

3. **(LO 3)** On January 20, 2029, Carlos Co. sold merchandise on account to Carson Co. for $20,000, n/30. On February 19, Carson Co. gave Carlos Co. an 8% promissory note in settlement of this account. Prepare the journal entry to record the sale and the settlement of the account receivable.

Solution

3. Jan. 20	Accounts Receivable	20,000	
	Sales Revenue		20,000
Feb. 19	Notes Receivable	20,000	
	Accounts Receivable		20,000

Practice Exercises

Journalize entries to record allowance for doubtful accounts using two different bases.

1. **(LO 2)** The ledger of Nuro Metalworks at the end of the current year shows Accounts Receivable £180,000, Sales Revenue £1,800,000, and Sales Returns and Allowances £60,000.

Instructions

a. If Nuro uses the direct write-off method to account for uncollectible accounts, journalize the adjusting entry at December 31, assuming Nuro determines that £2,900 of the accounts receivable is uncollectible.

b. If Allowance for Doubtful Accounts has a credit balance of £4,300 in the trial balance, journalize the adjusting entry at December 31, assuming bad debts are expected to be 10% of accounts receivable.

c. If Allowance for Doubtful Accounts has a debit balance of £410 in the trial balance, journalize the adjusting entry at December 31, assuming bad debts are expected to be 6% of accounts receivable.

Solution

1. a. Dec. 31	Bad Debt Expense	2,900	
	Accounts Receivable		2,900
b. Dec. 31	Bad Debt Expense	13,700	
	Allowance for Doubtful Accounts [(£180,000 × 10%) − £4,300]		13,700
c. Dec. 31	Bad Debt Expense	11,210	
	Allowance for Doubtful Accounts [(£180,000 × 6%) + £410]		11,210

Journalize entries for notes receivable transactions.

2. **(LO 3)** Sargeant Supply has the following transactions related to notes receivable during the last 2 months of 2029.

Nov. 1	Loaned CHF20,000 cash to Mary Hawkins on a 1-year, 12% note.
Dec. 11	Sold goods to Eminem, Inc., receiving a CHF9,000, 90-day, 8% note.
16	Received a CHF8,000, 6-month, 9% note in exchange for Rick DeLong's outstanding accounts receivable.
31	Accrued interest revenue on all notes receivable.

Instructions

a. Journalize the transactions for Sargeant Supply.

b. Record the collection of the Hawkins note at its maturity in 2030.

Solution

2. a. **2029**

Nov. 1	Notes Receivable	20,000	
	Cash		20,000
Dec. 11	Notes Receivable	9,000	
	Sales Revenue		9,000
16	Notes Receivable	8,000	
	Accounts Receivable		8,000
31	Interest Receivable	470	
	Interest Revenue*		470

*Calculation of interest revenue:

Hawkins' note:	CHF20,000 × 12% × 2/12 =	CHF400
Eminem's note:	9,000 × 8% × 20/360 =	40
DeLong's note:	8,000 × 9% × 15/360 =	30
Total accrued interest		CHF470

b. **2030**

Nov. 1	Cash	22,400	
	Interest Receivable		400
	Interest Revenue**		2,000
	Notes Receivable		20,000

**(CHF20,000 × 12% × 10/12)

Practice Problem

(LO 1, 2, 3) The following selected transactions relate to Dylan Confectioners (amounts in thousands).

Prepare entries for various receivables transactions.

Mar.	1	Sold ₩20,000 of merchandise to Hé Ltd., terms 2/10, n/30.
	11	Received payment in full from Hé for balance due from the March 1 transaction.
	12	Accepted Juno Company's ₩20,000, 6-month, 12% note for balance due on outstanding account receivable.
	13	Made Dylan credit card sales for ₩13,200.
	15	Made Visa credit card sales totaling ₩6,700. A 3% service fee is charged by Visa.
Apr.	11	Sold accounts receivable of ₩8,000 to Harcot Factor. Harcot assesses a service charge of 2% of the amount of receivables sold.
	13	Received collections of ₩8,200 on Dylan credit card sales and added finance charges of 1.5% to the remaining balances.
May	10	Wrote off as uncollectible ₩16,000 of accounts receivable. Dylan uses the percentage-of-receivables basis to estimate bad debts.
June	30	Accounts receivable total ₩2,000,000. The bad debt percentage is 1% of accounts receivable. At June 30, the balance in the allowance account is a credit balance of ₩3,500 before adjustment.
July	16	One of the accounts receivable written off in May was from Juli Chan, who pays the amount due, ₩4,000, in full.

Instructions

Prepare the journal entries for the transactions. (Ignore entries for cost of goods sold.)

Solution

Mar. 1	Accounts Receivable	20,000	
	Sales Revenue		20,000
	(To record sales on account)		
11	Cash	19,600	
	Sales Discounts (2% × ₩20,000)	400	
	Accounts Receivable		20,000
	(To record collection of accounts receivable)		
12	Notes Receivable	20,000	
	Accounts Receivable		20,000
	(To record acceptance of Juno Company note)		
13	Accounts Receivable	13,200	
	Sales Revenue		13,200
	(To record company credit card sales)		

15	Cash	6,499	
	Service Charge Expense (3% × ₩6,700)	201	
	Sales Revenue		6,700
	(To record credit card sales)		
Apr. 11	Cash	7,840	
	Service Charge Expense (2% × ₩8,000)	160	
	Accounts Receivable		8,000
	(To record sale of receivables to factor)		
13	Cash	8,200	
	Accounts Receivable		8,200
	(To record collection of accounts receivable)		
	Accounts Receivable [(₩13,200 − ₩8,200) × 1.5%]	75	
	Interest Revenue		75
	(To record interest on amount due)		
May 10	Allowance for Doubtful Accounts	16,000	
	Accounts Receivable		16,000
	(To record write-off of accounts receivable)		
June 30	Bad Debt Expense [(₩2,000,000 × 1%) − ₩3,500]	16,500	
	Allowance for Doubtful Accounts		16,500
	(To record estimate of uncollectible accounts)		
July 16	Accounts Receivable	4,000	
	Allowance for Doubtful Accounts		4,000
	(To reverse write-off of accounts receivable)		
	Cash	4,000	
	Accounts Receivable		4,000
	(To record collection of accounts receivable)		

Questions

1. What is the difference between an account receivable and a note receivable?

2. What are some common types of receivables other than accounts receivable and notes receivable?

3. **Texaco Oil Company** (USA) issues its own credit cards. Assume that Texaco charges you $40 interest on an unpaid balance. Prepare the journal entry that Texaco makes to record this revenue.

4. What are the essential features of the allowance method of accounting for bad debts?

5. Roger Holloway cannot understand why cash realizable value does not decrease when an uncollectible account is written off under the allowance method. Clarify this point for Roger.

6. What types of receivables does **TSMC** report on its statement of financial position (see Appendix A)? Does it use the allowance method or the direct write-off method to account for uncollectibles?

7. Borke Ltd. has a credit balance of NT$300,000 in Allowance for Doubtful Accounts before adjustment. The total estimated uncollectibles under the percentage-of-receivables basis is NT$580,000. Prepare the adjusting entry to record bad debt expense.

8. How are bad debts accounted for under the direct write-off method? What are the disadvantages of this method?

9. Regina Golden, the vice president of sales for Tropical Pools and Spas, wants the company's credit department to be less restrictive in granting credit. "How can we sell anything when you guys won't approve anybody?" she asks. Discuss the pros and cons of easy credit. What are the accounting implications?

10. Freida ASA accepts both its own and other credit cards. What are the advantages of accepting both types of cards?

11. An article recently appeared in the *Wall Street Journal* indicating that companies are selling their receivables at a record rate. Why are companies selling their receivables?

12. Westside Textiles decides to sell HK$8,000,000 of its accounts receivable to First Factors. First Factors assesses a service charge of 3% of the amount of receivables sold. Prepare the journal entry that Westside Textiles makes to record this sale.

13. Your roommate is uncertain about the advantages of a promissory note. Compare the advantages of a note receivable with those of an account receivable.

14. How may the maturity date of a promissory note be stated?

15. Indicate the maturity date of each of the following promissory notes:

Date of Note	Terms
a. March 13	one year after date of note
b. May 4	3 months after date
c. June 20	30 days after date
d. July 1	60 days after date

16. Compute the missing items for each of the following notes.

	Principal	Annual Interest Rate	Time	Total Interest
a.	?	9%	120 days	€ 450
b.	€30,000	10%	3 years	?
c.	€60,000	?	5 months	€1,500
d.	€45,000	8%	?	€1,200

17. Jana Company dishonors a note at maturity. What are the options available to the lender?

18. **Toyota Motor Company** (JPN) has accounts receivable and notes receivable. How should the receivables be reported on the statement of financial position?

19. The accounts receivable turnover is 8.14, and average net receivables during the period are ₺400,000. What is the amount of net credit sales for the period?

20. What percentage does **TSMC**'s 2020 allowance for doubtful accounts represent as a percentage of its gross receivables (see Appendix A)?

Brief Exercises

Identify different types of receivables.

BE8.1 (LO 1) Presented below are three receivables transactions. Indicate whether these receivables are reported as accounts receivable, notes receivable, or other receivables on a statement of financial position.

a. Sold merchandise on account for ₩64,000,000 to a customer.

b. Received a promissory note of ₩57,000,000 for services performed.

c. Advanced ₩10,000,000 to an employee.

Record basic accounts receivable transactions.

BE8.2 (LO 1) Record the following transactions on the books of RAS Co.

a. On July 1, RAS Co. sold merchandise on account to Waegelein Inc. for $17,200, terms 2/10, n/30.

b. On July 8, Waegelein Inc. returned merchandise worth $3,800 to RAS Co.

c. On July 11, Waegelein Inc. paid for the merchandise.

Prepare entry for allowance method and partial statement of financial position.

BE8.3 (LO 2, 4) During its first year of operations, Energy Solutions had credit sales of €3,000,000; €600,000 remained uncollected at year-end. The credit manager estimates that €31,000 of these receivables will become uncollectible.

a. Prepare the journal entry to record the estimated uncollectibles.

b. Prepare the current assets section of the statement of financial position for Energy Solutions. Assume that in addition to the receivables it has cash of €90,000, inventory of €130,000, and prepaid insurance of €7,500.

Prepare entry for write-off; determine cash realizable value.

BE8.4 (LO 2) At the end of 2029, Chin Appliances has accounts receivable of ¥700,000 and an allowance for doubtful accounts of ¥54,000 (amounts in thousands). On January 24, 2030, the company learns that its receivable from Megan Gray is not collectible, and management authorizes a write-off of ¥6,200.

a. Prepare the journal entry to record the write-off.

b. What is the cash realizable value of the accounts receivable (1) before the write-off and (2) after the write-off?

Prepare entries for collection of bad debt write-off.

BE8.5 (LO 2) Assume the same information as BE8.4. On March 4, 2030, Chin Appliances receives payment of ¥6,200 in full from Megan Gray. Prepare the journal entries to record this transaction.

Prepare entry using percentage-of-receivables method.

BE8.6 (LO 2) Kingston Publishers uses the percentage-of-receivables basis to record bad debt expense. It estimates that 1% of accounts receivable will become uncollectible. Accounts receivable are £420,000 at the end of the year, and the allowance for doubtful accounts has a credit balance of £1,500.

a. Prepare the adjusting journal entry to record bad debt expense for the year.

b. If the allowance for doubtful accounts had a debit balance of £800 instead of a credit balance of £1,500, determine the amount to be reported for bad debt expense.

Prepare entries to dispose of accounts receivable.

BE8.7 (LO 2) Presented below are two independent transactions.

a. Fiesta Restaurant accepted a Visa card in payment of a €175 lunch bill. The bank charges a 4% fee. What entry should Fiesta make?

b. St. Pierre AG sold its accounts receivable of €60,000. What entry should St. Pierre make, given a service charge of 3% on the amount of receivables sold?

Compute interest and determine maturity dates on notes.

BE8.8 (LO 3) Compute interest and find the maturity date for the following notes (NT$ in thousands).

	Date of Note	Principal	Interest Rate (%)	Terms
a.	June 10	NT$80,000	6%	60 days
b.	July 14	NT$64,000	7%	90 days
c.	April 27	NT$12,000	8%	75 days

Determine maturity dates and compute interest and rates on notes.

BE8.9 (LO 3) Presented below are data on three promissory notes. Determine the missing amounts.

	Date of Note	Terms	Maturity Date	Principal	Annual Interest Rate	Total Interest
a.	April 1	60 days	?	₺600,000	6%	?
b.	July 2	30 days	?	90,000	?	₺600
c.	March 7	6 months	?	120,000	10%	?

Prepare entry for notes receivable exchanged for account receivable.

BE8.10 (LO 3) On January 10, 2029, Wilfer Ltd. sold merchandise on account to Robertsen Co. for HK$84,600, n/30. On February 9, Robertsen Co. gave Wilfer Ltd. a 10% promissory note in settlement of this account. Prepare the journal entry to record the sale and the settlement of the account receivable. (Omit cost of goods sold entries.)

Prepare entry for estimated uncollectibles and classifications, and compute ratios.

BE8.11 (LO 2, 4) During its first year of operations, Fertig Retail had credit sales of R$3,000,000, of which R$400,000 remained uncollected at year-end. The credit manager estimates that R$18,000 of these receivables will become uncollectible.

a. Prepare the journal entry to record the estimated uncollectibles. (Assume an unadjusted balance of zero in Allowance for Doubtful Accounts.)

b. Prepare the current assets section of the statement of financial position for Fertig Retail, assuming that in addition to the receivables it has cash of R$90,000, merchandise inventory of R$180,000, and supplies of R$13,000.

c. Calculate the accounts receivable turnover and average collection period. Assume that average net accounts receivable were R$300,000. Explain what these measures tell us.

Compute ratios to analyze receivables.

BE8.12 (LO 4) The financial statements of **Minnesota Mining and Manufacturing Company (3M)** (USA) report net sales of $20.0 billion. Accounts receivable (net) are $2.7 billion at the beginning of the year and $2.8 billion at the end of the year. Compute 3M's accounts receivable turnover. Compute 3M's average collection period for accounts receivable in days.

DO IT! Exercises

Prepare entries to recognize accounts receivable.

DO IT! 8.1 (LO 1) On March 1, Lincoln sold merchandise on account to Amelia Stores for €28,000, terms 1/10, net 45. On March 6, Amelia returns merchandise with a sales price of €1,000. On March 11, Lincoln receives payment from Amelia for the balance due. Prepare journal entries to record the March transactions on Lincoln's books. (You may ignore cost of goods sold entries and explanations.)

Prepare entry for uncollectible accounts.

DO IT! 8.2a (LO 2) Gonzalez Fashions has been in business several years. At the end of the current year, the ledger shows the following:

Accounts Receivable	R$ 310,000 Dr.
Sales Revenue	2,200,000 Cr.
Allowance for Doubtful Accounts	6,100 Cr.

Bad debts are estimated to be 5% of accounts receivable. Prepare the entry to adjust Allowance for Doubtful Accounts.

Prepare entry for factored accounts.

DO IT! 8.2b (LO 2) Neumann Distributors is a growing company whose ability to raise capital has not been growing as quickly as its expanding assets and sales. Neumann's local banker has indicated that the company cannot increase its borrowing for the foreseeable future. Neumann's suppliers are demanding payment for goods acquired within 30 days of the invoice date, but Neumann's customers are slow in paying for their purchases (60–90 days). As a result, Neumann has a cash flow problem.

Neumann needs €160,000 to cover next Friday's payroll. Its balance of outstanding accounts receivable totals €800,000. To alleviate this cash crunch, the company sells €170,000 of its receivables. Record the entry that Neumann would make. (Assume a 2% service charge.)

Compute maturity date and interest on note.

DO IT! 8.3 (LO 3) Gentry Wholesalers accepts from Benton Stores a £6,200, 4-month, 9% note dated May 31 in settlement of Benton's overdue account. (a) What is the maturity date of the note? (b) What is the interest payable at the maturity date?

Compute ratios for receivables.

DO IT! 8.4 (LO 4) In 2029, Wainwright Drugstores has net credit sales of NT$1,300,000 for the year (amounts in thousands). It had a beginning accounts receivable (net) balance of NT$101,000 and an ending accounts receivable (net) balance of NT$107,000. Compute Wainwright Drugstore's (a) accounts receivable turnover and (b) average collection period in days.

Exercises

E8.1 (LO 1) On January 6, Malta Ltd. sells merchandise on account to Harley Inc. for £9,200, terms 1/10, n/30. On January 16, Harley pays the amount due.

Prepare entries for recognizing accounts receivable.

Instructions

Prepare the entries on Malta's books to record the sale and related collection. (Omit cost of goods sold entries.)

E8.2 (LO 1) Presented below are selected transactions of Federer Apparel. Federer sells in large quantities to other companies and also sells its product in a small retail outlet.

Journalize entries related to accounts receivable.

March	1	Sold merchandise on account to Lynda Company for CHF5,000, terms 2/10, n/30.
	3	Lynda Company returned merchandise worth CHF500 to Federer.
	9	Federer collected the amount due from Lynda Company from the March 1 sale.
	15	Federer sold merchandise for CHF400 in its retail outlet. The customer used his Federer credit card.
	31	Federer added 1.5% monthly interest to the customer's credit card balance.

Instructions

Prepare journal entries for the transactions above. (Ignore cost of goods sold entries and explanations.)

E8.3 (LO 1) Presented below are two independent situations.

Journalize entries for recognizing accounts receivable.

Instructions

a. On January 6, Brumbaugh Co. sells merchandise on account to Pryor Group for €7,000, terms 2/10, n/30. On January 16, Pryor pays the amount due. Prepare the entries on Brumbaugh's books to record the sale and related collection. (Omit cost of goods sold entries.)

b. On January 10, Andrew Farley uses his Paltrow Co. credit card to purchase merchandise from Paltrow Co. for €9,000. On February 10, Farley is billed for the amount due of €9,000. On February 12, Farley pays €5,000 on the balance due. On March 10, Farley is billed for the amount due, including interest at 1% per month on the unpaid balance as of February 12. Prepare the entries on Paltrow's books related to the transactions that occurred on January 10, February 12, and March 10. (Omit cost of goods sold entries.)

E8.4 (LO 1, 2) At the beginning of the current period, Coe Ltd. had balances in Accounts Receivable of £200,000 and in Allowance for Doubtful Accounts of £9,000 (credit). During the period, it had net credit sales of £800,000 and collections of £763,000. It wrote off as uncollectible accounts receivable of £7,300. However, a £3,100 account previously written off as uncollectible was recovered before the end of the current period. Uncollectible accounts are estimated to total £25,000 at the end of the period. (Omit cost of goods sold entries.)

Journalize receivables transactions.

Instructions

a. Prepare the entries to record sales and collections during the period.

b. Prepare the entry to record the write-off of uncollectible accounts during the period.

c. Prepare the entries to record the recovery of the uncollectible account during the period.

d. Prepare the entry to record bad debt expense for the period.

e. Determine the ending balances in Accounts Receivable and Allowance for Doubtful Accounts.

f. What is the net realizable value of the receivables at the end of the period?

E8.5 (LO 2) The ledger of Macarty Company at the end of the current year shows Accounts Receivable $78,000, Credit Sales $810,000, and Sales Returns and Allowances $40,000.

Journalize entries to record allowance for doubtful accounts using two different bases.

Instructions

a. If Macarty uses the direct write-off method to account for uncollectible accounts, journalize the entry at December 15 if Macarty determines that Matisse's $900 balance is uncollectible.

b. Assume Macarty uses the allowance method to account for uncollectible accounts. If Allowance for Doubtful Accounts has a credit balance of $1,100 in the trial balance, journalize the adjusting entry at December 31, assuming uncollectibles are expected to be 10% of accounts receivable.

c. Assume Macarty uses the allowance method to account for uncollectible accounts. If Allowance for Doubtful Accounts has a debit balance of $500 in the trial balance, journalize the adjusting entry at December 31, assuming uncollectibles are expected to be 8% of accounts receivable.

Determine bad debt expense, and prepare the adjusting entry.

E8.6 (LO 2) Min Yachts has accounts receivable of ₩95,400 at March 31, 2029 (amounts in thousands). Credit terms are 2/10, n/30. At March 31, 2029, there is a ₩2,100 credit balance in Allowance for Doubtful Accounts prior to adjustment. The company uses the percentage-of-receivables basis for estimating uncollectible accounts. The company's estimates of bad debts are as shown below.

	Balance, March 31		Estimated Percentage
Age of Accounts	**2029**	**2028**	**Uncollectible**
Current	₩65,000	₩75,000	2%
1–30 days past due	12,900	8,000	5
31–90 days past due	10,100	2,400	30
Over 90 days past due	7,400	1,100	50
	₩95,400	₩86,500	

Instructions

a. Determine the total estimated uncollectibles as of March 31, 2029.

b. Prepare the adjusting entry at March 31, 2029, to record bad debt expense.

c. Discuss the implications of the changes in the aging schedule from 2028 to 2029.

Journalize write-off and recovery.

E8.7 (LO 2) At December 31, 2028, Blanda Creations had a credit balance of €15,000 in Allowance for Doubtful Accounts. During 2029, Blanda wrote off accounts totaling €11,000. One of those accounts (€1,800) was later collected. At December 31, 2029, an aging schedule indicated that the balance in Allowance for Doubtful Accounts should be €19,000.

Instructions

Prepare journal entries to record the 2029 transactions of Blanda.

Journalize percentage-of-receivables basis, write-off, recovery.

E8.8 (LO 2) On December 31, 2029, Ling Industries estimated that 2% of its net accounts receivable of ¥450,000 will become uncollectible (amounts in thousands). The company recorded this amount as an addition to Allowance for Doubtful Accounts. The allowance account had a zero balance before adjustment at December 31, 2029. On May 11, 2030, Ling determined that the Jeff Shoemaker account was uncollectible and wrote off ¥1,100. On June 12, 2030, Shoemaker paid the amount previously written off.

Instructions

Prepare the journal entries on December 31, 2029, May 11, 2030, and June 12, 2030.

Journalize entries for the sale of accounts receivable.

E8.9 (LO 2) Presented below are two independent situations.

Instructions

a. On March 3, Kitselman Appliances sells $650,000 of its receivables to Ervay Factors Inc. Ervay Factors assesses a finance charge of 3% of the amount of receivables sold. Prepare the entry on Kitselman Appliances' books to record the sale of the receivables.

b. On May 10, Fillmore Company sold merchandise for $3,000 and accepted the customer's America Bank MasterCard. America Bank charges a 4% service charge for credit card sales. Prepare the entry on Fillmore Company's books to record the sale of merchandise.

Journalize entries for credit card sales.

E8.10 (LO 2) Presented as follows are two independent situations.

Instructions

a. On April 2, Jennifer Elston uses her **IKEA** (SWE) credit card to purchase merchandise from an IKEA store for €1,500. On May 1, Elston is billed for the €1,500 amount due. Elston pays €500 on the balance due on May 3. Elston receives a bill dated June 1 for the amount due, including interest at 1.0% per month on the unpaid balance as of May 3. Prepare the entries on IKEA's books related to the transactions that occurred on April 2, May 3, and June 1.

b. On July 4, Dupré Restaurant accepts a Visa card for a €200 dinner bill. Visa charges a 2% service fee. Prepare the entry on Dupré's books related to this transaction.

E8.11 (LO 2) Colaw Stores accepts both its own and national credit cards. During the year, the following selected summary transactions occurred (NT$ in thousands).

Journalize credit card sales.

Jan.	15	Made Colaw credit card sales totaling NT$18,000. (There were no balances prior to January 15.)
	20	Made Visa credit card sales (service charge fee 2%) totaling NT$4,500.
Feb.	10	Collected NT$10,000 on Colaw credit card sales.
	15	Added finance charges of 1.5% to Colaw credit card account balances.

Instructions

Journalize the transactions for Colaw Stores.

E8.12 (LO 3) Chang Supply has the following transactions related to notes receivable during the last 2 months of 2029. The company does not make entries to accrue interest except at December 31.

Journalize entries for notes receivable transactions.

Nov	1	Loaned HK$300,000 cash to Manny Shin on a 12 month, 10% note.
Dec.	11	Sold goods to Malcolm Inc., receiving a HK$67,500, 90-day, 8% note.
	16	Received a HK$400,000, 180 day, 9% note in exchange for Joe Fernetti's outstanding accounts receivable.
	31	Accrued interest revenue on all notes receivable.

Instructions

a. Journalize the transactions for Chang Supply. (Ignore cost of goods sold.)

b. Record the collection of the Shin note at its maturity in 2030.

E8.13 (LO 3) These transactions took place for Bramson Co.

Journalize notes receivable transactions.

2028		
May.	1	Received a $5,000, 12-month, 6% note in exchange for an outstanding account receivable from R. Stoney.
Dec.	31	Accrued interest revenue on the R. Stoney note.
2029		
May.	1	Received principal plus interest on the R. Stoney note. (No interest has been accrued since December 31, 2028.)

Instructions

Record the transactions in the general journal. The company does not make entries to accrue interest except at December 31.

E8.14 (LO 3) Vandiver Company had the following select transactions.

Prepare entries for note receivable transactions.

Apr. 1, 2029	Accepted Goodwin Company's 12-month, 6% note in settlement of a $30,000 account receivable.
July 1, 2029	Loaned $25,000 cash to Thomas Slocombe on a 9-month, 10% note.
Dec. 31, 2029	Accrued interest on all notes receivable.
Apr. 1, 2030	Received principal plus interest on the Goodwin note.
Apr. 1, 2030	Thomas Slocombe dishonored its note; Vandiver expects it will eventually collect.

Instructions

Prepare journal entries to record the transactions. Vandiver prepares adjusting entries once a year on December 31.

E8.15 (LO 3) On May 2, Ling Ltd. lends ¥9,000 to Chen, Inc., issuing a 6-month, 7% note (¥ in thousands). At the maturity date, November 2, Chen indicates that it cannot pay.

Journalize entries for dishonor of notes receivable.

Instructions

a. Prepare the entry to record the issuance of the note.

b. Prepare the entry to record the dishonor of the note, assuming that Ling expects collection will occur.

c. Prepare the entry to record the dishonor of the note, assuming that Ling does not expect collection in the future.

Prepare a statement of financial position presentation of receivables.

E8.16 (LO 4) Eileen Corp. had the following balances in receivable accounts at October 31, 2029 (in thousands): Allowance for Doubtful Accounts $52, Accounts Receivable $2,910, Other Receivables $189, and Notes Receivable $1,353.

Instructions

Prepare the statement of financial position presentation of Eileen Corp.'s receivables in good form.

Compute accounts receivable turnover and average collection period.

E8.17 (LO 4) Laskova A/S had accounts receivable of €100,000 on January 1, 2029. The only transactions that affected accounts receivable during 2029 were net credit sales of €1,000,000, cash collections of €920,000, and accounts written off of €30,000.

Instructions

a. Compute the ending balance of accounts receivable.
b. Compute the accounts receivable turnover for 2029.
c. Compute the average collection period in days.

Identify key terms.

E8.18 (LO 1, 2, 3, 4) The following words and phrases were discussed in this chapter.

1. Notes receivable.
2. Cash (net) realizable value.
3. Accounts receivable turnover.
4. Aging the accounts receivable.
5. Percentage-of-receivables basis.
6. Dishonored (defaulted) note.
7. Concentration of credit risk.
8. Allowance method.
9. Direct write-off method.
10. Factor.

Instructions

Match each word or phrase with its description below.

a. ________ Written promise (as evidenced by a formal instrument) for amounts to be received.
b. ________ A method of accounting for bad debts that involves estimating uncollectible accounts at the end of each period.
c. ________ A measure of the liquidity of accounts receivable, computed by dividing net credit sales by average net accounts receivable.
d. ________ A method of accounting for bad debts that involves charging receivable balances to Bad Debt Expense at the time receivables from a particular company are determined to be uncollectible.
e. ________ A finance company or bank that buys receivables from businesses for a fee and then collects the payments directly from the customers.
f. ________ The net amount a company expects to receive in cash from receivables.
g. ________ The threat of nonpayment from a single large customer or class of customers that could adversely affect the financial health of the company.
h. ________ A note that is not paid in full at maturity.
i. ________ A method of estimating the amount of bad debt expense whereby management establishes a percentage relationship between the amount of receivables and the expected losses from uncollectible accounts.
j. ________ A schedule of customer balances classified by the length of time they have been unpaid.

Problems

Prepare journal entries related to bad debt expense, and compute ratios.

P8.1 (LO 1, 2, 4) At December 31, 2028, Suisse Imports reported this information on its balance sheet.

Accounts receivable	$600,000
Less: Allowance for doubtful accounts	37,000

During 2029, the company had the following transactions related to receivables.

1. Sales on account	$2,500,000
2. Sales returns and allowances	50,000

3. Collections of accounts receivable 2,200,000
4. Write-offs of accounts receivable deemed uncollectible 41,000
5. Recovery of accounts previously written off as uncollectible 15,000

Instructions

a. Prepare the journal entries to record each of these five transactions. Assume that no cash discounts were taken on the collections of accounts receivable. (Omit cost of goods sold entries.)

b. Enter the January 1, 2029, balances in Accounts Receivable and Allowance for Doubtful Accounts, post the entries to the two accounts (use T-accounts), and determine the balances. b. A/R bal. $809,000

c. Prepare the journal entry to record bad debt expense for 2029, assuming that aging the accounts receivable indicates that estimated uncollectibles are $46,000.

d. Compute the accounts receivable turnover and average collection period.

P8.2 (LO 2) **Writing** Information related to Mingenback Ltd. for 2029 is summarized below. *Compute bad debt amounts.*

Total credit sales	£2,500,000
Accounts receivable at December 31	875,000
Bad debts written off	33,000

Instructions

a. What amount of bad debt expense will Mingenback Ltd. report if it uses the direct write-off method of accounting for bad debts?

b. Assume that Mingenback Ltd. estimates its bad debt expense based on 6% of accounts receivable. What amount of bad debt expense will Mingenback record if it has an Allowance for Doubtful Accounts credit balance of £3,000? b. £49,500

c. Assume the same facts as in (b), except that there is a £3,000 debit balance in Allowance for Doubtful Accounts. What amount of bad debt expense will Mingenback record?

d. What is the weakness of the direct write-off method of reporting bad debt expense?

P8.3 (LO 2) Presented below is an aging schedule for Sycamore AG. *Journalize entries to record transactions related to bad debts.*

Worksheet

	A	B	C	D	E	F	G
1				Number of Days Past Due			
2			Not				
3	Customer	Total	Yet Due	1–30	31–60	61–90	Over 90
4	Anders	€ 22,000		€10,000	€12,000		
5	Blake	40,000	€ 40,000				
6	Cyr	57,000	16,000	6,000		€35,000	
7	Deleon	34,000					€34,000
8	Others	132,000	96,000	16,000	14,000		6,000
9		€285,000	€152,000	€32,000	€26,000	€35,000	€40,000
10	Estimated Percentage Uncollectible		3%	6%	13%	25%	50%
11	Total Estimated Bad Debts	€ 38,610	€ 4,560	€ 1,920	€ 3,380	€ 8,750	€20,000
12							

At December 31, 2029, the unadjusted balance in Allowance for Doubtful Accounts is a credit of €12,000.

Instructions

a. Journalize and post the adjusting entry for bad debts at December 31, 2029. a. Bad debt expense €26,610

b. Journalize and post to the allowance account the following events and transactions in the year 2030.

1. On March 31, a €1,000 customer balance originating in 2029 is judged uncollectible.
2. On May 31, a check for €1,000 is received from the customer whose account was written off as uncollectible on March 31.

c. Journalize the adjusting entry for bad debts on December 31, 2030, assuming that the unadjusted balance in Allowance for Doubtful Accounts is a debit of €800 and the aging schedule indicates that total estimated bad debts will be €31,600. c. Bad debt expense €32,400

Journalize transactions related to bad debts.

P8.4 (LO 2) **Writing** Ho Publishers, uses the allowance method to estimate uncollectible accounts receivable. The company produced the following aging of the accounts receivable at year-end (¥ in thousands).

Worksheet

Home Insert Page Layout Formulas Data Review View

P18 fx

	A	B	C	D	E	F	G
1							
2			Number of Days Outstanding				
3		Total	0–30	31–60	61–90	91–120	Over 120
4	Accounts receivable	200,000	77,000	46,000	39,000	23,000	15,000
5	% uncollectible		1%	4%	5%	8%	20%
6	Estimated bad debts						
7							

Instructions

a. Tot. est. bad debts ¥9,400

a. Calculate the total estimated bad debts based on the above information.

b. Prepare the year-end adjusting journal entry to record the bad debts using the aged uncollectible accounts receivable determined in (a). Assume the current balance in Allowance for Doubtful Accounts is a ¥8,000 debit.

c. Of the above accounts, ¥5,000 is determined to be specifically uncollectible. Prepare the journal entry to write off the uncollectible account.

d. The company collects ¥5,000 subsequently on a specific account that had previously been determined to be uncollectible in (c). Prepare the journal entry(ies) necessary to restore the account and record the cash collection.

e. Comment on how your answers to (a)–(d) would change if Ho used 4% of **total** accounts receivable rather than aging the accounts receivable. What are the advantages to the company of aging the accounts receivable rather than applying a percentage to total accounts receivable?

Journalize entries to record transactions related to uncollectibles.

P8.5 (LO 2) **Writing** At December 31, 2029, the trial balance of Malone Company contained the following amounts before adjustment.

	Debit	Credit
Accounts Receivable	$180,000	
Allowance for Doubtful Accounts		$ 1,500
Sales Revenue		875,000

Instructions

a. Prepare the adjusting entry at December 31, 2029, to record bad debt expense, assuming that the aging schedule indicates that $10,200 of accounts receivable will be uncollectible.

b. Bad Debt Exp. $11,700

b. Repeat part (a), assuming that instead of a credit balance there is a $1,500 debit balance in Allowance for Doubtful Accounts.

c. During the next month, January 2030, a $2,100 account receivable is written off as uncollectible. Prepare the journal entry to record the write-off.

d. Repeat part (c), assuming that Malone Company uses the direct write-off method instead of the allowance method in accounting for uncollectible accounts receivable.

e. What are the advantages of using the allowance method in accounting for uncollectible accounts as compared to the direct write-off method?

Prepare entries for various credit card and notes receivable transactions.

P8.6 (LO 1, 2, 3, 4) Anping Enterprises closes its books on its July 31 year-end. The company does not make entries to accrue for interest except at its year-end. On June 30, the Notes Receivable account balance is NT$23,800 (amounts in thousands). Notes Receivable includes the following.

Date	Maker	Face Value	Term	Maturity Date	Interest Rate
April 21	Coote Inc.	NT$6,000	90 days	July 20	8%
May 25	Brady Co.	7,800	60 days	July 24	10%
June 30	BMG Corp.	10,000	6 months	December 31	6%

During July, the following transactions were completed.

July	5	Made sales of NT$4,500 on Anping credit cards.
	14	Made sales of NT$600 on Visa credit cards. The credit card service charge is 3%.
	20	Received payment in full from Coote Inc. on the amount due.
	24	Received payment in full from Brady Co. on the amount due.

Instructions

a. Journalize the July transactions and the July 31 adjusting entry for accrued interest receivable. (Interest is computed using 360 days; omit cost of goods sold entries.)

b. Enter the balances at July 1 in the receivable accounts and post the entries to all of the receivable accounts. (Use T-accounts.)

c. Show the statement of financial position presentation of the receivable accounts at July 31.

b. A/R bal. NT$4,500

c. Tot. receivables NT$14,550

Prepare entries for various receivable transactions.

P8.7 (LO 1, 2, 3) On January 1, 2029, Harter Wholesalers had Accounts Receivable €139,000, Notes Receivable €25,000, and Allowance for Doubtful Accounts €13,200. The note receivable is from Willingham Company. It is a 4-month, 9% note dated December 31, 2028. Harter prepares financial statements annually at December 31. During the year, the following selected transactions occurred.

Jan.	5	Sold €20,000 of merchandise to Sheldon Company, terms n/15.
	20	Accepted Sheldon's €20,000, 3-month, 8% note for balance due.
Feb.	18	Sold €8,000 of merchandise to Patwary Company and accepted Patwary's €8,000, 6-month, 9% note for the amount due.
Apr.	20	Collected Sheldon note in full.
	30	Received payment in full from Willingham Company on the amount due.
May	25	Accepted Potter Inc.'s €6,000, 3-month, 7% note in settlement of a past-due balance on account.
Aug.	18	Received payment in full from Patwary on note due.
	25	The Potter Inc. note was dishonored. Potter is not bankrupt; future payment is anticipated.
Sept.	1	Sold €12,000 of merchandise to Stanbrough Company and accepted a €12,000, 6-month, 10% note for the amount due.

Instructions

Journalize the transactions. (Omit cost of goods sold entries.)

Calculate and interpret various ratios.

P8.8 (LO 4) The amounts presented here are from recent annual reports of **Nike** (USA) and **adidas** (DEU). (All amounts are in millions.)

	Nike	adidas
Sales revenue	$37,403	€19,844
Allowance for doubtful accounts, beginning	30	189
Allowance for doubtful accounts, ending	214	267
Accounts receivable balance, beginning	4,302	2,814
Accounts receivable balance, ending	2,963	2,219

Instructions

Calculate the accounts receivable turnover and average collection period for both companies. Comment on the difference in their collection experiences.

Prepare financial statements.

P8.9 (LO 4) The adjusted trial balance of Yoon Imports for the year ended December 31, 2029, is as follows (amounts in thousands):

	Debit	Credit
Cash	¥ 6,400	
Accounts Receivable	2,700	
Notes Receivable	6,300	
Inventory	10,000	
Equipment	7,500	
Allowance for Doubtful Accounts		¥ 300
Accumulated Depreciation—Equipment		1,000
Notes Payable		1,100
Accounts Payable		600
Share Capital—Ordinary		16,000
Retained Earnings		12,000
Dividends	1,000	
Sales Revenue		13,000
Interest Revenue		100
Cost of Goods Sold	8,000	
Salary and Wages Expense	1,400	
Rent Expense	700	
Bad Debt Expense	60	
Service Charge Expense	40	
	¥44,100	¥44,100

Instructions

Net income ¥2,900

Prepare an income statement, retained earnings statement, and a classified statement of financial position. The notes payable is due on January 10, 2030.

Sales discounts, bad debt ratio, accounts receivable turnover.

P8.10 (LO 1, 2, 4) At January 1, 2029, Voung Company has a beginning accounts receivable balance of $600,000 and related transactions for year 2029:

1. In year 2029, it had credit sales of $3,060,000 with credit terms of 2/10, n/30, of which 80% were collected within the discount period.
2. In year 2029, it wrote off an allowance for doubtful accounts of $36,000, with part of the allowance written off in September being recovered in December.
3. It recognized bad debt expense of $44,940 in year 2029.
4. The allowance for doubtful accounts at the end of year 2029 was $13,740 greater than that at the end of year 2028.
5. The net balance of accounts receivable at the end of year 2029 was $261,060 greater than that at the end of year 2028.
6. Voung company adopted the percentage-of- receivables basis to estimate doubtful accounts, and the bad debt ratio is constant each year.

Instructions

a. What is the amount of cash discounts obtained from customers on credit sales in year 2029?

b. What amount was the allowance for doubt accounts at the beginning of year 2029?

c. What was the net balance of accounts receivable at the end of year 2029?

d. What amount was recovered from the allowance for doubt accounts written off in December year 2029?

e. What amount was collected in cash from accounts receivable in year 2029?

f. What is the bad debt ratio when using the percentage-of-receivables basis for estimating uncollectible accounts?

g. What was the accounts receivable turnover in year 2029?

Comprehensive Accounting Cycle Review

ACR8 Victoria Ltd.'s statement of financial position at December 31, 2028, is presented below.

Victoria Ltd.
Statement of Financial Position
December 31, 2028

Inventory	£ 9,400	Share capital—ordinary	£20,000
Accounts receivable	19,780	Retained earnings	12,730
Allowance for doubtful accounts	(800)	Accounts payable	8,750
Cash	13,100		£41,480
	£41,480		

During January 2029, the following transactions occurred. Victoria uses the perpetual inventory method.

Jan.	1	Victoria accepted a 4-month, 8% note from Merando Company in payment of Merando's £1,200 account.
	3	Victoria wrote off as uncollectible the accounts of Inwood Corporation (£450) and Goza Company (£280).
	8	Victoria purchased £17,200 of inventory on account.
	11	Victoria sold for £28,000 on account inventory that cost £19,600.
	15	Victoria sold inventory that cost £700 to Mark Lauber for £1,000. Lauber charged this amount on his Visa First Bank card. The service fee charged Victoria by First Bank is 3%.
	17	Victoria collected £22,900 from customers on account.
	21	Victoria paid £14,300 on accounts payable.
	24	Victoria received payment in full (£280) from Goza on the account written off on January 3.
	27	Victoria purchased supplies for £1,400 cash.
	31	Victoria paid other operating expenses, £3,718.

Adjustment data:

1. Interest is recorded for the month on the note from January 1.
2. Bad debts are expected to be 6% of the January 31, 2029, accounts receivable.
3. A count of supplies on January 31, 2029, reveals that £560 remains unused.

Instructions

(You may want to set up T-accounts to determine ending balances.)

a. Prepare journal entries for the above transactions and the adjusting entries. (Include entries for cost of goods sold using the perpetual system.)

b. Prepare an adjusted trial balance at January 31, 2029.

c. Prepare an income statement and a retained earnings statement for the month ending January 31, 2029, and a classified statement of financial position as of January 31, 2029.

Data Analytics in Action

Using Data Visualization to Understand Accounts Receivable and Bad Debts over Time

DA8.1 Data visualization can be used to understand accounts receivable and bad debts.

Excel

Example: Many stakeholders are interested in bad debt information. For example, under transparency rules in the United States, cities, states, and other governments publicize financial data. Using data visualization, we can see trends in the data from the city of Austin, Texas, regarding energy revenue and bad debt, as the following chart shows.

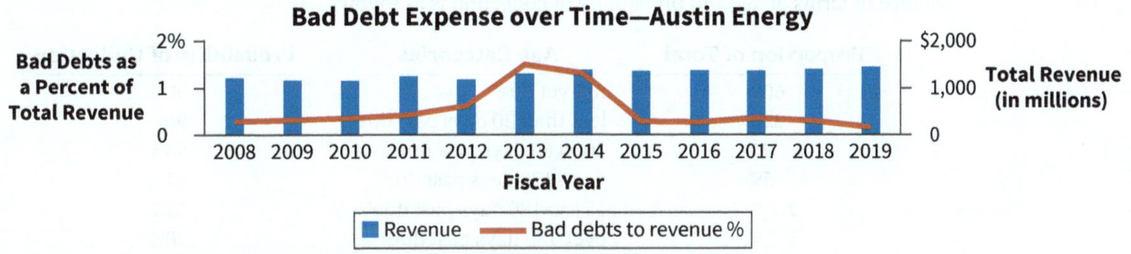

Source: Based on City of Austin open data portal.

The chart indicates a steady increase in bad debt expense as a percent of total revenue from 2008 to 2011, followed by a steep peak in 2014. The expense percentage declined sharply in 2015, followed by a slight increase in 2016 and a decline to the lowest level in 2019. Over the entire 12-year period, revenue increased steadily. However, the trend in revenue does not explain the spike in bad debt expense, so there is likely some other cause of the increase in bad debt expense from 2012 to 2013.

What conclusions can we make about the city of Austin's ability to collect amounts owed by energy customers? Except for the peak in 2013 and 2014, Austin appears to be efficient in collecting amounts due. While the highest percent uncollectible is 1.51%, this amount is relatively low compared to many industries, which experience higher rates of uncollectibility. Austin's lower bad debt expense rate may be due to the nature of the industry-providing service—viewed by most people as essential. Customers are more likely to pay their energy bills while foregoing payments to other obligations they may owe.

In this case, you will use the data to calculate the relationships of accounts receivable to revenue and assets, and prepare a combo column and line chart to visualize those relationships for each of the largest revenue-producing companies in the United States.

Go to the Wiley online course for complete case details and instructions.

Using Data Analytics to Understand Notes Receivable over Time

DA8.2 Banks have large loan portfolios that result from loans to customers. Analytics can help us understand the proportion of these notes receivables to the bank's total assets. For this case, you will

Excel

use the assets section of JPMorgan Chase's (USA) balance sheet (statement of financial position) for 2 years to (1) calculate the proportion of each asset as a percent of total assets for both years (this is often called common-size financial statements), (2) create pie charts, and (3) analyze the differences.

Go to the Wiley online course for complete case details and instructions.

Expand Your Critical Thinking

Financial Reporting Problem: CAF AG

CT8.1 CAF AG sells office equipment and supplies to many organizations in the city and surrounding area on contract terms of 2/10, n/30. In the past, over 75% of the credit customers have taken advantage of the discount by paying within 10 days of the invoice date.

The number of customers taking the full 30 days to pay has increased within the last year. Current indications are that less than 60% of the customers are now taking the discount. Bad debts as a percentage of gross credit sales have risen from the 2.5% provided in past years to about 4.5% in the current year.

The company's Finance Committee has requested more information on the collections of accounts receivable. The controller responded to this request with the report reproduced below.

CAF AG
Accounts Receivable Collections
May 31, 2029

The fact that some credit accounts will prove uncollectible is normal. Annual bad debt write-offs have been 2.5% of gross credit sales over the past 5 years. During the last fiscal year, this percentage increased to slightly less than 4.5%. The current Accounts Receivable balance is €1,400,000. The condition of this balance in terms of age and probability of collection is as follows.

Proportion of Total	Age Categories	Probability of Collection
60%	not yet due	98%
22%	less than 30 days past due	96%
9%	30 to 60 days past due	94%
5%	61 to 120 days past due	91%
$2^1/_2$%	121 to 180 days past due	75%
$1^1/_2$%	over 180 days past due	30%

Allowance for Doubtful Accounts had a credit balance of €29,500 on June 1, 2028. CAF has provided for a monthly bad debt expense accrual during the current fiscal year based on the assumption that 4.5% of gross credit sales will be uncollectible. Total gross credit sales for the 2028–2029 fiscal year amounted to €2,800,000. Write-offs of bad accounts during the year totaled €102,000.

Instructions

a. Prepare an accounts receivable aging schedule for CAF using the age categories identified in the controller's report to the Finance Committee showing the following.

1. The amount of accounts receivable outstanding for each age category and in total.
2. The estimated amount that is uncollectible for each category and in total.

b. Compute the amount of the year-end adjustment necessary to bring Allowance for Doubtful Accounts to the balance indicated by the age analysis. Then prepare the necessary journal entry to adjust the accounting records.

c. In a recessionary environment with tight credit and high interest rates:

1. Identify steps CAF might consider to improve the accounts receivable situation.
2. Then evaluate each step identified in terms of the risks and costs involved.

Comparative Analysis Problem: Nestlé SA (CHE) vs. Delfi Limited (SGP)

CT8.2 Nestlé's financial statements are presented in Appendix B. Financial statements of Delfi Limited are presented in Appendix C.

Instructions

a. Based on the information in these financial statements, compute the following ratios for each company for the most recent fiscal year shown. (Assume all sales are credit sales and that all receivables are trade receivables.)

1. Accounts receivable turnover.

2. Average collection period for receivables.

b. What conclusions about managing accounts receivable can you draw from these data?

Real-World Focus

CT8.3 Purpose: To learn more about factoring.

Instructions

Search the Internet under "commercial capital factoring" and then go to the corresponding **Commercial Capital LLC** website. Click on **Invoice Factoring** and answer the following questions.

a. What are some of the benefits of factoring?

b. What is the range of the percentages of the typical discount rate?

c. If a company factors its receivables, what percentage of the value of the receivables can it expect to receive from the factor in the form of cash, and how quickly will it receive the cash?

Decision-Making Across the Organization

CT8.4 Hilda and Tim Piwek own Campus Fashions. From its inception, Campus Fashions has sold merchandise on either a cash or credit basis, but no credit cards have been accepted. During the past several months, the Piweks have begun to question their sales policies. First, they have lost some sales because of refusing to accept credit cards. Second, representatives of two metropolitan banks have been persuasive in almost convincing them to accept their national credit cards. One bank, City National Bank, has stated that its credit card fee is 4%.

The Piweks decide that they should determine the cost of carrying their own credit sales. From the accounting records of the past 3 years, they accumulate the following data (amounts in thousands).

	2029	2028	2027
Net credit sales	NT$500,000	NT$650,000	NT$400,000
Collection agency fees for slow-paying customers	2,450	2,500	2,300
Salary of part-time accounts receivable clerk	4,100	4,100	4,100

Credit and collection expenses as a percentage of net credit sales are uncollectible accounts 1.6%, billing and mailing costs 0.5%, and credit investigation fee on new customers 0.15%.

Hilda and Tim also determine that the average accounts receivable balance outstanding during the year is 5% of net credit sales. The Piweks estimate that they could earn an average of 8% annually on cash invested in other business opportunities.

Instructions

With the class divided into groups, answer the following.

a. Prepare a table showing, for each year, total credit and collection expenses in New Taiwan dollars and as a percentage of net credit sales.

b. Determine the net credit and collection expense in New Taiwan dollars and as a percentage of sales after considering the revenue not earned from other investment opportunities.

c. Discuss both the financial and non-financial factors that are relevant to the decision.

Communication Activity

CT8.5 Lily Pao, a friend of yours, overheard a discussion at work about changes her employer wants to make in accounting for uncollectible accounts. Lily knows little about accounting, and she asks you to help make sense of what she heard. Specifically, she asks you to explain the differences between the percentage-of-receivables and the direct write-off methods for uncollectible accounts.

Instructions

In one page (or less), explain to Lily the two methods of accounting for uncollectibles. Be sure to discuss differences among these methods.

Ethics Case

CT8.6 The controller of Diaz Fashions believes that the yearly allowance for doubtful accounts for Diaz should be 2% of its accounts receivable balance at the end of the year. The president of Diaz, nervous that the shareholders might expect the company to sustain its 10% growth rate, suggests that the controller increase the allowance for doubtful accounts to 4%. The president thinks that the lower net income, which reflects a lower growth rate, will be a more sustainable rate for Diaz.

Instructions

a. Who are the stakeholders in this case?

b. Does the president's request pose an ethical dilemma for the controller?

c. Should the controller be concerned with Diaz's growth rate? Explain your answer.

Answers to Insight and Accounting Across the Organization Questions

They've Got Your Number Q: Why might a company want to consider a customer's social media network when deciding whether to grant the customer credit? **A:** A customer's social media network might indicate if the applicant's contacts have had some negative experiences with the applicant, such as the applicant having a history of paying very slowly or not at all.

Cookie Jar Allowances Q: How might investors determine that a company is managing its earnings? **A:** If the statement of financial position reflects an increase in Accounts Receivable and a decrease in the Allowance for Doubtful Accounts, this could indicate an attempt to manage earnings by reducing the estimated uncollectible percentage.

How Does a Credit Card Work? Q: Assume that Sogo prepares a bank reconciliation at the end of each month. If some credit card sales have not been processed by the bank, how should Sogo treat these transactions on its bank reconciliation? **A:** Sogo would treat the credit card receipts as deposits in transit. It has already recorded the receipts as cash. Its bank will increase Sogo's cash account when it receives the receipts.

Let the "Good Times" Roll Q: What factors should be considered in evaluating loan applications? **A:** At a minimum, the bank should request copies of recent tax forms and contact the listed employer to verify income. To verify ownership and value of assets, the bank should examine bank statements, investment statements, and title documents, and should employ appraisers.

A Look at U.S. GAAP

LEARNING OBJECTIVE 5

Compare the accounting for receivables under IFRS and U.S. GAAP.

The basic accounting and reporting issues related to the recognition, measurement, and disposition of receivables are essentially the same between IFRS and GAAP.

Key Points

Following are the key similarities and differences between GAAP and IFRS as related to the accounting for receivables.

Similarities

- The recording of accounts receivable, recognition of sales returns and allowances and sales discounts, and the allowance method to record bad debts are the same between IFRS and GAAP.
- Both IFRS and GAAP often use the term impairment to indicate that a receivable or a percentage of receivables may not be collected.

- The FASB and IASB have worked to implement fair value measurement (the amount they currently could be sold for) for financial instruments, such as receivables. Both Boards have faced bitter opposition from various factions.

Differences

- Although IFRS implies that receivables with different characteristics should be reported separately, there is no standard that mandates this segregation.
- IFRS and GAAP differ in the approach to estimating uncollectible accounts on receivables with a significant financing component (e.g., notes receivable). Under IFRS, long-term receivables that have not experienced a deterioration in credit quality after origination are estimated based on expected losses over the next 12 months. For long-term receivables that experience a credit quality decline, IFRS estimates uncollectible accounts based on lifetime expected losses. Under GAAP, only the second approach is used.
- IFRS and GAAP differ in the criteria used to determine how to record a factoring transaction. IFRS uses a combination approach focused on risks and rewards and loss of control. GAAP uses loss of control as the primary criterion. In addition, IFRS permits partial derecognition of receivables; GAAP does not.

GAAP Practice

GAAP Self-Test Questions

1. Under GAAP, receivables are reported on the balance sheet (statement of financial position) at:
   a. gross amount.
   b. gross amount less allowance for doubtful accounts.
   c. historical cost.
   d. replacement cost.

2. Which of the following statements is **false**?
   a. Receivables include equity securities purchased by the company.
   b. Receivables include credit card receivables.
   c. Receivables include amounts owed by employees as a result of company loans to employees.
   d. Receivables include amounts resulting from transactions with customers.

3. In recording a factoring transaction:
   a. IFRS focuses on loss of control.
   b. GAAP focuses on loss of control and risks and rewards.
   c. IFRS and GAAP allow partial derecognition.
   d. IFRS allows partial derecognition.

4. Under IFRS:
   a. the entry to record estimated uncollectible accounts is the same as GAAP.
   b. all impairments should be debited to Accounts Receivable.
   c. it is always acceptable to use the direct write-off method.
   d. all receivables are recorded at fair value.

GAAP Financial Reporting Problem: Apple Inc. (USA)

GAAP8.1 The financial statements of **Apple** are presented in Appendix D. The complete annual report, including the notes to its financial statements, is available at the company's website.

Instructions

Use the company's financial statements and notes to the financial statements to answer the following questions.

a. Calculate the accounts receivable turnover and average collection period for 2020 and 2019. Accounts receivable at September 29, 2018, was $23,186 (in millions).

b. What conclusions can you draw from the information in part (a)?

Answers to GAAP Self-Test Questions

1. b **2.** a **3.** d **4.** a

CHAPTER 9

Plant Assets, Natural Resources, and Intangible Assets

LEARNING OBJECTIVES After studying this chapter, you should be able to:

LO 1 Explain the accounting for plant asset expenditures.

LO 2 Apply depreciation methods to plant assets.

LO 3 Explain how to account for the disposal of plant assets.

LO 4 Describe how to account for natural resources and intangible assets.

LO 5 Discuss how plant assets, natural resources, and intangible assets are reported and analyzed.

Chapter Preview

The accounting for non-current assets has important implications for a company's reported results. In this chapter, we explain the application of the historical cost basis of accounting to property, plant, and equipment, such as **Rent-A-Wreck** (USA) or **Europcar** (FRA) vehicles, as well as to natural resources and intangible assets, such as the "Europcar" trademark. We also describe the methods that companies may use to allocate an asset's cost over its useful life. In addition, we discuss the accounting for expenditures incurred during the useful life of assets, such as the cost of replacing tires and brake pads on rental cars.

Plant Assets, Natural Resources, and Intangible Assets

Plant Asset Expenditures
- Determining the cost of plant assets
- Expenditures during useful life

Depreciation Methods
- Factors in computing depreciation
- Depreciation methods
- Component depreciation
- Depreciation and income taxes
- Revaluation of plant assets
- Revising periodic depreciation

Plant Asset Disposals
- Retirement of plant assets
- Sale of plant assets

Natural Resources and Intangible Assets
- Natural resources and depletion
- Intangible assets

Statement Presentation and Analysis
- Presentation
- Analysis

Practice

DO IT! 1 Cost of Plant Assets

DO IT! 2a Straight-Line Depreciation

2b Revised Depreciation

DO IT! 3 Plant Asset Disposal

DO IT! 4 Classification Concepts

DO IT! 5 Asset Turnover

Go to the Review and Practice section at the end of the chapter for a review of key concepts and practice applications with solutions.
Additional tutorials and practice opportunities are available in the Wiley online course.

Feature Story How Much for a Ride to the Beach?

It's summer vacation. Your plane has landed, you've finally found your bags, and you're dying to hit the Tylösand beach in Halmstad, Sweden—but first you need a "vehicular unit" to get you there. As you turn away from baggage claim, you see a long row of rental agency booths. First, you see booths for **Hertz** (USA) and **Europcar** (FRA). Then, a booth at the far end catches your eye—**Rent-A-Wreck** (USA). Now there's a company making a clear statement!

Any company that relies on equipment to generate revenues must make decisions about what kind of equipment to buy, how long to keep it, and how vigorously to maintain it. Rent-A-Wreck has decided to rent used rather than new cars and trucks. While Europcar emphasizes that all its vehicles are new, Rent-A-Wreck competes on price.

Rent-A-Wreck's message is simple: Rent a used car and save some cash. It's not a message that appeals to everyone. If you're a marketing executive wanting to impress a big client, you might choose Europcar instead of Rent-A-Wreck. But if you want to get from point A to point B for the minimum cash per mile, then Rent-A-Wreck is playing your tune. The company's message seems to be getting across to the right clientele. Revenues have increased significantly.

When you rent a car from Rent-A-Wreck or from Europcar, you are renting from an independent businessperson. This owner has paid a "franchise fee" for the right to use the Rent-A-Wreck or Europcar name. In order to gain a franchise, he or she must meet financial and other criteria, and must agree to run the rental agency according to prescribed rules. Some of these rules require that each franchise maintain its cars in a reasonable fashion. This ensures that, though you won't be cruising up to the Hotel Tylösand in a Mercedes convertible, you can be reasonably assured that you won't be calling a towtruck.

Monkey Business/Adobe Stock

9.1 Plant Asset Expenditures

LEARNING OBJECTIVE 1

Explain the accounting for plant asset expenditures.

Plant assets are resources that have three characteristics.

1. They have a physical substance (a definite size and shape).
2. They are used in the operations of a business.
3. They are not intended for sale to customers.

Plant assets are also called **property, plant, and equipment; plant and equipment**; and **fixed assets**. These assets are expected to be of use to the company for a number of years. Except for land, plant assets decline in service potential over their useful lives.

Because plant assets play a key role in ongoing operations, companies keep plant assets in good operating condition. They also replace worn-out or outdated plant assets, and expand productive resources as needed. Many companies have substantial investments in plant assets. **Illustration 9.1** shows the percentages of plant assets in relation to total assets of companies in a number of industries during a recent year.

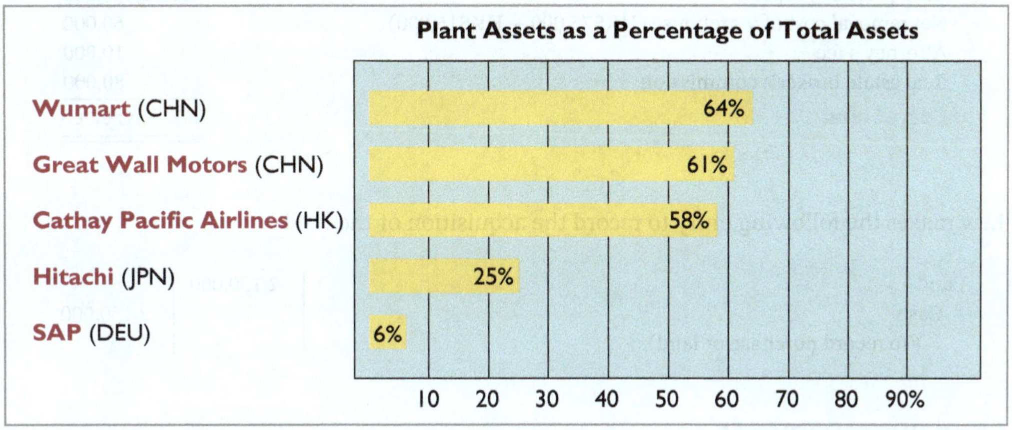

ILLUSTRATION 9.1

Percentages of plant assets in relation to total assets

Determining the Cost of Plant Assets

The historical cost basis requires that companies record plant assets at cost. Thus, **Europcar** (FRA) records its vehicles at cost. **Cost consists of all expenditures necessary to acquire the asset and make it ready for its intended use.** For example, the cost of factory machinery includes the purchase price, freight costs paid by the purchaser, and installation costs. Once cost is established, the company generally uses that amount as the basis of accounting for the plant asset over its useful life.

In the following sections, we explain the application of the historical cost basis to each of the major classes of plant assets.

Land

Companies often use **land** as a site for a manufacturing plant or office building. The cost of land includes:

1. The cash purchase price.
2. Closing costs such as title and attorney's fees.
3. Real estate brokers' commissions.
4. Accrued property taxes and other liens assumed by the purchaser.

For example, if the cash price is NT$50,000 and the purchaser agrees to pay accrued taxes of NT$5,000, the cost of the land is NT$55,000.

HELPFUL HINT

Management's intended use is important in applying the historical cost basis to plant assets.

Companies record as debits (increases) to the Land account all necessary costs incurred to make land **ready for its intended use** (see **Helpful Hint**). When a company acquires vacant land, these costs include expenditures for clearing, draining, filling, and grading. Sometimes, the land has a building on it that must be removed before construction of a new building. In this case, the company debits to the Land account all demolition and removal costs, less any proceeds from salvaged materials.

To illustrate, assume that Lew Ltd. acquires real estate at a cash cost of HK$2,000,000. The property contains an old warehouse that is razed at a net cost of HK$60,000 (HK$75,000 in costs less HK$15,000 in proceeds from salvaged materials). Additional expenditures are the attorney's fee, HK$10,000, and the real estate broker's commission, HK$80,000. The cost of the land is HK$2,150,000, as computed in **Illustration 9.2**.

ILLUSTRATION 9.2

Computation of cost of land

Land	
Cash price of property	HK$2,000,000
Net removal cost of warehouse (HK$75,000 − HK$15,000)	60,000
Attorney's fee	10,000
Real estate broker's commission	80,000
Cost of land	**HK$2,150,000**

Lew makes the following entry to record the acquisition of the land.

A	=	L	+	E
+2,150,000				
−2,150,000				

Cash Flows
−2,150,000

Land	2,150,000	
Cash		2,150,000
(To record purchase of land)		

Land Improvements

Land improvements are structural additions with limited lives that are made to land.

- Examples of land improvements are driveways, parking lots, fences, landscaping, and underground sprinklers.
- The cost of land improvements includes all expenditures necessary to make the improvements ready for their intended use.

For example, the cost of a new parking lot for a **Hero Supermarket** (IDN) includes the amount paid for paving, fencing, and lighting. Thus, Hero Supermarket debits to Land Improvements the total of all of these costs.

Land improvements have limited useful lives. Even when well-maintained, they will eventually be replaced. As a result, companies expense (depreciate) the cost of land improvements over their useful lives.

Buildings

Buildings are facilities used in operations, such as stores, offices, factories, warehouses, and airplane hangars. Companies debit to the Buildings account all necessary expenditures related to the purchase or construction of a building.

- When a building is **purchased**, such costs include the purchase price, closing costs (attorney's fees, title insurance, etc.), and the real estate broker's commission. Costs to make the building ready for its intended use include expenditures for remodeling and replacing or repairing the roof, floors, electrical wiring, and plumbing.
- When a new building is **constructed**, its costs consist of the contract price plus payments for architects' fees, building permits, and excavation costs.

In addition, companies charge certain interest costs to the Buildings account. Interest costs incurred to finance the project are included in the cost of the building when a significant period of time is required to get the building ready for use. In these circumstances, interest costs are considered as necessary as materials and labor.

However, the inclusion of interest costs in the cost of a constructed building is **limited to interest costs incurred during the construction period**. When construction has been completed, the company records subsequent interest payments on funds borrowed to finance the construction as debits (increases) to Interest Expense.

Equipment

Equipment includes assets used in operations, such as store check-out counters, factory machinery, delivery trucks, and airplanes.

- The cost of equipment, such as **Europcar** (FRA) vehicles, consists of the cash purchase price, sales taxes, freight charges, and insurance during transit paid by the purchaser.
- It also includes expenditures required in assembling, installing, and testing the unit.

However, Europcar does not include motor vehicle licenses and accident insurance on company vehicles in the cost of equipment. These costs represent **annual recurring expenditures and do not benefit future periods**. Thus, they are treated as **expenses** as they are incurred.

To illustrate, assume Zhang Ltd. purchases factory machinery at a cash price of HK$500,000. Related expenditures are for sales taxes HK$30,000, insurance during shipping HK$5,000, and installation and testing HK$10,000. The cost of the factory machinery is HK$545,000, computed in **Illustration 9.3**.

ILLUSTRATION 9.3

Computation of cost of factory machinery

Factory Machinery	
Cash price	HK$500,000
Sales taxes	30,000
Insurance during shipping	5,000
Installation and testing	10,000
Cost of factory machinery	**HK$545,000**

Zhang makes the following summary entry to record the purchase and related expenditures.

Equipment	545,000	
Cash		545,000
(To record purchase of factory machinery)		

A = L + E
+545,000
−545,000

Cash Flows
−545,000

For another example, assume that Huang Group purchases a delivery truck at a cash price of HK$420,000. Related expenditures consist of sales taxes HK$13,200, painting and lettering HK$5,000, motor vehicle license HK$800, and a three-year accident insurance policy HK$16,000. The cost of the delivery truck is HK$438,200, computed as shown in **Illustration 9.4**.

ILLUSTRATION 9.4

Computation of cost of delivery truck

Delivery Truck	
Cash price	HK$420,000
Sales taxes	13,200
Painting and lettering	5,000
Cost of delivery truck	**HK$438,200**

Huang treats the cost of the motor vehicle license as an expense and the cost of the insurance policy as a prepaid asset. Thus, Huang makes the following entry to record the purchase of the truck and related expenditures:

A	=	L	+	E
+438,200				
				−800 Exp
+16,000				
−455,000				

Cash Flows
−455,000

Equipment	438,200	
License Expense	800	
Prepaid Insurance	16,000	
Cash		455,000
(To record purchase of delivery truck and related expenditures)		

Expenditures During Useful Life

During the useful life of a plant asset, a company may incur costs for ordinary repairs, additions, or improvements.

- **Ordinary repairs** are expenditures to **maintain** the operating efficiency and productive life of the unit.
- They usually are fairly small amounts that occur frequently. Examples are motor tune-ups and oil changes, the painting of buildings, and the replacing of worn-out gears on machinery.

Companies record such repairs as debits to Maintenance and Repairs Expense as they are incurred. Because they are immediately charged as an expense against revenues, these costs are often referred to as **revenue expenditures**.

In contrast, **additions and improvements** are costs incurred to **increase** the operating efficiency, productive capacity, or useful life of a plant asset.

- They are usually material in amount and occur infrequently.
- Additions and improvements increase the company's investment in productive facilities.

Companies generally debit these amounts to the plant asset affected. They are often referred to as **capital expenditures**.

Companies must use good judgment in deciding between a revenue expenditure and capital expenditure. For example, assume that Rodriguez Co. purchases a number of wastepaper baskets. Although the proper accounting would appear to be to capitalize and then depreciate these wastepaper baskets over their useful lives, it would be more usual for Rodriguez to expense them immediately. This practice is justified on the basis of **materiality**. Materiality refers to the impact of an item's size on a company's financial operations. The **materiality concept** states that if an item would not make a difference in decision-making, the company does not have to follow IFRS in reporting that item.

Anatomy of a Fraud

Bernie Ebbers was the founder and CEO of the phone company **WorldCom** (USA). The company engaged in a series of increasingly large, debt-financed acquisitions of other companies. These acquisitions made the company grow quickly, which made the share price increase dramatically. However, because the acquired companies all had different accounting systems, WorldCom's financial records were a mess.

When WorldCom's performance started to flatten out, Bernie coerced WorldCom's accountants to engage in a number of fraudulent activities to make net income look better than it really was and thus prop up the share price. One of these frauds involved treating $7 billion of line costs as capital expenditures. The line costs, which were rental fees paid to other phone companies to use their phone lines, had always been properly expensed in previous years. Capitalization delayed expense recognition to future periods and thus boosted current-period profits.

Total take: $7 billion

The Missing Controls

Documentation procedures. The company's accounting system was a disorganized collection of non-integrated systems, which resulted from a series of business acquisitions. Top management took advantage of this disorganization to conceal its fraudulent activities.

Independent internal verification. A fraud of this size should have been detected by a routine comparison of the actual physical assets with the list of physical assets shown in the accounting records.

Accounting Across the Organization

Brian Raisbeck/
iStock.com

Many Firms Use Leases

Leasing is big business. Who does the most leasing? **AWAS** (IRL), **J.P. Morgan Leasing** (USA), and **ICBC** (CHN) are major lessors. Also, many companies have established separate leasing companies, such as **Boeing Capital Corporation** (USA), and **Mitsubishi Heavy Industries** (JPN).

As an excellent example of the magnitude of leasing, leased planes account for a high percentage of commercial airlines. Leasing is also becoming common in the hotel industry. **Marriott** (USA) and **InterContinental** (GBR) are choosing to lease hotels that are owned by someone else.

Why might airline managers choose to lease rather than purchase their planes? (Answer is available near the end of the chapter.)

DO IT! 1 | Cost of Plant Assets

Assume that Jing Feng Heating and Cooling purchases a delivery truck for ¥150,000 cash, plus sales taxes of ¥9,000 and delivery costs of ¥5,000. The buyer also pays ¥2,000 for painting and lettering, ¥6,000 for an annual insurance policy, and ¥800 for a motor vehicle license. Explain how each of these costs would be accounted for.

ACTION PLAN

- **Identify expenditures made in order to get delivery equipment ready for its intended use.**
- **Treat operating costs as expenses.**

Solution

The first four payments (¥150,000 purchase price, ¥9,000 sales taxes, ¥5,000 delivery costs, and ¥2,000 painting and lettering) are expenditures necessary to make the truck ready for its intended use. Thus, the cost of the truck is ¥166,000. The payments for insurance and the license are operating costs incurred annually and therefore are expensed.

Related exercise material: **BE9.1, BE9.2, BE9.3, DO IT! 9.1, E9.1, E9.2, and E9.3.**

9.2 Depreciation Methods

LEARNING OBJECTIVE 2

Apply depreciation methods to plant assets.

As explained in Chapter 3, **depreciation** is the **systematic allocation of the depreciable amount of an asset over its useful life.** Cost allocation enables companies to properly match expenses with revenues in accordance with the expense recognition principle, as shown in **Illustration 9.5**.

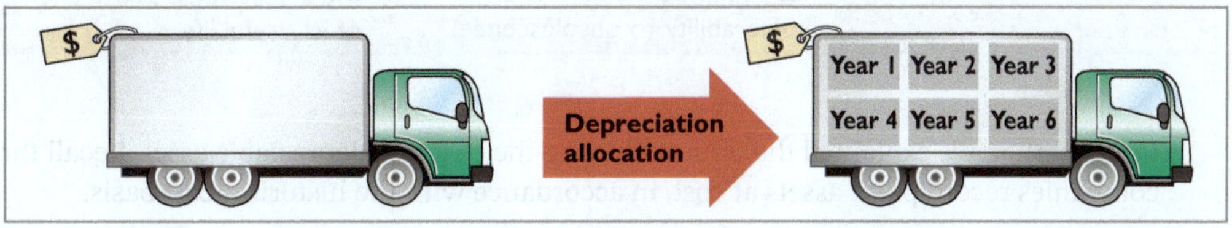

ILLUSTRATION 9.5

Depreciation as a cost allocation concept

It is important to understand that **depreciation is a process of cost allocation. It is not a process of asset valuation.** No attempt is made to measure the change in an asset's fair value during ownership.

- The **book value** (cost less accumulated depreciation) of a plant asset may be quite different from its **fair value**.
- If an asset is fully depreciated, it can have a zero book value but still have a positive fair value.

ETHICS NOTE

When a business is acquired, proper allocation of the purchase price to various asset classes is important since different depreciation treatments can materially affect income. For example, buildings are depreciated, but land is not.

Depreciation applies to three classes of plant assets: land improvements, buildings, and equipment (see **Ethics Note**). Each asset in these classes is considered to be a **depreciable asset**. Why? Because the usefulness to the company and revenue-producing ability of each asset will decline over the asset's useful life. Depreciation **does not apply to land** because its usefulness and revenue-producing ability generally remain intact over time. In fact, in many cases, the usefulness of land is greater over time because of the scarcity of good land sites. Thus, **land is not a depreciable asset**.

- During a depreciable asset's useful life, its revenue-producing ability declines because of **wear and tear**. A delivery truck that has been driven 100,000 miles will be less useful to a company than one driven only 800 miles.
- A decline in revenue-producing ability may also occur because of obsolescence. **Obsolescence** is the process of becoming out of date before the asset physically wears out.

For example, major airlines moved from Chicago's Midway Airport to Chicago-O'Hare International Airport in the United States because Midway's runways were too short for jumbo jets. Similarly, many companies replace their computers long before they originally planned to do so because technological improvements make the old computers obsolete.

Recognizing depreciation on an asset does not result in an accumulation of cash for replacement of the asset. The balance in Accumulated Depreciation represents the total amount of the asset's cost that the company has charged to expense. **It is not a cash fund.**

Note that the concept of depreciation is consistent with the going concern assumption.

- The **going concern assumption** states that the company will continue in operation for the foreseeable future.
- If a company does not use a going concern assumption, then plant assets should be stated at their fair value. In that case, depreciation of these assets is not needed.

Factors in Computing Depreciation

Three factors affect the computation of depreciation, as shown in **Illustration 9.6**.

ILLUSTRATION 9.6

Three factors in computing depreciation

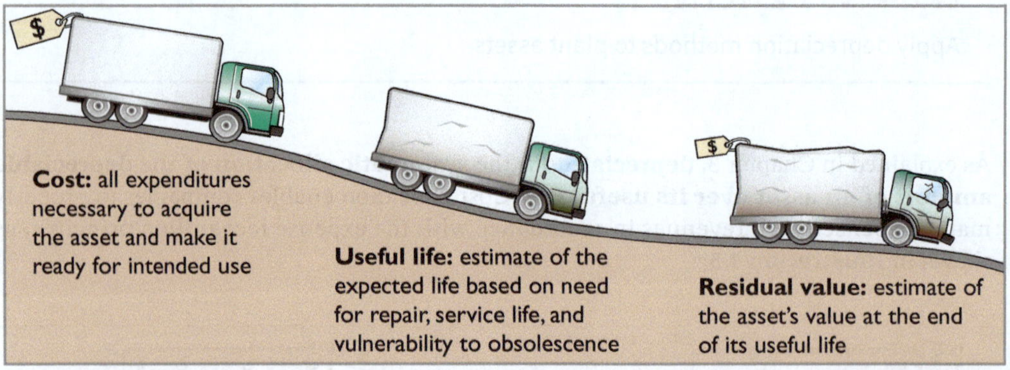

1. **Cost.** Earlier, we explained the issues affecting the cost of a depreciable asset. Recall that companies record plant assets at cost, in accordance with the historical cost basis.

2. **Useful life.** **Useful life** is an estimate of the expected productive life, also called service life, of the asset for its owner. Useful life may be expressed in terms of time, units of activity (such as machine hours), or units of output. Useful life is an estimate. In making the estimate, management considers such factors as the intended use of the asset, its expected repair and maintenance, and its vulnerability to obsolescence. Past experience with similar assets is often helpful in deciding on expected useful life. We might reasonably expect **Rent-A-Wreck** (USA) and **Europcar** (FRA) to use different estimated useful lives for their vehicles.
3. **Residual value.** **Residual value** is an estimate of the asset's value at the end of its useful life (see **Alternative Terminology**). This value may be based on the asset's worth as scrap or on its expected trade-in value. Like useful life, residual value is an estimate. In making the estimate, management considers how it plans to dispose of the asset and its experience with similar assets.

ALTERNATIVE TERMINOLOGY

Another term sometimes used for residual value is *salvage value*.

Depreciation Methods

Depreciation is generally computed using one of the following methods:

1. Straight-line
2. Units-of-activity
3. Declining-balance

Each method is acceptable under IFRS.

Management selects the method(s) it believes to be appropriate. The objective is to select the method that best measures an asset's contribution to revenue over its useful life. Once a company chooses a method, it should apply it consistently over the useful life of the asset. Consistency enhances the comparability of financial statements. Depreciation affects the statement of financial position through accumulated depreciation and the income statement through depreciation expense (see **Helpful Hint**).

HELPFUL HINT

Depreciation expense is reported on the income statement. Accumulated depreciation is reported on the statement of financial position as a deduction from plant assets.

We will compare the three depreciation methods using the following data for a small delivery truck purchased by Barb's Florists on January 1, 2029 (see **Illustration 9.7**).

ILLUSTRATION 9.7
Delivery truck data

Cost	€13,000
Expected residual value	€1,000
Estimated useful life in years	5
Estimated useful life in miles	100,000

No matter which method is used, the total amount depreciated over the useful life of the asset is its depreciable cost. **Depreciable cost** is equal to the cost of the asset less its residual value.

Straight-Line Method

Under the **straight-line method**, companies expense the same amount of depreciation for each year of the asset's useful life. It is measured solely by the passage of time.

To compute depreciation expense under the straight-line method, companies need to determine depreciable cost.

- As indicated above, **depreciable cost** is the cost of the asset less its residual value. It represents the total amount subject to depreciation.
- Under the straight-line method, to determine annual depreciation expense, we divide depreciable cost by the asset's useful life.

Illustration 9.8 shows the computation of the first year's depreciation expense for Barb's Florists.

ILLUSTRATION 9.8

Formula for straight-line method

Cost	−	Residual Value	=	Depreciable Cost
€13,000	−	€1,000	=	€12,000

Depreciable Cost	÷	Useful Life (in years)	=	Annual Depreciation Expense
€12,000	÷	5	=	€2,400

Alternatively, we also can compute an annual **rate** of depreciation. In this case, the rate is 20% (100% ÷ 5 years). When a company uses an annual straight-line rate, it applies the percentage rate to the depreciable cost of the asset. **Illustration 9.9** shows a **depreciation schedule** using an annual rate.

ILLUSTRATION 9.9

Straight-line depreciation schedule

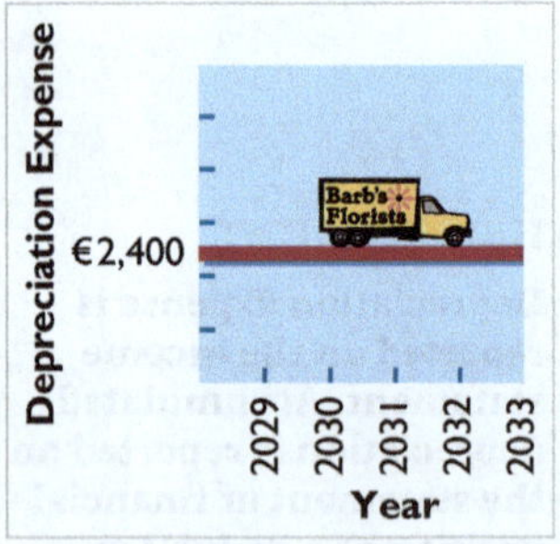

Barb's Florists

	Computation					End of Year	
Year	**Depreciable Cost**	×	**Depreciation Rate**	=	**Annual Depreciation Expense**	**Accumulated Depreciation**	**Book Value**
2029	€12,000		20%		€2,400	€ 2,400	€10,600*
2030	12,000		20		2,400	4,800	8,200
2031	12,000		20		2,400	7,200	5,800
2032	12,000		20		2,400	9,600	3,400
2033	12,000		20		2,400	12,000	1,000

*Book value = Cost − Accumulated depreciation = (€13,000 − €2,400).

Note that the depreciation expense of €2,400 is the same each year. The book value (computed as cost minus accumulated depreciation) at the end of the useful life is equal to the expected €1,000 residual value.

What happens to these computations for an asset purchased **during** the year, rather than on January 1? In that case, it is necessary to **prorate the annual depreciation** on a time basis. If Barb's Florists had purchased the delivery truck on April 1, 2029, the company would own the truck for nine months of the first year (April–December). Thus, depreciation for 2029 would be €1,800 (€12,000 × 20% × 9/12 of a year).

The straight-line method predominates in practice. Large companies such as **Daimler** (DEU), **Anheuser-Busch InBev** (BEL), and **Great Wall Motors** (CHN) use the straight-line method. It is simple to apply, and it matches expenses with revenues when the use of the asset is reasonably uniform throughout the service life.

ACTION PLAN

- **Calculate depreciable cost (Cost − Residual value).**
- **Divide the depreciable cost by the asset's estimated useful life.**

DO IT! 2a | Straight-Line Depreciation

On January 1, 2029, Iron Mountain Ski purchased a new snow-grooming machine for €50,000. The machine is estimated to have a 10-year life with a €2,000 residual value. What journal entry would Iron Mountain Ski make at December 31, 2029, if it uses the straight-line method of depreciation?

Solution

$$\text{Depreciation expense} = \frac{\text{Cost} - \text{Residual value}}{\text{Useful life}} = \frac{€50{,}000 - €2{,}000}{10} = €4{,}800$$

The entry to record the first year's depreciation would be:

Dec. 31	Depreciation Expense	4,800	
	Accumulated Depreciation—Equipment		4,800
	(To record annual depreciation on snow-grooming machine)		

Related exercise material: **BE9.4, BE9.5, DO IT! 9.2a, E9.4, E9.6, E9.7, and E9.10.**

Units-of-Activity Method

Under the **units-of-activity method**, useful life is expressed in terms of the total units of production or use expected from the asset, rather than as a time period (see **Alternative Terminology**). The units-of-activity method is ideally suited to factory machinery. Manufacturing companies can measure production in units of output or in machine hours. This method can also be used for such assets as delivery equipment (miles driven) and airplanes (hours in use). The units-of-activity method is generally not suitable for buildings or furniture because depreciation for these assets is more a function of time than of use.

ALTERNATIVE TERMINOLOGY

Another term often used is the *units-of-production method.*

- To use this method, companies estimate the total units of activity for the entire useful life and then divide these units into depreciable cost. The resulting number represents the depreciable cost per unit.
- The depreciable cost per unit is then applied to the units of activity during the year to determine the annual depreciation expense (see **Helpful Hint**).

HELPFUL HINT

Under any method, depreciation stops when the asset's book value equals expected residual value.

To illustrate, assume that Barb's Florists drives its delivery truck 15,000 miles in the first year. **Illustration 9.10** shows the units-of-activity formula and the computation of the first year's depreciation expense.

ILLUSTRATION 9.10

Formula for units-of-activity method

Depreciable Cost	÷	Total Units of Activity	=	Depreciable Cost per Unit
€12,000	÷	100,000 miles	=	€0.12

Depreciable Cost per Unit	×	Units of Activity during the Year	=	Annual Depreciation Expense
€0.12	×	15,000 miles	=	€1,800

Illustration 9.11 shows the units-of-activity depreciation schedule, using assumed mileage.

ILLUSTRATION 9.11

Units-of-activity depreciation schedule

Barb's Florists

	Computation				Annual	End of Year	
Year	Units of Activity	×	Depreciation Cost/Unit	=	Depreciation Expense	Accumulated Depreciation	Book Value
2029	15,000		€0.12		€1,800	€ 1,800	€11,200*
2030	30,000		0.12		3,600	5,400	7,600
2031	20,000		0.12		2,400	7,800	5,200
2032	25,000		0.12		3,000	10,800	2,200
2033	10,000		0.12		1,200	12,000	1,000

*(€13,000 – €1,800).

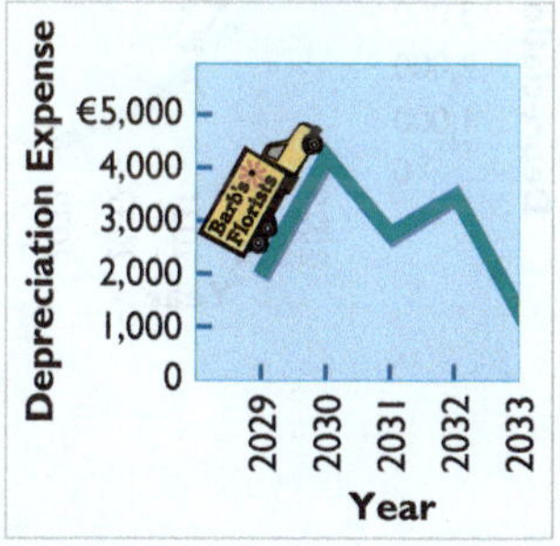

This method is easy to apply for assets purchased mid-year. In such a case, the company computes the depreciation using the productivity of the asset for the partial year.

The units-of-activity method is not nearly as popular as the straight-line method primarily because it is often difficult for companies to reasonably estimate total activity. However, some very large companies, such as **China Petroleum and Chemical Corporation** (CHN) and **British Petroleum** (GBR), do use this method. When the productivity of an asset varies significantly from one period to another, the units-of-activity method results in the best matching of expenses with revenues.

Declining-Balance Method

The **declining-balance method** produces a decreasing annual depreciation expense over the asset's useful life. The method is so named because the periodic depreciation is based on a **declining book value** (cost less accumulated depreciation) of the asset.

- With this method, companies compute annual depreciation expense by multiplying the book value at the beginning of the year by the declining-balance depreciation rate.
- **The depreciation rate remains constant from year to year, but the book value to which the rate is applied declines each year.**

At the beginning of the first year, book value is the cost of the asset. This is because the balance in accumulated depreciation at the beginning of the asset's useful life is zero. In subsequent years, book value is the difference between cost and accumulated depreciation to date.

- Unlike the other depreciation methods, the declining-balance method **ignores residual value in determining the amount to which the declining-balance rate is applied.**
- Residual value, however, does limit the total depreciation that can be taken. Depreciation stops when the asset's book value equals expected residual value.

A common declining-balance rate is double the straight-line rate. The method is often called the **double-declining-balance method.** If Barb's Florists uses the double-declining-balance method, it uses a depreciation rate of 40% (2 × the straight-line rate of 20%). **Illustration 9.12** shows the declining-balance formula and the computation of the first year's depreciation on the delivery truck.[1]

ILLUSTRATION 9.12

Formula for declining-balance method

Book Value at Beginning of Year	×	Declining-Balance Rate	=	Annual Depreciation Expense
€13,000	×	40%	=	€5,200

Illustration 9.13 shows the depreciation schedule under this method.

ILLUSTRATION 9.13

Double-declining-balance depreciation schedule

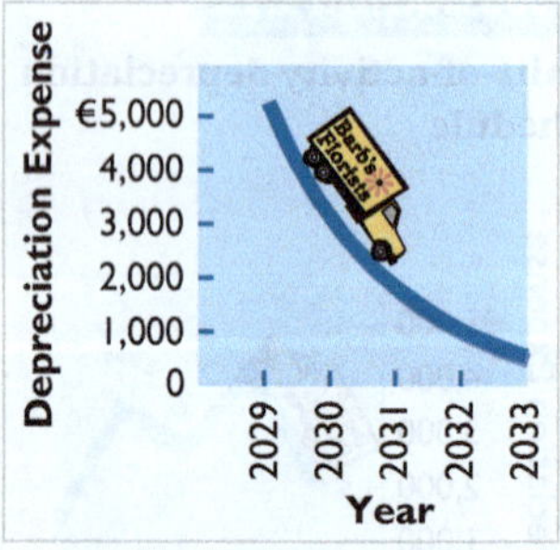

Barb's Florists

	Computation				Annual	End of Year	
Year	Book Value Beginning of Year	×	Depreciation Rate	=	Depreciation Expense	Accumulated Depreciation	Book Value
2029	€13,000		40%		€5,200	€ 5,200	€7,800
2030	7,800		40		3,120	8,320	4,680
2031	4,680		40		1,872	10,192	2,808
2032	2,808		40		1,123	11,315	1,685
2033	1,685		40		685*	12,000	1,000

*Computation of €674 (€1,685 × 40%) is adjusted to €685 in order for book value to equal residual value

The delivery equipment is 69% depreciated (€8,320 ÷ €12,000) at the end of the second year. Under the straight-line method, the truck would be depreciated 40% (€4,800 ÷ €12,000) at that time.

- Because the declining-balance method produces higher depreciation expense in the early years than in the later years, it is considered an **accelerated-depreciation method.**
- The declining-balance method is compatible with the expense recognition principle. It matches the higher depreciation expense in early years with the higher benefits received in these years. It also recognizes lower depreciation expense in later years, when the asset's contribution to revenue is less.

[1] IFRS refers to an alternative method of accelerated depreciation, called the *diminishing-balance method.* Under this method, a rate is multiplied by the remaining book value to determine depreciation. The rate is calculated using the formula Rate $= 1 - \left(\sqrt[n]{\frac{\text{Residual value}}{\text{Cost}}}\right)$, where n is the estimated useful life. Because financial calculators do not typically solve for the nth root, we have chosen to present the declining-balance method.

- Some assets lose usefulness rapidly because of obsolescence. In these cases, the declining-balance method provides the most appropriate depreciation amount (see **Helpful Hint**).

When a company purchases an asset during the year, it must prorate the first year's declining-balance depreciation on a time basis. For example, if Barb's Florists had purchased the truck on April 1, 2029, depreciation for 2029 would become €3,900 (€13,000 × 40% × 9/12). The book value at the beginning of 2030 is then €9,100 (€13,000 − €3,900), and the 2030 depreciation is €3,640 (€9,100 × 40%). Subsequent computations would follow from those amounts.

HELPFUL HINT

The method recommended for an asset that is expected to be significantly more productive in the first half of its useful life is the declining-balance method.

Comparison of Methods

Illustration 9.14 compares annual and total depreciation expense under each of the three methods for Barb's Florists.

ILLUSTRATION 9.14

Comparison of depreciation methods

Year	Straight-Line	Units-of-Activity	Declining-Balance
2029	€ 2,400	€ 1,800	€ 5,200
2030	2,400	3,600	3,120
2031	2,400	2,400	1,872
2032	2,400	3,000	1,123
2033	2,400	1,200	685
	€12,000	**€12,000**	**€12,000**

Annual depreciation varies considerably among the methods, but **total depreciation expense is the same (€12,000) for the five-year period** under all three methods. Each method is acceptable in accounting because each recognizes in a systematic manner the decline in service potential of the asset. **Illustration 9.15** graphs the depreciation expense pattern under each method.

ILLUSTRATION 9.15

Patterns of depreciation

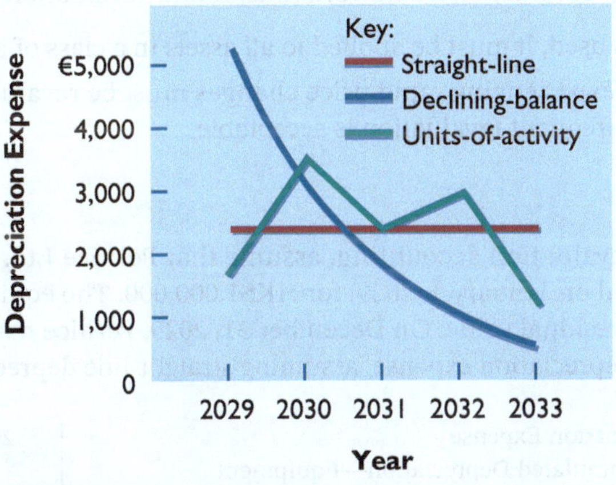

Component Depreciation

Thus far, we have assumed that plant assets use a single depreciation rate. However, IFRS requires component depreciation for plant assets. **Component depreciation** requires that any significant parts of a plant asset that have significantly different estimated useful lives should be separately depreciated.

To illustrate component depreciation, assume that Lexure Construction builds an office building for HK$4,000,000, not including the cost of the land. If the HK$4,000,000 is allocated over the 40-year useful life of the building, Lexure reports HK$100,000 (HK$4,000,000 ÷ 40) of depreciation per year, assuming straight-line depreciation and no residual value.

However, now assume that HK$320,000 of the cost of the building relates to a heating, ventilation, and air conditioning (HVAC) system and HK$600,000 relates to flooring. Because the HVAC system has a depreciable life of five years and the flooring has a depreciable life of 10 years, Lexure must use component depreciation. It must reclassify HK$320,000 of the cost of the building to the HVAC system and HK$600,000 to the cost of flooring. Assuming that Lexure uses straight-line depreciation, **Illustration 9.16** shows the computation of component depreciation for the first year of the office building.

ILLUSTRATION 9.16

Component depreciation computation

Building cost adjusted (HK$4,000,000 − HK$320,000 − HK$600,000)	HK$3,080,000
Building cost depreciation per year (HK$3,080,000 ÷ 40)	HK$ 77,000
HVAC system depreciation (HK$320,000 ÷ 5)	64,000
Flooring depreciation (HK$600,000 ÷ 10)	60,000
Total component depreciation in first year	**HK$ 201,000**

Depreciation and Income Taxes

Tax laws allow company taxpayers to deduct depreciation expense when they compute taxable income. However, tax laws often do not require taxpayers to use the same depreciation method on the tax return that is used in preparing financial statements.

- Many companies use straight-line in their financial statements to maximize net income.
- At the same time, they use an accelerated-depreciation method on their tax returns to minimize their income taxes.

Revaluation of Plant Assets

IFRS allows companies to revalue plant assets to fair value at the reporting date. Companies that choose to use the revaluation framework must follow revaluation procedures.

- If revaluation is used, it must be applied to all assets in a class of assets.
- Assets that are experiencing rapid price changes must be revalued on an annual basis. Otherwise, less frequent revaluation is acceptable.

Gain Situation

To illustrate asset revaluation accounting, assume that Pernice Ltd. applies revaluation to equipment purchased on January 1, 2029, for HK$1,000,000. The equipment has a useful life of five years and no residual value. On December 31, 2029, Pernice makes the following journal entry to record depreciation expense, assuming straight-line depreciation.

Dec. 31	Depreciation Expense	200,000	
	Accumulated Depreciation—Equipment		200,000
	(To record depreciation expense in 2029)		

After this entry, Pernice's equipment has a carrying amount of HK$800,000 (HK$1,000,000 − HK$200,000). At the end of 2029, independent appraisers determine that the asset has a fair value of HK$850,000. To report the equipment at its fair value of HK$850,000 on December 31, 2029, Pernice eliminates the Accumulated Depreciation—Equipment account, reduces Equipment to its fair value of HK$850,000, and records Revaluation Surplus of HK$50,000. The entry to record the revaluation is as follows.

Dec. 31	Accumulated Depreciation—Equipment	200,000	
	Equipment		150,000
	Revaluation Surplus		50,000
	(To adjust the equipment to its fair value)		

Thus, Pernice follows a two-step process.

1. Pernice records depreciation based on the cost basis of HK$1,000,000. As a result, it reports depreciation expense of HK$200,000 on the income statement.
2. Pernice records the revaluation. It does this by eliminating any accumulated depreciation, adjusting the recorded value of the equipment to its fair value, and crediting the revaluation surplus account.

In this example, the revaluation surplus is HK$50,000, which is the difference between the fair value of HK$850,000 and the book value of HK$800,000. Revaluation surplus is an example of an item reported as other comprehensive income, as discussed in Chapter 5. Pernice now reports the following information in its statement of financial position at the end of 2029 as shown in **Illustration 9.17**.

Equipment (HK$1,000,000 – HK$150,000)	HK$850,000
Accumulated depreciation—equipment	0
	HK$850,000
Revaluation surplus (equity)	HK$ 50,000

ILLUSTRATION 9.17

Statement presentation of plant assets (equipment) and revaluation surplus

Pernice reports depreciation expense of HK$200,000 in the income statement and HK$50,000 in other comprehensive income. As indicated, HK$850,000 is the new basis of the asset. Assuming no change in the total useful life, depreciation in 2030 will be HK$212,500 (HK$850,000 ÷ 4).

Loss Situation

Assume again that Pernice's equipment has a carrying amount of HK$800,000 (HK$1,000,000 – HK$200,000). However, at the end of 2029, independent appraisers determine that the asset has a fair value of HK$775,000, which results in an impairment loss of HK$25,000 (HK$800,000 – HK$775,000).

1. To record the equipment at fair value and to record this loss, Pernice first eliminates the balance in the Accumulated Depreciation—Equipment account of HK$200,000.
2. It reduces the Equipment account by HK$225,000 to report the equipment at HK$775,000 (HK$1,000,000 – HK$225,000).

The entry to record the equipment and report the impairment loss is as follows

Dec. 31	Accumulated Depreciation—Equipment	200,000	
	Impairment Loss	25,000	
	Equipment		225,000
	(To record impairment loss of equipment)		

The impairment loss of HK$25,000 reduces net income.

Comparison of this loss situation with the previous gain situation illustrates an important point. Losses are reported in net income, whereas gains are reported in other comprehensive income. The accounting for gains and losses continues this practice in subsequent periods with additional complications. As a result, the treatment of accounting for revaluation gains and losses in subsequent periods is addressed in advanced accounting classes.

Revising Periodic Depreciation

Depreciation is one example of the use of estimation in the accounting process. Management should periodically review annual depreciation expense. If wear and tear or obsolescence indicate that annual depreciation estimates are inadequate or excessive, the company should change the amount of depreciation expense.

When a change in an estimate is required, the company makes the change in **current and future years. It does not change depreciation in prior periods**. The rationale is that continual restatement of prior periods would adversely affect confidence in financial statements.

HELPFUL HINT

Use a step-by-step approach: (1) determine new depreciable cost; (2) divide by remaining useful life.

- To determine the new annual depreciation expense, the company first computes the asset's depreciable cost at the time of the revision.
- It then allocates the revised depreciable cost to the remaining useful life (see **Helpful Hint**).

To illustrate, assume that Barb's Florists decides on January 1, 2032, to extend the useful life of the truck by one year (a total life of six years) and increase its residual value to €2,200. The company has used the straight-line method to depreciate the asset to date. Depreciation per year was €2,400 [(€13,000 − €1,000) ÷ 5]. Accumulated depreciation after three years (2029–2031) is €7,200 (€2,400 × 3), and book value is €5,800 (€13,000 − €7,200). The new annual depreciation is €1,200, as shown in **Illustration 9.18**.

ILLUSTRATION 9.18

Revised depreciation computation

Book value, 1/1/32 (€13,000 - €7,200)	€5,800	
Less: New residual value	2,200	
Depreciable cost	€3,600	
Remaining useful life	3 years	(2032–2034)
Revised annual depreciation (€3,600 ÷ 3)	**€1,200**	

Barb's Florists makes no entry for the change in estimate. On December 31, 2032, during the preparation of adjusting entries, it records depreciation expense of €1,200. Companies must describe in the financial statements significant changes in estimates.

ACTION PLAN

- **Calculate depreciable cost.**
- **Divide depreciable cost by new remaining life.**

DO IT! 2b | Revised Depreciation

Chambers Landscaping purchased a piece of equipment for £36,000. It estimated a 6-year life and £6,000 residual value. Thus, straight-line depreciation was £5,000 per year [(£36,000 − £6,000) ÷ 6]. At the end of year three (before the depreciation adjustment), it estimated the new total life to be 10 years and the new residual value to be £2,000. Compute the revised depreciation.

Solution

Original depreciation expense = [(£36,000 − £6,000) ÷ 6] = £5,000
Accumulated depreciation after 2 years = 2 × £5,000 = £10,000
Book value = £36,000 − £10,000 = £26,000

Book value after 2 years of depreciation	£26,000
Less: New residual value	2,000
Depreciable cost	£24,000
Remaining useful life (10 − 2)	8 years
Revised annual depreciation (£24,000 ÷ 8)	£ 3,000

Related exercise material: **BE9.9, DO IT! 9.2b, and E9.9.**

9.3 Plant Asset Disposals

LEARNING OBJECTIVE 3

Explain how to account for the disposal of plant assets.

Companies dispose of plant assets that are no longer useful to them. **Illustration 9.19** shows the three ways in which companies make plant asset disposals.

ILLUSTRATION 9.19
Methods of plant asset disposal

Whatever the disposal method, the company must determine the book value of the plant asset at the disposal date to determine the gain or loss. Recall that the book value is the difference between the cost of the plant asset and the accumulated depreciation to date.

- If the disposal does not occur on the first day of the year, the company must record depreciation for the fraction of the year to the date of disposal.
- The company then eliminates the book value by reducing (debiting) Accumulated Depreciation for the total depreciation associated with that asset to the date of disposal and reducing (crediting) the asset account for the cost of the asset (see **Helpful Hint**).

HELPFUL HINT
When disposing of a plant asset, the company removes all amounts related to the asset. This includes the original cost and the total depreciation to date in the accumulated depreciation account.

In this chapter, we examine the accounting for the retirement and sale of plant assets. In the appendix to the chapter, we discuss and illustrate the accounting for exchanges of plant assets.

Retirement of Plant Assets

To illustrate the retirement of plant assets, assume that Hobart Publishing retires its computer printers, which cost €32,000. The accumulated depreciation on these printers is €32,000. The equipment, therefore, is fully depreciated (zero book value). The entry to record this retirement is as follows.

Accumulated Depreciation—Equipment	32,000	
Equipment		32,000
(To record retirement of fully depreciated equipment)		

A	=	L	+	E
+32,000				
−32,000				

Cash Flows
no effect

What happens if a fully depreciated plant asset is still useful to the company?

- In this case, the asset and its accumulated depreciation continue to be reported on the statement of financial position, without further depreciation adjustment, until the company retires the asset.
- Reporting the asset and related accumulated depreciation on the statement of financial position informs the financial statement reader that the asset is still in use.
- Once fully depreciated, no additional depreciation should be taken, even if an asset is still being used. In no situation can the accumulated depreciation on a plant asset exceed its cost.

If a company retires a plant asset before it is fully depreciated, and no cash is received for scrap or residual value, a loss on disposal occurs. For example, assume that Sunset Shipping discards delivery equipment that cost €18,000 and has accumulated depreciation of €14,000. The entry is as follows.

Accumulated Depreciation—Equipment	14,000	
Loss on Disposal of Plant Assets	4,000	
Equipment		18,000
(To record retirement of delivery equipment at a loss)		

A	=	L	+	E
+14,000				
				−4,000 Exp
−18,000				

Cash Flows
no effect

Under IFRS 18, a loss on the disposal of assets used in a company's core operating activities (such as property, plant and equipment or intangible assets) is classified within the operating category of the income statement and may be presented as other operating expenses.

Sale of Plant Assets

In a disposal by sale, the company compares the book value of the asset with the proceeds received from the sale.

- If the proceeds of the sale **exceed** the book value of the plant asset, **a gain on disposal occurs.**
- If the proceeds of the sale **are less than** the book value of the plant asset sold, **a loss on disposal occurs.**

Only by coincidence will the book value and the fair value of the asset be the same when the asset is sold. Gains and losses on sales of plant assets are therefore quite common. For example, **Delta Airlines** (USA) reported a $94 million gain on the sale of 10 aircraft.

Gain on Sale

To illustrate a gain on sale of plant assets, assume that on July 1, 2029, Wright Interiors sells office furniture for €16,000 cash. The office furniture originally cost €60,000. As of January 1, 2029, it had accumulated depreciation of €41,000. Depreciation for the first six months of 2029 is €8,000. Wright records depreciation expense and updates accumulated depreciation to July 1 with the following entry.

A	=	L	+	E
				−8,000 Exp
−8,000				

Cash Flows
no effect

July 1	Depreciation Expense	8,000	
	Accumulated Depreciation—Equipment		8,000
	(To record depreciation expense for the first 6 months of 2029)		

After the accumulated depreciation balance is updated, the company computes the gain or loss. The gain or loss is the difference between the proceeds from the sale and the book value at the date of disposal. **Illustration 9.20** shows this computation for Wright, which has a gain on disposal of €5,000.

ILLUSTRATION 9.20
Computation of gain on disposal

Cost of office furniture	€60,000
Less: Accumulated depreciation (€41,000 + €8,000)	49,000
Book value at date of disposal	11,000
Proceeds from sale	16,000
Gain on disposal of plant asset	**€ 5,000**

Wright records the sale and the gain on disposal of the plant asset as follows.

A	=	L	+	E
+16,000				
+49,000				
−60,000				
				+5,000 Rev

Cash Flows
+16,000

July 1	Cash	16,000	
	Accumulated Depreciation—Equipment	49,000	
	Equipment		60,000
	Gain on Disposal of Plant Assets		5,000
	(To record sale of office furniture at a gain)		

Under IFRS 18, a gain on the disposal of assets used in a company's core operating activities is classified within the operating category of the income statement and may be presented as other operating income.

Loss on Sale

Assume that instead of selling the office furniture for €16,000, Wright sells it for €9,000. In this case, Wright computes a loss of €2,000 as shown in **Illustration 9.21**.

Cost of office furniture	€60,000
Less: Accumulated depreciation	49,000
Book value at date of disposal	11,000
Proceeds from sale	9,000
Loss on disposal of plant asset	**€ 2,000**

ILLUSTRATION 9.21

Computation of loss on disposal

Wright records the sale and the loss on disposal of the plant asset as follows.

July 1	Cash	9,000	
	Accumulated Depreciation—Equipment	49,000	
	Loss on Disposal of Plant Assets	2,000	
	Equipment		60,000
	(To record sale of office furniture at a loss)		

A	=	L	+	E
+9,000				
+49,000				
				−2,000 Exp
−60,000				

Cash Flows
+9,000

Companies report a loss on the disposal of plant assets used in core operating activities within the operating category of the income statement and often present it as other operating expenses.

DO IT! 3 | Plant Asset Disposal

Overland Trucking decided to sell an old truck that cost £30,000 and has accumulated depreciation of £16,000. (a) What entry would Overland Trucking make to record the sale of the truck for £17,000 cash? (b) What entry would Overland Trucking make to record the sale of the truck for £10,000 cash?

ACTION PLAN

- **At the time of disposal, determine the book value of the asset.**
- **Compare the asset's book value with the proceeds received to determine whether a gain or loss has occurred.**

Solution

a. Sale of truck for cash at a gain:

Cash	17,000	
Accumulated Depreciation—Equipment	16,000	
Equipment		30,000
Gain on Disposal of Plant Assets [£17,000 − (£30,000 − £16,000)]		3,000
(To record sale of truck at a gain)		

b. Sale of truck for cash at a loss:

Cash	10,000	
Accumulated Depreciation—Equipment	16,000	
Loss on Disposal of Plant Assets [£10,000 − (£30,000 − £16,000)]	4,000	
Equipment		30,000
(To record sale of truck at a loss)		

Related exercise material: **BE9.11, BE9.12, DO IT! 9.3, E9.12, and E9.13.**

9.4 Natural Resources and Intangible Assets

LEARNING OBJECTIVE 4

Describe how to account for natural resources and intangible assets.

Natural Resources and Depletion

HELPFUL HINT

On a statement of financial position, natural resources may be described more specifically as *timberlands*, *mineral deposits*, *oil reserves*, and so on.

Common **natural resources** consist of standing timber and resources extracted from the ground, such as oil, gas, and minerals (see **Helpful Hint**). Standing timber is considered a biological asset under IFRS. In the years before they are harvested, the recorded value of biological assets is adjusted to fair value each period. The additional details of accounting for biological assets are beyond the scope of this text.

IFRS defines extractive industries as those businesses involved in finding and removing natural resources located in or near the earth's crust. The acquisition cost of an extractable natural resource is the price needed to acquire the resource **and** prepare it for its intended use. For an already-discovered resource, such as an existing coal mine, cost is the price paid for the property.

- The allocation of the cost of natural resources in a systematic manner over the resource's useful life is called **depletion**. (That is, depletion is to natural resources what depreciation is to plant assets.)
- **Companies generally use the units-of-activity method** (discussed earlier in the chapter) **to compute depletion**. The reason is that **depletion generally is a function of the units extracted during the year**.
- Under the units-of-activity method, companies divide the total cost of the natural resource minus residual value by the number of units estimated to be in the resource. The result is a **depletion cost per unit**. To compute depletion, the cost per unit is then multiplied by the number of units extracted.

To illustrate, assume that Lane Coal invests HK$50 million in a mine estimated to have 10 million tons of coal and no residual value. **Illustration 9.22** shows the computation of the depletion cost per unit.

ILLUSTRATION 9.22

Computation of depletion cost per unit

$$\frac{\textbf{Total Cost} - \textbf{Residual Value}}{\textbf{Total Estimated Units Available}} = \textbf{Depletion Cost per Unit}$$

$$\frac{\text{HK\$50,000,000}}{\text{10,000,000}} = \text{HK\$5.00 per ton}$$

If Lane extracts 250,000 tons in the first year, then the depletion for the year is HK$1,250,000 (250,000 tons × HK$5). It records the depletion as follows.

A	=	L	+	E
+1,250,000				
−1,250,000				

Cash Flows
no effect

Inventory (coal)	1,250,000	
Accumulated Depletion		1,250,000
(To record depletion of a coal mine)		

Lane debits Inventory for the total depletion for the year and credits Accumulated Depletion to reduce the carrying value of the natural resource. Accumulated Depletion is a contra asset similar to Accumulated Depreciation. Lane credits Inventory when it sells the inventory and debits Cost of Goods Sold. The amount not sold remains in inventory and is reported in the current assets section of the statement of financial position (see **Ethics Note**).

ETHICS NOTE

Investors were stunned at news that Royal Dutch Shell (NLD and GBR) had significantly overstated its reported oil reserves.

Some companies do not use an Accumulated Depletion account. In such cases, the company credits the amount of depletion directly to the natural resources account.

Environmental, Social, and Governance Insight — BHP Billiton

© Christian Uhrig/ iStockphoto

Sustainability Report Please

Sustainability reports identify how the company is meeting its social responsibilities. Many companies, both large and small, are now issuing these reports. For example, companies such as **Microsoft** (USA), **Tata** (IND), **BP** (GBR), **Nestlé** (CHE), and **Samsung** (KOR) issue these reports.

The following is an adapted section of a recent **BHP Billiton** (AUS) (a global mining, oil, and gas company) sustainability report on its environmental policies. These policies are to (1) take action to address the challenges of climate change, (2) set and achieve targets that reduce pollution, and (3) enhance biodiversity by assessing and considering ecological values and land-use aspects. Here is how BHP Billiton measures the success or failure of some of these policies:

Social Responsibility	Target	Target Date
Safety	• Zero work-related fatalities. • Year-on-year improvement of our total recordable injury frequency (TRIF).	Annual Annual
Health	For our most material exposures of respirable silica, diesel particulate and coal mine dust, we will achieve a 50 percent reduction in the number of workers potentially exposed as compared with the FY2021 baseline.	30 June 2026
Community	Zero significant community events.	Annual
	Our social investment will contribute to improved quality of life in host communities and support achievement of the UN Sustainable Development Goals. We will invest not less than one percent of pre-tax profit (three-year rolling average) in meeting these objectives.	30 June 2026
	Regional Indigenous Peoples Plans will be developed, which support implementation of BHP's Indigenous Peoples Strategy. Plans will include all geographically relevant assets.	30 June 2026
Climate change	Maintain FY2026 greenhouse gas (GHG) emissions at or below FY2021 levels while we continue to grow our business.	30 June 2026
	Longer-term goal: In line with international commitments, BHP aims to achieve net-zero operational GHG emissions in the second half of this century.	The second half of this century.

In addition to the environment, BHP Billiton has sections in its sustainability report that discuss people, safety, health, and community.

Why do you believe companies issue sustainability reports? (Answer is available near the end of the chapter.)

Intangible Assets

Intangible assets are rights, privileges, and competitive advantages that result from the ownership of long-lived assets that do not possess physical substance. Evidence of intangibles may exist in the form of contracts or licenses. Intangibles may arise from the following sources.

1. Government grants, such as patents, copyrights, licenses, trademarks, and trade names.
2. Acquisition of another business, in which the purchase price includes a payment for **goodwill**.
3. Private monopolistic arrangements arising from contractual agreements, such as franchises and leases.

Some widely known intangibles are **SAP**'s (DEU) patents, **Spar**'s (NLD) convenience store franchises, **Apple**'s (USA) trade name iPod, J.K. Rowlings' copyrights on the *Harry Potter* books, and the trademark **Europcar** (FRA) in the Feature Story.

Accounting for Intangible Assets

Companies record intangible assets at cost. This cost consists of all expenditures necessary for the company to acquire the right, privilege, or competitive advantage. Intangibles are categorized as having either a limited life or an indefinite life.

- If an intangible has a **limited life**, the company allocates its cost over the asset's useful life using a process similar to depreciation.
- The process of allocating the cost of intangibles is referred to as **amortization** (see **Helpful Hint**).
- The cost of intangible assets with **indefinite lives should not be amortized**.

> **HELPFUL HINT**
> ***Amortization* is to intangibles what *depreciation* is to plant assets and *depletion* is to extractable natural resources.**

To record amortization of an intangible asset, a company increases (debits) Amortization Expense and decreases (credits) the specific intangible asset. Alternatively, some companies choose to credit a contra account, such as Accumulated Amortization. *For homework purposes, you should directly credit the specific intangible asset.*

Intangible assets are typically amortized on a straight-line basis. For example, the legal life of a patent is 20 years in many countries. Companies **amortize the cost of a patent over its 20-year life or its useful life, whichever is shorter**. To illustrate the computation of patent amortization, assume that National Labs purchases a patent at a cost of NT$720,000. If National estimates the useful life of the patent to be eight years, the annual amortization expense is NT$90,000 (NT$720,000 ÷ 8). National records the annual amortization as follows.

A	=	L	+	E
				−90,000 Exp
−90,000				

Cash Flows
no effect

Dec. 31	Amortization Expense	90,000	
	Patents		90,000
	(To record patent amortization)		

Companies classify amortization expense as an operating expense in the income statement. Similar to property, plant, and equipment, IFRS permits revaluation of intangible assets to fair value, except for goodwill.

When intangible assets are acquired through a purchase, the determination of cost is similar to that of property, plant, and equipment. Cost includes the purchase price, as well as costs incurred to get the asset ready for use. However, special rules are used to determine cost when an intangible asset is generated internally, as a result of a company's own research and development efforts. These rules are discussed in a later section.

Patents A **patent** is an exclusive right issued by a patent office that enables the recipient to manufacture, sell, or otherwise control an invention for a specified number of years from the date of the grant. These "legal lives" sometimes vary across countries, but the legal life in many countries is 20 years. A patent is non-renewable. But, companies can extend the legal life of a patent by obtaining new patents for improvements or other changes in the basic design.

- **The initial cost of a patent is the cash or cash equivalent price paid to acquire the patent.**
- Many patents are subject to litigation by competitors. Any legal costs an owner incurs in successfully defending a patent in an infringement suit are considered necessary to establish the patent's validity. **The owner adds those costs to the Patents account and amortizes them over the remaining life of the patent.**

The patent holder amortizes the cost of a patent over its legal life or its useful life, whichever is shorter. Companies consider obsolescence and inadequacy in determining useful life. These factors may cause a patent to become economically ineffective before the end of its legal life.

Copyrights Governments grant **copyrights**, which give the owner the exclusive right to reproduce and sell an artistic or published work. Copyrights extend for the life of the creator plus a specified number of years, which can vary by country but is commonly 70 years.

- The cost of a copyright is the **cost of acquiring and defending it**.
- The cost may be only the small fee paid to a copyright office. Or, it may amount to much more if a copyright is acquired from another party.

The useful life of a copyright generally is significantly shorter than its legal life. Therefore, copyrights usually are amortized over a relatively short period of time.

Trademarks and Trade Names A **trademark** or **trade name** is a word, phrase, jingle, or symbol that identifies a particular enterprise or product. Trade names like Big Mac, Coca-Cola, and Jetta create immediate product identification. They also generally enhance the sale of the product. The creator or original user may obtain exclusive legal right to the trademark or trade name by registering it with a patent office or similar governmental agency. Such registration provides a specified number of years of protection, which can vary by country but is commonly 20 years. The registration may be renewed indefinitely as long as the trademark or trade name is in use.

- If a company purchases the trademark or trade name, its cost is the purchase price.
- If a company develops and maintains the trademark or trade name, any costs related to these activities are expensed as incurred.
- Because trademarks and trade names have indefinite lives, they are not amortized.

Franchises and Licenses When you fill up your tank at the **CPC** (TWN) station, eat lunch at **Subway** (USA), or rent a car from **Europcar** (FRA), you are dealing with franchises. A **franchise** is a contractual arrangement between a franchisor and a franchisee. The franchisor grants the franchisee the right to sell certain products, perform specific services, or use certain trademarks or trade names, usually within a designated geographic area.

Another type of franchise is that entered into between a governmental body (commonly municipalities) and a company. This franchise permits the company to use public property in performing its services. Examples are the use of city streets for a bus line or taxi service, use of public land for telephone and electric lines, and the use of airwaves for radio or TV broadcasting. Such operating rights are referred to as **licenses**. Franchises and licenses may be granted for a definite period of time, an indefinite period, or perpetually.

- **When a company incurs costs in connection with the purchase of a franchise or license, it should recognize an intangible asset.**
- Companies should amortize the cost of a limited-life franchise (or license) over its useful life.
- If the life is indefinite, the cost is not amortized.

Annual payments made under a franchise agreement are recorded as **operating expenses** in the period in which they are incurred.

Goodwill Usually, the largest intangible asset that appears on a company's statement of financial position is goodwill. **Goodwill** represents the value of all favorable attributes that relate to a company that is not tied to any other specific asset. These attributes include exceptional management, desirable location, good customer relations, skilled employees, high-quality products, and harmonious relations with labor unions. Goodwill is unique. Unlike assets such as investments and plant assets, which can be sold **individually** in the marketplace, goodwill can be identified only with the business **as a whole.**

If goodwill can be identified only with the business as a whole, how can its amount be determined? Management could try to put a monetary value on the factors listed above (exceptional management, desirable location, and so on). But, the results would be very subjective, and such subjective valuations would not contribute to the reliability of financial statements.

- **Therefore, companies record goodwill only when an entire business is purchased.**
- **In that case, goodwill is the excess of cost over the fair value of the net assets (assets less liabilities) acquired.**

In recording the purchase of a business, the company debits (increases) the identifiable acquired assets, credits liabilities at their fair values, credits cash for the purchase price, and records the difference as goodwill.

- **Goodwill is not amortized** because it is considered to have an indefinite life.
- However, goodwill must be written down if a company determines that its value has been permanently impaired.

Companies report goodwill in the statement of financial position under intangible assets.

Global Insight SoftBank Corp.

Pixtal/SuperStock

Should Companies Write Up Goodwill?

SoftBank Corp. (JPN) at one time was the country's largest Internet company. It boosted the profit margin of its mobile-phone unit from 3.2% to 11.2% through what appeared to some as accounting tricks. What did it do? It wrote down the value of its mobile-phone-unit assets by half. This would normally result in a huge loss.

But rather than take a loss, the company wrote up goodwill by the same amount. How did this move increase earnings? The assets were being depreciated over 10 years, but the company amortizes goodwill over 20 years. (Amortization of goodwill was allowed under the accounting standards it followed at that time.) While the new treatment did not break any rules, the company was criticized by investors for not providing sufficient justification or a detailed explanation for the sudden shift in policy.

Source: Adapted from Andrew Morse and Yukari Iwatani Kane, "SoftBank's Accounting Shift Raises Eyebrows," *Wall Street Journal* (August 28, 2007), p. C1.

Which aspects of this treatment are allowed under IFRS? (Answer is available near the end of the chapter.)

Research and Development Costs

Research and development costs are expenditures that may lead to patents, copyrights, new processes, and new products. Many companies spend considerable sums of money on research and development (R&D). For example, in a recent year **Samsung** (KOR) spent over ₩15 trillion on R&D.

Research and development costs present accounting problems as it is sometimes difficult to assign these costs to specific projects. Also, there are uncertainties in identifying the amount and timing of future benefits.

- Costs in the research phase are always expensed as incurred.
- Costs in the development phase are expensed until specific criteria are met, primarily that technological feasibility is achieved.
- Development costs incurred after technological feasibility has been achieved are capitalized to Development Costs, which is considered an intangible asset.

To illustrate, assume that Laser Scanner Ltd. spent NT$1 million on research and NT$2 million on development of new products. Of the NT$2 million in development costs, NT$400,000 was incurred prior to technological feasibility and NT$1,600,000 was incurred after technological feasibility had been demonstrated. The company would record these costs as follows.

A	=	L	+	E
				−1,400,000 Exp
+1,600,000				
−3,000,000				

Cash Flows
−3,000,000

Research and Development Expense	1,400,000	
Development Costs	1,600,000	
Cash		3,000,000
(To record research and development costs)		

ACTION PLAN

- **Know that the accounting for intangibles often depends on whether the item has a finite or indefinite life.**
- **Recognize the many similarities and differences between the accounting for natural resources, plant assets, and intangible assets.**

DO IT! 4 | Classification Concepts

Match the statement with the term most directly associated with it.

Copyrights	Depletion
Intangible assets	Franchises
Research costs	Trademarks and Trade names
Goodwill	

1. ______ The allocation of the cost of a natural resource in a systematic manner.
2. ______ Rights, privileges, and competitive advantages that result from the ownership of long-lived assets that do not possess physical substance.
3. ______ An exclusive right granted by a government to reproduce and sell an artistic or published work.

4. ______ A right to sell certain products or services or to use certain trademarks or trade names within a designated geographic area.
5. ______ Costs incurred by a company that often lead to patents or new products. These costs must be expensed as incurred.
6. ______ Because their lives are indefinite, they are not amortized.
7. ______ It is unique, can be identified only with the business as a whole.

Solution

1. Depletion.
2. Intangible assets.
3. Copyrights.
4. Franchises.
5. Research costs.
6. Trademarks and Trade names.
7. Goodwill.

Related exercise material: **BE9.13, BE9.14, BE9.15, DO IT! 9.4, E9.14, E9.15, and E9.16.**

9.5 Statement Presentation and Analysis

LEARNING OBJECTIVE 5

Discuss how plant assets, natural resources, and intangible assets are reported and analyzed.

Presentation

Usually, companies combine plant assets and natural resources under "Property, plant, and equipment" in the statement of financial position. They show intangibles assets separately. **Illustration 9.23** shows the assets section from the statement of financial position of Artex Enterprises, with emphasis on the reporting of plant assets.

ILLUSTRATION 9.23

Presentation of property, plant, and equipment, and intangible assets

Artex Enterprises
Statement of Financial Position (partial)
(in billions)

Property, plant, and equipment			
Gold mine	¥ 530		
Less: Accumulated depletion	210	¥ 320	
Land		600	
Buildings	7,600		
Less: Accumulated depreciation—buildings	500	7,100	
Equipment	3,870		
Less: Accumulated depreciation—equipment	620	3,250	
Total property, plant, and equipment			¥11,270
Intangible assets			
Patents		440	
Trademarks		180	
Goodwill		900	1,520
Total assets			¥12,790

Companies may disclose in the statement of financial position or the notes to the financial statements the major classes of assets such as land, land improvements, buildings and equipment, and accumulated depreciation (by major classes or in total). In addition, they should describe the depreciation and amortization methods that were used, as well as disclose the amount of depreciation and amortization expense for the period. *For homework purposes, use the format in Illustration 9.23 for preparing statement of financial position information.*

Analysis

Using ratios, we can analyze how efficiently a company uses its assets to generate sales. The **asset turnover** analyzes the productivity of a company's assets. It tells us, as shown below for **LG** (KOR), how many Korean won of sales the company generates for each Korean won invested in assets. This ratio is computed by dividing net sales by average total assets for the period, as shown in **Illustration 9.24**. LG's net sales for a recent year were ₩58,140 billion. Its total ending assets were ₩35,528 billion, and beginning assets were ₩34,766 billion.

ILLUSTRATION 9.24

Asset turnover formula and computation

Net Sales	÷	Average Total Assets	=	Asset Turnover
₩58,140	÷	$\frac{₩35,528 + ₩34,766}{2}$	=	1.65 times

Thus, each Korean won invested in assets produced ₩1.65 in sales for LG. If a company is using its assets efficiently, each investment in assets will create a high amount of sales. This ratio varies greatly among different industries—from those that are asset-intensive (utilities) to those that are not (services).

ACTION PLAN

- **Recognize that the asset turnover analyzes the productivity of a company's assets.**
- **Know the formula Net sales ÷ Average total assets = Asset turnover.**

DO IT! 5 | Asset Turnover

Paramour Company reported net income of $180,000, net sales of $420,000, and had total assets of $460,000 on January 1, 2029, and total assets on December 31, 2029, of $540,000 billion. Determine Paramour's asset turnover for 2029.

Solution

The asset turnover for Paramour Company is computed as follows.

Net Sales	÷	Average Total Assets	=	Asset Turnover
$420,000	÷	$\frac{\$460,000 + \$540,000}{2}$	=	.84 times

Related exercise material: **BE9.17, DO IT! 9.5, and E9.18.**

Appendix 9A Exchange of Plant Assets

LEARNING OBJECTIVE *6

Explain how to account for the exchange of plant assets.

Ordinarily, companies record a gain or loss on the exchange of plant assets.

- The rationale for recognizing a gain or loss is that most exchanges have **commercial substance.**
- An exchange has commercial substance if the future cash flows change as a result of the exchange.

To illustrate, Ramos Construction exchanges some of its equipment for land held by Brodhead Group. It is likely that the timing and amount of the cash flows arising from the land will differ significantly from the cash flows arising from the equipment. As a result, both Ramos and Brodhead are in different economic positions. Therefore, **the exchange has commercial substance**, and the companies recognize a gain or loss in the exchange. Because most exchanges have commercial substance (even when similar assets are exchanged), we illustrate only this type of situation for both a loss and a gain.

Loss Treatment

To illustrate an exchange that results in a loss, assume that Roland NV exchanged a set of used trucks plus cash for a new semi-truck. The used trucks have a combined book value of €42,000 (cost €64,000 less €22,000 accumulated depreciation). Roland's purchasing agent, experienced in the secondhand market, indicates that the used trucks have a fair value of €26,000. In addition to the trucks, Roland must pay €17,000 for the semi-truck. Roland computes the cost of the semi-truck as shown in **Illustration 9A.1**.

Fair value of used trucks	€26,000
Cash paid	17,000
Cost of semi-truck	€43,000

ILLUSTRATION 9A.1
Cost of semi-truck

Roland incurs a loss on disposal of plant assets of €16,000 on this exchange. The reason is that the book value of the used trucks is greater than the fair value of these trucks. **Illustration 9A.2** shows the computation.

Book value of used trucks (€64,000 − €22,000)	€42,000
Less: Fair value of used trucks	26,000
Loss on disposal of plant assets	**€16,000**

ILLUSTRATION 9A.2
Computation of loss on disposal

In recording an exchange at a loss, four steps are required:

1. Eliminate the book value of the asset given up.
2. Record the cost of the asset acquired.
3. Recognize the loss on disposal of plant assets.
4. Record the cash paid or received.

Roland thus records the exchange on the loss as follows.

	Debit	Credit	A = L + E
Equipment (new)	43,000		+43,000
Accumulated Depreciation—Equipment	22,000		+22,000
Loss on Disposal of Plant Assets	16,000		−16,000 Exp
Equipment (old)		64,000	−64,000
Cash		17,000	−17,000
(To record exchange of used trucks for semi-truck)			**Cash Flows** −17,000

Gain Treatment

To illustrate a gain situation, assume that Mark Express decides to exchange its old delivery equipment plus cash of €3,000 for new delivery equipment. The book value of the old delivery equipment is €12,000 (cost €40,000 less accumulated depreciation €28,000). The fair value of the old delivery equipment is €19,000.

The cost of the new asset is the fair value of the old asset exchanged plus any cash paid (or other consideration given up). The cost of the new delivery equipment is €22,000, computed as shown in **Illustration 9A.3**.

ILLUSTRATION 9A.3

Cost of new delivery equipment

Fair value of old delivery equipment	€19,000
Cash paid	3,000
Cost of new delivery equipment	**€22,000**

A gain results when the fair value of the old delivery equipment is greater than its book value. For Mark Express, there is a gain of €7,000 on disposal of plant assets, computed as shown in **Illustration 9A.4**.

ILLUSTRATION 9A.4

Computation of gain on disposal

Fair value of old delivery equipment	€19,000
Less: Book value of old delivery equipment (€40,000 – €28,000)	12,000
Gain on disposal of plant assets	**€ 7,000**

Mark Express records the exchange as follows.

A	= L +	E
+22,000		
+28,000		
−40,000		
		+7,000 Rev
−3,000		

Cash Flows
−3,000

Equipment (new)	22,000	
Accumulated Depreciation—Equipment (old)	28,000	
Equipment (old)		40,000
Gain on Disposal of Plant Assets		7,000
Cash		3,000
(To record exchange of old delivery equipment for new delivery equipment)		

In recording an exchange at a gain, the following four steps are involved.

1. Eliminate the book value of the asset given up.
2. Record the cost of the asset acquired.
3. Recognize the gain on disposal of plant assets.
4. Record the cash paid or received.

Accounting for exchanges of plant assets becomes more complex if the transaction does not have commercial substance. This issue is discussed in more advanced accounting classes.

Review and Practice

Learning Objectives Review

1 Explain the accounting for plant asset expenditures.

The cost of plant assets includes all expenditures necessary to acquire the asset and make it ready for its intended use. Once cost is established, the company uses that amount as the basis of accounting for a plant asset over its useful life.

Companies incur revenue expenditures to maintain the operating efficiency and productive life of an asset. They debit these expenditures to Maintenance and Repairs Expense as incurred. Capital expenditures increase the operating efficiency, productive capacity, or expected useful life of the asset. Companies generally debit these expenditures to the plant asset affected.

2 Apply depreciation methods to plant assets.

Depreciation is the allocation of the cost of a plant asset to expense over its useful (service) life in a systematic manner. Depreciation is not a process of valuation, nor is it a process that results in an accumulation of cash.

Three depreciation methods are:

Method	Effect on Annual Depreciation	Formula
Straight-line	Constant amount	Depreciable cost ÷ Useful life (in years)
Units-of-activity	Varying amount	Depreciable cost per unit × Units of activity during the year
Declining-balance	Decreasing amount	Book value at beginning of year × Declining-balance rate

Companies make revisions of periodic depreciation in present and future periods, not retroactively. They determine the new annual depreciation by dividing the depreciable cost at the time of the revision by the remaining useful life.

3 Explain how to account for the disposal of plant assets.

The accounting for disposal of a plant asset through retirement or sale is as follows. (a) Eliminate the book value of the plant asset at the date of disposal. (b) Record cash proceeds, if any. (c) Account for the difference between the book value and the cash proceeds as a gain or loss on disposal. (d) Record cash paid or received.

4 Describe how to account for natural resources and intangible assets.

Companies compute depletion cost per unit by dividing the total cost of the natural resource minus residual value by the number of units estimated to be in the resource. They then multiply the depletion cost per unit by the number of units extracted.

The process of allocating the cost of an intangible asset is referred to as amortization. The cost of intangible assets with indefinite lives is not amortized. Companies normally use the straight-line method for amortizing intangible assets.

5 Discuss how plant assets, natural resources, and intangible assets are reported and analyzed.

Companies usually combine plant assets and natural resources under property, plant, and equipment. They show intangibles separately under intangible assets. Either within the statement of financial position or in the notes, companies should disclose the balances of the major classes of assets, such as land, buildings, and equipment, and accumulated depreciation by major classes or in total. They also should describe the depreciation and amortization methods used, and should disclose the amount of depreciation and amortization expense for the period. The asset turnover measures the productivity of a company's assets in generating sales.

***6 Explain how to account for the exchange of plant assets.**

Ordinarily, companies record a gain or loss on the exchange of plant assets. The rationale for recognizing a gain or loss is that most exchanges have commercial substance. An exchange has commercial substance if the future cash flows change as a result of the exchange.

Glossary Review

Accelerated-depreciation method Depreciation method that produces higher depreciation expense in the early years than in the later years. (p. 9-12).

Additions and improvements Costs incurred to increase the operating efficiency, productive capacity, or useful life of a plant asset. (p. 9-6).

Amortization The allocation of the cost of an intangible asset to expense over its useful life in a systematic manner. (p. 9-21).

Asset turnover A measure of how efficiently a company uses its assets to generate sales; calculated as net sales divided by average total assets. (p. 9-26).

Capital expenditures Expenditures that increase the company's investment in productive facilities. (p. 9-6).

Component depreciation Depreciation method in which any significant parts of a plant asset that have significantly different useful lives are separately depreciated. (p. 9-13).

Copyrights Exclusive grant from the government that allows the owner to reproduce and sell an artistic or published work. (p. 9-22).

Declining-balance method Depreciation method that applies a constant rate to the declining book value of the asset and produces a decreasing annual depreciation expense over the useful life of the asset. (p. 9-11).

Depletion The allocation of the cost of an extractable natural resource to expense in a systematic manner over the resource's useful life. (p. 9-20).

Depreciable cost The cost of a plant asset less its residual value. (p. 9-9).

Depreciation The systematic allocation of the depreciable amount of an asset over its useful life. (p. 9-7).

Franchise (license) A contractual arrangement under which the franchisor grants the franchisee the right to sell certain products, perform specific services, or use certain trademarks or trade names, usually within a designated geographic area. (p. 9-23).

Going concern assumption States that the company will continue in operation for the foreseeable future. (p. 9-8).

Goodwill The value of all favorable attributes that relate to a company that is not attributable to any other specific asset. (p. 9-23).

Intangible assets Rights, privileges, and competitive advantages that result from the ownership of long-lived assets that do not possess physical substance. (p. 9-21).

Licenses Operating rights to use public property, granted to a business by a governmental agency. (p. 9-23).

Materiality concept If an item would not make a difference in decision-making, a company does not have to follow IFRS in reporting it. (p. 9-6).

Natural resources Assets that consist of standing timber and underground deposits of oil, gas, or minerals. (p. 9-20).

Ordinary repairs Expenditures to maintain the operating efficiency and productive life of the plant asset. (p. 9-6).

Patent An exclusive right issued by a patent office that enables the recipient to manufacture, sell, or otherwise control an invention for a specified number of years from the date of the grant. (p. 9-22).

Plant assets Tangible resources that are used in the operations of the business and are not intended for sale to customers. (p. 9-3).

Research and development (R&D) costs Expenditures that may lead to patents, copyrights, new processes, or new products. (p. 9-24).

Residual value An estimate of an asset's value at the end of its useful life. (p. 9-9).

Revenue expenditures Expenditures that are immediately charged against revenues as an expense. (p. 9-6).

Straight-line method Depreciation method in which periodic depreciation is the same for each year of the asset's useful life. (p. 9-9).

Trademark (trade name) A word, phrase, jingle, or symbol that identifies a particular enterprise or product. (p. 9-22).

Units-of-activity method Depreciation method in which useful life is expressed in terms of the total units of production or use expected from an asset. (p. 9-11).

Useful life An estimate of the expected productive life, also called service life, of an asset. (p. 9-9).

Practice Multiple-Choice Questions

1. (LO 1) Erin Danielle Electronics purchased equipment and incurred the following costs.

Cash price	€24,000
Sales taxes	1,200
Insurance during transit	200
Installation and testing	400
Total costs	€25,800

What amount should be recorded as the cost of the equipment?

a. €24,000. **c.** €25,400.
b. €25,200. **d.** €25,800.

2. (LO 1) Additions to plant assets are:

a. revenue expenditures.
b. debited to the Maintenance and Repairs Expense account.
c. debited to the Purchases account.
d. capital expenditures.

3. (LO 2) Depreciation is a process of:

a. valuation. **c.** cash accumulation.
b. cost allocation. **d.** appraisal.

4. (LO 2) Micah Bartlett Ltd. purchased equipment on January 1, 2028, at a total invoice cost of £400,000. The equipment has an estimated residual value of £10,000 and an estimated useful life of 5 years. The amount of accumulated depreciation at December 31, 2029, if the straight-line method of depreciation is used, is:

a. £80,000. **c.** £78,000.
b. £160,000. **d.** £156,000.

5. (LO 2) Ann Torbert purchased a truck for €11,000 on January 1, 2028. The truck will have an estimated residual value of €1,000 at the end of 5 years. Using the units-of-activity method, the balance in accumulated depreciation at December 31, 2029, can be computed by the following formula:

a. (€11,000 ÷ Total estimated activity) × Units of activity for 2029.
b. (€10,000 ÷ Total estimated activity) × Units of activity for 2029.
c. (€11,000 ÷ Total estimated activity) × Units of activity for 2028 and 2029.
d. (€10,000 ÷ Total estimated activity) × Units of activity for 2028 and 2029.

6. (LO 2) Chang Industries purchased a piece of equipment on January 1, 2029. The equipment cost HK$600,000 and has an estimated life of 8 years and a residual value of HK$80,000. What was the depreciation expense for the asset for 2030 under the double-declining-balance method?

a. HK$65,000. **c.** HK$150,000.
b. HK$112,500. **d.** HK$65,620.

7. (LO 2) When there is a change in estimated depreciation:

a. previous depreciation should be corrected.
b. current and future years' depreciation should be revised.
c. only future years' depreciation should be revised.
d. None of the answer choices is correct.

8. (LO 2) Able Towing purchased a tow truck for £60,000 on January 1, 2027. It was originally depreciated on a straight-line basis over 10 years with an assumed residual value of £12,000. On December 31, 2029, before adjusting entries had been made, the company decided to change the remaining estimated life to 4 years (including 2029) and the residual value to £2,000. What was the depreciation expense for 2029?

a. £6,000. **c.** £15,000.
b. £4,800. **d.** £12,100.

9. (LO 2) Wales Remodeling applies revaluation accounting to equipment that is recorded on its books at €800,000, with €100,000 of accumulated depreciation after depreciation for the year recorded. It has determined that the asset is now worth €775,000. The entry to record the revaluation would include a:

a. credit to Equipment of €25,000.
b. debit to Equipment of €75,000.
c. credit to Accumulated Depreciation of €100,000.
d. debit to Revaluation Surplus of €75,000.

10. (LO 3) Bennie Razors has decided to sell one of its old manufacturing machines on June 30, 2029. The machine was purchased for €80,000 on January 1, 2025, and was depreciated on a straight-line basis for 10 years assuming no residual value. If the machine was sold for €26,000, what was the amount of the gain or loss recorded at the time of the sale?

a. €18,000. **c.** €22,000.
b. €54,000. **d.** €46,000.

11. (LO 4) Maggie Sharrer Energy expects to extract 20 million tons of coal from a mine that cost NT$12 million. If no residual value is expected and 2 million tons are mined in the first year, the entry to record depletion will include a:

a. debit to Accumulated Depletion of NT$2,000,000.
b. credit to Depletion Expense of NT$1,200,000.
c. debit to Inventory of NT$1,200,000.
d. credit to Accumulated Depletion of NT$2,000,000.

12. (LO 4) Which of the following statements is **false**?

a. If an intangible asset has a finite life, it should be amortized.
b. The amortization period of an intangible asset can exceed 20 years.
c. Goodwill is recorded only when a business is purchased.
d. Development costs are always expensed when incurred.

13. (LO 5) Indicate which of the following statements is **true**.

a. Since intangible assets lack physical substance, they need be disclosed only in the notes to the financial statements.
b. Goodwill should be reported as a contra account in the equity section.
c. Totals of major classes of assets can be shown in the statement of financial position, with asset details disclosed in the notes to the financial statements.
d. Intangible assets are typically combined with plant assets and extractable natural resources and shown in the property, plant, and equipment section.

14. (LO 5) Tianzi Coffee reported net sales of HK$1,800,000, net income of HK$540,000, beginning total assets of HK$2,000,000, and ending total assets of HK$3,000,000. What was the company's asset turnover?

a. 0.90. **c.** 0.72.
b. 0.20. **d.** 1.39.

*15. **(LO 6)** Schopenhauer NV exchanged an old machine, with a book value of €39,000 and a fair value of €35,000, and paid €10,000 cash for a similar new machine. The transaction has commercial substance. At what amount should the machine acquired in the exchange be recorded on Schopenhauer's books?

a. €45,000. **c.** €49,000.
b. €46,000. **d.** €50,000.

*16. **(LO 6)** In exchanges of assets in which the exchange has commercial substance:

a. neither gains nor losses are recognized immediately.
b. gains, but not losses, are recognized immediately.
c. losses, but not gains, are recognized immediately.
d. both gains and losses are recognized immediately.

Solutions

1. **d.** All of the costs (€1,200 + €200 + €400) in addition to the cash price (€24,000) should be included in the cost of the equipment because they were necessary expenditures to acquire the asset and make it ready for its intended use. The other choices are therefore incorrect.

2. **d.** When an addition is made to plant assets, it is intended to increase productive capacity, increase the assets' useful life, or increase the efficiency of the assets. This is called a capital expenditure. The other choices are incorrect because (a) additions to plant assets are not revenue expenditures because the additions will have a long-term useful life whereas revenue expenditures are minor repairs and maintenance that do not prolong the life of the assets; (b) additions to plant assets are debited to Plant Assets, not Maintenance and Repairs Expense, because the Maintenance and Repairs Expense account is used to record expenditures not intended to increase the life of the assets; and (c) additions to plant assets are debited to Plant Assets, not Purchases, because the Purchases account is used to record assets intended for resale (inventory).

3. **b.** Depreciation is a process of allocating the cost of an asset over its useful life, not a process of (a) valuation, (c) cash accumulation, or (d) appraisal.

4. **d.** Accumulated depreciation will be the sum of 2 years of depreciation expense. Annual depreciation for this asset is (£400,000 − £10,000)/5 = £78,000. The sum of 2 years' depreciation is therefore £156,000 (£78,000 + £78,000), not (a) £80,000, (b) £160,000, or (c) £78,000.

5. **d.** The units-of-activity method takes residual value into consideration; therefore, the depreciable cost is €10,000. This amount is divided by total estimated activity. The resulting number is multiplied by the units of activity used in 2028 and 2029 to compute the accumulated depreciation at the end of 2029, the second year of the asset's use. The other choices are therefore incorrect.

6. **b.** For the double-declining method, the depreciation rate would be 25% or (1/8 × 2). For 2029, annual depreciation expense is HK$150,000 (HK$600,000 book value × 25%); for 2030, annual depreciation expense is HK$112,500 [(HK$600,000 − HK$150,000) × 25%], not (a) HK$65,000, (c) HK$150,000, or (d) HK$65,620.

7. **b.** When there is a change in estimated depreciation, the current and future years' depreciation computation should reflect the new estimates. The other choices are incorrect because (a) previous years' depreciation should not be adjusted when new estimates are made for depreciation, and (c) when there is a change in estimated depreciation, the current and future years' depreciation computation should reflect the new estimates. Choice (d) is wrong because there is a correct answer.

8. **d.** First, calculate accumulated depreciation from January 1, 2027, through December 31, 2028, which is £9,600 [[(£60,000 − £12,000)/10 years] × 2 years]. Next, calculate the revised depreciable cost, which is £48,400 (£60,000 − £9,600 − £2,000). Thus, the depreciation expense for 2029 is £12,100 (£48,400/4), not (a) £6,000, (b) £4,800, or (c) £15,000.

9. **a.** The entry to record the revaluation would include a credit to Equipment of €25,000 (€800,000 − €775,000), as well as a debit (not credit) to Accumulated Depreciation of €100,000 and a credit (not debit) to Revaluation Surplus of €75,000.

10. **a.** First, the book value needs to be determined. The accumulated depreciation as of June 30, 2029, is €36,000 [(€80,000/10) × 4.5 years]. Thus, the cost of the machine less accumulated depreciation equals €44,000 (€80,000 − €36,000). The loss recorded at the time of sale is €18,000 (€26,000 − €44,000), not (b) €54,000, (c) €22,000, or (d) €46,000.

11. **c.** The amount of depletion is determined by computing the depletion per unit (NT$12 million/20 million tons = NT$0.60 per ton) and then multiplying that amount times the number of units extracted during the year (2 million tons × NT$0.60 = NT$1,200,000). This amount is debited to Inventory and credited to Accumulated Depletion. The other choices are therefore incorrect.

12. **d.** Development costs are expensed when incurred until technological feasibility is achieved. After that point, development costs are capitalized. The other choices are true statements.

13. **c.** Reporting only totals of major classes of assets in the statement of financial position is appropriate. Additional details can be shown in the notes to the financial statements. The other choices are false statements.

14. **c.** Asset turnover = Net sales (HK$1,800,000)/Average total assets [(HK$2,000,000 + HK$3,000,000)/2] = 0.72 times, not (a) 0.90, (b) 0.20, or (d) 1.39 times.

*15. **a.** When an exchange has commercial substance, the debit to the new asset is equal to the fair value of the old asset plus the cash paid (€35,000 + €10,000 = €45,000), not (b) €46,000, (c) €49,000, or (d) €50,000.

*16. **d.** Both gains and losses are recognized immediately when an exchange of assets has commercial substance. The other choices are therefore incorrect.

Practice Brief Exercises

Compute straight-line and declining-balance depreciation.

1. **(LO 2)** Fulmer Express acquires a delivery truck at a cost of NT$50,000. The truck is expected to have a residual value of NT$5,000 at the end of its 5-year useful life. Compute annual depreciation expense for the first and second years using (a) the straight-line method and (b) the double-declining-balance method.

Solution

1. **a.** Depreciable cost is NT$45,000 (NT$50,000 − NT$5,000). With a 5-year useful life, annual depreciation is therefore NT$9,000 (NT$45,000 ÷ 5). Under the straight-line method, depreciation is the same each year. Thus, depreciation is NT$9,000 for both the first and second years.

   b. The declining balance rate is 40% (20% × 2), and this rate is applied to book value at the beginning of the year. The computations are:

	Book Value	×	Rate	=	Depreciation
Year 1	NT$50,000		40%		$20,000
Year 2	30,000*		40		12,000

*NT$50,000 − NT$20,000

Prepare entries for disposal by sale.

2. **(LO 3)** Giolito Farming sells equipment on August 31, 2029, for €20,000 cash. The equipment originally cost €60,000 and as of January 1, 2029, had accumulated depreciation of €38,000. Depreciation for the first 8 months of 2029 is €6,000. Prepare the journal entries to (a) update depreciation to August 31, 2029, and (b) record the sale of the equipment.

Solution

		Debit	Credit
2. a.	Depreciation Expense	6,000	
	Accumulated Depreciation—Equipment		6,000
b.	Cash	20,000	
	Accumulated Depreciation—Equipment	44,000	
	Equipment		60,000
	Gain on Disposal of Plant Assets		4,000

Cost of equipment	€60,000
Less: Accumulated depreciation	44,000*
Book value at date of disposal	16,000
Proceeds from sale	20,000
Gain on disposal	€ 4,000

*€38,000 + €6,000

Prepare entries for franchise.

3. **(LO 4)** Snow Restaurants acquires a limited-life franchise for ¥200,000 on January 2, 2029 (amounts in thousands). Its estimated useful life is 10 years. (a) Prepare the journal entry to record amortization expense for the first year. (b) Show how this franchise is reported on the statement of financial position at the end of the first year.

Solution

		Debit	Credit
3. a.	Amortization Expense (¥200,000 ÷ 10)	20,000	
	Franchises		20,000
b.	Intangible assets		
	Franchises		¥180,000

Practice Exercises

Determine depreciation for partial periods.

1. **(LO 2)** Winston Printing purchased a new machine on October 1, 2029, at a cost of £120,000. The company estimated that the machine will have a residual value of £12,000. The machine is expected to be used for 12,000 working hours during its 4-year life.

Instructions

Compute the depreciation expense under the following methods for the year indicated.

a. Straight-line for 2029.

b. Units-of-activity for 2029, assuming machine usage was 1,700 hours.

c. Declining-balance using double the straight-line rate for 2029 and 2030.

Solution

1. **a.** Straight-line method:

$$\left(\frac{£120{,}000 - £12{,}000}{4}\right) = £27{,}000 \text{ per year}$$

2029 depreciation = £27,000 × 3/12 = £6,750

b. Units-of-activity method:

$$\left(\frac{£120{,}000 - £12{,}000}{12{,}000}\right) = £9 \text{ per hour}$$

2029 depreciation = 1,700 hours × £9 = £15,300

c. Declining-balance method:

2029 depreciation = £120,000 × 50% × 3/12 = £15,000

Book value January 1, 2030 = £120,000 − £15,000 = £105,000

2030 depreciation = £105,000 × 50% = £52,500

2. **(LO 4)** Sun Moon Chemical, organized in 2029, has the following transactions related to intangible assets.

Prepare entries to set up appropriate accounts for different intangibles; amortize intangible assets.

1/2/29	Purchased patent (8-year life)	NT$560,000
4/1/29	Goodwill purchased (indefinite life)	360,000
7/1/29	10-year franchise; expiration date 7/1/2039	440,000
9/1/29	Research and development costs	185,000

Instructions

Prepare the necessary entries to record these intangibles. All costs incurred were for cash. Make the adjusting entries as of December 31, 2029, recording any necessary amortization and reflecting all balances accurately as of that date. Assume all development costs were incurred prior to technological feasibility.

Solution

2. 1/2/29	Patents	560,000	
	Cash		560,000
4/1/29	Goodwill	360,000	
	Cash		360,000
	(Part of the entry to record purchase of another company)		
7/1/29	Franchises	440,000	
	Cash		440,000
9/1/29	Research and Development Expense	185,000	
	Cash		185,000
12/31/29	Amortization Expense (NT$560,000 ÷ 8) + [(NT$440,000 ÷ 10) × 1/2]	92,000	
	Patents		70,000
	Franchises		22,000

Ending balances, 12/31/29:

Patents = NT$490,000 (NT$560,000 − NT$70,000)

Goodwill = NT$360,000

Franchises = NT$418,000 (NT$440,000 − NT$22,000)

Research and development expense = NT$185,000

Practice Problem

Compute depreciation under different methods.

1. **(LO 2)** DuPage Manufacturing purchases a factory machine at a cost of €18,000 on January 1, 2029. DuPage expects the machine to have a residual value of €2,000 at the end of its 4-year useful life.

During its useful life, the machine is expected to be used 160,000 hours. Actual annual hourly use was 2029, 40,000; 2030, 60,000; 2031, 35,000; and 2032, 25,000.

Instructions

Prepare depreciation schedules for the following methods: (a) straight-line, (b) units-of-activity, and (c) declining-balance using double the straight-line rate.

Solution

1. a.

Straight-Line Method

	Computation				Annual	End of Year	
Year	**Depreciable Cost***	×	**Depreciation Rate**	=	**Depreciation Expense**	**Accumulated Depreciation**	**Book Value**
2029	€16,000		25%		€4,000	€ 4,000	€14,000**
2030	16,000		25%		4,000	8,000	10,000
2031	16,000		25%		4,000	12,000	6,000
2032	16,000		25%		4,000	16,000	2,000

*€18,000 – €2,000.
**€18,000 – €4,000.

b.

Units-of-Activity Method

	Computation				Annual	End of Year	
Year	**Units of Activity**	×	**Depreciable Cost/Unit**	=	**Depreciation Expense**	**Accumulated Depreciation**	**Book Value**
2029	40,000		€0.10*		€4,000	€ 4,000	€14,000
2030	60,000		0.10		6,000	10,000	8,000
2031	35,000		0.10		3,500	13,500	4,500
2032	25,000		0.10		2,500	16,000	2,000

*(€18,000 – €2,000) ÷ 160,000.

c.

Declining-Balance Method

	Computation				Annual	End of Year	
Year	**Book Value Beginning of Year**	×	**Depreciation Rate***	=	**Depreciation Expense**	**Accumulated Depreciation**	**Book Value**
2029	€18,000		50%		€9,000	€ 9,000	€9,000
2030	9,000		50%		4,500	13,500	4,500
2031	4,500		50%		2,250	15,750	2,250
2032	2,250		50%		250**	16,000	2,000

*¼ × 2.
**Adjusted to €250 because ending book value should not be less than expected residual value.

Record disposal of plant asset.

2. **(LO 3)** On January 1, 2029, Hong Kong International Airport Limousine purchased a limo at an acquisition cost of HK$280,000. The vehicle has been depreciated by the straight-line method using a 4-year service life and a HK$40,000 residual value. The company's fiscal year ends on December 31.

Instructions

Prepare the journal entry or entries to record the disposal of the limousine assuming that it was:

a. Retired and scrapped on January 1, 2033.

b. Sold for HK$50,000 on July 1, 2032.

Solution

2. **a.** 1/1/33	Accumulated Depreciation—Equipment	240,000	
	Loss on Disposal of Plant Assets	40,000	
	Equipment		280,000
	(To record retirement of limousine)		
b. 7/1/32	Depreciation Expense*	30,000	
	Accumulated Depreciation—Equipment		30,000
	(To record depreciation to date of disposal)		
	Cash	50,000	
	Accumulated Depreciation—Equipment**	210,000	
	Loss on Disposal of Plant Assets	20,000	
	Equipment		280,000
	(To record sale of limousine)		

*[(HK$280,000 − HK$40,000) ÷ 4] × ½.
**[(HK$280,000 − HK$40,000) ÷ 4] × 3 = HK$180,000; HK$180,000 + HK$30,000.

Note: Asterisked Questions, Exercises, and Problems relate to material in the appendix to the chapter.

Questions

1. Rick Baden is uncertain about the applicability of the historical cost basis to plant assets. Explain the principle to Rick.

2. What are some examples of land improvements?

3. Lexa Company acquires the land and building owned by Malta Company. What types of costs may be incurred to make the asset ready for its intended use if Lexa Company wants to use (a) only the land, and (b) both the land and the building?

4. Distinguish between revenue expenditures and capital expenditures during an asset's useful life.

5. In a recent newspaper release, the president of Wanzo OAO asserted that something has to be done about depreciation. The president said, "Depreciation does not come close to accumulating the cash needed to replace the asset at the end of its useful life." What is your response to the president?

6. Jeremy is studying for the next accounting examination. He asks your help on two questions: (a) What is residual value? (b) Is residual value used in determining periodic depreciation under each depreciation method? Answer Jeremy's questions.

7. Contrast the straight-line method and the units-of-activity method as to (a) useful life, and (b) the pattern of periodic depreciation over useful life.

8. Contrast the effects of the three depreciation methods on annual depreciation expense.

9. What is component depreciation, and when must it be used?

10. In the fourth year of an asset's 5-year useful life, the company decides that the asset will have a 6-year service life. How should the revision of depreciation be recorded? Why?

11. What is revaluation of plant assets? When should revaluation be applied?

12. How is a gain or loss on the sale of a plant asset computed?

13. Luis Cycles owns a machine that is fully depreciated but is still being used. How should Luis account for this asset and report it in the financial statements?

14. What are extractable natural resources, and what are their distinguishing characteristics?

15. Explain the concept of depletion and how it is computed.

16. What are the similarities and differences between the terms depreciation, depletion, and amortization?

17. Spectrum Pharmaceuticals hires an accounting intern who says that intangible assets should always be amortized over their legal lives. Is the intern correct? Explain.

18. Goodwill has been defined as the value of all favorable attributes that relate to a business. What types of attributes could result in goodwill?

19. Mark Gannon, a business major, is working on a case problem for one of his classes. In the case problem, the company needs to raise cash to market a new product it developed. Sara Bates, an engineering major, takes one look at the company's statement of financial position and says, "This company has an awful lot of goodwill. Why don't you recommend that it sell some of it to raise cash?" How should Mark respond to Sara?

20. Under what conditions is goodwill recorded?

21. Often, research and development costs provide companies with benefits that last a number of years. (For example, these costs can lead to the development of a patent that will increase the company's income for many years.) However, IFRS requires that many such costs be recorded as an expense when incurred. Why?

22. Some product development expenditures are recorded as research and development expenses, and others as development costs. Explain the difference between these accounts, and how a company decides which classification is appropriate.

23. **McDonald's Corporation** (USA) reports total average assets of $28.9 billion and net sales of $20.5 billion. What is the company's asset turnover?

24. Alpha SE and Zito SE operate in the same industry. Alpha uses the straight-line method to account for depreciation; Zito uses an accelerated method. Explain what complications might arise in trying to compare the results of these two companies.

25. Wanzo ASA uses straight-line depreciation for financial reporting purposes but an accelerated method for tax purposes. Is it acceptable to use different methods for the two purposes? What is Wanzo's motivation for doing this?

26. You are comparing two companies in the same industry. You have determined that Lam Ltd. depreciates its plant assets over a 40-year life, whereas Shuey Ltd. depreciates its plant assets over a 20-year life. Discuss the implications this has for comparing the results of the two companies.

27. Zelm Company is doing significant work to revitalize its warehouses. It is not sure whether it should capitalize these costs or expense them. What are the implications for current-year net income and future net income of expensing versus capitalizing these costs?

*28. When assets are exchanged in a transaction involving commercial substance, how is the gain or loss on disposal of plant assets computed?

*29. Morris Refrigeration Company trades in an old machine on a new model when the fair value of the old machine is greater than its book value. The transaction has commercial substance. Should Morris recognize a gain on disposal of plant assets? If the fair value of the old machine is less than its book value, should Morris recognize a loss on disposal of plant assets?

Brief Exercises

Determine the cost of land.

BE9.1 (LO 1) The following expenditures were incurred by Rosenberg Construction in purchasing land: cash price €64,000, accrued taxes €3,000, attorneys' fees €2,500, real estate broker's commission €2,000, and clearing and grading €4,400. What is the cost of the land?

Determine the cost of a truck.

BE9.2 (LO 1) Jawson Repairs incurs the following expenditures in purchasing a truck: cash price £30,000, accident insurance £2,000, sales taxes £1,800, motor vehicle license £160, and painting and lettering £400. What is the cost of the truck?

Prepare entries for delivery truck costs.

BE9.3 (LO 1) Tong Pizza had the following two transactions related to its delivery truck.

1. Paid €45 for an oil change.
2. Paid €580 to install special gear unit, which increases the operating efficiency of the truck.

Prepare Tong's journal entries to record these two transactions.

Compute straight-line depreciation.

BE9.4 (LO 2) Weller Express acquires a delivery truck at a cost of €42,000. The truck is expected to have a residual value of €9,000 at the end of its 5-year useful life. Compute annual depreciation expense for the first and second years using the straight-line method.

Compute depreciation and evaluate treatment.

BE9.5 (LO 2) Kowloon Group purchased land and a building on January 1, 2029. Management's best estimate of the value of the land was HK$1,000,000 and of the building HK$2,000,000. However, management told the accounting department to record the land at HK$2,250,000 and the building at HK$750,000. The building is being depreciated on a straight-line basis over 20 years with no residual value. Why do you suppose management requested this accounting treatment? Is it ethical?

Compute declining-balance depreciation.

BE9.6 (LO 2) Depreciation information for Weller Express is given in BE9.4. Assuming the declining-balance depreciation rate is double the straight-line rate, compute annual depreciation for the first and second years under the declining-balance method.

Compute depreciation using the units-of-activity method.

BE9.7 (LO 2) Freemont Taxi Service uses the units-of-activity method in computing depreciation on its taxicabs. Each cab is expected to be driven 150,000 miles. Taxi no. 10 cost €33,500 and is expected to have a residual value of €500. Taxi no. 10 is driven 36,000 miles in year 1 and 22,000 miles in year 2. Compute the depreciation for each year.

Compute depreciation using component method.

BE9.8 (LO 2) Mandall Ltd. constructed a warehouse for £280,000. Mandall estimates that the warehouse has a useful life of 20 years and no residual value. Construction records indicate that £40,000 of the cost of the warehouse relates to its heating, ventilation, and air conditioning (HVAC) system, which has an estimated useful life of only 8 years. Compute the first year of depreciation expense using straight-line component depreciation.

Compute revised depreciation.

BE9.9 (LO 2) On January 1, 2029, the Vasquez SA ledger shows Equipment €32,000 and Accumulated Depreciation—Equipment €9,000. The depreciation resulted from using the straight-line method with a useful life of 10 years and residual value of €2,000. On this date, the company concludes that the equipment has a remaining useful life of only 4 years with the same residual value. Compute the revised annual depreciation.

BE9.10 (LO 2) At the end of its first year of operations, Brianna Industries chose to use the revaluation framework allowed under IFRS. Brianna's ledger shows Equipment £480,000 and Accumulated Depreciation—Equipment £60,000. Prepare journal entries to record the following.

Prepare entries for revaluation of plant assets.

a. Independent appraisers determine that the plant assets have a fair value of £468,000.

b. Independent appraisers determine that the plant assets have a fair value of £400,000.

BE9.11 (LO 3) Prepare journal entries to record the following.

Prepare entries for disposal by retirement.

a. Matterhorn AG retires its delivery equipment, which cost CHF44,000. Accumulated depreciation is also CHF44,000 on this delivery equipment. No residual value is received.

b. Assume the same information as (a), except that accumulated depreciation is CHF37,000, instead of CHF44,000, on the delivery equipment.

BE9.12 (LO 3) Arma Ltd. sells equipment on September 30, 2029, for £20,000 cash. The equipment originally cost £72,000 and as of January 1, 2029, had accumulated depreciation of £42,000. Depreciation for the first 9 months of 2029 is £4,800. Prepare the journal entries to (a) update depreciation to September 30, 2029, and (b) record the sale of the equipment.

Prepare entries for disposal by sale.

BE9.13 (LO 4) Jackie Chan Mining purchased for ¥7 million a mine that is estimated to have 28 million tons of ore and no residual value. In the first year, 4.7 million tons of ore are extracted.

Prepare depletion entry and statement of financial position presentation for natural resources.

a. Prepare the journal entry to record depletion for the first year.

b. Show how this mine is reported on the statement of financial position at the end of the first year.

BE9.14 (LO 4) Felipe Engineering purchases a patent for R$120,000 on January 2, 2029. Its estimated useful life is 8 years.

Prepare amortization expense entry and statement of financial position presentation for intangibles.

a. Prepare the journal entry to record amortization expense for the first year.

b. Show how this patent is reported on the statement of financial position at the end of the first year.

BE9.15 (LO 4) Newell Industries spent €260,000 on research and €600,000 on development of a new product. Of the €600,000 in development costs, €400,000 was incurred prior to technological feasibility and €200,000 after technological feasibility had been demonstrated. Prepare the journal entry to record research and development costs.

Prepare entry for research and development costs.

BE9.16 (LO 5) Information related to plant assets, extractable natural resources, and intangibles at the end of 2029 for Loomis Energy is as follows: buildings £1,300,000, accumulated depreciation—buildings £650,000, goodwill £410,000, coal mine £500,000, and accumulated depletion—coal mine £122,000. Prepare a partial statement of financial position of Loomis Energy for these items.

Classify long-lived assets on statement of financial position.

BE9.17 (LO 5) In a recent annual report, **Target** (USA) reported beginning total assets of $48.2 billion; ending total assets of $44.6 billion; and net sales of $72.6 billion. Compute Target's asset turnover.

Analyze long-lived assets.

***BE9.18 (LO 6)** Cordero Shipping exchanges old delivery equipment for new delivery equipment. The book value of the old delivery equipment is €33,000 (cost €61,000 less accumulated depreciation €28,000). Its fair value is €19,000, and cash of €5,000 is paid. Prepare the entry to record the exchange, assuming the transaction has commercial substance.

Prepare entry for disposal by exchange.

***BE9.19 (LO 6)** Assume the same information as BE9.18, except that the fair value of the old delivery equipment is €37,200. Prepare the entry to record the exchange.

Prepare entry for disposal by exchange.

DO IT! Exercises

DO IT! 9.1 (LO 1) Yockey HVAC purchased a delivery truck. The total cash payment was £28,220 including the following items.

Explain accounting for cost of plant assets.

Negotiated purchase price	£24,000
Installation of special shelving	1,200
Painting and lettering	780
Motor vehicle license	140
Annual insurance policy	800
Sales tax	1,300
Total paid	£28,220

Explain how each of these costs would be accounted for.

Calculate depreciation expense and make journal entry.

DO IT! 9.2a (LO 2) On January 1, 2029, Rolling Hills Country Club purchased a new riding mower for £18,000. The mower is expected to have an 8-year life with a £2,000 residual value. What journal entry would Rolling Hills make at December 31, 2029, if it uses straight-line depreciation?

Calculate revised depreciation.

DO IT! 9.2b (LO 2) Savin NV purchased a piece of equipment for €50,000. It estimated a 5-year life and €2,000 residual value. At the end of year four (before the depreciation adjustment), it estimated the new total life to be 8 years and the new residual value to be €4,000. Compute the revised depreciation.

Make journal entries to record plant asset disposal.

DO IT! 9.3 (LO 3) Forgetta Manufacturing has old equipment that cost €48,000. The equipment has accumulated depreciation of €28,000. Forgetta has decided to sell the equipment.

a. What entry would Forgetta make to record the sale of the equipment for €26,000 cash?

b. What entry would Forgetta make to record the sale of the equipment for €15,000 cash?

Match intangibles classifications concepts.

DO IT! 9.4 (LO 4) Match the statement with the term most directly associated with it.

a. Goodwill | **d.** Amortization
b. Intangible assets | **e.** Franchises
c. Development expenses | **f.** Development costs

1. ______ Rights, privileges, and competitive advantages that result from the ownership of long-lived assets that do not possess physical substance.
2. ______ The allocation of the cost of an intangible asset to expense in a systematic manner.
3. ______ A right to sell certain products or services, or use certain trademarks or trade names within a designated geographic area.
4. ______ Costs incurred after technological feasibility to complete the development of a new product.
5. ______ The excess of the cost of a company over the fair value of the net assets acquired.
6. ______ Costs incurred after research to bring a new product to a state of technological feasibility.

Calculate asset turnover.

DO IT! 9.5 (LO 5) For 2029, Sale Company reported beginning total assets of $300,000 and ending total assets of $340,000. Its net income for this period was $50,000, and its net sales were $400,000. Compute the company's asset turnover for 2029.

Exercises

Determine cost of plant acquisitions.

E9.1 (LO 1) **Writing** The following expenditures (in thousands) relating to plant assets were made by Lee Jung Ltd. during the first 2 months of 2029.

1. Paid ₩5,000 of accrued taxes at time plant site was acquired.
2. Paid ₩400 insurance to cover possible accident loss on new factory machinery while the machinery was in transit.
3. Paid ₩850 sales taxes on new delivery truck.
4. Paid ₩17,500 for parking lots and driveways on new plant site.
5. Paid ₩310 to have company name and advertising slogan painted on new delivery truck.
6. Paid ₩8,000 for installation of new factory machinery.
7. Paid ₩900 for one-year accident insurance policy on new delivery truck.
8. Paid ₩90 motor vehicle license fee on the new truck.

Instructions

a. Explain the application of the historical cost basis in determining the acquisition cost of plant assets.

b. List the numbers of the foregoing transactions, and opposite each indicate the account title to which each expenditure should be debited.

E9.2 (LO 1) Bliesmer Electronics incurred the following costs.

Determine property, plant, and equipment costs.

1. Sales tax on factory machinery purchased	€ 5,000
2. Painting of and lettering on truck immediately upon purchase	700
3. Installation and testing of factory machinery	2,000
4. Real estate broker's commission on land purchased	3,500
5. Insurance premium paid for first year's insurance on new truck	1,100
6. Cost of landscaping on property purchased	7,200
7. Cost of paving parking lot for new building constructed	17,900
8. Cost of clearing, draining, and filling land	12,600
9. Architect's fees on self-constructed building	10,000

Instructions

Indicate to which account Bliesmer would debit each of the costs.

E9.3 (LO 1) On March 1, 2029, Rollinger Group acquired real estate on which it planned to construct a small office building. The company paid €86,000 in cash. An old warehouse on the property was razed at a cost of €9,400; the salvaged materials were sold for €1,700. Additional expenditures before construction began included €1,100 attorney's fee for work concerning the land purchase, €5,100 real estate broker's fee, €7,800 architect's fee, and €12,700 to put in driveways and a parking lot.

Determine acquisition costs of land.

Instructions

a. Determine the amount to be reported as the cost of the land.

b. For each cost not used in part (a), indicate the account to be debited.

E9.4 (LO 2) Ann Tremel has prepared the following list of statements about depreciation.

Understand depreciation concepts.

1. Depreciation is a process of asset valuation, not cost allocation.
2. Depreciation provides for the proper matching of expenses with revenues.
3. The book value of a plant asset should approximate its fair value.
4. Depreciation applies to three classes of plant assets: land, buildings, and equipment.
5. Depreciation does not apply to a building because its usefulness and revenue-producing ability generally remain intact over time.
6. The revenue-producing ability of a depreciable asset will decline due to wear and tear and to obsolescence.
7. Recognizing depreciation on an asset results in an accumulation of cash for replacement of the asset.
8. The balance in accumulated depreciation represents the total cost that has been charged to expense.
9. Depreciation expense and accumulated depreciation are reported on the income statement.
10. Three factors affect the computation of depreciation: cost, useful life, and residual value.

Instructions

Identify each statement as true or false. If false, indicate how to correct the statement.

E9.5 (LO 2) Copacabana Bus Lines uses the units-of-activity method in depreciating its buses. One bus was purchased on January 1, 2029, at a cost of R$145,000. Over its 4-year useful life, the bus is expected to be driven 100,000 miles. Residual value is expected to be R$15,000.

Compute depreciation under units-of-activity method.

Instructions

a. Compute the depreciable cost per unit.

b. Prepare a depreciation schedule assuming actual mileage was 2029, 27,000; 2030, 32,000; 2031, 24,000; and 2032, 17,000.

E9.6 (LO 2) Rottino Company purchased a new machine on October 1, 2029, at a cost of $150,000. The company estimated that the machine will have a residual value of $12,000. The machine is expected to be used for 10,000 working hours during its 5-year life.

Determine depreciation for partial periods.

Instructions

Compute the depreciation expense under the following methods for the year indicated.

a. Straight-line for 2029.

b. Units-of-activity for 2029, assuming machine usage was 1,700 hours.

c. Declining-balance using double the straight-line rate for 2029 and 2030.

Compute depreciation using different methods.

E9.7 (LO 2) Tanger Interiors purchased a delivery truck for R$38,000 on January 1, 2029. The truck has an expected residual value of R$6,000, and is expected to be driven 100,000 miles over its estimated useful life of 8 years. Actual miles driven were 15,000 in 2029 and 12,000 in 2030.

Instructions

a. Compute depreciation expense for 2029 and 2030 using (1) the straight-line method, (2) the units-of-activity method, and (3) the double-declining-balance method.

b. Assume that Tanger uses the straight-line method.

1. Prepare the journal entry to record 2029 depreciation.
2. Show how the truck would be reported in the December 31, 2029, statement of financial position.

Compute depreciation under component method.

E9.8 (LO 2) Mooney Ltd. completed construction of an office building for £2,400,000 on December 31, 2028. The company estimated that the building would have a residual value of £0 and a useful life of 40 years. A more detailed review of the expenditures related to the building indicates that £300,000 of the total cost was used for personal property and £180,000 for land improvements. The personal property has a depreciable life of 5 years and land improvements have a depreciable life of 10 years.

Instructions

Compute depreciation expense for 2029 using component depreciation and the straight-line method.

Compute revised annual depreciation.

E9.9 (LO 2) Steve Grant, the new controller of Greenbriar Ltd., has reviewed the expected useful lives and residual values of selected depreciable assets at the beginning of 2029. His findings are as follows.

Type of Asset	Date Acquired	Cost	Accumulated Depreciation 1/1/29	Total Useful Life in Years Old	Total Useful Life in Years Proposed	Residual Value Old	Residual Value Proposed
Building	1/1/19	£800,000	£190,000	40	50	£40,000	£18,000
Warehouse	1/1/24	100,000	18,000	25	20	10,000	3,700

All assets are depreciated by the straight-line method. Greenbriar uses a calendar year in preparing annual financial statements. After discussion, management has agreed to accept Grant's proposed changes.

Instructions

a. Compute the revised annual depreciation on each asset in 2029. (Show computations.)

b. Prepare the entry (or entries) to record depreciation on the building in 2029.

Journalize entries for straight-line depreciation and revaluation.

E9.10 (LO 2) Barton Enterprises purchased equipment on January 1, 2029, at a cost of €350,000. Barton uses the straight-line depreciation method, a 5-year estimated useful life, and no residual value. At the end of 2029, independent appraisers determined that the assets have a fair value of €320,000.

Instructions

a. Prepare the journal entry to record 2029 depreciation using the straight-line method.

b. Prepare the journal entry to record the revaluation of the equipment.

c. Prepare the journal entry to record 2030 depreciation, assuming no additional revaluation.

Journalize entries for straight-line depreciation and revaluation.

E9.11 (LO 2) At December 31, 2029, the end of its first year of operations, Franklin SA chose to use the revaluation framework allowed under IFRS. Franklin's ledger shows Equipment €750,000 and Accumulated Depreciation—Equipment €150,000.

Instructions

a. Independent appraisers determine that the plant assets have a fair value of €660,000. Record the revaluation.

b. Using your answer from part (a), what would be the amount of Franklin's 2030 depreciation? Assume no change in the value of Franklin's equipment in 2030, a 4-year remaining life, and no residual value.

c. Independent appraisers determine that the plant assets have a fair value of €520,000. Record the revaluation. (Ignore your answers to parts (a) and (b).)

d. Using your answer from part (c), what would be the amount of Franklin's 2030 depreciation? Assume no change in the value of Franklin's equipment in 2030, a 4-year remaining life, and no residual value.

E9.12 (LO 3) Presented below are selected transactions at Ingles Company for 2029.

Journalize entries for disposal of plant assets.

Jan. 1	Retired a piece of machinery that was purchased on January 1, 2019. The machine cost £58,000 on that date. It had a useful life of 10 years with no residual value.
June 30	Sold a computer that was purchased on January 1, 2026. The computer cost £40,000. It had a useful life of 5 years with no residual value. The computer was sold for £14,600.
Dec. 31	Discarded a delivery truck that was purchased on January 1, 2025. The truck cost £34,000. It was depreciated based on a 6-year useful life with a £4,000 residual value.

Instructions

Journalize all entries required on the above dates, including entries to update depreciation, where applicable, on assets disposed of. Ingles Company uses straight-line depreciation. (Assume depreciation is up to date as of December 31, 2028.)

E9.13 (LO 3) Pryce Company owns equipment that cost $65,000 when purchased on January 1, 2026. It has been depreciated using the straight-line method based on an estimated residual value of $5,000 and an estimated useful life of 5 years.

Journalize entries for disposal of equipment.

Instructions

Prepare Pryce Company's journal entries to record the sale of the equipment in these four independent situations.

a. Sold for $31,000 on January 1, 2029.

b. Sold for $31,000 on May 1, 2029.

c. Sold for $11,000 on January 1, 2029.

d. Sold for $11,000 on October 1, 2029.

E9.14 (LO 4) On July 1, 2029, Ticino AG invested CHF736,000 in a mine estimated to have 800,000 tons of ore of uniform grade. During the last 6 months of 2029, 124,000 tons of ore were mined.

Journalize entries for natural resources depletion.

Instructions

a. Prepare the journal entry to record depletion.

b. Assume that the 124,000 tons of ore were mined, but only 90,000 units were sold. How are the costs applicable to the 34,000 unsold units reported?

E9.15 (LO 4) The following are selected 2029 transactions of Yosuke Ltd.

Prepare adjusting entries for amortization.

Jan. 1	Purchased a small company and recorded goodwill of €150,000. Its useful life is indefinite.
May 1	Purchased for €84,000 a patent with an estimated useful life of 5 years and a legal life of 20 years.

Instructions

Prepare necessary adjusting entries at December 31 to record amortization required by the events above.

E9.16 (LO 4) Nelson Company, organized in 2029, has the following transactions related to intangible assets.

Prepare entries to set up appropriate accounts for different intangibles; amortize intangible assets.

1/2/29	Purchased patent (7-year life)	$560,000
4/1/29	Goodwill purchased (indefinite life)	360,000
7/1/29	8-year franchise; expiration date 7/1/2037	440,000
11/1/29	Research and development costs incurred prior to technological feasibility	448,000

Instructions

Prepare the necessary entries to record these intangibles. All costs incurred were for cash. Make the adjusting entries as of December 31, 2029, recording any necessary amortization and reflecting all balances accurately as of that date.

Identify key terms.

E9.17 (LO 1, 2, 3, 4) The following is a list of words or phrases introduced in the chapter.

1. Capital expenditures.
2. Goodwill.
3. Plant assets.
4. Patent.
5. Copyright.
6. Impairment.
7. Accelerated-depreciation method.
8. Intangible assets.
9. Declining-balance method.
10. Amortization.
11. Trademark (trade name).
12. Ordinary repairs.
13. Units-of-activity method.

Instructions

Match the word or phrase above with its description below.

a. ______ Any depreciation method that produces higher depreciation expense in the early years than the straight-line approach.

b. ______ The process of allocating to expense the cost of an intangible asset.

c. ______ Expenditures that increase the company's investment in plant assets.

d. ______ A depreciation method that applies a constant rate to the declining book value of the asset and produces a decreasing annual depreciation expense over the asset's useful life.

e. ______ A permanent decline in the fair value of an asset.

f. ______ Rights, privileges, and competitive advantages that result from the ownership of long-lived assets that do not possess physical substance.

g. ______ Expenditures to maintain the operating efficiency and expected productive life of the asset.

h. ______ Resources that have physical substance, are used in the operations of a business, and are not intended for sale to customers.

i. ______ A depreciation method in which useful life is expressed in terms of the total units of production or use expected from the asset.

j. ______ An exclusive right granted by the government allowing the owner to reproduce and sell an artistic or published work.

k. ______ A word, phrase, jingle, or symbol that distinguishes or identifies a particular enterprise or product.

l. ______ An exclusive right issued by the Patent Office that enables the recipient to manufacture, sell, or otherwise control an invention for a period of 20 years from the date of the grant.

m. ______ The value of all favorable attributes that relate to a company that are not attributable to any other specific asset.

Calculate asset turnover.

E9.18 (LO 5) During 2029, Otaki Cellular reported net sales of €5,200,000 and net income of €1,500,000. Its statement of financial position reported average total assets of €1,600,000.

Instructions

Calculate the asset turnover.

Journalize entries for exchanges.

***E9.19 (LO 6)** Presented below are two independent transactions. Both transactions have commercial substance.

1. Global Co. exchanged old trucks (cost £64,000 less £22,000 accumulated depreciation) plus cash of £17,000 for new trucks. The old trucks had a fair value of £37,400.
2. Rijo Ltd. trades its used machine (cost £12,000 less £4,000 accumulated depreciation) for a new machine. In addition to exchanging the old machine (which had a fair value of £9,000), Rijo also paid cash of £3,200.

Instructions

a. Prepare the entry to record the exchange of assets by Global Co.

b. Prepare the entry to record the exchange of assets by Rijo Ltd.

Journalize entries for the exchange of plant assets.

***E9.20 (LO 6)** Jay's Delivery Company and Astro's Express Delivery exchanged delivery trucks on January 1, 2029. Jay's truck cost €22,000. It has accumulated depreciation of €16,000 and a fair value of €4,000. Astro's truck cost €10,000. It has accumulated depreciation of €7,000 and a fair value of €4,000. The transaction has commercial substance.

Instructions

a. Journalize the exchange for Jay's Delivery Company.

b. Journalize the exchange for Astro's Express Delivery.

Problems

Determine acquisition costs of land and building.

P9.1 (LO 1) Peete Company was organized on January 1. During the first year of operations, the following plant asset expenditures and receipts were recorded in random order.

	Debit
1. Excavation costs for new building	$ 23,000
2. Architect's fees on building plans	33,000
3. Full payment to building contractor	640,000
4. Cost of real estate purchased as a plant site	280,000
5. Cost of parking lots and driveways	29,000
6. Accrued real estate taxes paid at time of purchase of land	3,170
7. Installation cost of fences around property	6,800
8. Cost of demolishing building to make land suitable for construction of new building	31,000
9. Real estate taxes paid for the current year on land	6,400
	$1,052,370
	Credit
10. Proceeds from salvage of demolished building	$ 12,000

Instructions

Analyze the transactions using the following table column headings. Enter the number of each transaction in the Item column, and enter the amounts in the appropriate columns. For amounts in the Other Accounts column, also indicate the account title.

Item	Land	Buildings	Other Accounts

Land $302,170

Compute depreciation under different methods.

P9.2 (LO 2) In recent years, Freeman Transportation purchased three used buses. Because of frequent turnover in the accounting department, a different accountant selected the depreciation method for each bus, and various methods were selected. Information concerning the buses is summarized below.

Bus	Acquired	Cost	Residual Value	Useful Life in Years	Depreciation Method
1	1/1/27	£ 96,000	£ 6,000	5	Straight-line
2	1/1/27	140,000	10,000	4	Declining-balance
3	1/1/28	92,000	8,000	5	Units-of-activity

For the declining-balance method, the company uses the double-declining rate. For the units-of-activity method, total miles are expected to be 120,000. Actual miles of use in the first 2 years were 24,000 miles in 2028 and 36,000 miles in 2029.

Instructions

a. Compute the amount of accumulated depreciation on each bus at December 31, 2029.

b. If Bus 2 was purchased on April 1 instead of January 1, what is the depreciation expense for this bus in (1) 2027 and (2) 2028?

a. Bus 2, 12/31/28, £105,000

Compute depreciation under different methods.

P9.3 (LO 2) On January 1, 2029, Pele Industries purchased the following two machines for use in its production process.

Machine A: The cash price of this machine was R$35,000. Related expenditures included: sales tax R$2,200, shipping costs R$150, insurance during shipping R$80, installation and testing costs R$70, and R$100 of oil and lubricants to be used with the machinery during its first year of operations. Pele estimates that the useful life of the machine is 5 years with a R$5,000 residual value remaining at the end of that time period. Assume that the straight-line method of depreciation is used.

Machine B: The recorded cost of this machine was R$80,000. Pele estimates that the useful life of the machine is 4 years with a R$5,000 residual value remaining at the end of that time period.

Instructions

a. Prepare the following for Machine A.

1. The journal entry to record its purchase on January 1, 2029.
2. The journal entry to record annual depreciation at December 31, 2029.

b. Calculate the amount of depreciation expense that Pele should record for Machine B each year of its useful life under the following assumptions.

b. 2. 2029 DDB depreciation R$40,000

1. Pele uses the straight-line method of depreciation.
2. Pele uses the declining-balance method. The rate used is twice the straight-line rate.
3. Pele uses the units-of-activity method and estimates that the useful life of the machine is 125,000 units. Actual usage is as follows: 2029, 42,000 units; 2030, 37,000 units; 2031, 28,000 units; and 2032, 18,000 units.

c. Which method used to calculate depreciation on Machine B reports the highest amount of depreciation expense in year 1 (2029)? The highest amount in year 4 (2032)? The highest total amount over the 4-year period?

Calculate revisions to depreciation expense.

P9.4 (LO 2) At the beginning of 2027, Mansen Group acquired equipment costing £80,000. It was estimated that this equipment would have a useful life of 6 years and a residual value of £8,000 at that time. The straight-line method of depreciation was considered the most appropriate to use with this type of equipment. Depreciation is to be recorded at the end of each year.

During 2029 (the third year of the equipment's life), the company's engineers reconsidered their expectations, and estimated that the equipment's useful life would probably be 7 years (in total) instead of 6 years. The estimated residual value was not changed at that time. However, during 2032 the estimated residual value was reduced to £4,400.

Instructions

Indicate how much depreciation expense should be recorded each year for this equipment, by completing the following table.

Year	Depreciation Expense	Accumulated Depreciation
2027		
2028		
2029		
2030		
2031		
2032		
2033		

2033 depreciation expense, £11,400

Revising periodic depreciation.

P9.5 (LO 2) At the beginning of 2029, Dahua Company purchased an equipment costing $450,000. The equipment can be used for four years and has residual value of $50,000 at that time. At the beginning of 2031, the reassessment report of company's engineers found that the equipment still can be used for 3 years, and residual value became $40,000.

Instructions

What are the depreciation expense for 2031 at the straight-line method and double-declining-balance method?

Journalize a series of equipment transactions related to purchase, sale, retirement, and depreciation.

P9.6 (LO 2, 3, 5) At December 31, 2028, Jimenez Enterprises reported the following as plant assets.

Land		€ 3,000,000
Buildings	€26,500,000	
Less: Accumulated depreciation—buildings	12,100,000	14,400,000
Equipment	40,000,000	
Less: Accumulated depreciation—equipment	5,000,000	35,000,000
Total plant assets		€52,400,000

During 2029, the following selected cash transactions occurred.

April 1	Purchased land for €2,200,000.
May 1	Sold equipment that cost €750,000 when purchased on January 1, 2025. The equipment was sold for €466,000.
June 1	Sold land purchased on June 1, 2019 for €1,800,000. The land cost €300,000.
July 1	Purchased equipment for €2,450,000.
Dec. 31	Retired equipment that cost €500,000 when purchased on December 31, 2019. No residual value was received.

Instructions

a. Journalize the above transactions. The company uses straight-line depreciation for buildings and equipment. The buildings are estimated to have a 50-year life and no residual value. The equipment is estimated to have a 10-year useful life and no residual value. Update depreciation on assets disposed of at the time of sale or retirement.

b. Record adjusting entries for depreciation for 2029.

c. Prepare the plant assets section of Jimenez's statement of financial position at December 31, 2029.

b. Depreciation Expense—Buildings €530,000; Equipment €3,997,500
c. Total plant assets €51,722,500

P9.7 (LO 3) Yount Towing has equipment that cost €50,000 and that has been depreciated €22,000.

Record disposals.

Instructions

Record the disposal under the following assumptions.

a. It was scrapped as having no value.

b. It was sold for €25,000.

c. It was sold for €31,000.

P9.8 (LO 4, 5) The intangible assets section of Glover Restaurants at December 31, 2028, is presented below.

Prepare entries to record transactions related to acquisition and amortization of intangibles; prepare the intangible assets section.

Patents (£60,000 cost less £6,000 amortization)	£54,000
Franchises (£48,000 cost less £19,200 amortization)	28,800
Total	£82,800

The patent was acquired in January 2028 and has a useful life of 10 years. The franchise was acquired in January 2025 and also has a useful life of 10 years. The following cash transactions may have affected intangible assets during 2029.

Jan. 2	Paid £45,000 legal costs to successfully defend the patent against infringement by another company.
Jan.–June	Developed a new product, incurring £100,000 in research costs and £68,000 in development costs prior to technological feasibility. A patent was granted for the product on July 1. Its useful life is equal to its 20-year legal life.
Sept. 1	Paid £58,000 to an extremely large defensive lineman to appear in commercials advertising the company's products. The commercials will air in September and October.
Oct. 1	Acquired a franchise for £100,000. The franchise has a useful life of 40 years.

Instructions

a. Prepare journal entries to record the transactions above.

b. Prepare journal entries to record the 2029 amortization expense.

c. Prepare the intangible assets section of the statement of financial position at December 31, 2029.

b. Amortization Expense (patents) £11,000 Amortization Expense (franchises) £5,425
c. Total intangible assets £211,375

P9.9 (LO 4) Due to rapid turnover in the accounting department, a number of transactions involving intangible assets were improperly recorded by the Buek Industries in 2029.

Prepare entries to correct errors made in recording and amortizing intangible assets.

1. Buek developed a new manufacturing process, incurring research costs of €97,000 and development costs prior to technological feasibility of €50,000. The company also purchased a patent for €60,000. In early January, Buek capitalized €207,000 as the cost of the patents. Patent amortization expense of €10,350 was recorded based on a 20-year useful life.
2. On July 1, 2029, Buek purchased a small company and as a result acquired goodwill of €80,000. Buek recorded a half-year's amortization in 2029, based on a 50-year life (€800 amortization). The goodwill has an indefinite life.

Research and Develop. Exp. €147,000

Instructions

Prepare all journal entries necessary to correct any errors made during 2029. Assume the books have not yet been closed for 2029.

Calculate and comment on asset turnover.

P9.10 (LO 5) Writing LaPorta Company and Lott Corporation, two corporations of roughly the same size, are both involved in the manufacture of in-line skates. Each company depreciates its plant assets using the straight-line approach. An investigation of their financial statements reveals the following information.

	LaPorta Co.	Lott Corp.
Net income	$ 800,000	$1,000,000
Net sales	1,300,000	1,180,000
Average total assets	2,500,000	2,000,000
Average plant assets	1,800,000	1,000,000

Instructions

a. LaPorta .52 times

a. For each company, calculate the asset turnover.

b. Based on your calculations in part (a), comment on the relative effectiveness of the two companies in using their assets to generate net sales.

Comprehensive Accounting Cycle Review

ACR9 Raymond Construction's trial balance at December 31, 2029, is presented as follows. All 2029 transactions have been recorded except for the items described below.

	Debit	Credit
Cash	£ 28,000	
Accounts Receivable	36,800	
Notes Receivable	10,000	
Interest Receivable	–0–	
Inventory	36,200	
Prepaid Insurance	4,400	
Land	20,000	
Buildings	160,000	
Equipment	60,000	
Patents	8,000	
Allowance for Doubtful Accounts		£ 300
Accumulated Depreciation—Buildings		49,000
Accumulated Depreciation—Equipment		24,000
Accounts Payable		28,300
Income Taxes Payable		–0–
Salaries and Wages Payable		–0–
Unearned Rent Revenue		6,000
Notes Payable (due in 2030)		11,000
Interest Payable		–0–
Notes Payable (due after 2030)		35,000
Share Capital—Ordinary		50,000
Retained Earnings		63,600
Dividends	12,000	
Sales Revenue		910,000
Interest Revenue		–0–
Rent Revenue		–0–
Gain on Disposal of Plant Assets		–0–
Bad Debt Expense	–0–	
Cost of Goods Sold	630,000	

Depreciation Expense	–0–	
Income Tax Expense	–0–	
Insurance Expense	–0–	
Interest Expense	–0–	
Other Operating Expenses	61,800	
Amortization Expense	–0–	
Salaries and Wages Expense	110,000	
Total	£1,177,200	£1,177,200

Unrecorded transactions:

1. On May 1, 2029, Raymond purchased equipment for £13,000 plus sales taxes of £780 (all paid in cash).
2. On July 1, 2029, Raymond sold for £3,500 equipment which originally cost £5,000. Accumulated depreciation on this equipment at January 1, 2029, was £1,800; 2029 depreciation prior to the sale of the equipment was £450.
3. On December 31, 2029, Raymond sold on account £9,400 of inventory that cost £6,600.
4. Raymond estimates that uncollectible accounts receivable at year-end is £4,000.
5. The note receivable is a one-year, 8% note dated April 1, 2029. No interest has been recorded.
6. The balance in prepaid insurance represents payment of a £4,400 6-month premium on October 1, 2029.
7. The building is being depreciated using the straight-line method over 40 years. The residual value is £20,000.
8. The equipment owned prior to this year is being depreciated using the straight-line method over 5 years. The residual value is 10% of cost.
9. The equipment purchased on May 1, 2029, is being depreciated using the straight-line method over 5 years, with a residual value of £1,000.
10. The patent was acquired on January 1, 2029, and has a useful life of 10 years from that date.
11. Unpaid salaries and wages at December 31, 2029, total £2,200.
12. The unearned rent revenue of £6,000 was received on December 1, 2029, for 4 months rent.
13. Both the short-term and long-term notes payable are dated January 1, 2029, and carry a 9% interest rate. All interest is payable in the next 12 months.
14. Income tax expense was £17,000. It was unpaid at December 31.

Instructions

a. Prepare journal entries for the transactions listed above.

b. Prepare a December 31, 2029, adjusted trial balance.

c. Prepare a 2029 income statement and a 2029 retained earnings statement.

d. Prepare a December 31, 2029, classified statement of financial position.

b. Totals £1,228,294

c. Net income £68,256

d. Total assets £271,996

Data Analytics in Action

Using Data Visualization to Analyze Types of Assets

DA9 Data visualization can be used to identify changes in the composition of assets.

Example: Patents are often reported on companies' statements of financial position as intangible assets. For example, consider the following chart, which shows the countries that recently had at least 100,000 patents in force.

Excel

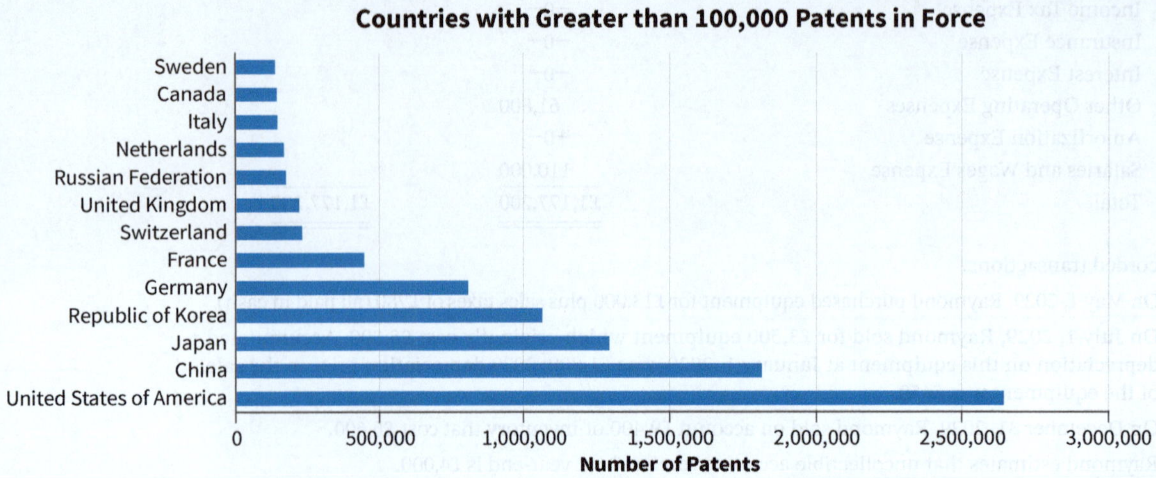

Source: Based on WIPO Statistics Database.

For U.S. companies that have many patents, U.S. accounting standards (GAAP) require the amounts to be valued at historical cost on the companies' statements of financial position (balance sheets). The market value of many of the patents owned by U.S. companies such as **Dropbox**, **Google**, and **Meta Platforms** is therefore much greater than the amount reported on a company's statement of financial position.

For this case, you will use data that shows the U.S. dollar value of intangible assets compared to tangible assets held by S&P 500 companies over the last 45 years. (The S&P 500 companies are a group of the largest 500 companies that trade shares on multiple U.S. exchanges, including the New York Stock Exchange and NASDAQ.) You will create and analyze a stacked column chart to identify trends in the types of assets held by these large U.S. companies over time.

Go to the Wiley online course for complete case details and instructions.

Expand Your Critical Thinking

Financial Reporting Problem: TSMC, Ltd. (TWN)

CT9.1 The financial statements of **TSMC** are presented in Appendix A. The complete annual report, including the notes to the financial statements, is available at the company's website.

Instructions

Refer to TSMC's financial statements and answer the following questions.

a. What was the total cost and book value of property, plant, and equipment at December 31, 2020?

b. What method or methods of depreciation are used by the company for financial reporting purposes?

c. What was the amount of depreciation expense for each of the years 2020 and 2019?

d. Using the statement of cash flows, what is the amount of capital spending in 2020 and 2019?

e. Where does the company disclose its intangible assets, and what types of intangibles did it have at December 31, 2020?

Comparative Analysis Problem: Nestlé SA (CHE) vs. Delfi Limited (SGP)

CT9.2 **Nestlé**'s financial statements are presented in Appendix B. Financial statements of **Delfi Limited** are presented in Appendix C.

Instructions

a. Compute the asset turnover for each company for the most recent fiscal year presented.

b. What conclusions concerning the efficiency of assets can be drawn from these data?

Real-World Focus

CT9.3 Financial statement readers use a company's annual report to identify its plant assets and the depreciation method used.

Instructions

Select a well-known company, do an Internet search by that company name, and then answer the following questions.

a. What is the name of the company?

b. What is the Internet address of the annual report?

c. At fiscal year-end, what is the net amount of its plant assets?

d. What is the accumulated depreciation?

e. Which method of depreciation does the company use?

Decision-Making Across the Organization

CT9.4 Givens Enterprises and Runge Group are two companies that are similar in many respects. One difference is that Givens uses the straight-line method, and Runge uses the declining-balance method at double the straight-line rate. On January 2, 2027, both companies acquired the following depreciable assets.

Asset	Cost	Residual Value	Useful Life
Buildings	£320,000	£20,000	40 years
Equipment	125,000	10,000	10 years

Including the appropriate depreciation charges, annual net income for the companies in the years 2027, 2028, and 2029 and total income for the 3 years were as follows.

	2027	2028	2029	Total
Givens Enterprises	£84,000	£88,400	£90,000	£262,400
Runge Group	68,000	76,000	85,000	229,000

At December 31, 2029, the statements of financial position of the two companies are similar except that Runge has more cash than Givens.

Linda Yanik is interested in buying one of the companies. She comes to you for advice.

Instructions

With the class divided into groups, answer the following.

a. Determine the annual and total depreciation recorded by each company during the 3 years.

b. Assuming that Runge also uses the straight-line method of depreciation instead of the declining-balance method as in (a), prepare comparative income data for the 3 years.

c. Which company should Linda Yanik buy? Why?

Communication Activity

CT9.5 The following was published with the financial statements to **American Exploration Company** (USA).

American Exploration Company
Notes to the Financial Statements

Property, Plant, and Equipment—The Company accounts for its oil and gas exploration and production activities using the successful efforts method of accounting. Under this method, acquisition costs for proved and unproved properties are capitalized when incurred. . . . The costs of drilling exploratory wells are capitalized pending determination of whether each well has discovered proved reserves. If proved reserves are not discovered, such drilling costs are charged to expense. . . . Depletion of the cost of producing oil and gas properties is computed on the units-of-activity method.

Instructions

Write a brief email to your instructor discussing American Exploration Company's note regarding property, plant, and equipment. Your email should address what is meant by the "successful efforts method" and "units-of-activity method."

Ethics Case

CT9.6 Dieker Containers is suffering declining sales of its principal product, non-biodegradeable plastic cartons. The president, Edward Mohling, instructs his controller, Betty Fetters, to lengthen asset lives to reduce depreciation expense. A processing line of automated plastic extruding equipment, purchased for €3.1 million in January 2029, was originally estimated to have a useful life of 8 years and a residual value of €300,000. Depreciation has been recorded for 2 years on that basis. Edward wants the estimated life changed to 12 years total, and the straight-line method continued. Betty is hesitant to make the change, believing it is unethical to increase net income in this manner. Edward says, "Hey, the life is only an estimate, and I've heard that our competition uses a 12-year life on their production equipment."

Instructions

a. Who are the stakeholders in this situation?

b. Is the change in asset life unethical, or is it simply a good business practice by an astute president?

c. What is the effect of Edward Mohling's proposed change on income before taxes in the year of change?

Answers to Insight and Accounting Across the Organization Questions

Many Firms Use Leases Q: Why might airline managers choose to lease rather than purchase their planes? **A:** The reasons for leasing include favorable tax treatment, better financing options, increased flexibility, reduced risk of obsolescence, and often less debt shown on the statement of financial position.

Sustainability Report Please Q: Why do you believe companies issue sustainability reports? **A:** It is important that companies clearly describe the things they value in addition to overall profitability. Most companies recognize that the health, safety, and environmental protections of their workforce and community are important components in developing strategies for continued growth and longevity. Without a strong commitment to the principles of corporate social responsibility, it is unlikely that a company will be able to maintain long-term stability and profitability. The development of a sustainability report helps companies to consider these issues and develop measures to assess whether they are meeting their goals in this area.

Should Companies Write Up Goodwill Q: Which aspects of this treatment are allowed under IFRS? **A:** Impairments are required for many assets, including inventories, property, plant, and equipment, as well as for intangible assets, including patents and goodwill. Under IFRS, when the value of these assets declines, they will be written down. However, unlike inventories, the impaired value of property, plant, equipment, and intangible assets (such as patents) may be recovered where permitted. Recoveries of goodwill are not permitted.

A Look at U.S. GAAP

LEARNING OBJECTIVE 7

Compare the accounting for long-lived assets under IFRS and U.S. GAAP.

GAAP follows most of the same principles as IFRS in the accounting for property, plant, and equipment. There are, however, some significant differences in the implementation: IFRS allows the use of revaluation of property, plant, and equipment, and it also requires the use of component depreciation. In addition, there are some significant differences in the accounting for both intangible assets and impairments.

Key Points

The following are the key similarities and differences between IFRS and U.S. GAAP related to the recording process for long-lived assets.

Similarities

- The definition for plant assets for both GAAP and IFRS is essentially the same.
- GAAP, like IFRS, capitalizes all direct costs in self-constructed assets such as raw materials and labor. IFRS does not address the capitalization of fixed overhead although in practice these costs are generally capitalized.
- GAAP, like IFRS, also capitalizes interest costs incurred during the construction period for self-constructed assets such as buildings.
- GAAP also views depreciation as an allocation of cost over an asset's useful life. GAAP permits the same depreciation methods (e.g., straight-line, accelerated, and units-of-activity) as IFRS.
- The accounting for subsequent expenditures, such as ordinary repairs and additions, are essentially the same under GAAP and IFRS.
- Under both GAAP and IFRS, changes in the depreciation method used and changes in useful life are handled in current and future periods. Prior periods are not affected. GAAP recently conformed to IFRS in the accounting for changes in depreciation methods.
- The accounting for plant asset disposals is essentially the same under GAAP and IFRS.
- Initial costs to acquire natural resources are recorded in essentially the same manner under GAAP and IFRS.
- The definition of intangible assets is essentially the same under GAAP and IFRS.
- The accounting for exchanges of non-monetary assets has converged between IFRS and GAAP. GAAP now requires that gains on exchanges of non-monetary assets be recognized if the exchange has commercial substance. This is the same framework used in IFRS.
- Both IFRS and GAAP record property, plant, and equipment at historical cost (also known as acquisition cost) when the asset is acquired. Acquisition cost consists of all expenditures necessary to acquire the asset and make it ready for its intended use.
- Under both GAAP and IFRS, interest costs incurred during construction are capitalized. Recently, IFRS converged to GAAP requirements in this area.

Differences

- Under GAAP, an item of property, plant, and equipment with multiple parts is generally depreciated over the useful life of the total asset. Thus, component depreciation is generally not used. However, GAAP permits companies to use component depreciation.
- GAAP uses the term **salvage value**, rather than residual value, to refer to an owner's estimate of an asset's value at the end of its useful life for that owner.
- While both IFRS and GAAP capitalize interest costs incurred during the construction period for self-constructed assets such as buildings, the method used to determine the amount of interest capitalized is different.
- IFRS allows companies to revalue plant assets to fair value at the reporting date.
- As in IFRS, under GAAP the costs associated with research and development are segregated into the two components. Costs in the research phase are always expensed under both GAAP and IFRS. Under IFRS, however, costs in the development phase are capitalized as Development Costs once technological feasibility is achieved. Under GAAP, all development costs are expensed as incurred.
- IFRS permits revaluation of intangible assets (except for goodwill). GAAP prohibits revaluation of intangible assets.
- IFRS requires an impairment test at each reporting date for plant assets and intangibles and records an impairment if the asset's carrying amount exceeds its recoverable amount. The recoverable amount is the higher of the asset's fair value less costs to sell or its value-in-use. Value-in-use is the future cash flows to be derived from the particular asset, discounted to present value. Under GAAP, impairment loss is measured as the excess of the carrying amount over the asset's fair value.
- IFRS allows reversal of impairment losses when there has been a change in economic conditions or in the expected use of the asset. Under GAAP, impairment losses cannot be reversed for assets to be held and used; the impairment loss results in a new cost basis for the asset. IFRS and GAAP are similar in the accounting for impairments of assets held for disposal.

GAAP Practice

GAAP Self-Test Questions

1. Which of the following statements is **correct**?
   a. Both IFRS and GAAP permit revaluation of property, plant, and equipment and intangible assets (except for goodwill).
   b. IFRS permits revaluation of property, plant, and equipment and intangible assets (except for goodwill).
   c. Both IFRS and GAAP permit revaluation of property, plant, and equipment but not intangible assets.
   d. GAAP permits revaluation of property, plant, and equipment but not intangible assets.

2. Rando Company has land that cost $450,000 but now has a fair value of $600,000. Rando Company follows GAAP to account for the land. Which of the following statements is **correct**?
   a. Rando Company must continue to report the land at $450,000.
   b. Rando Company would report a net income increase of $150,000 due to an increase in the value of the land.
   c. Rando Company would report the land at $600,000.
   d. Rando Company would credit Retained Earnings by $150,000.

3. Francisco Corporation is constructing a new building at a total initial cost of $10,000,000. The building is expected to have a useful life of 50 years with no salvage value. The building's finished surfaces (e.g., roof cover and floor cover) are 5% of this cost and have a useful life of 20 years. Building services systems (e.g., electric, heating, and plumbing) are 20% of the cost and have a useful life of 25 years. The depreciation in the first year using GAAP (without component depreciation), assuming straight-line depreciation with no salvage value, is:
   a. $200,000.
   b. $215,000.
   c. $255,000.
   d. None of the answer choices is correct.

4. Research and development costs are:
   a. expensed under GAAP.
   b. expensed under IFRS.
   c. expensed under both GAAP and IFRS.
   d. None of the answer choices is correct.

5. Value-in-use is defined as:
   a. net realizable value.
   b. fair value.
   c. future cash flows discounted to present value.
   d. total future undiscounted cash flows.

GAAP Exercises

GAAP9.1 Is component depreciation required under IFRS and GAAP? Explain.

GAAP9.2 What is revaluation of plant assets? Should revaluation be applied under GAAP?

GAAP9.3 Some product development expenditures are recorded as development expenses and others as development costs. Explain the difference between these accounts and how development costs are reported under GAAP.

GAAP9.4 Mandall Company constructed a warehouse for $280,000. Mandall estimates that the warehouse has a useful life of 20 years and no salvage (residual) value. Construction records indicate that $40,000 of the cost of the warehouse relates to its heating, ventilation, and air conditioning (HVAC) system, which has an estimated useful life of only 10 years. Compute the first year of depreciation expense using straight-line component depreciation using IFRS. How might GAAP differ from IFRS?

GAAP9.5 Newell Industries spent $300,000 on research and $600,000 on development of a new product. Of the $600,000 in development costs, $400,000 was incurred prior to technological feasibility and $200,000 after technological feasibility had been demonstrated. (a) Prepare the journal entry to record research and development costs under IFRS. (b) Prepare the journal entry to record research and development costs under GAAP.

GAAP Financial Statement Analysis: Apple Inc. (USA)

GAAP9.6 The financial statements of **Apple** are presented in Appendix D. The complete annual report, including the notes to the financial statements, is available at the company's website.

Instructions

Use the company's financial statements and notes to the financial statements, available at the company's website, to answer the following questions.

a. What were the total cost and book value of property, plant, and equipment at September 26, 2020?

b. What method or methods of depreciation are used by Apple for financial reporting purposes?

c. What was the amount of depreciation and amortization expense for each of the 3 years 2018–2020? (*Hint:* Use the statement of cash flows.)

d. Using the statement of cash flows, what are the amounts of property, plant, and equipment purchased (capital expenditures) in 2020 and 2019?

Answers to GAAP Self-Test Questions

1. b **2.** a **3.** a **4.** a **5.** c

CHAPTER **10**

Current Liabilities

LEARNING OBJECTIVES After studying this chapter, you should be able to:

LO 1 Explain how to account for current liabilities.

LO 2 Discuss how current liabilities are reported and analyzed.

Chapter Preview

Inventor-entrepreneur Wilbert Murdock, as the following Feature Story notes, had to use multiple credit cards to finance his business ventures. Murdock's credit card debts would be classified as **current liabilities** because they are due every month. Yet, by making minimal payments and paying high amounts of interest each month, Murdock used this credit source long-term. Some credit card balances remain outstanding for years as they accumulate interest.

Current Liabilities

Accounting for Current Liabilities

- What is a current liability?
- Notes payable
- Value-added and sales taxes payable
- Unearned revenues
- Salaries and wages
- Current maturities of long-term debt

Reporting and Analyzing Current Liabilities

- Reporting uncertainty
- Reporting of current liabilities
- Analysis of current liabilities

Practice

DO IT! 1 Current Liabilities

DO IT! 2 Reporting and Analyzing

Go to the Review and Practice section at the end of the chapter for a review of key concepts and practice applications with solutions.
Additional tutorials and practice opportunities are available in the Wiley online course.

Feature Story Financing His Dreams

What would you do if you had a great idea for a new product but couldn't come up with the cash to get the business off the ground? Small businesses often cannot attract investors. Nor can they obtain traditional debt financing through bank loans or bond issuances. Instead, they often resort to unusual, and costly, forms of non-traditional financing.

Such was the case for Wilbert Murdock. Murdock grew up in a New York housing project and always had great ambitions. His entrepreneurial spirit led him into some business ventures that failed: a medical diagnostic tool, a device to eliminate carpal tunnel syndrome, custom-designed sneakers, and a device to keep people from falling asleep while driving.

Another idea was computerized golf clubs that analyze a golfer's swing and provide immediate feedback. Murdock saw great potential in the idea. Many golfers are willing to shell out considerable sums of money for devices that might improve their game. But Murdock had no cash to develop his product, and banks and other lenders had shied away. Rather than give up, Murdock resorted to credit cards—in a big way. He quickly owed $25,000 to credit card companies.

While funding a business with credit cards might sound unusual, it isn't. A recent study found that one-third of businesses with fewer than 20 employees financed at least part of their operations with credit cards. As Murdock explained, credit cards are an appealing way to finance a start-up because "credit card companies don't care how the money is spent." However, they do care how they are paid. And so Murdock faced high interest charges and a number of credit card collection letters.

Murdock's debt forced him to sacrifice nearly everything in order to keep his business afloat. His car stopped running, he barely had enough money to buy food, and he lived and worked out of a dimly lit apartment in his mother's basement. Through it all he tried to maintain a positive spirit, joking that, if he becomes successful, he might some day get to appear in an **American Express** (USA) commercial.

Source: Rodney Ho, "Banking on Plastic: To Finance a Dream, Many Entrepreneurs Binge on Credit Cards," *Wall Street Journal* (March 9, 1998), p. A1.

TPG/Shutterstock

10.1 Accounting for Current Liabilities

LEARNING OBJECTIVE 1

Explain how to account for current liabilities.

What Is a Current Liability?

You have learned that liabilities are defined as "creditors' claims on total assets" and as "existing debts and obligations." Companies must settle or pay these claims, debts, and obligations at some time in the future by transferring assets or services. The future date on which they are due or payable (the maturity date) is a significant feature of liabilities.

Recall that a **current liability** is a debt that a company expects to pay within one year or the operating cycle, whichever is longer. Debts that do not meet this criterion are **non-current liabilities**.

- Financial statement users want to know whether a company's obligations are current or non-current. A company that has more current liabilities than current assets often lacks liquidity, or short-term debt-paying ability.

- In addition, users want to know the types of liabilities a company has. If a company declares bankruptcy, a specific, predetermined order of payment to creditors exists.

Thus, the amount and type of liabilities are of critical importance.

The different types of current liabilities include notes payable, accounts payable, unearned revenues, and accrued liabilities such as taxes, salaries and wages, and interest payable (see **Helpful Hint**). In the sections that follow, we discuss common types of current liabilities.

HELPFUL HINT

In previous chapters, we explained the entries for accounts payable and the adjusting entries for some current liabilities.

Notes Payable

Companies record obligations in the form of written notes as **notes payable**. Notes payable are often used instead of accounts payable because they give the lender formal proof of the obligation in case legal remedies are needed to collect the debt.

- Companies frequently issue notes payable to meet short-term financing needs. Notes payable usually require the borrower to pay interest.
- Notes are issued for varying periods of time. **Those due for payment within one year of the statement of financial position date are usually classified as current liabilities.**

To illustrate the accounting for notes payable, assume that First Hunan Bank agrees to lend ¥100,000 on September 1, 2029, if Yang Enterprises signs a ¥100,000, 12%, four-month note maturing on January 1 (amounts in thousands). When a company issues an interest-bearing note, the amount of assets it receives upon issuance of the note generally equals the note's face value. Yang therefore will receive ¥100,000 cash and will make the following journal entry.

Sept. 1	Cash	100,000	
	Notes Payable		100,000
	(To record issuance of 12%, 4-month note to First Hunan Bank)		

A = L + E
+100,000 | +100,000
Cash Flows
+100,000

Interest accrues over the life of the note, and the company must periodically record that accrual. If Yang prepares financial statements annually, it makes an adjusting entry at December 31 to recognize interest expense and interest payable of ¥4,000 (¥100,000 × 12% × 4/12). **Illustration 10.1** shows the formula for computing interest and its application to Yang's note.

Face Value of Note	×	Annual Interest Rate	×	Time in Terms of One Year	=	Interest
¥100,000	×	12%	×	4/12	=	¥4,000

ILLUSTRATION 10.1
Formula for computing interest

Yang makes an adjusting entry as follows.

Dec. 31	Interest Expense	4,000	
	Interest Payable		4,000
	(To accrue interest for 4 months on First Hunan Bank note)		

A = L + E
+4,000 | −4,000 Exp
Cash Flows
no effect

In the December 31 financial statements, the current liabilities section of the statement of financial position will show notes payable ¥100,000 and interest payable ¥4,000. In addition, the company will report interest expense of ¥4,000 in the financing category of the income statement. If Yang prepared financial statements monthly, the adjusting entry at the end of each month would be for ¥1,000 (¥100,000 × 12% × 1/12).

At maturity (January 1, 2030), Yang must pay the face value of the note (¥100,000) plus ¥4,000 interest (¥100,000 × 12% × 4/12). It records payment of the note and accrued interest as follows.

A	=	L	+	E
		−100,000		
		−4,000		
−104,000				

Cash Flows
−104,000

Jan. 1	Notes Payable	100,000	
	Interest Payable	4,000	
	Cash		104,000
	(To record payment of First Hunan Bank interest-bearing note and accrued interest at maturity)		

Value-Added and Sales Taxes Payable

Most countries have a consumption tax. Consumption taxes are generally either a value-added tax (VAT) or sales tax. The purpose of these taxes is to generate revenue for the government similar to the company or personal income tax. These two taxes accomplish the same objective—to tax the final consumer of the good or service. However, the two systems use different methods to accomplish this objective.

Value-Added Taxes Payable

Value-added taxes (VAT) are used by tax authorities more than sales taxes (over 100 countries require that companies collect a value-added tax). As indicated earlier, a **value-added tax** is a consumption tax. This tax is placed on a product or service whenever value is added at a stage of production and at final sale. A VAT is a cost to the end user, normally a private individual, similar to a sales tax.

- A VAT should not be confused with a sales tax. A sales tax is collected only once at the consumer's point of purchase. No one else in the production or supply chain is involved in the collection of the tax.
- In a VAT taxation system, the VAT is collected every time a business purchases products from another business in the product's supply chain.

To illustrate, assume that Hill Farms Wheat grows wheat and sells it to Sunshine Baking for €1,000. Hill Farms Wheat makes the following entry to record the sale, assuming the VAT is 10%.

A	=	L	+	E
+1,100				
				+1,000 Rev
		+100		

Cash Flows
+1,100

Cash	1,100	
Sales Revenue		1,000
Value-Added Taxes Payable		100
(To record sales and value-added taxes)		

Hill Farms Wheat then remits the €100 to the tax authority.[1]

Sales Taxes Payable

To illustrate the accounting for a sales tax, Cooley Grocery sells loaves of bread totaling €800 on a given day. Assuming a sales tax rate of 6%, Cooley make the following entry record the sale.

A	=	L	+	E
+848				
				+800 Rev
		+48		

Cash Flows
+848

Cash	848	
Sales Revenue		800
Sales Taxes Payable		48
(To record sales and sales taxes)		

When the company remits the taxes to the taxing agency, it debits Sales Taxes Payable and credits Cash. The company does not report sales taxes as an expense. It simply forwards to the government the amount paid by the customers. Thus, Cooley Grocery serves only as a **collection agent** for the taxing authority.

[1] In a VAT system, as the loaves of bread move from the manufacturer to the wholesaler, to the retailer, and finally the consumer, a VAT is incurred at each point. However, the cost to the end user (normally a consumer) is similar to the sales tax.

Sometimes companies do not enter sales taxes separately in the cash register. To determine the amount of sales in such cases, divide total receipts by 100% plus the sales tax percentage. For example, assume that Cooley Grocery enters total receipts of €10,600. The receipts from the sales are equal to the sales price (100%) plus the tax percentage (6% of sales), or 1.06 times the sales total. We can compute the sales amount as follows.

$$€10{,}600 \div 1.06 = €10{,}000$$

Thus, we can find the sales tax amount of €600 by either (1) subtracting sales from total receipts (€10,600 − €10,000) or (2) multiplying sales by the sales tax rate (€10,000 × .06).

Unearned Revenues

An airline company, such as **Qantas Airways** (AUS), often receives cash when it sells tickets for future flights. A magazine publisher, such as **Finance Asia** (HKG), receives customers' payments when they order magazines. Season tickets for concerts, sporting events, and theater programs are also paid for in advance. How do companies account for unearned revenues that are received before goods are delivered or services are performed?

1. When a company receives the advance payment, it debits Cash and credits a current liability account identifying the source of the unearned revenue.
2. When the company recognizes revenue, it debits an unearned revenue account and credits a revenue account.

To illustrate, assume that the **Liverpool F.C.** (GBR) sells 10,000 season soccer (football) tickets at £50 each for its five-game home schedule. The club makes the following entry for the sale of season tickets.

Aug. 6	Cash (10,000 × £50)	500,000	
	Unearned Ticket Revenue		500,000
	(To record sale of 10,000 season tickets)		

A = L + E
+500,000
+500,000
Cash Flows
+500,000

As each game is completed, Liverpool records the recognition of revenue with the following entry.

Sept. 7	Unearned Ticket Revenue	100,000	
	Ticket Revenue (£500,000 ÷ 5)		100,000
	(To record ticket revenue)		

A = L + E
−100,000
+100,000 Rev
Cash Flows
no effect

The account Unearned Ticket Revenue represents unearned revenue, and Liverpool reports it as a current liability. As the club recognizes revenue, it reclassifies the amount from unearned revenue to Ticket Revenue. Unearned revenue is substantial for some companies. In the airline industry, for example, tickets sold for future flights represent almost 50% of total current liabilities. At **United Airlines** (USA), unearned ticket revenue is its largest current liability, recently amounting to over $1 billion.

Illustration 10.2 shows specific unearned revenue and revenue accounts used in selected types of businesses.

ILLUSTRATION 10.2
Unearned revenue and revenue accounts

Type of Business	Account Title: Unearned Revenue	Account Title: Revenue
Airline	Unearned Ticket Revenue	Ticket Revenue
Magazine publisher	Unearned Subscription Revenue	Subscription Revenue
Hotel	Unearned Rent Revenue	Rent Revenue

Accounting Across the Organization SAP

Jerome Cid/123RF

SAP's Liabilities—Good or Bad?

Users of financial statements generally examine current liabilities to assess a company's liquidity and overall financial flexibility. Companies must pay many current liabilities, such as accounts payable, wages payable, and taxes payable, sooner rather than later. A substantial increase in these liabilities should therefore raise a red flag about a company's financial position. However, this is not the case for all current liabilities.

For example, **SAP** (DEU) has a current liability account entitled "Contract liabilities/deferred income" with a balance of €3.028 billion in the most recent period. This account, which has been increasing each year, is almost 24% of total current liabilities and over 13% of total liabilities. Deferred income is a liability account that arises from SAP sales of cloud subscription services and software support services where the payments are collected in advance.

Market analysts read such an increase in deferred income as a positive signal about SAP's sales and profitability. When SAP's sales are growing, its deferred income account increases. Thus, an increase in a liability is good news about SAP's sales. At the same time, a decline in deferred income is bad news. As one commentator noted, a slowdown or reversal of the growth in SAP's deferred income indicates slowing sales and also cash flows. Thus, financial statement readers have to carefully analyze increases in current liabilities to determine if it is a good or bad sign.

Source: Adapted from Glenn Wisegarver, "The SaaS Addiction to Deferred Revenue," *Forbes* (April 7, 2017).

What are some other companies where an increase in current liabilities, specifically deferred income, could be a good sign related to growth? Try to also think of companies not in the software and information technology industry. (Answer is available near the end of the chapter.)

Salaries and Wages

Companies report as a current liability the amounts owed to employees for salaries or wages at the end of an accounting period. In addition, they often also report as current liabilities the following items related to employee compensation.

1. Payroll deductions.
2. Bonuses.

Payroll Deductions

The most common types of payroll deductions are taxes, insurance premiums, employee savings, and union dues. **To the extent that a company has not remitted the amounts deducted to the proper authority at the end of the accounting period, it should recognize them as current liabilities.**

Social Security Taxes Most governments provide a level of social benefits (for retirement, unemployment, income, disability, and medical benefits) to individuals and families. The benefits are generally funded from taxes assessed on both the employer and the employees. These taxes are often referred to as **Social Security taxes** (or **Social Welfare taxes**).

Funds for these payments generally come from taxes levied on both the employer and the employee. Employers collect the employee's share of this tax by deducting it from the employee's gross pay, and remit it to the government along with their share. The government often taxes both the employer and the employee at the same rate. **Companies should report the amount of unremitted employee and employer Social Security tax on gross wages paid as a current liability.**

Income Tax Withholding Income tax laws generally require employers to withhold from each employee's pay the applicable income tax due on those wages. The employer computes the amount of income tax to withhold according to a government-prescribed formula or withholding tax table. That amount depends on the length of the pay period and each employee's taxable wages, marital status, and claimed dependents. **Illustration 10.3** summarizes payroll deductions and liabilities.

ILLUSTRATION 10.3
Summary of payroll liabilities

Item	Who Pays	
Income tax withholding Social Security taxes (employee share) Union dues	Employee	Employer reports these amounts as liabilities until remitted.
Social Security taxes (employer share)	Employer	

Payroll Deductions Example: Employee Assume that Cumberland Company has a weekly payroll of $10,000 (often referred to as **gross earnings**) entirely subject to Social Security taxes (8%), with income tax withholding of $1,320 and union dues of $88 deducted. If the weekly payroll is due on January 14, Cumberland records the salaries and wages payable (often referred to as **net pay**) and the **employee payroll deductions** as follows.

Jan. 14	Salaries and Wages Expense	10,000	
	Income Taxes Payable		1,320
	Social Security Taxes Payable		800
	Union Dues Payable		88
	Salaries and Wages Payable		7,792
	(To record payroll for the week ending January 14)		

A	=	L	+	E
				−10,000
		+1,320		
		+800		
		+88		
		+7,792		

Cash Flows
no effect

In many cases, employees ask the employer to withhold voluntary payments for contributions to other organizations, such as payments for additional insurance or charitable organizations, which requires the recording of additional withholding liabilities.

After recording the payroll for the week, Cumberland then records the payment of the payroll as follows.

Jan. 14	Salaries and Wages Payable	7,792	
	Cash		7,792
	(To record payment of payroll)		

A	=	L	+	E
		−7,792		
−7,792				

Cash Flows
−7,792

Payroll Deductions Example: Employer As the employer, Cumberland is also required to pay Social Security taxes and often other taxes as well (referred to as **employer payroll taxes**). It records payroll taxes related to the January 14 payroll as follows.

Jan. 14	Payroll Tax Expense	800	
	Social Security Taxes Payable		800

A	=	L	+	E
				−800
		+800		

Cash Flows
no effect

At the appropriate time, Cumberland then remits to the government Social Security taxes payable from both the employer and employee side as well as other withholding amounts.

Cumberland reports any withholding liabilities as a current liability because these amounts must be paid in the near future. Taxing authorities impose substantial penalties on employers if the withholding and payroll taxes are not computed correctly and not paid on time.[2]

Profit-Sharing and Bonus Plans Many companies give a **bonus** to certain or all employees in addition to their regular salaries or wages. Frequently, the bonus amount depends on the company's yearly profit. A company may consider **bonus payments to employees** as additional salaries and wages and should include them as a deduction in determining the net income for the year (see **Ethics Note**).

ETHICS NOTE

Bonuses often reward outstanding individual performance, but successful companies also need considerable teamwork. A challenge is to motivate individuals while preventing an unethical employee from taking another's idea for his or her own advantage.

To illustrate the entries for an employee bonus, assume that Palmer Group shows income for the year 2029 of NT$100,000. It will pay out bonuses of NT$10,700 in January 2030. Palmer makes an adjusting entry dated December 31, 2029, to record the bonuses as follows.

Salaries and Wages Expense	10,700	
Salaries and Wages Payable		10,700

In January 2030, when Palmer pays the bonus, it makes this journal entry:

Salaries and Wages Payable	10,700	
Cash		10,700

[2]This abbreviated and somewhat simplified discussion of payroll costs and deductions is not indicative of the volume of records and clerical work that may be involved in maintaining a sound and accurate payroll system.

Current Maturities of Long-Term Debt

Companies often have a portion of long-term debt that comes due in the current year. That amount is considered a current liability. As an example, assume that Wendy Construction issues a five-year, interest-bearing €25,000 note on January 1, 2029. This note specifies that each January 1, starting January 1, 2030, Wendy should pay €5,000 of the note. When the company prepares financial statements on December 31, 2029, it should report €5,000 as a current liability and €20,000 as a non-current liability. (The €5,000 amount is the portion of the note that is due to be paid within the next 12 months.)

Companies often identify current maturities of long-term debt on the statement of financial position as **long-term debt due within one year.**

- It is not necessary to prepare an adjusting entry to recognize the current maturity of long-term debt.
- At the statement of financial position date, all obligations due within one year are classified as current, and all other obligations as non-current.

ACTION PLAN

- **Use the interest formula: Face value of note × Annual interest rate × Time in terms of one year.**
- **Divide total receipts by 100% plus the tax rate to determine sales revenue; then subtract sales revenue from the total receipts.**
- **Determine what fraction of the total unearned rent should be recognized this year.**
- **Recognize that taxes withheld and Social Security costs are major payroll deductions.**

DO IT! 1 | Current Liabilities

You and several classmates are studying for the next accounting examination. They ask you to answer the following questions (amounts in thousands).

1. If cash is borrowed on a HK$50,000, 6-month, 12% note on September 1, how much interest expense would be incurred by December 31?
2. How is the sales tax amount determined when the cash register total includes sales taxes?
3. If HK$15,000 is collected in advance on November 1 for 3 months' rent, what amount of rent revenue is recognized by December 31?
4. Gross earnings for the month by employees is HK$80,000. All earnings are subject to an 8% Social Security tax and income taxes withheld of HK$15,600. What is the amount of net pay?
5. How should the current maturities of long-term debt be recognized ?

Solution

1. HK$50,000 × 12% × 4/12 = HK$2,000
2. First, divide the total cash register receipts by 100% plus the sales tax percentage to find the sales revenue amount. Second, subtract the sales revenue amount from the total cash register receipts to determine the sales taxes.
3. HK$15,000 × 2/3 = HK$10,000
4. HK$80,000 – (8% × HK$80,000) – HK$15,600 = HK$58,000
5. Companies should recognize the current maturities of long-term debt on the statement of financial position as long-term debt due within one year, and regard them as current liabilities at the statement of financial position date.

Related exercise material: **BE10.1, BE10.2, BE10.3, BE10.4, BE10.5, BE10.6, BE10.7, BE10.8, BE10.9, BE10.10, BE10.11, DO IT! 10.1, E10.1, E10.2, E10.3, E10.4, E10.5, E10.6, and E10.7.**

10.2 Reporting and Analyzing Current Liabilities

LEARNING OBJECTIVE 2

Discuss how current liabilities are reported and analyzed.

Reporting Uncertainty

With notes payable, interest payable, accounts payable, value-added and sales taxes payable, and salaries and wages payable, we know that an obligation to make a payment exists. Suppose, however, that your company is involved in a lawsuit which, if you lose, might result in bankruptcy. How should you report this major contingency? The answers to questions like this are difficult because these liabilities are dependent upon some future event.

- A **provision** is a liability of uncertain timing or amount (sometimes referred to as an (*estimated liability*).
- Provisions are very common and may be reported either as current or non-current depending on the date of expected payment.
- Common types of provisions are obligations related to litigation expense, warranty expense or product guarantees, and environmental damage.

For example, **Yancheng Petroleum** (CHN) reported HK$143 million related to provisions for decommissioning liabilities. **Sony** (JPN) reported ¥66,943 million for warranties of its products.

The difference between a provision and other liabilities (such as accounts or notes payable, salaries and wages payable, and dividends payable) is that **a provision has greater uncertainty about the timing or amount of the future expenditure required to settle the obligation**. For example, when **Giant Manufacturing** (TWN) reports an accounts payable, there is an invoice or formal agreement as to the existence and the amount of the liability. Similarly, when Giant accrues interest payable, the timing and the amount are known.

Recognition of a Provision

Companies accrue an expense and related liability for a provision only if the following three conditions are met.

1. A company has a present obligation as a result of a past event;
2. It is probable that an outflow of resources will be required to settle the obligation; and
3. A reliable estimate can be made of the amount of the obligation.

If these three conditions are not met, no provision is recognized.

In applying the second condition, the term **probable** is defined as "more likely than not to occur." This phrase is interpreted to mean the probability of occurrence is greater than 50%. If the probability is 50% or less, the provision is not recognized.

Reporting a Provision

Product warranties are an example of a provision that companies should record in the accounts. Warranty contracts result in future costs that companies may incur in replacing defective units or repairing malfunctioning units. Generally, a manufacturer, such as **Sony** (JPN), knows that it will incur some warranty costs on its most recent version of its Playstation. From prior experience with these products, the company usually can reasonably estimate the anticipated cost of servicing (honoring) the warranty.

- The accounting for warranty costs is based on the expense recognition principle.
- **The estimated cost of honoring product warranty contracts should be recognized as an expense in the period in which the sale occurs.**

To illustrate, assume that in 2029 Denson Manufacturing sells 10,000 washers and dryers at an average price of €600 each. The selling price includes a one-year warranty on parts. Denson expects that 500 units (5%) will be defective and that warranty repair costs will average €80 per unit. In 2029, the company honors warranty contracts on 300 units, at a total cost of €24,000.

Denson records those repair costs incurred in 2029 to honor warranty contracts on 2029 sales as shown below.

Jan. 1– Dec. 31	Warranty Expense	24,000	
	Repair Parts		24,000
	(To record honoring of 300 warranty contracts on 2029 sales)		

A	=	L	+	E
				−24,000
−24,000				

Cash Flows
no effect

At December 31, to accrue the estimated warranty costs on the 2029 sales less the amount already honored in 2029 of €24,000, Denson computes the estimated warranty liability as shown in **Illustration 10.4**.

ILLUSTRATION 10.4
Computation of estimated warranty liability

Number of units sold	10,000
Estimated rate of defective units	× 5%
Total estimated defective units	500
Average warranty repair cost	× €80
Estimated warranty liability	€40,000
Less: Warranty claims honored	24,000
Warranty liability at December 31, 2029	**€16,000**

The company makes the following adjusting entry for €16,000 after it adjusts for €24,000 of warranty claims honored during 2029.

A	=	L	+	E
				−16,000
		+16,000		

Cash Flows
no effect

	Debit	Credit
Warranty Expense	16,000	
Warranty Liability		16,000
(To record estimated warranty liability)		

The company reports warranty expense of €40,000 (€24,000 + €16,000) under selling expenses in the income statement. It classifies warranty liability of €16,000 (€40,000 − €24,000) as a current liability on the statement of financial position, assuming the warranty is estimated to be honored in the next year.

In the following year, Denson should debit to Warranty Liability all expenses incurred in honoring warranty contracts on 2029 sales. To illustrate, assume that the company replaces 20 defective units in January 2030, at an average cost of €80 in parts and labor. The summary entry for the month of January 2030 is as follows.

A	=	L	+	E
		−1,600		
−1,600				

Cash Flows
no effect

		Debit	Credit
Jan. 31	Warranty Liability	1,600	
	Repair Parts		1,600
	(To record honoring of 20 warranty contracts on 2029 sales)		

Reporting of Current Liabilities

Current liabilities are reported after non-current liabilities on the statement of financial position.

- Companies list each of the principal types of current liabilities separately within this category.
- In addition, companies disclose the terms of notes payable and other key information about the individual items in the notes to the financial statements.
- As a matter of custom, many companies show notes payable first and then accounts payable, regardless of amount. The current maturity of long-term debt is often shown last in the current liabilities section.

Illustration 10.5 provides an excerpt from Croix Beverages' statement of financial position, which is a common order of presentation among companies (see **Helpful Hint**).

ILLUSTRATION 10.5

Statement of financial position reporting of current liabilities

Croix Beverages
Statement of Financial Position
December 31, 2029
(partial, in thousands)

Current liabilities	
Notes payable	€ 4,157
Accounts payable	3,990
Accrued expenses	1,847
Salaries and wages payable	1,730
Unearned revenues	555
Income taxes payable	259
Warranty liability	141
Long-term debt due within one year	3,531
Total current liabilities	€16,210

HELPFUL HINT
For other examples of current liabilities sections, refer to the TSMC and Nestlé statements of financial position in Appendices A and B.

Analysis of Current Liabilities

Use of current and non-current classifications makes it possible to analyze a company's liquidity. **Liquidity** refers to the ability to pay maturing obligations and meet unexpected needs for cash.

- The relationship of current assets to current liabilities is critical in analyzing liquidity.
- We can express this relationship as a currency amount (working capital) and as a ratio (the current ratio).
- The excess of current assets over current liabilities is **working capital**.

Illustration 10.6 shows the formula for the computation of Croix Beverages' working capital, assuming current assets were €20,856 (euro amounts in thousands).

Current Assets	−	Current Liabilities	=	Working Capital
€20,856	−	€16,210	=	€4,646

ILLUSTRATION 10.6

Working capital formula and computation

As an absolute euro amount, working capital offers limited informational value. For example, €1 million of working capital may be far more than needed for a small company but inadequate for a large corporation. Also, €1 million of working capital may be adequate for a company at one time but inadequate at another time.

- The **current ratio** permits us to compare the liquidity of different-sized companies and of a single company at different times.
- The current ratio is calculated as current assets divided by current liabilities.

Illustration 10.7 shows the formula for this ratio, along with its computation using Croix's current asset and current liability data (euro amounts in thousands).

Current Assets	÷	Current Liabilities	=	Current Ratio
€20,856	÷	€16,210	=	1.29:1

ILLUSTRATION 10.7

Current ratio formula and computation

Historically, companies and analysts considered a current ratio of 2:1 to be the standard for a good credit rating. In recent years, however, many healthy companies have maintained ratios well below 2:1 by improving management of their current assets and liabilities. Croix's ratio of 1.29:1 is adequate but certainly below the standard of 2:1.

ACTION PLAN

- **Determine which liabilities will be paid within one year or the operating cycle and include those as current liabilities.**
- **If the provision is probable and reliably estimable, include it as a current liability.**
- **Use the formula for working capital: Current assets – Current liabilities.**
- **Use the formula for the current ratio: Current assets ÷ Current liabilities.**

DO IT! 2 | Reporting and Analyzing

Tron Cellular has the following account balances at December 31, 2029 (amounts in thousands).

Notes payable (NT$80,000 due after 12/31/30)	NT$200,000
Unearned service revenue	75,000
Other long-term debt (NT$30,000 due in 2030)	150,000
Salaries and wages payable	22,000
Other accrued expenses	15,000
Accounts payable	100,000

In addition, Tron is involved in a lawsuit. Legal counsel feels it is probable Tron will pay damages of NT$38,000 in 2030.

a. Prepare the current liabilities section of Tron's December 31, 2029, statement of financial position.

b. Tron's current assets are NT$504,000. Compute Tron's working capital and current ratio.

Solution

a. Current liabilities

Notes payable (NT$200,000 – NT$80,000)	NT$120,000
Accounts payable	100,000
Unearned service revenue	75,000
Lawsuit liability	38,000
Salaries and wages payable	22,000
Other accrued expenses	15,000
Long-term debt due within one year	30,000
Total current liabilities	NT$400,000

b. Working capital = Current assets – Current liabilities = NT$504,000 – NT$400,000 = NT$104,000

Current ratio = Current assets ÷ Current liabilities = NT$504,000 ÷ NT$400,000 = 1.26:1

Related exercise material: **BE10.12, BE10.13, BE10.14, DO IT! 10.2, E10.13, E10.14, and E10.15.**

Review and Practice

Learning Objectives Review

1 Explain how to account for current liabilities.

A current liability is a debt that a company expects to pay within one year or the operating cycle, whichever is longer. The major types of current liabilities are notes payable, accounts payable, value-added and sales taxes payable, unearned revenues, and accrued liabilities such as taxes, salaries and wages, and interest payable.

When a promissory note is interest-bearing, the amount of assets received upon the issuance of the note is generally equal to the face value of the note. Interest expense accrues over the life of the note. At maturity, the amount paid equals the face value of the note plus accrued interest.

Companies record value-added and sales taxes payable at the time the related sales occur. The company serves as a collection agent for the taxing authority. These taxes are not an expense to the company. Companies initially record unearned revenues in an Unearned Revenue account. As a company recognizes revenue, a transfer from unearned revenue to revenue occurs. Companies report related payroll liabilities such as Social Security taxes payable, income taxes payable, and salaries and wages payable as current liabilities. Companies report the current maturities of long-term debt as a current liability in the statement of financial position.

2 Discuss how current liabilities are reported and analyzed.

With notes payable, interest payable, accounts payable, and sales taxes payable, an obligation to make a payment exists. Companies report a provision, which is a liability of uncertain timing or amount (sometimes referred to as an estimated liability). Provisions are very common and may be reported either as current or non-current depending on the date of expected payment. Companies accrue an expense and related liability for a provision.

Companies should report the nature and amount of each current liability in the statement of financial position or in schedules in the notes accompanying the statements. The liquidity of a company may be analyzed by computing working capital and the current ratio.

Glossary Review

Bonus Compensation to management and other personnel, based on factors such as increased sales or the amount of net income. (p. 10-7).

Current liabilities Obligations that a company expects to pay within one year or the operating cycle, whichever is longer. (p. 10-2).

Current ratio A measure of a company's liquidity; computed as current assets divided by current liabilities. (p. 10-11).

Employee payroll deductions Deductions from gross earnings to determine the amount of a paycheck. (p. 10-7).

Employer payroll taxes Social Security taxes owed by employers. (p. 10-7).

Gross earnings Total compensation earned by an employee. (p. 10-7).

Net pay Gross pay less payroll deductions. (p. 10-7).

Notes payable Obligations in the form of written notes. (p. 10-3).

Provision Liability of uncertain timing or amount. (p. 10-9).

Social Security (Social Welfare) taxes Taxes assessed on employees and employers by the government to fund social costs. (p. 10-6).

Working capital A measure of a company's liquidity; computed as current assets minus current liabilities. (p. 10-11).

Practice Multiple-Choice Questions

1. **(LO 1)** The time period for classifying a liability as current is one year or the operating cycle, whichever is:

   a. longer.
   b. shorter.
   c. probable.
   d. possible.

2. **(LO 1)** To be classified as a current liability, a debt must be expected to be paid within:

   a. one year.
   b. the operating cycle.
   c. 2 years.
   d. one year or the operating cycle, whichever is longer.

3. **(LO 1)** Ong Imports borrows ₩88,500 (amounts in thousands) on September 1, 2029, from Seoul City Bank by signing an ₩88,500, 12%, one-year note. What is the accrued interest at December 31, 2029?

   a. ₩2,655.
   b. ₩3,540.
   c. ₩4,425.
   d. ₩10,620.

4. **(LO 1)** RS Company borrowed €70,000 on December 1 on a 6-month, 6% note. At December 31:

   a. neither the note payable nor the interest payable is a current liability.
   b. the note payable is a current liability, but the interest payable is not.
   c. the interest payable is a current liability but the note payable is not.
   d. both the note payable and the interest payable are current liabilities.

5. **(LO 1)** Becky Sherrick Company has total proceeds from sales of $4,515. If the proceeds include sales taxes of 5%, the amount to be credited to Sales Revenue is:

   a. $4,000.
   b. $4,300.
   c. $4,289.25.
   d. None of the answer choices is correct.

6. **(LO 1)** Sensible Insurance Company collected a premium of $18,000 for a 1-year insurance policy on April 1. What amount should Sensible report as a current liability for Unearned Service Revenue at December 31?

   a. $0.
   b. $4,500.
   c. $13,500.
   d. $18,000.

7. **(LO 1)** When recording the employer's payroll costs:

   a. gross earnings are recorded as salaries and wages payable.
   b. net pay is recorded as salaries and wages expense.
   c. payroll deductions are recorded as liabilities.
   d. more than one of the answer choices is correct.

8. **(LO 1)** Employers' payroll taxes include:

   a. salaries and wages expense.
   b. union dues payable.
   c. income taxes payable.
   d. Social Security taxes payable.

9. **(LO 2)** A provision should be recorded in the accounts when:

   a. it is probable the cash outflow will happen, but the amount cannot be reliably estimated.
   b. it is possible the cash outflow will happen, and the amount can be reliably estimated.
   c. it is probable the cash outflow will happen, and the amount can be reliably estimated.
   d. it is possible the contingency will happen, but the amount cannot be reliably estimated.

10. **(LO 2)** At December 31, Beijing Supply prepares an adjusting entry for a product warranty contract. Which of the following accounts is/are included in the entry?

    a. Miscellaneous Expense.
    b. Warranty Expense.
    c. Repair Parts.
    d. Both Miscellaneous Expense and Warranty Expense.

11. (LO 2) Working capital is calculated as:
   a. current assets minus current liabilities.
   b. total assets minus total liabilities.
   c. non-current liabilities minus current liabilities.
   d. either total assets minus total liabilities, or non-current liabilities minus current liabilities.

12. (LO 2) The current ratio is computed as:
   a. total assets divided by total liabilities.
   b. total assets divided by current liabilities.
   c. current assets divided by total liabilities.
   d. current assets divided by current liabilities.

Solutions

1. **a.** The time period for classifying a liability as current is one year or the operating cycle, whichever is longer, not (b) shorter, (c) probable, or (d) possible.

2. **d.** To be classified as a current liability, a debt must be expected to be paid within one year or the operating cycle, whichever is longer. Choices (a) and (b) are both correct, but (d) is the better answer. Choice (c) is incorrect.

3. **b.** Accrued interest at December 31, 2029, is computed as the face value (₩88,500) times the interest rate (12%) times the portion of the year the debt was outstanding (4 months out of 12), or ₩3,540 (₩88,500 × 12% × 4/12), not (a) ₩2,655, (c) ₩4,425, or (d) ₩10,620.

4. **d.** Both the note payable and interest payable are current liabilities. Notes due for payment within one year of the statement of financial position date are usually classified as current liabilities. The other choices are therefore incorrect.

5. **b.** Dividing the total proceeds ($4,515) by one plus the sales tax rate (1.05) will result in the amount of sales to be credited to the Sales Revenue account of $4,300 ($4,515 ÷ 1.05). The other choices are therefore incorrect.

6. **b.** The monthly premium is $1,500 or $18,000 divided by 12. Because Sensible has recognized 9 months of insurance revenue (April 1–December 31), 3 months' insurance premium is still unearned. The amount that will be reported as Unearned Service Revenue is therefore $4,500 (3 months × $1,500), not (a) $0, (c) $13,500, or (d) $18,000.

7. **c.** When recording payroll, payroll deductions are recorded as liabilities. The other choices are incorrect because (a) gross earnings are recorded as salaries and wages expense, (b) net pay is recorded as salaries and wages payable, and (d) only one of the answer choices is true concerning payroll.

8. **d.** The employer is generally required to pay Social Security taxes as well as deposit the employees' Social Security taxes. Employer payroll taxes do not include (a) salaries and wages expense, (b) union dues payable, or (c) income taxes payable.

9. **c.** A provision is recorded when the amount can be reliably estimated and the likelihood of the cash outflow is probable. The other choices are therefore incorrect.

10. **b.** The adjusting entry for product warranties includes a debit to Warranty Expense, not (a) Miscellaneous Expense, (c) Repair Parts, or (d) both Miscellaneous Expense and Warranty Expense.

11. **a.** Working capital is defined as current assets minus current liabilities. The other choices are therefore incorrect.

12. **d.** The current ratio is defined as current assets divided by current liabilities. The other choices are therefore incorrect.

Practice Brief Exercises

Compute value-added taxes payable.

1. (LO 1) Pond Discounts does not segregate sales and value-added taxes at the time of sale. The register total for March 16 is ¥19,928 (amounts in thousands). All sales are subject to a 6% value-added tax. Compute value-added taxes payable, and make the entry to record the company's sales for March 16.

Solution

1. Value-added taxes payable:
   1. Sales = ¥18,800 = (¥19,928 ÷ 1.06)
   2. Value-added taxes payable = ¥1,128 = (¥18,800 × 6%)

Mar. 16	Cash	19,928	
	Sales Revenue		18,800
	Value-Added Taxes Payable		1,128

Compute gross earnings and net pay.

2. (LO 1) Ben Borke's regular hourly wage rate is $20, and he receives an hourly rate of $30 for work in excess of 40 hours. During a January pay period, Ben works 46 hours. Ben's income tax withholding is $123, he has no voluntary deductions, and the Social Security tax rate is 7.65%. Compute Ben's gross earnings and net pay for the pay period.

Solution

2. Gross earnings:

Regular pay (40 × $20)	$800.00	
Overtime pay (6 × $30)	180.00	$980.00
Gross earnings		$980.00
Less: Social Security taxes payable ($980 × 7.65%)	$ 74.97	
Income taxes payable	123.00	197.97
Net pay		$782.03

3. **(LO 2)** On October 1, Oswald Electronics introduces a new product that includes a one-year warranty on parts. By year-end, 3,000 units are sold. Management believes that 6% of the units will be defective and that the average warranty costs will be €120 per unit. Prepare the adjusting entry at December 31 to accrue the estimated warranty cost. No warranties have been honored as of December 31.

Prepare adjusting entry for warranty costs.

Solution

3. Dec. 31	Warranty Expense	21,600	
	Warranty Liability		21,600
	[(3,000 × 6%) × €120]		

Practice Exercises

1. **(LO 1)** On June 1, Song Group borrows ¥150,000 from First Bank on a 6-month, ¥150,000, 8% note (amounts in thousands).

Prepare entries for interest-bearing notes.

Instructions

a. Prepare the entry on June 1.

b. Prepare the adjusting entry on June 30.

c. Prepare the entry at maturity (December 1), assuming monthly adjusting entries have been made through November 30.

d. What was the total financing cost (interest expense)?

Solution

1. a. June 1	Cash	150,000	
	Notes Payable		150,000
b. June 30	Interest Expense	1,000	
	Interest Payable		
	(¥150,000 × 8% × 1/12)		1,000
c. Dec. 1	Notes Payable	150,000	
	Interest Payable		
	(¥150,000 × 8% × 6/12)	6,000	
	Cash		156,000

d. ¥6,000

2. **(LO 1)** During the month of September, Lake Corporation's employees earned wages of $60,000. Withholdings related to these wages were $4,590 for Social Security, $6,500 for income tax, and $2,000 for union dues.

Record liabilities related to salaries and wages.

Prepare the September 30 journal entries for (a) salaries and wages expense and salaries and wages payable, (b) payment of salaries and wages, and (c) the company's payroll tax expense.

Solution

2.

			Debit	Credit
a.	Sept. 30	Salaries and Wages Expense	60,000	
		Social Security Taxes Payable		4,590
		Income Taxes Payable		6,500
		Union Dues Payable		2,000
		Salaries and Wages Payable		46,910
b.	Sept. 30	Salaries and Wages Payable	46,910	
		Cash		46,910
c.	Sept. 30	Payroll Tax Expense	4,590	
		Social Security Taxes Payable		4,590

Prepare current liabilities section of the statement of financial position and evaluate liquidity.

3. **(LO 2)** Kuo Theater has the following liability accounts after posting adjusting entries (amounts in thousands): Accounts Payable NT$77,000, Unearned Ticket Revenue NT$36,000, Warranty Liability NT$25,000, Interest Payable NT$10,000, Mortgage Payable NT$150,000, Notes Payable NT$100,000, and Sales Taxes Payable NT$14,000. Assume the company's operating cycle is less than 1 year, ticket revenue will be recognized within 1 year, warranty costs are expected to be incurred within 1 year, and the notes mature in 3 years.

Instructions

a. Prepare the current liabilities section of the statement of financial position, assuming NT$40,000 of the mortgage is payable next year.

b. Comment on Kuo's liquidity, assuming total current assets are NT$350,000.

Solution

3. a.

Kuo Theater
Partial Statement of Financial Position

Current liabilities	
Accounts payable	NT$ 77,000
Unearned ticket revenue	36,000
Warranty liability	25,000
Sales taxes payable	14,000
Interest payable	10,000
Long-term debt due within one year	40,000
Total current liabilities	NT$202,000

b. Kuo's working capital is NT$148,000 (NT$350,000 − NT$202,000), and its current ratio is 1.73:1 (NT$350,000 ÷ NT$202,000). Although a current ratio of 2:1 has been considered the standard for a good credit rating, many companies operate successfully with a current ratio well below 2:1.

Practice Problem

Record current liabilities and provisions.

(LO 1, 2) Boha Group had the following selected transactions (amounts in thousands).

Feb. 1 Signs a ¥50,000, 6-month, 9%-interest-bearing note payable to CitiBank and receives ¥50,000 in cash.

10 Cash register sales total ¥43,200, which includes an 8% value-added tax.

28 The payroll for the month consists of salaries and wages of ¥50,000. All wages are subject to 8% Social Security taxes. A total of ¥8,900 income taxes are withheld. The salaries are paid on March 1.

28 The company develops the following adjustment data.

1. Interest expense of ¥375 has been incurred on the note.
2. Employer payroll taxes include 8% Social Security taxes.
3. Some sales were made under warranty. Of the units sold under warranty, 350 are expected to become defective. Repair costs are estimated to be ¥40 per unit.

Instructions

a. Journalize the February transactions.

b. Journalize the adjusting entries at February 28.

Solution

a.	Feb. 1	Cash	50,000	
		Notes Payable		50,000
		(Issued 6-month, 9%-interest-bearing note to CitiBank)		
	10	Cash	43,200	
		Sales Revenue (¥43,200 ÷ 1.08)		40,000
		Value-Added Taxes Payable (¥40,000 × 8%)		3,200
		(To record sales revenue and value-added taxes payable)		
	28	Salaries and Wages Expense	50,000	
		Social Security Taxes Payable (8% × ¥50,000)		4,000
		Income Taxes Payable		8,900
		Salaries and Wages Payable		37,100
		(To record February salaries)		
b.	Feb. 28	Interest Expense	375	
		Interest Payable		375
		(To record accrued interest for February)		
	28	Payroll Tax Expense	4,000	
		Social Security Taxes Payable		4,000
		(To record employer's payroll taxes on February payroll)		
	28	Warranty Expense (350 × ¥40)	14,000	
		Warranty Liability		14,000
		(To record estimated warranty liability)		

Questions

1. Anjali Kumar believes a current liability is a debt that can be expected to be paid in one year. Is Anjali correct? Explain.

2. Petrocelli Foods obtains €40,000 in cash by signing a 7%, 6-month, €40,000 note payable to First Bank on July 1. Petrocelli's fiscal year ends on September 30. What information should be reported for the note payable in the annual financial statements?

3. **a.** Your roommate says, "Value-added taxes are reported as an expense in the income statement." Do you agree? Explain.

   b. Miaoli Company has cash proceeds from sales of NT$8,400 (amounts in thousands). This amount includes NT$400 of sales taxes. Give the entry to record the proceeds.

4. South Ulsan University sold 15,000 season football tickets at NT$80 (in thousands) each for its six-game home schedule. What entries should be made (a) when the tickets were sold, and (b) after each game?

5. What is liquidity? What are two measures of liquidity?

6. What is a provision? Give an example of a provision.

7. What is the difference between gross pay and net pay? Which amount should a company record as wages and salaries expense?

8. Which payroll tax is generally levied on both employers and employees?

9. Are the income taxes withheld from employee paychecks a payroll tax expense for the employer? Explain your answer.

10. How does working capital differ from the current ratio? How are they similar?

11. When should liabilities for each of the following items be recorded on the books of a company? (1) Warranty, (2) acquisition of goods by purchase on credit, and (3) profit-sharing bonus.

Brief Exercises

Identify whether obligations are current liabilities.

BE10.1 (LO 1) Jamison Company has the following obligations at December 31: (a) a note payable for $100,000 due in 2 years, (b) a 10-year mortgage payable of $300,000 payable in ten $30,000 annual payments, (c) interest payable of $15,000 on the mortgage, and (d) accounts payable of $60,000. For each obligation, indicate whether it should be classified as a current liability. (Assume an operating cycle of less than one year.)

Prepare entries for an interest-bearing note payable.

BE10.2 (LO 1) Pom Computers borrows HK$60,000 on July 1 from the bank by signing a HK$60,000, 10%, one-year note payable (amounts in thousands).

a. Prepare the journal entry to record the proceeds of the note.

b. Prepare the journal entry to record accrued interest at December 31, assuming adjusting entries are made only at the end of the year.

Compute and record sales taxes payable.

BE10.3 (LO 1) Coghlan Auto Supply does not segregate sales and sales taxes at the time of its cash sales. The register total for March 16 is €16,380. All sales are subject to a 5% sales tax. Compute sales taxes payable, and make the entry to record sales taxes payable and sales revenue.

Prepare entry for value-added taxes.

BE10.4 (LO 1) Dillons AS made credit sales of €30,000 which are subject to 6% VAT. The company also made cash sales which totaled €20,670 including the 6% VAT. (a) Prepare the entry to record Dillons' credit sales. (b) Prepare the entry to record Dillons' cash sales.

Prepare entries for liabilities related to salaries and wages.

BE10.5 (LO 1) Lexington AG's weekly payroll of €24,000 included Social Security taxes withheld of €1,920, income taxes withheld of €2,990, and insurance premiums withheld of €250. Prepare the journal entry to record Lexington's payroll.

Prepare entries for unearned revenues.

BE10.6 (LO 1) Sport Pro Magazine sold 12,000 annual subscriptions of its monthly magazine on August 1, 2029, for €18 each. Prepare Sport Pro's August 1, 2029, journal entry and the December 31, 2029, annual adjusting entry.

Prepare entries for unearned revenues.

BE10.7 (LO 1) Derby University sells 4,000 season basketball tickets at $210 each for its 12-game home schedule. Give the entry to record (a) the sale of the season tickets and (b) the revenue recognized by playing the first home game.

Prepare entries for liabilities related to salaries and wages.

BE10.8 (LO 1) Mayaguez Ltd. provides its officers with bonuses based on net income. For 2029, the bonuses total £350,000 and are paid on February 15, 2030. Prepare Mayaguez's December 31, 2029, adjusting entry and the February 15, 2030, entry.

Compute gross earnings and net pay.

BE10.9 (LO 1) Rachel Shinnar's gross earnings for the week are €800. Rachel's income tax withholding is €95, she has no voluntary deductions, and the Social Security tax rate is 6%. Compute Rachel's net pay for the pay period.

Record a payroll and the payment of wages.

BE10.10 (LO 1) Data for Rachel Shinnar are presented in BE10.9. Prepare the journal entries to record (a) Rachel's pay for the period and (b) the payment of Rachel's wages. Use January 15 for the end of the pay period and the payment date.

Record employer payroll taxes.

BE10.11 (LO 1) In January, gross earnings in Lugo Company totaled $80,000. All earnings are subject to 7.65% Social Security taxes and income taxes at 20%. Prepare the entry to record January payroll tax expense for the employer.

Prepare adjusting entry for warranty costs.

BE10.12 (LO 2) On December 1, New Belgium Appliances introduces a new product that includes a one-year warranty on parts. In December, 1,000 units are sold. Management believes that 5% of the units will be defective and that the average warranty costs will be €90 per unit. Prepare the adjusting entry at December 31 to accrue the estimated warranty cost.

Prepare entries related to provisions.

BE10.13 (LO 2) Scorcese A.Ş. is involved in a lawsuit at December 31, 2029. (a) Prepare the December 31 entry assuming it is probable that Scorcese will be liable for ₺900,000 as a result of this suit. (b) Prepare the December 31 entry, if any, assuming it is *not* probable that Scorcese will be liable for any payment as a result of this suit.

BE10.14 (LO 2) **Yahoo! Inc.**'s (USA) recent financial statements contain the following selected data (in thousands).

Analyze liquidity.

Current assets	$ 4,594,772	Current liabilities	$1,717,728
Total assets	14,936,030	Total liabilities	2,417,394

Compute (a) working capital and (b) current ratio.

DO IT! Exercises

DO IT! 10.1 (LO 1) You and several classmates are studying for the next accounting exam. They ask you to answer the following questions:

Answer questions about current liabilities.

1. If cash is borrowed on a €70,000, 9-month, 6% note on August 1, how much interest expense would be incurred by December 31?
2. The cash register total including sales taxes is €42,000, and the sales tax rate is 5%. What is the sales taxes payable?
3. If €45,000 is collected in advance on November 1 for 6-month magazine subscriptions, what amount of subscription revenue should be recognized by December 31?

DO IT! 10.2 (LO 2) Eslite Company, has the following account balances at December 31, 2029 (amounts in thousands).

Prepare current liabilities section and compute liquidity measures.

Notes payable (NT$60,000 due after 12/31/30)	NT$100,000
Unearned service revenue	70,000
Other long-term debt (NT$90,000 due in 2030)	250,000
Salaries and wages payable	32,000
Accounts payable	63,000

In addition, Eslite is involved in a lawsuit. Legal counsel feels it is probable Eslite will pay damages of NT$25,000 in 2030.

a. Prepare the current liabilities section of Eslite's December 31, 2029, statement of financial position.

b. Eslite's current assets are NT$570,000. Compute Eslite's working capital and current ratio.

Exercises

E10.1 (LO 1) Ang Hsu Enterprises had the following transactions involving notes payable (amounts in thousands).

Prepare entries for interest-bearing notes.

July 1, 2029	Borrows NT$50,000 from First Taiwan Bank by signing a 9-month, 8% note.
Nov. 1, 2029	Borrows NT$60,000 from Nantou City Bank by signing a 3-month, 6% note.
Dec. 31, 2029	Prepares adjusting entries.
Feb. 1, 2030	Pays principal and interest to Nantou City Bank.
Apr. 1, 2030	Pays principal and interest to First Taiwan Bank.

Instructions

Prepare journal entries for each of the transactions.

E10.2 (LO 1) On June 1, Merando Company borrows $90,000 from First Bank on a 6-month, $90,000, 8% note.

Prepare entries for interest-bearing notes.

Instructions

a. Prepare the entry on June 1.

b. Prepare the adjusting entry on June 30.

c. Prepare the entry at maturity (December 1), assuming monthly adjusting entries have been made through November 30.

d. What was the total financing cost (interest expense)?

Journalize sales and related taxes.

E10.3 (LO 1) In performing accounting services for small businesses, you encounter the following situations pertaining to cash sales.

1. Cerviq Company enters sales and sales taxes separately on its cash register. On April 10, the register totals are sales $22,000 and sales taxes $1,100.
2. Quartz Company does not segregate sales and sales taxes. Its register total for April 15 is $13,780, which includes a 6% sales tax.

Instructions

Prepare the entries to record the sales transactions and related taxes for (a) Cerviq Company and (b) Quartz Company.

Prepare entries for sales and value-added taxes.

E10.4 (LO 1) During the month of June, Danielle's Boutique had cash sales of £265,000 and credit sales of £153,700, both of which include the 6% sales tax that must be remitted to the government by July 15.

Instructions

a. Prepare the adjusting entry that should be recorded to fairly present the June 30 financial statements.
b. How would the adjusting entry change if the 6% tax was a VAT rather than a sales tax?

Journalize unearned subscription revenue.

E10.5 (LO 1) Cassini Company Ltd. publishes a monthly sports magazine, *Fishing Preview*. Subscriptions to the magazine cost $28 per year. During November 2029, Cassini sells 6,300 subscriptions for cash, beginning with the December issue. Cassini prepares financial statements quarterly and recognizes subscription revenue at the end of the quarter. The company uses the accounts Unearned Subscription Revenue and Subscription Revenue. The company has a December 31 year-end.

Instructions

a. Prepare the entry in November for the receipt of the subscriptions.
b. Prepare the adjusting entry at December 31, 2029, to record subscription revenue in December 2029.
c. Prepare the adjusting entry at March 31, 2030, to record subscription revenue in the first quarter of 2030.

Prepare entries related to salaries and wages.

E10.6 (LO 1) The payroll of Kee Ltd. for September 2029 is as follows (amounts in thousands): total payroll was ¥340,000; income taxes in the amount of ¥80,000 were withheld, as was ¥9,000 in union dues; and the current Social Security tax is 8% of an employee's wages. The employer must also remit 8% for employees' wages for Social Security taxes.

Instructions

Prepare the journal entries to record (a) salaries and wages payable, (b) salaries and wages paid, and (c) employer payroll taxes.

Prepare entries related to salaries and wages.

E10.7 (LO 1) Allison Hardware Ltd.'s payroll for November 2029 is €200,000. The Social Security rate is 8% on an employee's wages. Income tax withheld amounts to €29,000.

Instructions

Prepare the journal entries to record (a) salaries and wages payable and (b) Allison Hardware Ltd.'s payroll tax expense.

Prepare entries for warranties.

E10.8 (LO 2) Soundgarden Ltd. sold 200 color laser copiers on July 10, 2029, for £4,000 apiece, together with a 1-year warranty. Maintenance on each copier during the warranty period is estimated to be £330.

Instructions

Prepare entries to record the sale of the copiers, the related warranty costs, and any accrual on December 31, 2029. Actual warranty costs (inventory) incurred in 2029 were £17,000.

Record estimated liability and expense for warranties.

E10.9 (LO 2) Ting Manufacturing sells its products with a 75-day warranty for defective merchandise. Based on past experience, Ting estimates that 3% of the units sold will become defective during the warranty period. Management estimates that the average cost of replacing or repairing a defective unit is NT$15 (amounts in thousands). The units sold and units defective that occurred during the last 2 months of 2029 are as follows.

Month	Units Sold	Units Defective Prior to December 31
November	30,000	600
December	32,000	400

Instructions

a. Prepare the journal entries to record the provision for warranties and the costs incurred in honoring 1,000 warranty claims. (Assume actual costs of NT$15,000.)

b. Determine the estimated warranty liability at December 31 for the units sold in November and December.

c. Give the entry to record the honoring of 500 warranty contracts in January at an average cost of NT$15.

E10.10 (LO 2) Streep Factory provides a 2-year warranty with one of its products which was first sold in 2029. Streep sold $1,000,000 of products subject to the warranty. Streep expects $125,000 of warranty costs over the next 2 years. In 2029, Streep spent $70,000 servicing warranty claims. Prepare Streep's journal entries in 2029 to record the sales of its products, the costs incurred in honoring the warranties (assume expenditures are for repair costs), and the estimated liability for warranties at December 31, 2029.

Record expense for warranties.

E10.11 (LO 1) Gabrielle Osmon's hourly wage is €14. She receives a wage of €21 for work in excess of 40 hours. During a March weekly pay period, Gabrielle worked 46 hours. Gabrielle's income tax withholding is €135.

Compute and record net pay.

Instructions

a. Compute the following amounts for Gabrielle's wages for the current period: (1) gross earnings, (2) Social Security taxes (assume a 7.65% rate), and (3) net pay.

b. Record Gabrielle's pay.

E10.12 (LO 1) Selected data from a February payroll register for Saputra Group are presented below. Some amounts are intentionally omitted.

Compute missing payroll amounts and record payroll.

Gross earnings:		Medical insurance premium	Rp(3)
Regular	Rp9,100	Union dues	100
Overtime	(1)	Total deductions	(4)
Total	(2)	Net pay	Rp7,595
Deductions:		Account debited:	
Social Security taxes	Rp 765	Salaries and Wages Expense	(5)
Income taxes	1,140		

Social Security taxes are 7.65%. Medical insurance premium is 4% of gross earnings.

Instructions

a. Fill in the missing amounts.

b. Journalize (1) the February payroll and (2) the payment of the payroll.

E10.13 (LO 2) Gallardo Industries is involved in a lawsuit as a result of an accident that took place September 5, 2029. The lawsuit was filed on November 1, 2029, and claims damages of NT$1,000,000.

Record and disclose provisions.

Instructions

a. Assume that at December 31, 2029, Gallardo's attorneys feel that there is a greater than 50% chance that Gallardo will lose the lawsuit and be required to pay NT$1,000,000. How should the company account for this lawsuit?

b. Assume instead that at December 31, 2029, Gallardo's attorneys feel that there is a less than 50% chance that Gallardo could lose the lawsuit and be required to pay NT$1,000,000. How should the company account for this lawsuit?

Prepare the current liabilities section of the statement of financial position.

E10.14 (LO 2) Younger Online Company has the following liability accounts after posting adjusting entries: Accounts Payable $73,000, Unearned Ticket Revenue $24,000, Warranty Liability $18,000, Interest Payable $8,000, Mortgage Payable $120,000, Notes Payable $80,000, and Value-Added Taxes Payable $10,000. Assume the company's operating cycle is less than 1 year, ticket revenue will be recognized within 1 year, warranty costs are expected to be incurred within 1 year, and the notes mature in 3 years.

Instructions

a. Prepare the current liabilities section of the statement of financial position, assuming $30,000 of the mortgage is payable next year.

b. Comment on Younger Online Company's liquidity, assuming total current assets are $300,000.

Calculate current ratio and working capital before and after paying accounts payable.

E10.15 (LO 2) Suppose the following financial data were reported by **3M Company** (USA) for 2028 and 2029 (dollars in millions).

3M Company
Statement of Financial Position (partial)

	2029	2028
Current assets		
Cash and cash equivalents	$ 3,040	$1,849
Accounts receivable, net	3,250	3,195
Inventories	2,639	3,013
Other current assets	1,866	1,541
Total current assets	$10,795	$9,598
Current liabilities	$ 4,897	$5,839

Instructions

a. Calculate the current ratio and working capital for 3M for 2028 and 2029.

b. Suppose that at the end of 2029, 3M management used $200 million cash to pay off $200 million of accounts payable. How would its current ratio and working capital have changed?

Identify key terms.

E10.16 (LO 1, 2) The following is a list of words or phrases introduced in the chapter.

1. Current liability
2. Notes payable
3. Employee payroll deductions
4. Current ratio
5. Provision
6. Gross earnings
7. Social Security taxes
8. Working capital
9. Net pay
10. Employer payroll taxes

Instructions

Match the word or phrase above with its description below.

________ **a.** Total compensation earned by an employee.

________ **b.** An obligation in the form of a written note.

________ **c.** A liability of uncertain timing or amount.

________ **d.** A measure computed as current assets minus current liabilities.

________ **e.** A measure of a company's liquidity.

________ **f.** A debt that a company expects to pay within one year or the operating cycle.

________ **g.** Amounts withheld from gross earnings to determine the amount of a paycheck.

________ **h.** Benefits provided by a government that are funded from taxes assessed on both the employer and employees.

________ **i.** Gross pay less payroll deductions.

________ **j.** Social Security taxes owed by employers.

Problems

Prepare current liability entries, adjusting entries, and current liabilities section.

P10.1 (LO 1, 2) On January 1, 2029, the ledger of Chuan-Kwang Luggage contains the following liability accounts (amounts in thousands).

Accounts Payable	NT$52,000
Sales Taxes Payable	7,700
Unearned Service Revenue	16,000

During January, the following selected transactions occurred.

Jan.	5	Sold merchandise for cash totaling NT$20,520, which includes 8% sales taxes.
	12	Performed services for customers who had made advance payments of NT$10,000. (Credit Service Revenue.)
	14	Paid revenue department for sales taxes collected in December 2028 (NT$7,700).
	20	Sold 900 units of a new product on credit at NT$50 per unit, plus 8% sales tax. This new product is subject to a 1-year warranty.
	21	Borrowed NT$27,000 from First National Bank on a 3-month, 8%, NT$27,000 note.
	21	Sold merchandise for cash totaling NT$12,420, which includes 8% sales taxes.

Instructions

a. Journalize the January transactions.

b. Journalize the adjusting entries at January 31 for (1) the outstanding notes payable, and (2) estimated warranty liability, assuming warranty costs are expected to equal 7% of sales of the new product. (*Hint:* Use one-third of a month for the First National Bank note.)

c. Prepare the current liabilities section of the statement of financial position at January 31, 2029. Assume no change in accounts payable.

c. Current liability total NT$94,250

P10.2 (LO 1, 5) The following are selected transactions of Blanco Company. Blanco prepares financial statements **quarterly**. Interest on all notes is paid at maturity.

Journalize and post note transactions; show statement of financial position presentation.

Jan.	2	Purchased merchandise on account from Nunez Company, $30,000, terms 2/10, n/30. (Blanco uses the perpetual inventory system.)
Feb.	1	Issued a 9%, 2-month, $30,000 note to Nunez in payment of account.
Mar.	31	Accrued interest for 2 months on Nunez note.
Apr.	1	Paid face value and interest on Nunez note.
July	1	Purchased equipment from Marson Equipment, paying $11,000 in cash and signing a 10%, 3-month, $60,000 note.
Sept.	30	Accrued interest for 3 months on Marson note.
Oct.	1	Paid face value and interest on Marson note.
Dec.	1	Borrowed $24,000 from the Paola Bank by issuing a 3-month, 8% note with a face value of $24,000.
Dec.	31	Recognized interest expense for 1 month on Paola Bank note.

Instructions

a. Prepare journal entries for the listed transactions and events.

b. Post to the accounts Notes Payable, Interest Payable, and Interest Expense.

c. Show the statement of financial position presentation of notes and interest payable at December 31, 2029.

d. What is total interest expense for the year?

d. $2,110

P10.3 (LO 1) Cedarville Company pays its office employee payroll monthly. Below is a list of employees and their payroll data for August.

Record payroll expense.

Employee	Earnings for August
Mark Hamill	$4,200
Karen Robbins	3,500
Brent Kirk	2,700
Alec Guinness	7,400
Ken Sprouse	8,000

Assume that the income tax withheld is 10% of wages. Union dues withheld are 2% of wages. The Social Security rate is 8% on employee and employer.

Instructions

Make the journal entries necessary for the August payroll (assume the payroll is paid in August). The entries for the payroll and the company's payroll tax liability are made separately.

Cash credit $20,640

Record payroll expense.

P10.4 (LO 1) Below is a payroll sheet for Otis Import plc for the month of September 2029. Assume a 10% income tax rate for all employees and an 8% Social Security tax on employee and employer.

Name	Earnings to Aug. 31	September Earnings	Income Tax Withholding	Social Security
B.D. Williams	£ 6,800	£ 800		
D. Raye	6,500	700		
K. Baker	7,600	1,100		
F. Lopez	13,600	1,900		
A. Daniels	105,000	13,000		
B. Kingston	112,000	16,000		

Instructions

a. Salaries and Wages Payable £27,470

a. Make the necessary entries to record (1) salaries and wages expense and (2) the payment of the payroll.

b. Make the entry to record the payroll tax expenses of Otis Import.

Determine financial statement impact of current liabilities.

P10.5 (LO 1, 2) Presented below is a list of possible transactions.

1. Purchased inventory for €80,000 on account (assume perpetual system is used).

2. Issued an €80,000 note payable in payment on account (see item 1 above).

3. Recorded accrued interest on the note from item 2.

4. Recorded cash sales of €75,260, which includes 10% VAT.

5. Recorded wage expense of €35,000. The cash paid was €25,000; the difference was due to various amounts withheld.

6. Recorded employer's payroll taxes.

7. Recorded bonuses due to employees.

8. Recorded sales of product.

9. Honored warranty contracts in the period of sale, reducing the asset repair parts.

10. Recorded a liability on a lawsuit that the company will probably lose.

Instructions

Set up a table using the format shown below and analyze the effect of the above transactions on the financial statement categories indicated.

#	Assets	Liabilities	Equity	Net Income
1				

Use the following code:

I: Increase D: Decrease NE: No net effect

Compute current ratio and working capital.

P10.6 (LO 2) Chen Group has been operating for several years, and on December 31, 2029, presented the following statement of financial position (amounts in thousands).

Chen Group
Statement of Financial Position
December 31, 2029

Plant assets (net)	¥220,000	Share capital—ordinary	¥220,000
Inventory	95,000	Mortgage payable	140,000
Receivables	75,000	Accounts payable	70,000
Cash	40,000		
	¥430,000		¥430,000

The mortgage payable is due in 2032.

Instructions

Compute the current ratio and the working capital.

Distinguish current and non-current liabilities for warranty costs.

P10.7 (LO 1, 2) Liuhe Company provides a three-year warranty on all central air-conditioning equipment sold over 200 tons. Based on past experience, warranty costs account for approximately 12% of sales revenue, with 2% in the first year, 4% in the second year, and 6% in the third year. The following is detail data of sales revenue and actual warranty expenses for each year:

Year	Sales Revenue	Actual Warranty Expenses
X1	$20,000,000	$ 300,000
X2	50,000,000	1,500,000
X3	80,000,000	5,100,000

Instructions

a. What was the current liability balance for Liuhe Company's warranty service at the end of Year X3?

b. Prepare the necessary entries to accrue the estimated warranty costs.

Comprehensive Accounting Cycle Review

ACR10 Morgan Fashions' statement of financial position at December 31, 2028, is presented below.

Morgan Fashions
Statement of Financial Position
December 31, 2028

Equipment	€ 38,000	Share Capital—Ordinary	€ 20,750
Inventory	30,750	Retained Earnings	20,000
Prepaid Insurance	6,000	Accounts Payable	13,750
Cash	30,000	Interest Payable	250
		Notes Payable (long-term)	50,000
	€104,750		€104,750

During January 2029, the following transactions occurred. (Morgan uses the perpetual inventory system.)

1. Morgan paid €250 accrued interest on the note payable on January 1, 2029. The note is due December 31, 2030.
2. Morgan purchased €261,100 of inventory on account.
3. Morgan sold for €440,000 cash, inventory which cost €265,000. Morgan also collected €28,600 in sales taxes.
4. Morgan paid €230,000 in accounts payable.
5. Morgan paid €17,000 in sales taxes to the taxing authority.
6. Paid other operating expenses of €30,000.
7. On January 31, 2029, the payroll for the month consists of salaries and wages of €60,000. All salaries and wages are subject to 7.65% Social Security taxes. A total of €8,900 income taxes are withheld. The salaries and wages are paid on February 1.

Adjustment data:

8. Interest expense of €250 has been incurred on the notes payable.
9. The insurance for the year 2029 was prepaid on December 31, 2028.
10. The equipment was acquired on December 31, 2028, and will be depreciated on a straight-line basis over 5 years with a €2,000 residual value.
11. Employer's payroll taxes include 7.65% Social Security taxes.

Instructions

(You may need to set up T-accounts to determine ending balances.)

a. Prepare journal entries for the transactions listed above and the adjusting entries.

b. Prepare an adjusted trial balance at January 31, 2029.

c. Prepare an income statement and a retained earnings statement for the month ending January 31, 2029, and a classified statement of financial position as of January 31, 2029.

Expand Your Critical Thinking

Financial Reporting Problem: TSMC, Ltd. (TWN)

CT10.1 The financial statements of **TSMC** appear in Appendix A. The complete annual report, including the notes to the financial statements, is available at the company's website.

Instructions

Refer to TSMC's financial statements and answer the following questions about liabilities.

a. What were TSMC's total current liabilities at December 31, 2020? What was the increase/decrease in TSMC's total current liabilities from the prior year?

b. What were the components of total current liabilities on December 31, 2020?

c. What was TSMC's total non-current liabilities at December 31, 2020? What was the increase/decrease in total non-current liabilities from the prior year? What were the components of total non-current liabilities on December 31, 2020?

Comparative Analysis Problem: Nestlé SA (CHE) vs. Delfi Limited (SGP)

CT10.2 **Nestlé**'s financial statements are presented in Appendix B. Financial statements of **Delfi Limited** are presented in Appendix C.

Instructions

a. At the end of the most recent fiscal year reported, what was Nestlé's largest current liability account? What were its total current liabilities? What was Delfi Limited's largest current liability account? What were its total current liabilities?

b. Based on information contained in those financial statements, compute the following for each company for the most recent fiscal year reported.

1. Working capital.
2. Current ratio.

c. What conclusions concerning the relative liquidity of these companies can be drawn from these data?

Decision-Making Across the Organization

CT10.3 Cunningham Processing performs word-processing services for business clients and students in a university community. The work for business clients is fairly steady throughout the year. The work for students peaks significantly in December and May as a result of term papers, research project reports, and dissertations.

Two years ago, the company attempted to meet the peak demand by hiring part-time help. This led to numerous errors and much customer dissatisfaction. A year ago, the company hired four experienced employees on a permanent basis in place of part-time help. This proved to be much better in terms of productivity and customer satisfaction. But, it has caused an increase in annual payroll costs and a significant decline in annual net income.

Recently, Melissa Braun, a sales representative of Banister Services, has made a proposal to the company. Under her plan, Banister will provide up to four experienced workers at a daily rate of $80 per person for an 8-hour workday. Banister workers are not available on an hourly basis. Cunningham would have to pay only the daily rate for the workers used.

The owner of Cunningham Processing, Carol Holt, asks you, as the company's accountant, to prepare a report on the expenses that are pertinent to the decision. If the Banister plan is adopted, Carol will terminate the employment of two permanent employees and will keep two permanent employees. At the moment, each employee earns an annual income of $22,000. Cunningham pays 7.65% Social Security taxes. In addition, Cunningham pays $40 per month for each employee for medical and dental insurance. Carol indicates that if the Banister Services plan is accepted, her needs for temporary workers will be as follows.

Months	Number of Employees	Working Days per Month
January–March	2	20
April–May	3	25
June–October	2	18
November–December	3	23

Instructions

With the class divided into groups, answer the following.

a. Prepare a report showing the comparative payroll expense of continuing to employ permanent workers compared to adopting the Banister Services plan.

b. What other factors should Carol consider before finalizing her decision?

Communication Activity

CT10.4 Sammo Cheung, president of the Mui Consultants, has recently hired a number of additional employees. He recognizes that additional payroll tax will be due as a result of this hiring, and that the company will serve as the collection agent for other taxes.

Instructions

In an email to Sammo Cheung, explain each of the taxes, and identify the tax that results in payroll tax expense to Mui Consultants.

Ethics Case

CT10.5 Joko Saputra owns and manages Joko's Restaurant, a 24-hour restaurant near the city's medical complex. Joko employs 9 full-time employees and 16 part-time employees. He pays all of the full-time employees by check, the amounts of which are determined by Joko's public accountant, Acha Uwais. Joko pays all of his part-time employees in currency. He computes their wages and withdraws the cash directly from his cash register.

Acha has repeatedly urged Joko to pay all employees by check. But as Joko has told his competitor and friend, Iko Mahaffey, who owns the Senang Diner, "My part-time employees prefer the currency over a check. Also, I don't withhold or pay any taxes on those cash wages because they go totally unrecorded and unnoticed."

Instructions

a. Who are the stakeholders in this situation?

b. What are the legal and ethical considerations regarding Joko's handling of his payroll?

c. Acha Uwais is aware of Joko's payment of the part-time payroll in currency. What are her ethical responsibilities in this case?

d. What internal control principle is violated in this payroll process?

Considering Environmental, Social, and Governance Reporting

CT10.6 **Microfinance** is the process of lending small amounts of money to low-income or unemployed people who would otherwise not have access to banking services. It enables many of these people to operate small businesses. Recent challenges for microfinance are discussed in the *Economist* article, "For Microfinance Lenders, Covid-19 Is an Existential Threat."

Instructions

Read the article and then answer the following questions. (The article can be accessed by doing an online search that includes the title of the article and the magazine.)

a. Under normal circumstances, what is the default rate on small loans at **Dvara Trust** (IND)? What percent of borrowers were unable to pay their loans during the pandemic? Why were many borrowers unable to pay their loans even if they had money?

b. According to the World Bank, what percentage of the total number of global businesses do "MSMEs" represent? What percentage of employment does this represent? How many customers do microfinance institutions (MFIs) serve?

c. People who lack access to banking services are referred to as unbanked. What was the global change in the number of unbanked people between 2011 and 2017?

d. What is one step that could significantly reduce the default rate of loans (and thus sustain the businesses as well as lenders) during a pandemic?

Answers to Accounting Across the Organization Question

SAP's Liabilities—Good or Bad? Q: What are some other companies where an increase in current liabilities, specifically deferred income, could be a good sign related to growth? Try to also think of companies not in the software and information technology industry. **A:** Any company that is paid in advance before it provides a product or a service, such as newspapers, magazines, gift card programs, prepaid cell phone plans, and streaming services, would qualify.

A Look at U.S. GAAP

LEARNING OBJECTIVE 3

Compare the accounting for current liabilities under IFRS and U.S. GAAP.

IFRS and GAAP have similar definitions of liabilities. The general recording procedures for payroll are similar, although differences occur depending on the types of benefits that are provided in different countries. For example, companies in other countries often have different forms of pensions, unemployment benefits, welfare payments, and so on.

Key Points

Following are the key similarities and differences between GAAP and IFRS related to current liabilities and payroll.

Similarities

- The basic definition of a liability under GAAP and IFRS is very similar. In a more technical way, liabilities are defined by the IASB as a present obligation of the entity arising from past events, the settlement of which is expected to result in an outflow from the entity of resources embodying economic benefits.
- The accounting for current liabilities such as notes payable, unearned revenue, and payroll taxes payable are similar between IFRS and GAAP.
- Under both GAAP and IFRS, liabilities are classified as current if they are expected to be paid within 12 months or the operating cycle, whichever is longer.
- Both GAAP and IFRS require accrual of liabilities even when there is some uncertainty related to the liability as to its existence or amount. Specifically, both require that a liability should be accrued when it is probable that an outflow will occur and a reliable estimate can be made of the obligation.

Differences

- Companies using GAAP show assets before liabilities. Also, they will show current liabilities before non-current liabilities.
- While both GAAP and IFRS agree that when there is uncertainty about the existence of a liability, if it is probable that an outflow will occur, the liability should be accrued. However, while IFRS indicates that probable means more likely than not to occur, GAAP standards using the term probable are often interpreted as having a greater than 70% chance of occurring.
- Under GAAP, some contingent liabilities are recorded in the financial statements, others are disclosed, and in some cases no disclosure is required. IFRS uses the term **contingent liability** to refer only to possible obligations that are **not** recognized in the financial statements but may be disclosed if certain criteria are met.

GAAP Practice

GAAP Self-Test Questions

1. Which of the following is **false**?
   - **a.** Under GAAP, current liabilities are presented before non-current liabilities.
   - **b.** Under GAAP, an item is a current liability if it will be paid within the next 12 months.
   - **c.** Under GAAP, current liabilities are sometimes netted against current assets on the statement of financial position.
   - **d.** Under GAAP, a liability is only recognized if it is a present obligation.
2. How are contingent liabilities accounted for under GAAP?
   - **a.** Disclosed in the notes if it is probable that the company will incur a loss but the amount cannot be reasonably estimated.
   - **b.** Reported on the face of the financial statements if it is possible a loss will occur.
   - **c.** The same as a provision.
   - **d.** Defined in the same way as under IFRS.
3. Under GAAP, obligations related to warranties are considered:
   - **a.** contingent liabilities.
   - **b.** provisions.
   - **c.** possible obligations.
   - **d.** None of the answer choices is correct.
4. The joint projects of the FASB and IASB could potentially:
   - **a.** change the definition of liabilities.
   - **b.** change the definition of equity.
   - **c.** change the definition of assets.
   - **d.** All of the answer choices are correct.

GAAP Exercises

GAAP10.1 Define a contingent liability and give an example.

GAAP10.2 Briefly describe some of the similarities and differences between GAAP and IFRS with respect to the accounting for liabilities.

GAAP Financial Reporting Problem: Apple Inc. (USA)

GAAP10.3 The financial statements of **Apple** are presented in Appendix D. The complete annual report, including the notes to the financial statements, is available at the company's website.

Instructions

Refer to Apple's financial statements and answer the following questions about current and contingent liabilities and payroll costs.

- **a.** What were Apple's total current liabilities at September 26, 2020? What was the increase/decrease in Apple's total current liabilities from the prior year?
- **b.** In Apple's Note 10, the company explains the nature of its contingencies. Under what conditions does Apple recognize (record and report) liabilities for contingencies?
- **c.** What were the components of total current liabilities on September 26, 2020?

Answers to GAAP Self-Test Questions

1. c **2.** a **3.** a **4.** d

CHAPTER 11

Non-Current Liabilities

LEARNING OBJECTIVES After studying this chapter, you should be able to:

LO 1 Describe the major characteristics of bonds.
LO 2 Explain how to account for bond transactions.
LO 3 Explain how to account for other non-current liabilities.
LO 4 Discuss how non-current liabilities are reported and analyzed.

Chapter Preview

As you can see from the following Feature Story, having liabilities can be dangerous in difficult economic times. In this chapter, we will explain the accounting for the major types of non-current liabilities reported on the statement of financial position. Non-current liabilities are obligations that are expected to be paid more than one year in the future. These liabilities may be bonds, long-term notes, or lease obligations.

Non-Current Liabilities

Overview of Bonds	Accounting for Bond Transactions	Accounting for Non-Current Liabilities	Reporting and Analyzing Non-Current Liabilities
• Types of bonds • Issuing procedures • Bond trading • Determining the market price of a bond	• Issuing bonds at face value • Discount or premium on bonds • Issuing bonds at a discount • Issuing bonds at a premium • Redeeming bonds	• Long-term notes payable • Lease liabilities	• Presentation • Analysis • Debt and equity financing

Practice

DO IT! 1 Bond Terminology
DO IT! 2a Bond Issuance
2b Bond Redemption
DO IT! 3 Long-Term Notes
DO IT! 4 Analysis of Non-Current Liabilities

Go to the Review and Practice section at the end of the chapter for a review of key concepts and practice applications with solutions.
Additional tutorials and practice opportunities are available in the Wiley online course.

Feature Story Are We Living on Borrowed Time?

The fiscal crisis of 2008 was a classic credit crisis caused by excessive debt in the global economy. Share prices declined substantially, and a major recession occurred. Usually, after such a credit crisis, all sectors of the economy attempt to reduce their debt. But the exact opposite is happening as the buildup of debt in the global economy continues.

The reasons for this increase in debt issuance are many, but one important component is the lowering of interest rates. Companies, governments, and financial institutions can borrow at extremely low interest rates, and so they have. Here are some typical headlines that have appeared in the financial press recently:

- Global bond issuance is running at the fastest pace in nearly a decade as companies and countries binge on debt in an era of historically low interest rates.
- Global bond issuance volumes smash record in January.
- China just created a record $540 billion in debt in one month.
- A total of $4.88 trillion of debt has been sold since the year began (2016) as issuers take advantage of rock-bottom borrowing costs.

The importance of debt in a company's statement of financial position cannot be underestimated. Too much debt in a period of economic stagnation quickly leads to bankruptcy and business failure.

Source: Adapted from McKinsey Global Institute, *Debt and (Not Much) Deleveraging* (2015).

TPG/Shutterstock

11.1 Overview of Bonds

LEARNING OBJECTIVE 1

Describe the major characteristics of bonds.

Non-current liabilities are obligations that a company expects to pay more than one year in the future. In this chapter, we explain the accounting for the principal types of obligations reported in the non-current liabilities section of the statement of financial position. These obligations often are in the form of bonds or long-term notes.

Bonds are a form of interest-bearing note payable issued by companies, universities, and governmental agencies. Bonds are sold in relatively small denominations (for example,

€1,000 or multiples of €1,000). As a result, bonds attract many investors. When a company issues bonds, it is borrowing money. The person who buys the bonds (the bondholder) is lending money.

Types of Bonds

Secured Bonds

Unsecured Bonds

Bonds may have many different features. In the following sections, we describe the types of bonds commonly issued.

Secured and Unsecured Bonds

Secured bonds have specific assets of the issuer pledged as collateral for the bonds.

- A bond secured by real estate, for example, is called a **mortgage bond**.
- A bond secured by specific assets set aside to redeem (retire) the bonds is called a **sinking fund bond**.

Unsecured bonds, also called **debenture bonds**, are issued against the general credit of the borrower. Companies with good credit ratings use these bonds extensively. For example, at one time, **DuPont** (USA) reported over $2 billion of debenture bonds outstanding.

Convertible and Callable Bonds

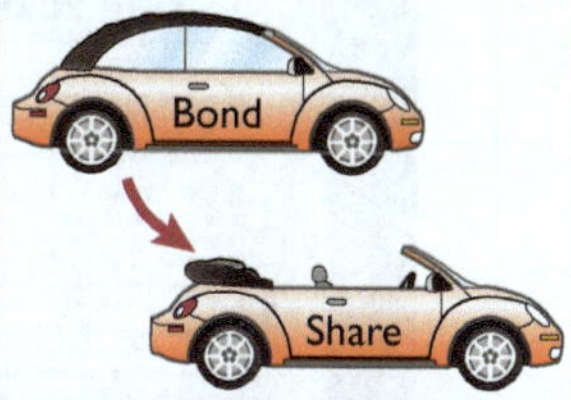

Convertible Bonds

Callable Bonds

Bonds that can be converted into ordinary shares at the bondholder's option are **convertible bonds**. The conversion feature generally is attractive to bond buyers. Bonds that the issuing company can redeem (buy back) at a stated currency amount (call price) prior to maturity are **callable bonds**. A call feature is included in nearly all company bond issues.

Issuing Procedures

Governmental laws grant companies the power to issue bonds. Both the board of directors and shareholders usually must approve bond issues. **In authorizing the bond issue, the board of directors must stipulate the number of bonds to be authorized, total face value, and contractual interest rate.** The total bond authorization often exceeds the number of bonds the company originally issues. This gives the company the flexibility to issue more bonds, if needed, to meet future cash requirements.

- The **face value** is the amount of principal the issuing company must pay at the maturity date.
- The **maturity date** is the date that the final payment is due to the investor from the issuing company.
- The **contractual interest rate**, often referred to as the **stated rate**, is the rate used to determine the amount of cash interest the issuing company pays and the investor receives. Usually, the contractual rate is stated as an annual rate.

The terms of the bond issue are set forth in a legal document called a **bond indenture**. The indenture shows the terms and summarizes the rights of the bondholders and their trustees, and the obligations of the issuing company. The **trustee** (usually a financial institution) keeps records of each bondholder, maintains custody of unissued bonds, and holds conditional title to pledged property.

In addition, the issuing company arranges for the printing of **bond certificates**. The indenture and the certificate are separate documents. As shown in **Illustration 11.1**, a bond certificate provides the following information: name of the issuer, face value, contractual interest rate, and maturity date. An investment company that specializes in selling securities generally sells the bonds for the issuing company.

ILLUSTRATION 11.1 **Bond certificate**

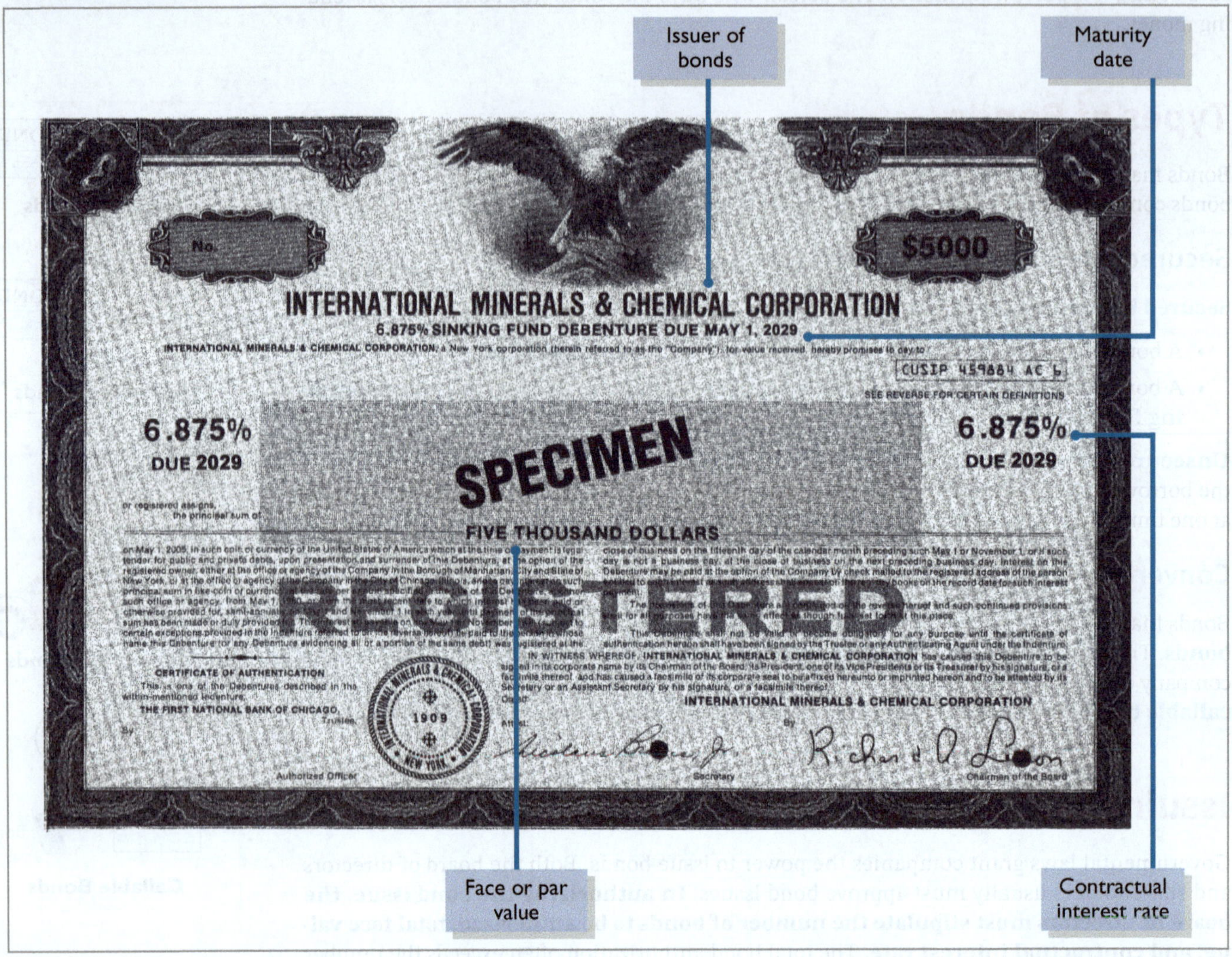

Bond Trading

> **HELPFUL HINT**
> **The price of a €1,000 bond trading at 95¼ is €952.50. The price of a €1,000 bond trading at 101⅞ is €1,018.75.**

Bondholders have the opportunity to convert their holdings into cash at any time by selling the bonds at the current market price on national securities exchanges. **Bond prices are quoted as a percentage of the face value of the bond, which is usually €1,000.** A €1,000 bond with a quoted price of 97 means that the selling price of the bond is 97% of face value, or €970 (see **Helpful Hint**). Newspapers and the financial press publish bond prices and trading activity daily as shown in **Illustration 11.2**.

ILLUSTRATION 11.2
Market information for bonds

Issuer	Contractual Interest Rate	Maturity	Close	Yield
Twitter, Inc.	3.875	Dec. 15, 2031	97.71	4.06

This bond listing indicates that **Twitter, Inc.** (USA) has outstanding 3.875% (contractual interest rate), $1,000 (face value) bonds that mature in 2031 (see **Helpful Hint**). The bonds currently yield a 4.06% return. At the close of trading, the price was 97.71% of face value, or $977.10.

A company makes journal entries **only when it issues or buys back bonds**, or when bondholders convert bonds into ordinary shares. For example, **Siemens** (DEU) **does not journalize** transactions between its bondholders and other investors. If Tom Smith sells his Siemens bonds to Faith Jones, Siemens does not journalize the transaction.

Environmental, Social, and Governance Insight

CarpathianPrince/
Shutterstock

How About Some Green Bonds?

Green bonds are debt used to fund activities such as renewable-energy projects. For example, a company may use the proceeds from the sale of green bonds to clean up its manufacturing operations and cut waste (such as related to energy consumption).

The use of green bonds has taken off as companies now have guidelines as to how to disclose and report on these green-bond proceeds. These standardized disclosures provide transparency as to how these bonds are used and their effect on overall profitability.

Investors are taking a strong interest in these bonds. Investing companies are installing socially responsible investing teams and have started to integrate sustainability into their investment processes. The disclosures of how companies are using the bond proceeds help investors to make better financial decisions.

Source: Based on Ben Edwards, "Green Bonds Catch On," *Wall Street Journal* (April 3, 2014), p. C5.

Why might standardized disclosure help investors to better understand how proceeds from the sale or issuance of bonds are used? (Answer is available near the end of the chapter.)

Determining the Market Price of a Bond

If you were an investor wanting to purchase a bond, how would you determine how much to pay? To be more specific, assume that Coronet AG issues a **zero-interest bond** (pays no interest) with a face value of €1,000,000 due in 20 years. For this bond, the only cash you receive is a million euros at the end of 20 years. Would you pay a million euros for this bond? We hope not! A million euros received 20 years from now is not the same as a million euros received today.

The term **time value of money** is used to indicate the relationship between time and money—that a euro received today is worth more than a euro promised at some time in the future.

Same euros at different times are not equal.

- If you had €1 million today, you would invest it.
- From that investment, you would earn interest such that at the end of 20 years, you would have much more than €1 million.
- Thus, if someone is going to pay you €1 million 20 years from now, you would want to find its equivalent today, or its present value.

In other words, you would want to determine the value today of the amount to be received in the future after taking into account current interest rates.

The current market price (present value) of a bond is the value at which it should sell in the marketplace. Market price therefore is a function of the three factors that determine present value:

1. The amounts to be received.
2. The length of time until the amounts are received.
3. The market interest rate. The **market interest rate** is the rate investors demand for loaning funds.

To illustrate, assume that Acropolis SA on January 1, 2029, issues €100,000 of 9% bonds, due in five years, with interest payable annually at year-end. The purchaser of the bonds would receive the following two types of cash payments:

1. **Principal** of €100,000 to be paid at maturity.
2. Five €9,000 **interest payments** (€100,000 × 9%) over the term of the bonds.

Illustration 11.3 shows a time diagram depicting both cash flows.

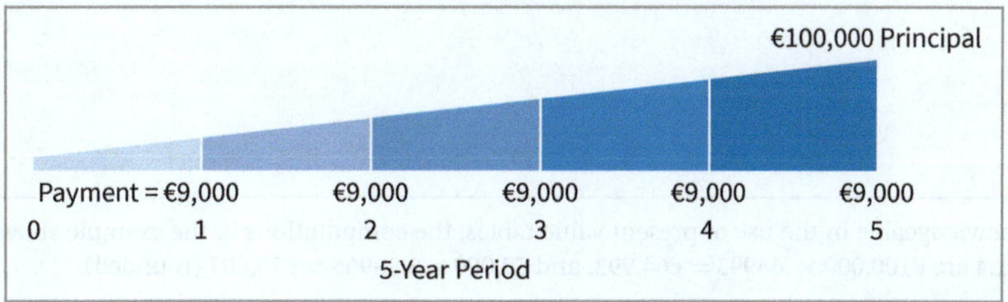

ILLUSTRATION 11.3

Time diagram depicting cash flows

The current market price of a bond is equal to the present value of all the future cash payments promised by the bond. **Illustration 11.4** lists and totals the present values of these amounts, assuming the market rate of interest is 9%.

ILLUSTRATION 11.4
Computing the market price of bonds

Present value of €100,000 received in 5 years	€ 64,993
Present value of €9,000 received annually for 5 years	35,007
Market price of bonds	**€100,000**

Tables are available to provide the present value numbers to be used, or these values can be determined mathematically or with financial calculators.[1] Appendix E provides further discussion of the concepts and the mechanics of the time value of money computations.

Investor Insight Volkswagen

phonlamaiphoto/Adobe Stock

Driving Up Debt

Imagine being an executive in the automotive industry. You are facing a generational change from internal combustion engines to electric power, which requires a great deal of capital. Then, you are dealing with a global pandemic that not only shuts downs many of your dealerships and sales outlets but also impacts your suppliers. When you are finally able to reopen your factories and assembly lines, key components needed to produce cars and trucks are not available or will be delayed. The lack of sales requires additional capital to keep your business open. Quite a challenging situation isn't it?

Fortunately, the manufacturers and their suppliers were able to raise $21.7 billion in extra long-term debt, which increased the total auto industry debt to over $1.1 trillion (see the chart). For example, **Volkswagen** (DEU) issued debt during this period. Analysts believe this inflow of cash will allow the industry breathing room until these companies are able to reopen plants and begin to recover lost sales.

However, more cash now means more debt later. Highly leveraged companies, that is, those with high debt levels, need to rely on best-case scenarios for sales. In the auto industry, there is a simple rule of thumb: New products drive profits, and Ford has several new product launches planned. Investors will need to monitor both sales and any future idle factories as they consider their investments in the auto industry.

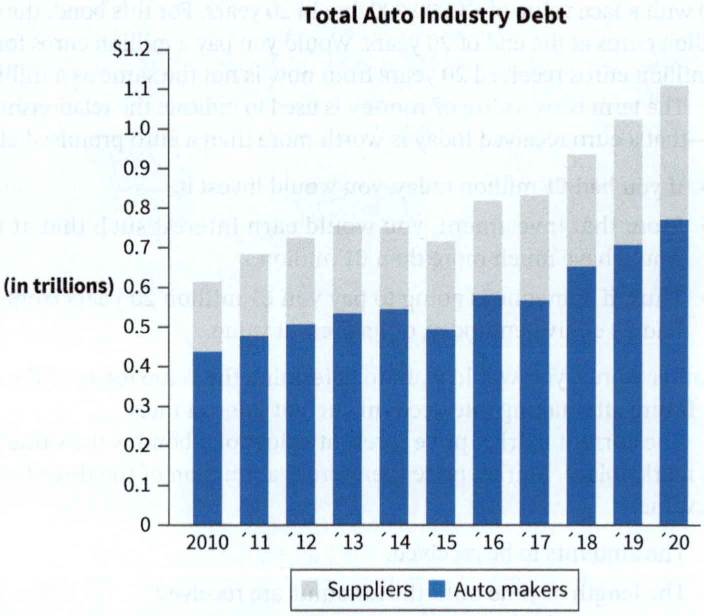

Source: Alix Partners.

Sources: Adapted from Molly Smith, "Ford Raises $8 Billion of Junk Bonds After Virus Spurs Loss," *bloomberg.com* (April 17, 2020); and Stephen Wilmot, "The Car Industry's $1.1 Trillion Debt Problem," *Wall Street Journal* (June 17, 2020).

When a company like Volkswagen issues debt to survive a challenging period, what risks does the company face in the future? How could issuing debt today reduce your options in the future? (Answer is available near the end of the chapter.)

[1] For those knowledgeable in the use of present value tables, the computations in the example shown in Illustration 11.4 are €100,000 × .64993 = €64,993, and €9,000 × 3.88965 = €35,007 (rounded).

DO IT! 1 | Bond Terminology

State whether each of the following statements is true or false. If false, indicate how to correct the statement.

_______ **1.** Mortgage bonds and sinking fund bonds are both examples of secured bonds.

_______ **2.** Unsecured bonds are also known as debenture bonds.

_______ **3.** The stated rate is the rate investors demand for loaning funds.

_______ **4.** The face value is the amount of principal the issuing company must pay at the maturity date.

_______ **5.** The bond issuer must make journal entries to record transfers of its bonds among investors.

_______ **6.** Time value of money means that a euro received today is worth more than a euro promised at some time in the future.

_______ **7.** The current market price of a bond is equal to the present value of all the future cash payments promised by the bonds.

ACTION PLAN

- **Review the types of bonds and the basic terms associated with bonds.**

Solution

1. True. **2.** True. **3.** False. The stated rate is the contractual interest rate used to determine the amount of cash interest the borrower pays. **4.** True. **5.** False. The bond issuer makes journal entries only when it issues or buys back bonds, when it records interest, and when convertible bonds are converted to shares. **6.** True. **7.** True.

Related exercise material: **DO IT! 11.1 and E11.1.**

11.2 Accounting for Bond Transactions

LEARNING OBJECTIVE 2

Explain how to account for bond transactions.

As indicated earlier, a company records bond transactions when it issues (sells) or redeems (buys back) bonds and when bondholders convert bonds into ordinary shares.

- If bondholders sell their bond investments to other investors, the issuing company receives no further money on the transaction.
- **The issuing company does not journalize the transaction** (although it does keep records of the names of bondholders in some cases).

Bonds may be issued at face value, below face value (discount), or above face value (premium). Bond prices for both new issues and existing bonds are quoted as **a percentage of the face value of the bond.**

Issuing Bonds at Face Value

To illustrate the accounting for bonds issued at face value, assume that on January 1, 2029, Candlestick AG issues €100,000, five-year, 10% bonds at 100 (100% of face value). The entry to record the sale is as follows.

Jan. 1	Cash	100,000	
	Bonds Payable		100,000
	(To record sale of bonds at face value)		

A	=	L	+	E
+100,000				
		+100,000		

Cash Flows
+100,000

Candlestick reports bonds payable in the non-current liabilities section of the statement of financial position because the maturity date is January 1, 2034 (more than one year away).

Over the term (life) of the bonds, companies make entries to record bond interest. Interest on bonds payable is computed in the same manner as interest on notes payable. Assume that interest is payable annually on January 1 on the Candlestick bonds. In that case, Candlestick accrues interest of €10,000 (€100,000 × 10%) on December 31. At December 31, Candlestick recognizes the €10,000 of interest expense incurred with the following entry.

A	=	L	+	E
				−10,000 Exp
		+10,000		

Cash Flows
no effect

Dec. 31	Interest Expense	10,000	
	Interest Payable		10,000
	(To accrue bond interest)		

The company classifies interest payable as a current liability because it is scheduled for payment within the next year. When Candlestick pays the interest on January 1, 2030, it debits (decreases) Interest Payable and credits (decreases) Cash for €10,000.

Candlestick records the payment on January 1 as follows.

A	=	L	+	E
		−10,000		
−10,000				

Cash Flows
−10,000

Jan. 1	Interest Payable	10,000	
	Cash		10,000
	(To record payment of bond interest)		

Discount or Premium on Bonds

The Candlestick example assumed that the contractual (stated) interest rate and the market (effective) interest rate paid on the bonds were the same.

- Recall that the **contractual interest rate** is the rate applied to the face (par) value to arrive at the interest paid in a year.
- The **market interest rate** is the rate investors demand for loaning funds to the company.
- When the contractual interest rate and the market interest rate are the same, bonds sell **at face value (par value)**.

However, market interest rates change daily. The type of bond issued, the state of the economy, current industry conditions, and the company's performance all affect market interest rates. As a result, contractual and market interest rates often differ. To make bonds salable when the two rates differ, bonds sell below or above face value.

To illustrate, suppose that a company issues 10% bonds at a time when other bonds of similar risk are paying 12%. Investors will not be interested in buying the 10% bonds, so their value will fall below their face value.

- When a bond is sold for less than its face value, the difference between the face value of a bond and its selling price is called a **discount**.
- As a result of the decline in the bonds' selling price, the actual interest rate incurred by the company increases to the level of the current market interest rate.

Conversely, if the market rate of interest is **lower than** the contractual interest rate, investors will have to pay more than face value for the bonds.

- When a bond is sold for more than its face value, the difference between its face value and selling price is called a **premium**.
- For example, if the market rate of interest is 8% but the contractual interest rate on the bonds is 10%, the price of the bonds will be bid up.

Illustration 11.5 shows these relationships.

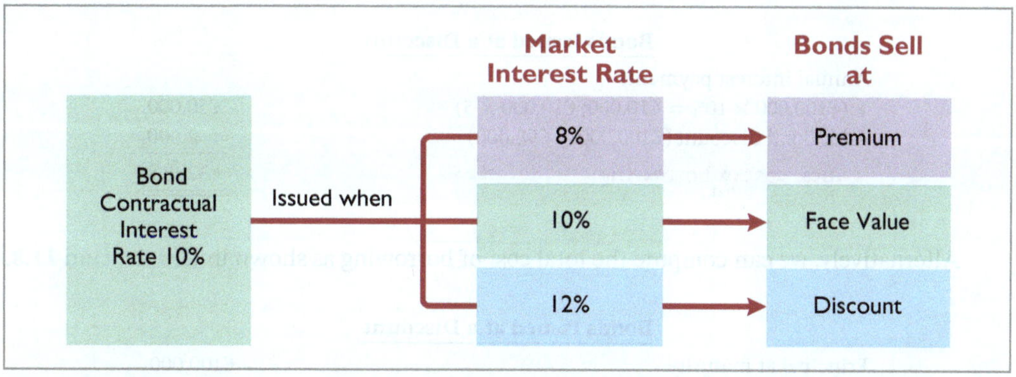

ILLUSTRATION 11.5

Interest rates and bond prices

Issuance of bonds at an amount different from face value is quite common. By the time a company prints the bond certificates and markets the bonds, it will be a coincidence if the market rate and the contractual rate are the same.

- The issuance of bonds at a discount does not mean that the issuer's financial strength is suspect.
- The sale of bonds at a premium does not indicate that the financial strength of the issuer is exceptional.

Issuing Bonds at a Discount

To illustrate issuance of bonds at a discount, assume that on January 1, 2029, Candlestick AG sells €100,000, five-year, 10% bonds for €98,000 (98% of face value). Interest is payable annually on January 1. The entry to record the issuance is as follows.

Jan. 1	Cash	98,000	
	Bonds Payable		98,000
	(To record sale of bonds at a discount)		

A = L + E
+98,000 = +98,000

Cash Flows
+98,000

Illustration 11.6 shows how the bonds payable of Candlestick AG would be presented on the statement of financial position if it was prepared on the day the bonds were issued.

ILLUSTRATION 11.6

Statement presentation of bonds issued at a discount

Candlestick AG Statement of Financial Position (partial)	
Non-current liabilities	
Bonds payable	€98,000

The €98,000 represents the **carrying (or book) value** of the bonds. On the date of issue, this amount equals the market price of the bonds.

The issuance of bonds below face value—at a discount—causes the total cost of borrowing to differ from the bond interest paid. That is, the issuing company must pay not only the contractual interest rate over the term of the bonds but also the face value (rather than the issuance price) at maturity.

- The difference between the issuance price and face value of the bonds—the discount—is an **additional cost of borrowing**.
- The company records this additional cost as **interest expense** over the life of the bonds.

The total cost of borrowing €98,000 for Candlestick is therefore €52,000, computed as shown in **Illustration 11.7**.

ILLUSTRATION 11.7

Total cost of borrowing—bonds issued at a discount

Bonds Issued at a Discount	
Annual interest payments	
(€100,000 × 10% = €10,000; €10,000 × 5)	€50,000
Add: Bond discount (€100,000 − €98,000)	2,000
Total cost of borrowing	**€52,000**

Alternatively, we can compute the total cost of borrowing as shown in **Illustration 11.8**.

ILLUSTRATION 11.8

Alternative computation of total cost of borrowing—bonds issued at a discount

Bonds Issued at a Discount	
Principal at maturity	€100,000
Annual interest payments (€10,000 × 5)	50,000
Cash to be paid to bondholders	150,000
Less: Cash received from bondholders	98,000
Total cost of borrowing	**€ 52,000**

To follow the expense recognition principle, companies allocate bond discount to expense in each period in which the bonds are outstanding. This is referred to as **amortizing the discount**.

- Amortization of the discount **increases** the amount of interest expense reported each period.
- That is, after the company amortizes the discount, the amount of interest expense it reports in a period will exceed the contractual amount.

As shown in Illustration 11.7, for the bonds issued by Candlestick, total interest expense will exceed the contractual interest by €2,000 over the life of the bonds.

As the discount is amortized, its balance declines. As a consequence, the carrying value of the bonds will increase, until at maturity the carrying value of the bonds equals their face amount. This is shown in **Illustration 11.9**. Appendices 11A and 11B discuss procedures for amortizing bond discount.

ILLUSTRATION 11.9

Amortization of bond discount

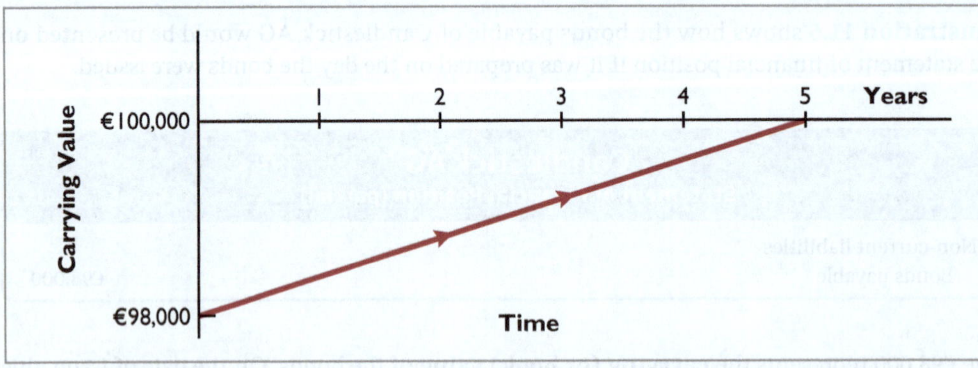

Issuing Bonds at a Premium

To illustrate the issuance of bonds at a premium, we now assume the Candlestick AG bonds described above sell for €102,000 (102% of face value) rather than for €98,000. The entry to record the sale is as follows.

Jan. 1	Cash	102,000	
	Bonds Payable		102,000
	(To record sale of bonds at a premium)		

A	=	L	+	E
+102,000				
		+102,000		

Cash Flows
+102,000

The **carrying value** of the bonds is the face value of the bonds adjusted for bond discount or bond premium amortized up to the redemption date.

To illustrate, assume that Candlestick AG has sold its bonds at a premium. At the end of the fourth period, Candlestick redeems these bonds at 103 after paying the annual interest. Assume that the carrying value of the bonds at the redemption date is €100,476. Candlestick makes the following entry to record the redemption at the end of the fourth interest period (January 1, 2033) as follows.

Jan. 1	Bonds Payable	100,476	
	Loss on Bond Redemption	2,524	
	Cash		103,000
	(To record redemption of bonds at 103)		

A	=	L	+	E
		−100,476		
				−2,524 Exp
−103,000				

Cash Flows
−103,000

Note that the loss of €2,524 is the difference between the cash paid of €103,000 and the carrying value of the bonds of €100,476.

DO IT! 2b | Bond Redemption

R & B Ltd. issued £500,000, 10-year bonds at a discount. Prior to maturity, when the carrying value of the bonds is £496,000, the company redeems the bonds at 98. Prepare the entry to record the redemption of the bonds.

ACTION PLAN

- **Determine and eliminate the carrying value of the bonds.**
- **Record the cash paid.**
- **Compute and record the gain or loss (the difference between the first two items).**

Solution

There is a gain on redemption: The cash paid, £490,000 (£500,000 × 98%), is less than the carrying value of £496,000. As a result, there is a gain on bond redemption of £6,000 (£496,000 – £490,000). The entry is:

Bonds Payable	496,000	
Gain on Bond Redemption		6,000
Cash		490,000
(To record redemption of bonds at 98)		

Related exercise material: **BE11.4, DO IT! 11.2b, E11.5, and E11.6.**

11.3 Accounting for Non-Current Liabilities

LEARNING OBJECTIVE 3

Explain how to account for other non-current liabilities.

Long-Term Notes Payable

Another type of long-term obligation is notes payable. **Long-term notes payable** are similar to short-term interest-bearing notes payable except that the term of the notes exceeds one year.

- A long-term note may be secured by a **mortgage** that pledges title to specific assets as security for a loan.
- Individuals widely use **mortgage notes payable** to purchase homes, and many small and some large companies use them to acquire plant assets.

At one time, approximately 18% of **McDonald's** (USA) long-term debt related to mortgage notes on land, buildings, and improvements.

Like other long-term notes payable, the mortgage loan terms may stipulate either a **fixed** or an **adjustable** interest rate. The interest rate on a fixed-rate mortgage remains the same over the life of the mortgage. The interest rate on an adjustable-rate mortgage is adjusted periodically to reflect changes in the market rate of interest. Typically, the terms require the borrower to make equal installment payments over the term of the loan. Each payment consists of:

1. Interest on the unpaid balance of the loan.
2. A reduction of loan principal.

While the total amount of the payment remains constant, the interest decreases each period, and the portion applied to the loan principal increases.

Companies initially record mortgage notes payable at face value. They subsequently make entries for each installment payment. To illustrate, assume that Mongkok Technology Ltd. issues a HK$500,000, 8%, 20-year mortgage note on December 31, 2029, to obtain needed financing for a new research laboratory. The terms provide for annual installment payments of HK$50,926. **Illustration 11.14** shows the installment payment schedule for the first four years.

ILLUSTRATION 11.14
Mortgage installment payment schedule

Interest Period	(A) Cash Payment	(B) Interest Expense (D) × 8%	(C) Reduction of Principal (A) − (B)	(D) Principal Balance (D) − (C)
Issue date				HK$500,000
1	HK$50,926	HK$40,000	HK$10,926	489,074
2	50,926	39,126	11,800	477,274
3	50,926	38,182	12,744	464,530
4	50,926	37,162	13,764	450,766

Mongkok records the mortgage loan on December 31, 2029, as follows.

A = L + E
+500,000
+500,000
Cash Flows
+500,000

Dec. 31, 2029	Cash	500,000	
	Mortgage Payable		500,000
	(To record mortgage loan)		

On December 31, 2030, Mongkok records the first installment payment as follows.

A = L + E
−40,000 Exp
−10,926
−50,926
Cash Flows
−50,926

Dec. 31, 2030	Interest Expense	40,000	
	Mortgage Payable	10,926	
	Cash		50,926
	(To record annual payment on mortgage)		

- In the statement of financial position, the company reports the reduction in principal for the next year as a current liability.
- It classifies the remaining unpaid principal balance as a non-current liability.

At December 31, 2030, the total liability is HK$489,074. Of that amount, HK$11,800 is current, and HK$477,274 (HK$489,074 − HK$11,800) is non-current.

Lease Liabilities

A **lease** is a contractual agreement between a lessor (owner of a property) and a lessee (renter of the property).

- This arrangement gives the lessee the right to use specific property, which is owned by the **lessor**, for a specified period of time.
- In return for the use of the property, the **lessee** makes rental payments over the lease term to the lessor.

Leasing has grown tremendously in popularity. Today, it is the fastest growing form of capital investment. Instead of borrowing money to buy an airplane, computer, nuclear core, or satellite, a company makes periodic payments to lease these assets. Even gambling casinos lease their slot machines. The global leasing-equipment market is over a $900 billion business, with Asia, Europe, and North America accounting for more than 80% of world volume.

Accounting for Lease Arrangements

A lessee recognizes a lease liability and a right-of-use asset for all leases with a term greater than one year. If the term of the lease is less than one year, no liability or asset is recognized and the rental payment is expensed as incurred.

- Companies recognize lease assets and lease liabilities on the statement of financial position, measured at the present value of the lease payments.
- Amortization of the leased asset and interest expense on the lease liability are reported on the income statement over the lease term.

To illustrate, assume that Gonzalez Construction decides to lease new equipment. The lease term is four years. The present value of the lease payments is €190,000. Gonzalez records the transaction as follows.

Right-of-Use Asset	190,000	
Lease Liability		190,000

Gonzalez reports a right-of-use asset on its statement of financial position under non-current assets. It reports the lease liability on the statement of financial position as a liability. The portion of the lease liability expected to be paid in the next year is a current liability. The remainder is classified as a non-current liability.

DO IT! 3 | Long-Term Notes

Cole Research issues a ₩250,000,000, 6%, 20-year mortgage note to obtain needed financing for a new lab. The terms call for annual payments of ₩21,796,000 each. Prepare the entries to record the mortgage loan and the first installment payment.

ACTION PLAN

- **Record the issuance of the note as a cash receipt and a liability.**
- **Each installment payment consists of interest and payment of principal.**

Solution

Cash	250,000,000	
Mortgage Payable		250,000,000
(To record mortgage loan)		
Interest Expense	15,000,000*	
Mortgage Payable	6,796,000	
Cash		21,796,000
(To record annual payment on mortgage)		

*Interest expense = ₩250,000,000 × 6%.

Related exercise material: **BE11.5, DO IT! 11.3, and E11.7.**

11.4 Reporting and Analyzing Non-Current Liabilities

LEARNING OBJECTIVE 4

Discuss how non-current liabilities are reported and analyzed.

Presentation

ALTERNATIVE TERMINOLOGY

Another term sometimes used for non-current liabilities is *long-term liabilities.*

Companies report non-current liabilities in a separate section of the statement of financial position immediately before current liabilities, as shown in **Illustration 11.15** (see **Alternative Terminology**). Alternatively, companies may present summary data in the statement of financial position, with detailed data (interest rates, maturity dates, conversion privileges, and assets pledged as collateral) shown in a supporting schedule.

ILLUSTRATION 11.15

Statement of financial position presentation of non-current liabilities

Guangzhou Ltd.
Statement of Financial Position (partial)
(in thousands)

Non-current liabilities	
Bonds payable 10% due in 2031	¥ 920,000
Mortgage payable, 11%, due in 2037 and secured by plant assets	300,000
Lease liabilities	200,000
Total non-current liabilities	¥1,420,000

Companies report the current maturities of long-term debt under current liabilities if they are to be paid within one year or the operating cycle, whichever is longer.

Analysis

ETHICS NOTE

Some companies try to minimize the amount of debt reported on their statement of financial position by not reporting certain types of commitments as liabilities. This subject is of intense interest in the financial community.

Long-term creditors and shareholders are interested in a company's long-run solvency (see **Ethics Note**). Of particular interest is the company's ability to pay interest as it comes due and to repay the face value of the debt at maturity. Here we look at two ratios that provide information about debt-paying ability and long-run solvency.

- The **debt to assets ratio** measures the percentage of the total assets provided by creditors. As shown in the formula in Illustration 11.16, it is computed by dividing total liabilities (both current and non-current liabilities) by total assets. The higher the percentage of debt to assets, the greater the risk that the company may be unable to meet its maturing obligations.
- **Times interest earned** indicates the company's ability to meet interest payments as they come due. It is computed by dividing the sum of net income, interest expense, and income tax expense by interest expense.

To illustrate these ratios, we will use data from an **LG** (KOR) annual report. The company had total liabilities of ₩22,839 billion, total assets of ₩35,528 billion, interest expense of ₩827 billion, income taxes of ₩354 billion, and net income of ₩223 billion. LG's debt to assets ratio and times interest earned are shown in **Illustration 11.16**.

Total Liabilities	÷	Total Assets	=	Debt to Assets Ratio
₩22,839	÷	₩35,528	=	64.3%
Net Income + Interest Expense + Income Tax Expense	÷	**Interest Expense**	=	**Times Interest Earned**
₩223 + ₩827 + ₩354	÷	₩827	=	1.70 times

ILLUSTRATION 11.16

Debt to assets and times interest earned ratios, with computations (in billions)

LG has a relatively high debt to assets percentage of 64.3%. Its times interest earned of 1.70 times might be considered low.

Debt and Equity Financing

To obtain large amounts of long-term capital, company management has to decide whether to issue additional ordinary shares (equity financing), bonds or notes (debt financing), or a combination of the two. This decision is important to both the company and to investors and creditors. The capital structure of a company provides clues as to the potential profit that can be achieved and the risks taken by the company. Debt financing offers these advantages over ordinary shares, as shown in **Illustration 11.17**.

Bond Financing	Advantages
	**1. Shareholder control is not affected.** Bondholders do not have voting rights, so current owners (shareholders) retain full control of the company.
	**2. Tax savings result.** Bond interest is deductible for tax purposes; dividends on shares are not.
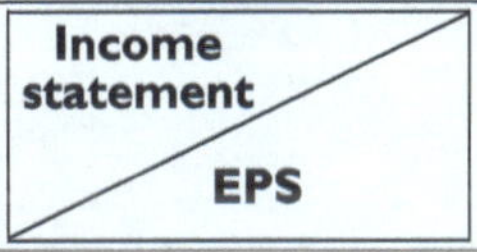	**3. Earnings per share (EPS) may be higher.** Although bond interest expense reduces net income, earnings per share is higher under bond financing because no additional shares are issued.

ILLUSTRATION 11.17

Advantages of bond financing over ordinary shares

As Illustration 11.17 shows, one reason to issue bonds is that they do not affect shareholder control.

- Because bondholders do not have voting rights, owners can raise capital with bonds and still maintain company control.
- In addition, bonds are attractive to companies because the cost of bond interest is tax-deductible.
- As a result of this tax treatment, which share dividends do not offer, bonds may result in lower cost of capital than equity financing.

To illustrate another advantage of bond financing, assume that Microsystems is considering two plans for financing the construction of a new €5 million plant. Plan A involves issuance of 200,000 ordinary shares at the current market price of €25 per share. Plan B involves issuance of €5 million, 8% bonds at face value. Income before interest and taxes on the new plant will be €1.5 million. Income taxes are expected to be 30%. Microsystems currently has 100,000 ordinary shares outstanding. **Illustration 11.18** shows the alternative effects on earnings per share.

ILLUSTRATION 11.18
Effects on earnings per share—equity vs. debt

	Plan A Issue Shares	Plan B Issue Bonds
Income before interest and taxes	€1,500,000	€1,500,000
Interest (8% × €5,000,000)	—	400,000
Income before income taxes	1,500,000	1,100,000
Income tax expense (30%)	450,000	330,000
Net income	€1,050,000	€ 770,000
Outstanding shares	300,000	100,000
Earnings per share	**€3.50**	**€7.70**

Note that net income is €280,000 less (€1,050,000 – €770,000) with long-term debt financing (bonds). However, earnings per share is higher because there are 200,000 fewer ordinary shares outstanding.

Major disadvantages of using debt financing include the following.

- A company must pay interest on a periodic basis. In addition, the company must also repay principal at the due date. A company with fluctuating earnings and a relatively weak cash position may have great difficulty making interest payments when earnings are low.
- When the economy, securities market, or a company's revenues stagnate, debt payments can gobble up cash quickly and limit a company's ability to meet its financial obligations.

Investment Insight

yenwen/Getty Images

Debt Masking

In the wake of the financial crisis of 2008, many financial institutions were wary of reporting too much debt on their financial statements, for fear that investors would consider them too risky. The Securities and Exchange Commission (SEC) was concerned that some companies engaged in "debt masking" to make it appear that they had less debt than they actually did.

With debt masking, companies enter into transactions at the end of the accounting period that essentially remove debt from their books. Shortly after the end of the period, they reverse the transaction and the debt goes back on their books. The *Wall Street Journal* reported that 18 large banks "had consistently lowered one type of debt at the end of each of the past five quarters, reducing it on average by 42% from quarterly peaks."

Source: Based on Tom McGinty et al., 2010.

What implications does debt masking have for an investor that is using the debt to assets ratio to evaluate a company's solvency? (Answer is available near the end of the chapter.)

ACTION PLAN

- **Use the formula for the debt to assets ratio (Total liabilities divided by Total assets).**

DO IT! 4 | Analysis of Non-Current Liabilities

As of December 31, 2029, FX Group has the following:

Assets	€2,000,000
Liabilities	1,200,000
Equity	800,000

Compute and discuss the debt to assets ratio at year-end.

Solution

The debt to assets ratio = €1,200,000 ÷ €2,000,000 = 60%. This means that 60% of its assets were provided by creditors. The higher the percentage of debt to assets, the greater the risk that the company may be unable to meet its maturing obligations.

Related exercise material: **DO IT! 11.4 and E11.10.**

Appendix 11A Effective-Interest Method of Bond Amortization

LEARNING OBJECTIVE *5

Apply the effective-interest method of amortizing bond discount and bond premium.

Financial liabilities, such as bonds, are to be accounted for at amortized cost. IFRS states that amortized cost is to be determined using the effective-interest method. Under the **effective-interest method of amortization**, the amortization of bond discount or bond premium results in periodic interest expense equal to a **constant percentage** of the carrying value of the bonds. The effective-interest method results in varying amounts of amortization and interest expense per period, but **a constant percentage rate**.

The following steps are required under the effective-interest method.

1. Compute the **bond interest expense** by multiplying the carrying value of the bonds at the beginning of the interest period by the effective-interest rate.
2. Compute the **bond interest paid** (or accrued) by multiplying the face value of the bonds by the contractual interest rate.
3. Compute the **amortization amount** by determining the difference between the amounts computed in steps (1) and (2).

Illustration 11A.1 depicts these steps.

ILLUSTRATION 11A.1

Computation of amortization—effective-interest method

(1) Bond Interest Expense		(2) Bond Interest Paid		(3)
(Carrying Value of Bonds at Beginning of Period × Effective-Interest Rate)	−	(Face Amount of Bonds × Contractual Interest Rate)	=	Amortization Amount

Amortizing Bond Discount

In the Candlestick AG example presented in the chapter, the company sold €100,000, five year, 10% bonds on January 1, 2029, for €98,000. This resulted in a €2,000 bond discount (€100,000 − €98,000). This discount results in an effective-interest rate of approximately 10.5348%. (The effective-interest rate can be computed using the techniques shown in Appendix E.)

Preparing a bond discount amortization schedule as shown in **Illustration 11A.2** facilitates the recording of interest expense and the discount amortization. Note that interest expense as a percentage of carrying value remains constant at 10.5348%.

ILLUSTRATION 11A.2 **Bond discount amortization schedule**

Candlestick AG
Bond Discount Amortization Schedule
Effective-Interest Method—Annual Interest Payments
10% Bonds Issued at 10.5348%

Interest Periods	(A) Interest to Be Paid (10% × €100,000)	(B) Interest Expense to Be Recorded (10.5348% × Preceding Bond Carrying Value)	(C) Discount Amortization (B) – (A)	(D) Unamortized Discount (D) – (C)	(E) Bond Carrying Value (€100,000 – D)
Issue date				€2,000	€ 98,000
1	€10,000	€10,324 (10.5348% × €98,000)	€ 324	1,676	98,324
2	10,000	10,358 (10.5348% × €98,324)	358	1,318	98,682
3	10,000	10,396 (10.5348% × €98,682)	396	922	99,078
4	10,000	10,438 (10.5348% × €99,078)	438	484	99,516
5	10,000	10,484 (10.5348% × €99,516)	484	-0-	100,000
	€50,000	€52,000	€2,000		

Column **(A)** remains constant because the face value of the bonds (€100,000) is multiplied by the annual contractual interest rate (10%) each period.
Column **(B)** is computed as the preceding bond carrying value times the annual effective-interest rate (10.5348%).
Column **(C)** indicates the discount amortization each period.
Column **(D)** decreases each period until it reaches zero at maturity.
Column **(E)** increases each period until it equals face value at maturity.

For the first interest period, the computations of bond interest expense and the bond discount amortization are as shown in **Illustration 11A.3**.

ILLUSTRATION 11A.3
Computation of bond discount amortization

Bond interest expense (€98,000 × 10.5348%)	€10,324
Less: Bond interest paid (€100,000 × 10%)	10,000
Bond discount amortization	**€ 324**

As a result, Candlestick records the accrual of interest and amortization of bond discount on December 31 as follows.

A = L + E
−10,324 Exp
+324
+10,000
Cash Flows
no effect

Dec. 31	Interest Expense	10,324	
	Bonds Payable		324
	Interest Payable		10,000
	(To record accrued interest and amortization of bond discount)		

For the second interest period, bond interest expense will be €10,358 (€98,324 × 10.5348%), and the discount amortization will be €358. At December 31, Candlestick makes the following adjusting entry.

A = L + E
−10,358 Exp
+358
+10,000
Cash Flows
no effect

Dec. 31	Interest Expense	10,358	
	Bonds Payable		358
	Interest Payable		10,000
	(To record accrued interest and amortization of bond discount)		

Amortizing Bond Premium

Continuing our example, assume Candlestick AG sells the bonds described above for €102,000 rather than €98,000. This would result in a bond premium of €2,000 (€102,000 − €100,000). This premium results in an effective-interest rate of approximately 9.4794%. (The effective-interest rate can be solved for using the techniques shown in Appendix E.) **Illustration 11A.4** shows the bond premium amortization schedule.

ILLUSTRATION 11A.4 **Bond premium amortization schedule**

Candlestick AG
Bond Premium Amortization Schedule
Effective-Interest Method—Annual Interest Payments
10% Bonds Issued at 9.4794%

Interest Periods	(A) Interest to Be Paid (10% × €100,000)	(B) Interest Expense to Be Recorded (9.4794% × Preceding Bond Carrying Value)	(C) Premium Amortization (A) − (B)	(D) Unamortized Premium (D) − (C)	(E) Bond Carrying Value (€100,000 + D)
Issue date				€2,000	€102,000
1	€10,000	€ 9,669 (9.4794% × €102,000)	€ 331	1,669	101,669
2	10,000	9,638 (9.4794% × €101,669)	362	1,307	101,307
3	10,000	9,603 (9.4794% × €101,307)	397	910	100,910
4	10,000	9,566 (9.4794% × €100,910)	434	476	100,476
5	10,000	9,524 * (9.4794% × €100,476)	476*	−0−	100,000
	€50,000	€48,000	€2,000		

Column **(A)** remains constant because the face value of the bonds (€100,000) is multiplied by the contractual interest rate (10%) each period.
Column **(B)** is computed as the carrying value of the bonds times the annual effective-interest rate (9.4794%).
Column **(C)** indicates the premium amortization each period.
Column **(D)** decreases each period until it reaches zero at maturity.
Column **(E)** decreases each period until it equals face value at maturity.

*Rounded to eliminate remaining premium resulting from rounding the effective rate.

For the first interest period, the computations of bond interest expense and the bond premium amortization are as shown in **Illustration 11A.5**.

Bond interest paid (€100,000 × 10%)	€10,000
Less: Bond interest expense (€102,000 × 9.4794%)	9,669
Bond premium amortization	**€ 331**

ILLUSTRATION 11A.5
Computation of bond premium amortization

The entry Candlestick makes on December 31 is as follows.

Date	Account	Debit	Credit
Dec. 31	Interest Expense	9,669	
	Bonds Payable	331	
	Interest Payable		10,000
	(To record accrued interest and amortization of bond premium)		

A = L + E
−9,669 Exp
−331
+10,000

Cash Flows
no effect

For the second interest period, interest expense will be €9,638, and the premium amortization will be €362. Note that the amount of periodic interest expense decreases over the life of the bond when companies apply the effective-interest method to bonds issued at a premium. The reason is that a constant percentage is applied to a decreasing bond carrying value to compute interest expense. The carrying value is decreasing because of the amortization of the premium.

Appendix 11B Straight-Line Amortization

LEARNING OBJECTIVE *6

Apply the straight-line method of amortizing bond discount and bond premium.

Amortizing Bond Discount

The effective-interest method presented in Appendix 11A is the method required by IFRS to determine amortized cost. Under U.S. GAAP, companies are allowed to use an alternative approach, straight-line amortization, when the results do not differ materially from the effective-interest method.

- Under the **straight-line method of amortization**, the amortization of bond discount or bond premium results in periodic interest expense of the same amount in each interest period.
- In other words, the straight-line method results in a constant amount of amortization and interest expense per period.

The amount is determined using the formula in **Illustration 11B.1**.

ILLUSTRATION 11B.1

Formula for straight-line method of bond discount amortization

Bond Discount	÷	Number of Interest Periods	=	Bond Discount Amortization

In the Candlestick AG example, the company sold €100,000, five-year, 10% bonds on January 1, 2029, for €98,000. This resulted in a €2,000 bond discount (€100,000 − €98,000). The bond discount amortization is €400 (€2,000 ÷ 5) for each of the five amortization periods. Candlestick records the first accrual of bond interest and the amortization of bond discount on December 31 as follows.

A	=	L	+	E
				−10,400 Exp
		+400		
		+10,000		

Cash Flows
no effect

Dec. 31	Interest Expense	10,400	
	Bonds Payable		400
	Interest Payable		10,000
	(To record accrued interest and amortization of bond discount)		

- Over the term of the bonds, the balance in Bonds Payable will increase annually by the same amount until the maturity date of the bonds.
- Thus, the carrying value of the bonds at maturity will be equal to the face value of the bonds.

Preparing a bond discount amortization schedule, as shown in **Illustration 11B.2**, is useful to determine interest expense, discount amortization, and the carrying value of the bond. As indicated, the interest expense recorded each period is €10,400. Also note that the carrying value of the bond increases €400 each period until it reaches its face value of €100,000 at the end of period 5.

ILLUSTRATION 11B.2

Bond discount amortization schedule

Candlestick AG
Bond Discount Amortization Schedule
Straight-Line Method—Annual Interest Payments
€100,000 of 10%, 5-Year Bonds

Interest Periods	(A) Interest to Be Paid (10% × €100,000)	(B) Interest Expense to Be Recorded (A) + (C)	(C) Discount Amortization (€2,000 ÷ 5)	(D) Unamortized Discount (D) – (C)	(E) Bond Carrying Value (€100,000 – D)
Issue date				€2,000	€ 98,000
1	€10,000	€10,400	€ 400	1,600	98,400
2	10,000	10,400	400	1,200	98,800
3	10,000	10,400	400	800	99,200
4	10,000	10,400	400	400	99,600
5	10,000	10,400	400	0	100,000
	€50,000	€52,000	€2,000		

Column (A) remains constant because the face value of the bonds (€100,000) is multiplied by the annual contractual interest rate (10%) each period.
Column (B) is computed as the interest paid (Column A) plus the discount amortization (Column C).
Column (C) indicates the discount amortization each period.
Column (D) decreases each period by the same amount until it reaches zero at maturity.
Column (E) increases each period by the amount of discount amortization until it equals the face value at maturity.

Amortizing Bond Premium

The amortization of bond premium parallels that of bond discount. **Illustration 11B.3** presents the formula for determining bond premium amortization under the straight-line method.

Bond Premium ÷ **Number of Interest Periods** = **Bond Premium Amortization**

ILLUSTRATION 11B.3

Formula for straight-line method of bond premium amortization

Continuing our example, assume Candlestick AG sells the bonds described previously for €102,000, rather than €98,000. This results in a bond premium of €2,000 (€102,000 – €100,000). The premium amortization for each interest period is €400 (€2,000 ÷ 5). Candlestick records the first accrual of interest on December 31 as follows.

Dec. 31	Interest Expense	9,600	
	Bonds Payable	400	
	Interest Payable		10,000
	(To record accrued bond interest and amortization of bond premium)		

A = L + E
−9,600 Exp
−400
+10,000
Cash Flows
no effect

Over the term of the bonds, the balance in Bonds Payable will decrease annually by the same amount until the maturity date of the bonds. Thus, the carrying value of the bonds at maturity will be equal to the face value of the bonds.

A bond premium amortization schedule, as shown in **Illustration 11B.4**, is useful to determine interest expense, premium amortization, and the carrying value of the bond. As indicated, the interest expense Candlestick records each period is €9,600. Note that the carrying value of the bond decreases €400 each period until it reaches its face value of €100,000 at the end of period 5.

ILLUSTRATION 11B.4

Bond premium amortization schedule

Candlestick AG
Bond Premium Amortization Schedule
Straight-Line Method—Annual Interest Payments
€100,000 of 10%, 5-Year Bonds

Interest Periods	(A) Interest to Be Paid (10% × €100,000)	(B) Interest Expense to Be Recorded (A) − (C)	(C) Premium Amortization (€2,000 ÷ 5)	(D) Unamortized Premium (D) − (C)	(E) Bond Carrying Value (€100,000 + D)
Issue date				€2,000	€102,000
1	€10,000	€ 9,600	€ 400	1,600	101,600
2	10,000	9,600	400	1,200	101,200
3	10,000	9,600	400	800	100,800
4	10,000	9,600	400	400	100,400
5	10,000	9,600	400	0	100,000
	€50,000	€48,000	€2,000		

Column (A) remains constant because the face value of the bonds (€100,000) is multiplied by the annual contractual interest rate (10%) each period.

Column (B) is computed as the interest paid (Column A) less the premium amortization (Column C).

Column (C) indicates the premium amortization each period.

Column (D) decreases each period by the same amount until it reaches zero at maturity.

Column (E) decreases each period by the amount of premium amortization until it equals the face value at maturity.

Review and Practice

Learning Objectives Review

1 Describe the major characteristics of bonds.

Bonds can have many different features and may be secured, unsecured, convertible, or callable. The terms of the bond issue are set forth in a bond indenture, and a bond certificate provides the specific information about the bond itself.

2 Explain how to account for bond transactions.

When companies issue bonds, they debit Cash for the cash proceeds and credit Bonds Payable for the face value of the bonds.

When bondholders redeem bonds at maturity, the issuing company credits Cash and debits Bonds Payable for the face value of the bonds. When bonds are redeemed before maturity, the issuing company (a) eliminates the carrying value of the bonds at the redemption date, (b) records the cash paid, and (c) recognizes the gain or loss on redemption.

3 Explain how to account for other non-current liabilities.

A typical non-current liability is mortgage notes payable. The terms of the loan generally require the borrower to make equal installment payments. Each payment consists of (1) interest on the unpaid balance of the loan and (2) a reduction of loan principal. The interest decreases each period, while the portion applied to the loan principal increases.

A lease grants the right to use specific property for a period of time in return for cash payments. For a lease, the lessee records the asset and related obligation at the present value of the future lease payments.

4 Discuss how non-current liabilities are reported and analyzed.

Companies should report the nature and amount of each long-term debt in the statement of financial position or in the notes accompanying the financial statements. Companies may sell bonds to investors to raise long-term capital. Bonds offer the following advantages over ordinary shares: (a) shareholder control is not affected, (b) tax savings result, and (c) earnings per share may be higher.

Shareholders and long-term creditors are interested in a company's long-run solvency. Debt to assets and times interest earned are two ratios that provide information about debt-paying ability and long-run solvency.

***5 Apply the effective-interest method of amortizing bond discount and bond premium.**

The effective-interest method results in varying amounts of amortization and interest expense per period but a constant percentage rate of interest.

***6 Apply the straight-line method of amortizing bond discount and bond premium.**

The straight-line method of amortization results in a constant amount of amortization and interest expense per period.

Glossary Review

Bond certificate A legal document that indicates the name of the issuer, the face value of the bonds, the contractual interest rate, and the maturity date of the bonds. (p. 11-3).

Bond indenture A legal document that sets forth the terms of the bond issue. (p. 11-3).

Bonds A form of interest-bearing notes payable. (p. 11-2).

Callable bonds Bonds that are subject to redemption at a stated currency amount prior to maturity at the option of the issuer. (p. 11-3).

Contractual interest rate Rate used to determine the amount of cash interest the borrower pays and the investor receives. (p. 11-3).

Convertible bonds Bonds that permit bondholders to convert them into ordinary shares at the bondholders' option. (p. 11-3).

Debenture bonds Bonds issued against the general credit of the borrower. Also called unsecured bonds. (p. 11-3).

Debt to assets ratio A solvency measure that indicates the percentage of total assets provided by creditors; computed as total liabilities divided by total assets. (p. 11-16).

Discount (on a bond) The difference between the face value of a bond and its selling price, when the bond is sold for less than its face value. (p. 11-8).

***Effective-interest method of amortization** A method of amortizing bond discount or bond premium that results in periodic interest expense equal to a constant percentage of the carrying value of the bonds. (p. 11-19).

Face value Amount of principal the issuer must pay at the maturity date of the bond. (p. 11-3).

Lease A lease is a contractual agreement between a lessor (owner of a property) and a lessee (renter of the property). (p. 11-15).

Market interest rate The rate investors demand for loaning funds to the company. (p. 11-5).

Maturity date The date on which the final payment on the bond is due from the bond issuer to the investor. (p. 11-3).

Mortgage bond A bond secured by real estate. (p. 11-3).

Mortgage notes payable A long-term note secured by a mortgage that pledges title to specific assets as security for a loan. (p. 11-13).

Non-current liabilities Obligations expected to be paid more than one year in the future. (p. 11-2).

Premium (on a bond) The difference between the selling price and the face value of a bond, when the bond is sold for more than its face value. (p. 11-8).

Secured bonds Bonds that have specific assets of the issuer pledged as collateral. (p. 11-3).

Sinking fund bonds Bonds secured by specific assets set aside to redeem them. (p. 11-3).

***Straight-line method of amortization** A method of amortizing bond discount or bond premium that results in allocating the same amount to interest expense in each interest period. (p. 11-22).

Times interest earned A solvency measure that indicates a company's ability to meet interest payments; computed by dividing the sum of net income, interest expense, and income tax expense by interest expense. (p. 11-16).

Time value of money The relationship between time and money. A euro received today is worth more than a euro promised at some time in the future. (p. 11-5).

Unsecured bonds Bonds issued against the general credit of the borrower. Also called debenture bonds. (p. 11-3).

Practice Multiple-Choice Questions

1. **(LO 1)** The market interest rate:
   a. is the contractual interest rate used to determine the amount of cash interest paid by the borrower.
   b. is listed in the bond indenture.
   c. is the rate investors demand for loaning funds.
   d. More than one of the answer choices is true.

2. **(LO 1)** The term used for bonds that are unsecured is:
   a. callable bonds. **c.** debenture bonds.
   b. indenture bonds. **d.** convertible bonds.

3. **(LO 2)** Karson Ltd. issues 10-year bonds with a maturity value of £200,000. If the bonds are issued at a premium, this indicates that:
   a. the contractual interest rate exceeds the market interest rate.
   b. the market interest rate exceeds the contractual interest rate.
   c. the contractual interest rate and the market interest rate are the same.
   d. no relationship exists between the two rates.

4. **(LO 2)** Four-Nine Shops issued bonds that pay interest every January 1. The entry to accrue bond interest at December 31 includes a:

a. debit to Interest Payable.

b. credit to Cash.

c. credit to Interest Expense.

d. credit to Interest Payable.

5. **(LO 2)** Gester Ltd. redeems its HK$1,000,000 face value bonds at 105 on January 1, following the payment of annual interest. The carrying value of the bonds at the redemption date is HK$1,037,450. The entry to record the redemption will include a:

a. credit of HK$37,450 to Loss on Bond Redemption.

b. debit of HK$1,037,450 to Bonds Payable.

c. credit of HK$12,550 to Gain on Bond Redemption.

d. debit of HK$50,000 to Bonds Payable.

6. **(LO 3)** Andrews Ltd. issues a €497,000, 10%, 3-year mortgage note on January 1. The note will be paid in three annual installments of €200,000, each payable at the end of the year. What is the amount of interest expense that should be recognized by Andrews in the second year?

a. €16,567. **c.** €34,670.

b. €49,700. **d.** €346,700.

7. **(LO 3)** Howard Ltd. issued a 20-year mortgage note payable on January 1, 2029. At December 31, 2029, the unpaid principal balance will be reported as:

a. a current liability.

b. a non-current liability.

c. part current and part non-current liability.

d. interest payable.

8. **(LO 4)** For 2029, Kim Ltd. reported net income of ₩300,000. Interest expense was ₩40,000 and income taxes were ₩100,000. The times interest earned was:

a. 3 times. **c.** 7.5 times.

b. 4.4 times. **d.** 11 times.

9. **(LO 4)** Which of the following statements is not true.

a. Capitalized leases should be reported on the statement of financial position.

b. All leases must be capitalized.

c. The lessor is the owner of the property in a lease arrangement.

d. The lease liability is determined by computing the present value of the lease payments.

*10. **(LO 5)** On January 1, Besalius plc issued £1,000,000, 9% bonds for £938,554. The market rate of interest for these bonds is 10%. Interest is payable annually on December 31. Besalius uses the effective-interest method of amortizing bond discount. At the end of the first year, Besalius should report unamortized bond discount of:

a. £54,900. **c.** £51,610.

b. £57,591. **d.** £51,000.

*11. **(LO 5)** On January 1, Dias SA issued R$1,000,000, 10%, 5-year bonds with interest payable annually on December 31. The bonds sold for R$1,072,096. The market rate of interest for these bonds was 12%. On the first interest date, using the effective-interest method, the debit entry to Interest Expense is for:

a. R$120,000. **c.** R$128,652.

b. R$125,581. **d.** R$140,000.

*12. **(LO 6)** On January 1, 2029, Hurley Ltd. issued NT$5,000,000, 5-year, 12% bonds at 96 with interest payable annually on December 31. The entry on December 31, 2030, to record payment of bond interest and the amortization of bond discount using the straight-line method will include a:

a. debit to Interest Expense NT$300,000.

b. debit to Interest Expense NT$600,000.

c. credit to Bonds Payable NT$40,000.

d. credit to Bonds Payable NT$20,000.

*13. **(LO 6)** For the bonds issued in Question 12 above, what is the carrying value of the bonds at the end of the third interest period?

a. NT$4,920,000. **c.** NT$4,860,000.

b. NT$4,880,000. **d.** NT$4,640,000.

Solutions

1. **c.** Market interest rate is the rate investors demand for loaning funds. The other choices are incorrect because (a) market interest rate is the same as contractual interest rate only if bonds sell at face value (par value) and (b) the contractual interest rate, not the market interest rate, is listed in the bond indenture. Choice (d) is wrong as there is only one correct answer.

2. **c.** Debenture bonds are not secured by any collateral. The other choices are incorrect because (a) callable bonds can be paid off or redeemed by the issuer before they reach their maturity date, (b) indenture bonds do not exist, and (d) convertible bonds permit bondholders to convert them into ordinary shares at the bondholders' option.

3. **a.** When bonds are issued at a premium, this indicates that the contractual interest rate is higher than the market interest rate. The other choices are incorrect because (b) when the market interest rate exceeds the contractual interest rate, bonds are sold at a discount; (c) when the contractual interest rate and the market interest rate are the same, bonds will be issued at par; and (d) the relationship between the market rate of interest and the contractual rate of interest determines whether bonds are issued at par, a discount, or a premium.

4. **d.** The adjusting entry to accrue bond interest at December 31 includes a debit to Interest Expense and credit to Interest Payable. The other choices are therefore incorrect.

5. **b.** The entry to record the redemption of bonds will include a debit to Bonds Payable of HK$1,037,450, a credit to Cash of HK$1,050,000 (HK$1,000,000 × 1.05) and a debit to Loss on Bond Redemption of HK$12,550 (HK$1,050,000 − HK$1,037,450). The other choices are therefore incorrect.

6. **c.** In the first year, Andrews will recognize €49,700 of interest expense (€497,000 × 10%). After the first payment is made, the amount remaining on the note will be €346,700 [€497,000 principal − (€200,000 payment − €49,700 interest)]. The remaining balance (€346,700) is multiplied by the interest rate (10%) to compute the interest expense to be recognized for the second year, €34,670 (€346,700 × 10%), not (a) €16,567, (b) €49,700, or (d) €346,700.

7. **c.** Howard Ltd. reports the reduction in principal for the next year as a current liability, and it classifies the remaining unpaid principal balance as a non-current liability. The other choices are therefore incorrect.

8. **d.** Times interest earned = Net income + Interest expense + Income tax expense (₩300,000 + ₩40,000 + ₩100,000 = ₩440,000) divided by Interest expense (₩40,000), which equals 11 times, not (a) 3, (b) 4.4, or (c) 7.5 times.

9. **b.** All leases must be capitalized is not true. Leases that have a term of less than one year are not capitalized but simply reported as rent expense on the income statement. The other three choices are true.

*10. **b.** The beginning balance of unamortized discount is £61,446 (£1,000,000 – £938,554). The discount amortization is £3,855, the difference between the cash interest payment of £90,000 (£1,000,000 × 9%) and the interest expense recorded of £93,855 (£938,554 × 10%). This discount amortization (£3,855) is then subtracted from the beginning balance of unamortized discount (£61,446), to arrive at a balance of £57,591 at the end of the first year, not (a) £54,900, (c) £51,610, or (d) £51,000.

*11. **c.** The debit to Interest Expense = R$1,072,096 (initial carrying value of bond) × 12% (market rate) = R$128,652, not (a) R$120,000, (b) R$125,581, or (d) R$140,000.

*12. **c.** [NT$5,000,000 – (96% × NT$5,000,000)] = NT$200,000; NT$200,000 ÷ 5 = NT$40,000 of discount to amortize annually. As a result, the entry would involve a credit to Bonds Payable of NT$40,000. The other choices are therefore incorrect.

*13. **a.** The carrying value of bonds increases by the amount of the periodic discount amortization. Discount amortization using the straight-line method is NT$40,000 each period. Total discount amortization for three periods is NT$120,000 (NT$40,000 × 3 periods) which is added to the initial carrying value (NT$4,800,000) to arrive at NT$4,920,000, the carrying value at the end of the third interest period, not (b) NT$4,880,000, (c) NT$4,860,000, or (d) NT$4,640,000.

Practice Brief Exercises

1. **(LO 2)** Kahnle Industries issued 3,000, 7%, 5-year, €1,000 bonds dated January 1, 2029, at 100. Interest is paid each January 1. (a) Prepare the journal entry to record the sale of these bonds on January 1, 2029. (b) Prepare the adjusting journal entry on December 31, 2029, to record interest expense. (c) Prepare the journal entry on January 1, 2030, to record interest paid.

Prepare entries for bands issued at face value.

Solution

1. **a.**

		Debit	Credit
2029			
Jan. 1	Cash	3,000,000	
	Bonds Payable (3,000 × €1,000)		3,000,000

b.

		Debit	Credit
2029			
Dec. 31	Interest Expense	210,000	
	Interest Payable (€3,000,000 × 7%)		210,000

c.

		Debit	Credit
2030			
Jan. 1	Interest Payable	210,000	
	Cash (€3,000,000 × 7%)		210,000

2. **(LO 3)** Tyler-Danish Inc. issues a $600,000, 10%, 10-year mortgage note on December 31, 2029, to obtain financing for a new building. The terms provide for annual installment payments of $97,647. Prepare the entry to record the mortgage loan on December 31, 2029, and the first installment payment on December 31, 2030.

Prepare entries for long-term notes payable.

Solution

2.

Semiannual Interest Period	(A) Cash Payment	(B) Interest Expense (D) × 10%	(C) Reduction of Principal (A) – (B)	(D) Principal Balance (D) – (C)
Issue Date				$600,000
1	$97,647	$60,000	$37,647	562,353

		Debit	Credit
2029			
Dec. 31	Cash	600,000	
	Mortgage Payable		600,000
2030			
Dec. 31	Interest Expense	60,000	
	Mortgage Payable	37,647	
	Cash		97,647

3. **(LO 4)** Presented below are liability items for Rymer Group at December 31, 2029. Prepare the non-current liabilities section of the statement of financial position for Rymer.

Prepare statement presentation of non-current liabilities.

Bonds payable, due 2031 (includes premium of £40,000)	£740,000
Accounts payable	100,000
Lease liability	120,000
Notes payable, due 2034	110,000

Solution

3. Non-current liabilities*

Bonds payable, due 2031	£740,000
Notes payable, due 2034	110,000
Lease liability	120,000
Total non-current liabilities	£970,000

*Accounts Payable is a current liability.

Practice Exercises

Prepare entries for bonds issued at face value.

1. **(LO 2)** Global Airlines Ltd. issued NT$900,000 of 8%, 10-year bonds on January 1, 2029, at face value. Interest is payable annually on January 1.

Instructions

Prepare the journal entries to record the following events.

a. The issuance of the bonds.

b. The accrual of interest on December 31.

c. The payment of interest on January 1, 2030.

d. The redemption of bonds at maturity, assuming interest for the last interest period has been paid and recorded.

Solution

1.

		Debit	Credit
	January 1, 2029		
a.	Cash	900,000	
	Bonds Payable		900,000
	December 31, 2029		
b.	Interest Expense	72,000	
	Interest Payable (NT$900,000 × 8%)		72,000
	January 1, 2030		
c.	Interest Payable	72,000	
	Cash		72,000
	January 1, 2039		
d.	Bonds Payable	900,000	
	Cash		900,000

Prepare entries to record mortgage note and installment payments.

2. **(LO 3)** Trawler SA borrowed €500,000 on December 31, 2029, by issuing a €500,000, 7% mortgage note payable. The terms call for annual installment payments of €80,000 on December 31.

Instructions

a. Prepare the journal entries to record the mortgage loan and the first two installment payments.

b. Indicate the amount of mortgage note payable to be reported as a current liability and as a non-current liability at December 31, 2030.

Solution

2.

		Debit	Credit
	December 31, 2029		
a.	Cash	500,000	
	Mortgage Payable		500,000
	December 31, 2030		
	Interest Expense (€500,000 × 7%)	35,000	
	Mortgage Payable	45,000	
	Cash		80,000

December 31, 2031

Interest Expense [(€500,000 – €45,000) × 7%]	31,850	
Mortgage Payable	48,150	
Cash		80,000

b. Current: €48,150
Non-current: €406,850 (€500,000 – €45,000 – €48,150)

Practice Problem

Prepare entries to record issuance of bonds and long-term notes, interest accrued, and bond redemption.

(LO 2, 3) Lee Software Ltd. has successfully developed a new spreadsheet program. To produce and market the program, the company needs additional financing. On January 1, 2029, Lee borrowed money as follows.

1. Lee issued NT$1 million, 10%, 10-year bonds at face value. Interest is payable annually on January 1.
2. Lee also issued a NT$400,000, 6%, 15-year mortgage payable. The terms provide for annual installment payments of NT$41,185 on December 31.

Instructions

a. For the 10-year, 10% bonds:

1. Journalize the issuance of the bonds on January 1, 2029.
2. Prepare the journal entries for interest expense in 2029.
3. Prepare the entry for the redemption of the bonds at 101 on January 1, 2032, after paying the interest due on this date.

b. For the mortgage payable:

1. Prepare the entry for the issuance of the note on January 1, 2029.
2. Prepare a payment schedule for the first four installment payments.
3. Indicate the current and non-current amounts for the mortgage payable at December 31, 2029.

Solution

a. 1. 2029

Jan. 1	Cash	1,000,000	
	Bonds Payable		1,000,000
	(To record issuance of bonds)		

2. 2029

Dec. 31	Interest Expense	100,000	
	Interest Payable (NT$1,000,000 × 10%)		100,000
	(To record accrual of annual bond interest)		

3. 2032

Jan. 1	Bonds Payable	1,000,000	
	Loss on Bond Redemption	10,000*	
	Cash		1,010,000
	(To record redemption of bonds at 101)		

*(NT$1,010,000 – NT$1,000,000)

b. 1. 2029

Jan. 1	Cash	400,000	
	Mortgage Payable		400,000
	(To record issuance of mortgage payable)		

2.

Annual Interest Period	Cash Payment	Interest Expense	Reduction of Principal	Principal Balance
Issue date				NT$400,000
1	NT$41,185	NT$24,000	NT$17,185	382,815
2	41,185	22,969	18,216	364,599
3	41,185	21,876	19,309	345,290
4	41,185	20,717	20,468	324,822

3. Current liability: NT$18,216
Non-current liability: NT$364,599

Note: Asterisked Questions, Exercises, and Problems relate to material in the appendices to the chapter.

Questions

1. (a) What are non-current liabilities? Give three examples. (b) What is a bond?

2. Contrast the following types of bonds: (a) secured and unsecured, and (b) convertible and callable.

3. The following terms are important in issuing bonds: (a) face value, (b) contractual interest rate, (c) bond indenture, and (d) bond certificate. Explain each of these terms.

4. Describe the two major obligations incurred by a company when bonds are issued.

5. Assume that Bedazzled Ltd. sold bonds with a face value of €100,000 for €104,000. Was the market interest rate equal to, less than, or greater than the bonds' contractual interest rate? Explain.

6. If a 6%, 10-year, R$800,000 bond is issued at face value and interest is paid annually, what is the amount of the interest payment at the end of the first period?

7. If the Bonds Payable account has a balance of HK$8,400,000 and the amount of the unamortized bond discount is HK$600,000, what is the face value of the bonds?

8. Which accounts are debited and which are credited if a bond issue originally sold at a premium is redeemed before maturity at 97 immediately following the payment of interest?

9. Roy Toth, a friend of yours, has recently purchased a home for €125,000, paying €25,000 down and the remainder financed by a 6.5%, 20-year mortgage, payable at €745.57 per month. At the end of the first month, Roy receives a statement from the bank indicating that only €203.90 of principal was paid during the month. At this rate, he calculates that it will take over 40 years to pay off the mortgage. Is he right? Discuss.

10. In general, what are the requirements for the financial statement presentation of non-current liabilities?

11. (a) As a source of long-term financing, what are the major advantages of bonds over ordinary shares? (b) What are the major disadvantages in using bonds for long-term financing?

12. What is a lease agreement?

13. Jhutti Company rents a warehouse for the storage of its excess inventory. In the months when its production greatly exceeds actual sales, the company rents the space. As a result, Jhutti does not have a long-term lease for warehouse space but instead rents it as needed. What is the nature of this type of lease agreement, and what accounting treatment should be used?

14. Benedict Production entered into an agreement to lease 12 computers from Haley Electronics. The present value of the lease payments is $186,300. What entry would Benedict make on the date of the lease agreement?

*15. Ginny Bellis is discussing the advantages of the effective-interest method of bond amortization with her accounting staff. What do you think Ginny is saying?

*16. Redbone AG issues CHF500,000 of 8%, 5-year bonds on January 1, 2029, at 104. If Redbone uses the effective-interest method in amortizing the premium, will the annual interest expense increase or decrease over the life of the bonds? Explain.

*17. Explain the straight-line method of amortizing discount and premium on bonds payable.

*18. Fleming Ltd. issues £400,000 of 7%, 5-year bonds on January 1, 2029, at 105. Assuming that the straight-line method is used to amortize the premium, what is the total amount of interest expense for 2029?

Brief Exercises

Prepare entries for bonds issued at face value.

BE11.1 (LO 2) Meera Ltd. issued 4,000, 8%, 5-year, £1,000 bonds dated January 1, 2029, at 100. Interest is paid each January 1.

a. Prepare the journal entry to record the sale of these bonds on January 1, 2029.
b. Prepare the adjusting journal entry on December 31, 2029, to record interest expense.
c. Prepare the journal entry on January 1, 2030, to record interest paid.

Prepare entries for bonds sold at a discount and a premium.

BE11.2 (LO 2) Nasreen Company issues €2 million, 10-year, 8% bonds at 97, with interest payable each January 1.

a. Prepare the journal entry to record the sale of these bonds on January 1, 2029.
b. Assuming instead that the above bonds sold for 104, prepare the journal entry to record the sale of these bonds on January 1, 2029.

Prepare entries for bonds issued.

BE11.3 (LO 2) Frankum SpA has issued three different bonds during 2029. Interest is payable annually on each of these bonds.

1. On January 1, 2029, 1,000, 8%, 5-year, €1,000 bonds dated January 1, 2029, were issued at face value.
2. On July 1, €900,000, 9%, 5-year bonds dated July 1, 2029, were issued at 102.
3. On September 1, €400,000, 7%, 5-year bonds dated September 1, 2029, were issued at 98.

Prepare the journal entry to record each bond transaction at the date of issuance.

BE11.4 (LO 2) The statement of financial position for Miley Consulting reports the following information on July 1, 2029.

Prepare entry for redemption of bonds.

Non-current liabilities	
Bonds payable	£940,000

Miley decides to redeem these bonds at 101 (face value of bonds £1,000,000) after paying annual interest. Prepare the journal entry to record the redemption on July 1, 2029.

BE11.5 (LO 3) Hanschu plc issues an £800,000, 10%, 10-year mortgage note on December 31, 2029, to obtain financing for a new building. The terms provide for annual installment payments of £130,196. Prepare the entry to record the mortgage loan on December 31, 2029, and the first installment payment on December 31, 2030.

Prepare entries for long-term notes payable.

BE11.6 (LO 4) Presented below are non-current liability items for Suarez AG at December 31, 2029. Prepare the non-current liabilities section of the statement of financial position for Suarez.

Prepare statement presentation of non-current liabilities.

Bonds payable, due 2031	CHF500,000
Lease liability	72,000
Notes payable, due 2034	80,000

BE11.7 (LO 4) Shaffer Ltd. is considering two alternatives to finance its construction of a new €2 million plant.

Compare debt versus equity financing.

a. Issuance of 200,000 ordinary shares at the market price of €10 per share.

b. Issuance of €2 million, 6% bonds at face value.

Complete the following table, and indicate which alternative is preferable.

	Issue Shares	Issue Bonds
Income before interest and taxes	€900,000	€900,000
Interest expense from bonds		
Income before income taxes		
Income tax expense (30%)		
Net income	€	€
Outstanding shares		500,000
Earnings per share	€	€

BE11.8 (LO 3) Imholf Company leases a new building from Noble Construction for 20 years. The present value of the lease payment is €700,000. Prepare the journal entry to record this transaction.

Record lease transaction.

***BE11.9 (LO 5)** Writing Presented below is the partial bond discount amortization schedule for Gomez SA. Gomez uses the effective-interest method of amortization.

Use effective-interest method of bond amortization.

Interest Periods	Interest to Be Paid	Interest Expense to Be Recorded	Discount Amortization	Unamortized Discount	Bond Carrying Value
Issue date				€38,609	€961,391
1	€45,000	€48,070	€3,070	35,539	964,461
2	45,000	48,223	3,223	32,316	967,684

a. Prepare the journal entry to record the payment of interest and the discount amortization at the end of period 1.

b. Explain why interest expense is greater than interest paid.

c. Explain why interest expense will increase each period.

***BE11.10 (LO 6)** Zhu Ltd. issues HK$5 million, 10-year, 9% bonds at 96, with interest payable annually on January 1. The straight-line method is used to amortize bond discount.

Prepare entries for bonds issued at a discount.

a. Prepare the journal entry to record the sale of these bonds on January 1, 2029.

b. Prepare the adjusting journal entry to record interest expense and bond discount amortization on December 31, 2029.

Prepare entries for bonds issued at a premium.

***BE11.11 (LO 6)** Golden plc issues £4 million, 5-year, 10% bonds at 102, with interest payable annually January 1. The straight-line method is used to amortize bond premium.

a. Prepare the journal entry to record the sale of these bonds on January 1, 2029.

b. Prepare the adjusting journal entry to record interest expense and bond premium amortization on December 31, 2029.

DO IT! Exercises

Evaluate statements about bonds.

DO IT! 11.1 (LO 1) State whether each of the following statements is true or false. If false, indicate how to correct the statement.

______ **1.** Mortgage bonds and sinking fund bonds are both examples of debenture bonds.

______ **2.** Convertible bonds are also known as callable bonds.

______ **3.** The market rate is the rate investors demand for loaning funds.

______ **4.** Annual interest paid on bonds is equal to the face value times the stated rate.

______ **5.** The present value of a bond is the value at which it should sell in the market.

Prepare journal entry for bond issuance and show statement of financial position presentation.

DO IT! 11.2a (LO 2) Jeon Enterprises, Ltd. issues ₩300,000,000 of bonds for ₩306,000,000. (a) Prepare the journal entry to record the issuance of the bonds, and (b) show how the bonds would be reported on the statement of financial position at the date of issuance.

Prepare entry for bond redemption.

DO IT! 11.2b (LO 2) Jeske Industries, SA issued €400,000 of 10-year bonds at a discount. Prior to maturity, when the carrying value of the bonds was €390,000, the company redeemed the bonds at 99. Prepare the entry to record the redemption of the bonds.

Prepare entries for mortgage note and installment payment on note.

DO IT! 11.3 (LO 3) Mattsen Orchard issues a R$700,000, 6%, 15-year mortgage note to obtain needed financing for a new lab. The terms call for annual payments of R$72,074 each. Prepare the entries to record the mortgage loan and the first installment payment.

Compute debt to assets ratio.

DO IT! 11.4 (LO 4) Huebner Hotels has assets of €1,800,000, liabilities of €1,100,000, and equity of €700,000 at December 31, 2029. Compute and discuss the debt to assets ratio at year-end.

Exercises

Evaluate statements about bonds.

E11.1 (LO 1) Liane Hansen has prepared the following list of statements about bonds.

1. Bonds are a form of interest-bearing notes payable.

2. When seeking long-term financing, an advantage of issuing bonds over issuing ordinary shares is that shareholder control is not affected.

3. When seeking long-term financing, an advantage of issuing ordinary shares over issuing bonds is that tax savings result.

4. Secured bonds have specific assets of the issuer pledged as collateral for the bonds.

5. Secured bonds are also known as debenture bonds.

6. A conversion feature may be added to bonds to make them more attractive to bond buyers.

7. The rate used to determine the amount of cash interest the borrower pays is called the stated rate.

8. Bond prices are usually quoted as a percentage of the face value of the bond.

9. The present value of a bond is the value at which it should sell in the marketplace.

Instructions

Identify each statement as true or false. If false, indicate how to correct the statement.

Prepare entries for issuance of bonds, and payment and accrual of bond interest.

E11.2 (LO 2) On January 1, 2029, Klosterman Ltd. issued £500,000, 10%, 10-year bonds at face value. Interest is payable annually on January 1.

Instructions

Prepare journal entries to record the following.

a. The issuance of the bonds.

b. The accrual of interest on December 31, 2029.

c. The payment of interest on January 1, 2030.

E11.3 (LO 2) On January 1, 2029, Forrester SA issued R$400,000, 8%, 5-year bonds at face value. Interest is payable annually on January 1.

Prepare entries for bonds issued at face value.

Instructions

Prepare journal entries to record the following.

a. The issuance of the bonds.

b. The accrual of interest on December 31, 2029.

c. The payment of interest on January 1, 2030.

E11.4 (LO 2) Pueblo Company issued €500,000 of 5-year, 8% bonds at 97 on January 1, 2029. The bonds pay interest annually.

Prepare entries to record issuance of bonds at discount and premium.

Instructions

a. 1. Prepare the journal entry to record the issuance of the bonds.

2. Compute the total cost of borrowing for these bonds.

b. Repeat the requirements from part (a), assuming the bonds were issued at 105.

E11.5 (LO 2) The following section is taken from Ohlman Ltd.'s. statement of financial position at December 31, 2028.

Prepare entries for bond interest and redemption.

Non-current liabilities	
Bonds payable, 7%, due January 1, 2033	HK$16,000,000
Current liabilities	
Interest payable	1,120,000

Bond interest is payable annually on January 1. The bonds are callable on any interest date.

Instructions

a. Journalize the payment of the bond interest on January 1, 2029.

b. Assume that on January 1, 2029, after paying interest, Ohlman calls bonds having a face value of HK$6,000,000. The call price is 103. Record the redemption of the bonds.

c. Prepare the entry to record the accrual of interest on December 31, 2029.

E11.6 (LO 2) The following situations are independent of each other.

Prepare journal entries for redemption of bonds.

Instructions

For each situation, prepare the appropriate journal entry for the redemption of the bonds.

a. Mikhail Corporation redeemed $140,000 face value, 9% bonds on April 30, 2029, at 101. The carrying value of the bonds at the redemption date was $126,500. The bonds pay annual interest, and the interest payment due on April 30, 2029, has been made and recorded.

b. Oldman, Inc., redeemed $170,000 face value, 12.5% bonds on June 30, 2029, at 98. The carrying value of the bonds at the redemption date was $184,000. The bonds pay annual interest, and the interest payment due on June 30, 2029, has been made and recorded.

E11.7 (LO 3) Yancey Co. receives $300,000 when it issues a $300,000, 10% mortgage note payable to finance the construction of a building at December 31, 2029. The terms provide for annual installment payments of $50,000 on December 31.

Prepare entries to record mortgage note and payments.

Instructions

Prepare the journal entries to record the mortgage loan and the first two payments.

E11.8 (LO 4) Global Car Rental is considering two alternatives for the financing of a purchase of a fleet of cars. These two alternatives are:

Compare two alternatives of financing—issuance of ordinary shares vs. issuance of bonds.

1. Issue 60,000 ordinary shares at ¥40 per share. (Cash dividends have not been paid nor is the payment of any contemplated.)

2. Issue 7%, 10-year bonds at face value for ¥2,400,000.

It is estimated that the company will earn ¥800,000 before interest and taxes as a result of this purchase. The company has an estimated tax rate of 30% and has 90,000 ordinary shares outstanding prior to the new financing.

Instructions

Determine the effect on net income and earnings per share for these two methods of financing.

Prepare non-current liabilities section.

E11.9 (LO 4) The adjusted trial balance for Zhang Ltd. at the end of 2029 contained the following accounts.

Interest Payable	HK$ 9,000
Lease Liability	59,500
Bonds Payable, due 2031	204,000

Instructions

Prepare the non-current liabilities section of the statement of financial position.

Calculate ratios; discuss impact of unrecorded obligations on liquidity and solvency.

E11.10 (LO 4) Suppose Lin Ltd.'s 2029 financial statements contain the following selected data (in millions).

Current assets	NT$ 3,416.3	Interest expense	NT$ 473.2
Total assets	30,224.9	Income taxes	1,936.0
Current liabilities	2,988.7	Net income	4,551.0
Total liabilities	16,191.0		

Instructions

Compute the following ratios and provide a brief interpretation of each.

a. Debt to assets ratio.

b. Times interest earned.

Prepare lease entries.

E11.11 (LO 3) Presented below are two independent situations.

1. Flinthills Car Rental leased a car to Jayhawk Company for 11 months. Terms of the lease agreement call for monthly payments of $500.
2. On January 1, 2029, Throm plc entered into an agreement to lease 20 computers from Drummond Electronics. The terms of the lease agreement require three annual rental payments of £20,000 (including 10% interest) beginning December 31, 2029. The present value of the three rental payments is £49,735.

Instructions

a. Prepare the appropriate journal entry to be made by Jayhawk for the first lease payment.

b. Prepare the journal entry to record the lease agreement on the books of Throm on January 1, 2029.

Prepare entries for issuance of bonds, payment of interest, and amortization of discount using effective-interest method.

***E11.12 (LO 5)** Lorance SpA issued €400,000, 7%, 20-year bonds on January 1, 2029, for €360,727. This price resulted in an effective-interest rate of 8% on the bonds. Interest is payable annually on January 1. Lorance uses the effective-interest method to amortize bond premium or discount.

Instructions

Prepare the journal entries to record the following. (Round to the nearest euro.)

a. The issuance of the bonds.

b. The accrual of interest and the discount amortization on December 31, 2029.

c. The payment of interest on January 1, 2030.

Prepare entries for issuance of bonds, payment of interest, and amortization of premium using effective-interest method.

***E11.13 (LO 5)** LRNA Ltd. issued £380,000, 7%, 10-year bonds on January 1, 2029, for £407,968. This price resulted in an effective-interest rate of 6% on the bonds. Interest is payable annually on January 1. LRNA uses the effective-interest method to amortize bond premium or discount.

Instructions

Prepare the journal entries to record the following. (Round to the nearest pound.)

a. The issuance of the bonds.

b. The accrual of interest and the premium amortization on December 31, 2029.

c. The payment of interest on January 1, 2030.

Prepare entries to record issuance of bonds, payment of interest, amortization of premium, and redemption at maturity.

***E11.14 (LO 6)** Adcock A/S issued €600,000, 9%, 20-year bonds on January 1, 2029, at 103. Interest is payable annually on January 1. Adcock uses straight-line amortization for bond premium or discount.

Instructions

Prepare the journal entries to record the following.

a. The issuance of the bonds.

b. The accrual of interest and the premium amortization on December 31, 2029.

c. The payment of interest on January 1, 2030.

d. The redemption of the bonds at maturity, assuming interest for the last interest period has been paid and recorded.

***E11.15 (LO 6)** Gridley Ltd. issued £800,000, 11%, 10-year bonds on December 31, 2028, for £730,000. Interest is payable annually on December 31. Gridley uses the straight-line method to amortize bond premium or discount.

Prepare entries to record issuance of bonds, payment of interest, amortization of discount, and redemption at maturity.

Instructions

Prepare the journal entries to record the following.

a. The issuance of the bonds.

b. The payment of interest and the discount amortization on December 31, 2029.

c. The redemption of the bonds at maturity, assuming interest for the last interest period has been paid and recorded.

E11.16 (LO 1, 2, 3, 4) The following are terms or phrases that were introduced in the chapter.

Identify key terms.

1. Bond certificate.
2. Premium (on a bond).
3. Discount (on a bond).
4. Times interest earned.
5. Present value.
6. Maturity date.
7. Callable bonds.
8. Market interest rate.
9. Secured bonds.
10. Contractual (stated) interest rate.
11. Unsecured bonds.
12. Face value.
13. Convertible bonds.

Instructions

Match the term or phrase with the appropriate description below.

a. ________ The value today of an amount to be received at some date in the future after taking into account current interest rates.

b. ________ Bonds that have specific assets of the issuer pledged as collateral.

c. ________ Bonds that can be converted into share capital—ordinary at the bondholder's option.

d. ________ A legal document that indicates the name of the issuer, the face value of the bonds, and other data such as the contractual interest rate and the maturity date of the bonds.

e. ________ Bonds that the issuing company can redeem (buy back) at a stated dollar amount prior to maturity.

f. ________ The date on which the final payment on a bond is due from the bond issuer to the investor.

g. ________ Rate used to determine the amount of interest the issuer pays and the investor receives.

h. ________ The difference between the face value of a bond and its selling price when a bond is issued for less than its face value.

i. ________ A measure of a company's solvency, calculated by dividing the sum of net income, interest expense, and income tax expense by interest expense.

j. ________ The rate investors demand for loaning funds to the corporation.

k. ________ Amount of principal due at the maturity date of the bond.

l. ________ Bonds issued against the general credit of the borrower.

m. ________ The difference between the selling price and the face value of a bond when a bond is sold for more than its face value.

Problems

P11.1 (LO 2, 4) On October 1, 2028, Kristal Corp. issued $700,000, 5%, 10-year bonds at face value. The bonds were dated October 1, 2028, and pay interest annually on October 1. Financial statements are prepared annually on December 31.

Prepare journal entries to record issuance of bonds, interest, statement of financial position presentation, and bond redemption.

Instructions

a. Prepare the journal entry to record the issuance of the bonds.

b. Prepare the adjusting entry to record the accrual of interest on December 31, 2028.

c. Show the statement of financial position presentation of bonds payable and bond interest payable on December 31, 2028.

d. Prepare the journal entry to record the payment of interest on October 1, 2029.

e. Prepare the adjusting entry to record the accrual of interest on December 31, 2029.

f. Loss $28,000

f. Assume that on January 1, 2030, Kristal pays the accrued bond interest and calls the bonds. The call price is 104. Record the payment of interest and redemption of the bonds.

Prepare entries to record issuance of bonds, interest accrual, and bond redemption.

P11.2 (LO 2, 4) Kershaw Electric Ltd. sold £6,000,000, 10%, 15-year bonds on January 1, 2029. The bonds were dated January 1, 2029, and paid interest on January 1. The bonds were sold at 98.

Instructions

a. Prepare the journal entry to record the issuance of the bonds on January 1, 2029.

b. At December 31, 2029, the amount of amortized bond discount is £8,000. Show the statement of financial position presentation of the bond liability at December 31, 2029.

c. Loss £224,000

c. On January 1, 2031, when the carrying value of the bonds was £5,896,000, the company redeemed the bonds at 102. Record the redemption of the bonds assuming that interest for the period has already been paid.

Prepare installment payments schedule and journal entries for a mortgage note payable.

P11.3 (LO 3, 4) Talkington Electronics issues a R$400,000, 8%, 10-year mortgage note on December 31, 2028. The proceeds from the note are to be used in financing a new research laboratory. The terms of the note provide for annual installment payments, exclusive of real estate taxes and insurance, of R$59,612. Payments are due on December 31.

Instructions

b. December 31 debit Mortgage Payable R$27,612
c. Current liability—2029 R$29,821

a. Prepare an installment payments schedule for the first 4 years.

b. Prepare the entries for (1) the loan and (2) the first installment payment.

c. Show how the total mortgage liability should be reported on the statement of financial position at December 31, 2029.

Analyze two different lease situations and prepare journal entries.

P11.4 (LO 3) Presented below are two different lease transactions that occurred for Ruggiero Inc. in 2029. Assume that all lease contracts start on January 1, 2029. In no case does Ruggiero receive title to the properties leased during or at the end of the lease term.

	Lessor	
	Judson Delivery	**Hester Co.**
Type of property	Computer	Delivery equipment
Yearly rental	$ 5,000	$ 4,200
Lease term	6 years	4 years
Estimated economic life	7 years	7 years
Present value of the lease rental payments	$26,000	$13,000

Instructions

a. How should the lease transaction with Hester Co. be recorded in 2029?

b. How should the lease transaction with Judson Delivery be recorded in 2029?

Prepare journal entries to record issuance of bonds, payment of interest, and amortization of bond discount using effective-interest method.

***P11.5 (LO 2, 5)** On January 1, 2029, Lock Industries Ltd. issued £1,800,000 face value, 5%, 10-year bonds at £1,667,518. This price resulted in an effective-interest rate of 6% on the bonds. Lock uses the effective-interest method to amortize bond premium or discount. The bonds pay annual interest January 1.

Instructions

(Round all computations to the nearest pound.)

a. Prepare the journal entry to record the issuance of the bonds on January 1, 2029.

b. Prepare an amortization table through December 31, 2031 (3 interest periods), for this bond issue.

c. Interest Expense £100,051

c. Prepare the journal entry to record the accrual of interest and the amortization of the discount on December 31, 2029.

d. Prepare the journal entry to record the payment of interest on January 1, 2030.

e. Prepare the journal entry to record the accrual of interest and the amortization of the discount on December 31, 2030.

***P11.6 (LO 2, 5)** Writing On January 1, 2029, Jade SA issued €2,000,000 face value, 7%, 10-year bonds at €2,147,202. This price resulted in a 6% effective-interest rate on the bonds. Jade uses the effective-interest method to amortize bond premium or discount. The bonds pay annual interest on each January 1.

Prepare journal entries to record issuance of bonds, payment of interest, and effective-interest amortization, and statement of financial position presentation.

Instructions

a. Prepare the journal entries to record the following transactions.

1. The issuance of the bonds on January 1, 2029.
2. Accrual of interest and amortization of the premium on December 31, 2029.
3. The payment of interest on January 1, 2030.
4. Accrual of interest and amortization of the premium on December 31, 2030.

a. 4. Interest Expense €128,162

b. Show the proper non-current liabilities statement of financial position presentation for the bond liability at December 31, 2030.

c. Provide the answers to the following questions in narrative form.

1. What amount of interest expense is reported for 2030?
2. Would the bond interest expense reported in 2030 be the same as, greater than, or less than the amount that would be reported if the straight-line method of amortization were used?

***P11.7 (LO 2, 6)** Paris Electric sold €3,000,000, 10%, 10-year bonds on January 1, 2029. The bonds were dated January 1 and pay interest annually on January 1. Paris Electric uses the straight-line method to amortize bond premium or discount. The bonds were sold at 104.

Prepare entries to record issuance of bonds, interest accrual, and straight-line amortization for 2 years.

Instructions

a. Prepare the journal entry to record the issuance of the bonds on January 1, 2029.

b. Prepare a bond premium amortization schedule for the first 4 interest periods.

b. Amortization €12,000

c. Prepare the journal entries for interest and the amortization of the premium in 2029 and 2030.

d. Show the statement of financial position presentation of the bond liability at December 31, 2030.

d. Bonds payable €3,096,000

***P11.8 (LO 2, 6)** Fong Corporation sold $2,000,000, 7%, 5-year bonds on January 1, 2029. The bonds were dated January 1, 2029, and pay interest each January 1. Fong Corporation uses the straight-line method to amortize bond premium or discount.

Prepare journal entries to record issuance of bonds, interest, and straight-line amortization, and show statement of financial position presentation.

Instructions

a. Prepare all the necessary journal entries to record the issuance of the bonds and bond interest expense for 2029, assuming that the bonds sold at 102.

b. Prepare journal entries as in part (a) assuming that the bonds sold at 97.

c. Show the statement of financial position presentation for the bond issue at December 31, 2029, for both requirements (a) and (b).

***P11.9 (LO 2, 6)** The following is taken from the Colaw SA statement of financial position.

Prepare entries to record interest payments, straight-line premium amortization, and redemption of bonds.

Colaw SA
Statement of Financial Position (partial)
December 31, 2029

Non-current liabilities	
Bonds payable (face value €3,000,000), 7% due January 1, 2040	€3,200,000
Current liabilities	
Interest payable (for 12 months from January 1 to December 31)	210,000

Interest is payable annually on January 1. The bonds are callable on any annual interest date. Colaw uses straight-line amortization for any bond premium or discount. From December 31, 2029, the bonds will be outstanding for an additional 10 years (120 months).

Instructions

a. Journalize the payment of bond interest on January 1, 2030.

b. Prepare the entry to amortize bond premium and to accrue the interest due on December 31, 2030.

c. Assume that on January 1, 2031, after paying interest, Colaw calls bonds having a face value of €1,200,000. The call price is 101. Record the redemption of the bonds.

d. Prepare the adjusting entry at December 31, 2031, to amortize bond premium and to accrue interest on the remaining bonds.

b. Amortization €20,000
c. Gain €60,000
d. Amortization €12,000

Identify coupon rate, premium or discount, what method is adopted, and redemption of bonds.

P11.10 (LO 2, 5, 6) On January 1, year X2, Dalin Company issued bonds with a face value of $1,000,000, with a term of five years, and the interest is paid on June 30 and December 31 each year. A table of future interest expenses and amortization of premiums and discounts presented by the company's accountants is as follows:

Interest Payment Date	Cash	Interest Expenses	Amortization Amount
X2/6/30	$30,000	$36,756	$6,756
X2/12/31	30,000	37,026	7,026
X3/6/30	30,000	37,307	7,307
X3/12/31	30,000	37,599	7,599
X4/6/30	30,000	37,903	7,903
X4/12/31	30,000	38,219	8,219
X5/6/30	30,000	38,548	8,548
X5/12/31	30,000	38,890	8,890
X6/6/30	30,000	39,246	9,246
X6/12/31	30,000	39,615	9,615

Instructions

a. What is the coupon rate and fair interest rate of the bonds?

b. Are the bonds issued at a premium or at a discount? What method is adopted to amortize the premium/discount?

c. If the company redeems half of the bonds at a call price of 98 after paying interest at the end of year X5, please make the redemption entry.

d. If the company adopts the straight-line method to amortize the premium/discount, please make the interest payment entry on X2/6/30.

Comprehensive Accounting Cycle Review

ACR11.1 James Ltd.'s statement of financial position at December 31, 2028, is presented below.

James Ltd.
Statement of Financial Position
December 31, 2028

Equipment	£ 43,000	Share capital—ordinary	£ 20,000
Prepaid insurance	5,600	Retained earnings	18,600
Inventory	25,750	Bonds payable	50,000
Cash	30,500	Accounts payable	13,750
	£104,850	Interest payable	2,500
			£104,850

During 2029, the following transactions occurred.

1. James paid £2,500 interest on the bonds on January 1, 2029.
2. James purchased £241,100 of inventory on account.
3. James sold for £450,000 cash inventory which cost £250,000. James also collected £31,500 sales taxes.
4. James paid £230,000 on accounts payable.
5. James paid £2,500 interest on the bonds on July 1, 2029.

6. The prepaid insurance (£5,600) expired on July 31.
7. On August 1, James paid £12,000 for insurance coverage from August 1, 2029, through July 31, 2030.
8. James paid £24,000 sales taxes to the government.
9. Paid other operating expenses, £91,000.
10. Redeemed the bonds on December 31, 2029, by paying £47,000 plus £2,500 interest.
11. Issued £90,000 of 8% bonds on December 31, 2029, at 104. The bonds pay interest every December 31.

Adjustment data:

1. Recorded the insurance expired from item 7.
2. The equipment was acquired on December 31, 2028, and will be depreciated on a straight-line basis over 5 years with a £3,000 residual value.
3. The income tax rate is 30%. (*Hint:* Prepare the income statement up to income before taxes and multiply by 30% to compute the amount.)

Instructions

(You may want to set up T-accounts to determine ending balances.)

a. Prepare journal entries for the transactions listed above and adjusting entries.
b. Prepare an adjusted trial balance at December 31, 2029.
c. Prepare an income statement and a retained earnings statement for the year ending December 31, 2029, and a classified statement of financial position as of December 31, 2029.

b. Totals £652,070
c. N.I. £61,880

ACR11.2 **Writing** Eastland AG and Westside AG are competing businesses. Both began operations 6 years ago and are quite similar in most respects. The current statements of financial position data for the two companies are shown below.

	Eastland AG	Westside AG
Plant and equipment	CHF255,300	CHF257,300
Accumulated depreciation—plant and equipment	(112,650)	(189,850)
Inventory	463,900	515,200
Accounts receivable	304,700	302,500
Allowance for doubtful accounts	(13,600)	–0–
Cash	63,300	48,400
Total assets	CHF960,950	CHF933,550
Equity	CHF442,750	CHF420,050
Non-current liabilities	78,000	82,000
Current liabilities	440,200	431,500
Total equity and liabilities	CHF960,950	CHF933,550

You have been engaged as a consultant to conduct a review of the two companies. Your goal is to determine which of them is in the stronger financial position.

Your review of their financial statements quickly reveals that the two companies have not followed the same accounting practices. The differences and your conclusions regarding them are summarized below.

1. Eastland has used the allowance method of accounting for bad debts. A review shows that the amount of its write-offs each year has been quite close to the allowances that have been provided. It therefore seems reasonable to have confidence in its current estimate of bad debts.

   Westside has used the direct write-off method for bad debts, and it has been somewhat slow to write off its uncollectible accounts. Based upon an aging analysis and review of its accounts receivable, it is estimated that CHF18,000 of its existing accounts will probably prove to be uncollectible.
2. Eastland estimated a useful life of 12 years and a residual value of CHF30,000 for its plant and equipment. It has been depreciating them on straight-line basis.

   Westside has the same type of plant and equipment. However, it estimated a useful life of 10 years and a residual value of CHF10,000. It has been depreciating its plant and equipment using the double-declining-balance method.

   Based upon engineering studies of these types of plant and equipment, you conclude that Westside's estimates and method for calculating depreciation are the more appropriate.
3. Among its current liabilities, Eastland has included the portions of non-current liabilities that become due within the next year. Westside has not done so.

You find that CHF16,000 of Westside's CHF82,000 of non-current liabilities are due to be repaid in the current year.

Instructions

a. Total assets:
Eastland CHF885,225
Westside CHF915,550

a. Revise the statements of financial position presented above so that the data are comparable and reflect the current financial position for each of the two companies.

b. Prepare a brief report to your client stating your conclusions.

Expand Your Critical Thinking

Financial Reporting Problem: TSMC, Ltd. (TWN)

CT11.1 The financial statements of **TSMC** appear in Appendix A. The complete annual report, including the notes to the financial statements, are available at the company's website.

Instructions

Refer to TSMC's financial statements and answer the following questions about liabilities.

a. What were TSMC's total non-current liabilities at December 31, 2020? What was the increase/decrease in total non-current liabilities from the prior year?

b. What were the components of total non-current liabilities on December 31, 2020?

Comparative Analysis Problem: Nestlé SA (CHE) vs. Delfi Limited (SGP)

CT11.2 Nestlé's financial statements are presented in Appendix B. Financial statements of **Delfi Limited** are presented in Appendix C.

Instructions

a. Based on the information contained in those financial statements, compute for the group the following ratios for each company for the most recent fiscal year reported.

1. Debt to assets ratio.
2. Times interest earned. Note that some companies, including Nestlé, refer to interest expense as financial expense.

b. What conclusions concerning the companies' long-run solvency can be drawn from these ratios?

Real-World Focus

CT11.3 Bond or debt securities pay a stated rate of interest. This rate of interest is dependent on the risk associated with the investment. **Fitch Ratings** provides ratings for companies that issue debt securities.

Instructions

Go to the Fitch Ratings website and then answer the following questions.

a. In what year did Fitch introduce its bond rating scale?

b. What letter values are assigned to debt investments that are considered "investment grade" and "speculative grade"? (See **Ratings Definitions**.)

c. Search the Internet to identify two other major credit rating agencies.

Decision-Making Across the Organization

***CT11.4** On January 1, 2027, Fleming Ltd. issued £2,400,000 of 5-year, 8% bonds at 95; the bonds pay interest annually on January 1. By January 1, 2029, the market rate of interest for bonds of risk similar to those of Fleming had risen. As a result, the market value of these bonds was £2,000,000 on January 1, 2029—below their carrying value. Debra Fleming, president of the company, suggests repurchasing all of these bonds in the open market at the £2,000,000 price. To do so, the company will have to issue £2,000,000 (face value) of new 10-year, 11% bonds at par. The president asks you, as controller, "What is the feasibility of my proposed repurchase plan?"

Instructions

With the class divided into groups, answer the following.

a. What is the carrying value of the outstanding Fleming 5-year bonds on January 1, 2029? (Assume straight-line amortization.)

b. Prepare the journal entry to redeem the 5-year bonds on January 1, 2029. Prepare the journal entry to issue the new 10-year bonds.

c. Prepare a short email to the president in response to her request for advice. List the economic factors that you believe should be considered for her repurchase proposal.

Communication Activity

CT11.5 Ron Seiser, president of Seiser AG, is considering the issuance of bonds to finance an expansion of his business. He has asked you to (1) discuss the advantages of bonds over equity financing, (2) indicate the types of bonds he might issue, and (3) explain the issuing procedures used in bond transactions.

Instructions

Write an email to the president, answering his request.

Ethics Case

CT11.6 Dylan Horn is the president, founder, and majority owner of Wesley Medical Ltd., an emerging medical technology products company. Wesley is in dire need of additional capital to keep operating and to bring several promising products to final development, testing, and production. Dylan, as owner of 51% of the outstanding shares, manages the company's operations. He places heavy emphasis on research and development and on long-term growth. The other principal shareholder is Mary Sommers who, as a non-employee investor, owns 40% of the shares. Mary would like to deemphasize the R&D functions and emphasize the marketing function, to maximize short-run sales and profits from existing products. She believes this strategy would raise the market price of Wesley's shares.

All of Dylan's personal capital and borrowing power is tied up in his 51% share ownership. He knows that any offering of additional shares will dilute his controlling interest because he won't be able to participate in such an issuance. But, Mary has money and would likely buy enough shares to gain control of Wesley. She then would dictate the company's future direction, even if it meant replacing Dylan as president and CEO.

The company already has considerable debt. Raising additional debt will be costly, will adversely affect Wesley's credit rating, and will increase the company's reported losses due to the growth in interest expense. Mary and the other minority shareholders express opposition to the assumption of additional debt, fearing the company will be pushed to the brink of bankruptcy. Wanting to maintain his control and to preserve the direction of "his" company, Dylan is doing everything to avoid a share issuance. He is contemplating a large issuance of bonds, even if it means the bonds are issued with a high effective-interest rate.

Instructions

a. Who are the stakeholders in this situation?

b. What are the ethical issues in this case?

c. What would you do if you were Dylan?

Answers to Insight and Accounting Across the Organization Questions

How About Some Green Bonds? Q: Why might standardized disclosure help investors to better understand how proceeds from the sale or issuance of bonds are used? **A:** By requiring transparency as to how a bond's proceeds are to be used and how it will affect a company's sustainable profitability, investors will make better financial decisions.

Driving Up Debt Q: When a company like Volkswagen issues debt to survive a challenging period, what risks does the company face in the future? How could issuing debt today reduce your options in the future? **A:** More cash now means more debt later. Without strong sales and profits, highly leveraged companies may have difficulties paying off debt as well as developing new products in the future. They may also have difficulty issuing additional debt, leaving the company potentially starved for cash.

Debt Masking Q: What implications does debt masking have for an investor that is using the debt to assets ratio to evaluate a company's solvency? **A:** Since the debt to assets ratio is calculated using financial statement numbers from the end of the accounting period, debt masking could result in investors making incorrect assumptions about a company's solvency. By engaging in debt masking, a company is misleading investors because what it is disclosing at the end of the period does not reflect what its normal financial position was during most of the accounting period.

A Look at U.S. GAAP

LEARNING OBJECTIVE 7

Compare the accounting for liabilities under IFRS and U.S. GAAP.

IFRS and GAAP have different definitions of liabilities. However, in practice, the liabilities reported will be the same in most cases. IFRSs related to reporting and recognition of liabilities are found in *IAS 1 (revised)* ("Presentation of Financial Statements") and *IAS 37* ("Provisions, Contingent Liabilities, and Contingent Assets").

Key Points

Similarities

- The basic definition of a liability under GAAP and IFRS is very similar. Liabilities may be legally enforceable via a contract or law but need not be; that is, they can arise due to normal business practice or customs.
- Both GAAP and IFRS classify liabilities as current or non-current on the face of the statement of financial position. IFRS specifically states, however, that industries where a *presentation* based on liquidity would be considered to **provide more** useful information (such as financial institutions) can use that format instead.
- The basic calculation for bond valuation is the same under GAAP and IFRS. In addition, the accounting for bond liability transactions is essentially the same between GAAP and IFRS.

Differences

- Under IFRS, companies sometimes show liabilities before assets. Also, they will sometimes show non-current liabilities before current liabilities. Neither of these presentations is used under GAAP.
- IFRS bases the determination of whether a liability is current or non-current on the facts that are present on the reporting date. GAAP, on the other hand, permits events that occur after the reporting date but before the financial statements are issued to impact the determination of current or non-current.
- IFRS requires use of the effective-interest method for amortization of bond discounts and premiums. GAAP allows use of the straight-line method where the difference is not material.
- GAAP often uses a separate discount or premium account to account for bonds payable. IFRS records discounts or premiums as direct increases or decreases to Bonds Payable. To illustrate, if a $100,000 bond was issued at 97, under GAAP a company would record:

Cash	97,000	
Discount on Bonds Payable	3,000	
Bonds Payable		100,000

Under IFRS, a company would record:

Cash	97,000	
Bonds Payable		97,000

- The accounting for convertible bonds differs between IFRS and GAAP. GAAP requires that the proceeds from the issuance of convertible debt be shown solely as debt. Unlike GAAP, IFRS splits the proceeds from the convertible bond between an equity component and a debt component. The equity conversion rights are reported in equity.

  To illustrate, assume that Harris Corp. issues convertible 7% bonds with a face value of $1,000,000 and receives $1,000,000. Comparable bonds without a conversion feature would have required a 9% rate of interest. To determine how much of the proceeds would be allocated to debt and how much to equity, the promised payments of the bond obligation would be discounted at the market rate of 9%. Suppose that this results in a present value of $850,000. The entry to record the issuance under GAAP would be:

Cash	1,000,000	
Bonds Payable		1,000,000

Under IFRS, the entry would be:

Cash	1,000,000	
Bonds Payable		850,000
Share Premium—Conversion Equity		150,000

- IFRS reserves the use of the term **contingent liability** to refer only to possible obligations that are **not** recognized in the financial statements but may be disclosed if certain criteria are met. Under GAAP, contingent liabilities are recorded in the financial statements if they are both probable and can be reasonably estimated. If only one of these criteria is met, then the item is disclosed in the notes.
- IFRS uses the term **provisions** to refer to liabilities of uncertain timing or amount. Examples of provisions would be provisions for warranties, employee vacation pay, or anticipated losses. Under GAAP, these are considered recordable **contingent liabilities**.
- Under IFRS, if there is a range of possible outcomes that are all equally likely related to a provision, the midpoint of the range should be used. Under GAAP, when there is a range of equally likely outcomes, the lower end of the range is used.

GAAP Practice

GAAP Self-Test Questions

1. Which of the following is **false**?
   a. Under GAAP, current liabilities are presented before non-current liabilities.
   b. Under GAAP, an item is a current liability if it will be paid within the next 12 months or the operating cycle, whichever is longer.
   c. Under GAAP, current liabilities can only arise due to normal business practices and customs.
   d. Under GAAP, a liability is only recognized if it is a present obligation.

2. The accounting for bonds payable is:
   a. essentially the same under IFRS and GAAP.
   b. different in that GAAP requires use of the straight-line method for amortization of bond premium and discount.
   c. the same except that market prices may be different because the present value calculations are different between IFRS and GAAP.
   d. not covered by IFRS.

3. Stevens Corporation issued 5% convertible bonds with a total face value of $3,000,000 for $3,000,000. If the bonds had not had a conversion feature, they would have sold for $2,600,000. Under GAAP, the entry to record the transaction would require a credit to:
   a. Bonds Payable for $3,000,000.
   b. Bonds Payable for $400,000.
   c. Share Premium—Conversion Equity for $400,000.
   d. Discount on Bonds Payable for $400,000.

4. Which of the following is **true** regarding accounting for amortization of bond discount and premium?
   a. Both IFRS and GAAP must use the effective-interest method.
   b. GAAP must use the effective-interest method, but IFRS may use either the effective-interest method or the straight-line method.
   c. IFRS is required to use the effective-interest method.
   d. GAAP is required to use the straight-line method.

5. A company is involved in a lawsuit where it is probable that it will have to pay a fine. The company does not dispute the facts, only the amount it should be required to pay. At year-end, the attorneys involved in the case estimate that the fine will be somewhere between €1,000,000 and €3,000,000, with each amount in the range equally likely. Which of the following statements is **correct**?
   a. Under both IFRS and GAAP, the maximum of the range (€3,000,000) should be reported.
   b. Under both IFRS and GAAP, the minimum of the range (€1,000,000) should be reported.
   c. Under both IFRS and GAAP, the midpoint of the range (€2,000,000) should be reported.
   d. Under IFRS, the midpoint of the range (€2,000,000) should be reported. Under GAAP, the minimum of the range (€1,000,000) should be reported.

GAAP Exercises

GAAP11.1 Briefly describe some of the similarities and differences between GAAP and IFRS with respect to the accounting for liabilities.

GAAP11.2 Ratzlaff Company issues $2 million, 10-year, 8% bonds at 97, with interest payable on January 1.

Instructions

a. Prepare the journal entry to record the sale of these bonds on January 1, 2029, using GAAP.

b. Assuming instead that the above bonds sold for 104, prepare the journal entry to record the sale of these bonds on January 1, 2029, using GAAP.

GAAP11.3 Archer Company issued £4,000,000 par value, 7% convertible bonds at 99 for cash. The net present value of the debt without the conversion feature is £3,800,000. Prepare the journal entry to record the issuance of the convertible bonds (a) under GAAP and (b) under IFRS.

GAAP Financial Statement Analysis: Apple Inc. (USA)

GAAP11.4 The financial statements of **Apple** are presented in Appendix D. The complete annual report, including the notes to its financial statements, is available at the company's website.

Instructions

Use the company's financial statements and notes to the financial statements to answer the following questions.

a. What were Apple's total non-current liabilities at September 26, 2020? What was the increase/decrease in Apple's total non-current liabilities from the prior year?

b. How much was the long-term debt at September 26, 2020?

c. What were the components of total non-current liabilities on September 26, 2020?

Answers to GAAP Self-Test Questions

1. c **2.** a **3.** a **4.** c **5.** d

CHAPTER **12**

Corporations: Organization, Share Transactions, and Equity

LEARNING OBJECTIVES After studying this chapter, you should be able to:

LO 1 Discuss the major characteristics of a corporation.

LO 2 Explain how to account for ordinary, preference, and treasury shares.

LO 3 Explain how to account for cash dividends, share dividends, and share splits.

LO 4 Discuss how equity is reported and analyzed.

Chapter Preview

Corporations like **adidas** (DEU) have substantial resources at their disposal. In fact, the corporation is the dominant form of business organization in the world in terms of sales, earnings, and number of employees. In this chapter, we will explain the essential features of a corporation and the accounting for a corporation's share capital transactions.

Corporations: Organization, Share Transactions, and Equity

The Corporate Form of Organization
- Characteristics of a corporation
- Forming a corporation
- Shareholder rights
- Share issue considerations
- Corporate capital

Accounting for Share Transactions
- Accounting for ordinary shares
- Accounting for preference shares
- Accounting for treasury shares

Accounting for Dividends and Splits
- Accounting for cash dividends
- Dividend preferences
- Accounting for share dividends
- Accounting for share splits

Reporting and Analyzing Equity
- Retained earnings
- Presentation of statement of financial position
- Analysis

Practice

DO IT! 1a Corporate Organization
1b Corporate Capital

DO IT! 2a Issuance of Shares
2b Treasury Shares

DO IT! 3a Dividends on Preference and Ordinary Shares
3b Share Dividends and Share Splits

DO IT! 4a Equity Section
4b Return on Shareholders' Equity

Go to the Review and Practice section at the end of the chapter for a review of key concepts and practice applications with solutions.
Additional tutorials and practice opportunities are available in the Wiley online course.

Feature Story To the Victor Go the Spoils

You never know where a humble start might take you. One of the most recognized brands in the world began in 1924 when Adolf "Adi" Dassler became committed to the idea of providing high-quality, sport-specific shoes to athletes. He and his brother stitched together canvas and whatever else he could find in post-World War I Germany to create his shoes. They were so dedicated to their company that they sometimes ran their equipment with electricity generated by riding an exercise bicycle.

Just like today, success in the early years of the **Dassler Brothers Shoe Company** (DEU) hinged on affiliations with famous athletes. So it was very fortunate for the brothers that in the 1936 Olympics, their shoes were worn by the famous African-American runner Jesse Owens. After World War II, as a result of a family quarrel, Adi's brother left and formed his own shoe company, **Puma** (DEU). Adi renamed his company using a combination of his nickname "Adi" and the first part of his last name, Dassler, to create the now famous name **adidas** (DEU). In the 1990s, adidas became a publicly traded company for the first time when its shares began to trade on both German and French exchanges.

By becoming a public company, adidas increased its ability to raise funds. It would need these funds in order to compete in the increasingly competitive world of sports apparel. Within two years of going public, adidas AG acquired the **Salomon Group** (FRA). This acquisition brought in the brands Salomon, TaylorMade, Mavic, and Bonfire. Less than 10 years later, adidas acquired **Reebok** (GBR). The combination of Reebok and adidas created a company with a global footprint large enough to compete with **Nike** (USA).

The shoe market is fickle, with new styles becoming popular almost daily and vast international markets still lying untapped. Whether one of these two giants does eventually take control of the pedi-planet remains to be seen. Meanwhile, the shareholders of each company sit anxiously in the stands as this Olympic-size drama unfolds.

TPG/Shutterstock

12.1 The Corporate Form of Organization

LEARNING OBJECTIVE 1

Discuss the major characteristics of a corporation.

Many years ago, a noted scholar defined a corporation as "an artificial being, invisible, intangible, and existing only in contemplation of law." This definition is the foundation for the prevailing legal interpretation in many countries that a **corporation** is an **entity separate and distinct from its owners.**

A corporation is created by law, and its continued existence depends upon the statutes of the jurisdiction in which it is incorporated.

- As a legal entity, a corporation has most of the rights and privileges of a person.
- The major exceptions relate to privileges that only a living person can exercise, such as the right to vote or to hold public office.
- A corporation is subject to the same duties and responsibilities as a person. For example, it must abide by the laws, and it must pay taxes.

Two common ways to classify corporations are by **purpose** and by **ownership**. A corporation may be organized for the purpose of making a profit, or it may be not-for-profit.

- For-profit corporations include such well-known companies as **BHP Billiton** (AUS), **Hyundai Motors** (KOR), **LUKOIL** (RUS), and **Microsoft** (USA).
- Not-for-profit corporations are organized for charitable, medical, or educational purposes. Examples are the **International Committee of the Red Cross** (CHE) and the **Bill & Melinda Gates Foundation** (USA).

Classification by ownership differentiates publicly held and privately held corporations.

- A **publicly held corporation** may have thousands of shareholders. Its shares are regularly traded on a national securities exchange such as the **São Paùlo Stock Exchange** (BRA). Examples are **Toyota** (JPN), **Siemens** (DEU), **Sinopec** (CHN), and **General Electric** (USA).
- In contrast, a **privately held corporation** usually has only a few shareholders, and does not offer its shares for sale to the general public (see **Alternative Terminology**).

ALTERNATIVE TERMINOLOGY

Privately held corporations are also referred to as *closely held corporations.*

Privately held companies are generally much smaller than publicly held companies, although some notable exceptions exist. **Cargill Inc.** (USA), a private corporation that trades in grain and other commodities, is one of the largest companies in the world.

Characteristics of a Corporation

A number of characteristics distinguish corporations from proprietorships and partnerships. However, since corporations are created by national laws, corporations in each country will have their own unique characteristics. We explain the most important characteristics that are common or typical of corporations around the world in this section.

Separate Legal Existence

Legal existence separate from owners

In most countries, a corporate entity is separate and distinct from its owners. The corporation acts under its own name rather than in the name of its shareholders. **Volvo** (SWE) may buy, own, and sell property. It may borrow money, and it may enter into legally binding contracts in its own name. It may also sue or be sued, and it pays its own taxes.

In a partnership, the acts of the owners (partners) bind the partnership. In contrast, the acts of its owners (shareholders) do not bind the corporation unless such owners are **agents** of the corporation. For example, if you owned shares of Volvo, you would not have the right to purchase inventory for the company unless you were designated as an agent of the corporation.

Limited Liability of Shareholders

Limited liability of shareholders

Since a corporation is a separate legal entity, in most countries creditors have recourse only to corporate assets to satisfy their claims. The liability of shareholders is normally limited to their investment in the corporation. Creditors have no legal claim on the personal assets of the owners unless fraud has occurred. Even in the event of bankruptcy, shareholders' losses are generally limited to their capital investment in the corporation.

Transferable Ownership Rights

Transferable ownership rights

Ordinary shares give ownership in a corporation. These shares are transferable units. Shareholders may dispose of part or all of their interest in a corporation simply by selling their shares. The transfer of an ownership interest in a partnership requires the consent of each owner. In contrast, the transfer of shares is entirely at the discretion of the shareholder. It does not require the approval of either the corporation or other shareholders.

The transfer of ownership rights between shareholders normally has no effect on the daily operating activities of the corporation. Nor does it affect the corporation's assets, liabilities, and total equity. The transfer of these ownership rights is a transaction between individual owners. The company does not participate in the transfer of these ownership rights after the original sale of the ordinary shares.

Ability to Acquire Capital

Ability to acquire capital

It is relatively easy for a corporation to obtain capital through the issuance of shares. Investors buy shares in a corporation to earn money over time as the share price grows. Investors also like to invest in shares because they have limited liability and shares are readily transferable. Also, individuals can become shareholders by investing relatively small amounts of money. In sum, the ability of a successful corporation to obtain capital is virtually unlimited.

Continuous Life

Continuous life

The life of a corporation is stated in its charter. The life may be perpetual, or it may be limited to a specific number of years. If it is limited, the company can extend the life through renewal of the charter. Since a corporation is a separate legal entity, its continuance as a going concern is not affected by the withdrawal, death, or incapacity of a shareholder, employee, or officer. As a result, a successful company can have a continuous and perpetual life.

Corporation Management

Shareholders legally own the corporation. However, they manage the corporation indirectly through a board of directors they elect. The board, in turn, formulates the operating policies for the company. The board also selects officers, such as a president and one or more vice presidents, to execute policy and to perform daily management functions.

Illustration 12.1 presents a typical organization chart showing the delegation of responsibility. The chief executive officer (CEO) has overall responsibility for managing the business. As the organization chart shows, the CEO delegates responsibility to other officers. The chief accounting officer is the **controller**. The controller's responsibilities include:

1. Maintaining the accounting records.
2. Ensuring an adequate system of internal control.
3. Preparing financial statements, tax returns, and internal reports.

The **treasurer** has custody of the corporation's financial resources and is responsible for maintaining the company's cash position.

The organizational structure of a corporation enables a company to hire professional managers to run the business (see **Ethics Note**). On the other hand, the separation of ownership and management often reduces an owner's ability to actively manage the company.

ETHICS NOTE

Managers who are not owners are often compensated based on the performance of the firm. They thus may be tempted to exaggerate firm performance by inflating income figures.

Government Regulations

A corporation is subject to governmental regulations. Laws prescribe the requirements for issuing shares, the distributions of earnings permitted to shareholders, and the effects of retiring shares. Securities laws govern the sale of shares to the general public. Also, most

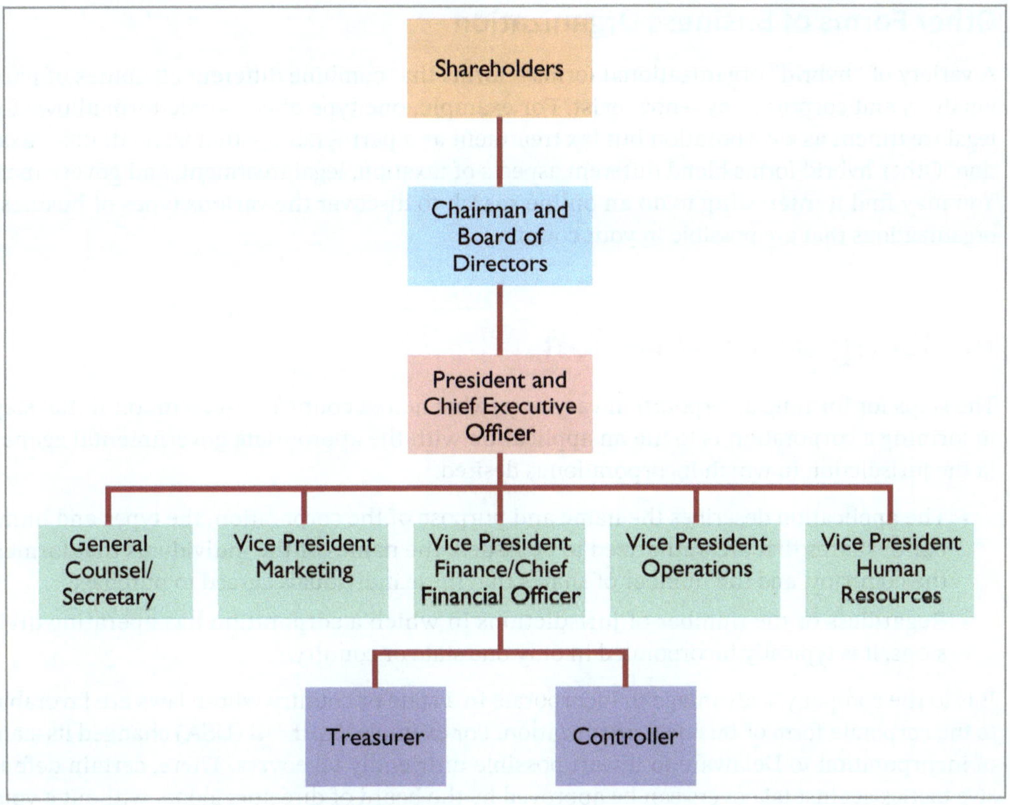

ILLUSTRATION 12.1

Corporation organization chart

publicly held corporations are required to make extensive disclosure of their financial affairs to securities regulators through quarterly and annual reports. In addition, when a corporation lists its shares on organized securities exchanges, it must comply with the reporting requirements of these exchanges. Government regulations are designed to protect the owners of the corporation.

Additional Taxes

Additional taxes

In most countries, owners of proprietorships and partnerships report their share of earnings on their personal income tax returns. The individual owner then pays taxes on this amount. Corporations, on the other hand, must pay government taxes **as a separate legal entity**. These taxes can be substantial.

In addition, shareholders must pay taxes on cash dividends (pro rata distributions of net income). Thus, many argue that the government taxes corporate income **twice (double taxation)**—once at the corporate level, and again at the individual level.

In summary, **Illustration 12.2** shows the advantages and disadvantages of a corporation compared to a proprietorship and a partnership.

ILLUSTRATION 12.2

Advantages and disadvantages of a corporation

Advantages	Disadvantages
Separate legal existence	Corporation management—separation of ownership and management
Limited liability of shareholders	Government regulations
Transferable ownership rights	Additional taxes
Ability to acquire capital	
Continuous life	
Corporation management—professional managers	

Other Forms of Business Organization

A variety of "hybrid" organizational forms—forms that combine different attributes of partnerships and corporations—now exist. For example, one type of corporate form allows for legal treatment as a corporation but tax treatment as a partnership—that is, no double taxation. Other hybrid forms blend different aspects of taxation, legal treatment, and governance. You may find it interesting to do an online search to discover the various types of business organizations that are possible in your country.

Forming a Corporation

The steps for forming a corporation vary somewhat across countries. A common initial step in forming a corporation is to file an application with the appropriate governmental agency in the jurisdiction in which incorporation is desired.

- The application describes the name and purpose of the corporation, the types and number of shares that are authorized to be issued, the names of the individuals that formed the company, and the number of shares that these individuals agreed to purchase.
- Regardless of the number of jurisdictions in which a corporation has operating divisions, it is typically incorporated in only one state or country.

It is to the company's advantage to incorporate in a state or country whose laws are favorable to the corporate form of business organization. For example, **Gulf Oil** (USA) changed its state of incorporation to Delaware to thwart possible unfriendly takeovers. There, certain defensive tactics against takeovers can be approved by the board of directors alone, without a vote by shareholders.

After the government approves the application, it grants a **charter** (see **Alternative Terminology**). The charter may be an approved copy of the application form, or it may be a separate document containing the same basic data. Upon receipt of its charter, the corporation establishes **by-laws**.

ALTERNATIVE TERMINOLOGY

The charter is often referred to as the *articles of incorporation*.

- The by-laws establish the internal rules and procedures for conducting the affairs of the corporation.
- Corporations engaged in commerce outside their state or country must also obtain a **license** from each of those governments in which they do business. The license subjects the corporation's operating activities to the general corporation laws of that state or country.

Costs incurred in the formation of a corporation are called **organization costs**. These costs include legal and government fees, and promotional expenditures involved in the organization of the business.

- **Corporations expense organization costs as incurred**.
- Determining the amount and timing of future benefits is so difficult that it is standard procedure to take a conservative approach of expensing these costs immediately.

Shareholder Rights

When chartered, the corporation may begin selling ownership rights in the form of shares. When a corporation has only one class of shares, it is **ordinary shares**. Each ordinary share gives the shareholder the ownership rights pictured in **Illustration 12.3**. The articles of incorporation or the by-laws state the ownership rights of a share.

Proof of share ownership is evidenced by a form known as a **share certificate**. As **Illustration 12.4** shows, the face of the certificate shows the name of the corporation, the

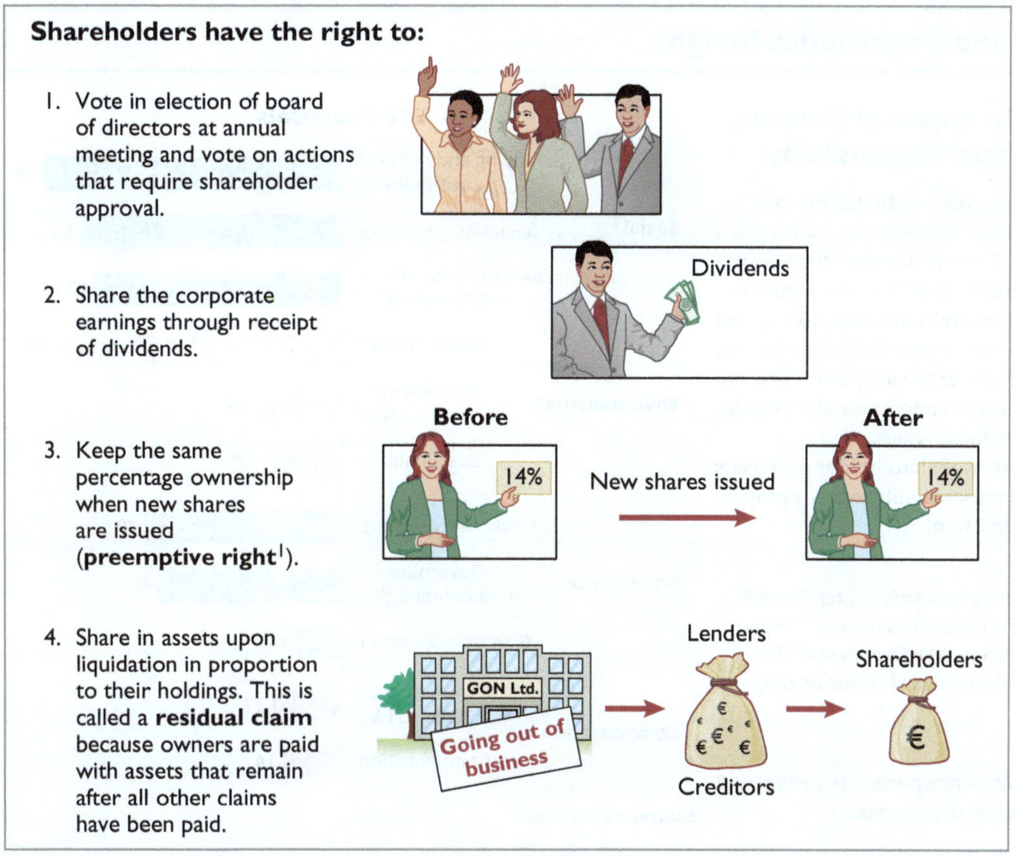

ILLUSTRATION 12.3

Ownership rights of shareholders

shareholder's name, the class and special features of the share, the number of shares owned, and the signatures of authorized corporate officials. Prenumbered certificates facilitate accountability. They may be issued for any quantity of shares.

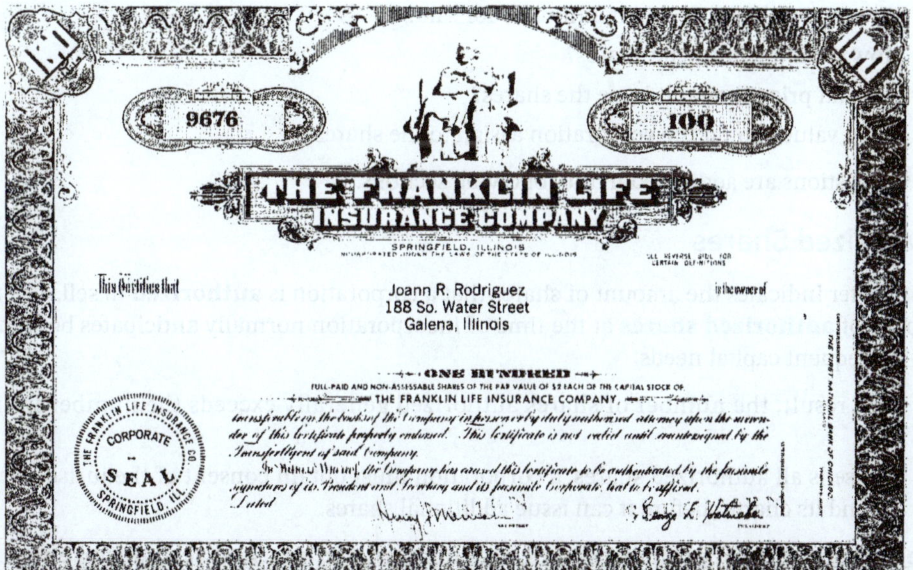

ILLUSTRATION 12.4

A share certificate

[1]A number of companies have eliminated the preemptive right because they believe it makes an unnecessary and cumbersome demand on management. For example, by shareholder approval, IBM (USA) has dropped its preemptive right for shareholders.

Environmental, Social, and Governance Insight

Rawpixel.com/Adobe Stock

The Impact of Company Social Responsibility

A survey conducted by **Institutional Shareholder Services**, a U.S. proxy advisory firm, found that 83% of investors now believe environmental, social, and governance (ESG) factors can significantly impact shareholder value over the long term. This belief is clearly visible in the rising level of support for shareholder proposals requesting action related to these issues.

The chart shows that the number of shareholder proposals related to social and environmental responsibility exceeds proposals related to governance and compensation.

ESG Proposals

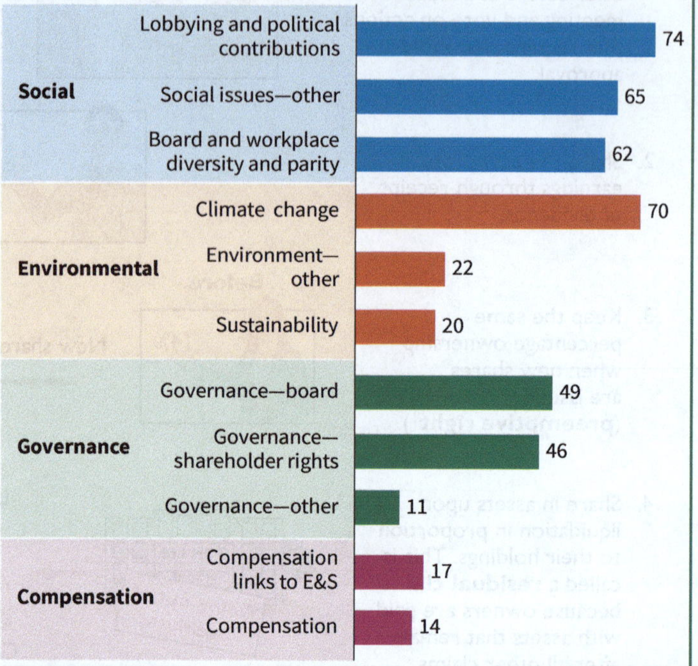

Source: ISS Analytics.

Sources: Based on Investor Responsibility Research Center, Ernst & Young, *Seven Questions CEOs and Boards Should Ask About: "Triple Bottom Line" Reporting*; and Subodh Mishra, "An Overview of U.S. Shareholder Proposal Filings," *Harvard Law School Forum on Corporate Governance* (February 28, 2018).

Why are ESG-related shareholder proposals increasing? (Answer is available near the end of the chapter.)

Share Issue Considerations

In considering the issuance of shares, a corporation must resolve a number of basic questions:

- How many shares should it authorize for sale?
- How should it issue the shares?
- At what price should it issue the shares?
- What value should the corporation assign to the shares?

These questions are addressed in the following sections.

Authorized Shares

The charter indicates the amount of shares that a corporation is **authorized** to sell. The total amount of **authorized shares** at the time of incorporation normally anticipates both initial and subsequent capital needs.

- As a result, the number of shares authorized generally exceeds the number initially sold.
- If it sells all authorized shares, a corporation must obtain consent of the jurisdiction to amend its charter before it can issue additional shares.

The authorization of ordinary shares does not result in a formal accounting entry. The reason is that the event has no immediate effect on either corporate assets or equity.

However, the number of authorized shares is often reported in the equity section. It is then simple to determine the number of unissued shares that the corporation can issue without amending the charter: subtract the total shares issued from the total authorized. For example, if **Quanta Computer** (TWN) was authorized to sell 100,000 ordinary shares and issued 80,000 shares, 20,000 shares would remain unissued.

Issuance of Shares

A corporation can issue ordinary shares **directly** to investors. Alternatively, it can issue the shares **indirectly** through an investment banking firm that specializes in bringing securities to the attention of prospective investors. Direct issue is typical in closely held companies. Indirect issue is customary for a publicly held corporation.

In an indirect issue, the investment banking firm may agree to **underwrite** the entire share issue. In this arrangement, the investment banker buys the shares from the corporation at a stipulated price and resells them to investors. The corporation thus avoids any risk of being unable to sell the shares. Also, it obtains immediate use of the cash received from the underwriter. The investment banking firm, in turn, assumes the risk of reselling the shares, in return for an underwriting fee.[2] For example, **Google** (USA) (the world's number-one Internet search engine) used underwriters when it issued a highly successful initial public offering, raising $1.67 billion. The underwriters charged a 3% underwriting fee (approximately $50 million) on Google's share offering.

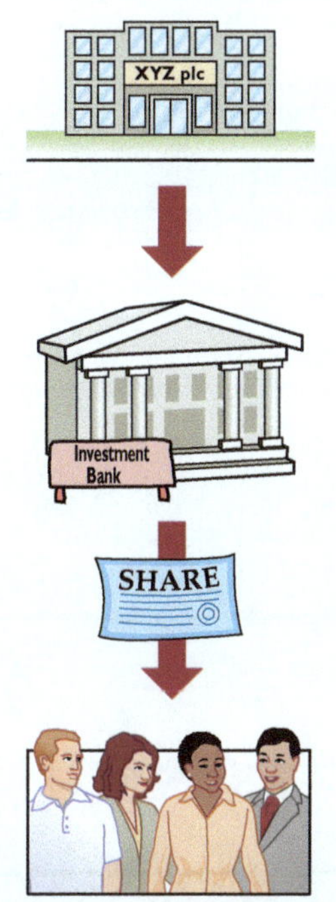

Indirect issuance

How does a corporation set the price for a new issue of shares? Among the factors to be considered are:

1. The company's anticipated future earnings.
2. Its expected dividend rate per share.
3. Its current financial position.
4. The current state of the economy.
5. The current state of the securities market.

The calculation can be complex and is properly the subject of a finance course.

Market Price of Shares

The shares of publicly held companies are traded on organized exchanges. The interaction between buyers and sellers determines the prices per share. In general, the prices set by the marketplace tend to follow the trend of a company's earnings and dividends. But, factors beyond a company's control, such as an oil embargo, changes in interest rates, or the outcome of a presidential election, may cause day-to-day fluctuations in market prices.

Investor Insight adidas

pidjoe/Getty Images

How to Read Share Quotes

Organized exchanges trade the shares of publicly held companies at prices per share established by the interaction between buyers and sellers. For each listed security, the financial press reports the high and low prices of the shares during the year, the total volume of shares traded on a given day, the high and low prices for the day, and the closing market price, with the net change for the day.

adidas (DEU) is listed on a number of exchanges. Here is a listing for adidas (prices are in euros).

	52 Weeks						
Company	**High**	**Low**	**Volume**	**High**	**Low**	**Close**	**Net Change**
adidas	113.38	70.61	61,753	113.38	111.18	113.07	1.20

These numbers indicate the following. The high and low market prices for the previous 52 weeks were €113.38 and €70.61. The trading volume for the day was 61,753 shares. The high, low, and closing prices for that date were €113.38, €111.18, and €113.07, respectively. The net change for the day was an increase of €1.20 per share.

For shares traded on organized exchanges, how are the prices per share established? What factors might influence the price of shares in the marketplace? (Answer is available near the end of the chapter.)

[2] Alternatively, the investment banking firm may agree only to enter into a **best-efforts contract** with the corporation. In such cases, the banker agrees to sell as many shares as possible at a specified price. The corporation bears the risk of unsold shares. Under a best-efforts arrangement, the banking firm is paid a fee or commission for its services.

The trading of ordinary shares on securities exchanges involves the transfer of **already issued shares** from an existing shareholder to another investor. These transactions have **no impact** on a corporation's equity.

Par and No-Par Value Shares

Par value shares (or **nominal value shares**) are ordinary shares to which the charter has assigned a value per share. Years ago, par value determined the **legal capital** per share that a company must retain in the business for the protection of corporate creditors; that amount was not available for withdrawal by shareholders. Thus, in the past, most governments required the corporation to sell its shares at par or above.

However, par value was often immaterial relative to the value of the company's shares—even at the time of issue. Thus, its usefulness as a protective device to creditors was questionable. For example, one French company's par value is €1 per share, yet a new issue in 2022 would have sold at a **market price** in the €27 per share range. Thus, par has no relationship with market price. In the vast majority of cases, it is an immaterial amount. As a consequence, today many governments do not require a par value. Instead, they use other means to protect creditors.

No-par value shares are ordinary shares to which the charter has not assigned a value. No-par value shares are fairly common today. For example, **Carrefour** (FRA) and **Anheuser-Busch InBev** (BEL) both have no-par shares. In many countries, the board of directors assigns a **stated value** to no-par shares.

ACTION PLAN

- **Review the characteristics of a corporation and understand which are advantages and which are disadvantages.**
- **Understand that corporations raise capital through the issuance of shares, which can be par or no-par.**

DO IT! 1a | Corporate Organization

Indicate whether each of the following statements is true or false. If false, indicate how to correct the statement.

________ 1. Similar to partners in a partnership, shareholders of a corporation have unlimited liability.

________ 2. It is relatively easy for a corporation to obtain capital through the issuance of shares.

________ 3. The separation of ownership and management is an advantage of the corporate form of business.

________ 4. The journal entry to record the authorization of ordinary shares includes a credit to the appropriate share capital account.

________ 5. Par value shares are ordinary shares to which the charter has assigned a value per share.

________ 6. No-par value shares are fairly common today. In many countries, the board of directors assigns a stated value to no-par shares.

Solution

1. False. The liability of shareholders is normally limited to their investment in the corporation. **2.** True. **3.** False. The separation of ownership and management is a disadvantage of the corporate form of business. **4.** False. The authorization of ordinary shares does not result in a formal accounting entry. **5.** True. **6.** True.

Related exercise material: **BE12.1, DO IT! 12.1a, E12.1, and E12.2.**

Corporate Capital

Equity is identified by various names: **stockholders' equity**, **shareholders' equity**, or **corporate capital**. The equity section of a corporation's statement of financial position consists of two parts:

1. Share capital.
2. Retained earnings (earned capital).

The distinction between **share capital** and **retained earnings** is important from both a legal and a financial point of view. Legally, corporations can make distributions of earnings (declare dividends) out of retained earnings in most countries. However, they often cannot declare dividends out of share capital. Management, shareholders, and others often look to retained earnings for the continued existence and growth of the corporation.

Share Capital

Share capital is the total amount of cash and other assets paid in to the corporation by shareholders in exchange for shares. As noted earlier, when a corporation has only one class of shares, they are **ordinary shares**.

Retained Earnings

Retained earnings is net income that a corporation retains for future use. Net income is recorded in Retained Earnings by a closing entry that debits Income Summary and credits Retained Earnings. For example, assuming that net income for Delta Robotics in its first year of operations is HK$1,300,000, the closing entry is:

Income Summary	1,300,000	
Retained Earnings		1,300,000
(To close Income Summary and transfer net income to Retained Earnings)		

A	=	L	+	E
				−1,300,000 Inc
				+1,300,000 RE

Cash Flows
no effect

If Delta Robotics has a balance of HK$8,000,000 in Share Capital—Ordinary at the end of its first year, its equity section is as shown in **Illustration 12.5**.

ILLUSTRATION 12.5
Equity section

Delta Robotics
Statement of Financial Position (partial)

Equity		
Share capital—ordinary	HK$8,000,000	
Retained earnings	1,300,000	
Total equity		**HK$9,300,000**

Illustration 12.6 compares the equity accounts reported on a statement of financial position for a proprietorship and a corporation.

ILLUSTRATION 12.6
Comparison of equity accounts

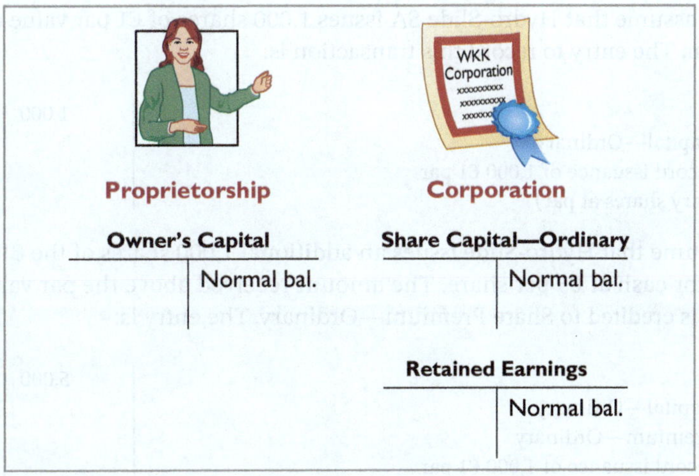

ACTION PLAN

- **Record net income in Retained Earnings by a closing entry in which Income Summary is debited and Retained Earnings is credited.**
- **In the equity section, show (1) share capital—ordinary and (2) retained earnings.**

DO IT! 1b | Corporate Capital

At the end of its first year of operation, Doral AG has €750,000 of ordinary shares and net income of €122,000. Prepare (a) the closing entry for net income and (b) the equity section at year-end.

Solution

a.

Income Summary	122,000	
Retained Earnings		122,000
(To close Income Summary and transfer net income to Retained Earnings)		

b. Equity

Share capital—ordinary	€750,000
Retained earnings	122,000
Total equity	€872,000

Related exercise material: **DO IT! 12.1b.**

12.2 Accounting for Share Transactions

LEARNING OBJECTIVE 2

Explain how to account for ordinary, preference, and treasury shares.

Accounting for Ordinary Shares

Let's now look at how to account for issues of ordinary shares. The primary objective in accounting for the issuance of ordinary shares is to identify the specific sources of capital.

Issuing Par Value Ordinary Shares for Cash

As discussed earlier, par value does not indicate a share's market price. Therefore, the cash proceeds from issuing par value shares may be equal to, greater than, or less than par value.

- When the company records issuance of ordinary shares for cash, it credits the par value of the shares to Share Capital—Ordinary.
- It records in a separate account the portion of the proceeds that is above or below par value.

To illustrate, assume that Hydro-Slide SA issues 1,000 shares of €1 par value ordinary shares at par for cash. The entry to record this transaction is:

A = L + E
+1,000 | +1,000 OS
Cash Flows
+1,000

Cash	1,000	
Share Capital—Ordinary		1,000
(To record issuance of 1,000 €1 par ordinary shares at par)		

Now assume that Hydro-Slide issues an additional 1,000 shares of the €1 par value ordinary shares for cash at €5 per share. The amount received above the par value, in this case €4 (€5 – €1), is credited to Share Premium—Ordinary. The entry is:

A = L + E
+5,000 | +1,000 OS
+4,000 OS
Cash Flows
+5,000

Cash	5,000	
Share Capital—Ordinary		1,000
Share Premium—Ordinary		4,000
(To record issuance of 1,000 €1 par ordinary shares)		

The total capital from these two transactions is €6,000, and the legal capital is €2,000. Assuming Hydro-Slide has retained earnings of €27,000, **Illustration 12.7** shows the company's equity section.

ILLUSTRATION 12.7

Share premium

Hydro-Slide SA
Statement of Financial Position (partial)

Equity	
Share capital—ordinary	€ 2,000
Share premium—ordinary	**4,000**
Retained earnings	27,000
Total equity	€33,000

When a corporation issues shares for less than par value, it debits the account Share Premium—Ordinary if a credit balance exists in this account. If a credit balance does not exist, then the corporation debits to Retained Earnings the amount less than par. This situation occurs only rarely. Most jurisdictions do not permit the sale of ordinary shares below par value because shareholders may be held personally liable for the difference between the price paid upon original sale and par value.

Issuing No-Par Ordinary Shares for Cash

When no-par ordinary shares have a stated value, the entries are similar to those illustrated for par value shares.

- The corporation credits the stated value to Share Capital—Ordinary.
- Also, when the selling price of no-par shares exceeds stated value, the corporation credits the excess to Share Premium—Ordinary.

For example, assume that instead of €1 par value shares, Hydro-Slide SA has €5 stated value no-par shares and the company issues 5,000 shares at €8 per share for cash. The entry is:

Cash	40,000	
Share Capital—Ordinary		25,000
Share Premium—Ordinary		15,000
(To record issuance of 5,000 €5 stated value no-par shares)		

A = L + E
+40,000
+25,000 OS
+15,000 OS
Cash Flows
+40,000

Hydro-Slide reports Share Premium—Ordinary below Share Capital—Ordinary in the equity section.

What happens when no-par shares do not have a stated value? In that case, the corporation credits the entire proceeds to Share Capital—Ordinary. Thus, if Hydro-Slide does not assign a stated value to its no-par shares, it records the issuance of the 5,000 shares at €8 per share for cash as follows.

Cash	40,000	
Share Capital—Ordinary		40,000
(To record issuance of 5,000 no-par shares)		

A = L + E
+40,000
+40,000 OS
Cash Flows
+40,000

Issuing Ordinary Shares for Services or Non-Cash Assets

Corporations also may issue shares for services (compensation to attorneys or consultants) or for non-cash assets (land, buildings, and equipment). In such cases, what cost should be recognized in the exchange transaction?

- To comply with the **historical cost basis**, in a non-cash transaction **cost is the cash equivalent price.**

- Thus, **cost is either the fair value of the consideration given up or the fair value of the consideration received,** whichever is more clearly determinable.

To illustrate, assume that attorneys have helped Jordan Company incorporate. They have billed the company €5,000 for their services. They agree to accept 4,000 shares of €1 par value ordinary shares in payment of their bill. At the time of the exchange, there is no established market price for the shares. In this case, the fair value of the consideration received, €5,000, is more clearly evident. Accordingly, Jordan makes the following entry.

A = L + E
−5,000 Exp
+4,000 OS
+1,000 OS

Cash Flows
no effect

Organization Expense	5,000	
Share Capital—Ordinary		4,000
Share Premium—Ordinary		1,000
(To record issuance of 4,000 €1 par value shares to attorneys)		

As explained previously, organization costs are expensed as incurred.

In contrast, assume that Athletic Research AG is an existing publicly held corporation. Its €5 par value shares are actively traded at €8 per share. The company issues 10,000 shares to acquire land recently advertised for sale at €90,000. The most clearly evident value in this non-cash transaction is the market price of the consideration given, €80,000. The company records the transaction as follows.

A = L + E
+80,000
+50,000 OS
+30,000 OS

Cash Flows
no effect

Land	80,000	
Share Capital—Ordinary		50,000
Share Premium—Ordinary		30,000
(To record issuance of 10,000 €5 par value shares for land)		

As illustrated in these examples, **the par value of the shares is never a factor in determining the cost of the assets received.** This is also true of the stated value of no-par shares.

Accounting for Preference Shares

To appeal to more investors, a corporation may issue an additional class of shares, called preference shares. **Preference shares** have contractual provisions that give them some preference or priority over ordinary shares. Typically, preference shareholders have a priority as to (1) distributions of earnings (dividends) and (2) assets in the event of liquidation. However, they generally do not have voting rights.

Like ordinary shares, corporations may issue preference shares for cash or for non-cash assets.

- The entries for these transactions are similar to the entries for ordinary shares.
- When a corporation has more than one class of shares, each capital account title should identify the shares to which it relates. A company might have the following accounts: Share Capital—Preference, Share Capital—Ordinary, Share Premium—Preference, and Share Premium—Ordinary.

For example, if Florence SpA issues 10,000 shares of €10 par value preference shares for €12 cash per share, the entry to record the issuance is:

A = L + E
+120,000
+100,000 PS
+20,000 PS

Cash Flows
+120,000

Cash	120,000	
Share Capital—Preference		100,000
Share Premium—Preference		20,000
(To record issuance of 10,000 €10 par value preference shares)		

Preference shares may have either a par value or no-par value. In the equity section of the statement of financial position, companies list preference shares first because of their dividend and liquidation preferences over ordinary shares.

DO IT! 2a | Issuance of Shares

Hefei Ltd. begins operations on March 1 by issuing 1,000,000 of ¥10 par value ordinary shares for cash at ¥12 per share. On March 15, it issues 50,000 ordinary shares to attorneys in settlement of their bill of ¥600,000 for organization costs. On March 28, Hefei issues 15,000 shares of ¥100 par value preference shares for cash at ¥250 per share. Journalize the issuance of the shares, assuming the shares are not publicly traded.

ACTION PLAN

- In issuing shares for cash, credit Share Capital—Ordinary (Preference) for par value per share.
- Credit any additional proceeds in excess of par to Share Premium—Ordinary (Preference).
- When shares are issued for services, use the cash equivalent price.
- For the cash equivalent price, use either the fair value of what is given up or the fair value of what is received, whichever is more clearly determinable.

Solution

Mar. 1	Cash	12,000,000	
	Share Capital—Ordinary		10,000,000
	Share Premium—Ordinary		2,000,000
	(To record issuance of 1,000,000 shares at ¥12 per share)		
Mar. 15	Organization Expense	600,000	
	Share Capital—Ordinary		500,000
	Share Premium—Ordinary		100,000
	(To record issuance of 50,000 shares for attorneys' fees)		
Mar. 28	Cash	3,750,000	
	Share Capital—Preference (15,000 × ¥100)		1,500,000
	Share Premium—Preference (15,000 × ¥150)		2,250,000
	(To record issuance of 15,000 shares at ¥250 per share)		

Related exercise material: **BE12.2, BE12.3, BE12.4, BE12.6, DO IT! 12.2a, E12.3, E12.4, and E12.7.**

Accounting for Treasury Shares

Treasury shares are a corporation's own shares that it has issued and subsequently reacquired from shareholders but not retired (see **Helpful Hint**). A corporation may acquire treasury shares for various reasons:

HELPFUL HINT

Treasury shares do not have dividend rights or voting rights.

1. To reissue the shares to officers and employees under bonus and share compensation plans.
2. To signal to the securities market that management believes the shares are underpriced, in the hope of enhancing its market price.
3. To have additional shares available for use in the acquisition of other companies.
4. To reduce the number of shares outstanding and thereby increase earnings per share.

Another infrequent reason for purchasing treasury shares is that management may want to eliminate hostile shareholders by buying them out.

Many corporations have treasury shares. As examples, **adidas** (DEU) and **Lenovo** (CHN) report purchasing treasury shares in recent years.

Purchase of Treasury Shares

Companies generally account for treasury shares by **the cost method.** This method uses the cost of the shares purchased to value the treasury shares.

- Under the cost method, the company debits **Treasury Shares** for the **price paid to reacquire the shares.**
- When the company disposes of the shares, it credits to Treasury Shares **the same amount** it paid to reacquire the shares.

To illustrate, assume that on January 1, 2029, the equity section of Mead, Ltd. has 100,000 HK$50 par value ordinary shares outstanding (all issued at par value) and Retained Earnings of HK$2,000,000. The equity section before purchase of treasury shares is as shown in **Illustration 12.8**.

ILLUSTRATION 12.8

Equity section with no treasury shares

Mead, Ltd.
Statement of Financial Position (partial)

Equity	
Share capital—ordinary, HK$50 par value, 100,000 shares issued and outstanding	HK$5,000,000
Retained earnings	2,000,000
Total equity	HK$7,000,000

On February 1, 2029, Mead acquires 4,000 of its shares at HK$80 per share. The entry is:

A	=	L	+	E
				−320,000 TS
−320,000				

Cash Flows
−320,000

Feb. 1	Treasury Shares	320,000	
	Cash		320,000
	(To record purchase of 4,000 treasury shares at HK$80 per share)		

Mead debits Treasury Shares for the cost of the shares purchased. Is the original Share Capital—Ordinary account affected? No, because **the number of issued shares does not change.**

- In the equity section of the statement of financial position, Mead deducts treasury shares after retained earnings to determine total equity.
- Treasury Shares is a **contra equity account**.
- Thus, the acquisition of treasury shares reduces equity.

The equity section of Mead after purchase of treasury shares is as shown in **Illustration 12.9**.

ILLUSTRATION 12.9

Equity section with treasury shares

Mead, Ltd.
Statement of Financial Position (partial)

Equity	
Share capital—ordinary, HK$50 par value, 100,000 shares issued and 96,000 shares outstanding	HK$5,000,000
Retained earnings	2,000,000
	7,000,000
Less: Treasury shares (4,000 shares)	**320,000**
Total equity	HK$6,680,000

ETHICS NOTE

The purchase of treasury shares reduces the cushion for creditors and preference shareholders. A restriction for the cost of treasury shares purchased is often required. The restriction is usually applied to retained earnings.

Mead discloses in the statement of financial position both the number of shares issued (100,000) and the number in the treasury (4,000). The difference is the number of shares outstanding (96,000). The term **outstanding shares** means the number of issued shares that are being held by shareholders.

Some maintain that companies should report treasury shares as an asset because they can be sold for cash. But under this reasoning, companies would also show unissued shares as an asset, which is clearly incorrect. Rather than being an asset, treasury shares reduce shareholder claims on corporate assets (see **Ethics Note**). This effect is correctly shown by reporting treasury shares as a deduction from equity.

Disposal of Treasury Shares

Treasury shares are usually sold or retired. The accounting for their sale differs when treasury shares are sold above cost than when they are sold below cost (see **Helpful Hint**).

> **HELPFUL HINT**
> **Treasury share transactions are classified as equity transactions. As in the case when shares are issued, the income statement is not involved.**

Sale of Treasury Shares Above Cost If the selling price of the treasury shares is equal to their cost, the company records the sale of the shares by a debit to Cash and a credit to Treasury Shares. When the selling price of the shares is greater than their cost, the company credits the difference to Share Premium—Treasury.

To illustrate, assume that on July 1, Mead, Ltd. sells for HK$100 per share 1,000 of the 4,000 treasury shares previously acquired at HK$80 per share. The entry is as follows.

July 1	Cash	100,000	
	Treasury Shares		80,000
	Share Premium—Treasury		20,000
	(To record sale of 1,000 treasury shares above cost)		

A = L + E
+100,000
+80,000 TS
+20,000 TS
Cash Flows
+100,000

Mead does not record a HK$20,000 gain on sale of treasury shares.

1. Gains on sales occur when **assets** are sold, and treasury shares are not an asset.
2. A corporation does not realize a gain or suffer a loss from share transactions with its own shareholders.

Thus, companies should **not** include in net income any capital arising from the sale of treasury shares. Instead, they report Share Premium—Treasury separately on the statement of financial position, as a part of equity.

Sale of Treasury Shares Below Cost When a company sells treasury shares below their cost, it usually debits to Share Premium—Treasury the excess of cost over selling price. Thus, if Mead sells an additional 800 treasury shares on October 1 at HK$70 per share, it makes the following entry.

Oct. 1	Cash (800 × HK$70)	56,000	
	Share Premium—Treasury	8,000	
	Treasury Shares		64,000
	(To record sale of 800 treasury shares below cost)		

A = L + E
+56,000
−8,000 TS
+64,000 TS
Cash Flows
+56,000

Observe the following from the two sales entries.

1. Mead credits Treasury Shares at cost in each entry.
2. Mead uses Share Premium—Treasury for the difference between cost and the resale price of the shares.
3. The original Share Capital—Ordinary account is not affected.

The sale of treasury shares increases both total assets and total equity.

After posting the foregoing entries, the treasury share accounts will have the balances as shown in **Illustration 12.10** on October 1.

Treasury Shares

	Debit		Credit
Feb. 1	320,000	July 1	80,000
		Oct. 1	64,000
Oct. 1 Bal.	176,000		

Share Premium—Treasury

	Debit		Credit
Oct. 1	8,000	July 1	20,000
		Oct. 1 Bal.	12,000

ILLUSTRATION 12.10
Treasury share accounts

When a company fully depletes the credit balance in Share Premium—Treasury, it debits to Retained Earnings any additional excess of cost over selling price. To illustrate, assume that Mead sells its remaining 2,200 shares at HK$70 per share on December 1. The excess of cost over selling price is HK$22,000 [2,200 × (HK$80 − HK$70)]. In this case, Mead debits HK$12,000 of the excess to Share Premium—Treasury. It debits the remainder to Retained Earnings. The entry is:

A	=	L	+	E
+154,000				
				−12,000 TS
				−10,000 RE
				+176,000 TS

Cash Flows
+154,000

Dec. 1	Cash (2,200 × HK$70)	154,000	
	Share Premium—Treasury	12,000	
	Retained Earnings	10,000	
	Treasury Shares		176,000
	(To record sale of 2,200 treasury shares at HK$70 per share)		

Accounting Across the Organization Reebok

Paul Vidler/Alamy Stock Photo

Why Would a Company Buy Its Own Shares?

In a bold (and some would say risky) move, **Reebok** (DEU) at one time bought back nearly a third of its shares. This repurchase of shares dramatically reduced Reebok's available cash. In fact, the company borrowed significant funds to accomplish the repurchase.

In a press release, management stated that it was repurchasing the shares because it believed its shares were severely underpriced. The repurchase of so many shares was meant to signal management's belief in good future earnings.

Skeptics, however, suggested that Reebok's management was repurchasing shares to make it less likely that another company would acquire Reebok (in which case Reebok's top managers would likely lose their jobs). By depleting its cash, Reebok became a less likely acquisition target. Acquiring companies like to purchase companies with large cash balances so they can pay off debt used in the acquisition.

As noted in the Feature Story, Reebok was eventually acquired by **adidas** (DEU). In 2014, adidas announced a program to buy back up to 10% of its shares. This was done to appease shareholders who were disappointed with the company's results in recent years.

What signal might a large share repurchase send to investors regarding management's belief about the company's growth opportunities? (Answer is available near the end of the chapter.)

ACTION PLAN

- **Record the purchase of treasury shares at cost.**
- **When treasury shares are sold above cost, credit the excess of the selling price over cost to Share Premium—Treasury.**
- **When treasury shares are sold below cost, debit the excess of cost over selling price to Share Premium—Treasury.**

DO IT! 2b | Treasury Shares

Salvador SA purchases 3,000 shares of its R$50 par value ordinary shares for R$180,000 cash on July 1. It will hold the shares in the treasury until resold. On November 1, the corporation sells 1,000 treasury shares for cash at R$70 per share. Journalize the treasury share transactions.

Solution

July 1	Treasury Shares	180,000	
	Cash		180,000
	(To record purchase of 3,000 treasury shares at R$60 per share)		
Nov. 1	Cash	70,000	
	Treasury Shares		60,000
	Share Premium—Treasury		10,000
	(To record sale of 1,000 treasury shares at R$70 per share)		

Related exercise material: **BE12.5, DO IT! 12.2b, E12.5, E12.6, and E12.8.**

12.3 Accounting for Dividends and Splits

LEARNING OBJECTIVE 3

Explain how to account for cash dividends, share dividends, and share splits.

A dividend **is a corporation's distribution of cash or shares to its shareholders on a pro rata (proportional to ownership) basis**. Pro rata means that if you own 10% of the ordinary shares, you will receive 10% of the dividend.

- Dividends can take four forms: cash, property, scrip (a promissory note to pay cash), or shares.
- Cash dividends predominate in practice although companies also declare share dividends with some frequency.

These two forms of dividends are therefore the focus of discussion in this chapter.

Investors are very interested in a company's dividend practices. In the financial press, **dividends are generally reported quarterly as a currency amount per share**. (Sometimes they are reported on an annual basis.) For example, in a recent year, **BASF**'s (DEU) dividend rate was €1.95 a share. **The Hershey Company**'s (USA) was $1.19, and **Marks and Spencer plc**'s (GBR) was 22.5p.

Accounting for Cash Dividends

A cash dividend is a pro rata distribution of cash to shareholders. Cash dividends are not paid on treasury shares. For a corporation to pay a cash dividend, it must have the following.

1. **Retained earnings.** The legality of a cash dividend depends on the laws of the country in which the company is incorporated. Payment of cash dividends from retained earnings is legal in all jurisdictions. In general, cash dividend distributions from only the balance in share capital—ordinary (legal capital) are illegal.

   A dividend declared out of share capital or share premium is termed a liquidating dividend. Such a dividend reduces or "liquidates" the amount originally paid in by shareholders.

2. **Adequate cash.** The legality of a dividend and the ability to pay a dividend are two different things. For example, **adidas** (DEU), with retained earnings of over €5.0 billion, could legally declare a dividend of at least €5.0 billion. But adidas's cash balance is only €1.6 billion.

   Before declaring a cash dividend, a company's board of directors must carefully consider both current and future demands on the company's cash resources. In some cases, current liabilities may make a cash dividend inappropriate. In other cases, a major plant expansion program may warrant only a relatively small dividend.

3. **Declaration of dividends.** A company does not pay dividends unless its board of directors decides to do so, at which point the board "declares" the dividend. The board of directors has full authority to determine the amount of income to distribute in the form of a dividend and the amount to retain in the business. Dividends do not accrue like interest on a note payable, and they are not a liability until declared.

The amount and timing of a dividend are important issues for management to consider. The payment of a large cash dividend could lead to liquidity problems for the company. On the other hand, a small dividend or a missed dividend may cause unhappiness among shareholders.

Many shareholders expect to receive a reasonable cash payment from the company on a periodic basis. Many companies declare and pay cash dividends quarterly. On the other hand, a number of high-growth companies pay no dividends, preferring to conserve cash to finance future capital expenditures.

Entries for Cash Dividends

Three dates are important in connection with dividends:

1. The declaration date.
2. The record date.
3. The payment date.

Normally, there are two to four weeks between each date. Companies make accounting entries on the declaration date and the payment date.

On the **declaration date**, the board of directors formally declares (authorizes) the cash dividend and announces it to shareholders. The declaration of a cash dividend **commits the corporation to a legal obligation**. The company must make an entry to recognize the increase in Cash Dividends and the increase in the liability Dividends Payable.

To illustrate, assume that on December 1, 2029, the directors of Media General declare a €0.50 per share cash dividend on 100,000 shares of €10 par value ordinary shares. The dividend is €50,000 (100,000 × €0.50). The entry to record the declaration is as follows.

A	=	L	+	E
				−50,000 Div
		+50,000		

Cash Flows
no effect

Declaration Date

Dec. 1	Cash Dividends	50,000	
	Dividends Payable		50,000
	(To record declaration of cash dividend)		

Cash dividends decrease retained earnings. We use the specific title Cash Dividends to differentiate it from other types of dividends, such as share dividends. Dividends Payable is a current liability. It will normally be paid within the next several months. *For homework problems, you should use the Cash Dividends account for recording cash dividend declarations.*

> **HELPFUL HINT**
> **The purpose of the record date is to identify the persons or entities that will receive the dividend, not to determine the amount of the dividend liability.**

At the **record date**, the company determines ownership of the outstanding shares for dividend purposes (see **Helpful Hint**). The shareholders' records maintained by the corporation supply this information. In the interval between the declaration date and the record date, the corporation updates its share ownership records. For Media General, the record date is December 22. No entry is required on this date because the corporation's liability recognized on the declaration date is unchanged.

Record Date

Dec. 22	No entry		

On the **payment date**, the company makes cash dividend payments to the shareholders of record (as of December 22) and records the payment of the dividend. If January 20 is the payment date for Media General, the entry on that date is as follows.

A	=	L	+	E
		−50,000		
−50,000				

Cash Flows
−50,000

Payment Date

Jan. 20	Dividends Payable	50,000	
	Cash		50,000
	(To record payment of cash dividend)		

- Note that payment of the dividend reduces both current assets and current liabilities. It has no effect on equity.
- The cumulative effect of the declaration and payment of a cash dividend is to **decrease both equity and total assets.**

Illustration 12.11 summarizes the three important dates associated with dividends for Media General.

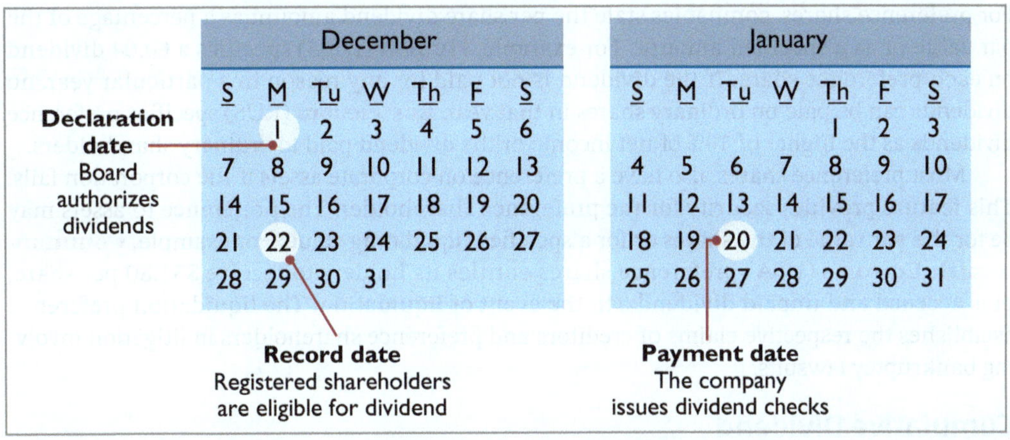

ILLUSTRATION 12.11
Key dividend dates

When using a Cash Dividends account, Media General should transfer the balance of the Cash Dividends account to Retained Earnings at the end of the year by a closing entry. The entry for Media General at closing is as follows.

Retained Earnings	50,000	
Cash Dividends		50,000
(To close Cash Dividends to Retained Earnings)		

Investor Insight

JHVEPhoto/Adobe Stock

Dividend Aristocrats

Many shares pay regular and sometimes increasing dividends. For example, in a recent post, 30 different European companies, called the **dividend aristocrats**, were identified that had paid either sustained or increased dividends over the past 20 years. Think of that—these companies have gone through both the global recession of 2008–2009 and the global Covid-19 pandemic that began in 2019 without decreasing their dividend payments. Sounds like a solid return for the shareholders.

This kind of return can really add up. In a review of data from 1927 to 2014, dividend payers outperformed non-dividend payers, averaging 10.4% annual growth versus 8.5%. If you do not think that difference is much, the following table indicates how an annual investment of €10,000 would grow at each of these rates.

Growth Over	8.5% Annual Growth Rate	10.4% Annual Growth Rate
10 years	€ 161,000	€ 179,400
20 years	524,900	661,800
30 years	1,300,000	2,000,000

The dividend aristocrats included **Air Liquide** (FRA), **SAP** (DEU), and **Unilever** (GBR). Happy investing!

Sources: Adapted from "30 Real European Dividend Aristocrats in 2021," *The European Dividend Growth Investor* (May 20, 2021); and Selena Maranjian, "Dividend Stocks in 2017: 7 Stats Everyone Should Know," *The Motley Fool* (December 14, 2016).

Why is a company's dividend policy so important to shareholders? (Answer is available near the end of the chapter.)

Dividend Preferences

Preference shareholders have the right to receive dividends before ordinary shareholders. For example, if the dividend rate on preference shares is £5 per share, ordinary shareholders cannot receive any dividends in the current year until preference shareholders have received £5 per share. The first claim to dividends does not, however, **guarantee** the payment of dividends.

- Dividends depend on many factors, such as adequate retained earnings and availability of cash.
- If a company does not pay dividends to preference shareholders, it cannot pay dividends to ordinary shareholders.

Dividend preferences

For preference shares, companies state the per share dividend amount as a percentage of the par value or as a specified amount. For example, **Henkel** (DEU) specifies a €0.04 dividend on each preference share. If the dividend is not paid for any reason in a particular year, no dividends can be paid on ordinary shares in that year. **Rostelecom** (RUS) specifies preference dividends as the higher of 10% of net income or the dividend paid to ordinary shareholders.

Most preference shares also have a preference on corporate assets if the corporation fails. This feature provides security for the preference shareholder. The preference to assets may be for the par value of the shares or for a specified liquidating value. For example, **Commonwealth Edison**'s (USA) preference shares entitles its holders to receive $31.80 per share, plus accrued and unpaid dividends, in the event of liquidation. The liquidation preference establishes the respective claims of creditors and preference shareholders in litigation involving bankruptcy lawsuits.

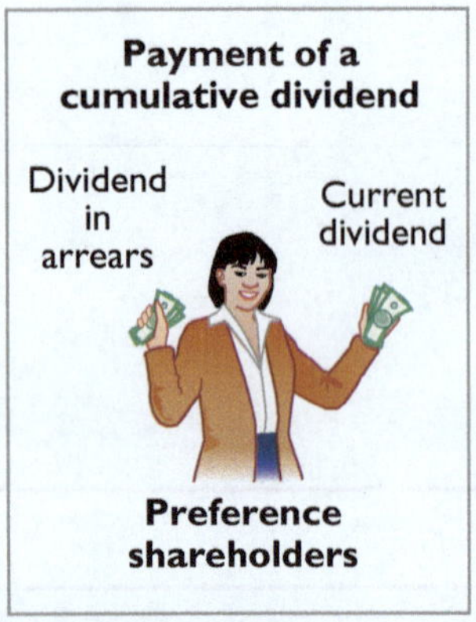

Cumulative Dividend

Preference shares often contain a **cumulative dividend** feature.

- This feature stipulates that preference shareholders must be paid both current-year dividends and any unpaid prior-year dividends before ordinary shareholders are paid dividends.
- When preference shares are cumulative, preference dividends not declared in a given period are called **dividends in arrears**.

To illustrate, assume that Scientific Leasing has 5,000 shares of 7%, €100 par value, cumulative preference shares outstanding. Each €100 share pays a €7 dividend (.07 × €100). The annual dividend is €35,000 (5,000 × €7 per share). If dividends are two years in arrears, preference shareholders are entitled to receive the dividends shown in **Illustration 12.12**.

ILLUSTRATION 12.12
Computation of total dividends to preference shares

Dividends in arrears (€35,000 × 2)	€ 70,000
Current-year dividends	35,000
Total preference dividends	**€105,000**

The company cannot pay dividends to ordinary shareholders until it pays the entire preference dividend. In other words, companies cannot pay dividends to ordinary shareholders while any preference dividends are in arrears.

- Dividends in arrears are not considered a liability. **No obligation exists until the board of directors formally declares that the corporation will pay a dividend.**
- However, companies should disclose in the notes to the financial statements the amount of dividends in arrears. Doing so enables investors to assess the potential impact of this commitment on the corporation's financial position.

The investment community does not look favorably on companies that are unable to meet their dividend obligations. As a financial officer noted in discussing one company's failure to pay its cumulative preference dividend for a period of time, "Not meeting your obligations on something like that is a major black mark on your record."

Allocating Cash Dividends between Preference and Ordinary Shares

As indicated, preference shares have priority over ordinary shares in regard to dividends. Holders of cumulative preference shares must be paid any unpaid prior-year dividends and their current year's dividend before ordinary shareholders receive dividends.

To illustrate, assume that at December 31, 2028, IBR Industries has 1,000 shares of 8%, €100 par value cumulative preference shares. It also has 50,000 shares of €10 par value ordinary shares outstanding. The dividend per share for preference shares is €8 (€100 par value × 8%). The required annual dividend for preference shares is therefore €8,000 (1,000 shares × €8). At December 31, 2028, the directors declare a €6,000 cash dividend. In this case, the entire dividend amount goes to preference shareholders because of their dividend preference. The entry to record the declaration of the dividend is as follows.

Dec. 31	Cash Dividends	6,000	
	Dividends Payable		6,000
	(To record €6 per share cash dividend to preference shareholders)		

A = L + E
−6,000 Div
+6,000
Cash Flows
no effect

Because of the cumulative feature, dividends of €2 (€8 − €6) per share are in arrears on preference shares for 2028. IBR must pay these dividends to preference shareholders before it can pay any future dividends to ordinary shareholders. IBR should disclose dividends in arrears in the financial statements.

At December 31, 2029, IBR declares a €50,000 cash dividend. The allocation of the dividend to the two classes of shares is as shown in **Illustration 12.13**.

ILLUSTRATION 12.13
Allocating dividends to preference and ordinary shares

Total dividend		€50,000
Allocated to preference shares		
Dividends in arrears, 2028 (1,000 × €2)	**€2,000**	
2029 dividend (1,000 × €8)	**8,000**	**10,000**
Remainder allocated to ordinary shares		€40,000

The entry to record the declaration of the dividend is as follows.

Dec. 31	Cash Dividends	50,000	
	Dividends Payable		50,000
	(To record declaration of cash dividends of €10,000 to preference shares and €40,000 to ordinary shares)		

A = L + E
−50,000 Div
+50,000
Cash Flows
no effect

If IBR's preference shares are not cumulative, preference shareholders receive only €8,000 in dividends in 2029. Ordinary shareholders receive €42,000.

DO IT! 3a | Dividends on Preference and Ordinary Shares

MasterMind Gaming has 2,000 shares of 6%, ¥100 par value preference shares outstanding at December 31, 2029 (¥ in thousands). At December 31, 2029, the company declared a ¥60,000 cash dividend. Determine the dividend paid to preference shareholders and ordinary shareholders under each of the following scenarios.

1. The preference shares are non-cumulative, and the company has not missed any dividends in previous years.
2. The preference shares are non-cumulative, and the company did not pay a dividend in each of the two previous years.
3. The preference shares are cumulative, and the company did not pay a dividend in each of the two previous years.
4. The preference shares are cumulative, and the company did not pay a dividend only one year of the two previous years.

ACTION PLAN

- **Determine dividends on preference shares by multiplying the dividend rate times the par value of the share times the number of preference shares.**
- **Understand the cumulative feature. If preference shares are cumulative, then any missed dividends (dividends in arrears) and the current year's dividend must be paid to preference shareholders before dividends are paid to ordinary shareholders.**

Solution

1. The company has not missed past dividends and the preference shares are non-cumulative. Thus, the preference shareholders are paid only this year's dividend. The dividend paid to preference shareholders would be ¥12,000 (2,000 × .06 × ¥100). The dividend paid to ordinary shareholders would be ¥48,000 (¥60,000 − ¥12,000).

2. The preference shares are non-cumulative. Thus, past unpaid dividends do not have to be paid. The dividend paid to preference shareholders would be ¥12,000 (2,000 × .06 × ¥100). The dividend paid to ordinary shareholders would be ¥48,000 (¥60,000 − ¥12,000).
3. The preference shares are cumulative. Thus, dividends that have been missed (dividends in arrears) must be paid. The dividend paid to preference shareholders would be ¥36,000 (3 × 2,000 × .06 × ¥100). Of the ¥36,000, ¥24,000 relates to dividends in arrears and ¥12,000 relates to the current dividend on preference shares. The dividend paid to ordinary shareholders would be ¥24,000 (¥60,000 − ¥36,000).
4. The preference shares are cumulative. Thus, dividends that have been missed (dividends in arrears) must be paid. The dividend paid to preference shareholders would be ¥24,000 (2 × 2,000 × 0.06 × ¥100). Of the ¥24,000, ¥12,000 relates to dividends in arrears and ¥12,000 relates to the current dividend on preference shares. The dividend paid to ordinary shareholders would be ¥36,000 (¥60,000 − ¥24,000).

Related exercise material: **BE12.7, BE12.8, DO IT! 12.3a, E12.10, and E12.11.**

Accounting for Share Dividends

A **share dividend** is a pro rata (proportional to ownership) distribution to shareholders of the corporation's own shares. Whereas a company pays cash in a cash dividend, a company issues shares in a share dividend.

- **A share dividend results in a decrease in retained earnings and an increase in share capital and share premium.**
- Unlike a cash dividend, a share dividend does not decrease total equity or total assets.

To illustrate, assume that you have a 2% ownership interest in Cetus Group. That is, you own 20 of its 1,000 ordinary shares. If Cetus declares a 10% share dividend, it would issue 100 shares (1,000 × 10%). You would receive two shares (20 × 10%). Would your ownership interest change? No, it would remain at 2% (22 ÷ 1,100). **You now own more shares, but your ownership interest has not changed.**

Cetus has disbursed no cash and has assumed no liabilities. What, then, are the purposes and benefits of a share dividend? Corporations issue share dividends generally for one or more of the following reasons.

1. To satisfy shareholders' dividend expectations without using up cash.
2. To increase the marketability of the corporation's shares. When the number of shares outstanding increases, the market price per share decreases. Decreasing the market price of the shares makes it easier for smaller investors to purchase the shares.
3. To emphasize that a portion of equity has been permanently reinvested in the business (and is unavailable for cash dividends).

When the dividend is declared, the board of directors determines the size of the share dividend and the value assigned to each dividend.

IFRS is silent regarding the accounting for share dividends. One approach used in some countries is that if the company issues a **small share dividend** (less than 20–25% of the corporation's issued shares), the value assigned to each share is the fair value (market price) per share. This treatment is based on the assumption that a small share dividend will have little effect on the market price of the shares previously outstanding. Thus, many shareholders consider small share dividends to be distributions of earnings equal to the market price of the shares distributed.

If a company issues a **large share dividend** (greater than 20–25%), the price assigned to the dividend is the par or stated value. Small share dividends predominate in practice. Thus, we will illustrate only entries for small share dividends.

Entries for Share Dividends

To illustrate the accounting for small share dividends, assume that Danshui Ltd. has a balance of NT$3,000,000 in retained earnings. It declares a 10% share dividend on its 50,000 shares of NT$100 par value ordinary shares. The current fair value of its shares is NT$150 per share. The number of shares to be issued is 5,000 (10% × 50,000). Therefore, the total amount to be debited to Share Dividends is NT$750,000 (5,000 × NT$150). The entry to record the declaration of the share dividend is as follows.

Share Dividends	750,000	
Ordinary Share Dividends Distributable		500,000
Share Premium—Ordinary		250,000
(To record declaration of 10% shares dividend)		

A	=	L	+	E
				−750,000 Div
				+500,000 OS
				+250,000 OS

Cash Flows
no effect

Danshui debits Share Dividends for the fair value of the shares issued (NT$150 × 5,000). (Similar to cash dividends, share dividends decrease retained earnings.) Danshui also credits Ordinary Share Dividends Distributable for the par value of the dividend shares (NT$100 × 5,000) and credits Share Premium—Ordinary for the excess over par (NT$50 × 5,000).

- Ordinary Share Dividends Distributable is an **equity account.**
- It is not a liability because assets will not be used to pay the dividend.

If the company prepares a statement of financial position before it issues the dividend shares, it reports the distributable account as shown in **Illustration 12.14**.

ILLUSTRATION 12.14

Statement presentation of ordinary share dividends distributable

Share capital—ordinary	NT$5,000,000
Ordinary share dividends distributable	**500,000**
	NT$5,500,000

When Danshui issues the dividend shares, it debits Ordinary Share Dividends Distributable and credits Share Capital—Ordinary as follows.

Ordinary Share Dividends Distributable	500,000	
Share Capital—Ordinary		500,000
(To record issuance of 5,000 shares in a share dividend)		

A	=	L	+	E
				−500,000 OS
				+500,000 OS

Cash Flows
no effect

Effects of Share Dividends

How do share dividends affect equity? They **change the composition of equity** because they transfer a portion of retained earnings to share capital and share premium. However, **total equity remains the same**. Share dividends also have no effect on the par or stated value per share, but the number of shares outstanding increases. **Illustration 12.15** shows these effects for Danshui.

ILLUSTRATION 12.15

Share dividend effects

	Before Dividend	Change	After Dividend
Equity			
Share capital—ordinary	NT$5,000,000	NT$500,000	NT$5,500,000
Share premium—ordinary	—	250,000	250,000
Total share capital	5,000,000	+750,000	5,750,000
Retained earnings	3,000,000	−750,000	2,250,000
Total equity	**NT$8,000,000**	**NT$ 0**	**NT$8,000,000**
Outstanding shares	**50,000**	**+5,000**	**55,000**
Par value per share	**NT$100.00**	**NT$0.00**	**NT$100.00**

In this example, the total of share capital—ordinary and share premium—ordinary increases by NT$750,000 (50,000 shares × 10% × NT$150) and retained earnings decreases by the same amount. Note also that total equity remains unchanged at NT$8,000,000. The number of shares increases by 5,000 (50,000 × 10%).

Accounting for Share Splits

HELPFUL HINT

A share split changes the par value per share but does not affect any balances in equity.

A **share split**, like a share dividend, involves issuance of additional shares to shareholders according to their percentage ownership. **However, a share split results in a reduction in the par or stated value per share** (see **Helpful Hint**).

- The purpose of a share split is to increase the marketability of the shares by lowering the market price per share.
- This, in turn, makes it easier for the corporation to issue additional shares.

The effect of a split on market price is generally **inversely proportional** to the size of the split.

For example, after a 2-for-1 share split, the market price of **Nike**'s (USA) shares fell from $111 to approximately $55. The lower market price stimulated market activity. Within one year, the shares were trading above $100 again. **Illustration 12.16** shows the effect of a 4-for-1 share split for shareholders.

ILLUSTRATION 12.16

Effect of share split for shareholders

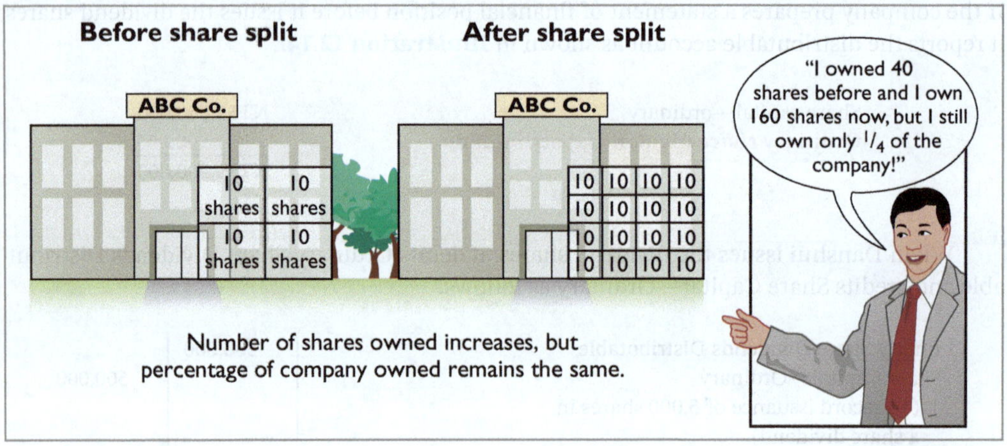

In a share split, the company increases the number of shares in the same proportion that par or stated value per share decreases. For example, in a 2-for-1 split, the company exchanges one $10 par value share for two $5 par value shares.

- **A share split does not have any effect on share capital, share premium, retained earnings, or total equity.**
- However, the number of shares outstanding increases, and par value per share decreases.

Illustration 12.17 shows these effects for Danshui Ltd., assuming that it splits its 50,000 ordinary shares on a 2-for-1 basis.

ILLUSTRATION 12.17

Share split effects

	Before Share Split	Change	After Share Split
Equity			
Share capital—ordinary	NT$5,000,000	NT$ -0-	NT$5,000,000
Share premium—ordinary	-0-	-0-	-0-
Retained earnings	3,000,000	-0-	3,000,000
Total equity	**NT$8,000,000**	**NT$ -0-**	**NT$8,000,000**
Outstanding shares	**50,000**	**+50,000**	**100,000**
Par value per share	**NT$100.00**	**−NT$50.00**	**NT$50.00**

A share split does not affect the balances in any equity accounts. Therefore, **a company does not need to journalize a share split.**

Illustration 12.18 summarizes the differences between share dividends and share splits.

Item	Share Dividend	Share Split
Total retained earnings	Decrease	No change
Total par value (ordinary shares)	Increase	No change
Par value per share	No change	Decrease
Outstanding shares	Increase	Increase
Total equity	No change	No change

ILLUSTRATION 12.18

Differences between the effects of share dividends and share splits

Investor Insight Berkshire Hathaway

Dietmar Klement/ Getty Images

Split or Not?

Warren Buffett's **Berkshire Hathaway Inc.** (USA) Class A shares closed above $250,000 recently. Given the high price, Mr. Buffett is often asked why the shares have never been split. One reason given is pride, as Berkshire Hathaway's share price is the second-highest per share price in the world. What company wouldn't like to be able to make that claim?

A second reason is that Mr. Buffett wants to attract sophisticated investors to his company, who recognize that splitting the shares does nothing to increase value. He worries that splitting the shares will lead to speculation and hurt the stability of the share price. He also notes that an alternative now exists for shareholders who would like to own Berkshire Hathaway, called Class B shares.

Class B shares are 1/30th the value of the Class A shares. Class B shares were created because various financial companies were attempting to replicate the Class A shares by creating mutual funds for smaller investors for a substantial fee. Mr. Buffett objected to these companies charging high fees to smaller investors and therefore created the Class B shares to accommodate these individuals.

One thing is certain—it is a great investment. The shares are up three million percent since Mr. Buffett bought shares in the company!

Source: Based on Erik Holm, "Three Reasons Berkshire Never Split A Shares," *The Wall Street Journal* (February 16, 2017), p. B13.

Why does Warren Buffett oppose share splits? (Answer is available near the end of the chapter.)

DO IT! 3b | Share Dividends and Share Splits

Sing CD has had five years of record earnings. Due to this success, the market price of its 500,000 shares of £2 par value ordinary shares has tripled from £15 per share to £45. During this period, the sum of share capital and share premium remained the same at £2,000,000. Retained earnings increased from £1,500,000 to £10,000,000. CEO Joan Elbert is considering either a 10% share dividend or a 2-for-1 share split. She asks you to show the before-and-after effects of each option on retained earnings, total equity, shares outstanding, and par value per share.

ACTION PLAN

- **Calculate the share dividend's effect on retained earnings by multiplying the number of new shares times the market price of the shares (or par value for a large share dividend).**
- **Recall that a share dividend increases the number of shares without affecting total equity.**
- **Recall that a share split only increases the number of shares outstanding and decreases the par value per share.**

Solution

The share dividend amount is £2,250,000 [(500,000 × 10%) × £45]. The new balance in retained earnings is £7,750,000 (£10,000,000 − £2,250,000). The retained earnings balance after the share split is the same as it was before the split: £10,000,000. Total equity does not change. The effects on the equity accounts are as follows.

	Original Balances	After Dividend	After Split
Share capital/premium	£ 2,000,000	£ 4,250,000	£ 2,000,000
Retained earnings	10,000,000	7,750,000	10,000,000
Total equity	£12,000,000	£12,000,000	£12,000,000
Shares outstanding	500,000	550,000	1,000,000
Par value per share	£2.00	£2.00	£1.00

Related exercise material: **BE12.9, BE12.10, DO IT! 12.3b, E12.12, E12.13, E12.14, and E12.15.**

12.4 Reporting and Analyzing Equity

LEARNING OBJECTIVE 4

Discuss how equity is reported and analyzed.

Retained Earnings

Recall that retained earnings is net income that a company retains in the business.

- The balance in retained earnings is part of the shareholders' claim on the total assets of the corporation.
- It does not, however, represent a claim on any specific asset.
- Nor can the amount of retained earnings be associated with the balance of any asset account.

For example, a NT$10,000,000 balance in retained earnings does not mean that there should be NT$10,000,000 in cash. The reason is that the company may have used the cash resulting from the excess of revenues over expenses to purchase buildings, equipment, and other assets.

To demonstrate that retained earnings and cash may be quite different, Illustration 12.19 shows recent amounts of retained earnings and cash in selected companies.

ILLUSTRATION 12.19
Retained earnings and cash balances

	(in millions)	
Company	**Retained Earnings**	**Cash**
Stora Ensa (FIN)	€3,197	€2,065
Cathay Pacific (HKG)	HK$40,320	HK$12,359
Orion (KOR)	₩457,219	₩223,179
China Mobile Limited (CHN)	¥44,931	¥786,631

HELPFUL HINT
Remember that Retained Earnings is an equity account, whose normal balance is a credit.

- When a company has net income, it closes net income to retained earnings. The closing entry is a debit to Income Summary and a credit to Retained Earnings (see **Helpful Hint**).
- When a company has a **net loss** (expenses exceed revenues), it also closes this amount to retained earnings. The closing entry is a debit to Retained Earnings and a credit to Income Summary.

To illustrate, assume that Chen Company has a net loss of HK$400,000 in 2029. The closing entry to record this loss is as follows.

Retained Earnings	400,000	
Income Summary		400,000
(To close net loss to Retained Earnings)		

This closing entry is prepared even if it results in a debit balance in Retained Earnings. **Companies do not debit net losses to Share Capital or Share Premium.** If cumulative losses exceed cumulative income over a company's life, a debit balance in Retained Earnings results. A debit balance in Retained Earnings is identified as a **deficit**. A company reports a deficit as a deduction in the equity section, as shown in Illustration 12.20.

ILLUSTRATION 12.20
Equity with deficit

Statement of Financial Position (partial)	
Equity	
Share capital—ordinary	€800,000
Retained earnings (deficit)	**(50,000)**
Total equity	€750,000

The balance in retained earnings is generally available for dividend declarations. In some cases, however, there may be **retained earnings restrictions**.

- Retained earnings restrictions make a portion of the retained earnings balance currently unavailable for dividends.
- Companies generally disclose **retained earnings restrictions** in the notes to the financial statements.

For example, as shown in **Illustration 12.21**, **Tektronix Inc.** (USA), a manufacturer of electronic measurement devices, had total retained earnings of $774 million, but the unrestricted portion was only $223.8 million.

ILLUSTRATION 12.21
Disclosure of restriction

Real World

Tektronix Inc.
Notes to the Financial Statements

Certain of the Company's debt agreements require compliance with debt covenants. Management believes that the Company is in compliance with such requirements. The Company had unrestricted retained earnings of $223.8 million after meeting those requirements.

A retained earnings statement for Graber SA, based on assumed data, is shown in **Illustration 12.22**.

ILLUSTRATION 12.22
Retained earnings statement

Graber SA
Retained Earnings Statement
For the Year Ended December 31, 2029

Balance, January 1, as reported			€1,050,000
Add: Net income			410,000
			1,460,000
Less:	Cash dividends	€100,000	
	Share dividends	200,000	300,000
Balance, December 31			€1,160,000

Presentation of Statement of Financial Position

Illustration 12.23 presents the equity section of Graber SA's statement of financial position. Note the following.

1. "Ordinary share dividends distributable" is shown under "Share capital—ordinary."
2. A note (Note R) discloses a retained earnings restriction.

Note that instead of presenting a detailed equity section in the statement of financial position and a retained earnings statement, many companies prepare a **statement of changes in equity**. This statement shows the changes (1) in each equity account and (2) in total that occurred during the year.

ILLUSTRATION 12.23

Comprehensive equity section

Graber SA
Statement of Financial Position (partial)

Equity		
Share capital—preference, 9% €100 par value, cumulative, callable at €120, 10,000 shares authorized, 6,000 shares issued and outstanding		€ 600,000
Share capital—ordinary, no-par, €5 stated value, 500,000 shares authorized, 400,000 shares issued and 390,000 outstanding	€2,000,000	
Ordinary share dividends distributable	**50,000**	2,050,000
Share premium—preference	30,000	
Share premium—ordinary	1,050,000	1,080,000
Retained earnings (**see Note R**)		1,160,000
Less: Treasury shares (10,000 shares)		80,000
Total equity		€4,810,000

Note R: Retained earnings is restricted for the cost of treasury shares, €80,000.

The equity section of Graber SA in Illustration 12.23 includes most of the accounts previously discussed. The disclosures pertaining to Graber's ordinary shares indicate that the company issued 400,000 shares; 100,000 shares are unissued (500,000 authorized less 400,000 issued); and 390,000 shares are outstanding (400,000 issued less 10,000 shares in treasury).

Under IFRS, companies often use the term "Reserves" for forms of equity other than that contributed by shareholders. Reserves sometimes includes retained earnings. More commonly, this line item is used to report the equity impact of comprehensive income items, such as the Revaluation Surplus that resulted from the revaluation of property, plant, and equipment.

ACTION PLAN

- **Present share capital first; list preference shares before ordinary shares.**
- **Present share premium after share capital.**
- **Report retained earnings after share capital and share premium.**

DO IT! 4a | Equity Section

Jennifer NV has issued 300,000 shares of €3 par value ordinary shares. It authorized 600,000 shares. The share premium on the ordinary shares is €380,000. The corporation has reacquired 15,000 shares at a cost of €50,000 and is currently holding those shares. Treasury shares were reissued in prior years for €72,000 more than their cost.

The company also has 4,000 shares issued and outstanding of 8%, €100 par value preference shares. It authorized 10,000 shares. The share premium on the preference shares is €25,000. Retained earnings is €610,000.

Prepare the equity section of the statement of financial position.

Solution

Jennifer NV
Statement of financial position (partial)

Equity		
Share capital, preference 8%, €100 par value, 10,000 shares authorized, 4,000 shares issued and outstanding		€ 400,000
Share capital, ordinary, €3 par value, 600,000 shares authorized, 300,000 shares issued, and 285,000 shares outstanding		900,000
Share premium—preference	€ 25,000	
Share premium—ordinary	380,000	
Share premium—treasury	72,000	477,000
Retained earnings		610,000
Less: Treasury shares (15,000 shares)		50,000
Total equity		€2,337,000

Related exercise material: **BE12.13, DO IT! 12.4a, E12.18, E12.19, E12.20, E12.21, and E12.22.**

Analysis

Analysts can measure profitability from the viewpoint of the investor in ordinary shares by the **return on ordinary shareholders' equity**.

- This ratio indicates how many euros of net income the company earned for each euro invested by the ordinary shareholders.
- It is computed by dividing **net income available to ordinary shareholders** (which is net income minus preference dividends) by average ordinary shareholders' equity.

To illustrate, **Carrefour**'s (FRA) beginning-of-the-year and end-of-the-year ordinary shareholders' equity was €8,047 and €8,597 million, respectively. Its net income was €1,263 million, and no preference shares were outstanding. The return on ordinary shareholders' equity is computed as shown in **Illustration 12.24**.

Net Income minus Preference Dividends	÷	Average Ordinary Shareholders' Equity	=	Return on Ordinary Shareholders' Equity
(€1,263 − €0)	÷	$\frac{(€8{,}047 + €8{,}597)}{2}$	=	15.2%

ILLUSTRATION 12.24
Return on ordinary shareholders' equity computation

As shown above, if a company has preference shares, we would deduct the amount of **preference dividends** from the company's net income to compute income available to ordinary shareholders. Also, the par value of preference shares is deducted from total shareholders' equity when computing the average ordinary shareholders' equity.

DO IT! 4b | Return on Shareholders' Equity

On January 1, 2029, Siena purchased 2,000 treasury shares. Other information regarding Siena is provided below.

	2028	2029
Net income	€110,000	€110,000
Dividends on preference shares	€10,000	€10,000
Dividends on ordinary shares	€2,000	€1,600
Weighted-average number of shares outstanding	10,000	8,000*
Ordinary shareholders' equity, beginning of year	€500,000	€400,000*
Ordinary shareholders' equity, end of year	€500,000	€400,000

*Adjusted for purchase of treasury shares.

Compute (a) return on ordinary shareholders' equity for each year and (b) discuss the changes in the amount of the ratio.

ACTION PLAN

- **Determine return on ordinary shareholders' equity by dividing net income available to ordinary shareholders by the average ordinary shareholders' equity.**

Solution

a.

	2028	2029
Return on ordinary shareholders' equity	$\frac{(€110{,}000 - €10{,}000)}{(€500{,}000 + €500{,}000)/2} = 20\%$	$\frac{(€110{,}000 - €10{,}000)}{(€400{,}000 + €400{,}000)/2} = 25\%$

b. Between 2028 and 2029, return on ordinary shareholders' equity improved from 20% to 25%. While this would appear to be good news for the company's ordinary shareholders, these increases should be carefully evaluated. It is important to note that net income did not change during this period. The increase in this ratio was due to the purchase of treasury shares, which reduced the denominator of the ratio. As the company repurchases its own shares, it becomes more reliant on debt and thus increases its risk.

Related exercise material: **BE12.14, DO IT! 12.4b, E12.23, and E12.24.**

Appendix 12A Statement of Changes in Equity

LEARNING OBJECTIVE *5

Describe the use and content of the statement of changes in equity.

In addition to the statement of financial position and income statement, a statement of changes in equity is also presented each period.

- The statement shows the changes in **each** equity account and in **total** equity during the year.
- Disclosure of such changes is necessary to make the financial statements sufficiently informative for users.

As shown in **Illustration 12A.1**, the statement is prepared in columnar form. It contains columns for each account and for total equity. The transactions are then identified and their effects are shown in the appropriate columns.

In practice, additional columns are usually provided to show the number of issued shares and the number of treasury shares. **When a statement of changes in equity is presented, a retained earnings statement is not necessary** because the retained earnings column explains the changes in this account.

ILLUSTRATION 12A.1 Statement of changes in equity

Hampton AG
Statement of Changes in Equity
For the Year Ended December 31, 2029

	Share Capital (€5 Par)	Share Premium	Retained Earnings	Treasury Shares	Total
Balance January 1	€300,000	€200,000	€650,000	€(34,000)	€1,116,000
Issued 5,000 ordinary shares at €15	25,000	50,000			75,000
Declared a €40,000 cash dividend			(40,000)		(40,000)
Purchased 2,000 shares for treasury at €16				(32,000)	(32,000)
Net income for year			240,000		240,000
Balance December 31	€325,000	€250,000	€850,000	€(66,000)	€1,359,000

Appendix 12B Book Value—Another per Share Amount

LEARNING OBJECTIVE *6

Compute book value per share.

Book Value per Share

You have learned about a number of per share amounts in this chapter. Another per share amount of some importance is **book value per share**. It represents **the equity an ordinary shareholder has in the net assets of the corporation** from owning one share. Remember that the net assets (total assets minus total liabilities) of a corporation must be equal to total equity. Therefore, the formula for computing book value per share when a company has only one class of shares outstanding is shown in **Illustration 12B.1**.

Total Ordinary Shareholders' Equity	÷	Number of Ordinary Shares Outstanding	=	Book Value per Share

ILLUSTRATION 12B.1
Book value per share formula

Thus, if Marlo Corporation has total ordinary shareholders' equity of $1,500,000 (share capital—ordinary $1,000,000 and retained earnings $500,000) and 50,000 shares of ordinary shares outstanding, book value per share is $30 ($1,500,000 ÷ 50,000).

When a company has both preference and ordinary shares, the computation of book value is more complex. Since preference shareholders have a prior claim on net assets over ordinary shareholders, their equity must be deducted from total equity. Then we can determine the equity that applies to the ordinary shares. The computation of book value per share involves the following steps.

1. **Compute the preference share equity.** This equity is equal to the sum of the call price of preference shares plus any cumulative dividends in arrears. If the preference shares do not have a call price, the par value of the shares is used.
2. **Determine the ordinary shareholders' equity.** Subtract the preference share equity from total equity.
3. **Determine book value per share.** Divide ordinary shareholders' equity by ordinary shares.

Example

We will use the equity section of Graber SA shown in Illustration 12.23. Graber's preference shares are callable at €120 per share and are cumulative. Assume that dividends on Graber's preference shares were in arrears for one year, €54,000 (6,000 × €9). The computation of preference share equity (Step 1 in the preceding list) is shown in **Illustration 12B.2**.

Call price (6,000 shares × €120)	€720,000
Dividends in arrears (6,000 shares × €9)	54,000
Preference share equity	€774,000

ILLUSTRATION 12B.2
Computation of preference share equity—Step 1

The computation of book value per share (Steps 2 and 3) is as shown in **Illustration 12B.3**.

ILLUSTRATION 12B.3

Computation of book value per share with preference shares—Steps 2 and 3

Total equity	€4,810,000
Less: **Preference share equity**	**774,000**
Ordinary shareholders' equity	**€4,036,000**
Ordinary shares outstanding	**390,000**
Book value per share (€4,036,000 ÷ 390,000)	**€10.35**

Note that we used the call price of €120 instead of the par value of €100. Note also that share premium—preference, €30,000, **is not assigned to the preference share equity.** Preference shareholders ordinarily do not have a right to amounts contributed in excess of par value. Therefore, such amounts are assigned to the ordinary shareholders' equity in computing book value.

Book Value versus Market Price

Be sure you understand that **book value per share may not equal market price per share.**

- Book value generally is based on recorded costs.
- Market price reflects the subjective judgments of thousands of shareholders and prospective investors about a company's potential for future earnings and dividends.
- Market price per share may exceed book value per share, but that fact does not necessarily mean that the shares are overpriced.

The correlation between book value and the annual range of a company's market price per share is often remote, as indicated in **Illustration 12B.4** for some U.S. companies.

ILLUSTRATION 12B.4

Book value and market price compared

Company	Book Value (year-end)	Market Range (for the year)
The Limited, Inc.	$13.38	$22.89–$31.03
H. J. Heinz Company	$ 7.48	$34.53–$40.61
Cisco Systems	$ 3.66	$17.01–$21.24
Walmart Inc.	$12.79	$42.31–$50.87

Book value per share is useful in determining the trend of a shareholder's per share equity in a corporation. It is also significant in many contracts and in court cases where the rights of individual parties are based on cost information.

Review and Practice

Learning Objectives Review

1 Discuss the major characteristics of a corporation.

The major characteristics of a corporation are separate legal existence, limited liability of shareholders, transferable ownership rights, ability to acquire capital, continuous life, corporation management, government regulations, and additional taxes.

2 Explain how to account for ordinary, preference, and treasury shares.

When the issuance of ordinary shares for cash is recorded, the par value of the shares is credited to Share Capital—Ordinary. The portion of the proceeds that is above or below par value is recorded in a separate account. When no-par ordinary shares have a stated value, the entries are similar to those for par value shares. When no-par shares do not have a stated value, the entire proceeds are credited to Share Capital—Ordinary.

Preference shares have contractual provisions that give them priority over ordinary shares in certain areas. Typically, preference shareholders have a preference to (1) dividends and (2) assets in liquidation. They generally do not have voting rights.

The cost method is generally used in accounting for treasury shares. Under this approach, Treasury Shares is debited at the price paid to reacquire the shares. The same amount is credited to Treasury Shares when the shares are sold. The difference between the sales price and cost is recorded in equity accounts, not in income statement accounts.

3 Explain how to account for cash dividends, share dividends, and share splits.

Companies make entries for cash dividends at the declaration date and at the payment date. At the **declaration date**, the entry is debit Cash Dividends and credit Dividends Payable. At the **payment date**, the entry is debit Dividends Payable and credit Cash.

At the declaration date, the entry for a small share dividend is debit Share Dividends, credit Share Premium—Ordinary, and credit Ordinary Share Dividends Distributable.

At the payment (distribution) date, the entry for a small share dividend is debit Ordinary Share Dividends Distributable and credit Share Capital—Ordinary. A share split reduces the par or stated value per share and increases the number of shares but does not affect balances in equity accounts.

4 Discuss how equity is reported and analyzed.

Companies report each of the individual debits and credits to retained earnings in the retained earnings statement. Additions and deductions consist generally of net income or net loss, cash and share dividends, and some disposals of treasury shares.

A comprehensive equity section includes all equity accounts. It consists of two sections: share capital and retained earnings. It should also include notes to the financial statements that explain any restrictions on retained earnings and any dividends in arrears. One measure of profitability is the return on ordinary shareholders' equity. It is calculated by dividing net income minus preference share dividends by average ordinary shareholders' equity.

*5 Describe the use and content of the statement of changes in equity.

Corporations must prepare a statement of changes in equity each period. This statement, prepared in columnar form, shows changes in each equity account and in total equity during the accounting period.

*6 Compute book value per share.

Book value per share represents the equity an ordinary shareholder has in the net assets of a corporation from owning one share. When there are only ordinary shares outstanding, the formula for computing book value is: Total ordinary shareholders' equity ÷ Number of ordinary shares outstanding.

Glossary Review

Authorized shares The amount of shares that a corporation is authorized to sell as indicated in its charter. (p. 12-8).

***Book value per share** The equity an ordinary shareholder has in the net assets of the corporation from owning one share. (p. 12-33).

Cash dividend A pro rata distribution of cash to shareholders. (p. 12-19).

Charter A document that sets forth important terms and features regarding the creation of a corporation. (p. 12-6).

Corporation A business organized as a legal entity separate and distinct from its owners under corporation law. (p. 12-3).

Cumulative dividend A feature of preference shares entitling the shareholder to receive current and unpaid prior-year dividends before ordinary shareholders receive any dividends. (p. 12-22).

Declaration date The date the board of directors formally declares the dividend and announces it to shareholders. (p. 12-20).

Deficit A debit balance in retained earnings. (p. 12-28).

Dividend A corporation's distribution of cash or shares to its shareholders on a pro rata (proportional) basis. (p. 12-19).

Liquidating dividend A dividend declared out of share capital or share premium. (p. 12-19).

No-par value shares Shares that have not been assigned a value in the corporate charter. (p. 12-10).

Organization costs Costs incurred in the formation of a corporation. (p. 12-6).

Outstanding shares Shares that have been issued and are being held by shareholders. (p. 12-16).

Par value shares (or **nominal value shares**) Capital shares that have been assigned a value per share in the corporate charter. (p. 12-10).

Payment date The date dividends are transferred to shareholders. (p. 12-20).

Preference shares Shares that have some contractual preferences over ordinary shares. (p. 12-14).

Privately held corporation A corporation that has only a few shareholders and whose shares are not available for sale to the general public. (p. 12-3).

Publicly held corporation A corporation that may have thousands of shareholders and whose shares are regularly traded on a national securities exchange. (p. 12-3).

Record date The date when ownership of outstanding shares is determined for dividend purposes. (p. 12-20).

Retained earnings Net income that a corporation retains for future use. (p. 12-11).

Retained earnings restrictions Circumstances that make a portion of retained earnings currently unavailable for dividends. (p. 12-29).

Return on ordinary shareholders' equity A ratio that measures profitability from the shareholders' point of view. It is computed by dividing net income available to ordinary shareholders by average ordinary shareholders' equity. (p. 12-31).

Share capital Cash and other assets paid into the corporation by shareholders in exchange for shares. (p. 12-11).

Share dividend A pro rata distribution of the corporation's own shares to shareholders. (p. 12-24).

Share split The issuance of additional shares to shareholders accompanied by a reduction in the par or stated value per share. (p. 12-26).

Stated value The amount per share assigned by the board of directors to no-par shares that become legal capital per share. (p. 12-10).

Statement of changes in equity A statement that shows the changes in each equity account and in total equity during the year. (p. 12-29).

Treasury shares A corporation's own shares that the corporation has issued and reacquired but not retired. (p. 12-15).

Practice Multiple-Choice Questions

1. **(LO 1)** Which of the following is **not** a major advantage of the corporate form of organization?
   - **a.** Separate legal existence.
   - **b.** Continuous life.
   - **c.** Government regulations.
   - **d.** Transferable ownership rights.

2. **(LO 1)** A major disadvantage of a corporation is:
   - **a.** limited liability of shareholders.
   - **b.** additional taxes.
   - **c.** transferable ownership rights.
   - **d.** separate legal existence.

3. **(LO 1)** Which of the following statements is **false**?
   - **a.** Ownership of ordinary shares gives the owner a voting right.
   - **b.** The equity section begins with a share capital section.
   - **c.** The authorization of share capital does not result in a formal accounting entry.
   - **d.** Par value and market price of a company's shares are always the same.

4. **(LO 2)** ABC Industries issues 1,000 €10 par ordinary shares value at €12 per share. In recording the transaction, credits are made to:
   - **a.** Share Capital—Ordinary €10,000 and Share Premium—Ordinary €2,000.
   - **b.** Share Capital—Ordinary €12,000.
   - **c.** Share Capital—Ordinary €10,000 and Gain from Sale of Shares €2,000.
   - **d.** Share Capital—Ordinary €10,000 and Retained Earnings €2,000.

5. **(LO 2)** Lucroy AG issues 100 shares of €10 par value preference shares at €12 per share. In recording the transaction, credits are made to:
   - **a.** Share Capital—Preference €1,200.
   - **b.** Share Capital—Preference €1,000 and Retained Earnings €200.
   - **c.** Share Capital—Preference €1,000 and Share Premium—Ordinary €200.
   - **d.** Share Capital—Preference €1,000 and Share Premium—Preference €200.

6. **(LO 2)** Treasury shares may be repurchased:
   - **a.** to reissue the shares to officers and employees under bonus and share compensation plans.
   - **b.** to signal to the securities market that management believes the shares are underpriced.
   - **c.** to have additional shares available for use in the acquisition of other companies.
   - **d.** More than one of the answer choices is correct.

7. **(LO 2)** XYZ Ltd. sells 100 of its £5 par value treasury shares at £13 per share. If the cost of acquiring the shares was £10 per share, the entry for the sale should include credits to:
   - **a.** Treasury Shares 1,000 and Share Premium—Treasury 300.
   - **b.** Treasury Shares 500 and Share Premium—Treasury 800.
   - **c.** Treasury Shares 1,000 and Retained Earnings 300.
   - **d.** Treasury Shares 500 and Gain from Sale of Treasury Shares 800.

8. **(LO 2)** In the statement of financial position, the cost of treasury shares is deducted in:
   - **a.** expenses.
   - **b.** revenues.
   - **c.** equity.
   - **d.** liabilities.

9. **(LO 3)** Entries for cash dividends are required on the:
   - **a.** declaration date and the payment date.
   - **b.** record date and the payment date.
   - **c.** declaration date, record date, and payment date.
   - **d.** declaration date and the record date.

10. **(LO 3)** Preference shares may have priority over ordinary shares **except** in:
    - **a.** dividends.
    - **b.** assets in the event of liquidation.
    - **c.** cumulative dividend features.
    - **d.** voting.

11. **(LO 3)** Encore Ltd. declared an £80,000 cash dividend. It currently has 3,000 shares of 7%, £100 par value cumulative preference shares outstanding. It is one year in arrears on its preference shares. How much cash will Encore distribute to the ordinary shareholders?
    - **a.** £38,000.
    - **b.** £42,000.
    - **c.** £59,000.
    - **d.** None of the answer choices is correct.

12. **(LO 3)** Which of the following statements about small share dividends is **true**?
    - **a.** A debit to Retained Earnings should be made for the par value of the shares issued.
    - **b.** A small share dividend decreases total equity.
    - **c.** Market price per share should be assigned to the dividend shares.
    - **d.** A small share dividend ordinarily will have an effect on par value per share.

13. **(LO 3)** Which of the following statements about a 3-for-1 share split is **true**?

a. It will triple the market price of the share.
b. It will triple the amount of total equity.
c. It will have no effect on total equity.
d. It requires the company to distribute cash.

14. **(LO 3)** Raptor NV has retained earnings of €500,000 and total equity of €2,000,000. It has 100,000 shares of €8 par value ordinary shares outstanding, which is currently selling for €30 per share. If Raptor declares a 10% ordinary share dividend:

a. net income will decrease by €80,000.
b. retained earnings will decrease by €80,000 and total equity will increase by €80,000.
c. retained earnings will decrease by €300,000 and total equity will increase by €300,000.
d. retained earnings will decrease by €300,000 and total share capital will increase by €300,000.

15. **(LO 4)** All **but one** of the following is reported in a retained earnings statement. The exception is:

a. share dividends.
b. net income and net loss.
c. sales revenue.
d. cash dividends.

16. **(LO 4)** In the equity section, Ordinary Share Dividends Distributable is reported as a(n):

a. deduction from share capital and retained earnings.
b. addition to share premium.
c. deduction from retained earnings.
d. addition to share capital.

17. **(LO 4)** The return on ordinary shareholders' equity is defined as:

a. net income divided by total assets.
b. cash dividends divided by average ordinary shareholders' equity.
c. income available to ordinary shareholders divided by average ordinary shareholders' equity.
d. None of the answer choices is correct.

18. **(LO 4)** Katie Ltd. reported net income of NT$186,000 during 2029 and paid dividends of NT$26,000 on ordinary shares. It also has 10,000 shares of 6%, NT$100 par value, non-cumulative preference shares outstanding and paid dividends of NT$60,000 on preference shares. Ordinary shareholders' equity was NT$1,200,000 on January 1, 2029, and NT$1,600,000 on December 31, 2029 (amounts in thousands). The company's return on ordinary shareholders' equity for 2029 is:

a. 10.0%. **c.** 7.1%.
b. 9.0%. **d.** 13.3%.

*19. **(LO 5)** Since a statement of changes in equity is required, it is **not** necessary to prepare a(n):

a. retained earnings statement.
b. statement of financial position.
c. income statement.
d. statement of cash flows.

*20. **(LO 6)** The ledger of JFK, plc shows share capital—ordinary, treasury shares—ordinary, and no preference shares. For this company, the formula for computing book value per share is:

a. total equity divided by the number of ordinary shares issued.
b. share capital—ordinary divided by the number of ordinary shares issued.
c. total equity divided by the number of ordinary shares outstanding.
d. share capital—ordinary divided by the number of ordinary shares outstanding.

Solutions

1. **c.** Government regulations are a disadvantage of a corporation. The other choices are advantages of a corporation.

2. **b.** Additional taxes are a disadvantage of a corporation. The other choices are advantages of a corporation.

3. **d.** Par value has no relationship with market price, and many governments today do not require a par value. The other choices are true statements.

4. **a.** Share Capital—Ordinary should be credited for €10,000 and Share Premium—Ordinary should be credited for €2,000. The shares are par value, so the excess above par is reported separately. This excess is contributed, not earned, capital. The other choices are therefore incorrect.

5. **d.** Share Capital—Preference should be credited for €1,000 and Share Premium—Preference should be credited for €200. The other choices are incorrect because (a) a total credit for the entire proceeds to Share Capital—Preference is incorrect because Share Capital—Preference has a total par value that is different than total proceeds; (b) this is contributed capital, not earned capital, so a credit to Retained Earnings is not correct; and (c) the account Share Premium—Ordinary is not an appropriate account title.

6. **d.** Corporations repurchase treasury shares to have additional shares available for use in acquisition, to reissue shares under bonus and share compensation plans, and to signal to the securities share market that management believes the shares are underpriced. Although the other choices are true statements, choice (d) is the better answer.

7. **a.** Treasury Shares should be credited for £1,000 (100 shares × £10, the acquisition price). Share Premium—Treasury should be credited for the difference between the £1,000 and the cash received of £1,300 (100 shares × £13), or £300. The other choices are therefore incorrect.

8. **c.** The cost of treasury shares is deducted in equity accounts. The other choices are therefore incorrect.

9. **a.** Entries are required for dividends on the declaration date and the payment date, but not the record date. The other choices are therefore incorrect.

10. **d.** Preference shares usually do not have voting rights and therefore do not have priority over ordinary shares on this issue. The other choices are true statements.

11. **a.** The preference shareholders will receive a total of £42,000 in dividends (3,000 × .07 × £100 × 2 years). The ordinary shareholders will receive £38,000 (£80,000 − £42,000), not (b) £42,000, (c) £59,000, or (d) none.

12. **c.** Because the share dividend is considered small, the fair value (market price), not the par value, is assigned to the shares. The other choices are incorrect because (a) a debit to Retained Earnings for the fair value of the shares issued should be made; (b) a small share div-

idend changes the composition of total equity, but does not change the total; and (d) a small share dividend will have no effect on par value per share.

13. c. Share splits have no effect on total share capital, retained earnings, or total equity. The other choices are incorrect because (a) share splits reduce the market price per share, (b) share splits have no effect on total equity, and (d) the company will distribute additional shares, not cash.

14. d. Retained earnings will decrease by €300,000 and total share capital will increase by €300,000. The other choices are therefore incorrect because (a) net income is not affected, (b) retained earnings decreases by €300,000, and (c) total equity does not change.

15. c. Sales revenue is not reported on the retained earnings statement. The other choices are true statements.

16. d. Ordinary Share Dividends Distributable is reported as an addition to share capital not (a) as a deduction from share capital and retained earnings, (b) as an addition to share premium, or (c) as a deduction from retained earnings.

17. c. Return on ordinary shareholders' equity equals Net income less Preference dividends (income available to ordinary shareholders) divided by Average ordinary shareholders' equity. The other choices are therefore incorrect.

18. b. Return on ordinary shareholders' equity is Net income available to ordinary shareholders divided by Average ordinary shareholders' equity. Net income available to ordinary shareholders is Net income less Preference dividends = NT$126,000 [NT$186,000 – (10,000 × .06 × NT$100)]. The company's return on ordinary shareholders' equity for the year is therefore 9.0% [NT$126,000/(NT$1,200,000 + NT$1,600,000)/2)], not (a) 10.0%, (c) 7.1%, or (d) 13.3%.

***19. a.** Since a statement of changes in equity is required, a retained earnings statement is unnecessary as the information would be redundant. Choices (b) statement of financial position, (c) income statement, and (d) statement of cash flows are also required statements.

***20. c.** When a company has only one class of shares outstanding, Book value per share is Total equity divided by Number of ordinary shares outstanding. The other choices are therefore incorrect.

Practice Brief Exercises

Prepare entries for issuance of shares.

1. (LO 2) On April 10, Leury SE issues 3,000 shares of €5 par value ordinary shares for cash at €14 per share. Journalize the issuance of the shares.

Solution

1.

April 10	Cash (3,000 × €14)	42,000	
	Share Capital—Ordinary (3,000 × €5)		15,000
	Share Premium—Ordinary (3,000 × €9)		27,000

Prepare entries for treasury share transactions.

2. (LO 2) On June 1, Omar Group purchases 600 shares of its £5 par value ordinary shares for the treasury at a cash price of £10 per share. On August 15, it sells 400 treasury shares for cash at £13 per share. Journalize the two treasury share transactions.

Solution

2.

June 1	Treasury Shares (600 × £10)	6,000	
	Cash		6,000
Aug. 15	Cash (400 × £13)	5,200	
	Treasury Shares (400 × £10)		4,000
	Share Premium—Treasury (400 × £3)		1,200

Prepare entries for a cash dividend.

3. (LO 3) Teng Electronics has 70,000 ordinary shares outstanding. It declares a ¥2 per share cash dividend on November 15 to shareholders of record on December 15 (¥ in thousands). The dividend is paid on December 31. Prepare the entries on the appropriate dates to record the declaration and payment of the cash dividend.

Solution

3.

Nov. 15	Cash Dividends (70,000 × ¥2/share)	140,000	
	Dividends Payable		140,000
Dec. 31	Dividends Payable	140,000	
	Cash		140,000

4. **(LO 3)** The equity section of Ynoa plc consists of share capital—ordinary (£5 par) £3,000,000 and retained earnings £1,000,000. A 15% share dividend (90,000 shares) is declared when the market price per share is £11. Show the before-and-after effects of the dividend on the following.

Show the before-and-after effects of a share dividend.

a. The components of equity.

b. Shares outstanding.

c. Par value per share.

Solution

4.

	Before Dividend	After Dividend
a. Equity		
Share capital—ordinary, £5 par	£3,000,000	£3,450,000
Share premium—ordinary	—	540,000
Retained earnings	1,000,000	10,000
Total equity	£4,000,000	£4,000,000
b. Outstanding shares	600,000	690,000
c. Par value per share	£5.00	£5.00

5. **(LO 4)** The balance in retained earnings on January 1, 2029, for ChrisBeck Ltd. was HK$400,000 (amounts in thousands). During the year, the company paid cash dividends of HK$50,000 and distributed a share dividend of HK$10,000. Net income for 2029 was HK$107,000. Prepare the retained earnings statement for 2029.

Prepare a retained earnings statement.

Solution

5.

ChrisBeck Ltd.
Retained Earnings Statement
For the Year Ended December 31, 2029
(amounts in thousands)

Balance, January 1		HK$400,000
Add: Net income		107,000
		507,000
Less: Cash dividends	HK$50,000	
Share dividends	10,000	60,000
Balance, December 31		HK$447,000

6. **(LO 4)** Phoa Enterprises has the following accounts at December 31: Ordinary Shares, HK$2 par, 50,000 shares issued, HK$100,000; Share Premium—Ordinary HK$40,000; Retained Earnings HK$65,000; and Treasury Shares, 2,000 shares, HK$17,000 (HK$ in thousands). Prepare the equity section of the statement of financial position.

Prepare equity section.

Solution

6.

Phoa Enterprises
Statement of Financial Position (partial)
(HK$ in thousands)

Equity	
Share capital—ordinary, HK$2 par value,	
50,000 shares issued and 48,000 shares outstanding	HK$100,000
Share premium—ordinary	40,000
Retained earnings	65,000
Less: Treasury shares (2,000 shares)	17,000
Total equity	HK$188,000

Practice Exercises

Journalize issuance of ordinary and preference shares and purchase of treasury shares.

1. **(LO 2)** Maci plc had the following transactions during the current period.

Mar. 2	Issued 5,000 shares of £5 par value ordinary shares to attorneys in payment of a bill for £35,000 for services performed in helping the company to incorporate.
June 12	Issued 60,000 shares of £5 par value ordinary shares for cash of £370,000.
July 11	Issued 1,000 shares of £100 par value preference shares for cash at £112 per share.
Nov. 28	Purchased 2,000 shares of treasury shares for £70,000.

Instructions

Journalize the transactions.

Solution

1.

Mar. 2	Organization Expense	35,000	
	Share Capital—Ordinary (5,000 × £5)		25,000
	Share Premium—Ordinary		10,000
June 12	Cash	370,000	
	Share Capital—Ordinary (60,000 × £5)		300,000
	Share Premium—Ordinary		70,000
July 11	Cash (1,000 × £112)	112,000	
	Share Capital—Preference (1,000 × £100)		100,000
	Share Premium—Preference (1,000 × £12)		12,000
Nov. 28	Treasury Shares	70,000	
	Cash		70,000

Journalize treasury share transactions.

2. **(LO 2)** Star Industries purchased from its shareholders 5,000 shares of its own previously issued shares for €250,000. It later resold 2,000 shares for €53 per share, then 2,000 more shares for €48 per share, and finally 1,000 shares for €43 per share.

Instructions

Prepare journal entries for the purchase of the treasury shares and the three sales of treasury shares.

Solution

2.

Treasury Shares	250,000	
Cash		250,000
Cash (2,000 × €53)	106,000	
Treasury Shares (2,000 × €50)		100,000
Share Premium—Treasury		6,000
Cash (2,000 × €48)	96,000	
Share Premium—Treasury	4,000	
Treasury Shares (2,000 × €50)		100,000
Cash (1,000 × €43)	43,000	
Share Premium—Treasury (€6,000 – €4,000)	2,000	
Retained Earnings	5,000	
Treasury Shares (1,000 × €50)		50,000

3. **(LO 3)** At December 31, 2029, Lebron Athletics distributes €50,000 of cash dividends. Its outstanding ordinary shares have a par value of €400,000, and its 6% preference shares have a par value of €100,000 at December 31, 2029.

Allocate cash dividends to preference and ordinary shares.

Instructions

a. Show the allocation of dividends to each class of shares, assuming that the preference share dividend is 6% and not cumulative.

b. Show the allocation of the dividends to each class of shares, assuming the preference share dividend of 6% is cumulative and Lebron did not pay any dividends on the preference shares in the preceding 2 years.

c. Journalize the declaration of the cash dividend at December 31, 2029, assuming the requirements in part (b).

Solution

3. **a.**

	2029
Total dividend declaration	€50,000
Allocation to preference shares (6% × €100,000)	(6,000)
Remainder to ordinary shares	€44,000

b.

	2029
Total dividend declaration	€50,000
Allocation to preference shares (6% × €100,000 × 3)	(18,000)
Remainder to ordinary shares	€32,000

c.

Dec. 31	Cash Dividends	50,000	
	Dividends Payable		50,000

4. **(LO 3, 4)** On January 1, Chong Ltd. had 95,000 shares of no-par ordinary shares issued and outstanding. The shares have a stated value of NT$60 per share (amounts in thousands). During the year, the following occurred.

Journalize cash dividends; indicate statement presentation.

Apr.	1	Issued 25,000 additional ordinary shares for NT$170 per share.
June	15	Declared a cash dividend of NT$10 per share to shareholders of record on June 30.
July	10	Paid the NT$10 cash dividend.
Dec.	1	Issued 2,000 additional ordinary shares for NT$190 per share.
	15	Declared a cash dividend on outstanding shares of NT$12 per share to shareholders of record on December 31.

Instructions

a. Prepare the entries, if any, on each of the three dividend dates.

b. How are dividends and dividends payable reported in the financial statements prepared at December 31?

Solution

4. a.

June 15	Cash Dividends (120,000 × NT$10)	1,200,000	
	Dividends Payable		1,200,000
July 10	Dividends Payable	1,200,000	
	Cash		1,200,000
Dec. 15	Cash Dividends (122,000 × NT$12)	1,464,000	
	Dividends Payable		1,464,000

b. In the retained earnings statement, dividends of NT$2,664,000 will be deducted. In the statement of financial position, Dividends Payable of NT$1,464,000 will be reported as a current liability.

Prepare a retained earnings statement.

5. **(LO 4)** Rabb AG reported retained earnings of €400,000 and 200,000 shares outstanding at January 1, 2029.

The following transactions occurred during 2029.

1. A cash dividend of €0.50 per share was declared and paid.
2. A 5% share dividend was declared and distributed when the market price per share was €18 per share.
3. Net income was €340,000.

Instructions

Prepare a retained earnings statement for 2029.

Solution

5.

Rabb AG
Retained Earnings Statement
For the Year Ended December 31, 2029

Balance, January 1		€400,000
Add: Net income		340,000
		740,000
Less: Cash dividends	€100,000*	
Share dividends	180,000**	280,000
Balance, December 31		€460,000

*(200,000 × €.50/sh); **(200,000 × .05 × €18/sh)

Practice Problems

Journalize transactions and prepare equity section.

1. **(LO 2, 4)** Cabral SA is authorized to issue 1,000,000 R$5 par value ordinary shares. In its first year, the company has the following share transactions.

Jan. 10	Issued 400,000 ordinary shares at R$8 per share.
July 1	Issued 100,000 ordinary shares for land. The land had an asking price of R$900,000. The shares are currently selling on a national exchange at R$8.25 per share.
Sept. 1	Purchased 10,000 ordinary shares for the treasury at R$9 per share.
Dec. 1	Sold 4,000 treasury shares at R$10 per share.

Instructions

a. Journalize the transactions.

b. Prepare the equity section assuming the company had retained earnings of R$200,000 at December 31.

Solution

1. a. Jan. 10	Cash	3,200,000	
	Share Capital—Ordinary		2,000,000
	Share Premium—Ordinary		1,200,000
	(To record issuance of 400,000 R$5 par value shares)		
July 1	Land	825,000	
	Share Capital—Ordinary		500,000
	Share Premium—Ordinary		325,000
	(To record issuance of 100,000 R$5 par value shares for land)		
Sept. 1	Treasury Shares	90,000	
	Cash		90,000
	(To record purchase of 10,000 treasury shares at cost)		
Dec. 1	Cash	40,000	
	Treasury Shares		36,000
	Share Premium—Treasury		4,000
	(To record sale of 4,000 treasury shares above cost)		

b.

Cabral SA
Statement of Financial Position (partial)

Equity		
Share capital—ordinary, R$5 par value, 1,000,000 shares authorized, 500,000 shares issued, 494,000 shares outstanding		R$2,500,000
Share premium—ordinary	R$1,525,000	
Share premium—treasury	4,000	1,529,000
Retained earnings		200,000
Less: Treasury shares (6,000 shares)		54,000
Total equity		R$4,175,000

2. (LO 3, 4) On January 1, 2029, Hayslett AG had the following equity accounts.

Prepare dividend entries and equity section.

Share Capital—Ordinary (€10 par value, 260,000 shares issued and outstanding)	€2,600,000
Share Premium—Ordinary	1,500,000
Retained Earnings	3,200,000

During the year, the following transactions occurred.

April 1	Declared a €1.50 cash dividend per share to shareholders of record on April 15, payable May 1.
May 1	Paid the dividend declared in April.
June 1	Announced a 2-for-1 share split. Prior to the split, the market price per share was €24.
Aug. 1	Declared a 10% share dividend to shareholders of record on August 15, distributable August 31. On August 1, the market price of the shares was €10 per share.
31	Issued the shares for the share dividend.
Dec. 1	Declared a €1.50 per share dividend to shareholders of record on December 15, payable January 5, 2030.
31	Determined that net income for the year was €600,000.

Instructions

a. Journalize the transactions and the closing entries for net income, share dividends, and cash dividends.

b. Prepare an equity section at December 31.

Solution

2. a.

Date	Account	Debit	Credit
Apr. 1	Cash Dividends (260,000 × €1.50)	390,000	
	Dividends Payable		390,000
May 1	Dividends Payable	390,000	
	Cash		390,000
June 1	No journal entry needed for share split		
Aug. 1	Share Dividends (52,000* × €10)	520,000	
	Ordinary Share Dividends Distributable (52,000 × €5)		260,000
	Share Premium—Ordinary (52,000 × €5)		260,000
	*520,000 × .10		
31	Ordinary Share Dividends Distributable	260,000	
	Share Capital—Ordinary		260,000
Dec. 1	Cash Dividends (572,000** × €1.50)	858,000	
	Dividends Payable		858,000
	**(260,000 × 2) + 52,000		
31	Income Summary	600,000	
	Retained Earnings		600,000
	Retained Earnings	1,768,000	
	Share Dividends		520,000
	Cash Dividends (€390,000 + €858,000)		1,248,000

b.

Hayslett AG
Statement of Financial Position (partial)

Equity	
Share capital—ordinary, €5 par value, 572,000 shares issued and outstanding	€2,860,000
Share premium—ordinary	1,760,000
Retained earnings	2,032,000*
Total equity	€6,652,000

*€3,200,000 + €600,000 − €390,000 − €520,000 − €858,000

Note: Asterisked Questions, Exercises, and Problems relate to material in the appendices to the chapter.

Questions

1. Mark Adler, a student, asks your help in understanding the following characteristics of a corporation: (a) separate legal existence, (b) limited liability of shareholders, and (c) transferable ownership rights. Explain these characteristics to Mark.

2. a. Your friend Paula Leuck cannot understand how the characteristic of corporation management is both an advantage and a disadvantage. Clarify this problem for Paula.

   b. Identify and explain two other disadvantages of a corporation.

3. The following terms pertain to the forming of a corporation: (1) charter, (2) by-laws, and (3) organization costs. Explain the terms.

4. What are the basic ownership rights of ordinary shareholders in the absence of restrictive provisions?

5. A corporation has been defined as an entity separate and distinct from its owners. In what ways is a corporation a separate legal entity?

6. a. What are the two principal components of equity?

   b. What is share capital? Give three examples.

7. The corporate charter of Keller Ltd. allows the issuance of a maximum of 100,000 ordinary shares. During its first two years of operations, Keller sold 70,000 shares and reacquired 7,000 of these shares. After these transactions, how many shares are authorized, issued, and outstanding?

8. Which is the better investment—ordinary shares with a par value of ₩5,000 per share, or ordinary shares with a par value of ₩20,000 per share? Why?

9. What factors help determine the market price of shares?

10. Why are ordinary shares usually not issued at a price that is less than par value?

11. Land appraised at £84,000 is purchased by issuing 1,000 £10 par value ordinary shares. The market price of the shares at the time of the exchange, based on active trading in the securities market, is £95 per share. Should the land be recorded at £10,000, £84,000, or £95,000? Explain.

12. For what reasons might a company like **Wesfarmers** (AUS) repurchase some of its shares (treasury shares)?

13. Luz A/S purchases 1,000 shares of its own previously issued €5 par value ordinary shares for €9,000. Assuming the shares are held in

the treasury, what effect does this transaction have on (a) net income, (b) total assets, (c) retained earnings, and (d) total equity?

14. The treasury shares purchased in Question 13 are resold by Luz A/S for €13,000. What effect does this transaction have on (a) net income, (b) total assets, (c) retained earnings, and (d) total equity?

15. What are the principal differences between ordinary shares and preference shares?

16. **a.** What is a dividend?
b. "Dividends must be paid in cash." Do you agree? Explain.

17. Tim Miotke maintains that adequate cash is the only requirement for the declaration of a cash dividend. Is Tim correct? Explain.

18. **a.** Three dates are important in connection with cash dividends. Identify these dates, and explain their significance to the corporation and its shareholders.
b. Identify the accounting entries that are made for a cash dividend and the date of each entry.

19. Farley Farms declares a €55,000 cash dividend on December 31, 2029. The required annual dividend on preference shares is €10,000. Determine the allocation of the dividend to preference and ordinary shareholders assuming the preference shares are cumulative and dividends are 1 year in arrears.

20. Contrast the effects of a cash dividend and a share dividend on a company's statement of financial position.

21. Travis Mordica asks, "Since share dividends don't change anything, why declare them?" What is your answer to Travis?

22. Gorton Ltd. has 30,000 shares of £10 par value ordinary shares outstanding when it announces a 2-for-1 share split. Before the split, the shares had a market price of £120 per share. After the split, how many shares will be outstanding? What will be the approximate market price per share?

23. The board of directors is considering either a share split or a share dividend. They understand that total equity will remain the same under either action. However, they are not sure of the different effects of the two types of actions on other aspects of equity. Explain the differences to the directors.

24. How are retained earnings restrictions generally reported in the financial statements?

25. Rafy Furcal believes that both the beginning and ending balances in retained earnings are shown in the equity section. Is Rafy correct? Discuss.

26. Dean Percival, who owns many investments in ordinary shares, says, "I don't care what a company's net income is. The share price tells me everything I need to know!" How do you respond to Dean?

*27. What is the formula for computing book value per share when a corporation has only ordinary shares?

*28. Bihar Ltd.'s ordinary shares have a par value of Rs10, a book value of Rs240, and a current market price of Rs180. Explain why these amounts are all different (amounts in thousands).

Brief Exercises

BE12.1 (LO 1) Kari Home is studying for her accounting midterm examination. Identify for Kari the advantages and disadvantages of the corporate form of business organization.

List the advantages and disadvantages of a corporation.

BE12.2 (LO 2) On May 10, Chen Co. issues 2,000 €6 par value ordinary shares for cash at €13 per share. Journalize the issuance of the shares.

Prepare entries for issuance of par value ordinary shares.

BE12.3 (LO 2) On June 1, Federia Ltd. issues 4,500 no-par ordinary shares at a cash price of HK$600 per share. Journalize the issuance of the shares assuming the shares have a stated value of HK$200 per share.

Prepare entries for issuance of no-par value ordinary shares.

BE12.4 (LO 2) Alou Ltd.'s £10 par value ordinary shares are actively traded at a market price of £15 per share. Alou issues 5,000 shares to purchase land advertised for sale at £81,000. Journalize the issuance of the shares in acquiring the land.

Prepare entries for issuance of shares in a non-cash transaction.

BE12.5 (LO 2) On July 1, Pearl River Industries purchases 500 of its HK$20 par value ordinary shares for the treasury at a cash price of HK$80 per share. On September 1, it sells 350 treasury shares for cash at HK$90 per share. Journalize the two treasury share transactions.

Prepare entries for treasury share transactions.

BE12.6 (LO 2) Chard Ltd. issues 5,000 £100 par value preference shares for cash at £118 per share. Journalize the issuance of the preference shares.

Prepare entries for issuance of preference shares.

BE12.7 (LO 3) Greenwood Enterprises has 80,000 ordinary shares outstanding. It declares a €1 per share cash dividend on November 1 to shareholders of record on December 1. The dividend is paid on December 31. Prepare the entries on the appropriate dates to record the declaration and payment of the cash dividend.

Prepare entries for a cash dividend.

BE12.8 (LO 3) M. Bot Ltd. has 10,000 shares of 8%, €100 par value, cumulative preference shares outstanding at December 31, 2029. No dividends were declared in 2027 or 2028. If M. Bot wants to pay €375,000 of dividends in 2029, what amount of dividends will ordinary shareholders receive?

Determine dividends paid to ordinary shareholders.

BE12.9 (LO 3) Langley Ltd. has 50,000 shares of £10 par value ordinary shares outstanding. It declares a 15% share dividend on December 1 when the market price per share is £16. The dividend shares are issued on December 31. Prepare the entries for the declaration and issuance of the share dividend.

Prepare entries for a share dividend.

Show before-and-after effects of a share dividend.

BE12.10 (LO 3) The equity section of Pretzer plc consists of ordinary shares (£10 par) £2,000,000 and retained earnings £500,000. A 15% share dividend (30,000 shares) is declared when the market price per share is £16. Show the before-and-after effects of the dividend on the following.

a. The components of equity.

b. Shares outstanding.

c. Par value per share.

Prepare a retained earnings statement.

BE12.11 (LO 4) For the year ending December 31, 2029, Soto Ltd. reports net income ¥170,000 and dividends ¥85,000 (amounts in thousands). Prepare the retained earnings statement for the year assuming the balance in retained earnings on January 1, 2029, was ¥220,000.

Prepare a retained earnings statement.

BE12.12 (LO 4) The balance in retained earnings on January 1, 2029, for Palmer Cosmetic was €800,000. During the year, the company paid cash dividends of €90,000 and distributed a share dividend of €8,000. Net income for 2029 was €120,000. Prepare the retained earnings statement for 2029.

Prepare equity section.

BE12.13 (LO 4) Garcia Enterprises has the following accounts at December 31: Share Capital—Ordinary, €10 par, 5,000 shares issued, €50,000; Share Premium—Ordinary €32,000; Retained Earnings €45,000; and Treasury Shares, 500 shares, €9,000. Prepare the equity section of the statement of financial position.

Compute the return on ordinary shareholders' equity.

BE12.14 (LO 4) Whetzel Imports reported net income of NT$152,000, declared dividends on ordinary shares of NT$50,000, and had an ending balance in retained earnings of NT$360,000. Ordinary shareholders' equity was NT$700,000 at the beginning of the year and NT$820,000 at the end of the year. Compute the return on ordinary shareholders' equity.

Compute book value per share.

***BE12.15 (LO 6)** The statement of financial position for Lauren Ltd. shows the following: total equity £817,000, ordinary shares issued 44,000 shares, and ordinary shares outstanding 35,000 shares. Compute the book value per share. (No preference shares are outstanding.)

DO IT! Exercises

Analyze statements about corporate organization.

DO IT! 12.1a (LO 1) Indicate whether each of the following statements is true or false. If false, indicate how to correct the statement.

_______ **1.** The corporation is an entity separate and distinct from its owners.

_______ **2.** The liability of shareholders is normally limited to their investment in the corporation.

_______ **3.** The relative lack of government regulation is an advantage of the corporate form of business.

_______ **4.** There is no journal entry to record the authorization of ordinary shares.

_______ **5.** No-par value shares are quite rare today.

Close net income and prepare equity section.

DO IT! 12.1b (LO 1) At the end of its first year of operation, Jaeger Industries has €1,000,000 of ordinary shares and net income of €228,000. Prepare (a) the closing entry for net income and (b) the equity section at year-end.

Journalize issuance of shares.

DO IT! 12.2a (LO 2) Zermatt AG began operations on April 1 by issuing 50,000 of CHF2 par value ordinary shares for cash at CHF13 per share. On April 19, it issued 2,000 ordinary shares to attorneys in settlement of their bill of CHF27,100 for organization costs. On April 27, Zermatt issues 1,000 of CHF100 par value preference shares for cash at CHF110 per share. Journalize the issuance of shares, assuming the shares are not publicly traded.

Journalize treasury share transactions.

DO IT! 12.2b (LO 2) Delsman Limited purchased 2,000 of its £5 par value ordinary shares for £128,000 on August 1. It will hold these shares in the treasury until resold. On December 1, the corporation sold 1,200 treasury shares for cash at £72 per share. Journalize the treasury share transactions.

Determine dividends paid to preference and ordinary shareholders.

DO IT! 12.3a (LO 3) Herr Fashions has 2,000 shares of 7%, €100 par value preference shares outstanding at December 31, 2029. At December 31, 2029, the company declared a €110,000 cash dividend. Determine the dividend paid to preference shareholders and ordinary shareholders under each of the following scenarios.

1. The preference shares are non-cumulative, and the company has not missed any dividends in previous years.

2. The preference shares are non-cumulative, and the company did not pay a dividend in each of the two previous years.
3. The preference shares are cumulative, and the company did not pay a dividend in each of the two previous years.

Determine effects of share dividend and share split.

DO IT! 12.3b (LO 3) Jurgens AG has had 4 years of net income. Due to this success, the market price of its 400,000 shares of £2 par value ordinary shares has increased from £12 per share to £49. During this period, total share capital and share premium remained the same at £2,400,000. Retained earnings increased from £1,800,000 to £12,000,000. CEO E. Rife is considering either a 15% share dividend or a 2-for-1 share split. He asks you to show the before-and-after effects of each option on (a) retained earnings and (b) total equity.

Prepare equity section.

DO IT! 12.4a (LO 4) Anders SA has issued 100,000 shares of €5 par value ordinary shares. It authorized 500,000 shares. The share premium on the ordinary shares is €240,000. The corporation has reacquired 7,000 shares at a cost of €46,000 and is currently holding those shares. Treasury shares were reissued in prior years for €47,000 more than their cost.

The company also has 2,000 shares issued and outstanding of 7%, €100 par value preference shares. It authorized 10,000 shares. The share premium on the preference shares is €23,000. Retained earnings is €372,000.

Prepare the equity section of the statement of financial position.

Compute return on ordinary shareholders' equity.

DO IT! 12.4b (LO 4) On January 1, 2029, Vahsholtz Automotive purchased 5,000 treasury shares. Other information regarding Vahsholtz Automotive is provided as follows.

	2028	2029
Net income	€100,000	€110,000
Dividends on preference shares	€30,000	€30,000
Dividends on ordinary shares	€20,000	€25,000
Weighted-average number of ordinary shares outstanding	50,000	45,000
Ordinary shareholders' equity beginning of year	€600,000	€750,000
Ordinary shareholders' equity end of year	€750,000	€830,000

Compute return on ordinary shareholders' equity for each year.

Exercises

Identify characteristics of a corporation.

E12.1 (LO 1) Victoria has prepared the following list of statements about corporations.

1. A corporation is an entity separate and distinct from its owners.
2. As a legal entity, a corporation has most of the rights and privileges of a person.
3. Most of the largest corporations are privately held corporations.
4. Corporations may buy, own, and sell property; borrow money; enter into legally binding contracts; and sue and be sued.
5. The net income of a corporation is not taxed as a separate entity.
6. Creditors have a legal claim on the personal assets of the owners of a corporation if the corporation does not pay its debts.
7. The transfer of shares from one owner to another requires the approval of either the corporation or other shareholders.
8. The board of directors of a corporation legally owns the corporation.
9. The chief accounting officer of a corporation is the controller.
10. Corporations are subject to fewer regulations than partnerships or proprietorships.

Instructions

Identify each statement as true or false. If false, indicate how to correct the statement.

Identify characteristics of a corporation.

E12.2 (LO 1, 2) Victoria (see E12.1) has studied the information you gave her in that exercise and has come to you with more statements about corporations.

1. Corporation management is both an advantage and a disadvantage of a corporation compared to a proprietorship or a partnership.
2. Limited liability of shareholders, government regulations, and additional taxes are the major disadvantages of a corporation.

3. When a corporation is formed, organization costs are recorded as an asset.
4. Each ordinary share gives the shareholder the ownership rights to vote at shareholder meetings, share in corporate earnings, keep the same percentage ownership when new shares are issued, and share in assets upon liquidation.
5. The number of issued shares is always greater than or equal to the number of authorized shares.
6. A journal entry is required for the authorization of ordinary shares.
7. Publicly held corporations usually issue shares directly to investors.
8. The trading of shares on a securities exchange involves the transfer of already issued shares from an existing shareholder to another investor.
9. The market price of ordinary shares is usually the same as its par value.
10. Retained earnings is the total amount of cash and other assets paid in to the corporation by shareholders in exchange for shares.

Instructions

Identify each statement as true or false. If false, indicate how to correct the statement.

Journalize issuance of ordinary shares.

E12.3 (LO 2) During its first year of operations, Mona Corporation had these transactions pertaining to its ordinary shares.

Jan. 10	Issued 30,000 shares for cash at $5 per share.
July 1	Issued 60,000 shares for cash at $7 per share.

Instructions

a. Journalize the transactions, assuming that the ordinary shares has a par value of $5 per share.
b. Journalize the transactions, assuming that the ordinary shares is no-par with a stated value of $1 per share.

Journalize issuance of ordinary shares.

E12.4 (LO 2) Luis SLU issued 1,000 ordinary shares.

Instructions

Prepare the entry for the issuance under the following assumptions.

a. The shares had a par value of €5 per share and were issued for a total of €48,000.
b. The shares had a stated value of €5 per share and were issued for a total of €48,000.
c. The shares had no par or stated value and were issued for a total of €48,000.
d. The shares had a par value of €5 per share and were issued to attorneys for services during incorporation valued at €48,000.
e. The shares had a par value of €5 per share and were issued for land worth €48,000.

Journalize treasury share transactions.

E12.5 (LO 2) Nanjing Ltd. purchased from its shareholders 5,000 shares of its own previously issued shares for ¥250,000. It later resold 1,300 shares for ¥54 per share, then 2,000 more shares for ¥49 per share, and finally 1,700 shares for ¥40 per share.

Instructions

Prepare journal entries for the purchase of the treasury shares and the three sales of treasury shares.

Journalize issuance of ordinary and preference shares and purchase of treasury shares.

E12.6 (LO 2) Sorocaba Co. had the following transactions during the current period.

Mar. 2	Issued 5,000 R$1 par value ordinary shares to attorneys in payment of a bill for R$44,000 for services performed in helping the company to incorporate.
June 12	Issued 60,000 R$1 par value ordinary shares for cash of R$468,000.
July 11	Issued 1,000 R$100 par value preference shares for cash at R$110 per share.
Nov. 28	Purchased 2,000 treasury shares for R$18,000.

Instructions

Journalize the transactions.

Journalize non-cash ordinary shares transactions.

E12.7 (LO 2) As an auditor for the CPA firm of Hinkson and Calvert, you encounter the following situations in auditing different clients.

1. LR Corporation is a closely held corporation whose shares are not publicly traded. On December 5, the corporation acquired land by issuing 5,000 $20 par value ordinary shares. The owners' asking price for the land was $120,000, and the fair value of the land was $110,000.

2. Vera Corporation is a publicly held corporation whose ordinary shares are traded on the securities markets. On June 1, it acquired land by issuing 20,000 $10 par value ordinary shares. At the time of the exchange, the land was advertised for sale at $250,000. The shares were selling at $11 per share.

Instructions

Prepare the journal entries for each of the situations above.

Journalize treasury share transactions.

E12.8 (LO 2) On January 1, 2029, the equity section of Bergin Stores shows share capital—ordinary (£5 par value) £1,500,000; share premium—ordinary £1,000,000; and retained earnings £1,200,000. During the year, the following treasury share transactions occurred.

Mar. 1	Purchased 50,000 shares for cash at £12 per share.
July 1	Sold 10,000 treasury shares for cash at £14 per share.
Sept. 1	Sold 8,000 treasury shares for cash at £10 per share.

Instructions

a. Journalize the treasury share transactions.

b. Restate the entry for September 1, assuming the treasury shares were sold at £9 per share.

Prepare correct entries for share capital transactions.

E12.9 (LO 2) Anya OAO recently hired a new accountant with extensive experience in accounting for partnerships. Because of the pressure of the new job, the accountant was unable to review his textbooks on the topic of corporation accounting. During the first month, the accountant made the following entries for the corporation's share capital.

May 2	Cash	130,000	
	Share Capital—Ordinary		130,000
	(Issued 10,000 €10 par value ordinary shares at €13 per share)		
10	Cash	580,000	
	Share Capital—Ordinary		580,000
	(Issued 10,000 €50 par value preference shares at €58 per share)		
15	Share Capital—Ordinary	18,000	
	Cash		18,000
	(Purchased 1,200 ordinary shares for the treasury at €15 per share)		
31	Cash	8,000	
	Share Capital—Ordinary		5,000
	Gain on Sale of Shares		3,000
	(Sold 500 treasury shares at €16 per share)		

Instructions

On the basis of the explanation for each entry, prepare the entry that should have been made for the share capital transactions.

Journalize cash dividends; indicate statement presentation.

E12.10 (LO 3, 4) On January 1, Chevon Enterprises had 95,000 no-par ordinary shares issued and outstanding. The shares have a stated value of €5 per share. During the year, the following occurred.

Apr. 1	Issued 25,000 additional ordinary shares for €17 per share.
June 15	Declared a cash dividend of €1 per share to shareholders of record on June 30.
July 10	Paid the €1 cash dividend.
Dec. 1	Issued 2,000 additional ordinary shares for €19 per share.
15	Declared a cash dividend on outstanding shares of €1.20 per share to shareholders of record on December 31.

Instructions

a. Prepare the entries to record these transactions.

b. How are dividends and dividends payable reported in the financial statements prepared at December 31?

Allocate cash dividends to preference and ordinary shares.

E12.11 (LO 3) Knudsen Bakeries was organized on January 1, 2028. During its first year, the company issued 2,000 shares of HK$50 par value preference shares and 100,000 shares of HK$10 par value ordinary shares. At December 31, the company declared the following cash dividends: 2028, HK$5,000; 2029, HK$12,000; and 2030, HK$28,000 (HK$ in thousands).

Instructions

a. Show the allocation of dividends to each class of shares, assuming the preference share dividend is 6% and non-cumulative.

b. Show the allocation of dividends to each class of shares, assuming the preference share dividend is 7% and cumulative.

c. Journalize the declaration of the cash dividend at December 31, 2030, under part (b).

Journalize share dividends.

E12.12 (LO 3) On January 1, 2029, Lenne Corporation had $1,200,000 of share capital—ordinary outstanding that was issued at par and retained earnings of $750,000. The company issued 30,000 ordinary shares at par on July 1 and earned net income of $400,000 for the year.

Instructions

Journalize the declaration of a 15% share dividend on December 10, 2029, for the following two independent assumptions.

a. Par value is $10 and market price is $15.

b. Par value is $5 and market price is $8.

Compare effects of a share dividend and a share split.

E12.13 (LO 3) On October 31, the equity section of Lucerne AG consists of share capital—ordinary CHF500,000 and retained earnings CHF900,000. Lucerne is considering the following two courses of action: (1) declaring a 5% share dividend on the 50,000, CHF10 par value shares outstanding, or (2) effecting a 2-for-1 share split that will reduce par value to CHF5 per share. The current market price is CHF14 per share.

Instructions

Prepare a tabular summary of the effects of the alternative actions on the components of equity, outstanding shares, and par value per share. Use the following column headings: Before Action, After Share Dividend, and After Share Split.

Indicate account balances after a share dividend.

E12.14 (LO 3) On October 1, Little Bobby Company's equity is as follows.

Share capital—ordinary, €5 par value	€400,000
Share premium—ordinary	25,000
Retained earnings	155,000
Total equity	€580,000

On October 1, Little Bobby declares and distributes a 10% share dividend when the market price is €15 per share.

Instructions

a. Determine the par value per share (1) before the share dividend and (2) after the share dividend.

b. Indicate the balances in the three equity accounts after the share dividend shares have been distributed.

Prepare correcting entries for dividends and a share split.

E12.15 (LO 3) Before preparing financial statements for the current year, the chief accountant for Toso Shipping discovered the following errors in the accounts.

1. The declaration and payment of NT$50,000 cash dividend was recorded as a debit to Interest Expense NT$50,000 and a credit to Cash NT$50,000.
2. A 10% share dividend (1,000 shares) was declared on the NT$20 par value shares when the market price per share was NT$36. The only entry made was Share Dividends (Dr.) NT$20,000 and Dividend Payable (Cr.) NT$20,000. The shares have not been issued.
3. A 4-for-1 share split involving the issue of 400,000 shares of NT$5 par value ordinary shares for 100,000 shares of NT$20 par value ordinary shares was recorded as a debit to Retained Earnings NT$2,000,000 and a credit to Share Capital—Ordinary NT$2,000,000.

Instructions

Prepare the correcting entries at December 31.

E12.16 (LO 4) On January 1, 2029, Eddy Industries had retained earnings of £650,000. During the year, Eddy had the following selected transactions.

Prepare a retained earnings statement.

1. Declared cash dividends £120,000.
2. Earned net income £350,000.
3. Declared share dividends £90,000.

Instructions

Prepare a retained earnings statement for the year.

E12.17 (LO 4) Bindra A.Ş. reported retained earnings at December 31, 2028, of ₺310,000. Bindra had 200,000 shares outstanding at the beginning of 2029.

Prepare a retained earnings statement.

The following transactions occurred during 2029.

1. A cash dividend of ₺0.50 per share was declared and paid.
2. A 5% share dividend was declared and distributed when the market price per share was ₺15 per share.
3. Net income was ₺285,000.

Instructions

Prepare a retained earnings statement for 2029.

E12.18 (LO 4) Dirk SA reported the following balances at December 31, 2028: share capital—ordinary €500,000, share premium—ordinary €100,000, and retained earnings €250,000. During 2029, the following transactions affected equity.

Prepare an equity section.

1. Issued preference shares with a par value of €125,000 for €200,000.
2. Purchased treasury shares (ordinary) for €40,000.
3. Earned net income of €180,000.
4. Declared and paid cash dividends of €56,000.

Instructions

Prepare the equity section of Dirk SA's December 31, 2029, statement of financial position.

E12.19 (LO 4) The following accounts appear in the ledger of Tiger Ltd. after the books are closed at December 31 (¥ in thousands).

Prepare an equity section.

Share Capital—Ordinary, no par, ¥1 stated value, 400,000 shares authorized; 300,000 shares issued	¥ 300,000
Ordinary Share Dividends Distributable	30,000
Share Premium—Ordinary	1,200,000
Share Capital—Preference, ¥5 par value, 8%, 40,000 shares authorized; 30,000 shares issued	150,000
Retained Earnings	800,000
Treasury Shares—Ordinary (10,000 shares)	74,000
Share Premium—Preference	344,000

Instructions

Prepare the equity section at December 31, assuming retained earnings is restricted for plant expansion in the amount of ¥100,000.

E12.20 (LO 4) The equity section of Atrio Ltd. showed the following: share premium €6,101, share capital—ordinary €925, share capital—preference €58, retained earnings €7,420, and treasury shares €2,828. (All amounts are in millions.)

Prepare an equity section.

The preference shares have 577,740 shares authorized, with a par value of €100 and an annual €3.50 per share cumulative dividend preference. At December 31, 577,649 preference shares are issued and 546,024 shares are outstanding. There are 1.8 billion shares of €1 par value ordinary shares authorized, of which 924.6 million are issued and 844.8 million are outstanding at December 31.

Instructions

Prepare the equity section, including disclosure of all relevant data.

Prepare an equity section.

E12.21 (LO 4) The following equity accounts are in the ledger of Eudaley Group at December 31, 2029.

Share Capital—Ordinary (€5 stated value)	€1,500,000
Share Premium—Preference	280,000
Share Premium—Ordinary	900,000
Share Capital—Preference (8%, €100 par)	500,000
Retained Earnings	1,234,000
Treasury Shares (10,000 ordinary shares)	120,000

Instructions

Prepare the equity section of the statement of financial position at December 31, 2029.

Answer questions about equity section.

E12.22 (LO 2, 4) Writing The equity section of Ahab SA at December 31 is as follows.

Ahab SA
Statement of Financial Position (partial)

Equity	
Share capital—preference, cumulative, 10,000 shares authorized, 5,000 shares issued and outstanding	€ 300,000
Share capital—ordinary, no par, 750,000 shares authorized, 600,000 shares issued	1,200,000
Retained earnings	1,858,000
Less: Treasury shares—ordinary (75,000 shares)	75,000
Total equity	€3,283,000

Instructions

From a review of the equity section, as chief accountant, write a memo to the president of the company answering the following questions.

a. How many ordinary shares are outstanding?

b. Assuming there is a stated value, what is the stated value of the ordinary shares?

c. What is the par value of the preference shares?

Calculate ratio to evaluate earnings performance.

E12.23 (LO 4) The following financial information is available for Plummer SA.

	2029	2028
Average ordinary shareholders' equity	€1,200,000	€900,000
Dividends paid to ordinary shareholders	50,000	30,000
Dividends paid to preference shareholders	20,000	20,000
Net income	290,000	200,000
Market price of ordinary shares	20	15

The weighted-average number of ordinary shares outstanding was 80,000 for 2028 and 100,000 for 2029.

Instructions

Calculate return on ordinary shareholders' equity for 2029 and 2028.

Compute return on equity.

E12.24 (LO 4) In 2029, Orasco SA had net sales of R$600,000 and cost of goods sold of R$360,000. Operating expenses were R$153,000, and interest expense was R$7,500. The corporation's tax rate is 30%. The corporation declared preference dividends of R$15,000 in 2029, and its average ordinary shareholders' equity during the year was R$200,000.

Instructions

Compute Orasco's return on ordinary shareholders' equity for 2029.

Prepare an equity section.

***E12.25 (LO 4, 6)** The equity section of Santano Group showed the following: share premium €6,101, share capital—ordinary €925, share capital—preference €58, retained earnings €7,420, and treasury shares €2,828. (All amounts are in millions.)

The preference shares have 577,740 shares authorized, with a par value of €100 and an annual €3.50 per share cumulative dividend preference. At December 31, 577,649 preference shares are issued and 546,024 shares are outstanding. There are 1.8 billion shares of €1 par value ordinary shares authorized, of which 924.6 million are issued and 844.8 million are outstanding at December 31.

Instructions

a. Compute the book value per share of ordinary shares, assuming there are no preference dividends in arrears. (Round to two decimals.)

b. Compute the book value per share of ordinary shares, assuming there is one year of preference dividends in arrears. (Round to two decimals.)

***E12.26 (LO 4, 6)** At December 31, Gorden Limited has total equity of £3,200,000. Included in this total are share capital—preference £500,000 and share premium—preference £50,000. There are 10,000 shares of £50 par value, 8% cumulative preference shares outstanding. At year-end, 200,000 ordinary shares are outstanding.

Compute book value per share with preference shares.

Instructions

Compute the book value per share of ordinary shares, under each of the following assumptions.

a. There are no preference dividends in arrears, and the preference shares do not have a call price.

b. Preference dividends are one year in arrears, and the preference shares have a call price of £60 per share.

***E12.27 (LO 3, 6)** On October 1, Venden Holdings' equity is as follows.

Compute book value per share; indicate account balances after a share dividend.

Share capital—ordinary, £5 par value	£400,000
Share premium—ordinary	25,000
Retained earnings	225,000
Total equity	£650,000

On October 1, Venden declares and distributes a 12% share dividend when the market price of the shares is £14 per share.

Instructions

a. Compute the book value per share (1) before the share dividend and (2) after the share dividend. (Round to two decimals.)

b. Indicate the balances in the three equity accounts after the dividend shares have been distributed.

Problems

P12.1 (LO 2, 4) Gão Limited was organized on January 1, 2029. It is authorized to issue 10,000 8%, HK$1,000 par value preference shares, and 500,000 no-par ordinary shares with a stated value of HK$20 per share. The following share transactions were completed during the first year.

Journalize share transactions, post, and prepare share capital section.

Jan. 10	Issued 100,000 ordinary shares for cash at HK$48 per share.
Mar. 1	Issued 5,000 preference shares for cash at HK$1,050 per share.
Apr. 1	Issued 18,000 ordinary shares for land. The asking price of the land was HK$980,000. The fair value of the land was HK$920,000.
May 1	Issued 80,000 ordinary shares for cash at HK$45 per share.
Aug. 1	Issued 10,000 ordinary shares to attorneys in payment of their bill of HK$320,000 for services provided in helping the company organize.
Sept. 1	Issued 10,000 ordinary shares for cash at HK$50 per share.
Nov. 1	Issued 1,000 preference shares for cash at HK$1,060 per share.

Instructions

a. Journalize the transactions.

b. Post to the equity accounts. (Use J5 as the posting reference.)

c. Prepare the share capital section of the statement of financial position at December 31, 2029.

c. Total equity HK$16,450,000

Journalize and post treasury share transactions, and prepare equity section.

P12.2 (LO 2, 4) Elston Limited had the following equity accounts on January 1, 2029: Share Capital—Ordinary (£5 par) £400,000, Share Premium—Ordinary £200,000, and Retained Earnings £100,000. In 2029, the company had the following treasury share transactions.

Mar.	1	Purchased 5,000 shares at £9 per share.
June	1	Sold 500 shares at £12 per share.
Sept.	1	Sold 2,500 shares at £10 per share.
Dec.	1	Sold 1,000 shares at £6 per share.

Elston uses the cost method of accounting for treasury shares. In 2029, the company reported net income of £34,000.

Instructions

a. Journalize the treasury share transactions, and prepare the closing entry at December 31, 2029, for net income.

b. Treasury Shares £9,000

b. Open accounts for (1) Share Premium—Treasury, (2) Treasury Shares, and (3) Retained Earnings. Post to these accounts using J10 as the posting reference.

c. Total equity £726,000

c. Prepare the equity section for Elston Limited at December 31, 2029.

Journalize and post transactions, prepare equity section.

P12.3 (LO 2, 4) The equity accounts of Terrell SE on January 1, 2029, were as follows.

Share Capital—Preference (9%, €50 par, cumulative, 10,000 shares authorized)	€ 400,000
Share Capital—Ordinary (€1 stated value, 2,000,000 shares authorized)	1,000,000
Share Premium—Preference	100,000
Share Premium—Ordinary	1,450,000
Retained Earnings	1,816,000
Treasury Shares—Ordinary (20,000 shares)	50,000

During 2029, the company had the following transactions and events pertaining to its equity.

Feb.	1	Issued 30,000 ordinary shares for €120,000.
Apr.	14	Sold 9,000 treasury shares—ordinary for €42,000.
Sept.	3	Issued 7,000 ordinary shares for a patent valued at €32,000.
Nov.	10	Purchased 1,000 ordinary shares for the treasury at a cost of €6,000.
Dec.	31	Determined that net income for the year was €452,000.

No dividends were declared during the year.

Instructions

a. Journalize the transactions and the closing entry for net income.

b. Enter the beginning balances in the accounts, and post the journal entries to the equity accounts. (Use J5 for the posting reference.)

c. Total equity €5,356,000

c. Prepare an equity section at December 31, 2029, including the disclosure of the preference dividends in arrears.

Prepare dividend entries and equity section.

P12.4 (LO 3, 4) On January 1, 2029, Prasad SpA had the following equity accounts.

Share Capital—Ordinary (€25 par value, 48,000 shares issued and outstanding)	€1,200,000
Share Premium—Ordinary	200,000
Retained Earnings	600,000

During the year, the following transactions occurred.

Feb.	1	Declared a €1 cash dividend per share to shareholders of record on February 15, payable March 1.
Mar.	1	Paid the dividend declared in February.
Apr.	1	Announced a 5-for-1 share split. Prior to the split, the market price per share was €36.
July	1	Declared a 10% share dividend to shareholders of record on July 15, distributable July 31. On July 1, the market price was €7 per share.
July	31	Issued the shares for the share dividend.
Dec.	1	Declared a €0.40 per share dividend to shareholders of record on December 15, payable January 5, 2030.
	31	Determined that net income for the year was €350,000.

Instructions

a. Journalize the transactions and the closing entries for net income and dividends.

b. Enter the beginning balances, and post the entries to the equity accounts. (*Note:* Open additional equity accounts as needed.)

c. Prepare an equity section at December 31.

c. Total equity €2,196,400

Prepare retained earnings statement and equity section, and allocation of dividends.

P12.5 (LO 3, 4) The post-closing trial balance of Russo SpA at December 31, 2029, contains the following equity accounts.

Share Capital—Preference (12,000 shares issued)	€ 600,000
Share Capital—Ordinary (250,000 shares issued)	2,500,000
Share Premium—Preference	250,000
Share Premium—Ordinary	425,000
Ordinary Share Dividends Distributable	250,000
Retained Earnings	1,078,000

A review of the accounting records reveals the following.

1. No errors have been made in recording 2029 transactions or in preparing the closing entry for net income.
2. Preference shares are €50 par, 8%, and cumulative; 12,000 shares have been outstanding since January 1, 2028.
3. Authorized shares are 20,000 preference shares, 500,000 ordinary shares with a €10 par value.
4. The January 1 balance in Retained Earnings was €1,158,000.
5. On July 1, 20,000 ordinary shares were issued for cash at €16 per share.
6. A cash dividend of €240,000 was declared and properly allocated to preference and ordinary shares on October 1. No dividends were paid to preference shareholders in 2028.
7. On December 31, a 10% ordinary share dividend was declared out of retained earnings on ordinary shares when the market price per share was €17.
8. Net income for the year was €585,000.
9. On December 31, 2029, the directors authorized disclosure of a €200,000 restriction of retained earnings for plant expansion. (Use Note X.)

Instructions

a. Reproduce the Retained Earnings account for 2029.

b. Prepare a retained earnings statement for 2029.

c. Prepare an equity section at December 31, 2029.

d. Compute the allocation of the cash dividend to preference and ordinary shares.

c. Total equity €5,103,000

Prepare entries for share transactions and prepare equity section.

P12.6 (LO 3, 4) Jude Limited has been authorized to issue 20,000 £100 par value, 10%, non-cumulative preference shares and 1,000,000 no-par ordinary shares. The company assigned a £2.50 stated value to the ordinary shares. At December 31, 2029, the ledger contained the following balances pertaining to equity.

Share Capital—Preference	£ 120,000
Share Premium—Preference	12,000
Share Capital—Ordinary	1,000,000
Share Premium—Ordinary	1,600,000
Treasury Shares—Ordinary (1,000 shares)	9,000
Share Premium—Treasury	1,000
Retained Earnings	82,000

The preference shares were issued for land having a fair value of £132,000. All ordinary shares issued were for cash. In November, 1,500 ordinary shares were purchased for the treasury at a per share cost of £9. In December, 500 treasury shares were sold for £11 per share. No dividends were declared in 2029.

Instructions

a. Prepare the journal entries for the:

1. Issuance of preference shares for land.
2. Issuance of ordinary shares for cash.

3. Purchase of treasury shares (ordinary) for cash.
4. Sale of treasury shares for cash.

b. Total equity £2,806,000

b. Prepare the equity section at December 31, 2029.

Prepare dividend entries and equity section.

P12.7 (LO 3, 4) On January 1, 2029, Primo plc had the following equity accounts.

Share Capital—Ordinary (£10 par value, 75,000 shares issued and outstanding)	£750,000
Share Premium—Ordinary	200,000
Retained Earnings	540,000

During the year, the following transactions occurred.

Jan. 15	Declared a £2 cash dividend per share to shareholders of record on January 31, payable February 15.
Feb. 15	Paid the dividend declared in January.
Apr. 15	Declared a 10% share dividend to shareholders of record on April 30, distributable May 15. On April 15, the market price of the shares was £15 per share.
May 15	Issued the shares for the share dividend.
July 1	Announced a 2-for-1 share split. The market price per share prior to the announcement was £15. (The new par value is £5.)
Dec. 1	Declared a £0.60 per share cash dividend to shareholders of record on December 15, payable January 10, 2030.
31	Determined that net income for the year was £260,000.

Instructions

a. Journalize the transactions and the closing entries for net income and dividends.

b. Enter the beginning balances, and post the entries to the equity accounts. (*Note:* Open additional equity accounts as needed.)

c. Total equity £1,501,000

c. Prepare an equity section at December 31.

Prepare equity section; compute book value per share.

***P12.8 (LO 4, 6)** The following equity accounts are in the ledger of Westin SE at December 31, 2029.

Share Capital—Ordinary (€10 stated value)	€1,500,000
Share Premium—Treasury	6,000
Share Premium—Ordinary	690,000
Share Premium—Preference	42,400
Share Capital—Preference (8%, €100 par, non-cumulative)	360,000
Retained Earnings	776,000
Treasury Shares—Ordinary (7,000 shares)	92,000

Instructions

a. Total equity €3,282,400

a. Prepare an equity section at December 31, 2029.

b. Compute the book value per share of the ordinary shares, assuming the preference shares have a call price of €110 per share.

Prepare statement of changes in equity

***P12.9 (LO 2, 3, 5)** On January 1, 2029, Goodhue Inc. had the following equity balances.

Share Capital—Ordinary (400,000 shares issued)	$800,000
Share Premium—Ordinary	500,000
Ordinary Share Dividends Distributable	120,000
Retained Earnings	600,000

During 2029, the following transactions and events occurred.

1. Issued 60,000 $2 par value ordinary shares as a result of 15% share dividend declared on December 15, 2028.
2. Issued 30,000 ordinary shares for cash at $4 per share.
3. Purchased 25,000 ordinary shares for the treasury at $5 per share.
4. Declared and paid a cash dividend of $111,000.
5. Sold 8,000 treasury shares for cash at $5 per share.
6. Earned net income of $360,000.

Instructions

Total equity $2,304,000

Prepare a statement of changes in equity for the year.

***P12.10 (LO 4, 6)** On January 1, 2029, Renai Company had the following equity accounts.

Prepare equity section; compute book value per share.

Share Capital—Preference (12%, $100 par, cumulative, authorized 10,000 shares)	$ 800,000
Share Capital—Ordinary ($10 par, authorized 400,000 shares)	2,000,000
Share Premium—Preference	160,000
Share Premium—Ordinary	2,800,000
Retained Earnings	3,632,000
Treasury Shares—Ordinary (2,000 shares)	80,000

During the year, the following transactions occurred:

Feb. 15	Issued 4,000 $10 par value ordinary shares and received cash $200,000.
Apr. 18	Sold 1,200 treasury shares for cash $56,000.
Aug. 31	Issued 1,000 ordinary shares in exchange for a patent valued at $50,000.
Dec. 5	Repurchase 200 ordinary treasury shares from the market for cash $12,000.
Dec. 31	Determined that net income for the year was $753,640.

Assume the call price of preference shares is $125, and that Renai Company did not have any cumulative dividends in arrears before January 1, 2029.

Instructions

a. Explain the meanings of the book value per share of the ordinary shares.

b. Prepare an equity section of statement of financial position at December 31, 2029.

c. Compute the book value per share of the ordinary shares.

b. Total equity $10,359,640

Accounting Cycle Review

ACR12 Voltaire SA's statement of financial position at December 31, 2028, is presented as follows.

Voltaire SA
Statement of Financial Position
December 31, 2028

Land	€ 40,000	Share capital—ordinary	
Buildings	130,000	(€1 par)	€ 50,000
Accumulated depreciation—buildings	(20,000)	Retained earnings	147,400
Supplies	4,400	Accounts payable	25,600
Accounts receivable	45,500		€223,000
Allowance for doubtful accounts	(1,500)		
Cash	24,600		
	€223,000		

During 2029, the following transactions occurred.

1. On January 1, 2029, Voltaire issued 1,500 €20 par, 6% preference shares for €33,000.
2. On January 1, 2029, Voltaire also issued 900 €1 par value ordinary shares for €6,300.
3. Voltaire performed services for €276,000 on account.
4. On April 1, 2029, Voltaire collected fees of €36,000 in advance for services to be performed from April 1, 2029, to March 31, 2030.
5. Voltaire collected €267,000 from customers on account.
6. Voltaire bought €26,100 of supplies on account.
7. Voltaire paid €32,200 on accounts payable.
8. Voltaire reacquired 400 ordinary shares on June 1, 2029, for €8 per share.
9. Paid other operating expenses of €188,200.
10. On December 31, 2029, Voltaire declared the annual preference share dividend and a €0.50 per share dividend on the outstanding ordinary shares, all payable on January 15, 2030.
11. An account receivable of €1,300 which originated in 2028 is written off as uncollectible.

Adjustment data:

1. A count of supplies indicates that €5,900 of supplies remain unused at year-end.
2. Recorded revenue recognized from item 4 above.
3. The allowance for doubtful accounts should have a balance of €3,500 at year-end.
4. Depreciation is recorded on the building on a straight-line basis based on a 30-year life and a residual value of €10,000.
5. The income tax rate is 30%. (*Hint:* Prepare the income statement up to income before taxes and multiply by 30% to compute the amount of taxes.)

Instructions

(You may want to set up T-accounts to determine ending balances.)

a. Prepare journal entries for the transactions listed above and adjusting entries.

b. Prepare an adjusted trial balance at December 31, 2029.

c. Prepare an income statement and a retained earnings statement for the year ending December 31, 2029, and a classified statement of financial position as of December 31, 2029.

b. Totals €647,620
c. Net income €58,030
Tot. assets €344,900

Data Analytics in Action

Using Data Visualization to Analyze Dividends

DA12.1 Data visualization can be used to compare dividends and share prices.

Excel

Example: The dividend yield ratio is the annual dividend per share divided by the market price per share. Two factors can contribute to a high dividend yield: (1) the payment of a large dividend, which causes the numerator to be large, or (2) having a low market share price, which causes the denominator to be small.

Ford Motor Company (USA) is considered to have a high dividend yield. But how does Ford's dividend yield compare to its competitors? Consider the following chart, which presents the dividends per share and dividend yields for Ford, **General Motors** (USA), **Toyota** (JPN), and **Tesla** (USA).

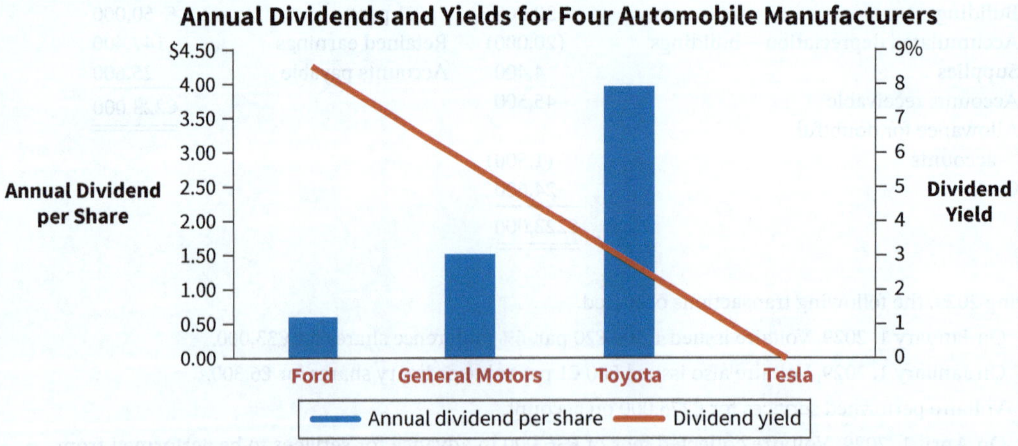

Source: Based on MarketBeat and Nasdaq.

If you examine the pattern of dividend yields, observe that both General Motors and Toyota have higher dividends than Ford, while Tesla currently pays no dividends. The dividend yields are much higher for Ford than those of General Motors and Toyota, while Tesla has a zero yield due to not paying dividends.

For this case, you will review data for these four companies to determine how the effect of market share prices can help explain the dividend yield. You will create and analyze a combo column and line chart to determine how an investor might balance share prices and dividend yields when deciding which shares to buy.

Go to the Wiley online course for complete case details and instructions.

Using Data Analytics to Compare the Effect of Share Splits

DA12.2 As noted in the chapter, Warren Buffet, the CEO of **Berkshire Hathaway** (USA), does not believe in share splits. On the other hand, **The Walt Disney Company** (USA) shares have been split a few times. For this case, you will use share prices from both companies to create and analyze a line chart and a combo clustered column and line chart.

Excel

Go to the Wiley online course for complete case details and instructions.

Expand Your Critical Thinking

Financial Reporting Problem: TSMC, Ltd. (TWN)

CT12.1 The equity section for **TSMC** is shown in Appendix A. The complete annual report, including the notes to the financial statements (use Note 22), is available at the company's website.

Instructions

a. What is the par or stated value per share of TSMC's ordinary shares?

b. What percentage of TSMC's authorized ordinary shares was issued at December 31, 2020?

c. How many ordinary shares were outstanding at December 31, 2020, and at December 31, 2019?

Comparative Analysis Problem: Nestlé SA (CHE) vs. Delfi Limited (SGP)

CT12.2 **Nestlé**'s financial statements are presented in Appendix B. Financial statements of **Delfi Limited** are presented in Appendix C. The complete annual reports of Nestlé and Delfi, including the notes to the financial statements, are available at each company's respective website.

Instructions

a. What is the par or stated value of Nestlé's (Note 17) and Delfi's (Note 28) ordinary shares?

b. How many shares were issued by Nestlé at December 31, 2020, and by Delfi at December 31, 2020?

c. How many treasury shares are held by Nestlé at December 31, 2020, and by Delfi at December 31, 2020?

d. How many Nestlé ordinary shares are outstanding at December 31, 2020? How many Delfi ordinary shares are outstanding at December 31, 2020?

Real-World Focus

CT12.3 Use the equity section of an annual report and identify the major components.

Instructions

Select a well-known company, search the Internet for its most recent annual report, and then answer the following questions.

a. What is the company's name?

b. What classes of share capital has the company issued?

c. For each class:

1. How many shares are authorized, issued, and/or outstanding?
2. What is the par value?

d. What are the company's retained earnings?

e. Has the company acquired treasury shares? How many?

Decision-Making Across the Organization

CT12.4 The shareholders' meeting for Kissinger SE has been in progress for some time. The chief financial officer for Kissinger is presently reviewing the company's financial statements and is explaining the items that comprise the equity section of the statement of financial position for the current year. The equity section of Kissinger at December 31, 2029, is as follows.

Kissinger SE
Statement of Financial Position (partial)
December 31, 2029

Share capital—preference, authorized 1,000,000 shares cumulative, €100 par value, €8 per share, 6,000 shares issued and outstanding	€ 600,000
Share capital—ordinary, authorized 5,000,000 shares, €1 par value, 3,000,000 shares issued, and 2,700,000 outstanding	3,000,000
Share premium—preference	50,000
Share premium—ordinary	25,000,000
Retained earnings	900,000
Less: Treasury shares (300,000 shares)	9,300,000
Total equity	€20,250,000

At the meeting, shareholders have raised a number of questions regarding the equity section.

Instructions

With the class divided into groups, answer the following questions as if you were the chief financial officer for Kissinger SE.

a. "What does the cumulative provision related to the preference shares mean?"

b. "I thought the ordinary shares were presently selling at €29.75, but the company has the shares stated at €1 per share. How can that be?"

c. "Why is the company buying back its ordinary shares? Furthermore, the treasury shares have a debit balance because they are subtracted from equity. Why are treasury shares not reported as an asset if they have a debit balance?"

Communication Activity

CT12.5 Jerrod Platt, your uncle, is an inventor who has decided to incorporate. Uncle Jerrod knows that you are an accounting major at U.N.O. In a recent email to you, he ends with the question, "I'm filling out an incorporation application. Can you tell me the difference in the following terms: (1) authorized shares, (2) issued shares, (3) outstanding shares, and (4) preference shares?"

Instructions

In a brief email, differentiate for Uncle Jerrod among the four different share terms. Write the email to be friendly, yet professional.

Ethics Case

CT12.6 The R&D division of Hancock Chemical Ltd. has just developed a chemical for sterilizing the vicious Brazilian "killer bees" which are invading Mexico and the southern states of the United States. The president of Hancock is anxious to get the chemical on the market to boost the company's profits. He believes his job is in jeopardy because of decreasing sales and profits. Hancock has an opportunity to sell this chemical in Central American countries, where the laws are much more relaxed than in the United States.

The director of Hancock's R&D division strongly recommends further testing in the laboratory for side-effects of this chemical on other insects, birds, animals, plants, and even humans. He cautions the president, "We could be sued from all sides if the chemical has tragic side-effects that we didn't even test for in the labs." The president answers, "We can't wait an additional year for your lab tests. We can avoid losses from such lawsuits by establishing a separate wholly owned corporation to shield Hancock Ltd. from such lawsuits. We can't lose any more than our investment in the new corporation, and we'll invest in just the patent covering this chemical. We'll reap the benefits if the chemical works and is safe, and avoid the losses from lawsuits if it's a disaster." The following week, Hancock creates a new wholly owned corporation called Badell Ltd., sells the chemical patent to it for $10, and watches the spraying begin.

Instructions

a. Who are the stakeholders in this situation?

b. Are the president's motives and actions ethical?

c. Can Hancock shield itself against losses of Badell Ltd.?

Answers to Insight and Accounting Across the Organization Questions

The Impact of Company Social Responsibility Q: Why are ESG-related shareholder proposals increasing? **A:** These proposals are increasing as more and more investors believe that environmental, social, and governance factors can significantly impact shareholder value over the long term.

How to Read Share Quotes Q: For shares traded on organized exchanges, how are the prices per share established? What factors might influence the price of shares in the marketplace? **A:** The prices per share are established by the interaction between buyers and sellers of the shares. Factors that might influence share prices include a company's anticipated future earnings, its current financial position, and the current state of the economy.

Why Would a Company Buy Its Own Shares? Q: What signal might a large share repurchase send to investors regarding management's belief about the company's growth opportunities? **A:** A large share repurchase might signal that management believes that future strong earnings are likely and that the current share price is undervalued.

Dividend Aristocrats Q: Why is a company's dividend policy so important to shareholders? **A:** Consistent dividend payers have achieved a higher growth rate than non-dividend payers, which can significantly impact investors' returns.

Split or Not? Q: Why does Warren Buffett oppose share splits? **A:** Buffett prefers to attract shareholders who will make a long-term commitment to his company, as opposed to traders who will only hold their investment for a short period of time. He believes that a high share price discourages short-term investment.

A Look at U.S. GAAP

LEARNING OBJECTIVE 7

Compare the accounting for equity under IFRS and U.S. GAAP.

The accounting for transactions related to equity, such as issuance of shares, purchase of treasury shares, and cash and share (stock) dividends, are similar under both IFRS and GAAP. Major differences relate to terminology used, introduction of items such as revaluation surplus, and presentation of equity information.

Key Points

Following are the key similarities and differences between IFRS and GAAP as related to equity.

Similarities

- Aside from terminology used, the accounting transactions for the issuance of shares and the purchase of treasury shares are similar.
- Like IFRS, GAAP does not allow a company to record gains or losses on purchases of its own shares.

Differences

- Under IFRS, the term **reserves** is used to describe all equity accounts other than those arising from contributed (paid-in) capital. This would include, for example, reserves related to retained earnings, asset revaluations, and fair value differences.
- Many countries have a different mix of investor groups than in the United States. For example, in Germany, financial institutions like banks are not only major creditors of corporations but often are the largest corporate shareholders as well. In the United States, Asia, and the United Kingdom, many companies rely on substantial investment from private investors.
- There are often terminology differences for equity accounts. The following summarizes some of the common differences in terminology.

GAAP	IFRS
Common stock	Share capital—ordinary
Stockholders	Shareholders
Par value	Nominal or face value
Authorized stock	Authorized share capital
Preferred stock	Share capital—preference
Paid-in capital	Issued/allocated share capital
Paid-in capital in excess of par—common stock	Share premium—ordinary
Paid-in capital in excess of par—preferred stock	Share premium—preference
Retained earnings	Retained earnings or Retained profits
Retained earnings deficit	Accumulated losses
Accumulated other comprehensive income	General reserve and other reserve accounts

As an example of how similar transactions use different terminology under GAAP, consider the accounting for the issuance of 1,000 shares of $1 par value share capital for $5 per share. Under GAAP, the entry is as follows.

Cash	5,000	
Common Stock		1,000
Paid-in Capital in Excess of Par		4,000

- A major difference between IFRS and GAAP relates to the account Revaluation Surplus. Revaluation surplus arises under IFRS because companies are permitted to revalue their property, plant, and equipment to fair value under certain circumstances. This account is part of general reserves under IFRS and is not considered contributed capital.
- IFRS often uses terms such as **retained profits** or **accumulated profit or loss** to describe retained earnings. The term **retained earnings** is also often used.
- Equity is given various descriptions under GAAP, such as shareholders' equity, owners' equity, and stockholders' equity.

GAAP Practice

GAAP Self-Test Questions

1. Which of the following is **true**?
   a. In the United States, the primary corporate shareholders are financial institutions.
   b. Share capital means total assets under GAAP.
   c. Under both IFRS and GAAP, the accounting for the issuance of shares and the purchases of treasury shares are similar.
   d. The accounting for treasury shares differs extensively between GAAP and IFRS.

2. Under GAAP, the amount of capital received in excess of par value would be credited to:
   a. Retained Earnings.
   b. Paid-in Capital in Excess of Par.
   c. Share Premium.
   d. Par value is not used under GAAP.

3. Which of the following is **false**?
   a. Under GAAP, companies cannot record gains on transactions involving their own shares.
   b. Under IFRS, companies cannot record gains on transactions involving their own shares.
   c. Under IFRS, the statement of changes in equity is a required statement.
   d. Under GAAP, a company records a revaluation surplus when it experiences an increase in the price of its ordinary shares.

4. Which of the following does **not** represent a pair of GAAP/IFRS-comparable terms?
   a. Paid-in capital in excess of par/Share premium.
   b. Treasury stock/Repurchase reserve.
   c. Common stock/Share capital.
   d. Preferred stock/Preference shares.

5. The basic accounting for cash dividends and share dividends:
   a. is different under IFRS versus GAAP.
   b. is the same under IFRS and GAAP.
   c. differs only for the accounting for cash dividends between GAAP and IFRS.
   d. differs only for the accounting for share dividends between GAAP and IFRS.

GAAP Exercises

GAAP12.1 On May 10, Jaurez Corporation issues 1,000 shares of $10 par value common stock for cash at $18 per share. Journalize the issuance of the shares.

GAAP12.2 Meenen Corporation has the following accounts at December 31, 2029: Common Stock, $10 par, 5,000 shares issued, $50,000; Paid-in Capital in Excess of Par, $10,000; Retained Earnings, $45,000; and Treasury Stock, 500 shares, $11,000. Prepare the stockholders' equity section of the balance sheet. For an example of a stockholders' equity section, see the **Apple** financial statements in Appendix D.

GAAP12.3 Overton Co. had the following transactions during the current period.

Mar. 2	Issued 5,000 shares of $1 par value common stock to attorneys in payment of a bill for $30,000 for services performed in helping the company to incorporate.
June 12	Issued 60,000 shares of $1 par value common stock for cash of $375,000.
July 11	Issued 1,000 shares of $100 par value preferred stock for cash at $110 per share.
Nov. 28	Purchased 2,000 treasury shares for $80,000.

Instructions

Journalize the above transactions.

GAAP Financial Reporting Problem: Apple Inc. (USA)

GAAP12.4 The financial statements of **Apple** are presented in Appendix D. The complete annual report, including the notes to its financial statements, is available at the company's website.

Instructions

Use the company's annual report to answer the following questions.

a. Determine the following amounts at September 26, 2020: (1) total stockholders' equity and (2) number of treasury shares.

b. Did the company declare and pay any dividends for the year ended September 26, 2020?

c. Examine the stockholders' equity section of the company's balance sheet. For each of the following, provide the comparable label that would be used under IFRS: (1) common stock and (2) additional paid-in capital.

Answers to GAAP Self-Test Questions

1. c **2.** b **3.** d **4.** b **5.** b

CHAPTER **13**

Investments

LEARNING OBJECTIVES After studying this chapter, you should be able to:

LO 1 Explain how to account for debt investments.

LO 2 Explain how to account for equity investments.

LO 3 Indicate how debt and equity investments are reported in financial statements.

Chapter Preview

As indicated in the following Feature Story, **Sony**'s (JPN) management believes in aggressive growth through investing in the shares of existing companies. Besides purchasing shares, companies also purchase other securities such as bonds issued by companies or by governments. Companies can make investments for a short or long period of time, as a passive investment, or with the intent to control another company. As you will see in this chapter, the way in which a company accounts for its investments is determined by a number of factors.

Investments

Debt Investments	Accounting for Equity Investments	Financial Statements Presentation
• Why companies invest • Classification of financial assets • Accounting for debt investments	• Insignificant influence • Significant influence • Controlling interest	• Statement of financial position presentation • Presentation of realized and unrealized gain or loss • Classified statement of financial position

Practice

DO IT! 1 Debt Investments

DO IT! 2a Trading and Non-Trading Securities

2b Equity Investments

DO IT! 3 Financial Statement Presentation of Investments

Go to the Review and Practice section at the end of the chapter for a review of key concepts and practice applications with solutions.

Feature Story Playing for Fun and Profit

Sony (JPN) has thrived for decades despite being engaged in lines of business that are constantly changing. It is not an environment for the timid. Sony began in 1945 as a radio repair shop in Tokyo. Soon, it was making Japan's first tape recorders. Long before **Apple**'s (USA) iPod, Sony changed the way the world listened to music by developing high-quality, low-cost transistor radios, which enabled people to listen to music on the go. Over the years as technologies, tastes, and lifestyles changed, Sony adapted and invested.

Much of Sony's success in electronics is due to the innovative spirit within the Sony Electronics division. As a result of this innovative spirit, Sony has invented many game-changing new products. However, despite its internal successes, Sony has not been afraid to invest in other companies when it saw strategic advantages and opportunities. For example, Sony Electronics recently acquired **Som Livre** (BRA) and **Crunchyroll** (USA) to enhance the competitiveness of its product lines.

One of Sony's most well-known recent successes is the PlayStation video-gaming console and PlayStationVR. PlayStations have outsold all competitors. Yet, even in this case, Sony has made strategic investments to strengthen its position. To stay on top, Sony's Computer Entertainment Division has invested in numerous other video-gaming companies including **Bluepoint Games** (USA), **Fabrik Games** (GBR), and **Nixxes Software** (NED).

Although Sony is probably best known for technology, the reality is that it engages in many different business lines. Much of its growth outside of electronics has resulted from major strategic acquisitions. Two of its biggest acquisitions occurred when Sony Music Entertainment acquired **CBS Records** (USA) and when Sony Pictures Entertainment acquired **Columbia Pictures Entertainment** (USA). In both instances, Sony became a major player by boldly acquiring a large, established business.

Sony has also made investments that were less than 100% acquisitions. For example, it partnered with **Ericsson** (SWE) in a 50% joint venture called Sony Ericsson to make cell phones. It also has investments with a smaller ownership interest. For example, it has less than a 20% interest in **Japan Advanced Semiconductor Manufacturing** (JPN) and a 30% interest in **EMI Music Publishing** (USA/GBR). To succeed in an ever-changing world, Sony will need to continue to innovate internally as well as make smart investments.

Courtesy of Brian Yu

13.1 Debt Investments

LEARNING OBJECTIVE 1

Explain how to account for debt investments.

Why Companies Invest

Corporations purchase investments in debt or equity securities generally for one of three reasons.

1. As a temporary investment for excess cash.
2. To obtain earnings from investment income.
3. For strategic reasons.

Excess Cash

A corporation may **have excess cash** that it does not need for the immediate purchase of operating assets. For example, many companies experience seasonal fluctuations in sales. A marina has more sales in the spring and summer than in the fall and winter. (The reverse is true for many ski shops.) At the end of an operating cycle, the marina may have cash on hand that is temporarily idle until the start of another operating cycle. It may invest the excess funds to earn a greater return—interest and dividends—than it would get by just holding the funds in the bank. **Illustration 13.1** depicts the role that such temporary investments play in the operating cycle.

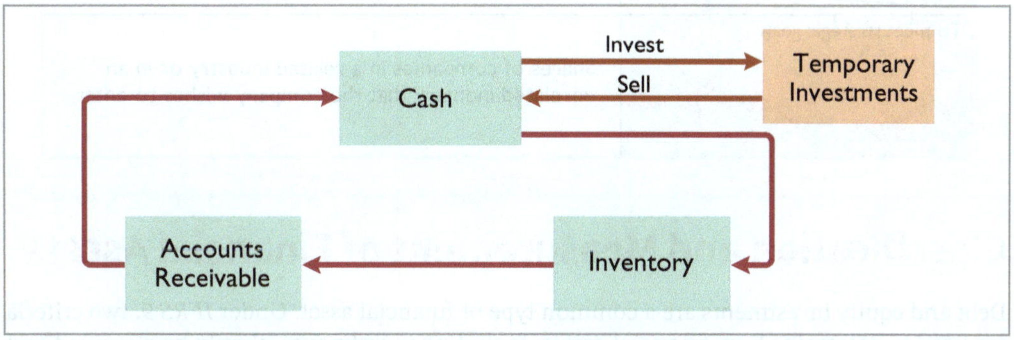

ILLUSTRATION 13.1
Temporary investments and the operating cycle

Excess cash may also result from economic cycles. For example, when the economy is booming, **Siemens** (DEU) generates considerable excess cash. It uses some of this cash to purchase new plant and equipment, and pays out some of the cash in dividends. But, it may also invest excess cash in liquid assets in anticipation of a future downturn in the economy. It can then liquidate these investments during a recession, when sales are slow and cash is scarce.

- When investing excess cash for short periods of time, corporations invest in low-risk, highly liquid securities—most often short-term government securities. It is generally not wise to invest short-term excess cash in ordinary shares because equity investments can experience rapid price changes.
- If you did invest your short-term excess cash in shares and the price of the shares declined significantly just before you needed cash again, you would be forced to sell your investment at a loss.

Earnings from Investment Income

A second reason some companies purchase investments is to generate **earnings from investment income.** For example, banks make most of their earnings by lending money, but they also generate earnings by investing primarily in debt securities. Conversely, mutual share funds invest primarily in equity securities in order to benefit from share-price appreciation and dividend revenue.

Strategic Reasons

Companies also invest for **strategic reasons**. A company can exercise some influence over a customer or supplier by purchasing a significant, but not controlling, interest in that company. Or, a company may purchase a non-controlling interest in another company in a related industry in which it wishes to establish a presence. A corporation may also choose to purchase a controlling interest in another company. For example, **Kraft** (USA) purchased **Cadbury** (GBR) to expand its presence in the food industry.

In summary, businesses invest in other companies for the reasons shown in **Illustration 13.2**.

ILLUSTRATION 13.2

Why companies invest

Reason	Typical Investment
To house excess cash until needed 	Low-risk, high-liquidity, short-term securities such as government-issued securities
To generate earnings 	Debt securities (banks and other financial institutions) and equity securities (mutual funds and pension funds)
To meet strategic goals 	Shares of companies in a related industry or in an unrelated industry that the company wishes to enter

Classification and Measurement of Financial Assets

Debt and equity investments are a common type of financial asset. Under *IFRS 9*, two criteria are used to determine how financial assets, including investments, should be classified and measured.

1. **What is the company's business model for managing the financial asset?** Is the company's business model to hold the financial asset to collect contractual cash flows rather than to sell the financial asset prior to its contractual maturity, to realize its fair value changes?
2. **What are the contractual cash flow characteristics of the financial investment?** Do the contractual terms of the financial asset give rise on specified dates to cash flows that are solely payments of principal and interest?

Based on applying the two criteria, investment securities are generally classified as **held-for-collection**, **held-for-collection and selling**, **trading**, or **non-trading**. A company will then measure a specific financial asset using either amortized cost, fair value through other comprehensive income, or fair value through profit and loss.

Debt Investments

Debt investments are investments in government and company bonds. For purposes of valuation and reporting at a financial statement date, companies classify debt investments into three categories.

1. **Financial assets measured at amortized cost**: A debt instrument that meets the following two conditions is measured at amortized cost: (a) the objective of the entity's business model is to hold the financial asset to collect the contractual cash flows; and (b) the contractual terms of the financial asset give rise on specified dates to cash flows that are solely payments of principal and interest on the principal amount outstanding.
2. **Financial assets at fair value through other comprehensive income (FVTOCI)**: A debt instrument that meets the following two conditions is measured at fair value through other comprehensive income: (a) the financial asset is held within a business model whose objective is achieved by both collecting contractual cash flows and selling financial assets; and (b) the contractual terms of the financial asset give rise on specified dates to cash flows that are solely payments of principal and interest on the principal amount outstanding. On derecognition, the cumulative gain or loss previously recognized in OCI is reclassified from equity to profit or loss.
3. **Financial assets at fair value through profit or loss (FVTPL)**: Debt instruments that do not meet the conditions mentioned in the above categories (measured at amortized cost or FVTOCI) are measured at fair value through profit or loss. *IFRS 9* contains an op-

tion that an entity may, at initial recognition, irrevocably designate a financial asset to be measured at FVTPL if doing so would eliminate or significantly reduce a measurement or recognition inconsistency (sometimes referred to as an accounting mismatch) or otherwise result in more relevant information.

Equity Investments

Equity instruments are likely to be shares that have been purchased in a company, but not enough to give the investee significant influence (associate), control (subsidiary) or joint control (joint venture). Equity investments or share investments do not have fixed interest or principal payment and therefore are never classified as held-for-collection securities. The default category is fair value through profit or loss; measurement at fair value through other comprehensive income only occurs if specified criteria are met.

1. **Financial assets at fair value through profit or loss (FVTPL):** When an equity investment that is held for trading, it is measured at fair value with changes reported in net income. Trading securities are bought and held primarily for sale in the near term to generate a profit from short-term fluctuations in price.
2. **Financial assets at fair value through other comprehensive income (FVTOCI):** When an equity investment is not held for trading, an entity can make an irrevocable election at initial recognition to measure it at fair value through other comprehensive income. Upon sale of the equity investment, the cumulative changes in other comprehensive income will never be recognized in profit or loss (i.e. there is no recycling of gains or losses).
3. **Equity method:** The equity method is used when one company has **significant influence**, but not control, **over** another company. Unless evidence is presented that significant influence does not exist, the equity method is generally used when an investment results in a 20% to 50% ownership in another company.
4. **Consolidated financial statements:** Consolidated financial statements are the financial statements prepared by a company (the parent) that has investments in more than 50% of the ordinary shares of other companies (called subsidiaries). At 50% or more ownership, investor controls the investee's business and financing decisions effectively making the investee (now called a subsidiary) just an extension of its organization. In accordance with the substance over form principle of accounting, the parent and the subsidiary must be presented as a single economic entity.

Illustration 13.3 summarizes the classification and measurement of debt and equity investments.

ILLUSTRATION 13.3 Classification and measurement

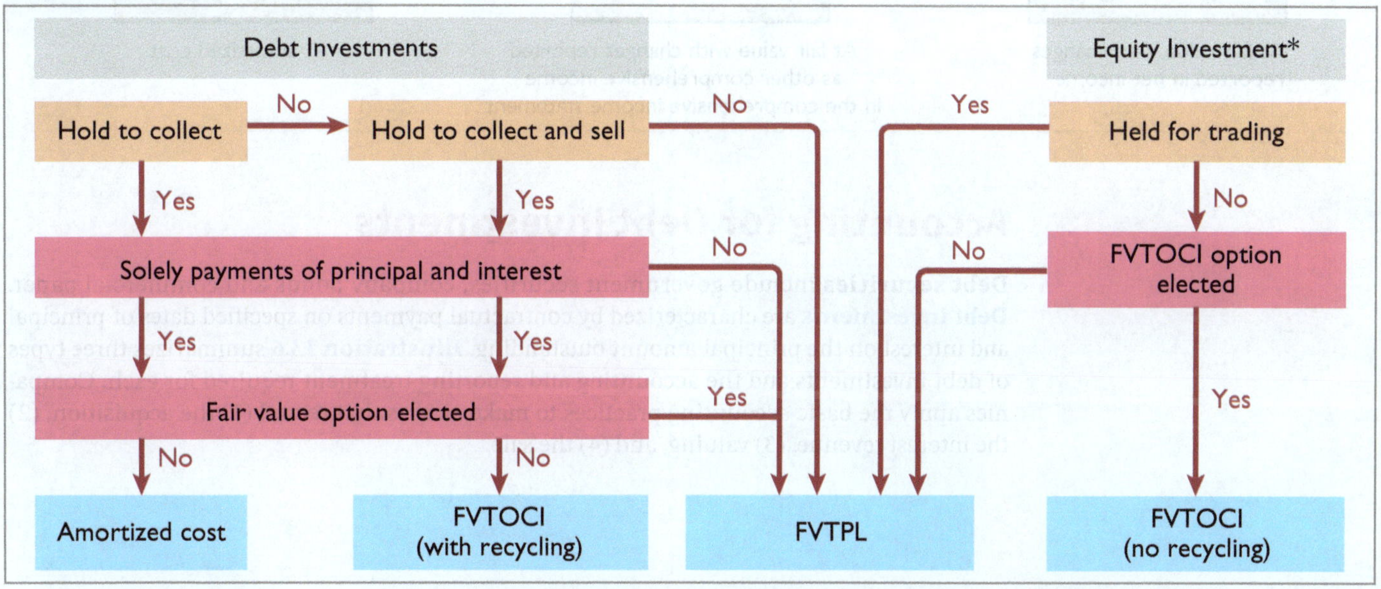

*For equity investments for which the investor has significant influence over the investee, the equity method is used.

ILLUSTRATION 13.4

Accounting guidelines for investments

Type of Financial Instrument	Category	Fair Value Gains/Losses	Recycling from OCI to P/L	Income from Investments
Debt	Amortized cost	–	–	Interest when earned
	FVTOCI	OCI	Yes	Interest when earned
	FVTPL	Profit or loss	–	Interest when earned
Equity				
Little or no influence	FVTPL	Profit or loss	–	Dividends declared
	FVTOCI	OCI	No	Dividends declared
Significant influence	Equity method	–	–	Proportionate share of investee's net income
Controlling	Consolidation	–	–	–

Illustration 13.3 summarizes the classification and measurement of debt and equity investments. For purposes of valuation and reporting at a financial statement date, debt investments may be classified as at amortized cost ("held-for-collection" business model), as an FVTOCI financial asset ("held-for-collection and selling" business model), or as an FVTPL financial asset ("held-for-trading" business model). Equity investments do not have fixed interest or principal payment schedules and therefore are never classified as held-for-collection securities. An equity investment that does not enable an investor to exercise significant influence over the investee has two classifications: an FVTPL financial asset or an FVTOCI financial asset. **Illustration 13.4** and **Illustration 13.5** summarize the accounting and valuation guidelines for these securities. **These guidelines apply to all debt securities and to equity investments representing less than 20% holdings.**

ILLUSTRATION 13.5 **Valuation guidelines**

FVTPL
(both debt and shares)

At fair value with changes reported in net income

FVTOCI
(both debt and shares)

At fair value with changes reported as other comprehensive income in the comprehensive income statement

Amortized Cost
(debt only)

At amortized cost

Accounting for Debt Investments

Debt securities include government securities, company bonds and commercial paper. **Debt investments** are characterized by contractual payments on specified dates of principal and interest on the principal amount outstanding. **Illustration 13.6** summarizes three types of debt investments and the accounting and reporting treatment required for each. Companies apply the basic accounting practices to make entries that record (1) the acquisition, (2) the interest revenue, (3) valuing, and (4) the sale.

ILLUSTRATION 13.6
Accounting for debt investments by business model

Business Model	Valuation	Unrealized Gains or Losses	Income from Investments
1. Held for collection	Amortized cost	Not recognized	Interest revenue; gains and losses from sale.
2. Held for collection and selling	FVTOCI	Recognized as other comprehensive income and as a separate component of equity	Interest revenue; gains or losses are reclassified from equity to current profits or losses from sale. (debt investments only)
3. Held for trading	FVTPL	Recognized in net income	Interest revenue; no gains or losses recognized from sale.

Debt Investments: Financial Assets at Amortized Cost

According to *IFRS 9*, if the objective of a company's business model is to hold debt investments to collect the contractual cash flows, the debt investment is measured at **amortized cost**. Amortized cost is the initial cost of the investment, minus any repayments received, and plus or minus cumulative amortization of discounts or premiums. When a debt investment measured at amortized cost, any discount or premium arising on acquisition should be amortized using the effective interest method which is discussed in Appendix 11A.

Recording Acquisition of Bonds at Face Value When the market interest rate and the stated rate on the bond are the same, the market price of the bond equals its face value. That is, the bond investments are purchased at a face value. At acquisition, investments in financial assets at amortized cost are recorded at cost. Cost includes all expenditures necessary to acquire these investments, such as the price paid plus brokerage fees (commissions), if any.

Assume, for example, that Kuhl NV acquires 100 Doan SA 8%, 5-year, €1,000 bonds on January 1, 2029, at a cost of €100,000. Interest is payable each July 1 and January 1. The market interest rate is 8%. This bond investment is classified as financial assets at amortized cost. The entry to record the investment is:

Jan. 1	Financial Assets at Amortized Cost	100,000	
	Cash		100,000
	(To record purchase of 100 Doan SA bonds)		

A = L + E
+100,000
−100,000
Cash Flows
−100,000

Recording Bond Interest Kuhl NV records the receipt of the first semiannual interest payment on July 1, 2029, as follows.

Jan. 1	Cash (€100,000 × 8% × 1/2)	4,000	
	Interest Revenue		4,000
	(To record receipt of interest on Doan SA bonds)		

A = L + E
+4,000 +4,000 Rev
Cash Flows
+4,000

If Kuhl NV's fiscal year ends on December 31, it accrues the interest of €4,000 earned since July 1. The adjusting entry is:

Dec. 31	Interest Receivable	4,000	
	Interest Revenue		4,000
	(To accrue interest on Doan SA bonds)		

A = L + E
+4,000 +4,000 Rev
Cash Flows
no effect

Kuhl NV presents its investment in Doan SA bonds in its December 31, 2029, financial statements, as shown in **Illustration 13.7**.[1]

[1] Under *IFRS 18*, companies must classify their income and expenses into five categories—operating, investing, financing, income tax, and discontinued operations—with interest revenue from debt investments classified under the investing category.

ILLUSTRATION 13.7

Reporting debt investments at amortized cost

	Statement of Financial Position	
	Non-current assets	
	Financial assets at amortized cost	**€100,000**
	Current assets	
	Interest receivable	**€ 4,000**
	Statement of Comprehensive Income	
	Operating income	€ **XXX**
Investing	**Interest revenue (€4,000 + €4,000)**	€ **8,000**

At financial report date, the investments are not to adjust to fair values. The financial assets which are classified to amortized cost are usual to hold for a long time and are not viewed as a temporary. The fair value of the financial investment is only disclosed and not recognized on financial statement. When the maturity date of the bonds is within one year, then financial assets at amortized cost should be reclassified as current assets.

Kuhl NV reports receipt of the interest on January 1, 2030 as follows.

A = L + E
+4,000
−4,000
Cash Flows
+4,000

Jan. 1	Cash	4,000	
	Interest Receivable		4,000
	(To record receipt of accrued interest)		

A credit to Interest Revenue at this time is incorrect because the company earned and accrued interest revenue in the **preceding** accounting period.

Recording Bonds Repayment at Maturity Regardless of the acquisition price of bonds, the carrying amount of the bond at maturity will equal their face value. Assume that Kuhl NV holds the bonds until the maturity date of January 1, 2034. The journal entry is:

A = L + E
+100,000
−100,000
Cash Flows
+100,000

Jan. 1	Cash	100,000	
	Financial Assets at Amortized Cost		100,000
	(To record repayment of Doan SA bonds)		

Recording the Sale of Bonds before Maturity Assume that Kuhl NV sells the bonds on October 1, 2033 (three months before the maturity date of January 1, 2034) for $101,500 plus accrued interest. The journal entry is:

A = L + E
+103,500
−100,000 +3,500
Cash Flows
+103,500

Oct. 1	Interest Receivable	2,000	
	Interest Revenue (€100,000 × 8% × 3/12)		2,000
	(To accrue interest on Doan SA bonds)		
Oct. 1	Cash	103,500	
	Interest Receivable		2,000
	Financial Assets at Amortized Cost		100,000
	Gain on Sale of Financial Assets at Amortized Cost		1,500
	(To record the sale of Doan SA bonds)		

Recording Acquisition of Bonds at a Discount When the market interest rate differs from the stated rate on the bond, the market price of the bond will not be equal to its face value. To make bonds salable when the two rates differ, bonds sell below or above face value.

Assume, for example, that Kuhl NV acquires 100 Doan SA 8%, 5-year, €1,000 bonds on January 1, 2029, at a discount, paying €92,278. Interest is payable on July 1 and January 1. The market interest rate is 10%. This bond investment is classified as a financial asset measured at amortized cost. The entry to record the investment is:

A = L + E
+92,278
−92,278
Cash Flows
−92,278

Jan. 1	Financial Assets at Amortized Cost	92,278	
	Cash		92,278
	(To record purchase of 100 Doan SA bonds)		

As indicated in Appendix 11A, companies must amortize premiums or discounts using the **effective-interest method**. They apply the effective-interest method to bond investments in a way similar to that for bonds payable. To compute interest revenue, companies compute the effective-interest rate or yield at the time of investment and apply that rate to the beginning carrying amount (book value) for each interest period. The investment carrying amount is increased by the amortized discount or decreased by the amortized premium in each period.

Illustration 13.8 shows the effect of the discount amortization on the interest revenue that Kuhl NV records each period for its investment in Doan SA bonds.

ILLUSTRATION 13.8

Schedule of interest revenue and bond discount amortization—effective-interest method

8% Bonds Purchased to Yield 10%

Date	Cash Received	Interest Revenue	Bond Discount Amortization	Carrying Amount of Bonds
1/1/29				€92,278
7/1/29	€ 4,000[a]	€ 4,614[b]	€ 614[c]	92,892[d]
1/1/30	4,000	4,645	645	93,537
7/1/30	4,000	4,677	677	94,214
1/1/31	4,000	4,711	711	94,925
7/1/31	4,000	4,746	746	95,671
1/1/32	4,000	4,783	783	96,454
7/1/32	4,000	4,823	823	97,277
1/1/33	4,000	4,864	864	98,141
7/1/33	4,000	4,907	907	99,048
1/1/34	4,000	4,952	952	100,000
	€40,000	€47,722	€7,722	

[a] €4,000 = €100,000 × .08 × 6/12
[b] €4,614 = €92,278 × .10 × 6/12
[c] €614 = €4,614 − €4,000
[d] €92,892 = €92,278 + €614

Recording Bond Interest Kuhl NV records the receipt of the first semiannual interest payment on July 1, 2029, as follows.

July 1	Cash	4,000	
	Financial Assets at Amortized Cost	614	
	Interest Revenue		4,614
	(To record receipt of interest on Doan SA bonds)		

A = L + E
+4,614 +4,614 Rev
Cash Flows
+4,000

Because Kuhl NV is on a calendar-year basis, it accrues interest and amortizes the discount at December 31, 2029, as follows.

Dec. 31	Interest Receivable	4,000	
	Financial Assets at Amortized Cost	645	
	Interest Revenue		4,645
	(To accrue interest on Doan SA bonds)		

A = L + E
+4,645 +4,645 Rev
Cash Flows
no effect

Kuhl NV reports its investment in Doan SA bonds in its December 31, 2029, financial statements, as shown in **Illustration 13.9**.

ILLUSTRATION 13.9

Reporting debt investments at a discount

Statement of Financial Position

	Non-current assets	
	Financial assets at amortized cost	**€93,537**
	Current assets	
	Interest receivable	**€ 4,000**

Statement of Comprehensive Income

	Operating income	€ XXX
Investing	**Interest revenue (€4,614 + €4,645)**	**€ 9,259**

Recording the Sale of Bonds before Maturity Assume that Kuhl NV sells its investment in Doan SA bonds on November 1, 2031, at 99¾ plus accrued interest. The discount amortization from July 1, 2031, to November 1, 2031, is €522 (4/6 × €783). Kuhl NV records this discount amortization as follows.

A	=	L	+	E
+3,189				
				+3,189 Rev

Cash Flows
no effect

Nov. 1	Interest Receivable (€100,000 × 8% × 4/12)	2,667	
	Financial Assets at Amortized Cost	522	
	Interest Revenue (€95,671 × 10% × 4/12)		3,189
	(To accrue interest on Doan SA bonds)		

Kuhl NV records the sale of the bonds as follows.

A	=	L	+	E
+102,417				
−98,860				
				+3,557 Gain

Cash Flows
+102,417

Nov. 1	Cash (€99,750 + €2,667)	102,417	
	Interest Receivable		2,667
	Financial Assets at Amortized Cost		96,193
	Gain on Sale of Financial Assets at Amortized Cost		3,557
	(To record the sale of Doan SA bonds)		

The credit to Interest Receivable represents accrued interest for 4 months, for which the purchaser pays cash. The debit to Cash represents the selling price of the bonds plus accrued interest (€99,750 + €2,667). The credit to Financial Assets at Amortized Cost represents the book value of the bonds on the date of sale. The credit to Gain on Sale of Investments represents the excess of the selling price over the book value of the bonds.

Investor Insight

Jane0606/Shutterstock

Hey, I Thought It Was Safe!

It is often stated that bond investments are safer than share investments. After all, with an investment in bonds, you are guaranteed return of principal and interest payments over the life of the bonds. However, here are some other factors you may want to consider:

- In 2013, the value of bonds fell by 2% due to interest rate risk. That is, when interest rates rise, it makes the yields paid on existing bonds less attractive. As a result, the price of the existing bond you are holding falls.
- While interest rates are currently low, it is likely that they will increase in the future. If you hold bonds, there is a real possibility that the value of your bonds will be reduced.
- Credit risk also must be considered. Credit risk means that a company may not be able to pay back what it borrowed. Former bondholders in companies that declared bankruptcy saw their bond values drop substantially.

An advantage of a bond investment over shares is that if you hold it to maturity, you will receive your principal and also interest payments over the life of the bond. But if you have to sell your bond investment before maturity, you may be facing a roller coaster regarding its value.

Why is the fluctuating value of bonds of concern if a company intends to hold them until maturity? (Answer is available near the end of the chapter.)

ACTION PLAN

- **Record bond investments at cost.**
- **Record interest when accrued.**
- **When bonds are sold, credit the investment account for the amortized cost of the bonds.**
- **Record any difference between the amortized cost and the net proceeds as a gain or loss.**

DO IT! 1 | Debt Investments

Waldo AG had the following transactions pertaining to debt investments classified as held-for-collection.

Jan. 1, 2029	Purchased 30, €1,000 Hillary AG 10% bonds for €30,000. Interest is payable annually on January 1.
Dec. 31, 2029	Accrued interest on Hillary AG bonds in 2029.
Jan. 1, 2030	Received interest on Hillary AG bonds.
Jan. 1, 2030	Sold 15 Hillary AG bonds for €14,600.
Dec. 31, 2030	Accrued interest on Hillary AG bonds in 2030.

Journalize the transactions.

Solution

Jan. 1 (2029)	Financial Assets at Amortized Cost	30,000	
	Cash		30,000
	(To record purchase of 30 Hillary AG bonds)		
Dec. 31 (2029)	Interest Receivable	3,000	
	Interest Revenue (€30,000 × 10%)		3,000
	(To accrue interest on Hillary AG bonds)		
Jan. 1 (2030)	Cash	3,000	
	Interest Receivable		3,000
	(To record receipt of interest on Hillary AG bonds)		
Jan. 1 (2030)	Cash	14,600	
	Loss on Sale of Financial Assets at Amortized Cost	400	
	Financial Assets at Amortized Cost (€30,000 × 15/30)		15,000
	(To record sale of 15 Hillary AG bonds)		
Dec. 31 (2030)	Interest Receivable	1,500	
	Interest Revenue (€15,000 × 10%)		1,500
	(To accrue interest on Hillary AG bonds)		

Related exercise material: **BE13.1, DO IT! 13.1, E13.2, and E13.3.**

Debt Investments: Financial Assets at Fair Value through Other Comprehensive Income (FVTOCI)

Under *IFRS 9*, if the objective of the business model is not only to collect contractual cash flows but also to sell debt securities, then the debt investment is measured at fair value through other comprehensive income (FVTOCI).

Recording Acquisition of Bonds at Face Value At acquisition, debt investments classified as FVTOCI are recorded at cost. Transaction costs that are directly attributable to the acquisition of financial assets should be added to the cost of the investments.

For example, assume that Kuhl NV acquires 100 Doan SA 8%, 5-year, €1,000 bonds on January 1, 2029, at a cost of €100,000. Interest is payable each July 1 and January 1. The market interest rate is 8%. This bond investment is measured at FVTOCI. The entry to record the investment is:

Jan. 1	Debt Investments at FVTOCI	100,000	
	Cash		100,000
	(To record purchase of 100 Doan SA bonds)		

A = L + E
+100,000
−100,000
Cash Flows
−100,000

Recording Bond Interest Kuhl NV records interest revenue on July 1, 2029, as follows.

July 1	Cash (€100,000 × 8% × 1/2)	4,000	
	Interest Revenue		4,000
	(To record receipt of interest on Doan SA bonds)		

A = L + E
+4,000 +4,000 Rev
Cash Flows
+4,000

At December 31, 2029, Kuhl NV accrues the interest of €4,000 earned since July 1. The adjusting entry is:

Dec. 31	Interest Receivable	4,000	
	Interest Revenue		4,000
	(To accrue interest on Doan SA bonds)		

A = L + E
+4,000 +4,000 Rev
Cash Flows
no effect

Adjusting Investments to Fair Value A financial asset measured at FVTOCI is reported at fair value, so its carrying amount must be adjusted to fair value at the end of each reporting period. Changes in fair value are recognized as an unrealized gain or loss in other comprehensive income rather than in net income. **Note that unrealized gains or losses on debt investments at FVTOCI are recognized in other comprehensive income (OCI) which is an equity account, and its balance is to be carried forward from period to period until such investments are sold.** Depending on the length of holding time period, financial assets at FVTOCI can be classified as current or non-current assets in the investments section of the statement of financial position.

To illustrate, assume that at the end of 2029, the fair value of Doan bonds is €102,500 and the carrying amount of the investments is €100,000. That is, the fair value of FVTOCI securities is €2,500 higher than its amortized cost. Kuhl makes the following adjusting entry.

A	=	L	+	E
+2,500				
				+2,500

Cash Flows
no effect

Dec. 31	Fair Value Adjustment—Debt Investments at FVTOCI	2,500	
	OCI—Unrealized Gain or Loss on Debt Investments at FVTOCI		2,500
	(To record unrealized gain on Doan SA bonds)		

The use of a Fair Value Adjustment account enables the company to maintain a record of its amortized cost. Because the adjustment account has a debt balance in this case, Kuhl adds it to the balance of the investments to arrive at a **fair value** for the FVTOCI securities. At December 31, 2029, Kuhl reports on its statement of financial position Debt Investments at FVTOCI of €102,500 (€100,000 + €2,500). Because Debt Investments at FVTOCI are likely to be held for more than one year, it is often classified under non-current assets. The amount of the current period adjustment to the OCI—Unrealized Gain or Loss on Debt Investments at FVTOCI is €2,500, and is presented in the other comprehensive income section of the statement of comprehensive income. Recall that companies exclude from net income any unrealized gains and losses related to FVTOCI securities.

The closing entry to transfer the OCI—Unrealized Gain or Loss on Debt Investments at FVTOCI to Accumulated Other Comprehensive Income is as follows.

A	=	L	+	E
				−2,500
				+2,500

Cash Flows
no effect

Dec. 31	OCI—Unrealized Gain or Loss on Debt Investments at FVTOCI	2,500	
	Accumulated Other Comprehensive Income		2,500
	(To close unrealized gain or loss to equity)		

The Accumulated Other Comprehensive Income account aggregates the change in the OCI—Unrealized Gain or Loss on Debt Investments at FVTOCI and is reported as part of equity in the statement of financial position. Since this was Kuhl's first year of operations, it started with a balance of zero. Kuhl reports accumulated other comprehensive income of €2,500.

Kuhl reports its debt investments at FVTOCI in its December 31, 2029, financial statements, as shown in **Illustration 13.10**.

ILLUSTRATION 13.10

Reporting debt investments at FVTOCI

Statement of Financial Position	
Non-current assets	
Debt investments at FVTOCI	**€ 100,000**
Add: Fair value adjustment—FVTOCI	**2,500**
	€ 102,500
Current assets	
Interest receivable	**€ 4,000**
Equity	
Accumulated other comprehensive income	**€ 2,500**

ILLUSTRATION 13.10

(Continued)

Statement of Comprehensive Income		
Operating income	€	XXX
Interest revenue (€4,000 + €4,000)		8,000
Income before financing and income taxes		XXX
Interest expense		(XXX)
Net income		XXX
Other comprehensive income		
Unrealized gain or loss on financial assets at FVTOCI		2,500
Comprehensive income	€	XXX

Kuhl reports receipt of the interest on January 1, 2030, as follows.

Jan. 1	Cash	4,000	
	Interest Receivable		4,000
	(To record receipt of accrued interest)		

A	=	L	+	E
+4,000				
−4,000				

Cash Flows
+4,000

Recording Sale of Bonds When a company sells a debt investment at FVTOCI, it revalues the investment before making the journal entry for the sale. As a result, there is no additional gain or loss when a company makes the sale journal entry, because the market price of the bonds is equal to the sum of the carrying amount of bonds and valuation adjustment.

Suppose that Kuhl sold all Doan bonds for €102,500 on January 1, 2030, after receiving the interest due. Kuhl records the receipt of cash for selling of FVTOCI securities as follows:

Jan. 1	Cash	102,500	
	Debt Investments at FVTOCI		100,000
	Fair Value Adjustment—Debt Investments at FVTOCI		2,500
	(To record sale of Doan SA bonds)		

A	=	L	+	E
+102,500				
−100,000				
−2,500				

Cash Flows
+102,500

Reclassification Adjustment When a debt investment at FVTOCI is sold, **the cumulative gain or loss previously recognized in other comprehensive income is reclassified from equity to profit or loss** as a reclassification adjustment. Since Kuhl has disposed all of Doan bonds, we need to close the "OCI—Unrealized Gain or Loss on Debt Investments at FVTOCI" in the equity section by reclassifying €2,500 into net income and record it as "Gain on Sale of Debt Investments at FVTOCI."

Jan. 1	OCI—Unrealized Gain or Loss on Debt Investments at FVTOCI	2,500	
	Gain on Sale of Debt Investments at FVTOCI		2,500
	(To reclassify from equity to profit or loss)		

A	=	L	+	E
				+2,500
				+2,500

Cash Flows
no effect

At year-end OCI—Unrealized Gain or Loss on Debt Investments at FVTOCI is closed to Accumulated Other Comprehensive Income as shown in the following entry.

Dec. 31	Accumulated Other Comprehensive Income	2,500	
	OCI—Unrealized Gain or Loss on Debt Investments at FVTOCI		2,500
	(To close unrealized gain or loss to equity)		

A	=	L	+	E
				−2,500
				+2,500

Cash Flows
no effect

Debt Investments: Financial Assets at Fair Value through Profit or Loss (FVTPL)

Some companies often hold debt investments with the intention of selling them in a short period of time to generate profits from short-term differences in price as opposed to holding the asset to collect contractual cash flows. These debt investments are often referred to as trading investments. **Trading** means frequent buying and selling. **Trading securities** is measured at **fair value through profit or loss** (FVTPL). That is, companies adjust trading securities to fair value at the end of each period (an approach referred to as mark-to-market accounting), with **gains and losses reported as part of net income**. Companies classify trading securities as current assets (see **Helpful Hint**). A company may, at initial recognition, designate a financial asset as measured at fair value through profit or loss (FVTPL) to eliminate or significantly reduce a measurement or recognition inconsistency (sometimes referred to as an 'accounting mismatch').

HELPFUL HINT

The fact that trading securities are short-term investments increases the likelihood that they will be sold at fair value (the company may not be able to time their sale) and the likelihood that there will be realized gains or losses.

Recording Acquisition of Bonds At acquisition, debt investments classified as FVTPL are recorded at cost. For investments accounted for at FVTPL, IFRS requires that brokerage and transaction costs shall be expensed and reported in the investing category of the income statement.

For example, on January 1, 2029, Kehaur Company acquires $300,000 of Jinshiuh, Inc., 9% bonds at par. The interest is payable each December 31, and the bonds mature December 31, 2031. The bonds are classified as trading securities and measured at fair value through profit or loss (FVTPL). The entry to record the investment is as follows.

A = L + E
+300,000
−300,000
Cash Flows
−300,000

Jan. 1	Financial Assets at FVTPL	300,000	
	Cash		300,000
	(To record purchase of Jinshiuh bonds)		

Recording Bond Interest Kehaur records the receipt of interest is:

A = L + E
+27,000 +27,000 Rev
Cash Flows
+27,000

Dec. 31	Cash	27,000	
	Interest Revenue		27,000
	(To record receipt of interest on Jinshiuh bonds)		

Kehaur reports Interest Revenue under "the investing category, rather than including it within operating income and expenses" in the statement of comprehensive income.

Adjusting Investments to Fair Value Assume that at the end of 2029 the fair value of Jinshiuh bonds is $292,000 and the carrying amount of the investments is $300,000. Kehaur records fair value and gain or loss through an adjusting entry at the time it prepares financial statements. In this entry, the company uses a valuation allowance account, Fair Value Adjustment—FVTPL, to record the difference between the total cost of trading securities and their total fair value. The adjusting entry for Kehaur is:

A = L + E
−8,000 −8,000
Cash Flows
no effect

Dec. 31	Loss on Financial Assets at FVTPL	8,000	
	Fair Value Adjustment—FVTPL		8,000
	(To record loss on Jinshiuh bonds)		

This journal entry recognizes the $8,000 decrease in the value of debt investments measured at FVTPL. Why not adjust the financial assets account directly instead of creating the valuation account? The use of a Fair Value Adjustment account enables Kehaur to maintain a record of the investment cost. Kehaur subtracts a credit balance (or adds a debit balance) of the Fair Value Adjustment—FVTPL account to the cost of the investments to arrive at a fair value for the trading securities. Over time, the valuation account is adjusted to reflect the difference between the cost and the fair value of the financial assets.

The fair value of the securities is the amount Kehaur reports on its statement of financial position. It includes the Loss on Financial Assets at FVTPL in determining net income and does not affect other comprehensive income. Kehaur reports Loss on Financial Assets at FVTPL in the investing category of the income statement.

The Fair Value Adjustment—FVTPL account is carried forward into future accounting periods. For trading securities, the company closes the Loss on Financial Assets at FVTPL account at the end of the reporting period.

Recording Sale of Bonds Suppose that Kehaur sold all of its investment in Jinshiuh bonds for $295,000 on March 1, 2030. As the bonds were valued for $292,000 on December 31, 2029, the securities have increased in value and that increase must be valued before making the journal entry for sales.

A = L + E
+3,000 +3,000
Cash Flows
no effect

March 1	Fair Value Adjustment—FVTPL	3,000	
	Gain on Financial Assets at FVTPL		3,000
	(To record gain on Jinshiuh bonds)		

Kehaur reports any gains or losses on the sale of debt investments in the investing category of the income statement. After making the valuation adjustment, Kehaur records the sale of the Jinshiuh bonds as follows.

March 1	Cash	295,000	
	Fair Value Adjustment—FVTPL	5,000	
	Financial Assets at FVTPL		300,000
	(To record sale of Jinshiuh bonds)		

A	=	L	+	E
+295,000				
+5,000				
−300,000				

Cash Flows
+295,000

13.2 Accounting for Equity Investments

LEARNING OBJECTIVE 2

Explain how to account for equity investments.

Equity investments are investments in the shares of other companies. When a company holds shares (and/or debt) of several different companies, the group of securities is identified as an **investment portfolio**.

The accounting for investments in shares depends on the extent of the investor's influence over the operating and financial affairs of the issuing company (the investee). Under *IAS 28*, if an investor holds 20% or more of the voting shares of the investee, it is presumed that the investor has significant influence, unless it can be clearly demonstrated that this is not the case. Conversely, if the investor holds less than 20% of the voting shares of the investee, it is presumed that the investor does not have significant influence, unless such influence can be clearly demonstrated. Significant influence is the power to participate in the financial and operating policy decisions of the investee[2]. Usually, having more members on the board of directors suggests greater influence over the operating and financial affairs of the investee.

The accounting and reporting for equity investments therefore depend on the level of influence and the type of security involved, as shown in **Illustration 13.11**.

Companies are required to use judgment instead of blindly following the guidelines. We explain the application of each guideline next.

ILLUSTRATION 13.11

Accounting guidelines for equity investments

	Percentage of Ownership	Board Representation	Level of Influence	Accounting Guidelines
	Less than 20%	Non member	Insignificant	Fair value
	Between 20% and 50%	Minority members	Significant	Equity method
	More than 50%	Majority members	Controlling	Consolidated financial statements

[2] The existence of significant influence by a company is usually evidenced in one or more of the following ways: (a) representation on the board of directors or equivalent governing body of the investee; (b) participation in policy-making processes, including participation in decisions about dividends or other distributions; (c) material transactions between the entity and its investee; (d) interchange of managerial personnel; or (e) provision of essential technical information.

Insignificant Influence

When an investor has an interest of less than 20%, it is presumed that the investor has little or no influence over the investee. Under *IFRS 9*, the presumption is that equity investments are held-for-trading. That is, companies hold these securities to profit from price changes. As with debt investments that are held-for-trading, the general accounting and reporting rule for these investments is to value the securities at **fair value** with changes in value reported in **profit or loss** (FVTPL).

However, some equity investments are held for purposes other than trading. For example, a company may be required to hold an equity investment in order to sell its products in a particular area. As a result, IFRS allows companies to classify some equity investments as non-trading. **Non-trading equity investments** are recorded at **fair value** on the statement of financial position, with unrealized gains and losses reported in **other comprehensive income** (FVTOCI). In both classifications (i.e., FVTPL and FVTOCI), cash dividends received are always recognized as income (see **Helpful Hint**).

HELPFUL HINT
The entries for investments in ordinary shares also apply to investments in preference shares.

Equity Investments: Financial Assets at Fair Value through Profit or Loss (FVTPL)

Equity investments are commonly held-for-trading and measured at fair value through profit or loss (FVTPL). Companies adjust FVTPL securities to fair value at the end of each period (an approach referred to as mark-to-market accounting). Changes in the fair value between accounting periods are reported in the investing category of the income statement and are included in the net income. Companies often classify FVTPL securities as current assets.

Recording Acquisition of Shares At acquisition, equity investments are recorded at cost. The cost of equity investments is measured at the purchase price of the security. For equity investments measured at FVTPL, brokerage and other transaction costs incidental to the purchase are recorded as expense.

For example, assume that on July 1, 2029, Lee Ltd. acquires 1,000 shares (10%, ownership with insignificant influence on the investee) of Beal Ltd. Lee pays HK$405 per share. Lee measures the equity investments as fair value through profit or loss (FVTPL). The entry for the purchase is:

A = L + E
+405,000
−405,000
Cash Flows
−405,000

July 1	Financial Assets at FVTPL	405,000	
	Cash		405,000
	(To record purchase of 1,000 ordinary shares of Beal Ltd.)		

Recording Dividends During the time Lee owns the shares, it makes entries for any cash dividends received. If Lee receives a HK$20 per share dividend on October 1, the entry is:

A = L + E
+20,000
+20,000 Rev
Cash Flows
+20,000

Oct. 1	Cash (1,000 × HK$20)	20,000	
	Dividend Revenue		20,000
	(To record receipt of cash dividend)		

Lee reports Dividend Revenue in the investing category of the income statement. Unlike interest on notes and bonds, dividends do not accrue. Therefore, companies do not make adjusting entries to accrue dividends.

Adjusting Investments to Fair Value Assume that on December 31, 2029, the fair value of Beal Ltd. is HK$450 per share. The fair value of Lee's equity investments exceeds its cost by HK$45,000. The adjusting entry for Lee is:

A = L + E
+45,000
+45,000
Cash Flows
no effect

Dec. 31	Fair Value Adjustment—FVTPL	45,000	
	Gain on Financial Assets at FVTPL		45,000
	(To record gain on Beal shares)		

because the adjustment account, Fair Value Adjustment—FVTPL, has a debit balance in this case, Lee adds it to the Financial Assets at FVTPL account to determine fair value.

Under IFRS 18, Gain on Financial Assets at FVTPL is classified in the investing category of the income statement.

Recording Sale of Shares When a company sells an equity investment, it revalues the investment before making the journal entry for the sale. As a result, there is no additional gain or loss when a company makes the sale journal entry, because the sales price is equal to the sum of the cost of the shares and valuation adjustment.

Assume that Lee Ltd. sold all of its Beal shares for HK$395,000 on February 10, 2030. As the shares was valued for HK$450,000 on December 31, 2029, the securities have decreased in value and Lee decreases the value of the shares by the following journal entry:

Feb. 10	Loss on Financial Assets at FVTPL	55,000	
	Fair Value Adjustment—FVTPL		55,000
	(To record loss on Beal shares)		

A = L + E
−55,000 (A); −55,000 (E)
Cash Flows
no effect

Lee reports the Loss on Financial Assets at FVTPL in the investing category of the income statement.

After making the valuation adjustment, Lee records the receipt of net proceeds for the sale:

Feb. 10	Cash	395,000	
	Fair Value Adjustment—FVTPL	10,000	
	Financial Assets at FVTPL		405,000
	(To record sale of Beal shares)		

A = L + E
+395,000
+10,000
−405,000
Cash Flows
+395,000

DO IT! 2a | Trading and Non-Trading Securities

Some of Chengdu Ltd.'s investment securities are classified as trading securities and some are classified as non-trading. The cost and fair value of each category at December 31, 2029, are as follows.

	Cost	Fair value	Unrealized Gain (Loss)
Trading securities	¥936,000	¥949,000	¥13,000
Non-trading securities	¥488,000	¥514,000	¥26,000

At December 31, 2028, the Fair Value Adjustment—FVTPL account had a debit balance of ¥92,000, and the Fair Value Adjustment—FVTOCI account had a credit balance of ¥57,500. Prepare the required journal entries for each group of securities for December 31, 2029.

ACTION PLAN

- **Adjust trading securities to fair value and report the adjustment in current-period income.**
- **Adjust non-trading securities to fair value and report the adjustment as a separate component of equity.**

Solution

Trading securities:

Loss on Financial Assets at FVTPL (¥92,000 − ¥13,000)	79,000	
Fair Value Adjustment—FVTPL		79,000
(To record loss on trading securities)		

Non-trading securities:

Fair Value Adjustment—FVTOCI	83,500	
OCI—Unrealized Gain or Loss on Financial Assets at FVTOCI (¥57,500 + ¥26,000)		83,500
(To record unrealized gain on non-trading securities)		

Related exercise material: **BE13.4, BE13.5, BE13.6, BE13.7, DO IT! 13.2a, E13.10 and E13.11.**

Equity Investments: Financial Assets at Fair Value through Other Comprehensive Income (FVTOCI)

Under *IFRS 9*, at initial recognition, companies may make an **irrevocable election** for particular equity investments (e.g. for non-trading reasons) to present subsequent changes in fair value in other comprehensive income (FVTOCI). This option only applies to equity instruments that are held for purposes other than trading. The accounting entries to record non-trading equity investments measured at fair value through other comprehensive income (FVTOCI) are the same as for trading equity investments (FVTPL), except for recording the unrealized holding gain or loss. Companies reports **non-trading equity investments** at **fair value** on the statement of financial position, with unrealized gain or loss reported in **other comprehensive income**. Dividend are recognized in profit or loss. When equity investments measured at FVTOCI are sold, the cumulative unrealized gains or losses previously recognized in accumulated other comprehensive income are directly transferred to retained earnings (never reclassified from equity to current profit or loss). Depending on the length of holding time period, equity investments measured at FVTOCI can be classified as current or non-current assets in the investments section of the statement of financial position.

Recording Acquisition of Shares At acquisition, equity investments are recorded at cost. For equity investments measured at FVTOCI, cost includes all expenditures necessary to acquire these investments, such as the brokerage and other transaction costs.

For example, assume that on May 1, 2029, Su Company purchased 1,000 shares of Taur Inc. for $20 per share. The investment represents less than 20% interest. Su makes an irrevocable election to measure the equity investments as fair value through other comprehensive income (FVTOCI). Su records this investment as follows.

A	=	L	+	E
+20,000				
−20,000				

Cash Flows
−20,000

May 1	Equity Investments at FVTOCI	20,000	
	Cash		20,000
	(To record purchase of 1,000 ordinary shares of Taur Inc.)		

Recording Dividends On November 30, 2029, Su received a cash dividend of $400 on its investment in the shares of Taur Inc. It records the cash dividend as follows.

A	=	L	+	E
+400				+400 Rev

Cash Flows
+400

Nov. 30	Cash	400	
	Dividend Revenue		400
	(To record receipt of cash dividend)		

Similar to the accounting for trading investments, when an investor owns less than 20% of the ordinary shares of another company, it is presumed that the investor has relatively little influence on the investee. Therefore, **the investor earns income when the investee declares cash dividends.**

Adjusting Investments to Fair Value A financial asset measured at FVTOCI is reported at fair value. For non-trading equity investments, companies **report the unrealized gain or loss on FVTOCI equity investments as other comprehensive income (OCI).**

At December 31, 2029, Su's investment in Taur has the fair value of $23,000. The fair value of the equity investment exceeds cost by $3,000. Su increases the value of the shares by the following entry:

A	=	L	+	E
+3,000				+3,000

Cash Flows
no effect

Dec. 31	Fair Value Adjustment—Equity Investments at FVTOCI	3,000	
	OCI—Unrealized Gain or Loss on Equity Investments at FVTOCI		3,000
	(To record unrealized gain on Taur shares)		

The closing entry to transfer the OCI—Unrealized Gain or Loss on Equity Investments at FVTOCI to Accumulated Other Comprehensive Income is as follows.

A	=	L	+	E
				−3,000
				+3,000

Cash Flows
no effect

Dec. 31	OCI—Unrealized Gain or Loss on Equity Investments at FVTOCI	3,000	
	Accumulated Other Comprehensive Income		3,000
	(To close unrealized gain or loss to equity)		

Su records the unrealized gains or losses arising from changes in the fair value of this non-trading equity investments in an OCI—Unrealized Gain or Loss on Equity Investments at FVTOCI account. Su reports this amount as **a part of other comprehensive income and as a component of accumulated other comprehensive income (reported in equity).**

At December 31, 2029, Su reports on its statement of financial position equity investments at FVTOCI of $23,000 (cost of $20,000 + $3,000). In its equity section, it reports accumulated other comprehensive income of $3,000.

Su reports its equity investments in its December 31, 2029, financial statements as shown in **Illustration 13.12**.

ILLUSTRATION 13.12

Reporting equity investments at FVTOCI

Statement of Financial Position

Non-current assets	
Equity investments at FVTOCI	**$20,000**
Add: Fair value adjustment—FVTOCI	**3,000**
	$23,000
Equity	
Accumulated other comprehensive income	**$ 3,000**

Statement of Comprehensive Income

Operating income	€ XXX
Dividend revenue	**400**
Income before financing and income taxes	XXX
Interest expense	(XXX)
Net income	XXX
Other comprehensive income	
Unrealized gain or loss on equity investments at FVTOCI	**3,000**
Comprehensive income	**€ XXX**

Recording Sale of Shares On February 1, 2030, Su sold all of its Taur Inc. shares, receiving proceeds of $22,500. Before Su records the sale, it first updates the carrying amount of the Taur Inc. equity investment to fair value and recognizes any unrealized gain or loss as shown in **Illustration 13.13** (see **Ethics Note**).

ETHICS NOTE

Some managers seem to hold their non-trading securities that have experienced losses, while selling those that have gains, thus increasing income. Do you think this is ethical?

ILLUSTRATION 13.13

Adjustment to fair value of investment

Non-Trading Equity Investment (FVTOCI)	
Fair value of Taur equity investment (February 1, 2030)	$22,500
Fair value of Taur equity investment (December 31, 2029)	23,000
OCI—Unrealized gain or loss on equity investments at FVTOCI	**$ (500)**

Su makes the following entry to reduce the equity investment and recognize the unrealized loss for Taur shares as follows.

Feb. 1	OCI—Unrealized Gain or Loss on Equity Investments at FVTOCI	500	
	Fair Value Adjustment—Equity Investments at FVTOCI		500
	(To record unrealized loss on Taur shares)		

A = L + E
−500 (A); −500 (E)
Cash Flows
no effect

The following entry is then made to record the sale of the investment.

Feb. 1	Cash	22,500	
	Equity Investments at FVTOCI		20,000
	Fair Value Adjustment—Equity Investments at FVTOCI		2,500
	(To record sale of Taur shares)		

A = L + E
+22,500
−20,000
−2,500
Cash Flows
+22,500

The entry to transfer OCI—Unrealized Gain or Loss on Equity Investments at FVTOCI to Accumulated Other Comprehensive Income is as follows.

Feb. 1	Accumulated Other Comprehensive Income	500	
	OCI—Unrealized Gain or Loss on Equity Investments at FVTOCI		500
	(To close unrealized gain or loss to equity)		

A = L + E
−500 (E)
+500 (E)
Cash Flows
no effect

Reclassification Adjustment When an equity investment classified as FVTOCI is sold, the cumulative gain or loss previously recognized in other comprehensive income (OCI) is

never reclassified from equity to profit or loss. The balance of unrealized gains or losses in accumulated other comprehensive income may be transferred to **retained earnings.**

Since Su Company has sold all of Taur Inc. shares, it transfers the balance of unrealized gain on equity investments at FVTOCI ($3,000 – $500) in accumulated other comprehensive income to retained earnings as follows.

A	=	L	+	E
				−2,500
				+2,500

Cash Flows
no effect

Feb. 1	Accumulated Other Comprehensive Income	2,500	
	Retained Earnings		2,500
	(To transfer from AOCI to retained earnings)		

Significant Influence

When an investor company owns only a small portion of the ordinary shares of another company, the investor cannot exercise control over the investee. But, when an investor owns between 20% and 50% of the voting shares of a company, it is presumed that the investor has significant influence over the financial and operating activities of the investee. When an investor has significant influence but not control over an investee, it refers to the investee as an **associate**. The investor probably has a representative on the associate's board of directors and, through that representative, may exercise some control over the associate. The associate company in some sense becomes part of the investor company. **Note that the percentage ownership criterion serves only as a guideline; the ability to influence is the key criterion.**

Equity Method

HELPFUL HINT
Under the equity method, the investor recognizes revenue on the accrual basis, i.e., when it is earned by the associate.

In instances of "significant influence" (generally an investment of 20% or more), the investor must account for the equity investment using the **equity method**. Under the equity method, **the investor records its share of the net income of the associate in the year when it is earned** (see **Helpful Hint**). Under the equity method, the investor company initially records the investment in ordinary shares of an associate at cost. After that, it **adjusts** the investment account annually to show the investor's equity in the associate. Each year, the investor does the following.

1. It increases (debits) the investment account and increases (credits) revenue for its share of the associate's net income.[3]
2. The investor also decreases (credits) the investment account for the amount of dividends received. The investment account is reduced for dividends received because payment of a dividend decreases the net assets of the associate.

An alternative might be to delay recognizing the investor's share of net income until the associate declares a cash dividend. But, that approach would ignore the fact that the investor and associate are, in some sense, one company, making the investor better off by the associate's earned income.

Recording Acquisition of Shares Assume that Milar plc acquires 30% of the ordinary shares of Beck plc for £120,000 on January 1, 2029. The entry to record this transaction is:

A	=	L	+	E
+120,000				
−120,000				

Cash Flows
−120,000

Jan. 1	Equity Method Investments	120,000	
	Cash		120,000
	(To record purchase of Beck ordinary shares)		

Recording Revenue and Dividends For 2029, Beck reports net income of £100,000. It declares and pays a £40,000 cash dividend. Milar records (1) its share of Beck's income, £30,000 (30% × £100,000), and (2) the reduction in the investment account for the dividends received, £12,000 (£40,000 × 30%). The entries are:

A	=	L	+	E
+30,000				+30,000 Rev

Cash Flows
no effect

(1)

Dec. 31	Equity Method Investments	30,000	
	Revenue from Equity Method Investments		30,000
	(To record 30% equity in Beck's 2029 net income)		

[3]Conversely, the investor increases (debits) a loss account and decreases (credits) the investment account for its share of the associate's net loss.

(2)

Dec. 31	Cash	12,000	
	Equity Method Investments		12,000
	(To record dividends received)		

A	=	L	+	E
+12,000				
−12,000				

Cash Flows
+12,000

Illustration 13.14 shows Milar's investment and revenue accounts after it posts the transactions for the year.

ILLUSTRATION 13.14
Investment and revenue accounts after posting

Equity Method Investments

Jan. 1	120,000	Dec. 31	12,000
Dec. 31	30,000		
Dec. 31	Bal. 138,000		

Revenue from Equity Method Investments

		Dec. 31	30,000

During the year, the investment account increased £18,000. This increase of £18,000 is explained as follows:

1. Milar records a £30,000 increase in revenue from its equity investment in Beck.
2. Milar records a £12,000 decrease due to dividends received from its equity investment in Beck.

Note that the difference between reported revenue under the fair value method and reported revenue under the equity method can be significant. For example, Milar would report only £12,000 (30% × £40,000) of dividend revenue if it used the fair value method.

Controlling Interest

A company that owns more than 50% of the ordinary shares of another entity is known as the **parent company**.

- The entity whose shares the parent company owns is called the **subsidiary (affiliated) company**.
- Because of its share ownership, the parent company has a **controlling interest** in the subsidiary.

Consolidated Financial Statements

When a company owns more than 50% of the ordinary shares of another company, it usually prepares **consolidated financial statements** (See **Helpful Hint**).

- Consolidated financial statements present the total assets and liabilities controlled by the parent company.
- They also present the total revenues and expenses of the subsidiary companies.

HELPFUL HINT
If parent (A) has three wholly owned subsidiaries (B, C, and D), there are four separate legal entities. From the viewpoint of the shareholders of the parent company, there is only one economic entity.

Companies prepare consolidated statements **in addition to** the financial statements for the parent and individual subsidiary companies. Whether or not consolidated financial statements are prepared, the parent company generally accounts for the investment in the subsidiary using the equity method as explained in the previous section of this chapter.

Consolidated statements are useful to the shareholders, board of directors, and managers of the parent company. These statements indicate the magnitude and scope of operations of the companies under common control. For example, regulators and the courts undoubtedly used the consolidated statements of **AT&T** (USA) to determine whether a breakup of the company was in the public interest. **Illustration 13.15** lists three companies that prepare consolidated statements and some of the companies they have owned. Appendix 13A discusses how to prepare consolidated financial statements.

ILLUSTRATION 13.15
Examples of consolidated companies and their subsidiaries

Unilever (NLD)	**Alibaba** (CHN)	**The Disney Company** (USA)
Hellmann's	Taobao	Capital Cities/ABC, Inc.
Dove	Lazada	Disneyland, Disney World
Rexona	DingTalk	Mighty Ducks
Knorr	TMall	Anaheim Angels
		ESPN

Accounting Across the Organization adidas

Who's in Control?

adidas (DEU) owns 100% of the shares of **Rockport** (USA). The ordinary shareholders of adidas elect the board of directors of the company, who, in turn, select the officers and managers. The board of directors also controls the property owned by adidas, which includes the ordinary shares of Rockport.

Svenni/Adobe stock

Thus, the shareholders of adidas are in control of the operations of Rockport. These relationships are illustrated below.

Where on adidas's statement of financial position will you find its investment in Rockport? (Answer is available near the end of the chapter.)

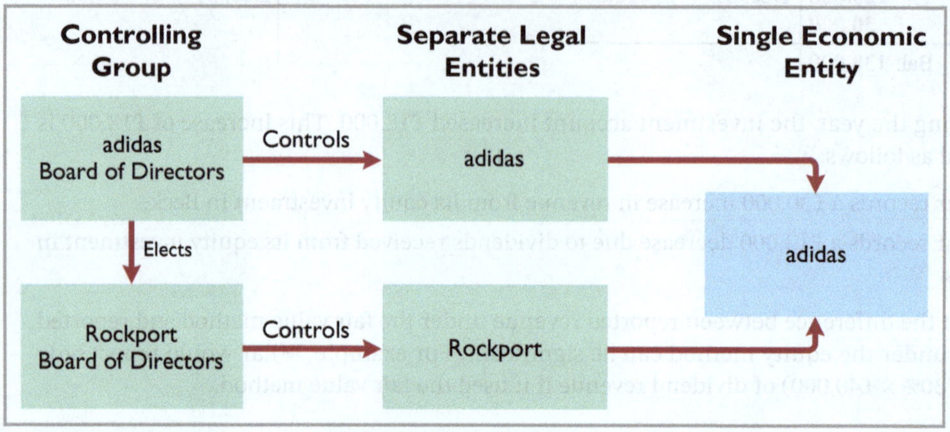

ACTION PLAN

- **Presume that the investor has relatively little influence over the investee when an investor owns less than 20% of the ordinary shares of another company. In this case, net income earned by the investee is not considered a proper basis for recognizing income from the investment by the investor.**
- **Presume significant influence for investments of 20%–50%. Therefore, record the investor's share of the net income of the associate.**

DO IT! 2b | Equity Investments

Presented below are two independent situations.

1. Rho Jean Ltd. acquired 5% of the 400,000 ordinary shares of Stillwater Ltd. at a total cost of NT$60 per share on May 18, 2029. These shares are classified as trading securities. On August 30, Stillwater declared and paid a NT$750,000 dividend. On December 31, Stillwater reported net income of NT$2,440,000 for the year.
2. Natal, Ltd. obtained significant influence over North Sails by buying 40% of North Sails' 60,000 outstanding ordinary shares at a cost of NT$120 per share on January 1, 2029. On April 15, North Sails declared and paid a cash dividend of NT$450,000. On December 31, North Sails reported net income of NT$1,200,000 for the year.

Prepare all necessary journal entries for 2029 for (1) Rho Jean and (2) Natal.

Solution

1.	May 18	Financial Assets at FVTPL (400,000 × 5% × NT$60) Cash (To record purchase of 20,000 shares of Stillwater)	1,200,000	1,200,000
	Aug. 30	Cash Dividend Revenue (NT$750,000 × 5%) (To record receipt of cash dividend)	37,500	37,500
2.	Jan. 1	Equity Method Investments (60,000 × 40% × NT$120) Cash (To record purchase of 24,000 shares of North Sails)	2,880,000	2,880,000
	Apr. 15	Cash Equity Method Investments (NT$450,000 × 40%) (To record receipt of cash dividend)	180,000	180,000
	Dec. 31	Equity Method Investments (NT$1,200,000 × 40%) Revenue from Equity Method Investments (To record 40% equity in North Sails' net income)	480,000	480,000

Related exercise material: **BE13.2, BE13.3, DO IT! 13.2b, E13.4, E13.5, E13.6, E13.7, and E13.8.**

13.3 Financial Statements Presentation

LEARNING OBJECTIVE 3

Indicate how debt and equity investments are reported in financial statements.

Statement of Financial Position Presentation

In the statement of financial position, companies classify investments as either current assets (i.e., short-term) or non-current assets (i.e., long-term). Financial assets at FVTPL (i.e., trading securities) are always classified as current assets. Financial assets at FVTOCI and financial assets at amortized cost can be either current assets or non-current assets depending on the circumstances. (See **Helpful Hint**.)

HELPFUL HINT

Short-term investments (also called marketable securities) are securities held by a company that are:

1. **Readily marketable.**
2. **Intended to be converted into cash within the next year or operating cycle, whichever is longer.**

Investments that do not meet both criteria are classified as long-term investments.

Presentation of Realized and Unrealized Gain or Loss

Companies must present in the financial statements gains and losses on investments, whether realized or unrealized. In the income statement, companies report the gains and losses listed in **Illustration 13.16** within the investing category. Interest and dividend revenue are also reported in the investing category of the income statement.

ILLUSTRATION 13.16

Income and expenses related to investments

Investing Category Income and Expenses	
Interest Revenue	Gain on Sale of Financial Assets at Amortized Cost
Dividend Revenue	Loss on Sale of Financial Assets at Amortized Cost
Revenue from Equity Method Investments	Gain on Sale of Debt Investments at FVTOCI
	Loss on Sale of Debt Investments at FVTOCI
	Gain on Financial Assets at FVTPL
	Loss on Financial Assets at FVTPL

- In a comprehensive income statement, companies report unrealized gains or losses on financial assets at FVTOCI as other comprehensive income or loss.
- In the statement of financial position, companies report in the equity section accumulated other comprehensive income or loss.

Illustration 13.17 shows the statement of financial position of equity assuming that Dawson plc has share capital—ordinary of £3,000,000, retained earnings of £1,500,000, and an accumulated other comprehensive loss of £100,000.

ILLUSTRATION 13.17

Accumulated other comprehensive loss

Dawson plc
Statement of Financial Position (partial)

Equity	
Share capital—ordinary	£3,000,000
Retained earnings	1,500,000
Accumulated other comprehensive loss	**(100,000)**
Total equity	£4,400,000

Note that the presentation of accumulated other comprehensive loss is similar to the presentation of the cost of treasury shares in the equity section (it decreases equity). Accumulated other comprehensive income is added to equity. Reporting the unrealized gain or loss as components of other comprehensive income and in the equity section serves two purposes:

1. It reduces the volatility of net income due to fluctuations in fair value.
2. It informs the financial statement user of the gain or loss that would occur if the securities were sold at fair value.

Companies must report items such as unrealized gains or losses on financial assets at FVTOCI as part of comprehensive income. Unrealized gains and losses on financial assets at FVTOCI therefore affect comprehensive income (and equity) but are not included in the computation of net income.

Classified Statement of Financial Position

We have presented many sections of classified statements of financial position in this and preceding chapters.

The classified statement of financial position in **Illustration 13.18** includes, in one place, key topics from previous chapters: the issuance of par value ordinary shares, restrictions of retained earnings, and issuance of bonds. From this chapter, the statement includes (highlighted in red) short-term and long-term investments.

- The investments under current assets are considered financial assets at FVTPL.
- The long-term investments in shares of less than 20% owned companies are considered equity investments at FVTOCI.
- **Illustration 13.18** also includes a long-term investment reported using the equity method and descriptive notations within the statement, such as the cost flow method for valuing inventory and one note to the statement.

ILLUSTRATION 13.18

Classified statement of financial position

Pace SA
Statement of Financial Position
December 31, 2029

Assets			
Intangible assets			
Goodwill			€ 270,000
Property, plant, and equipment			
Land		€ 200,000	
Buildings	€ 800,000		
Less: Accumulated depreciation—buildings	200,000	600,000	
Equipment	180,000		
Less: Accumulated depreciation—equipment	54,000	126,000	
Total property, plant, and equipment			926,000
Investments			
Financial assets at amortized cost		**20,000**	
Financial assets at fair value through other comprehensive income		**30,000**	
Investments accounted for using equity method		**150,000**	200,000
Current assets			
Prepaid insurance		23,000	
Inventory, at FIFO cost		43,000	
Accounts receivable	84,000		
Less: Loss allowance	4,000	80,000	
Financial assets at fair value through profit or loss		**147,000**	
Cash		21,000	314,000
Total assets			€ 1,710,000

ILLUSTRATION 13.18
(Continued)

Equity and Liabilities		
Equity		
Share capital—ordinary, €10 par value, 200,000 shares authorized, 80,000 shares issued and outstanding	€800,000	
Share premium—ordinary	100,000	
Retained earnings (Note 1)	255,000	
Accumulated other comprehensive income	**10,000**	€1,165,000
Non-current liabilities		
Bonds payable, 10%, due 2033		290,000
Current liabilities		
Accounts payable	185,000	
Income taxes payable	60,000	
Interest payable	10,000	255,000
Total equity and liabilities		€1,710,000

Note 1. Retained earnings of €100,000 is restricted for plant expansion.

DO IT! 3 | Financial Statement Presentation of Investments

Identify where each of the following items would be reported in the financial statements.

1. Interest earned on investments in bonds.
2. Fair value adjustment—FVTOCI.
3. Unrealized loss on financial assets at FVTOCI.
4. Gain on sale of debt investments at FVTOCI.
5. Gain on financial assets at FVTPL.

Use the following possible categories:

Statement of financial position:

Intangible assets	Equity
Property, plant, and equipment	Non-current liabilities
Investments	Current liabilities
Current assets	

Income statement:

Investing category income and expenses

Comprehensive income statement:

Other comprehensive income

ACTION PLAN

- **Classify investments as current assets if they will be held for less than one year.**
- **Report gains or losses on financial assets at FVTPL in income.**
- **Report unrealized gains or losses on financial assets at FVTOCI in other comprehensive income.**
- **Report realized earnings on investments in the investing category of the income statement.**

Solution

Item	Financial Statement	Category
1. Interest earned on investments in bonds	Income statement	Investing category income and expenses
2. Fair value adjustment—FVTOCI	Statement of financial position	Investments
3. Unrealized loss on financial assets at FVTOCI	Comprehensive income statement	Other comprehensive income
4. Gain on sale of debt investments at FVTOCI	Income statement	Investing category income and expenses
5. Gain on financial assets at FVTPL	Income statement	Investing category income and expenses

Related exercise material: **BE13.7, BE13.8, DO IT! 13.3, E13.10 and E13.11.**

Appendix 13A Preparing Consolidated Financial Statements

LEARNING OBJECTIVE *4

Describe the form and content of consolidated financial statements as well as how to prepare them.

Most of the large businesses are holding companies that own other companies. They therefore prepare **consolidated** financial statements that combine the separate companies.

Consolidated Statement of Financial Position

Companies prepare consolidated statements of financial position from the individual statements of their affiliated companies. They do not prepare consolidated statements from ledger accounts kept by the consolidated entity because only the separate legal entities maintain accounting records.

All items in the individual statements of financial position are included in the consolidated statement except amounts that pertain to transactions between the affiliated companies.

- Transactions between the affiliated companies are identified as **intercompany transactions**.
- The process of excluding these transactions in preparing consolidated statements is referred to as **intercompany eliminations** (see **Helpful Hint**).
- These eliminations are necessary to avoid overstating assets, liabilities, and equity in the consolidated statement of financial position.

HELPFUL HINT

Eliminations are aptly named because they eliminate duplicate data. They are not adjustments.

For example, amounts owed by a subsidiary to a parent company and the related receivable reported by the parent company would be eliminated. The objective in a consolidated statement is to show only obligations to and receivables from parties who are not part of the affiliated group of companies.

To illustrate, assume that on January 1, 2029, Powers plc pays £150,000 in cash for 100% of Serto plc's ordinary shares. Powers records the investment at cost. **Illustration 13A.1** presents the separate statements of financial position of the two companies immediately after the purchase, together with combined and consolidated data.[4] Powers obtains the balances in the "combined" column by adding the items in the separate statements of the affiliated companies. The combined totals do not represent a consolidated statement of financial position because there has been a double-counting of assets and equity in the amount of £150,000.

ILLUSTRATION 13A.1

Combined and consolidated data

Powers plc and Serto plc
Statement of Financial Position
January 1, 2029

Assets	Powers plc	Serto plc	Combined Data	Consolidated Data
Plant and equipment (net)	£325,000	£145,000	£470,000	£470,000
Investment in Serto plc ordinary shares	150,000		150,000	-0-
Current assets	50,000	80,000	130,000	130,000
Total assets	£525,000	£225,000	£750,000	£600,000
Equity and Liabilities				
Share capital—ordinary	£300,000	£100,000	£400,000	£300,000
Retained earnings	175,000	50,000	225,000	175,000
Current liabilities	50,000	75,000	125,000	125,000
Total equity and liabilities	£525,000	£225,000	£750,000	£600,000

[4] We use condensed data throughout this material to keep details at a minimum.

The Investment in Serto ordinary shares that appears on the statement of financial position of Powers represents an interest in the net assets of Serto. As a result, there has been a double-counting of assets. Similarly, there has been a double-counting in equity because the ordinary shares of Serto are completely owned by the shareholders of Powers.

The balances in the consolidated data column are the amounts that should appear in the consolidated statement of financial position. The double-counting has been eliminated by showing Investment in Serto at zero and by reporting only the share capital and retained earnings of Powers as equity.

Use of a Worksheet—Cost Equal to Book Value

The preparation of a consolidated statement of financial position is usually facilitated by the use of a worksheet (see **Helpful Hint**). As shown in **Illustration 13A.2**, the worksheet for a consolidated statement of financial position contains columns for:

1. the statement of financial position data for the separate legal entities,
2. intercompany eliminations, and
3. consolidated data.

HELPFUL HINT

As in the case of the worksheets explained earlier in this text, consolidated worksheets are also optional.

All data in the worksheet relate to the preceding example in which Powers plc acquires 100% ownership of Serto plc for £150,000. In this case, the cost of the investment, £150,000, is equal to the book value [£150,000 (£225,000 − £75,000)] of the subsidiary's net assets. The intercompany elimination results in a credit to the investment account maintained by Powers for its balance, £150,000, and debits to the Share Capital and Retained Earnings accounts of Serto for their respective balances, £100,000 and £50,000.

As in the case of the worksheets explained earlier in this text, consolidated worksheets are also optional.

It is important to recognize that companies make intercompany eliminations solely on the worksheet to present correct consolidated data. Neither of the affiliated companies journalizes or posts the eliminations. Therefore, eliminations do not affect the ledger accounts. Powers' investment account and Serto's share capital and retained earnings accounts are reported by the separate entities in preparing their own financial statements.

ILLUSTRATION 13A.2

Worksheet—cost equal to book value

Powers plc

Home Insert Page Layout Formulas Data Review View

P18 fx

	A	B	C	D	E	F
1	**Powers plc and Subsidiary**					
2	**Worksheet—Consolidated Statement of Financial Position**					
3	**January 1, 2029 (Acquisition Date)**					
4		**Powers**	**Serto**	**Eliminations**		**Consolidated**
5	**Assets**	**plc**	**plc**	**Dr.**	**Cr.**	**Data**
6	Plant and equipment (net)	325,000	145,000			470,000
7	Investment in Serto plc ordinary					
8	shares	150,000			150,000	-0-
9	Current assets	50,000	80,000			130,000
10	Totals	525,000	225,000			600,000
11						
12						
13	**Equity and Liabilities**					
14	Share capital—Powers plc	300,000				300,000
15	Share capital—Serto plc		100,000	100,000		-0-
16	Retained earnings—Powers plc	175,000				175,000
17	Retained earnings—Serto plc		50,000	50,000		-0-
18	Current liabilities	50,000	75,000			125,000
19	Totals	525,000	225,000	150,000	150,000	600,000
20						

Use of a Worksheet—Cost Above Book Value

The cost of acquiring the ordinary shares of another company may be above or below its book value. The management of the parent company may pay more than book value for the shares, generally for one of two reasons:

1. It believes the fair values of identifiable assets such as land, buildings, and equipment are higher than their recorded book values.
2. It believes the subsidiary's future earnings prospects warrant a payment for goodwill.

To illustrate, assume the same data used above, except that Powers plc pays £165,000 in cash for 100% of Serto's ordinary shares. The excess of cost over book value is £15,000 (£165,000 − £150,000). Powers recognizes this amount separately in eliminating the parent company's investment account, as shown in **Illustration 13A.3**.

Total assets and total equity and liabilities are the same as in the preceding example (£600,000). However, in this case, total assets include £15,000 of Excess of Cost Over Book Value of Subsidiary and current assets are £15,000 less due to the higher price paid to Serto. The disposition of the excess is explained in the next section.

ILLUSTRATION 13A.3

Worksheet—cost above to book value

Powers plc

Home Insert Page Layout Formulas Data Review View

P18 fx

	A	B	C	D	E	F
1	**Powers plc and Subsidiary**					
2	**Worksheet—Consolidated Statement of Financial Position**					
3	**January 1, 2029 (Acquisition Date)**					
4		**Powers**	**Serto**	**Eliminations**		**Consolidated**
5	**Assets**	**plc**	**plc**	**Dr.**	**Cr.**	**Data**
6	Plant and equipment (net)	325,000	145,000			470,000
7	Investment in Serto plc ordinary					
8	shares	165,000			165,000	-0-
9	Current assets	35,000	80,000			115,000
10	Excess of cost over book value of					
11	subsidiary			15,000		15,000
12	Totals	525,000	225,000			600,000
13						
14						
15	**Equity and Liabilities**					
16	Share capital—Powers plc	300,000				300,000
17	Share capital—Serto plc		100,000	100,000		-0-
18	Retained earnings—Powers plc	175,000				175,000
19	Retained earnings—Serto plc		50,000	50,000		-0-
20	Current liabilities	50,000	75,000			125,000
21	Totals	525,000	225,000	165,000	165,000	600,000
22						
23						
24	Note that a separate line is added to the worksheet for the excess of cost over book value of subsidiary.					

Content of a Consolidated Statement of Financial Position

HELPFUL HINT
The consolidated worksheet is another useful spreadsheet application. This is an easier worksheet to attempt since the required instructions are very straightforward.

To illustrate a consolidated statement of financial position, we will use the worksheet shown in Illustration 13A.3 (see **Helpful Hint**). This worksheet shows an excess of cost over book value of £15,000.

- In the consolidated statement of financial position, Powers first allocates this amount to specific assets, such as plant and equipment and inventory, if their fair values on the acquisition date exceed their book values.
- Any remainder is considered to be goodwill. For Serto, assume that the fair value of the plant and equipment is £155,000. Thus, Powers allocates £10,000 of the excess of cost over book value to plant and equipment, and the remainder, £5,000, to goodwill.

Illustration 13A.4 shows the condensed consolidated statement of financial position of Powers plc.

Through innovative financial restructuring, **The Coca-Cola Company** (USA) at one time eliminated a substantial amount of non-intercompany debt. It sold to the public 51% of two bottling companies. The "49% solution," as insiders call the strategy, enabled Coca-Cola to keep effective control over the businesses. It also swept $3 billion of debt from its consolidated statement of financial position because it no longer consolidated the two bottling companies. Finally, the new companies obtained independent access to equity markets to satisfy their own large appetites for capital.

ILLUSTRATION 13A.4
Consolidated statement of financial position

Powers plc
Consolidated Statement of Financial Position
January 1, 2029

Assets		
Goodwill		£ 5,000
Plant and equipment (net)		480,000
Current assets		115,000
Total assets		£600,000
Equity and Liabilities		
Equity		
Share capital—ordinary	£300,000	
Retained earnings	175,000	£475,000
Current liabilities		125,000
Total equity and liabilities		£600,000

Consolidated Income Statement

Affiliated companies also prepare a consolidated income statement.

- This statement shows the results of operations of affiliated companies as though they are one economic unit.
- This means that the statement shows only revenue and expense transactions between the consolidated entity and companies and individuals who are outside the affiliated group.

Consequently, all intercompany revenue and expense transactions must be eliminated. Intercompany transactions such as sales between affiliates and interest on loans charged by one affiliate to another must be eliminated. A worksheet facilitates the preparation of consolidated income statements in the same manner as it does for the statement of financial position.

Review and Practice

Learning Objectives Review

1 Explain how to account for debt investments.

Companies record investments in debt securities when they purchase bonds, receive or accrue interest, and sell the bonds. When debt investments are classified as held-for-collection, they are accounted for based on amortized cost. They report gains or losses on the sale of bonds in the investing category of the income statement.

2 Explain how to account for equity investments.

Companies record investments in shares when they purchase the shares, receive dividends, and sell the shares. When ownership is less than 20%, fair value method is used. When ownership is between 20% and 50%, the equity method should be used. When ownership is more than 50%, companies prepare consolidated financial statements.

When a company owns more than 50% of the shares of another company, it prepares consolidated financial statements. These statements indicate the magnitude and scope of operations of the companies under common control.

3 Indicate how debt and Equity investments are reported in financial statements.

Investments in debt securities are classified as trading, held-for-collection, or held-for-collection and selling securities for valuation and reporting purposes. Equity investments are classified either as trading or non-trading. Equity investments have no maturity date and therefore are never classified as held-for-collection. Trading securities are reported as current assets at fair value, with changes from cost reported in net income. Non-trading securities are also reported at fair value, with the changes from cost reported in other comprehensive income. Non-trading equity investments and both held-for-collection and held-for-collection and selling debt investments are classified as short-term or long-term, depending on their expected future sale or maturity date.

Short-term investments are securities that are (a) readily marketable and (b) intended to be converted to cash within the next year or operating cycle, whichever is longer. Investments that do not meet both criteria are classified as long-term investments.

*4 Describe the form and content of consolidated financial statements as well as how to prepare them.

Consolidated financial statements are similar in form and content to the financial statements of an individual company. A consolidated statement of financial position shows the assets and liabilities controlled by the parent company. A consolidated income statement shows the results of operations of affiliated companies as though they are one economic unit. The worksheet for a consolidated statement of financial position contains columns for (a) the statement of financial position data for the separate entities, (b) intercompany eliminations, and (c) consolidated data.

Glossary Review

Amortized cost Investments in debt securities held for collection are initially recorded at cost. Interest revenue including the amortization of any discount or premium is recorded each period. (p. 13-7).

Associate An investee company that an investor has significant influence over but does not control. (p. 13-20).

Consolidated financial statements Financial statements that present the assets and liabilities controlled by the parent company and the total revenues and expenses of the subsidiary companies. (p. 13-5).

Controlling interest Ownership of more than 50% of the ordinary shares of another entity. (p. 13-21).

Debt investments Investments in government and company bonds. (p. 13-4).

Effective-interest method A method of amortizing bond discount or bond premium that results in periodic interest revenue equal to a constant percentage of the carrying value of the bonds. (p. 13-9)

Equity investments Investments in shares of other company. (p. 13-15).

Equity method An accounting method in which the investment in ordinary shares is initially recorded at cost, and the investment account is then adjusted annually to show the investor's equity in the associate. (p. 13-5).

Fair value Amount for which a security could be sold in a normal market. (p. 13-12).

Financial assets measured at amortized cost The financial asset is held within a business model whose objective is to hold financial assets to collect their contractual cash flows and the cash flows from the asset are only the payments of principal and interest. (p. 13-4).

Financial assets at fair value through other comprehensive income (FVTOCI) The financial asset is held within a business model whose objective is to both collect contractual cash flows and sell the financial asset. (p. 13-4).

Financial assets at fair value through profit or loss (FVTPL) Financial assets that do not qualify to be measured at amortized cost or FVTOCI. (p. 13-4).

Held-for-collection and selling securities Debt investments that are held both to collect contractual cash flows and to sell. (p. 13-4)

Held-for-collection securities Debt investments that are held to collect contractual cash flows. (p. 13-4)

***Intercompany eliminations** Eliminations made to exclude the effects of intercompany transactions when preparing consolidated statements. (p. 13-26).

***Intercompany transactions** Transactions between affiliated companies. (p. 13-26).

Investment portfolio A group of shares and/or debt securities in different companies held for investment purposes. (p. 13-15).

Long-term investments Investments that are not readily marketable or that management does not intend to convert into cash within the next year or operating cycle, whichever is longer. (p. 13-23).

Non-trading equity investments Equity investments held for purposes other than trading. (p. 13-16).

Parent company A company that owns more than 50% of the ordinary-shares of another entity. (p. 13-21).

Short-term investments Investments that are readily marketable and intended to be converted into cash within the next year or operating cycle, whichever is longer. (p. 13-23).

Subsidiary (affiliated) company A company with more than 50% of its shares is owned by another company. (p. 13-21).

Trading securities Securities bought and held primarily for sale in the near term to generate income from short-term price differences. (p. 13-13).

Practice Multiple-Choice Questions

1. **(LO 1)** Which of the following is **not** a primary reason why companies invest in debt and equity securities?
   - **a.** They wish to gain control of a competitor.
   - **b.** They have excess cash.
   - **c.** They wish to move into a new line of business.
   - **d.** They are required to by law.

2. **(LO 1)** Debt investments are initially recorded at:
   - **a.** cost.
   - **b.** cost plus dividends.
   - **c.** par value.
   - **d.** face value.

3. **(LO 1)** Hanes Group sells debt investments at FVTOCI costing £26,000 for £28,000, plus accrued interest that has been recorded. In journalizing the sale, credits are to:
   - **a.** Debt Investments at FVTOCI and Loss on Sale of Debt Investments at FVTOCI.
   - **b.** Debt Investments at FVTOCI, Gain on Sale of Debt Investments at FVTOCI, and Interest Receivable.
   - **c.** Equity Investments and Interest Receivable.
   - **d.** No correct answer is given.

4. **(LO 2)** Anatolian A.Ş. receives net proceeds of ₺42,000 on the sale of FVTPL equity investments that cost ₺39,500. This transaction will result in reporting in the income statement a:
   - **a.** loss of ₺2,500 in the investing category of the income statement.
   - **b.** loss of ₺2,500 in operating expenses.
   - **c.** gain of ₺2,500 in the investing category of the income statement.
   - **d.** gain of ₺2,500 in operating expenses.

5. **(LO 2)** The equity method of accounting for long-term investments in shares should be used when the investor has significant influence over an associate and owns:
   - **a.** between 20% and 50% of the associate's ordinary shares.
   - **b.** 30% or more of the associate's ordinary shares.
   - **c.** more than 50% of the associate's ordinary shares.
   - **d.** less than 20% of the associate's ordinary shares.

6. **(LO 2)** Assume that Horicon NV acquired 25% of the ordinary shares of Sheboygan NV on January 1, 2029, for €300,000. During 2029, Sheboygan reported net income of €160,000 and paid total dividends of €60,000. If Horicon uses the equity method to account for its investment, the balance in the investment account on December 31, 2029, will be:
   - **a.** €300,000.
   - **b.** €325,000.
   - **c.** €400,000.
   - **d.** €340,000.

7. **(LO 2)** Using the information in Question 6, what entry would Horicon make to record the receipt of the dividend from Sheboygan?
   - **a.** Debit Cash and credit Revenue from Equity Investments.
   - **b.** Debit Cash Dividends and credit Revenue from Equity Investments.
   - **c.** Debit Cash and credit Equity Method Investments.
   - **d.** Debit Cash and credit Dividend Revenue.

8. **(LO 2)** You have a controlling interest if:
   - **a.** you own more than 20% of a company's ordinary shares.
   - **b.** you are the president of the company.
   - **c.** you use the equity method.
   - **d.** you own more than 50% of a company's ordinary shares.

9. **(LO 2)** Which of the following statements is **false**? Consolidated financial statements are useful to:
   - **a.** determine the profitability of specific subsidiaries.
   - **b.** determine the total profitability of companies under common control.
   - **c.** determine the breadth of a parent company's operations.
   - **d.** determine the full extent of total obligations of companies under common control.

10. **(LO 3)** At the end of the first year of operations, the total cost of the trading securities (financial assets at FVTPL) portfolio is ₩120,000,000. Total fair value is ₩115,000,000. The financial statements should show:
    - **a.** a reduction of an asset of ₩5,000,000 and an other comprehensive loss of ₩5,000,000.
    - **b.** a reduction of an asset of ₩5,000,000 and an unrealized loss of ₩5,000,000 in the equity section.
    - **c.** a reduction of an asset of ₩5,000,000 in the current assets section and a loss of ₩5,000,000 in the investing category of the income statement.
    - **d.** an increment of an asset of ₩5,000,000 in the current assets section and a gain of ₩5,000,000 in the investing category of the income statement.

11. **(LO 3)** At December 31, 2029, the fair value of non-trading securities (equity investments at FVTOCI) is €41,300 and the cost is €39,800. At January 1, 2029, there was a credit balance of €900 in the Fair Value Adjustment—Equity Investments at FVTOCI account. The required adjusting entry would be:
    - **a.** Debit Fair Value Adjustment—Equity Investments at FVTOCI for €1,500 and credit OCI—Unrealized Gain or Loss on Equity Investments at FVTOCI for €1,500.
    - **b.** Debit Fair Value Adjustment—Equity Investments at FVTOCI for €600 and credit OCI—Unrealized Gain or Loss on Equity Investments at FVTOCI for €600.
    - **c.** Debit Fair Value Adjustment—Equity Investments at FVTOCI for €2,400 and credit OCI—Unrealized Gain or Loss on Financial Assets at FVTOCI for €2,400.
    - **d.** Debit OCI—Unrealized Gain or Loss on Equity Investments at FVTOCI for €2,400 and credit Fair Value Adjustment—Equity Investments at FVTOCI for €2,400.

12. **(LO 3)** In the statement of financial position, a debit balance in OCI—Unrealized Gain or Loss on Financial Assets at FVTOCI results in a(n):
    - **a.** increase to equity.
    - **b.** decrease to equity.
    - **c.** loss in the income statement.
    - **d.** loss in the retained earnings statement.

13. **(LO 3)** Short-term debt investments must be readily marketable and expected to be sold within:
    - **a.** 3 months from the date of purchase.
    - **b.** the next year or operating cycle, whichever is shorter.
    - **c.** the next year or operating cycle, whichever is longer.
    - **d.** the operating cycle.

*14. **(LO 4)** Pate Ltd. pays £175,000 for 100% of Sinko's ordinary shares when Sinko's equity consists of Share Capital—Ordinary £100,000 and Retained Earnings £60,000. In the worksheet for the consolidated statement of financial position, the eliminations will include a:

a. credit to Investment in Sinko Share Capital—Ordinary £160,000.

b. credit to Excess of Book Value over Cost of Subsidiary £15,000.

c. debit to Retained Earnings £75,000.

d. debit to Excess of Cost over Book Value of Subsidiary £15,000.

*15. **(LO 4)** Which of the following statements about intercompany eliminations is **true**?

a. They are not journalized or posted by any of the subsidiaries.

b. They do not affect the ledger accounts of any of the subsidiaries.

c. They are made solely on the worksheet to arrive at correct consolidated data.

d. All of these answer choices are correct.

*16. **(LO 4)** Which one of the following statements about consolidated income statements is **false**?

a. A worksheet facilitates the preparation of the statement.

b. The consolidated income statement shows the results of operations of affiliated companies as a single economic unit.

c. All revenue and expense transactions between parent and subsidiary companies are eliminated.

d. When a subsidiary is wholly owned, the form and content of the statement will differ from the income statement of an individual company.

Solutions

1. **d.** Companies are not required to by law to invest in debt and equity securities. The other choices are reasons why companies invest in debt and equity securities.

2. **a.** When debt investments are purchased, they are recorded at cost, not (b) cost plus dividends, (c) par value, or (d) face value.

3. **b.** Credits are made to Debt Investments at FVTOCI, Gain on Sale of Debt Investments at FVTOCI, and Interest Receivable. The other choices are therefore incorrect.

4. **c.** Because the cash received (₺42,000) is greater than the cost (₺39,500), this sale results in a gain, not a loss, which will be reported in the investing category of the income statement. The other choices are therefore incorrect.

5. **a.** The equity method is used when the investor can exercise significant influence and owns between 20% and 50% of the associate's ordinary shares. The other choices are therefore incorrect.

6. **b.** Horicon records the acquisition of the share investment by debiting Equity Investments €300,000 and crediting Cash €300,000. Then, Horicon records (1) its share in Sheboygan's net income (€160,000 × .25) by debiting Equity Method Investments €40,000 and crediting Income from Equity Investments €40,000 and (2) the reduction in the investment account for the dividends received (€60,000 × .25) by debiting Cash €15,000 and crediting Equity Method Investments €15,000. Thus, the balance in the investment account on December 31 will be €325,000 (€300,000 + €40,000 − €15,000), not (a) €300,000, (c) €400,000, or (d) €340,000.

7. **c.** Horicon records the receipt of the dividend from Sheboygan by debiting Cash and crediting Equity Method Investments. The other choices are therefore incorrect.

8. **d.** You have a controlling interest if you own more than 50% of a company's shares, not (a) 20% of a company's shares, (b) are president of the company, or (c) use the equity method.

9. **a.** Consolidated financial statements are not useful in determining the profitability of specific subsidiaries (legal entities) because consolidated financial statements represent the result of the single economic entity. The other choices are true statements.

10. **c.** The difference between the fair value (₩115,000,000) and total cost (₩120,000,000) of trading securities (financial assets at FVTPL) at the end of the first year would result in a reduction of an asset of ₩5,000,000 through the valuation allowance account in the current assets section and a loss of ₩5,000,000 in the investing category of the income statement. The other choices are therefore incorrect.

11. **c.** In this case, there is an unrealized gain of €1,500 because total fair value of €41,300 is €1,500 greater than the total cost of €39,800. The desired balance in the fair value adjustment account is €1,500 debit. The required adjusting entry considers the existing credit balance of €900 and is a debit to Fair Value Adjustment—Equity Investments at FVTOCI for €2,400 (€1,500 + €900) and a credit to OCI—Unrealized Gain or Loss on Equity Investments at FVTOCI for €2,400 (€1,500 + €900). The other choices are therefore incorrect.

12. **b.** A debit balance in OCI—Unrealized Gain or Loss on Financial Assets at FVTOCI decreases equity. The other choices are therefore incorrect.

13. **c.** Short-term debt investments are current assets that are expected to be consumed, sold, or converted to cash within one year or the operating cycle, whichever is longer. The other choices are therefore incorrect.

*14. **d.** The eliminations will include a debit to Excess of Cost over Book Value of Subsidiary £15,000 (£175,000 − £160,000). The other choices are therefore incorrect.

*15. **d.** All of the statements in choices (a), (b), and (c) are correct, so (d) is the best answer.

*16. **d.** When a subsidiary is wholly owned, the form and content of the statement will be the same as, not different from, the income statement of an individual company. The other choices are true statements.

Practice Brief Exercises

Journalize debt investments transactions.

1. **(LO 1)** Liriano SpA purchased debt investments measured at FVTPL for €85,000 on January 1, 2029. On July 1, 2029, Liriano received cash interest of €6,800. Journalize the purchase and the receipt of interest. Assume that no interest has been accrued.

Solution

1. Jan. 1	Financial Assets at FVTPL	85,000	
	Cash		85,000
July 1	Cash	6,800	
	Interest Revenue		6,800

2. **(LO 2)** On June 1, Meng Group buys 2,000 ordinary shares of Minaya Ltd. for ¥570,000 cash. On October 15, Meng sells the equity investments measured at FVTPL for ¥540,000 in cash. Journalize the purchase and sale of the ordinary shares.

Journalize equity investments transactions.

Solution

2. June 1	Financial Assets at FVTPL	570,000	
	Cash		570,000
Oct. 15	Loss on Financial Assets at FVTPL	30,000	
	Fair Value Adjustment—FVTPL		30,000
Oct. 15	Cash	540,000	
	Fair Value Adjustment—FVTPL	30,000	
	Financial Assets at FVTPL		570,000

3. **(LO 3)** The cost of the trading securities of Dylan Company at December 31, 2029, is $46,000. At December 31, 2029, the fair value of the securities is $50,000. (a) Prepare the adjusting entry to record the securities at fair value. (b) Show the financial statement presentation at December 31, 2029.

Prepare an adjusting entry for fair value and indicate statement presentation.

Solution

3. a. Dec. 31	Fair Value Adjustment—FVTPL	4,000	
	Gain on Financial Assets at FVTPL ($50,000 – $46,000)		4,000

b. **Statement of Financial Position**

Current assets
Financial Assets at FVTPL $50,000

Income Statement

Investing category income and expenses
Gain on Financial Assets at FVTPL $4,000

Practice Exercises

1. **(LO 1)** Chen Enterprises purchased 70 Feng Company 6%, 10-year, NT$10,000 bonds on January 1, 2029, for NT$700,000. The bonds pay interest annually on January 1. On January 1, 2030, after receipt of interest, Chen sold 42 of the bonds for NT$391,000. The bonds are held to collect contractual cash flows.

Journalize debt investment transactions, accrue interest, and record sale.

Instructions

Prepare the journal entries to record the transactions described above.

Solution

1. **January 1, 2029**

Financial Assets at Amortized Cost	700,000	
Cash		700,000

December 31, 2029

Interest Receivable	42,000	
Interest Revenue (NT$700,000 × 6%)		42,000

January 1, 2030

Cash	42,000	
Interest Receivable		42,000

January 1, 2030

Cash	391,000	
Loss on Sale of Financial Assets at Amortized Cost	29,000	
Financial Assets at Amortized Cost (42/70 × NT$700,000)		420,000

Journalize share investment transactions.

2. **(LO 2)** Cannon AG had the following transactions in 2029 pertaining to equity investments.

Feb. 1	Purchased 600 of Ronin ordinary shares (2% interest) for €6,000 cash.
July 1	Received cash dividends of €1 per share on Ronin shares.
Sept. 1	Sold 300 shares of Ronin shares for €4,200.
Dec. 1	Received cash dividends of €1 per share on Ronin shares.

Instructions

Journalize the transactions, assuming the equity investments are classified as trading securities.

Solution

2.

February 1, 2029

Financial Assets at FVTPL (600 × €10)	6,000	
Cash		6,000

July 1, 2029

Cash (600 × €1)	600	
Dividend Revenue		600

September 1, 2029

Fair Value Adjustment—FVTPL	1,200	
Gain on Financial Assets at FVTPL		1,200
Cash	4,200	
Financial Assets at FVTPL (€6,000 × 300/600)		3,000
Fair Value Adjustment—FVTPL		1,200

December 1, 2029

Cash (300 × €1)	300	
Dividend Revenue		300

Prepare adjusting entries for fair value, and indicate statement presentation for two classes of securities.

3. **(LO 3)** Sunshine Ltd. started business on January 1, 2029, and has the following data at December 31, 2029.

Securities	Cost	Fair Value
Trading	£120,000	£125,000
Non-trading	100,000	96,000

The non-trading securities are held as a long-term investment.

Instructions

a. Prepare the adjusting entries to report each class of securities at fair value.

b. Indicate the statement presentation of each class of securities and the related unrealized gain (loss) accounts.

Solution

3. **a.**

December 31, 2029

Fair Value Adjustment—FVTPL (£125,000 – £120,000)	5,000	
Gain on Financial Assets at FVTPL		5,000
OCI—Unrealized Gain or Loss on Financial Assets at FVTOCI (£100,000 – £96,000)	4,000	
Fair Value Adjustment—FVTOCI		4,000

b. **Statement of Financial Position**

Current assets	
Financial Assets at FVTPL	£125,000
Investments	
Financial Assets at FVTOCI	96,000
Equity	
Accumulated other comprehensive loss	£ 4,000

Income Statement

Investing category income and expenses	
Gain on Financial Assets at FVTPL	£ 5,000

Comprehensive Income Statement

Other comprehensive income	
Unrealized loss on Financial Assets at FVTOCI	£ 4,000

Practice Problem

(LO 2, 3) In its first year of operations, DeMarco plc had the following selected transactions in equity investments that are considered trading securities.

Journalize transactions and prepare adjusting entry to record fair value.

June 1	Purchased for cash 600 shares of Sanburg for £24.50 per share.
July 1	Purchased for cash 800 shares of Cey plc at £33.75 per share.
Sept. 1	Received a £1 per share cash dividend from Cey plc.
Nov. 1	Sold 200 shares of Sanburg for cash at £26.25 per share.
Dec. 15	Received a £0.50 per share cash dividend on Sanburg shares.

At December 31, the fair values per share were Sanburg £25 and Cey £30.

Instructions

a. Journalize the transactions.

b. Prepare the adjusting entry at December 31 to report the securities at fair value.

Solution

a. June 1	Financial Assets at FVTPL—Equity	14,700	
	Cash (600 × £24.50)		14,700
	(To record purchase of 600 shares of Sanburg)		
July 1	Financial Assets at FVTPL—Equity	27,000	
	Cash (800 × £33.75)		27,000
	(To record purchase of 800 shares of Cey)		
Sept. 1	Cash (800 × £1.00)	800	
	Dividend Revenue		800
	(To record receipt of £1 per share cash dividend from Cey)		
Nov. 1	Fair Value Adjustment—FVTPL	350	
	Gain on Financial Assets at FVTPL		350
	(To record gain on trading securities)		
	Cash (200 × £26.25)	5,250	
	Financial Assets at FVTPL—Equity		4,900
	Fair Value Adjustment—FVTPL		350
	(To record sale of 200 shares of Sanburg)		
Dec. 15	Cash [(600 − 200) × £0.50]	200	
	Dividend Revenue		200
	(To record receipt of £0.50 per share dividend from Sanburg)		
b. Dec. 31	Loss on Financial Assets at FVTPL	2,800	
	Fair Value Adjustment—FVTPL		2,800
	(To record loss on trading securities)		

Investment	Cost	Fair Value	Unrealized Gain (Loss)
Sanburg shares	£ 9,800	£10,000	£ 200
Cey shares	27,000	24,000	(3,000)
Total	£36,800	£34,000	£ (2,800)

Note: All asterisked Questions, Exercises, and Problems relate to material in the appendix to the chapter.

Questions

1. What are the reasons that companies invest in securities?

2. **a.** What is the cost of an investment in bonds classified as held-for-collection?

 b. When is interest on bonds recorded?

3. Tino Martinez is confused about losses and gains on the sale of debt investments at FVTOCI. Explain to Tino (a) how the gain or loss is computed, and (b) the statement presentation of the gains and losses.

4. Kolkata Ltd. sells Gish's bonds classified as Financial Assets at Amortized Cost, with an amortized cost of Rs40,000 for Rs45,000, including Rs500 of accrued interest. In recording the sale, Kolkata books a Rs5,000 gain. Is this correct? Explain.

5. What is the cost of an equity investment at FVTOCI?

6. To acquire Kinston plc shares, R. Neal pays £63,200. What entry should be made for this investment that is held for trading?

7. (a) When should a long-term investment in ordinary shares be accounted for by the equity method? (b) When is revenue recognized under this method?

8. Rijo SA uses the equity method to account for its ownership of 30% of the ordinary shares of Pippen Packing. During 2029, Pippen reported a net income of €80,000 and declares and pays cash dividends of €10,000. What recognition should Rijo give to these events?

9. What constitutes "significant influence" when an investor's financial interest is below the 50% level?

10. Distinguish between the fair value and equity methods of accounting for investments in shares.

11. What are consolidated financial statements?

12. What are the classification guidelines for investments at a statement of financial position date?

13. Tina Eddings is the controller of Mendez SLU. At December 31, the company's investments in trading securities cost €74,000. They have a fair value of €70,000. Indicate how Tina would report these data in the financial statements prepared on December 31.

14. Using the data in Question 13, how would Tina report the data if the investment were long-term and the securities were classified as non-trading?

15. Hashmi Group's investments in non-trading securities at December 31 show total cost of £195,000 and total fair value of £205,000. Prepare the adjusting entry.

16. Using the data in Question 15, prepare the adjusting entry assuming the securities are classified as trading securities.

17. What is the year-end accounting treatment of the account OCI—Unrealized Gain or Loss on Financial Assets at FVTOCI?

18. What purposes are served by reporting OCI—Unrealized Gain or Loss on Financial Assets at FVTOCI in the equity section rather than including it in income?

19. Altoona Wholesale Supply owns shares in Key Ltd. Altoona intends to hold the shares indefinitely because of some negative tax consequences if sold. Should the investment in Key be classified as a short-term investment? Why or why not?

*20. (a) What asset and equity balances are eliminated in preparing a consolidated statement of financial position for a parent and a wholly owned subsidiary? (b) Why are they eliminated?

*21. Yinhu Finance pays HK$318,000,000 to purchase all the outstanding ordinary shares of Lia Ltd. At the date of purchase, the net assets of Lia have a book value of HK$290,000,000. Yinhu's management allocates HK$20,000,000 of the excess cost to undervalued land on the books of Lia. What should be done with the rest of the excess?

Brief Exercises

Journalize entries for debt investments.

BE13.1 (LO 1) Kimmel Industries AG purchased debt investments for CHF50,000 on January 1, 2029. On July 1, 2029, Kimmel received cash interest of CHF1,600. Journalize the purchase and the receipt of interest. Assume that no interest has been accrued. The debt investments were held to collect contractual cash flows.

Journalize entries for equity investments.

BE13.2 (LO 2) On August 1, Paul Holdings buys 1,000 ordinary shares of Merlynn for €35,700. On December 1, Paul sells the equity investments for €40,000 in cash. Journalize the purchase and sale of the ordinary shares.

Record transactions under the equity method of accounting.

BE13.3 (LO 2) Kayser SE owns 25% of Plano Company. For the current year, Plano reports net income of €190,000 and declares and pays a €40,000 cash dividend. Record Kayser's equity in Plano's net income and the receipt of dividends from Plano.

Prepare adjusting entry using fair value.

BE13.4 (LO 3) The cost of the trading securities (financial assets at FVTPL) of Hardy Company at December 31, 2029, is £62,000. At December 31, 2029, the fair value of the securities is £59,000. Prepare the adjusting entry to record the securities at fair value. This is the company's first year of operations.

Indicate statement presentation using fair value.

BE13.5 (LO 3) For the data presented in BE13.4, show the financial statement presentation of the trading securities and related accounts.

Prepare adjusting entry using fair value.

BE13.6 (LO 3) Amazonas SA holds as a long-term investment non-trading share securities (equity investments at FVTOCI) costing R$72,000. At December 31, 2029, the fair value of the securities is R$66,000. Prepare the adjusting entry to record the securities at fair value. This is the company's first year of operations.

BE13.7 (LO 3) For the data presented in BE13.6, show the financial statement presentation of the non-trading securities and related accounts. Assume the non-trading securities (equity investments at FVTOCI) are non-current.

Indicate statement presentation using fair value.

BE13.8 (LO 3) Gurnee Limited has the following long-term investments: (1) Ordinary shares of Kornas Co. (10% ownership) held as non-trading securities (equity investments at FVTOCI), cost £108,000, fair value £115,000. (2) Ordinary shares of Kozanecki OAO. (30% ownership), cost £210,000, equity £270,000. Prepare the investments section of the statement of financial position.

Prepare investments section of statement of financial position.

***BE13.9 (LO 4)** Paula Company acquires 100% of the ordinary shares of Shannon Company for €190,000 cash. On the acquisition date, Shannon's ledger shows Share Capital—Ordinary €120,000 and Retained Earnings €70,000. Complete the worksheet for the following accounts: Paula–Investment in Shannon Ordinary Shares, Shannon–Share Capital—Ordinary, and Shannon–Retained Earnings.

Prepare partial consolidated worksheet when cost equals book value.

***BE13.10 (LO 4)** Data for the Paula and Shannon companies are given in BE13.9. Instead of paying €190,000, assume that Paula pays €200,000 to acquire the 100% interest in Shannon Company. Complete the worksheet for the accounts identified in BE13.9 and for the excess of cost over book value.

Prepare partial consolidated worksheet when cost exceeds book value.

DO IT! Exercises

DO IT! 13.1 (LO 1) Kurtyka Ltd. had the following transactions relating to debt investments classified as held-for-collection:

Make journal entries for bond investment.

Jan. 1, 2029	Purchased 50, £1,000, 8% Nordica Company bonds for £50,000. Interest is payable annually on January 1.
Dec. 31, 2029	Accrued interest on the Nordica Company bonds.
Jan. 1, 2030	Received interest from Nordica Company bonds.
Jan. 1, 2030	Sold 30 Nordica Company bonds for £28,700.

Journalize the above transactions, including the journal entry for the accrual of interest on December 31, 2030.

DO IT! 13.2a (LO 2) Some of Quinghai Lake Limited's investment securities are classified as trading securities and some are classified as non-trading. The cost and fair value of each category at December 31, 2029, were as follows.

Make journal entries for trading and non-trading securities.

	Cost	Fair Value	Unrealized Gain (Loss)
Trading securities	¥96,000	¥84,900	¥(11,100)
Non-trading securities	¥59,100	¥63,200	¥ 4,100

At December 31, 2028, the Fair Value Adjustment—FVTPL account had a debit balance of ¥2,200, and the Fair Value Adjustment—FVTOCI account had a credit balance of ¥7,750. Prepare the required journal entries for each group of securities for December 31, 2029.

DO IT! 13.2b (LO 2) The following are two independent situations:

Make journal entries for equity investments.

1. Lorfeld Ltd. acquired 10% of the 500,000 ordinary shares of Northbrook Enterprises at a total cost of €11 per share on June 17, 2029. These shares are classified as trading securities. On September 3, Northbrook declared and paid a €160,000 dividend. On December 31, Northbrook reported net income of €550,000 for the year.
2. Saa Ltd. obtained significant influence over McCarthy Company by buying 30% of McCarthy's 100,000 outstanding ordinary shares at a cost of €18 per share on January 1, 2029. On May 15, McCarthy declared and paid a cash dividend of €150,000. On December 31, McCarthy reported net income of €270,000 for the year.

Prepare all necessary journal entries for 2029 for (a) Lorfeld and (b) Saa.

DO IT! 13.3 (LO 3) Identify where each of the following items would be reported in the financial statements.

Indicate financial statement presentation of investments.

1. Loss on sale of debt investments at FVTOCI.
2. Unrealized gain on financial assets at FVTOCI.
3. Fair value adjustment—FVTPL.
4. Interest earned on investments in bonds.
5. Loss on financial assets at FVTPL.

Use the following possible categories:

Statement of financial position:

Intangible assets	Equity
Property, plant, and equipment	Non-current liabilities
Investments	Current liabilities
Current assets	

Income statement:

Investing category income and expenses

Comprehensive income statement:

Other comprehensive income

Exercises

Understand debt and equity investments.

E13.1 (LO 1) Mr. Wellington is studying for an accounting test and has developed the following questions about investments.

1. What are three reasons why companies purchase investments in debt or equity securities?
2. Why would a company have excess cash that it does not need for operations?
3. What is the typical investment when investing cash for short periods of time?
4. What are the typical investments when investing cash to generate earnings?
5. Why would a company invest in securities that provide no current cash flows?
6. What is the typical equity investment when investing cash for strategic reasons?

Instructions

Provide answers for Mr. Wellington.

Journalize debt investment transactions and accrue interest.

E13.2 (LO 1) Floyd Limited had the following transactions pertaining to debt investments.

Jan. 1, 2029	Purchased 50 £1,000 Petal Co. 8% bonds for £50,000 cash and classified as financial assets at amortized cost. Interest is payable annually on January 1.
Dec. 31, 2029	Accrued interest on the Petal Co. bonds.
Jan. 1, 2030	Received interest on Petal Co. bonds.
Jan. 1, 2030	Sold 30 Petal Co. bonds for £33,500.

Instructions

a. Journalize the transactions.

b. Prepare the adjusting entry for the accrual of interest at December 31, 2030.

Journalize debt investment transactions, accrue interest, and record sale.

E13.3 (LO 1) Brook Ltd. purchased 70 Meissner AG 9%, 10-year, €1,000 bonds on January 1, 2029, for €70,000. The bonds pay interest annually on January 1. Brook's business model is to hold these bonds to collect contractual cash flows and sell. The market value of the bonds was €70,525 at the end of 2029. On January 1, 2030, after receipt of interest, Brook sold 40 of the bonds for €40,300.

Instructions

Prepare the journal entries to record the transactions described above.

Journalize equity investment transactions.

E13.4 (LO 2) Diann Ltd. had the following transactions pertaining to equity investments classified as trading securities.

Feb. 1	Purchased 600 ordinary shares of Ronn (2%) for £6,200.
July 1	Received cash dividends of £1 per share on Ronn ordinary shares.
Sept. 1	Sold 300 ordinary shares of Ronn for £4,300.
Dec. 1	Received cash dividends of £1 per share on Ronn ordinary shares.

Instructions

a. Journalize the transactions.

b. Explain how dividend revenue and the gain (loss) on sale should be reported in the income statement.

E13.5 (LO 2) Spring Ltd. had the following transactions pertaining to investments in ordinary shares. The investment is classified as trading.

Journalize transactions for investments in shares.

Jan.	1	Purchased 2,500 ordinary shares of Angeltide Limited (5%) for €142,000.
July	1	Received a cash dividend of €2.80 per share.
Dec.	1	Sold 500 ordinary shares of Angeltide Limited for €31,200.
Dec.	31	Received a cash dividend of €2.90 per share. The market value of Angeltide shares was €62 per share.

Instructions

Journalize the transactions.

E13.6 (LO 2) On February 1, Minitori SpA purchased 500 ordinary shares (2% ownership) of Becker Company for €15,400 and paid a brokerage fee of €100. Minitori classified the investment as a trading investment. On March 20, Minitori sold 100 shares of Becker for €2,850. Minitori received a dividend of €1.00 per share on April 25. On June 15, Minitori sold 200 shares of Becker for €7,300. On July 28, Minitori received a dividend of €1.3 per share. The market value of Becker shares was €35 per share at December 31.

Journalize transactions for investments in shares.

Instructions

Prepare the journal entries to record the transactions described above.

E13.7 (LO 2) On January 1, Vince SpA purchased a 25% equity in Morelli SpA for £180,000. At December 31, Morelli declared and paid a £36,000 cash dividend and reported net income of £160,000.

Journalize and post transactions under the equity method.

Instructions

a. Journalize the transactions.

b. Determine the amount to be reported as an investment in Morelli at December 31.

E13.8 (LO 2, 3) Presented below are two independent situations.

Journalize entries under cost and equity methods.

1. On March 18, 2029, Chicory Cosmetics acquired 15% of the 200,000 ordinary shares of Racine Fashion at a cost of €13 per share and paid a brokerage fee of €6,000. On June 30, Racine declared and paid a €60,000 dividend. On December 31, Racine reported net income of €122,000 for the year. At December 31, the market price of Racine Fashion was €15 per share. The shares are classified as non-trading.
2. On January 1, 2029, Frank Ltd. obtained significant influence over Nowak Industries by buying 30% of Nowak's 30,000 outstanding ordinary shares at a cost of €9 per share and paid transaction costs of €270. On June 15, Nowak declared and paid a cash dividend of €30,000. On December 31, Nowak reported a net income of €80,000 for the year.

Instructions

Prepare all the necessary journal entries for 2029 for (a) Chicory Cosmetics and (b) Frank Ltd.

E13.9 (LO 2) On January 1, 2029, Roosevelt Company purchased 12% bonds having a maturity value of $500,000 for $537,907. The bonds provide the bondholders with a 10% yield. They are dated January 1, 2029, and mature January 1, 2034, with interest received December 31 of each year. Roosevelt's business model is to hold these bonds to collect contractual cash flows.

Journalize debt investment transactions.

Instructions

a. Prepare the journal entry at the date of the bond purchase.

b. Prepare a bond amortization schedule.

c. Prepare the journal entry to record the interest received and the amortization for 2029.

d. Prepare the journal entry to record the interest received and the amortization for 2030.

E13.10 (LO 3) At December 31, 2029, the end of its first year of operations, the trading securities (financial assets at FVTPL) for Geneva AG are as follows.

Prepare adjusting entry to record fair value, and indicate statement presentation.

Security	Cost	Fair Value
A	CHF17,500	CHF16,000
B	12,500	14,000
C	23,000	19,000
	CHF53,000	CHF49,000

Instructions

a. Prepare the adjusting entry at December 31, 2029, to report the securities at fair value.

b. Show the statement of financial position and income statement presentation at December 31, 2029, after adjustment to fair value.

Prepare adjusting entry to record fair value, and indicate statement presentation.

E13.11 (LO 3) **Writing** Data for investments in shares classified as trading securities are presented in E13.10. Assume instead that the investments are classified as non-trading securities (equity investments at FVTOCI). They have the same cost and fair value. The securities are considered to be a long-term investment.

Instructions

a. Prepare the adjusting entry at December 31, 2029, to report the securities at fair value.

b. Show the statement of financial position presentation at December 31, 2029, after adjustment to fair value.

c. E. Devonshire, a member of the board of directors, does not understand the reporting of the unrealized gains or losses. Write a letter to Ms. Devonshire explaining the reporting and the purposes that it serves.

Journalize debt investment transactions and record sale.

E13.12 (LO 1) On January 1, 2029, Enda Company purchased €1,000,000, 3-year, 6% bonds of Naihui AG for €948,458. The bonds were purchased to yield 8% interest. Interest is payable annually on December 31. Enda Company plans to hold the bonds to collect contractual cash flows and sell. The fair values of the bonds were €1,037,722 on December 31, 2029, and €990,654 on December 31, 2030.

On December 31, 2030, after receiving the annual interest payment, Enda Company sold one-half of the bonds at their fair value of €495,327.

Instructions

a. Prepare a bond amortized schedule.

b. Prepare the journal entries for this debt investment for the years 2029 and 2030. Omit closing entries.

Prepare consolidated worksheet when cost equals book value.

***E13.13 (LO 4)** On January 1, 2029, Lennon Enterprises acquires 100% of Ono Ltd. for £220,000 in cash. The condensed statements of financial position of the two companies immediately following the acquisition are as follows.

	Lennon Enterprises	Ono Ltd.
Plant and equipment (net)	£300,000	£220,000
Investment in Ono Ltd. ordinary shares	220,000	
Current assets	60,000	50,000
	£580,000	£270,000
Share capital—ordinary	£230,000	£ 80,000
Retained earnings	170,000	140,000
Current liabilities	180,000	50,000
	£580,000	£270,000

Instructions

Prepare a worksheet for a consolidated statement of financial position.

Prepare consolidated worksheet when cost exceeds book value.

***E13.14 (LO 4)** Data for the Lennon and Ono companies are presented in E13.13. Assume that instead of paying £220,000 in cash for Ono Ltd., Lennon Enterprises pays £225,000 in cash. Thus, at the acquisition date, the assets of Lennon Enterprises are current assets £55,000, investment in Ono Ltd. ordinary shares £225,000, and plant and equipment (net) £300,000.

Instructions

Prepare a worksheet for a consolidated statement of financial position.

Problems

P13.1 (LO 1, 2, 3) Yuen Long Carecenters Ltd. provides financing and capital to the healthcare industry, with a particular focus on nursing homes for the elderly. The following selected transactions relate to bonds acquired as an investment by Yuen Long, whose fiscal year ends on December 31. Yuen Long plans to hold the bonds to collect contractual cash flows.

Journalize debt investment transactions and show financial statement presentation.

2029

Jan. 1 Purchased at face value HK$2,000,000 of Franco Nursing Centers, 10-year, 7% bonds dated January 1, 2029, directly from Franco. Interest is paid on January 1 of each year.
Dec. 31 Accrual of interest at year-end on the Franco bonds.

(Assume that all intervening transactions and adjustments have been properly recorded and that the number of bonds owned has not changed from December 31, 2029, to December 31, 2031.)

2032

Jan. 1 Received the annual interest on the Franco bonds.
Jan. 1 Sold HK$1,000,000 Franco bonds at 105.
Dec. 31 Accrual of interest at year-end on the Franco bonds.

Instructions

a. Journalize the listed transactions for the years 2029 and 2032.

b. Show the statement of financial position presentation of the bonds and interest receivable at December 31, 2029. Assume the investments are classified as held-for-collection.

a. Gain on sale of Financial Assets at Amortized Cost HK$50,000

P13.2 (LO 1, 2) Presented below is an amortization schedule related to Spangler Company's 5-year, $100,000 bond with a 7% interest rate and a 5% yield, purchased on December 31, 2029, for $108,660.

Journalize debt investment transactions.

Date	Cash Received	Interest Revenue	Bond Premium Amortization	Carrying Amount of Bonds
12/31/29				$108,660
12/31/30	$7,000	$5,433	$1,567	107,093
12/31/31	7,000	5,354	1,646	105,447
12/31/32	7,000	5,272	1,728	103,719
12/31/33	7,000	5,186	1,814	101,905
12/31/34	7,000	5,095	1,905	100,000

The following schedule presents a comparison of the amortized cost and fair value of the bonds at year-end.

	12/31/30	12/31/31	12/31/32	12/31/33	12/31/34
Amortized cost	$107,093	$105,447	$103,719	$101,905	$100,000
Fair value	106,500	107,500	105,650	103,000	100,000

Instructions

a. Prepare the journal entry to record the purchase of these bonds on December 31, 2029, assuming the bonds are classified as held-for-collection investments.

b. Prepare the journal entry or entries related to the held-for-collection bonds for 2030.

c. Prepare the journal entry or entries related to the held-for-collection bonds for 2032.

d. Prepare the journal entry or entries to record the purchase of these bonds, assuming they are classified as trading.

e. Prepare the journal entry or entries related to the bonds for 2030, assuming they are classified: (1) trading, and (2) held-for-collection and selling.

f. Prepare the journal entry or entries related to the trading bonds for 2032.

P13.3 (LO 1, 2) Presented below is information taken from a bond investment amortization schedule with related fair values provided. These bonds are managed to profit from changes in market interest rates.

Journalize debt investment transactions.

	12/31/29	12/31/30	12/31/31
Amortized cost	€491,150	€519,442	€550,000
Fair value	497,000	509,000	550,000

Instructions

a. Indicate whether the bonds were purchased at a discount or at a premium.

b. Prepare the adjusting entry to record the bonds at fair value at December 31, 2029. The Fair Value Adjustment account has a debit balance of €1,000 prior to adjustment.

c. Prepare the adjusting entry to record the bonds at fair value at December 31, 2030.

d. Repeat the requirements for (c), assuming the investments are held under a held-for-collection and selling strategy.

Journalize investment transactions, prepare adjusting entry, and show statement presentation.

P13.4 (LO 2, 3) In January 2029, the management of Stefan SE concludes that it has sufficient cash to permit some short-term investments in debt and equity securities. All securities are considered to be trading securities (financial assets at FVTPL). During the year, the following transactions occurred.

Feb.	1	Purchased 600 ordinary shares of Superior for €32,400.
Mar.	1	Purchased 800 ordinary shares of Pawlik for €20,400.
Apr.	1	Purchased 50 €1,000, 7% Venice bonds for €50,000. Interest is payable semiannually on October 1 and April 1.
July	1	Received a cash dividend of €0.60 per share on the Superior ordinary shares.
Aug.	1	Sold 200 ordinary shares of Superior at €57 per share.
Sept.	1	Received a €1 per share cash dividend on the Pawlik ordinary shares.
Oct.	1	Received the interest on the Venice bonds.
Oct.	1	Sold the Venice bonds for €49,000.

At December 31, the fair value of the Superior ordinary shares was €55 per share. The fair value of the Pawlik ordinary shares was €24 per share.

Instructions

a. Gain on Financial Assets at FVTPL €600

a. Journalize the transactions and post to the accounts Financial Assets at FVTPL—Debt and Financial Assets at FVTPL—Equity. (Use the T-account form.)

b. Prepare the adjusting entry at December 31, 2029, to report the investment securities at fair value.

c. Show the statement of financial position presentation of investment securities at December 31, 2029.

d. Identify the income statement accounts and give the statement classification of each account.

Journalize transactions and adjusting entry for equity investments.

P13.5 (LO 2, 3) On December 31, 2028, Ogallala Associates owned the following securities, held as a long-term investment. The securities are not held for influence or control of the investee.

Ordinary Shares	Shares	Cost
Carlene Co.	2,000	£60,000
Riverdale Co.	5,000	45,000
Raczynski Co.	1,500	30,000

Ogallala made an irrevocable option to measure the equity investment as fair value through other comprehensive income. On December 31, 2028, the total fair value of the securities was equal to its cost. In 2029, the following transactions occurred.

Aug.	1	Received £0.70 per share cash dividend on Carlene Co. ordinary shares.
Sept.	1	Sold 2,000 ordinary shares of Riverdale Co. for cash at £8 per share.
Oct.	1	Sold 800 ordinary shares of Carlene Co. for cash at £33 per share.
Nov.	1	Received £1 per share cash dividend on Raczynski Co. ordinary shares.
Dec.	15	Received £0.70 per share cash dividend on Carlene Co. ordinary shares.
	31	Received £1 per share semiannual cash dividend on Riverdale Co. ordinary shares.

At December 31, the fair values per share of the ordinary shares were Carlene Co. £32, Riverdale Co. £8, and Raczynski Co. £18.

Instructions

a. Journalize the 2029 transactions and post to the account Equity Investments at FVTOCI. (Use the T-account form.)

b. Unrealized loss £3,600

b. Prepare the adjusting entry at December 31, 2029, to show the securities at fair value. The shares should be classified as non-trading securities.

c. Show the statement of financial position presentation of the investments at December 31, 2029. At this date, Ogallala Associates has share capital—ordinary £1,500,000 and retained earnings £1,000,000.

P13.6 (LO 2, 3) Control Alt Design Ltd. acquired 30% of the outstanding ordinary shares of Walter Company on January 1, 2029, by paying £800,000 for the 45,000 shares. Walter declared and paid £0.30 per share cash dividends on March 15, June 15, September 15, and December 15, 2029. Walter reported net income of £320,000 for the year. At December 31, 2029, the market price of Walter ordinary shares was £24 per share.

Prepare entries under the fair value and equity methods, and tabulate differences.

Instructions

a. Prepare the journal entries for Control Alt Design for 2029, assuming Control Alt Design cannot exercise significant influence over Walter. Use fair value method and assume that Walter ordinary shares should be classified as trading securities.

a. Total dividend revenue £54,000

b. Prepare the journal entries for Control Alt Design for 2029, assuming Control Alt Design can exercise significant influence over Walter. Use the equity method.

b. Revenue from share investments £96,000

c. Indicate the statement of financial position and income statement account balances at December 31, 2029, under each method of accounting.

P13.7 (LO 2, 3) The following securities are in Pascual SA's portfolio of long-term non-trading securities measured at fair value through other comprehensive income at December 31, 2028.

Journalize equity investment transactions and show statement presentation.

	Cost
1,000 shares of Reginald SA ordinary shares	R$52,000
1,400 shares of Elderberry A/S ordinary shares	84,000
1,200 shares of Mattoon AG preference shares	33,600

On December 31, 2028, the total cost of the portfolio equaled total fair value. Pascual had the following transactions related to the securities during 2025.

Jan.	20	Sold all 1,000 ordinary shares of Reginald at R$54.80 per share.
	28	Purchased 400 R$70 par value ordinary shares of Hachito Ltd. at R$79.20 per share.
	30	Received a cash dividend of R$1.05 per share on Elderberry ordinary shares.
Feb.	8	Received cash dividends of R$0.40 per share on Mattoon preference shares.
	18	Sold all 1,200 preference shares of Mattoon at R$26.30 per share.
July	30	Received a cash dividend of R$1.00 per share on Elderberry ordinary shares.
Sept.	6	Purchased an additional 600 R$70 par value ordinary shares of Hachito at R$82 per share.
Dec.	1	Received a cash dividend of R$1.35 per share on Hachito ordinary shares.

At December 31, 2029, the fair values of the securities were:

Elderberry A/S ordinary shares	R$64 per share
Hachito Ltd. ordinary shares	R$72 per share

Instructions

a. Prepare journal entries to record the transactions. Pascual has no significant influence over its equity investments.

a. OCI—Unrealized Gain on Equity Investments at FVTOCI R$2,800

b. Post to the account Equity Investments at FVTOCI. (Use T-account.)

c. Prepare the adjusting entry at December 31, 2029 to report the portfolio at fair value. Also prepare the required closing entry related to the investment securities.

c. Unrealized loss R$3,280

d. Show the statement of financial position presentation at December 31, 2029, for the investment related accounts.

P13.8 (LO 3) The following data, presented in alphabetical order, are taken from the records of Radar Industries Ltd.

Prepare a statement of financial position.

Accounts payable	€ 240,000
Accounts receivable	140,000
Accumulated depreciation—buildings	180,000
Accumulated depreciation—equipment	52,000
Loss allowance	6,000
Bonds payable (10%, due 2032)	540,000
Buildings	950,000
Cash	42,000
Dividends payable	80,000
Equipment	275,000
Fair value adjustment—FVTOCI (Dr.)	8,000
Goodwill	200,000
Income taxes payable	120,000

Inventory	170,000
Investment in Mara ordinary shares (30% ownership), at equity	380,000
Equity Investments at FVTOCI (10% ownership), at cost	278,000
Land	390,000
Notes payable (due 2030)	70,000
Prepaid insurance	16,000
Retained earnings	103,000
Share capital—ordinary (€10 par value; 500,000 shares authorized, 150,000 shares issued)	1,500,000
Share premium—ordinary	130,000
Financial assets at fair value through profit or loss	180,000
OCI—Unrealized gain or loss on financial assets at FVTOCI	8,000

The investment in Sasse ordinary shares is considered to be a long-term non-trading security.

Instructions

Total assets €2,791,000

Prepare a classified statement of financial position at December 31, 2029.

Prepare consolidated worksheet and statement of financial position when cost exceeds book value.

***P13.9 (LO 4)** Liu Limited purchased all the outstanding ordinary shares of Yang Plastics on December 31, 2029. Just before the purchase, the condensed statements of financial position of the two companies appeared as follows (amounts in thousands).

	Liu Limited	Yang Plastics
Plant and equipment (net)	¥2,100,000	¥ 676,000
Current assets	1,480,000	435,500
	¥3,580,000	¥1,111,500
Share capital—ordinary	¥1,950,000	¥ 525,000
Retained earnings	1,052,000	494,000
Current liabilities	578,000	92,500
	¥3,580,000	¥1,111,500

Liu used current assets of ¥1,218,000 to acquire the shares of Yang Plastics. The excess of this purchase price over the book value of Yang Plastics' net assets is determined to be attributable ¥84,000 to Yang Plastics' plant and equipment and the remainder to goodwill.

Instructions

a. Prepare the entry for Liu Limited's acquisition of Yang Plastics shares.

b. Excess of cost over book value ¥199,000

b. Prepare a consolidated worksheet at December 31, 2029.

c. Prepare a consolidated statement of financial position at December 31, 2029.

Comprehensive Accounting Cycle Review

ACR13 Writing **Part I** Mindy Feldkamp and her two colleagues, Oscar Lopez and Lori Melton, are personal trainers at an upscale health spa/resort in Madrid. They want to start a health club that specializes in health plans for people in the 50+ age range. The growing population in this age range and strong consumer interest in the health benefits of physical activity have convinced them they can profitably operate their own club. In addition to many other decisions, they need to determine what type of business organization they want. Oscar believes there are more advantages to the corporate form than a partnership, but he hasn't yet convinced Mindy and Lori. They have come to you, a small-business consulting specialist, seeking information and advice regarding the choice of starting a partnership versus a corporation.

Instructions

a. Prepare a memo (dated May 26, 2028) that describes the advantages and disadvantages of both partnerships and corporations. Advise Mindy, Oscar, and Lori regarding which organizational form you believe would better serve their purposes. Make sure to include reasons supporting your advice.

Part II After deciding to incorporate, each of the three investors receives 20,000 €2 par ordinary shares on June 12, 2028, in exchange for their co-owned building (€200,000 fair value) and €100,000 total cash they contributed to the business. The next decision that Mindy, Oscar, and Lori need to make is how to obtain financing for renovation and equipment. They understand the difference between equity securities and debt securities, but do not understand the tax, net income, and earnings per share consequences of equity versus debt financing on the future of their business.

Instructions

b. Prepare notes for a discussion with the three entrepreneurs in which you will compare the consequences of using equity versus debt financing. As part of your notes, show the differences in interest and tax expense assuming €1,400,000 is financed with ordinary shares, and then alternatively with debt. Assume that when ordinary shares are used, 140,000 shares will be issued. When debt is used, assume the interest rate on debt is 9%, the tax rate is 32%, and income before interest and taxes is €300,000. (You may want to use an electronic spreadsheet.)

Part III During the discussion about financing, Lori mentions that one of her clients, Roberto Marino, has approached her about buying a significant interest in the new club. Having an interested investor sways the three to issue equity securities to provide the financing they need. On July 21, 2028, Mr. Marino buys 90,000 shares at a price of €10 per share.

The club, LifePath Fitness, opens on January 12, 2029, and after a slow start begins to produce the revenue desired by the owners. The owners decide to pay themselves a share dividend since cash has been less than abundant since they opened their doors. The 10% share dividend is declared by the owners on July 27, 2029. The market price of the shares is €3 on the declaration date. The date of record is July 31, 2029 (there have been no changes in share ownership since the initial issuance), and the issue date is August 15, 2029. By the middle of the fourth quarter of 2029, the cash flow of LifePath Fitness has improved to the point that the owners feel ready to pay themselves a cash dividend. They declare a €0.05 cash dividend per share on December 4, 2029. The record date is December 14, 2029, and the payment date is December 24, 2029.

Instructions

c. (1) Record all of the transactions related to the ordinary shares of LifePath Fitness during the years 2028 and 2029. (2) Indicate how many shares are issued and outstanding after the share dividend is issued.

Part IV Since the club opened, a major concern has been the pool facilities. Although the existing pool is adequate, Mindy, Oscar, and Lori all desire to make LifePath a cutting-edge facility. Until the end of 2029, financing concerns prevented this improvement. However, because there has been steady growth in clientele, revenue, and income since the third quarter of 2029, the owners have explored possible financing options. They are hesitant to issue shares and change the ownership mix because they have been able to work together as a team with great effectiveness. They have formulated a plan to issue secured term bonds to raise the needed €600,000 for the pool facilities. By the end of December 2029, everything was in place for the bond issue to go ahead. On January 1, 2030, the €600,000 face value of bonds were issued for €548,000. The bonds pay annual interest of 6% on January 1 of each year. The bonds mature in 10 years, and amortization is computed using the straight-line method.

Instructions

d. Record (1) the issuance of the secured bonds, (2) the adjusting entry required on December 31, 2030, (3) the interest payment made on January 1, 2031, and (4) the interest accrual on December 31, 2031.

Expand Your Critical Thinking

Financial Reporting Problem: TSMC, Ltd. (TWN)

CT13.1 The financial statements of TSMC are presented in Appendix A. The complete annual report, including the notes to the financial statements, is available at the company's website.

Instructions

a. See Note 4 to the financial statements and indicate what the consolidated financial statements include.

b. Using TSMC's consolidated statement of cash flows, determine how much was spent for capital acquisitions during the current year.

Comparative Analysis Problem: Nestlé SA (CHE) vs. Delfi Limited (SGP)

CT13.2 **Nestlé**'s financial statements are presented in Appendix B. Financial statements of **Delfi Limited** are presented in Appendix C. Complete annual reports, including notes to the financial statements, are available at each company's respective website.

Instructions

a. Based on the information contained in these financial statements, determine the following for each company.

1. Net cash provided (used) for investing (investment) activities for the current year (from the statement of cash flows).

2. Cash used for capital expenditures during the current year.

b. Each of Nestlé's financial statements is labeled "consolidated." What has been consolidated? That is, from the contents of Nestlé's annual report, identify by name the divisions that have been consolidated.

Real-World Focus

CT13.3 Most publicly traded companies are examined by numerous analysts. These analysts often don't agree about a company's future prospects. In this exercise, you will find analysts' ratings about companies and make comparisons over time and across companies in the same industry. You will also see to what extent the analysts experienced "earnings surprises." Earnings surprises can cause changes in share prices.

Instructions

Go to the **Yahoo! Finance** website and then choose a company or use the index to find the company's name. Choose **Research** and then answer the following questions.

a. How many analysts rated the company?

b. What percentage rated it a strong buy?

c. What was the average rating for the week?

d. Did the average rating improve or decline relative to the previous week?

e. What was the amount of the earnings surprise percentage during the last quarter?

Decision-Making Across the Organization

CT13.4 At the beginning of the question-and-answer portion of the annual shareholders' meeting of Kemper Ltd., shareholder Mike Kerwin asks, "Why did management sell the holdings in UMW Company at a loss when this company has been very profitable during the period Kemper held its shares?"

Since president Tony Chavez has just concluded his speech on the recent success and bright future of Kemper, he is taken aback by this question and responds, "I remember we paid £1,300,000 for those shares some years ago. I am sure we sold these shares at a much higher price. You must be mistaken."

Kerwin retorts, "Well, right here in footnote number 7 to the annual report it shows that 240,000 shares, a 30% interest in UMW, were sold on the last day of the year. Also, it states that UMW earned £520,000 this year and paid out £160,000 in cash dividends. Further, a summary statement indicates that in past years, while Kemper held UMW shares, UMW earned £1,240,000 and paid out £440,000 in dividends. Finally, the income statement for this year shows a loss on the sale of UMW shares of £180,000. So, I doubt that I am mistaken."

Red-faced, president Chavez turns to you.

Instructions

With the class divided into groups, answer the following.

a. What amount (in pounds) did Kemper receive upon the sale of the UMW shares?

b. Explain why both shareholder Kerwin and president Chavez are correct.

Communication Activity

CT13.5 Bunge Ltd. has purchased two securities for its portfolio. The first is an equity investment in Longley Industries, one of its suppliers. Bunge purchased 10% of Longley with the intention of holding it for a number of years but has no intention of purchasing more shares. The second investment was a purchase of debt securities. Bunge purchased the debt securities because its analysts believe that changes in market interest rates will cause these securities to increase in value in a short period of time. Bunge intends to sell the debt securities as soon as they have increased in value.

Instructions

Write an email to Max Scholes, the chief financial officer, explaining how to account for each of these investments. Explain what the implications for reported income are from this accounting treatment.

Ethics Case

CT13.6 Bartlet Financial Services holds a large portfolio of debt and equity securities as an investment. The total fair value of the portfolio at December 31, 2029, is greater than total cost. Some securities have increased in value and others have decreased. Deb Faust, the financial vice president, and Jan McCabe, the controller, are in the process of classifying for the first time the securities in the portfolio.

Faust suggests classifying the securities that have increased in value as trading securities in order to increase net income for the year. She wants to classify the securities that have decreased in value as long-term non-trading securities, so that the decreases in value will not affect 2029 net income.

McCabe disagrees. She recommends classifying the securities that have decreased in value as trading securities and those that have increased in value as long-term non-trading securities. McCabe argues that the company is having a good earnings year and that recognizing the losses now will help to smooth income for this year. Moreover, for future years, when the company may not be as profitable, the company will have built-in gains.

Instructions

a. Will classifying the securities as Faust and McCabe suggest actually affect earnings as each says it will?

b. Is there anything unethical in what Faust and McCabe propose? Who are the stakeholders affected by their proposals?

c. Assume that Faust and McCabe properly classify the portfolio. At year-end, Faust proposes to sell the securities that will increase 2029 net income, and McCabe proposes to sell the securities that will decrease 2029 net income. Is this unethical?

Answers to Insight and Accounting Across the Organization Questions

Hey, I Thought It Was Safe! Q: Why is the fluctuating value of bonds of concern if a company intends to hold them until maturity? **A:** While changes in the value of a bond based on changes in interest rates do not impact future cash flows, changes in the credit risk of the bond can have an impact on future cash flows.

Who's in Control? Q: Where on adidas's statement of financial position will you find its investment in Rockport? **A:** Since adidas owns 100% of Rockport, you will not find that investment on its statement of financial position. Instead, Rockport's financial information is combined together with adidas, to produce consolidated financial statements.

A Look at U.S. GAAP

LEARNING OBJECTIVE 5

Compare the accounting for investments under IFRS and U.S. GAAP.

The accounting and reporting for investments under IFRS and GAAP are very similar.

Key Points

Similarities

- The basic accounting entries to record the acquisition of debt securities, the receipt of interest, and the sale of debt securities are the same under IFRS and GAAP.

- The basic accounting entries to record the acquisition of equity investments, the receipt of dividends, and the sale of equity securities are the same under IFRS and GAAP.
- Both IFRS and GAAP classify investments into categories having different measurement and reporting methods. IFRS focuses on the business model and the nature of the securities cash flows to determine the category, whereas GAAP focuses on the nature of the security and management's intent. The result, in many cases, will be the same.

  For example, assume that **Mitsubishi** (JPN) purchases a bond investment that it intends to hold to maturity (held-for-collection). Its business model for this type of investment is to collect interest and then principal at maturity. The payment dates for the interest rate and principal are stated on the bond. In this case, Mitsubishi accounts for the investment at amortized cost. If, on the other hand, Mitsubishi purchased the bonds as part of a trading strategy to speculate on interest rate changes (a trading investment), then the debt investment is reported at fair value. As a result, only debt investments such as receivables, loans, and bond investments that meet the two criteria above are recorded at amortized cost. All other debt investments are recorded and reported at fair value.
- Both IFRS and GAAP use the same criteria to determine whether the equity method of accounting should be used—that is, significant influence with a general guide of over 20% ownership. IFRS uses the term **associate investment** rather than equity investment to describe its investment under the equity method.
- Both IFRS and GAAP account for investments in debt securities classified as held-for-collection (IFRS) and held-to-maturity (GAAP) using amortized cost.
- Both IFRS and GAAP account for equity investments classified as trading securities using fair value with changes in fair value recorded in net income.

Differences

- GAAP permits equity investments that do not have a readily determinable fair value to be recorded at cost with certain adjustments. IFRS does not have a similar alternative.
- IFRS permits equity investments that are not designated as held for trading at the time of purchase to be recorded at fair value with changes in fair value recorded in other comprehensive income. GAAP does not have a similar accounting policy election.
- The basis for consolidation under IFRS is control. Under GAAP, a bipolar approach is used, which is a risk-and-reward model (often referred to as a variable-entity approach) and a voting-interest approach. However, under both systems, for consolidation to occur, the investor company must generally own 50% of another company.
- Under IFRS, both the investor and an associate company should follow the same accounting policies. As a result, in order to prepare financial information, adjustments are made to the associate's policies to conform to the investor's books. GAAP does not have that requirement.

GAAP Practice

GAAP Self-Test Questions

1. The following asset is **not** considered a financial asset under both GAAP and IFRS:

   a. trading securities.
   b. equity securities.
   c. held-for-collection securities.
   d. inventories.

2. Under GAAP, the equity method of accounting for long-term investments in ordinary shares should be used when the investor has significant influence over an investee and owns:

   a. between 20% and 50% of the investee's ordinary shares.
   b. 30% or more of the investee's ordinary shares.
   c. more than 50% of the investee's ordinary shares.
   d. less than 20% of the investee's ordinary shares.

3. At the end of the first year of operations, the total cost of the trading investments portfolio is $120,000. Total fair value is $115,000. The financial statements under GAAP should show:

   a. a reduction in the carrying value of the asset of $5,000 in current assets and an unrealized loss of $5,000 in other expenses and losses.
   b. a reduction in the carrying value of the asset of $5,000 in current assets and an unrealized loss of $5,000 in the equity section of the balance sheet (statement of financial position).
   c. a reduction in the carrying value of the asset of $5,000 in current assets and an unrealized loss of $5,000 in other comprehensive income.
   d. a reduction in the carrying value of the asset $5,000 in current assets and a realized loss of $5,000 in other expenses and losses.

4. Under GAAP, unrealized gains on non-trading share investments should:

   a. be reported as other revenues and gains in the income statement as part of net income.
   b. be reported as other gains on the income statement as part of net income.
   c. not be reported on the income statement or balance sheet (statement of financial position).
   d. be reported as other comprehensive income.

5. Under GAAP, the unrealized loss on trading investments should be reported:
   a. as part of other comprehensive loss reducing net income.
   b. on the income statement reducing net income.
   c. as part of other comprehensive loss not affecting net income.
   d. directly to equity bypassing the income statement.

GAAP Financial Reporting Problem: Apple Inc. (USA)

GAAP13.1 The financial statements of **Apple** are available in Appendix D. The complete annual report, including the notes to the financial statements, is available at the company's website.

Instructions

a. Determine the percentage increase for (1) short-term marketable securities from 2019 to 2020, and (2) long-term marketable securities from 2019 to 2020.

b. Using Apple's consolidated statement of cash flows, determine:

1. Purchases of marketable securities during the current year.
2. How much was spent for business acquisitions, net of cash acquired during the current year.

Answers to GAAP Self-Test Questions

1. d **2.** a **3.** a **4.** d **5.** b

CHAPTER **14**

Statement of Cash Flows

LEARNING OBJECTIVES After studying this chapter, you should be able to:

LO 1 Discuss the usefulness and format of the statement of cash flows.

LO 2 Prepare a statement of cash flows using the indirect method.

LO 3 Analyze the statement of cash flows.

Chapter Preview

The statement of financial position, income statement, and retained earnings statement do not always show the whole picture of the financial condition of a company or institution. In fact, looking at the financial statements of some well-known companies, a thoughtful investor might ask questions like these: How did **Anheuser-Busch InBev** (BEL) finance cash dividends of €2.1 billion in a year? How could **Cathay Pacific Airways** (HKG) purchase new assets that cost HK$9.2 billion in a year in which it reported a net loss of over HK$8.6 billion? How did the companies that spent a combined fantastic $3.4 trillion on mergers and acquisitions in a recent year finance those deals? Answers to these and similar questions can be found in this chapter, which presents the statement of cash flows.

Statement of Cash Flows

Statement of Cash Flows: Usefulness and Format

- Usefulness of the statement of cash flows
- Classification of cash flows
- Significant non-cash activities
- Format of the statement of cash flows

Preparing the Statement of Cash Flows—Indirect Method

- Indirect and direct methods
- Indirect method—Computer Services International
- Step 1: Operating activities
- Summary of conversion to net cash provided by operating activities
- Step 2: Investing and financing activities
- Step 3: Net change in cash

Using Cash Flows to Evaluate a Company

- Free cash flow

Practice

DO IT! 1 Cash Flow Activities

DO IT! 2a Net Cash Provided by Operating Activities

DO IT! 2b Indirect Method

DO IT! 3 Free Cash Flow

Go to the Review and Practice section at the end of the chapter for a review of key concepts and practice applications with solutions.
Additional tutorials and practice opportunities are available in the Wiley online course.

Feature Story What Should We Do with This Cash?

In today's environment, companies must be ready to respond to changes quickly in order to survive and thrive. This requires that they manage their cash very carefully. A company's cash needs, and how it addresses them, depend on many factors. For example, many high-tech companies need significant cash in order to grow, especially in their early years. To conserve cash, some young companies pay their employees with company shares, or share options. Not only does this conserve cash, but it creates an incentive for employees to work hard. If the company succeeds, then the value of its company shares will increase.

Successful mature companies frequently generate lots of cash—often exceeding their immediate needs. This excess cash is often referred to as "free cash flow." A company with significant free cash flow must decide what to do with this cash. If it doesn't want to expand its capacity in its existing product lines, it might decide to acquire businesses in other industries. Or, it might increase its dividend payments, buy back shares, or pay down its debt.

In some instances, management will simply accumulate massive amounts of cash, which can result in shareholder criticism. For example, **Keyence** (JPN), a manufacturer of sensors and measuring instruments, generated significant amounts of cash for many years. The company is debt-free and not inclined toward acquisitions. But, it also has been reluctant to pay out dividends. Some have suggested that its aversion to dividend payments is due to the fact that the company's chairman and largest shareholder does not want to incur the personal income tax that would result if he received dividends on his 25% share ownership. At a recent shareholder meeting, many of the company's other shareholders complained loudly that the company's returns were being dragged down because it was accumulating so much cash and investing it in low-paying government securities. They demanded that the company increase its dividend.

It appears that there is a general movement in Japan and other maturing Asian economies to begin to pay higher dividends. Many companies suffer from excess productive capacity, so it makes sense for them to use their excess cash to either pay higher dividends or buy back shares. As this occurs, the percentage of cash flow paid out in dividends may well begin to approach about 50%, which is common in mature markets such as Europe.

After the financial crisis of 2007–2008, emerging-market companies and developed-market companies had quite different philosophies regarding cash flows. Companies in developed countries accumulated cash and paid down debt. In contrast, companies in developing countries continued to spend cash to expand operations as well as borrow it to finance their expansion.

Courtesy of Brian Yu

14.1 Statement of Cash Flows: Usefulness and Format

LEARNING OBJECTIVE 1

Discuss the usefulness and format of the statement of cash flows.

The statement of financial position, income statement, and retained earnings statement provide only limited information about a company's cash flows (cash receipts and cash payments).

- Comparative statements of financial position show the increase in property, plant, and equipment during the year. But, they do not show how the additions were financed or paid for.
- The income statement shows net income. But, it does not indicate the amount of cash generated by operating activities.
- The retained earnings statement shows cash dividends declared but not the cash dividends paid during the year.

None of these statements presents a detailed summary of where cash came from and how it was used.

Usefulness of the Statement of Cash Flows

The **statement of cash flows** reports the cash receipts, cash payments, and net change in cash resulting from operating, investing, and financing activities during a period. The information in a statement of cash flows should help investors, creditors, and others assess the following.

1. **The entity's ability to generate future cash flows.** By examining relationships among items in the statement of cash flows, investors can make predictions of the amounts, timing, and uncertainty of future cash flows better than they can from accrual-basis data.
2. **The entity's ability to pay dividends and meet obligations.** If a company does not have adequate cash, it cannot pay employees, settle debts, or pay dividends. Employees, creditors, and shareholders should be particularly interested in this statement because it alone shows the flows of cash in a business.
3. **The reasons for the difference between net income and net cash provided (used) by operating activities.** Net income provides information on the success or failure of a business. However, some financial statement users are critical of accrual-basis net income because it requires many estimates. As a result, users often challenge the reliability of the number. Such is not the case with cash. Many readers of the statement of cash flows want to know the reasons for the difference between net income and net cash provided by operating activities. Then, they can assess for themselves the reliability of the income number (see **Ethics Note**).
4. **The cash investing and financing transactions during the period.** By examining a company's investing and financing transactions, a financial statement reader can better understand why assets and liabilities changed during the period.

ETHICS NOTE

Though we would discourage reliance on cash flows to the exclusion of accrual accounting, comparing net cash provided by operating activities to net income can reveal important information about the "quality" of reported net income. Such a comparison can reveal the extent to which net income provides a good measure of actual performance.

Classification of Cash Flows

The statement of cash flows classifies cash receipts and cash payments as operating, investing, and financing activities. Transactions and other events characteristic of each kind of activity are as follows.

1. **Operating activities** include the cash effects of main business activities that create revenues and expenses. They thus enter into the determination of operating income.
2. **Investing activities** include (a) acquiring and disposing of investments and property, plant, and equipment, and (b) lending money and collecting the loans.

3. **Financing activities** include (a) obtaining cash from issuing debt and repaying the amounts borrowed, and (b) obtaining cash from shareholders, repurchasing shares, and paying dividends.

The operating activities category is the most important. It shows the cash provided by company operations. This source of cash is generally considered to be the best measure of a company's ability to generate sufficient cash to continue as a going concern.

Illustration 14.1 lists typical cash receipts and cash payments within each of the three classifications. **Study the list carefully**. It will prove very useful in solving homework exercises and problems.[1]

ILLUSTRATION 14.1 Typical receipt and payment classifications

Operating activities

Investing activities

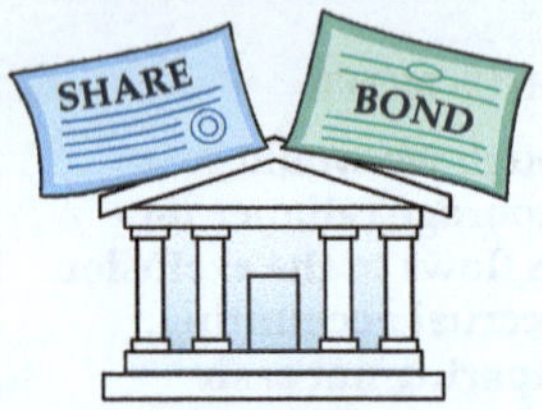

Financing activities

TYPES OF CASH INFLOWS AND OUTFLOWS

Operating activities—Income statement items

Cash inflows:

From sale of goods or services.

Cash outflows:

To suppliers for inventory.
To employees for wages.
To others for expenses.
To government for taxes.

Investing activities—Changes in investments and non-current assets

Cash inflows:

From interest received and dividends received.
From sale of property, plant, and equipment.
From sale of investments in debt or equity securities of other entities.
From collection of principal on loans to other entities.

Cash outflows:

To purchase property, plant, and equipment.
To purchase investments in debt or equity securities of other entities.
To make loans to other entities.

Financing activities—Changes in non-current liabilities and equity

Cash inflows:

From sale of ordinary shares.
From issuance of long-term debt (bonds and notes).

Cash outflows:

To lenders for interest.
To shareholders as dividends.
To redeem long-term debt or reacquire ordinary shares (treasury shares).

Note the following general guidelines:

1. Operating activities involve income statement items.
2. Investing activities involve cash flows resulting from changes in investments and non-current asset items.
3. Financing activities involve cash flows resulting from changes in non-current liability and equity items.

---

[1] Before the issue of *IFRS 18*, *IAS 7* allows companies some flexibility regarding the classification of certain items. Interest and dividends paid can be classified as either operating or financing, depending on what treatment the company thinks is most appropriate. Similarly, interest and dividends received can be classified as either operating or investing. Taxes paid are classified as operating except in circumstances where they can be identified with specific investing or financing activities. In order to comply with the amended *IAS 7*, we have identified the specific treatment for each of these items in Illustration 14.1, rather than allowing alternative options. *All assignment and testing material is based on this treatment. IFRS 18 'Presentation and Disclosure in Financial Statements'* introduces consequential amendments to *IAS 7 'Statement of Cash Flows'*, effective January 1, 2027, eliminating the options for presenting cash flows related to interest and dividends paid and received. Dividends paid are always classified as cash flows from financing. For entities that do not invest in assets or provide financing to customers as a main business activity, interest paid is classified as cash flows from financing activities, and interest and dividends received are classified as cash flows from investing. Entities whose main business is lending (e.g., banks) may classify interest and dividends received as operating activities because they are a primary source of revenue.

IFRS requires that the amount of cash paid for taxes, as well as cash flows from interest and dividends received and paid, be disclosed. The category (operating, investing, or financing) that each item was included in must be disclosed as well. An example of such a disclosure from the notes to **Daimler**'s (DEU) financial statements is provided in **Illustration 14.2**.

ILLUSTRATION 14.2

Daimler's statement of cash flows note

Real World

Daimler
Annual Report

Cash provided by operating activities includes the following cash flows:

	2020	2019	2018
(in millions of €)			
Interest paid	(158)	(725)	(678)
Interest received	179	337	257
Dividends received	1,808	1,296	1,429

Source: Modified from Daimler Annual Report 2020.

Significant Non-Cash Activities

Not all of a company's significant activities involve cash. Examples of significant non-cash activities are as follows.

1. Direct issuance of ordinary shares to purchase assets.
2. Conversion of bonds into ordinary shares.
3. Direct issuance of debt to purchase assets.
4. Exchanges of plant assets.

Companies do not report in the body of the statement of cash flows significant financing and investing activities that do not affect cash. Instead, they report these activities in either a **separate note or supplementary schedule** to the financial statements.

In solving homework assignments, you should present significant non-cash investing and financing activities in a separate note to the financial statements. (See the last entry in Illustration 14.3 for an example.)

Accounting Across the Organization Target Corporation

BCFC/Shutterstock

Net *What*?

Net income is not the same as net cash provided by operating activities. The table shows some results from recent annual reports (dollars in millions), including **Target Corporation** (USA). Note how the numbers differ greatly across the list even though all these companies engage in retail merchandising.

Company	Net Income	Net Cash Provided by Operating Activities
Kohl's Corporation	$ 889	$ 1,884
Walmart Inc.	16,669	25,591
J. C. Penney Company, Inc.	(1,388)	(1,814)
Costco Wholesale Corp.	4,002	8,861
Target Corporation	1,971	6,520

In general, why do differences exist between net income and net cash provided by operating activities? (Answer is available near the end of the chapter.)

Format of the Statement of Cash Flows

The general format of the statement of cash flows presents the results of the three activities discussed previously—operating, investing, and financing—plus the significant non-cash investing and financing activities. **Illustration 14.3** shows a widely used form of the statement of cash flows.

ILLUSTRATION 14.3

Format of statement of cash flows

Company Name
Statement of Cash Flows
For the Period Covered

Cash flows from operating activities		
(List of individual items)	XX	
Net cash provided (used) by operating activities		XXX
Cash flows from investing activities		
(List of individual inflows and outflows)	XX	
Net cash provided (used) by investing activities		XXX
Cash flows from financing activities		
(List of individual inflows and outflows)	XX	
Net cash provided (used) by financing activities		XXX
Net increase (decrease) in cash		XXX
Cash at beginning of period		XXX
Cash at end of period		XXX
Note xx		
Non-cash investing and financing activities		
(List of individual non-cash transactions)		XXX

The cash flows from operating activities section always appears first, followed by the investing activities section, and then the financing activities section. The sum of the operating, investing, and financing sections equals the net increase or decrease in cash for the period. This amount is added to the beginning cash balance to arrive at the ending cash balance—the same amount reported on the statement of financial position.

ACTION PLAN

- **Identify the three types of activities used to report all cash inflows and outflows.**
- **Report as operating activities the cash effects of transactions that create revenues and expenses and enter into the determination of operating income.**
- **Report as investing activities transactions that (a) acquire and dispose of investments and non-current assets and (b) lend money and collect loans.**
- **Report as financing activities transactions that (a) obtain cash from issuing debt and repay the amounts borrowed and (b) obtain cash from shareholders and pay them dividends.**

DO IT! 1 | Cash Flow Activities

During its first week, Hu Na Ltd. had these transactions.

1. Issued 100,000 HK$50 par value ordinary shares for HK$8,000,000 cash.
2. Borrowed HK$2,000,000 from Castle Bank, signing a 5-year note bearing 8% interest.
3. Purchased two semi-trailer trucks for HK$1,700,000 cash.
4. Paid employees HK$120,000 for salaries and wages.
5. Collected HK$200,000 cash for services performed.

Classify each of these transactions by type of cash flow activity.

Solution

1. Financing activity
2. Financing activity
3. Investing activity
4. Operating activity
5. Operating activity

Related exercise material: **BE14.1, BE14.2, BE14.3, DO IT! 14.1, E14.1, E14.2, and E14.3.**

14.2 Preparing the Statement of Cash Flows—Indirect Method

LEARNING OBJECTIVE 2

Prepare a statement of cash flows using the indirect method.

Companies prepare the statement of cash flows differently from the three other basic financial statements. First, it is not prepared from an adjusted trial balance. It requires detailed information concerning the changes in account balances that occurred between two points in time. An adjusted trial balance will not provide the necessary data. Second, the statement of cash flows deals with cash receipts and payments. As a result, the company **adjusts** the effects of the use of accrual accounting **to determine cash flows.**

The information to prepare this statement usually comes from three sources:

1. **Comparative statements of financial position.** Information in the comparative statements of financial position indicates the amount of the changes in assets, liabilities, and equities from the beginning to the end of the period.
2. **Current income statement.** Information in this statement helps determine the amount of net cash provided or used by operating activities during the period.
3. **Additional information.** Such information includes transaction data that are needed to determine how cash was provided or used during the period.

Preparing the statement of cash flows from these data sources involves three major steps as explained in **Illustration 14.4**.

ILLUSTRATION 14.4

Three major steps in preparing the statement of cash flows

STEP 1: Determine net cash provided/used by operating activities by converting operating income from an accrual basis to a cash basis.

This step involves analyzing not only the current year's income statement but also comparative statements of financial position and selected additional data.

STEP 2: Analyze changes in non-current asset and liability accounts and record as investing and financing activities, or disclose as non-cash transactions.

This step involves analyzing comparative statements of financial position data and selected additional information for their effects on cash.

STEP 3: Compare the net change in cash on the statement of cash flows with the change in the Cash account reported on the statement of financial position to make sure the amounts agree.

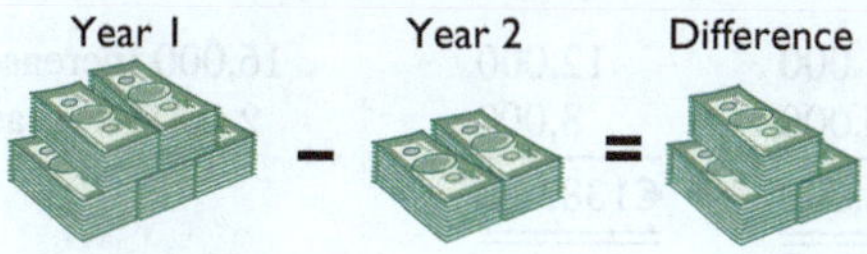

The difference between the beginning and ending cash balances can be easily computed from comparative statements of financial position.

Indirect and Direct Methods

In order to perform Step 1, a company **must convert operating income from an accrual basis to a cash basis**. This conversion may be done by either of two methods: (1) the indirect method or (2) the direct method. **Both methods arrive at the same amount** for "Net cash provided by operating activities." They differ in **how** they arrive at the amount.

- The **indirect method** adjusts operating income for items that do not affect cash.[2] A great majority of companies use this method. Companies favor the indirect method for two reasons:
  1. It is easier and less costly to prepare.
  2. It focuses on the differences between operating income and net cash flow from operating activities.
- The **direct method** shows operating cash receipts and payments, making it more consistent with the objective of a statement of cash flows. The IASB has expressed a preference for the direct method but allows the use of either method.

The next section illustrates the more popular indirect method. Appendix 14A illustrates the direct method.

Indirect Method—Computer Services International

To explain how to prepare a statement of cash flows using the indirect method, we use financial information from Computer Services International. **Illustration 14.5** presents Computer Services' current- and previous-year statements of financial position, its current-year income statement, and related financial information for the current year.

ILLUSTRATION 14.5

Comparative statements of financial position, income statement, and additional information for Computer Services International

Computer Services International
Comparative Statements of Financial Position
December 31

Assets	2029	2028	Change in Account Balance Increase/Decrease
Property, plant, and equipment			
Land	€130,000	€ 20,000	€110,000 Increase
Buildings	160,000	40,000	120,000 Increase
Accumulated depreciation—buildings	(11,000)	(5,000)	6,000 Increase
Equipment	27,000	10,000	17,000 Increase
Accumulated depreciation—equipment	(3,000)	(1,000)	2,000 Increase
Current assets			
Prepaid expenses	5,000	1,000	4,000 Increase
Inventory	15,000	10,000	5,000 Increase
Accounts receivable	20,000	30,000	10,000 Decrease
Cash	55,000	33,000	22,000 Increase
Total assets	€398,000	€138,000	
Equity and Liabilities			
Equity			
Share capital—ordinary	€ 70,000	€ 50,000	€ 20,000 Increase
Retained earnings	164,000	48,000	116,000 Increase
Non-current liabilities			
Bonds payable	130,000	20,000	110,000 Increase
Current liabilities			
Accounts payable	28,000	12,000	16,000 Increase
Income taxes payable	6,000	8,000	2,000 Decrease
Total equity and liabilities	€398,000	€138,000	

[2] Amendments to *IAS 7* require all companies to use the operating profit subtotal, as defined in *IFRS 18*, as the starting point for the indirect method of reporting cash flows from operating activities. In addition, the presentation alternatives for cash flows related to interest and dividends paid and received have been removed.

ILLUSTRATION 14.5
(Continued)

Computer Services International
Income Statement
For the Year Ended December 31, 2029

Sales revenue		€507,000
Cost of goods sold	€150,000	
Operating expenses (excluding depreciation)	111,000	
Depreciation expense	9,000	
Loss on disposal of plant	3,000	273,000
Operating income		234,000
Interest expense		42,000
Income before income tax		192,000
Income tax expense		47,000
Net income		€145,000

Additional information for 2029:

1. Depreciation expense was comprised of €6,000 for building and €3,000 for equipment.
2. The company sold equipment with a book value of €7,000 (cost €8,000, less accumulated depreciation €1,000) for €4,000 cash.
3. Issued €110,000 of long-term bonds in direct exchange for land.
4. A building costing €120,000 was purchased for cash. Equipment costing €25,000 was also purchased for cash.
5. Issued ordinary shares for €20,000 cash.
6. The company declared and paid a €29,000 cash dividend.

Step 1: Operating Activities

Determine Net Cash Provided/Used by Operating Activities by Converting Operating Income from an Accrual Basis to a Cash Basis

To reduce diversity in the classification and presentation of cash flows and to improve comparability across entities, the amended *IAS 7* requires all entities to use the **'operating profit or loss'** subtotal as the starting point when determining cash flows from operating activities under the indirect method. A useful starting point is to understand **why** operating income must be converted to net cash provided by operating activities.

Under IFRS, companies use the accrual basis of accounting.

- This basis requires that companies record revenue when their performance obligation is satisfied and record expenses when incurred.
- Revenues may include credit sales for which the company has not yet collected cash.
- Expenses incurred may include some items that the company has not yet paid in cash.

Thus, under the accrual basis, operating income is not the same as net cash provided by operating activities.

IAS 7 requires that companies must separately disclose **cash flows arising from income taxes and cash flows from interest and dividends received and paid.** The amendments require entities to classify interest and dividend cash flows based on their **main business activities.** Entities that do not have a specified main business activity of investing in assets or providing financing to customers are required to classify **interest and dividends paid** as cash flows from **financing activities**, and **interest and dividends received** as cash flows from **investing activities.**[3] Generally, cash flows arising from income taxes are

[3] For entities with specified main business activities of investing in assets or providing financing to customers, dividends received, interest received, and interest paid are classified in a single category of the statement of cash flows, determined by how the related income or expenses are classified in the income statement. Dividends paid are classified as cash flows from financing activities.

classified as operating activities, unless they can be identified specifically with financing or investing activities. Therefore, under the indirect method, when reporting cash flows from operating activities, companies start with **operating income** and then adjust it for the effects of:

- Non-cash items such as depreciation, amortization, impairment, gains or losses on the disposal of property, plant and equipment.
- Changes during the period in inventories and operating receivables and payables.
- Items of income or expense associated with investing or financing cash flows.

The indirect method (or reconciliation method) starts with accrual basis **operating income** and converts it to net cash provided by operating activities. **Illustration 14.6** lists the three types of adjustments.

ILLUSTRATION 14.6

Three types of adjustments to convert operating income to net cash provided by operating activities

Operating Income +/–	Adjustments	=	Net Cash Provided/Used by Operating Activities
	• **Add back non-cash expenses**, such as depreciation expense and amortization expense. • **Deduct gains and add losses** that resulted from investing and financing activities. • **Analyze changes** to non-cash current asset and current liability accounts.		

We explain the three types of adjustments in the next three sections.

Depreciation Expense

HELPFUL HINT

Depreciation is similar to any other expense in that it reduces operating income. It differs in that it does not involve a current cash outflow. That is why it must be added back to operating income to arrive at net cash provided by operating activities.

Computer Services' income statement reports depreciation expense of €9,000. Although depreciation expense reduces operating income, it does not reduce cash.

- In other words, depreciation expense is a non-cash charge (see **Helpful Hint**).
- The company must add it back to income before income tax to arrive at net cash provided by operating activities.

Computer Services reports depreciation expense in the statement of cash flows as shown in **Illustration 14.7**.

ILLUSTRATION 14.7

Adjustment for depreciation

Cash flows from operating activities	
Operating income	€234,000
Adjustments to reconcile operating income to net cash provided by operating activities:	
Depreciation expense	**9,000**
Net cash provided by operating activities	€243,000

As the first adjustment to operating income in the statement of cash flows, companies frequently list depreciation and similar non-cash charges such as amortization of intangible assets.

Loss on Disposal of Plant Assets

Illustration 14.1 states that cash received from the sale (disposal) of plant assets should be reported in the investing activities section. Because of this, **companies must eliminate from operating income all gains and losses related to the disposal of plant assets, to arrive at net cash provided by operating activities.**

In our example, Computer Services' income statement reports a €3,000 loss on disposal of plant assets (book value €7,000, less €4,000 cash received from disposal of plant assets). The company's loss of €3,000 should not be included in net cash provided by operating activities. **Illustration 14.8** shows that the €3,000 loss is eliminated by adding €3,000 back to operating income to arrive at net cash provided by operating activities.

ILLUSTRATION 14.8

Adjustment for loss on disposal of plant assets

Cash flows from operating activities		
Operating income		€234,000
Adjustments to reconcile operating income to net cash provided by operating activities:		
Depreciation expense	€ 9,000	
Loss on disposal of plant assets	**3,000**	12,000
Net cash provided by operating activities		€246,000

- If a gain on disposal occurs, the company deducts the gain from its operating income in order to determine net cash provided by operating activities.
- **In the case of either a gain or a loss, companies report as a source of cash in the investing activities section of the statement of cash flows the actual amount of cash received from the sale.**

Changes to Non-Cash Current Asset and Current Liability Accounts

A final adjustment in reconciling operating income to net cash provided by operating activities involves examining all changes in current asset and current liability accounts. The accrual-accounting process records revenues in the period in which the performance obligation is satisfied and expenses in the period in which they are incurred.

- Companies use Accounts Receivable to record amounts owed to the company for sales that have been made but for which cash collections have not yet been received.
- They use the Prepaid Insurance account to reflect insurance that has been paid for but which has not yet expired and therefore has not been expensed.
- The Salaries and Wages Payable account reflects salaries and wages expense that has been incurred by the company but has not been paid.

As a result, companies need to adjust operating income for these accruals and prepayments to determine net cash provided by operating activities. Thus, they must analyze the change in each current asset and current liability account to determine its impact on net income and cash.

Changes in Non-Cash Current Assets The adjustments required for changes in non-cash current asset accounts are as follows. **Deduct from operating income increases in current asset accounts, and add to operating income decreases in current asset accounts, to arrive at net cash provided by operating activities.** We observe these relationships by analyzing the accounts of Computer Services.

Decrease in Accounts Receivable Computer Services' accounts receivable decreased by €10,000 (from €30,000 to €20,000) during the period. For Computer Services, this means that cash receipts were €10,000 higher than sales revenue. The Accounts Receivable account in **Illustration 14.9** shows that Computer Services had €507,000 in sales revenue (as reported on the income statement), but it collected €517,000 in cash.

ILLUSTRATION 14.9

Analysis of accounts receivable

Accounts Receivable				
1/1/29	Balance	30,000	Receipts from customers	517,000
	Sales revenue	507,000		
12/31/29	Balance	20,000		

As shown in **Illustration 14.10**, to adjust operating income to net cash provided by operating activities, the company adds to operating income the decrease of €10,000 in accounts receivable. When the Accounts Receivable balance increases, cash receipts are lower than sales revenue recognized under the accrual basis. Therefore, the company deducts from operating income the amount of the increase in accounts receivable, to arrive at net cash provided by operating activities.

Increase in Inventory Computer Services' inventory increased €5,000 (from €10,000 to €15,000) during the period. The change in the Inventory account reflects the difference between the amount of inventory purchased and the amount sold. For Computer Services, this means that the cost of merchandise purchased exceeded the cost of goods sold by €5,000. As a result, cost of goods sold does not reflect €5,000 of cash payments made for merchandise.

The company deducts from operating income this inventory increase of €5,000 during the period, to arrive at net cash provided by operating activities (see Illustration 14.11). If inventory decreases, the company adds to operating income the amount of the change, to arrive at net cash provided by operating activities.

Increase in Prepaid Expenses Computer Services' prepaid expenses increased during the period by €4,000. This means that cash paid for expenses is higher than expenses reported on an accrual basis. In other words, the company has made cash payments in the current period but will not charge expenses to income until future periods (as charges to the income statement). To adjust operating income to net cash provided by operating activities, the company deducts from operating income the €4,000 increase in prepaid expenses (see Illustration 14.10).

ILLUSTRATION 14.10

Adjustments for changes in current asset accounts

Cash flows from operating activities		
Operating income		€234,000
Adjustments to reconcile operating income to net cash provided by operating activities:		
Depreciation expense	€ 9,000	
Loss on disposal of plant assets	3,000	
Decrease in accounts receivable	**10,000**	
Increase in inventory	**(5,000)**	
Increase in prepaid expenses	**(4,000)**	13,000
Net cash provided by operating activities		€247,000

If prepaid expenses decrease, reported expenses are higher than the expenses paid. Therefore, the company adds to operating income the decrease in prepaid expenses, to arrive at net cash provided by operating activities.

Changes in Current Liabilities The adjustments required for changes in current liability accounts are as follows. **Add to operating income increases in current liability accounts, and deduct from operating income decreases in current liability accounts, to arrive at net cash provided by operating activities.**

Increase in Accounts Payable For Computer Services, Accounts Payable increased by €16,000 (from €12,000 to €28,000) during the period. That means the company received €16,000 more in goods than it actually paid for. As shown in **Illustration 14.11**, to adjust operating income to determine net cash provided by operating activities, the company adds to operating income the €16,000 increase in Accounts Payable.

ILLUSTRATION 14.11

Adjustments for changes in current liability accounts

Cash flows from operating activities		
Operating income		€234,000
Adjustments to reconcile operating income to net cash provided by operating activities:		
Depreciation expense	€ 9,000	
Loss on disposal of plant assets	3,000	
Decrease in accounts receivable	10,000	
Increase in inventory	(5,000)	
Increase in prepaid expenses	(4,000)	
Increase in accounts payable	**16,000**	29,000
Net cash provided by operating activities		€263,000

Cash Payments for Income Taxes *IAS 7* requires that income tax payments are separately disclosed and generally classified as operating activities, unless they can be specifically identified with financing or investing activities. Computer Services' Income Taxes Payable account decreased by €2,000. That means the €47,000 of income tax expense reported on the income statement was €2,000 less than the amount of taxes paid during the period of €49,000. As shown in **Illustration 14.12**, the company discloses the amount of income taxes paid of €49,000 as a separate line item after the subtotal for **cash from operating activities before income taxes**, to arrive at net cash provided by operating activities.

ILLUSTRATION 14.12

Reporting of taxes in the operating section

Cash flows from operating activities		
Operating income		€234,000
Adjustments to reconcile operating income to net cash provided by operating activities:		
Depreciation expense	€ 9,000	
Loss on disposal of plant assets	3,000	
Decrease in accounts receivable	10,000	
Increase in inventory	(5,000)	
Increase in prepaid expenses	(4,000)	
Increase in accounts payable	16,000	29,000
Cash from operating activities before income taxes		€263,000
Income taxes paid		**(49,000)**
Net cash provided by operating activities		€214,000

Illustration 14.12 shows that, after starting with operating income of €234,000, the sum of all of the adjustments to operating income was €(20,000). This resulted in net cash provided by operating activities of €214,000.

Summary of Conversion to Net Cash Provided by Operating Activities—Indirect Method

As shown in the previous illustrations, the statement of cash flows prepared by the indirect method starts with operating income. It then adds or deducts items to arrive at net cash provided by operating activities. The required adjustments are as follows:

1. Non-cash charges such as depreciation and amortization.
2. Gains and losses on the disposal of plant assets.
3. Changes in non-cash current asset and current liability accounts.
4. Cash flows related to taxes paid.

Illustration 14.13 provides a summary of these changes.

ILLUSTRATION 14.13

Adjustments required to convert operating income to net cash provided by operating activities

		Adjustments Required to Convert Operating Income to Net Cash Provided by Operating Activities
Non-Cash Charges	Depreciation expense	Add
	Patent amortization expense	Add
Gains and Losses	Loss on disposal of plant assets	Add
	Gain on disposal of plant assets	Deduct
Changes in Current Assets and Current Liabilities	Increase in current asset account	Deduct
	Decrease in current asset account	Add
	Increase in current liability account	Add
	Decrease in current liability account	Deduct
Taxes Paid	Taxes paid	Deduct

ACTION PLAN

- **Add non-cash charges such as depreciation back to net income to compute net cash provided by operating activities.**
- **Deduct from net income gains on the disposal of plant assets, or add losses back to net income, to compute net cash provided by operating activities.**
- **Use changes in non-cash current asset and current liability accounts to compute net cash provided by operating activities.**

DO IT! 2a | Net Cash Provided by Operating Activities

Josh's PhotoPlus reported net income of £73,000 for 2029. Included in the income statement were depreciation expense of £7,000 and a gain on disposal of plant assets of £2,500. Josh's comparative statements of financial position show the following balances.

	12/31/28	12/31/29
Accounts receivable	£17,000	£21,000
Accounts payable	6,000	2,200

Calculate net cash provided by operating activities for Josh's PhotoPlus.

Solution

Cash flows from operating activities		
Net income		£73,000
Adjustments to reconcile net income to net cash provided by operating activities:		
Depreciation expense	£ 7,000	
Gain on disposal of plant assets	(2,500)	
Increase in accounts receivable	(4,000)	
Decrease in accounts payable	(3,800)	(3,300)
Net cash provided by operating activities		£69,700

Related exercise material: **BE14.4, BE14.5, BE14.6, DO IT! 14.2, E14.4, E14.5, E14.6, E14.7, and E14.8.**

Step 2: Investing and Financing Activities

Analyze Changes in Non-Current Asset and Liability Accounts and Record as Investing and Financing Activities, or Disclose as Non-Cash Transactions

Increase in Land As indicated from the change in the Land account and the additional information, the company purchased land of €110,000 through the issuance of long-term bonds. The issuance of bonds payable for land has no effect on cash. But, it is a significant non-cash investing and financing activity that merits disclosure in a separate schedule. (See Illustration 14.15.)

Increase in Buildings As the additional data indicate, Computer Services acquired a building for €120,000 cash. This is a cash outflow reported in the investing section. (See Illustration 14.15.)

Increase in Equipment The Equipment account increased €17,000. The additional information explains that this net increase resulted from two transactions: (1) a purchase of equipment of €25,000, and (2) the sale for €4,000 of equipment costing €8,000. These transactions are investing activities.

The company should report each transaction separately. Thus, it reports the purchase of equipment as an outflow of cash for €25,000. It reports the sale as an inflow of cash for €4,000. The T-account in Illustration 14.14 shows the reasons for the change in this account during the year.

ILLUSTRATION 14.14
Analysis of equipment

Equipment				
1/1/29	Balance	10,000	Cost of equipment sold	8,000
	Purchase of equipment	25,000		
12/31/29	Balance	27,000		

The following entry shows details of the equipment sale transaction.

Cash	4,000	
Accumulated Depreciation—Equipment	1,000	
Loss on Disposal of Plant Assets	3,000	
Equipment		8,000

A	=	L	+	E
+4,000				
+1,000				
				−3,000 Exp
−8,000				

Cash Flows
+4,000

Increase in Bonds Payable The Bonds Payable account increased €110,000. As indicated in the additional information, the company acquired land from the issuance of these bonds.

Cash Payments for Interest Under the amended *IAS 7*, entities that do not have investing in assets or providing financing to customers as a main business activity are required to classify interest paid as cash flows from financing activities. For Computer Services, the statement of financial position did not include an accrual for interest payable for 2028 or 2029; the amount reported as expense is the same as the amount of interest paid. Illustration 14.15 shows the reporting of interest paid of €42,000 as a separate line item to arrive at net cash provided by financing activities.

Increase in Share Capital—Ordinary The statement of financial position reports an increase in Share Capital—Ordinary of €20,000. The additional information section notes that this increase resulted from the issuance of new shares (see **Helpful Hint**). This is a cash inflow reported in the financing section.

HELPFUL HINT

When companies issue shares or bonds for cash, the actual proceeds will appear in the statement of cash flows as a financing inflow (rather than the par value of the shares or face value of bonds).

Increase in Retained Earnings Retained earnings increased €116,000 during the year. This increase can be explained by two factors: (1) net income of €145,000 increased retained earnings, and (2) dividends of €29,000 decreased retained earnings. The company adjusts operating income to net cash provided by operating activities in the operating activities section. Payment of the dividends (not the declaration) is a **cash outflow that the company reports as a financing activity**.

Statement of Cash Flows—2029

Using the previous information, we can now prepare a statement of cash flows for 2029 for Computer Services International as shown in **Illustration 14.15**. Note that in the investing and financing activities sections, positive numbers indicate cash inflows (receipts), and negative numbers indicate cash outflows (payments).

Step 3: Net Change in Cash

Compare the Net Change in Cash on the Statement of Cash Flows with the Change in the Cash Account Reported on the Statement of Financial Position to Make Sure the Amounts Agree

Illustration 14.15 indicates that the net change in cash during the period was an increase of €22,000. This agrees with the change in the Cash account reported on the statement of financial position in Illustration 14.5.

ILLUSTRATION 14.15

Statement of cash flows, 2029—indirect method

Computer Services International

Statement of Cash Flows—Indirect Method

For the Year Ended December 31, 2029

Cash flows from operating activities		
Operating income		€234,000
Adjustments to reconcile operating income to net cash provided by operating activities:		
Depreciation expense	€ 9,000	
Loss on disposal of plant assets	3,000	
Decrease in accounts receivable	10,000	
Increase in inventory	(5,000)	
Increase in prepaid expenses	(4,000)	
Increase in accounts payable	16,000	29,000
Cash from operating activities before income taxes		€263,000
Income taxes paid		(49,000)
Net cash provided by operating activities		€214,000
Cash flows from investing activities		
Purchase of building	(120,000)	
Purchase of equipment	(25,000)	
Disposal of plant assets	4,000	
Net cash used by investing activities		(141,000)
Cash flows from financing activities		
Interest paid	(42,000)	
Issuance of ordinary shares	20,000	
Payment of cash dividends	(29,000)	
Net cash used by financing activities		(51,000)
Net increase in cash		22,000
Cash at beginning of period		33,000
Cash at end of period		€ 55,000
Note 1		
Non-cash investing and financing activities		
Issuance of bonds payable to purchase land		€110,000

Accounting Across the Organization

Soubrette/iStockphoto

Burning Through Our Cash

A once popular method of growth seems to be ending. Companies, including a number of technology-focused companies, used to raise large amount of cash and invest it in a strategy of rapid grown. The strategy was called blitzscaling. The idea was that by growing large quickly, a company could capture the market.

For example, **WeWork** (USA) and **Ucommune** (CHN) focused on hyper-growth to snap up office space for co-working facilities. From shared mobility companies like **Ofo** (CHN), to smartphone makers like **Smartisan** (CHN), cash was raised and then spent quickly to chase the prospect of rapid growth.

The market now seems to be drawn to companies that can actually grow profits and cash flows. Seasoned investors understand that both growth and profits must be kept in balance in the early stages of a company's life. Focusing too much on growth without considering profits and cash flows can lead to bankruptcy. Focusing just on profits and cash flows can slow down growth and lead to being passed by another more growth-oriented company. Add finding this balance to the list of the many difficult but important challenges face by entrepreneurs!

Source: Based on Iris Deng, "China's Tech Start-Ups Kiss Goodbye to Cash Burning As Investors Focus on Profits," *South China Morning Post* (December 24, 2019).

What implications does a company's cash burn rate have for its survival? (Answer is available near the end of the chapter.)

DO IT! 2b | Indirect Method

Use the following information to prepare a statement of cash flows using the indirect method.

Dragon Ltd.
Comparative Statements of Financial Position
December 31
(NT$ in thousands)

Assets	**2029**	**2028**	**Change Increase/Decrease**
Land	NT$ 75,000	NT$ 70,000	NT$ 5,000 Increase
Buildings	200,000	200,000	–0–
Accumulated depreciation—buildings	(21,000)	(11,000)	10,000 Increase
Equipment	193,000	68,000	125,000 Increase
Accumulated depreciation—equipment	(28,000)	(10,000)	18,000 Increase
Prepaid expenses	4,000	6,000	2,000 Decrease
Inventory	54,000	–0–	54,000 Increase
Accounts receivable	68,000	26,000	42,000 Increase
Cash	54,000	37,000	17,000 Increase
Totals	NT$599,000	NT$386,000	
Equity and Liabilities			
Share capital—ordinary (NT$1 par)	NT$220,000	NT$ 60,000	NT$160,000 Increase
Retained earnings	206,000	136,000	70,000 Increase
Bonds payable	140,000	150,000	10,000 Decrease
Accounts payable	23,000	40,000	17,000 Decrease
Accrued expenses payable	10,000	–0–	10,000 Increase
Totals	NT$599,000	NT$386,000	

Dragon Ltd.
Income Statement
For the Year Ended December 31, 2029
(NT$ in thousands)

Sales revenue		NT$890,000
Cost of goods sold	NT$465,000	
Operating expenses	221,000	
Loss on disposal of plant assets	2,000	688,000
Operating income		202,000
Interest expense		(12,000)
Income before income tax		190,000
Income tax expense		(65,000)
Net income		NT$125,000

Additional information (all amounts in thousands of NT$):

1. Operating expenses include depreciation expense of NT$33,000.
2. Equipment with a cost of NT$41,000 and a book value of NT$36,000 was sold for NT$34,000 cash.
3. Land was sold at its book value for cash.
4. Interest expense of NT$12,000 was paid in cash.
5. Equipment with a cost of NT$166,000 was purchased for cash.

ACTION PLAN

- **Determine net cash provided/used by operating activities by adjusting operating income for items that did not affect cash.**
- **Determine net cash provided/used by investing activities and financing activities.**
- **Determine the net increase/decrease in cash.**

6. Bonds of NT$10,000 were redeemed at their face value for cash.
7. Ordinary shares (NT$1 par) of NT$130,000 were issued for cash.
8. Cash dividends of NT$55,000 were declared and paid in 2029.
9. Ordinary shares of NT$30,000 were issued in exchange for land.

Solution

Dragon Ltd.
Statement of Cash Flows—Indirect Method
For the Year Ended December 31, 2029
(NT$ in thousands)

Cash flows from operating activities		
Operating income		NT$202,000
Adjustments to reconcile operating income to net cash provided by operating activities:		
Depreciation expense	NT$ 33,000	
Loss on disposal of plant assets	2,000	
Increase in accounts receivable	(42,000)	
Increase in inventory	(54,000)	
Decrease in prepaid expenses	2,000	
Decrease in accounts payable	(17,000)	
Increase in accrued expenses payable	10,000	(66,000)
Cash from operating activities before income taxes		136,000
Income taxes paid		(65,000)
Net cash provided by operating activities		71,000
Cash flows from investing activities		
Sale of land	25,000	
Disposal of plant assets	34,000	
Purchase of equipment	(166,000)	
Net cash used by investing activities		(107,000)
Cash flows from financing activities		
Interest Paid	(12,000)	
Redemption of bonds	(10,000)	
Sale of ordinary shares	130,000	
Payment of dividends	(55,000)	
Net cash provided by financing activities		53,000
Net increase in cash		17,000
Cash at beginning of period		37,000
Cash at end of period		NT$ 54,000
Note 1		
Non-cash investing and financing activities		
Issued ordinary shares in exchange for land		NT$ 30,000

Related exercise material: **BE14.4, BE14.5, BE14.6, BE14.7, E14.4, E14.5, E14.6, E14.7, E14.8, and E14.9.**

14.3 Using Cash Flows to Evaluate a Company

LEARNING OBJECTIVE 3

Analyze the statement of cash flows.

Traditionally, investors and creditors used ratios based on accrual accounting. These days, cash-based ratios are gaining increased acceptance among analysts.

Free Cash Flow

In the statement of cash flows, net cash provided by operating activities is intended to indicate the cash-generating capability of a company. Analysts have noted, however, that **net cash provided by operating activities fails to take into account that a company must invest in new fixed assets** just to maintain its current level of operations. Companies also must at least **maintain dividends at current levels** to satisfy investors.

- The measurement of free cash flow provides additional insight regarding a company's cash-generating ability.
- **Free cash flow** describes the net cash provided by operating activities after adjustment for capital expenditures and dividends.

Consider the following example. Suppose that MPC produced and sold 10,000 personal computers this year. It reported HK$1,000,000 net cash provided by operating activities. In order to maintain production at 10,000 computers, MPC invested HK$150,000 in equipment. It chose to pay HK$50,000 in dividends. Its free cash flow was HK$800,000 (HK$1,000,000 – HK$150,000 – HK$50,000). The company could use this HK$800,000 either to purchase new assets to expand the business or to pay an HK$800,000 dividend and continue to produce 10,000 computers.

In practice, free cash flow is often calculated with the formula in **Illustration 14.16**. (Alternative definitions also exist.)

ILLUSTRATION 14.16

Free cash flow

Free Cash Flow = Net Cash Provided by Operating Activities − Capital Expenditures − Cash Dividends

Illustration 14.17 provides basic information (in millions) excerpted from a recent statement of cash flows of **Anheuser-Busch InBev** (BEL).

ILLUSTRATION 14.17

Anheuser-Busch InBev cash flow information ($ in millions)

Real World

Anheuser-Busch InBev
Statement of Cash Flows (partial)

Cash provided by operating activities		$ 17,451
Cash flows from investing activities		
Additions to property and equipment and intangibles	$ (3,869)	
Purchases of non-controlling interests	(99)	
Sale of property, plant, and equipment	4,002	
Acquisitions of companies	(17,439)	
Other	7,124	
Cash used by investing activities		(10,281)
Cash paid for dividends		(6,253)

Anheuser-Busch InBev's free cash flow is calculated as shown in **Illustration 14.18**.

ILLUSTRATION 14.18

Calculation of Anheuser-Busch InBev's free cash flow ($ in millions)

Cash provided by operating activities	$17,451
Less: Expenditures on property and equipment	3,869
Dividends paid	6,253
Free cash flow	$ 7,329

The company generated a significant amount of cash from its operations, but it spent most of it to buy property, plant, and equipment, and to pay dividends.

ACTION PLAN

- **Compute free cash flow as Net cash provided by operating activities – Capital expenditures – Cash dividends.**

DO IT! 3 | Free Cash Flow

Luó Ltd. issued the following statement of cash flows for 2029.

Luó Ltd.
Statement of Cash Flows—Indirect Method
For the Year Ended December 31, 2029
(¥ in thousands)

Cash flows from operating activities		
Net income		¥19,000
Adjustments to reconcile net income to net cash provided by operating activities:		
Depreciation expense	¥ 8,100	
Loss on disposal of plant assets	1,300	
Decrease in accounts receivable	6,900	
Increase in inventory	(4,000)	
Decrease in accounts payable	(2,000)	10,300
Net cash provided by operating activities		29,300
Cash flows from investing activities		
Sale of investments	1,100	
Purchase of equipment	(19,000)	
Net cash used by investing activities		(17,900)
Cash flows from financing activities		
Issuance of ordinary shares	10,000	
Payment on long-term note payable	(5,000)	
Payment of dividends	(9,000)	
Net cash used by financing activities		(4,000)
Net increase in cash		7,400
Cash at beginning of year		10,000
Cash at end of year		¥17,400

(a) Compute free cash flow for Luó. (b) Explain why free cash flow often provides better information than "Net cash provided by operating activities."

Solution

a. Free cash flow (¥ in thousands) = ¥29,300 − ¥19,000 − ¥9,000 = ¥1,300

b. Net cash provided by operating activities fails to take into account that a company must invest in new plant assets just to maintain the current level of operations. Companies must also maintain dividends at current levels to satisfy investors. The measurement of free cash flow provides additional insight regarding a company's cash-generating ability.

Related exercise material: **BE14.8, BE14.9, BE14.10, BE14.11, DO IT! 14.3, E14.7, and E14.9.**

Appendix 14A Statement of Cash Flows—Direct Method

LEARNING OBJECTIVE *4

Prepare a statement of cash flows using the direct method.

To explain and illustrate the direct method for preparing a statement of cash flows, we will use the transactions of Computer Services International for 2029. **Illustration 14A.1** presents information related to 2029 for the company.

ILLUSTRATION 14A.1

Comparative statements of financial position, income statement, and additional information for Computer Services International

Computer Services International
Comparative Statements of Financial Position
December 31

Assets	**2029**	**2028**	**Change in Account Balance Increase/Decrease**
Property, plant, and equipment			
Land	€130,000	€ 20,000	€110,000 Increase
Buildings	160,000	40,000	120,000 Increase
Accumulated depreciation—buildings	(11,000)	(5,000)	6,000 Increase
Equipment	27,000	10,000	17,000 Increase
Accumulated depreciation—equipment	(3,000)	(1,000)	2,000 Increase
Current assets			
Prepaid expenses	5,000	1,000	4,000 Increase
Inventory	15,000	10,000	5,000 Increase
Accounts receivable	20,000	30,000	10,000 Decrease
Cash	55,000	33,000	22,000 Increase
Total assets	€398,000	€138,000	
Equity and Liabilities			
Equity			
Share capital—ordinary	€ 70,000	€ 50,000	€ 20,000 Increase
Retained earnings	164,000	48,000	116,000 Increase
Non-current liabilities			
Bonds payable	130,000	20,000	110,000 Increase
Current liabilities			
Accounts payable	28,000	12,000	16,000 Increase
Income taxes payable	6,000	8,000	2,000 Decrease
Total equity and liabilities	€398,000	€138,000	

Computer Services International
Income Statement
For the Year Ended December 31, 2029

Sales revenue		€507,000
Cost of goods sold	€150,000	
Operating expenses (excluding depreciation)	111,000	
Depreciation expense	9,000	
Loss on disposal of plant	3,000	273,000
Operating income		234,000
Interest expense		42,000
Income before income tax		192,000
Income tax expense		47,000
Net income		€145,000

Additional information for 2029:

1. Depreciation expense was comprised of €6,000 for building and €3,000 for equipment.
2. The company sold equipment with a book value of €7,000 (cost €8,000, less accumulated depreciation €1,000) for €4,000 cash.
3. Issued €110,000 of long-term bonds in direct exchange for land.
4. A building costing €120,000 was purchased for cash. Equipment costing €25,000 was also purchased for cash.
5. Issued ordinary shares for €20,000 cash.
6. The company declared and paid a €29,000 cash dividend.

To prepare a statement of cash flows under the direct approach, we will apply the three steps outlined in Illustration 14.4.

Step 1: Operating Activities

Determine Net Cash Provided/Used by Operating Activities by Converting Operating Income from an Accrual Basis to a Cash Basis

Under the **direct method**, companies compute net cash provided by operating activities by **adjusting each item in the income statement** from the accrual basis to the cash basis.

- To simplify and condense the operating activities section, companies **report only major classes of operating cash receipts and cash payments.**
- For these major classes, the difference between cash receipts and cash payments is the net cash provided by operating activities.

These relationships are as shown in **Illustration 14A.2**.

ILLUSTRATION 14A.2 **Major classes of cash receipts and payments**

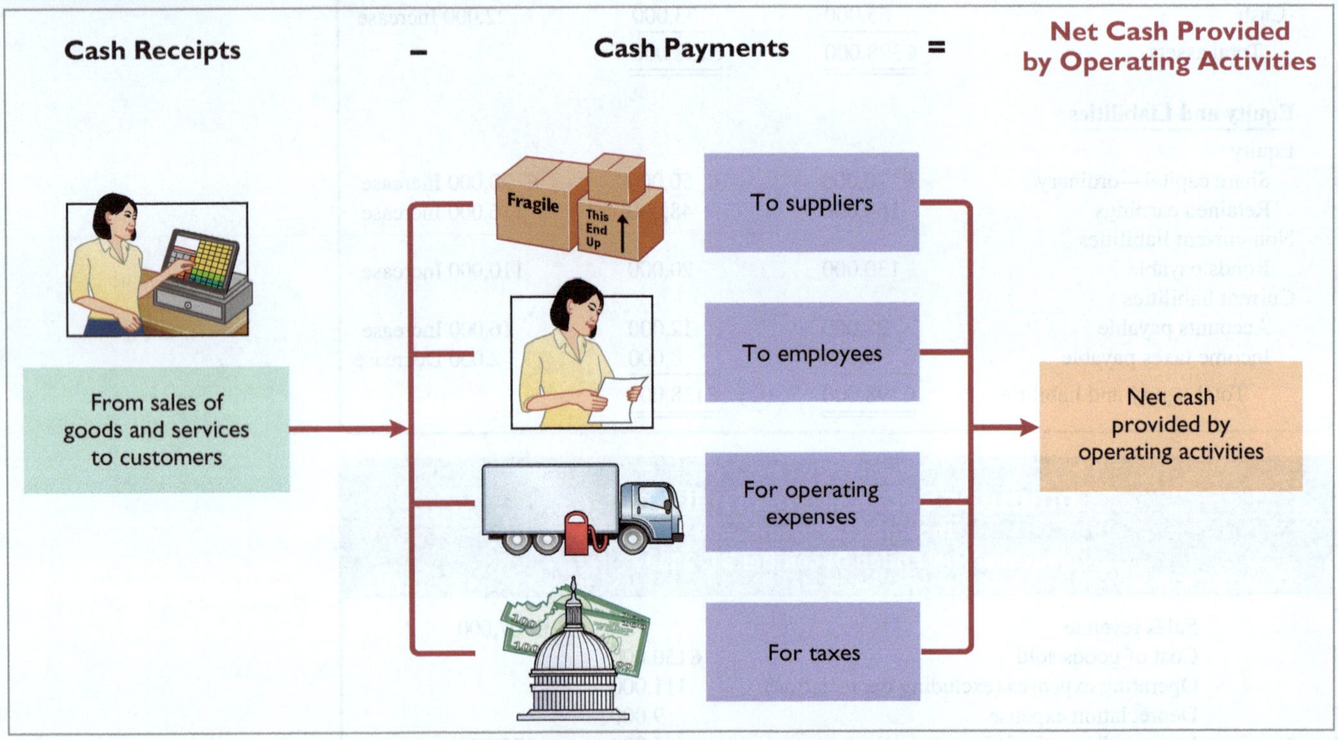

An efficient way to apply the direct method is to analyze the items reported in the income statement in the order in which they are listed. We then determine cash receipts and cash payments related to these revenues and expenses. The following presents the adjustments required to prepare a statement of cash flows for Computer Services using the direct approach.

Cash Receipts from Customers The income statement for Computer Services reported revenue from customers of €507,000. How much of that was cash receipts? To answer that, a company needs to consider the change in accounts receivable during the year. When accounts receivable increase during the year, revenues on an accrual basis are higher than cash receipts from customers. Operations led to revenues, but not all of those revenues resulted in cash receipts.

- To determine the amount of cash receipts, a company deducts from sales revenue the increase in accounts receivable.

- On the other hand, there may be a decrease in accounts receivable. That would occur if cash receipts from customers exceeded sales revenue. In that case, a company adds to sales revenue the decrease in accounts receivable.

For Computer Services, accounts receivable decreased €10,000. Thus, cash receipts from customers were €517,000, computed as shown in **Illustration 14A.3**.

ILLUSTRATION 14A.3

Computation of cash receipts from customers

Sales revenue	€507,000
Add: Decrease in accounts receivable	10,000
Cash receipts from customers	**€517,000**

Computer Services can also determine cash receipts from customers from an analysis of the Accounts Receivable account, as shown in **Illustration 14A.4** (see **Helpful Hint**).

HELPFUL HINT

The T-account shows that revenue plus decrease in receivables equals cash receipts.

ILLUSTRATION 14A.4

Analysis of accounts receivable

Accounts Receivable

1/1/29	Balance	30,000	**Receipts from customers**	**517,000**
	Sales revenue	507,000		
12/31/29	Balance	20,000		

Illustration 14A.5 shows the relationships among cash receipts from customers, sales revenue, and changes in accounts receivable.

ILLUSTRATION 14A.5

Formula to compute cash receipts from customers—direct method

Cash Receipts from Customers	=	**Sales Revenue**	+	**Decrease in Accounts Receivable**
				or
			−	**Increase in Accounts Receivable**

Cash Payments to Suppliers Computer Services reported cost of goods sold of €150,000 on its income statement. How much of that was cash payments to suppliers? To answer that, it is first necessary to find purchases for the year. To find purchases, a company adjusts cost of goods sold for the change in inventory. When inventory increases during the year, purchases for the year have exceeded cost of goods sold. As a result, to determine the amount of purchases, a company adds to cost of goods sold the increase in inventory.

In 2029, Computer Services' inventory increased €5,000. It computes purchases as shown in **Illustration 14A.6**.

ILLUSTRATION 14A.6

Computation of purchases

Cost of goods sold	€150,000
Add: Increase in inventory	5,000
Purchases	**€155,000**

After computing purchases, a company can determine cash payments to suppliers. This is done by adjusting purchases for the change in accounts payable. When accounts payable increase during the year, purchases on an accrual basis are higher than they are on a cash basis.

- As a result, to determine cash payments to suppliers, a company deducts from purchases the increase in accounts payable.
- On the other hand, if cash payments to suppliers exceed purchases, there will be a decrease in accounts payable. In that case, a company adds to purchases the decrease in accounts payable.

For Computer Services, cash payments to suppliers were €139,000, computed as shown in **Illustration 14A.7**.

ILLUSTRATION 14A.7

Computation of cash payments to suppliers

Purchases	€155,000
Deduct: Increase in accounts payable	16,000
Cash payments to suppliers	**€139,000**

Computer Services also can determine cash payments to suppliers from an analysis of the Accounts Payable account, as shown in **Illustration 14A.8** (see **Helpful Hint**).

ILLUSTRATION 14A.8

Analysis of accounts payable

HELPFUL HINT

The T-account shows that purchases less increase in accounts payable equal payments to suppliers.

Accounts Payable				
Payments to suppliers	**139,000**	1/1/29	Balance	12,000
			Purchases	155,000
		12/31/29	Balance	28,000

Illustration 14A.9 shows the relationships among cash payments to suppliers, cost of goods sold, changes in inventory, and changes in accounts payable.

ILLUSTRATION 14A.9

Formula to compute cash payments to suppliers—direct method

Cash Payments to Suppliers = **Cost of Goods Sold** { **+ Increase in Inventory** or **− Decrease in Inventory** } { **+ Decrease in Accounts Payable** or **− Increase in Accounts Payable** }

Cash Payments for Operating Expenses Computer Services reported on its income statement operating expenses of €111,000. How much of that amount was cash paid for operating expenses? To answer that, we need to adjust this amount for any changes in prepaid expenses and accrued expenses payable.

For example, if prepaid expenses increased during the year, cash paid for operating expenses is higher than operating expenses reported on the income statement. To convert operating expenses to cash payments for operating expenses, a company adds the increase in prepaid expenses to operating expenses. On the other hand, if prepaid expenses decrease during the year, it deducts the decrease from operating expenses.

Companies must also adjust operating expenses for changes in accrued expenses payable. When accrued expenses payable increase during the year, operating expenses on an accrual basis are higher than they are on a cash basis.

- As a result, to determine cash payments for operating expenses, a company deducts from operating expenses an increase in accrued expenses payable.
- On the other hand, a company adds to operating expenses a decrease in accrued expenses payable because cash payments exceed operating expenses.

Computer Services' cash payments for operating expenses were €115,000, computed as shown in **Illustration 14A.10**.

ILLUSTRATION 14A.10

Computation of cash payments for operating expenses

Operating expenses	€111,000
Add: Increase in prepaid expenses	4,000
Cash payments for operating expenses	**€115,000**

Illustration 14A.11 shows the relationships among cash payments for operating expenses, changes in prepaid expenses, and changes in accrued expenses payable.

ILLUSTRATION 14A.11

Formula to compute cash payments for operating expenses—direct method

Cash Payments for Operating Expenses = **Operating Expenses** { **+ Increase in Prepaid Expenses** or **− Decrease in Prepaid Expenses** } { **+ Decrease in Accrued Expenses Payable** or **− Increase in Accrued Expenses Payable** }

Depreciation Expense and Loss on Disposal of Plant Assets Computer Services' depreciation expense in 2029 was €9,000. Depreciation expense is not shown on a statement of cash flows under the direct method because it is a non-cash charge. If the amount for operating expenses includes depreciation expense, operating expenses must be reduced by the amount of depreciation to determine cash payments for operating expenses.

The loss on disposal of plant assets of €3,000 is also a non-cash charge. The loss on disposal of plant assets reduces operating income, but it does not reduce cash. Thus, the loss on disposal of plant assets is not shown on the statement of cash flows under the direct method.

Other charges to expense that do not require the use of cash, such as the amortization of intangible assets and expected credit loss, are treated in the same manner as depreciation.

Cash Payments for Income Taxes Computer Services reported income tax expense of €47,000 on the income statement. Income taxes payable, however, decreased €2,000. This decrease means that income taxes paid were more than income taxes reported in the income statement. Cash payments for income taxes were therefore €49,000, as **Illustration 14A.12** shows.

ILLUSTRATION 14A.12

Computation of cash payments for income taxes

Income tax expense	€47,000
Add: Decrease in income taxes payable	2,000
Cash payments for income taxes	**€49,000**

Illustration 14A.13 shows the relationships among cash payments for income taxes, income tax expense, and changes in income taxes payable.

ILLUSTRATION 14A.13

Formula to compute cash payments for income taxes—direct method

Cash Payments for Income Taxes	=	**Income Tax Expense**	**+ Decrease in Income Taxes Payable** **or** **− Increase in Income Taxes Payable**

The operating activities section of the statement of cash flows of Computer Services is shown in **Illustration 14A.14**.

ILLUSTRATION 14A.14

Operating activities section of the statement of cash flows

Cash flows from operating activities		
Cash receipts from customers		€517,000
Less: Cash payments:		
To suppliers	€139,000	
For operating expenses	115,000	
For income taxes	49,000	303,000
Net cash provided by operating activities		€214,000

When a company uses the direct method, it must also provide in a **separate schedule** (not shown here) the net cash flows from operating activities as computed under the indirect method.

Step 2: Investing and Financing Activities

Analyze Changes in Non-Current Asset and Liability Accounts and Record as Investing and Financing Activities, or Disclose as Non-Cash Transactions

Increase in Land As indicated from the change in the Land account and the additional information, the company purchased land of €110,000 by directly exchanging bonds for land. The exchange of bonds payable for land has no effect on cash. But, it is a significant non-cash investing and financing activity that merits disclosure in a note to the financial statements (see **Helpful Hint**). (See Illustration 14A.16.)

HELPFUL HINT

The investing and financing activities are measured and reported the same under both the direct and indirect methods.

Increase in Buildings As the additional data indicate, Computer Services acquired a building for €120,000 cash. This is a cash outflow reported in the investing activities section. (See Illustration 14A.16.)

Increase in Equipment The Equipment account increased €17,000. The additional information explains that this was a net increase that resulted from two transactions: (1) a purchase of equipment of €25,000, and (2) the sale for €4,000 of equipment costing €8,000. These transactions are investing activities. The company should report each transaction separately.

The statement in Illustration 14A.16 reports the purchase of equipment as an outflow of cash for €25,000. It reports the sale as an inflow of cash for €4,000. The T-account in Illustration 14A.15 shows the reasons for the change in this account during the year.

ILLUSTRATION 14A.15

Analysis of equipment

Equipment

1/1/29	Balance	10,000	Cost of equipment sold	8,000
	Purchase of equipment	25,000		
12/31/29	Balance	27,000		

The following entry shows the details of the equipment sale transaction.

Cash	4,000	
Accumulated Depreciation—Equipment	1,000	
Loss on Disposal of Plant Assets	3,000	
Equipment		8,000

A	=	L	+	E
+4,000				
+1,000				
				−3,000 Exp
−8,000				

Cash Flows
+4,000

Increase in Bonds Payable The Bonds Payable account increased €110,000. As indicated in the additional information, the company acquired land by directly exchanging bonds for land. Illustration 14A.16 reports this non-cash transaction in a separate note.

Cash Payments for Interest Computer Services reported on the income statement interest expense of €42,000. Since the statement of financial position did not include an accrual for interest payable for 2028 or 2029, the amount reported as expense is the same as the amount of interest paid.

Increase in Share Capital—Ordinary The statement of financial position reports an increase in Share Capital—Ordinary of €20,000. The additional information section notes that this increase resulted from the issuance of new shares (see **Helpful Hint**). This is a cash inflow reported in the financing section in Illustration 14A.16.

HELPFUL HINT

When companies issue shares or bonds for cash, the actual proceeds will appear in the statement of cash flows as a financing inflow (rather than the par value of the shares or face value of bonds).

Increase in Retained Earnings Retained earnings increased €116,000 during the year. This increase can be explained by two factors: (1) net income of €145,000 increased retained earnings, and (2) dividends of €29,000 decreased retained earnings. The company adjusts net income to net cash provided by operating activities in the operating activities section. Payment of the dividends (not the declaration) is a **cash outflow that the company reports as a financing activity in Illustration 14A.16.**

Statement of Cash Flows—2029

Illustration 14A.16 shows the statement of cash flows for Computer Services.

ILLUSTRATION 14A.16

Statement of cash flows, 2029 — direct method

Computer Services International
Statement of Cash Flows—Direct Method
For the Year Ended December 31, 2029

Cash flows from operating activities		
Cash receipts from customers		€517,000
Less: Cash payments:		
To suppliers	€ 139,000	
For operating expenses	115,000	
For income taxes	49,000	303,000
Net cash provided by operating activities		214,000
Cash flows from investing activities		
Purchase of building	(120,000)	
Purchase of equipment	(25,000)	
Disposal of plant assets	4,000	
Net cash used by investing activities		(141,000)
Cash flows from financing activities		
Interest paid	(42,000)	
Issuance of ordinary shares	20,000	
Payment of cash dividends	(29,000)	
Net cash used by financing activities		(51,000)
Net increase in cash		22,000
Cash at beginning of period		33,000
Cash at end of period		€ 55,000
Note 1		
Non-cash investing and financing activities		
Issuance of bonds payable to purchase land		€110,000

Step 3: Net Change in Cash

Compare the Net Change in Cash on the Statement of Cash Flows with the Change in the Cash Account Reported on the Statement of Financial Position to Make Sure the Amounts Agree

Illustration 14A.16 indicates that the net change in cash during the period was an increase of €22,000. This agrees with the change in balances in the Cash account reported on the statements of financial position in Illustration 14A.1.

Appendix 14B Statement of Cash Flows—T-Account Approach

LEARNING OBJECTIVE *5

Use the T-account approach to prepare a statement of cash flows.

Many people like to use T-accounts to provide structure to the preparation of a statement of cash flows. The use of T-accounts is based on the accounting equation that you learned in Chapter 1. The basic equation is:

Assets = Liabilities + Equity

Now, let's rewrite the left-hand side as:

Cash + Non-Cash Assets = Liabilities + Equity

Next, rewrite the equation by subtracting Non-Cash Assets from each side to isolate Cash on the left-hand side:

Cash = Liabilities + Equity − Non-Cash Assets

Finally, if we insert the Δ symbol (which means "change in"), we have:

Δ Cash = Δ Liabilities + Δ Equity − Δ Non-Cash Assets

What this means is that the change in cash is equal to the change in all of the other statement of financial position accounts. Another way to think about this is that if we analyze the changes in all of the non-cash statement of financial position accounts, we will explain the change in the Cash account. This, of course, is exactly what we are trying to do with the statement of cash flows.

To implement this approach:

- Prepare a large Cash T-account, with sections for operating, investing, and financing activities.
- Then, prepare smaller T-accounts for all of the other non-cash statement of financial position accounts. Insert the beginning and ending balances for each of these accounts.
- Once you have done this, then walk through the steps outlined in Illustration 14.4.

As you walk through the steps, enter debit and credit amounts into the affected accounts. When all of the changes in the T-accounts have been explained, you are done.

To demonstrate, we will apply this approach to the example of Computer Services International that is presented in the chapter. Each of the adjustments in **Illustration 14B.1** is numbered so you can follow them through the T-accounts.

1. Post net income by adding back interest expense as a debit to the operating section of the Cash T-account and a credit to Retained Earnings. Make sure to label all adjustments to the Cash T-account. It also helps to number each adjustment so you can trace all of them if you make an error.
2. Post depreciation expense as a debit to the operating section of Cash and a credit to each of the appropriate accumulated depreciation accounts.
3. Post any gains or losses on the sale of property, plant, and equipment. To do this, it is best to first prepare the journal entry that was recorded at the time of the sale and then post each element of the journal entry. For example, for Computer Services the entry was as follows.

Cash	4,000	
Accumulated Depreciation—Equipment	1,000	
Loss on Disposal of Plant Assets	3,000	
Equipment		8,000

The €4,000 cash entry is a source of cash in the investing section of the Cash account. Accumulated Depreciation—Equipment is debited for €1,000. The Loss on Disposal of Plant Assets is a debit to the operating section of the Cash T-account. Finally, Equipment is credited for €8,000.

4-8. Next, post each of the changes to the non-cash current asset and current liability accounts. For example, to explain the €10,000 decline in Computer Services' Accounts Receivable, credit Accounts Receivable for €10,000 and debit the operating section of the Cash T-account for €10,000.

ILLUSTRATION 14B.1 **T-account approach**

Cash

Operating			
(1) Operating income	187,000	(5) Inventory	5,000
(2) Depreciation expense	9,000	(6) Prepaid expenses	4,000
(3) Loss on disposal of plant assets	3,000	(8) Income taxes payable	2,000
(4) Accounts receivable	10,000		
(7) Accounts payable	16,000		
Net cash provided by operating activities	214,000		
Investing			
(3) Disposal of plant assets	4,000	(10) Purchased building	120,000
		(11) Purchased equipment	25,000
		Net cash used by investing activities	141,000
Financing			
(13) Issued ordinary shares	20,000	(12) Interest paid	42,000
		(14) Dividend paid	29,000
		Net cash used by financing activities	51,000
	22,000		

Accounts Receivable

Debit	Credit
30,000	(4) 10,000
20,000	

Inventory

Debit	Credit
10,000	
(5) 5,000	
15,000	

Prepaid Expenses

Debit	Credit
1,000	
(6) 4,000	
5,000	

Land

Debit	Credit
20,000	
(9) 110,000	
130,000	

Buildings

Debit	Credit
40,000	
(10) 120,000	
160,000	

Accumulated Depreciation—Buildings

Debit	Credit
	5,000
	(2) 6,000
	11,000

Equipment

Debit	Credit
10,000	
(11) 25,000	(3) 8,000
27,000	

Accumulated Depreciation—Equipment

Debit	Credit
	1,000
(3) 1,000	(2) 3,000
	3,000

Accounts Payable

Debit	Credit
	12,000
	(7) 16,000
	28,000

Income Taxes Payable

Debit	Credit
	8,000
(8) 2,000	
	6,000

Bonds Payable

Debit	Credit
	20,000
	(9) 110,000
	130,000

Share Capital—Ordinary

Debit	Credit
	50,000
	(13) 20,000
	70,000

Retained Earnings

Debit	Credit
	48,000
	(1) 187,000
(12) 42,000	
(14) 29,000	
	164,000

9. Analyze the changes in the non-current accounts. Land was purchased by issuing Bonds Payable. This requires a debit to Land for €110,000 and a credit to Bonds Payable for €110,000. Note that this is a significant non-cash event that requires disclosure in a note at the bottom of the statement of cash flows.
10. Buildings is debited for €120,000, and the investing section of the Cash T-account is credited for €120,000 as a use of cash from investing.
11. Equipment is debited for €25,000 and the investing section of the Cash T-account is credited for €25,000 as a use of cash from investing.
12. Post interest expense as a debit to Retained Earnings and a credit to the financing section of the Cash T-account.
13. Share Capital—Ordinary is credited for €20,000 for the issuance of ordinary shares, and the financing section of the Cash T-account is debited for €20,000.
14. Retained Earnings is debited to reflect the payment of the €29,000 dividend, and the financing section of the Cash T-account is credited to reflect the use of Cash.

At this point, all of the changes in the non-cash accounts have been explained. All that remains is to subtotal each section of the Cash T-account and agree the total change in cash with the change shown on the statement of financial position. Once this is done, the information in the Cash T-account can be used to prepare a statement of cash flows.

Review and Practice

Learning Objectives Review

1 Discuss the usefulness and format of the statement of cash flows.

The statement of cash flows provides information about the cash receipts, cash payments, and net change in cash resulting from the operating, investing, and financing activities of a company during the period.

Operating activities include the cash effects of transactions that enter into the determination of operating income. Investing activities involve cash flows resulting from changes in investments and non-current asset items. Financing activities involve cash flows resulting from changes in non-current liability and equity items.

2 Prepare a statement of cash flows using the indirect method.

The preparation of a statement of cash flows involves three major steps. (1) Determine net cash provided/used by operating activities by converting operating income from an accrual basis to a cash basis. (2) Analyze changes in non-current asset and liability accounts and record as investing and financing activities, or disclose as non-cash transactions. (3) Compare the net change in cash on the statement of cash flows with the change in the Cash account reported on the statement of financial position to make sure the amounts agree.

3 Analyze the statement of cash flows.

Free cash flow indicates the amount of cash a company generated during the current year that is available for the payment of dividends or for expansion.

*4 Prepare a statement of cash flows using the direct method.

The preparation of the statement of cash flows involves three major steps. (1) Determine net cash provided/used by operating activities by converting operating income from an accrual basis to a cash basis. (2) Analyze changes in non-current asset and liability accounts and record as investing and financing activities, or disclose as non-cash transactions. (3) Compare the net change in cash on the statement of cash flows with the change in the Cash account reported on the statement of financial position to make sure the amounts agree. The direct method reports cash receipts less cash payments to arrive at net cash provided by operating activities.

*5 Use the T-account approach to prepare a statement of cash flows.

To use T-accounts to prepare the statement of cash flows: (1) prepare a large Cash T-account with sections for operating, investing, and financing activities; (2) prepare smaller T-accounts for all other non-cash accounts; (3) insert beginning and ending balances for all accounts; and (4) follows the steps in Illustration 14B.1, entering debit and credit amounts as needed.

Glossary Review

Direct method A method of preparing a statement of cash flows that shows operating cash receipts and payments, making it more consistent with the objective of the statement of cash flows. (p. 14-8, 14-22).

Financing activities Cash flow activities that include (a) obtaining cash from issuing debt and repaying the amounts borrowed, and (b) obtaining cash from shareholders, repurchasing shares, and paying dividends. (p. 14-4).

Free cash flow Net cash provided by operating activities adjusted for capital expenditures and dividends paid. (p. 14-19).

Indirect method A method of preparing a statement of cash flows in which net income is adjusted for items that do not affect cash, to determine net cash provided by operating activities. (p. 14-8).

Investing activities Cash flow activities that include (a) acquiring and disposing of investments and property, plant, and equipment using cash, and (b) lending money and collecting the loans. (p. 14-3).

Operating activities Cash flow activities that include the cash effects of transactions that create revenues and expenses and thus enter into the determination of operating income. (p. 14-3).

Statement of cash flows A basic financial statement that provides information about the cash receipts, cash payments, and net change in cash during a period, resulting from operating, investing, and financing activities. (p. 14-3).

Practice Multiple-Choice Questions

1. **(LO 1)** Which of the following is **incorrect** about the statement of cash flows?
   - **a.** It is a fourth basic financial statement.
   - **b.** It provides information about cash receipts and cash payments of an entity during a period.
   - **c.** It reconciles the ending Cash account balance to the balance per the bank statement.
   - **d.** It provides information about the operating, investing, and financing activities of the business.

2. **(LO 1)** Which of the following will **not** be reported in the statement of cash flows?
   - **a.** The net change in plant assets during the year.
   - **b.** Cash payments for plant assets during the year.
   - **c.** Cash receipts from sales of plant assets during the year.
   - **d.** Cash payments for dividends.

3. **(LO 1)** The statement of cash flows classifies cash receipts and cash payments by these activities:
   - **a.** operating and non-operating.
   - **b.** investing, financing, and operating.
   - **c.** financing, operating, and non-operating.
   - **d.** investing, financing, and non-operating.

4. **(LO 1)** Which is an example of a cash flow from an operating activity?
   - **a.** Payment of cash to suppliers for inventory.
   - **b.** Receipt of cash from the issuance of ordinary shares.
   - **c.** Payment of cash dividends to the company's shareholders.
   - **d.** None of the above.

5. **(LO 1)** Which is an example of a cash flow from an investing activity?
   - **a.** Receipt of cash from the issuance of bonds payable.
   - **b.** Payment of cash to repurchase outstanding ordinary shares.
   - **c.** Receipt of cash from the sale of equipment.
   - **d.** Payment of cash to suppliers for inventory.

6. **(LO 1)** Cash dividends paid to shareholders are classified on the statement of cash flows as:
   - **a.** an operating activity.
   - **b.** an investing activity.
   - **c.** a combination of an operating activity and an investing activity.
   - **d.** a financing activity.

7. **(LO 1)** Which is an example of a cash flow from a financing activity?
   - **a.** Receipt of cash from sale of land.
   - **b.** Issuance of debt for cash.
   - **c.** Purchase of equipment for cash.
   - **d.** Receipt of interest.

8. **(LO 1)** Which of the following is **incorrect** about the statement of cash flows?
   - **a.** The direct method may be used to report net cash provided by operating activities.
   - **b.** The statement shows the net cash provided (used) for three categories of activity.
   - **c.** The operating section is the last section of the statement.
   - **d.** The indirect method may be used to report net cash provided by operating activities.

Use the indirect method to solve Questions 9 through 10.

9. **(LO 2)** Net income is £132,000, accounts payable increased £10,000 during the year, inventory decreased £6,000 during the year, and accounts receivable increased £12,000 during the year. Under the indirect method, what is net cash provided by operating activities?
   - **a.** £102,000.
   - **b.** £112,000.
   - **c.** £124,000.
   - **d.** £136,000.

10. **(LO 2)** Items that are added back to net income in determining net cash provided by operating activities under the indirect method do **not** include:
    - **a.** depreciation expense.
    - **b.** an increase in inventory.
    - **c.** amortization expense.
    - **d.** loss on disposal of equipment.

11. **(LO 2)** The following data are available for Allen Clapp Ltd.

Net income	HK$2,000,000
Depreciation expense	400,000
Dividends paid	600,000
Gain on disposal of land	100,000
Decrease in accounts receivable	200,000
Decrease in accounts payable	300,000

Net cash provided by operating activities is:
   - **a.** HK$1,600,000.
   - **b.** HK$2,200,000.
   - **c.** HK$2,400,000.
   - **d.** HK$2,800,000.

12. **(LO 2)** The following data are available for Orange Peels Ltd.

Sale of land	NT$1,000,000
Sale of equipment	500,000
Issuance of ordinary shares	700,000
Purchase of equipment	300,000
Payment of cash dividends	600,000

Net cash provided by investing activities is:
   - **a.** NT$1,200,000.
   - **b.** NT$1,300,000.
   - **c.** NT$1,500,000.
   - **d.** NT$1,900,000.

13. **(LO 2)** The following data are available for Something Strange!

Increase in accounts payable	€ 40,000
Increase in bonds payable	100,000
Sale of investment	50,000
Issuance of ordinary shares	60,000
Payment of cash dividends	30,000

Net cash provided by financing activities is:

a. €90,000.
b. €130,000.
c. €160,000.
d. €170,000.

14. (LO 3) The statement of cash flows should **not** be used to evaluate an entity's ability to:

a. earn net income.
b. generate future cash flows.
c. pay dividends.
d. meet obligations.

15. (LO 3) Free cash flow provides an indication of a company's ability to:

a. generate net income.
b. generate cash to pay additional dividends.
c. generate cash to invest in new capital expenditures.
d. generate both cash to pay additional dividends and to invest in new capital expenditures.

Use the direct method to solve Questions 16 and 17.

*16. (LO 4) The beginning balance in accounts receivable is €44,000, the ending balance is €42,000, and sales during the period are €129,000. What are cash receipts from customers?

a. €127,000.
b. €129,000.
c. €131,000.
d. €141,000.

*17. (LO 4) Which of the following items is reported on a statement of cash flows prepared by the direct method?

a. Loss on disposal of building.
b. Increase in accounts receivable.
c. Depreciation expense.
d. Cash payments to suppliers.

Solutions

1. **c.** The statement of cash flows does not reconcile the ending cash balance to the balance per the bank statement. The other choices are true statements.

2. **a.** The net change in plant assets during the year is not reported in the statement of cash flows. The other choices are true statements.

3. **b.** Operating, investing, and financing activities are the three classifications of cash receipts and cash payments used in the statement of cash flows. The other choices are therefore incorrect.

4. **a.** Payment of cash to suppliers for inventory is an operating activity. The other choices are incorrect because (b) receipt of cash from the issuance of ordinary shares is a financing activity, (c) payment of cash dividends to the company's shareholders is a financing activity, and (d) there is a correct answer.

5. **c.** Receipt of cash from the sale of equipment is an investing activity. The other choices are incorrect because (a) the receipt of cash from the issuance of bonds payable is a financing activity, (b) payment of cash to repurchase outstanding ordinary shares is a financing activity, and (d) payment of cash to suppliers for inventory is an operating activity.

6. **d.** Cash dividends paid to shareholders are classified as a financing activity, not (a) an operating activity, (b) an investing activity, or (c) a combination of (a) and (b).

7. **b.** Issuance of debt for cash is a financing activity. The other choices are incorrect because (a) the receipt of cash for the sale of land is an investing activity, (c) the purchase of equipment for cash is an investing activity, and (d) receipt of interest is an investing activity.

8. **c.** The operating section of the statement of cash flows is the first, not the last, section of the statement. The other choices are true statements.

9. **d.** Net cash provided by operating activities is computed by adjusting net income for the changes in the three current asset/current liability accounts listed. An increase in accounts payable (£10,000) and a decrease in inventory (£6,000) are added to net income (£132,000), while an increase in accounts receivable (£12,000) is subtracted from net income, or £132,000 + £10,000 + £6,000 − £12,000 = £136,000, not (a) £102,000, (b) £112,000, or (c) £124,000.

10. **b.** An increase in inventory is subtracted, not added, to net income in determining net cash provided by operating activities. The other choices are incorrect because (a) depreciation expense, (c) amortization expense, and (d) loss on disposal of equipment are all added back to net income in determining net cash provided by operating activities.

11. **b.** Net cash provided by operating activities is HK$2,200,000 (Net income HK$2,000,000 + Depreciation expense HK$400,000 − Gain on disposal of land HK$100,000 + Decrease in accounts receivable HK$200,000 − Decrease in accounts payable HK$300,000), not (a) HK$1,600,000, (c) HK$2,400,000, or (d) HK$2,800,000.

12. **a.** Net cash provided by investing activities is NT$1,200,000 (Sale of land NT$1,000,000 + Sale of equipment NT$500,000 − Purchase of equipment NT$300,000), not (b) NT$1,300,000, (c) NT$1,500,000, or (d) NT$1,900,000. Issuance of ordinary shares and payment of cash dividends are financing activities.

13. **b.** Net cash provided by financing activities is €130,000 (Increase in bonds payable €100,000 + Issuance of ordinary shares €60,000 − Payment of cash dividends €30,000), not (a) €90,000, (c) €160,000, or (d) €170,000. Increase in accounts payable is an operating activity and sale of investment is an investing activity.

14. **a.** The statement of cash flows is not used to evaluate an entity's ability to earn net income. The other choices are true statements.

15. **d.** Free cash flow provides an indication of a company's ability to generate cash to pay additional dividends and to invest in new capital expenditures. Choice (a) is incorrect because other measures besides free cash flow provide the best measure of a company's ability to earn net income. Choices (b) and (c) are true statements, but (d) is the better answer.

*16. **c.** Cash collections from customers amount to €131,000 (€129,000 + €2,000). The other choices are therefore incorrect.

*17. **d.** Cash payments to suppliers are reported on a statement of cash flows prepared by the direct method. The other choices are incorrect because (a) loss on disposal of building, (b) increase in accounts receivable, and (c) depreciation expense are reported in the operating activities section of the statement of cash flows when the indirect, not direct, method is used.

Practice Brief Exercises

Identify investing activity transactions.

1. The following is a summary of the Cash account of Covey AG (amounts in euros).

Cash (Summary Form)

Balance, Jan. 1	8,000		
Receipts from customers	364,000	Payments for goods	200,000
Dividends on share investments	6,000	Payments for operating expenses	140,000
Proceeds from sale of land	96,000	Purchase of equipment	70,000
Proceeds from issuance of bonds payable	300,000	Taxes paid	8,000
		Dividends paid	50,000
Balance, Dec. 31	306,000		

What amount of net cash provided (used) by investing activities should be reported in the statement of cash flows?

Solution

1. Cash flows from investing activities

Cash received from dividends	€ 6,000
Proceeds from sale of land	96,000
Purchase of equipment	(70,000)
Net cash provided by financing activities	€32,000

Compute net cash provided by operating activities—indirect method.

2. Engel Inc. reported net income of $1.6 million in 2029. Depreciation for the year was $140,000, accounts receivable increased $250,000, and accounts payable increased $210,000. The company also had a gain on disposal of plant assets of $19,000. Compute net cash provided by operating activities using the indirect method.

Solution

2. Net income		$1,600,000
Adjustments to reconcile net income to net cash provided by operating activities		
Depreciation expense	$ 140,000	
Gain on disposal of plant assets	(19,000)	
Accounts receivable increase	(250,000)	
Accounts payable increase	210,000	81,000
Net cash provided by operating activities		$1,681,000

Calculate free cash flow.

3. Goldberg plc reported net cash provided by operating activities of £410,000, net cash used by investing activities of £200,000 (including cash spent for equipment of £160,000), and net cash provided by financing activities of £60,000. Dividends of £110,000 were paid. Calculate free cash flow.

Solution

3. Free cash flow = £410,000 – £160,000 – £110,000 = £140,000

Practice Exercises

Prepare journal entries to determine effect on statement of cash flows.

1. **(LO 2)** Furst Ltd. had the following transactions.
   1. Paid salaries of NT$140,000.
   2. Issued 1,000 shares of NT$10 par value ordinary shares for equipment worth NT$160,000.
   3. Sold equipment (cost NT$100,000, accumulated depreciation NT$60,000) for NT$30,000.
   4. Sold land (cost NT$120,000) for NT$160,000.
   5. Issued another 1,000 shares of NT$10 par ordinary shares for NT$180,000.
   6. Recorded depreciation of NT$200,000.

Instructions

For each transaction above, (a) prepare the journal entry, and (b) indicate how it would affect the statement of cash flows. Assume the indirect method.

Solution

1. 1. a.

Salaries and Wages Expense	140,000	
Cash		140,000

b. Salaries and wages expense is not reported separately on the statement of cash flows. It is part of the computation of net income in the income statement and is included in the net income amount on the statement of cash flows (operating section).

2. a.

Equipment	160,000	
Ordinary Shares		10,000
Share Premium—Ordinary		150,000

b. The issuance of ordinary shares for equipment (NT$160,000) is reported as a non-cash financing and investing activity in a note to the financial statements.

3. a.

Cash	30,000	
Loss on Disposal of Plant Assets	10,000	
Accumulated Depreciation—Equipment	60,000	
Equipment		100,000

b. The cash receipt (NT$30,000) is reported in the investing section. The loss (NT$10,000) is added to net income in the operating section.

4. a.

Cash	160,000	
Land		120,000
Gain on Disposal of Plant Assets		40,000

b. The cash receipt (NT$160,000) is reported in the investing section. The gain (NT$40,000) is deducted from net income in the operating section.

5. a.

Cash	180,000	
Ordinary Shares		10,000
Share Premium—Ordinary		170,000

b. The cash receipt (NT$180,000) is reported in the financing section.

6. a.

Depreciation Expense	200,000	
Accumulated Depreciation—Equipment		200,000

b. Depreciation expense (NT$200,000) is added to net income in the operating section.

Prepare statement of cash flows and compute free cash flow.

2. **(LO 2, 3)** Strong AG's comparative statements of financial position are presented below.

Strong AG
Comparative Statements of Financial Position
December 31

	2029	2028
Investments	€ 23,000	€ 16,000
Equipment	60,000	70,000
Accumulated depreciation—equipment	(14,000)	(10,000)
Accounts receivable	24,200	22,300
Cash	28,200	17,700
Total	€121,400	€116,000
Ordinary shares	€ 60,000	€ 45,000
Retained earnings	31,800	29,900
Bonds payable	10,000	30,000
Accounts payable	19,600	11,100
Total	€121,400	€116,000

Additional information:

1. Net income was €28,300. Dividends declared and paid were €26,400.
2. Equipment which cost €10,000 and had accumulated depreciation of €1,200 was sold for €4,300.

3. All other changes in non-current account balances had a direct effect on cash flows, except the change in accumulated depreciation.

Instructions

a. Prepare a statement of cash flows for 2029 using the indirect method.

b. Compute free cash flow.

Solution

2. **a.**

Strong AG
Statement of Cash Flows
For the Year Ended December 31, 2029

Cash flows from operating activities		
Net income		€ 28,300
Adjustments to reconcile net income to net cash provided by operating activities:		
Depreciation expense	€ 5,200*	
Loss on sale of equipment	4,500**	
Increase in accounts payable	8,500	
Increase in accounts receivable	(1,900)	16,300
Net cash provided by operating activities		44,600
Cash flows from investing activities		
Sale of equipment	4,300	
Purchase of investments	(7,000)	
Net cash used by investing activities		(2,700)
Cash flows from financing activities		
Issuance of ordinary shares	15,000	
Retirement of bonds	(20,000)	
Payment of dividends	(26,400)	
Net cash used by financing activities		(31,400)
Net increase in cash		10,500
Cash at beginning of period		17,700
Cash at end of period		€ 28,200

*[€14,000 – (€10,000 – €1,200)]; **[€4,300 – (€10,000 – €1,200)]

b. €44,600 – €0 – €26,400 = €18,200

Practice Problem

(LO 2, 4) The income statement for the year ended December 31, 2029, for Kosinski AG contains the following condensed information.

Prepare statement of cash flows using indirect and direct methods.

Kosinski AG
Income Statement
For the Year Ended December 31, 2029

Sales revenue		€6,583,000
Operating expenses (excluding depreciation)	€4,920,000	
Depreciation expense	880,000	5,800,000
Operating income		783,000
Income tax expense		353,000
Net income		€ 430,000

Included in operating expenses is a €24,000 loss resulting from the sale of machinery for €270,000 cash. Machinery was purchased at a cost of €750,000.

The following balances are reported on Kosinski's comparative statements of financial position at December 31.

Kosinski AG
Comparative Statements of Financial Position (partial)

	2029	2028
Inventory	€834,000	€867,000
Accounts receivable	775,000	610,000
Cash	672,000	130,000
Accounts payable	521,000	501,000

Income tax expense of €353,000 represents the amount paid in 2029. Dividends declared and paid in 2029 totaled €200,000.

Instructions

a. Prepare the statement of cash flows for 2029 using the indirect method.

***b.** Prepare the statement of cash flows for 2029 using the direct method.

Solution

a.

Kosinski AG
Statement of Cash Flows—Indirect Method
For the Year Ended December 31, 2029

Cash flows from operating activities		
Operating income		€ 783,000
Adjustments to reconcile operating income to net cash provided by operating activities:		
Depreciation expense	€ 880,000	
Loss on disposal of plant assets	24,000	
Increase in accounts receivable	(165,000)	
Decrease in inventory	33,000	
Increase in accounts payable	20,000	792,000
Cash from operating activities before income taxes		1,575,000
Income taxes paid		(353,000)
Net cash provided by operating activities		1,222,000
Cash flows from investing activities		
Disposal of plant assets	270,000	
Purchase of machinery	(750,000)	
Net cash used by investing activities		(480,000)
Cash flows from financing activities		
Payment of cash dividends	(200,000)	
Net cash used by financing activities		(200,000)
Net increase in cash		542,000
Cash at beginning of period		130,000
Cash at end of period		€ 672,000

*b.

Kosinski AG
Statement of Cash Flows—Direct Method
For the Year Ended December 31, 2029

Cash flows from operating activities		
Cash collections from customers		€6,418,000*
Cash payments:		
For operating expenses	€4,843,000**	
For income taxes	353,000	5,196,000
Net cash provided by operating activities		1,222,000
Cash flows from investing activities		
Disposal of plant assets	270,000	
Purchase of machinery	(750,000)	
Net cash used by investing activities		(480,000)
Cash flows from financing activities		
Payment of cash dividends	(200,000)	
Net cash used by financing activities		(200,000)
Net increase in cash		542,000
Cash at beginning of period		130,000
Cash at end of period		€ 672,000

Direct-Method Computations:

*Computation of cash collections from customers:	
Sales revenue	€6,583,000
Deduct: Increase in accounts receivable	165,000
Cash collections from customers	€6,418,000
**Computation of cash payments for operating expenses:	
Operating expenses	€4,920,000
Deduct: Loss on disposal of plant assets	24,000
Deduct: Decrease in inventories	33,000
Deduct: Increase in accounts payable	20,000
Cash payments for operating expenses	€4,843,000

Note: All asterisked Questions, Exercises, and Problems relate to material in the appendices to the chapter.

Questions

1. a. What is a statement of cash flows?
   b. Nick Johns maintains that the statement of cash flows is an optional financial statement. Do you agree? Explain.
2. What questions about cash are answered by the statement of cash flows?
3. Distinguish among the three types of activities reported in the statement of cash flows.
4. a. What are the major sources (inflows) of cash in a statement of cash flows?
   b. What are the major uses (outflows) of cash?
5. Why is it important to disclose certain non-cash transactions? How should they be disclosed?
6. Wilma Flintstone and Barny Rublestone were discussing the format of the statement of cash flows of Saltwater Candy Co. At the bottom of Saltwater Candy's statement of cash flows was a note entitled "Non-cash investing and financing activities." Give three examples of significant non-cash transactions that would be reported in this manner.
7. Why is it necessary to use comparative statements of financial position, a current income statement, and certain transaction data in preparing a statement of cash flows?
8. Distinguish between the direct and indirect methods of preparing the statement of cash flows. Are both methods acceptable? Which method is preferred by the IASB? Which method is more popular?

9. When the total cash inflows exceed the total cash outflows in the statement of cash flows, how and where is this excess identified?

10. Describe the indirect method for determining net cash provided (used) by operating activities.

11. Why is it necessary to convert accrual-based net income to cash-basis income when preparing a statement of cash flows?

12. The president of Ferneti A/S is puzzled. During the last year, the company experienced a net loss of £800,000, yet its cash increased £300,000 during the same period of time. Explain to the president how this could occur.

13. Identify five items that are adjustments to convert operating income to net cash provided by operating activities under the indirect method.

14. Why and how is depreciation expense reported in a statement prepared using the indirect method?

15. Why is the statement of cash flows useful?

*16. Describe the direct method for determining net cash provided by operating activities.

*17. Give the formulas under the direct method for computing (a) cash receipts from customers and (b) cash payments to suppliers.

*18. Aloha Ltd. reported sales revenue of NT$2 million for 2029. Accounts receivable decreased NT$140,000 and accounts payable increased NT$300,000. Compute cash receipts from customers, assuming that the receivable and payable transactions related to operations.

*19. In the direct method, why is depreciation expense not reported in the cash flows from operating activities section?

Brief Exercises

Indicate statement presentation of selected transactions.

BE14.1 (LO 1) Each of the items below must be considered in preparing a statement of cash flows for Aksu A.Ş. for the year ended December 31, 2029. For each item, state how it should be shown in the statement of cash flows for 2029.

a. Issued bonds for ₺150,000 cash.

b. Purchased equipment for ₺200,000 cash.

c. Sold land costing ₺50,000 for ₺50,000 cash.

d. Declared and paid a ₺18,000 cash dividend.

Classify items by activities.

BE14.2 (LO 1) Classify each item as an operating, investing, or financing activity. Assume all items involve cash unless there is information to the contrary.

a. Purchase of equipment.

b. Proceeds from sale of building.

c. Redemption of bonds.

d. Depreciation.

e. Payment of dividends.

f. Issuance of ordinary shares.

Identify financing activity transactions.

BE14.3 (LO 1) The following T-account is a summary of the Cash account of Wiegman Ltd.

Cash (Summary Form)

Balance, Jan. 1	8,000		
Receipts from customers	364,000	Payments for goods	200,000
Dividends on share investments	6,000	Payments for operating expenses	140,000
Proceeds from sale of equipment	36,000	Interest paid	10,000
Proceeds from issuance of		Taxes paid	8,000
bonds payable	460,000	Dividends paid	40,000
Balance, Dec. 31	476,000		

What amount of net cash (in £) provided (used) by financing activities should be reported in the statement of cash flows?

Compute net cash provided by operating activities—indirect method.

BE14.4 (LO 2) Mokena Ltd. reported net income of €2.0 million in 2029. Depreciation for the year was €160,000, accounts receivable increased €350,000, and accounts payable increased €280,000. Compute net cash provided by operating activities using the indirect method.

Compute net cash provided by operating activities—indirect method.

BE14.5 (LO 2) The net income for Lodi Ltd. for 2029 was £250,000. For 2029, depreciation on plant assets was £65,000, and the company incurred a gain on disposal of plant assets of £12,000. Compute net cash provided by operating activities under the indirect method.

Compute net cash provided by operating activities—indirect method.

BE14.6 (LO 2) The comparative statements of financial position for Sergipe SA show these changes in non-cash current asset accounts: accounts receivable increase R$80,000, prepaid expenses decrease R$28,000, and inventories decrease R$30,000. Compute net cash provided by operating activities using the indirect method assuming that net income is R$250,000.

Determine cash received from sale of equipment.

BE14.7 (LO 2) The T-accounts for Equipment and the related Accumulated Depreciation—Equipment for Gao Ltd. at the end of 2029 are shown here.

Equipment				Accumulated Depreciation—Equipment			
Beg. bal.	800,000	Disposals	220,000	Disposals	85,000	Beg. bal.	445,000
Acquisitions	410,600					Depr. exp.	120,000
End. bal.	990,600					End. bal.	480,000

In addition, Gao's income statement reported a loss on disposal of plant assets of HK$63,000. What amount was reported on the statement of cash flows as "cash flow from disposal of plant assets"?

Calculate free cash flow.

BE14.8 (LO 3) In a recent year, **Cypress Semiconductor Corporation** (USA) reported net cash provided by operating activities of $155,397,000, net cash used in investing of $207,628,000, and net cash used in financing of $33,372,000. In addition, cash spent for fixed assets during the period was $130,820,000. No dividends were paid. Calculate free cash flow.

Calculate free cash flow.

BE14.9 (LO 3) Wruck Company reported net cash provided by operating activities of £420,000, net cash used by investing activities of £150,000, and net cash provided by financing activities of £80,000. In addition, cash spent for capital assets during the period was £250,000. No dividends were paid. Calculate free cash flow.

Calculate free cash flow.

BE14.10 (LO 3) Suppose in a recent quarter that **Alliance Atlantis Communications Inc.** (USA) reported net cash provided by operating activities of $45,000,000 and revenues of $265,800,000. Cash spent on plant asset additions during the quarter was $1,400,000. No dividends were paid. Calculate free cash flow.

Calculate and analyze free cash flow.

BE14.11 (LO 3) The management of Russel Ltd. is trying to decide whether it can increase its dividend. During the current year, it reported net income of €875,000. It had net cash provided by operating activities of €643,000, paid cash dividends of €80,000, and had capital expenditures of €274,000. Compute the company's free cash flow, and discuss whether an increase in the dividend appears warranted. What other factors should be considered?

Compute receipts from customers—direct method.

***BE14.12 (LO 4)** Suppose **Columbia Sportswear Company** (USA) had accounts receivable of $205,025,000 at the beginning of a recent year and $267,653,000 at year end. Sales revenue was $1,085,307,000 for the year. What is the amount of cash receipts from customers?

Compute cash payments for income taxes—direct method.

***BE14.13 (LO 4)** Kinsey Ltd. reported income taxes of £360,000,000 on its 2029 income statement, income taxes payable of £277,000,000 at December 31, 2028, and £525,000,000 at December 31, 2029. What amount of cash payments were made for income taxes during 2029?

Compute cash payments for operating expenses—direct method.

***BE14.14 (LO 4)** Yaddof SE reports operating expenses of €70,000 excluding depreciation expense of €19,000 for 2029. During the year, prepaid expenses decreased €6,800 and accrued expenses payable increased €4,100. Compute the cash payments for operating expenses in 2029.

DO IT! Exercises

Classify transactions by type of cash flow activity.

DO IT! 14.1 (LO 1) Piekarski OAO had the following transactions.

1. Issued €200,000 of bonds payable.
2. Paid utilities expense.
3. Issued 500 shares of preference shares for €45,000.
4. Sold land and a building for €250,000.
5. Loaned €30,000 to Zarembski Company, receiving Zarembski's 1-year, 12% note.

Classify each of these transactions by type of cash flow activity (operating, investing, or financing).

Calculate net cash from operating activities.

DO IT! 14.2 (LO 2) Muniz Photography SA reported net income of R$100,000 for 2029. Included in the income statement were depreciation expense of R$4,000, amortization expense of R$3,000, and a gain on disposal of plant assets of R$3,900. Muniz's comparative statements of financial position show the following balances.

	12/31/28	12/31/29
Accounts receivable	R$27,000	R$21,000
Accounts payable	6,000	9,200

Calculate net cash provided by operating activities for Muniz Photography SA.

Compute and discuss free cash flow.

DO IT! 14.3 (LO 3) Zielinski OAO issued the following statement of cash flows for 2029.

Zielinski OAO
Statement of Cash Flows—Indirect Method
For the Year Ended December 31, 2029

Cash flows from operating activities		
Net income		€ 59,000
Adjustments to reconcile net income to net cash provided by operating activities:		
Depreciation expense	€ 9,400	
Loss on disposal of plant assets	3,300	
Decrease in accounts receivable	8,500	
Increase in inventory	(5,000)	
Decrease in accounts payable	(2,500)	13,700
Net cash provided by operating activities		72,700
Cash flows from investing activities		
Sale of investments	3,100	
Purchase of equipment	(26,000)	
Net cash used by investing activities		(22,900)
Cash flows from financing activities		
Issuance of shares	20,000	
Payment on long-term note payable	(10,000)	
Payment for dividends	(16,000)	
Net cash used by financing activities		(6,000)
Net increase in cash		43,800
Cash at beginning of year		13,000
Cash at end of year		€ 56,800

(a) Compute free cash flow for Zielinski. (b) Explain why free cash flow often provides better information than "Net cash provided by operating activities."

Exercises

Classify transactions by type of activity.

E14.1 (LO 1) Laurent AG had these transactions during 2029.

a. Issued CHF50,000 par value ordinary shares for cash.

b. Purchased a machine for CHF30,000, giving a long-term note in exchange.

c. Issued CHF200,000 par value ordinary shares to purchase land worth CHF200,000.

d. Declared and paid a cash dividend of CHF18,000.

e. Sold a long-term investment with a cost of CHF15,000 for CHF15,000 cash.

f. Collected CHF16,000 of accounts receivable.

g. Paid CHF18,000 on accounts payable.

Instructions

Analyze the transactions and indicate whether each transaction resulted in a cash flow from operating activities, investing activities, financing activities, or non-cash investing and financing activities.

Classify transactions by type of activity.

E14.2 (LO 1) An analysis of comparative statements of financial position, the current year's income statement, and the general ledger accounts of Solomon Co. uncovered the following items. Assume all items involve cash unless there is information to the contrary.

a. Payment of interest on notes payable.

b. Exchange of land for patent.

c. Sale of building at book value.

d. Payment of dividends.

e. Depreciation.

f. Receipt of dividends on investment in shares.

g. Receipt of interest on notes receivable.

h. Issuance of ordinary shares.

i. Amortization of patent.
j. Issuance of bonds for land.
k. Purchase of land.
l. Conversion of bonds into ordinary shares.
m. Loss on sale of land.
n. Retirement of bonds.

Instructions

Indicate how each item should be classified in the statement of cash flows using these four major classifications: operating activity (indirect method), investing activity, financing activity, and significant noncash investing and financing activity.

E14.3 (LO 1) Tim Latimer Ltd. had the following transactions.

Prepare journal entry and determine effect on cash flows.

1. Sold land (cost £12,000) for £10,000.
2. Issued ordinary shares at par value for £18,000.
3. Recorded depreciation on buildings for £14,000.
4. Paid salaries of £7,000.
5. Issued 1,000 shares of £1 par value ordinary shares for equipment worth £9,000.
6. Sold equipment (cost £10,000, accumulated depreciation £8,000) for £3,500.

Instructions

For each transaction above, (a) prepare the journal entry, and (b) indicate how it would affect the statement of cash flows under the indirect method.

E14.4 (LO 2) Bracewell Ltd. reported net income of £195,000 for 2029. Bracewell also reported depreciation expense of £40,000 and a gain of £5,000 on disposal of plant assets. The comparative statements of financial position show an increase in accounts receivable of £15,000 for the year, a £17,000 increase in accounts payable, and a £4,000 decrease in prepaid expenses.

Prepare the operating activities section—indirect method.

Instructions

Prepare the operating activities section of the statement of cash flows for 2029. Use the indirect method.

E14.5 (LO 2) The current sections of Nasreen SA's statements of financial position at December 31, 2028 and 2029, are presented here. Nasreen's net income for 2029 was €147,000. Depreciation expense was €21,000.

Prepare the operating activities section—indirect method.

	2029	2028
Current assets		
Prepaid expenses	€ 27,000	€ 25,000
Inventory	158,000	172,000
Accounts receivable	110,000	79,000
Cash	105,000	99,000
Total current assets	€400,000	€375,000
Current liabilities		
Accrued expenses payable	€ 15,000	€ 9,000
Accounts payable	85,000	95,000
Total current liabilities	€100,000	€104,000

Instructions

Prepare the net cash provided by operating activities section of the company's statement of cash flows for the year ended December 31, 2029, using the indirect method.

E14.6 (LO 2) The three accounts shown below appear in the general ledger of Chaudry NV during 2029.

Prepare partial statement of cash flows—indirect method.

Equipment

Date		Debit	Credit	Balance
Jan. 1	Balance			160,000
July 31	Purchase of equipment	70,000		230,000
Sept. 2	Cost of equipment constructed	53,000		283,000
Nov. 10	Cost of equipment sold		49,000	234,000

Accumulated Depreciation—Equipment

Date		Debit	Credit	Balance
Jan. 1	Balance			71,000
Nov. 10	Accumulated depreciation on equipment sold	28,000		43,000
Dec. 31	Depreciation for year		23,000	66,000

Retained Earnings

Date		Debit	Credit	Balance
Jan. 1	Balance			105,000
Aug. 23	Dividends (cash)	17,000		88,000
Dec. 31	Net income		67,000	155,000

Instructions

From the postings in the accounts, indicate how the information is reported on a statement of cash flows using the indirect method. The loss on disposal of plant assets was €5,000. (*Hint:* Cost of equipment constructed is reported in the investing activities section as a decrease in cash of €53,000.)

Prepare statement of cash flows and compute free cash flow.

E14.7 (LO 2, 3) Meera Ltd.'s comparative statements of financial position are presented below.

Meera Ltd.
Comparative Statements of Financial Position
December 31

	2029	2028
Land	£ 20,000	£ 26,000
Buildings	70,000	70,000
Accumulated depreciation—buildings	(15,000)	(10,000)
Accounts receivable	20,800	23,400
Cash	17,660	10,700
Total	£113,460	£120,100
Share capital—ordinary	£ 75,000	£ 72,000
Retained earnings	26,090	20,000
Accounts payable	12,370	28,100
Total	£113,460	£120,100

Additional information:

1. Net income was £22,590. Income tax expense and paid were £5,600. Dividends declared and paid were £16,500.
2. All other changes in non-current account balances had a direct effect on cash flows, except the change in accumulated depreciation. The land was sold for £5,000.

Instructions

a. Prepare a statement of cash flows for 2029 using the indirect method.
b. Compute free cash flow.

Prepare a statement of cash flows—indirect method.

E14.8 (LO 2) Here are comparative statements of financial position for Syal SE.

Syal SE
Comparative Statements of Financial Position
December 31

Assets	2029	2028
Land	€ 73,000	€100,000
Equipment	260,000	200,000
Accumulated depreciation—equipment	(66,000)	(34,000)
Inventory	170,000	187,000
Accounts receivable	85,000	71,000
Cash	73,000	33,000
Total	€595,000	€557,000

Equity and Liabilities		
Share capital—ordinary (€1 par)	€216,000	€174,000
Retained earnings	194,000	136,000
Bonds payable	150,000	200,000
Accounts payable	35,000	47,000
Total	€595,000	€557,000

Additional information:

1. Net income for 2029 was €103,000.
2. Income tax expense and paid were €25,750.
3. Depreciation expense was €32,000.
4. Cash dividends of €45,000 were declared and paid.
5. Bonds payable amounting to €50,000 were redeemed for cash €50,000.
6. Ordinary shares were issued for €42,000 cash.
7. No equipment was sold during 2029.
8. Land was sold for its book value of €27,000.

Instructions

Prepare a statement of cash flows for 2029 using the indirect method.

E14.9 (LO 2, 3) Cassandra SA's comparative statements of financial position are presented below.

Prepare statement of cash flows and compute free cash flow.

Cassandra SA
Comparative Statements of Financial Position
December 31

	2029	2028
Equipment	€ 60,000	€ 70,000
Accumulated depreciation—equipment	(14,000)	(10,000)
Investments	20,000	13,000
Accounts receivable	25,200	22,300
Cash	17,000	17,700
Total	€108,200	€113,000
Share capital—ordinary	€ 50,000	€ 45,000
Retained earnings	33,600	24,900
Bonds payable	10,000	30,000
Accounts payable	14,600	13,100
Total	€108,200	€113,000

Additional information:

1. Net income was €23,300. Income tax expense and paid were €5,800. Dividends declared and paid were €14,600.
2. Equipment that cost €10,000 and had accumulated depreciation of €1,800 was sold for €3,500.
3. All other changes in non-current account balances had a direct effect on cash flows, except the change in accumulated depreciation.

Instructions

a. Prepare a statement of cash flows for 2029 using the indirect method.
b. Compute free cash flow.

***E14.10 (LO 4)** Recife Company completed its first year of operations on December 31, 2029. Its initial income statement showed that Recife had revenues of R$195,000 and operating expenses of R$78,000. Accounts receivable and accounts payable at year-end were R$48,000 and R$25,000, respectively. Assume that accounts payable related to operating expenses. (Ignore income taxes.)

Compute net cash provided by operating activities—direct method.

Instructions

Compute net cash provided by operating activities using the direct method.

***E14.11 (LO 4)** Suppose a recent income statement for **McDonald's Corporation** (USA) shows cost of goods sold $4,527.8 million and operating expenses (including depreciation expense of $1,120 million)

Compute cash payments—direct method.

$10,517.6 million. The comparative statements of financial position for the year show that inventory increased $17.1 million, prepaid expenses increased $65.3 million, accounts payable (merchandise suppliers) increased $139.6 million, and accrued expenses payable increased $190.6 million.

Instructions

Using the direct method, compute (a) cash payments to suppliers and (b) cash payments for operating expenses.

Compute cash flow from operating activities—direct method.

***E14.12 (LO 4)** The 2029 accounting records of Liz Ten Transport Ltd. reveal these transactions and events.

Payment of interest	£10,000	Collection of accounts receivable	£190,000
Cash sales	54,000	Payment of salaries and wages	55,000
Receipt of dividend revenue	18,000	Depreciation expense	16,000
Payment of income taxes	16,000	Proceeds from disposal of plant assets	12,000
Net income	38,000	Purchase of equipment for cash	22,000
Payment of accounts payable for merchandise	115,000	Loss on disposal of plant assets	3,000
		Payment of dividends	14,000
Payment for land	74,000	Payment of operating expenses	28,000

Instructions

Prepare the cash flows from operating activities section using the direct method. (Not all of the items will be used.)

Calculate cash flows—direct method.

***E14.13 (LO 4)** The following information is taken from the 2029 general ledger of Okonedo ASA.

Rent	Rent expense	€ 40,000
	Prepaid rent, January 1	5,600
	Prepaid rent, December 31	9,000
Salaries	Salaries and wages expense	€ 65,000
	Salaries and wages payable, January 1	10,000
	Salaries and wages payable, December 31	8,000
Sales	Sales revenue	€170,000
	Accounts receivable, January 1	19,000
	Accounts receivable, December 31	7,000

Instructions

In each case, compute the amount that should be reported in the operating activities section of the statement of cash flows under the direct method.

Prepare the operating activities section—indirect method.

E14.14 (LO 2) The following are selected data taken from the records of Kehaur AG at December 31, 2029, and the increases or decreases in each statement of financial position account from 2028 to 2029.

Selected statement of financial position accounts	Increase (Decrease)
Accounts receivable	(13,000)
Inventory	8,000
Accounts payable	(3,400)
Interest payable	(10,000)
Income tax payable	10,000

Selected income statement information for the year ended December 31, 2029.	
Sales revenue	$500,000
Cost of goods sold	(300,000)
Depreciation	(60,000)
Gain on sale of equipment	15,000
Interest expense	(14,000)
Income tax expense	(50,000)
Net Income	$ 91,000

Instructions

Prepare the operating activities section of the statement of cash flows for the year ended December 31, 2029, using the indirect method.

E14.15 (LO 2) Su Inc. has prepared the following comparative statement of financial position for 2028 and 2029:

Prepare a statement of cash flows—indirect method.

	12/31/29	12/31/28
Equipment	€1,060,000	€850,000
Accumulated depreciation	(450,000)	(375,000)
Patent	153,000	174,000
Prepaid rent	18,000	27,000
Inventory	150,000	180,000
Accounts receivables	159,000	117,000
Cash	297,000	153,000
	€1,387,000	€1,126,000
Share capital—ordinary (€10 par)	€ 297,000	€ 234,000
Share premium—ordinary	510,000	-0-
Retained earnings	400,000	383,000
Mortgage payable	-0-	450,000
Accounts payable	120,000	-0-
Income taxes payable	24,000	28,000
Interest payable	36,000	31,000
	€1,387,000	€1,126,000

The income statement for 2029 is as follows:

Sales	€1,980,000
Cost of goods sold	1,089,000
Gross profit	891,000
Operating expenses	600,000
Operating income	291,000
Interest expense	50,000
Income before income tax	241,000
Income tax expense	40,000
Net income	€ 201,000

Additional information:

1. The Accumulated Depreciation account has been credited only for the depreciation expense for the period.
2. The Retained Earnings account has been charged for dividends of €184,000 and credited for the net income for the year.

Instructions

Prepare a statement of cash flows for the year 2029 using the indirect method.

***E14.16 (LO 4)** Data for Su Inc. are presented in E14.15.

Prepare the operating activities section—direct method.

Instructions

Prepare a schedule of cash provided by operating activities using the direct method.

Problems

P14.1 (LO 1) You are provided with the following transactions that took place during a recent fiscal year.

Distinguish among operating, investing, and financing activities.

Transaction	Statement of Cash Flow Activity Affected	Cash Inflow, Outflow, or No Effect?
a. Recorded depreciation expense on the plant assets.		
b. Recorded and paid interest expense.		
c. Recorded cash proceeds from a sale of plant assets.		
d. Acquired land by issuing ordinary shares.		
e. Paid a cash dividend to preference shareholders.		

f. Issuance of ordinary shares to purchase land.

g. Recorded cash sales.

h. Recorded sales on account.

i. Purchased inventory for cash.

j. Purchased inventory on account.

Instructions

Complete the table indicating whether each item (1) affects operating (O) activities, investing (I) activities, financing (F) activities, or is a non-cash (NC) transaction reported in a separate schedule, and (2) represents a cash inflow or cash outflow or has no cash flow effect. Assume use of the indirect approach.

Determine cash flow effects of changes in equity accounts.

P14.2 (LO 2) The following account balances relate to the equity accounts of Chipo Ltd. at year-end.

	2029	2028
Share capital—ordinary, 10,500 and 10,000 shares, respectively, for 2029 and 2028	£155,000	£130,000
Share capital—preference, 5,000 shares	125,000	125,000
Retained earnings	300,000	250,000

A small share dividend was declared and issued in 2029. The market value of the shares was £11,200. Cash dividends were £16,000 in both 2029 and 2028. The ordinary shares have no par or stated value.

Instructions

a. Net income £77,200

a. What was the amount of net income reported by Chipo Ltd. in 2029?

b. Determine the amounts of any cash inflows or outflows related to the ordinary shares and dividend accounts in 2029.

c. Indicate where each of the cash inflows or outflows identified in (b) would be classified on the statement of cash flows.

Prepare the operating activities section—direct method.

P14.3 (LO 2) The income statement of Toby Zed NV is presented here. (Ignore income taxes.)

Toby Zed NV
Income Statement
For the Year Ended November 30, 2029

Sales revenue		€7,500,000
Cost of goods sold		
Beginning inventory	€1,900,000	
Purchases	4,400,000	
Goods available for sale	6,300,000	
Ending inventory	1,400,000	
Total cost of goods sold		4,900,000
Gross profit		2,600,000
Operating expenses		1,150,000
Net income		€1,450,000

Additional information:

1. Accounts receivable increased €200,000 during the year, and inventory decreased €500,000.
2. Prepaid expenses increased €175,000 during the year.
3. Accounts payable to suppliers of merchandise decreased €340,000 during the year.
4. Accrued expenses payable decreased €105,000 during the year.
5. Operating expenses include depreciation expense of €85,000.

Instructions

Cash from oper. €1,215,000

Prepare the operating activities section of the statement of cash flows for the year ended November 30, 2029, for Toby Zed, using the indirect method.

Prepare the operating activities section—direct method.

***P14.4 (LO 4)** Data for Toby Zed NV are presented in P14.3.

Instructions

Cash from oper. €1,215,000

Prepare the operating activities section of the statement of cash flows using the direct method.

P14.5 (LO 2) Rattigan plc's income statement contained the condensed information below.

Prepare the operating activities section—indirect method.

Rattigan plc
Income Statement
For the Year Ended December 31, 2029

Service revenue		£970,000
Operating expenses, excluding depreciation	£624,000	
Depreciation expense	55,000	
Loss on disposal of plant assets	25,000	704,000
Income before income taxes		266,000
Income tax expense		40,000
Net income		£226,000

Rattigan's statement of financial position contained the comparative data at December 31, shown below.

	2029	2028
Accounts receivable	£75,000	£60,000
Accounts payable	41,000	27,000
Income taxes payable	13,000	7,000

Accounts payable pertain to operating expenses.

Instructions

Prepare the operating activities section of the statement of cash flows using the indirect method.

Cash from operations £311,000

***P14.6 (LO 4)** Data for Rattigan plc are presented in P14.5.

Prepare the operating activities section—direct method.

Instructions

Prepare the operating activities section of the statement of cash flows using the direct method.

Cash from oper. £311,000

P14.7 (LO 2, 3) Presented below are the financial statements of Rajesh Ltd.

Prepare a statement of cash flows—indirect method, and compute free cash flow.

Rajesh Ltd.
Comparative Statements of Financial Position
December 31

Assets	**2029**	**2028**
Equipment	£ 60,000	£ 78,000
Accumulated depreciation—equipment	(29,000)	(24,000)
Inventory	30,000	20,000
Accounts receivable	33,000	14,000
Cash	37,000	20,000
Total	£131,000	£108,000
Equity and Liabilities		
Share capital—ordinary	£ 18,000	£ 14,000
Retained earnings	50,000	38,000
Bonds payable	27,000	33,000
Accounts payable	29,000	15,000
Income taxes payable	7,000	8,000
Total	£131,000	£108,000

Rajesh Ltd.
Income Statement
For the Year Ended December 31, 2029

Sales revenue	£242,000
Cost of goods sold	175,000
Gross profit	67,000
Operating expenses	24,000
Income from operations	43,000
Interest expense	3,000
Income before income taxes	40,000
Income tax expense	8,000
Net income	£ 32,000

Additional data:

1. Depreciation expense is £13,300.
2. Dividends declared and paid were £20,000.
3. During the year, equipment was sold for £9,700 cash. This equipment cost £18,000 originally and had accumulated depreciation of £8,300 at the time of sale.

Instructions

a. Cash from operations £29,300

a. Prepare a statement of cash flows using the indirect method.

b. Compute free cash flow.

Prepare a statement of cash flows—direct method, and compute free cash flow.

***P14.8 (LO 3, 4)** Data for Rajesh Ltd. are presented in P14.7. Further analysis reveals the following.

1. Accounts payable pertain to merchandise suppliers.
2. All operating expenses except for depreciation were paid in cash.
3. All depreciation expense is in the operating expenses.
4. All sales and purchases are on account.

Instructions

a. Cash from operations £29,300

a. Prepare a statement of cash flows for Rajesh using the direct method.

b. Compute free cash flow.

Prepare a statement of cash flows—indirect method.

P14.9 (LO 2) Condensed financial data of Sinjh SA follow.

Sinjh SA
Comparative Statements of Financial Position
December 31

Assets	**2029**	**2028**
Equipment	€265,000	€242,500
Accumulated depreciation—equipment	(47,000)	(52,000)
Long-term investments	140,000	114,000
Prepaid expenses	29,300	26,000
Inventory	112,500	102,850
Accounts receivable	92,800	33,000
Cash	100,350	48,400
Total	€692,950	€514,750
Equity and Liabilities		
Share capital—ordinary	€220,000	€175,000
Retained earnings	234,450	105,450
Bonds payable	110,000	150,000
Accounts payable	112,000	67,300
Accrued expenses payable	16,500	17,000
Total	€692,950	€514,750

Sinjh SA
Income Statement
For the Year Ended December 31, 2029

Sales revenue	€392,780	
Gain on disposal of plant assets	5,000	€397,780
Less:		
Cost of goods sold	135,460	
Operating expenses, excluding depreciation	12,410	
Depreciation expense	45,000	
Income tax expense	27,280	
Interest expense	4,730	224,880
Net income		€172,900

Additional information:

1. New equipment costing €80,000 was purchased for cash during the year.
2. Old equipment having an original cost of €57,500 and accumulated depreciation of €50,000 was sold for €12,500 cash.
3. Bonds payable matured and were paid off at face value for cash.
4. A cash dividend of €43,900 was declared and paid during the year.

Instructions

Prepare a statement of cash flows using the indirect method.

Cash from operations €184,350

***P14.10 (LO 4)** Data for Sinjh SA are presented in P14.9. Further analysis reveals that accounts payable pertain to merchandise creditors.

Prepare a statement of cash flows—direct method.

Instructions

Prepare a statement of cash flows for Sinjh using the direct method.

Cash from operations €184,350

P14.11 (LO 2) The comparative statements of financial position for Amaral Reis SA as of December 31 are presented as follows.

Prepare a statement of cash flows—indirect method.

Amaral Reis SA
Comparative Statements of Financial Position
December 31

Assets	**2029**	**2028**
Land	R$145,000	R$130,000
Equipment	228,000	155,000
Accumulated depreciation—equipment	(45,000)	(35,000)
Buildings	200,000	200,000
Accumulated depreciation—buildings	(60,000)	(40,000)
Prepaid expenses	18,280	21,000
Inventory	154,550	142,000
Accounts receivable	46,000	62,000
Cash	62,520	45,000
Total	R$749,350	R$680,000
Equity and Liabilities		
Share capital—ordinary, R$1 par	R$195,000	R$160,000
Retained earnings	208,000	180,000
Bonds payable	300,000	300,000
Accounts payable	46,350	40,000
Total	R$749,350	R$680,000

Additional information:

1. Operating expenses include depreciation expense of R$40,000.
2. Land was sold for cash at book value of R$20,000.
3. Cash dividends of R$20,000 were paid.
4. Net income for 2029 was R$48,000. Income tax expense and paid were R$12,000.
5. Equipment was purchased for R$95,000 cash. In addition, equipment costing R$22,000 with a book value of R$12,000 was sold for R$6,000 cash.
6. Issued 35,000 shares of R$1 par value ordinary shares in exchange for land with a fair value of R$35,000.

Instructions

Prepare a statement of cash flows for the year ended December 31, 2029, using the indirect method.

Cash from operations R$106,520

P14.12 (LO 2) Comparative statement of financial position accounts of Naihui Group are presented below.

Prepare a statement of cash flows—indirect method.

Naihui Group
Comparative Statement of Financial Position Accounts
As of December 31

Debit Balances	**2029**	**2028**
Cash	$ 75,000	$ 51,000
Accounts receivable	155,000	130,000
Inventory	75,000	61,000
Financial assets at amortized cost	50,000	85,000
Equipment	70,000	48,000
Buildings	145,000	145,000
Land	40,000	25,000
Totals	$610,000	$545,000
Credit Balances		
Allowance for doubtful accounts	$ 10,000	$ 8,000
Accumulated depreciation—Equipment	21,000	14,000
Accumulated depreciation—Buildings	37,000	28,000
Accounts payable	66,000	60,000
Income taxes payable	12,000	10,000
Long-term notes payable	62,000	70,000
Share capital—ordinary	310,000	260,000
Retained earnings	92,000	95,000
Totals	$610,000	$545,000

Additional data:

1. Equipment that cost $10,000 and was 60% depreciated was sold in 2029.
2. Cash dividends were declared and paid during the year.
3. Ordinary shares were issued in exchange for land.
4. Financial assets at amortized cost having a carrying amount of $35,000 were sold during the year.
5. There were no write-offs of uncollectible accounts during the year.

Naihui's 2029 income statement is as follows.

Sales revenue	$950,000
Cost of goods sold	(600,000)
Gross profit	350,000
Operating expenses (includes depreciation expense and expected credit loss)	(250,000)
Gain on sale of financial assets at amortized cost	15,000
Loss on sale of equipment	(3,000)
Income before taxes	112,000
Income taxes	(45,000)
Net income	$ 67,000

Instructions

Prepare a statement of cash flows using the indirect method.

Prepare a statement of cash flows—direct and indirect method.

P14.13 (LO 2, 4) The comparative statement of financial position and the income statement for Taur Company as of May 31, 2029, are as follows. The company is preparing its statement of cash flows.

Taur Company
Comparative Statements of Financial Position
As of May 31

Assets	**2029**	**2028**
Plant assets	$600,000	$502,000
Less: Accumulated depreciation—plant assets	(150,000)	(125,000)
	450,000	377,000
Inventory	220,000	250,000
Prepaid expenses	9,000	7,000
Accounts receivable	75,000	58,000
Cash	28,250	20,000
Total assets	$782,250	$712,000

Share capital—ordinary, $10 par	$370,000	$280,000
Retained earnings	145,000	120,000
Bonds payable	70,000	100,000
Accounts payable	123,000	115,000
Salaries and wages payable	47,250	72,000
Interest payable	27,000	25,000
Total equity and liabilities	$782,250	$712,000

Taur Company
Income Statement
For the Year Ended May 31, 2029

Sales revenue		$1,255,250
Cost of merchandise sold		(722,000)
Gross profit		533,250
Operating Expenses		
Salaries and wages expense	252,100	
Depreciation expense	25,000	
Other expenses	8,150	(285,250)
Operating income		248,000
Interest expense		(75,000)
Income before income tax		173,000
Income tax expense		(43,000)
Net income		$ 130,000

The following is additional information concerning Taur's transactions during the year ended May 31, 2029.

1. All sales during the year were made on account.
2. All merchandise was purchased on account, comprising the total accounts payable account.
3. Plant assets costing $98,000 were purchased by paying $28,000 in cash and issuing 7,000 ordinary shares.
4. The "other expenses" are related to prepaid items.
5. All income taxes incurred during the year were paid during the year.
6. In order to supplement its cash, Taur issued 2,000 ordinary shares at par value.
7. There were no penalties assessed for the retirement of bonds.
8. Cash dividends of $105,000 were declared and paid at the end of the fiscal year.

Instructions

a. Using the indirect method, calculate only the net cash flow from operating activities for Taur Company for the year ended May 31, 2029.

b. Prepare a statement of cash flows for Taur Company for the year ended May 31, 2029, using the direct method. Be sure to support the statement with appropriate calculations.

Data Analytics in Action

Using Data Visualization to Analyze Cash Flows

DA14.1 Data visualization can be used to illustrate cash flows.

Excel

Example: Consider three U.S. tech companies, **Box**, **FireEye**, and **MobileIron**, which have all issued shares to the public. As mentioned, prior to making investments in these companies, the investors most likely closely examined each respective company's cash flows. The investors want to be sure that these companies are able to generate enough cash to satisfy liabilities, pay dividends, and grow the company.

We can use data visualization to understand the pattern of cash flows for companies such as these. For example, consider the following chart.

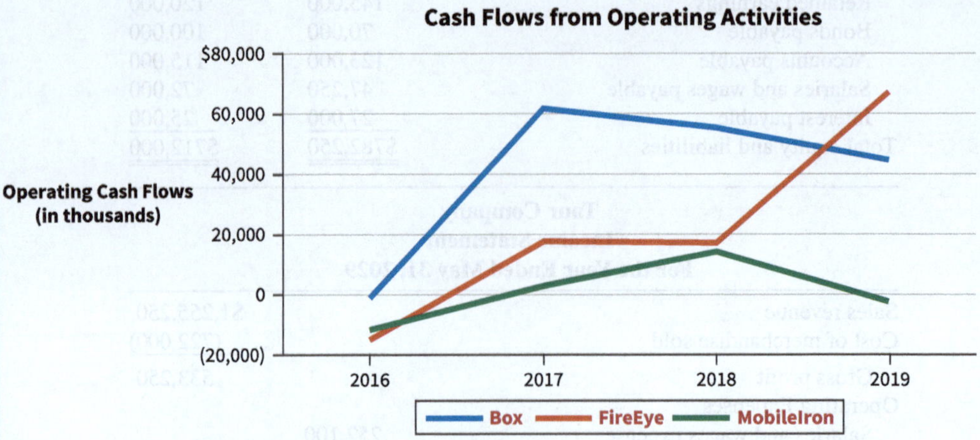

Source: Based on yahoo! finance website.

FireEye has an upward sloping trajectory, making its operating cash flows appear more promising than the others. Box's operating cash flows have the steepest downward trend beginning in 2017, making it the company with the biggest concerns. MobileIron had a steady increase for the first two years but has taken a recent downturn, making it a second company that investors should monitor closely.

For this case, you will look more closely at the statement of cash flow data for these three companies. You will then create and analyze clustered column charts to determine what helpful information these visualizations might provide to investors.

Go to the Wiley online course for complete case details and instructions.

Using Data Analytics to Evaluate Industry Cash Flows

Excel

DA14.2 By evaluating the cash flows of top competitors within an industry, financial statement users can make certain generalizations about that industry overall. This will help them to better analyze the cash flows of another company within that industry. For this case, you will use cash flow information from four leading U.S. pharmaceutical companies to create and analyze waterfall charts, and then make generalizations about this industry's cash flows.

Go to the Wiley online course for complete case details and instructions.

Expand Your Critical Thinking

Financial Reporting Problem: TSMC, Ltd. (TWN)

CT14.1 Refer to the financial statements of TSMC presented in Appendix A to answer the following questions. The complete annual report, including notes to the financial statements, is available at the company's website.

a. What was the amount of net cash provided by operating activities for the year ended December 31, 2020? For the year ended December 31, 2019?

b. What was the amount of increase or decrease in cash and cash equivalents for the year ended December 31, 2020? For the year ended December 31, 2019?

c. Which method of computing net cash provided by operating activities does TSMC use?

d. From your analysis of the 2020 statement of cash flows, did the change in accounts and notes receivable decrease or increase cash? Did the change in inventories decrease or increase cash? Did the change in accounts payable and other current liabilities decrease or increase cash?

e. What was the net outflow or inflow of cash from investing activities for the year ended December 31, 2020?

f. What was the amount of interest paid in the year ended December 31, 2020? What was the amount of income taxes paid in the year ended December 31, 2020?

Comparative Analysis Problem: Nestlé SA (CHE) vs. Delfi Limited (SGP)

CT14.2 Refer to the financial statements of **Nestlé** (Appendix B) and **Delfi Limited** (Appendix C) to answer the following questions. Complete annual reports, including notes to the financial statements, are available at each company's respective website.

Instructions

a. Based on the information contained in these financial statements, compute free cash flow for each company for the most recent fiscal year shown.

b. What conclusions concerning the management of cash can be drawn from these data?

Decision-Making Across the Organization

CT14.3 Norman Roads and Sara Mesa are examining the following statement of cash flows for Del Carpio, SLU for the year ended January 31, 2029.

Del Carpio SLU
Statement of Cash Flows
For the Year Ended January 31, 2029

Sources of cash	
From sales of merchandise	€350,000
From sale of ordinary shares	405,000
From sale of investment (purchased below)	85,000
From depreciation	75,000
From issuance of note for truck	25,000
From interest on investments	6,000
Total sources of cash	946,000
Uses of cash	
For purchase of fixtures and equipment	320,000
For merchandise purchased for resale	245,000
For operating expenses (including depreciation)	160,000
For purchase of investment	75,000
For purchase of truck by issuance of note	25,000
For purchase of ordinary shares	15,000
For interest on note payable	5,000
Total uses of cash	845,000
Net increase in cash	€101,000

Norman claims that Del Carpio's statement of cash flows is an excellent portrayal of a superb first year with cash increasing €101,000. Sara replies that it was not a superb first year. Rather, she says, the year was an operating failure, the statement is presented incorrectly, and €101,000 is not the actual increase in cash. The cash balance at the beginning of the year was €140,000.

Instructions

With the class divided into groups, answer the following.

a. Using the data provided, prepare a statement of cash flows in proper form using the indirect method. The only non-cash items in the income statement are depreciation and the gain from the sale of the investment.

b. With whom do you agree, Norman or Sara? Explain your position.

Real-World Focus

CT14.4 Purpose: Learn about the **U.S. Securities and Exchange Commission (SEC)**.

Instructions

Go to the U.S. SEC website and then choose **About** to answer the following questions.

a. How many enforcement actions does the SEC take each year against securities law violators? What are typical infractions?

b. After the Depression, Congress passed the Securities Acts of 1933 and 1934 to improve investor confidence in the markets. What two "common sense" notions are these laws based on?

c. Who was the President of the United States at the time of the creation of the SEC? Who was the first SEC Chairperson?

CT14.5 Purpose: Use the Internet to view U.S. SEC filings.

Instructions

Select a well-known U.S. company, such as **McDonald's** or **Starbucks**. Do an Internet search for "Yahoo-Edgar Online" to access the website for easily locating U.S. SEC filings for your chosen company and then answer the following questions.

a. What company did you select?

b. Which filing is the most recent? What is the date?

c. What other recent U.S. SEC filings are available for your viewing?

Communication Activity

CT14.6 Bart Sampson, the owner-president of Computer Services International, is unfamiliar with the statement of cash flows that you, as his accountant, prepared. He asks for further explanation.

Instructions

Write him a brief memo explaining the form and content of the statement of cash flows as shown in Illustration 14.15.

Ethics Case

CT14.7 Babbit Ltd. is a medium-sized wholesaler of automotive parts. It has 10 shareholders who have been paid a total of £1 million in cash dividends for 8 consecutive years. The board's policy requires that, for this dividend to be declared, net cash provided by operating activities as reported in Babbit's current year's statement of cash flows must exceed £1 million. President and CEO Milton Williams' job is secure so long as he produces annual operating cash flows to support the usual dividend.

At the end of the current year, controller Jerry Roberts presents president Milton Williams with some disappointing news: The net cash provided by operating activities is calculated by the indirect method to be only £970,000. The president says to Jerry, "We must get that amount above £1 million. Isn't there some way to increase operating cash flow by another £30,000?" Jerry answers, "These figures were prepared by my assistant. I'll go back to my office and see what I can do." The president replies, "I know you won't let me down, Jerry."

Upon close scrutiny of the statement of cash flows, Jerry concludes that he can get the operating cash flows above £1 million by reclassifying a £60,000, 2-year note payable listed in the financing activities section as "Proceeds from bank loan—£60,000." He will report the note instead as "Increase in payables—£60,000" and treat it as an adjustment of net income in the operating activities section. He returns to the president, saying, "You can tell the board to declare their usual dividend. Our net cash flow provided by operating activities is £1,030,000." "Good man, Jerry! I knew I could count on you," exults the president.

Instructions

a. Who are the stakeholders in this situation?

b. Was there anything unethical about the president's actions? Was there anything unethical about the controller's actions?

c. Are the board members or anyone else likely to discover the misclassification?

Answers to Insight and Accounting Across the Organization Questions

Net *What?* Q: In general, why do differences exist between net income and net cash provided by operating activities? **A:** The differences are explained by differences in the timing of the reporting of revenues and expenses under accrual accounting versus the cash basis. Under accrual accounting, companies report revenues when the performance obligation is satisfied, even if cash has not been received. They report expenses when incurred, even if cash has not been paid.

Burning Through Our Cash Q: What implications does a company's cash burn rate have for its survival? **A:** The cash burn rate is measured by the amount that cash disbursements exceed cash receipts during a year. If a company doesn't have a sufficient cash cushion to weather bad times, it will be unable to pay its liabilities as they come due and will cease to exist.

A Look at U.S. GAAP

LEARNING OBJECTIVE 6

Compare the procedures for the statement of cash flows under IFRS and U.S. GAAP.

As in IFRS, the statement of cash flows is a required statement for GAAP. In addition, the content and presentation of a GAAP statement of cash flows is similar to the one used for IFRS. However, the disclosure requirements related to the statement of cash flows are more extensive under GAAP. *IAS 7* ("Cash Flow Statements") provides the overall IFRS requirements for cash flow information.

Key Points

Similarities

- Companies preparing financial statements under both GAAP and IFRS must prepare a statement of cash flows as an integral part of the financial statements.
- Both IFRS and GAAP require that the statement of cash flows should have three major sections—operating, investing, and financing—along with changes in cash and cash equivalents.
- Similar to IFRS, the statement of cash flows can be prepared using either the indirect or direct method under GAAP. Companies choose for the most part to use the indirect method for reporting net cash flows from operating activities.

Differences

- The definition of cash equivalents used in GAAP is similar to that used in IFRS. A major difference is that in certain situations, bank overdrafts are considered part of cash and cash equivalents under IFRS (which is not the case in GAAP). Under GAAP, bank overdrafts are classified as financing activities in the statement of cash flows and are reported as liabilities on the statement of financial position.
- IFRS requires that non-cash investing and financing activities be excluded from the statement of cash flows. Instead, these non-cash activities should be reported elsewhere. This requirement is interpreted to mean that non-cash investing and financing activities should be disclosed in the notes to the financial statements instead of in the financial statements. Under GAAP, companies may present this information on the face of the statement of cash flows.
- One area where there can be substantial differences between IFRS and GAAP relates to the classification of interest, dividends, and taxes. The following table indicates the differences between the two approaches.

Item	IFRS	GAAP
Interest paid	Financing	Operating
Interest received	Investing	Operating
Dividends paid	Financing	Financing
Dividends received	Investing	Operating
Taxes paid	Operating—unless specific identification with financing or investing activity	Operating

- Under IFRS, some companies present the operating section in a single line item, with a full reconciliation provided in the notes to the financial statements. This presentation is not seen under GAAP.
- Similar to IFRS, under GAAP companies must disclose the amount of taxes and interest paid. Under GAAP, companies disclose this in the notes to the financial statements. Under the amended *IAS 7*, companies that do not have a specified main business activity of investing in assets or providing financing to customers are required to classify interest paid as cash flows from financing activities, and interest and dividends received as cash flows from investing activities.

GAAP Practice

GAAP Self-Test Questions

1. Under GAAP interest paid can be reported as:

   a. only a financing element.

   b. a financing element or an investing element.

   c. a financing element or an operating element.

   d. only an operating element.

2. IFRS requires that non-cash items:

   a. be reported in the section to which they relate, that is, a non-cash investing activity would be reported in the investing section.

   b. be disclosed in the notes to the financial statements.

   c. do not need to be reported.

   d. be treated in a fashion similar to cash equivalents.

3. Which of the following statements is **false**?

   a. Bank overdrafts are treated in a similar manner under GAAP and IFRS.

   b. GAAP and IFRS use the same three sections in the statement of cash flows.

   c. A single line item for operating cash flows, with a full reconciliation in the notes, is sometimes presented under IFRS.

   d. Both GAAP and IFRS require the disclosure of the amount of cash used to pay interest and taxes.

4. Under GAAP:

   a. taxes are always treated as an operating item.

   b. the income statement uses the headings operating, investing, and financing.

   c. dividends received can be either an operating or investing item.

   d. dividends paid can be either an operating or investing item.

5. Which of the following is **correct**?

   a. Under GAAP, the statement of cash flows is optional.

   b. GAAP requires use of the direct approach in preparing the statement of cash flows.

   c. The majority of companies following GAAP and the majority following IFRS employ the indirect approach to the statement of cash flows.

   d. Cash and cash equivalents are reported as separate line items under GAAP.

GAAP Exercises

GAAP14.1 Discuss the differences that exist in the treatment of bank overdrafts under GAAP and IFRS.

GAAP14.2 Describe the treatment of each of the following items under IFRS versus GAAP.

a. Interest paid.
b. Interest received.
c. Dividends paid.
d. Dividends received.

GAAP14.3 Explain how the treatment of cash equivalents differs between IFRS and GAAP.

GAAP Financial Reporting Problem: Apple Inc. (USA)

GAAP14.4 The financial statements of **Apple** are presented in Appendix D. The complete annual report, including the notes to its financial statements, is available at the company's website.

Instructions

Use the company's financial statements to answer the following questions.

a. What was the amount of net cash provided by operating activities for 2020? For 2019?

b. What was the amount of increase or decrease in cash and cash equivalents for the year ended September 26, 2020?

c. Which method of computing net cash provided by operating activities does Apple use?

d. From your analysis of the 2020 statement of cash flows, was the change in accounts receivable a decrease or an increase in cash? Was the change in inventories a decrease or an increase in cash? Was the change in accounts payable a decrease or an increase in cash?

e. What was the net cash used by investing activities for 2020?

f. What was the amount of income taxes paid in 2020?

Answers to GAAP Self-Test Questions

1. d **2.** b **3.** a **4.** a **5.** c

CHAPTER 15

Financial Analysis: The Big Picture

LEARNING OBJECTIVES After studying this chapter, you should be able to:

LO 1 Apply horizontal analysis and vertical analysis to financial statements.

LO 2 Analyze a company's performance using ratio analysis.

LO 3 Apply the concept of sustainable income.

Chapter Preview

We can learn an important lesson from Li Ka-shing: Study companies carefully if you wish to invest. Do not get caught up in fads but instead find companies that are financially healthy. Using some of the basic decision tools presented in this text, you can perform a rudimentary analysis on any company and draw basic conclusions about its financial health. Although it would not be wise for you to bet your life savings on a company's shares relying solely on your current level of knowledge, we strongly encourage you to practice your new skills wherever possible. Only with practice will you improve your ability to interpret financial numbers.

Before unleashing you on the world of high finance, we will present a few more important concepts and techniques, as well as provide you with one more comprehensive review of company financial statements. We use all of the decision tools presented in this text to analyze a single company.

Financial Analysis: The Big Picture

Basics of Financial Statement Analysis
- Need for comparative analysis
- Tools of analysis
- Horizontal analysis
- Vertical analysis

Ratio Analysis
- Liquidity ratios
- Profitability ratios
- Solvency ratios
- Summary of ratios

Sustainable Income
- Discontinued operations
- Changes in accounting principle
- Comprehensive income

Practice

DO IT! 1 Horizontal Analysis
DO IT! 2 Ratio Analysis
DO IT! 3 Unusual Items

Go to the Review and Practice section at the end of the chapter for a review of key concepts and practice applications with solutions.
Additional tutorials and practice opportunities are available in the Wiley online course.

Feature Story: Making Money the Old-Fashioned Way

Li Ka-shing likes things simple. He wears a basic electronic wristwatch, basic black dress shoes, and basic business suits. He lives by the philosophy that "If you keep a good reputation, work hard, be nice to people, keep your promises, your business will be much easier." It seems to have worked for him. Business has been good. Li Ka-shing is one of Asia's richest men, with a net worth of over US$30 billion. That placed him in the top 20 on a recent list of the richest people in the world.

Li was not born rich. His family fled to Hong Kong from mainland China during the upheavals of war in 1940. His father died when Li was in his teens, forcing him to quit school and take a job at a plastics trading company. Within a few years, Li had started his own plastics company. One of his early businesses produced plastic flowers. He produced the parts for the flowers and then paid people to assemble the flowers in their homes. This saved him the cost of additional factory space (space being in short supply in Hong Kong).

Over the years, Li also invested in Hong Kong properties. One long-time business associate recalls that Li was very disciplined when bidding on investments in businesses and properties. He didn't like debt, and he would never bid above a predetermined number. He knew precisely what it would take for his investments to be profitable.

Today, Li's business interests span many industries and virtually all parts of the world. His companies operate in 55 countries with approximately 250,000 employees. He owns ports, retail companies, electricity companies and energy interests such as oil sands in Canada, shipping companies, and telecom companies. He describes his criteria for doing business in a country as "rule of law, political stability that safeguards investments, ease of doing business and good tax structures."

How can you enjoy similar success? There are no guarantees, but honing your financial analysis skills would be a start. A good way for you to begin your career as a successful investor is to master the fundamentals of financial analysis discussed in this chapter.

Sources: Tom Mitchell and Robin Kwong, "Breaking the Mould," *Financial Times Online* (October 26, 2007); and Michael Schuman, "The Miracle of Asia's Richest Man," *Forbes.com* (February 24, 2010).

TPG/Shutterstock

15.1 Basics of Financial Statement Analysis

LEARNING OBJECTIVE 1

Apply horizontal analysis and vertical analysis to financial statements.

Analyzing financial statements involves evaluating three characteristics: a company's liquidity, profitability, and solvency.

- A **short-term creditor**, such as a bank, is primarily interested in liquidity—the ability of the borrower to pay obligations when they come due. The liquidity of the borrower is extremely important in evaluating the safety of a loan.

- A **long-term creditor**, such as a bondholder, looks to profitability and solvency measures that indicate the company's ability to survive over a long period of time. Long-term creditors consider such measures as the amount of debt in the company's capital structure and its ability to meet interest payments.

Similarly, **shareholders** look at the profitability and solvency of the company. They want to assess the likelihood of dividends and the growth potential of their investment.

Need for Comparative Analysis

Every item reported in a financial statement has significance. When **Marks and Spencer plc (M&S)** (GBR) reports cash and cash equivalents of £422.9 million on its statement of financial position, we know the company had that amount of cash on the report date. But, we do not know whether the amount represents an increase over prior years, or whether it is adequate in relation to the company's need for cash. To obtain such information, we need to compare the amount of cash with other financial statement data.

Comparisons can be made on a number of different bases. Three are illustrated in this chapter.

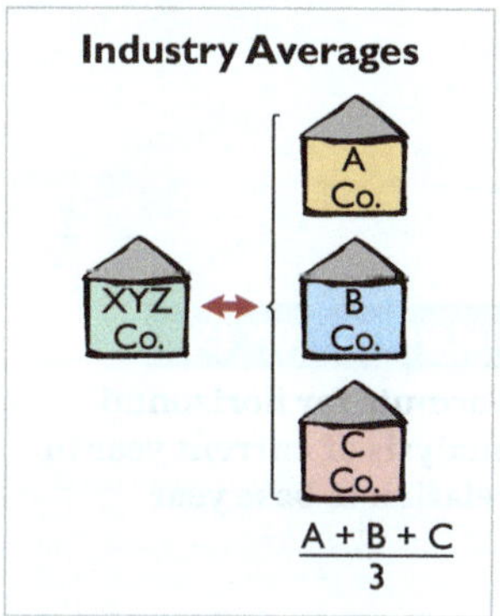

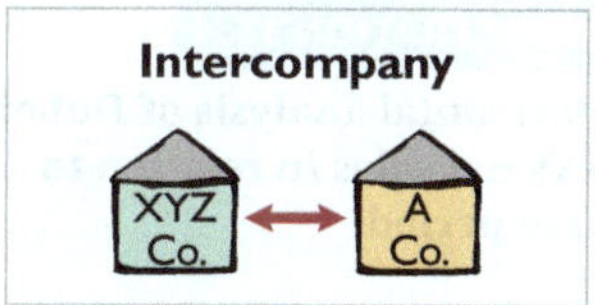

1. **Intracompany basis.** Comparisons within a company are often useful to detect changes in financial relationships and significant trends. For example, a comparison of **M&S**'s current year's cash amount with the prior year's cash amount shows either an increase or a decrease. Likewise, a comparison of M&S's year-end cash amount with the amount of its total assets at year-end shows the proportion of total assets in the form of cash.
2. **Industry averages.** Comparisons with industry averages provide information about a company's relative position within the industry. For example, financial statement readers can compare M&S's financial data with the averages for its industry compiled by financial rating organizations such as the U.S. companies **Dun & Bradstreet, Moody's**, and **Standard & Poor's**, or with information provided on the Internet by organizations such as **Yahoo!** on its financial site.
3. **Intercompany basis.** Comparisons with other companies provide insight into a company's competitive position. For example, investors can compare M&S's total sales for the year with the total sales of its competitors in retail, such as **Carrefour** (FRA).

Tools of Analysis

We use various tools to evaluate the significance of financial statement data. Three commonly used tools are as follows.

1. **Horizontal analysis** evaluates a series of financial statement data over a period of time.
2. **Vertical analysis** evaluates financial statement data by expressing each item in a financial statement as a percentage of a base amount.
3. **Ratio analysis** expresses the relationship among selected items of financial statement data.

Horizontal analysis is used primarily in intracompany comparisons. Two features in published financial statements and annual report information facilitate this type of comparison. First, each of the basic financial statements presents comparative financial data for a minimum of two years. Second, a summary of selected financial data is presented for a series of five to 10 years or more. Vertical analysis is used in both intra- and intercompany comparisons. Ratio analysis is used in all three types of comparisons. In the following sections, we explain and illustrate each of the three types of analysis.

Horizontal Analysis

Horizontal analysis, also called **trend analysis**, is a technique for evaluating a series of financial statement data over a period of time. Its purpose is to determine the increase or decrease that has taken place. This change may be expressed as either an amount or a percentage. For example, **Illustration 15.1** shows recent net sales figures of Dubois SA.

ILLUSTRATION 15.1
Dubois SA's net sales

Dubois SA Net Sales (in thousands)		
2029	2028	2027
€19,860	€19,903	€18,781

If we assume that 2027 is the base year, we can measure all percentage increases or decreases from this base period amount, as shown in **Illustration 15.2**.

ILLUSTRATION 15.2
Formula for horizontal analysis of changes since base period

$$\text{Change Since Base Period} = \frac{\text{Current Year Amount} - \text{Base Year Amount}}{\text{Base Year Amount}}$$

For example, we can determine that net sales for Dubois increased from 2027 to 2028 approximately 6% [(€19,903 − €18,781) ÷ €18,781]. Similarly, we can determine that net sales increased from 2027 to 2029 approximately 5.7% [(€19,860 − €18,781) ÷ €18,781].

Alternatively, we can express current year sales as a percentage of the base period. We do this by dividing the current year amount by the base year amount, as shown in **Illustration 15.3**.

ILLUSTRATION 15.3
Formula for horizontal analysis of current year in relation to base year

$$\text{Current Results in Relation to Base Period} = \frac{\text{Current Year Amount}}{\text{Base Year Amount}}$$

Illustration 15.4 presents this analysis for Dubois for a three-year period using 2027 as the base period.

ILLUSTRATION 15.4
Horizontal analysis of Dubois SA's net sales in relation to base period

Dubois SA Net Sales (in thousands) in Relation to Base Period 2027		
2029	2028	2027
€19,860	€19,903	€18,781
105.7%	106.0%	100%

Statement of Financial Position

To further illustrate horizontal analysis, we will use the financial statements of Quality Department Store, a fictional retailer. **Illustration 15.5** presents a horizontal analysis of its two-year condensed statements of financial position, showing euro and percentage changes.

ILLUSTRATION 15.5
Horizontal analysis of statements of financial position

Quality Department Store
Condensed Statements of Financial Position
December 31

	2029	2028	Increase or (Decrease) During 2029: Amount	Percent
Assets				
Intangible assets	€ 15,000	€ 17,500	€ (2,500)	(14.3%)
Plant assets (net)	800,000	632,500	167,500	26.5%
Current assets	1,020,000	945,000	75,000	7.9%
Total assets	€1,835,000	€1,595,000	€240,000	15.0%

ILLUSTRATION 15.5

(continued)

	2029	2028	Increase or (Decrease) During 2029 Amount	Percent
Equity				
Share capital—ordinary, €1 par	€ 275,400	€ 270,000	€ 5,400	2.0%
Retained earnings	727,600	525,000	202,600	38.6%
Total equity	1,003,000	795,000	208,000	26.2%
Liabilities				
Non-current liabilities	€ 487,500	€ 497,000	€ (9,500)	(1.9%)
Current liabilities	344,500	303,000	41,500	13.7%
Total liabilities	832,000	800,000	32,000	4.0%
Total equity and liabilities	€1,835,000	€1,595,000	€240,000	15.0%

The comparative statements of financial position in Illustration 15.5 show that a number of significant changes have occurred in Quality Department Store's financial structure from 2028 to 2029:

- In the assets section, plant assets (net) increased €167,500, or 26.5%.
- In the equity section, retained earnings increased €202,600, or 38.6%.
- In the liabilities section, current liabilities increased €41,500, or 13.7%.

These changes suggest that the company expanded its asset base during 2029 and **financed this expansion primarily by retaining income** rather than assuming additional long-term debt.

Income Statement

Illustration 15.6 presents a horizontal analysis of the two-year condensed income statements of Quality Department Store for the years 2029 and 2028 (see **Helpful Hint**). Horizontal analysis of the income statements shows the following changes.

- Net sales increased €260,000, or 14.2% (€260,000 ÷ €1,837,000).
- Cost of goods sold increased €141,000, or 12.4% (€141,000 ÷ €1,140,000).
- Total operating expenses increased €37,000, or 11.6% (€37,000 ÷ €320,000).

HELPFUL HINT

Note that though the amount column is additive (the total is €55,300), the percentage column is not additive (26.5% is not the column total). A separate percentage has been calculated for each item.

ILLUSTRATION 15.6

Horizontal analysis of income statements

Quality Department Store
Condensed Income Statements
For the Years Ended December 31

	2029	2028	Increase or (Decrease) During 2029 Amount	Percent
Sales revenue	€2,195,000	€1,960,000	€235,000	12.0%
Sales returns and allowances	98,000	123,000	(25,000)	(20.3%)
Net sales	2,097,000	1,837,000	260,000	14.2%
Cost of goods sold	1,281,000	1,140,000	141,000	12.4%
Gross profit	816,000	697,000	119,000	17.1%
Selling expenses	253,000	211,500	41,500	19.6%
Administrative expenses	104,000	108,500	(4,500)	(4.1%)
Total operating expenses	357,000	320,000	37,000	11.6%
Operating income	459,000	377,000	82,000	21.8%
Interest and dividends	9,000	11,000	(2,000)	(18.2%)
Income before financing and income taxes	468,000	388,000	80,000	20.6%
Interest expense	36,000	40,500	(4,500)	(11.1%)
Income before income taxes	432,000	347,500	84,500	24.3%
Income tax expense	168,200	139,000	29,200	21.0%
Net income	€ 263,800	€ 208,500	€ 55,300	26.5%

Overall, gross profit and net income were up substantially. Gross profit increased 17.1%, and net income, 26.5%. Quality's profit trend appears favorable.

Retained Earnings Statement

Illustration 15.7 presents a horizontal analysis of Quality Department Store's comparative retained earnings statements. Analyzed horizontally, net income increased €55,300, or 26.5%, whereas dividends on the share capital—ordinary increased only €1,200, or 2%. We saw in the horizontal analysis of the statement of financial position that ending retained earnings increased 38.6%. As indicated earlier, the company retained a significant portion of net income to finance additional plant facilities.

ILLUSTRATION 15.7

Horizontal analysis of retained earnings statements

Quality Department Store
Retained Earnings Statements
For the Years Ended December 31

	2029	2028	Increase or (Decrease) During 2029 Amount	Percent
Retained earnings, Jan. 1	€525,000	€376,500	€148,500	39.4%
Add: Net income	263,800	208,500	55,300	26.5%
	788,800	585,000	203,800	
Deduct: Dividends	61,200	60,000	1,200	2.0%
Retained earnings, Dec. 31	€727,600	€525,000	€202,600	38.6%

Horizontal analysis of changes from period to period is relatively straightforward and is quite useful. But, complications can occur in making the computations. If an item has no value in a base year or preceding year but does have a value in the next year, we cannot compute a percentage change. Similarly, if a negative amount appears in the base or preceding period and a positive amount exists the following year (or vice versa), no percentage change can be computed.

Vertical Analysis

Vertical analysis, also called **common-size analysis**, is a technique that expresses each financial statement item as a percentage of a base amount. On a statement of financial position, we might say that current assets are 22% of total assets—total assets being the base amount. Or on an income statement, we might say that selling expenses are 16% of net sales—net sales being the base amount.

Statement of Financial Position

Illustration 15.8 presents the vertical analysis of Quality Department Store's comparative statements of financial position. The base for the asset items is **total assets**. The base for the equity and liability items is **total equity and liabilities**.

- Vertical analysis shows the relative size of each category in the statement of financial position.
- It also can show the **percentage change** in the individual asset, liability, and equity items (see **Helpful Hint**).

HELPFUL HINT

The formula for calculating these statement of financial position percentages is:

$$\frac{\text{Each item}}{\text{Total assets}} = \%$$

For example, we can see that current assets decreased from 59.2% of total assets in 2028 to 55.6% in 2029 (even though the absolute euro amount increased €75,000 in that time). Plant assets (net) have increased from 39.7% to 43.6% of total assets. Retained earnings have increased from 32.9% to 39.7% of total equity and liabilities. These results reinforce the earlier observations that **Quality Department Store is choosing to finance its growth through retention of earnings rather than through issuing additional debt**.

ILLUSTRATION 15.8

Vertical analysis of statements of financial position

Quality Department Store
Condensed Statements of Financial Position
December 31

	2029		2028	
	Amount	**Percent**	**Amount**	**Percent**
Assets				
Intangible assets	€ 15,000	0.8%	€ 17,500	1.1%
Plant assets (net)	800,000	43.6%	632,500	39.7%
Current assets	1,020,000	55.6%	945,000	59.2%
Total assets	€1,835,000	100.0%	€1,595,000	100.0%
Equity				
Share capital—ordinary, €1 par	€ 275,400	15.0%	€ 270,000	16.9%
Retained earnings	727,600	39.7%	525,000	32.9%
Total equity	1,003,000	54.7%	795,000	49.8%
Liabilities				
Non-current liabilities	€ 487,500	26.5%	€ 497,000	31.2%
Current liabilities	344,500	18.8%	303,000	19.0%
Total liabilities	832,000	45.3%	800,000	50.2%
Total equity and liabilities	€1,835,000	100.0%	€1,595,000	100.0%

Income Statement

Illustration 15.9 shows vertical analysis of Quality Department Store's income statements. Cost of goods sold as a percentage of net sales declined 1% (62.1% vs. 61.1%), and total operating expenses declined 0.4% (17.4% vs. 17.0%). As a result, it is not surprising to see net income as a percentage of net sales increase from 11.4% to 12.6% (see **Helpful Hint**). Quality Department Store appears to be a profitable business that is becoming even more successful.

HELPFUL HINT

The formula for calculating these income statement percentages is:

$$\frac{\text{Each item on I/S}}{\text{Net sales}} = \%$$

ILLUSTRATION 15.9

Vertical analysis of income statements

Quality Department Store
Condensed Income Statements
For the Years Ended December 31

	2029		2028	
	Amount	**Percent**	**Amount**	**Percent**
Sales revenue	€2,195,000	104.7%	€1,960,000	106.7%
Sales returns and allowances	98,000	4.7%	123,000	6.7%
Net sales	2,097,000	100.0%	1,837,000	100.0%
Cost of goods sold	1,281,000	61.1%	1,140,000	62.1%
Gross profit	816,000	38.9%	697,000	37.9%
Selling expenses	253,000	12.0%	211,500	11.5%
Administrative expenses	104,000	5.0%	108,500	5.9%
Total operating expenses	357,000	17.0%	320,000	17.4%
Operating income	459,000	21.9%	377,000	20.5%
Interest and dividends	9,000	0.4%	11,000	0.6%
Income before financing and income taxes	468,000	22.3%	388,000	21.1%
Interest expense	36,000	1.7%	40,500	2.2%
Income before income taxes	432,000	20.6%	347,500	18.9%
Income tax expense	168,200	8.0%	139,000	7.5%
Net income	€ 263,800	12.6%	€ 208,500	11.4%

An associated benefit of vertical analysis is that it enables you to compare companies of different sizes. For example, Quality Department Store's main competitor is a Park Street store in a nearby town. Using vertical analysis, we can compare the condensed income statements of Quality Department Store (a small retail company) with Park Street (a giant global retailer), as shown in **Illustration 15.10**.

ILLUSTRATION 15.10

Intercompany income statement comparison

Condensed Income Statements

For the Year Ended December 31, 2029
(in thousands)

	Quality Department Store		Park Street	
	Amount	**Percent**	**Amount**	**Percent**
Net sales	€2,097	100.0%	€17,556,000	100.7%
Cost of goods sold	1,281	61.1%	10,646,000	60.6%
Gross profit	816	38.9%	6,910,000	39.4%
Selling and administrative expenses	357	17.0%	6,247,000	35.6%
Operating income	459	21.9%	663,000	3.8%
Interest and dividends	9	0.4%	88,000	0.5%
Income before financing and income taxes	468	22.3%	751,000	4.3%
Interest expense	36	1.7%	140,000	0.8%
Income before income taxes	432	20.6%	611,000	3.5%
Income tax expense	168	8.0%	360,000	2.1%
Net income	€ 264	12.6%	€ 251,000	1.4%

Park Street's net sales are 8,372 times greater than the net sales of relatively tiny Quality Department Store. But vertical analysis eliminates this difference in size. The percentages show that Quality's and Park Street's gross profit rates were comparable at 38.9% and 39.4%. However, the percentages related to operating income were significantly different at 21.9% and 3.8%. This disparity can be attributed to Quality's selling and administrative expense percentage (17%), which is much lower than Park Street's (35.6%). Although Park Street earned net income more than 951 times larger than Quality's, Park Street's net income as a **percentage of each sales euro** (1.4%) is only 11% of Quality's (12.6%).

ACTION PLAN

- **Find the percentage change by dividing the amount of the increase by the 2028 amount (base year).**

DO IT! 1 | Horizontal Analysis

Summary financial information for Rosepatch NV is as follows.

	December 31, 2029	December 31, 2028
Plant assets (net)	€756,000	€420,000
Current assets	234,000	180,000
Total assets	€990,000	€600,000

Compute the amount and percentage changes in 2029 using horizontal analysis, assuming 2028 is the base year.

Solution

	Increase in 2029	
	Amount	**Percent**
Plant assets (net)	€336,000	80% [(€756,000 − €420,000) ÷ €420,000]
Current assets	54,000	30% [(€234,000 − €180,000) ÷ €180,000]
Total assets	€390,000	65% [(€990,000 − €600,000) ÷ €600,000]

Related exercise material: **BE15.2, BE15.3, BE15.6, BE15.7, DO IT! 15.1, E15.1, E15.3, and E15.4.**

15.2 Ratio Analysis

LEARNING OBJECTIVE 2

Analyze a company's performance using ratio analysis.

Ratio analysis expresses the relationship among selected items of financial statement data.

- A **ratio** expresses the mathematical relationship between one quantity and another.
- The relationship is expressed in terms of either a percentage, a rate, or a simple proportion.

To illustrate, **Marks and Spencer plc (M&S)** recently had current assets of £1,267.9 million and current liabilities of £2,238.3 million. We can find the relationship between these two measures by dividing current assets by current liabilities. The alternative means of expression are:

Percentage:	Current assets are 57% of current liabilities.
Rate:	Current assets are .57 times current liabilities.
Proportion:	The relationship of current assets to liabilities is .57:1.

To analyze the primary financial statements, we can use ratios to evaluate liquidity, profitability, and solvency. **Illustration 15.11** describes these classifications.

ILLUSTRATION 15.11

Financial ratio classifications

Liquidity Ratios

Measure short-term ability of the company to pay its maturing obligations and to meet unexpected needs for cash

Profitability Ratios

Measure the income or operating success of a company for a given period of time

Solvency Ratios

Measure the ability of the company to survive over a long period of time

Ratios can provide clues to underlying conditions that may not be apparent from individual financial statement components. However, a single ratio by itself is not very meaningful. Thus, in the discussion of ratios we will use the following types of comparisons.

1. **Intracompany comparisons** for two years for Quality Department Store.
2. **Industry average comparisons** based on median ratios for department stores.
3. **Intercompany comparisons** based on Park Street as Quality Department Store's principal competitor.

Liquidity Ratios

Liquidity ratios measure the short-term ability of the company to pay its maturing obligations and to meet unexpected needs for cash. Short-term creditors such as bankers and suppliers are particularly interested in assessing liquidity. The ratios we can use to determine the company's short-term debt-paying ability are the current ratio, the acid-test ratio, accounts receivable turnover, and inventory turnover.

1. Current Ratio

The **current ratio** is a widely used measure for evaluating a company's liquidity and short-term debt-paying ability. The ratio is computed by dividing current assets by current liabilities. **Illustration 15.12** shows the 2029 and 2028 current ratios for Quality Department Store and comparative data.

ILLUSTRATION 15.12

Current ratio

$$\text{Current Ratio} = \frac{\text{Current Assets}}{\text{Current Liabilities}}$$

Quality Department Store

2029	**2028**
$\frac{€1,020,000}{€344,500} = 2.96:1$	$\frac{€945,000}{€303,000} = 3.12:1$
Industry average **1.70:1**	Park Street **2.05:1**

What does the ratio actually mean? The 2029 ratio of 2.96:1 means that for every euro of current liabilities, Quality has €2.96 of current assets. Quality's current ratio has decreased in the current year. But, compared to the industry average of 1.70:1, Quality appears to be very liquid. Park Street has a current ratio of 2.05:1, which indicates it has adequate current assets relative to its current liabilities.

HELPFUL HINT

Any company can operate successfully without working capital if it has very predictable cash flows and solid earnings. A number of U.S. companies (e.g., Whirlpool, American Standard, and Campbell's Soup) are pursuing this goal as less money tied up in working capital means more money to invest in the business.

- The current ratio is sometimes referred to as the **working capital ratio. Working capital** is current assets minus current liabilities.
- The current ratio is a more dependable indicator of liquidity than working capital (see **Helpful Hint**).
- Two companies with the same amount of working capital may have significantly different current ratios.

The current ratio is only one measure of liquidity. It does not take into account the **composition** of the current assets. For example, a satisfactory current ratio does not disclose the fact that a portion of the current assets may be tied up in slow-moving inventory. A euro of cash would be more readily available to pay the bills than a euro of slow-moving inventory.

Investor Insight

NovaStock/SuperStock

How to Manage the Current Ratio

The apparent simplicity of the current ratio can have real-world limitations because adding equal amounts to both the numerator and the denominator causes the ratio to decrease if it exceeds 1:1.

Assume, for example, that a company has $2,000,000 of current assets and $1,000,000 of current liabilities; its current ratio is 2:1. If it purchases $1,000,000 of inventory on account, it will have $3,000,000 of current assets and $2,000,000 of current liabilities; its current ratio decreases to 1.5:1. If, instead, the company pays off $500,000 of its current liabilities, it will have $1,500,000 of current assets and $500,000 of current liabilities; its current ratio increases to 3:1.

Thus, any trend analysis should be done with care because the ratio is susceptible to quick changes and is easily influenced by management.

How might management influence a company's current ratio? (Answer is available near the end of the chapter.)

2. Acid-Test Ratio

The **acid-test (quick) ratio** is a measure of a company's immediate short-term liquidity.

- We compute the acid-test ratio by dividing the sum of cash, financial assets at FVTPL, and net accounts receivable by current liabilities.
- Thus, it is an important complement to the current ratio.

For example, assume that the current assets of Quality Department Store for 2029 and 2028 consist of the items shown in **Illustration 15.13**.

ILLUSTRATION 15.13

Current assets of Quality Department Store

Quality Department Store
Statement of Financial Position (partial)

	2029	2028
Current assets		
Prepaid expenses	€ 50,000	€ 40,000
Inventory	620,000	500,000
Accounts receivable (net*)	**230,000**	**180,000**
Financial assets at FVTPL	**20,000**	**70,000**
Cash	**100,000**	**155,000**
Total current assets	€1,020,000	€945,000

*Allowance for doubtful accounts is €10,000 at the end of each year.

Cash, financial assets at FVTPL, and accounts receivable (net) are highly liquid compared to inventory and prepaid expenses. The inventory may not be readily saleable, and the prepaid expenses may not be transferable to others. Thus, the acid-test ratio measures **immediate** liquidity. The 2029 and 2028 acid-test ratios for Quality Department Store and comparative data are as shown in **Illustration 15.14**.

ILLUSTRATION 15.14

Acid-test ratio

$$\text{Acid-Test Ratio} = \frac{\text{Cash + Financial Assets at FVTPL + Accounts Receivable (Net)}}{\text{Current Liabilities}}$$

Quality Department Store

2029		2028	
$\frac{€100{,}000 + €20{,}000 + €230{,}000}{€344{,}500}$	= 1.02:1	$\frac{€155{,}000 + €70{,}000 + €180{,}000}{€303{,}000}$	= 1.34:1
Industry average		Park Street	
0.70:1		**1.05:1**	

The ratio has declined in 2029. Is an acid-test ratio of 1.02:1 adequate? This depends on the industry and the economy. When compared with the industry average of 0.70:1 and Park Street's of 1.05:1, Quality's acid-test ratio seems adequate.

3. Accounts Receivable Turnover

We can measure liquidity by how quickly a company can convert certain assets to cash. How liquid, for example, are the accounts receivable? The ratio used to assess the liquidity of the receivables is the **accounts receivable turnover**.

- It measures the number of times, on average, the company collects receivables during the period.
- We compute the accounts receivable turnover by dividing net credit sales (net sales less cash sales) by the average net accounts receivable.
- Unless seasonal factors are significant, average net accounts receivable can be computed from the beginning and ending balances of the net accounts receivable.[1]

[1] If seasonal factors are significant, the average accounts receivable balance might be determined by using monthly amounts.

For example, assume that all Quality Department Store's sales are credit sales. The balance of net accounts receivable at the beginning of 2028 is €200,000. **Illustration 15.15** shows the accounts receivable turnover for Quality Department Store and comparative data. Quality's accounts receivable turnover improved in 2029. The turnover of 10.2 times is substantially lower than Park Street's 37.2 times, and is also lower than the department store industry's average of 46.4 times.

ILLUSTRATION 15.15

Accounts receivable turnover

$$\text{Accounts Receivable Turnover} = \frac{\text{Net Credit Sales}}{\text{Average Net Accounts Receivable}}$$

Quality Department Store

2029	2028
$\frac{€2{,}097{,}000}{\left[\frac{€180{,}000 + €230{,}000}{2}\right]} = 10.2 \text{ times}$	$\frac{€1{,}837{,}000}{\left[\frac{€200{,}000 + €180{,}000}{2}\right]} = 9.7 \text{ times}$
Industry average	Park Street
46.4 times	**37.2 times**

Average Collection Period A popular variant of the accounts receivable turnover is to convert it to an **average collection period** in terms of days. To do so, we divide the accounts receivable turnover into 365 days. For example, the accounts receivable turnover of 10.2 times divided into 365 days gives an average collection period of approximately 36 days. This means that accounts receivable are collected on average every 36 days, or about every 5 weeks.

- Analysts frequently use the average collection period to assess the effectiveness of a company's credit and collection policies.
- The general rule is that the collection period should not greatly exceed the credit term period (the time allowed for payment).

4. Inventory Turnover

Inventory turnover measures the number of times, on average, the inventory is sold during the period.

- Its purpose is to measure the liquidity of the inventory.
- We compute the inventory turnover by dividing cost of goods sold by the average inventory.
- Unless seasonal factors are significant, we can use the beginning and ending inventory balances to compute average inventory.

Assuming that the inventory balance for Quality Department Store at the beginning of 2028 was €450,000, its inventory turnover and comparative data are as shown in **Illustration 15.16**. Quality's inventory turnover declined slightly in 2029. The turnover of 2.3 times is low compared with the industry average of 4.3 and Park Street's 3.1. Generally, the faster the inventory turnover, the less cash a company has tied up in inventory and the less chance a company has of inventory obsolescence.

ILLUSTRATION 15.16

Inventory turnover

$$\text{Inventory Turnover} = \frac{\text{Cost of Goods Sold}}{\text{Average Inventory}}$$

Quality Department Store

2029	2028
$\frac{€1{,}281{,}000}{\left[\frac{€500{,}000 + €620{,}000}{2}\right]} = 2.3 \text{ times}$	$\frac{€1{,}140{,}000}{\left[\frac{€450{,}000 + €500{,}000}{2}\right]} = 2.4 \text{ times}$
Industry average	Park Street
4.3 times	**3.1 times**

Days in Inventory A variant of inventory turnover is the **days in inventory**. We calculate it by dividing the inventory turnover into 365. For example, Quality's 2029 inventory turnover of 2.3 times divided into 365 is approximately 159 days. An average selling time of 159 days is also high compared with the industry average of 84.9 days (365 ÷ 4.3) and Park Street's 117.7 days (365 ÷ 3.1).

Inventory turnovers vary considerably among industries. For example, grocery store chains have a turnover of 17.1 times and an average selling period of 21 days. In contrast, jewelry stores have an average turnover of 0.80 times and an average selling period of 456 days.

Profitability Ratios

Profitability ratios measure the income or operating success of a company for a given period of time. Income, or the lack of it, affects the company's ability to obtain debt and equity financing. It also affects the company's liquidity position and the company's ability to grow. As a consequence, both creditors and investors are interested in evaluating earning power—profitability. Analysts frequently use profitability as the ultimate test of management's operating effectiveness.

5. Profit Margin

Profit margin is a measure of the percentage of each euro of sales that results in net income (see **Alternative Terminology**). We can compute it by dividing net income by net sales. **Illustration 15.17** shows Quality Department Store's profit margin and comparative data.

ALTERNATIVE TERMINOLOGY

Profit margin is also called the *rate of return on sales*.

ILLUSTRATION 15.17

Profit margin

$$\text{Profit Margin} = \frac{\text{Net Income}}{\text{Net Sales}}$$

Quality Department Store

2029	2028
$\frac{€263,800}{€2,097,000} = 12.6\%$	$\frac{€208,500}{€1,837,000} = 11.4\%$
Industry average	**Park Street**
8.0%	**1.4%**

Quality experienced an increase in its profit margin from 2028 to 2029. Its profit margin is unusually high in comparison with the industry average of 8% and Park Street's 1.4%.

High-volume (high inventory turnover) businesses, such as grocery stores and discount stores, generally experience low profit margins. In contrast, low-volume businesses, such as jewelry stores or airplane manufacturers, have high profit margins.

6. Asset Turnover

Asset turnover measures how efficiently a company uses its assets to generate sales.

- It is determined by dividing net sales by average total assets.
- The resulting number shows the euros of sales produced by each euro invested in assets.
- Unless seasonal factors are significant, we can use the beginning and ending balance of total assets to determine average total assets.

Assuming that total assets at the beginning of 2028 were €1,446,000, the 2029 and 2028 asset turnover for Quality Department Store and comparative data are shown in **Illustration 15.18**.

Asset turnover shows that in 2029 Quality generated sales of approximately €1.20 for each euro it had invested in assets. The ratio did not change from 2028 to 2029. Quality's asset turnover is below both the industry average of 1.4 times and Park Street's ratio of 1.4 times.

ILLUSTRATION 15.18

Asset turnover

$$\text{Asset Turnover} = \frac{\text{Net Sales}}{\text{Average Total Assets}}$$

Quality Department Store

2029	2028
$\frac{€2{,}097{,}000}{\left[\frac{€1{,}595{,}000 + €1{,}835{,}000}{2}\right]} = 1.2 \text{ times}$	$\frac{€1{,}837{,}000}{\left[\frac{€1{,}446{,}000 + €1{,}595{,}000}{2}\right]} = 1.2 \text{ times}$
Industry average	**Park Street**
1.4 times	**1.4 times**

Asset turnovers vary considerably among industries. For example, a large utility company might have a ratio of 0.4 times, and a large grocery chain might have a ratio of 3.4 times.

7. Return on Assets

An overall measure of profitability is **return on assets**. We compute this ratio by dividing net income by average total assets. The 2029 and 2028 return on assets for Quality Department Store and comparative data are shown in **Illustration 15.19**.

ILLUSTRATION 15.19

Return on assets

$$\text{Return on Assets} = \frac{\text{Net Income}}{\text{Average Total Assets}}$$

Quality Department Store

2029	2028
$\frac{€263{,}800}{\left[\frac{€1{,}595{,}000 + €1{,}835{,}000}{2}\right]} = 15.4\%$	$\frac{€208{,}500}{\left[\frac{€1{,}446{,}000 + €1{,}595{,}000}{2}\right]} = 13.7\%$
Industry average	**Park Street**
8.9%	**2.4%**

Quality's return on assets improved from 2028 to 2029. Its return of 15.4% is very high compared with the department store industry average of 8.9% and Park Street's 2.4%.

8. Return on Ordinary Shareholders' Equity

Another widely used profitability ratio is **return on ordinary shareholders' equity**.

- It measures profitability from the ordinary shareholders' viewpoint.
- This ratio shows how many euros of net income the company earned for each euro invested by the owners.
- We compute it by dividing net income available to ordinary shareholders by average ordinary shareholders' equity.

When a company has preference shares, we must deduct **preference dividend** requirements from net income to compute income available to ordinary shareholders. Similarly, we deduct the par value of preference shares (or call price, if applicable) from total equity to determine the amount of ordinary shareholders' equity used in this ratio.

Assuming that ordinary shareholders' equity at the beginning of 2028 was €667,000, **Illustration 15.20** shows the 2029 and 2028 ratios for Quality Department Store and comparative data.

Quality's rate of return on ordinary shareholders' equity is high at 29.3%, considering an industry average of 18.3% and a rate of 6.4% for Park Street.

ILLUSTRATION 15.20

Return on ordinary shareholders' equity

$$\text{Return on Ordinary Shareholders' Equity} = \frac{\text{Net Income} - \text{Preference Dividends}}{\text{Average Ordinary Shareholders' Equity}}$$

Quality Department Store

2029

$$\frac{€263{,}800 - €0}{\left[\dfrac{€795{,}000 + €1{,}003{,}000}{2}\right]} = 29.3\%$$

2028

$$\frac{€208{,}500 - €0}{\left[\dfrac{€667{,}000 + €795{,}000}{2}\right]} = 28.5\%$$

Industry average	Park Street
18.3%	**6.4%**

Note also that Quality's rate of return on ordinary shareholders' equity (29.3%) is substantially higher than its rate of return on assets (15.4%). The reason is that Quality has made effective use of **leverage**.

- **Leveraging** or **trading on the equity** at a gain means that the company has borrowed money at a lower rate of interest than it is able to earn by using the borrowed money.
- Leverage enables Quality Department Store to use money supplied by non-owners to increase the return to the owners.
- A comparison of the rate of return on total assets with the rate of interest paid for borrowed money indicates the profitability of trading on the equity.

Quality Department Store earns more on its borrowed funds than it has to pay in the form of interest. Thus, the return to shareholders exceeds the return on the assets, due to benefits from the positive leveraging.

9. Earnings per Share (EPS)

Earnings per share (EPS) is a measure of the net income earned on each ordinary share.

- It is computed by dividing net income available to ordinary shareholders by the number of weighted-average ordinary shares outstanding during the year.
- A measure of net income earned on a per share basis provides a useful perspective for determining profitability.

Assuming that there is no change in the number of outstanding shares during 2028 and that the 2029 increase occurred midyear, **Illustration 15.21** shows the net income per share for Quality Department Store for 2029 and 2028.

ILLUSTRATION 15.21

Earnings per share

$$\text{Earnings per Share} = \frac{\text{Net Income} - \text{Preference Dividends}}{\text{Weighted-Average Ordinary Shares Outstanding}}$$

Quality Department Store

2029

$$\frac{€263{,}800 - €0}{\left[\dfrac{270{,}000 + 275{,}400}{2}\right]} = €0.97$$

2028

$$\frac{€208{,}500 - €0}{270{,}000} = €0.77$$

Note that no industry or specific competitive data are presented. Such comparisons are not meaningful because of the wide variations in the number of shares outstanding among companies. The only meaningful EPS comparison is an intracompany trend comparison. Here, Quality's earnings per share increased 20 cents per share in 2029. This represents a 26% increase over the 2028 earnings per share of 77 cents.

The terms "earnings per share" and "net income per share" refer to the amount of net income applicable to each ordinary share. Therefore, in computing EPS, if there are preference dividends declared for the period, we must deduct them from net income to determine income available to the ordinary shareholders.

10. Price-Earnings Ratio

The **price-earnings (P-E) ratio** is a widely used measure of the ratio of the market price of each ordinary share to the earnings per share.

- The price-earnings (P-E) ratio reflects investors' assessments of a company's future earnings.
- We compute it by dividing the market price per share by earnings per share.

Assuming that the market price of Quality Department Store shares is €8 in 2028 and €12 in 2029, the price-earnings ratio computation is as shown in **Illustration 15.22**.

ILLUSTRATION 15.22
Price-earnings ratio

$$\text{Price-Earnings Ratio} = \frac{\text{Market Price per Share}}{\text{Earnings per Share}}$$

Quality Department Store

2029	2028
$\frac{€12.00}{€0.97} = 12.4$ times	$\frac{€8.00}{€0.77} = 10.4$ times
Industry average	Park Street
21.3 times	**17.2 times**

In 2029, each Quality Department Store share sold for 12.4 times the amount that the company earned on each share. Quality's price-earnings ratio is lower than the industry average of 21.3 times, and also lower than the ratio of 17.2 times for Park Street.

11. Payout Ratio

The **payout ratio** measures the percentage of earnings distributed in the form of cash dividends.

- We compute it by dividing cash dividends paid on ordinary shares by net income.
- Companies that have high growth rates generally have low payout ratios because they reinvest most of their net income into the business.

The 2029 and 2028 payout ratios for Quality Department Store are computed as shown in **Illustration 15.23**.

ILLUSTRATION 15.23
Payout ratio

$$\text{Payout Ratio} = \frac{\text{Cash Dividends Paid on Ordinary Shares}}{\text{Net Income}}$$

Quality Department Store

2029	2028
$\frac{€61,200}{€263,800} = 23.2\%$	$\frac{€60,000}{€208,500} = 28.8\%$
Industry average	Park Street
16.1%	**63.0%**

Quality's payout ratio decreased from 2028 to 2029, but is higher than the industry average payout ratio of 16.1%. Park Street's ratio is very high because its net income in 2029 was quite low.

Solvency Ratios

Solvency ratios measure the ability of a company to survive over a long period of time. Long-term creditors and shareholders are particularly interested in a company's ability to pay interest as it comes due and to repay the face value of debt at maturity. Debt to assets and times interest earned are two ratios that provide information about debt-paying ability.

12. Debt to Assets Ratio

The **debt to assets ratio** measures the percentage of the total assets that creditors provide.

- We compute it by dividing total liabilities (both current and non-current liabilities) by total assets.
- This ratio indicates the company's degree of leverage.
- It also provides some indication of the company's ability to withstand losses without impairing the interests of creditors. The higher the percentage of total liabilities to total assets, the greater the risk that the company may be unable to meet its maturing obligations.

The 2029 and 2028 ratios for Quality Department Store and comparative data are as shown in **Illustration 15.24**.

ILLUSTRATION 15.24
Debt to assets ratio

$$\text{Debt to Assets Ratio} = \frac{\text{Total Liabilities}}{\text{Total Assets}}$$

Quality Department Store

2029	2028
$\frac{€832{,}000}{€1{,}835{,}000} = 45.3\%$	$\frac{€800{,}000}{€1{,}595{,}000} = 50.2\%$
Industry average	Park Street
34.2%	**62.0%**

A ratio of 45.3% means that creditors have provided 45.3% of Quality Department Store's total assets. Quality's 45.3% is above the industry average of 34.2%. It is considerably below the high 62.0% ratio of Park Street. The lower the ratio, the more equity "buffer" there is available to the creditors. Thus, from the creditors' point of view, a low ratio of debt to assets is usually desirable. Therefore, the decrease in Quality's debt to assets ratio from 2028 to 2029 would be viewed as a favorable trend.

The adequacy of this ratio is often judged in the light of the company's earnings. Generally, companies with relatively stable earnings (such as public utilities) have higher debt to assets ratios than cyclical companies with widely fluctuating earnings (such as many high-tech companies).

13. Times Interest Earned

Times interest earned provides an indication of the company's ability to meet interest payments as they come due (see **Alternative Terminology**). We compute it by dividing the sum of net income, interest expense, and income tax expense by interest expense. **Illustration 15.25** shows the 2029 and 2028 ratios for Quality Department Store and comparative data.

ALTERNATIVE TERMINOLOGY

Times interest earned is also called *interest coverage*.

- Note that times interest earned uses net income before interest expense and income tax expense.
- This represents the amount available to cover interest.

ILLUSTRATION 15.25
Times interest earned

$$\text{Times Interest Earned} = \frac{\text{Net Income} + \text{Interest Expense} + \text{Income Tax Expense}}{\text{Interest Expense}}$$

Quality Department Store

2029	2028
$\frac{€263{,}800 + €36{,}000 + €168{,}200}{€36{,}000} = 13 \text{ times}$	$\frac{€208{,}500 + €40{,}500 + €139{,}000}{€40{,}500} = 9.6 \text{ times}$
Industry average	Park Street
16.1 times	**2.9 times**

For Quality Department Store, the 2029 amount of €468,000 is computed by taking net income of €263,800 and adding back the €36,000 of interest expense and the €168,200 of income tax expense.

Quality's interest expense is well covered at 13 times. It is less than the industry average of 16.1 times but significantly exceeds Park Street's 2.9 times and is an improvement over the 2028 ratio of 9.6 times.

Summary of Ratios

Illustration 15.26 summarizes the ratios discussed in this chapter. The summary includes the formula and purpose or use of each ratio.

ILLUSTRATION 15.26 Summary of liquidity, profitability, and solvency ratios

Ratio	Formula	Purpose or Use
Liquidity Ratios		
1. Current ratio	$\frac{\text{Current assets}}{\text{Current liabilities}}$	Measures short-term debt-paying ability.
2. Acid-test (quick) ratio	$\frac{\text{Cash + Financial assets at FVTPL + Accounts receivable (net)}}{\text{Current liabilities}}$	Measures immediate short-term liquidity.
3. Accounts receivable turnover	$\frac{\text{Net credit sales}}{\text{Average net accounts receivable}}$	Measures liquidity of accounts receivable.
4. Inventory turnover	$\frac{\text{Cost of goods sold}}{\text{Average inventory}}$	Measures liquidity of inventory.
Profitability Ratios		
5. Profit margin	$\frac{\text{Net income}}{\text{Net sales}}$	Measures net income generated by each currency unit of sales.
6. Asset turnover	$\frac{\text{Net sales}}{\text{Average total assets}}$	Measures how efficiently assets are used to generate sales.
7. Return on assets	$\frac{\text{Net income}}{\text{Average total assets}}$	Measures overall profitability of assets.
8. Return on ordinary shareholders' equity	$\frac{\text{Net income − Preference dividends}}{\text{Average ordinary shareholders' equity}}$	Measures profitability of owners' investment.
9. Earnings per share (EPS)	$\frac{\text{Net income − Preference dividends}}{\text{Weighted-average ordinary shares outstanding}}$	Measures net income earned on each ordinary share.
10. Price-earnings (P-E) ratio	$\frac{\text{Market price per share}}{\text{Earnings per share}}$	Measures the ratio of the market price per share to earnings per share.
11. Payout ratio	$\frac{\text{Cash dividends paid on ordinary shares}}{\text{Net income}}$	Measures percentage of earnings distributed in the form of cash dividends.
Solvency Ratios		
12. Debt to assets ratio	$\frac{\text{Total liabilities}}{\text{Total assets}}$	Measures the percentage of total assets provided by creditors.
13. Times interest earned	$\frac{\text{Net income + Interest expense + Income tax expense}}{\text{Interest expense}}$	Measures ability to meet interest payments as they come due.

DO IT! 2 | Ratio Analysis

The condensed financial statements of John Cully Group, for the years ended June 30, 2029 and 2028, are presented below.

John Cully Group
Statements of Financial Position
June 30

	(in thousands)			
	2029		2028	
Assets				
Intangibles and other assets		€ 876.7		€ 849.3
Property, plant, and equipment (net)		694.2		647.0
Financial assets at amortized cost		12.3		12.6
Current assets				
Prepaid expenses and other current assets	€204.4		€269.2	
Inventory	768.3		653.5	
Accounts receivable (net)	776.6		664.9	
Cash	553.3	2,302.6	611.6	2,199.2
Total assets		€3,885.8		€3,708.1
Equity and Liabilities				
Shareholders' equity—ordinary		€1,708.6		€1,749.0
Non-current liabilities		679.5		637.1
Current liabilities		1,497.7		1,322.0
Total equity and liabilities		€3,885.8		€3,708.1

John Cully Group
Income Statements
For the Year Ended June 30

	(in thousands)	
	2029	2028
Sales revenue	€6,336.3	€5,790.4
Cost of goods sold	1,617.4	1,476.3
Gross profit	4,718.9	4,314.1
Selling and administrative expenses	4,007.6	3,679.0
Operating income	711.3	635.1
Interest expense	13.9	27.1
Income before income taxes	697.4	608.0
Income tax expense	291.3	232.6
Net income	€ 406.1	€ 375.4

Compute the following ratios for 2029 and 2028.

a. Current ratio.

b. Inventory turnover. (Inventory on 6/30/27 was €599.0.)

c. Profit margin.

d. Return on assets. (Assets on 6/30/27 were €3,349.9.)

e. Return on ordinary shareholders' equity. (Equity on 6/30/27 was €1,795.9.)

f. Debt to assets ratio.

g. Times interest earned.

ACTION PLAN

- **Remember that the current ratio includes all current assets. The acid-test ratio uses only cash, financial assets at FVTPL, and net accounts receivable.**
- **Use average balances for turnover ratios like inventory, accounts receivable, as well as return on assets.**

Solution

	2029	2028
a. Current ratio:		
€2,302.6 ÷ €1,497.7 =	1.5:1	
€2,199.2 ÷ €1,322.0 =		1.7:1
b. Inventory turnover:		
€1,617.4 ÷ [(€768.3 + €653.5) ÷ 2] =	2.3 times	
€1,476.3 ÷ [(€653.5 + €599.0) ÷ 2] =		2.4 times
c. Profit margin:		
€406.1 ÷ €6,336.3 =	6.4%	
€375.4 ÷ €5,790.4 =		6.5%
d. Return on assets:		
€406.1 ÷ [(€3,885.8 + €3,708.1) ÷ 2] =	10.7%	
€375.4 ÷ [(€3,708.1 + €3,349.9) ÷ 2] =		10.6%
e. Return on ordinary shareholders' equity:		
(€406.1 − €0) ÷ [(€1,708.6 + €1,749.0) ÷ 2] =	23.5%	
(€375.4 − €0) ÷ [(€1,749.0 + €1,795.9) ÷ 2] =		21.2%
f. Debt to assets ratio:		
(€1,497.7 + €679.5) ÷ €3,885.8 =	56.0%	
(€1,322.0 + €637.1) ÷ €3,708.1 =		52.8%
g. Times interest earned:		
(€406.1 + €291.3 + €13.9) ÷ €13.9 =	51.2 times	
(€375.4 + €232.6 + €27.1) ÷ €27.1 =		23.4 times

Related exercise material: **BE15.9, BE15.10, BE15.11, BE15.12, BE15.13, DO IT! 15.2, E15.5, E15.6, E15.7, E15.8, E15.9, E15.10, and E15.11.**

15.3 Sustainable Income

LEARNING OBJECTIVE 3

Apply the concept of sustainable income.

The value of a company like **Google** (USA) is a function of the amount, timing, and uncertainty of its future cash flows. Google's current and past income statements are particularly useful in helping analysts predict these future cash flows. In using this approach, analysts must make sure that Google's past income numbers reflect its **sustainable income**, that is, do not include unusual (out-of-the-ordinary) revenues, expenses, gains, and losses.

- **Sustainable income** is, therefore, the most likely level of income to be obtained by a company in the future.
- Sustainable income differs from actual net income by the amount of unusual revenues, expenses, gains, and losses included in the current year's income.
- Analysts are interested in sustainable income because it helps them derive an estimate of future earnings without the "noise" of unusual items.

Fortunately, an income statement provides information on sustainable income by separating operating transactions from non-operating transactions. This statement also highlights intermediate components of income such as operating income, income before financing and income taxes, income before income taxes, and income from continuing operations. In addition, information on unusual items such as gains or losses on discontinued items and components of other comprehensive income are disclosed.

Illustration 15.27 presents a statement of comprehensive income for Cruz Textiles for the year 2029. A statement of comprehensive income includes not only net income but a

ILLUSTRATION 15.27

Statement of comprehensive income

Cruz Textiles Statement of Comprehensive Income For the Year Ended 2029	
Sales revenue	$900,000
Cost of goods sold	650,000
Gross profit	250,000
Operating expenses	100,000
Operating income	**150,000**
Other investment income	30,000
Income before financing and income taxes	**180,000**
Interest expense	10,000
Income before income taxes	**170,000**
Income tax expense	24,000
Income from continuing operations	**146,000**
Discontinued operations (net of tax)	**30,000**
Net income	176,000
Other comprehensive income items (net of tax)	**10,000**
Comprehensive income	$186,000

broader measure of income called comprehensive income. The two major unusual items in this statement are discontinued operations and other comprehensive income (highlighted in red). When estimating future cash flows, analysts must consider the implications of each of these components.

In looking at Illustration 15.27, note that Cruz Textiles' two major types of unusual items, discontinued operations and other comprehensive income, are reported net of tax. That is, Cruz first calculates income tax expense before income from continuing operations. Then, it calculates income tax expense related to the discontinued operations and other comprehensive income. The general concept is, "Let the tax follow the income or loss." We discuss discontinued operations and other comprehensive income in more detail next.

Discontinued Operations

Discontinued operations refers to the disposal of a major line of business or geographical area of operations of a business, such as the elimination of a major class of customers or an entire geographic region. For example, to downsize its operations, **General Dynamics Corp.** (USA) sold its missile business to **Hughes Aircraft Co.** (USA) for $450 million. In its income statement, General Dynamics reported the sale in a separate section entitled "Discontinued operations."

- Following the disposal of a major component, the company should report on its income statement both income from continuing operations and income (or loss) from discontinued operations.
- **The income (loss) from discontinued operations consists of two parts: the income (loss) from operations** and **the gain (loss) on disposal of the component.**

To illustrate, assume that during 2029 Acro Energy Ltd. has income before income taxes of NT$800,000. During 2029, Acro discontinued and sold its unprofitable chemical division. The loss in 2029 from chemical operations (net of NT$60,000 taxes) was NT$140,000. The loss on disposal of the chemical division (net of NT$30,000 taxes) was NT$70,000. Assuming a 30% tax rate on income, **Illustration 15.28** shows Acro's statement of comprehensive income presentation (see **Helpful Hint**).

HELPFUL HINT

Observe the dual disclosures: (1) the results of operations of the discontinued division must be eliminated from the results of continuing operations, and (2) the company must also report the disposal of the operation.

Note that the statement uses the caption "Income from continuing operations" and adds a new section "Discontinued operations."

- **The new section reports both the operating loss and the loss on disposal net of applicable income taxes.**
- This presentation clearly indicates the separate effects of continuing operations and discontinued operations on net income.

ILLUSTRATION 15.28

Statement presentation of discontinued operations

Acro Energy Ltd.
Statement of Comprehensive Income (partial)
For the Year Ended December 31, 2029

Income before income taxes		NT$800,000
Income tax expense		240,000
Income from continuing operations		560,000
Discontinued operations		
Loss from operations of chemical division, net of NT$60,000 income tax savings	**NT$140,000**	
Loss from disposal of chemical division, net of NT$30,000 income tax savings	**70,000**	**210,000**
Net income		NT$350,000

Investor Insight Procter & Gamble Co.

Kenneth C. Zirkel/iStockphoto

What Does "Non-Recurring" Really Mean?

Many companies incur restructuring charges as they attempt to reduce costs. They often label these items in the income statement as "non-recurring" charges to suggest that they are isolated events which are unlikely to occur in future periods.

The question for analysts is, are these costs really one-time, "non-recurring" events, or do they reflect problems that the company will be facing for many periods in the future? If they are one-time events, they can be largely ignored when trying to predict future earnings.

But some companies report "one-time" restructuring charges over and over again. For example, toothpaste and other consumer-goods giant **Procter & Gamble Co.** (USA) reported a restructuring charge in 12 consecutive quarters. **Motorola** (USA) had "special" charges in 14 consecutive quarters.

On the other hand, other companies have a restructuring charge only once in a five- or ten-year period. There appears to be no substitute for careful analysis of the numbers that comprise net income.

If a company takes a large restructuring charge, what is the effect on the company's current income statement versus future ones? (Answer is available near the end of the chapter.)

Changes in Accounting Principle

ETHICS NOTE

Changes in accounting principle should result in financial statements that are more informative for statement users. They should *not* be used to artificially improve the reported performance or financial position of the company.

For ease of comparison, users of financial statements expect companies to prepare such statements on a basis **consistent** with the preceding period.

- A **change in accounting principle** occurs when the principle used in the current year is different from the one used in the preceding year.
  - Accounting rules permit a change when management can show that the new principle is preferable to the old principle (see **Ethics Note**). An example is a change in inventory costing methods (such as FIFO to average-cost).

Companies report most changes in accounting principle retroactively. That is, they report both the current period and previous periods using the new principle. As a result, the same principle applies in all periods. This treatment improves the ability to compare results across years.

Comprehensive Income

Most revenues, expenses, gains, and losses are included in net income. However, certain gains and losses bypass net income. Instead, these items are reported as part of a more inclusive earnings measure called comprehensive income. The IASB requires companies to report not only net income but also comprehensive income. **Comprehensive income** is the sum of net income and other comprehensive income items.

Illustration of Comprehensive Income

Accounting standards require that companies adjust most investments in shares and bonds up or down to their market price at the end of each accounting period. For example, assume that during 2029 Stassi AG purchased shares for €10,000 as an investment. At the end of 2029, Stassi was still holding the investment, but the shares' market price was now €8,000. In this case, Stassi is required to reduce the recorded value of its investment by €2,000. The €2,000 difference is an unrealized loss.

Should Stassi include this €2,000 unrealized loss in net income? It depends on whether Stassi classifies the shares as financial assets at FVTPL or FVTOCI.

- A **financial assets at FVTPL** is bought and held primarily for sale in the near term to generate income on short-term price differences.
- Companies report unrealized losses on financial assets at FVTPL in the "Investing" section of the income statement.
- The rationale: It is likely that the company will realize the unrealized loss (or an unrealized gain), so the company should report the loss (gain) as part of net income.

If Stassi did not purchase the investment for trading purposes, it is classified as financial assets at FVTOCI.

- **Financial assets at FVTOCI** are held with the intent of selling them sometime in the future.
- Companies do not include unrealized gains or losses on financial assets at FVTOCI in net income. Instead, they report them as part of "Other comprehensive income."
- Other comprehensive income is not included in net income. It bypasses net income and is recorded as a direct adjustment to equity.

Format

One format for reporting other comprehensive income is to report a statement of comprehensive income. For example, assuming that Stassi AG has a net income of €300,000, the unrealized loss would be reported below net income as shown in **Illustration 15.29**.

ILLUSTRATION 15.29

Lower portion of statement of comprehensive income

Stassi AG
Statement of Comprehensive Income (partial)
For the Year Ended 2029

Net income	€300,000
Other comprehensive income	
Unrealized loss on financial assets at FVTOCI (net of tax)	2,000
Comprehensive income	**€298,000**

Companies also report the unrealized loss as a separate component of equity. To illustrate, assume Stassi AG has ordinary shares of €3,000,000, retained earnings of €1,500,000, and accumulated other comprehensive loss of €2,000. **Illustration 15.30** shows the statement of financial position presentation of the unrealized loss.

ILLUSTRATION 15.30

Unrealized loss in equity section

Stassi AG
Statement of Financial Position (partial)

Equity	
Share capital—ordinary	€3,000,000
Retained earnings	1,500,000
Accumulated other comprehensive loss	**2,000**
Total equity	€4,498,000

Note that the presentation of the accumulated other comprehensive loss is similar to the presentation of the cost of treasury shares in the equity section. (An unrealized gain would be added in this section of the statement of financial position.) Reporting the unrealized gain or loss in the equity section serves two important purposes:

1. It reduces the volatility of net income due to fluctuations in fair value.
2. It informs the financial statement user of the gain or loss that would occur if the company sold the securities at fair value.

Complete Statement of Comprehensive Income

The statement of comprehensive income for Pace AG in **Illustration 15.31** presents the types of items found on this statement, such as net sales, cost of goods sold, operating expenses, and income taxes. In addition, it shows how companies report discontinued operations and other comprehensive income (highlighted in red).

ILLUSTRATION 15.31

Complete statement of comprehensive income

Pace AG
Statement of Comprehensive Income
For the Year Ended December 31, 2029

Net sales		€440,000
Cost of goods sold		260,000
Gross profit		180,000
Operating expenses		110,000
Operating income		70,000
Interest revenue		5,600
Income before financing and income taxes		75,600
Interest expense		9,600
Income before income taxes		66,000
Income tax expense (€66,000 × 30%)		19,800
Income from continuing operations		46,200
Discontinued operations		
Loss from operation of plastics division, net of income tax savings €18,000 (€60,000 × 30%)	**€42,000**	
Gain on disposal of plastics division, net of €15,000 income taxes (€50,000 × 30%)	**35,000**	**7,000**
Net income		**39,200**
Other comprehensive income		
Unrealized gain on financial assets at FVTOCI, net of income taxes (€15,000 × 30%)		**10,500**
Comprehensive income		**€ 49,700**

ACTION PLAN

- **Disclose the income tax effect of each component of income, beginning with income from continuing operations.**

DO IT! 3 | Unusual Items

In its proposed 2029 statement of comprehensive income, AIR plc reports income before income taxes £400,000, loss on operation of discontinued flower division £50,000, and loss on disposal of discontinued flower division £90,000. The income tax rate is 30%. Prepare a correct statement of comprehensive income, beginning with "Income before income taxes."

Solution

AIR plc
Statement of Comprehensive Income (partial)
For the Year Ended December 31, 2029

Income before income taxes		£400,000
Income tax expense (£400,000 × 30%)		120,000
Income from continuing operations		280,000
Discontinued operations		
Loss from operation of flower division, net of £15,000 tax savings	£35,000	
Loss on disposal of flower division, net of £27,000 tax savings	63,000	98,000
Net income		£182,000

Related exercise material: **BE15.14, BE15.15, DO IT! 15.3, E15.12, and E15.13.**

Review and Practice

Learning Objectives Review

1 Apply horizontal analysis and vertical analysis to financial statements.

There are three bases of comparison: (1) intracompany, which compares an item or financial relationship with other data within a company; (2) industry, which compares company data with industry averages; and (3) intercompany, which compares an item or financial relationship of a company with data of one or more competing companies.

Horizontal analysis is a technique for evaluating a series of data over a period of time to determine the increase or decrease that has taken place, expressed as either an amount or a percentage. Vertical analysis is a technique that expresses each item within a financial statement in terms of a percentage of a relevant total or a base amount.

2 Analyze a company's performance using ratio analysis.

The formula and purpose of each ratio is presented in Illustration 15.26.

3 Apply the concept of sustainable income.

Sustainable income analysis is useful in evaluating a company's performance. Sustainable income is the most likely level of income to be obtained by the company in the future. Discontinued operations and other comprehensive income are presented on the statement of comprehensive income to highlight their unusual nature. Items below income from continuing operations must be presented net of tax.

Glossary Review

Accounts receivable turnover A measure of the liquidity of accounts receivable; computed by dividing net credit sales by average net accounts receivable. (p. 15-11).

Acid-test (quick) ratio A measure of a company's immediate short-term liquidity; computed by dividing the sum of cash, financial assets at FVTPL, and net accounts receivable by current liabilities. (p. 15-10).

Asset turnover A measure of how efficiently a company uses its assets to generate sales; computed by dividing net sales by average total assets. (p. 15-13).

Change in accounting principle The use of a principle in the current year that is different from the one used in the preceding year. (p. 15-22).

Comprehensive income The sum of net income and other comprehensive income items. (p. 15-22).

Current ratio A measure used to evaluate a company's liquidity and short-term debt-paying ability; computed by dividing current assets by current liabilities. (p. 15-10).

Debt to assets ratio Measures the percentage of assets provided by creditors; computed by dividing total liabilities by total assets. (p. 15-17).

Discontinued operations The disposal of a separate major line of business or geographical area of operations. (p. 15-21).

Earnings per share (EPS) The net income earned on each ordinary share; computed by dividing net income minus preference dividends (if any) by the number of weighted-average ordinary shares outstanding. (p. 15-15).

Horizontal analysis A technique for evaluating a series of financial statement data over a period of time, to determine the increase (decrease) that has taken place, expressed as either an amount or a percentage. (p. 15-3).

Inventory turnover A measure of the liquidity of inventory; computed by dividing cost of goods sold by average inventory. (p. 15-12).

Leveraging See *Trading on the equity*. (p. 15-15).

Liquidity ratios Measures of the short-term ability of the company to pay its maturing obligations and to meet unexpected needs for cash. (p. 15-9).

Payout ratio Measures the percentage of earnings distributed in the form of cash dividends; computed by dividing cash dividends paid on ordinary shares by net income. (p. 15-16).

Price-earnings (P-E) ratio Measures the ratio of the market price of each ordinary share to the earnings per share; computed by dividing the market price per share by earnings per share. (p. 15-16).

Profitability ratios Measures of the income or operating success of a company for a given period of time. (p. 15-13).

Profit margin Measures the percentage of each currency unit of sales that results in net income; computed by dividing net income by net sales. (p. 15-13).

Ratio An expression of the mathematical relationship between one quantity and another. The relationship may be expressed either as a percentage, a rate, or a simple proportion. (p. 15-9).

Ratio analysis A technique for evaluating financial statements that expresses the relationship between selected financial statement data. (p. 15-9).

Return on assets An overall measure of profitability; computed by dividing net income by average total assets. (p. 15-14).

Return on ordinary shareholders' equity Measures the currency units of net income earned for each currency unit invested by the owners; computed by dividing net income minus preference dividends (if any) by average ordinary shareholders' equity. (p. 15-14).

Solvency ratios Measures of the ability of the company to survive over a long period of time. (p. 15-16).

Sustainable income The most likely level of income to be obtained by a company in the future. (p. 15-20).

Times interest earned Measures a company's ability to meet interest payments as they come due; computed by dividing the sum of net income, interest expense, and income tax expense by interest expense. (p. 15-17).

Trading on the equity Borrowing money at a lower rate of interest than can be earned by using the borrowed money. (p. 15-15).

Vertical analysis A technique for evaluating financial statement data that expresses each item within a financial statement as a percentage of a base amount. (p. 15-6).

Practice Multiple-Choice Questions

1. **(LO 1)** Comparisons of data within a company are an example of the following comparative basis:
   a. Industry averages.
   b. Intracompany.
   c. Intercompany.
   d. Both intracompany and intercompany.

2. **(LO 1)** In horizontal analysis, each item is expressed as a percentage of the:
   a. net income amount.
   b. equity amount.
   c. total assets amount.
   d. base year amount.

3. **(LO 1)** Sammy plc reported net sales of £300,000, £330,000, and £360,000 in the years, 2027, 2028, and 2029, respectively. If 2027 is the base year, what is the trend percentage for 2029?
   a. 77%.
   b. 108%.
   c. 120%.
   d. 130%.

4. **(LO 1)** The following schedule is a display of what type of analysis?

	Amount	Percent
Property, plant, and equipment	€600,000	75%
Current assets	200,000	25%
Total assets	€800,000	

   a. Horizontal analysis.
   b. Differential analysis.
   c. Vertical analysis.
   d. Ratio analysis.

5. **(LO 1)** In vertical analysis, the base amount for depreciation expense is generally:
   a. net sales.
   b. depreciation expense in a previous year.
   c. gross profit.
   d. fixed assets.

6. **(LO 2)** Which of the following measures is an evaluation of a firm's ability to pay current liabilities?
   a. Acid-test ratio.
   b. Current ratio.
   c. Both acid-test and current ratios.
   d. None of the answer choices is correct.

7. **(LO 2)** A measure useful in evaluating the efficiency in managing inventories is:
   a. inventory turnover.
   b. days in inventory.
   c. either the inventory turnover or days in inventory.
   d. None of the answer choices is correct.

Use the following financial statement information as of the end of each year to answer Questions 8–12.

	2029	2028
Inventory	£ 54,000	£ 48,000
Current assets	81,000	106,000
Total assets	382,000	326,000
Current liabilities	27,000	36,000
Total liabilities	102,000	88,000
Share capital—preference	40,000	40,000
Ordinary shareholders' equity	240,000	198,000
Net sales	784,000	697,000
Cost of goods sold	306,000	277,000
Net income	134,000	90,000
Income tax expense	22,000	18,000
Interest expense	12,000	12,000
Dividends paid to preference shareholders	4,000	4,000
Dividends paid to ordinary shareholders	15,000	10,000

8. **(LO 2)** Compute the days in inventory for 2029.
   a. 64.4 days.
   b. 60.8 days.
   c. 6 days.
   d. 24 days.

9. **(LO 2)** Compute the current ratio for 2029.
   a. 1.26:1.
   b. 3.0:1.
   c. 0.80:1.
   d. 3.75:1.

10. **(LO 2)** Compute the profit margin for 2029.
   a. 17.1%.
   b. 18.1%.
   c. 37.9%.
   d. 5.9%.

11. **(LO 2)** Compute the return on ordinary shareholders' equity for 2029.
   a. 47.9%.
   b. 51.7%.
   c. 61.2%.
   d. 59.4%.

12. **(LO 2)** Compute the times interest earned for 2029.
   a. 11.2 times.
   b. 65.3 times.
   c. 14.0 times.
   d. 13.0 times.

13. **(LO 3)** In reporting discontinued operations, the statement of comprehensive income should show in a special section:
   a. gains and losses on the disposal of the discontinued component.
   b. gains and losses from operations of the discontinued component.
   c. gains and losses from operations and the disposal of the discontinued component.
   d. None of the answer choices is correct.

14. **(LO 3)** Scout Ltd. has income before taxes of £400,000, loss on operation of a discontinued division of £40,000, and a £60,000 loss on disposal of a division. If the income tax rate is 25% on all items, the statement of comprehensive income should show income from continuing operations and discontinued operations, respectively, of:

a. £400,000 and £100,000.
b. £400,000 and £75,000.
c. £300,000 and £100,000.
d. £300,000 and £75,000.

Solutions

1. **b.** Comparisons of data within a company are called intracompany comparisons, not (a) industry averages, (c) intercompany comparisons, or (d) both intracompany and intercompany comparisons. Intercompany comparisons are among companies.

2. **d.** Horizontal analysis converts each succeeding year's balance to a percentage of the base year amount, not (a) net income amount, (b) equity amount, or (c) total assets amount.

3. **c.** The trend percentage for 2029 is 120% (£360,000/£300,000), not (a) 77%, (b) 108%, or (d) 130%.

4. **c.** The data in the schedule is a display of vertical analysis because the individual asset items are expressed as a percentage of total assets. The other choices are therefore incorrect. Horizontal analysis is a technique for evaluating a series of data over a period of time.

5. **a.** In vertical analysis, net sales is used as the base amount for income statement items, not (b) depreciation expense in a previous year, (c) gross profit, or (d) fixed assets.

6. **c.** Both the acid-test ratio and the current ratio measure a firm's ability to pay current liabilities. Choices (a) and (b) are correct but (c) is the better answer. Choice (d) is incorrect because there is a correct answer.

7. **c.** Both inventory turnover and days in inventory measure a firm's efficiency in managing inventories. Choices (a) and (b) are correct but (c) is the better answer. Choice (d) is incorrect because there is a correct answer.

8. **b.** Inventory turnover = Cost of goods sold/Average inventory [£306,000/(£54,000 + £48,000/2)] = 6 times. Thus, days in inventory = 60.8 (365/6), not (a) 64.4, (c) 6, or (d) 24 days.

9. **b.** Current ratio = Current assets/Current liabilities (£81,000/£27,000) = 3.0:1, not (a) 1.26:1, (c) 0.80:1, or (d) 3.75:1.

10. **a.** Profit margin = Net income/Net sales (£134,000/£784,000) = 17.1%, not (b) 18.1%, (c) 37.9%, or (d) 5.9%.

11. **d.** Return on ordinary shareholders' equity = Net income (£134,000) − Preference dividends (£4,000)/Average ordinary shareholders' equity [(£240,000 + £198,000)/2] = 59.4%, not (a) 47.9%, (b) 51.7%, or (c) 61.2%.

12. **c.** Times interest earned = Net income + Interest expense + Income tax expense divided by Interest expense [(£134,000 + £12,000 + £22,000)/£12,000] = 14.0 times, not (a) 11.2, (b) 65.3, or (d) 13.0 times.

13. **c.** Gains and losses on the disposal of the discontinued component and gains and losses from operations of the discontinued component are shown in the special section titled discontinued operations. Other comprehensive income items are reported in a separate section after net income on the statement of comprehensive income. Choices (a) and (b) are therefore correct but (c) is the better answer. Choice (d) is incorrect as there is a correct answer.

14. **d.** Income tax expense = 25% × £400,000 = £100,000; therefore, income from continuing operations = £400,000 − £100,000 = £300,000. The loss on discontinued operations is shown net of tax, (£60,000 + £40,000) × 75% = £75,000. The other choices are therefore incorrect.

Practice Brief Exercises

1. **(LO 1)** Using the following data from the comparative statements of financial position of Alfredo SpA, illustrate horizontal analysis. *Prepare horizontal analysis.*

	December 31, 2029	December 31, 2028
Share capital—ordinary	€ 700,000	€ 600,000
Accounts payable	300,000	200,000
Total equity and liabilities	2,000,000	1,800,000

Solution

1.

			Increase or (Decrease)	
	December 31, 2029	December 31, 2028	Amount	Percentage
Share capital—ordinary	€ 700,000	€ 600,000	€100,000	17%*
Accounts payable	300,000	200,000	100,000	50
Total equity and liabilities	2,000,000	1,800,000	200,000	11

*100/600 = 16.7%; 100/200 = 50%; 200/1,800 = 11.1%

Calculate ratios.

2. **(LO 2)** Gonzalez Sports has beginning inventory of £400,000, cost of goods sold of £2,200,000, and days in inventory of 73. What is Gonzalez's inventory turnover and ending inventory?

Solution

2. Days in inventory = 365/Inventory turnover

73 = 365/Inventory turnover

Therefore, inventory turnover = 365/73 = 5.

Inventory turnover = Cost of goods sold/Average inventory

5 = £2,200,000/Average inventory

Therefore, average inventory = £2,200,000/5 = £440,000.

Since beginning inventory is £400,000, ending inventory must be £480,000 because average inventory is £440,000 [(£400,000 + £480,000)/2].

Prepare a discontinued operations section.

3. **(LO 3)** On September 30, Teng Group discontinued its operations in Africa. During the year, the operating gain was ¥100,000 before taxes. On September 1, Teng disposed of its African facilities at a pretax loss of ¥350,000. The applicable tax rate is 30%. Show the discontinued operations section of the income statement (amounts in thousands).

Solution

3.

Teng Group
Income Statement (partial)

Discontinued operations		
Gain from operations of discontinued division, net of ¥30,000 income taxes (¥100,000 × 30%)	¥ 70,000	
Loss from disposal of discontinued division, net of ¥105,000 income tax saving (¥350,000 × 30%)	(245,000)	¥(175,000)

Practice Exercises

Prepare horizontal and vertical analysis.

1. **(LO 1)** The comparative condensed statements of financial position of Roadway Ltd. are presented as follows.

Roadway Ltd.
Condensed Statements of Financial Position
December 31
(in thousands)

	2029	2028
Assets		
Intangibles	NT$ 25,000	NT$ 40,000
Property, plant, and equipment (net)	99,000	90,000
Current assets	76,000	80,000
Total assets	NT$200,000	NT$210,000
Equity and Liabilities		
Equity	NT$ 16,200	NT$ 12,000
Non-current liabilities	143,000	150,000
Current liabilities	40,800	48,000
Total equity and liabilities	NT$200,000	NT$210,000

Instructions

a. Prepare a horizontal analysis of the statement of financial position data for Roadway Ltd. using 2028 as a base.

b. Prepare a vertical analysis of the statement of financial position data for Roadway Ltd. in columnar form for 2029.

Solution

1. a.

Roadway Ltd.
Condensed Statements of Financial Position
December 31
(in thousands)

	2029	2028	Increase (Decrease)	Percent Change from 2028
Assets				
Intangibles	NT$ 25,000	NT$ 40,000	NT$(15,000)	(37.5%)
Property, plant, and equipment (net)	99,000	90,000	9,000	10.0%
Current assets	76,000	80,000	(4,000)	(5.0%)
Total assets	NT$200,000	NT$210,000	NT$(10,000)	(4.8%)
Equity and liabilities				
Equity	NT$ 16,200	NT$ 12,000	NT$ 4,200	35.0%
Non-current liabilities	143,000	150,000	(7,000)	(4.7%)
Current liabilities	40,800	48,000	(7,200)	(15.0%)
Total equity and liabilities	NT$200,000	NT$210,000	NT$(10,000)	(4.8%)

b.

Roadway Ltd.
Condensed Statement of Financial Position
December 31, 2029

	Amount	Percent
Assets		
Intangibles	NT$ 25,000	12.5%
Property, plant, and equipment (net)	99,000	49.5%
Current assets	76,000	38.0%
Total assets	NT$200,000	100.0%
Equity and liabilities		
Equity	NT$ 16,200	8.1%
Non-current liabilities	143,000	71.5%
Current liabilities	40,800	20.4%
Total equity and liabilities	NT$200,000	100.0%

2. **(LO 2)** Rondo plc's comparative statements of financial position are presented below. *Compute ratios.*

Rondo plc
Statements of Financial Position
December 31

	2029	2028
Land	£ 20,000	£ 26,000
Buildings	70,000	70,000
Accumulated depreciation—buildings	(15,000)	(10,000)
Inventory	9,000	7,000
Accounts receivable	21,200	23,400
Cash	5,300	3,700
Total	£110,500	£120,100
Share capital—ordinary	£ 75,000	£ 69,000
Retained earnings	25,130	20,000
Accounts payable	10,370	31,100
Total	£110,500	£120,100

Rondo's 2029 income statement included net sales of £120,000, cost of goods sold of £70,000, and net income of £14,000.

Instructions

Compute the following ratios for 2029.

a. Current ratio.
b. Acid-test ratio.
c. Accounts receivable turnover.
d. Inventory turnover.
e. Profit margin.
f. Asset turnover.
g. Return on assets.
h. Return on ordinary shareholders' equity.
i. Debt to assets ratio.

Solution

2. **a.** (£5,300 + £21,200 + £9,000)/£10,370 = 3.42
   b. (£5,300 + £21,200)/£10,370 = 2.56
   c. £120,000/[(£21,200 + £23,400)/2] = 5.38
   d. £70,000/[(£9,000 + £7,000)/2] = 8.8
   e. £14,000/£120,000 = 11.7%
   f. £120,000/[(£110,500 + £120,100)/2] = 1.04
   g. £14,000/[(£110,500 + £120,100)/2] = 12.1%
   h. £14,000/[(£75,000 + £25,130 + £69,000 + £20,000)/2] = 14.8%
   i. £10,370/£110,500 = 9.4%

Practice Problem

Prepare a statement of comprehensive income.

(LO 3) The events and transactions of Dever SA for the year ending December 31, 2029, resulted in the following data.

Cost of goods sold	R$2,600,000
Net sales	4,400,000
Interest expense	(4,000)
Selling and administrative expenses	1,100,000
Income from operations of plastics division	70,000
Gain from disposal of plastics division	500,000
Unrealized loss on financial assets at FVTOCI	60,000

Analysis reveals that:

1. All items are before the applicable income tax rate of 30%.
2. The plastics division was sold on July 1.
3. All operating data for the plastics division have been segregated.

Instructions

Prepare a statement of comprehensive income for the year.

Solution

Dever SA
Statement of Comprehensive Income
For the Year Ended December 31, 2029

Net sales		R$4,400,000
Cost of goods sold		2,600,000
Gross profit		1,800,000
Selling and administrative expenses		1,100,000
Operating income		700,000
Interest expense		4,000
Income before income taxes		696,000
Income tax expense (R$696,000 × 30%)		208,800
Income from continuing operations		487,200
Discontinued operations		
Income from operations of plastics division, net of R$21,000 income taxes (R$70,000 × 30%)	R$ 49,000	
Gain from disposal of plastics division, net of R$150,000 income taxes (R$500,000 × 30%)	350,000	399,000
Net income		886,200
Other comprehensive income		
Unrealized loss on financial assets at FVTOCI, net of R$18,000 income tax savings (R$60,000 × 30%)		42,000
Comprehensive income		R$ 844,200

Questions

1. **a.** Kurt Gibson believes that the analysis of financial statements is directed at two characteristics of a company: liquidity and profitability. Is Kurt correct? Explain.
   b. Are short-term creditors, long-term creditors, and shareholders interested primarily in the same characteristics of a company? Explain.

2. **a.** Distinguish among the following bases of comparison: (1) intracompany, (2) industry averages, and (3) intercompany.
   b. Give the principal value of using each of the three bases of comparison.

3. Two popular methods of financial statement analysis are horizontal analysis and vertical analysis. Explain the difference between these two methods.

4. **a.** If Nimoy SA had net income of €350,000 in 2028 and it experienced a 22.4% increase in net income for 2029, what is its net income for 2029?
   b. If five cents of every euro of Nimoy revenue is net income in 2028, what is the euro amount of 2028 revenue?

5. What is a ratio? What are the different ways of expressing the relationship of two amounts? What information does a ratio provide?

6. Name the major ratios useful in assessing (a) liquidity and (b) solvency.

7. Maribel Ortiz is puzzled. Her company had a profit margin of 10% in 2029. She feels that this is an indication that the company is doing well. Gordon Liddy, her accountant, says that more information is needed to determine the firm's financial well-being. Who is correct? Why?

8. What do the following classes of ratios measure? (a) Liquidity ratios. (b) Profitability ratios. (c) Solvency ratios.

9. What is the difference between the current ratio and the acid-test ratio?

10. Monte Company, a retail store, has an accounts receivable turnover of 4.5 times. The industry average is 12.5 times. Does Monte have a collection problem with its accounts receivable?

11. Which ratios should be used to help answer the following questions?
    a. How efficient is a company in using its assets to produce sales?
    b. How near to sale is the inventory on hand?
    c. How many dollars of net income were earned for each dollar invested by the owners?
    d. How able is a company to meet interest charges as they come due?

12. The price-earnings ratio of **General Motors** (USA) (automobile builder) was 8, and the price-earnings ratio of **Microsoft** (USA) (computer software) was 38. Which company did the securities market favor? Explain.

13. What is the formula for computing the payout ratio? Would you expect this ratio to be high or low for a growth company?

14. Holding all other factors constant, indicate whether each of the following changes generally signals good or bad news about a company.

a. Increase in profit margin.

b. Decrease in inventory turnover.

c. Increase in the current ratio.

d. Decrease in earnings per share.

e. Increase in price-earnings ratio.

f. Increase in debt to assets ratio.

g. Decrease in times interest earned.

15. The return on assets for Miller Limited is 7.6%. During the same year, Miller's return on ordinary shareholders' equity is 12.8%. What is the explanation for the difference in the two rates?

16. Which two ratios do you think should be of greatest interest to:

a. A pension fund considering the purchase of 20-year bonds?

b. A bank contemplating a short-term loan?

c. An ordinary shareholder?

17. Why must preference dividends be subtracted from net income in computing earnings per share?

18. a. What is meant by trading on the equity?

b. How would you determine the profitability of trading on the equity?

19. Tillman SA has net income of R$160,000, weighted-average ordinary shares outstanding of 50,000, and preference dividends for the period of R$30,000. What is Tillman's earnings per share? Pat Tillman, the president of Tillman SA, believes the computed EPS of the company is high. Comment.

20. Why is it important to report discontinued operations separately from income from continuing operations?

21. You are considering investing in Cherokee Transportation. The company reports 2029 earnings per share of €6.50 on income from continuing operations and €4.75 on net income. Which EPS figure would you consider more relevant to your investment decision? Why?

22. MRT Ltd. reported 2028 earnings per share of £3.20 and had no discontinued operations. In 2029, EPS on income from continuing operations was £2.99, and EPS on net income was £3.49. Is this a favorable trend?

Brief Exercises

Follow the rounding procedures used in the chapter.

Discuss need for comparative analysis.

BE15.1 (LO 1) **Writing** You recently received an email from your Uncle Liam. A portion of the email is as follows.

You know that I have a significant amount of money I saved over the years. I am thinking about starting an investment program. I want to do the investing myself, based on my own research and analysis of financial statements. I know that you are studying accounting, so I have a couple of questions for you. I have heard that different users of financial statements are interested in different characteristics of companies. Is this true, and, if so, why? Also, some of my friends, who are already investing, have told me that comparisons involving a company's financial data can be made on a number of different bases. Can you explain these bases to me?

Instructions

Write an email to your Uncle Liam that answers his questions.

Identify and use tools of financial statement analysis.

BE15.2 (LO 1, 2) Maria Fierro SpA reported the following amounts in 2027, 2028, and 2029.

	2027	2028	2029
Current assets	€220,000	€230,000	€240,000
Current liabilities	€160,000	€170,000	€184,000
Total assets	€500,000	€600,000	€630,000

Instructions

(a) Identify and describe the three tools of financial statement analysis. (b) Perform each of the three types of analysis on Maria Fierro's current assets.

Prepare horizontal analysis.

BE15.3 (LO 1) Using the following data from the comparative statements of financial position of Dotte NV, illustrate horizontal analysis.

	December 31, 2029	December 31, 2028
Inventory	€ 840,000	€ 500,000
Accounts receivable	€ 520,000	€ 350,000
Total assets	€2,500,000	€3,000,000

BE15.4 (LO 1) Using the same data presented above in BE15.3 for Dotte NV, illustrate vertical analysis.

Prepare vertical analysis.

BE15.5 (LO 1) Net income was €550,000 in 2027, €500,000 in 2028, and €525,000 in 2029. What is the percentage of change from (a) 2027 to 2028 and (b) 2028 to 2029? Is the change an increase or a decrease?

Calculate percentage of change.

BE15.6 (LO 1) If Valdamorte plc had net income of £560,000 in 2029 and it experienced a 40% increase in net income over 2028, what was its 2028 net income?

Calculate net income.

BE15.7 (LO 1) Horizontal analysis (trend analysis) percentages for Kemplar Company's sales revenue, cost of goods sold, and expenses are shown below.

Calculate change in net income.

Horizontal Analysis	**2029**	**2028**	**2027**
Sales revenue	97.8	103.3	100.0
Cost of goods sold	103.0	96.0	100.0
Expenses	105.2	99.3	100.0

Did Kemplar's net income increase, decrease, or remain unchanged over the 3-year period?

BE15.8 (LO 1) Vertical analysis (common size) percentages for Dagman Company's sales revenue, cost of goods sold, and expenses are shown below.

Calculate change in net income.

Vertical Analysis	**2029**	**2028**	**2027**
Sales revenue	100.0	100.0	100.0
Cost of goods sold	59.2	62.4	64.5
Expenses	25.0	25.6	27.5

Did Dagman's net income as a percentage of sales increase, decrease, or remain unchanged over the 3-year period? Provide numerical support for your answer.

BE15.9 (LO 2) Selected condensed data taken from a recent statement of financial position of Morino Ltd. are as follows.

Calculate liquidity ratios.

Morino Ltd.
Statement of Financial Position (partial)

Other current assets	£ 6,271,000
Inventory	14,814,000
Accounts receivable (net)	12,545,000
Financial assets at FVTPL	4,947,000
Cash	8,113,000
Total current assets	£46,690,000
Total current liabilities	£41,200,000

What are the (a) working capital, (b) current ratio, and (c) acid-test ratio?

BE15.10 (LO 2) Huntsinger SE has net income of €12.76 million and net revenue of €88 million in 2029. Its assets are €14 million at the beginning of the year and €18 million at the end of the year. What are Huntsinger's (a) asset turnover and (b) profit margin?

Calculate profitability ratios.

BE15.11 (LO 2) Writing The following data are taken from the financial statements of Gladow Company.

Evaluate collection of accounts receivable.

	2029	**2028**
Accounts receivable (net), end of year	€ 550,000	€ 520,000
Net sales on account	3,680,000	3,000,000
Terms for all sales are 1/10, n/60.		

a. Compute for each year (1) the accounts receivable turnover and (2) the average collection period. At the end of 2027, accounts receivable (net) was €480,000.

b. What conclusions about the management of accounts receivable can be drawn from these data?

Evaluate management of inventory.

BE15.12 (LO 2) **Writing** The following data are from the income statements of Charles A.Ş.

	2029	2028
Sales revenue	₺6,420,000	₺6,240,000
Beginning inventory	980,000	860,000
Purchases	4,440,000	4,720,000
Ending inventory	1,020,000	980,000

a. Compute for each year (1) the inventory turnover and (2) the days in inventory.

b. What conclusions concerning the management of the inventory can be drawn from these data?

Calculate amounts from profitability ratios.

BE15.13 (LO 2) Feng Company has equity of HK$4,000,000 and net income of HK$680,000. It has a payout ratio of 22% and a return on assets of 16%. How much did Feng pay in cash dividends, and what were its average assets?

Prepare discontinued operations section of statement of comprehensive income.

BE15.14 (LO 3) On June 30, Blevins ASA discontinued its operations in Europe. During the year, the operating loss was €320,000 before taxes. On September 1, Blevins disposed of its European facilities at a pretax loss of €150,000. The applicable tax rate is 30%. Show the discontinued operations section of the statement of comprehensive income.

Prepare partial statement of comprehensive income.

BE15.15 (LO 3) An inexperienced accountant for Silva AG showed the following in the income statement: income before income taxes €450,000 and unrealized gain on financial assets at FVTOCI (before taxes) €70,000. The unrealized gain on financial assets at FVTOCI and income before income taxes are both subject to a 25% tax rate. Prepare a correct partial statement of comprehensive income, beginning with income before income taxes.

DO IT! Exercises

Prepare horizontal analysis.

DO IT! 15.1 (LO 1) Summary financial information for Rapture Limited is as follows.

	December 31, 2029	December 31, 2028
Plant assets	£ 821,000	£750,000
Current assets	188,000	225,000
Total assets	£1,009,000	£975,000

Compute the amount and percentage changes in 2029 using horizontal analysis, assuming 2028 is the base year.

Compute ratios.

DO IT! 15.2 (LO 2) The condensed financial statements of Soule SpA for the years 2028 and 2029 are presented as follows.

Soule SpA
Statements of Financial Position
December 31

		2029		2028
Intangibles and other assets		€ 530		€ 510
Property, plant, and equipment		420		380
Financial assets at amortized cost		10		10
Current assets				
Prepaid expenses	€120		€160	
Inventory	430		390	
Accounts receivable (net)	470		433	
Cash and cash equivalents	330	1,350	360	1,343
Total assets		€2,310		€2,243
Equity		€1,020		€1,040
Non-current liabilities		390		393
Current liabilities		900		810
Total equity and liabilities		€2,310		€2,243

Soule SpA Income Statements For the Years Ended December 31		
	2029	2028
Sales revenue	€4,000	€3,600
Cost of goods sold	984	895
Gross profit	3,016	2,705
Selling and administrative expenses	2,400	2,330
Operating income	616	375
Interest expense	10	20
Income before income taxes	606	355
Income tax expense	242	142
Net income	€ 364	€ 213

Compute the following ratios for 2029 and 2028.

a. Current ratio.

b. Inventory turnover. (Inventory on 12/31/27 was €326.)

c. Profit margin.

d. Return on assets. (Assets on 12/31/27 were €2,100.)

e. Return on ordinary shareholders' equity. (Equity on 12/31/27 was €960.)

f. Debt to assets ratio.

g. Times interest earned.

Prepare statement of comprehensive income including unusual items.

DO IT! 15.3 (LO 3) In its proposed 2029 income statement, Grinders Limited reports income before income taxes £500,000, income taxes £160,000 (not including unusual items), loss on operation of discontinued music division £60,000, and gain on disposal of discontinued music division £50,000, and unrealized loss on financial assets at FVTOCI of £30,000. The income tax rate is 32%. Prepare a correct partial statement of comprehensive income beginning with income before income taxes.

Exercises

Follow the rounding procedures used in the chapter.

Prepare horizontal analysis.

E15.1 (LO 1) Financial information for Gallup SA is presented below.

	December 31, 2029	December 31, 2028
Plant assets (net)	€396,000	€320,000
Current assets	128,000	110,000
Share capital—ordinary, €1 par	159,000	115,000
Retained earnings	135,300	150,000
Non-current liabilities	138,700	95,000
Current liabilities	91,000	70,000

Instructions

Prepare a schedule showing a horizontal analysis for 2029 using 2028 as the base year.

Prepare vertical analysis.

E15.2 (LO 1) Operating data for Conard Limited are presented below.

	2029	2028
Net sales	£750,000	£600,000
Cost of goods sold	480,000	408,000
Selling expenses	105,000	84,000
Administrative expenses	75,000	54,000
Income tax expense	36,000	18,000
Net income	54,000	36,000

Instructions

Prepare a schedule showing a vertical analysis for 2029 and 2028.

Prepare horizontal and vertical analyses.

E15.3 (LO 1) The comparative condensed statements of financial position of Garcia SLU are presented below.

Garcia SLU
Comparative Condensed Statements of Financial Position
December 31

	2029	2028
Assets		
Intangibles	€ 24,000	€ 40,000
Property, plant, and equipment (net)	100,000	92,000
Current assets	76,000	82,000
Total assets	€200,000	€214,000
Equity and liabilities		
Equity	€ 20,000	€ 16,000
Non-current liabilities	140,000	150,000
Current liabilities	40,000	48,000
Total equity and liabilities	€200,000	€214,000

Instructions

a. Prepare a horizontal analysis of the statement of financial position data for Garcia using 2028 as a base.

b. Prepare a vertical analysis of the statement of financial position data for Garcia in columnar form for 2029.

Prepare horizontal and vertical analyses.

E15.4 (LO 1) Here are the comparative condensed income statements of Delaney Corporation.

Delaney Corporation
Condensed Income Statements
For the Years Ended December 31

	2029	2028
Net sales	$598,000	$500,000
Cost of goods sold	477,000	420,000
Gross profit	121,000	80,000
Operating expenses	80,000	44,000
Net income	$ 41,000	$ 36,000

Instructions

a. Prepare a horizontal analysis of the income statement data for Delaney Corporation, using 2028 as a base. (Show the amounts of increase or decrease.)

b. Prepare a vertical analysis of the income statement data for Delaney Corporation for both years.

Compute liquidity ratios and compare results.

E15.5 (LO 2) Nordstrom, Inc. (USA), operates department stores in numerous states. The following is selected financial statement data for a recent year.

Nordstrom, Inc.
Statement of Financial Position (partial)

(in millions)	End-of-Year	Beginning-of-Year
Other current assets	$ 239	$ 227
Prepaid expenses	87	80
Merchandise inventory	1,531	1,360
Accounts receivable (net)	2,177	2,129
Cash and cash equivalents	1,194	1,285
Total current assets	$5,228	$5,081
Total current liabilities	$2,541	$2,226

For the year, net sales were $12,166 and cost of goods sold was $7,737 (in millions).

Instructions

a. Compute the four liquidity ratios at the end of the year.

b. Using the data in the chapter, compare Nordstrom's liquidity with (1) that of Park Street, and (2) the industry averages for department stores.

E15.6 (LO 2) Bennis SA had the following transactions occur involving current assets and current liabilities during February 2029.

Perform current and acid-test ratio analysis.

Feb.	3	Accounts receivable of R$15,000 are collected.
	7	Equipment is purchased for R$28,000 cash.
	11	Paid R$3,000 for a 1-year insurance policy.
	14	Accounts payable of R$12,000 are paid.
	18	Cash dividends of R$5,000 are declared.

Additional information:

1. As of February 1, 2029, current assets were R$140,000, and current liabilities were R$50,000.

2. As of February 1, 2029, current assets included R$10,000 of inventory and R$5,000 of prepaid expenses.

Instructions

a. Compute the current ratio as of the beginning of the month and after each transaction.

b. Compute the acid-test ratio as of the beginning of the month and after each transaction.

E15.7 (LO 2) Willingham Ltd. has the following comparative statements of financial position data.

Compute selected ratios.

Willingham Ltd.
Statements of Financial Position
December 31

	2029	2028
Plant assets (net)	£205,000	£190,000
Inventory	60,000	50,000
Accounts receivable (net)	70,000	50,000
Cash	10,000	30,000
	£345,000	£320,000
Share capital—ordinary, £10 par	£140,000	£120,000
Retained earnings	55,000	40,000
Mortgage payable (6%)	100,000	100,000
Accounts payable	50,000	60,000
	£345,000	£320,000

Additional information for 2029:

1. Net income was £28,000.

2. Sales on account were £418,000. Sales returns and allowances were £22,000.

3. Cost of goods sold was £190,000.

Instructions

Compute the following ratios at December 31, 2029.

a. Current ratio.

b. Acid-test ratio.

c. Accounts receivable turnover.

d. Inventory turnover.

E15.8 (LO 2) Selected comparative statement data for Molini Products are presented below. All statement of financial position data are as of December 31.

Compute selected ratios.

	2029	2028
Net sales	£700,000	£680,000
Cost of goods sold	480,000	400,000
Interest expense	7,000	5,000
Net income	42,000	34,000
Accounts receivable	120,000	100,000
Inventory	85,000	75,000
Total assets	580,000	540,000
Total ordinary shareholders' equity	425,000	325,000

Instructions

Compute the following ratios for 2029.

a. Profit margin.

b. Asset turnover.

c. Return on assets.

d. Return on ordinary shareholders' equity.

Compute selected ratios.

E15.9 (LO 2) The income statement for Christiansen A/S appears below.

Christiansen A/S
Income Statement
For the Year Ended December 31, 2029

Net sales	€400,000
Cost of goods sold	235,000
Gross profit	165,000
Expenses (including €14,000 interest and €17,000 income taxes)	105,000
Net income	€ 60,000

Additional information:

1. The weighted-average ordinary shares outstanding in 2029 were 32,000 shares.
2. The market price of Christiansen A/S was €10.80 per share at December 31, 2029.
3. Cash dividends of €20,000 were paid, €5,000 of which were to preference shareholders.

Instructions

Compute the following ratios for 2029.

a. Earnings per share.

b. Price-earnings ratio.

c. Payout ratio.

d. Times interest earned.

Compute amounts from ratios.

E15.10 (LO 2) Rees Company experienced a fire on December 31, 2029, in which its financial records were partially destroyed. It has been able to salvage some of the records and has ascertained the following balances.

	December 31, 2029	December 31, 2028
Inventory	€200,000	€180,000
Accounts receivable (net)	73,000	126,000
Cash	30,000	10,000
Share capital—ordinary, €100 par	400,000	400,000
Retained earnings	134,000	122,000
Accounts payable	50,000	90,000
Notes payable	30,000	60,000

Additional information:

1. The inventory turnover is 3.4 times.
2. The return on ordinary shareholders' equity is 25%.
3. The accounts receivable turnover is 8.8 times.
4. The return on assets is 20%.
5. Total assets at December 31, 2028, were €650,000.

Instructions

Compute the following for Rees Company.

a. Cost of goods sold for 2029.

b. Net sales (credit) for 2029.

c. Net income for 2029.

d. Total assets at December 31, 2029.

E15.11 (LO 2) Yadier NV's comparative statements of financial position are presented below.

Compute ratios.

Yadier NV
Statements of Financial Position
December 31

	2029	2028
Land	€ 20,000	€ 26,000
Buildings	70,000	70,000
Accumulated depreciation—buildings	(15,000)	(10,000)
Inventory	10,000	7,000
Accounts receivable	22,000	24,000
Cash	4,300	3,700
Total assets	€111,300	€120,700
Share capital—ordinary	€ 72,000	€ 69,000
Retained earnings	24,300	20,600
Accounts payable	15,000	31,100
Total equity and liabilities	€111,300	€120,700

Yadier's 2029 income statement included net sales of €100,000, cost of goods sold of €60,350, and net income of €14,000.

Instructions

Compute the following ratios for 2029.

a. Current ratio.

b. Acid-test ratio.

c. Accounts receivable turnover.

d. Inventory turnover.

e. Profit margin.

f. Asset turnover.

g. Return on assets.

h. Return on ordinary shareholders' equity.

i. Debt to assets ratio.

E15.12 (LO 3) **Writing** For its fiscal year ending October 31, 2029, Douglas Limited reports the following partial data shown below.

Prepare an income statement.

Income before income taxes	£550,000
Income tax expense (30% × £400,000)	120,000
Income before discontinued operations	430,000
Loss on discontinued division	150,000
Net income	£280,000

The loss on discontinued division consists of £60,000 loss from operations of the division and £90,000 loss on disposal of the division. The income tax rate is 30% on all items.

Instructions

a. Prepare a correct statement of comprehensive income, beginning with income before income taxes.

b. Explain in an email why the income statement data are misleading.

E15.13 (LO 3) Trayer plc has income from continuing operations of £290,000 for the year ended December 31, 2029. It also has the following items (before considering income taxes).

Prepare statement of comprehensive income.

1. An unrealized loss of £80,000 on financial assets at FVTOCI.
2. A gain of £30,000 on the discontinuance of a division (comprised of a £10,000 loss from operations and a £40,000 gain on disposal).
3. A correction of an error in last year's financial statements that resulted in a £20,000 understatement of 2028 income before income taxes.

Assume all items are subject to income taxes at a 20% tax rate.

Instructions

Prepare a statement of comprehensive income, beginning with income from continuing operations.

Common-size analysis and trend analysis.

E15.14 (LO 1) The relevant data of Jiajia Company for the past three years are as follows:

	Common-size analysis			Trend analysis		
	2028	**2029**	**2030**	**2028**	**2029**	**2030**
Sales revenue	100	100	100	100	110	120
Cost of goods sold	50	75	80	100	?	?
Operating expenses	10	?	?	100	143	210

Instructions

Compute the missing data and explain the Jiajia company's profit trend over the past three years?

Compute current ratio and quick ratio.

E15.15 (LO 2) Dongshan Company managed its inventory using the perpetual inventory system and had three independent purchase/sale inventory situations as follow:

Instructions

a. Dongshan Company had $540,000 in working capital at the end of 2029. On January 1, 2030, it purchased goods $600,000 on credit and sold them on credit at cost plus a 30% profit. After these two transactions were included at the beginning of 2030, its current ratio was 2. What was the company's current ratio at the end of 2029 ?

b. Before the $200,000 credit purchase transaction, Dongshan Company had a current ratio of 2.5 and a quick ratio of 1.5. However, after the credit purchase transaction, the current ratio became 2. What would the quick ratio become after the credit purchase transaction?

c. If the original current ratio is 1.13 and quick ratio is 0.93, and a $100 inventory is purchased on credit, and half of the inventory is immediately sold on credit for $70, what is the impact of these transactions on the current ratio and quick ratio?

Problems

Follow the rounding procedures used in the chapter.

Prepare vertical analysis and comment on profitability.

P15.1 (LO 1, 2) Writing Comparative statement data for Lionel Company and Barrymore Company, two competitors, appear below. All statement of financial position data are as of December 31, 2029, and December 31, 2028.

	Lionel Company		Barrymore Company	
	2029	**2028**	**2029**	**2028**
Net sales	£1,549,035		£339,038	
Cost of goods sold	1,053,345		237,325	
Operating expenses	263,336		77,979	
Interest expense	7,745		2,034	
Income tax expense	61,960		8,476	
Plant assets (net)	596,920	£575,610	142,842	£128,927
Current assets	401,584	388,020	86,450	82,581
Share capital—ordinary, £5 par	578,765	578,765	137,435	137,435
Retained earnings	252,224	225,358	55,528	47,430
Non-current liabilities	102,500	84,000	16,711	11,989
Current liabilities	65,015	75,507	19,618	14,654

Instructions

a. Prepare a vertical analysis of the 2029 income statement data for Lionel Company and Barrymore Company in columnar form.

b. Comment on the relative profitability of the companies by computing the return on assets and the return on ordinary shareholders' equity for both companies.

b. Return on assets—Lionel 16.6%

P15.2 (LO 2) The comparative statements of Larker Tool SA are presented below.

Compute ratios from statement of financial position and income statement.

Larker Tool SA
Income Statement
For the Years Ended December 31

	2029	2028
Net sales	R$1,818,500	R$1,750,500
Cost of goods sold	1,011,500	996,000
Gross profit	807,000	754,500
Selling and administrative expense	516,000	479,000
Income from operations	291,000	275,500
Interest expense	15,000	14,000
Income before income taxes	276,000	261,500
Income tax expense	84,000	77,000
Net income	R$ 192,000	R$ 184,500

Larker Tool SA
Statements of Financial Position
December 31

	2029		2028	
Assets				
Plant assets (net)		R$600,300		R$520,300
Current assets				
Inventory	R$110,950		R$115,500	
Accounts receivable (net)	105,750		102,800	
Financial assets at FVTPL	69,000		50,000	
Cash	60,100	345,800	64,200	332,500
Total assets		R$946,100		R$852,800
Equity and Liabilities				
Equity				
Share capital—ordinary (R$5 par)		R$300,000		R$300,000
Retained earnings		242,600		165,400
Total equity		542,600		465,400
Bonds payable		200,000		200,000
Current liabilities				
Accounts payable		160,000		145,400
Income taxes payable		43,500		42,000
Total current liabilities		203,500		187,400
Total liabilities		403,500		387,400
Total equity and liabilities		R$946,100		R$852,800

All sales were on account.

Instructions

Compute the following ratios for 2029. (Weighted-average ordinary shares in 2029 were 60,000.)

a. Earnings per share.
b. Return on ordinary shareholders' equity.
c. Return on assets.
d. Current ratio.
e. Acid-test ratio.
f. Accounts receivable turnover.
g. Inventory turnover.
h. Times interest earned.
i. Asset turnover.
j. Debt to assets ratio.

c. Return on assets 21.3%

Perform ratio analysis, and evaluate financial position and operating results.

P15.3 (LO 2) **Writing** Condensed statement of financial position and income statement data for Clarence Limited appear below.

Clarence Limited
Statements of Financial Position
December 31

	2029	2028	2027
Plant and equipment (net)	£400,000	£370,000	£358,000
Financial assets at amortized cost	75,000	70,000	45,000
Other current assets	90,000	95,000	64,000
Accounts receivable (net)	50,000	45,000	48,000
Cash	25,000	20,000	18,000
Total assets	£640,000	£600,000	£533,000
Share capital—ordinary, £10 par	£345,000	£315,000	£300,000
Retained earnings	145,000	123,000	113,000
Non-current liabilities	80,000	87,000	50,000
Current liabilities	70,000	75,000	70,000
Total equity and liabilities	£640,000	£600,000	£533,000

Clarence Limited
Income Statement
For the Years Ended December 31

	2029	2028
Sales revenue	£740,000	£700,000
Less: Sales returns and allowances	40,000	60,000
Net sales	700,000	640,000
Cost of goods sold	420,000	400,000
Gross profit	280,000	240,000
Operating expenses (including income taxes)	236,000	210,000
Net income	£ 44,000	£ 30,000

Additional information:

1. The market price of Clarence's ordinary shares was £4.00, £5.00, and £7.00 for 2027, 2028, and 2029, respectively.
2. All dividends were paid in cash.

Instructions

a. Compute the following ratios for 2028 and 2029.
   1. Profit margin.
   2. Asset turnover.
   3. Earnings per share. (Weighted-average ordinary shares in 2029 were 32,000 and in 2028 were 31,000.)
   4. Price-earnings ratio.
   5. Payout ratio.
   6. Debt to assets ratio.

b. Based on the ratios calculated, discuss briefly the improvement or lack thereof in financial position and operating results from 2028 to 2029 of Clarence Limited.

a. 2. Asset turnover 1.1 times both years

Compute ratios, and comment on overall liquidity and profitability.

P15.4 (LO 2) Financial information for Ernie Bishop Company is presented below.

Ernie Bishop Company
Statements of Financial Position
December 31

Assets	**2029**	**2028**
Land	€130,000	€130,000
Building and equipment (net)	168,000	175,000
Prepaid expenses	29,000	23,000
Inventory	125,000	135,000
Accounts receivable (net)	98,000	80,000
Financial assets at FVTPL	52,000	40,000
Cash	70,000	65,000
Total assets	€672,000	€648,000
Equity and Liabilities		
Share capital—ordinary, €10 par	€200,000	€200,000
Retained earnings	130,000	116,000
Bonds payable, due 2032	150,000	150,000
Notes payable (long-term)	100,000	100,000
Accounts payable	48,000	42,000
Accrued liabilities	44,000	40,000
Total equity and liabilities	€672,000	€648,000

Ernie Bishop Company
Income Statement
For the Years Ended December 31

	2029	**2028**
Net sales	€858,000	€798,000
Cost of goods sold	611,000	575,000
Gross profit	247,000	223,000
Operating expenses	204,500	181,000
Net income	€ 42,500	€ 42,000

Additional information:

1. Inventory at the beginning of 2028 was €118,000.
2. Total assets at the beginning of 2028 were €632,000.
3. No ordinary share transactions occurred during 2028 or 2029.
4. All sales were on account.
5. Accounts receivable (net) at the beginning of 2028 were €88,000.
6. Notes payable are classified as a current liability.

Instructions

a. Indicate, by using ratios, the change in liquidity and profitability of Ernie Bishop Company from 2028 to 2029. (*Note:* Not all profitability ratios can be computed.)

b. Given below are three independent situations and a ratio that may be affected. For each situation, compute the affected ratio (1) as of December 31, 2029, and (2) as of December 31, 2030, after giving effect to the situation.

b. 1. Return on equity: 2029 13.2%, 2030 11.2%

Situation	Ratio
1. 18,000 ordinary shares were sold at par on July 1, 2030. Net income for 2030 was €50,000.	Return on ordinary shareholders' equity
2. All of the notes payable were paid in 2030. The only change in liabilities was that the notes payable were paid. Total assets on December 31, 2030, were €700,000.	Debt to assets ratio
3. Market price of ordinary shares was €9 on December 31, 2029, and €12.50 on December 31, 2030. Net income for 2030 was €50,000.	Price-earnings ratio

Compute selected ratios, and compare liquidity, profitability, and solvency for two companies.

P15.5 (LO 2) Selected financial data of **Target** (USA) and **Walmart Inc.** (USA) for a recent year are presented below (in millions).

	Target	Walmart
	Income Statement Data for Year	
Net sales	$72,596	$476,294
Cost of goods sold	51,160	358,069
Selling and administrative expenses	16,816	91,353
Other operating income (expenses)	(391)	(410)
Interest expense	1,126	2,335
Income tax expense	1,132	8,105
Net income	$ 1,971	$ 16,022
	Statement of Financial Position Data (End of Year)	
Non-current assets	$32,980	$143,566
Current assets	11,573	61,185
Total assets	$44,553	$204,751
Total equity	$16,231	$ 81,339
Non-current liabilities	15,545	54,067
Current liabilities	12,777	69,345
Total equity and liabilities	$44,553	$204,751
	Beginning-of-Year Balances	
Total assets	$48,163	$203,105
Total equity	16,558	81,738
Current liabilities	14,031	71,818
Total liabilities	31,605	131,287
	Other Data	
Average net accounts receivable	$2,921	$ 6,723
Average inventory	8,335	44,331
Net cash provided by operating activities	6,520	23,257

Instructions

a. For each company, compute the following ratios.

a. 4. Inventory turnover Target 6.1

1. Current ratio.
2. Accounts receivable turnover.
3. Average collection period.
4. Inventory turnover.
5. Days in inventory.
6. Profit margin.
7. Asset turnover.
8. Return on assets.
9. Return on ordinary shareholders' equity.
10. Debt to assets ratio.
11. Times interest earned.

b. Compare the liquidity, profitability, and solvency of the two companies.

P15.6 (LO 2) The comparative statements of Beulah Limited are presented below.

Compute numerous ratios.

Beulah Limited
Income Statement
For the Years Ended December 31

	2029	2028
Net sales (all on account)	£500,000	£420,000
Expenses		
Cost of goods sold	315,000	254,000
Selling and administrative	120,800	114,800
Interest expense	7,500	6,500
Income tax expense	20,000	15,000
Total expenses	463,300	390,300
Net income	£ 36,700	£ 29,700

Beulah Limited
Statements of Financial Position
December 31

	2029	2028
Assets		
Plant assets (net)	£423,000	£383,000
Current assets		
Inventory	80,000	60,000
Accounts receivable (net)	85,000	75,000
Financial assets at FVTPL	18,000	15,000
Cash	21,000	18,000
Total current assets	204,000	168,000
Total assets	£627,000	£551,000
Equity and Liabilities		
Equity		
Share capital—ordinary (£5 par)	£150,000	£150,000
Retained earnings	223,000	200,000
Total equity	373,000	350,000
Non-current liabilities		
Bonds payable	120,000	80,000
Current liabilities		
Accounts payable	122,000	110,000
Income taxes payable	12,000	11,000
Total current liabilities	134,000	121,000
Total liabilities	254,000	201,000
Total equity and liabilities	£627,000	£551,000

Additional data:

The ordinary shares recently sold at £19.50 per share.

Instructions

Compute the following ratios for 2029.

a. Current ratio.
b. Acid-test ratio.
c. Accounts receivable turnover.
d. Inventory turnover.
e. Profit margin.
f. Asset turnover.
g. Return on assets.
h. Return on ordinary shareholders' equity.
i. Earnings per share.
j. Price-earnings ratio.
k. Payout ratio.
l. Debt to assets ratio.
m. Times interest earned.

f. Asset turnover 0.85 times

Compute missing information given a set of ratios.

P15.7 (LO 2) Presented below is an incomplete income statement and incomplete comparative statements of financial position of Bondi ASA.

Bondi ASA
Income Statement
For the Year Ended December 31, 2029

Net sales	€10,500,000
Cost of goods sold	?
Gross profit	?
Operating expenses	1,500,000
Income from operations	?
Interest expense	?
Income before income taxes	?
Income tax expense	550,000
Net income	€ ?

Bondi ASA
Statements of Financial Position
December 31

	2029	2028
Assets		
Plant assets (net)	€4,620,000	€4,355,000
Current assets		
Inventory	?	1,720,000
Accounts receivable (net)	?	1,050,000
Cash	480,000	375,000
Total current assets	?	3,145,000
Total assets	€ ?	€7,500,000
Equity and Liabilities		
Share capital—ordinary, €1 par	€3,000,000	€3,000,000
Retained earnings	400,000	375,000
Total equity	3,400,000	3,375,000
Long-term notes payable	?	3,300,000
Current liabilities	?	825,000
Total liabilities	?	4,125,000
Total equity and liabilities	€ ?	€7,500,000

Additional information:

1. The accounts receivable turnover for 2029 is 8 times.
2. All sales are on account.
3. The profit margin for 2029 is 14.5%.
4. Return on assets is 20% for 2029.
5. The current ratio on December 31, 2029, is 2.5.
6. The inventory turnover for 2029 is 4.9 times.

Instructions

Compute the missing information given the ratios above. Show computations. (*Note:* Start with one ratio and derive as much information as possible from it before trying another ratio. List all missing amounts under the ratio used to find the information.)

Prepare statement of comprehensive income with discontinued operations.

P15.8 (LO 3) Violet Bick SA owns a number of cruise ships and a chain of hotels. The hotels, which have not been profitable, were discontinued on September 1, 2029. The 2029 operating results for the company were as follows.

Operating revenues	€12,900,000
Operating expenses	8,700,000
Operating income	€ 4,200,000

Analysis discloses that these data include the operating results of the hotel chain, which were operating revenues €2,000,000 and operating expenses €2,500,000. The hotels were sold at a gain of €300,000 before taxes. This gain is not included in the operating results. During the year, the company had an unrealized gain on financial assets at FVTOCI of €150,000. In 2029, the company had other expense of €200,000, which is not included in the operating results. The company is in the 30% income tax bracket.

Instructions

Prepare a condensed statement of comprehensive income.

Comprehensive income €3,115,000

Prepare statement of comprehensive income.

P15.9 (LO 3) The ledger of Gower Limited at December 31, 2029, contains the following summary data.

Net sales	£1,580,000	Cost of goods sold	£1,100,000
Selling expenses	70,000	Administrative expenses	90,000
Interest expense	(6,000)		

Your analysis reveals the following additional information that is not included in the above data.

1. The entire puzzles division was discontinued on August 31. The income from operations for this division before income taxes was £15,000. The puzzles division was sold at a loss of £74,000 before income taxes.
2. The company had an unrealized gain on financial assets at FVTOCI of £120,000 before income taxes for the year.
3. The income tax rate on all items is 30%.

Instructions

Prepare a statement of comprehensive income for the year ended December 31, 2029. Use the format illustrated in the Practice Problem.

Comprehensive income £262,500

Error correction and ratio computation.

P15.10 (LO 2) Company A uses a calendar year system and a periodic inventory system. The following is a partial financial statement of Company A for years X4 and X5:

	Year X4	Year X5
Sales Revenue (all on credit)	$1,000,000	$1,200,000
Gross Profit	550,000	600,000
Operating Profit	200,000	300,000
Net Income	100,000	140,000
Beginning Inventory	220,000	300,000
Ending Inventory	300,000	420,000
Beginning Accounts Receivable	150,000	250,000
Ending Accounts Receivable	250,000	350,000

Instructions

(The following questions are independent and do not affect each other.)

a. Assume Company A undervalued its beginning inventory by $40,000 in year X5 and overvalued its ending inventory by $60,000. If the above inventory error had not occurred, what would the inventory turnover be for year X5?

b. Assume Company A undervalued its sales revenue by $50,000 in year X4, and this amount was collected in year X5. In year X5, sales revenue was overvalued by $100,000. If the above error had not occurred, what would the average collection days for accounts receivable in year X5 (assuming a year has 360 days) be?

c. Assume there was an accounts receivable of $60,000 in year X5 that was confirmed uncollectible due to the customer's bankruptcy, but the company negligently failed to write off the allowance for doubtful accounts. How would the above error affect the net accounts receivable turnover (increase, decrease, or remain unchanged)? Please provide reasons to support your answer.

Compute financial ratios and assess financial position.

P15.11 (LO 2) The following is a partial financial record of Bali Company for 2030:

	12/31/2029	12/31/2030		2030
Quick assets	$300,000	$280,000	Net sales	$1,050,000
Current liability	400,000	400,000	Selling expense	120,000
Inventory	300,000	350,000	Gross profit	400,000
Bank deposits	180,000	130,000	Income before income taxes	100,000
Fixed assets (net)	250,000	450,000	Interest expense	200,000
Accumulated depreciation	120,000	140,000	Income tax expense	25,000
Total assets	900,000	1,100,000		
Prepaid expense	50,000	20,000		
Equity	450,000	550,000		

Instructions

a. Based on the above information, compute the following financial ratios of Bali Company for 2030.

1. Times interest earned.
2. Return on assets.
3. Current ratio.
4. Financial leverage index.
5. Fixed asset turnover.

b. Based on the above financial ratios, assess the financial condition of Bali Company in 2030.

Expand Your Critical Thinking

Financial Reporting Problem: TSMC, Ltd. (TWN)

CT15.1 Your parents are considering investing in **TSMC** ordinary shares. They ask you, as an accounting expert, to make an analysis of the company for them. TSMC's financial statements are presented in Appendix A. The complete annual report, including the notes to the financial statements, is available at the company's website.

The company's 2018 ending total assets are NT$2,090,128.0 and its ending ordinary share equity is NT$1,677,496.4 (all amounts in millions).

Instructions

(Follow the approach in the chapter for rounding numbers.)

a. Compute for 2020 and 2019 the (1) profit margin, (2) asset turnover, (3) return on assets, and (4) return on ordinary shareholders' equity. How would you evaluate TSMC's profitability?

b. Compute for 2020 and 2019 the (1) debt to assets ratio and (2) times interest earned. How would you evaluate TSMC's long-term solvency?

c. What information outside the annual report may also be useful to your parents in making a decision about TSMC?

Comparative Analysis Problem: Nestlé SA (CHE) vs. Delfi Limited (SGP)

CT15.2 **Nestlé**'s financial statements are presented in Appendix B. Financial statements of **Delfi Limited** are presented in Appendix C.

Instructions

a. Based on the information contained in the 2020 financial statements, determine each of the following for each company for the most recent fiscal year shown.

1. The percentage increase (decrease) in (i) net sales and (ii) net income.
2. The percentage increase in (i) total assets and (ii) total ordinary shareholders' equity.

b. What conclusions concerning the two companies can be drawn from these data?

Decision-Making Across the Organization

CT15.3 As the chartered public accountant for Bonita Ltd., you have been asked to develop some key ratios from the comparative financial statements. This information is to be used to convince creditors that the company is solvent and will continue as a going concern. The data requested and the computations developed from the financial statements follow.

	2029	2028
Current ratio	3.4 times	2.1 times
Acid-test ratio	.8 times	1.3 times
Asset turnover	2.6 times	2.2 times
Net income	Up 32%	Down 9%
Earnings per share	$3.30	$2.50

Instructions

With the class divided into groups, complete the following.

Bonita Ltd. asks you to prepare a list of brief comments stating how each of these items supports the solvency and going-concern potential of the business. The company wishes to use these comments to support its presentation of data to its creditors. You are to prepare the comments as requested, giving the implications and the limitations of each item separately. Then prepare a collective inference that may be drawn from the individual items about Bonita's solvency and going-concern potential.

Ethics Case

CT15.4 Robert Turnbull, president of Turnbull Industries, wishes to issue a press release to bolster his company's image and maybe even its share price, which has been gradually falling. As controller, you have been asked to provide a list of 20 financial ratios along with some other operating statistics relative to Turnbull Industries' first quarter financials and operations.

Two days after you provide the ratios and data requested, Perry Jarvis, the public relations director of Turnbull, asks you to prove the accuracy of the financial and operating data contained in the press release written by the president and edited by Perry. In the press release, the president highlights the sales increase of 25% over last year's first quarter and the positive change in the current ratio from 1.5:1 last year to 3:1 this year. He also emphasizes that production was up 50% over the prior year's first quarter.

You note that the press release contains only positive or improved ratios and none of the negative or deteriorated ratios. For instance, no mention is made that the debt to assets ratio has increased from 35% to 55%, that inventories are up 89%, and that while the current ratio improved, the acid-test ratio fell from 1:1 to .5:1. Nor is there any mention that the reported profit for the quarter would have been a loss had not the estimated lives of Turnbull's plant and machinery been increased by 30%. Perry emphasizes, "The prez wants this release by early this afternoon."

Instructions

a. Who are the stakeholders in this situation?

b. Is there anything unethical in president Turnbull's actions?

c. Should you as controller remain silent? Does Perry have any responsibility?

Answers to Insight and Accounting Across the Organization Questions

How to Manage the Current Ratio Q: How might management influence a company's current ratio? **A:** Management can affect the current ratio by speeding up or withholding payments on accounts payable just before the statement of financial position date. Management can alter the cash balance by increasing or decreasing non-current assets or long-term debt, or by issuing or purchasing ordinary shares.

What Does "Non-Recurring" Really Mean? Q: If a company takes a large restructuring charge, what is the effect on the company's current income statement versus future ones? **A:** The current period's net income can be greatly diminished by a large restructuring charge. The net incomes in future periods can be enhanced because they are relieved of costs (e.g., depreciation and labor expenses) that would have been charged to them.

A Look at U.S. GAAP

LEARNING OBJECTIVE 4

Compare financial statement analysis and income statement presentation under IFRS and U.S. GAAP.

The tools of financial analysis are the same throughout the world. Techniques such as vertical and horizontal analysis, for example, are tools used by analysts regardless of whether GAAP- or IFRS-related financial statements are being evaluated. In addition, the ratios provided in the text are the same ones that are used globally.

Key Points

- The tools of financial statement analysis covered in this chapter are universal and therefore no significant differences exist in the analysis methods used.
- The basic objectives of the income statement are the same under both GAAP and IFRS. As indicated in the text, a very important objective is to ensure that users of the income statement can evaluate the earning power of the company. Earning power is the normal level of income to be obtained in the future. Thus, both the IASB and the FASB are interested in distinguishing normal levels of income from unusual items in order to better predict a company's future profitability.
- The basic accounting for discontinued operations is the same under GAAP and IFRS.
- The accounting for changes in accounting principles and changes in accounting estimates are the same for both GAAP and IFRS.
- Both IFRS and GAAP follow the same approach in reporting comprehensive income. The statement of comprehensive income can be prepared under the one-statement approach or the two-statement approach.

  Under the one-statement approach, all components of revenue and expense are reported in a statement of income. This combined statement of comprehensive income first computes net income or loss, which is then followed by components of other comprehensive income or loss items to arrive at comprehensive income. An example appears below.

Walter Company
Statement of Comprehensive Income
For the Year Ended December 31, 2029

Sales revenue	$5,100,000
Cost of goods sold	3,800,000
Gross profit	1,300,000
Operating expenses	700,000
Net income	600,000
Other comprehensive income	
Unrealized gain on non-trading securities (net of taxes)	75,000
Comprehensive income	$ 675,000

Under the two-statement approach, all the components of revenues and expenses are reported in a traditional income statement except for other comprehensive income or loss. In addition, a second statement (the comprehensive income statement) is then prepared, starting with net income and followed by other comprehensive income or loss items to arrive at comprehensive income. An example of the two-statement approach, using the same data as that used above for Walter Company, is as follows.

Walter Company Income Statement For the Year Ended December 31, 2029	
Sales revenue	$5,100,000
Cost of goods sold	3,800,000
Gross profit	1,300,000
Operating expenses	700,000
Net income	$ 600,000

Walter Company Comprehensive Income Statement For the Year Ended December 31, 2029	
Net income	$600,000
Other comprehensive income	
Unrealized gain on non-trading securities (net of taxes)	75,000
Comprehensive income	$675,000

- The issues related to quality of earnings are the same under both GAAP and IFRS. It is hoped that by adopting a more principles-based approach, as found in IFRS, many of the earnings quality issues will disappear.

GAAP Practice

GAAP Self-Test Questions

1. The basic tools of financial analysis are the same under both GAAP and IFRS **except** that:
   - **a.** horizontal analysis cannot be done because the format of the statements is sometimes different.
   - **b.** analysis is different because vertical analysis cannot be done under GAAP.
   - **c.** the current ratio cannot be computed because current liabilities are often reported before current assets in GAAP statements of position.
   - **d.** None of the answer choices is correct.

2. Under GAAP:
   - **a.** the reporting of discontinued items is different than IFRS.
   - **b.** the reporting of other comprehensive income is prohibited.
   - **c.** the reporting of changes in accounting principles is different than under IFRS.
   - **d.** None of the answer choices is correct.

3. Presentation of comprehensive income must be reported under GAAP in:
   - **a.** the statement of stockholders' equity.
   - **b.** the income statement before net income.
   - **c.** the notes to the financial statements.
   - **d.** a statement of comprehensive income.

4. Parmalane reports the following information:

Sales revenue	$500,000
Cost of goods sold	200,000
Operating expense	40,000
Unrealized loss on non-trading securities	10,000

   Parmalane should report the following under the two-statement approach using GAAP:
   - **a.** net income of $260,000 and comprehensive income of $270,000.
   - **b.** net income of $270,000 and comprehensive income of $260,000.
   - **c.** other comprehensive income of $10,000 and comprehensive income of $270,000.
   - **d.** other comprehensive loss of $10,000 and comprehensive income of $250,000.

5. Assuming the same information as in Question 4, Parmalane should report the following using a one-statement approach under GAAP:
   - **a.** net income of $260,000 and comprehensive income of $270,000.
   - **b.** net income of $270,000 and comprehensive income of $260,000.
   - **c.** other comprehensive income of $10,000 and comprehensive income of $270,000.
   - **d.** other comprehensive loss of $10,000 and comprehensive income of $250,000.

GAAP Exercises

GAAP15.1 Chen Company reports the following information for the year ended December 31, 2029: sales revenue $1,000,000, cost of goods sold $700,000, operating expenses $200,000, and an unrealized gain on non-trading securities of $75,000. Prepare a statement of comprehensive income using the one-statement approach.

GAAP15.2 Assume the same information for Chen Company as in GAAP15.1. Prepare the income statement and comprehensive income statement using the two-statement approach.

GAAP Financial Reporting Problem: Apple Inc. (USA)

GAAP15.3 Your parents are considering investing in **Apple** common stock. They ask you, as an accounting expert, to make an analysis of the company for them. The financial statement of Apple are presented in Appendix D. The complete annual report, including the notes to the financial statements, is available at the company's website.

Instructions

a. Make a 3-year trend analysis, using 2018 as the base year, of (1) net sales and (2) net earnings. Comment on the significance of the trend results.

b. Compute for 2020 and 2019 the (1) debt to assets ratio and (2) times interest earned. (See Note 6 for interest expense.) How would you evaluate Apple's long-term solvency?

c. Compute for 2020 and 2019 the (1) profit margin, (2) asset turnover, (3) return on assets, and (4) return on common stockholders' equity. How would you evaluate Apple's profitability? Total assets at September 29, 2018, were $365,725 million, and total stockholders' equity at September 29, 2018, was $107,147 million.

d. What information outside the annual report may also be useful to your parents in making a decision about Apple?

Answers to GAAP Self-Test Questions

1. d **2.** d **3.** d **4.** d **5.** d

APPENDIX A

Specimen Financial Statements: Taiwan Semiconductor Manufacturing Company, Limited

Taiwan Semiconductor Manufacturing Company Limited and Subsidiaries

CONSOLIDATED STATEMENTS OF FINANCIAL POSITION
(In Millions of New Taiwan Dollars)

	Notes	December 31, 2019	December 31, 2020
		NT$	NT$
ASSETS			
CURRENT ASSETS			
Cash and cash equivalents	7	$ 455,399.3	$ 660,170.6
Financial assets at fair value through profit or loss	8	326.8	2,259.4
Financial assets at fair value through other comprehensive income	9	127,396.6	122,448.5
Financial assets at amortized cost	10	299.9	6,598.0
Hedging financial assets	11	25.9	0.1
Notes and accounts receivable, net	12	138,908.6	145,480.3
Receivables from related parties	34	862.1	558.1
Other receivables from related parties	34	51.6	50.6
Inventories	6, 13, 37	82,981.2	137,353.4
Other financial assets	35	11,041.1	10,676.1
Other current assets		5,320.8	6,590.2
Total current assets		822,613.9	1,092,185.3
NONCURRENT ASSETS			
Financial assets at fair value through other comprehensive income	9	4,124.3	4,514.9
Financial assets at amortized cost	10	7,348.9	4,372.2
Investments accounted for using equity method	14	18,618.8	18,730.2
Property, plant and equipment	6, 15	1,352,377.4	1,555,589.1
Right-of-use assets	6, 16	17,232.4	27,728.5
Intangible assets	6, 17	20,653.0	25,768.1
Deferred income tax assets	6, 28	17,928.4	25,958.2
Refundable deposits		2,085.0	1,343.0
Other noncurrent assets		1,742.9	4,411.0
Total noncurrent assets		1,442,111.1	1,668,415.2
TOTAL		$2,264,725.0	$2,760,600.5

(Continued)

Taiwan Semiconductor Manufacturing Company Limited and Subsidiaries

CONSOLIDATED STATEMENTS OF FINANCIAL POSITION
(In Millions of New Taiwan Dollars)

	Notes	December 31, 2019 NT$	December 31, 2020 NT$
LIABILITIES AND EQUITY			
CURRENT LIABILITIES			
Short-term loans	18, 31	$ 118,522.3	$ 88,559.0
Financial liabilities at fair value through profit or loss	8	982.3	94.1
Hedging financial liabilities	11	1.8	1.2
Accounts payable		38,771.1	38,987.3
Payables to related parties	34	1,434.9	2,107.7
Salary and bonus payable		16,272.3	20,071.2
Accrued profit sharing bonus to employees and compensation to directors and supervisors	30	23,648.9	35,681.0
Payables to contractors and equipment suppliers		140,810.7	157,805.0
Cash dividends payable	23	129,652.0	129,652.0
Income tax payable	6, 28	40,094.3	68,656.7
Long-term liabilities - current portion	19, 31	31,800.0	2,600.0
Accrued expenses and other current liabilities	6, 16, 22, 24,31	56,373.2	87,683.2
Total current liabilities		598,363.8	631,898.4
NONCURRENT LIABILITIES			
Bonds payable	19, 31	25,100.0	254,105.1
Long-term bank loans	20, 31	—	1,967.6
Deferred income tax liabilities	6, 28	344.4	1,729.9
Lease liabilities	6, 16, 31	15,041.8	20,560.6
Net defined benefit liability	21	9,182.5	11,914.1
Guarantee deposits	22, 31	176.9	265.6
Others		2,128.3	2,395.4
Total noncurrent liabilities		51,973.9	292,938.3
Total liabilities		650,337.7	924,836.7
EQUITY ATTRIBUTABLE TO SHAREHOLDERS OF THE PARENT			
Capital stock	23	259,303.8	259,303.8
Capital surplus	23	56,339.7	56,347.2
Retained earnings	23		
Appropriated as legal capital reserve		311,147.0	311,147.0
Appropriated as special capital reserve		10,675.1	42,259.1
Unappropriated earnings		1,003,808.3	1,220,434.0
		1,325,630.4	1,573,840.1
Others	23	(27,568.3)	(54,679.8)
Equity attributable to shareholders of the parent		1,613,705.6	1,834,811.3
NON - CONTROLLING INTERESTS		681.7	952.5
Total equity		1,614,387.3	1,835,763.8
TOTAL		$2,264,725.0	$2,760,600.5

The accompanying notes are an integral part of the consolidated financial statements.

Taiwan Semiconductor Manufacturing Company Limited and Subsidiaries

CONSOLIDATED STATEMENTS OF PROFIT OR LOSS AND OTHER COMPREHENSIVE INCOME
(In Millions of New Taiwan Dollars, Except Earnings Per Share that are in New Taiwan Dollars)

	Notes	2018	2019	2020
		NT$	NT$	NT$
NET REVENUE	6, 24, 34, 38	$1,031,473.6	$1,069,985.4	$1,339,254.8
COST OF REVENUE	6, 13, 30, 34, 37	533,487.5	577,286.9	628,108.4
GROSS PROFIT BEFORE REALIZED (UNREALIZED) GROSS PROFIT ON SALES TO ASSOCIATES		497,986.1	492,698.5	711,146.4
REALIZED (UNREALIZED) GROSS PROFIT ON SALES TO ASSOCIATES		(111.8)	3.4	(16.3)
GROSS PROFIT		497,874.3	492,701.9	711,130.1
OPERATING EXPENSES	6, 30, 34			
Research and development		85,895.6	91,418.7	109,486.0
General and administrative		20,265.9	21,737.2	28,457.6
Marketing		5,987.8	6,348.6	7,112.8
Total operating expenses		112,149.3	119,504.5	145,056.4
OTHER OPERATING INCOME AND EXPENSES, NET	15, 16, 30	(2,101.5)	(496.3)	710.0
INCOME FROM OPERATIONS	38	383,623.5	372,701.1	566,783.7
NON-OPERATING INCOME AND EXPENSES				
Share of profits of associates		3,090.6	2,861.0	3,562.0
Interest Income	25	14,694.4	16,189.4	9,018.4
Other income		158.4	417.3	660.6
Foreign exchange gain (loss), net		2,438.2	2,095.2	(3,303.3)
Finance costs	26	(3,051.2)	(3,250.9)	(2,081.5)
Other gains and losses, net	27	(3,410.8)	(1,151.0)	10,106.4
Total non-operating income and expenses		13,919.6	17,161.0	17,962.6
INCOME BEFORE INCOME TAX		397,543.1	389,862.1	584,746.3
INCOME TAX EXPENSE	6, 28	34,436.9	35,835.1	73,738.3
NET INCOME		363,106.2	354,027.0	511,008.0
OTHER COMPREHENSIVE INCOME (LOSS)	6, 21, 23, 28			
Items that will not be reclassified subsequently to profit or loss:				
Remeasurement of defined benefit obligation		(861.2)	253.9	(3,516.8)
Unrealized gain/(loss) on investments in equity instruments at fair value through other comprehensive income		(3,309.1)	334.3	423.7
Gain (loss) on hedging instruments		41.0	(109.6)	24.1
Share of other comprehensive loss of associates		(14.2)	(18.2)	(11.6)
Income tax benefit (expense) related to items that will not be reclassified subsequently		195.7	(21.0)	422.7
		(3,947.8)	439.4	(2,657.9)

(Continued)

Taiwan Semiconductor Manufacturing Company Limited and Subsidiaries

CONSOLIDATED STATEMENTS OF PROFIT OR LOSS AND OTHER COMPREHENSIVE INCOME
(In Millions of New Taiwan Dollars, Except Earnings Per Share that are in New Taiwan Dollars)

	Notes	2018	2019	2020
		NT$	NT$	NT$
Items that may be reclassified subsequently to profit or loss:				
Exchange differences arising on translation of foreign operations		$ 14,562.4	$ (14,689.1)	$ (29,847.2)
Unrealized gain/(loss) on investments in debt instruments at fair value through other comprehensive income		(870.9)	2,566.4	2,466.7
Share of other comprehensive income (loss) of associates		93.3	(140.2)	(283.4)
		13,784.8	(12,262.9)	(27,663.9)
Other comprehensive income (loss) for the year, net of income tax		9,837.0	(11,823.5)	(30,321.8)
TOTAL COMPREHENSIVE INCOME FOR THE YEAR		$ 372,943.2	$ 342,203.5	$ 480,686.2
NET INCOME ATTRIBUTABLE TO:				
Shareholders of the parent		$ 363,052.7	$ 353,948.0	$ 510,744.0
Non-controlling interests		53.5	79.0	264.0
		$ 363,106.2	$ 354,027.0	$ 511,008.0
TOTAL COMPREHENSIVE INCOME ATTRIBUTABLE TO:				
Shareholders of the parent		$ 372,886.8	$ 342,124.9	$ 480,422.1
Non-controlling interests		56.4	78.6	264.1
		$ 372,943.2	$ 342,203.5	$ 480,686.2

		2018	2019	2020
		Income Attributable to Shareholders of the Parent	Income Attributable to Shareholders of the Parent	Income Attributable to Shareholders of the Parent
		NT$	NT$	NT$
EARNINGS PER SHARE	29			
Basic earnings per share		$ 14.00	$ 13.65	$ 19.70
Diluted earnings per share		$ 14.00	$ 13.65	$ 19.70
EARNINGS PER EQUIVALENT ADS				
Basic earnings per share		$ 70.01	$ 68.25	$ 98.48
Diluted earnings per share		$ 70.01	$ 68.25	$ 98.48

The accompanying notes are an integral part of the consolidated financial statements.

Taiwan Semiconductor Manufacturing Company Limited and Subsidiaries

CONSOLIDATED STATEMENTS OF CHANGES IN EQUITY
(In Millions of New Taiwan Dollars)

	Equity Attributable to Shareholders of the Parent														
	Capital Stock - Common Stock			Retained Earnings				Others							
	Shares (In Millions)	Amount	Capital Surplus	Legal Capital Reserve	Special Capital Reserve	Un-appropriated Earnings	Total	Foreign Currency Translation Reserve	Unrealized Gain (Loss) on Financial Assets at Fair Value Through Other Comprehensive Income	Gain (Loss) on Hedging Instruments	Unearned Stock-Based Employee Compensation	Total	Total	Non-controlling Interests	Total Equity
BALANCE, JANUARY 1, 2018	25,930.3	$ 259,303.8	$ 56,309.6	$ 241,722.7	$ —	$ 964,884.9	$1,206,607.6	$(26,697.7)	$ (524.9)	$ 4.2	$(10.3)	$(27,228.7)	$1,494,992.3	$700.0	$1,495,692.3
Appropriations of earnings															
Legal capital reserve	—	—	—	34,311.2	—	(34,311.2)	—	—	—	—	—	—	—	—	—
Special capital reserve	—	—	—	—	26,907.5	(26,907.5)	—	—	—	—	—	—	—	—	—
Cash dividends to shareholders	—	—	—	—	—	(207,443.0)	(207,443.0)	—	—	—	—	—	(207,443.0)	—	(207,443.0)
Total	—	—	—	34,311.2	26,907.5	(268,661.7)	(207,443.0)	—	—	—	—	—	(207,443.0)	—	(207,443.0)
Net income in 2018	—	—	—	—	—	363,052.7	363,052.7	—	—	—	—	—	363,052.7	53.5	363,106.2
Other comprehensive income (loss) in 2018, net of income tax	—	—	—	—	—	(765.3)	(765.3)	14,655.3	(4,097.5)	41.6	—	10,599.4	9,834.1	2.9	9,837.0
Total comprehensive income (loss) in 2018	—	—	—	—	—	362,287.4	362,287.4	14,655.3	(4,097.5)	41.6	—	10,599.4	372,886.8	56.4	372,943.2
Disposal of investments in equity instruments at fair value through other comprehensive income	—	—	—	—	—	(1,193.1)	(1,193.1)	—	1,193.1	—	—	1,193.1	—	—	—
Basis adjustment for loss on hedging instalments	—	—	—	—	—	—	—	—	—	(22.2)	—	(22.2)	(22.2)	—	(22.2)
Adjustments to share of changes in equities of associates	—	—	(6.4)	—	—	—	—	—	—	—	8.5	8.5	2.1	—	2.1
From share of changes in equities of subsidiaries	—	—	2.7	—	—	—	—	—	—	—	—	—	2.7	(2.7)	—
Donation from shareholders	—	—	10.1	—	—	—	—	—	—	—	—	—	10.1	—	10.1
Decrease in non-controlling interests	—	—	—	—	—	—	—	—	—	—	—	—	—	(77.4)	(77.4)
BALANCE, DECEMBER 31, 2018	25,930.3	$ 259,303.8	$ 56,316.0	$ 276,033.9	$ 26,907.5	$ 1,057,317.5	$1,360,258.9	$(12,042.4)	$ (3,429.3)	$ 23.6	$ (1.8)	$(15,449.9)	$1,660,428.8	$676.3	$1,661,105.1
Appropriations of earnings															
Legal capital reserve	—	—	—	35,113.1	—	(35,113.1)	—	—	—	—	—	—	—	—	—
Special capital reserve	—	—	—	—	(16,232.4)	16,232.4	—	—	—	—	—	—	—	—	—
Cash dividends to shareholders	—	—	—	—	—	(388,955.7)	(388,955.7)	—	—	—	—	—	(388,955.7)	—	(388,955.7)
Total	—	—	—	35,113.1	(16,232.4)	(407,836.4)	(388,955.7)	—	—	—	—	—	(388,955.7)	—	(388,955.7)
Net income in 2019	—	—	—	—	—	353,948.0	353,948.0	—	—	—	—	—	353,948.0	79.0	354,027.0
Other comprehensive income (loss) in 2019, net of income tax	—	—	—	—	—	217.1	217.1	(14,829.0)	2,898.5	(109.7)	—	(12,040.2)	(11,823.1)	(0.4)	(11,823.5)
Total comprehensive income (loss) in 2019	—	—	—	—	—	354,165.1	354,165.1	(14,829.0)	2,898.5	(109.7)	—	(12,040.2)	342,124.9	78.6	342,203.5
Disposal of investments in equity instruments at fair value through other comprehensive income	—	—	—	—	—	162.1	162.1	—	(162.1)	—	—	(162.1)	—	—	—
Basis adjustment for gain on hedging instruments	—	—	—	—	—	—	—	—	—	82.3	—	82.3	82.3	—	82.3
Adjustments to share of changes in equities of associates	—	—	19.4	—	—	—	—	—	—	—	1.6	1.6	21.0	0.2	21.2
From share of changes in equities of subsidiaries	—	—	0.3	—	—	—	—	—	—	—	—	—	0.3	(0.3)	—
Donation from shareholders	—	—	4.0	—	—	—	—	—	—	—	—	—	4.0	—	4.0
Decrease in non-controlling interests	—	—	—	—	—	—	—	—	—	—	—	—	—	(73.1)	(73.1)
BALANCE, DECEMBER 31, 2019	25,930.3	$ 259,303.8	$ 56,339.7	$ 311,147.0	$ 10,675.1	$ 1,003,808.3	$1,325,630.4	$ (26,871.4)	$ (692.9)	$ (3.8)	$ (0.2)	$(27,568.3)	$1,613,705.6	$681.7	$1,614,387.3

(Continued)

Taiwan Semiconductor Manufacturing Company Limited and Subsidiaries

CONSOLIDATED STATEMENTS OF CHANGES IN EQUITY
(In Millions of New Taiwan Dollars)

	Equity Attributable to Shareholders of the Parent														
	Capital Stock - Common Stock			Retained Earnings				Others							
	Shares (In Millions)	Amount	Capital Surplus	Legal Capital Reserve	Special Capital Reserve	Un-appropriated Earnings	Total	Foreign Currency Translation Reserve	Unrealized Gain (Loss) on Financial Assets at Fair Value Through Other Comprehensive Income	Gain (Loss) on Hedging Instruments	Unearned Stock-Based Employee Compensation	Total	Total	Non-controlling Interests	Total Equity
Appropriations of earnings															
Special capital reserve	—	—	—	—	31,584.0	(31,584.0)	—	—	—	—	—	—	—	—	—
Cash dividends to shareholders	—	—	—	—	—	(259,303.8)	(259,303.8)	—	—	—	—	—	(259,303.8)	—	(259,303.8)
Total	—	—	—	—	31,584.0	(290,887.8)	(259,303.8)	—	—	—	—	—	(259,303.8)	—	(259,303.8)
Net income in 2020	—	—	—	—	—	510,744.0	510,744.0	—	—	—	—	—	510,744.0	264.0	511,008.0
Other comprehensive income (loss) in 2020, net of income tax	—	—	—	—	—	(3,121.8)	(3,121.8)	(30,130.2)	2,906.0	24.1	—	(27,200.1)	(30,321.9)	0.1	(30,321.8)
Total comprehensive income (loss) in 2020	—	—	—	—	—	507,622.2	507,622.2	(30,130.2)	2,906.0	24.1	—	(27,200.1)	480,422.1	264.1	480,686.2
Disposal of investments in equity instruments at fair value through other comprehensive income	—	—	—	—	—	(108.7)	(108.7)	—	108.7	—	—	108.7	—	—	—
Basis adjustment for loss on hedging instruments	—	—	—	—	—	—	—	—	—	(20.3)	—	(20.3)	(20.3)	—	(20.3)
Adjustments to share of changes in equities of associates	—	—	0.3	—	—	—	—	—	—	—	0.2	0.2	0.5	—	0.5
Donation from shareholders	—	—	7.2	—	—	—	—	—	—	—	—	—	7.2	—	7.2
Increase in non-controlling interests	—	—	—	—	—	—	—	—	—	—	—	—	—	6.7	6.7
BALANCE, DECEMBER 31, 2020	25,930.3	$ 259,303.8	$ 56,347.2	$ 311,147.0	$ 42,259.1	$ 1,220,434.0	$1,573,840.1	$(57,001.6)	$ 2,321.8	$ —	$ —	$(54,679.8)	$1,834,811.3	$952.5	$1,835,763.8
BALANCE, DECEMBER 31, 2020 (IN MILLIONS OF US$ - Note 3)		$ 9,234.5	$ 2,006.7	$ 11,080.7	$ 1,505.0	$ 43,462.7	$ 56,048.4	$ (2,030.0)	$ 82.7	$ —	$ —	$ (1,947.3)	$ 65,342.3	$ 33.9	$ 65,376.2

The accompanying notes are an integral part of the consolidated financial statements.

Taiwan Semiconductor Manufacturing Company Limited and Subsidiaries

CONSOLIDATED STATEMENTS OF CASH FLOWS
(In Millions of New Taiwan Dollars)

	2018	2019	2020
	NT$	NT$	NT$
CASH FLOWS FROM OPERATING ACTIVITIES			
Income before income tax	$ 397,543.1	$ 389,862.1	$584,746.3
Adjustments for:			
Depreciation expense	288,124.9	281,411.8	324,538.4
Amortization expense	4,421.4	5,472.4	7,186.2
Expected credit losses recognized (reversal) on investments in debt instruments	(2.4)	1.7	3.7
Finance costs	3,051.2	3,250.9	2,081.5
Share of profits of associates	(3,090.6)	(2,861.0)	(3,562.0)
Interest income	(14,694.4)	(16,189.4)	(9,018.4)
Share-based compensation	—	2.8	6.6
Loss (gain) on disposal or retirement of property, plant and equipment, net	1,005.6	950.0	(188.9)
Loss (gain) on disposal of intangible assets, net	(0.4)	2.4	0.6
Impairment loss (reversal of impairment loss) on property, plant and equipment	423.5	(301.4)	10.2
Loss (gain) on financial instruments at fair value through profit or loss, net	358.2	955.7	(3.0)
Loss (gain) on disposal of investments in debt instruments at fair value through other comprehensive income, net	989.1	(537.8)	(1,439.4)
Loss from disposal of subsidiaries	—	4.6	—
Unrealized (realized) gross profit on sales to associates	111.8	(3.4)	16.3
Loss (gain) on foreign exchange, net	2,916.7	(5,228.2)	(1,372.6)
Dividend income	(158.4)	(417.3)	(637.6)
Loss (gain) arising from fair value hedges, net	2.3	(13.1)	—
Gain on lease modification	—	(2.1)	(2.8)
Changes in operating assets and liabilities:			
Financial instruments at fair value through profit or loss	480.1	848.8	(2,965.2)
Notes and accounts receivable, net	(13,271.3)	(18,119.6)	(8,082.7)
Receivables from related parties	599.7	(277.7)	304.0
Other receivables from related parties	106.1	13.4	7.6
Inventories	(29,370.0)	20,249.8	(54,372.2)
Other financial assets	(4,601.3)	3,383.5	1,389.5
Other current assets	(513.0)	(76.3)	(1,358.1)
Other noncurrent assets	152.6	—	—
Accounts payable	4,540.6	5,860.1	404.6
Payables to related parties	(279.9)	58.4	672.8
Salary and bonus payable	216.5	1,800.9	3,798.9
Accrued profit sharing bonus to employees and compensation to directors and supervisors	562.0	(332.2)	12,032.1
Accrued expenses and other current liabilities	(20,226.4)	(2,372.0)	20,617.4
Net defined benefit liability	(60.5)	(215.0)	(785.2)
Cash generated from operations	619,336.8	667,182.8	874,028.6
Income taxes paid	(45,382.5)	(52,044.1)	(51,362.4)
Net cash generated by operating activities	573,954.3	615,138.7	822,666.2
CASH FLOWS FROM INVESTING ACTIVITIES			
Acquisitions of:			
Financial instruments at fair value through profit or loss – debt instruments	$ (310.5)	$ (124.7)	$ —
Financial assets at fair value through other comprehensive income	(96,412.8)	(257,558.2)	(262,637.5)
Financial assets at amortized cost	(2,294.1)	(313.9)	(4,302.8)
Property, plant and equipment	(315,581.9)	(460,422.2)	(507,238.7)
Intangible assets	(7,100.3)	(9,329.9)	(9,542.4)

(Continued)

Taiwan Semiconductor Manufacturing Company Limited and Subsidiaries

CONSOLIDATED STATEMENTS OF CASH FLOWS
(In Millions of New Taiwan Dollars)

	2018	2019	2020
	NT$	NT$	NT$
Proceeds from disposal or redemption of:			
Financial instruments at fair value through profit or loss – debt instruments	487.2	2,418.2	30.0
Financial assets at fair value through other comprehensive income	86,639.3	230,444.5	266,931.9
Financial assets at amortized cost	2,032.4	14,349.2	285.2
Property, plant and equipment	181.5	287.3	606.7
Intangible assets	0.5	—	—
Proceeds from return of capital of investments in equity instruments at fair value through other comprehensive income	127.9	1.1	51.1
Derecognition of hedging financial instruments	250.5	(436.6)	(308.8)
Interest received	14,660.4	16,875.0	9,775.1
Proceeds from government grants - property, plant and equipment		2,565.3	1,044.3
Proceeds from government grants - land use right and others	—	850.6	25.4
Other dividends received	158.4	320.2	735.1
Dividends received from investments accounted for using equity method	3,262.9	1,719.0	2,752.1
Increase in prepayments for leases			(4,693.4)
Refundable deposits paid	(2,227.5)	(1,465.8)	(726.9)
Refundable deposits refunded	1,857.2	1,019.3	1,431.9
Net cash used in investing activities	(314,268.9)	(458,801.6)	(505,781.7)
CASH FLOWS FROM FINANCING ACTIVITIES			
Increase (decrease) in short-term loans	23,923.0	31,804.3	(31,571.6)
Proceeds from short-term bills payable	—	—	7,485.3
Repayments of short-term bills payable	—	—	(7,500.0)
Proceeds from issuance of bonds	—	—	236,725.7
Repayment of bonds	(58,024.9)	(34,900.0)	(31,800.0)
Proceeds from long-term bank loans	—	—	2,000.0
Payments for transaction costs attributable to the issuance of bonds	—	—	(390.7)
Repayment of the principal portion of lease liabilities	—	(2,930.6)	(2,615.7)
Interest paid	(3,233.4)	(3,597.1)	(1,781.1)
Guarantee deposits received	1,668.9	62.2	145.6
Guarantee deposits refunded	(1,948.1)	(701.3)	(16.1)
Cash dividends	(207,443.0)	(259,303.8)	(259,303.8)
Donation from shareholders	10.1	4.0	7.3
Decrease in non-controlling interests	(77.4)	(75.9)	—
Net cash used in financing activities	(245,124.8)	(269,638.2)	(88,615.1)
EFFECT OF EXCHANGE RATE CHANGES ON CASH AND CASH EQUIVALENTS	$ 9,862.3	$ (9,114.2)	$ (23,498.1)
NET INCREASE (DECREASE) IN CASH AND CASH EQUIVALENTS	24,422.9	(122,415.3)	204,771.3
CASH AND CASH EQUIVALENTS, BEGINNING OF YEAR	553,391.7	577,814.6	455,399.3
CASH AND CASH EQUIVALENTS, END OF YEAR	$ 577,814.6	$ 455,399.3	$660,170.6

The accompanying notes are an integral part of the consolidated financial statements.

APPENDIX B

Specimen Financial Statements: Nestlé SA

Consolidated Income Statement for the Year Ended December 31, 2020

In millions of CHF

	Notes	2020	2019
Sales	3	**84 343**	**92 568**
Other revenue		338	297
Cost of goods sold		(42 971)	(46 647)
Distribution expenses		(7 861)	(8 496)
Marketing and administration expenses		(17 370)	(19 790)
Research and development costs		(1 576)	(1 672)
Other trading income	4	238	163
Other trading expenses	4	(908)	(2 749)
Trading operating profit	3	**14 233**	**13 674**
Other operating income	4	1 919	3 717
Other operating expenses	4	(1 356)	(1 313)
Operating profit		**14 796**	**16 078**
Financial income	5	109	200
Financial expense	5	(983)	(1 216)
Profit before taxes, associates and joint ventures		**13 922**	**15 062**
Taxes	13	(3 365)	(3 159)
Income from associates and joint ventures	14	1 815	1 001
Profit for the year		**12 372**	**12 904**
of which attributable to non-controlling interests		140	295
of which attributable to shareholders of the parent (Net profit)		12 232	12 609

(continues)

(continued)

In millions of CHF

	Notes	2020	2019
As percentages of sales			
Trading operating profit		16.9%	14.8%
Profit for the year attributable to shareholders of the parent (Net profit)		14.5%	13.6%
Earnings per share (in CHF)			
Basic earnings per share	15	4.30	4.30
Diluted earnings per share	15	4.29	4.30

Consolidated Statement of Comprehensive Income for the Year Ended December 31, 2020

In millions of CHF

	Notes	2020	2019
Profit for the year recognized in the income statement		**12 372**	**12 904**
Currency retranslations, net of taxes	17	(2 931)	(1 050)
Changes in cash flow hedge and cost of hedge reserves, net of taxes		(54)	(66)
Share of other comprehensive income of associates and joint ventures	14/17	(265)	49
Items that are or may be reclassified subsequently to the income statement		(3 250)	(1 067)
Remeasurement of defined benefit plans, net of taxes	10/17	(166)	(320)
Fair value changes on equity instruments, net of taxes	17	124	(4)
Share of other comprehensive income of associates and joint ventures	14/17	(340)	337
Items that will never be reclassified to the income statement		(382)	13
Other comprehensive income for the year	17	**(3 632)**	**(1 054)**
Total comprehensive income for the year		**8 740**	**11 850**
of which attributable to non-controlling interests		76	317
of which attributable to shareholders of the parent		8 664	11 533

Consolidated Balance Sheet as at December 31, 2020

In millions of CHF

	Notes	2020	2019
Assets			
Current assets			
Cash and cash equivalents	12/16	5 235	7 469
Short-term investments	12	3 374	2 794
Inventories	6	10 101	9 343
Trade and other receivables	7/12	10 746	11 766
Prepayments and accrued income		477	498
Derivative assets	12	310	254
Current income tax assets		708	768
Assets held for sale	2	3 117	2 771
Total current assets		**34 068**	**35 663**
Non-current assets			
Property, plant and equipment	8	25 840	28 762
Goodwill	9	27 620	28 896
Intangible assets	9	20 148	17 824
Investments in associates and joint ventures	14	12 005	11 505
Financial assets	12	2 594	2 611
Employee benefits assets	10	468	510
Current income tax assets		—	55
Deferred tax assets	13	1 285	2 114
Total non-current assets		**89 960**	**92 277**
Total assets		**124 028**	**127 940**

(continues)

(continued)

In millions of CHF	Notes	2020	2019
Liabilities and equity			
Current liabilities			
Financial debt	12	12 019	14 032
Trade and other payables	7/12	18 515	18 803
Accruals and deferred income		4 917	4 492
Provisions	11	508	802
Derivative liabilities	12	254	420
Current income tax liabilities		2 661	2 673
Liabilities directly associated with assets held for sale	2	848	393
Total current liabilities		**39 722**	**41 615**
Non-current liabilities			
Financial debt	12	27 928	23 132
Employee benefits liabilities	10	5 118	6 151
Provisions	11	1 029	1 162
Deferred tax liabilities	13	2 636	2 589
Other payables	12	1 081	429
Total non-current liabilities		**37 792**	**33 463**
Total liabilities		**77 514**	**75 078**
Equity	17		
Share capital		288	298
Treasury shares		(6 643)	(9 752)
Translation reserve		(24 397)	(21 526)
Other reserves		(365)	(45)
Retained earnings		76 812	83 060
Total equity attributable to shareholders of the parent		**45 695**	**52 035**
Non-controlling interests		819	827
Total equity		**46 514**	**52 862**
Total liabilities and equity		**124 028**	**127 940**

Consolidated Cash Flow Statement for the Year Ended December 31, 2020

In millions of CHF

	Notes	2020	2019
Operating activities			
Operating profit	16	14 796	16 078
Depreciation and amortization	16	3 465	3 713
Impairment		711	2 336
Net result on disposal of businesses	4	(1 678)	(3 416)
Other non-cash items of income and expense	16	248	(28)
Cash flow before changes in operating assets and liabilities		**17 542**	**18 683**
Decrease/(increase) in working capital	16	314	349
Variation of other operating assets and liabilities	16	(699)	(94)
Cash generated from operations		**17 157**	**18 938**
Interest paid		(815)	(1 028)
Interest and dividend received		76	162
Taxes paid		(2 645)	(2 854)
Dividends and interest from associates and joint ventures	14	604	632
Operating cash flow		**14 377**	**15 850**
Investing activities			
Capital expenditure	8	(4 076)	(3 695)
Expenditure on intangible assets	9	(288)	(516)
Acquisition of businesses, net of cash acquired	2	(4 520)	(125)
Disposal of businesses, net of cash disposed of	2	3 916	9 959
Investments (net of divestments) in associates and joint ventures	14	(182)	(540)
Inflows/(outflows) from treasury investments		(749)	2 978
Other investing activities		232	295
Investing cash flow		**(5 667)**	**8 356**

(continues)

(continued)

In millions of CHF

	Notes	2020	2019
Financing activities			
Dividend paid to shareholders of the parent	17	(7 700)	(7 230)
Dividends paid to non-controlling interests		(268)	(463)
Acquisition (net of disposal) of non-controlling interests		(1)	(16)
Purchase (net of sale) of treasury shares [(a)]		(6 814)	(9 773)
Inflows from bonds and other non-current financial debt	12	10 330	57
Outflows from bonds and current portion of other non-current financial debt	12	(3 182)	(3 287)
Inflows/(outflows) from current financial debt	12	(2 747)	(444)
Financing cash flow		**(10 382)**	**(21 156)**
Currency retranslations		(562)	(221)
Increase/(decrease) in cash and cash equivalents		**(2 234)**	**2 829**
Cash and cash equivalents at beginning of year		7 469	4 640
Cash and cash equivalents at end of year	16	**5 235**	**7 469**

(a) Mostly relates to share buyback programs launched in 2017 and in 2020.

Consolidated Statement of Changes in Equity for the Year Ended December 31, 2020

In millions of CHF

	Share capital	Treasury shares	Translation reserve	Other reserves	Retained earnings	Total equity attributable to shareholders of the parent	Non-controlling interests	Total equity
Equity as at January 1, 2019	**306**	**(6 948)**	**(20 432)**	**(183)**	**84 620**	**57 363**	**1 040**	**58 403**
Profit for the year	—	—	—	—	12 609	**12 609**	295	**12 904**
Other comprehensive income for the year	—	—	(1 094)	(7)	25	**(1 076)**	22	**(1 054)**
Total comprehensive income for the year	—	—	(1 094)	(7)	12 634	**11 533**	317	**11 850**
Dividends	—	—	—	—	(7 230)	**(7 230)**	(463)	**(7 693)**
Movement of treasury shares	—	(9 946)	—	—	175	**(9 771)**	—	**(9 771)**
Equity compensation plans	—	280	—	—	(142)	**138**	(1)	**137**
Changes in non-controlling interests	—	—	—	—	4	**4**	(68)	**(64)**
Reduction in share capital [(a)]	(8)	6 862	—	—	(6 854)	**—**	—	**—**
Total transactions with owners	(8)	(2 804)	—	—	(14 047)	**(16 859)**	(532)	**(17 391)**
Other movements [(b)]	—	—	—	145	(147)	**(2)**	2	**—**
Equity as at December 31, 2019	**298**	**(9 752)**	**(21 526)**	**(45)**	**83 060**	**52 035**	**827**	**52 862**
Equity as at January 1, 2020	**298**	**(9 752)**	**(21 526)**	**(45)**	**83 060**	**52 035**	**827**	**52 862**
Profit for the year	—	—	—	—	12 232	**12 232**	140	**12 372**
Other comprehensive income for the year	—	—	(2 871)	(321)	(376)	**(3 568)**	(64)	**(3 632)**
Total comprehensive income for the year	—	—	(2 871)	(321)	11 856	**8 664**	76	**8 740**
Dividends	—	—	—	—	(7 700)	**(7 700)**	(268)	**(7 968)**
Movement of treasury shares	—	(6 911)	—	—	7	**(6 904)**	—	**(6 904)**
Equity compensation plans	—	360	—	—	(227)	**133**	(3)	**130**
Changes in non-controlling interests [(c)]	—	—	—	—	(394)	**(394)**	186	**(208)**
Reduction in share capital [(a)]	(10)	9 660	—	—	(9 650)	**—**	—	**—**
Total transactions with owners	(10)	3 109	—	—	(17 964)	**(14 865)**	(85)	**(14 950)**
Other movements [(b)]	—	—	—	1	(140)	**(139)**	1	**(138)**
Equity as at December 31, 2020	**288**	**(6 643)**	**(24 397)**	**(365)**	**76 812**	**45 695**	**819**	**46 514**

(a) Reduction in share capital, see Note 17.1.

(b) Other movements in Retained earnings is explained further in Note 14 in the table of movement of carrying value of Associates and joint ventures.

(c) Movements reported under Retained earnings include put options for the acquisition of non-controlling interests.

Specimen Financial Statements: Delfi Limited

CONSOLIDATED INCOME STATEMENT

FOR THE FINANCIAL YEAR ENDED 31 DECEMBER 2020

	Note	The Group 2020 US$'000	2019 US$'000
Revenue	4	**385,120**	440,692[1]
Cost of sales		**(275,007)**	(307,543)[1]
Gross profit		**110,113**	133,149
Other operating income	4	**2,280**	3,150
Selling and distribution costs		**(55,406)**	(59,599)[1]
Administrative expenses		**(24,596)**	(27,062)
Finance costs	6	**(3,153)**	(3,670)
Other operating expenses		**(1,200)**	(1,314)
Exceptional items	9	**–**	(256)
Share of results of associated companies and joint ventures	16	**(391)**	(821)
Profit before income tax		**27,647**	43,577
Income tax expense	8(a)	**(10,170)**	(15,361)
Total profit		**17,477**	28,216
Profit/(loss) attributable to:			
Equity holders of the Company		**17,477**	28,218
Non-controlling interest		**–**	(2)
		17,477	28,216
Earnings per ordinary share [2] (expressed in US cents per share)			
Basic and Diluted	10	**2.86**	4.62

Note:

(1) Reclassification has been made between selling and distribution costs, revenue and cost of sales for the financial year ended 31 December 2019 as disclosed in Note 39.

(2) Diluted earnings per share for financial years 2020 and 2019 are the same as basic earnings per share as there were no potentially dilutive ordinary shares.

The accompanying notes form an integral part of these financial statements.

CONSOLIDATED STATEMENT OF COMPREHENSIVE INCOME

FOR THE FINANCIAL YEAR ENDED 31 DECEMBER 2020

	The Group	
	2020	2019
	US$'000	US$'000
Profit for the year	**17,477**	28,216
Other comprehensive (loss)/income:		
Items that may be reclassified subsequently to profit or loss:		
Foreign currency translation reserve		
– Currency translation differences arising from consolidation	**(3,858)**	6,491
Items that will not be reclassified subsequently to profit or loss:		
Defined pension benefits obligation		
– Remeasurements of defined pension benefits obligation (Note 26(b))	**(1,257)**	(1,049)
– Tax on remeasurements (Note 8(b))	**296**	285
	(961)	(764)
Other comprehensive (loss)/income, net of tax	**(4,819)**	5,727
Total comprehensive income for the year	**12,658**	33,943
Total comprehensive income attributable to:		
Equity holders of the Company	**12,656**	33,943
Non-controlling interest	**2**	–
	12,658	33,943

The accompanying notes form an integral part of these financial statements.

BALANCE SHEETS

AS AT 31 DECEMBER 2020

	Note	The Group 2020 US$'000	The Group 2019 US$'000	The Company 2020 US$'000	The Company 2019 US$'000
ASSETS					
Current assets					
Cash and cash equivalents	11	**65,522**	57,558	**52,063**	44,955
Trade receivables	12	**81,690**	89,787	**1,274**	1,471
Loan to joint venture	17	**60**	60	**60**	60
Inventories	13	**76,847**	87,401	**9**	–
Rights to returned goods	4(a)	**2,815**	3,169	**–**	–
Income tax recoverable	8(a)	**6,888**	4,627	**–**	–
Other current assets	14	**11,030**	12,430	**540**	465
		244,852	255,032	**53,946**	46,951
Non-current assets					
Investments in subsidiaries	15	**–**	–	**41,097**	40,992
Investments in associated companies and joint ventures	16	**2,425**	2,869	**3,900**	3,900
Loans to associated company and joint venture	17	**967**	915	**–**	–
Property, plant and equipment	18	**107,180**	116,983	**2,358**	2,276
Intangible assets	20	**20,916**	21,576	**18,017**	17,871
Deferred income tax assets	8(b)	**3,174**	1,771	**–**	–
Income tax recoverable	8(a)	**1,939**	2,212	**–**	–
Other non-current assets	22	**1,035**	937	**–**	–
		137,636	147,263	**65,372**	65,039
Total assets		**382,488**	402,295	**119,318**	111,990
LIABILITIES					
Current liabilities					
Trade payables	23	**29,900**	37,153	**1,295**	986
Refund liabilities	4(a)	**7,854**	4,838	**–**	–
Other payables	24	**52,171**	55,982	**3,934**	3,452
Current income tax liabilities		**1,014**	2,420	**–**	–
Derivative liabilities		**30**	53	**–**	37
Borrowings	25	**48,748**	58,315	**–**	–
		139,717	158,761	**5,229**	4,475
Non-current liabilities					
Other payables	24	**540**	1,765	**358**	1,140
Deferred income tax liabilities	8(b)	**246**	1,063	**–**	–
Provisions for other liabilities and charges	26	**16,236**	13,106	**–**	–
		17,022	15,934	**358**	1,140
Total liabilities		**156,739**	174,695	**5,587**	5,615
NET ASSETS		**225,749**	227,600	**113,731**	106,375
EQUITY					
Capital and reserves attributable to equity holders of the Company					
Share capital	27	**95,936**	95,936	**95,936**	95,936
Foreign currency translation reserve	28(a)	**(7,413)**	(3,553)	**–**	–
Other reserves	28(b)	**994**	1,887	**–**	–
Retained earnings	29	**136,113**	133,213	**17,795**	10,439
		225,630	227,483	**113,731**	106,375
Non-controlling interest		**119**	117	**–**	–
TOTAL EQUITY		**225,749**	227,600	**113,731**	106,375

The accompanying notes form an integral part of these financial statements.

CONSOLIDATED STATEMENT OF CHANGES IN EQUITY

FOR THE FINANCIAL YEAR ENDED 31 DECEMBER 2020

		Attributable to equity holders of the Company							
	Note	Share capital US$'000	Foreign currency translation reserve US$'000	General reserve US$'000	Defined pension benefits obligation US$'000	Retained earnings US$'000	Total US$'000	Non-controlling interest US$'000	Total equity US$'000
The Group									
Balance at 1 January 2020		**95,936**	**(3,553)**	**2,437**	**(550)**	**133,213**	**227,483**	**117**	**227,600**
Profit for the year		–	–	–	–	17,477	17,477	–	17,477
Other comprehensive (loss)/income for the year		–	(3,860)	–	(961)	–	(4,821)	2	(4,819)
Total comprehensive (loss)/income for the year		**–**	**(3,860)**	**–**	**(961)**	**17,477**	**12,656**	**2**	**12,658**
Transfer to general reserve	29(a)	–	–	68	–	(68)	–	–	–
Final dividend relating to 2019 paid	30	–	–	–	–	(6,600)	(6,600)	–	(6,600)
Interim dividend relating to 2020 paid	30	–	–	–	–	(7,909)	(7,909)	–	(7,909)
Total transactions with owners, recognised directly in equity		**–**	**–**	**68**	**–**	**(14,577)**	**(14,509)**	**–**	**(14,509)**
Balance at 31 December 2020		**95,936**	**(7,413)**	**2,505**	**(1,511)**	**136,113**	**225,630**	**119**	**225,749**
Balance at 1 January 2019		**95,936**	**(10,042)**	**2,366**	**214**	**117,656**	**206,130**	**117**	**206,247**
Profit/(loss) for the year		–	–	–	–	28,218	28,218	(2)	28,216
Other comprehensive income/(loss) for the year		–	6,489	–	(764)	–	5,725	2	5,727
Total comprehensive income/(loss) for the year		**–**	**6,489**	**–**	**(764)**	**28,218**	**33,943**	**–**	**33,943**
Transfer to general reserve	29(a)	–	–	71	–	(71)	–	–	–
Final dividend relating to 2018 paid	30	–	–	–	–	(4,950)	(4,950)	–	(4,950)
Interim dividend relating to 2019 paid	30	–	–	–	–	(7,640)	(7,640)	–	(7,640)
Total transactions with owners, recognised directly in equity		**–**	**–**	**71**	**–**	**(12,661)**	**(12,590)**	**–**	**(12,590)**
Balance at 31 December 2019		**95,936**	**(3,553)**	**2,437**	**(550)**	**133,213**	**227,483**	**117**	**227,600**

The accompanying notes form an integral part of these financial statements.

CONSOLIDATED STATEMENT OF CASH FLOWS

FOR THE FINANCIAL YEAR ENDED 31 DECEMBER 2020

	Note	**2020 US$'000**	2019 US$'000
Cash flows from operating activities			
Total profit		**17,477**	28,216
Adjustments:			
Income tax expense		**10,170**	15,361
Depreciation and amortisation		**13,771**	13,420
Gain on disposal of property, plant and equipment		**(52)**	(179)
Interest income		**(683)**	(1,282)
Interest expense		**3,153**	3,670
Fair value gain on derivatives		**(23)**	(4)
Share of results of associated companies and joint ventures		**391**	821
Operating cash flow before working capital changes		**44,204**	60,023
Changes in working capital			
Inventories		**10,554**	(11,186)
Trade and other receivables		**10,448**	(16,095)
Rights to returned goods		**354**	(1,086)
Trade and other payables		**(11,417)**	15,931
Refund liabilities		**3,016**	1,381
Cash generated from operations		**57,159**	48,968
Interest received		**683**	1,282
Income tax paid, net of tax refund received		**(15,437)**	(18,164)
Net cash provided by operating activities		**42,405**	32,086
Cash flows from investing activities			
Purchases of property, plant and equipment		**(3,706)**	(10,003)
Advances for purchase of property, plant and equipment		**(776)**	(182)
Purchases of intangible assets		**(439)**	(473)
Proceeds from disposal of property, plant and equipment		**79**	239
Net cash used in investing activities		**(4,842)**	(10,419)
Cash flows from financing activities			
Proceeds from bank loans		**–**	19,797
Repayment of trade finance		**(931)**	(1,318)
Repayment of bank loans		**(7,431)**	(5,394)
Repayment of lease liabilities		**(2,184)**	(1,578)
Interest paid		**(3,153)**	(3,670)
Dividends paid to equity holders of the Company		**(14,509)**	(12,590)
Net cash used in financing activities		**(28,208)**	(4,753)
Net increase in cash and cash equivalents		**9,355**	16,914
Cash and cash equivalents			
Beginning of financial year		**55,689**	38,214
Effects of currency translation on cash and cash equivalents		**(254)**	561
End of financial year	11	**64,790**	55,689

The accompanying notes form an integral part of these financial statements.

Specimen Financial Statements: Apple Inc.

Apple Inc.

CONSOLIDATED STATEMENTS OF OPERATIONS

(In millions, except number of shares which are reflected in thousands and per share amounts)

	Years ended September 26, 2020	Years ended September 28, 2019	Years ended September 29, 2018
Net sales:			
Products	$ 220,747	$ 213,883	$ 225,847
Services	53,768	46,291	39,748
Total net sales	274,515	260,174	265,595
Cost of sales:			
Products	151,286	144,996	148,164
Services	18,273	16,786	15,592
Total cost of sales	169,559	161,782	163,756
Gross margin	104,956	98,392	101,839
Operating expenses:			
Research and development	18,752	16,217	14,236
Selling, general and administrative	19,916	18,245	16,705
Total operating expenses	38,668	34,462	30,941
Operating income	66,288	63,930	70,898
Other income/(expense), net	803	1,807	2,005
Income before provision for income taxes	67,091	65,737	72,903
Provision for income taxes	9,680	10,481	13,372
Net income	$ 57,411	$ 55,256	$ 59,531
Earnings per share:			
Basic	$ 3.31	$ 2.99	$ 3.00
Diluted	$ 3.28	$ 2.97	$ 2.98
Shares used in computing earnings per share:			
Basic	17,352,119	18,471,336	19,821,510
Diluted	17,528,214	18,595,651	20,000,435

See accompanying Notes to Consolidated Financial Statements.

Apple Inc.

CONSOLIDATED STATEMENTS OF COMPREHENSIVE INCOME
(In millions)

	Years ended September 26, 2020	September 28, 2019	September 29, 2018
Net income	$ 57,411	$ 55,256	$ 59,531
Other comprehensive income/(loss):			
Change in foreign currency translation, net of tax	88	(408)	(525)
Change in unrealized gains/losses on derivative instruments, net of tax:			
Change in fair value of derivatives	79	(661)	523
Adjustment for net (gains)/losses realized and included in net income	(1,264)	23	382
Total change in unrealized gains/losses on derivative instruments	(1,185)	(638)	905
Change in unrealized gains/losses on marketable debt securities, net of tax:			
Change in fair value of marketable debt securities	1,202	3,802	(3,407)
Adjustment for net (gains)/losses realized and included in net income	(63)	25	1
Total change in unrealized gains/losses on marketable debt securities	1,139	3,827	(3,406)
Total other comprehensive income/(loss)	42	2,781	(3,026)
Total comprehensive income	$ 57,453	$ 58,037	$ 56,505

See accompanying Notes to Consolidated Financial Statements.

Apple Inc.

CONSOLIDATED BALANCE SHEETS
(In millions, except number of shares which are reflected in thousands and par value)

	September 26, 2020	September 28, 2019
ASSETS:		
Current assets:		
Cash and cash equivalents	$ 38,016	$ 48,844
Marketable securities	52,927	51,713
Accounts receivable, net	16,120	22,926
Inventories	4,061	4,106
Vendor non-trade receivables	21,325	22,878
Other current assets	11,264	12,352
Total current assets	143,713	162,819
Non-current assets:		
Marketable securities	100,887	105,341
Property, plant and equipment, net	36,766	37,378
Other non-current assets	42,522	32,978
Total non-current assets	180,175	175,697
Total assets	$ 323,888	$ 338,516
LIABILITIES AND SHAREHOLDERS' EQUITY:		
Current liabilities:		
Accounts payable	$ 42,296	$ 46,236
Other current liabilities	42,684	37,720
Deferred revenue	6,643	5,522
Commercial paper	4,996	5,980
Term debt	8,773	10,260
Total current liabilities	105,392	105,718
Non-current liabilities:		
Term debt	98,667	91,807
Other non-current liabilities	54,490	50,503
Total non-current liabilities	153,157	142,310
Total liabilities	258,549	248,028
Commitments and contingencies		
Shareholders' equity:		
Common stock and additional paid-in capital, $0.00001 par value: 50,400,000 shares authorized; 16,976,763 and 17,772,945 shares issued and outstanding, respectively	50,779	45,174
Retained earnings	14,966	45,898
Accumulated other comprehensive income/(loss)	(406)	(584)
Total shareholders' equity	65,339	90,488
Total liabilities and shareholders' equity	$ 323,888	$ 338,516

See accompanying Notes to Consolidated Financial Statements.

Apple Inc.

CONSOLIDATED STATEMENTS OF SHAREHOLDERS' EQUITY
(In millions, except per share amounts)

	Years ended		
	September 26, 2020	**September 28, 2019**	**September 29, 2018**
Total shareholders' equity, beginning balances	$ 90,488	$ 107,147	$ 134,047
Common stock and additional paid-in capital:			
Beginning balances	45,174	40,201	35,867
Common stock issued	880	781	669
Common stock withheld related to net share settlement of equity awards	(2,250)	(2,002)	(1,778)
Share-based compensation	6,975	6,194	5,443
Ending balances	50,779	45,174	40,201
Retained earnings:			
Beginning balances	45,898	70,400	98,330
Net income	57,411	55,256	59,531
Dividends and dividend equivalents declared	(14,087)	(14,129)	(13,735)
Common stock withheld related to net share settlement of equity awards	(1,604)	(1,029)	(948)
Common stock repurchased	(72,516)	(67,101)	(73,056)
Cumulative effects of changes in accounting principles	(136)	2,501	278
Ending balances	14,966	45,898	70,400
Accumulated other comprehensive income/(loss):			
Beginning balances	(584)	(3,454)	(150)
Other comprehensive income/(loss)	42	2,781	(3,026)
Cumulative effects of changes in accounting principles	136	89	(278)
Ending balances	(406)	(584)	(3,454)
Total shareholders' equity, ending balances	$ 65,339	$ 90,488	$ 107,147
Dividends and dividend equivalents declared per share or RSU	$ 0.795	$ 0.75	$ 0.68

See accompanying Notes to Consolidated Financial Statements.

Apple Inc.

CONSOLIDATED STATEMENTS OF CASH FLOWS
(In millions)

	Years ended		
	September 26, 2020	September 28, 2019	September 29, 2018
Cash, cash equivalents and restricted cash, beginning balances	$ 50,224	$ 25,913	$ 20,289
Operating activities:			
Net income	57,411	55,256	59,531
Adjustments to reconcile net income to cash generated by operating activities:			
Depreciation and amortization	11,056	12,547	10,903
Share-based compensation expense	6,829	6,068	5,340
Deferred income tax benefit	(215)	(340)	(32,590)
Other	(97)	(652)	(444)
Changes in operating assets and liabilities:			
Accounts receivable, net	6,917	245	(5,322)
Inventories	(127)	(289)	828
Vendor non-trade receivables	1,553	2,931	(8,010)
Other current and non-current assets	(9,588)	873	(423)
Accounts payable	(4,062)	(1,923)	9,175
Deferred revenue	2,081	(625)	(3)
Other current and non-current liabilities	8,916	(4,700)	38,449
Cash generated by operating activities	80,674	69,391	77,434
Investing activities:			
Purchases of marketable securities	(114,938)	(39,630)	(71,356)
Proceeds from maturities of marketable securities	69,918	40,102	55,881
Proceeds from sales of marketable securities	50,473	56,988	47,838
Payments for acquisition of property, plant and equipment	(7,309)	(10,495)	(13,313)
Payments made in connection with business acquisitions, net	(1,524)	(624)	(721)
Purchases of non-marketable securities	(210)	(1,001)	(1,871)
Proceeds from non-marketable securities	92	1,634	353
Other	(791)	(1,078)	(745)
Cash generated by/(used in) investing activities	(4,289)	45,896	16,066
Financing activities:			
Proceeds from issuance of common stock	880	781	669
Payments for taxes related to net share settlement of equity awards	(3,634)	(2,817)	(2,527)
Payments for dividends and dividend equivalents	(14,081)	(14,119)	(13,712)
Repurchases of common stock	(72,358)	(66,897)	(72,738)
Proceeds from issuance of term debt, net	16,091	6,963	6,969
Repayments of term debt	(12,629)	(8,805)	(6,500)
Repayments of commercial paper, net	(963)	(5,977)	(37)
Other	(126)	(105)	—
Cash used in financing activities	(86,820)	(90,976)	(87,876)
Increase/(Decrease) in cash, cash equivalents and restricted cash	(10,435)	24,311	5,624
Cash, cash equivalents and restricted cash, ending balances	$ 39,789	$ 50,224	$ 25,913
Supplemental cash flow disclosure:			
Cash paid for income taxes, net	$ 9,501	$ 15,263	$ 10,417
Cash paid for interest	$ 3,002	$ 3,423	$ 3,022

See accompanying Notes to Consolidated Financial Statements.

APPENDIX E

Time Value of Money

Appendix Preview

Would you rather receive NT$1,000 today or a year from now? You should prefer to receive the NT$1,000 today because you can invest the NT$1,000 and earn interest on it. As a result, you will have more than NT$1,000 a year from now. What this example illustrates is the concept of the **time value of money**. Everyone prefers to receive money today rather than in the future because of the interest factor.

Appendix Outline

LEARNING OBJECTIVES	REVIEW
LO 1 Compute interest and future values.	• Nature of interest • Future value of a single amount • Future value of an annuity
LO 2 Compute present values.	• Present value variables • Present value of a single amount • Present value of an annuity • Time periods and discounting • Present value of a long-term note or bond
LO 3 Use a financial calculator to solve time value of money problems.	• Present value of a single sum • Present value of an annuity • Useful financial calculator applications

E.1 Interest and Future Values

LEARNING OBJECTIVE 1

Compute interest and future values.

Nature of Interest

Interest is payment for the use of another person's money.

- Interest is the difference between the amount borrowed or invested (called the **principal**) and the amount repaid or collected.
- The amount of interest to be paid or collected is usually stated as a rate over a specific period of time.
- The rate of interest is generally stated as an annual rate.

The amount of interest involved in any financing transaction is based on three elements:

1. **Principal (*p*):** The original amount borrowed or invested.
2. **Interest Rate (*i*):** An annual percentage of the principal.
3. **Time (*n*):** The number of periods that the principal is borrowed or invested.

Simple Interest

Simple interest is computed on the principal amount only.

- Simple interest is the return on the principal for one period.
- Simple interest is usually expressed as shown in **Illustration E.1**.

ILLUSTRATION E.1
Interest computation

$$\text{Interest} = \underset{p}{\text{Principal}} \times \underset{i}{\text{Rate}} \times \underset{n}{\text{Time}}$$

For example, if you borrowed NT$5,000 for 2 years at a simple interest rate of 6% annually, you would pay NT$600 in total interest, computed as follows.

$$\begin{aligned} \text{Interest} &= p \times i \times n \\ &= \text{NT\$5,000} \times .06 \times 2 \\ &= \text{NT\$600} \end{aligned}$$

Compound Interest

Compound interest is computed on principal **and** on any interest earned that has not been paid or withdrawn.

- Compound interest is the return on (or growth of) the principal for two or more time periods.
- Compounding computes interest not only on the principal but also on the interest earned to date on that principal, assuming the interest is left on deposit.

To illustrate the difference between simple and compound interest, assume that you deposit €1,000 in Bank Two, where it will earn simple interest of 9% per year, and you deposit another €1,000 in Citizens Bank, where it will earn compound interest of 9% per year compounded annually. Also assume that in both cases you will not withdraw any cash until three years from the date of deposit. **Illustration E.2** shows the computation of interest to be received and the accumulated year-end balances.

ILLUSTRATION E.2 **Simple versus compound interest**

Bank Two

Simple Interest Calculation	Simple Interest	Accumulated Year-End Balance
Year 1 €1,000.00 × 9%	€ 90.00	€1,090.00
Year 2 €1,000.00 × 9%	90.00	€1,180.00
Year 3 €1,000.00 × 9%	90.00	€1,270.00
	€ 270.00	

Citizens Bank

Compound Interest Calculation	Compound Interest	Accumulated Year-End Balance
Year 1 €1,000.00 × 9%	€ 90.00	€1,090.00
Year 2 €1,090.00 × 9%	98.10	€1,188.10
Year 3 €1,188.10 × 9%	106.93	€1,295.03
	€ 295.03	

€25.03 Difference

Note the following in Illustration E.2.

- Simple interest uses the initial principal of €1,000 to compute the interest in all three years.
- Compound interest uses the accumulated balance (principal plus interest to date) at each year-end to compute interest in the succeeding year—which explains why your compound interest account is larger.

Obviously, if you had a choice between investing your money at simple interest or at compound interest, you would choose compound interest, all other things—especially risk—being equal. In the example, compounding provides €25.03 of additional interest income. For practical purposes, compounding assumes that unpaid interest earned becomes a part of the principal, and the accumulated balance at the end of each year becomes the new principal on which interest is earned during the next year.

Illustration E.2 indicates that you should invest your money at the bank that compounds interest. Most business situations use compound interest. Simple interest is generally applicable only to short-term situations of one year or less.

Future Value of a Single Amount

The **future value of a single amount** is the value at a future date of a given amount invested, assuming compound interest. For example, in Illustration E.2, €1,295.03 is the future value of the €1,000 investment earning 9% for three years. The €1,295.03 is determined more easily by using the formula shown in **Illustration E.3**.

$$FV = p \times (1 + i)^n$$

ILLUSTRATION E.3

Formula for future value

where:

FV = future value of a single amount
p = principal (or present value; the value today)
i = interest rate for one period
n = number of periods

The €1,295.03 is computed as follows.

$$\begin{aligned} FV &= p \times (1+i)^n \\ &= €1,000 \times (1 + .09)^3 \\ &= €1,000 \times 1.29503 \\ &= €1,295.03 \end{aligned}$$

The 1.29503 is computed by multiplying (1.09 × 1.09 × 1.09). The amounts in this example can be depicted in the time diagram shown in **Illustration E.4**.

ILLUSTRATION E.4 **Time diagram**

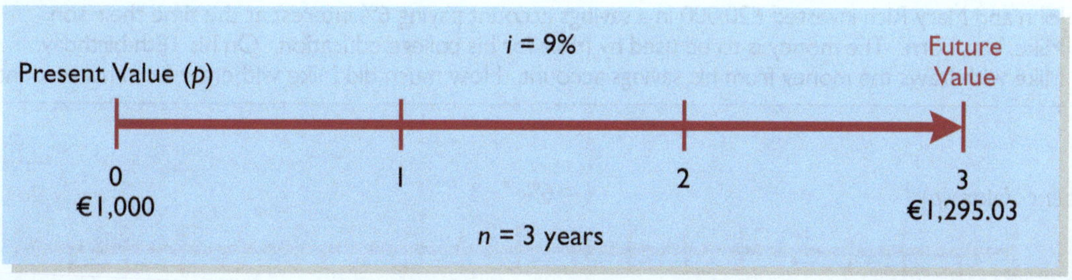

Another method used to compute the future value of a single amount involves a compound interest table. This table shows the future value of 1 for n periods. **Table 1** is such a table.

In Table 1, n is the number of compounding periods, the percentages are the periodic interest rates, and the 5-digit decimal numbers in the respective columns are the future value of 1 factors. To use Table 1, you multiply the principal amount by the future value factor for the specified number of periods and interest rate. For example, the future value factor for two periods at 9% is 1.18810. Multiplying this factor by €1,000 equals €1,188.10—which

TABLE 1 Future Value of 1

(*n*) Periods	4%	5%	6%	7%	8%	9%	10%	11%	12%	15%
0	1.00000	1.00000	1.00000	1.00000	1.00000	1.00000	1.00000	1.00000	1.00000	1.00000
1	1.04000	1.05000	1.06000	1.07000	1.08000	1.09000	1.10000	1.11000	1.12000	1.15000
2	1.08160	1.10250	1.12360	1.14490	1.16640	1.18810	1.21000	1.23210	1.25440	1.32250
3	1.12486	1.15763	1.19102	1.22504	1.25971	1.29503	1.33100	1.36763	1.40493	1.52088
4	1.16986	1.21551	1.26248	1.31080	1.36049	1.41158	1.46410	1.51807	1.57352	1.74901
5	1.21665	1.27628	1.33823	1.40255	1.46933	1.53862	1.61051	1.68506	1.76234	2.01136
6	1.26532	1.34010	1.41852	1.50073	1.58687	1.67710	1.77156	1.87041	1.97382	2.31306
7	1.31593	1.40710	1.50363	1.60578	1.71382	1.82804	1.94872	2.07616	2.21068	2.66002
8	1.36857	1.47746	1.59385	1.71819	1.85093	1.99256	2.14359	2.30454	2.47596	3.05902
9	1.42331	1.55133	1.68948	1.83846	1.99900	2.17189	2.35795	2.55803	2.77308	3.51788
10	1.48024	1.62889	1.79085	1.96715	2.15892	2.36736	2.59374	2.83942	3.10585	4.04556
11	1.53945	1.71034	1.89830	2.10485	2.33164	2.58043	2.85312	3.15176	3.47855	4.65239
12	1.60103	1.79586	2.01220	2.25219	2.51817	2.81267	3.13843	3.49845	3.89598	5.35025
13	1.66507	1.88565	2.13293	2.40985	2.71962	3.06581	3.45227	3.88328	4.36349	6.15279
14	1.73168	1.97993	2.26090	2.57853	2.93719	3.34173	3.79750	4.31044	4.88711	7.07571
15	1.80094	2.07893	2.39656	2.75903	3.17217	3.64248	4.17725	4.78459	5.47357	8.13706
16	1.87298	2.18287	2.54035	2.95216	3.42594	3.97031	4.59497	5.31089	6.13039	9.35762
17	1.94790	2.29202	2.69277	3.15882	3.70002	4.32763	5.05447	5.89509	6.86604	10.76126
18	2.02582	2.40662	2.85434	3.37993	3.99602	4.71712	5.55992	6.54355	7.68997	12.37545
19	2.10685	2.52695	3.02560	3.61653	4.31570	5.14166	6.11591	7.26334	8.61276	14.23177
20	2.19112	2.65330	3.20714	3.86968	4.66096	5.60441	6.72750	8.06231	9.64629	16.36654

is the accumulated balance at the end of year 2 in the Citizens Bank example in Illustration E.2. The €1,295.03 accumulated balance at the end of the third year is calculated from Table 1 by multiplying the future value factor for three periods (1.29503) by the €1,000.

The demonstration problem in **Illustration E.5** shows how to use Table 1.

ILLUSTRATION E.5 Demonstration problem—Using Table 1 for *FV* of 1

John and Mary Rich invested £20,000 in a savings account paying 6% interest at the time their son, Mike, was born. The money is to be used by Mike for his college education. On his 18th birthday, Mike withdraws the money from his savings account. How much did Mike withdraw from his account?

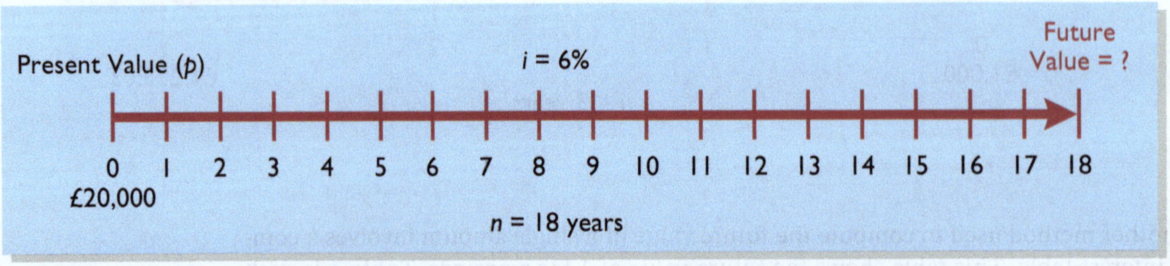

Answer: The future value factor from Table 1 is 2.85434 (18 periods at 6%). The future value of £20,000 earning 6% per year for 18 years is **£57,086.80** (£20,000 × 2.85434).

Future Value of an Annuity

The preceding discussion involved the accumulation of only a single principal sum. Individuals and businesses frequently encounter situations in which a **series** of equal amounts are to be paid or received at evenly spaced time intervals (periodically), such as loans or lease (rental) contracts.

- A series of payments or receipts of equal amounts is referred to as an **annuity**.
- The **future value of an annuity** is the sum of all the payments (receipts) plus the accumulated compound interest on them.
- In computing the future value of an annuity, it is necessary to know:
  1. The interest rate.
  2. The number of payments (receipts).
  3. The amount of the periodic payments (receipts).

To illustrate the computation of the future value of an annuity, assume that you invest HK$2,000 at the end of each year for three years at 5% interest compounded annually. This situation is depicted in the time diagram in **Illustration E.6**.

ILLUSTRATION E.6 **Time diagram for a three-year annuity**

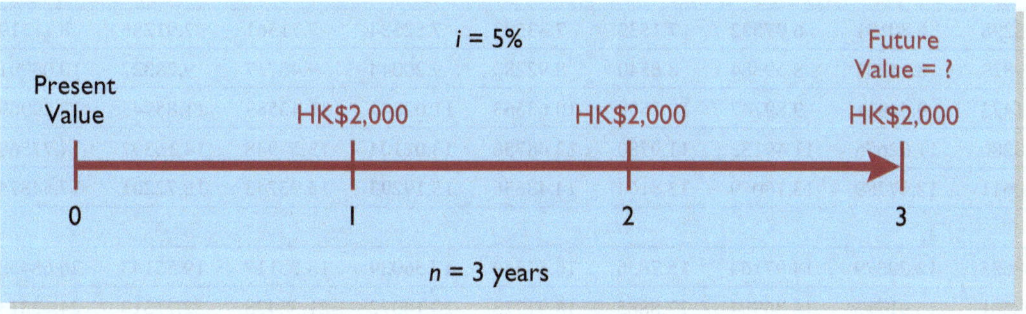

The HK$2,000 invested at the end of year 1 will earn interest for two years (years 2 and 3), and the HK$2,000 invested at the end of year 2 will earn interest for one year (year 3). However, the last HK$2,000 investment (made at the end of year 3) will not earn any interest. Using the future value factors from Table 1, the future value of these periodic payments is computed as shown in **Illustration E.7**.

ILLUSTRATION E.7 **Future value of periodic payment computation**

Invested at End of Year	Number of Compounding Periods	Amount Invested	×	Future Value of 1 Factor at 5%	=	Future Value
1	2	HK$2,000	×	1.10250		HK$2,205
2	1	HK$2,000	×	1.05000		2,100
3	0	HK$2,000	×	1.00000		2,000
				3.15250		HK$6,305

- The first HK$2,000 investment is multiplied by the future value factor for two periods (1.1025) because two years' interest will accumulate on it (in years 2 and 3).
- The second HK$2,000 investment will earn only one year's interest (in year 3) and therefore is multiplied by the future value factor for one year (1.0500).

- The final HK$2,000 investment is made at the end of the third year and will not earn any interest. Thus, $n = 0$ and the future value factor is 1.00000. Consequently, the future value of the last HK$2,000 invested is only HK$2,000 since it does not accumulate any interest.

Calculating the future value of each individual cash flow is required when the periodic payments or receipts are not equal in each period. However, when the periodic payments (receipts) are **the same in each period**, the future value can be computed by using a future value of an annuity of 1 table. **Table 2** is such a table.

TABLE 2 Future Value of an Annuity of 1

(n) Payments	4%	5%	6%	7%	8%	9%	10%	11%	12%	15%
1	1.00000	1.00000	1.00000	1.0000	1.00000	1.00000	1.00000	1.00000	1.00000	1.00000
2	2.04000	2.05000	2.06000	2.0700	2.08000	2.09000	2.10000	2.11000	2.12000	2.15000
3	3.12160	3.15250	3.18360	3.2149	3.24640	3.27810	3.31000	3.34210	3.37440	3.47250
4	4.24646	4.31013	4.37462	4.4399	4.50611	4.57313	4.64100	4.70973	4.77933	4.99338
5	5.41632	5.52563	5.63709	5.7507	5.86660	5.98471	6.10510	6.22780	6.35285	6.74238
6	6.63298	6.80191	6.97532	7.1533	7.33592	7.52334	7.71561	7.91286	8.11519	8.75374
7	7.89829	8.14201	8.39384	8.6540	8.92280	9.20044	9.48717	9.78327	10.08901	11.06680
8	9.21423	9.54911	9.89747	10.2598	10.63663	11.02847	11.43589	11.85943	12.29969	13.72682
9	10.58280	11.02656	11.49132	11.9780	12.48756	13.02104	13.57948	14.16397	14.77566	16.78584
10	12.00611	12.57789	13.18079	13.8164	14.48656	15.19293	15.93743	16.72201	17.54874	20.30372
11	13.48635	14.20679	14.97164	15.7836	16.64549	17.56029	18.53117	19.56143	20.65458	24.34928
12	15.02581	15.91713	16.86994	17.8885	18.97713	20.14072	21.38428	22.71319	24.13313	29.00167
13	16.62684	17.71298	18.88214	20.1406	21.49530	22.95339	24.52271	26.21164	28.02911	34.35192
14	18.29191	19.59863	21.01507	22.5505	24.21492	26.01919	27.97498	30.09492	32.39260	40.50471
15	20.02359	21.57856	23.27597	25.1290	27.15211	29.36092	31.77248	34.40536	37.27972	47.58041
16	21.82453	23.65749	25.67253	27.8881	30.32428	33.00340	35.94973	39.18995	42.75328	55.71747
17	23.69751	25.84037	28.21288	30.8402	33.75023	36.97351	40.54470	44.50084	48.88367	65.07509
18	25.64541	28.13238	30.90565	33.9990	37.45024	41.30134	45.59917	50.39593	55.74972	75.83636
19	27.67123	30.53900	33.75999	37.3790	41.44626	46.01846	51.15909	56.93949	63.43968	88.21181
20	29.77808	33.06595	36.78559	40.9955	45.76196	51.16012	57.27500	64.20283	72.05244	102.44358

Table 2 shows the future value of 1 to be received periodically for a given number of payments. It assumes that each payment is made at the **end** of each period. We can see from Table 2 that the future value of an annuity of 1 factor for three payments at 5% is 3.15250. The future value factor is the total of the three individual future value factors as shown in Illustration E.7. Multiplying this amount by the annual investment of HK$2,000 produces a future value of HK$6,305.

The demonstration problem in **Illustration E.8** shows how to use Table 2.

ILLUSTRATION E.8 **Demonstration problem—Using Table 2 for *FV* of an annuity of 1**

John and Char Lewis' daughter, Debra, has just started high school. They decide to start a college fund for her and will invest £2,500 in a savings account at the end of each year she is in high school (4 payments total). The account will earn 6% interest compounded annually. How much will be in the college fund at the time Debra graduates from high school?

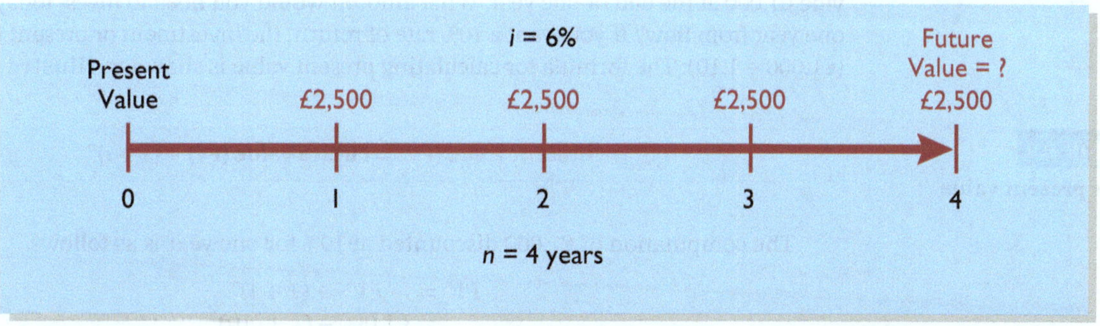

Answer: The future value factor from Table 2 is 4.37462 (4 payments at 6%). The future value of £2,500 invested each year for 4 years at 6% interest is **£10,936.55** (£2,500 × 4.37462).

Note that we can apply the same concepts in situations where the future value and interest rate are known, but the payment must be calculated. Suppose, for example, that in Illustration E.8 that the amount that Debra needs to accumulate in her college fund by the end of four years is £10,936.55. If Debra earns 6% on her four annual payments, we can solve for the amount of the annuity payments by dividing £10,936.55 by the future value factor of 4.37462 to determine the payment amount of £2,500.

E.2 Present Value Concepts

LEARNING OBJECTIVE 2

Compute present values.

Present Value Variables

The **present value** is the value now of a given amount to be paid or received in the future, assuming compound interest.

- The present value, like the future value, is based on three variables:
  1. The dollar amount to be received (future amount).
  2. The length of time until the amount is received (number of periods).
  3. The interest rate (the discount rate).
- The process of determining the present value is referred to as **discounting the future amount**.

Present value computations are used in measuring many items. For example, the present value of principal and interest payments is used to determine the market price of a bond.

Determining the amount to be reported for notes payable and lease liabilities also involves present value computations. Finally, all rate of return and internal rate of return computations involve present value techniques.

Present Value of a Single Amount

To illustrate present value, assume that you want to invest a sum of money today that will provide €1,000 at the end of one year. What amount would you need to invest today to have €1,000 one year from now? If you want a 10% rate of return, the investment or present value is €909.09 (€1,000 ÷ 1.10). The formula for calculating present value is shown in **Illustration E.9**.

ILLUSTRATION E.9

Formula for present value

$$\text{Present Value (PV)} = \text{Future Value (FV)} \div (1 + i)^n$$

The computation of €1,000 discounted at 10% for one year is as follows.

$$\begin{aligned} PV &= \quad FV \div (1 + i)^n \\ &= €1{,}000 \div (1 + .10)^1 \\ &= €1{,}000 \div 1.10 \\ &= €909.09 \end{aligned}$$

The future amount (€1,000), the discount rate (10%), and the number of periods (1) are known. The variables in this situation can be depicted in the time diagram in **Illustration E.10**.

ILLUSTRATION E.10

Finding present value if discounted for one period

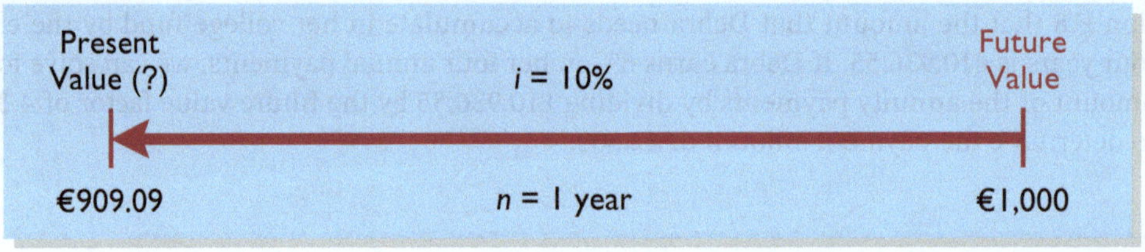

If the single amount of €1,000 is to be received **in two years** and discounted at 10% [PV = €1,000 ÷ (1 + .10)^2], its present value is €826.45 [(€1,000 ÷ 1.21), depicted in **Illustration E.11**.

ILLUSTRATION E.11

Finding present value if discounted for two periods

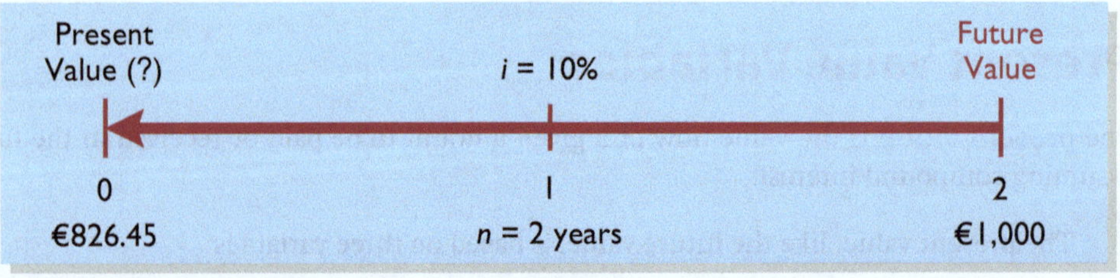

The present value of 1 may also be determined through tables that show the present value of 1 for n periods. In **Table 3** below, n is the number of discounting periods involved. The percentages are the periodic interest rates or discount rates, and the 5-digit decimal numbers in the respective columns are the present value of 1 factors.

When using Table 3, the future value is multiplied by the present value factor specified at the intersection of the number of periods and the discount rate.

TABLE 3 **Present Value of 1**

(*n*) Periods	4%	5%	6%	7%	8%	9%	10%	11%	12%	15%
1	.96154	.95238	.94340	.93458	.92593	.91743	.90909	.90090	.89286	.86957
2	.92456	.90703	.89000	.87344	.85734	.84168	.82645	.81162	.79719	.75614
3	.88900	.86384	.83962	.81630	.79383	.77218	.75132	.73119	.71178	.65752
4	.85480	.82270	.79209	.76290	.73503	.70843	.68301	.65873	.63552	.57175
5	.82193	.78353	.74726	.71299	.68058	.64993	.62092	.59345	.56743	.49718
6	.79031	.74622	.70496	.66634	.63017	.59627	.56447	.53464	.50663	.43233
7	.75992	.71068	.66506	.62275	.58349	.54703	.51316	.48166	.45235	.37594
8	.73069	.67684	.62741	.58201	.54027	.50187	.46651	.43393	.40388	.32690
9	.70259	.64461	.59190	.54393	.50025	.46043	.42410	.39092	.36061	.28426
10	.67556	.61391	.55839	.50835	.46319	.42241	.38554	.35218	.32197	.24719
11	.64958	.58468	.52679	.47509	.42888	.38753	.35049	.31728	.28748	.21494
12	.62460	.55684	.49697	.44401	.39711	.35554	.31863	.28584	.25668	.18691
13	.60057	.53032	.46884	.41496	.36770	.32618	.28966	.25751	.22917	.16253
14	.57748	.50507	.44230	.38782	.34046	.29925	.26333	.23199	.20462	.14133
15	.55526	.48102	.41727	.36245	.31524	.27454	.23939	.20900	.18270	.12289
16	.53391	.45811	.39365	.33873	.29189	.25187	.21763	.18829	.16312	.10687
17	.51337	.43630	.37136	.31657	.27027	.23107	.19785	.16963	.14564	.09293
18	.49363	.41552	.35034	.29586	.25025	.21199	.17986	.15282	.13004	.08081
19	.47464	.39573	.33051	.27615	.23171	.19449	.16351	.13768	.11611	.07027
20	.45639	.37689	.31180	.25842	.21455	.17843	.14864	.12403	.10367	.06110

For example, the present value factor for one period at a discount rate of 10% is .90909, which equals the €909.09 (€1,000 × .90909) computed in Illustration E.10. For two periods at a discount rate of 10%, the present value factor is .82645, which equals the €826.45 (€1,000 × .82645) computed previously.

- Note that a higher discount rate produces a smaller present value. For example, using a 15% discount rate, the present value of €1,000 due one year from now is €869.57, versus €909.09 at 10%.
- Also note that the further removed from the present the future value is, the smaller the present value. For example, using the same discount rate of 10%, the present value of €1,000 due in **five years** is €620.92. The present value of €1,000 due in **one year** is €909.09, a difference of €288.17.

The following two demonstration problems (**Illustrations E.12** and **E.13**) illustrate how to use Table 3.

ILLUSTRATION E.12

Demonstration problem—Using Table 3 for *PV* of 1

Suppose you have a winning lottery ticket. You have the option of taking NT$100,000 three years from now or taking the present value of NT$100,000 now. Assuming an 8% rate in discounting, how much will you receive if you accept your winnings now?

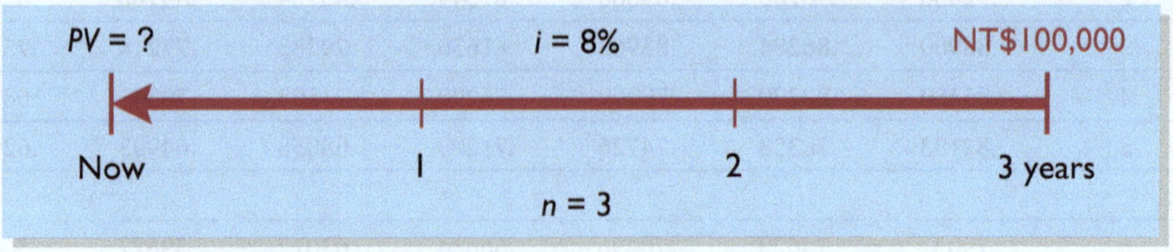

Answer: The present value factor from Table 3 is .79383 (3 periods at 8%). The present value of NT$100,000 to be received in 3 years discounted at 8% is **NT$79,383** (NT$100,000 × .79383).

ILLUSTRATION E.13

Demonstration problem—Using Table 3 for *PV* of 1

Determine the amount you must deposit today in your super savings account, paying 9% interest, in order to accumulate £5,000 for a down payment 4 years from now on a new car.

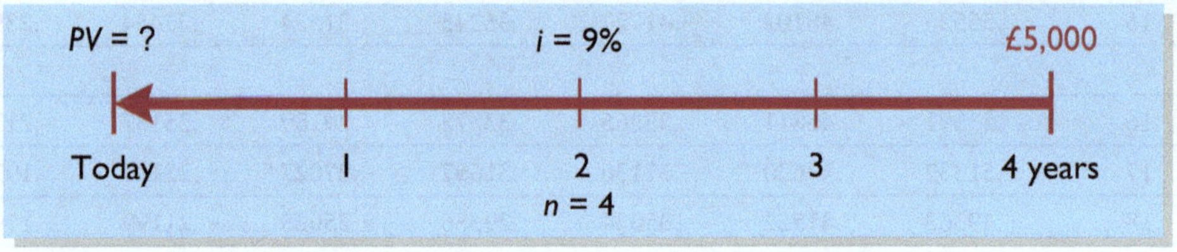

Answer: The present value factor from Table 3 is .70843 (4 periods at 9%). The present value of £5,000 to be received in 4 years discounted at 9% is **£3,542.15** (£5,000 × .70843).

Present Value of an Annuity

The preceding discussion involved the discounting of only a single future amount. Businesses and individuals frequently engage in transactions in which a series of equal amounts are to be received or paid at evenly spaced time intervals (periodically). Examples of a series of periodic receipts or payments are loan agreements, installment sales, mortgage notes, lease (rental) contracts, and pension obligations. As discussed earlier, these periodic receipts or payments are **annuities**.

- The **present value of an annuity** is the value now of a series of future receipts or payments, discounted assuming compound interest.
- In computing the present value of an annuity, it is necessary to know:
  1. The discount rate.
  2. The number of payments (receipts).
  3. The amount of the periodic payments or receipts.

To illustrate the computation of the present value of an annuity, assume that you will receive €1,000 cash annually for three years at a time when the discount rate is 10%. This situation is depicted in the time diagram in Illustration E.14. Illustration E.15 shows the computation of its present value in this situation.

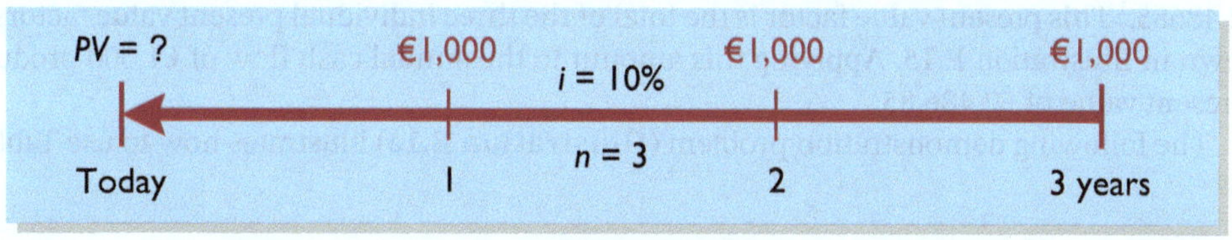

ILLUSTRATION E.14

Time diagram for a three-year annuity

Future Amount	×	Present Value of 1 Factor at 10%	=	Present Value
€1,000 (one year away)		.90909		€ 909.09
1,000 (two years away)		.82645		826.45
1,000 (three years away)		.75132		751.32
		2.48686		**€2,486.86**

ILLUSTRATION E.15

Present value of a series of future amounts computation

This method of calculation is required when the periodic cash flows are not uniform in each period. However, when the future receipts are the same in each period, an annuity table can be used. As illustrated in **Table 4**, an annuity table shows the present value of 1 to be received periodically for a given number of payments. It assumes that each payment is made at the end of each period.

TABLE 4 **Present Value of an Annuity of 1**

(*n*) Payments	4%	5%	6%	7%	8%	9%	10%	11%	12%	15%
1	.96154	.95238	.94340	.93458	.92593	.91743	.90909	.90090	.89286	.86957
2	1.88609	1.85941	1.83339	1.80802	1.78326	1.75911	1.73554	1.71252	1.69005	1.62571
3	2.77509	2.72325	2.67301	2.62432	2.57710	2.53130	2.48685	2.44371	2.40183	2.28323
4	3.62990	3.54595	3.46511	3.38721	3.31213	3.23972	3.16986	3.10245	3.03735	2.85498
5	4.45182	4.32948	4.21236	4.10020	3.99271	3.88965	3.79079	3.69590	3.60478	3.35216
6	5.24214	5.07569	4.91732	4.76654	4.62288	4.48592	4.35526	4.23054	4.11141	3.78448
7	6.00205	5.78637	5.58238	5.38929	5.20637	5.03295	4.86842	4.71220	4.56376	4.16042
8	6.73274	6.46321	6.20979	5.97130	5.74664	5.53482	5.33493	5.14612	4.96764	4.48732
9	7.43533	7.10782	6.80169	6.51523	6.24689	5.99525	5.75902	5.53705	5.32825	4.77158
10	8.11090	7.72173	7.36009	7.02358	6.71008	6.41766	6.14457	5.88923	5.65022	5.01877
11	8.76048	8.30641	7.88687	7.49867	7.13896	6.80519	6.49506	6.20652	5.93770	5.23371
12	9.38507	8.86325	8.38384	7.94269	7.53608	7.16073	6.81369	6.49236	6.19437	5.42062
13	9.98565	9.39357	8.85268	8.35765	7.90378	7.48690	7.10336	6.74987	6.42355	5.58315
14	10.56312	9.89864	9.29498	8.74547	8.24424	7.78615	7.36669	6.98187	6.62817	5.72448
15	11.11839	10.37966	9.71225	9.10791	8.55948	8.06069	7.60608	7.19087	6.81086	5.84737
16	11.65230	10.83777	10.10590	9.44665	8.85137	8.31256	7.82371	7.37916	6.97399	5.95424
17	12.16567	11.27407	10.47726	9.76322	9.12164	8.54363	8.02155	7.54879	7.11963	6.04716
18	12.65930	11.68959	10.82760	10.05909	9.37189	8.75563	8.20141	7.70162	7.24967	6.12797
19	13.13394	12.08532	11.15812	10.33560	9.60360	8.95012	8.36492	7.83929	7.36578	6.19823
20	13.59033	12.46221	11.46992	10.59401	9.81815	9.12855	8.51356	7.96333	7.46944	6.25933

Table 4 shows that the present value of an annuity of 1 factor for three payments at 10% is 2.48685.[1] This present value factor is the total of the three individual present value factors, as shown in Illustration E.15. Applying this amount to the annual cash flow of €1,000 produces a present value of €2,486.85.

The following demonstration problem (**Illustration E.16**) illustrates how to use Table 4.

ILLUSTRATION E.16

Demonstration problem—Using Table 4 for *PV* of an annuity of 1

Kildare Construction has just signed a finance lease contract for equipment that requires rental payments of €6,000 each, to be paid at the end of each of the next 5 years. The appropriate discount rate is 12%. What is the present value of the rental payments—that is, the amount used to finance the leased equipment?

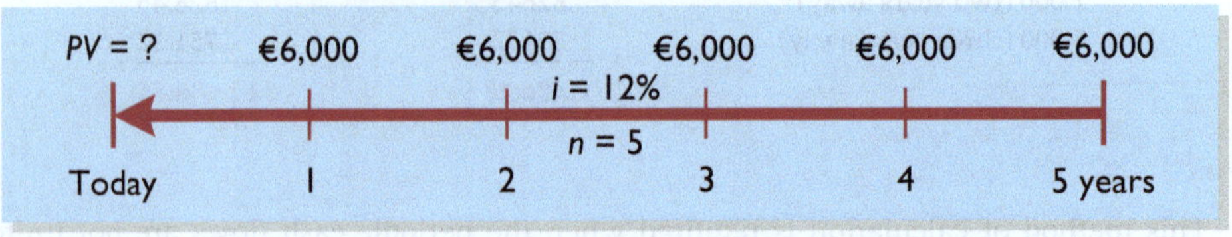

Answer: The present value factor from Table 4 is 3.60478 (5 payments at 12%). The present value of 5 payments of €6,000 each discounted at 12% is **€21,628.68** (€6,000 × 3.60478).

Note that the same concepts apply in situations when the price and interest rate are known, but the payment must be calculated. Suppose, for example, that in Illustration E.16 that the price of the lease contract is €21,628.68 and that Kildare Construction wants to finance the lease contract by making five annual lease payments when the annual rate of interest is 12%. In this case, rather than solving for the present value, we need to solve for the amount of the annual payment. To do this, we divide the price (the present value) of £21,628.68 by the present value factor of 3.60478 to arrive at an annual payment of £6,000.

Time Periods and Discounting

In the preceding calculations, the discounting was done on an annual basis using an annual interest rate.

- Discounting may also be done over shorter periods of time such as monthly, quarterly, or semiannually.
- When the time frame is less than one year, it is necessary to convert the annual interest rate to the applicable time frame.

Assume, for example, that the investor in Illustration E.14 received €500 **semiannually** for three years instead of €1,000 annually. In this case, the number of periods becomes six (3 × 2), the discount rate is 5% (10% ÷ 2), the present value factor from Table 4 is 5.07569 (6 periods at 5%), and the present value of the future cash flows is €2,537.85 (5.07569 × €500). This amount is slightly higher than the €2,486.86 computed in Illustration E.15 because interest is computed twice during the same year. That is, during the second half of the year, interest is earned on the first half-year's interest.

Present Value of a Long-Term Note or Bond

The present value (or market price) of a long-term note or bond is a function of three variables: (1) the payment amounts, (2) the length of time until the amounts are paid, and (3) the discount rate. Our example uses a five-year bond issue.

[1]The difference of .00001 between 2.48686 and 2.48685 is due to rounding.

The first variable (amounts to be paid) is made up of two elements:

1. A series of interest payments (an annuity).
2. The principal amount (a single sum).

To compute the present value of the bond, both the interest payments and the principal amount must be discounted—two different computations. The time diagrams for a bond due in five years are shown in **Illustration E.17**.

ILLUSTRATION E.17 **Present value of a bond time diagram**

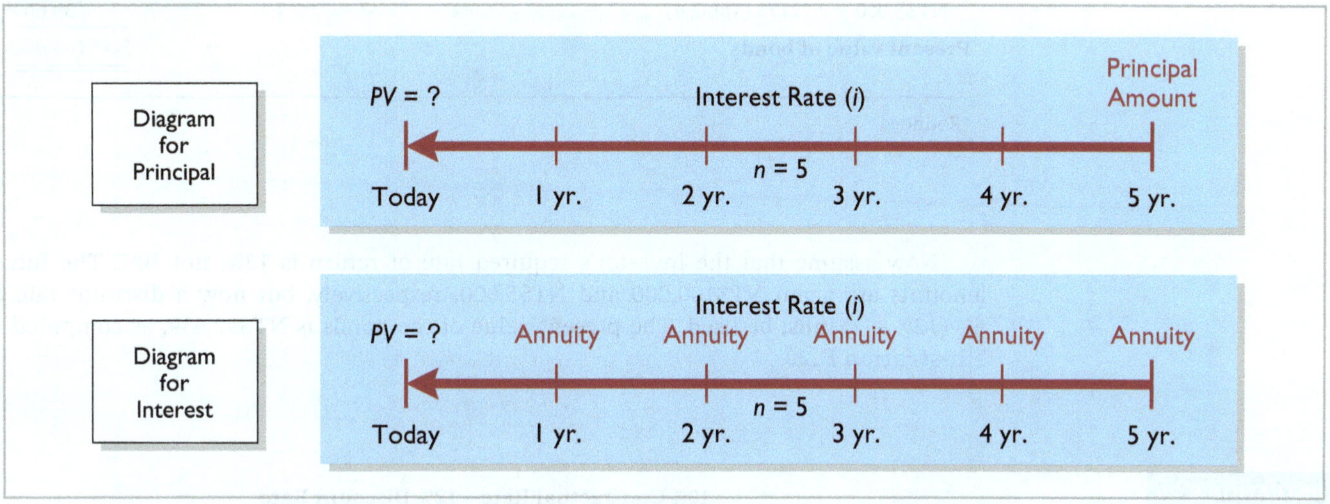

When the investor's market interest rate is equal to the bond's contractual interest rate, the present value of the bonds will equal the face value of the bonds. To illustrate, assume a bond issue of 10%, five-year bonds with a face value of NT$100,000 with interest payable **semiannually** on January 1 and July 1. If the discount rate is the same as the contractual rate, the bonds will sell at face value. In this case, the investor will receive (1) NT$100,000 at maturity and (2) a series of ten NT$5,000 interest payments [(NT$100,000 × 10%) ÷ 2] over the term of the bonds. The length of time is expressed in terms of interest periods—in this case—10, and the discount rate per interest period, 5%. The following time diagram (**Illustration E.18**) depicts the variables involved in this discounting situation.

ILLUSTRATION E.18 **Time diagram for present value of a 10%, five-year bond paying interest semiannually**

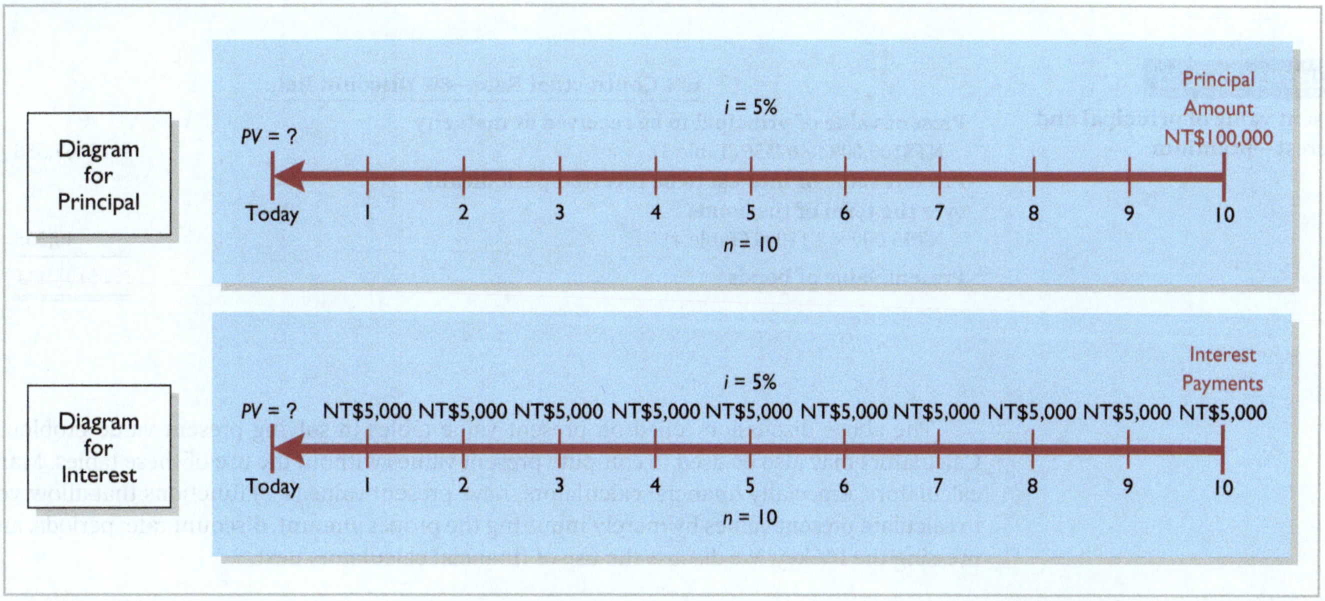

Illustration E.19 shows the computation of the present value of these bonds.

ILLUSTRATION E.19

Present value of principal and interest—face value

10% Contractual Rate—10% Discount Rate	
Present value of principal to be received at maturity	
NT$100,000 × *PV* of 1 due in 10 periods at 5%	
NT$100,000 × .61391 (Table 3)	NT$ 61,391
Present value of interest to be received periodically over the term of the bonds	
NT$5,000 × *PV* of 1 due periodically for 10 periods at 5%	
NT$5,000 × 7.72173 (Table 4)	38,609*
Present value of bonds	**NT$100,000**

*Rounded

Now assume that the investor's required rate of return is 12%, not 10%. The future amounts are again NT$100,000 and NT$5,000, respectively, but now a discount rate of 6% (12% ÷ 2) must be used. The present value of the bonds is NT$92,639, as computed in **Illustration E.20**.

ILLUSTRATION E.20

Present value of principal and interest—discount

10% Contractual Rate—12% Discount Rate	
Present value of principal to be received at maturity	
NT$100,000 × .55839 (Table 3)	NT$55,839
Present value of interest to be received periodically over the term of the bonds	
NT$5,000 × 7.36009 (Table 4)	36,800
Present value of bonds	**NT$92,639**

Conversely, if the discount rate is 8% and the contractual rate is 10%, the present value of the bonds is NT$108,111, computed as shown in **Illustration E.21**.

ILLUSTRATION E.21

Present value of principal and interest—premium

10% Contractual Rate—8% Discount Rate	
Present value of principal to be received at maturity	
NT$100,000 × .67556 (Table 3)	NT$ 67,556
Present value of interest to be received periodically over the term of the bonds	
NT$5,000 × 8.11090 (Table 4)	40,555
Present value of bonds	**NT$108,111**

The above discussion relied on present value tables in solving present value problems. Calculators may also be used to compute present values without the use of these tables. Many calculators, especially financial calculators, have present value (*PV*) functions that allow you to calculate present values by merely inputting the proper amount, discount rate, periods, and pressing the PV key. We discuss the use of financial calculators next.

E.3 Using Financial Calculators

LEARNING OBJECTIVE 3

Use a financial calculator to solve time value of money problems.

Business professionals, once they have mastered the underlying time value of money concepts, often use a financial calculator to solve these types of problems. In most cases, they use calculators if interest rates or time periods do not correspond with the information provided in the compound interest tables.

To use financial calculators, you enter the time value of money variables into the calculator. **Illustration E.22** shows the five most common keys used to solve time value of money problems.[2]

ILLUSTRATION E.22
Financial calculator keys

where:

N = number of periods
I = interest rate per period (some calculators use I/YR or i)
PV = present value (occurs at the beginning of the first period)
PMT = payment (all payments are equal, and none are skipped)
FV = future value (occurs at the end of the last period)

In solving time value of money problems in this appendix, you will generally be given three of four variables and will have to solve for the remaining variable. The fifth key (the key not used) is given a value of zero to ensure that this variable is not used in the computation.

Present Value of a Single Sum

To illustrate how to solve a present value problem using a financial calculator, assume that you want to know the present value of €84,253 to be received in five years, discounted at 11% compounded annually. **Illustration E.23** depicts this problem.

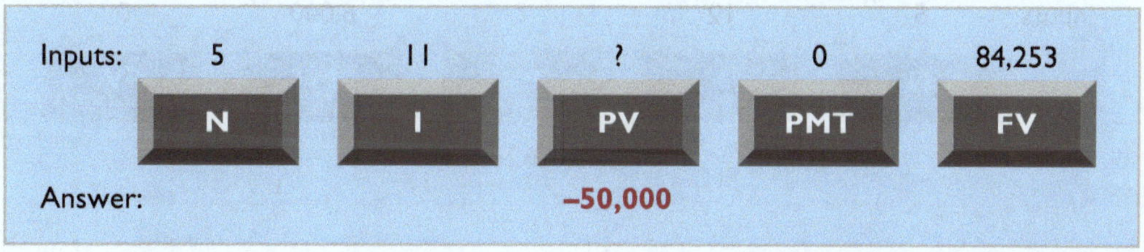

ILLUSTRATION E.23
Calculator solution for present value of a single sum

[2]On many calculators, these keys are actual buttons on the face of the calculator; on others, they appear on the display after the user accesses a present value menu.

Illustration E.23 shows you the information (inputs) to enter into the calculator: N = 5, I = 11, PMT = 0, and FV = 84,253. You then press PV for the answer: −€50,000. As indicated, the PMT key was given a value of zero because a series of payments did not occur in this problem.

Plus and Minus

The use of plus and minus signs in time value of money problems with a financial calculator can be confusing. Most financial calculators are programmed so that the positive and negative cash flows in any problem offset each other. In the present value problem above, we identified the €84,253 future value initial investment as a positive (inflow); the answer −€50,000 was shown as a negative amount, reflecting a cash outflow. If the 84,253 were entered as a negative, then the final answer would have been reported as a positive 50,000.

Hopefully, the sign convention will not cause confusion. If you understand what is required in a problem, you should be able to interpret a positive or negative amount in determining the solution to a problem.

Compounding Periods

In the previous problem, we assumed that compounding occurs once a year. Some financial calculators have a default setting, which assumes that compounding occurs 12 times a year. You must determine what default period has been programmed into your calculator and change it as necessary to arrive at the proper compounding period.

Rounding

Most financial calculators store and calculate using 12 decimal places. As a result, because compound interest tables generally have factors only up to five decimal places, a slight difference in the final answer can result. In most time value of money problems, the final answer will not include more than two decimal places.

Present Value of an Annuity

To illustrate how to solve a present value of an annuity problem using a financial calculator, assume that you are asked to determine the present value of rental receipts of €6,000 each to be received at the end of each of the next five years, when discounted at 12%, as pictured in Illustration E.24.

ILLUSTRATION E.24

Calculator solution for present value of an annuity

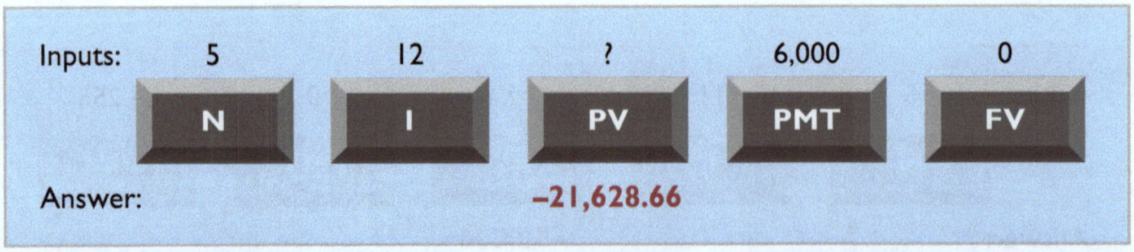

In this case, you enter N = 5, I = 12, PMT = 6,000, FV = 0, and then press PV to arrive at the answer of −€21,628.66.

Useful Applications of the Financial Calculator

With a financial calculator, you can solve for any interest rate or for any number of periods in a time value of money problem. Here are some examples of these applications.

Auto Loan

Assume you are financing the purchase of a used car with a three-year loan. The loan has a 9.5% stated annual interest rate, compounded monthly. The price of the car is €6,000, and you want to determine the monthly payments, assuming that the payments start one month after the purchase. This problem is pictured in **Illustration E.25**.

ILLUSTRATION E.25
Calculator solution for auto loan payments

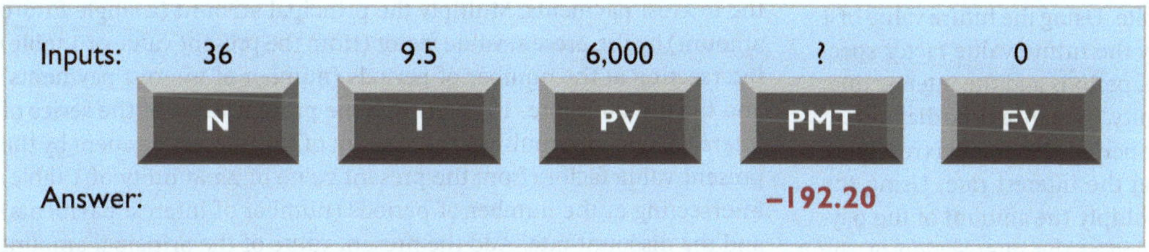

To solve this problem, you enter N = 36 (12 × 3), I = 9.5, PV = 6,000, FV = 0, and then press PMT. You will find that the monthly payments will be €192.20. Note that the payment key is usually programmed for 12 payments per year. Thus, you must change the default (compounding period) if the payments are other than monthly.

Mortgage Loan Amount

Say you are evaluating financing options for a loan on a house (a mortgage). You decide that the maximum mortgage payment you can afford is €700 per month. The annual interest rate is 8.4%. If you get a mortgage that requires you to make monthly payments over a 15-year period, what is the maximum home loan you can afford? **Illustration E.26** depicts this problem.

ILLUSTRATION E.26
Calculator solution for mortgage amount

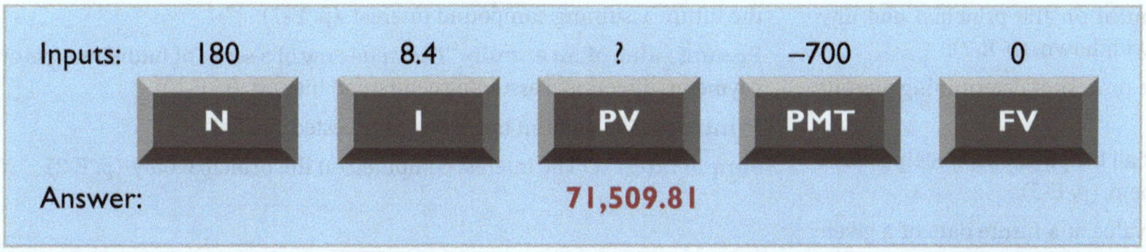

You enter N = 180 (12 × 15 years), I = 8.4, PMT = −700, FV = 0, and press PV. With the payments-per-year key set at 12, you find a present value of €71,509.81— the maximum home loan you can afford, given that you want to keep your mortgage payments at €700. Note that by changing any of the variables, you can quickly conduct "what-if" analyses for different situations.

Review

Learning Objectives Review

1 Compute interest and future values.

Simple interest is computed on the principal only, while compound interest is computed on the principal and any interest earned that has not been withdrawn.

To solve for future value of a single amount, prepare a time diagram of the problem. Identify the principal amount, the number of compounding periods, and the interest rate. Using the future value of 1 table, multiply the principal amount by the future value factor specified at the intersection of the number of periods and the interest rate.

To solve for future value of an annuity, prepare a time diagram of the problem. Identify the amount of the periodic payments (receipts), the number of payments (receipts), and the interest rate. Using the future value of an annuity of 1 table, multiply the amount of the payments by the future value factor specified at the intersection of the number of periods and the interest rate.

2 Compute present values.

The following three variables are fundamental to solving present value problems: (1) the future amount, (2) the number of periods, and (3) the interest rate (the discount rate).

To solve for present value of a single amount, prepare a time diagram of the problem. Identify the future amount, the number of discounting periods, and the discount (interest) rate. Using the present value of a single amount table, multiply the future amount by the present value factor specified at the intersection of the number of periods and the discount rate.

To solve for present value of an annuity, prepare a time diagram of the problem. Identify the amount of future periodic receipts or payments (annuities), the number of payments (receipts), and the discount (interest) rate. Using the present value of an annuity of 1 table, multiply the amount of the annuity by the present value factor specified at the intersection of the number of payments and the interest rate.

To compute the present value of notes and bonds, determine the present value of the principal amount and the present value of the interest payments. Multiply the principal amount (a single future amount) by the present value factor (from the present value of 1 table) intersecting at the number of periods (number of interest payments) and the discount rate. To determine the present value of the series of interest payments, multiply the amount of the interest payment by the present value factor (from the present value of an annuity of 1 table) intersecting at the number of periods (number of interest payments) and the discount rate. Add the present value of the principal amount to the present value of the interest payments to arrive at the present value of the note or bond.

3 Use a financial calculator to solve time value of money problems.

Financial calculators can be used to solve the same and additional problems as those solved with time value of money tables. Enter into the financial calculator the amounts for all of the known elements of a time value of money problem (periods, interest rate, payments, future or present value), and it solves for the unknown element. Particularly useful situations involve interest rates and compounding periods not presented in the tables.

Glossary Review

Annuity A series of equal amounts to be paid or received at evenly spaced time intervals (periodically). (p. E-5).

Compound interest The interest computed on the principal and any interest earned that has not been paid or withdrawn. (p. E-2).

Discounting the future amount(s) The process of determining present value. (p. E-7).

Future value of an annuity The sum of all the payments (receipts) plus the accumulated compound interest on them. (p. E-5).

Future value of a single amount The value at a future date of a given amount invested, assuming compound interest. (p. E-3).

Interest Payment for the use of another person's money. (p. E-1).

Present value The value now of a given amount to be paid or received in the future assuming compound interest. (p. E-7).

Present value of an annuity The value now of a series of future receipts or payments, discounted assuming compound interest. (p. E-10).

Principal The amount borrowed or invested. (p. E-1).

Simple interest The interest computed on the principal only. (p. E-2).

Brief Exercises

(Use tables to solve exercises BEE.1 to BEE.23.)

Compute the future value of a single amount.

BEE.1 (LO 1) Randy Owen invested €9,000 at 5% annual interest, and left the money invested without withdrawing any of the interest for 15 years. At the end of the 15 years, Randy withdrew the accumulated amount of money. (a) What amount did Randy withdraw, assuming the investment earns simple interest? (b) What amount did Randy withdraw, assuming the investment earns interest compounded annually?

BEE.2 (LO 1) For each of the following cases, indicate (a) to what interest rate columns and (b) to what number of periods you would refer in looking up the future value factor.

Use future value tables.

(1) In Table 1 (future value of 1):

	Annual Rate	Number of Years Invested	Compounded
Case A	5%	3	Annually
Case B	12%	4	Semiannually

(2) In Table 2 (future value of an annuity of 1):

	Annual Rate	Number of Years Invested	Compounded
Case A	3%	8	Annually
Case B	8%	6	Semiannually

BEE.3 (LO 1) Joyce Ltd. signed a lease for an office building for a period of 8 years. Under the lease agreement, a security deposit of £8,400 is made. The deposit will be returned at the expiration of the lease with interest compounded at 4% per year. What amount will Joyce receive at the time the lease expires?

Compute the future value of a single amount.

BEE.4 (LO 1) Bates Company issued $1,000,000, 12-year bonds and agreed to make annual sinking fund deposits of $60,000. The deposits are made at the end of each year into an account paying 6% annual interest. What amount will be in the sinking fund at the end of 12 years?

Compute the future value of an annuity.

BEE.5 (LO 1) Frank and Maureen Fantazzi invested €8,000 in a savings account paying 5% annual interest when their daughter, Angela, was born. They also deposited €1,000 on each of her birthdays until she was 18 (including her 18th birthday). How much was in the savings account on her 18th birthday (after the last deposit)?

Compute the future value of a single amount and of an annuity.

BEE.6 (LO 1) Hugh Curtin borrowed $35,000 on July 1, 2025. This amount plus accrued interest at 8% compounded annually is to be repaid on July 1, 2030. How much will Hugh have to repay on July 1, 2030?

Compute the future value of a single amount.

BEE.7 (LO 2) For each of the following cases, indicate (a) to what interest rate columns and (b) to what number of periods you would refer in looking up the discount rate.

Use present value tables.

(1) In Table 3 (present value of 1):

	Annual Rate	Number of Years Involved	Discounts per Year
Case A	12%	7	Semiannually
Case B	8%	11	Annually
Case C	6%	8	Semiannually

(2) In Table 4 (present value of an annuity of 1):

	Annual Rate	Number of Years Involved	Number of Payments Involved	Frequency of Payments
Case A	10%	20	20	Annually
Case B	10%	7	7	Annually
Case C	8%	5	10	Semiannually

BEE.8 (LO 2) **a.** What is the present value of $25,000 due 9 periods from now, discounted at 10%?
b. What is the present value of $25,000 to be received at the end of each of 6 periods, discounted at 9%?

Determine present values.

BEE.9 (LO 2) Pingtung Ltd. is considering an investment that will return a lump sum of NT$750,000 eight years from now. What amount should Pingtung pay for this investment to earn an 5% return?

Compute the present value of a single amount investment.

BEE.10 (LO 2) Lloyd Company earns 6% on an investment that will return $450,000 eight years from now. What is the amount Lloyd should invest now to earn this rate of return?

Compute the present value of a single amount investment.

BEE.11 (LO 2) Arthur plc is considering investing in an annuity contract that will return £46,000 annually at the end of each year for 12 years. What amount should Arthur pay for this investment if it earns an 7% return?

Compute the present value of an annuity investment.

BEE.12 (LO 2) Kaehler Enterprises earns 5% on an investment that pays back $80,000 at the end of each of the next 6 years. What is the amount Kaehler invested to earn the 5% rate of return?

Compute the present value of an annual investment.

Compute the present value of bonds.

BEE.13 (LO 2) Hanna Railroad is about to issue €300,000 of 10-year bonds paying an 11% interest rate, with interest payable semiannually. The discount rate for such securities is 10%. How much can Hanna expect to receive for the sale of these bonds?

Compute the present value of bonds.

BEE.14 (LO 2) Assume the same information as BEE.13 except that the discount rate is 12% instead of 10%. In this case, how much can Hanna expect to receive from the sale of these bonds?

Compute the present value of a note.

BEE.15 (LO 2) Yilan Ltd. receives a NT$48,000, 5-year note bearing interest of 4% (paid annually) from a customer at a time when the discount rate is 6%. What is the present value of the note received by Yilan?

Compute the present value of bonds.

BEE.16 (LO 2) Gleason Enterprises issued 6%, 8-year, $2,500,000 par value bonds that pay interest semi-annually on October 1 and April 1. The bonds are dated April 1, 2025, and are issued on that date. The discount rate of interest for such bonds on April 1, 2025, is 8%. What cash proceeds did Gleason receive from issuance of the bonds?

Compute the present value of a machine for purposes of making a purchase decision.

BEE.17 (LO 2) Mark Barton owns a garage and is contemplating purchasing a tire retreading machine for $20,000. After estimating costs and revenues, Mark projects a net cash flow from the retreading machine of $3,200 annually for 8 years. Mark hopes to earn a return of 7% on such investments. What is the present value of the retreading operation? Should Mark purchase the retreading machine?

Compute the present value of a note.

BEE.18 (LO 2) Frazier Company issues a 10%, 5-year mortgage note on January 1, 2025, to obtain financing for new equipment. Land is used as collateral for the note. The terms provide for semian-nual installment payments of $48,850. What were the cash proceeds received from the issuance of the note?

Compute the maximum price to pay for a machine.

BEE.19 (LO 2) Wei Ltd. is considering purchasing equipment. The equipment will produce the follow-ing cash flows: Year 1, ¥40,000; Year 2, ¥43,000; and Year 3, ¥45,000. Wei requires a minimum rate of return of 8%. What is the maximum price Wei should pay for this equipment?

Compute the interest rate on a single amount.

BEE.20 (LO 2) If Colleen Mooney invests $4,765.50 now and she will receive $12,000 at the end of 12 years, what annual rate of interest will Colleen earn on her investment? (*Hint:* Use Table 3.)

Compute the number of periods of a single amount.

BEE.21 (LO 2) Wayne Kurt has been offered the opportunity of investing $31,681 now. The investment will earn 9% per year and at the end of that time will return Wayne $75,000. How many years must Wayne wait to receive $75,000? (*Hint:* Use Table 3.)

Compute the interest rate on an annuity.

BEE.22 (LO 2) Joanne Quick made an investment of $10,271.38. From this investment, she will receive $1,200 annually for the next 15 years starting one year from now. What rate of interest will Joanne's investment be earning for her? (*Hint:* Use Table 4.)

Compute the number of payments of an annuity.

BEE.23 (LO 2) Patty Schleis invests €6,673.16 now for a series of €1,400 annual returns beginning one year from now. Patty will earn a return of 7% on the initial investment. How many annual payments of €1,400 will Patty receive? (*Hint:* Use Table 4.)

Determine interest rate.

BEE.24 (LO 3) Carly Simon wishes to invest $18,000 on July 1, 2025, and have it accumulate to $50,000 by July 1, 2035. Use a financial calculator to determine at what exact annual rate of interest Carly must invest the $18,000.

Determine interest rate.

BEE.25 (LO 3) On July 17, 2025, James Taylor borrowed $66,000 from his grandfather to open a clothing store. Starting July 17, 2026, James has to make 8 equal annual payments of $11,225 each to repay the loan. Use a financial calculator to determine what interest rate James is paying.

Determine interest rate.

BEE.26 (LO 3) As the purchaser of a new house, Carrie Underwood has signed a mortgage note to pay the Nashville National Bank and Trust Co. $8,400 every 6 months for 20 years, at the end of which time she will own the house. At the date the mortgage is signed, the purchase price was $198,000 and Underwood made a down payment of $20,000. The first payment will be made 6 months after the date the mortgage is signed. Using a financial calculator, compute the exact rate of interest earned on the mortgage by the bank.

BEE.27 **(LO 3)** Using a financial calculator, solve for the unknowns in each of the following situations.

Various time value of money situations.

a. On June 1, 2024, Holly Golightly purchases lakefront property from her neighbor, George Peppard, and agrees to pay the purchase price in seven payments of $22,000 each, the first payment to be payable June 1, 2025. (Assume that interest compounded at an annual rate of 5.4% is implicit in the payments.) What is the purchase price of the property?

b. On January 1, 2024, Sammis Corporation purchased 200 of the $1,000 face value, 7% coupon, 10-year bonds of Malone Inc. The bonds mature on January 1, 2034, and pay interest annually beginning January 1, 2025. Sammis purchased the bonds to yield 8.65%. How much did Sammis pay for the bonds?

BEE.28 **(LO 3)** Using a financial calculator, provide a solution to each of the following situations.

Various time value of money situations.

a. Lynn Anglin owes a debt of $42,000 from the purchase of her new sport utility vehicle. The debt bears annual interest of 7.8% compounded monthly. Lynn wishes to pay the debt and interest in equal monthly payments over 8 years, beginning one month hence. What equal monthly payments will pay off the debt and interest?

b. On January 1, 2025, Roger Molony offers to buy Dave Feeney's used snowmobile for $8,000, payable in five equal annual installments, which are to include 7.25% interest on the unpaid balance and a portion of the principal. If the first payment is to be made on December 31, 2025, how much will each payment be?

APPENDIX F

Accounting for Partnerships

Appendix Preview

In this appendix, we discuss reasons why businesses select the partnership form of organization. We also explain the major issues in accounting for partnerships.

Appendix Outline

LEARNING OBJECTIVES	REVIEW
LO 1 Discuss and account for the formation of a partnership.	• Characteristics of partnerships • Organizations with partnership characteristics • Advantages and disadvantages of partnerships • The partnership agreement • Accounting for a partnership formation
LO 2 Explain how to account for net income or net loss of a partnership.	• Dividing net income or net loss • Partnership financial statements
LO 3 Explain how to account for the liquidation of a partnership.	• No capital deficiency • Capital deficiency
LO 4 Prepare journal entries when a partner is either admitted or withdraws.	• Admission of a partner • Withdrawal of a partner

F.1 Forming a Partnership

LEARNING OBJECTIVE 1

Discuss and account for the formation of a partnership.

A **partnership** is an association of two or more persons to carry on as co-owners of a business for profit. Partnerships are sometimes used in small retail, service, or manufacturing companies. Accountants, lawyers, and doctors also find it desirable to form partnerships with other professionals in the field.

Characteristics of Partnerships

Partnerships are fairly easy to form. People form partnerships simply by a verbal agreement or more formally by written agreement.

- The formation of a business entity is determined by the laws of each country.
- As a result, each country determines the types of entities that can be formed and the legal rights of the owners.

The following sections explain partnership characteristics from a general perspective.

Association of Individuals

Association of Individuals

A partnership is a legal entity. A partnership can own property (land, buildings, equipment) and can sue or be sued. **A partnership also is an accounting entity.** Thus, the personal assets, liabilities, and transactions of the partners are excluded from the accounting records of the partnership.

The net income of a partnership is not taxed as a separate entity. But, a partnership must file an information tax return showing partnership net income and each partner's share of that net income. Each partner's share is taxable at **personal tax rates**, regardless of the amount of net income each withdraws from the business during the year.

Mutual Agency

Mutual Agency

Mutual agency means that each partner acts on behalf of the partnership when engaging in partnership business. The act of any partner is binding on all other partners. This is true even when partners act beyond the scope of their authority, so long as the act appears to be appropriate for the partnership.

For example, a partner of a grocery store who purchases a delivery truck creates a binding contract in the name of the partnership, even if the partnership agreement denies this authority. On the other hand, if a partner in a law firm purchased a snowmobile for the partnership, such an act would not be binding on the partnership. The purchase is clearly outside the scope of partnership business.

Limited Life

Limited Life

Corporations have unlimited life. Partnerships do not. A partnership may be ended voluntarily at any time through the acceptance of a new partner or the withdrawal of a partner. It may be ended involuntarily by the death or incapacity of a partner.

Partnership dissolution occurs whenever a partner withdraws or a new partner is admitted. Dissolution does not necessarily mean that the business ends. If the continuing partners agree, operations can continue without interruption by forming a new partnership.

Unlimited Liability

Unlimited Liability

Each partner is **personally and individually liable** for all partnership liabilities. Creditors' claims attach first to partnership assets. If these are insufficient, the claims then attach to the personal resources of any partner, irrespective of that partner's equity in the partnership. Because each partner is responsible for all the debts of the partnership, each partner is said to have **unlimited liability**.

Co-Ownership of Property

Partners jointly own partnership assets. If the partnership is dissolved, each partner has a claim on total assets equal to the balance in his or her respective capital account. This claim does not attach to **specific assets** that an individual partner contributed to the firm. Similarly, if a partner invests a building in the partnership valued at €100,000 and the building is later sold at a gain of €20,000, the partners all share in the gain.

Partnership net income (or net loss) is also co-owned. **If the partnership contract does not specify to the contrary, all net income or net loss is shared equally by the partners.** As you will see later, though, partners may agree to unequal sharing of net income or net loss.

Organizations with Partnership Characteristics

If you are starting a business with a friend, each of you has little capital, and your business is not risky, you probably want to use a partnership. As indicated above, the partnership is easy to establish and its cost is minimal. These types of partnerships are often called **regular partnerships**.

- However, if your business is risky—say, roof repair or performing some type of professional service—you will want to limit your liability and not use a regular partnership.
- As a result, special forms of business organizations with partnership characteristics are now often used to provide protection from unlimited liability for people who wish to work together in some activity.

The special partnership forms are limited partnerships, limited liability partnerships, and limited liability companies. These special forms use the same accounting procedures as those described for a regular partnership. In addition, for taxation purposes, all the profits and losses pass through these organizations (similar to the regular partnership) to the owners, who report their share of partnership net income or losses on their personal tax returns.

Limited Partnerships

In a **limited partnership**, one or more partners have **unlimited liability** and one or more partners have **limited liability** for the debts of the firm. Those with unlimited liability are **general partners**. Those with limited liability are **limited partners**. Limited partners are responsible for the debts of the partnership up to the limit of their investment in the firm.

The words "Limited Partnership," "Ltd.," or "LP" identify this type of organization. For the privilege of limited liability, the limited partner usually accepts less compensation than a general partner and exercises less influence in the affairs of the firm. If the limited partners get involved in management, they risk their liability protection.

Limited Liability Partnership

A **limited liability partnership** or "LLP" is designed to protect innocent partners from malpractice or negligence claims resulting from the acts of another partner (see **Helpful Hint**). LLPs generally carry large insurance policies as protection against malpractice suits. These professional partnerships vary in size from a medical partnership of three to five doctors, to 150 to 200 partners in a large law firm, to more than 2,000 partners in an international accounting firm.

> **HELPFUL HINT**
>
> **In an LLP, *all* partners have limited liability. There are no general partners.**

Limited Liability Companies

A hybrid form of business organization with certain features like a corporation and others like a limited partnership is the **limited liability company** or "LLC." An LLC usually has a limited life. The owners, called **members**, have limited liability like owners of a corporation. Whereas limited partners do not actively participate in the management of a limited partnership (LP), the members of a limited liability company (LLC) can assume an active management role. Most taxing authorities usually classify an LLC as a partnership.

Illustration F.1 summarizes different forms of organizations that have partnership characteristics.

ILLUSTRATION F.1

Different forms of organizations with partnership characteristics

	Major Advantages	Major Disadvantages
Regular Partnership  General Partners	Simple and inexpensive to create and operate.	Owners (partners) personally liable for business debts.
Limited Partnership  General Partner, Limited Partners	Limited partners have limited personal liability for business debts as long as they do not participate in management. General partners can raise cash without involving outside investors in management of business.	General partners personally liable for business debts. More expensive to create than regular partnership. Suitable mainly for companies that invest in real estate.
Limited Liability Partnership 	Mostly of interest to partners in old-line professions such as law, medicine, and accounting. Owners (partners) are not personally liable for the malpractice of other partners.	Unlike a limited liability company, owners (partners) remain personally liable for many types of obligations owed to business creditors, lenders, and landlords. Often limited to a short list of professions.
Limited Liability Company 	Owners have limited personal liability for business debts even if they participate in management.	More expensive to create than regular partnership.

Source: Based on Nolo website.

Advantages and Disadvantages of Partnerships

Why do people choose partnerships? One major advantage of a partnership is to combine the skills and resources of two or more individuals. In addition, partnerships are easily formed and are relatively free from government regulations and restrictions. A partnership does not have to contend with the "red tape" that a larger company must face. Also, partners generally can make decisions quickly on substantive business matters without having to consult a board of directors.

On the other hand, partnerships also have some major disadvantages. **Unlimited liability** is particularly troublesome. Many individuals fear they may lose not only their initial investment but also their personal assets if those assets are needed to pay partnership creditors.

Illustration F.2 summarizes the advantages and disadvantages of the regular partnership form of business organization. As indicated previously, different types of partnership forms have evolved to reduce some of the disadvantages.

ILLUSTRATION F.2

Advantages and disadvantages of a partnership

Advantages	Disadvantages
Combining skills and resources of two or more individuals	Mutual agency
Ease of formation	Limited life
Freedom from governmental regulations and restrictions	Unlimited liability
Ease of decision-making	

The Partnership Agreement

Ideally, the agreement of two or more individuals to form a partnership should be expressed in a written contract, called the **partnership agreement** or **articles of co-partnership**. The partnership agreement contains such basic information as the name and principal location of the firm, the purpose of the business, and date of inception. In addition, it should specify relationships among the partners, such as:

1. Names and capital contributions of partners.
2. Rights and duties of partners.
3. Basis for sharing net income or net loss.
4. Provision for withdrawals of assets.
5. Procedures for submitting disputes to arbitration.
6. Procedures for the withdrawal or addition of a partner.
7. Rights and duties of surviving partners in the event of a partner's death.

We cannot overemphasize the importance of a written contract. The agreement should attempt to anticipate all possible situations, contingencies, and disagreements (see **Ethics Note**). The help of a lawyer is highly desirable in preparing the agreement.

ETHICS NOTE

A well-developed partnership agreement specifies in clear and concise language the process by which the partners will resolve ethical and legal problems. This issue is especially significant when the partnership experiences financial distress.

Accounting for a Partnership Formation

We now turn to the basic accounting for partnerships. The major accounting issues relate to forming the partnership, dividing income or loss, and preparing financial statements.

- When forming a partnership, each partner's initial investment in a partnership is entered in the partnership records.
- The partnership should record these investments at the **fair value of the assets at the date of their transfer to the partnership**.
- All partners must agree to the values assigned.

To illustrate, assume that A. Lau and T. Song combine their proprietorships to start a partnership named Lau-Song Software. The firm will specialize in developing financial modeling software. Lau and Song have the assets listed in **Illustration F.3** prior to the formation of the partnership (amounts in thousands).

ILLUSTRATION F.3

Book and fair values of assets invested

	Book Value		Fair Value	
	A. Lau	T. Song	A. Lau	T. Song
Cash	¥ 8,000	¥ 9,000	¥ 8,000	¥ 9,000
Accounts receivable		4,000		4,000
Allowance for doubtful accounts		(700)		(1,000)
Equipment	5,000		4,000	
Accumulated depreciation—equipment	(2,000)			
	¥11,000	¥12,300	¥12,000	¥12,000

The partnership records the investments as follows.

Investment of A. Lau

Cash	8,000	
Equipment	4,000	
A. Lau, Capital		12,000
(To record investment of Lau)		

A = L + E
+8,000
+4,000
+12,000
Cash Flows
+8,000

Investment of T. Song

Cash	9,000	
Accounts Receivable	4,000	
Allowance for Doubtful Accounts		1,000
T. Song, Capital		12,000
(To record investment of Song)		

A = L + E
+9,000
+4,000
−1,000
+12,000
Cash Flows
+9,000

Note that the partnership records neither the original cost of the equipment (¥5,000) nor its book value (¥5,000 − ¥2,000). It records the equipment at its fair value, ¥4,000. The partnership does not carry forward any accumulated depreciation from the books of previous entities (in this case, the two proprietorships).

In contrast, the gross claims on customers (¥4,000) are carried forward to the partnership. The partnership adjusts the allowance for doubtful accounts to ¥1,000, to arrive at a cash (net) realizable value of ¥3,000. A partnership may start with an allowance for doubtful accounts because it will continue to collect existing accounts receivable, some of which are expected to be uncollectible. In addition, this procedure maintains the control and subsidiary relationship between Accounts Receivable and the accounts receivable subsidiary ledger.

- After formation of the partnership, the accounting for transactions is similar to any other type of business organization. For example, the partners record all transactions with outside parties, such as the purchase or sale of inventory and the payment or receipt of cash, the same as for a corporation.
- The steps in the accounting cycle described in Chapter 4 also apply to a partnership. For example, the partnership prepares a trial balance and journalizes and posts adjusting entries. A worksheet may be used.

There are minor differences in journalizing and posting closing entries and in preparing financial statements, as we explain in the following sections.

F.2 Accounting for Net Income or Net Loss

LEARNING OBJECTIVE 2

Explain how to account for net income or net loss of a partnership.

Dividing Net Income or Net Loss

Partners equally share partnership net income or net loss unless the partnership contract indicates otherwise. The same basis of division usually applies to both net income and net loss. It is customary to refer to this basis as the **income ratio**, the **income and loss ratio**, or the **profit and loss (P&L) ratio.**

- Because of its wide acceptance, we use the term **income ratio** to identify the basis for dividing net income and net loss.
- The partnership recognizes a partner's share of net income or net loss in the accounts through closing entries.

Closing Entries

A partnership must make four entries in preparing closing entries. The entries are:

1. Debit each revenue account for its balance, and credit Income Summary for total revenues.
2. Debit Income Summary for total expenses, and credit each expense account for its balance.
3. Debit Income Summary for its balance, and credit each partner's capital account for his or her share of net income. Or, credit Income Summary, and debit each partner's capital account for his or her share of net loss.
4. Debit each partner's capital account for the balance in that partner's drawings account, and credit each partner's drawings account for the same amount.

The first two entries are the same as in a corporation. The last two entries are different because (1) there are two or more owners' capital and drawings accounts, and (2) it is necessary to divide net income (or net loss) among the partners.

To illustrate the last two closing entries, assume that AB Company has net income of €32,000 for 2025. The partners, L. Arbor and D. Barnett, share net income and net loss equally. Drawings for the year were Arbor €8,000 and Barnett €6,000. The last two closing entries are as follows.

Dec. 31	Income Summary	32,000	
	L. Arbor, Capital (€32,000 × 50%)		16,000
	D. Barnett, Capital (€32,000 × 50%)		16,000
	(To transfer net income to partners' capital accounts)		

A	=	L	+	E
				−32,000
				+16,000
				+16,000

Cash Flows
no effect

Dec. 31	L. Arbor, Capital	8,000	
	D. Barnett, Capital	6,000	
	L. Arbor, Drawings		8,000
	D. Barnett, Drawings		6,000
	(To close drawings accounts to capital accounts)		

A	=	L	+	E
				−8,000
				−6,000
				+8,000
				+6,000

Cash Flows
no effect

Assume that the beginning capital balance is €47,000 for Arbor and €36,000 for Barnett. After posting the closing entries, the capital and drawings accounts will appear as shown in **Illustration F.4**.

ILLUSTRATION F.4
Partners' capital and drawings accounts after closing

L. Arbor, Capital

12/31	Clos.	8,000	1/1	Bal.	47,000
			12/31	Clos.	16,000
			12/31	Bal.	55,000

D. Barnett, Capital

12/31	Clos.	6,000	1/1	Bal.	36,000
			12/31	Clos.	16,000
			12/31	Bal.	46,000

L. Arbor, Drawings

12/31	Bal.	8,000	12/31	Clos.	8,000

D. Barnett, Drawings

12/31	Bal.	6,000	12/31	Clos.	6,000

The partners' capital accounts are permanent accounts. Their drawings accounts are temporary accounts. Normally, the capital accounts will have credit balances, and the drawings accounts will have debit balances. Drawings accounts are debited when partners withdraw cash or other assets from the partnership for personal use.

Income Ratios

As noted earlier, the partnership agreement should specify the basis for sharing net income or net loss. The following are typical income ratios.

1. A fixed ratio, expressed as a proportion (6:4), a percentage (70% and 30%), or a fraction (2/3 and 1/3) (see **Helpful Hint**).
2. A ratio based either on capital balances at the beginning of the year or on average capital balances during the year.
3. Salaries to partners and the remainder on a fixed ratio.

HELPFUL HINT
A proportion such as 4:4:2 has a denominator of 10 (4 + 4 + 2). Thus, the basis for sharing net income or loss is 4/10, 4/10, and 2/10.

4. Interest on partners' capital balances and the remainder on a fixed ratio.
5. Salaries to partners, interest on partners' capital, and the remainder on a fixed ratio.

The objective is to settle on a basis that will equitably reflect the partners' capital investment and service to the partnership.

A **fixed ratio** is easy to apply, and it may be an equitable basis in some circumstances. Assume, for example, that Hei and Li are partners. Each contributes the same amount of capital, but Hei expects to work full-time in the partnership and Li expects to work only half-time. Accordingly, the partners agree to a fixed ratio of 2/3 to Hei and 1/3 to Li.

A **ratio based on capital balances** may be appropriate when the funds invested in the partnership are considered the critical factor. Capital ratios may also be equitable when the partners hire a manager to run the business and do not plan to take an active role in daily operations.

The three remaining ratios (items 3, 4, and 5) give specific recognition to differences among partners. These ratios provide salary allowances for time worked and interest allowances for capital invested. Then, the partnership allocates any remaining net income or net loss on a fixed ratio.

Salaries to partners and interest on partners' capital are not expenses of the partnership. Therefore, these items do not enter into the matching of expenses with revenues and the determination of net income or net loss. For a partnership, as for other entities, salaries and wages expense pertains to the cost of services performed by employees. Likewise, interest expense relates to the cost of borrowing from creditors. But partners, as owners, are not considered either **employees** or **creditors**. When the partnership agreement permits the partners to make monthly withdrawals of cash based on their "salary," the partnership debits these withdrawals to the partner's drawings account.

Salaries, Interest, and Remainder on a Fixed Ratio

Under income ratio (5) in the list above, the partnership must apply salaries and interest **before** it allocates the remainder on the specified fixed ratio. **This is true even if the provisions exceed net income. It is also true even if the partnership has suffered a net loss for the year.** The partnership's income statement should show, below net income, detailed information concerning the division of net income or net loss.

To illustrate, assume that Sara King and Ray Lee are co-partners in the Kingslee Company. The partnership agreement provides for (1) salary allowances of $8,400 to King and $6,000 to Lee, (2) interest allowances of 10% on capital balances at the beginning of the year, and (3) the remaining income to be divided equally. Capital balances on January 1 were King $28,000, and Lee $24,000. In 2025, partnership net income is $22,000. The division of net income is as shown in **Illustration F.5**.

ILLUSTRATION F.5

Division of net income schedule

Kingslee Company
Division of Net Income
For the Year Ended December 31, 2025

	Net income	$22,000	

Division of Net Income

	Sara King	Ray Lee	Total
Salary allowance	$ 8,400	$6,000	$14,400
Interest allowance on partners' capital			
Sara King ($28,000 × 10%)	2,800		
Ray Lee ($24,000 × 10%)		2,400	
Total interest allowance			5,200
Total salaries and interest	11,200	8,400	19,600
Remaining income, $2,400 ($22,000 − $19,600)			
Sara King ($2,400 × 50%)	1,200		
Ray Lee ($2,400 × 50%)		1,200	
Total remainder			2,400
Total division of net income	**$12,400**	**$9,600**	**$22,000**

Kingslee records the division of net income as follows.

Dec. 31	Income Summary	22,000	
	Sara King, Capital		12,400
	Ray Lee, Capital		9,600
	(To close net income to partners' capital)		

A	=	L	+	E
				−22,000
				+12,000
				+9,600

Cash Flows
no effect

Now let's look at a situation in which the salary and interest allowances **exceed** net income. Assume that Kingslee Company's net income is only $18,000. In this case, the salary and interest allowances will create a deficiency of $1,600 ($18,000 − $19,600). The computations of the allowances are the same as those in the preceding example. Beginning with total salaries and interest, we complete the division of net income as shown in **Illustration F.6**.

ILLUSTRATION F.6
Division of net income—income deficiency

	Sara King	Ray Lee	Total
Total salaries and interest	$11,200	$8,400	$19,600
Remaining deficiency ($1,600)			
($18,000 − $19,600)			
Sara King ($1,600 × 50%)	(800)		
Ray Lee ($1,600 × 50%)		(800)	
Total remainder			(1,600)
Total division	**$10,400**	**$7,600**	**$18,000**

Partnership Financial Statements

The financial statements of a partnership are similar to those of a corporation. The income statement for a partnership is identical to the income statement for a corporation except for the division of net income, as shown earlier.

- The statement of changes in equity for a partnership is called the **partners' capital statement**.
- It explains the changes in each partner's capital account and in total partnership capital during the year.

Illustration F.7 shows the partners' capital statement for Kingslee Company. It is based on the division of $22,000 of net income in Illustration F.5. The statement includes assumed data for the additional investment and drawings. The partnership prepares the partners' capital statement from the income statement and the partners' capital and drawings accounts (see **Helpful Hint**).

ILLUSTRATION F.7
Partners' capital statement

Kingslee Company
Partners' Capital Statement
For the Year Ended December 31, 2025

	Sara King	Ray Lee	Total
Capital, January 1	$ 28,000	$ 24,000	$ 52,000
Add: Additional investment	2,000		2,000
Net income	12,400	9,600	22,000
	42,400	33,600	76,000
Less: Drawings	7,000	5,000	12,000
Capital, December 31	**$35,400**	**$28,600**	**$64,000**

HELPFUL HINT
Partners' capital may change due to (1) additional investment, (2) drawings, and (3) net income or net loss.

The statement of financial position for a partnership is the same as for a corporation except for the equity section. For a partnership, the statement of financial position shows the capital balances of each partner. **Illustration F.8** shows the equity section for Kingslee Company.

ILLUSTRATION F.8

Equity section of a partnership statement of financial position

Kingslee Company
Statement of Financial Position (partial)
December 31, 2025

Equity		
Sara King, capital	$35,400	
Ray Lee, capital	28,600	
Total equity		$ 64,000
Total liabilities (assumed amount)		115,000
Total equity and liabilities		$179,000

F.3 Liquidation of a Partnership

LEARNING OBJECTIVE 3

Explain how to account for the liquidation of a partnership.

Liquidation of a business involves selling the assets of the firm, paying liabilities, and distributing any remaining assets. Liquidation may result from the sale of the business by mutual agreement of the partners, from the death of a partner, or from bankruptcy. **Partnership liquidation** ends both the legal and economic life of the entity.

- From an accounting standpoint, the partnership should complete the accounting cycle for the final operating period prior to liquidation.
- This includes preparing adjusting entries and financial statements.
- It also involves preparing closing entries and a post-closing trial balance.

Thus, only statement of financial position accounts should be open as the liquidation process begins.

ETHICS NOTE

The process of selling non-cash assets and then distributing the cash reduces the likelihood of partner disputes. If instead the partnership distributes non-cash assets to partners to liquidate the firm, the partners would need to agree on the value of the non-cash assets, which can be very difficult to determine.

In liquidation, the sale of non-cash assets for cash is called **realization**. Any difference between book value and the cash proceeds is called the **gain or loss on realization**. To liquidate a partnership, it is necessary to:

1. Sell non-cash assets for cash and recognize a gain or loss on realization.
2. Allocate gain/loss on realization to the partners based on their income ratios.
3. Pay partnership liabilities in cash.
4. Distribute remaining cash to partners on the basis of their **capital balances**.

Each of the steps must be performed in sequence. The partnership must pay creditors **before** partners receive any cash distributions. Also, an accounting entry must record each step (see **Ethics Note**).

When a partnership is liquidated, all partners may have credit balances in their capital accounts. This situation is called **no capital deficiency**. Or, one or more partners may have a debit balance in the capital account. This situation is termed a **capital deficiency**. To illustrate each of these conditions, assume that KSW Company is liquidated when its ledger shows the assets, liabilities, and equity accounts presented in **Illustration F.9** (amounts in thousands).

ILLUSTRATION F.9

Account balances prior to liquidation

Assets		Equity and Liabilities	
Equipment	HK$35,000	R. Kwok, Capital	HK$15,000
Accum. Depr.—Equipment	(8,000)	P. Shiu, Capital	17,800
Inventory	18,000	W. Wong, Capital	1,200
Accounts Receivable	15,000	Notes Payable	15,000
Cash	5,000	Accounts Payable	16,000
	HK$65,000		HK$65,000

No Capital Deficiency

The partners of KSW Company agree to liquidate the partnership on the following terms. (1) The partnership will sell its non-cash assets to Yam Enterprises for HK$75,000 cash. (2) The partnership will pay its partnership liabilities. The income ratios of the partners are 3:2:1, respectively (see **Helpful Hint**). The steps in the liquidation process are as follows.

> **HELPFUL HINT**
> **The income ratios' denominator for KSW Company is 6 (3 + 2 + 1).**

1. KSW sells the non-cash assets (accounts receivable, inventory, and equipment) for HK$75,000. The book value of these assets is HK$60,000 (HK$15,000 + HK$18,000 + HK$35,000 − HK$8,000). Thus, KSW realizes a gain of HK$15,000 on the sale. The entry is:

(1)

Cash	75,000	
Accumulated Depreciation–Equipment	8,000	
Accounts Receivable		15,000
Inventory		18,000
Equipment		35,000
Gain on Realization		15,000
(To record realization of non-cash assets)		

A	=	L	+	E
+75,000				
+8,000				
−15,000				
−18,000				
−35,000				
				+15,000

Cash Flows
+75,000

2. KSW allocates the HK$15,000 gain on realization to the partners based on their income ratios, which are 3:2:1. The entry is:

(2)

Gain on Realization	15,000	
R. Kwok, Capital (HK$15,000 × 3/6)		7,500
P. Shiu, Capital (HK$15,000 × 2/6)		5,000
W. Wong, Capital (HK$15,000 × 1/6)		2,500
(To allocate gain to partners' capital accounts)		

A	=	L	+	E
				−15,000
				+7,500
				+5,000
				+2,500

Cash Flows
no effect

3. Partnership liabilities consist of Notes Payable HK$15,000 and Accounts Payable HK$16,000. KSW pays creditors in full by a cash payment of HK$31,000. The entry is:

(3)

Notes Payable	15,000	
Accounts Payable	16,000	
Cash		31,000
(To record payment of partnership liabilities)		

A	=	L	+	E
		−15,000		
		−16,000		
−31,000				

Cash Flows
−31,000

4. KSW distributes the remaining cash to the partners on the basis of **their capital balances**. After posting the entries in the first three steps, all partnership accounts, including Gain on Realization, will have zero balances except for four accounts: Cash HK$49,000; R. Kwok, Capital HK$22,500; P. Shiu, Capital HK$22,800; and W. Wong, Capital HK$3,700, as shown in **Illustration F.10**.

ILLUSTRATION F.10 **Ledger balances before distribution of cash**

Cash				R. Kwok, Capital				P. Shiu, Capital				W. Wong, Capital			
Bal.	5,000	(3)	31,000			Bal.	15,000			Bal.	17,800			Bal.	1,200
(1)	75,000					(2)	7,500			(2)	5,000			(2)	2,500
Bal.	**49,000**					**Bal.**	**22,500**			**Bal.**	**22,800**			**Bal.**	**3,700**

KSW records the distribution of cash as follows.

(4)

R. Kwok, Capital	22,500	
P. Shiu, Capital	22,800	
W. Wong, Capital	3,700	
Cash		49,000
(To record distribution of cash to partners)		

A	=	L	+	E
				−22,500
				−22,800
				−3,700
−49,000				

Cash Flows
−49,000

After posting this entry, all partnership accounts will have zero balances.

A word of caution: **Partnerships should not distribute remaining cash to partners on the basis of their income-sharing ratios.** On this basis, Kwok would receive three-sixths, or HK$24,500, which would produce an erroneous debit balance of HK$2,000. The income ratio is the proper basis for allocating net income or loss. **It is not a proper basis for making the final distribution of cash to the partners.**

Schedule of Cash Payments

> **ALTERNATIVE TERMINOLOGY**
>
> **The schedule of cash payments is sometimes called a *safe cash payments schedule*.**

The **schedule of cash payments** shows the distribution of cash to the partners in a partnership liquidation (see **Alternative Terminology**). The schedule of cash payments is organized around the basic accounting equation. **Illustration F.11** shows the schedule for KSW Company. The numbers in parentheses in column B refer to the four required steps in the liquidation of a partnership. They also identify the accounting entries that KSW must make. The cash payments schedule is especially useful when the liquidation process extends over a period of time.

ILLUSTRATION F.11 **Schedule of cash payments, no capital deficiency**

KSW Company

KSW Company
Schedule of Cash Payments

	Item	B	Cash	+	Non-Cash Assets	=	Liabilities	+	R. Kwok, Capital	+	P. Shiu, Capital	+	W. Wong, Capital
3	Balances before liquidation		5,000	+	60,000	=	31,000	+	15,000	+	17,800	+	1,200
4	Sale of non-cash assets and allocation of gain	(1)&(2)	75,000	+	(60,000)	=			7,500	+	5,000	+	2,500
5	New balances		80,000	+	–0–	=	31,000	+	22,500	+	22,800	+	3,700
6	Pay liabilities		(31,000)			=	(31,000)						
7	New balances	(3)	49,000	+	–0–	=	–0–	+	22,500	+	22,800	+	3,700
8	Cash distribution to partners	(4)	(49,000)			=			(22,500)	+	(22,800)	+	(3,700)
9	Final balances		–0–		–0–		–0–		–0–		–0–		–0–
10													
11													

Capital Deficiency

A capital deficiency may result from recurring net losses, excessive drawings, or losses from realization suffered during liquidation. To illustrate, assume that KSW Company is on the brink of bankruptcy. The partners decide to liquidate by having a "going-out-of-business" sale. They sell merchandise at substantial discounts, and sell the equipment at auction. Cash proceeds from these sales and collections from customers total only HK$42,000. Thus, the loss from liquidation is HK$18,000 (HK$60,000 – HK$42,000). The steps in the liquidation process are as follows.

1. The entry for the realization of non-cash assets is:

A	=	L	+	E
+42,000				
+8,000				
				−18,000
−15,000				
−18,000				
−35,000				

Cash Flows
+42,000

(1)

Cash	42,000	
Accumulated Depreciation—Equipment	8,000	
Loss on Realization	18,000	
Accounts Receivable		15,000
Inventory		18,000
Equipment		35,000
(To record realization of non-cash assets)		

2. KSW allocates the loss on realization to the partners on the basis of their income ratios. The entry is:

(2)		
R. Kwok, Capital (HK$18,000 × 3/6)	9,000	
P. Shiu, Capital (HK$18,000 × 2/6)	6,000	
W. Wong, Capital (HK$18,000 × 1/6)	3,000	
Loss on Realization		18,000
(To allocate loss on realization to partners)		

A	=	L	+	E
				−9,000
				−6,000
				−3,000
				+18,000

Cash Flows
no effect

3. KSW pays the partnership liabilities. This entry is the same as the previous one.

(3)		
Notes Payable	15,000	
Accounts Payable	16,000	
Cash		31,000
(To record payment of partnership liabilities)		

A	=	L	+	E
		−15,000		
		+16,000		
−31,000				

Cash Flows
−31,000

4. After posting the three entries, two accounts will have debit balances—Cash HK$16,000 and W. Wong, Capital HK$1,800. Two accounts will have credit balances—R. Kwok, Capital HK$6,000 and P. Shiu, Capital HK$11,800. **Illustration F.12** shows all four accounts.

ILLUSTRATION F.12 **Ledger balances before distribution of cash**

Cash				R. Kwok, Capital				P. Shiu, Capital				W. Wong, Capital			
Bal.	5,000	(3)	31,000	(2)	9,000	Bal.	15,000	(2)	6,000	Bal.	17,800	(2)	3,000	Bal.	1,200
(1)	42,000					**Bal.**	**6,000**			**Bal.**	**11,800**	**Bal.**	**1,800**		
Bal.	**16,000**														

Wong has a capital deficiency of HK$1,800 and so owes the partnership HK$1,800. Kwok and Shiu have a legally enforceable claim for that amount against Wong's personal assets. Note that the distribution of cash is still made on the basis of capital balances. But, the amount will vary depending on how Wong settles the deficiency. Two alternatives are presented in the following sections.

Payment of Deficiency

If the partner with the capital deficiency pays the amount owed the partnership, the deficiency is eliminated. To illustrate, assume that Wong pays HK$1,800 to the partnership. The entry is:

(a)		
Cash	1,800	
W. Wong, Capital		1,800
(To record payment of capital deficiency by Wong)		

A	=	L	+	E
+1,800				
				+1,800

Cash Flows
+1,800

After posting this entry, account balances are as shown in **Illustration F.13**.

ILLUSTRATION F.13 **Ledger balances after paying capital deficiency**

Cash				R. Kwok, Capital				P. Shiu, Capital				W. Wong, Capital			
Bal.	5,000	(3)	31,000	(2)	9,000	Bal.	15,000	(2)	6,000	Bal.	17,800	(2)	3,000	Bal.	1,200
(1)	42,000					**Bal.**	**6,000**			**Bal.**	**11,800**			Bal.	1,800
(a)	1,800													**Bal.**	**-0-**
Bal.	**17,800**														

The cash balance of HK$17,800 is now equal to the credit balances in the capital accounts (Kwok HK$6,000 + Shiu HK$11,800). KSW now distributes cash on the basis of these balances. The entry is:

A	=	L	+	E
				−6,000
				−11,800
−17,800				

Cash Flows
−17,800

R. Kwok, Capital	6,000	
P. Shiu, Capital	11,800	
Cash		17,800
(To record distribution of cash to the partners)		

After posting this entry, all accounts will have zero balances.

Non-Payment of Deficiency

> **HELPFUL HINT**
> The ratios with all three partners were 3:2:1 and the denominator was therefore 6. Leaving out Wong, the denominator changes to 5 (3 + 2).

If a partner with a capital deficiency is unable to pay the amount owed to the partnership, the partners with credit balances must absorb the loss. The partnership allocates the loss on the basis of the income ratios that exist between the partners with credit balances.

The income ratios of Kwok and Shiu are 3:2, or 3/5 and 2/5, respectively (see **Helpful Hint**). Thus, KSW would make the following entry to remove Wong's capital deficiency.

A	=	L	+	E
				−1,080
				+720
				+1,800

Cash Flows
no effect

(a)

R. Kwok, Capital (HK$1,800 × 3/5)	1,080	
P. Shiu, Capital (HK$1,800 × 2/5)	720	
W. Wong, Capital		1,800
(To record write-off of capital deficiency)		

After posting this entry, the cash and capital accounts will have the balances shown in **Illustration F.14**.

ILLUSTRATION F.14 Ledger balances after non-payment of capital deficiency

Cash				R. Kwok, Capital				P. Shiu, Capital				W. Wong, Capital			
Bal.	5,000	(3)	31,000	(2)	9,000	Bal.	15,000	(2)	6,000	Bal.	17,800	(2)	3,000	Bal.	1,200
(1)	42,000			(a)	1,080			(a)	720					(a)	1,800
Bal.	**16,000**					**Bal.**	**4,920**			**Bal.**	**11,080**			**Bal.**	**-0-**

The cash balance (HK$16,000) now equals the sum of the credit balances in the capital accounts (Kwok HK$4,920 + Shiu HK$11,080). KSW records the distribution of cash as:

A	=	L	+	E
				−4,920
				−11,080
−16,000				

Cash Flows
−16,000

R. Kwok, Capital	4,920	
P. Shiu, Capital	11,080	
Cash		16,000
(To record distribution of cash to the partners)		

After posting this entry, all accounts will have zero balances.

F.4 Admissions and Withdrawals of Partners

LEARNING OBJECTIVE 4

Prepare journal entries when a partner is either admitted or withdraws.

The chapter explained how the basic accounting for a partnership works. We now look at how to account for a common occurrence in partnerships—the addition or withdrawal of a partner.

Admission of a Partner

The admission of a new partner results in the **legal dissolution** of the existing partnership and the beginning of a new one.

- From an economic standpoint, however, the admission of a new partner (or partners) may be of minor significance in the continuity of the business. For example, in large public accounting or law firms, partners are admitted annually without any change in operating policies.
- **To recognize the economic effects, it is necessary only to open a capital account for each new partner.** In the entries illustrated in this appendix, we assume that the accounting records of the predecessor firm will continue to be used by the new partnership.

A new partner may be admitted either by (1) purchasing the interest of one or more existing partners or (2) investing assets in the partnership. The former affects only the capital accounts of the partners who are parties to the transaction. The latter increases both net assets and total capital of the partnership.

Purchase of a Partner's Interest

> **HELPFUL HINT**
> **In a purchase of an interest, the partnership is not a participant in the transaction. In this transaction, the new partner contributes *no* cash to the partnership.**

The **admission** of a partner **by purchase of an interest** is a personal transaction between one or more existing partners and the new partner. Each party acts as an individual separate from the partnership entity. The individuals involved negotiate the price paid. It may be equal to or different from the capital equity acquired. The purchase price passes directly from the new partner to the partners who are giving up part or all of their ownership claims (see **Helpful Hint**).

- Any money or other consideration exchanged is the personal property of the participants and **not** the property of the partnership.
- Upon purchase of an interest, the new partner acquires each selling partner's capital interest and income ratio.

Accounting for the purchase of an interest is straightforward. The partnership records only the changes in partners' capital. **Partners' capital accounts are debited for any ownership claims sold.** At the same time, the new partner's capital account is credited for the capital equity purchased. Total assets, total liabilities, and total capital remain unchanged, as do all individual asset and liability accounts.

To illustrate, assume that L. Carson agrees to pay €10,000 each to C. Ames and D. Barker for $33^1/_3$% (one-third) of their interest in the Ames–Barker partnership. At the time of the admission of Carson, each partner has a €30,000 capital balance. Both partners, therefore, give up €10,000 of their capital equity. The entry to record the admission of Carson is:

C. Ames, Capital	10,000	
D. Barker, Capital	10,000	
L. Carson, Capital		20,000
(To record admission of Carson by purchase)		

Illustration F.15 shows the effect of this transaction on net assets and partners' capital.

ILLUSTRATION F.15 **Ledger balances after purchase of a partner's interest**

Net Assets		C. Ames, Capital			D. Barker, Capital			L. Carson, Capital	
60,000		10,000		30,000	10,000		30,000		20,000
			Bal.	20,000		Bal.	20,000		

Note that net assets remain unchanged at €60,000, and each partner has a €20,000 capital balance. Ames and Barker continue as partners in the firm, but the capital interest of each has changed. The cash paid by Carson goes directly to the individual partners and not to the partnership.

Regardless of the amount paid by Carson for the one-third interest, the entry is exactly the same. If Carson pays €12,000 each to Ames and Barker for one-third of the partnership, the partnership still makes the entry shown above.

Investment of Assets in a Partnership

The admission of a partner by an investment of assets is a transaction between the new partner and the partnership. Often referred to simply as **admission by investment**, the transaction **increases both the net assets and total capital of the partnership.**

Assume, for example, that instead of purchasing an interest, Carson invests €30,000 in cash in the Ames-Barker partnership for a $33^1/_3$% capital interest. In such a case, the entry is:

Cash	30,000	
L. Carson, Capital		30,000
(To record admission of Carson by investment)		

Illustration F.16 shows the effects of this transaction on the partnership accounts.

ILLUSTRATION F.16 **Ledger balances after investment of assets**

Net Assets		C. Ames, Capital		D. Barker, Capital		L. Carson, Capital	
60,000			30,000		30,000		**30,000**
30,000							
Bal. 90,000							

Note that both net assets and total capital have increased by €30,000.

Remember that Carson's one-third capital interest might not result in a one-third income ratio. The new partnership agreement should specify Carson's income ratio, and it may or may not be equal to the one-third capital interest.

The comparison of the net assets and capital balances in **Illustration F.17** shows the different effects of the purchase of an interest and admission by investment.

ILLUSTRATION F.17

Comparison of purchase of an interest and admission by investment

Purchase of an Interest		Admission by Investment	
Net assets	**€60,000**	**Net assets**	**€90,000**
Capital		Capital	
C. Ames	€20,000	C. Ames	€30,000
D. Barker	20,000	D. Barker	30,000
L. Carson	20,000	L. Carson	30,000
Total capital	**€60,000**	**Total capital**	**€90,000**

When a new partner purchases an interest, the total net assets and total capital of the partnership **do not change**. When a partner is admitted by investment, both the total net assets and the total capital **change** by the amount of the new investment.

In the case of admission by investment, further complications occur when the new partner's investment differs from the capital equity acquired. When those amounts are not the same, the difference is considered a **bonus** either to (1) the existing (old) partners or (2) the new partner.

Bonus to Old Partners For both personal and business reasons, the existing partners may be unwilling to admit a new partner without receiving a bonus. In an established firm, existing partners may insist on a bonus as compensation for the work they have put into the company over the years. Two accounting factors underlie the business reason.

1. Total partners' capital equals the book value of the recorded net assets of the partnership. When the new partner is admitted, the fair values of assets such as land and buildings may be higher than their book values. The bonus will help make up the difference between fair value and book value.
2. When the partnership has been profitable, goodwill may exist. But, the partnership statement of financial position does not report goodwill. The new partner is usually willing to pay the bonus to become a partner.

A bonus to old partners results when the new partner's investment in the firm is greater than the capital credit on the date of admittance. The bonus results in **an increase in the capital balances of the old partners. The partnership allocates the bonus to them on the basis of their income ratios before the admission of the new partner.**

To illustrate, assume that the Yoo-Hyuk partnership, owned by Ahn Yoo and Joo Hyuk, has total capital of ₩120,000 (amounts in thousands). Jang Sung acquires a 25% ownership (capital) interest in the partnership by making a cash investment of ₩80,000. The procedure for determining Sung's capital credit and the bonus to the old partners is as follows.

1. **Determine the total capital of the new partnership.** Add the new partner's investment to the total capital of the old partnership. In this case, the total capital of the new firm is ₩200,000, computed as follows.

Total capital of existing partnership	₩120,000
Investment by new partner, Sung	80,000
Total capital of new partnership	₩200,000

2. **Determine the new partner's capital credit.** Multiply the total capital of the new partnership by the new partner's ownership interest. Sung's capital credit is ₩50,000 (₩200,000 × 25%).
3. **Determine the amount of bonus.** Subtract the new partner's capital credit from the new partner's investment. The bonus in this case is ₩30,000 (₩80,000 − ₩50,000).
4. **Allocate the bonus to the old partners on the basis of their income ratios.** Assuming the ratios are Yoo 60%, and Hyuk 40%, the allocation is Yoo ₩18,000 (₩30,000 × 60%) and Hyuk ₩12,000 (₩30,000 × 40%).

The entry to record the admission of Sung is:

Cash	80,000	
Ahn Yoo, Capital		18,000
Joo Hyuk, Capital		12,000
Jang Sung, Capital		50,000
(To record admission of Sung and bonus to old partners)		

A	=	L	+	E
+80,000				
				+18,000
				+12,000
				+50,000

Cash Flows
+80,000

Bonus to New Partner A bonus to a new partner results when the new partner's investment in the firm is less than his or her capital credit. This may occur when the new partner possesses special attributes that the partnership wants. For example, the new partner may be able to supply cash that the firm needs for expansion or to meet maturing debts. Or the new partner may be a recognized expert in a relevant field. Thus, an engineering firm may be willing to give a renowned engineer a bonus to join the firm. The partners of a restaurant may offer a bonus to a sports celebrity in order to add the athlete's name to the partnership. A bonus to a new partner may also result when recorded book values on the partnership books are higher than their fair values.

A bonus to a new partner results in a **decrease in the capital balances of the old partners. The amount of the decrease for each partner is based on the income ratios before the admission of the new partner.** To illustrate, assume that Jang Sung invests ₩20,000 in cash for a 25% ownership interest in the Yoo-Hyuk partnership. **Illustration F.18** shows the computations for Sung's capital credit and the bonus, using the four procedures described in the preceding section.

ILLUSTRATION F.18

Computation of capital credit and bonus to new partner

1.	Total capital of Yoo-Hyuk partnership		₩120,000
	Investment by new partner, Sung		20,000
	Total capital of new partnership		₩140,000
2.	**Sung's capital credit** (25% × ₩140,000)		**₩ 35,000**
3.	**Bonus to Sung** (₩35,000 − ₩20,000)		**₩ 15,000**
4.	Allocation of bonus to old partners:		
	Yoo (₩15,000 × 60%)	₩9,000	
	Hyuk (₩15,000 × 40%)	6,000	₩ 15,000

A = L + E
+20,000
+9,000
+6,000
+35,000
Cash Flows
+20,000

The partnership records the admission of Sung as follows.

Cash	20,000	
Ahn Yoo, Capital	9,000	
Joo Hyuk, Capital	6,000	
Jang Sung, Capital		35,000
(To record Sung's admission and bonus)		

Withdrawal of a Partner

Now let's look at the opposite situation–the withdrawal of a partner.

- A partner may withdraw from a partnership **voluntarily**, by selling his or her equity in the firm.
- Or, a partner may withdraw **involuntarily**, by reaching mandatory retirement age or by dying.

The withdrawal of a partner, like the admission of a partner, legally dissolves the partnership. The legal effects may be recognized by dissolving the firm. However, it is customary to record only the economic effects of the partner's withdrawal, while the firm continues to operate and reorganizes itself legally.

As indicated earlier, the partnership agreement should specify the terms of withdrawal. The withdrawal of a partner may be accomplished by (1) payment from partners' personal assets or (2) payment from partnership assets. The former affects only the partners' capital accounts. The latter decreases total net assets and total capital of the partnership.

Payment from Partners' Personal Assets

Withdrawal by payment from partners' personal assets is a personal transaction between the partners.

- **It is the direct opposite of admitting a new partner who purchases a partner's interest.**
- The remaining partners pay the retiring partner directly from their personal assets.
- **Partnership assets are not involved in any way, and total capital does not change.** The effect on the partnership is limited to changes in the partners' capital balances.

To illustrate, assume that partners Ma, Wenyin, and Hejun have capital balances of ¥25,000, ¥15,000, and ¥10,000, respectively (amounts in thousands). Ma and Wenyin agree to buy out Hejun's interest. Each of them agrees to pay Hejun ¥8,000 in exchange for one-half of Hejun's total interest of ¥10,000. The entry to record the withdrawal is:

A = L + E
−10,000
+5,000
+5,000
Cash Flows
no effect

Z. Hejun, Capital	10,000	
W. Ma, Capital		5,000
L. Wenyin, Capital		5,000
(To record purchase of Hejun's interest)		

The effect of this entry on the partnership accounts is shown in **Illustration F.19**.

ILLUSTRATION F.19 **Ledger balances after payment from partners' personal assets**

Net Assets		W. Ma, Capital		L. Wenyin, Capital		Z. Hejun, Capital	
50,000			25,000		15,000	**10,000**	10,000
			5,000		**5,000**		Bal. -0-
			Bal. 30,000		Bal. 20,000		

Note that net assets and total capital remain the same at ¥50,000.

What about the ¥16,000 paid to Hejun? You've probably noted that it is not recorded. The entry debited Hejun's capital only for ¥10,000, not for the ¥16,000 that she received. Similarly, both Ma and Wenyin credit their capital accounts for only ¥5,000, not for the ¥8,000 they each paid.

After Hejun's withdrawal, Ma and Wenyin will share net income or net loss equally unless they indicate another income ratio in the partnership agreement.

Payment from Partnership Assets

Withdrawal by payment from partnership assets is a transaction that involves the partnership.

- **Both partnership net assets and total capital decrease as a result.**
- Using partnership assets to pay for a withdrawing partner's interest is the **reverse** of admitting a partner through the investment of assets in the partnership.

Many partnership agreements provide that the amount paid should be based on the fair value of the assets at the time of the partner's withdrawal. When this basis is required, some maintain that any differences between recorded asset balances and their fair values should be (1) recorded by an adjusting entry, and (2) allocated to all partners on the basis of their income ratios.

This position has serious flaws. Recording the revaluations violates the historical cost basis, which requires that assets be stated at original cost. It also violates the going-concern assumption, which assumes the entity will continue indefinitely. The terms of the partnership contract should not dictate the accounting for this event.

In accounting for a withdrawal by payment from partnership assets, the partnership should not record asset revaluations. Instead, it should consider any difference between the amount paid and the withdrawing partner's capital balance as **a bonus** to the retiring partner or to the remaining partners.

Bonus to Retiring Partner A partnership may pay a bonus to a retiring partner when:

1. The fair value of partnership assets is more than their book value,
2. There is unrecorded goodwill resulting from the partnership's superior earnings record, or
3. The remaining partners are eager to remove the partner from the firm.

The partnership deducts the bonus from the remaining partners' capital balances on the basis of their income ratios at the time of the withdrawal.

To illustrate, assume that the following capital balances exist in the RST partnership: Roman €50,000, Sand €30,000, and Terk €20,000. The partners share income in the ratio of 3:2:1, respectively. Terk retires from the partnership and receives a cash payment of €25,000 from the firm. The procedure for determining the bonus to the retiring partner and the allocation of the bonus to the remaining partners is as follows.

1. **Determine the amount of the bonus.** Subtract the retiring partner's capital balance from the cash paid by the partnership. The bonus in this case is €5,000 (€25,000 – €20,000).
2. **Allocate the bonus to the remaining partners on the basis of their income ratios.** The ratios of Roman and Sand are 3:2. Thus, the allocation of the €5,000 bonus is: Roman €3,000 (€5,000 × 3/5) and Sand €2,000 (€5,000 × 2/5).

A	=	L	+	E
				−20,000
				−3,000
				−2,000
−25,000				

Cash Flows
−25,000

The partnership records the withdrawal of Terk as follows (see **Helpful Hint**).

B. Terk, Capital	20,000	
F. Roman, Capital	3,000	
D. Sand, Capital	2,000	
Cash		25,000
(To record withdrawal of and bonus to Terk)		

The remaining partners, Roman and Sand, will recover the bonus given to Terk as the partnership sells or uses the undervalued assets.

HELPFUL HINT

Compare this entry to the next one.

Bonus to Remaining Partners The retiring partner may give a bonus to the remaining partners when:

1. Recorded assets are overvalued.
2. The partnership has a poor earnings record.
3. The partner is eager to leave the partnership.

In such cases, the cash paid to the retiring partner will be less than the retiring partner's capital balance. **The partnership allocates (credits) the bonus to the capital accounts of the remaining partners on the basis of their income ratios.**

To illustrate, assume instead that the partnership pays Terk only €16,000 for her €20,000 equity when she withdraws from the partnership. In that case:

1. The bonus to remaining partners is €4,000 (€20,000 − €16,000).
2. The allocation of the €4,000 bonus is Roman €2,400 (€4,000 × 3/5) and Sand €1,600 (€4,000 × 2/5).

Under these circumstances, the entry to record the withdrawal is as follows (see **Helpful Hint**).

A	=	L	+	E
				−20,000
				+2,400
				+1,600
−16,000				

Cash Flows
−16,000

B. Terk, Capital	20,000	
F. Roman, Capital		2,400
D. Sand, Capital		1,600
Cash		16,000
(To record withdrawal of Terk and bonus to remaining partners)		

Note that if Sand had withdrawn from the partnership, Roman and Terk would divide any bonus on the basis of their income ratio, which is 3:1 or 75% and 25%.

HELPFUL HINT

Compare this entry to the one above.

Death of a Partner

The death of a partner dissolves the partnership. However, partnership agreements usually contain a provision for the surviving partners to continue operations. When a partner dies, it usually is necessary to determine the partner's equity at the date of death. This is done by:

1. Determining the net income or loss for the year to date.
2. Closing the books.
3. Preparing financial statements.

The partnership agreement may also require an independent audit and a revaluation of assets.

The surviving partners may agree to purchase the deceased partner's equity from their personal assets. Or they may use partnership assets to settle with the deceased partner's estate. In both instances, the entries to record the withdrawal of the partner are similar to those presented earlier.

To facilitate payment from partnership assets, some partnerships obtain life insurance policies on each partner, with the partnership named as the beneficiary. The partnership then uses the proceeds from the insurance policy on the deceased partner to settle with the estate.

Review

Learning Objectives Review

1 Discuss and account for the formation of a partnership.

The principal characteristics of a partnership are (a) association of individuals, (b) mutual agency, (c) limited life, (d) unlimited liability, and (e) co-ownership of property. When formed, a partnership records each partner's initial investment at the fair value of the assets at the date of their transfer to the partnership.

2 Explain how to account for net income or net loss of a partnership.

Partnerships divide net income or net loss on the basis of the income ratio, which may be (a) a fixed ratio, (b) a ratio based on beginning or average capital balances, (c) salaries to partners and the remainder on a fixed ratio, (d) interest on partners' capital and the remainder on a fixed ratio, and (e) salaries to partners, interest on partners' capital, and the remainder on a fixed ratio.

The financial statements of a partnership are similar to those of a corporation. The principal differences are as follows. (a) The partnership shows the division of net income on the income statement. (b) The statement of changes in equity is called a partners' capital statement. (c) The partnership reports each partner's capital on the statement of financial position.

3 Explain how to account for the liquidation of a partnership.

When a partnership is liquidated, it is necessary to record the (a) sale of non-cash assets, (b) allocation of the gain or loss on realization, (c) payment of partnership liabilities, and (d) distribution of cash to the partners on the basis of their capital balances.

4 Prepare journal entries when a partner is either admitted or withdraws.

The entry to record the admittance of a new partner by purchase of a partner's interest affects only partners' capital accounts. The entries to record the admittance by investment of assets in the partnership (a) increase both net assets and total capital and (b) may result in recognition of a bonus to either the old partners or the new partner.

The entry to record a withdrawal from the firm when the partners pay from their personal assets affects only partners' capital accounts. The entry to record a withdrawal when payment is made from partnership assets (a) decreases net assets and total capital and (b) may result in recognizing a bonus either to the retiring partner or the remaining partners.

Glossary Review

Admission by investment Admission of a partner by investing assets in the partnership, causing both partnership net assets and total capital to increase. (p. F-16).

Admission by purchase of an interest Admission of a partner in a personal transaction between one or more existing partners and the new partner; does not change total partnership assets or total capital. (p. F-15).

Capital deficiency A debit balance in a partner's capital account after allocation of gain or loss. (p. F-10).

General partners Partners who have unlimited liability for the debts of the firm. (p. F-3).

Income ratio The basis for dividing net income and net loss in a partnership. (p. F-6).

Limited liability company A form of business organization, usually classified as a partnership for tax purposes and usually with limited life, in which partners, who are called members, have limited liability. (p. F-3).

Limited liability partnership A partnership of professionals in which partners are given limited liability and the public is protected from malpractice by insurance carried by the partnership. (p. F-3).

Limited partners Partners whose liability for the debts of the firm is limited to their investment in the firm. (p. F-3).

Limited partnership A partnership in which one or more general partners have unlimited liability and one or more partners have limited liability for the obligations of the firm. (p. F-3).

No capital deficiency All partners have credit balances after allocation of gain or loss. (p. F-10).

Partners' capital statement The statement of changes in equity for a partnership which shows the changes in each partner's capital account and in total partnership capital during the year. (p. F-9).

Partnership An association of two or more persons to carry on as co-owners of a business for profit. (p. F-1).

Partnership agreement A written contract expressing the voluntary agreement of two or more individuals in a partnership. (p. F-5).

Partnership dissolution A change in partners due to withdrawal or admission, which does not necessarily terminate the business. (p. F-2).

Partnership liquidation An event that ends both the legal and economic life of a partnership. (p. F-10).

Schedule of cash payments A schedule showing the distribution of cash to the partners in a partnership liquidation. (p. F-12).

Withdrawal by payment from partners' personal assets Withdrawal of a partner in a personal transaction between partners; does not change total partnership assets or total capital. (p. F-18).

Withdrawal by payment from partnership assets Withdrawal of a partner in a transaction involving the partnership, causing both partnership net assets and total capital to decrease. (p. F-19).

Questions

1. The characteristics of a partnership include the following: (a) association of individuals, (b) limited life, and (c) co-ownership of property. Explain each of these terms.

2. Yuen Sheng is confused about the partnership characteristics of (a) mutual agency and (b) unlimited liability. Explain these two characteristics for Yuen.

3. Joe Lee and Lin Qi are considering a business venture. They ask you to explain the advantages and disadvantages of the partnership form of organization.

4. Why might a company choose to use a limited partnership?

5. Cho and Su form a partnership. Cho contributes land with a book value of NT$50,000 and a fair value of NT$60,000. Cho also contributes equipment with a book value of NT$52,000 and a fair value of NT$57,000. The partnership assumes a NT$20,000 mortgage on the land. What should be the balance in Cho's capital account upon formation of the partnership?

6. W. Jenson, N. Emch, and W. Gilligan have a partnership. A dispute has arisen among the partners. Jenson has invested twice as much in assets as the other two partners, and he believes net income and net losses should be shared in accordance with the capital ratios. The partnership agreement does not specify the division of profits and losses. How will net income and net loss be divided?

7. Smita and Swati are discussing how income and losses should be divided in a partnership they plan to form. What factors should be considered in determining the division of net income or net loss?

8. M. Lin and R. Chow have partnership capital balances of HK$40,000 and HK$80,000, respectively (amounts in thousands). The partnership agreement indicates that net income or net loss should be shared equally. If net income for the partnership is HK$42,000, how should the net income be divided?

9. S. Pletcher and F. Holt share net income and net loss equally. (a) Which account(s) is (are) debited and credited to record the division of net income between the partners? (b) If S. Pletcher withdraws €30,000 in cash for personal use instead of salary, which account is debited and which is credited?

10. Partners T. Kher and R. Puri are provided salary allowances of INR30,000 and INR25,000, respectively (amounts in thousands). They divide the remainder of the partnership income in a ratio of 3:2. If partnership net income is INR40,000, how much is allocated to Kher and Puri?

11. Are the financial statements of a partnership similar to those of a corporation? Discuss.

12. How does the liquidation of a partnership differ from the dissolution of a partnership?

13. Roger Fuller and Mike Rangel are discussing the liquidation of a partnership. Roger maintains that all cash should be distributed to partners on the basis of their income ratios. Is he correct? Explain.

14. In continuing their discussion from Question 13, Mike says that even in the case of a capital deficiency, all cash should still be distributed on the basis of capital balances. Is Mike correct? Explain.

15. Norris, Madson, and Howell have income ratios of 5:3:2 and capital balances of $34,000, $31,000, and $28,000, respectively. Non-cash assets are sold at a gain and allocated to the partners. After creditors are paid, $103,000 of cash is available for distribution to the partners. How much cash should be paid to Madson?

16. Before the final distribution of cash, account balances are Cash ¥27,000; S. Hui, Capital ¥19,000 (Cr.); L. Song, Capital ¥12,000 (Cr.); and M. Li, Capital ¥4,000 (Dr.) (amounts in thousands). Li is unable to pay any of the capital deficiency. If the income-sharing ratios are 5:3:2, respectively, how much cash should be paid to L. Song?

17. Why is **TSMC** not a partnership?

18. Susan Turnbull decides to purchase from an existing partner for €50,000 a one-third interest in a partnership. What effect does this transaction have on partnership net assets?

19. James Park decides to invest €25,000 in a partnership for a one-sixth capital interest. How much do the partnership's net assets increase? Does Park also acquire a one-sixth income ratio through this investment?

20. Chuling Chow purchases for HK$72,000 Meng's interest in the Ng-Meng partnership (amounts in thousands). Assuming that Meng has a HK$68,000 capital balance in the partnership, what journal entry is made by the partnership to record this transaction?

21. K. Boo-jin has a ¥41,000 capital balance in a partnership (amounts in thousands). She sells her interest to P. Beom-Su for ¥45,000 cash. What entry is made by the partnership for this transaction?

22. Andrea Riley retires from the partnership of Jaggard, Pester, and Riley. She receives €85,000 of partnership assets in settlement of her capital balance of €81,000. Assuming that the income-sharing ratios are 5:3:2, respectively, how much of Riley's bonus is debited to Pester's capital account?

23. Your roommate argues that partnership assets should be revalued in situations like those in Question 21. Why is this generally not done?

24. How is a deceased partner's equity determined?

Brief Exercises

Journalize entries in forming a partnership.

BEF.1 (LO 1) Barbara Ripley and Fred Nichols decide to organize the ALL-Star partnership. Ripley invests $15,000 cash, and Nichols contributes $10,000 cash and equipment having a book value of $3,500. Prepare the entry to record Nichols's investment in the partnership, assuming the equipment has a fair value of $4,000.

Prepare portion of opening statement of financial position for partnership.

BEF.2 (LO 1) Wang and Qinghou decide to merge their proprietorships into a partnership called WQ Company. The statement of financial position of WQ Co. shows (amounts in thousands):

Accounts receivable	¥16,000	
Less: Allowance for doubtful accounts	1,200	¥14,800
Equipment	20,000	
Less: Accumulated depreciation—equip.	7,000	13,000

The partners agree that the net realizable value of the receivables is ¥14,500 and that the fair value of the equipment is ¥11,000. Indicate how the accounts should appear in the opening statement of financial position of the partnership.

BEF.3 (LO 2) Rod Darling Co. reports net income of €75,000. The income ratios are Rod 60% and Darling 40%. Indicate the division of net income to each partner, and prepare the entry to distribute the net income.

Journalize the division of net income using fixed income ratios.

BEF.4 (LO 2) PFW Co. reports net income of €45,000. Partner salary allowances are Pitts €15,000, Filbert €5,000, and Witten €5,000. Indicate the division of net income to each partner, assuming the income ratio is 50:30:20, respectively.

Compute division of net income with a salary allowance and fixed ratios.

BEF.5 (LO 2) Kun-Hee & Jae-Chul Co. reports net income of ₩31,000 (amounts in thousands). Interest allowances are Kun-Hee ₩7,000 and Jae-Chul ₩5,000, salary allowances are Kun-Hee ₩15,000 and Jae-Chul ₩10,000, and the remainder is shared equally. Show the distribution of income.

Show division of net income when allowances exceed net income.

BEF.6 (LO 3) After liquidating non-cash assets and paying creditors, account balances in the Fan Co. are Cash HK$21,000; A, Capital (Cr.) HK$8,000; B, Capital (Cr.) HK$9,000; and C, Capital (Cr.) HK$4,000 (amounts in thousands). The partners share income equally. Journalize the final distribution of cash to the partners.

Journalize final cash distribution in liquidation.

BEF.7 (LO 4) 3C Co. capital balances are Chu ¥30,000, Cho ¥25,000, and Chow ¥22,000 (amounts in thousands). The partners share income equally. Cheng is admitted to the firm by purchasing one-half of Chow's interest for ¥13,000. Journalize the admission of Cheng to the partnership.

Journalize admission by purchase of an interest.

BEF.8 (LO 4) In Eastwood Co., capital balances are Irey $40,000 and Pedigo $50,000. The partners share income equally. Vernon is admitted to the firm with a 45% interest by an investment of cash of $58,000. Journalize the admission of Vernon.

Journalize admission by investment.

BEF.9 (LO 4) Capital balances in Pelmar Co. are Lang €40,000, Oslo €30,000, and Fernetti €20,000. Lang and Oslo each agree to pay Fernetti €12,000 from their personal assets. Lang and Oslo each receive 50% of Fernetti's equity. The partners share income equally. Journalize the withdrawal of Fernetti.

Journalize withdrawal paid by personal assets.

BEF.10 (LO 4) Data pertaining to Pelmar Co. are presented in BEF.9. Instead of payment from personal assets, assume that Fernetti receives €24,000 from partnership assets in withdrawing from the firm. Journalize the withdrawal of Fernetti.

Journalize withdrawal paid by partnership assets.

Exercises

EF.1 (LO 1) Xia Chow has prepared the following list of statements about partnerships.

Identify characteristics of partnership.

1. A partnership is an association of three or more persons to carry on as co-owners of a business for profit.
2. The legal requirements for forming a partnership can be quite burdensome.
3. A partnership is not an entity for financial reporting purposes.
4. The net income of a partnership is taxed as a separate entity.
5. The act of any partner is binding on all other partners, even when partners perform business acts beyond the scope of their authority.
6. Each partner is personally and individually liable for all partnership liabilities.
7. When a partnership is dissolved, the assets legally revert to the original contributor.
8. In a limited partnership, one or more partners have unlimited liability and one or more partners have limited liability for the debts of the firm.
9. Mutual agency is a major advantage of the partnership form of business.

Instructions

Identify each statement as true or false. If false, indicate how to correct the statement.

EF.2 (LO 1) K. Yi, S. Lun, and E. Gao are forming a partnership. Yi is transferring NT$50,000 of personal cash to the partnership (amounts in thousands). Lun owns land worth NT$15,000 and a small building worth NT$80,000, which she transfers to the partnership. Gao transfers to the partnership cash of

Journalize entry for formation of a partnership.

NT$9,000, accounts receivable of NT$32,000, and equipment worth NT$39,000. The partnership expects to collect NT$29,000 of the accounts receivable.

Instructions

a. Prepare the journal entries to record each of the partners' investments.

b. What amount would be reported as total equity immediately after the investments?

Journalize entry for formation of a partnership.

EF.3 (LO 1) Zhang Li has owned and operated a proprietorship for several years. On January 1, she decides to terminate this business and become a partner in the firm of Li and Xuan. Li's investment in the partnership consists of ¥12,000 in cash, and the following assets of the proprietorship: accounts receivable ¥14,000 less allowance for doubtful accounts of ¥2,000, and equipment ¥30,000 less accumulated depreciation of ¥4,000 (amounts in thousands). It is agreed that the allowance for doubtful accounts should be ¥3,000 for the partnership. The fair value of the equipment is ¥23,500.

Instructions

Journalize Li's admission to the firm of Li and Xuan.

Prepare schedule showing distribution of net income and closing entry.

EF.4 (LO 2) McGill and Smyth have capital balances on January 1 of €50,000 and €40,000, respectively. The partnership income-sharing agreement provides for (1) annual salaries of €22,000 for McGill and €13,000 for Smyth, (2) interest at 10% on beginning capital balances, and (3) remaining income or loss to be shared 60% by McGill and 40% by Smyth.

Instructions

a. Prepare a schedule showing the distribution of net income, assuming net income is (1) €50,000 and (2) €36,000.

b. Journalize the allocation of net income in each of the situations above.

Prepare journal entries to record allocation of net income.

EF.5 (LO 2) Tsang (beginning capital, HK$60,000) and Woo (beginning capital HK$90,000) are partners (amounts in thousands). During 2025, the partnership earned net income of HK$80,000, and Tsang made drawings of HK$18,000 while Woo made drawings of HK$24,000.

Instructions

a. Assume the partnership income-sharing agreement calls for income to be divided 45% to Tsang and 55% to Woo. Prepare the journal entry to record the allocation of net income.

b. Assume the partnership income-sharing agreement calls for income to be divided with a salary of HK$30,000 to Tsang and HK$25,000 to Woo, with the remainder divided 45% to Tsang and 55% to Woo. Prepare the journal entry to record the allocation of net income.

c. Assume the partnership income-sharing agreement calls for income to be divided with a salary of HK$40,000 to Tsang and HK$35,000 to Woo, interest of 10% on beginning capital, and the remainder divided 50%–50%. Prepare the journal entry to record the allocation of net income.

d. Compute the partners' ending capital balances under the assumption in part (c).

Prepare partners' capital statement and partial statement of financial position.

EF.6 (LO 2) For KDK Co., beginning capital balances on January 1, 2025, are Deepika Kapoor INR20,000 and Kareena Dutt INR18,000 (amounts in thousands). During the year, drawings were Kapoor INR8,000 and Dutt INR5,000. Net income was INR40,000, and the partners share income equally.

Instructions

a. Prepare the partners' capital statement for the year.

b. Prepare the equity section of the statement of financial position at December 31, 2025.

Prepare a classified statement of financial position of a partnership.

EF.7 (LO 2) Arif, Falel, and Bayu are forming The Doctor Partnership. Arif is transferring Rs30,000 of personal cash and equipment worth Rs25,000 to the partnership (amounts in thousands). Falel owns land worth Rs28,000 and a small building worth Rs75,000, which he transfers to the partnership. There is a long-term mortgage of Rs20,000 on the land and building, which the partnership assumes. Bayu transfers cash of Rs7,000, accounts receivable of Rs36,000, supplies worth Rs3,000, and equipment worth Rs27,000 to the partnership. The partnership expects to collect Rs32,000 of the accounts receivable.

Instructions

Prepare a classified statement of financial position for the partnership after the partners' investments on December 31, 2025.

EF.8 (LO 3) Wenyou Company at December 31 has (amounts in thousands) cash ¥20,000, non-cash assets ¥100,000, liabilities ¥55,000, and the following capital balances: Wen ¥45,000 and You ¥20,000. The firm is liquidated, and ¥105,000 in cash is received for the non-cash assets. Wen and You income ratios are 60% and 40%, respectively.

Prepare cash payments schedule.

Instructions

Prepare a schedule of cash payments.

EF.9 (LO 3) Data for Wenyou Company are presented in EF.8. Wenyou Company now decides to liquidate the partnership.

Journalize transactions in a liquidation.

Instructions

Prepare the entries to record:

a. The sale of non-cash assets.

b. The allocation of the gain or loss on realization to the partners.

c. Payment of creditors.

d. Distribution of cash to the partners.

EF.10 (LO 3) Prior to the distribution of cash to the partners, the accounts in the VUP Company are Cash $24,000; Vogel, Capital (Cr.) $17,000; Utech, Capital (Cr.) $15,000; and Pena, Capital (Dr.) $8,000. The income ratios are 5:3:2, respectively. VUP Company decides to liquidate the company.

Journalize transactions with a capital deficiency.

Instructions

a. Prepare the entry to record (1) Pena's payment of $8,000 in cash to the partnership and (2) the distribution of cash to the partners with credit balances.

b. Prepare the entry to record (1) the absorption of Pena's capital deficiency by the other partners and (2) the distribution of cash to the partners with credit balances.

EF.11 (LO 4) K. Kolmer, C. Eidman, and C. Ryno share income on a 5:3:2 basis. They have capital balances of $34,000, $26,000, and $21,000, respectively, when Don Jernigan is admitted to the partnership.

Journalize admission of a new partner by purchase of an interest.

Instructions

Prepare the journal entry to record the admission of Don Jernigan under each of the following assumptions.

a. Purchase of 50% of Kolmer's equity for $19,000.

b. Purchase of 50% of Eidman's equity for $12,000.

c. Purchase of $33^1/_3$% of Ryno's equity for $9,000.

EF.12 (LO 4) S. Bo and T. Mi share income on a 3:2 basis. They have capital balances of ¥100,000 and ¥60,000, respectively, when W. Jin is admitted to the partnership (amounts in thousands).

Journalize admission of a new partner by investment.

Instructions

Prepare the journal entry to record the admission of W. Jin under each of the following assumptions.

a. Investment of ¥90,000 cash for a 30% ownership interest with bonuses to the existing partners.

b. Investment of ¥50,000 cash for a 30% ownership interest with a bonus to the new partner.

EF.13 (LO 4) N. Kim, C. Hae-jin, and C. Ki-Won have capital balances of ₩50,000, ₩40,000, and ₩30,000, respectively (amounts in thousands). Their income ratios are 4:4:2. Ki-Won withdraws from the partnership under each of the following independent conditions.

Journalize withdrawal of a partner with payment from partners' personal assets.

1. Kim and Hae-jin agree to purchase Ki-won's equity by paying ₩17,000 each from their personal assets. Each purchaser receives 50% of Ki-won's equity.

2. Hae-jin agrees to purchase all of Ki-won's equity by paying ₩22,000 cash from her personal assets.

3. Kim agrees to purchase all of Ki-won's equity by paying ₩26,000 cash from his personal assets.

Instructions

Journalize the withdrawal of Ki-won under each of the assumptions above.

Journalize withdrawal of a partner with payment from partnership assets.

EF.14 (LO 4) B. Yam, J. Koo, and N. Hui have capital balances of HK$95,000, HK$75,000, and HK$60,000, respectively (amounts in thousands). They share income or loss on a 5:3:2 basis. Hui withdraws from the partnership under each of the following conditions.

1. Hui is paid HK$64,000 in cash from partnership assets, and a bonus is granted to the retiring partner.
2. Hui is paid HK$52,000 in cash from partnership assets, and bonuses are granted to the remaining partners.

Instructions

Journalize the withdrawal of Hui under each of the assumptions above.

Journalize entry for admission and withdrawal of partners.

EF.15 (LO 4) Foss, Albertson, and Espinosa are partners who share profits and losses 50%, 30%, and 20%, respectively. Their capital balances are €100,000, €60,000, and €40,000, respectively.

Instructions

a. Assume Garrett joins the partnership by investing €88,000 for a 25% interest with bonuses to the existing partners. Prepare the journal entry to record his investment.

b. Assume instead that Foss leaves the partnership. Foss is paid €110,000 with a bonus to the retiring partner. Prepare the journal entry to record Foss's withdrawal.

Problems

Prepare entries for formation of a partnership and a statement of financial position.

PF.1 (LO 1, 2) The post-closing trial balances of two proprietorships on January 1, 2025, are presented below (amounts in thousands).

	Bon-Joon Company		Joon-Ho Company	
	Dr.	**Cr.**	**Dr.**	**Cr.**
Cash	₩ 14,000		₩12,000	
Accounts receivable	17,500		26,000	
Allowance for doubtful accounts		₩ 3,000		₩ 4,400
Inventory	26,500		18,400	
Equipment	45,000		29,000	
Accumulated depreciation—equipment		24,000		11,000
Notes payable		18,000		15,000
Accounts payable		22,000		31,000
Bon-Joon, capital		36,000		
Joon-Ho, capital				24,000
	₩103,000	₩103,000	₩85,400	₩85,400

Bon-Joon and Joon-Ho decide to form a partnership, BJH Company, with the following agreed upon valuations for non-cash assets.

	Bon-Joon Company	Joon-Ho Company
Accounts receivable	₩17,500	₩26,000
Allowance for doubtful accounts	4,500	4,000
Inventory	28,000	20,000
Equipment	25,000	15,000

All cash will be transferred to the partnership, and the partnership will assume all the liabilities of the two proprietorships. Further, it is agreed that Bon-Joon will invest an additional ₩5,000 in cash, and Joon-Ho will invest an additional ₩19,000 in cash.

Instructions

a. Bon-Joon, Capital ₩40,000
Joon-Ho, Capital ₩23,000

c. Total assets ₩173,000

a. Prepare separate journal entries to record the transfer of each proprietorship's assets and liabilities to the partnership.

b. Journalize the additional cash investment by each partner.

c. Prepare a classified statement of financial position for the partnership on January 1, 2025.

PF.2 (LO 2) At the end of its first year of operations on December 31, 2025, LWC Company's accounts show the following (amounts in thousands).

Journalize divisions of net income and prepare a partners' capital statement.

Partner	Drawings	Capital
A. Lingyu	¥23,000	¥48,000
J. Woo	14,000	30,000
K. Cheng	10,000	25,000

The capital balance represents each partner's initial capital investment. Therefore, net income or net loss for 2025 has not been closed to the partners' capital accounts.

Instructions

a. Journalize the entry to record the division of net income for the year 2025 under each of the following independent assumptions.

1. Net income is ¥30,000. Income is shared 6:3:1.
2. Net income is ¥40,000. Lingyu and Woo are given salary allowances of ¥15,000 and ¥10,000, respectively. The remainder is shared equally.
3. Net income is ¥19,000. Each partner is allowed interest of 10% on beginning capital balances. Lingyu is given a ¥15,000 salary allowance. The remainder is shared equally.

b. Prepare a schedule showing the division of net income under assumption (3) above.

c. Prepare a partners' capital statement for the year under assumption (3) above.

a. 1. Lingyu ¥18,000
2. Lingyu ¥20,000
3. Lingyu ¥17,700

c. Lingyu ¥42,700

PF.3 (LO 3) The partners in Crawford Company decide to liquidate the firm when the statement of financial position shows the following.

Prepare entries with a capital deficiency in liquidation of a partnership.

Crawford Company
Statement of Financial Position
May 31, 2025

Assets		Equity and Liabilities	
Equipment	€ 21,000	A. Jamison, capital	€ 33,000
Accumulated depreciation—equipment	(5,500)	S. Moyer, capital	21,000
Inventory	34,500	P. Roper, capital	3,000
Accounts receivable	25,000	Notes payable	13,500
Allowance for doubtful accounts	(1,000)	Accounts payable	27,000
Cash	27,500	Salaries and wages payable	4,000
	€101,500		€101,500

The partners share income and loss 5:3:2. During the process of liquidation, the following transactions were completed in the following sequence.

1. A total of €51,000 was received from converting non-cash assets into cash.
2. Gain or loss on realization was allocated to partners.
3. Liabilities were paid in full.
4. P. Roper paid his capital deficiency.
5. Cash was paid to the partners with credit balances.

Instructions

a. Prepare the entries to record the transactions.

b. Post to the cash and capital accounts.

c. Assume that Roper is unable to pay the capital deficiency.

1. Prepare the entry to allocate Roper's debit balance to Jamison and Moyer.
2. Prepare the entry to record the final distribution of cash.

a. Loss on realization €23,000
Cash paid: to Jamison €21,500; to Moyer €14,100

PF.4 (LO 4) At April 30, partners' capital balances in PDL Company are G. Donley $52,000, C. Lamar $48,000, and J. Pinkston $18,000. The income sharing ratios are 5:4:1, respectively. On May 1, the PDLT Company is formed by admitting J. Terrell to the firm as a partner.

Journalize admission of a partner under different assumptions.

Instructions

a. Journalize the admission of Terrell under each of the following independent assumptions.

1. Terrell purchases 50% of Pinkston's ownership interest by paying Pinkston $16,000 in cash.
2. Terrell purchases $33^1/_3$% of Lamar's ownership interest by paying Lamar $15,000 in cash.

a. 1. Terrell $9,000
2. Terrell $16,000

3. Terrell $54,000
4. Terrell $48,000

3. Terrell invests $62,000 for a 30% ownership interest, and bonuses are given to the old partners.
4. Terrell invests $42,000 for a 30% ownership interest, which includes a bonus to the new partner.

b. Lamar's capital balance is $32,000 after admitting Terrell to the partnership by investment. If Lamar's ownership interest is 20% of total partnership capital, what were (1) Terrell's cash investment and (2) the bonus to the new partner?

Journalize withdrawal of a partner under different assumptions.

PF.5 (LO 4) On December 31, the capital balances and income ratios in MSY Company are as follows (amounts in thousands).

Partner	Capital Balance	Income Ratio
Mui	HK$60,000	50%
Sang	40,000	30%
Yen	30,000	20%

Instructions

a. Journalize the withdrawal of Yen under each of the following assumptions.

a. 1. Sang, Capital HK$15,000

1. Each of the continuing partners agrees to pay HK$18,000 in cash from personal funds to purchase Yen's ownership equity. Each receives 50% of Yen's equity.

2. Sang, Capital HK$30,000
3. Bonus HK$4,000
4. Bonus HK$8,000

2. Sang agrees to purchase Yen's ownership interest for HK$25,000 cash.
3. Yen is paid HK$34,000 from partnership assets, which includes a bonus to the retiring partner.
4. Yen is paid HK$22,000 from partnership assets, and bonuses to the remaining partners are recognized.

b. If Sang's capital balance after Yen's withdrawal is HK$43,600, what were (1) the total bonus to the remaining partners and (2) the cash paid by the partnership to Yen?

APPENDIX **G**

Subsidiary Ledgers and Special Journals

Appendix Preview

A reliable information system is a necessity for any company. Whether companies use pen, pencil, or computers in maintaining accounting records, certain principles and procedures apply. The purpose of this appendix is to explain and illustrate two components of an accounting information system: subsidiary ledgers and special journals.

Appendix Outline

LEARNING OBJECTIVES	REVIEW
LO 1 Describe the nature and purpose of a subsidiary ledger.	• Subsidiary ledger example • Advantages of subsidiary ledgers
LO 2 Record transactions in special journals.	• Sales journal • Cash receipts journal • Purchases journal • Cash payments journal • Effects of special journals • Cybersecurity

G.1 Subsidiary Ledgers

LEARNING OBJECTIVE 1

Describe the nature and purpose of a subsidiary ledger.

Imagine a business that has several thousand charge (credit) customers and shows the transactions with these customers in only one general ledger account—Accounts Receivable. It would be nearly impossible to determine the balance owed by an individual customer at any specific time. Similarly, the amount payable to one creditor would be difficult to locate quickly from a single Accounts Payable account in the general ledger.

Instead, companies use subsidiary ledgers to keep track of individual balances.

- A **subsidiary ledger** is a group of accounts with a common characteristic (for example, all accounts receivable).
- It is an addition to and an expansion of the general ledger.
- The subsidiary ledger frees the general ledger from the details of individual balances.

Two common subsidiary ledgers are as follows.

1. The **accounts receivable** (or **customers'**) **subsidiary ledger**, which collects transaction data of individual customers.
2. The **accounts payable** (or **creditors'**) **subsidiary ledger**, which collects transaction data of individual creditors.

In each of these subsidiary ledgers, companies usually arrange individual accounts in alphabetical order.

A general ledger account summarizes the detailed data from a subsidiary ledger. For example, the detailed data from the accounts receivable subsidiary ledger are summarized in Accounts Receivable in the general ledger. The general ledger account that summarizes subsidiary ledger data is called a **control account**.

Illustration G.1 presents an overview of the relationship of subsidiary ledgers to the general ledger. There, the general ledger control accounts and subsidiary ledger accounts are in green. Note that Cash and Share Capital—Ordinary in this illustration are not control accounts because there are no subsidiary ledger accounts related to these accounts.

ILLUSTRATION G.1 **Relationship of general ledger and subsidiary ledgers**

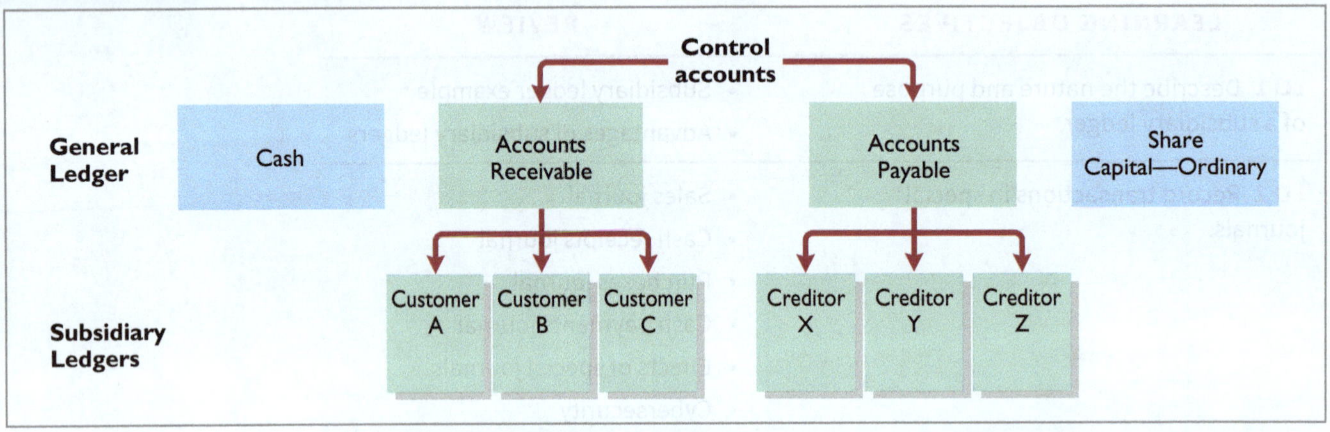

At the end of an accounting period, each general ledger control account balance must equal the composite balance of the individual accounts in the related subsidiary ledger. For example, the balance in Accounts Payable in Illustration G.1 must equal the total of the subsidiary balances of Creditors X + Y + Z.

Subsidiary Ledger Example

Illustration G.2 lists credit sales and collections on account for Pujols Company.

ILLUSTRATION G.2

Sales and collection transactions

Credit Sales			Collections on Account		
Jan. 10	Aaron Co.	$ 6,000	Jan. 19	Aaron Co.	$4,000
12	Branden Inc.	3,000	21	Branden Inc.	3,000
20	Caron Co.	3,000	29	Caron Co.	1,000
		$12,000			$8,000

Illustration G.3 provides an example of a control account and subsidiary ledger for Pujols Company. (Due to space considerations, the explanation column in these accounts is not shown in this and subsequent illustrations.) Illustration G.3 is based on the transactions listed in Illustration G.2.

Pujols can reconcile the total debits ($12,000) and credits ($8,000) in Accounts Receivable in the general ledger to the detailed debits and credits in the subsidiary accounts. Also, the

ILLUSTRATION G.3 **Relationship between general and subsidiary ledgers**

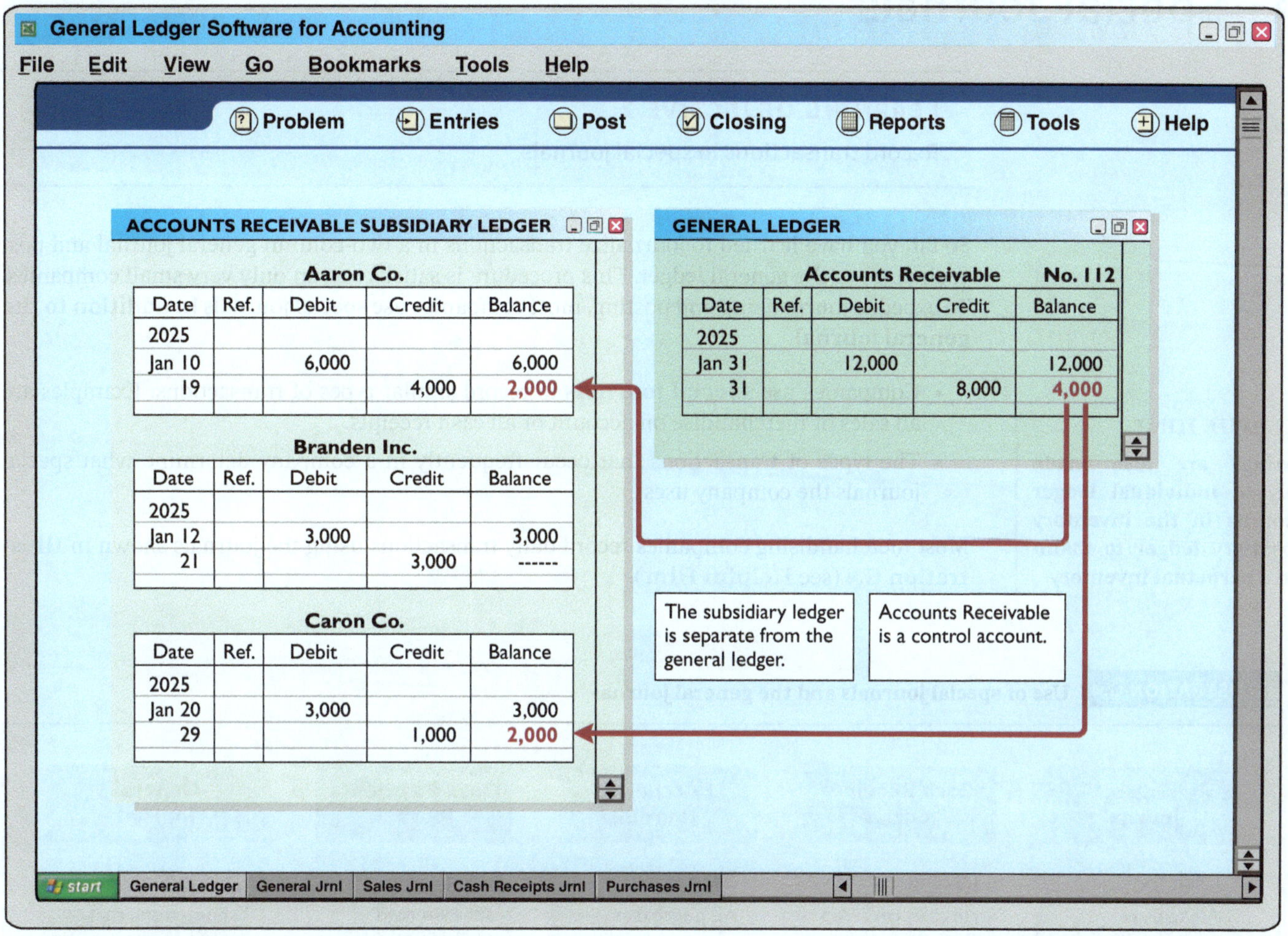

balance of $4,000 in the control account agrees with the total of the balances in the individual accounts (Aaron Co. $2,000 + Branden Inc. $0 + Caron Co. $2,000) in the subsidiary ledger.

- As Illustration G.3 shows, companies make monthly postings to the control accounts in the general ledger. This practice allows them to prepare monthly financial statements.
- Companies post to the individual accounts in the subsidiary ledger daily. Daily posting ensures that account information is current. This enables the company to monitor credit limits, bill customers, and answer inquiries from customers about their account balances.

Advantages of Subsidiary Ledgers

Subsidiary ledgers have several advantages:

1. **They show in a single account transactions affecting one customer or one creditor,** thus providing up-to-date information on specific account balances.
2. **They free the general ledger of excessive details.** As a result, a trial balance of the general ledger does not contain vast numbers of individual account balances.
3. **They help locate errors in individual accounts** by reducing the number of accounts in one ledger and by using control accounts.
4. **They make possible a division of labor** in posting. One employee can post to the general ledger while someone else posts to the subsidiary ledgers.

G.2 Special Journals

LEARNING OBJECTIVE 2

Record transactions in special journals.

So far, you have learned to journalize transactions in a two-column general journal and post each entry to the general ledger. This procedure is satisfactory in only very small companies. To expedite journalizing and posting, most companies use special journals **in addition to the general journal**.

- Companies use **special journals** to record similar types of transactions. Examples are all sales of merchandise on account or all cash receipts.
- The types of transactions that occur frequently in a company determine what special journals the company uses.

HELPFUL HINT

Postings are also made daily to individual ledger accounts in the inventory subsidiary ledger to maintain a perpetual inventory.

Most merchandising companies record daily transactions using the journals shown in **Illustration G.4** (see **Helpful Hint**).

ILLUSTRATION G.4 **Use of special journals and the general journal**

Sales Journal	Cash Receipts Journal	Purchases Journal	Cash Payment Journal	General Journal
Used for: All sales of merchandise on account	Used for: All cash received (including cash sales)	Used for: All purchases of merchandise on account	Used for: All cash paid (including cash purchases)	Used for: Transactions that cannot be entered in a special journal, including correcting, adjusting, and closing entries

If a transaction cannot be recorded in a special journal, the company records it in the general journal. For example, if a company had special journals for only the four types of transactions listed above, it would record purchase returns and allowances that do not affect cash in the general journal. Similarly, **correcting, adjusting, and closing entries are recorded in the general journal.** In some situations, companies might use special journals other than those listed above. For example, when sales returns and allowances that do not affect cash are frequent, a company might use a special journal to record these transactions.

- Special journals **permit greater division of labor** because several people can record entries in different journals at the same time. For example, one employee may journalize all cash receipts, and another may journalize all credit sales.
- Also, the use of special journals **reduces the time needed to complete the posting process**. With special journals, companies may post some accounts monthly instead of daily, as we will illustrate later in the appendix.

On the following pages, we discuss the four special journals shown in Illustration G.4.

Sales Journal

In the **sales journal**, companies record **sales of merchandise on account**. Cash sales of merchandise go in the cash receipts journal. Credit sales of assets other than merchandise go in the general journal.

Journalizing Credit Sales

To demonstrate use of a sales journal, we will use data for Karns Wholesale Supply, which uses a **perpetual inventory system**. Under this system, each entry in the sales journal results in one entry **at selling price** and another entry **at cost**. The entry at selling price is a debit to Accounts Receivable (a control account) and a credit of equal amount to Sales Revenue. The entry at cost is a debit to Cost of Goods Sold and a credit of equal amount to Inventory (a control account).

Using a sales journal with two amount columns, the company can show on only one line a sales transaction at both selling price and cost. **Illustration G.5** shows this two-column sales journal of Karns Wholesale Supply, using assumed credit sales transactions, for sales invoices 101–107.

ILLUSTRATION G.5 **Journalizing the sales journal—perpetual inventory system**

General Ledger Software for Accounting

SALES JOURNAL S1

Date	Account Debited	Invoice No.	Ref.	Accts. Receivable Dr. Sales Revenue Cr.	Cost of Goods Sold Dr. Inventory Cr.
2025					
May 3	Abbot Sisters	101		10,600	6,360
7	Babson Co.	102		11,350	7,370
14	Carson Bros.	103		7,800	5,070
19	Deli Co.	104		9,300	6,510
21	Abbot Sisters	105		15,400	10,780
24	Deli Co.	106		21,210	15,900
27	Babson Co.	107		14,570	10,200
				90,230	62,190

Note that, unlike the general journal, an explanation is not required for each entry in a special journal. Also, the use of prenumbered invoices ensures that all invoices are journalized and no invoices are duplicated. Finally, the reference (Ref.) column is not used in journalizing. It is used in posting the sales journal, as explained in the next section.

Posting the Sales Journal

Companies make daily postings from the sales journal **to the individual accounts receivable** in the subsidiary ledger. Posting **to the general ledger** is done **monthly**. **Illustration G.6** shows both the daily and monthly postings.

ILLUSTRATION G.6 **Posting the sales journal**

General Ledger Software for Accounting

File Edit View Go Bookmarks Tools Help

Problem Entries Post Closing Reports Tools Help

SALES JOURNAL S1

Date	Account Debited	Invoice No.	Ref.	Accts. Receivable Dr. Sales Revenue Cr.	Cost of Goods Sold Dr. Inventory Cr.
2025					
May 3	Abbot Sisters	101	√	10,600	6,360
7	Babson Co.	102	√	11,350	7,370
14	Carson Bros.	103	√	7,800	5,070
19	Deli Co.	104	√	9,300	6,510
21	Abbot Sisters	105	√	15,400	10,780
24	Deli Co.	106	√	21,210	15,900
27	Babson Co.	107	√	14,570	10,200
				90,230	62,190
				(112) / (401)	(505) / (120)

At the end of the accounting period, the company posts totals to the general ledger.

The company posts individual amounts to the subsidiary ledger daily.

ACCOUNTS RECEIVABLE SUBSIDIARY LEDGER

Abbot Sisters

Date	Ref.	Debit	Credit	Balance
2025				
May 3	S1	10,600		10,600
21	S1	15,400		26,000

Babson Co.

Date	Ref.	Debit	Credit	Balance
2025				
May 7	S1	11,350		11,350
27	S1	14,570		25,920

Carson Bros.

Date	Ref.	Debit	Credit	Balance
2025				
May 14	S1	7,800		7,800

Deli Co.

Date	Ref.	Debit	Credit	Balance
2025				
May 19	S1	9,300		9,300
24	S1	21,210		30,510

GENERAL LEDGER

Accounts Receivable **No. 112**

Date	Ref.	Debit	Credit	Balance
2025				
May 31	S1	90,230		90,230

Inventory **No. 120**

Date	Ref.	Debit	Credit	Balance
2025				
May 31	S1		62,190	62,190[1]

Sales Revenue **No. 401**

Date	Ref.	Debit	Credit	Balance
2025				
May 31	S1		90,230	90,230

Cost of Goods Sold **No. 505**

Date	Ref.	Debit	Credit	Balance
2025				
May 31	S1	62,190		62,190

The subsidiary ledger is separate from the general ledger.

Accounts Receivable is a control account.

[1]The normal balance for Inventory is a debit. But because of the sequence in which we have posted the special journals, with the sales journal first, the credits to Inventory are posted before the debits. This posting sequence explains the credit balance in Inventory, which exists only until the other journals are posted.

start General Ledger General Jrnl Sales Jrnl Cash Receipts Jrnl Purchases Jrnl

A check mark (✓) is inserted in the reference column to indicate that the daily posting to the customer's account has been made. If the subsidiary ledger accounts were numbered, the account number would be entered in place of the check mark.

At the end of the month, Karns posts the column totals of the sales journal to the general ledger. Here, the column totals are posted as follows. From the selling-price column, a debit of $90,230 to Accounts Receivable (account No. 112), and a credit of $90,230 to Sales Revenue (account No. 401). From the cost column, a debit of $62,190 to Cost of Goods Sold (account No. 505), and a credit of $62,190 to Inventory (account No. 120).

Karns inserts the account numbers below the column totals to indicate that the postings have been made. In both the general ledger and subsidiary ledger accounts, the reference **S1** indicates that the posting came from page 1 of the sales journal.

Proving the Ledgers

The next step is to "prove" the ledgers. To do so, Karns must determine two things:

1. The total of the general ledger debit balances must equal the total of the general ledger credit balances.
2. The sum of the subsidiary ledger balances must equal the balance in the control account.

Illustration G.7 shows the proof of the postings from the sales journal to the general and subsidiary ledgers.

ILLUSTRATION G.7

Proving the equality of the postings from the sales journal

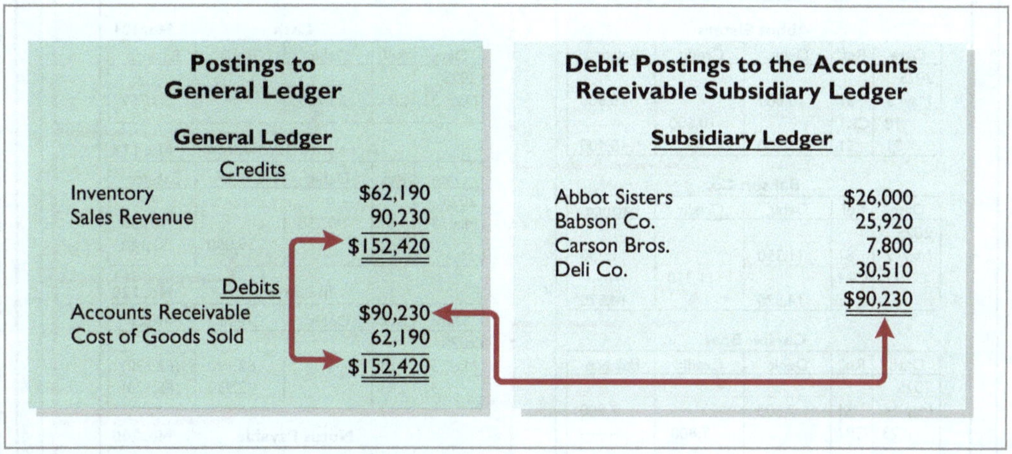

Advantages of the Sales Journal

The use of a special journal to record sales on account has a number of advantages.

- The one-line entry for each sales transaction saves time. In the sales journal, it is not necessary to write out the four account titles for each transaction.
- Only totals, rather than individual entries, are posted to the general ledger. This saves posting time and reduces the possibilities of errors in posting.
- A division of labor results because one individual can take responsibility for the sales journal.

Cash Receipts Journal

In the **cash receipts journal**, companies record all receipts of cash. The most common types of cash receipts are cash sales of merchandise and collections of accounts receivable. Many other possibilities exist, such as receipt of money from bank loans and cash proceeds from disposal of equipment. A one- or two-column cash receipts journal would not have space enough for all possible cash receipt transactions. Therefore, companies use a multiple-column cash receipts journal.

Generally, a cash receipts journal includes the following columns: debit columns for Cash and Sales Discounts, and credit columns for Accounts Receivable, Sales Revenue, and "Other Accounts." Companies use the Other Accounts category when the cash receipt does not involve a cash sale or a collection of accounts receivable. Under a perpetual inventory system, each sales entry also is accompanied by an entry that debits Cost of Goods Sold and credits Inventory for the cost of the merchandise sold. **Illustration G.8** shows a six-column cash receipts journal.

ILLUSTRATION G.8

Journalizing and posting the cash receipts journal

General Ledger Software for Accounting

File Edit View Go Bookmarks Tools Help

Problem Entries Post Closing Reports Tools Help

CASH RECEIPTS JOURNAL CR1

Date	Account Credited	Ref.	Cash Dr.	Sales Discounts Dr.	Accounts Receivable Cr.	Sales Revenue Cr.	Other Accounts Cr.	Cost of Goods Sold Dr. Inventory Cr.
2025								
May 1	Share Capital—Ordinary	311	5,000				5,000	
7			1,900			1,900		1,240
10	Abbot Sisters	√	10,388	212	10,600			
12			2,600			2,600		1,690
17	Babson Co.	√	11,123	227	11,350			
22	Notes Payable	200	6,000				6,000	
23	Carson Bros.	√	7,644	156	7,800			
28	Deli Co.	√	9,114	186	9,300			
			53,769	781	39,050	4,500	11,000	2,930
			(101)	(414)	(112)	(401)	(x)	(505)/(120)

The company posts individual amounts to the subsidiary ledger daily.

At the end of the accounting period, the company posts totals to the general ledger.

ACCOUNTS RECEIVABLE SUBSIDIARY LEDGER

Abbot Sisters

Date	Ref.	Debit	Credit	Balance
2025				
May 3	S1	10,600		10,600
10	CR1		10,600	--------
21	S1	15,400		15,400

Babson Co.

Date	Ref.	Debit	Credit	Balance
2025				
May 7	S1	11,350		11,350
17	CR1		11,350	--------
27	S1	14,570		14,570

Carson Bros.

Date	Ref.	Debit	Credit	Balance
2025				
May 14	S1	7,800		7,800
23	CR1		7,800	-------

Deli Co.

Date	Ref.	Debit	Credit	Balance
2025				
May 19	S1	9,300		9,300
24	S1	21,210		30,510
28	CR1		9,300	21,210

The subsidiary ledger is separate from the general ledger.

Accounts Receivable is a control account.

GENERAL LEDGER

Cash No. 101

Date	Ref.	Debit	Credit	Balance
2025				
May 31	CR1	53,769		53,769

Accounts Receivable No. 112

Date	Ref.	Debit	Credit	Balance
2025				
May 31	S1	90,230		90,230
31	CR1		39,050	51,180

Inventory No. 120

Date	Ref.	Debit	Credit	Balance
2025				
May 31	S1		62,190	(62,190)
31	CR1		2,930	(65,120)

Notes Payable No. 200

Date	Ref.	Debit	Credit	Balance
2025				
May 22	CR1		6,000	6,000

Share Capital—Ordinary No. 311

Date	Ref.	Debit	Credit	Balance
2025				
May 1	CR1		5,000	5,000

Sales Revenue No. 401

Date	Ref.	Debit	Credit	Balance
2025				
May 31	S1		90,230	90,230
31	CR1		4,500	94,730

Sales Discounts No. 414

Date	Ref.	Debit	Credit	Balance
2025				
May 31	CR1	781		781

Cost of Goods Sold No. 505

Date	Ref.	Debit	Credit	Balance
2025				
May 31	S1	62,190		62,190
31	CR1	2,930		65,120

start General Ledger General Jrnl Sales Jrnl Cash Receipts Jrnl Purchases Jrnl

Companies may use additional credit columns if these columns significantly reduce postings to a specific account. For example, a loan company receives thousands of cash collections from customers. Using separate credit columns for Loans Receivable and Interest Revenue, rather than the Other Accounts credit column, would reduce postings.

Journalizing Cash Receipts Transactions

To illustrate the journalizing of cash receipts transactions, we examine the May transactions of Karns Wholesale Supply. Collections from customers relate to the entries recorded in the sales journal in Illustration G.5. The entries in the cash receipts journal are based on the following cash receipts.

May	1	D. A. Karns makes an investment of $5,000 in the business.
	7	Cash sales of merchandise total $1,900 (cost, $1,240).
	10	Received a check for $10,388 from Abbot Sisters in payment of invoice No. 101 for $10,600 less a 2% discount.
	12	Cash sales of merchandise total $2,600 (cost, $1,690).
	17	Received a check for $11,123 from Babson Co. in payment of invoice No. 102 for $11,350 less a 2% discount.
	22	Received cash by signing a note for $6,000.
	23	Received a check for $7,644 from Carson Bros. in full for invoice No. 103 for $7,800 less a 2% discount.
	28	Received a check for $9,114 from Deli Co. in full for invoice No. 104 for $9,300 less a 2% discount.

Further information about the columns in the cash receipts journal is discussed below.

Debit Columns:

1. **Cash.** Karns enters in this column the amount of cash actually received in each transaction. The column total indicates the total cash receipts for the month.
2. **Sales Discounts.** Karns includes a Sales Discounts column in its cash receipts journal. By doing so, it does not need to enter sales discount items in the general journal. As a result, the cash receipts journal shows on one line the collection of an account receivable within the discount period.

Credit Columns:

3. **Accounts Receivable.** Karns uses the Accounts Receivable column to record cash collections on account. The amount entered here is the amount to be credited to the individual customer's account (see **Helpful Hint**).
4. **Sales Revenue.** The Sales Revenue column records all cash sales of merchandise. Cash sales of other assets (plant assets, for example) are not reported in this column.
5. **Other Accounts.** Karns uses the Other Accounts column whenever the credit is other than to Accounts Receivable or Sales Revenue. For example, in the first entry, Karns enters $5,000 as a credit to Share Capital—Ordinary. This column is often referred to as the sundry accounts column.

Debit and Credit Column:

6. **Cost of Goods Sold and Inventory.** This column records debits to Cost of Goods Sold and credits to Inventory.

HELPFUL HINT

A *subsidiary ledger* account is credited when the entry involves a collection of accounts receivable. A *general ledger* account is credited when the account is not shown in a special column (and an amount must be entered in the Other Accounts column). Otherwise, no account is shown in the "Account Credited" column.

In a multi-column journal, generally only one line is needed for each entry. Debit and credit amounts for each line must be equal. When Karns journalizes the collection from Abbot Sisters on May 10, for example, three amounts are indicated. Note also that the Account Credited column identifies both general ledger and subsidiary ledger account titles. General ledger accounts are illustrated in the May 1 and May 22 entries. A subsidiary account is illustrated in the May 10 entry for the collection from Abbot Sisters.

When Karns has finished journalizing a multi-column journal, it totals the amount columns and compares the totals to prove the equality of debits and credits. **Illustration G.9** shows the proof of the equality of Karns's cash receipts journal.

Totaling the columns of a journal and proving the equality of the totals is called **footing** and **cross-footing** a journal.

ILLUSTRATION G.9

Proving the equality of the cash receipts journal

Debits		Credits	
Cash	$53,769	Accounts Receivable	$39,050
Sales Discounts	781	Sales Revenue	4,500
Cost of Goods Sold	2,930	Other Accounts	11,000
	$57,480	Inventory	2,930
			$57,480

Posting the Cash Receipts Journal

Posting a multi-column journal (Illustration G.8) involves the following steps.

1. **At the end of the month**, the company posts all column totals, except for the Other Accounts total, to the account title(s) specified in the column heading (such as Cash or Accounts Receivable). The company then enters account numbers below the column totals to show that they have been posted. For example, Karns has posted Cash to account No. 101, Accounts Receivable to account No. 112, Inventory to account No. 120, Sales Revenue to account No. 401, Sales Discounts to account No. 414, and Cost of Goods Sold to account No. 505.
2. The company **separately posts the individual amounts comprising the Other Accounts total** to the general ledger accounts specified in the Account Credited column. See, for example, the credit posting to Share Capital—Ordinary. The total amount of this column has not been posted. The symbol (X) is inserted below the total to this column to indicate that the amount has not been posted.
3. The individual amounts in a column, posted in total to a control account (Accounts Receivable, in this case), are posted **daily to the subsidiary ledger** account specified in the Account Credited column. See, for example, the credit posting of $10,600 to Abbot Sisters.

The symbol **CR**, used in both the subsidiary and general ledgers, identifies postings from the cash receipts journal.

Proving the Ledgers

After posting of the cash receipts journal is completed, Karns proves the ledgers. As shown in **Illustration G.10**, the general ledger totals agree. Also, the sum of the subsidiary ledger balances equals the control account balance.

ILLUSTRATION G.10

Proving the ledgers after posting the sales and the cash receipts journals

Schedule of Accounts Receivable (from accounts receivable subsidiary ledger)	
Abbot Sisters	$15,400
Babson Co.	14,570
Deli Co.	21,210
	$51,180

General Ledger	
Debits	
Cash	$ 53,769
Accounts Receivable	51,180
Sales Discounts	781
Cost of Goods Sold	65,120
	$170,850
Credits	
Notes Payable	$ 6,000
Share Capital—Ordinary	5,000
Sales Revenue	94,730
Inventory	65,120
	$170,850

Purchases Journal

In the **purchases journal**, companies record all purchases of merchandise on account. Each entry in this journal results in a debit to Inventory and a credit to Accounts Payable. For example, consider the following credit purchase transactions for Karns Wholesale Supply in **Illustration G.11**.

ILLUSTRATION G.11
Credit purchase transactions

Date	Supplier	Amount
5/6	Jasper Manufacturing Inc.	$11,000
5/10	Eaton and Howe Inc.	7,200
5/14	Fabor and Son	6,900
5/19	Jasper Manufacturing Inc.	17,500
5/26	Fabor and Son	8,700
5/29	Eaton and Howe Inc.	12,600

Illustration G.12 shows the purchases journal for Karns Wholesale Supply (see **Helpful Hint**). When using a one-column purchases journal (as in Illustration G.12), a company cannot journalize other types of purchases on account or cash purchases in it. For example, if the company used the purchases journal in Illustration G.12, Karns would have to record credit purchases of equipment or supplies in the general journal. Likewise, all cash purchases would be entered in the cash payments journal.

HELPFUL HINT

A single-column purchases journal needs only to be footed to prove the equality of debits and credits.

Journalizing Credit Purchases of Merchandise

The journalizing procedure is similar to that for a sales journal.

- Companies make entries in the purchases journal from purchase invoices.
- In contrast to the sales journal, the purchases journal may not have an invoice number column because invoices received from different suppliers will not be in numerical sequence.
- To ensure that they record all purchase invoices, some companies consecutively number each invoice upon receipt and then use an internal document number column in the purchases journal.

The entries for Karns Wholesale Supply are based on the assumed credit purchases listed in Illustration G.11.

Posting the Purchases Journal

The procedures for posting the purchases journal are similar to those for the sales journal.

- In this case, Karns makes **daily** postings to the **accounts payable ledger** (see **Helpful Hint**).
- It makes **monthly** postings to Inventory and Accounts Payable in the general ledger.
- In both ledgers, Karns uses **P1** in the reference column to show that the postings are from page 1 of the purchases journal.

HELPFUL HINT

Postings to subsidiary ledger accounts are done daily because it is often necessary to know a current balance for the subsidiary accounts.

Proof of the equality of the postings from the purchases journal to both ledgers is shown in **Illustration G.13**.

Expanding the Purchases Journal

Some companies expand the purchases journal to include all types of purchases on account, not just merchandise. Instead of one column for inventory and accounts payable, they use a multiple-column format. This format usually includes a credit column for Accounts Payable and debit columns for purchases of Inventory, Supplies, and Other Accounts. **Illustration G.14** shows a multi-column purchases journal for Hanover Co. The posting procedures are similar to those shown earlier for posting the cash receipts journal. *For homework problems, assume the use of a single-column purchases journal unless instructed otherwise.*

ILLUSTRATION G.12 **Journalizing and posting the purchases journal**

General Ledger Software for Accounting

File Edit View Go Bookmarks Tools Help

Problem Entries Post Closing Reports Tools Help

PURCHASES JOURNAL P1

Date	Account Credited	Terms	Ref.	Inventory Dr. Accounts Payable Cr.
2025				
May 6	Jasper Manufacturing Inc.	2/10, n/30	√	11,000
10	Eaton and Howe Inc.	3/10, n/30	√	7,200
14	Fabor and Son	1/10, n/30	√	6,900
19	Jasper Manufacturing Inc.	2/10, n/30	√	17,500
26	Fabor and Son	1/10, n/30	√	8,700
29	Eaton and Howe Inc.	3/10, n/30	√	12,600
				63,900
				(120)/(201)

The company posts individual amounts to the subsidiary ledger daily.

At the end of the accounting period, the company posts totals to the general ledger.

ACCOUNTS PAYABLE SUBSIDIARY LEDGER

Eaton and Howe Inc.

Date	Ref.	Debit	Credit	Balance
2025				
May 10	P1		7,200	7,200
29	P1		12,600	19,800

Fabor and Son

Date	Ref.	Debit	Credit	Balance
2025				
May 14	P1		6,900	6,900
26	P1		8,700	15,600

Jasper Manufacturing Inc.

Date	Ref.	Debit	Credit	Balance
2025				
May 6	P1		11,000	11,000
19	P1		17,500	28,500

GENERAL LEDGER

Inventory **No. 120**

Date	Ref.	Debit	Credit	Balance
2025				
May 31	S1		62,190	(62,190)
31	CR1		2,930	(65,120)
31	P1	63,900		(1,220)

Accounts Payable **No. 201**

Date	Ref.	Debit	Credit	Balance
2025				
May 31	P1		63,900	63,900

The subsidiary ledger is separate from the general ledger.

Accounts Payable is a control account.

start General Ledger General Jrnl Sales Jrnl Cash Receipts Jrnl Purchases Jrnl

Postings to General Ledger	
Inventory (debit)	$63,900
Accounts Payable (credit)	$63,900

Credit Postings to Accounts Payable Ledger	
Eaton and Howe Inc.	$19,800
Fabor and Son	15,600
Jin Manufacturing Inc.	28,500
	$63,900

ILLUSTRATION G.13 Proving the equality of the purchases journal

ILLUSTRATION G.14 Multi-column purchases journal

General Ledger Software for Accounting

File Edit View Go Bookmarks Tools Help

Problem Entries Post Closing Reports Tools Help

PURCHASES JOURNAL PI

Date	Account Credited	Ref.	Accounts Payable Cr.	Inventory Dr.	Supplies Dr.	Other Accounts Dr. Account	Ref.	Amount
2025								
June 1	Signe Audio	√	2,000		2,000			
3	Wight Co.	√	1,500	1,500				
5	Orange Tree Co.	√	2,600			Equipment	157	2,600
30	Sue's Business Forms	√	800		800			
			56,600	43,000	8,700			4,900

start General Ledger General Jrnl Sales Jrnl Cash Receipts Jrnl Purchases Jrnl

Cash Payments Journal

In a **cash payments (cash disbursements) journal**, companies record all disbursements of cash. Entries are made from prenumbered checks. Because companies make cash payments for various purposes, the cash payments journal has multiple columns. **Illustration G.15** shows a four-column journal.

ILLUSTRATION G.15 Journalizing and posting the cash payments journal

General Ledger Software for Accounting

File Edit View Go Bookmarks Tools Help

Problem Entries Post Closing Reports Tools Help

CASH PAYMENTS JOURNAL CP1

Date	Ck. No.	Account Debited	Ref.	Other Accounts Dr.	Accounts Payable Dr.	Inventory Cr.	Cash Cr.
2025							
May 1	101	Prepaid Insurance	130	1,200			1,200
3	102	Inventory	120	100			100
8	103	Inventory	120	4,400			4,400
10	104	Jasper Manuf. Inc.	√		11,000	220	10,780
19	105	Eaton & Howe Inc.	√		7,200	216	6,984
23	106	Fabor and Son	√		6,900	69	6,831
28	107	Jasper Manuf. Inc.	√		17,500	350	17,150
30	108	Cash Dividends	332	500			500
				6,200	42,600	855	47,945
				(x)	(201)	(120)	(101)

The company posts individual amounts to the subsidiary ledger daily.

At the end of the accounting period, the company posts totals to the general ledger.

ACCOUNTS PAYABLE SUBSIDIARY LEDGER

Eaton and Howe Inc.

Date	Ref.	Debit	Credit	Balance
2025				
May 10	P1		7,200	7,200
19	CP1	7,200		-------
29	P1		12,600	12,600

Fabor and Son

Date	Ref.	Debit	Credit	Balance
2025				
May 14	P1		6,900	6,900
23	CP1	6,900		-------
26	P1		8,700	8,700

Jasper Manufacturing Inc.

Date	Ref.	Debit	Credit	Balance
2025				
May 6	P1		11,000	11,000
10	CP1	11,000		--------
19	P1		17,500	17,500
28	CP1	17,500		--------

The subsidiary ledger is separate from the general ledger.

Accounts Payable is a control account.

GENERAL LEDGER

Cash No. 101

Date	Ref.	Debit	Credit	Balance
2025				
May 31	CR1	53,769		53,769
31	CP1		47,945	5,824

Inventory No. 120

Date	Ref.	Debit	Credit	Balance
2025				
May 3	CP1	100		100
8	CP1	4,400		4,500
31	S1		62,190	57,690
31	CR1		2,930	60,620
31	P1	63,900		3,280
31	CP1		855	2,425

Prepaid Insurance No. 130

Date	Ref.	Debit	Credit	Balance
2025				
May 1	CP1	1,200		1,200

Accounts Payable No. 201

Date	Ref.	Debit	Credit	Balance
2025				
May 31	P1		63,900	63,900
31	CP1	42,600		21,300

Cash Dividends No. 332

Date	Ref.	Debit	Credit	Balance
2025				
May 30	CP1	500		500

start General Ledger General Jrnl Sales Jrnl Cash Receipts Jrnl Purchases Jrnl

Journalizing Cash Payments Transactions

The procedures for journalizing transactions in this journal are similar to those for the cash receipts journal. Karns records each transaction on one line, and for each line there must be equal debit and credit amounts. The entries in the cash payments journal in Illustration G.15 are based on the following transactions for Karns Wholesale Supply.

May	1	Issued check No. 101 for $1,200 for the annual premium on a fire insurance policy.
	3	Issued check No. 102 for $100 in payment of freight when terms were FOB shipping point.
	8	Issued check No. 103 for $4,400 for the purchase of merchandise.
	10	Sent check No. 104 for $10,780 to Jasper Manufacturing Inc. in payment of May 6 invoice for $11,000 less a 2% discount.
	19	Mailed check No. 105 for $6,984 to Eaton and Howe Inc. in payment of May 10 invoice for $7,200 less a 3% discount.
	23	Sent check No. 106 for $6,831 to Fabor and Son in payment of May 14 invoice for $6,900 less a 1% discount.
	28	Sent check No. 107 for $17,150 to Jasper Manufacturing Inc. in payment of May 19 invoice for $17,500 less a 2% discount.
	30	Issued check No. 108 for $500 to D. A. Karns as a cash withdrawal for personal use.

Note that whenever Karns enters an amount in the Other Accounts column, it must identify a specific general ledger account in the Account Debited column. The entries for checks No. 101, 102, 103, and 108 illustrate this situation. Similarly, Karns must identify a subsidiary account in the Account Debited column whenever it enters an amount in the Accounts Payable column. See, for example, the entry for check No. 104.

After Karns journalizes the cash payments journal, it totals the columns. The totals are then balanced to prove the equality of debits and credits.

Posting the Cash Payments Journal

The procedures for posting the cash payments journal are similar to those for the cash receipts journal.

- Karns posts the amounts recorded in the Accounts Payable column individually to the subsidiary ledger and in total to the control account.
- It posts Inventory and Cash only in total at the end of the month.
- Transactions in the Other Accounts column are posted individually to the appropriate account(s) affected. The company does not post totals for the Other Accounts column.

Illustration G.15 shows the posting of the cash payments journal. Note that Karns uses the symbol **CP** as the posting reference. After postings are completed, the company proves the equality of the debit and credit balances in the general ledger. In addition, the control account balances should agree with the subsidiary ledger total balance. **Illustration G.16** shows the agreement of these balances.

Schedule of Accounts Payable
(from accounts payable subsidiary ledger)

Eaton and Howe Inc.	$12,600
Fabor and Son	8,700
	$21,300

General Ledger

Debits

Cash	$ 5,824
Accounts Receivable	51,180
Inventory	2,425
Prepaid Insurance	1,200
Cash Dividends	500
Sales Discounts	781
Cost of Goods Sold	65,120
	$127,030

Credits

Notes Payable	$ 6,000
Accounts Payable	21,300
Share Capital—Ordinary	5,000
Sales Revenue	94,730
	$127,030

ILLUSTRATION G.16

Proving the ledgers after postings from the sales, cash receipts, purchases, and cash payments journals

Effects of Special Journals on the General Journal

Special journals for sales, purchases, and cash substantially reduce the number of entries that companies make in the general journal. **Only transactions that cannot be entered in a special journal are recorded in the general journal.** For example, a company may use the general journal to record such transactions as granting of credit to a customer for a sales return or allowance, granting of credit from a supplier for purchases returned, acceptance of a note receivable from a customer, and purchase of equipment by issuing a note payable. Also, **correcting, adjusting, and closing entries are made in the general journal**.

The general journal has columns for date, account title and explanation, reference, and debit and credit amounts. When control and subsidiary accounts are not involved, the procedures for journalizing and posting of transactions are the same as those described in earlier chapters. When control and subsidiary accounts are involved, companies make two changes from the earlier procedures:

1. In **journalizing**, they identify both the control and the subsidiary accounts.
2. In **posting**, there must be a **dual posting**: once to the control account and once to the subsidiary account.

To illustrate, assume that on May 31, Karns Wholesale Supply returns $500 of merchandise for credit to Fabor and Son. **Illustration G.17** shows the entry in the general journal and the posting of the entry.

ILLUSTRATION G.17 Journalizing and posting the general journal

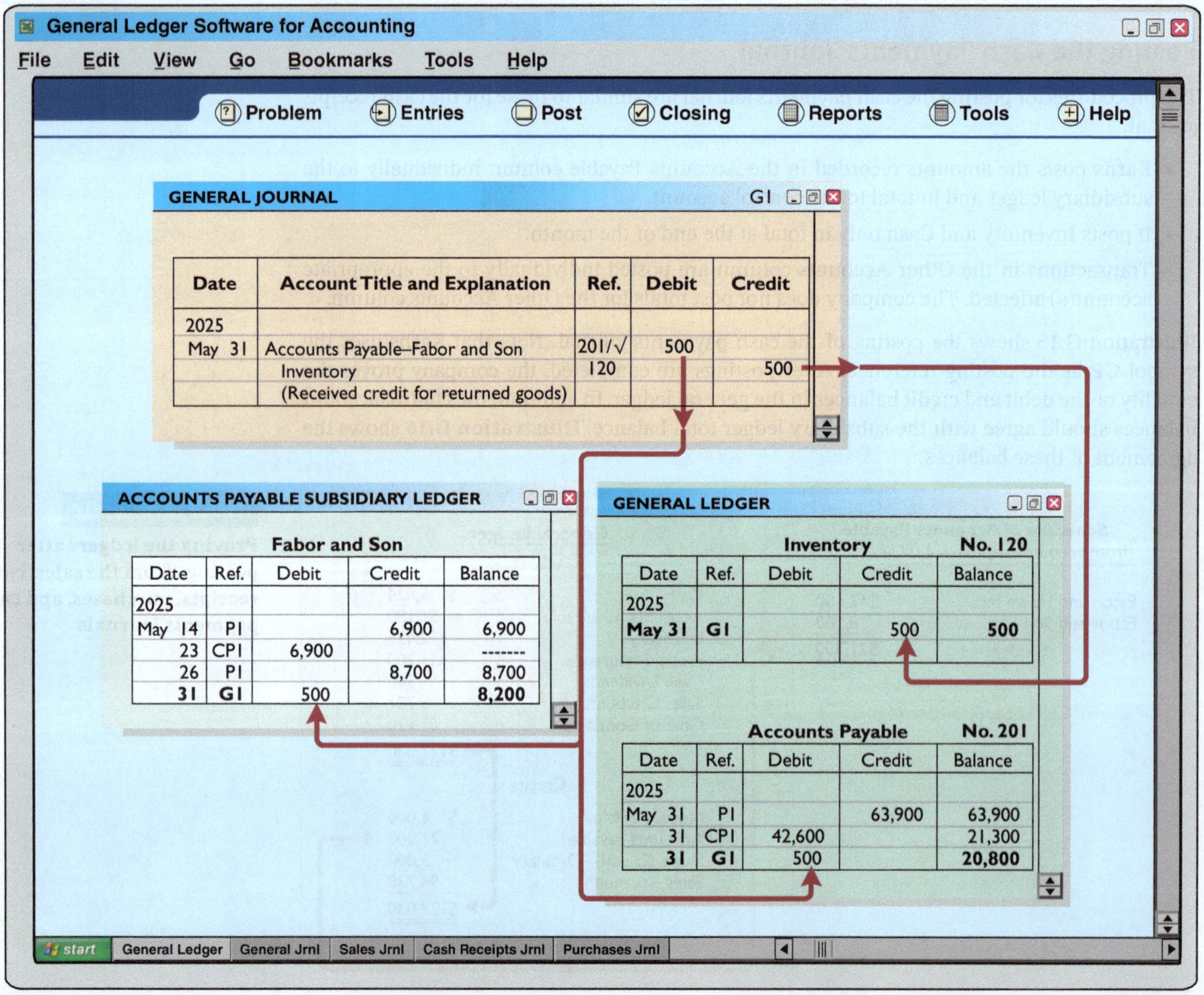

GENERAL JOURNAL G1

Date	Account Title and Explanation	Ref.	Debit	Credit
2025				
May 31	Accounts Payable–Fabor and Son	201/√	500	
	Inventory	120		500
	(Received credit for returned goods)			

ACCOUNTS PAYABLE SUBSIDIARY LEDGER

Fabor and Son

Date	Ref.	Debit	Credit	Balance
2025				
May 14	P1		6,900	6,900
23	CP1	6,900		-------
26	P1		8,700	8,700
31	**G1**	500		**8,200**

GENERAL LEDGER

Inventory No. 120

Date	Ref.	Debit	Credit	Balance
2025				
May 31	**G1**		500	**500**

Accounts Payable No. 201

Date	Ref.	Debit	Credit	Balance
2025				
May 31	P1		63,900	63,900
31	CP1	42,600		21,300
31	**G1**	500		**20,800**

Note that the general journal indicates two accounts (Accounts Payable, and Fabor and Son) for the debit, and two postings ("201/✓") in the reference column. One debit is posted to the control account and another debit is posted to the creditor's account in the subsidiary ledger. If Karns receives cash instead of credit on this return, then it would record the transaction in the cash receipts journal.

Cybersecurity: A Final Comment

Have you ever been hacked? With the increasing use of cell phones, tablets, and social media, a real risk exists that your confidential information may be stolen and used illegally. Companies, individuals, and even nations have all been victims of **cybercrime**—a crime that involves the Internet, a computer system, or computer technology.

For companies, cybercrime is clearly a major threat as the hacking of employees' or customers' records can cost millions of dollars. Unfortunately, the number of security breaches is increasing. For example, shares of **SK Communications** (KOR) dropped 6% after the company reported that hackers stole the personal information of 35 million users of social network Cyworld (now Cyhome) and search engine Nate. Fortunately, since access was free, no financial data was taken.

Here are three reasons for the rise in the successful hacks of company computer records.

1. Companies and their employees continue to increase their activity on the Internet, primarily due to the use of mobile devices and cloud computing.
2. Companies today collect and store unprecedented amounts of personal data on customers and employees.
3. Companies often take measures to protect themselves from cybersecurity attacks but then fail to check if employees are carrying out the proper security guidelines.

Note that cybersecurity risks extend far beyond company operations and compliance. Many hackers target highly sensitive intellectual information or other strategic assets. **Illustration G.18** highlights the type of hackers and their motives, targets and impacts.

ILLUSTRATION G.18 **Profiles of hackers**

Malicious Actors	Motives	Targets	Impacts
Nation-state	• Economic, political, and/or military advantage	• Trade secrets • Sensitive business information • Emerging technologies • Critical infrastructure	• Loss of competitive advantage • Disruption to critical infrastructure
Organized crime	• Immediate financial gain • Collect information for future financial gains	• Financial/payment systems • Personally identifiable information • Payment card information • Protected health information	• Costly regulatory inquiries and penalties • Consumer and shareholder lawsuits • Loss of consumer confidence
Hacktivists	• Influence political and/or social change • Pressure businesses to change their practices	• Company secrets • Sensitive business information • Information related to key executives, employees, customers, and business partners	• Disruption of business activities • Harm to brand and reputation • Loss of consumer confidence
Insiders	• Personal advantage, monetary gain • Professional revenge • Patriotism	• Sales, deals, market strategies • Company secrets, intellectual property • Business operations • Personnel information	• Trade secret disclosure • Operational disruption • Harm to brand and reputation • National security impact

Source: PriceWaterhouseCoopers, "Answering Your Cybersecurity Questions" (January 2014).

Companies now recognize that cybersecurity systems that protect confidential data must be implemented. It follows that companies (as well as nations and individuals) must continually verify that their cybersecurity defenses are sound and uncompromised.

Review

Learning Objectives Review

1 Describe the nature and purpose of a subsidiary ledger.

A subsidiary ledger is a group of accounts with a common characteristic. It facilitates the recording process by freeing the general ledger from details of individual balances.

2 Record transactions in special journals.

Companies use special journals to group similar types of transactions. In a special journal, generally only one line is used to record a complete transaction.

Glossary Review

Accounts payable (creditors') subsidiary ledger A subsidiary ledger that collects transaction data of individual creditors. (p. G-2).

Accounts receivable (customers') subsidiary ledger A subsidiary ledger that collects transaction data of individual customers. (p. G-2).

Cash payments (cash disbursements) journal A special journal that records all disbursements of cash. (p. G-13).

Cash receipts journal A special journal that records all cash received. (p. G-7).

Control account An account in the general ledger that summarizes subsidiary ledger data. (p. G-2).

Cybercrime A crime that involves the Internet, a computer system, or computer technology. (p. G-17).

Purchases journal A special journal that records all purchases of merchandise on account. (p. G-11).

Sales journal A special journal that records all sales of merchandise on account. (p. G-5).

Special journals Journals that record similar types of transactions, such as all credit sales. (p. G-4).

Subsidiary ledger A group of accounts with a common characteristic. (p. G-1).

Questions

1. What are the advantages of using subsidiary ledgers?

2. (a) When do companies normally post to (1) the subsidiary accounts and (2) the general ledger control accounts? (b) Describe the relationship between a control account and a subsidiary ledger.

3. Identify and explain the four special journals discussed in the appendix. List an advantage of using each of these journals rather than using only a general journal.

4. Kim Sports uses special journals. It recorded in a sales journal a sale made on account to R. Yang Co. for ¥435 (amounts in thousands). A few days later, Yang returns ¥70 worth of merchandise for credit. Where should Kim record the sales return? Why?

5. A €500 purchase of merchandise on account from Loire Gourmet Shops was properly recorded in the purchases journal. When posted, however, the amount recorded in the subsidiary ledger was €50. How might this error be discovered?

6. Why would special journals used in different businesses not be identical in format? What type of business would maintain a cash receipts journal but not include a column for accounts receivable?

7. The cash and the accounts receivable columns in the cash receipts journal were mistakenly over-added by €4,000 at the end of the month. (a) Will the accounts receivable ledger agree with the Accounts Receivable control account? (b) Assuming no other errors, will the trial balance totals be equal?

8. One column total of a special journal is posted at month-end to only two general ledger accounts. One of these two accounts is Accounts Receivable. What is the name of this special journal? What is the other general ledger account to which that same month-end total is posted?

9. In what journal would the following transactions be recorded? (Assume that a two-column sales journal and a single-column purchases journal are used.)

   a. Recording of depreciation expense for the year.

   b. Credit given to a customer for merchandise purchased on credit and returned.

   c. Sales of merchandise for cash.

d. Sales of merchandise on account.

e. Collection of cash on account from a customer.

f. Purchase of office supplies on account.

10. In what journal would the following transactions be recorded? (Assume that a two-column sales journal and a single-column purchases journal are used.)

a. Cash received from signing a note payable.

b. Investment of cash by shareholders.

c. Closing of the expense accounts at the end of the year.

d. Purchase of merchandise on account.

e. Credit received for merchandise purchased and returned to supplier.

f. Payment of cash on account due a supplier.

11. What transactions might be included in a multiple-column purchases journal that would not be included in a single-column purchases journal?

12. Give an example of a transaction in the general journal that causes an entry to be posted twice (i.e., to two accounts), one in the general ledger, the other in the subsidiary ledger. Does this affect the debit/credit equality of the general ledger?

13. Give some examples of appropriate general journal transactions for an organization using special journals.

Brief Exercises

BEG.1 (LO 1) Presented below is information related to Anping Manufacturing for its first month of operations. Identify the balances that appear in the accounts receivable subsidiary ledger and the accounts receivable balance that appears in the general ledger at the end of January.

Identify subsidiary ledger balances.

Credit Sales			Cash Collections		
Jan. 7	Ling Ltd.	NT$10,000	Jan. 17	Ling Ltd.	NT$7,000
15	TMC Co.	8,000	24	TMC Co.	4,000
23	Wong Co.	9,000	29	Wong Co.	9,000

BEG.2 (LO 1) Identify in what ledger (general or subsidiary) each of the following accounts is shown.

Identify subsidiary ledger accounts.

a. Rent Expense.

b. Accounts Receivable—Cabrera.

c. Notes Payable.

d. Accounts Payable—Pacheco.

BEG.3 (LO 2) Identify the journal in which each of the following transactions is recorded.

Identify special journals.

a. Cash sales.

b. Payment of cash dividends.

c. Cash purchase of land.

d. Credit sales.

e. Purchase of merchandise on account.

f. Receipt of cash for services performed.

BEG.4 (LO 2) Indicate whether each of the following debits and credits is included in the cash receipts journal. (Use "Yes" or "No" to answer this question.)

Identify entries to cash receipts journal.

a. Debit to Sales Revenue.

b. Credit to Inventory.

c. Credit to Accounts Receivable.

d. Debit to Accounts Payable.

BEG.5 (LO 2) Hallasan Shoes uses special journals and a general journal. Identify the journal in which each of the following transactions is recorded.

Identify transactions for special journals.

a. Purchased equipment on account.

b. Purchased merchandise on account.

c. Paid utility expense in cash.

d. Sold merchandise on account.

BEG.6 (LO 2) Identify the special journal(s) in which the following column headings appear.

Identify transactions for special journals.

a. Sales Discounts Dr.

b. Accounts Receivable Cr.

c. Cash Dr.

d. Sales Revenue Cr.

e. Inventory Dr.

BEG.7 (LO 2) Papha Computer Components uses a multi-column cash receipts journal. Indicate which column(s) is/are posted only in total, only daily, or both in total and daily.

Indicate postings for cash receipts journal.

a. Accounts Receivable.

b. Sales Discounts.

c. Cash.

d. Other Accounts.

Exercises

Determine control account balances, and explain posting of special journals.

EG.1 (LO 1, 2) Semora Textiles uses both special journals and a general journal as described in this appendix. On June 30, after all monthly postings had been completed, the Accounts Receivable control account in the general ledger had a debit balance of ₩340,000; the Accounts Payable control account had a credit balance of ₩77,000 (amounts in thousands).

The July transactions recorded in the special journals are summarized below. No entries affecting accounts receivable and accounts payable were recorded in the general journal for July.

Sales journal	Total sales ₩161,400
Purchases journal	Total purchases ₩66,400
Cash receipts journal	Accounts receivable column total ₩131,000
Cash payments journal	Accounts payable column total ₩47,500

Instructions

a. What is the balance of the Accounts Receivable control account after the monthly postings on July 31?

b. What is the balance of the Accounts Payable control account after the monthly postings on July 31?

c. To what account(s) is the column total of ₩161,400 in the sales journal posted?

d. To what account(s) is the accounts receivable column total of ₩131,000 in the cash receipts journal posted?

Explain postings to subsidiary ledger.

EG.2 (LO 1) **Writing** Presented below is the subsidiary accounts receivable account of Kam-Bo Hung.

Date	Ref.	Debit	Credit	Balance
2025				
Sept. 2	S31	61,000		61,000
9	G4		14,000	47,000
27	CR8		47,000	—

Instructions

Write an email to Lilly Cheung, chief financial officer, that explains each transaction.

Post various journals to control and subsidiary accounts.

EG.3 (LO 1, 2) On September 1, the balance of the Accounts Receivable control account in the general ledger of Zhao Foods was ¥10,960 (amounts in thousands). The customers' subsidiary ledger contained account balances as follows: Chang ¥1,440, Wu ¥2,640, Fung ¥2,060, and Tumen ¥4,820. At the end of September, the various journals contained the following information.

Sales journal: Sales to Tumen ¥800, to Chang ¥1,260, to Tamsui ¥1,330, and to Fung ¥1,600.
Cash receipts journal: Cash received from Fung ¥1,310, from Tumen ¥3,300, from Tamsui ¥380, from Wu ¥1,800, and from Chang ¥1,240.
General journal: An allowance is granted to Tumen ¥220.

Instructions

a. Set up control and subsidiary accounts and enter the beginning balances. Do not construct the journals.

b. Post the various journals. Post the items as individual items or as totals, whichever would be the appropriate procedure. (No sales discounts given.)

c. Prepare a schedule of accounts receivable and prove the agreement of the controlling account with the subsidiary ledger at September 30, 2025.

Determine control and subsidiary ledger balances for accounts receivable.

EG.4 (LO 1) Feng Decorators Company has a balance in its Accounts Receivable control account of ¥10,000 on January 1, 2025 (amounts in thousands). The subsidiary ledger contains three accounts: Long Company, balance ¥4,000; Chu Company, balance ¥2,500; and Fan Company. During January, the following receivable-related transactions occurred.

	Credit Sales	Collections	Returns
Long Company	¥9,000	¥8,000	¥ -0-
Chu Company	7,000	2,500	3,000
Fan Company	8,500	9,000	-0-

Instructions

a. What is the January 1 balance in the Fan Company subsidiary account?

b. What is the January 31 balance in the control account?

c. Compute the balances in the subsidiary accounts at the end of the month.

d. Which January transaction would not be recorded in a special journal?

EG.5 (LO 1) Pennington SA has a balance in its Accounts Payable control account of €9,250 on January 1, 2025. The subsidiary ledger contains three accounts: Hale Co., balance €3,000; Janish Co., balance €1,875; and Valdez Co., balance unknown. During January, the following payable-related transactions occurred.

Determine control and subsidiary ledger balances for accounts payable.

	Purchases	Payments	Returns
Hale Co.	€6,750	€6,000	€ -0-
Janish Co.	5,250	1,875	2,250
Valdez Co.	6,375	6,750	-0-

Instructions

a. What is the January 1 balance in the Valdez subsidiary account?

b. What is the January 31 balance in the control account?

c. Compute the balances in the subsidiary accounts at the end of the month.

d. Which January transaction would not be recorded in a special journal?

EG.6 (LO 2) Seo-hyeon's Auto Supply uses special journals and a general journal. The following transactions occurred during September 2025 (amounts in thousands).

Record transactions in sales and purchases journal.

Sept.	2	Sold merchandise on account to A. Jinwoo, invoice no. 101, NT$620, terms n/30. The cost of the merchandise sold was NT$420.
	10	Purchased merchandise on account from Jeju Company NT$650, terms 2/10, n/30.
	12	Purchased office equipment on account from C. Song NT$6,500.
	21	Sold merchandise on account to New Taiwan Supply Co., invoice no. 102 for NT$800, terms 2/10, n/30. The cost of the merchandise sold was NT$480.
	25	Purchased merchandise on account from Leung Sisters NT$860, terms n/30.
	27	Sold merchandise to Ulsan Company for NT$700 cash. The cost of the merchandise sold was NT$400.

Instructions

a. Prepare a sales journal (see Illustration G.6) and a single-column purchases journal (see Illustration G.12). (Use page 1 for each journal.)

b. Record the transaction(s) for September that should be journalized in the sales journal and the purchases journal.

EG.7 (LO 2) R. Lawrence Luggage uses special journals and a general journal. The following transactions occurred during May 2025.

Record transactions in cash receipts and cash payments journal.

May	1	R. Lawrence invested €40,000 cash in the business.
	2	Sold merchandise to Crapsky Co. for €6,300 cash. The cost of the merchandise sold was €4,200.
	3	Purchased merchandise for €7,700 from J. Mosca using check no. 101.
	14	Paid salary to K. Eyre €700 by issuing check no. 102.
	16	Sold merchandise on account to Stanton Company for €900, terms n/30. The cost of the merchandise sold was €630.
	22	A check of €9,000 is received from C. Galatoire in full for invoice 101; no discount given.

Instructions

a. Prepare a multiple-column cash receipts journal (see Illustration G.8) and a multiple-column cash payments journal (see Illustration G.15). (Use page 1 for each journal.)

b. Record the transaction(s) for May that should be journalized in the cash receipts journal and cash payments journal.

EG.8 (LO 2) Shou Computers uses the columnar cash journals illustrated in the text. In April, the following selected cash transactions occurred.

Explain journalizing in cash journals.

1. Made a refund to a customer as an allowance for damaged goods.
2. Received collection from customer within the 3% discount period.

3. Purchased merchandise for cash.
4. Paid a creditor within the 3% discount period.
5. Received collection from customer after the 3% discount period had expired.
6. Paid freight on merchandise purchased.
7. Paid cash for office equipment.
8. Received cash refund from supplier for merchandise returned.
9. Paid cash dividend to shareholders.
10. Made cash sales.

Instructions

Indicate (a) the journal, and (b) the columns in the journal that should be used in recording each transaction.

Journalize transactions in general journal and explain postings.

EG.9 (LO 2) **Writing** Mama Liana Cakes has the following selected transactions during March (amounts in thousands).

Mar.	2	Purchased equipment costing Rp7,400 from Hasan Company on account.
	5	Received credit of Rp410 from Kusuma Company for merchandise damaged in shipment to Mama Liana.
	7	Issued credit of Rp400 to Bambang Company for merchandise the customer returned. The returned merchandise had a cost of Rp260.

Mama Liana uses a one-column purchases journal, a sales journal, the columnar cash journals used in the text, and a general journal.

Instructions

a. Journalize the transactions in the general journal.
b. In a brief email to the president of Mama Liana Cakes, explain the postings to the control and subsidiary accounts from each type of journal.

Indicate journalizing in special journals.

EG.10 (LO 2) Below are some typical transactions incurred by Cheung Publishers.

1. Payment of creditors on account.
2. Return of merchandise sold for credit.
3. Collection on account from customers.
4. Sale of land for cash.
5. Sale of merchandise on account.
6. Sale of merchandise for cash.
7. Received credit for merchandise purchased on credit.
8. Sales discount taken on goods sold.
9. Payment of employee wages.
10. Payment of cash dividend to shareholders.
11. Depreciation on building.
12. Purchase of office supplies for cash.
13. Purchase of merchandise on account.

Instructions

For each transaction, indicate whether it would normally be recorded in a cash receipts journal, cash payments journal, sales journal, single-column purchases journal, or general journal.

Explain posting to control account and subsidiary ledger.

EG.11 (LO 1, 2) The general ledger of Huang Marine Supply contained the following Accounts Payable control account (in T-account form). Also shown is the related subsidiary ledger (amounts in thousands of yen).

GENERAL LEDGER

Accounts Payable

Feb. 15	General journal	1,400	Feb. 1	Balance	26,025
28	?	?	5	General journal	265
			11	General journal	550
			28	Purchases	13,400
			Feb. 28	Balance	10,500

ACCOUNTS PAYABLE LEDGER

Bak

	Feb. 28 Bal. 4,600

Zhao

	Feb. 28 Bal. 2,300

Poon

	Feb. 28 Bal. ?

Instructions

a. Indicate the missing posting reference and amount in the control account, and the missing ending balance in the subsidiary ledger.

b. Indicate the amounts in the control account that were dual-posted (i.e., posted to the control account and the subsidiary accounts).

EG.12 (LO 1, 2) Selected accounts from the ledgers of Youngblood Company at July 31 showed the following.

Prepare purchases and general journals.

GENERAL LEDGER

Equipment No. 157

Date	Explanation	Ref.	Debit	Credit	Balance
July 1		G1	3,900		3,900

Inventory No. 120

Date	Explanation	Ref.	Debit	Credit	Balance
July 15		G1	400		400
18		G1		100	300
25		G1		200	100
31		P1	9,300		9,400

Accounts Payable No. 201

Date	Explanation	Ref.	Debit	Credit	Balance
July 1		G1		3,900	3,900
15		G1		400	4,300
18		G1	100		4,200
25		G1	200		4,000
31		P1		9,300	13,300

ACCOUNTS PAYABLE LEDGER

Bernardo Inc.

Date	Explanation	Ref.	Debit	Credit	Balance
July 15		G1		400	400

Marsh Co.

Date	Explanation	Ref.	Debit	Credit	Balance
July 3		P1		2,400	2,400
20		P1		1,700	4,100

Flaherty Equipment Co.

Date	Explanation	Ref.	Debit	Credit	Balance
July 1		G1		3,900	3,900

Weller Co.

Date	Explanation	Ref.	Debit	Credit	Balance
July 14		P1		1,100	1,100
25		G1	200		900

Lange Corp.

Date	Explanation	Ref.	Debit	Credit	Balance
July 17		P1		1,400	1,400
18		G1	100		1,300
29		P1		1,600	2,900

Yates Co.

Date	Explanation	Ref.	Debit	Credit	Balance
July 12		P1		500	500
21		P1		600	1,100

Instructions

From the data prepare:

a. The single-column purchases journal for July.

b. The general journal entries for July.

EG.13 (LO 1, 2) Zhao Products uses both special journals and a general journal as described in this appendix. Zhao also posts customers' accounts in the accounts receivable subsidiary ledger. The postings for the most recent month are included in the subsidiary T-accounts below (amounts in thousands of yen).

Determine correct posting amount to control account.

Baak				Liang		
Bal.	-0-	145		Bal.	120	120
	145				190	
					150	

Faan				So		
Bal.	150	150		Bal.	340	250
	290				200	

Instructions

Determine the correct amount of the end-of-month posting from the sales journal to the Accounts Receivable control account.

Compute balances in various accounts.

EG.14 (LO 2) Selected account balances for Hallasan Ltd. at January 1, 2025, are presented below (amounts in thousands).

Accounts Payable	₩14,000
Accounts Receivable	22,000
Cash	17,000
Inventory	13,500

Hallasan's sales journal for January shows a total of ₩110,000 in the selling-price column, and its one-column purchases journal for January shows a total of ₩77,000.

The column totals in Hallasan's cash receipts journal are Cash Dr. ₩61,000, Sales Discounts Dr. ₩1,100, Accounts Receivable Cr. ₩45,000, Sales Revenue Cr. ₩6,000, and Other Accounts Cr. ₩11,100.

The column totals in Hallasan's cash payments journal for January are Cash Cr. ₩55,000, Inventory Cr. ₩1,000, Accounts Payable Dr. ₩46,000, and Other Accounts Dr. ₩10,000. Hallasan's total cost of goods sold for January is ₩63,600.

Accounts Payable, Accounts Receivable, Cash, Inventory, and Sales Revenue are not involved in the Other Accounts column in either the cash receipts or cash payments journal, and are not involved in any general journal entries.

Instructions

Compute the January 31 balance for Hallasan in the following accounts.

a. Accounts Payable.
b. Accounts Receivable.
c. Cash.
d. Inventory.
e. Sales Revenue.

Problems

Journalize transactions in cash receipts journal; post to control account and subsidiary ledger.

PG.1 (LO 1, 2) Yansheng Market's chart of accounts includes the following selected accounts.

101	Cash	401	Sales Revenue
112	Accounts Receivable	414	Sales Discounts
120	Inventory	505	Cost of Goods Sold
311	Share Capital—Ordinary		

On April 1, the accounts receivable ledger of Yansheng Market showed the following balances (amounts in thousands): Lau HK$1,550, Gong HK$1,200, Chan Co. HK$2,900, and Chiu-Wai HK$2,200. The April transactions involving the receipt of cash were as follows.

Apr.	1	Shareholders invested additional cash in the business HK$7,200.
	4	Received check for payment of account from Chiu-Wai less 2% cash discount.
	5	Received check for HK$920 in payment of invoice no. 307 from Chan Co.
	8	Made cash sales of merchandise totaling HK$7,245. The cost of the merchandise sold was HK$4,347.
	10	Received check for HK$600 in payment of invoice no. 309 from Lau.
	11	Received cash refund from a supplier for damaged merchandise HK$740.
	23	Received check for HK$1,000 in payment of invoice no. 310 from Chan Co.
	29	Received check for payment of account from Gong (no cash discount allowed).

Instructions

a. Journalize the transactions above in a six-column cash receipts journal with columns for Cash Dr., Sales Discounts Dr., Accounts Receivable Cr., Sales Revenue Cr., Other Accounts Cr., and Cost of Goods Sold Dr./Inventory Cr. Foot and cross-foot the journal.

b. Insert the beginning balances in the Accounts Receivable control and subsidiary accounts, and post the April transactions to these accounts.

c. Prove the agreement of the control account and subsidiary account balances.

a. Balancing totals HK$25,452

c. Accounts Receivable HK$1,930

Journalize transactions in cash payments journal; post to control account and subsidiary ledgers.

PG.2 (LO 1, 2) Reineke Construction's chart of accounts includes the following selected accounts.

101	Cash	201	Accounts Payable
120	Inventory	332	Cash Dividends
130	Prepaid Insurance	505	Cost of Goods Sold
157	Equipment		

On October 1, the accounts payable ledger of Reineke Company showed the following balances: Uggla Company €2,700, Orr Co. €2,500, Rosenthal Co. €1,800, and Clevenger Company €3,700. The October transactions involving the payment of cash were as follows.

Oct. 1	Purchased merchandise, check no. 63, €300.
3	Purchased equipment, check no. 64, €800.
5	Paid Uggla Company balance due of €2,700, less 2% discount, check no. 65, €2,646.
10	Purchased merchandise, check no. 66, €2,550.
15	Paid Rosenthal Co. balance due of €1,800, check no. 67.
16	Paid cash dividend of €400, check no. 68.
19	Paid Orr Co. in full for invoice no. 610, €2,000 less 2% cash discount, check no. 69, €1,960.
29	Paid Clevenger Company in full for invoice no. 264, €2,500, check no. 70.

Instructions

a. Journalize the transactions above in a four-column cash payments journal with columns for Other Accounts Dr., Accounts Payable Dr., Inventory Cr., and Cash Cr. Foot and cross-foot the journal.

b. Insert the beginning balances in the Accounts Payable control and subsidiary accounts, and post the October transactions to these accounts.

c. Prove the agreement of the control account and the subsidiary account balances.

a. Balancing totals €13,050

c. Accounts Payable €1,700

Journalize transactions in multi-column purchases journal and sales journal; post to the general and subsidiary ledgers.

PG.3 (LO 1, 2) The chart of accounts of LR Scooters includes the following selected accounts.

112	Accounts Receivable	401	Sales Revenue
120	Inventory	412	Sales Returns and Allowances
126	Supplies	505	Cost of Goods Sold
157	Equipment	610	Advertising Expense
201	Accounts Payable		

In July, the following transactions were completed (amounts in thousands). All purchases and sales were on account. The cost of all merchandise sold was 70% of the sales price.

July 1	Purchased merchandise from Oong Company NT$8,000.
2	Received freight bill from Laau Shipping on Oong purchase NT$400.
3	Made sales to Choi Company NT$1,300 and to Huang Bros. NT$1,500.
5	Purchased merchandise from Goo Company NT$3,200.
8	Received credit on merchandise returned to Goo Company NT$300.
13	Purchased store supplies from Ngg Supply NT$720.
15	Purchased merchandise from Oong Company NT$3,600 and from Soxng Company NT$4,300.
16	Made sales to Aang Company NT$3,450 and to Huang Bros. NT$1,870.
18	Received bill for advertising from Viun Advertisements NT$600.
21	Sales were made to Choi Company $310 and to Zafn Company NT$2,800.
22	Granted allowance to Choi Company for merchandise damaged in shipment NT$40.
24	Purchased merchandise from Goo Company NT$3,000.
26	Purchased equipment from Ngg Supply NT$900.
28	Received freight bill from Laau Shipping on Goo purchase of July 24, NT$380.
30	Sales were made to Aang Company NT$5,600.

a. Purchases journal—Accounts Payable NT$25,100
Sales journal—Sales Revenue NT$16,830
c. Accounts Receivable NT$16,790
Accounts Payable NT$24,800

Instructions

a. Journalize the transactions above in a purchases journal, a sales journal, and a general journal. The purchases journal should have the following column headings: Date, Account Credited (Debited), Ref., Accounts Payable Cr., Inventory Dr., and Other Accounts Dr.

b. Post to both the general and subsidiary ledger accounts. (Assume that all accounts have zero beginning balances.)

c. Prove the agreement of the control and subsidiary accounts.

Journalize transactions in special journals.

PG.4 (LO 1, 2) Selected accounts from the chart of accounts of Meng Enterprises are shown below.

101	Cash	401	Sales Revenue
112	Accounts Receivable	412	Sales Returns and Allowances
120	Inventory	414	Sales Discounts
126	Supplies	505	Cost of Goods Sold
157	Equipment	726	Salaries and Wages Expense
201	Accounts Payable		

The cost of all merchandise sold was 60% of the sales price. During January, Meng completed the following transactions (amounts in thousands).

Jan.	3	Purchased merchandise on account from Gum Co. ¥9,000.
	4	Purchased supplies for cash ¥80.
	4	Sold merchandise on account to Wei ¥5,250, invoice no. 371, terms 1/10, n/30.
	5	Returned ¥300 worth of damaged goods purchased on account from Gum Co. on January 3.
	6	Made cash sales for the week totaling ¥3,150.
	8	Purchased merchandise on account from Pang Co. ¥4,500.
	9	Sold merchandise on account to Loeng Corp. ¥5,400, invoice no. 372, terms 1/10, n/30.
	11	Purchased merchandise on account from Che Co. ¥3,700.
	13	Paid in full Gum Co. on account less a 2% discount.
	13	Made cash sales for the week totaling ¥6,260.
	15	Received payment from Loeng Corp. for invoice no. 372.
	15	Paid semi-monthly salaries of ¥14,300 to employees.
	17	Received payment from Wei for invoice no. 371.
	17	Sold merchandise on account to Dyun Co. ¥1,200, invoice no. 373, terms 1/10, n/30.
	19	Purchased equipment on account from Ziu Corp. ¥5,500.
	20	Cash sales for the week totaled ¥3,200.
	20	Paid in full Pang Co. on account less a 2% discount.
	23	Purchased merchandise on account from Gum Co. ¥7,800.
	24	Purchased merchandise on account from Yap Corp. ¥5,100.
	27	Made cash sales for the week totaling ¥4,230.
	30	Received payment from Dyun Co. for invoice no. 373.
	31	Paid semi-monthly salaries of ¥13,200 to employees.
	31	Sold merchandise on account to Wei ¥9,330, invoice no. 374, terms 1/10, n/30.

Meng uses the following journals.

1. Sales journal.
2. Single-column purchases journal.
3. Cash receipts journal with columns for Cash Dr., Sales Discounts Dr., Accounts Receivable Cr., Sales Revenue Cr., Other Accounts Cr., and Cost of Goods Sold Dr./Inventory Cr.
4. Cash payments journal with columns for Other Accounts Dr., Accounts Payable Dr., Inventory Cr., and Cash Cr.
5. General journal.

a. Sales journal ¥21,180
Purchases journal ¥30,100
Cash receipts journal balancing total ¥38,794
Cash payments journal balancing total ¥40,780

Instructions

Using the selected accounts provided:

a. Record the January transactions in the appropriate journal noted.

b. Foot and cross-foot all special journals.

c. Show how postings would be made by placing ledger account numbers and checkmarks as needed in the journals. (Actual posting to ledger accounts is not required.)

PG.5 (LO 1, 2) Presented below are the purchases and cash payments journals for Adhikari Group for its first month of operations (amounts in thousands).

Journalize in sales and cash receipts journals; post; prepare a trial balance; prove control to subsidiary; prepare adjusting entries; prepare an adjusted trial balance.

PURCHASES JOURNAL **P1**

Date	Account Credited	Ref.	Inventory Dr. Accounts Payable Cr.
July 4	N. Akhand		6,800
5	Pai Co.		8,100
11	J. Gupta		5,920
13	Huq Co.		15,300
20	M. Maji		7,900
			44,020

CASH PAYMENTS JOURNAL **CP1**

Date	Account Debited	Ref.	Other Accounts Dr.	Accounts Payable Dr.	Inventory Cr.	Cash Cr.
July 4	Supplies		600			600
10	Pai Co.			8,100	81	8,019
11	Prepaid Rent		6,000			6,000
15	N. Akhand			6,800		6,800
19	Cash Dividends		2,500			2,500
21	Huq Co.			15,300	153	15,147
			9,100	30,200	234	39,066

In addition, the following transactions have not been journalized for July. The cost of all merchandise sold was 65% of the sales price.

July 1	The founder, A. Adhikari, invests ₹80,000 in cash.
6	Sell merchandise on account to Chatterjee Co. $6,200 terms 1/10, n/30.
7	Make cash sales totaling ₹8,000.
8	Sell merchandise on account to S. Garga ₹4,600, terms 1/10, n/30.
10	Sell merchandise on account to Kutsa Co. ₹4,900, terms 1/10, n/30.
13	Receive payment in full from S. Garga.
16	Receive payment in full from Kutsa Co.
20	Receive payment in full from Chatterjee Co.
21	Sell merchandise on account to R. Kumar ₹5,000, terms 1/10, n/30.
29	Returned damaged goods to N. Akhand and received cash refund of ₹420.

Instructions

a. Open the following accounts in the general ledger.

101	Cash	332	Cash Dividends
112	Accounts Receivable	401	Sales Revenue
120	Inventory	414	Sales Discounts
126	Supplies	505	Cost of Goods Sold
131	Prepaid Rent	631	Supplies Expense
201	Accounts Payable	729	Rent Expense
311	Share Capital—Ordinary		

b. Journalize the transactions that have not been journalized in the sales journal and the cash receipts journal (see Illustration G.8).

b. Sales journal total ₹20,700
Cash receipts journal balancing total ₹109,320

c. Post to the accounts receivable and accounts payable subsidiary ledgers. Follow the sequence of transactions as shown in the problem.

d. Post the individual entries and totals to the general ledger.

e. Prepare a trial balance at July 31, 2025.

e. Totals ₹122,520

f. Determine whether the subsidiary ledgers agree with the control accounts in the general ledger.

f. Accounts Receivable ₹5,000
Accounts Payable ₹13,820

g. The following adjustments at the end of July are necessary.

1. A count of supplies indicates that ₹140 is still on hand.
2. Recognize rent expense for July, ₹500.

Prepare the necessary entries in the general journal. Post the entries to the general ledger.

h. Prepare an adjusted trial balance at July 31, 2025.

h. Totals ₹122,520

Journalize in special journals; post; prepare a trial balance.

PG.6 (LO 1, 2) The post-closing trial balance for Horner Autos is shown below.

Horner Autos
Post-Closing Trial Balance
December 31, 2024

	Debit	Credit
Cash	€ 41,500	
Accounts Receivable	15,000	
Notes Receivable	45,000	
Inventory	23,000	
Equipment	6,450	
Accumulated Depreciation—Equipment		€ 1,500
Accounts Payable		43,000
Share Capital—Ordinary		60,000
Retained Earnings		26,450
	€130,950	€130,950

The subsidiary ledgers contain the following information: (1) accounts receivable—B. Hannigan €2,500, I. Kirk €7,500, and T. Hodges €5,000; (2) accounts payable—T. Igawa €12,000, D. Danford €18,000, and K. Thayer €13,000. The cost of all merchandise sold was 60% of the sales price.

The transactions for January 2025 are as follows.

Jan.	3	Sell merchandise to M. Ziesmer €8,000, terms 2/10, n/30.
	5	Purchase merchandise from E. Pheatt €2,000, terms 2/10, n/30.
	7	Receive a check from T. Hodges €3,500.
	11	Pay freight on merchandise purchased €300.
	12	Pay rent of €1,000 for January.
	13	Receive payment in full from M. Ziesmer.
	14	Post all entries to the subsidiary ledgers. Issued credit of €300 to B. Hannigan for returned merchandise.
	15	Send K. Thayer a check for €12,870 in full payment of account, discount €130.
	17	Purchase merchandise from G. Roland €1,600, terms 2/10, n/30.
	18	Pay sales salaries of €2,800 and office salaries €2,000.
	20	Give D. Danford a 60-day note for €18,000 in full payment of account payable.
	23	Total cash sales amount to €9,100.
	24	Post all entries to the subsidiary ledgers. Sell merchandise on account to I. Kirk €7,400, terms 1/10, n/30.
	27	Send E. Pheatt a check for €950.
	29	Receive payment on a note of €40,000 from B. Stout.
	30	Post all entries to the subsidiary ledgers. Return merchandise of €300 to G. Roland for credit.

Instructions

a. Open general and subsidiary ledger accounts for the following.

101	Cash	311	Share Capital—Ordinary
112	Accounts Receivable	401	Sales Revenue
115	Notes Receivable	412	Sales Returns and Allowances
120	Inventory	414	Sales Discounts
157	Equipment	505	Cost of Goods Sold
158	Accumulated Depreciation—Equipment	726	Salaries and Wages Expense
200	Notes Payable	729	Rent Expense
201	Accounts Payable		

b. Sales journal €15,400
Purchases journal €3,600
Cash receipts journal (balancing) €66,060
Cash payments journal (balancing) €20,050

b. Record the January transactions in a sales journal, a single-column purchases journal, a cash receipts journal (see Illustration G.8), a cash payments journal (see Illustration G.15), and a general journal.

d. Totals €144,800

c. Post the appropriate amounts to the general ledger.

e. Accounts Receivable €18,600
Accounts Payable €14,350

d. Prepare a trial balance at January 31, 2025.

e. Determine whether the subsidiary ledgers agree with controlling accounts in the general ledger.

Comprehensive Accounting Cycle Review

ACRG.1 (Perpetual Method) Koto Merchants uses a perpetual inventory system and both an accounts receivable and an accounts payable subsidiary ledger. Balances related to both the general ledger and the subsidiary ledgers for Koto are indicated (amounts in thousands). Also following are a series of transactions for Koto for the month of January. Credit sales terms are 2/10, n/30. The cost of all merchandise sold was 60% of the sales price.

GENERAL LEDGER

Account Number	Account Title	January 1 Opening Balance
101	Cash	Rp35,750
112	Accounts Receivable	13,000
115	Notes Receivable	39,000
120	Inventory	18,000
126	Supplies	1,000
130	Prepaid Insurance	2,000
157	Equipment	6,450
158	Accumulated Depreciation—Equip.	1,500
201	Accounts Payable	35,000
311	Share Capital—Ordinary	50,000
320	Retained Earnings	28,700

Schedule of Accounts Receivable
(from accounts receivable subsidiary ledger)

Customer	January 1 Opening Balance
Bodi Co.	Rp1,500
Mohede Co.	4,000
Sueba Co.	7,500

Schedule of Accounts Payable
(from accounts payable subsidiary ledger)

Creditor	January 1 Opening Balance
R. Manuwa	Rp15,000
Medan Co.	9,000
Shihab Co.	11,000

Jan. 3 Sell merchandise on account to B. Chen Rp3,600, invoice no. 510, and to Tjong Company Rp1,800, invoice no. 511.

5 Purchase merchandise from Goh Co. Rp5,000 and D. Phe Rp2,200, terms n/30.

7 Receive checks from Mohede Rp4,000 and Sueba Rp2,000 after discount period has lapsed.

8 Pay freight on merchandise purchased Rp235.

9 Send checks to Medan for Rp9,000 less 2% cash discount, and to Shihab for Rp11,000 less 1% cash discount.

9 Issue credit of Rp300 to Tjong for merchandise returned.

10 Daily cash sales from January 1 to January 10 total Rp15,500. Make one journal entry for these sales.

11 Sell merchandise on account to Bodi Rp1,600, invoice no. 512, and to Mohede Rp900, invoice no. 513.

12 Pay rent of Rp1,000 for January.

13 Receive payment in full from B. Chen and Tjong less cash discounts.

15 Paid dividend of Rp800 cash.

15 Post all entries to the subsidiary ledgers.

16 Purchase merchandise from Shihab Rp15,000, terms 1/10, n/30; Medan Rp14,200, terms 2/10, n/30; and Goh Rp1,500, terms n/30.

17 Pay Rp400 cash for office supplies.

18 Return Rp200 of merchandise to Medan and receive credit.

20 Daily cash sales from January 11 to January 20 total Rp20,100. Make one journal entry for these sales.

21 Issue Rp15,000 note, maturing in 90 days, to R. Manuwa in payment of balance due.

21 Receive payment in full from Mohede less cash discount.

Jan.	22	Sell merchandise on account to B. Chen Rp2,700, invoice no. 514, and to Bodi Rp2,300, invoice no. 515.
	22	Post all entries to the subsidiary ledgers.
	23	Send checks to Shihab and Medan for full payment less cash discounts.
	25	Sell merchandise on account to Sueba Rp3,500, invoice no. 516, and to Tjong Rp6,100, invoice no. 517.
	27	Purchase merchandise from Shihab Rp14,500, terms 1/10, n/30; D. Phe Rp3,200, terms n/30; and Goh Rp5,400, terms n/30.
	27	Post all entries to the subsidiary ledgers.
	28	Pay Rp200 cash for office supplies.
	31	Daily cash sales from January 21 to January 31 total Rp21,300. Make one journal entry for these sales.
	31	Pay sales salaries Rp4,300 and office salaries Rp3,800.

Instructions

a. Record the January transactions in a sales journal, a single-column purchases journal, a cash receipts journal as shown in Illustration G.8, a cash payments journal as shown in Illustration G.15, and a two-column general journal.

b. Post the journals to the general ledger.

c. Prepare a trial balance at January 31, 2025, in the trial balance columns of the worksheet. Complete the worksheet using the following additional information.

1. Office supplies at January 31 total Rp900.
2. Insurance coverage expires on October 31, 2025.
3. Annual depreciation on the equipment is Rp1,500.
4. Interest of Rp50 has accrued on the note payable.

d. Prepare an income statement and a retained earnings statement for January and a classified statement of financial position at January 31, 2025.

e. Prepare and post adjusting and closing entries.

f. Prepare a post-closing trial balance for January 31, 2025, and determine whether the subsidiary ledgers agree with the control accounts in the general ledger.

ACRG.2 (Periodic Inventory) Yi Ltd. has the following opening account balances in its general and subsidiary ledgers on January 1 and uses the periodic inventory system. All accounts have normal debit and credit balances (amounts in thousands).

GENERAL LEDGER

Account Number	Account Title	January 1 Opening Balance
101	Cash	₩33,750
112	Accounts Receivable	13,000
115	Notes Receivable	39,000
120	Inventory	20,000
126	Supplies	1,000
130	Prepaid Insurance	2,000
157	Equipment	6,450
158	Accumulated Depreciation—Equip.	1,500
201	Accounts Payable	35,000
311	Share Capital—Ordinary	60,000
320	Retained Earnings	18,700

Schedule of Accounts Receivable
(from accounts receivable subsidiary ledger)

Customer	January 1 Opening Balance
Au & Sons	₩4,000
B. Bak	7,500
R. Kang	1,500

Schedule of Accounts Payable
(from accounts payable subsidiary ledger)

Creditor	January 1 Opening Balance
Bai Co.	₩11,000
Oe Sisters	9,000
R. Ryu	15,000

In addition, the following transactions have not been journalized for January 2025.

Jan.	3	Sell merchandise on account to Baozi Co. ₩3,600, invoice no. 510, and Lim Co. ₩1,800, invoice no. 511.
	5	Purchase merchandise on account from S. Chen ₩5,000 and Koh Co. ₩2,700.
	7	Receive checks for ₩4,000 from Au & Sons and ₩2,000 from B. Bak.
	8	Pay freight on merchandise purchased ₩180.
	9	Send checks to Oe Sisters for ₩9,000 and Bai Co. for ₩11,000.
	9	Issue credit of ₩300 to Lim Co. for merchandise returned.
	10	Cash sales from January 1 to January 10 total ₩15,500. Make one journal entry for these sales.
	11	Sell merchandise on account to R. Kang for ₩2,900, invoice no. 512, and to Au & Sons ₩900, invoice no. 513.
		Post all entries to the subsidiary ledgers.
	12	Pay rent of ₩1,000 for January.
	13	Receive payment in full from Baozi Co. and Lim Co.
	15	Pay ₩800 cash dividends.
	16	Purchase merchandise on account from Bai Co. for ₩12,000, from Oe Sisters for ₩13,900, and from S. Chen for ₩1,500.
	17	Pay ₩400 cash for supplies.
	18	Return ₩200 of merchandise to Oe Sisters and receive credit.
	20	Cash sales from January 11 to January 20 total ₩17,500. Make one journal entry for these sales.
	21	Issue ₩15,000 note to R. Ryu in payment of balance due.
	21	Receive payment in full from Au & Sons.
		Post all entries to the subsidiary ledgers.
	22	Sell merchandise on account to Baozi Co. for ₩3,700, invoice no. 514, and to R. Kang for ₩800, invoice no. 515.
	23	Send checks to Bai Co. and Oe Sisters in full payment.
	25	Sell merchandise on account to B. Bak for ₩3,500, invoice no. 516, and to Lim Co. for ₩6,100, invoice no. 517.
	27	Purchase merchandise on account from Bai Co. for ₩12,500, from Koh Co. for ₩1,200, and from S. Chen for ₩2,800.
	28	Pay ₩200 cash for office supplies.
	31	Cash sales from January 21 to January 31 total ₩22,920. Make one journal entry for these sales.
	31	Pay sales salaries of ₩4,300 and office salaries of ₩3,600.

Instructions

a. Record the January transactions in the appropriate journal—sales, purchases, cash receipts, cash payments, and general.

b. Post the journals to the general and subsidiary ledgers. Add and number new accounts in an orderly fashion as needed.

c. Prepare a trial balance at January 31, 2025, using a worksheet. Complete the worksheet using the following additional information.

1. Supplies at January 31 total ₩700.
2. Insurance coverage expires on October 31, 2025.
3. Annual depreciation on the equipment is ₩1,500.
4. Interest of ₩30 has accrued on the note payable.
5. Inventory at January 31 is ₩15,000.

d. Prepare an income statement and a retained earnings statement for January 2025 and a classified statement of financial position at January 31, 2025.

e. Prepare and post the adjusting and closing entries.

f. Prepare a post-closing trial balance for January 31, 2025, and determine whether the subsidiary ledgers agree with the control accounts in the general ledger.

SUBJECT INDEX

B

C

F

T

U

V

W

Y

Z

COMPANY INDEX